NINETEENTH CENTURY MIRACLES;

OR,

SPIRITS AND THEIR WORK IN EVERY COUNTRY

OF THE EARTH.

A COMPLETE HISTORICAL COMPENDIUM

OF THE GREAT MOVEMENT KNOWN AS

"MODERN SPIRITUALISM."

———————

BY

EMMA HARDINGE BRITTEN,

AUTHOR OF

History of Modern American Spiritualism ;" " Wildfire Club ;" " Faiths, Facts, and Frauds of Religious
History ;" "On the Road : or, a Manual for Spiritual Investigators ;" "The Electric Physician ;"
"The Western Star Magazine ;" and numerous Lectures on Religion,
Theology, Science and Reform

———————

PUBLISHED BY WILLIAM BRITTEN.
NEW YORK: LOVELL & CO., 14, VESEY STREET.
1884.

DEDICATION.

———◆———

To W. S. and C. B.

Whose Names, unknown on Earth, shine in Immortal Types

in the Archives of Eternity,

This Humble Record of the Mightiest Work ever

Performed on Earth,

Is Gratefully Inscribed by

The Author.

TABLE OF CONTENTS.

SPIRITUALISM IN THE DUTCH INDIES.

SPIRITUALISM IN RUSSIA.

SPIRITUALISM IN SCANDINAVIA, NORWAY, SWEDEN, &c,, &c.

SPIRITUALISM IN SWITZERLAND.

SPIRITUALISM IN ITALY.

SPIRITUALISM IN SPAIN.

SPIRITUALISM IN EUROPE CONCLUDED—AUSTRIA, BELGIUM, AND TURKEY.

SPIRITUALISM IN AMERICA.

TABLE OF REFERENCE ON SPECIAL SUBJECTS.

The following Table of References, although by no means designed to fill the place of a complete index, will be found serviceable to those who desire to refer to prominent cases on special subjects :—

INTRODUCTION.

ETERNITY and INFINITY are the only words that seem, in our imperfect forms of speech, to embody the conditions of spiritual existence. TIME and SPACE are equally apposite to the state of being we call "material." Whilst therefore, we essay to write of a dispensation which manifests the characteristics of the endless and illimitable, it must not be forgotten that we are yet denizens of a material sphere, bounded in on every side by the limitations of time and space.

The author of these pages would press the above propositions upon the reader's attention, because they may serve to excuse the necessity of *secularizing* a subject, the high religious import of which should command the most sublime forms of expression that language can supply. But as the inspiring intelligences who prompt the production of this volume, mark out the beaten path of verbal simplicity as the best that can be adopted for the reader's benefit, and charge the author to leave to posterity only a brief compendious record of the footprints made by an invisible world of being in this, the nineteenth century, so must our chief aim be to reduce to the plainest possible mode of expression the tale we have to tell. The reader will find then in the following pages, nothing more than a concise historical summary of the spiritual movement as it has transpired in various countries of the earth, from the commencement of the nineteenth century.

There have been certain features of specialty in this "cause" in America, which have given it a prominence there unparalleled in any other country. This remarkable distinctiveness the author has already testified to by publishing a voluminous work embodying the history of the first twenty years of American Spiritualism.* Any student endowed with ordinary powers of observation will soon discover that "the modern outpouring of the spirit" has been just as full in other lands as in America, but no where else has the same freedom of speech been allowed to testify to the facts of spirit communion. No other people have so fully organised the propaganda of the movement by the aid of professional media as the Americans, neither have the inhabitants of any other country so universally systematized the use and culture of "spiritual gifts." It must also be remembered, that the immense mass of spiritual literature put forth through the American press has contributed largely to the popular understanding of the subject. Considering however, the world-wide character of the spiritual outpouring in the nineteenth century, the author has been urgently entreated—by such

---

* "Modern American Spiritualism: a twenty years' record of the open communion between spirits and mortals." By Emma Hardinge Britten. Published by Colby and Rich, office of the *Banner of Light*, Boston, Mass., U.S.A.

I

dwellers of the life beyond as can make their wishes understood—to supplement the History of American Spiritualism, by one which shall include compendious sketches of the movement all over the earth, as well as continue the record in America from its first twenty years of action to the present date. In carrying out this plan of the work, the author has been strongly counselled by the same intelligences as prompt the undertaking, to write of what pertains to the history of Spiritualism without fear or favour, but to omit, as far as possible, all notice of those excrescences which invariably fasten on the armies of reform, in the shape of fraud, imbecility, or such evidences of human selfishness as represent what Spiritualism *is not*—not what it really is. Whilst then, we would "nothing extenuate, or set down aught in malice," we shall unhesitatingly point to any breaches made in the spiritual garrison by human intervention, but carefully avoid giving to the worthless interloper, that notoriety which so many seek to obtain, even at the price of tampering with "the life lightnings," through which the angels telegraph to man; in a word, the cheat, swindler, and parasite, whose genius it is to prey upon any cause strong enough to bear them along on the broad current of progress, may look in vain for opportunities to make capital out of this volume. Whether we send it down the stream of time to the one or the many, we do not propose to disgrace its pages with names which simply represent the darker features of humanity, not the light destined to be shed abroad by the great nineteenth-century spiritual outpouring.

With these impelling motives to our undertaking, we essay its commencement, committing the result to God and the angels, whose work it is, and under whose guidance the author reverently attempts the record.

CONCERNING THE WORKERS AND THEIR WORK.

How far disembodied spirits are the authors of the startling phenomena which have obtained the name of "Modern Spiritualism," how much of the reported marvels are due to the spirit within man himself, or owe their colouring to exaggeration on the part of the narrator, and easy credulity on that of the observer, are questions which are agitating thoughtful minds everywhere, both within and without the ranks of Spiritualism.

That fraudulent manifestations have been given, and in many instances publicly represented as proceeding from spirits, none can deny; but the question of how to discern the true from the false, is of the most vital importance, especially to a writer, whose sole aim is to present a worthy record of a sublime truth, yet to free it from all the misrepresentation which would render such a record valueless.

The chief obstacles which intervene between this purpose and its accomplishment, are the manifestations of partisan spirit, which find their readiest sphere of representation in the columns of the spiritual journals. One set of writers determinately upholds every asserted claim to mediumship, however flimsy, and hurls denunciation against every individual who either presumes to question the validity of that claim, or draws attention to the most palpable evidence of imposture. This injurious spirit of credulity, so often mistaken by the world for complicity with the impostor, is met on the other hand by equally violent denunciation of all which the denouncer cannot himself fully apprehend.

The editors of the spiritual journals are besieged with demands to make their columns the arena of this unseemly warfare. If they comply, they disgust and offend the impartial, whilst their refusals to do so, are regarded as tantamount to partisanship, to be construed at the pleasure of the belligerents. But a still worse result of this quarrelsome and self-assertive spirit, is the difficulty which it interposes of arriving at any reliable representation of a communion, which depends wholly for its acceptance on the validity of the facts claimed for it.

The philosophy of Spiritualism, however beautiful in theory, or true in principle, *grows out of its facts*, for, if spirits are not the authors of the communications received in their names, the whole theory of a hereafter— as demonstrated by Spiritualism—crumbles into the dust and ashes which underlie the unsustained assertions of theology.

To place religion upon the assured foundation of knowledge, and redeem mankind from the tempest-tossed ocean of speculative opinion, we have nothing, unless we have facts and basic fundamental principles. To demonstrate these, and guide our drifting souls into the ports of eternity by the infallible compass of truth, spirits have come to earth.

What then can we say of the remorseless swindlers, who would simulate the personality of these angelic pilots, or the imbecile credulity of those who allow themselves to be duped by their shallow pretences?

Testimony on so weighty and solemn a question as Spiritual existence, can only be admissible when it is proven beyond the peradventure of one or two interested witnesses; in short, the entire intercommunion between the two worlds, must be based on the impregnable rock of truth, or it can never shake the earth with the birth throes of a religion, which claims to demonstrate immortality, as the corner-stone upon which man's faith may rest unmoved.

On the other hand, psychological conditions are subtle, and as yet often incomprehensible, in their working.

Those who attempt to deal with them, whilst they should observe their modes with the closest scrutiny, should yet approach the subject in a considerate and even reverential spirit; always remembering, that they may break or destroy, whilst they endeavour to bend and shape, the invisible force, to suit man's ignorance and presumption. It is certain, however, that discourteous treatment and rude denunciation are not the methods best calculated to evolve psychic phenomena, or ensure results which obviously require calm and harmonious mental conditions. Dean Swift was not far wrong when he said, that "it required a man with brains to write a book, but any brainless ass could criticise it." And this is true of all intellectual processes, Spiritualism not excepted. Whilst the wise and philosophical investigator may take much pains to study out the best means of evolving phenomena, the presence of the boorish ignoramus may be quite sufficient to mar its production. At present, we are profoundly ignorant of all the laws and forces concerned in the evolution of spiritual phenomena; hence, we should be prepared to extend an equal amount of charity both to the medium and the investigator, confident that the spirit of partizanship will never favour the discovery of truth, or promote the integrity of righteous judgment. Many attempts have been made to draw unfavourable comparisons between the value of testimony received from paid or professional mediums, and that obtained through persons whose rank and wealth might be supposed to exclude the hypothesis of *motives* for practising deception.

Unfortunately for the theory that non-professional mediums alone are reliable, the assumption is not based upon admissible facts, for it can be shown, that a large percentage of the alleged spirit communications received through non-professional mediumship, is often tinctured by hallucination, self-deception, and prepossession of opinion, especially upon religious subjects, whilst some of the most notorious *exposés* that have occurred in connexion with physical mediumship, have involved *ladies and gentlemen*, whose positions in society, were assumed to be sufficient warranty, to exclude all idea of fraud or deception.

If the difficulty also of testing mediums, when the investigators are simply *guests*, and the slightest appearance of suspicion would be resented as a mortal affront, be taken into account, the balance, as a whole, may be struck in favour of maintaining professional mediumship, especially for the purposes of investigation and the more general advancement of Spiritualism amongst the masses. In the meantime, there are two forms of spiritual manifestation which are not open to any of the objections above suggested; manifestations, which can be criticised and examined at pleasure, and which always present testimony of an indisputable character. These are, first; spontaneous or unevoked phenomena, occurring without preparation; and next, all such forms of *intelligence* as cannot be traced, either to the knowledge of the communicants or the mentality of the recipients. Multitudes of both these forms of spiritual agency will be found detailed in this volume; in fact, the author has given the preference, wherever possible, to the records of spontaneous phenomena, because its production is freed from all those equivocal conditions which surround invocatory processes These, together with the vast mass of supra-mundane intelligence which has been given during the modern spiritual dispensation, are quite sufficient to demonstrate the facts of spiritual agency, and place the cause on a basis of proof, that rises triumphantly over the most injudicious partisanship, or the most bigoted antagonism.

We now trust our readers will understand in what spirit this volume is written, and why its author has withheld a large mass of offered testimony, extravagantly lauded by one party, and equally extravagantly denounced by another. Also, why those names are omitted from the roll-call of the grand spiritual army that have been made the Shibboleth of contending parties, to prove or disprove imposture.

We may often err in the conclusions we attempt to draw, and utterly fail to do justice to the stupendous theme we treat of, but we will never wilfully aid in deluding a generation, seeking to find in Spiritualism, the path to Heaven that no merely speculative faith can point out.

In endeavouring to trace out with all fidelity, the origin of the great modern spiritual movement, it will soon become apparent that though very momentous results were obtained in the Hydesville investigations of 1848— especially in the discovery of a systematic mode of communing with spirits through a set of concerted signals—yet even in America, the land in which Spiritualism has attained to a pre-eminent degree of popularity, spirit communion was demonstrated, long prior to the "Hydesville disturbances"; in fact, it is obvious that this century in the New, as well as the Old World, has been remarkable for the persistence with which spirits have endeavoured to effect a direct method of intercourse with mortals.

The causes before alluded to, which have favoured the marked publicity to which Spiritualism has attained in America, should be carefully considered, and will be found explanatory of the custom of dating the commencement of the modern movement, from the "Rochester knockings" in 1848. One great diffiuclty in attempting to chronicle the details of this movement, is the very fact that it did not originate in any special locality, or at any given time, inasmuch as it manifested its influence in a sponta-neous and universal outpouring all over the world, coming and going like the wind—few, if any, could say whence, or whitherward.   Again; it is because we cannot trace up the history of modern Spiritualism consecutively from point to point, either in time or place, that we find it expedient to take the commencement of this century for our data, and propose to treat of the manifestations as they occurred, independently, in the various countries of earth from which authentic records are obtainable.   In pursuance of this plan, we shall commence our researches in Germany, where we shall find abundant testimony to the supra-mundane character of the intelligence derivable from spirit sources, as well as proof positive, that spirits have manifested their presence on earth through spontaneous action and wholly unprepared conditions.

"NINETEENTH CENTURY MIRACLES;"

OR,

SPIRITS AND THEIR WORK IN EVERY COUNTRY OF THE WORLD.

CHAPTER I.

SPIRITUALISM IN GERMANY.

(FROM THE CLOSE OF THE 18TH TO THE BEGINNING OF THE 19TH CENTURY.)

WILLIAM HOWITT, that most indefatigable student of every subject on which he chose to exercise his facile pen, in his "History of the Supernatural," writes in strong terms against the custom of identifying the modern Spiritual movement with America as its birth place, or the "Rochester knockings," as the opening of intelligent communication between mortals and spirits.

We have already pointed to the reasons which have tended to popularize Spiritualism in America, but we must add, that the very methods so favourable to the diffusion of knowledge on Spiritual subjects, are not in accordance with the conservatism of older countries, especially in Germany, where the prevailing policy has been to discountenance and even forbid associations, having for their aim the investigation of subjects not immediately fostered by the government.

In America, the investigator finds his best opportunities for gathering up knowledge concerning the status of Spiritualism, in public meetings, Sunday services, conferences, children's lyceums, and the columns of journals specially devoted to the interests of the Spiritual cause.

In Germany, Spiritualism has no publicly defined status. It is not known as a movement, and until the last few years, has had no periodicals devoted to its exposition; yet the higher class of German literature, redolent of Spiritual facts and philosophy, is most voluminous, and a long and brilliant array of eminent German writers could be mentioned, whose works are almost entirely devoted to Spiritualistic subjects.

Take for example the history of Jüng Stilling, the famous pneumatologist, whose life-long experiences in seership, inspiration, prophecy, and the gift of healing, no bigot, however prejudiced, can deny. Cotemporary with this celebrated phenomenal character, was the noble Swiss philosopher Lavater, whilst the literature of the period was enriched by the writings of

Eschenmayer, Mayer, Gorres, Schubert, Werner, Kant, Dr. Ennemoser, the author of the most exhaustive treatise on magic, extant; Dr. Justinius Kerner, the renowned magnetist and biographer of the life and experiences of "the Seeress of Prevorst"; Zschocke, the famous seer and mystic; and many others, whose works connect the close of the last century with the opening of the present, and by the profusion of spiritual evidences they bring, unite in one unbroken chain, the modern outpouring, with the Swedenborgian and Paracelsian period; with mediæval spiritualism, or those forms of influx stigmatised by the ignorance of the times as "Witchcraft and Sorcery"; whilst again; the ghastly records of those dark days reach back in continuous links of connection with the more sublime, because more distant revelations of the Christian, Hebraic, and those other ancient dispensations, during which the foundations of world-wide religious systems were laid.

To return to the immediate subject of this chapter. Germany has made no sensational mark in the form of popular spiritualism, but she has contributed to the age a wealth of recorded facts, philosophy, and high-toned spiritual literature, unmatched by any other nation of our own times. It is to Germany too, that the world owes one of the mightiest discoveries that has ever been made in spiritual science, for Germany was the birth-place of ANTON MESMER, a pioneer in the realms of the imponderable, through whose stupendous revelations, miracle became converted into law, the supernatural into the spiritual, and ancient alchemy into modern magnetism; in a word, it is only in contemplating the great and revolutionary work effected by Mesmer, that we can begin to appreciate the influence of the German mind upon the movement we now assume to be of purely spiritual authorship.

SEERS, PROPHETS, AND MEDIUMS.

A close observer of all phenomena of a spiritualistic character, will recognise, that they require for their production the presence of certain exceptional persons, such as in ancient time were termed seers and prophets; in the middle ages, witches and wizards; and in our own time, magnetic subjects, or spirit mediums.

In the mystic writings of the Orientalists, it is intimated that the wonder-working element displayed in special individuals is latent in the whole human race, and can be brought into action by certain elaborate methods of culture. Now, although the Mediæval Mystics, especially Cornelius Agrippa, Van Helmont, and Jacob Böhmen, have professed to give instructions for the unfoldment of magical power, the readers of their treatises have seldom profited by them; in fact, so vast have been the claims for what might be done, and so futile the attempts to realize these claims, that magical processes have long been relegated to the realms of shadowy superstition. Not so however, the study of those mysterious forces with which the visible universe is teeming. Whether the affinities of chemistry, and the potencies of light, heat, and magnetism, &c., had anything to do with the "vital principle" in animated bodies, has been a question which often obtruded itself upon the philosopher, though never in such a shape as admitted of practical analysis. Paracelsus, Van Helmont, and Böhmen, have hinted at the existence of such a connection, and the first named, professed to have made cures by discovering the assimilation of the magnet to the human system. Still the great problems of the vital forces or the *Elixir Vitœ*, have remained unsolved, and would have continued to do so but for the timely appearance of Anton Mesmer, who, about the middle of the last century, brought the wand of science to bear upon the enchantments of ignorance, and in a single lifetime, broke that spell of mystery which had enshrouded the hidden secrets of life, and the correlation of all forces in the universe. These may seem large claims to make for one who, in his own day, was denounced as an impostor by the scientific world, misunderstood and deserted even by those he had most benefited, and suffered to die in obscurity by the very followers who should have placed him on the highest pinnacle of fame. But Anton Mesmer is no exception to human procedures in every case, where the mind leaps before its age. Slowly but surely, the world recognises its benefactors, though it may be too late to return their benefits. To those who believe that the immortal spirit is the real man, acknowledgment of blessings received, will never seem too late, even if they are only sped by grateful memory and the pen of posterity, across the pathless realms which separate men from the land of ascended spirits.

In considering the life, work, and influence of Dr. Mesmer, it would seem as if he had been providentially born and prepared for the part he was destined to fill in the history of human progress.

Even in his eighth year, he would absent himself from home and school, to trace up the source of streams, and wander far to collect stones, shells, and minerals, which he would pore over with strange and unchildlike interest.

Educated as a physician, he took his degree as a doctor of medicine, at the Vienna University, where he attracted universal attention by the curious nature of his inaugural thesis, the subject of which was, "The influence of the planets on the human body."

During his residence at Vienna, he became acquainted with the professor of astronomy at the University, Father Hehl, a learned Jesuit, who claimed to be the inventor of certain steel plates, in which he could conserve the virtues of the magnet, so as to apply them successfully to the cure of disease.

Whatever might have been the original merit of Father Hehl's discovery, his friend Mesmer soon improved upon it, and by his own superadded methods, produced such astonishing results in the cure of diseases, that he excited the spirit of rivalry, not only in the mind of his former friend, but also in the entire medical faculty of Vienna.

The strife thus commenced was fanned into fury by Mesmer's continued successes, and though the machinations of his enemies ultimately obliged him to quit the city, opposition only had the effect of stimulating him to fresh energy in pursuing his path of discovery ; in fact, from the time when, in 1772, his attention was first called to the curative effects of the magnet, up to the date of his death, in 1815, he never ceased to study, improve in, and practise the art of healing, which has been justly called, after its great discoverer, "Mesmerism."

In his new mode of practice, Dr. Mesmer's earliest efforts were directed towards the utilization of the magnet, and his first cures were effected by the aid of magnetic machines, together with a *baquet* or bath, in which various mineral substances, immersed in water, were brought into connection with his patients. In a very short time, Mesmer discovered that which he had previously assumed, namely, that the chief virtue in his experiments resided in his own organism. It was from the point when he commenced the application of magnetic passes with his own hands, and found that he could transfer the life principle from himself to his patients, under the direction of his will, that his system obtained the now familiar name of "animal magnetism." Our purpose is not to write the biography of Anton Mesmer; we simply aim to point out the gradations of unfoldment, by which the true knowledge of occult life forces was obtained. This stupendous result does not appear to have been known to, or anticipated by Mesmer, although it undoubtedly became familiar to many of his followers. The extent of this great man's discoveries, and the theorems upon which he based his whole system, are succinctly described by one of his most eminent biographers, Dr. Justinius Kerner, from whose admirable work, "The Life of Mesmer," we shall epitomize the summary of his views in the following chapter.

CHAPTER II.

SPIRITUALISM IN GERMANY (CONTINUED).

Dr. Anton Mesmer.

IN the *London Spiritual Magazine*, Mr. Wm. Howitt, one of its ablest and most constant contributors, gives a series of papers translated from Dr. Kerner's life of Mesmer, from which the following extracts are taken :—

"During his fifteen years medical practice in Vienna, Mesmer came upon his new art of healing through observing the origin and career of diseases in connection with the great changes in our solar system and the universe; in short, with what he termed 'Universal Magnetism.' He sought for this magnetism originally in electricity and subsequently in mineral magnetism. . . . . It was after this manner Mesmer reasoned. There must exist a power which permeates the universe and binds together all bodies upon earth; and it must be possible for man to bring this influence under his command.

"This power he first sought for in the magnet. He then pondered upon it in regard to man and applied it successfully to the cure of the sick. This remarkable result would, in any other investigator, have brought him to the end of his experiments. Not so with Mesmer. Ever accompanied by the idea of a primal power, which must pervade the universe, the thought occurred to him that the influence must exist yet more powerfully in man than in the magnet. . . He thus perceived that he could not ascribe alone to the magnet which he held in his hands the effects produced, since he must also, in his turn, influence the magnet.

"Upon this, he cast aside his magnet, and with his hands alone, brought forth similar and unadulterated effects."

Seifert, another of Mesmer's biographers, affirms that he wore beneath his vest a shirt of leather, lined with silk, to prevent the escape of the magnetic fluid.

He also believed that Mesmer wore magnets about his person, with a view of strengthening his own magnetism.

The following description is given by Seifert of the *Baquet* which Mesmer used in the early days of his magnetic practice —

"This receptacle was a large pan, tub, or pool of water, filled with various magnetic substances, such as water, sand, stone, glass bottles (filled with magnetic water), &c. It was a focus within which the magnetism was concentrated, and out of which proceeded a number of conductors. These being bent pointed iron wands, one end was retained in the *baquet*, whilst the other was connected with the patient and applied to the seat of the disease. This arrangement might be made use of by any number of persons seated round the *baquet*, and thus a fountain, or any receptacle in a garden, as in a room, would answer for the purpose desired."

MESMER'S THEOREMS.

The following summary of the twenty-seven theorems which Mesmer published when the French Academy refused to indorse his discovery, are taken from *Mémoire sur la Découverte du Magnetisme Animal, par M. Mesmer. Paris,* 1779 :—

"Animal magnetism is a fluid universally diffused.

"It is the medium of a mutual influence between the heavenly bodies, the earth, and animated bodies.

"It is continuous, so as to leave no void. Its subtility admits of no comparison.

"It is capable of receiving, propagating, and communicating all the impressions of motion. It is susceptible of flux and reflux.

"The animal body experiences the effect of this agent by insinuating itself into the substance of the nerves—it affects them immediately.

"There are observed, particularly in the human body, properties analogous to those of the magnet, and in it are observed poles equally different and opposite.

"The action and the virtues of animal magnetism, may be communicated from one body to other bodies, animate and inanimate.

"This action may take place at a remote distance, without the aid of any intermediate body.

"It is increased, reflected by mirrors; communicated, propagated, augmented by sound. Its virtues may be accumulated, concentrated, transported.

"Although this fluid is universal, all animal bodies are not equally susceptible of it. There are even some—though a very small number—which have properties so opposite, that their very presence destroys all the effects of this fluid on other bodies.

"Animal magnetism is capable of healing diseases of the nerves immediately, and others mediately.

"It perfects the action of medicines, excites and directs salutary crises in such a manner, that the physician may render himself master of them. By its means, he may know the state of each individual's health, judge the most complicated diseases, prevent their increase, and heal them without dangerous effects or troublesome consequences, whatever be the age, sex, or temperament of the patient.

"In animal magnetism, nature presents an universal method of healing and preserving mankind." . . .

Nothing in the history of the race is more admirably illustrative of providential methods, than the succession of steps through which great ideas are perfected, from their inception to their fruitage.

Thus it is that we find the grand discovery of Mesmer, interpreting the dreams of the mystics concerning the "Philosopher's Stone" and "Elixir Vitæ"; illustrating the theories of Galileo and Newton, and converting the universal realm of gravitation which they perceived, into the soul-force of the universe, which could be made the instrument of annihilating disease and indefinitely extending the life of man. But though Mesmer capped the climax of philosophic research in the direction of blind, non-intelligent forces, his powers of observation extended no farther. He himself perceived that there were unknown realms of knowledge yet to be traversed;

and that as the element with which he was attempting to deal, was itself illimitable, so the paths of new discovery must also be boundless. It has often been urged that Mesmer dared not advance to the verification of the hypotheses which he perceived—let us grant this—still it must be remembered that it was his bold hand which opened the temple door of LIFE FORCES; also, that the great discoverer laboured at first alone and unaided; and when at last he succeeded in drawing round him a cordon of sympathetic minds, he had to bear the brunt of all the persecution, scorn, and even martyrdom, which ignorance and bigotry ever launch against the pioneers of new ideas and progress.

In process of time, the very bitterness of the denunciations that were visited upon the discoverer of animal magnetism, wrought their usual effect of provoking general investigation, and winning over numerous converts to the new system of cure.

Amongst the most enthusiastic of Mesmer's early followers, was the Marquis de Puységur, a wealthy and influential nobleman of Strasbourg, who, in carrying out the instructions of the great mesmerist, chanced to hit upon the still more remarkable and interesting sequence of clairvoyance, evolved through the mesmeric sleep.

At first, the discovery of a highly-exalted intelligential state in connection with somnambulism, was so amazing to M. de Puységur, that he was inclined to suppose the principle of cure itself, must result from the effect of magnetism upon the spirit. Like Mesmer, he immediately began to put forth theories in this direction, and, like Mesmer, he lived to realise that he had as yet attained only to the first glimmering of truth on these wonderful and occult subjects.

Puységur's views upon the new discovery, as being connected with phenomena of the most curious and interesting nature, soon began to supersede those of Mesmer, and amongst his most devoted adherents, he had the good fortune to include the celebrated Lavater, through whose talents and influence, many other persons of eminence were attracted to the marquis's experiments.

Thus it happened, that after the noble-minded Mesmer had laid his theory before the French Academy of Sciences, only to find it scornfully rejected, he returned to Germany, to experience neglect and ingratitude, and find the laurels he had so justly earned, already encircling the brow of another. The truth is, Puységur's experiments challenged from all observers, the deepest and most absorbing attention.

Mesmer seems to have been aware that sleep-waking intelligence was not unfrequently a result of animal magnetism, but he affirmed this state was full of danger, and he not only steadily discountenanced the practice of deepening the magnetic sleep into waking trance, but he bitterly opposed the new sect formed by Puységur, and disclaimed all alliance with his followers.

It might have been partly as the result of this feud, and partly in contemptible subservience to the opinions of the French *savants*, that the name of Mesmer, was for a time almost tabooed from the literature of the subject, and it became fashionable to speak of, and investigate the wonders of "Somnambulism," but carefully to avoid all allusion to the unpopular theme of *animal magnetism.*

Time, the immutable touchstone of truth, has at length rendered justice to all sides of this vexed question. Puységur, Barberini, Kerner, Cahagnet, Dupotet, Deleuze, and all who have written on, or experimented with these

MESMER

wondrous occult life forces, have each had their day, commanded the fickle mind of the populace for the time being, and aided in compelling the world to acknowledge the facts which were being daily enacted.

Even the verdict of the French Academy has done a work for truth, by proving the incapacity of stereotyped associations to deal with matters outside the grooves laid down for their own action. In the mean time, the rival claims of Mesmer's various followers, have all been merged in the value of the great fundamental discovery of a demonstrable vital force, and the possibility of its utilization and transfer, as originally proved by Mesmer. Every other name takes rank—where it justly belongs—as secondary to his. Animal magnetism, and all the marvels which follow in its train, are now synonymous with the equally popular term, "Mesmerism," and the founder of the system, silently but inevitably, takes his place in the annals of fame, as the true alchemist, who discovered and applied to the use of humanity, the "Philosopher's Stone," and the "Elixir Vitæ."

CHAPTER III.

SPIRITUALISM IN GERMANY (CONTINUED).

THE PHILOSOPHER'S STONE IN ACTION.

DURING Mesmer's visit to Paris, and pending his efforts to obtain recognition for his new curative process from the French Academy of Sciences, he drew around him many interested followers, amongst whom was M. d'Eslon, a physician of great eminence. This gentleman, who was highly enthusiastic in his adherence to the new science, during Mesmer's absence from Paris conducted experiments himself, with more *éclat* than skill, and more display than judgment.

It was under the advice of d'Eslon that Mesmer was induced to challenge the French Academicians, and urge them to investigate the working of "animal magnetism." It was also by aid of his indomitable energy, that the new methods of cure retained their hold upon the popular mind after the unfavourable verdict of the *savants* had condemned it.

M. Bailly, the French astronomer, justly celebrated in his particular sphere of knowledge, but wholly incapable of pronouncing upon psychological phenomena, was one of those, whose opinions were most adverse to the claims of Mesmer. He gives the following account of the methods pursued by d'Eslon; we quote them here, to show how purely physical they were, and how thoroughly they disregarded all those conditions, which we now believe to be essential to the production of psychological phenomena. Bailly says :—

"The sick persons, arranged in great numbers, and in several rows around the *baquet* (bath), received the magnetism by means of the iron rods, which conveyed it to them from the *baquet* by the cords wound round their bodies, by the thumb which connected them with their neighbours, and by the sounds of a pianoforte, or an agreeable voice, diffusing magnetism in the air.

" The patients were also directly magnetised by means of the finger and wand of the magnetiser, moved slowly before their faces, above or behind their heads, or on the diseased parts.

" The magnetiser acts also by fixing his eyes on the subjects; by the application of his hands on the region of the solar plexus; an application which sometimes continues for hours.

" Meanwhile the patients present a very varied picture.

" Some are calm, tranquil, and experience no effect. Others cough and spit, fee pains, heat, or perspiration. Others, again, are convulsed.

" As soon as one begins to be convulsed, it is remarkable that others are immediately affected.

" The Commissioners have observed some of these convulsions last more than three hours. They are often accompanied with expectorations of a violent character, often streaked with blood. The convulsions are marked with involuntary motions of the throat, limbs, and sometimes the whole body; by dimness of the eyes, shrieks, sobs, laughter, and the wildest hysteria. These states are often followed by langour and depression. The smallest noise appears to aggravate the symptoms, and often to occasion shudderings and terrible cries. It was noticeable that a sudden change in the air or time of the music had a great influence on the patients, and soothed or accelerated the convulsions, stimulating them to ecstacy, or moving them to floods of tears.

" Nothing is more astonishing than the spectacle of these convulsions.

" One who has not seen them can form no idea of them. The spectator is as much astonished at the profound repose of one portion of the patients as at the agitation of the rest.

" Some of the patients may be seen rushing towards each other with open arms, and manifesting every symptom of attachment and affection.

" All are under the power of the magnetizer; it matters not what state of drowsiness they may be in, the sound of his voice, a look, a motion of his hands, spasmodically affects them.*

Let it be remembered that besides the official investigations of the Commissioners, numerous private experiments were instituted separately amongst them, the result of which brought conviction to *their* minds at least, that "hysteria and imagination," not animal magnetism, *as an actual force*, were the sources of the effects they observed.

Dr. Mackay, LL.D., in his work on " Popular Delusions," says :—

" The report of the Commissioners was drawn up by the unfortunate and illustrious Bailly. After detailing the experiments made, and their results, they came to the conclusion that the only proof advanced in support of 'animal magnetism' was its effects on the human body; that those effects could be produced without magnetic passes or manipulations, and that *such effects never transpired without the patient's knowledge, hence*, that imagination did, and animal magnetism did not, account for all that transpired."

In justice to the cause of truth it should be observed, that none of that intelligence which often accompanies somnambulic states, such as clairvoyance, &c., seems to have been manifested before the French *savants*. Possibly the heterogeneous character of the assemblage organised by d'Eslon, forbade the unfoldment of psychological phenomena, or any of those curative results which had been claimed for Mesmer's practice. When these disadvantageous concomitants are borne in mind—and we remember the effect produced upon modern witnesses by the spasmodic jerks, gasps, shudderings, &c., not unfrequently exhibited in nineteenth century spirit circles, our astonishment at the imbecility of the verdict pronounced against animal magnetism by the French Academicians may be considerably modified, indeed we may wish we had a few of those illustrious observers present to criticise the reports so freely and unconditionally published to-day, as " notes of *spiritualistic* phenomena."

---

* Rapporte des Commissionaires. Redigé par M. Bailly, Paris, 1784.

The chief difficulty in sifting and describing occult phenomena was then, and is now, the distinction between mere nervous irritability and the genuine effect produced in the physical system by magnetism, or upon the mind by the psychological impress of a second mind, no matter whether that be by a disembodied or embodied operator.

The force which can change a diseased tissue into a healthy one must be a genuine, substantial element, and the transmission of thought from one mind to another, so as to enable an entranced subject to render such intelligence as is wholly foreign to that subject's previous knowledge, is an objective proof of an outside power from which no candid observer can dissent.

It does not appear, from a careful study of M. Bailly's report, that any such testimony was afforded. Tears, laughter, hysteria, and convulsions were prominent amongst the effects produced, and these were naturally enough deemed by superficial observers, to be the result of foreknowledge amongst the patients, who, in a state of expectancy, might quite as well have been under the influence of excited imagination as animal magnetism. It is scarcely to be wondered at therefore, that mesmeric experiments conducted on the crude and wholesale methods described by Bailly, produced no results that might not have been readily ascribed to the influence of diseased imaginations.

Had no other methods been practised by Mesmer himself in the treatment of private patients, his reputation would never have survived the shock produced by d'Eslon's injudicious exhibitions.

But more fortunate results *did* attend Mesmer's practice, and the many remarkable cures he was known to have effected, served in some degree to counteract the injurious report of the French Academy.

Still more productive of sensational public interest were the phenomena evolved by the magnetic experiments of M. de Puységur.

According to Dr. Mackay's statement in his sketch of the French Magnetizers, M. de Puységur's discovery of the sleep-waking state in connection with animal magnetism, appears to have resulted more from accident than design.

Mackay says :—

"The Marquis de Puységur had one day magnetized his gardener, and observing that he had fallen into a very profound sleep, it occurred to him to address questions to him as he would have done to a natural somnambulist. To his great delight, the man answered him with such surprising lucidity, that he was encouraged to renew his experiments, when he found that *the soul of the speaker was enlarged, and brought into more intimate connexion with the hidden things of life and nature, and with himself, M. de Puységur.* Very soon too, he discovered that all farther manipulations were needless.

"Without speaking or making a sign, he could mentally impart his will to the patient; in fact, he could converse with him soul to soul, without the employment of any physical methods whatever."

M. de Puységur, who was evidently feeling his way blindly along the new path of occult force, also discovered, that he could impart his own magnetic power to inanimate objects, which, thus charged, would re-act upon those brought into contact with them. Thus, in order to reserve as much as possible the mysterious power with which he felt himself possessed, he proceeded to magnetize a tree, in contact with which he claimed, that any number of patients could receive all the benefit which could be imparted by personal manipulations.

Now, although the unthinking "great public" were of course sufficiently prompt to cast all manner of derision upon M. de Puységur's "magical tree," and "the man with the enlarged soul," even the most ill-natured criticisms could not disguise the fact that veritable results of healing and clairvoyance were evolved. M. Dupotet's *Histoire de Magnétisme* bears witness to the multitude of remarkable cures effected by Puységur, whilst his one clairvoyant soon multiplied into vast numbers, from whose entranced lips the most marvellous results of lucidity were constantly obtained. Writing of his first and most celebrated "lucid," the Marquis says, in letters to his friend, M. Cloquet, the Receiver of Finance, and one of his great sympathisers :—

" It is from this simple man that I receive the wisest counsel and the most prudent directions in all great emergencies. Himself one of the most ignorant rustics of the country, in the magnetic sleep he is a peasant no longer. A being who awake, can scarcely utter a sentence, commonplace, illiterate and timid, when magnetized he is a poet, philosopher, and physician. I need not speak either. I have only to think before him and he instantly understands and answers me."

Much more of the same nature M. de Puységur pours forth concerning his clairvoyants, but as the powers then deemed so extraordinary, are now familiar enough to the reader, it would be unnecessary to pursue these quotations farther. Whilst the Marquis de Puységur was making converts in every direction, by his wonderful somnambulists, a magnetizer of a still higher tone appeared on the scene in the person of the Chevalier de Barberini, a gentleman of Lyons, whose magnetic processes, associated with prayer, produced results even more extraordinary than the clairvoyants of Puységur. The Chevalier de Barberini magnetized his subjects both by manipulations and will, but in most instances, the effects he produced, threw the patients into that state now known as trance and ecstasy. Visions of the most exalted character followed. The "lucids" described scenes and persons in the other world ; traversed the regions of disembodied souls, and only returned to earth reluctantly, to relate their aerial flights to wondering listeners, and describe to bereaved mourners, the apparitions of friends who had long since passed beyond the grave. *The Continental Miscellany and Foreign Review*, describes "The New Sect of Barberinists," and affirms that in Sweden and Germany, where they were very numerous, "these fanatics were called *Spiritualists*, to distinguish them from the followers of M. de Puységur, who were termed *Experimentalists*." In this miscellany an account of the magnetic state by one of the subjects, is given in these words :—

"In such an one, animal instinct ascends to the highest degree admissible in this world. The clairvoyant is then similar to God : his eye penetrates all the secrets of nature ; in spirit, he sees through all space ; friends, enemies, spirits. He sees all actions, penetrates into all causes ; he becomes a physician, a prophet, a divine."

We shall now proceed to consider the final results achieved by Mesmer and his followers in Germany. In such a review we may regard Mesmer, Puységur, Barberini, and their various adherents, as so many index fingers pointing on the well-defined path which leads the investigator through the newly discovered fields of occult force ; from mineral to animal magnetism ; from their effects upon the body to those of the nerves, soul, and spirit ; from the clairvoyant flights of the spirit upon earth to the life beyond, and into realms of being, peopled by spirits with spiritual entities.

From the time of Mesmer up to the present date, the practices of the Mesmerists have been continuous, and the results, though variable with the characteristics both of operators and subjects, may be classified after the following manner :—

1. We have unmistakable effects produced in the physical organism, sometimes modifying, and at others curing diseases of various types.

2. Magnetized subjects, when questioned during their sleep, sometimes describe their own states ; prescribe remedies of a more effective nature than their physicians could do for them, and occasionally delineate the nature of disease, and prescribe remedies for others.

3. Some magnetic subjects can describe distant scenes, objects, and persons ; traverse space spiritually, find lost property, and occasionally, describe past and future events ; speak in languages they have not studied, play on instruments of which they have had no previous knowledge, and exhibit other supra-mundane powers.

4. The magnetized subject not unfrequently quits the realms of earth and descends into dark spheres, and ascends into bright ones inhabited by spiritual beings, the descriptions of whom, correspond perfectly with the identity of those who have once been known as dwellers on earth.

5. Besides the effects proceeding as above described from magnetic manipulations, thousands of instances are recorded of persons manifesting one or more, and sometimes all the phenomena described in these speci-fications, without the agency of any human magnetizer at all. As these persons have claimed that they were under the control of a Spiritual magnetizer, or a soul who had once inhabited the human form, and as the phenomena they exhibited, paralleled in all respects those evolved by the agency of a human magnetizer, the conclusion is inevitable, that the Spirit of the magnetizer, when disembodied, can produce the same effects as when on earth, and that those who are susceptible to animal magnetism, may become equally receptive of the same influence, projected by a Spiritual magnetizer. Finally, it is proved, that a certain class of individuals are not receptive to the influence of magnetism at all, whilst others are by predisposition, operators rather than subjects ; and others again, erect psychological barriers of dislike or antagonism to the whole subject, thereby actively repelling the influence. It has also been demonstrated that, whilst some magnetized subjects cannot attain to more than one, two, or three of the states above specified, others may attain to them all ; thus the several states may be recognized as degrees to which differently constituted subjects attain, by laws at present but little known or understood by man.

Experience has shown, that the presence of disease, which at one stage of the enquiry was deemed a necessary element for the receptivity oi magnetic influence, is now only one of its contingents ; hundreds of robust and healthful persons having exhibited all the phases of somnambulic power above described, both with human and spiritual magnetizers.

It will appear evident, that in these successive states, we first trace out what effects animal magnetism can produce when both operator and subject are mortals, and next, show that precisely the same results are obtained when the operator is a spirit and the subject only is a mortal. Whilst spirits, from their superior conditions of knowledge, can effect more wonderful results by magnetism and psychology than mortals, we may assure ourselves that the *modus operandi* is in each case one and the same thing. Magnetic subjects are the mediums for spirits still in the body, and mediums are the subjects of spirits out of the body. The one is the stepping-stone to the other. Animal magnetism is the body of the science; spiritual magnetism the soul; but as animal magnetism most generally prepares the organism of the subject for the reception of the higher and more subtle force of spiritual magnetism, so it is evident, that the universality with which animal magnetism has been practised all over the civilised world, during the last century, has prepared the organisms of multitudes of susceptible persons for the influx of spiritual magnetism, besides stimulating and preparing the minds of men for the unfoldment of occult phenomena. In this view of the question, the great alchemist, Anton Mesmer, may well be regarded as the human founder of the New Spiritual Dispensation; whilst the work he has effected has already advanced from matter to force, from thence to mind, and from mind again onward to spirit, and realms of purely spiritual existence.

AUTHOR'S DEFINITION OF BODY, SOUL, AND SPIRIT.

BODY—MATTER. SOUL—FORCE. SPIRIT—INTELLIGENCE.

MAN—a Trinity of Body, Soul, and Spirit.

A SPIRIT from the earth spheres—a duality of Soul and Spirit.

AN ANGEL from the celestial heavens—Pure Spirit.

(Teachings of some Oriental occultists.)

CHAPTER IV.

SPIRITUALISM IN GERMANY (CONTINUED).

WONDERFUL NARRATIVES BY DR. JUSTINIUS KERNER.

AMONGST the most important contributions to modern German spiritual literature are the writings of Dr. Justinius Kerner, especially a volume published in 1834, entitled " *Geschichten Besessener neurerer Zeit.*"

This work contains numerous narratives of what is commonly called "obsession," but what the learned writer uncompromisingly designates as *"Demoniacal Possession."*

Taking the ground that all haunting spirits have once inhabited the human form, Dr. Kerner throws an immense flood of light upon the dark regions of "supernaturalism," proving conclusively the modes in which unhappy earth-bound spirits afflict mediumistic sensitives, and by their strange and repulsive acts of possession, give rise to the frightful superstitions that have heretofore been called " Witchcraft and Diabolism."

Many of the cases narrated by Dr. Kerner came immediately under his own supervision.

It was to his residence, that the afflicted peasant Grombach brought his unfortunate daughter Magdalene, a young girl who, from the weird notoriety obtained by her state of obsession, was named in the records of the time, "The Maid of Orlach." Of this case we must now give some details, as they afford a striking evidence of the difficulties which attend the investigation of psychological phenomena, unless it be understood that spirits can control susceptible human beings magnetically as well as mortals.

Kerner's narrative, considerably condensed, is as follows :—

"In the small village of Orlach, in Wurtemburg, lived a peasant named Grombach. He was a good Lutheran Protestant, and an honest, respectable man. He had four children, of whom his daughter, Magdalene—a lively, healthy, industrious girl—was one. In February, 1831, strange disturbances began to occur in the cow-house. The cows were found tied up in unusual ways and places. Sometimes their tails would be found plaited all together, and that with as much skill as if the finest lace weaver had executed the work. For some weeks these occurrences were repeated, but the most incessant watchfulness could never detect any human agency at work. About this time, Magdalene, whilst sitting milking, received a smart box on the ear, and her cap was struck off with so much violence, by invisible hands, that it flew against her father, who was attracted towards her by her cry. On several occasions, strange cats and birds came and went in the cow-house, no one knew from whence or whither.

"On the 8th of February, 1832, whilst Magdalene and her brother were cleaning out the cow-house, a clear fire was suddenly found to be burning in it. No combustible matter whatever was known to have been near the building; and though the flames were soon extinguished by the help of the neighbours, the origin of the fire was entirely unknown.

"The sudden bursting out of flames was repeated on the 9th, 10th and 11th of February, until—at the urgent request of Grombach—watchers were stationed in and around the premises day and night, notwithstanding which, flames broke out in different parts of the dwelling, obliging the poor family to empty it of all furniture; still the burning continued from time to time in the dismantled cottage.

"A few days after the last burning, Magdalene saw in the cow-shed, about eight in the evening, the grey shadowy form of a woman, whose head and body appeared closely swathed. Before she had time to cry for help, the figure said to her—in a strange, distant, though clear voice—'Remove the house; remove the house! If it be not removed before the 5th of March of next year, great misfortune will befal you. The house has been set on fire by an evil spirit; but unless it be pulled down before the 5th of March next year, I cannot protect you from great misfortune. Promise that the house shall be destroyed.'

"The girl, who seems to have rallied under the sense of a benign and protecting influence in this apparition, gave a promise to that effect. Grombach and his son were present at this interview. They heard Magdalene's words, and the sound of some distant voice as if in conversation with her, but they could neither distinguish what was said nor did they see the apparition. From this time, the female spirit frequently appeared to Magdalene, and always brought with her a sense of strange strength and protection. Magdalene loved her, and conversed with her without the slightest sentiment of fear. The spirit said she had been born at Orlach, in 1412; that she had been made a nun against her will, and had been guilty of many crimes, of which she could not then speak. She seemed very religious, but very sorrowful. She could read the girl's thoughts, but refused to tell why the house should be pulled down, or what was the cause of her grief. She often referred to a 'black spirit,' by whom she was bound in some mysterious way, and alleged that he was endeavouring to work great evil to the family, which she desired to prevent. This 'white spirit,' as Magdalene called her, often foretold events truly, and manifested a tender interest in all that concerned Magdalene.

"On St. John's day, when all the family were at church except Magdalene, who remained at home to prepare the dinner, she was startled by a loud explosion in the cow-house. She was about to rush out to see what had occurred, when she beheld close to her, on the hearth, a heap of yellow frogs.

"She was on the point of gathering them up in her apron, as a curiosity to show her parents on their return, when she heard a voice seeming to call up to her from the ground, 'Magdalene, let the frogs go,' when instantly they vanished.

"After this, a terrible time of persecution ensued. Magdalene was pursued everywhere by voices, scornful laughter, and frightful apparitions of animals of different kinds.

"At length, in mid-day, whilst she was haymaking, she encountered the apparition of a black man, who said to her, 'What does she want who comes to thee? Do not thou speak to her; but speak to me, and I will give thee the key to the cellar beneath thy house. There are eight firkins of wine there, and many rich things.' Then he laughed contemptuously and vanished. For several days during the season of haymaking, this black spirit appeared to the girl, trying to tempt her to answer him, and threatening her with all sorts of woes if she conversed any more with the white spirit, whom he spoke of as that 'bag of bones.' He tried to induce her to have mass said to keep the weather fine, though Magdalene and her family were all Protestants. He seemed to be dressed as a monk, and often alleged that he was one. He could imitate the voices of her neighbours, and often did so to induce her to answer him when he called her, but she was always conscious of his presence and mockery, and by the advice of her 'white angel' never answered him. He often jeered about her old father carrying a bible with him, and told her 'the mass was much finer and grander.'

"No language can do justice to the persecutions which the poor girl suffered from this terrible spirit. His voice was frequently heard by others as well as herself, mimicking the tones of her family or friends, and always calling upon her for answers: but her peculiar sensitiveness enabled her so to distinguish his voice, that she never answered him. He often predicted the future truly, and on one occasion promised to give her some money in proof of his friendship. The next evening, Magdalene and her sister being in the cow-house, a small bag fell suddenly from a beam, and on opening it they discovered several thalers and eleven gulden. No one could give any account of how the money came there, or who owned it. In the evening of the next day, the white spirit told Magdalene that her persecutor had placed the money there in fulfilment of one of his promises, but that she must not keep it, but give it to various charities.

"The spirit then added, that she should be rewarded for her obedience by having money really given her, with which she advised her to buy a hymn book. The day after this interview, Magdalene, with her father, hastened to the town of Hall to dispose of the money to the orphanage, and as she returned she was accosted by a shopkeeper, who enquired if she were not the wonderful peasant girl of whom he had heard so much.

"Magdalene modestly informed him of her name, when he begged her acceptance of a gulden *to buy a new hymn book with.*"

Many incidents of this kind are given in Kerner's narrative, showing the singular and antagonistic intelligences by which the young girl was besieged.

"At length her persecutor appeared to her in such frightful and monstrous shapes, that she frequently swooned from excessive fear, and it was in one of these cataleptic attacks that a new and most distressing phase of her enemy's power was made manifest. The girl affirmed, that a black and frightful monster would come and lay a cold icy hand on the back of her neck previous to the attacks, which now became frequent. Sometimes she would remain unconscious, cold, and rigid for hours. At others, she would strike violently at everyone who approached her, with the *left hand and foot*, which were icy cold, whilst the entire right side of her body was warm and quiescent.

"Her parents sent for doctors and clergymen, but all without effect. When questioned she would cry out, 'The black spirit! it is he that plagues me.' 'Where is he then?' the doctor would enquire; for answer, she would invariably strike at her left side with her right hand. That some most inexplicable but powerful effect was produced in the girl's system, all the reports of the medical men who were called in to attend her testify. Generally, the left side was cold, stiff, and unmanageable; the right warm, and perfectly natural. These states increased in strangeness and violence as the year progressed, until at last, according to her own account, the black spirit would enter her lifeless body, and cause her to rise up and speak in a hoarse bass voice, language that was only worthy of a demon.

"The doctors who were first called to attend her, treated her according to their custom with bleeding and leeches. In her somnambulic states she would frequently say to them, 'This will do no good. I am not ill. No physician can help me.' It was asked, 'Who then can help thee?' Then she would awake suddenly, and joyfully cry, 'I am helped; the white lady has helped me.' "

Dr. Kerner's report on this extraordinary case seems free from the exaggerated horrors of other narrators; yet his descriptions are sufficiently appalling. We quote his own words literally in the following statements.

" From this time "—about the 25th of August—" the white spirit told her in connection with many comforting texts of Scripture, that the black spirit must for a time gain full possession of her body, but that she would always be with her and conduct her soul to a place of safety, whilst the black spirit remained.

" Magdalene's own account of her frightful persecution was this:—She would see, even in the midst of her work, the outline of a monk's form, clothed in black; the face she could never clearly discern. Then she would hear him say, 'Wilt thou still give me no answer? Take care, I shall plague thee.' Then she would feel him press against her left side, and seize the back of her neck with five cold fingers.

" This was always her last conscious memory. From this time, she only spoke with the hoarse man's voice, and demoniacal speech of her tormentor. Generally, she lay with a face as livid as death—her eyes closed, the pupils when examined turned inwards, and the left foot and hand constantly moving up and down or extended to strike or menace. These attacks lasted from four to five hours, and on awakening a struggle of an extraordinary character would appear to ensue between her right and left sides. It must be noticed that the left side was always icy cold, though in constant motion, whilst the right was warm and quiescent.

" She never seemed to have any knowledge of the language used on these occasions, but would declare that she had been to church, and prayed and sung with the congregation.

"After this condition had lasted five months without alleviation, at my request, the poor girl was brought to my house.

" Whatever I might myself have thought, I never encouraged the idea to her parents, or the various physicians who examined her case, of 'demoniacal possession.'

" Still I felt compelled to pronounce her sufferings beyond the ordinary means of relief from medical treatment.

" I only prescribed for her myself, prayer, and spare diet. The magnetic passes which on a few occasions I tried to make, were immediately neutralized by the demoniacal power which impelled her to make counter-passes with her own hand.

" Thus mesmeric, and indeed every other mode of treatment, were unemployed by me, who recognized in her a *demoniacal magnetic* condition, and confided in the divination of the white spirit, who foretold her recovery on the 5th of March.

" Thus believing, I allowed her without anxiety, to return to her parents, convinced by long and careful observation, that there was not the slightest shadow of dissimulation about the young girl, nor was it possible to exaggerate the extraordinary, and obvious character of her attacks. I earnestly advised the parents to make no exhibition of their daughter's preternatural condition ; to keep her attacks as secret as possible, and call no one in to witness them. I believe it was not owing to any negligence on the part of the parents, to whom their daughter's condition was a great loss, as well as a serious affliction, but to the curiosity of the outer world, that crowds of inquisitive people streamed to the hitherto unknown village of Orlach, to see and hear the miraculous girl. In this, there was at least one good result, which was, the observation and testimony of so many astonished witnesses.

" One of these was an intelligent and scientific man, Pastor Gerber, who saw Magdalene in several of her attacks, and printed his observations on her case in the *Didaskalia.*

" On the 4th of March, whilst workmen were in course of pulling down the house, as the white spirit had incessantly commanded, that apparition suddenly stood before Magdalene. This time she was so radiant, and attired in such dazzling white robes, that the poor girl could scarcely dare to look upon her. She made a confession of her earthly sins through Magdalene's lips, alleging that she had been seduced by a monk, the 'black spirit,' and become the partner of his fearful crimes. She spoke through the entranced lips of Magdalene, of her centuries of suffering, penitence, firm reliance on the atonement of her Saviour, and the final termination of her long and weary penance. After a most affecting and ecstatic prayer, the White Spirit left her, and for the last time as it seemed she was possessed bodily by her foul tormentor. . . . From Sunday night until Tuesday at noon, the girl took no food, and remained unchanged, with the same signs of demoniacal possession before described.

During the Tuesday, an immense multitude assembled in Orlach, to witness the final demolition of the house, and question the demon. His language though still uttered in a man's bass voice, was religious and full of hope of redemption. He prayed in affecting terms, acknowledged that he had committed fearful crimes, but his term of earthly imprisonment was nearly ended.

" He described castles, and scenes in the country, of which the girl could have had no knowledge, and the accurate description he gave of the ancient monastery of Krailsheim, on the site of which Grombach's cottage and farm had stood, was pronounced by an antiquary present, to be perfectly correct. It was half-past eleven in the morning when the workmen engaged in the demolition of the house, came to an extremely ancient piece of masonry, which, on being removed, disclosed a large dry well, filled with rubbish, mixed with human bones, amongst which were the remains of several infants. These tokens, coupled with the confessions of the spirits speaking through Magdalene excited the most profound interest in the community at large.

" Magdalene herself had been removed to the house of a neighbour at some distance from the scene of her former home, but the crisis of her attack kept constant and faithful pace with the progress of the work, and just as the above-named ancient piece of masonry was discovered, the livid appearance of her face entirely changed to a bright and healthful glow. Her eyes opened, and never shall I forget the astonishing transformation she exhibited. Confused and amazed at seeing herself surrounded by so many strangers, the poor girl covered her face with her hands, and began to weep ; she soon recovered however, and became at once and entirely free from the monstrous obsession to which she had been subject for more than eighteen months.

"No return either of this obsession, nor the faculty of ghost-seeing was ever experienced. Mind and body alike were instantaneously restored to their normal condition of health and strength, and but for the theory of demoniacal possession, the case has been and must ever remain a paradox which the ordinary experiences of the physician can never explain."

Besides the curious facts connected with this case, Dr. Kerner relates many others of an equally striking character.

Of course it will be understood by every well-informed reader of Spiritual literature, that the most extraordinary illustration on record of German Spiritualism, or indeed of any country, is to be found in the history of Kerner's renowned "Seeress," Madame Frederica Hauffe of Prevorst, whose mediumship was not only spontaneous and wholly undesired, but whose philosophic teachings and doctrine of the spheres, deserve far more attention than has been generally accorded to them ; in fact, they antedate in some respects, and far excel in others, all that has since been demonstrated in the modern Spiritual movement.

The continual recurrence to the experiences of this famed Prevorst Seeress, in the writings of nearly all Spiritualistic authors, would render their repetition here tedious and unnecessary. We cannot close Dr. Kerner's invaluable record however, without adding one more narrative in which he was interested, although for special and private reasons it was not published among his other collected cases : —

SCENES FROM BEYOND THE VEIL.

" Some ten years ago there resided in New York, U.S.A., an aged lady of German birth the widow of an eminent American merchant, by name Madame Walter. This lady having become deeply interested in Spiritualism, communicated to Mrs. Hardinge Britten the particulars of her own early experience, at a period of her life when she had been a patient of the renowned German physician, philosopher, and writer, Dr. Justinius Kerner. The circumstances of her case were so remarkable that Dr. Kerner had noted them down with a view of incorporating them with other narratives of a kindred character, in a forthcoming volume. At Madame Walter's earnest request, her experiences, which seemed to her at that time too sacred to be entrusted to a cold materialistic world, were simply recorded in MSS. but not published. At the time when the strange tale was communicated to Mrs. Britten, the narrator deemed it her solemn duty to offer her record as a contribution to an age, better prepared than formerly to receive it. It need only be added, that in addition to the high and unimpeachable character of the venerable lady from whom Mrs. Britten received the history orally, she is also in possession of Dr. Kerner's MSS., from which she has already drawn some details for her published sketches, and which she now deems worthy of being presented in more complete form.

"Dr. Kerner stated that it was in the year 1827 that a medical friend of his, residing in the neighbourhood of Weinsberg, expressed a wish that he, Dr. Kerner, would take charge of a singular and interesting patient, a young lady who had been placed under his care for medical treatment.

"To this proposition Dr. Kerner assented, and thus he became acquainted with Mdlle. Olga Schwartzenberg, the daughter of the Baroness M——, of Vienna.

"At the age of twenty, Mdlle. Olga had become the victim of a severe nervous and epigastric disorder, which had determined her mother to send her to Weinsberg, to the care of her trusty family physician.

"The mother herself was a gay, heartless, fashionable widow, who had just contracted a second marriage with an immensely wealthy, but very aged man, the Baron M——, who had become captivated with the fair widow's remarkable personal attractions.

"Under the treatment of Drs. Kerner and Moran, Mdlle. Olga not only began to recover her health, but she displayed to a wonderful degree, the faculty of clairvoyance, and by the magnetic passes administered to her, became a somnambulist of extraordinary lucidity.

"In the magnetic sleep she could speak in several foreign tongues she had not studied; play on any instrument presented to her, though entirely unacquainted with music, and discourse most eloquently on various scientific subjects. Besides these interesting results of the sleep-waking condition, Mdlle. Olga, in her normal state, could see, and actually describe, the spirits of many deceased persons known to those around her, yet wholly strange to herself. Notwithstanding the peculiar excellence and accuracy of these descriptions, Mdlle. Olga treated the whole subject of spiritual existence with the utmost scorn and derision, and insisted on attributing the apparitions she perceived, to the reflex action of the minds of those with whom she came in contact.

"As this young lady had been brought up by a worldly-minded, atheistical mother, Dr. Kerner was at no loss to account for her total disbelief in immortality, and her contempt of all religious ideas; still it pained him to perceive that her rare gifts of seership made no other impression on her mind than to furnish food for ridicule, and denial of spiritual agency.

"It was on a certain night in October, 1827, that Mdlle. Olga was left by her physician in a peaceful magnetic sleep, her maid, Anna Matterlich, occupying a couch in an adjoining apartment, to restrain—as her mistress gaily alleged—any undue flights of her somnambulistic wanderings 'beyond the confined earth.'

"At a very early hour the next morning, Dr. Kerner was summoned in haste to attend his patient, and he then received from her pale lips the following astounding statement:—

"'Dr. Kerner,' she said, 'the sleep in which you left me must have been of very short duration, for the moment after your departure I became so wide awake that I heard, and could have counted the number of your retreating footsteps. At the instant that you closed the door behind you, I felt irresistibly impelled to rise from my bed, throw on a dressing gown, and seat myself by my writing-table. Whilst I sat, abstractedly gazing at the still blazing fire, to my unspeakable astonishment, my door was opened noiselessly and my mother entered the room, and without attempting to salute me, took a chair, and sat down by the fire on the opposite side to myself.'

"'If I was astonished at her unexpected appearance, I was still more so at the extraordinary change manifested in her person.'

"'Her dress—the splendid lace in which she was married to the Baron M——gave me the idea of a cold so intense that it froze my very marrow to look at her; indeed, I felt—though she did not complain, or shiver—that she was perishing with cold. I had always been accustomed to hear my mother spoken of as a very beautiful woman, and I had often gazed at her myself with admiring wonder; but oh! what a contrast did she now present to the loveliness which had so fascinated all beholders! Her hair was loose and hanging around her shoulders in disorder; but to my amazement I perceived that it was nearly all false, and from its lack of arrangement failed to conceal the grey locks which it was designed to hide. One cheek was coarsely patched with rouge, whilst the other was deadly pale. A set of false teeth was in her hand, and her neck and arms were only half smeared with enamel.'

"'I had never seen my mother at her toilette, and these disclosures fairly overwhelmed me, yet all this was forgotten, totally overlooked, whilst gazing on the unutterable expression of woe which marked every lineament of that wretched face. I had never seen despair, rage, and remorse so awfully depicted on a human countenance, nor did I deem it possible that those passions could find such a fearfully vivid expression.'

" ' I seemed to see, moreover,—and wonderful it was for me to perceive it,—my mother's entire past history, all written,—I could not tell how or where,—yet impressèd clearly upon her, and obvious to every eye. And, oh Heaven! may I never again witness the naked deformity of an ill-spent life, thus indelibly imprinted on the form!'

" ' Aghast and speechless, I listened in silence, whilst my mother spoke to me! but her very tones were changed, and instead of the soft silvery accents of other days, her voice was hollow and faint, and seemed to come from an illimitable distance off, and in no way to proceed from the forlorn figure that sat before me. It said: "Olga! I have come to tell you of a very, very terrible dream I have had, a dream you ought to know, and one which, if I had realised *before*, I should have been happier—happier now!" She sighed; —and oh, what a sigh of anguish was that!—then motioning me to the writing table by my side, she bade me take down the words she was going to speak.'

" ' Mechanically I obeyed her, when she continued as follows, speaking so slowly and with so many pauses, that, though I never seemed to possess the courage to address her, I was enabled to transcribe her words faster than she uttered them :—

" ' I was dressing, as you see, to go to court, when a sudden faintness seized me, memory fled, and consciousness only returned in the form of this horrible dream.'

" Here a shudder of agony seemed to shake her frame, and a long pause ensued.

" ' I found myself on the brink of a dreary, high cliff, overhanging a wild and stormy sea. The air was thicker and heavier than night; yet it was not night. All was lonely, wild, black, and dreary. It seemed as if I had stood in that awful solitude for ages, yet why or how I came there, I knew not.

" ' Suddenly, the ground rocked and parted beneath my feet. Shrieking in mortal terror. I caught at the earth, blades of grass, the very motes in the air, to stay my fall, but all in vain. Down—down—I was hurled! oh, how long I was in falling! Surely I must have spent years in that awful descent, for the whole of my past life, even to its minutest details, passed in solemn march before me as I fell. Not the vivid flashes of sudden remembrance, but the stately panorama of every year, hour, and minute unrolled itself before me as clearly as in the time when each event was enacted. I saw my own pale mother sinking into an early grave, but the bitter causes of that untimely death came with her; my disobedience, ingratitude, and desertion. Every unkind word or act of folly I had committed against her, was engraved on the funeral pall from which her faded form seemed to emerge.

" ' I saw dim effigies of young, timid hearts that my idle coquetries had broken. I saw the charms of beauty and intellect with which God had endowed me, first adorning, then disfiguring my own phantom likeness, with the semblance of reptiles and loathsome animals. I saw faces of many a weary drudge whom I had sacrificed to my service; and those who had bowed to me and cringed before me, now reviled me and pointed with foul grimaces to my unfinished toilette.

" ' All this and more, more than tongue can speak, I saw, and knew, and felt, during that tremendous fall.

" ' I tell you, girl, a thousand years must have passed in that downward flight. At length I landed—landed on a distant shore, where thick haze clouded at first my straining vision, and the cold winds swept around me with such a piercing, icy chill as I never dreamed to exist before.

" ' As I shrank and shivered in their tempestuous cruelty, myriads of ragged forms flitted before me, and I knew they were wretched creatures whom I had passed by unnoticed in my town drives, and then I wept to think I had never done anything to alleviate their misery. They mocked at me now, and then they passed away. I would have helped them, but the bitter blast sighed out, " *Too late! Too late!* "

" ' Lies I had spoken, and trivial follies long since forgotten, seemed now to assume tangible shapes, and rose up to meet me so palpably that I felt with shame and horror they were fastening themselves upon my form—my very dress, and would be seen and known by all beholders.

" ' I strove to hide myself for very shame, but millions of eyes were upon me, and all seemed to read me through and through.

" ' Then arose the wild and agonising wish, since I could not conceal my true self, that I were changed.

" ' I screamed aloud a frantic prayer to return to earth and lead a new life—do something, everything, over again, and be a better, truer, and purer woman. But again the bitter winds sighed out the doleful cry, ' *Too late! Too late!* ' In my despair I cried to those who surrounded me that I was not fit to be seen. I must and would be something better. And then I remembered what the priests had taught—how they had preached that the blood of Christ would cleanse the worst of sinners, and redeem all who believed in Him from the penalty so justly due to ill-spent lives. I had never believed this. I had never been taught to believe, but I would do so now; and then with frantic haste I sped on to find a priest. With the wish came the realisation. A celebrated minister of the Christian Church, long dead and gone, started up suddenly in my path, alive again, and offered me a crucifix. But, oh, horror! As I gazed upon this man I saw he was worse than I was. He was a hypocrite, a base deceiver, and his changing form was marred by the wild, despairing images of thousands of shipwrecked souls whom his false teachings had misled. Still, a shadowy hope was left. I would cling to the crucifix. Pictures of faithful believers thus redeemed flitted before my eyes; but even as with out-stretched arms I strove to clasp the image, it *spoke*, and in sweet, though relentless, tones it said, "Not everyone who saith unto me, Lord, Lord! but he who doeth the will of my Father, who is in heaven, he shall be saved." Then I shrieked out, "Is there then no salva-tion?" The answer came, "Work out thine own salvation." "But how?" "In action." "But," I cried again, "I am dead. There is no hope, no repentance after death." "There is no death," answered the voice, so still, so soft, yet so full of power that it seemed to fill the spaces of infinity. Confused and overwhelmed, yet still aroused and stirred by the strange new thought that there *might be progress* even beyond the grave, I asked, "Where, then, is hell?" No answer came, but yet I felt that answer, and it impelled me to look around through the murky air on the bleak and barren prospect, and the dreary stunted forms of beings on whose faces I read images of mis-spent lives like my own. Then I cried, "Lo, I am in hell, and I myself have made it!"

"'Then I *thought*, but did not dare to ask, of Heaven.

"'Thought in spirit life is action, reality, and with the thought came a view! Oh, that I could speak of the radiant visions that one brief glance presented!

"'The brightest and highest flights of ideality on earth fall short, far short, of that blooming, sunlit land, and the happy, lovely people that inhabit it. And yet I saw what they had been, as clearly as I saw the evil lives of *my* associates. Some had been crippled, blind, starved, worked to death, or worn out with cares and toils, but all had been true and faithful unto death, and good to one another. All those that dwell in those heavenly spheres, those lands of light and beauty, that even to look at for a single instant is worth a thousand years of suffering, had been kind, patient, brave, or helpful.

"'Oh, what a glory it was to look upon the good! Oh, that I had been good, ever so little! Oh, that I had left some record behind, to bless mankind! that single blessing would have saved me! But whilst I sighed in heaviness, with Milton's fallen angel, "Me miserable!" the sweet soft voice breathed in my ear: "Up and be doing! prepare, and commence thy life anew. Work out thine own salvation. Arise, and go to thy Father." I thought, for it was but a dream, Olga—I thought, and said, *I will arise:* and I did go, and I came here, as the first fruit of my new life and new resolution, for I found, that is, I *thought* I found, that the only way to help myself was by helping others, and so I came hither to warn my child; to tell her that not in church, in pulpit, or in the good deeds of another, does the path to heaven lie, but in her own strivings after good; in her deeds to her fellow mortals; in pure thoughts, good acts, kind words, and the motives for good which move us through every second of our mortal pilgrimage. Heaven and hell are states, my child. No foot can tread the path by which we reach them but our own; no mouthing hypocrite can teach us how to find the way, or save, or guide us, only the im-pulses to good and truth which God has given to every human soul, if we would but heed them. These are our saviours, Olga. Arise! and save thyself!"

"'She ceased, and gaining self-possession from the cessation of the agonising tones that had so long rung in my ear, I cried out—

"'Oh, mother! tell me one thing more. In the name of heaven, tell me how and when you came here!'

"'Raising my eyes as I spoke, I sought to meet her glance, but I gazed on vacancy. The empty chair alone remained; the pen, ink, and *wet writing* inscribed with the fearful tale were the only mementos that remained of that awful interview!'

"The lady concluded her narrative by adding, that after the disappearance of the appari-tion, she remembered no more until she found Dr. Kerner and her maid bending anxiously over her. As a sequel to this terrible vision, Dr. Kerner stated that the Baroness M—— died at Vienna, on the very night in question; she had been found at her toilet half dressed, but covered with blood. The sudden rupture of a blood vessel had robbed her of life, in the very act of preparing to ensnare all hearts in the meshes of her unreal charms.

"The appearance of the corpse in all respects corresponded to the apparition witnessed by the daughter, *even to the set of false teeth* still clutched in the hand of the mute but eloquent dead. It need only be added that to the last day of her earthly life Madame Walter's terrible vision bore fruits in her chastened spirit, by inciting her to ceaseless acts of benevolence, holy thoughts, and words of tender sympathy, which made all who knew her in life, and remembered her after death, 'rise up and call her blessed.'"

CHAPTER V.

SPIRITUALISM IN GERMANY (CONTINUED).

WONDERFUL PHENOMENAL PERSONAGES.

DURING the progress of the Spiritual movement, the desire to satisfy the many marvel seekers who crowd its ranks has no doubt induced those journalists whose business it is to administer to popular taste, to ransack the literature of the past for proofs of Spirit intercourse.

Thus there are very few well-attested cases but what have already found their way into print, and helped to feed man's craving appetite for additional wonders from the Spirit world.

At the risk of reiterating some experiences that have been already worn threadbare, the scope of this compendium obliges us to reprint such cases as will illustrate various phases of our subject occurring in different countries.

It is with this view that we now proceed to give a brief notice of the remarkable cures effected through the instrumentality of the celebrated Prince Hohenlohe, Archbishop of Grosswardein, in Hungary, and Abbot of St. Michael's Monastery at Gaborjan.

It must be understood that this eminent ecclesiastic attributed his great powers of healing to the special interposition of his "Lord and Saviour Jesus Christ." The excellent and amiable Arabian gentleman, Nathaniel Aymar, of whom Bayard Taylor and other Eastern travellers make mention, attributed cures just as remarkable as those of which we are about to write, to the influence of Mahomet. A very successful Chinese doctor of California, "Ah Sing," claimed to heal diseases only under the influence of Fo, and Dr. Valmour, a negro, of New Orleans, performed the most astonishing feats of healing solely through what he assured the author, was the influence of his father's spirit, who was a physician before him. The most renowned healers of America cite the names of divers spirits as the sources of their astonishing powers, and any number of Buddhists of whom the author has cognizance make cures by the influence of their God-man Buddha. To the one-idead sectarian of any shade of opinion it is necessary to preface our account of Prince Hohenlohe's cures with these remarks, lest we should be instrumental in deluding our readers concerning the real sources of that remarkable man's beneficent powers. The true scientist will be at no loss to find a common origin for all spiritual and magnetic potencies, and that independent of sect, creed, or clime.

The following particulars are taken from the autobiography of Prince Hohenlohe, of which a fine translation has been rendered by William Howitt. From this we learn that the Prince was born in 1794, and being destined for the church, filled many clerical positions of distinction in Olmütz, Munich, and Bamberg.

In 1820 he became acquainted with a peasant named Martin Michel, whom he met at a watering-place in the Duchy of Baden, and from whom he learned that the power of healing, "*through the name of Christ,*" was constantly practised by him, and could be exercised equally well by any other true Christian. The Prince relates the first cure he effected under the influence of his new friend Martin in the following terms :—

"At the commencement of the year 1826, I proceeded to Hapfort, to pay a visit to Prince Louis, heir to the crown of Bavaria. There finding Martin, I invited him to journey with me in my carriage to Würtzburg. On the morrow I paid a visit to Baron von Reinach, and when we were about to dine, the domestics carried in the young Princess Matilda of Schwartzenburg, who for eight years had not the power of walking, through paralysis. Touched with compassion for the poor cripple, who was placed at my side, I bethought me of Martin, who had cured me of a violent sore throat, and I said within myself that probably, if the Princess had firm confidence in the help of the Saviour, Martin could cure her likewise.

"On the 21st of June, after performing mass, I felt myself irresistibly impelled to hasten to the Princess, and tell her that if she had a firm reliance on the promise of Jesus Christ she could be healed. I went to the Princess, accompanied by Martin Michel, and leaving him in the ante-chamber, was shown into the apartment of the Princess, whom I found reclining on a bed, enveloped as it were in a mass of machinery. After the usual salutations I said to her, 'My dear cousin, God is able to help you through Jesus Christ His Son, and I have brought with me a pious peasant, at whose prayer God has already succoured the afflicted. If you are willing I will call him in, that he may pray for you.'

" 'With all my heart,' replied the Princess, whereupon I called Michel.

"After some words addressed to the invalid, Martin commenced praying, but it is necessary to have seen him to have a just idea of the depth of fervour with which he prayed. I avow on my own part that I threw myself on the ground in supplication also. The prayers ended, I felt a secret power which I could not explain nor resist, which impelled me to say in a loud voice to the Princess, 'In the name of Jesus Christ arise and walk !'

"As I pronounced these words, ever memorable to me, the Princess was not only able to rise, which she had not done for eight years, but to walk with perfect ease and strength.

"The rumour of this event was quickly spread, and I was surrounded by invalids. I say nothing of the number of such facts as then took place, for it is not for me to speak of them."

The Princess it seems walked to church on the following Sunday, to the astonishment of the whole community, and in sight of multitudes who for years had been accustomed only to see her reclining in a carriage, or borne in the arms of attendants.

The next notable cure was performed by the Prince alone, and it took place on the person of Louis, Crown Prince of Bavaria, the well-known monarch of that country, and the liberal patron of arts and sciences in Munich.

The following letter, although it has often appeared in print before, is selected for quotation in this place, because it bears a testimony which none can question to the powers of the celebrated Therapeutist. It was written by Prince Louis of Bavaria, and is as follows :—

"TO THE COUNT VON SINSHEIM.

"MY DEAR COUNT,—There are still miracles. The last ten days of the month the people of Würtzburg might believe themselves in the days of the Apostles.

"The deaf hear, the blind see, the lame freely walk, not by the aid of art, but by means of a few short prayers, and the invocation of the name of Jesus Christ. The Prince of Hohenlohe demanded only faith in Jesus Christ to heal the sick ; but this faith was an indispensable condition.

"On the evening of the 28th the number of persons cured amounted to more than seventy. These were of all classes, from the humblest to a prince of the blood, who, without any exterior means, recovered the hearing which he had lost from his infancy.* This cure was effected by a prayer made during some minutes by Prince Hohenlohe, a priest of only twenty-seven years of age.

---

*Prince Louis here speaks of himself and his own cure.

" . . . In my ante-chanber, the Prince twice unsuccessfully pronounced his prayer for a woman who had been blind for twenty-five years, but at the pressing solicitation of the woman, he prayed a third time, and she recovered her sight.   . . .

"The inhabitants of Würtzburg have testified by the most lively acclamations the pleasure which my cure has given them.   You are at liberty to communicate this letter, and to allow any one who wishes it to take a copy of it."

"Louis, Prince Royal.

"Bruckenau, July 3rd, 1822. "

Whilst no honest reader can fail to admire the manly candour with which Prince Louis testified to those marvels, which many a cowardly ingrate would have kept secret, and many an interested bigot would have tried to smother up, the scientist might suggest the pertinent enquiry, why the Prince's prayers could not cure the blind woman mentioned in the above letter until the third repetition.

It could not have been for lack of *faith* on the part of the patient, because it was at her pressing entreaty that the third prayer was offered.

Was the good healer's "Saviour" harder to be entreated in this poor woman's case than in that of the Crown Prince, who was cured instantane-ously, and upon the strength of the first prayer offered ?

If we were called upon to solve such a problem through magnetic and psychologic laws our difficulties would be explained at once.   We should perceive in this, as in many other instances, that special and continuous applications of the good healer's force were required, whilst in the Prince's case a mere shock, or primary exertion of will, was all that was needed.

Meantime, those who insist upon calling in "the Lord Jesus" as the sole agent of cure, could not deny that he was somewhat partial, and not always just, for the memoirs of Prince Hohenlohe prove that there were occa-sional failures, although all that came appeared to have been "full of faith and the holy spirit."

Professor Onymus, of the University of Würzburg, himself an eye-witness of Prince Hohenlohe's wonderful operations, has given the following account of them :—

" Prince Hohenlohe cures the sick by his prayers.   From all sides they bring the sick, the blind, the lame, deaf, and dumb to his door.   The victims of every evil that afflict humanity besiege the house where he stays, and it is not without great trouble, and by the assistance of the police, that you are able to get to him.   Notwithstanding, he never seems fatigued.

" He never refuses his aid to any one, even to the poor, or mendicants with the most disgusting complaints.

" When he quits the house, it is not to carry alleviation to the palaces of the great ; he goes in preference to the cabins of the poor.   When he prays we see that the prayer comes from the bottom of his heart, and that with so much fervour, that he oftentimes seems ready to sink with exhaustion."

As we cannot do justice to one tenth of the laudatory notices that were written of the Prince's marvellous cures, we must conclude by selecting a few of the notable cases recorded by Legation Councillor Scharold, who, like many other distinguished personages of the time, wrote of what he himself was an eye-witness to.

" Elizabeth Laner, cured of a rheumatic affection of the nerves, which made her a helpless cripple of twenty-five years' standing.

" Captain Ruthlein, of Thundorf, seventy years of age, and Fraülein Fegelim, upwards of seventy, both cured of total paralysis, and able to use every limb and organ freely.

" Michal Dinsenbacher, aged twenty-four, for three years suffered dreadful agonies with an abscess of the chest, and caries of bones. Patient of hospital, cured on the spot, and at work in the fields the next day.

"Two lame men, carried in arms into the house of Aulic Councillor Martin, total paralysis,—cured on the spot.

"The widow Balzano, and another woman of Narstadt, blind ; one for twenty-five, another, nineteen years ; cured at the Legation office of Counsellor Scharold."

It would be needless to pursue this list farther.

Prince Charles of Bartenstein, in a letter to his father, dated August 18, 1821, expresses his amazement at the cures which he himself had witnessed in the chapel at Bruckenau, where he declares, "four hundred blind, deaf, dumb, and paralytic people &c., &c., were instantaneously and completely cured." A vast number of thoroughly attested cases were collected and published in 1825 in the German papers.

At the solicitation of *the medical faculty of Germany* however, the Government at length *forbade these operations ;* and Prince Hohenlohe retired to Austria, where he continued his divine work until his death, which took place in his fifty-fifth year, at Böslon, near Vienna.

Among the great variety of manifestations recorded by the American Spiritual journals, none have excited more interest than the appearance of letters, names, and figures on the flesh of the mediums, thus affording incontrovertible evidence both of the intelligence which arranges the characters, and of a new and wonderful phase of chemistry, involved in their production.

Not to depreciate the value of such a curious form of supra-mundane agency, but to show its accordance with some unknown law at work in various directions, we point to one or two remarkable cases of " stigmata," many of which have been indisputably attested on the Continent of Europe. Our German illustration of this singular phase is the celebrated Katherine Emerick, the nun of Dülmen, of whom we give the account published by Herr Clemens Von Brentano, who visited the Ecstatic, and observed her case for many years. He says—

" The most remarkable features of this case were—a bloody crown encircling the head ; marks of wounds in the hands, feet and side, and two or three crosses on the breast. These, and the mark round her forehead, often bled, the latter usually on Wednesday, and the former on Friday, and with such obstinacy, that very often heavy drops ran down. This statement has been subscribed to by numerous physicians, and others also who have visited her.

" In 1820 the Ecclesiastical Board visited Dülmen several times, and found the facts more or less to agree with the published reports.

" On the breast was found a double cross, in red connected lines. The bleedings had developed for years, and all accounts agree that they could not have been produced by any known applications from without. They have been continually watched for days, and washed by physicians, but never varied in appearance, nor could they be accounted for on any known physiological cause. Katherine appeared to have been a highly sensitive devout person from childhood.

" In one of her numerous visions she informed her confessor that she had a vision of the Saviour, who appeared to her as a radiant youth, offering her a garland with the left hand and a crown of thorns with the right. She seized the latter, and pressed it to her brow, but on regaining outward consciousness she felt a severe pain encircling her head, accompanied by drops of blood. Soon after this, in 1802, she entered the convent at Dülmen.

" About 1814 her case became generally known, through a pamphlet published by her attending physician. Still later she submitted — though reluctantly — to an official investigation, and though she always desired most earnestly to be left in strict retirement, she yielded patiently to any form of investigation that could throw light on her wonderful case."

The celebrated naturalist, Count Stolberg, visited Katherine in 1821, and from his account we learn that for many months at a time, her whole nourishment consisted of water and small portions of an apple, plum, or cherry, daily. She was subject to trances, and fasts prolonged for incredible periods of time. She often spoke in trance, in strange and beautiful language. Her prevision, knowledge of character, distant events and places, was astonishing, and her cheerfulness, piety, and resignation excited the admiration of all around her. Early on the Friday morning, the thorn wounds on her head began to bleed; later in the day the eight wounds on her hands and feet commenced bleeding. No artist could have more accurately painted the crown and crosses, and no matter what pains were taken to wipe off the drops of blood, they continued to flow throughout the entire day. She had many remarkable spiritual gifts, and besides the phenomena already described, her clairvoyant perceptions were constant and most penetrating. Ennemoser, in his "History of Magic," relates many other equally remarkable and well attested cases of Stigmata, none of which are more striking in the persons of religious ecstatics than that which has recently attracted the attention of the Continental world, in the person of a poor servant girl of Belgium, of whom the following account is rendered by Father Johann Weber, a Dominican physician, who was sent by the Bishop of the Diocese to the village of Bois d'Haisne, in Belgium, to investigate the case :—

The Dominican's visit is described in the Roman Catholic *Tablet* of 1869 in the following words :—

"He arrived at the village of Bois d'Haisne, at the house of the Lafans, about one o'clock in the day. Louisa was at that very moment in one of her mysterious trances; but the venerable Provincial was only disposed to doubt, since her appearance was perfectly natural. However, the parish priest who accompanied him soon convinced him of the reality, by shaking her violently, and then sticking pins into her arms and legs without producing the smallest effect upon her; nor did blood flow from the punctures, though they were deep. Finding that she was entirely insensible, they proceeded to examine her hands and feet, in which they found the distinct marks of the *stigmata*. There were also marks of the crown of thorns round her head, but there was no trace of blood in any of the wounds. After about a quarter of an hour's observation, the priest recalled her to consciousness by the simple words, "Well, Louisa." She opened her eyes quite naturally, and then saw the Provincial. The priest explained to her that he had been sent by the bishop to investigate the matter. In answer to his enquiry as to what she had seen in her ecstacy, she replied that she had been assisting in the bearing of the cross. He was very much struck both with her simplicity and ignorance. She was merely a peasant girl, and nothing more. The priest having left the house, the Provincial resolved to remain and watch the case; but that he might not appear to be doing so, he took out his breviary and began to say his office. He remarked only that she turned to the east, and that her expression was one of singular modesty and reflection. At a little before two o'clock she gave a deep sigh and lifted up her hands. Soon her watcher perceived a stream of blood to issue from the wound in her left hand, which could not have been caused by any instrument or other agency, as she had not moved from her arm-chair, and her hands did not touch each other. Tears flowed from her eyes and fell unheeded on her cheek. Her expression changed to one expressing great anguish, a kind of foam escaped from her lips and filled her mouth. At a quarter to three she fell, her arms being extended in the shape of a cross. Her sister ran to put cloths under her head and feet, the former being lifted with great difficulty. Her face was warm, but her hands and feet were icy cold as if dead, while the pulse apparently ceased to beat. At three o'clock she moved, crossing her feet a little, and assuming exactly the attitude of Christ on the cross. Thus she remained until four o'clock, when she suddenly rose, knelt with clasped hands, and seemed to pray with the utmost fervour. Her body during this time appeared as if it scarcely touched the ground. After about ten minutes she seated herself again in the arm chair, resuming her attitude of modest recollection, and the Provincial thought she would soon be herself again; but the most curious phenomena were yet to come. After a few seconds her expression became painfully distressed; she lifted her arms again in the shape of a cross, sighing heavily, and greenish foam again escaping from her mouth, while the mark of the crown of thorns on her head became more and more distinct. Suddenly she burst forth in a loud cry, and bowed her head. At that moment her body had all the appearance of death; her face was deadly pale, and even cadaverous; her lips were black and livid; her eyes glassy, open, and apparently without life. A few moments after, the colour returned to her cheeks, and her face assumed an expression of intense beatitude. The parish priest came back at this moment, and taking a lamp of petroleum, put it close to her eyes without her perceiving it. The Provincial pricked her feet, both on the soles and on the upper parts, without her feeling it in the smallest degree. At a quarter past six she suddenly became perfectly natural, the pulse began to beat as usual, and she was "herself" again. She had no recollection of anything she had herself done during her ecstacy. She seemed to think little or nothing of these extraordinary visions, and did not attribute to herself any merit or holiness in consequence. She is a tertiary of St. Francis, but knows very little of his history. In answer to some questions which were put to her, she replied that she had never been spoken to by Our Lord, and that she had seen the evil one under various forms; when she mentioned him she was filled with great fear.

"The following morning she was at the parish church, and received the communion at the hands of the Provincial with great reverence. The priest's housekeeper being absent, she came to the presbytery to prepare breakfast. The Provincial was struck with her brisk, healthy appearance, and could scarcely imagine that he beheld in the bright, simple servant girl the Extatica who, in a few hours, probably, would be again undergoing the mysterious conformity to the Passion above described."

Of stone-throwing, hauntings, or the disturbances which in Germany are commonly attributed to the "Polter Gheist," we have so many accounts, and the manifestations so nearly resemble each other, that it would be tedious to repeat them.

Almost every reader of Spiritual literature is familiar with the accounts published by Brevior, Howitt, Owen, Mrs. Crowe, &c., concerning the hauntings in the Castle of Slawensik, in Upper Silesia, especially those which occurred to Councillor Hahn and his friend Cornet Kern.

Dr. Dörfel, a physician resident at Hamburgh, quite recently sent the author a numerously-signed document, containing accounts, known to and witnessed personally by the signers, of manifestations which tally almost exactly with those in the Castle of Slawensik. These hauntings followed the family of Dr. Dörfel for a period of more than three years, during which he removed from Darmstadt, Berlin, and Bonn, in the hope of avoiding them. They came in the shape of frightful apparitions, groanings, shrieks, poundings, throwing of missiles, movements of heavy furniture, &c., and had been witnessed by Madame Dörfel and her two daughters, besides about one hundred different persons, neighbours of the suffering and afflicted family, who had been called in at various times and places in the vain hope of exorcising the persecutors who tormented them.

In answer to Dörfel's statement sent to the author, the latter advised him to form circles, and endeavour to communicate with the invisible persecutors, on the generally pursued system of American Spiritualists. This advice being followed, proved successful.

During the year 1870, the harassed family succeeded in communicating by raps and planchette writing, with the Polter Gheist, and a number of his weird associates. In this way they learned a terrible history of crime and wrong, involving persons of high position, of whom it would now be injudicious to write. The spirits represented that they only attached themselves to the doctor's family because they found in its members the requisite medium power. The communications soon grew orderly; the criminal spirits manifested penitence and desire for progress, after which the hauntings entirely ceased. In all probability, hundreds of similar cases would be thus explained and terminated, if those who are cognisant of them, would only enter upon a systematic method of communing with the invisibles, on the plan of the modern spirit circle.

From the reports of M. Kalodzy, the author of several valuable works on mineralogy, mining, engineering, &c., we have received a curious collection of narratives concerning the knockings which are so common in Hungarian and Bohemian mines. M. Kalodzy says, these knockings have been repeatedly heard by him and the pupils that he—as a teacher in the Hungarian School of Mines—has introduced there, and that many of the miners are so accustomed to the signals of their "Kobolds" that they would not like to work in any direction against which the knockers warn them. In Northern Germany, these knockings are quite common in mines, and are attributed to the *Berg-geister*, or spirits of mountains and mines.

From Mdme. Kalodzy, the writer of "Rambles in the Hartz Mountains," and "The Clock Makers of the Forest," &c., the author of this work has received the following account of these "Kobolds" or spirits, as witnessed by Madame Kalodzy and three companions, who spent a week in the hut of a peasant, one Michael Engelbrecht, in whose family the Kobolds seem to have been perfectly familiar :—

"On the three first days after our arrival," said Madame K——, "we only heard a few dull knocks, sounding in and about the mouth of the mine, as if produced by some vibrations of very distant blows, but when on the third evening Michael came home from work, he brought us the welcome intelligence that his friends, the Kobolds, had promised by knockings to make us a visit. This we were right glad of, as Dorothea, our Michael's wife, had expressed her fears that they might be shy of so many strangers, and would not appear, unless we spent some hours in the mine.

"We were about to sit down to tea when Mdlle. Gronin called our attention to a steady light, round, and about the size of a cheese plate, which appeared suddenly on the wall of the little garden directly opposite the door of the hut in which we sat.

"Before any of us could rise to examine it, four more lights appeared almost simultaneously, about the same shape, and varying only in size. Surrounding each one was the dim outline of a small human figure, black and grotesque, more like a little image carved out of black shining wood, than anything else I can liken them to. Dorothea kissed her hands to these dreadful little shapes, and Michael bowed with great reverence. As for me and my companions, we were so awe-struck yet amused at these comical shapes, that we could not move or speak until they themselves seemed to flit about in a sort of wavering dance, and then vanish, one by one."

The narrator went on to say, that she and her husband have since both heard and seen these little men, who always come and go very suddenly ; appear as above described in the shadowy image of diminutive black dwarfs about two or three feet in height, and at that part which in the human being is occupied by the heart, they carry the round luminous circle first described, an appearance which is much more frequently seen than the little black men themselves.

Mr. Weske, a wealthy and intelligent German gentleman of San Francisco, has related to the author a graphic account of his discovering a fine gold lode by aid of these knocking mining spirits. Mr. William Howitt, in an article on the *Berg-Geister*, written some years ago for the *London Spiritual Magazine*, says :—

"We know that the miners of Germany and the North have always asserted, and do still assert, the existence of Kobolds and other *Berg-geister* or spirits of the mountains and mines, and that they assist or thwart their exertions in quest of ore, as they are irritated or placated."

The miners describe them as short, black, and declare that when they are attached to certain miners they go before them in the solid subterranean rock, knocking with their hammers, and thus indicating the presence of metal and the devious course of the vein. If it is lost by a break in the strata, or "fault" as they call it, the sound of the *Berg-geister's* hammer directs where again to seek it, and when there is a busy and energetic thumping of many hammers, it is the certain announcement of abundant ore. Not caring in this plain matter of fact compendium to enter more fully into the vexed question of sub-human spiritual intelligences, we shall treat no more on what is termed by the Occultists "elementary existences." As abundance of testimony on this question can be found in other writings, we must return to our narrative of phenomena which may be attributed to the agency of human spirits, or originate in the realms of magnetism and psychology.

It may not be uninteresting to the student of Spiritualistic phenomena to learn, that besides the instances of levitation recorded of Mr. D. D. Home, and other physical media of the New Dispensation, several spontaneous cases of this kind are on record.

The following brief article is selected from many other illustrations of this phase of sptrit power, because it comes from respectable and authentic sources.

A correspondent in the *Journal de Frankfort*, of September, 1861, writes as follows :—

To the Editor of the "Spiritual Magazine."

"We read in the *Gegenwart of Vienna* that a Catholic Priest was preaching before his congregation last Sunday in the Church of St. Mary, at Vienna, on the subject of the constant protection of angels over the faithful committed to their charge, and this in words of great exaltation, and with an unction and eloquence which touched profoundly the hearts of numbers of the congregation. Soon after the commencement of the sermon, a girl of about twenty years of age showed all the signs of ecstacy, and soon, her arms crossed upon her bosom, and with her eyes fixed on the preacher, she was seen by the whole congregation to be raised gradually from the floor into the air, and there to rest at an elevation, of more than a foot, to the end of the sermon. We are assured that the same phenomenon had happened several days previously at the moment of her receiving the communion."—*Journal de Frankfort*, Sept. 6, 1861.

This remarkable occurrence was also testified of by the late Baron de Palm, who was present on the occasion, and himself related it to the author. In connection with this event, Baron Kirkup, of Florence, a well known and esteemed correspondent of the *London Spiritual Magazine*, writes to the Editor in the following terms :—

"This is a confirmation of my friend Mr. Home's repeated elevation, of which there are a thousand witnesses. I possess eight engravings from different copperplates of a similar elevation of Pope Pius VII. There is this inscription :

"' *Pius Sept. Pont. Max.*
Savonæ in Ecstasim iterum raptus die Assumptionis B. V. M.
15*th Augusti*, 1811.'

"I have two ancient prints of different risings in the air of St. Catherine of Sienna ; one inscriptisn is :

"' *Sublime per echstasim rapta divina arcana contemplatur,*' &c.

"I believe many of your friends know

"Your obedient servant,

"Florence, 15 October, 1861.   SEYMOUR KIRKUP."

From the letters of an esteemed Spiritualist of Baden Baden, Col. Kyd, a gentleman who, in connection with his amiable lady's Planchette writing, has done much to stimulate investigation into Spiritual matters throughout many of the most fashionable circles of Germany, the author learned accounts concerning a certain Pastor Blumhard, which have since been verified by several persons who have visited that gentleman, and published details of his wonderful achievements. Pastor Blumhard resides at Boll, near Gappingen in Würtemberg, and is a noble-minded enthusiast, whose life, in a more limited sphere than that of the excellent Pastor Oberlin, still greatly resembles it. M. Blumhard performs many marvellous cures by the laying on of hands, having in one instance cured completely an unfortunate woman, a parishioner of his, of an immense wen. The report of this extraordinary case attracted so much attention to the good Pastor, that he was visited from far and near, by great numbers both of the curious and afflicted of earth. M. Blumhard not only cures the sick, but he administers to the miserably poor, of whom his parish is full, by presents of fruit, vegetables, wine, and provisions of all kinds. These his narrow means could never enable him to purchase, but all his great benefactions, though procured through human means, are generally brought to him by entire strangers, and always in answer to prayer. Hundreds of persons report that they have been compelled by a power they could not resist, to send presents of clothes, or food, to Pastor Blumhard. On these occasions it is invariably found that some poor needy parishioner has besought the prayers of the good Pastor for precisely the articles sent in. Like Müller, of Bristol, England, the philosophy of this life of prayer and faith is easily understood by the student of magnetism and psychology, but as in Müller's case, Pastor Blumhard's religion alone is held responsible for the Divine response. Be it as it may, a good work is accomplished, and an humble German priest is the instrument through whom it is wrought. A few such evidences of Christian faith in action, would do more to prove the truth and value of Christianity, than the Pope of Rome and all his Cardinals, or the barren fruitless sermons of the whole Bench of English Bishops.

CHAPTER VI.

SPIRITUALISM IN GERMANY (CONCLUDED.)

To the writings of Kerner, Ennemoser, Eschenmayer, and their cotemporaries, we must refer our readers for further details concerning the subjects treated of in the last chapter, meantime it needs no reiteration to show that all the spiritual phenomena now so generally known throughout the world, were quite familiar amongst the Germans during the entire of this century

Even the inspiration exhibited on the public rostrum, for which American Spiritualism has been so specially and justly celebrated, has not been wanting in the nineteenth-century marvels of German Spiritualism. In proof of this we cite the case of the celebrated Baroness Von Krüdener, a Prussian lady of high birth, who for more than twenty years, during the stormiest days of revolutionary strife on the Continent of Europe, that is, from 1793 to the period of her death in 1824, deemed herself called upon to quit the brilliant life of the *salon*, and the attractions which her rank and station offered, in order that she might preach a gospel of peace and purity, in the presence of warlike and violent men, many of them the contending generals, princes, and potentates who ruled the destinies of Europe.

A prophetess and orator of the most remarkable power, this beautiful and accomplished lady pursued her mission in despite of threats, dangers, and captivity.

The following anecdote will suffice to show the great power she wielded over the most influential personages of her time.

In William Howitt's charming biography of the Baroness Von Krüdener, when describing the chaotic state of Europe during the Napoleonic wars, he says :—

"One evening the Emperor Alexander of Russia who had been making his way across Bavaria wearily for days, through crowds of exulting people who looked upon him as a saviour, entered an hotel at Heilbronn borne down by fatigue." "He shut himself up in his room, filled with deep and painful reflections.

"Alexander is supposed to have been aware of the intended murder of his father, the Emperor Paul, and despite his wish to become his people's benefactor, he could not rise above the dark memories that haunted him.

"He himself relates that he had just exclaimed aloud, "Oh, that some holy soul might be sent to me, who could solve the great enigma of my life and destiny!" when the door opened, and Prince Wollonsky, entreating pardon for the intrusion, announced, that Madame Krüdener waited without, and would insist upon seeing His Imperial Highness.

"'Madame Krüdener!' replied the Emperor, 'then surely she comes in answer to my prayer; let her enter.' Madam Krüdener had met the Emperor before, and won his confidence by her marvellous spirit of prophecy, fearless love of truth, and simple piety.

"For three long hours the noble lady counselled with the tempest-tossed soul of the monarch.

"He himself declared, 'she spoke music to his spirit, and brought him a peace which no other on earth could give.' Before she quitted him, she declared, she had come to plead the cause of the starving peasantry of Russia, famine-stricken and perishing, from the ravages of the armies that had passed through the land, and consumed all their means of subsistence.

"The representations of this admirable woman were effectual, as Alexander exhausted his resources in sending provisions to the sufferers, and relieving to the utmost extent of his power those, for whom the good Baroness had so ably pleaded."

Referring to Madame Krüdener's subsequent residence in Paris, in the eventful year 1815, her biographer says :—

"Here then we reach a point in our heroine's life, which fixed upon her the eyes and wonder of all Europe.

"Three times a week, she held religious meetings, which were attended by all the princes, nobles, and great generals of Europe. There, in a simple black, or dark blue dress, with her hair cut close, and although past fifty, retaining traces of her former singular beauty, she addressed the assembled potentates in the most exalted strains of eloquence.

"She exhorted them to put an end to the horrors of war, and inaugurate true Christianity, by peace on earth, and good will to men.

"It was a strange spectacle, to see those who commanded the destinies of Europe sitting humbly at the feet of this inspired woman.

"Madame Von Krüdener, by the wonderful fulfilment of her predictions, and the inspiration of her preaching, had herself become one of the powers of Europe, and for a time, there is no doubt, that she actually directed the movements of the allied princes."

Few who read this description will fail to recognize in it, the characteristics which—with all due allowance for difference in surrounding circumstances—distinguish the "trance-speaking mediums" of America, who, like Madame Krüdener, have become an irresistible power in the circle of their special ministrations.

Up to the last quarter of a century, despite the universality with which spiritual gifts were manifested in individual cases, the tendency to materialism on the one hand, and intolerance on the other, succeeded in repressing the public advance of Spiritualism in Germany. No better illustration of this Teutonic conservatism can be given, than the antagonistic reception that was accorded to Baron Von Reichenbach's brilliant discoveries, in what he termed " Odylic or Od Force."

Although Reichenbach's treatises on "Od Force," have been made familiar to English readers by Dr. Ashburner's fine translation, it may not be amiss to explain in brief the nature of Reichenbach's discoveries. This indefatigable scientist procured the aid of a large number of " Sensitives," or what would now be termed, clairvoyants or spirit mediums.

These persons he placed in dark rooms, and then submitted to their spiritual sight, magnets, shells, crystals, minerals, animals, human hands, and a great variety of animate and inanimate objects, known only to himself, but detected by the Sensitives, through the flames or luminous appearances, that each substance gave forth.

These flames differed in colour, size, and intensity, according to the nature of the object examined, but as large numbers of persons fully corroborated each other's observations, and the Baron's experiments were conducted for years, with the most persevering attention, he conceived himself justified in arriving at the conclusion, that from every object in the human, animal, vegetable, and mineral kingdoms, there emanated a force which could be detected under favourable conditions, as flames, or luminous appearances, and whilst some observers were disposed to regard these as the universal life of things, he (Reichenbach) for special reasons defined them in his writings as " Odyle," or " Od Force."

Whatever name or style Von Reichenbach, Mesmer, Galvani, Volta, Newton, Paracelsus the Rosicrucian, or Geber the Alchemist, may have thought proper to give to the "force," or "element," of which they discoursed, the intelligent reader will be at no loss to correlate all such forces, and resolve them into the one all-pervading *life principle of the Universe.*

It would be needless to enter upon further details of Von Reichenbach's discovery, to which no mere summary could do justice; it is enough to say that when he first gave the result of his researches to the world, instead of winning the applause and gratitude of his countrymen, he simply drew down upon himself an amount of insult and contempt, of which the most unenlightened age might have been ashamed.

In 1865, the first regular journal devoted to Spiritualism was published in Germany, under the title of *Psyche.* A contemporary French paper makes the following notice of this periodical in connection with the Baron Von Reichenbach's discoveries.

"*Psyche* is the only German paper treating of Spiritualism, odic force, and other kindred subjects. It is published monthly, and its chief editor is H. A. Berthelea, D.M., Zittan, Saxony. Since this excellent little periodical was commenced, many fine works have been contributed to the treasury of spiritual literature, prominent amongst which stands a noble spiritual journal conducted by the eminent Russian Councillor Hon. Alexander Aksakof, entitled, *Psychische Studien.* It was first published at Leipzig, in 1874, since when it numbers amongst its contributors the honoured names of the Baron and Baroness von Vay, Prince Emil Wittgenstein; Professors Maximilian Perty, Wagner, Fichte, and a long list of potentates and scientists of high standing and distinguishad ability."

For a more detailed account of its editor Alexander Aksakof, and the great services he has rendered to the cause of human progress, we must refer our readers to our section on Russian Spiritualism.

Amongst the most distinguished supporters of the movement in Germany, we would again mention the Baroness von Vay, a highly-gifted seeress; also Colonel and Mrs. Kyd, of Baden Baden; His Imperial Highness Nicholas, Duke of Leuchtenberg; the late amiable and lamented Princess Alice of Darmstadt, the Barons Holmfeld, Guldenstubbe, and de Palm, and many other celebrated Spiritualists of distinction.

Still, Spiritualism as a cause, made but little public progress until the advent of the Davenports, Henry Slade, and other mediums from America, who, by their professional announcements, compelled the press to notice the subject, and draw forth investigators from the privacy of the *salon*, to the arena of public discussion.

There are many reasons for believing that the demonstrations that had already been published abroad, in the shape of hauntings, obsessions, &c., had tended to repel rather than attract investigators.

Thus, about 1865, when Spiritualism had completely captivated the American, and British mind, and in France, no less than six spiritual journals were liberally supported, Germany could only boast of the periodical before mentioned, called *Psyche*.

About 1867, several works in exposition of Spiritualism were put forth at Vienna, and found a rapid sale in the establishments of Lechner and Wenedikt.

Reports of American spirit photographs being taken, and stirring accounts of the phenomena produced through the mediumship of the celebrated Mr. D. D. Home, and Rollin Squire of America, were published in tract form, and widely circulated.

The *séances* of the above named gentlemen being given non-professionally, were of course limited only to the favoured few with whom they were guests. Still the accounts of the marvels enacted in their presence, stimulated public curiosity to the highest pitch. About this time, several other works on the subject of Spiritualism were put forth, amongst them, a fine treatise on the Science of Soul, by Dr. Epps. This *brochure* became so popular, that the publishers could hardly keep pace with the demand.

Private circles too began to multiply rapidly, but the chief impetus given to a wide-spread interest in the cause of Spiritualism, was unquestionably due to the agency so much, and so unwisely denounced by many leaders of the Spiritual ranks, namely, professional mediumship.

The distinguished services rendered to the cause by Mr. D. D. Home, were, as above remarked, confined to such influential personages as sought this gentleman's society, in the character of a friend and equal.

The deliberate investigation of the subject, requisite for scientific experiments, could not be conducted in the presence of monarchs and princes, neither could the guest of such exalted personages be examined, with the severe scrutiny to which the Davenports, Messrs. Foster, Slade, and other professional mediums, have felt called upon to submit.

Strictly speaking then, it is in a great measure due to the services of professional media, that Spiritualism has at last conquered the stolidity of

German conservatism, and made itself known and acknowledged through-out the length and breadth of the land.

With a view of rendering equal justice to both sides of the question, and to show how both public and private mediumship appeals each, to its appropriate class of minds, we shall present notices of each phase, commencing with a sketch taken from the book reviewer's notice in a recent number of the *Banner of Light*, concerning the mediumship of the gifted Baroness von Vay. The extract is as follows:—

"VISIOÑEN IM WASSERGLASE," ETC.

" We have received from Baroness Adelma von Vay, of Gonobitz, Austria, a copy of a work of some hundred pages, printed in the German tongue, in which a marked and novel phase of her mediumship is practically set forth to the reading world. In her preface, this talented writer and worthy lady presents the object of the *brochure* as follows:—

" ' In my book, " Studies of the Spirit-World," I have mentioned my visions wit-nessed in a glass of water. For the benefit of the reader who has not perused that work, I here present the following explanation of those visions from the " Studies," page 85:—

" ' Our spirit guides advised me to make the attempt to see visions in a glass of water. They disclosed to me one day that I possessed the gift of being able to see spirits without becoming somnambulic. They said I was to fill a glass with water, and look therein, and they would then produce spiritual representations in the same. Upon making the trial, I immediately saw all kinds of objects in the water. At first the water seemed to be agitated ; by degrees the pictures appeared at the brim of the glass. I perceive these visions only in the evening, never by day, and I must feel dis-posed thereto through an earnest desire for the same. I am in a normal condition—*i. e.*, in full consciousness of what I observe and say. The desire of others to see this or that picture has absolutely no influence upon me. These pictures often remain a long time in the same place, others again disappear instantaneously. They often appear to be much larger than the surface of the glass would seem to permit ; some-times appear like photographs, then again in colors, or like brilliant light cloud-pictures. As I perceive the visions in the water I dictate the view to my husband, Baron Eugene von Vay, who transcribes it, and it is then explained by my guides.

' ADELMA VAY.' "

For some time previous to the breaking out of the Russian war with Turkey, Professor Boutlerof, and M. Aksakof, both eminent Russian scien-tists, had agreed with their immediate friends, to engage Dr. Slade, of America, to assist them in a series of experiments on the subject of physical force mediumship, in which direction, Dr. Slade bore a high reputation.

The disturbed state of Russia in consequence of the late war, measu-rably interfered with this project, and though some satisfactory *séances* were conducted, the investigation did not assume the character originally intended.

During Dr. Slade's tour through Europe however, he was induced to give a special course of *séances*, to some of the Professors of the Leipzig University, the result of which was, that six of that distinguished body, gave in their testimony to the truthfulness of Dr. Slade, and signed a docu-ment, absolving him from the slightest implication of fraud or personal agency in the manifestations.

Now if report speaks truly, at least five of the *savants* have yielded assent to the claim of a spiritual origin for the marvellous effects they witnessed, whilst the sixth, now to the grief of his many friends *the late* Professor Zoellner, issued a work, entitled " Transcendental Physics," in which, though attempting to show that the wondrous phenomena he described, were due to the interference of "a force," which he vaguely defined, as, "a fourth dimension in space," he yet fully endorsed the truthfulness of Slade, acquitted him of any attempt at imposition; described the super-mundane character of the results produced, and challenged the world of science to account for the same, on any hypothesis, save the spiritual one alleged by the Medium, or his own (Zoellner's) theory of "a fourth dimension in space."

The amazing statements put forth by authorities so eminent as Zoellner, and the other Leipzig professors, have not only awakened universal interest throughout Germany, but they have also attracted world-wide attention, and amongst other unlooked for effects, provoked a curious discussion in America, to which it will now be in order to make some allusion.

A certain blatant preacher and lecturer, one, Rev. Joseph Cook, of Boston, America, during a course of what he announced as "Scientific Religious Lectures," made the Leipzig professor's investigations, the subject of several addresses. In these, he read aloud, numerous extracts from Professor Zoellner's book, and commented freely on the astonishing phenomena there recorded.

Whilst the Rev. Joseph Cook was thus making converts to the Spiritual cause, of all those listeners who were prone to believe on the authority of others, he seemed to have forgotten, how far he was committing himself, in the opinion of those clerical brethren, to whom Spiritualism has been the grand *bête noir* of the age. Beginning to realize possibly that he had gone too far, yet unable to unsay what he had already said, or explain away the marvels on which he had so freely descanted, he undertook to beat a retreat in the following *creditable* (?) fashion.

In a lecture to be given by him at Saratoga, New York, for the benefit of some Christian Church, Mr. Cook announced, that he would *take that opportunity of setting himself right, on the question of Spiritualism.* Feeling possibly, that the "ism" itself, as underlying the entire structure of the religion he, and all other Christians profess, was too much for him to grapple with, Mr. Cook proceeded *to set himself right*, before an immense audience, including a large number of highly respectable Spiritualists, by pouring forth upon the latter, as a class, such a string of vituperation, and abuse, as to call the blush of shame to the cheeks of every listener present.

At the request of the indignant Spiritualists of the place, the author, who was one of the Rev. Joseph Cook's audience, gave a review of, and answer to this address, in a lecture delivered the following evening. Thus the whole subject was re-opened, and from the reports taken down on that occasion, graphic accounts of what actually occurred in the presence of the Leipzig professors, as detailed by Mr. Cook himself, were placed side by side, with the vituperations which he had just poured out against those who believed in the facts he had been at such pains to relate. Without any farther preface we shall quote as much of the author's lecture, as will re-state Cook's account of the Leipzig investigations. Mrs. Hardinge Britten said :—

" In the *Journal* of February 21st, of this year, I find a report of a lecture delivered by Mr. Joseph Cook in Boston, on the 3rd of that month, in which he gives a full account of some noteworthy experiments of six distinguished German scientists, whose spiritual investigations with Henry Slade, the American medium, were published in a work written quite recently by Prof. Zoellner, Professor of Physical Astronomy at Leipzig University. Without attempting to reiterate experiments which seemed as amazing to Mr. Cook and the Leipzig scientists, as they are familiar, and their recital stale and uninteresting to experienced Spiritualists, I must still commend to your attention the following extracts from Mr. Cook's lecture.   He says:—

"'Six renowned German names to their own credit or discredit can now be quoted in the list of believers in the reality of the alleged facts of the modern psychical or spiritual manifestations.   They are Profs. Zoellner, Fechner, and Scheibner, of Leipzig University; Prof. Weber, of Gottingen University; Prof. Fichte, of Stuttgart, and Prof. Ulrici, of Halle University.'

"After detailing minutely what is the standing and reputation of these eminent scholars, and describing with equal care the phenomena they witnessed, he, Mr. Cook, goes on to descant on the high moral character and intellectual ability of a certain Signor Bellachini, Court Conjurer of Germany.   This gentleman, he shows, having called on Henry Slade, and witnessed many of his manifestations, given both at Slade's lodgings and the conjurer's own apartments, tendered to Slade a sworn affidavit to the effect that no conjuration known to him could account for the extraordinary demonstrations of occult power and intelligence he had thus witnessed. Bellachini, like a true man, as well as a true artist, commends Mr. Slade's manifestations to the respectful consideration of science, and deprecates any unfavourable judgments that may be passed upon it hastily, or without thorough investigation, This manly testimonial, legally witnessed and duly filed, Mr. Cook read out in full.

" His next noteworthy remarks are as follows, and are given verbatim from a work on 'Psychography' recently published in London by M. A. Oxon.

"'Henry Slade having proceeded to St. Petersburg to fulfill his engagement with Mr. Aksakof and Prof. Boutlerof, and to present the phenomena of psychography to the scrutiny of a committee of scientific experts, has had a series of successful sittings in the course of which writing has been obtained ln the Prussian language.   At one recent sitting, writing in six different languages was obtained on a single slate.

"'On Wednesday, February 20th, accompanied by Mr. Aksakof and Prof. Boutlerof, Slade had a most successful sitting with the Grand Duke Constantine, who received them cordially, and himself obtained writing on a new slate held by himself alone.'

"Mr. Cook next goes on to describe a fresh set of experiments, remarkable enough to early investigators, but sufficiently familiar to us as the phenomenon of writing obtained in closed slates, &c.   Mr. Cook also read out in detail the account of a very curious phenomenon, being no other than the sudden disappearance of a small table in a light room, which for several minutes was thoroughly searched in vain to find it. Whilst the amazed Prof. Zoellner, was continuing his fruitless attempts to account for the disappearance of this ponderable body, it appeared as suddenly as it had disappeared, floating in the air just below the ceiling—the legs upwards.   From thence, it floated down and was laid by invisible hands gently on another piece of furniture.   In commenting upon this extraordinary manifestation Mr. Cook says:—

"'The mechanical theory of matter is exploded if Zoellner's alleged facts can be proved to be real, but here are grave experts who unite in assuring the world that these events occurred under their own eyesight.   [Then how dare Mr. Cook insert his presumption *if* in this category?]   Here is the Court Conjurer who says he can do nothing of the kind.   I hold in my hand a volume by Fichte, and he says, quoting these experiments, and naming the professors who witnessed them, that he could himself, if he were authorised, give in addition to these names many others in Germany who by the experiments at Leipzig, have been convinced of the reality of the facts and of their worthiness to be made the subject of scientific research.'

" But Mr. Cook does not stop here.   He gives yet more facts, details yet more of the Leipzig experiments and after the recital of one remarkable bomb-shell thrown into the camp of materialism, breaks forth into the following bombastic burst of oratory:—

"'If this single circumstance attested by the Leipzig professors is a fact, it blows to the four moons of Jupiter the whole materialistic mechanical theory of matter. The materialism of ages is answered by a simple fact like this.   But here we have these six men agreeing these Leipzig assertions are worthy of credence.'   Save and except the insolent imbecile *if*, with which Mr. Cook commences this paragraph, and the possibility which that *if* implies, that the six Leipzig professors who have investigated, don't know as much by aid of their senses, as he, Cook, does, who had not then investigated, without the aid of his senses; this paragraph alone shows that when he was dealing with grand dukes, eminent professors and men of higher rank than he could have ever before dealt with, the manifestations were worthy of all credence, and blew opposing theories to the four moons of Jupiter.   But when he, Cook, feels the hand of clerical pressure hard upon him, and he is in his own country, and amongst his own circle of grundy-worshipping priests and deacons, he is accused of believing that which his spiritual pastors and masters desire him not to believe, grand dukes, emperors, statesmen, kings, queens, princes and princesses; nobles, potentates, professors without end; magistrates, lawyers, doctors, ladies, gentlemen, mechanics, operatives, clergymen, peasants, for all these grades and every other unnamed, make up the tens of millions of European, Asiatic, Australian, Indian, and American Spiritualism—all these become at once vermin, reptiles, toads, frogs, snakes, monsters, wretches, &c., together with every other hard and vulgar name, which this truly Christian man's vocabulary can supply."

We must apologize to our readers for the insertion of the above *choice collection of epithets.* All we can say is, that the language—although strangely out of place in this book—was used by one who called himself a "gentleman," and a *Christian minister*; the author only repeats it, for the sake of giving the paragraph, in which the present status of Spiritualism, is summed up, in its entirety.

We have now brought to a close, all that our space will allow us to give, concerning the progress of Spiritualism in Germany, during the nineteenth century, up to the present date.

Germany! The land of Anton Mesmer, the modern discoverer of the true *Elixir Vitæ,* and the master mind from whom Puységur, and Barberini, derived that inspiration, which proclaimed to the world the power of the soul to transcend the barriers of time and space! Land of Zschocke, whose sensitive spirit detected the invisible soul of things; of Kerner, that brave and good physician, who dared the sneers of materialism, and the threats of dogmatism, in proclaiming abroad the stupendous facts of the soul's return, beyond the grave. Land of Schubert, Werner, Kant, and Fichte! Land where the soul enfranchised by the wand of magnetism, was first made free to soar away into the realms of the illimitable, and bring back tidings from the shores of the eternal beyond!

Germany! The country from which the noble Aksakof could freely send abroad the message of spiritual light and life through the columns of a high-toned press! where sages and schoolmen, princes and potentates, listen in reverend silence, to the oracles of inspired utterances. Germany! The land bound up in the external fetters of cold materialism, but inwardly illuminated by spiritual gifts of such wondrous potency, that it only needs to remove the barriers of social and conventional restraint, liberate the mind, and permit the soul and its possibilities free expression, to make it' the church of humanity, from which all the rays of spiritual sunlight shall stream forth, to illuminate, bless, and elevate, the entire family of mankind.

CHAPTER VII.

SPIRITUALISM IN FRANCE.

ALTHOUGH the sameness which prevails in reports of all phenomena arising from a common source, must to a great extent mar the interest of the present record, there are two features of compensation even in this respect which must not be overlooked. The first is, the circumstantial evidence which this very sameness affords, to the unity of the source from whence "Spiritual manifestations" are derived. And next; we cannot fail to observe, that certain characteristic features of variety are impressed upon those manifestations by the peculiarities of the people to whom they are addressed.

Turning our lens of observation from Germany to France, we find the same historical proofs that the phenomena derived from the practices of animal magnetism, which antedated the unfoldment of Spiritualism in the one country, are just as strikingly demonstrated in the other. The impressions produced upon the people of these two lands, however, were totally different.

In Germany, the physical and scientific aspects of Spiritualism have found more favour than its religious tendencies. In France it is otherwise. There, the national characteristics are impulsive, and emotional, hence Spiritualistic teachings have promoted the formation of new sects, and inspired its votaries with a deep religious sentiment. Mesmer, with characteristic caution, never sanctioned any advance beyond the physical results of his discoveries, whilst his followers Puységur, and Barberini, soared away into the spiritual realms to which the enfranchised souls of their somnambulists pointed the way.

Very soon after public attention had been drawn to the subject of magnetism in France, by Drs. Mesmer and d'Eslon, several gentlemen distinguished for learning and scientific attainments, followed up their experiments with great success.

Amongst these was the Baron Dupotet whose deep interest in the subject of magnetism induced him to publish a fine periodical which, under the title of *Journal du Magnétisme*—still forms a complete treasury of well collated facts, and curious experiments in occult force.

From this work we learn, that the Baron's investigations commenced in the year 1836, since which period up to 1848, he chronicled the production of the following remarkable phases of phenomena, the occurrence of which is testified to by numerous scientific and eminent witnesses.

Through the Baron's magnetized subjects was evolved, clairvoyance, trance-speaking, and healing ; the *stigmata* or raised letters and figures on the subject's body ; elevation of somnambulists into the air ; insensibility to fire, injury, or touch. In the presence of the magnetized subjects also, heavy bodies were moved without human contact, and objects were brought from distant places through walls and closed doors. Sometimes the " Lucides " described scenes in the spirit world, found lost property, prophesied and spoke in foreign languages.

In these *séances*, styled by the Baron in later years, *magical*, apparitions presented themselves in crystals, water, mirrors, and often in *forms, tangible alike to the sight and touch of all present.*

Amongst the witnesses to these *séances* were Messrs. Bertrand, d'Hunin, Seguin, and Morin ; men whose position in the world of science rendered their testimony absolutely unquestionable.

In 1840, Baron Dupotet writes that he had " rediscovered in magnetism the magic of antiquity." " Let the *savants*," he says, " reject the doctrine of spiritual appearances ; the enquirer of to-day is compelled to believe it, from an examination of undeniable facts." . . . " If the knowledge of ancient magic is lost, all the facts remain on which to reconstruct it."

The Baron after summing up the phenomena named above, challenges the world of science either to account for, or disprove them.

But of all the revelators to whom French Spiritualists are indebted for indubitable proof of super-mundane intercourse, none stands more prominent in truthfulness and worth, than M. Cahagnet, the well-known author of "The Celestial Telegraph," a work translated into English in 1848.

M. Cahagnet was an unlearned mechanic, a man of the people, and though a sensible and interesting writer, was neither well read, nor highly educated. He affirms that he was a "Materialist" when first his attention was attracted to the subject of animal magnetism, but being of a thoughtful nature, he determined to devote all the leisure he could spare to a thorough examination of its possibilities. When he found that he possessed the power to induce the magnetic sleep in others, he proceeded on the plan then generally adopted by mesmerists, namely, to try how far he could succeed in biologizing his subjects, that is to say, to substitute his own senses, mind, and will, for those of the sleeper.

In the course of these experiments M. Cahagnet discovered, that he could effect remarkable cures of disease, and being naturally of a benevolent disposition, he determined to bend all his energies in this desirable direction.

He soon found however, that he was destined to realize the aphorism, "he builded wiser than he knew." A new and most perplexing obstacle arose to confound his philosophy and scatter his theories to the winds; this was the fact, that some of his subjects, instead of representing what simply he willed, or manifesting—in accordance with his views of biology—merely the influence of his mind, began to transcend both will and mind, and wander off in space, to regions they persisted in calling the "land of spirits," and to describe people, whom they emphatically affirmed to be the souls of those, *the world called dead.*

For a long time M. Cahagnet strove vehemently to combat what he termed these "wild hallucinations," but when he found them constantly recurring, and vast numbers of those who had come to witness the experiments in magnetism, recognizing in the descriptions given by the somnambulists, the spirits of those whom they had known on earth, and mourned as dead, conviction became inevitable, and the magnetizer, like his visitors, was compelled to admit a new and wonderful phase of lucidity, and one which carried the vision of the clairvoyant from earth to heaven, and pierced the veil which separated the mortal from the realms of immortality.

It was after a long series of carefully conducted experiments of the above description, that M. Cahagnet was finally persuaded to give the results of his wonderful *séances* to the world, under the name and style of "The Celestial Telegraph," or, "Secrets of the Life to Come."

The following extract from the introduction to the second volume of these "Secrets," will give the reader some idea of the cautious spirit in which this excellent investigator established the authenticity of his revelations. He says:

"When in January 1848, I presented the public with the first volume of the 'Secrets,' I was unable to verify the facts therein contained by any testimony but my own.

"My position as a simple workman—my very confined social relations, absolutely null in the scientific world,—could give no weight to the statements I had propounded. I felt that despite their truth, I ought to support these revelations by honourable testimonials. To attain this end, I have given apparition sittings to persons who solicited them, and now I can surround my own name with multitudes of others whom the public venerate as authorities. In this second volume, I present to the world a vast number of testimonials to apparitions obtained, recognized, and testified of in writing, as true, by princes, nobles, generals, pastors of many creeds, merchants, men of letters, artisans, personages of all classes, and many nations, all of whom are ready to confirm by verbal testimony the acknowledgments signed at my abode."

About the year 1848, M. Cahagnet, having become very familiar with somnambulic revelations from the world of spirits, through several of the most remarkable and lucid subjects of the age, received a number of communications affirming the fact of the soul's existence anterior to its appearance upon earth. Whilst denying emphatically any belief in the doctrine of Re-incarnation and declaring against it in the most positive terms, the communicating spirits uniformly alleged that, when freed from the trammels of matter, they all remembered having lived in an anterior state of purity and innocence as spirits ; that they perceived how truly and wisely their earthly lives were designed for probationary purposes, and meant to impart vigour and knowledge to the soul ; but that once undergone, it was never again repeated, and the return of the soul to its former spiritual state was never interrupted by re-incarnations on earth. These spirits, too, alleged that the sphere of eternity afforded the souls of evil or unprogressed men all the opportunities necessary to purify them from sin and its effects, through innumerable stages of progress.

As being peculiarly apposite to the subject discussed in this chapter, especially in commenting on the great French magnetists, who may be justly ranked as the *John Baptists*, who ushered in the Messianic Spiritual movement of the nineteenth century, we call attention to the following quotations from the recondite work entitled " Art Magic." On page 433 the author says :

" The narrow conservatism of the age, and the pitiful jealousy of the Medical Faculty, rendered it difficult and harassing to conduct magnetic experiments openly in Europe within several years of Mesmer's decease. Still such experiments were not wanting, and to show their results, we give a few excerpts from the correspondence between the famous French Magnetists, MM. Deleuze and Billot, from the years 1829 to 1840. By these letters, published in 1836, it appears that M. Billot commenced his experiments in magnetizing as early as 1789, and that during forty years, he had an opportunity of witnessing facts in clairvoyance, ecstasy, and somnambulism, which at the time of their publication transcended the belief of the general mass of readers. On many occasions in the presence of entranced subjects, spirits recognized as having once lived on earth in mortal form—would come *in bodily presence* before the eyes of an assembled company and at request, bring flowers, fruits, and objects, removed by distance from the scene of the experiments.

" M. Deleuze frankly admits that his experience was more limited to those phases of somnambulism in which his subjects submitted to amputations and severe surgical operations without experiencing the slightest pain. . . . In a letter dated 1831 M. Billot writing to Deleuze says :—

" ' I repeat, I have seen and known all that is permitted to man. I have seen the stigmata arise on magnetized subjects ; I have dispelled obsessions of evil spirits with a single word. I have seen spirits bring those material objects I told you of, and when requested, make them so light that they would float, and, again a small *boiteau de bonbons* was rendered so heavy, that I failed to move it an inch until the power was removed."

" ' To those who enjoyed the unspeakable privilege of listening to the " somnambules " of Billot, Deleuze, and Cahagnet, another and yet more striking feature of unanimous revelation was poured forth. Spirits of those who had passed away from earth strong in the faith of Roman Catholicism—often priests and dignitaries of that conservative Church, addressing prejudiced believers in their former doctrine, asserted that there was no creed in Heaven—no sectarian worship, or ecclesiastical dogmatism there prevailing.

" ' They taught that God was a grand Spiritual Sun—life on earth a probation ;— the spheres, different degrees of compensative happiness or states of retributive suffering ;—each appropriate to the good or evil deeds done on earth. They described the ascending changes open to every soul in proportion to its own efforts to improve.

" ' They all insisted that man was his own judge, incurred a penalty or reward for which there was no substitution. They taught nothing of Christ, absolutely denied the idea of vicarious atonement—and represented man as his own Saviour or destroyer.

" ' They spoke of arts, sciences, and continued activities, as if the life beyond was but an extension of the present on a greatly improved scale. Descriptions of the radiant beauty, supernal happiness, and ecstatic sublimity manifested by the blest spirits who had risen to the spheres of paradise, Heaven, and the glory of Angelic companionship, melts the heart, and fills the soul with irresistible yearnings to lay down life's weary burdens and be at rest with them.' "

It seems unfortunate for the good people who insist upon making a heaven or hell to suit themselves, and whose strong sectarian bias, induces them to banish every spirit from their presence who presumes to deny their views, that Cahagnet's revelating angels would neither endorse Catholicism, Protestantism, or Re-incarnation.

Having shown that Spiritualism arose in France as in Germany from the awakening of soul powers evolved by magnetism and traced the footprints of the great temple builders who have laid the foundation stones of the mighty Spiritual edifice in the human system, and steadily worked upwards from matter to force, and from thence to spirit in every gradation of sphere, life and progress, we recall the pithy words of the Baron Dupotet, who, addressing the would-be leaders of public opinion in his splendid essay on the " Philosophical Teaching of Magnetism," says :

" You *savants* of our country ; you have not shown yourselves better informed than the Siamese.

" For these sixty years it has been shouted in your ears, *The magnetizers march to the discovery of a moral world ;* all the phenomena they produce indisputably prove its existence.

" You have declared that they were impostors, imbeciles, and the most illustrious amongst you, have only pronounced a verdict which will attest to future ages your ignorance or your insincerity.

" Before the soul is disengaged from matter, it can, and does, converse with pure spirits. Already it can gaze prophetically on its own future destiny, by regarding the condition of those who have gone before ;—but a step ;—yet one, which the eye of spirit alone can measure, and if men are spirits already, who can stay the eagle glance of the soul into the land of its own inheritance ? "

In following up the history of Spiritualism in France, although we find it has gained an immense foothold, and exerted a wide-spread influence upon the popular mind, it is nevertheless evident, that one of the chief obstacles to its general acceptance has been its lack of internal unity, and the antagonistic sentiments which have prevailed amongst its acknowledged leaders.

Two of those who have figured most prominently in the grand drama of French Spiritualism, and in all probability exerted more influence upon public opinion than any other members of its *dramatis personæ*, were MM. Allan Kardec and Pierart the respective editors of the two leading Spiritual journals entitled *La Revue Spirite* and *La Revue Spiritualiste*. These gentlemen may be also regarded as the representatives of the two opposing factions known as

SPIRITUALISTS AND SPIRITISTS

the former teaching, that the soul of man undergoes but one mortal birth, and continues its progress through eternity in spiritual states, the latter affirming the doctrine of Re-incarnation, and alleging that the one spirit in man can and does undergo many incarnations in different mortal forms.

It will be understood that M. Kardec and his followers represent the " Spiritists " or re-incarnationists—M. Pierart leading the ranks of the opposing faction most commonly called Spiritualists.

To M. Kardec has been generally attributed the merit or demerit—as the case may be—of originating the doctrine of Re-incarnation,—at least as that doctrine is taught in this century. This is quite a mistake, as will be shown by the following extracts, taken from a paper published in the *London Spiritualist* of 1875, and written by the accomplished scholar and statesman, the Hon. Alexander Aksakof. As the duty of a faithful historian is rather to record facts, than enunciate opinions, we shall make no apology for introducing M. Aksakof's paper to the attention of the reader, however much it may seem to savour of partisanship. It is entitled

"RESEARCHES ON THE HISTORICAL ORIGIN OF THE RE-INCARNATION

SPECULATIONS OF FRENCH SPIRITUALISTS :—

" In view of the approaching publication of translations in the English language of the works of Allan Kardec, of which the principal volume, "The Spirits' Book," is already out, I feel it my duty to lay before the English public the result of my researches in the direction of the origin of the dogma of Reincarnation. When "Spiritism," newly baptised with this name, and embodied in the form of a doctrine by Kardec, began to spread in France, nothing astonished me more than the divergence of this doctrine from that of "Spiritualism," touching the point of Reincarnation. This divergence was the more strange because the sources of the contradictory affirmations claim to be the same, namely the spirit-world and communications given by spirits. As Spiritism was born in 1856 with the publication of the "Book of Spirits," it is clear that to solve this enigma it was necessary to begin with the historical origin of this book. It is remarkable that nowhere, either in this volume or in any of his others, does Kardec give upon this head the slightest detail. And why was this? the essential point in all serious criticisms being to know before all things how such a book came into existence? As I did not live in Paris, it was difficult for me to procure the necessary information; all that I could learn was that a certain somnambulist, known by the name of Celina Japhet, had contributed largely to the work, but that she had been dead for a long time. During my stay in Paris in 1873, I explained to a Spiritualistic friend my regret that I had never met this somnambulist in life, to which he replied that he had also heard that she was dead, but he doubted whether the rumour was true; also that he had reason to suppose that this was nothing but a rumour spread abroad by the Spiritists, and that it would be well if I made further personal inquiry.

"He gave me the former address of Madame Japhet, and what was my astonishment and joy to find her in perfect health. When I told her of my surprise she replied, that it was nothing new to her, for the *Spiritists* were actually making her pass for a dead person.

" Here is the substance of what she was obliging enough to give me.

" Mdlle. Celina Bequet was a natural somnambulist from childhood. About sixteen years of age she was mesmerised for the first time by Ricard. In 1841 she was attacked with a serious illness which confined her to her bed for twenty-seven months.

"Finding no relief from medicine, she was put into the mesmeric sleep by her brother. She then prescribed the necessary remedies, and after six weeks, could leave her bed, and walk by aid of crutches. At last, after about eleven months, she entirely recovered her health.

"In 1845, she went to Paris to search for M. Ricard, and made the acquaintance of M. Roustan at the house of M. Millet a mesmerist.

"She then, for family reasons, took the name of Japhet, and became a professional somnambulist under the control of M. Roustan. In this position she remained till about 1848. Under her assumed name, she gave medical advice by the direction of the *spirits* of her grandfather, Hahnemann, and Mesmer, from each of whom she received a great many communications.

"In this manner also the doctrine of re-incarnation was given her, *by the spirits of her grandfather, St. Teresa and others.* As the somnambulic powers of Madame Japhet were developed under the mesmeric influence of M. Roustan, it may be well to remark in this place, that M. Roustan himself believed in the plurality of terrestrial existences. (See Cahagnet's *Sanctuaire au Spiritualisme.* Paris, 1850. p. 164. Since dated—1848.

"In 1849, Madame d'Abnour on her return from America, desired to form a circle for spiritual phenomena, of which she had lately been a witness. For this purpose, she called upon M. de Guldenstubbe, by whom M. Roustan and Celina Japhet were asked to become members of his spirit circle.

"This circle was joined by the Abbé Chatel, and the three Demoiselles Bauvrais; it consisted of nine persons, and met once a week at the house of *Madame Japhet*, 46, *Rue des Martyrs*, afterwards, almost up to the time of the war of 1870, it met twice a week.

"In 1855, the circle was composed of M. Taillandier, M. Tillman, M. Sagia (since dead) Messrs. Sardou father and son, Madame Japhet, and M. Roustan, who continued a member of it until about 1864. They began by making a chain, American fashion, in form of a horse-shoe, round Madame Celina, and they obtained spiritual phenomena more or less remarkable; but soon Madame Celina developed as a writing medium, and it was through that channel that the greater part of the communications were obtained.

"In 1856 she met M. Denizard Rivail, introduced by M. Victorien Sardou. He correlated the materials by a number of questions; himself arranged the whole in systematic order, and published 'The Spirits' Book' without ever mentioning the name of Madame C. Japhet, although three-quarters of this book had been given through her mediumship. The rest was obtained from communications through Madame Bodin, who belonged to another spirit-circle. She is not mentioned except on the last page of the first number of the *Revue Spirite*, where, in consequence of the number of reproaches that were addressed to him, he makes a short mention of her. As he was also attached to an important journal, *L'Univers*, he published his book under the names which he had borne in his two previous existences. One of these names was Allan—a fact revealed to him by Madame Japhet, and the other name of Kardec was revealed to him by the medium Roze. After the publication of the 'Book of Spirits,' of which Kardec did not even present one copy to Madame Japhet, he quitted the circle and arranged another in his own house, M. Roze being the medium. When he thus left, he possessed a mass of manuscript which he had carried off from the house of Madame Japhet, and he availed himself of the right of an editor by never giving it back again. To the numerous requests for its return which were made to him, he contented himself by replying, 'Let her go to law with me.' These manuscripts were to some extent useful in the compilation of the 'Book of Mediums,' of which all the contents, so says Madame Japhet, had been obtained through medial communications.

"It would be essential in order to complete this article to review the ideas on pre-existence and on reincarnation which were strongly in vogue in France just before 1850. An abstract of these will be found in the work of M. Pezzani on 'The Plurality of Existences.' The works of Cahagnet should also be consulted. As I am now away from my library, it is impossible for me to give the relative points exactly.

"In addition to the foregoing supplementary details, bearing upon the origin of "The Book of Spirits" and the different points connected therewith, testimony ought to be obtained from living witnesses to throw light upon the conception and birth of this book, such as Madame Japhet, Mdlle. de Guldenstubbe, M. Sardou, and M. Tallandier. The last continues up to the present time to work with Madame Japhet as a medium; she is still in possession of her somnambulic powers, and continues to give consultations. She sends herself off to sleep *by means of objects which have been mesmerised by M. Roustan*. I think it a duty on this occasion to testify to the excellence of her lucidity. I consulted her about myself, and she gave me exact information as to a local malady, and as to the state of my health in general. Now is it not astonishing that this remarkable person, who has done so much for French Spiritism, should be living entirely unknown for twenty years, and no notice or remark made about her? Instead of being the centre of public attention she is totally ignored; in fact, they have buried her alive! Let us hope that reparation which is due to her will be made one day. "Spiritualism" might, in this matter, offer a noble example to "Spiritism."

"Now to return to the question of Reincarnation. I leave it to English critics to draw their deductions from the facts which I unravelled by my researches, incomplete though they be; I will do no more than throw out the following ideas: That the propagation of this doctrine by Kardec was a matter of strong predilection is clear; from the beginning, Reincarnation has not been presented as an object of study, but as a dogma. To sustain it he has always had resource to writing mediums, who it is well known pass so easily under the psychological influence of preconceived ideas; and Spiritism has engendered such in profusion; whereas through physical mediums the communications are not only more objective, but always contrary to the doctrine of Reincarnation. Kardec adopted the plan of always disparaging this kind of mediumship, alleging as a pretext its moral inferiority, Thus the experimental method is altogether unknown in Spiritism; for twenty years it has not made the slightest intrinsic progress, and it has remained in total ignorance of Anglo-American Spiritualism! The few French physical mediums who developed their power in spite of Kardec, were never mentioned by him in the *Revue*; they remained almost unknown to Spiritists, and only because their spirits did not support the doctrine of Reincarnation! Thus Camile Bredif, a very good physical medium, acquired celebrity only in consequence of his visit to St. Petersburg. I do not remember ever to have seen in the *Revue Spirite* the slightest notice of him, still less any descriptions of manifestations produced in his presence. Knowing the reputation of Mr. Home, Kardec made several overtures to get him upon his side; he had two interviews with him for this purpose, but as Mr. Home told him that spirits who had communicated through him never endorsed the idea of Reincarnation, he thenceforth ignored him, thereby disregarding the value of the manifestations which were produced in his presence. I have upon this head a letter from Mr. Home, although at the present moment it is not within reach.

"In conclusion; it is scarcely necessary to point out that all that I have herein stated does not affect the question of Reincarnation, considered upon its own merits, but only concerns the causes of its origin and of its propagation as Spiritism."

"Chateau de Krotofka, Russia, July 24, 1875."

Without attempting to offer any comments on M. Aksakof's narrative—the plain facts of which speak for themselves—it may be remarked, that in most magnetic operations, it is generally found that the first effects produced, are deep somnolency, or a sleep-waking state. The next is most commonly the biological condition, in which the subject represents the mind, will, sense, &c., of the magnetizer; and the next succeeding that, is a condition beyond and independent of the operator, in which an *invisible spirit* often takes control, and substitudes *his* mind, will, and sense, for that of the earthly magnetizer. This last named degree is now recognised, as "Spirit Mediumship." It is one which may or may not be induced by human magnetism, but whenever it does ensue, the power of the human mind ceases to operate, and that of the spirit controlling takes its place. Now whilst we have abundant historical testimony to show that this condition of spiritual control was attained by the "lucides" of Messrs. Billot, Dupotet, and Cahagnet, we have no such evidence of independent spiritual influence operating upon Madame Japhet, whilst she was the magnetic subject of M. Roustan. How powerful this gentleman's magnetism must have been, and how completely Madame Japhet was dependent upon his control, we learn from her own acknowledgment to M. Aksakof, namely, that she still gives consultations, *and sends herself off to sleep, by means of objects which have been mesmerized by M. Roustan.*

What stronger proof can we have that the controlling spirit of Madame Japhet was M. Roustan? and that "The Book of Spirits," emanated far more reasonably from his biological impression, than from the saints, apostles, martyrs, and other historical celebrities, to whom it has been attributed?

Still it may be asked by the devotees of the re-incarnation theory, of what consequence is it whether this doctrine was first taught by Roustan, or Kardec, so long as it is true? Aye even so! *So long as it is true!* That indeed is the main question; but ere it can be answered, another arises, and that is, How can the truth of this doctrine be tested? and again; Can we arrive at any veritable knowledge of spiritual existence except from spirits themselves, and that in communications given under conditions which preclude the possibility of human interference or bias?

To this it may be objected, that no such independent conditions exist, the general opinion being, that spirit communications are always more or less tinctured by the characteristics of the medium through whom the intelligence is given.

Whilst we admit the force of this objection *to a certain extent*, we still insist that there are some conditions far more favourable for the transmission of spiritual revelations than others; such for example, were the circumstances under which spirits influenced the visions of Messrs. Puységur and Barberini's clairvoyants, and subsequently gave direct communications through the "lucides" of Messrs. Dupotet, Billot, and Cahagnet. In all these cases, the magnetizers themselves were wholly unprepared for the nature of the intelligence rendered, in fact they were at first disposed to reject it, because it conflicted so strongly with their own preconceived opinions. The same independent character pervaded the spirit communications first received in America, they being in general, not only new and strange, but totally opposed to the views of many of those who received them, and it is a fact worthy of the gravest consideration, that in all these EARLY AND UNBIASSED REVELATIONS, no word of the doctrine of re-incarnation was ever given, except to individuals who had already cherished the belief.

If we add, that in the most independent form of spiritual revelation, namely through physical mediumship, few if any instances are known wherein spirits have taught the doctrine of re-incarnation, we deem we have proved that the theory in question has not originated from authentic and reliable spiritual sources, but is in reality one of those Oriental ideas which other philosophers besides M. Roustan cherish. The author is even now well acquainted with a gentleman who appeals to every person inhuman enough to ill-treat dumb animals, imploring them to desist, on the plea, that they may, in all probability be abusing *one of their own ancestors*. Thousands of such erratic opinions have been in vogue and that without any reason for attributing them to spiritual sources.

As a result of M. Aksakof's researches into the origin of the modern French re-incarnation doctrine, those readers who have had any experience in psychological experiments, will neither be surprised to find Madame Japhet reflecting the powerful idiosyncrasies of M. Roustan, or M. Kardec impressing his equally strong opinions upon the susceptible individuals with whom he came in contact.

It must be remembered also, to account for the great prevalence of this remarkable man's doctrines on the Continent—that he was the only notable writer who distributed works in the French language on this subject, and maintained its propagandism with untiring zeal.

In respect to the question of testimony, it must be remembered that M. Kardec derived his communications chiefly from those writing and trance mediums who might have proved the most susceptible to his influence, and is said to have persistently banished from his circles, not only Mr. Home, M. Bredif, and other physical mediums, but all those who did not endorse his favourite dogma through their communications. Having now presented the historical view of one side of the question, it becomes necessary to call attention to some of the representative writings of the opposite faction, distinguished from the followers of M. Kardec by the soubriquet of "Spiritualists."

To do justice to this portion of our subject, we must now introduce M. Pierart, the editor of the opposition paper published in Paris, of which mention has already been made, under the title of *La Revue Spiritualiste*.

Although it seems something of an anomaly to commence our record of a noble life by treating of its close, we find we cannot present to our readers a more compendious view of M. Pierart's good service in the cause

4

of Spiritualism, than by republishing his obituary notice, written by M. F. Clavairoz, Consul General of France at Trieste, and copied into most of the English and American Spiritual journals. This gentleman says:

"The valiant champion whose last work, 'The Primitive World,' I noticed a short time ago, has been struck down by death. It was, alas! so to speak, the last flame bursting forth from the soul of this apostle. He corrected the proofs upon his bed of suffering, where my hand pressed his. M. Pierart succumbed to the malady with which he had been afflicted for several months, but of which he had hoped to be cured. The cause of Spiritualism has suffered a great loss; but progress is not arrested because a combatant falls in the strife. Without being in any way discouraged in our aspirations, our regrets follow beyond the grave those whom we have known and loved, and whose courage has sustained us in our efforts in the struggle. He whom we have just lost is stamped with the seal of brave soldiers of the truth. Born in an humble condition, he valiantly made himself what he afterwards became. M. Pierart received his first education at the College of Avanes; entered the grammar school of Douai, which he quitted with the diploma of teacher, and subsequently became professor at the College of Maubenge. While there he was chosen by Baron Dupotet to be his secretary, and they worked together several years. In 1858 he founded *La Revue Spiritualiste*, at which time it required courage to propagate the new facts which had opened up an unknown field for speculation concerning the soul. His magazine reported the psychological phenomena which began in America, and it was continued by M. Pierart until he substituted for it the *Concile de la Libre Pensée*, which was stopped in 1873, in consequence of clerical influence. Afterwards he resumed his spiritual labours by publishing the *Benedictin de St. Maur*, which he continued until the last. It is not only in the treatment of spiritual phenomena that M. Pierart has shown the power of his ardent soul, which was so captivated by all that is great and generous, for he published a number of historical works. No labour was too great for him when what seemed doubtful required investigation, and no consideration ever caused him to hesitate to divulge what he considered to be true. An indefatigable worker and careful investigator, history and archæology attracted him as much as mesmerism and the occult sciences. He penetrated the arcana of Druidism, and studied the origin of the most ancient religions. His style—always precise, clear, and enlightened by clairvoyance—gave to his words a real authority. No one had more knowledge than he of the mysteries of the past, and death came upon him just as he was preparing to publish the result of his investigations. M. Pierart has for twenty years fought for the cause of Spiritualism, loved by all who knew him, and appreciated by all who read him. His death will leave a great gap, and the work he has left undone will be difficult for another to accomplish. His faith supported him in his earthly struggle against poverty, and the secret persecutions by which he was beset. As for Spiritualists, who know that death is only a transformation, we believe that Pierart's soul will be with us and continue to interest itself in a cause which so occupied him during his earthly sojourn."

In order to make our readers still better acquainted with this admirable champion of Spiritualism, and show some of the curious intrigues by which a great cause may be sacrificed to human ambition, and selfishness, we shall present a few extracts from an article published by M. Pierart in 1878, a translation of which was sent to the English *Medium* of London, by F. Tennyson, Esq., of St. Ewolds, Jersey.

The article is headed—

APPEAL OF M. PIERART.

To the old readers of the Revue Spiritualiste, and the Concile de Libre Pensée, and all those who love the truth, in connexion with Morality and Philosophy.

"FRIENDS AND BROTHERS,—It is now many years since our voice which won your sympathies, has made itself heard, but the day has come when we entertain the hope that its tones will once again rally you round the banner of truth which for fifteen years we upheld with unflinching resolution and zeal.

"In the year 1858, when we started our journal, we also established a focus of re-union where you could all meet for the discussion of those consoling verities which were our delight, and the common subject of our most earnest meditations. This association continued until 1864.

" It was then that we quitted Paris, and withdrew into the country keeping up however at intervals our intercourse with those who remained faithful to us, and our cause.

"Many among you have asked why we quitted the capital, to bury ourselves in the woods, and we have given reasons which we must now reproduce, for doing so.

" Paris is a sink of corruption, and the man who does not lend himself to it, leads a life anything but agreeable. There is no room in this Babylon for upright, courageous, and liberal ministers of Truth. To obtain intellectual distinction, one must cringe ' to the powers that be,' a degradation we would not sink to.

" Besides, we encountered not a few such men as are described in the gospel of St. Matthew—chap. 10, ver. 17 to 27.

" We were desirous of resting the question of Spiritualism on the ground of facts, and critical analysis, trusting that the phenomena would eventually prove themselves. But in this we were unsupported, left alone, and misunderstood. Clever pychagogues launched out into wild guesses; published catechisms, and foolish articles of belief, the results of ill-digested compilations, yet of a nature to impress the simple-minded. . . . What is more, the enemy wormed himself into the heart of our unpretending society in order to paralyze its action.

" Mediums deceived us. Others introducing themselves through our journal, availed themselves of this opportunity to alienate our readers and set up opposition organs.

" It was then, that profoundly discouraged, we proceeded to take up our permanent abode in the country; to live the life of a hermit, alone in the society of our beloved books, in presence of the works of God, and the surroundings of Nature, which, at any rate, do not sadden or deceive the spirit open to their influences.

'· At length the Jesuits interfered to obstruct our work. In 1873, about the time the 'Gouvernement de Combat " was installed; in direct violation of all law, our journal, which had never busied itself with politics, was suppressed. It seems that, in spite of its obscurity and slight importance, it troubled the slumbers of the ecclesiastics. It was regarded by the prelates and politicians of this same "Gouvernement de Combat" as extremely dangerous. Our just appeals for its reinstatement were disregarded. Even to this day the suppressed numbers are in the office of the Minister of the Interior, and we have never been able to recover them. Our letters have received no answers. Thereby hangs a tale which may be better understood by the following letter, sent to the republican journals in the month of February, 1876:—

"'Saint Maur des Fosses, Jan. 6th, 1876.

"' Mr. Editor,—The abuse of the state of siege in regard to the political press, has been recently animadverted upon from the tribune and in the journals: but nothing has been said of the outrages which the periodical and non-political press has had to endure. I am myself a victim of this new-fangled torture; and my case is so perfectly unprecedented, that I can no longer keep silence.

"' In 1858 I started a journal, which I called the *Revue Spiritualiste*, devoted to the examination of philosophical questions and religious exegesis. This paper was succeeded in 1870 by the *Concile de Libre Pensée*, which continued to discuss the same subjects. It cannot be alleged that this publication was atheistical, or that it propagated evil principles, or stimulated bad passions.

"' Unceasingly it pleaded the being of a God, the immortality of the soul, and carefully avoided entering upon political and social questions. The Empire, though by no means favourably disposed towards the Press, had left it alone. Not so the men of the 'Gouvernement de Combat,' whose rise, three years since, France beheld with astonishment. It was then that my journal was suppressed.

"' When I requested an explanation they did not deign to answer me. After waiting two years, I wrote to the Director of the Press to know whether, if I bound myself by entering into recognisances and agreed to publish my paper in a department not subject to the state of siege, I might be permitted to continue it. The answer was that under no conditions whatsoever, and in no part of France, would it be suffered to appear. Why? Not the shadow of a reason was assigned on this any more than on the previous occasion.

"' I began to publish, about this time, a work entitled "Revelations and Commentaries on the History of the Early World." I found that after several pages had been printed, the proofs were seized at the post-office, and I never heard any more of them, so that I was constrained to discontinue the work.

"'Now, what elements of sedition were there to be found in my work on "The Early World"? They could not assert that it was the spark to fire the powder magazine of social and political passions. But it opposed the cosmogony and chronology of the Bible. Besides, it demonstrated the wide difference between actual Catholicism and primitive Christianity, and had perpetrated the unforgivable sin of exhibiting in new points of view the abuses of the confessional and the celibacy of the priesthood.

"'Such are the noted facts, as unquestionable as they are incredible.'"

It would be unnecessary to republish M. Pierart's eloquent comments on what he considers these "incredible" facts in farther detail, there being few Spiritualists of any experience who could not parallel, and in some respects exceed them; but we shall yet claim the reader's attention for a few more extracts from this gentleman's voluminous writings. The following sketches of his power as a prophetic Seer being both original in style and characteristic of French Spiritualism :—

EXTRACTS FROM THE "CONCILE DE LIBRE PENSÉE"

(Books 8th and 9th).

"The year in which visions of great cotemporary events followed close upon one another was 1860.

"I anticipated the war which terminated in the bloody battle of Sadowa. The night before the battle, I had a vision of a Lancer whom I recognised by his uniform to be an Austrian Uhlan. He held a lance with a *black* pennant, and was singing a mournful air which I remember to have heard in my youth sung by the veterans who witnessed the disaster of 1812 and 1813. It commenced thus—

> 'They lie and sleep on the ground,
> And the drum shall wake them no more!'

This vision made a painful impression upon me in my waking hours, but its significance was soon explained by the arrival of the telegram which announced the defeat and slaughter of Sadowa.

"Towards the end of 1867, I saw in vision vast multitudes of armed men approaching Paris from Germany, and the French Empire tottering beneath their heavy tread.

"This prophecy was soon sadly realized in the fall of the Second Empire, already often predicted by a host of mediums.

"Before the advance of the Black Prussians and the carnage of Champigny and Villiers-sur-Marne, I saw their approach in a cloud of black ravens which swooped down before the place where I was sitting.

"Shortly after this, I had a distinct vision of myself returning from the north of France to Paris. On the way I encountered cavalry officers in foreign uniforms, one of whom thrust me aside with the point of his sabre, ordering me in an imperious voice to stand off. Very soon after, this scene was enacted in all its minutiæ, for on quitting my native place to return to Paris, I encountered suddenly a party of Prussian soldiers who represented exactly the persons and scenes of my vision.

"Just before the war, when all was apparently peaceful and calm, for more than fifteen days, every morning quite early, as I was dressing, I heard a dull sound as of a cannonade, which seemed to come from Paris, and its environs. At first I imagined there was some émeute in the great city, to the tune of artillery practice on the esplanade at Vincennes, but I soon learnt that there was nothing of the kind. Whence came this noise of cannon firing, which only I myself could hear, but at regular intervals, and unmistakably? I could not account for it. It was not hallucination; I was in perfect possession of my senses, and laying my ear to the ground I heard the sound intensified. Even now I ask myself how ever this audible phenomenon could be. Was I to understand it as a prophecy of the dreadful cannonade which was soon to thunder in Paris and its environs? At this present date I should so explain it. About this time I had a letter from my friend M. Clavairoz. He asked me what my spirits said about the war. As for his spirit, in whom he had perfect confidence he announced nothing but disaster.

" A few days after this an English friend of mine paid me a visit. It was Mr. S. Chinnery, a very sensitive man, and good seer, whose presentiments rarely deceived him. He, no more than myself, had faith in the coming triumphs of France. He related to me a scene he had just witnessed in the gardens of the Tuileries, by the fountain nearest the Palace. A man—his dress in disorder, wild-looking, and hollow-eyed—had come there to weave a sort of incantation and denounce prophetically the potentate who resided close by. Laying coals on the edge of the basin and turning toward the Tuileries in an attitude of malediction, he thundered out these words : ' Napoleon, thy days are numbered, thy kingdom is coming to an end. Witness these coals, which have been sent me by one in the last stage of phthisis, whose death is close at hand.'

" After giving the particulars of this scene, which had made a strong impression on him, Mr. Chinnery recounted various prophecies and presentiments, of which he had made a collection, and which convinced him that France was about to pass through a very lamentable crisis.

" I was in Belgium at the time of the disaster at Sedan. Before leaving, I had offered to the Flamant family, who dwelt at Joinville-le-Pont, on the other side of the Marne, the use of my apartment, in case the tide of war should reach Paris and its environs. I knew the enemy would not cross this stream in the teeth of the forts which protected it, but the left bank was in great danger of being ravaged. The members of this family, though they had no faith in my predictions, were very soon only too glad to accept my offer.

" But I have now to relate the most wondrous of all the phenomena of that grievous period of terror. I was far away, but my good genius guarded my home. As I had quitted home in a hurry, everything had been left in confusion; but when they took possession, everything was found in the most perfect order. Certainly no mortal hand could have acomplished this in an apartment under lock and key. Who then, could have put everything to rights? If it was a spirit, the new occupiers saw nothing of him; but their dog no doubt saw him, for no sooner had the animal entered than he began to tremble all over, and to howl, so that they were obliged to open the door for him, and find him quarters in the garden. A luminous spirit was seen to go out from the house and to soar over it in the open air, with outstretched arms in sign of protection, at the moment when the enemy's cannon announced the investment of the Marne.

" From that time I pursued in the journals every detail of the siege with the greatest anxiety. As the enemy's projectiles were aimed at the heights which crowned the approaches to the river, I dreaded lest they should force the passage, or a cannonade come down upon the lofty building that contained my apartment, which was close by the church, on the highest point of the locality, and therefore could not fail to be a target for them. One morning I had a vision—it seemed to me that a bombardment had commenced, and they were stowing away my books in safe hiding places. I afterwards ascertained that this vision was true.

" I had had a thousand proofs of the action of the spiritual world on the natural. My good genius over and over again had saved me from great misfortunes. To turn aside the balls once fired off seemed to me impossible even for him, but I believed it might be in his power to act on the organs of a human being, so I besought him, in case the house should be in danger of bombardment, to exercise his influence on the visual organs of the artillery officers who pointed the cannon. I had no hope except in this.

" I was not deceived. For six weeks an iron hail of shells hurled over the centre of the village of St. Maur. The houses all round mine were burnt, but mine remained intact. This so astonished the Wurtemburg artillery officer who directed the firing, that at the time of the armistice he came to see it, and declared, in presence of the assembled villagers who had returned, and the brave Flamant family, that 'the house must either be the devil's house or the dwelling of a sorcerer, as he had tried to set fire to it for six weeks, and had not succeeded.' At the same time it cannot be denied that the good dames of the neighbourhood attributed this fact to the agency of 'Our Lady of Miracles' of St. Maur; but, at all events, Our Lady might as well have preserved the other burnt houses while she was about it.

" Whether people believe in these things or not, and howsoever they explain them it is not the less certain that they are facts; and we have our own way of looking at them, undreamt of in their philosophy."   " Z. T. PJERART."

CHAPTER VIII.

SPIRITUALISM IN FRANCE.

SPIRITISM AND SPIRITUALISM (CONTINUED).

IT must not be supposed that the schism which divided the two leaders of French Spiritualism was confined to the immediate sphere of action in which they moved. Scattered sympathisers with the writings of Allan Kardec may be found all over the Continent of Europe and in small numbers in America also. Few people who read works put forth with authoritative pretentions, have the faculty of thoroughly digesting what they read, hence, when M. Kardec's books were translated into the English language, and it became the publisher's interest to aid in their circulation, they found more readers than thinkers, and their plausible style attracted more admiration than sincere convicton. In France, no doubt M. Kardec's personal influence and strong psychological power, admirably fitted him for a propagandist, and when we remember how readily any doctrines eloquently advocated will command adherents, especially amongst restless and excitable natures, we need be at no loss to discover why M. Kardec's writings have become so popular and his opinions so generally accepted by his readers. Little or no Spiritual literature was disseminated in the French language when Allan Kardec's works were first published. He possessed that indomitable energy and psychological influence in which his much harassed rival Pierart was wanting. Thus in a measure, the field of Continental Spiritual propagandism was his own, nor did he fail to make use of his great opportunities.

The successes achieved by Kardec's journal *La Revue Spirite*, communicated a wave of influence also, which propagated journals of a similar character all over the country. Thus in 1864, there were no less than ten Spiritualistic periodicals published in France, under the following titles : *La Revue Spirite, La Revue Spiritualiste,* and *L'Avenir,* PARIS; four *Spiritist* journals published in Bordeaux, which, in 1865, became merged into *L'Union Spirite Bordelaise; La Medium Evangélique,* TOULOUSE; *L'Echo d'outre Tombe,* MARSEILLES; and *La Vérité,* LYONS.

The editors of these journals are said to have been all followers of Allan Kardec, with the exception of M. Pierart, editor of *La Revue Spiritualiste.*

How far the Re-incarnationists were in sympathy with Spiritualism proper, may be gathered from the fact, that they never noticed an opera published in 1865 in M. Pierart's paper, said to be the production of spirits, through the mediumship of Dr. C. Maldigny, entitled "Swedenborg."

Several persons of literary talent pronounced this opera a very meritorious work, but as its publisher M. Pierart was a Spiritualist, amongst a host of *Spiritist* journalists, not one contributed to popularize it, by a single word of comment.

This is but one out of many kindred facts which tend to prove the total lack of sympathy existing between the opposing parties.

It must be remarked that the doctrines of the Re-incarnationists, although defended with great ability by their propagandists, who included many of the most capable minds of France, were not suffered to pass without severe castigation on the part of their English neighbours; and as we are pledged to represent the history of the movement, rather than our own personal predilections, it becomes necessary to note how the French spiritual schism was received on the other side of the Channel.

In the *London Spiritual Magazine* of 1865, the editor, in commenting on the ominous silence of the *Spirite* journals concerning Dr. Maldigny's opera of Swedenborg says :—

"It is worthy of note that the journals of the Kardec school, so far as we have seen them, do not take the least notice of this opera. The *Avenir* of Paris which appears weekly, but greatly wants facts, has not a word to say about it. . . . It is greatly to be regretted that the main object of the Kardecian journals, seems to be, not the demonstration of the constantly recurring facts of Spiritualism, but the deification of Kardec's absurd doctrine of Re-incarnation.

"To this doctrine—which has nothing to do with Spiritualism, even if it had a leg of reason or fact to stand on—all the strength, and almost all the space of these journals is devoted.

"These are the things which give the enemies of Spiritualism a real handle against it, and bring it into contempt with sober minds. Re-incarnation is a doctrine which cuts up by the roots all individual identity in the future existence. It desolates utterly that dearest yearning of the human heart for reunion with its loved ones in a permanent world. If some are to go back into fresh physical bodies, and bear new names, and new natures, if they are to become respectively Tom Styles, Ned Snooks, and a score of other people, who shall ever hope to meet again with his friends, wife, children, brothers and sisters? When he enters the spirit-world and enquires for them, he will have to learn that they are already gone back to earth, and are somebody else, the sons and daughters of other people, and will have to become over and over the kindred of a dozen other families in succession! Surely no such most cheerless crotchet could bewitch the intellects of any people, except under the most especial bedevilment of the most sarcastic and mischievous of devils."

In the January number for 1866, a still stronger article on this subject appears from the pen of Wm. Howitt, who writes the following fearless words of protest against the doctrine of Re-incarnation :—

"In the *Avenir* of November 2nd, M. Pezzani thinks he has silenced M. Pierart, by asserting that without Re-incarnation all is chaos and injustice in God's creation—'In this world there are rich and poor, oppressed and oppressors, and without Re-incarnation God's justice could not be vindicated.' That is to say, in M. Pezzani's conception, God has not room in the infinite future to punish and redress every wrong, without sending back souls again and again into the flesh. M. Pezzani's idea, and that of his brother Re-incarnationists is, that the best way to get from Paris to London is to travel any number of times from Paris to Calais and back again. We English that the only way is to go on to London at once. . . . As to M. Pezzani's notions of God's injustice without Re-incarnation, if souls were re-incarnated a score of times, injustice between man and man, riches and poverty, oppression and wrong, all the enigmas of social inequality would remain just then as now.

"In noticing these movements in the Spiritist camp in France, we should be doing a great injustice if we did not refer to the zealous, eloquent, and unremitting exertions of M. Pierart in the *Revue Spiritualiste*, to expose and resist the errors of the *Spirites* to which we have alluded. The doctrine of Re-incarnation M. Pierart has persistently resisted and denounced as at once false, unfounded on any evidence, and most pernicious to the character of Spiritualism."

Again he adds :—

"What are the fruits which this serpent doctrine of Re-incarnation have already begun to produce in the South of France? There the medium Hillaire, having run away with his neighbour's wife, it is stated that the unhappy husband appealed to their leader Kardec to use his influence to bring back the fugitive wife with the money which she and her paramour had carried off.

"But the answer is stated to have been from Kardec, that he could do no such thing, as the husband was no doubt punished for a similar crime in some former state of existence."

M. Pierart in commenting on this notorious case says in the *Revue Spiritualiste*, 8th vol. :—

"In the south of France a people has only awakened from the death of materialistic belief, to the death of all virtue, sense, morality, and reason.

"There a tribunal has lately heard enunciated the doctrine, that it is necessary to tolerate theft and adultery, because these crimes can only happen as the punishment of like sins in a former existence."

M. Pierart concludes a scathing article on this case in the following words :—

"Away then, with these doctrines destructive of progress, negative of the spirit which ought to reign in humanity! Away! and it is high time; for seduction and blind error are arising and spreading themselves on all sides like a leprosy, which it will soon be too late to attempt to cure. They go on originating fanatical impulses, made obstinate by the force of ignorance and the absence of a critical spirit. And no one calls attention to the danger! and we ourselves stand nearly alone and unable to vanquish the hydra. But we shall at least have done our part. Our warnings have been heard from time to time, and if they remain without response, we shall at least enjoy the consciousness of having performed a great duty."

Again William Howitt writes :—

"We may regret the necessity,—one which amounts to a duty,—of devoting so much space to a doctrine which assails, and would uproot if permitted to flourish, the most vital principles of Spiritualism, amongst which are—

"1. THE IMMORTALITY OF THE SOUL—utterly annihilated if an individual known as such on earth, is not himself at all but somebody else in past life and will be somebody else in the future.

"2. It negatives ETERNAL PROGRESS, if the soul is to return to this weary earth for endless births as somebody else, instead of marching on through the decades of eternity in unchanged, and ever strengthening individuality.

"3. It crushes out for ever the sweet ties of FAMILY AFFECTION—if, for example ;— the blessed mother whom we have known and adored, is not our mother, but we are perchance her great grandfather, and she may be presently born again as the child of our worst enemy!

"4. It wholly discredits the facts of SPIRIT COMMUNION upon which alone, the foundations of Spiritualism rest; because Spiritualism came to us a stranger, and before we had begun to pervert its revealments or interpolate them with our own wild theories, it declared that the soul moved on for ever, but never retrogressed back into its rudimental shell of mortal mould. It showed us the worst of spirits, progressing through the spheres of Spiritual existence, growing brighter and fairer beneath our very eyes, but never returning to be re-born in strange households, to the distraction of all kindred ties, and the annihilation of that divine sentiment of love for one another, which is the redeeming element in the lowest depths of humanity."

"Can you give me any INDISPUTABLE PROOF that the doctrine of the soul's Re-incarnation in matter is true?" asked the author of a Spirit, communicating under test conditions so well defined, as to render doubt touching that spirit's personality impossible. "Can you give me any indisputable proof," replied the spirit, "that an acorn having once grown to be an oak, ever becomes an acorn again, or the eagle having once given birth to its young, ever becomes again a germ egg?"

Who cannot follow out these living pictures of Nature's harmonious and unbroken laws, from plant and animal life to man, nor dwarf the intellect down to the measure of M. Roustan's dreams, filtered through the lips of his somnambulic subject, even though they be stamped with the mighty genius of M. Allan Kardec?

And now that same Allan Kardec is a spirit! He passed from the scene of his earthly pilgrimage on the 31st of March, 1869.

Whatever might have been the impulse that led him to promulgate a doctrine fraught with so much that many Spiritualists deem false and injurious, it is impossible that he could have exerted over his own imme-diate sympathizers so unbounded an influence as he wielded, without being a man of powerful intellect, and indomitable energy. It is also impossible that he could so long have remained the centre of a large circle, without becoming known for what he truly was, and as all his most intimate associates pronounce upon him the verdict of superior excellence, who shall venture to visit a stupendous intellectual misconception, upon the heart and intention of the man?

That he had the elements of greatness, let us cordially acknowledge. Meantime, whatever he may now be in sentiment and knowledge, we are assured he is in the land of light, where he will no more "see as in a glass darkly, but face to face," with divine truth.

Were it not for the vice of the age, which rejoices to represent greatness through the shams of mediocrity, we might hope to learn from the lips of the enfranchised spirit himself, how it fares with him, and how far his spiritual eyes have been opened, to the realities of his new sphere of existence. Still again, we are consoled by the assurance, that all progress for all living souls, is but a question of time, and that sooner or later, he will join the mighty armies of progression, whose watchword through eternity is, Excelsior!

It should be stated in this brief notice of a memorable man, that the followers of Allan Kardec are accustomed to assemble annually at his tomb in Père La Chaise and celebrate with all the love and interest which his memory excites, their continued affiliation, in spirit at least, with their great leader. Until within the last twelvemonth, these touching anniversary services have been participated in by the venerable Madame Kardec. Quite recently however, the noble widow has gone to join—as we faith-fully believe—the husband to whom she seemed to be bound by ties of tenderness and personal affection which strangely contradict her cherished philosophy of Re-incarnation.

Madame Kardec leaves a munificent bequest behind, in aid of the fund designed to publish and disseminate her husband's writings, and it seems to have been in view of her noble character and earnest endeavour to act out her highest sense of right, that her obsequies were attended by crowds of persons distinguished alike for their literary and social eminence. The reader cannot fail to be interested in the following excerpts which give brief accounts of one of the anniversary gatherings held at the tomb of the celebrated French Spiritist.

The *Daily News* of London says :—

"The other day a solemn conclave met in Paris to do honour to a name which, although a borrowed one, has in the space of less than twenty years made the circuit of the globe, and founded a school of religious philosophy in which its adepts seem to find the meeting point of Mysticism and Methodism. Allan Kardec, whose imposing tomb at Père La Chaise cannot fail to have attracted the attention of the most careless visitor to that city of the dead, was the son of a French lawyer, and was born at Lyons in the early years of the century. His real name was Hippolyte Léon Denizard Rivail, and with it for more than fifty years he was content to live a life of obscurity. Some few years however, after the establishment of the Second Empire, Spiritualistic manifestations were imported into France from across the Atlantic. It fascinated Rivail's mind, long given up to the study of the mediæval Mystics. In 1858 he had gathered around him so many fellow-believers that a ' Société des Etudes Spirites ' was constituted, and a few months later their organ, the *Revue Spirite*, appeared. Both the Association and the organ still survive, and claim to be making important progress, not only in France, but in every Continental country."

Writing of the same occasion, one of the American papers remarks :—

" There was a large gathering of Continental Spiritualists around the tomb of Allan Kardec in the cemetery of Père La Chaise, Paris, on the occasion of the recent anniversary of his death. Speeches in honour of him and his work were delivered by prominent disciples. One of the floral crowns to decorate his tomb was brought from America. Madame Kardec was present, and received the sympathetic salutations of the assemblage.

" In the evening many were present at a banquet and concert. About three hundred brothers and sisters in belief met at the rooms of the Society for continuing Allan Kardec's work, in the Rue des Petits-Champs. The rooms are now too small for the growing Society. The evening was devoted to oratorical, poetical, and musical tributes to the memory of the venerated founder."

Those who are familiar with the writings of R. D. Owen, Shorter, Howitt, and other celebrated European Spiritualists, will have read with absorbing interest, accounts of the marvellous phenomena which frequently occurred in the presence of the late Baron de Guldenstubbe, and his gifted sister. The speciality of the Baron's mediumship was, the production of writings executed by the hands of spirits themselves. These writings the Baron, Mdlle. Guldenstubbe, and their friends, obtained in the following way. According to certain theories of his own, the Baron de Guldenstubbe believed, that tombs, altars, statues, and other objects consecrated to the memory of the illustrious deceased, were imbued with special magnetic properties, which aided in attracting the spirits to whose memory they were dedicated. With this impression he was in the habit of placing blank papers in concealed niches of remarkable monuments, and under the most crucial test conditions, obtained spirit writings, drawings, and hieroglyphics of the rarest interest. A volume could be filled with descriptions of these wonderful productions, the genuine character of which it is impossible to question. As some facsimiles and elaborate accounts have been published by several well-known authors, of these writings, we shall ask our readers to satisfy themselves on the present occasion, with two short narratives, both of which are selected, as much for their unquestionable authenticity, as for their rarity. The first is written by Dr. G. L. Ditson for the *Banner of Light* of 1881, and reads thus :—

" Following the above is an account, from the pen of Mons. Leymarie, of a visit made, by order of the spirits, by Baron Guldenstubbe to Versailles. He was required to go with certain ladies named, whom he was to invite, and evidently for a special purpose. While in the gallery at V. the Bishop of Orleans, M. Dupanloup, passed on his way to celebrate mass in the chapel. Knowing the ladies referred to above, he stopped and addressed them, and also the Baron, to whom he expressed his regrets that he was a follower of Luther, who would suffer in purgatory for the division he had caused in the true Church. The Baron replied that he did not think that Luther was in purgatory or in hell, and as a proof of it, if the Bishop would place a blank piece of paper on Luther's portrait, there would come some evidence of his (the Baron's) belief. The Bishop tore a piece of paper from his register, and placed it as suggested. After a few moments he took it down and found written upon it:

‘In vitâ pestis eram Papœ,
In morte mors ero. LUTHER.'

(Living, I was a flail to the Pope; dead, I will be his death.) They were all greatly astonished. The Bishop extended his hand to the Baron and his sisters (both mediums), asking permission to visit them in Paris. The permission was obtained, and he frequently availed himself of it subsequently.

"Among the signatures of royalty which the Baron obtained by direct writing in the crypt of St. Denis was that of Marie Antoinette, which resembled hers while she was in the flesh, as the Director of the Gobelin tapestry manufactory declared—for he had some of her letters. Baron Guldenstubbe, as is well-known, held a high position among men of science, and his sister is perhaps hardly less distinguished. The Baron healed the sick, also, by animal magnetism. M. Leymarie refers to the Baroness Guldenstubbe as a lady devoted to the cause of Spiritualism as well as to the sciences in general."

The second and last notice which we can give of Baron de Guldenstubbe was first printed in the *Daily News*, of London, in 1859, and has been since copied into some of the Spiritual papers. It reads as follows :—

"Among the most famous ‘mediums’ now here [Paris] is a German, the Baron Guldenstubbe, and his sister. The Baron is a nobleman of well-known *status* and good fortune; his wife is a firm believer, but is not a ‘medium,' while his sister—said to be very clever and amiable, but the most weird, unearthly, elfin-looking little creature imaginable—shares her brother's gifts, and even surpasses him in this line. The Baron and his sister, with a number of friends, have been in the habit for two years past, of going to the churches here, placing bits of paper and pencil on the tombs, and finding messages written on the papers by the spirits of those whose mortal remains lie beneath the marble. Those who have been to the scene of operations say that the Baron lays a bit of paper and pencil on each tomb from whose occupant they desire to hear, and retires a few paces from them; that in the course of ten minutes the friends approach the tombs and take up their papers, when messages are found written on the latter. The papers are examined carefully before they are laid on the tomb, and are known to be innocent of all trace of writing; the visitors remain within a few paces of them, so that no one could approach without being seen; and yet when the papers are taken up, they are found to contain writing, always distinctly visible. A week or so ago Madame S—— caught a violent cold; the white of her eye changed, as it were, to a piece of red cornelian. It was frightful to look at, and she fully expected that she would find herself "in for a long and painful attack." Before the attack had come on Madame S—— had been desired (by the "spirit" of some old Norman knight, with a very romantic name, who came to her one evening at the Baron's house) to go on the following Friday to Sèvres, to place a paper and pencil in the middle of the public road, at thirty paces from the entrance to the famous china manufactory, and to wait there for a message from him. Though her eye was so inflamed as to compel her to relinquish all invitations, Madame S—— did not hesitate, protected by a thick veil, to go to Sèvres at the time appointed. She and a friend, having counted off the thirty paces, held a bit of blank paper over the spot indicated for a few minutes, "to magnetise it," and then laid it on the ground with a pencil, covering them with some stones, so as to prevent the wind (which was high and cold) from blowing the paper away. Madame S—— says that she hardly ventured to hope the writing would take place, as Baron Guldenstubbe, who had been told to accompany her, took no part in the thing, but walked about with his sister in various directions, looking at the building and fine prospect. Presently the two came up to Madame S—— and offered to place the paper for her.

"‘Thank you,’ she said, ‘I have placed it myself; it is under those stones yonder.

"‘But you will probably have no message,’ returned the Baron; ‘you are not yet a medium, and it would have been better to allow me to help you.'

"'Perhaps so,' replied Madame S——, 'but I felt an impulse prompting me to try my own power. I have magnetised the paper before putting it under the stones, and by-and-bye we shall see what is the result.' At that moment Mdlle. Guldenstubbe suddenly went off into a sort of cataleptic vision, throwing up her arms, which grew rigid, and declaring, with a face of horror that she saw a man in armour where the stones were; a javelin had struck him under the arm, between the joints of his mail, and the blood was flowing in torrents.

"'He will not die of his wound,' she cried, 'but he suffers dreadfully; he begs Madame S—— to take the paper from under the stones; he has written upon it, and says she must place the paper, as though it were a plaster, on her eye to-night when she goes to bed, and it will cure her.'

"On going to the spot, and lifting off the stones that covered the paper, the latter was found to be marked with a single letter—an L or an S—very indistinct, but so firmly traced, that the paper was raised by the pressure of the pencil, and under it was a queer mark, much better traced, which appeared to be not a letter, but a cabalistic sign. Intensely delighted with the success of the experiment, the party returned to Paris; and on retiring for the night, Madame S—— laid the paper on her inflamed eye, tying it carefully in place with a handkerchief. Next morning, to her great satisfaction, the eye was cured! Now, it is certain that Madame S——, however much she may unconsciously deceive herself, is quite incapable of attempting to deceive others; and as to the fact of the sudden and inexplicable cure of her eye, numbers of her friends, are witnesses to its reality; but what is one to think of such an occurrence? In this case good seems to have been done."

We shall close this chapter by a brief account of a wonderful healer who is even now effecting cures by spirit power, as remarkable as any one recorded during the present century.

Our subject is an excellent mechanic;—a watchmaker by trade, by the name of Hyppolite;—and the following sketch of his noble work is translated for the columns of *Light* (London) of this current year, 1883, from an account written by M. Ch. Fauvety, President of the "Scientific Psychological Society" of Paris.

M. Fauvety says in the Society's Bulletin, for the new year:

"In one of the poorer quarters of Paris, cures have been, and are still being, performed, by imposition of hands, &c. The subjects, many of them have been treated unsuccessfully at hospitals. The healer asks for no payment. What good he does is, he says, for the love of God and humanity. Orthodox practitioners could gain nothing by prosecuting a heterodox therapeutist like this, so he goes on in his work unmolested.

"The healer's name is Hippolyte. He is between forty and fifty, and is in the business of a watchmaker with his father, a hale and upright man of eighty.

"In the room at the back of the shop early every morning Hippolyte's daughter is ready to receive sick visitors, giving to each a number in the order of which each will be attended to. At nine o'clock Hippolyte begins and keeps at his work of healing until past noon, and then he goes to the watchmaking and mending by which the household is supported.

"With respect to his method of treatment, Hippolyte says that as soon as *rapport* is established between the patient and himself—which seems to be pre-requisite—he has impressions as to what is out of order and what he has to do; sometimes his hands are used to make passes; sometimes somnambulic sleep comes on, in which communications are made through the patient about his case, to help in the cure. In chronic cases the method generally pursued is evidently calculated to rouse into activity the will and organic forces of the patient, in aid of which Hippolyte uses manipulations. In these he declares he is moved by his 'spirit guides.'

"Various persons have watched Hippolyte's treatment, and all concur in recognising positive cures or palpable amelioration.

"The maladies we saw cured included paralyses, neuralgia, gouty and rheumatic affections, diseases of joints,—some condemned to amputation at hospitals,—spinal disorders, &c. As many as thirty patients came some days, of both sexes and all ages. The following few cases will illustrate some of Hippolyte's modes of proceeding; they are from a note containing more written for me by him :—

"'A youth suffering from epilepsy was brought to me after much orthodox treatment. As I spoke to him he went into a fit of fearful severity. I felt myself moved to lay my hands upon him, my right to his heart, my left to his head, and to direct my gaze to his throat. He presently came out of the fit, passing into the somnambulic sleep. Then, in answer to questions, he said, that the exciting cause of his fits was fright occasioned by some mischievous companions; he then predicted the day and hour of the next fit, and said he would be well and would not need treatment until then. When he returned to ordinary consciousness he had no memory of what had been said through him. I got his promise to come on the day named. He came in accordance with the promise and went into a similar fit, but less strong, exactly at the predicted hour. My hands were applied as before; the fit lasted but a few minutes, he passing again into the somnambulic sleep; in it came another prediction that the next fit would not be until after twenty-one weeks, and date and hour were named; that the fit following that would be at a still longer interval and would be the last. The fulfilment of these predictions is looked forward to with complete confidence.

" ' A. Delavigne came, after long and fruitless treatment by the faculty, with chronic articular rheumatism and cold swelling of wrist, and hand, and fingers, quite disabling her from her work of lace-making. While treating her I felt the impulse to put a wooden roller under her hand, and upon this roller, without her own volition, and without any aid from me, her hand was exercised for three hours with intervals of rest. This was repeated at every treatment. Sometimes the bare hand would be made to beat the table forcibly with blow after blow, without any effort of her own, as if to rouse the internal parts of the limb into action. She completely recovered and returned to work.

" ' A neighbouring tradesman asked my attention to the case of a lady-customer of his. Three weeks previously she came to his shop to make purchases, and while doing so her little boy, who accompanied her, fell down some cellar-steps. Thinking he must be killed—but he was not hurt—she fainted and fell. She was carried home, for it was found that all power had left her lower limbs. She had been under medical treatment ever since, but with no good result; she was getting very weak, had lost desire for food, and was almost sleepless. She came in an invalid's chair and was carried in.

" ' After the first treatment of twenty minutes she was able to walk to her little carriage. The next day, while under treatment, she passed into somnambulic sleep. In it she spoke of her internal condition and predicted coming pains, from reaction, and their duration. At every subsequent treatment she passed into the sleep, assisted with directions, and predicted her full restoration. At the end of a few weeks, her visits having become less and less frequent, she felt quite well. Her last visit was to tell me, with radiant and grateful countenance, that she had been invited to a *soirée dansante*, and had found that her limbs had entirely regained their full strength and activity.

" M. Fauvety says that although people not poor find their way to Hippolyte, the greater number are very poor, as may be judged from the circumstance that on the table were always tickets for bread placed at Hippolyte's disposal by the *Conseil de Bienfaisance* of his district; there was also a wooden bowl to receive the small contributions of the less poor for him to distribute among those who needed better nourishment than their own means afforded, or to pay omnibus fares for those unable to walk."

A large number of additional testimonials both printed and in MSS., have been sent to the author concerning the beneficent gifts of this noble healer, and the excellent uses to which he devotes his powers. Our space forbids any more extended notice than a hearty " God speed," words which will find an echo in the hearts of hundreds, whom this man's Christ-like work has already blessed and benefited.

CHAPTER IX.

SPIRITUALISM IN FRANCE (CONTINUED).

OF

PHENOMENAL AND EXPERIMENTAL SPIRITUALISM.

The Curé D'Ars, Jacob the Zouave, and Our Lady of Lourdes.

NOTWITHSTANDING the fact that the experimental method of receiving communications through physical mediumship was not in favour with M. Allan Kardec and his followers, (the ruling party in the modern movement in France), there is an abundant amount of phenomena of all kinds recorded in M. Pierart's excellent journal *La Revue Spiritualiste,* also in many other European journals devoted to the subject. From this treasury we are about to select such facts of a representative character as will give a general view of French Spiritualism in the nineteenth century.

Pursuant to the plan of this work, we shall first record a case of spontaneous spirit power or one which gives unmistakable proof of spiritual influence without the aid of invocatory processes, and the illustration we are about to introduce, is the celebrated "Curé D'Ars," the founder of the D'Ars "Providence," and many other noble works of charity.

Jean Baptiste Vianney, was born in the vicinity of Lyons in 1786, in an humble sphere of life.

His natural capacity was by no means remarkable, and at school he was only remembered as a somewhat dull scholar.

Circumstances having opened up the way for his becoming a priest, although he had only Latin enough to say mass, and no learning beyond the routine of his profession, yet his amiable nature and unaffected piety won him friends wherever he went. After some changes of fortune and the rejection of two good offers of rich positions, which in his extreme humility he did not deem himself fit for, he accepted the pastoral charge of the little agricultural village of D'Ars, now in the arrondisement of Trevoux.

This place, the scene of his life-long labours was almost as stagnant and full of ignorance as good Pastor Oberlin's famous valley of *Ban de la Roche.*

When M. Vianney became its Curé, his deep devotion, fervent preaching, and the genuine interest he displayed in the happiness and welfare of his flock, soon won their confidence, and placed him in the very centre of their hearts and affections.

Although he was wholly dependent for subsistence upon the small pittance he received for his pastoral services, he managed to live upon such meagre fare that he was enabled to disburse nearly all his salary in charity.

Very soon his reputation for beneficence drew around him a much larger circle of poor dependents than he could provide for, and then it was that he commenced his extraordinary life of faith, supplicating in fervent prayer for whatever means were necessary to carry out his divine mission of blessing to his unfortunate fellow creatures. In this way the sphere of his benevolence and the wonderful results of the means he employed to maintain it, reached proportions that could scarcely be credited.

Amongst other great undertakings he built three chapels, and established a " Providence " or home for destitute children, to which he added another for friendless women. When the number of his poor pensioners exceeded his means of accommodation, he devoted one room after another of his own humble dwelling to their use, reserving only the garret for himself. All these undertakings involved not only incessant labour but vast expense. The Curé had not a franc of his own to devote to these purposes, for he gave away in casual and daily charities nearly all his means, sometimes even depriving himself of his small allowance of bread and milk to feed the hungry.

He gave away the bed on which he lay and cheerfully substituted for it a couch of straw, which he declared was quite good enough for him. He often robbed himself of the decent clothes provided for him by admiring friends and administered to the wants of others in fluttering rags.

Always cheerful, contented, indomitably active; planning his own buildings and helping to raise them himself; preaching incessantly and never weary of speaking words of good cheer and consolation, this wonderful being became the life and soul as well as the founder of the most gigantic enterprises.

When the orphans of poor dependents wanted bread he prayed for it, and it was sure to come. When the treasury was empty and food and fuel must be purchased he prayed and the money came pouring in from all quarters. When the work on his buildings came to a standstill and the workmen would not tease the good father for help, he knew exactly what they wanted—and prayed accordingly—food, money, building materials, and clothes, were sent just as certainly as they were needed, but not until the good pastor had put up his fervent petition for the same.

Kind helpful women tendered their services as teachers and seamstresses, whereupon he opened schools for the children and established clothing depôts for the destitute.

The idea of his " Providence " too became contagious, and numbers of other institutions of a similar kind began to spring up in different provinces of France.

M. l'Abbé Monnin, whose biography of this wonderful man occupies two bulky volumes avers, that his " Providence " was established fifteen years before that of Müller in Bristol, England, both being supported in the same miraculous way by faith and prayer.

M. Monnin relates endless miracles of the good Curé, the recital of which could add but little to the reader's interest in the astonishing facts already narrated. Here were three chapels erected, four or five houses built and endowed, countless numbers relieved, and upwards of one hundred poor women and children regularly maintained, and all by a man without a penny in the world, and a stipend barely sufficient to provide for the daily wants of one person.

But now a still more wonderful thing was to happen in the enchanted region of D'Ars.

Persons afflicted with disease began to experience sudden cures, whilst praying before the altar, or making confessions to the Curé.

The fame of this new miracle soon spread abroad, until the Abbé Monnin declares, that upwards of 20,000 persons annually came from Germany, Italy, Belgium, all parts of France, and even from England, and that in less than six years, this number increased to an average of 80,000.

Diseases of every kind that had been pronounced incurable were dissipated at once.

The indefatigable Curé gave himself up to the work heart and soul.

His church stood open day and night, and the immense crowds that surrounded it, were obliged to wait for hours and sometimes days to reach the good healer.

No one was allowed to take precedence of the rest, except in cases of extreme poverty or extreme suffering. Princes, nobles, and great ladies, often drove up as near as they could to the church in grand carriages, and manifested the utmost astonishment when informed, that notwithstanding their rank, they could not be admitted except in turn.

The Curé only permitted himself to take four hours sleep, namely from eleven to three, and when he came to the confessional again, the church and all the approaches to it were crowded with those who had waited all night to secure their places.

Omnibuses were established to convey patients from Lyons to D'Ars, and the Saône was covered with boats full of anxious pilgrims.

Amongst thousands of reported cases of wonderful cures, there was one which Mr. Wm. Howitt, another of the Curé D'Ars' biographers, relates in the following touching terms. He says:

"A poor woman came from a great distance, carrying on her back a boy of eight years old who had no use in his legs whatever. For four-and-twenty hours the poor mother perseveringly endeavoured to get near the Curé. At length he put his hands on the child and blessed him, saying some words of comfort to the mother. On entering their lodgings for the night the boy said, 'Mother, buy my sabots, for M. the Curé has promised that I shall walk to-morrow.' The words of the Curé had not been quite so positive, but the child had such faith in him that he felt confident of his cure. The mother went and bought the sabots, and sure enough, on the morrow the child was cured and ran through the church crying joyfully, "I am cured! I am cured!' The mother was overwhelmed with tears and emotion."

We cannot conclude this brief notice which does but poor justice to the subject as detailed by the Abbé Monnin, without making the following additional extracts from Mr. Howitt's interesting accouut of the Curé. He says:

"Numerous letters are found in these volumes [Abbé Monnins' biography] from people, detailing the circumstances of their ailments and their cures, and many others from well-known persons soliciting the prayers of the Curé for themselves and friends. All this time the Curé was not only expending superhuman exertions in church services, from year to year, giving himself but a short pause for a very meagre breakfast and dinner. but he was receiving large sums from all sides and bestowing them as promptly in relieving distress, assisting poor pilgrims, and sending relief to distant places. When somebody asked him the secret of obtaining such great supplies of money, he replied that it was by simply giving it away again as fast as he could, to those who needed it. Nobody at the same time could be more unassuming, unostentatious, or unselfish. He expended everything he had, money, prayers, strength, as long as he had any: and this life he continued till within four days of his death, in August, 1859, at the age of 73.

One of the most remarkable features of the Curé d'Ars was the condition of spiritual clairvoyance to which he had attained. By his extreme abstemiousness, his intense exertions, and his ardent piety, he seemed to have purged away almost all fleshly impediments betwixt the invisible world and himself. Notwithstanding the constant throng of people that surrounded him so that he had difficulty to pass amongst them in his church, or to and from his house; though they were coming and going continually, he seemed to know them, their names, their connections, and circumstances as soon as he cast his eyes on them. He would pick out particular individuals in the crowd, tell them the cases he knew were pressing, take them into his confessional and speak to them of their wants in a manner that filled them with astonishment.

"Seeing a young Savoyard lady in the congregation, he told her in passing, that he would see her on the morrow. As she had but just arrived and was a perfect stranger she thought he had mistaken her for some one else, but on the morrow when she was admitted to his confessional, he told her her most secret thoughts; amongst other things of which she had never spoken, of her desire to enter a religious house, of the sisters she had left at home, and their special characters, all of which was perfectly correct.

"Another lady from a distance, he advised to look after her property and dispose of it at once to her relatives as she had no time to lose. Although in middle life and perfect health apparently, she died suddenly, almost immediately after following his advice. This lady's relations, grateful for his judicious council, informed him of.

"Le Père Nigre who was planning in his own mind a soldier's home at Tourbières, when preaching there, stated in the pulpit, that he had just been to D'Ars, when the Curé, to whom he was a stranger, accosted him by saying, 'Well, father, how go on your plans for the soldiers' home? Come; when will you have done thinking of it, and begin building it.' 'Now,' said the preacher, 'though this thing was in my mind, I had never spoken of it to a living creature, yet he knew all about it.'

"During the excitement of the Revolution of 1848, many persons consulted him about the safety of their families. He bade them rest in peace for there would be no blood spilled except in and just round Paris.

"During the Crimean war he was asked to pray for the safety of a soldier there, and a sister ill at home. He replied, 'The soldier will return quite safe; the sister is ripe for heaven.' He was quite right in both cases. A young lady, during the Italian war, was in great terror for her husband. 'Tell her,' said the Curé, 'that she has nothing to fear. Peace will be made directly.' This was on the 25th June. The news of the interview of Villafranca came directly afterwards.

"A man who had a little land, offered it for sale to the Curé; he advised him whatever he did not to part with it. Very soon after, a mine was discovered in it, which secured the proprietor two thousand francs annually. On the other hand, a director of mines consulted him on investing in a new mine lately opened, and which promised to pay richly. He counselled him by no means to do it. Twelve days after, the mine was flooded with water and became unworkable, besides causing the death of various persons.

"The Curé, like many of the old saints, believed himself terribly assailed by the devil, and no doubt he was, but perhaps not to the extent that he supposed. But let us see what phenomena surrounded him, for actual spirits were busy about him; and let us take their proceedings from his own point of view. From the moment that the Curé opened the orphan house at D'Ars, six years after his going there, and thence to the end of his life, he was beset by the continual evidences of what he deemed satanic influence. At nine o'clock one evening, as he retired to rest, he was startled by three loud knocks at his outer gate, as if they would drive it in with a huge club. He arose, threw open the window, and asked who was there. No answer was given. He returned to bed, but was scarcely asleep when he was roused again by other blows, this time not on the outer gate, but on that of the staircase leading to his chamber. He arose and called out, but again there was no answer. Imagining that they were thieves who came to steal some valuables belonging to the Viscomte d'Ars, he had two stout men to come and sleep at the parsonage; these men heard the same noises, but were unable to discover any one, and soon came to the conclusion that they were produced by no human power. They continued their watch for several nights, still hearing the noises, but discovering no one. A snow fell in the night, and the blows coming on the front door, the Curé descended quickly, thinking this time he should be able to trace them by their footmarks in the snow. To his astonishment there were no marks at all. He was now quite satisfied that the men were right, that they were no mortal disturbers. Some young men of the village, however, formed themselves into a guard over the house during the night, and a party of his neighbours came and slept in the room adjoining his own. The cartwright of the village came, carrying his loaded gun with him. At midnight there came a terrific noise, and the furniture of the room in which this poor man was stationed, resounded as if with a storm of blows. The cries for help caused the Curé and other watchers to rush in, but nothing was either to be seen or heard.

"These disturbances continued with more or less violence for a period of over *thirty-five years.* Sometimes there were heard sounds as if a wild horse were rearing

5

in the hall below the Curé's room throwing his hoofs to the ceiling and then plunging with all four feet on the tiled floor.

"At other times a gendarme seemed to be ascending the stairs in his boots, and stamping loudly as he ascended. Again it seemed like a great flock of sheep passing above his head, and making sleep impossible by that monotonous patter of hoofs. Catherine Lassagne in her notes of her life at the Providence at Ars, relates many such things, and says that every one who knew the Curé, knew that he would sooner suffer death than state an untruth. He said to her one day that when the flock of sheep seemed running over his head, he has taken a stick and struck smart blows on the ceiling to cause them to be silent, but to no purpose. Just as he would be dropping asleep, 'Grappin,' as he called the devil, or the grappling iron, would begin, as it were anew, hooping a cask with iron hoops, and with a tremendous din.

"All this things, remarks the Abbe Monnin, are precisely what happened to the ancient saints, and which are to be found in abundance in the *Diabolische Mystik*, of Göres, B.V., chapters xxi. and xxii. On the occasion of the Curé going to Saint Trivier-sur-Moignans to preach, at a great jubilee held by the missionaries, he was much teased by his brother clergymen about these hauntings. They were very witty about them, telling him they all came of not living well enough; that they were rats, and a dozen other things. The Curé took it all in good part, bade them good night, and went to bed. At midnight these gentlemen came rushing to his room in terrible affright. The house seemed turned topsy-turvy; the doors banged, the windows rattled, the walls shook, and ominous cracks appeared to announce their fall. 'Rise! rise!' they cried to the Curé, who was lying quietly, 'the house falls.' 'Oh!' said he, 'I know very well what it is; go to your beds: you have nothing to fear.' An hour after a bell rung: there was a man at the gate who had come several leagues to confess to the Curé. He always expected when these disturbances took place that some one was on his way to seek consolation from him; and it never failed to prove so. He believed the demons made the uproar out of envy of the good he was about to do. The clergy, however, were cured of laughing at him, and one of them made a vow never again to jest on apparitions and nocturnal noises. Another night the devil, the Curé said, had amused himself by pushing him about his chamber all night on a bed on castors; and the next day when he entered his confessional, he felt himself lifted up and tossed about as though he had been in a boat on a rough sea.

"But was the devil really engaged in all these transactions? The truth probably is, that M. Vianney had so reduced his body by fasting, penance and enormous exertion, that he had opened himself to all kinds of spiritual impressions, in which the devil was sure to have his share. But most likely many of these ghostly visitors were merely spirits of a low order who liked to amuse themselves, as they found the Curé accessible to them. Many, no doubt, like those who visited the Seeress of Prevorst, would have been glad of his prayers, had he not been so completely shut up on that head, by his catholic demonophobia.

"Nothing, however, is more certain than that the worthy Curé d'Ars was actively beset by spirits of one kind or another for upwards of thirty years. He exorcised several persons who were possessed, and records dialogues with these demons in which they assured him that they often said mass.

"Altogether the biography of the Curé d'Ars is one of the most remarkable of modern times. Miracles of the highest and lowest kinds were in active operation round him for a long course of years. They were exhibited before thousands and tens of thousands of people of all classes and ranks and of many countries.

"What had been reported from all past ages by men of the highest character for veracity learning and talent, was repeated at Ars for thirty-five years in all its powers. . . . Yet we are told that all this time the press of France preserved a profound silence on the matter as though no such things were taking place."

To the well-informed Spiritualist, all comment on this strange history is unnecessary. The greatest miracle of the good man's life is the fact that the stolid scepticism of a cold materialistic age can still exist, after events of such astonishing and world-wide celebrity have testified to divine and spiritual interposition in human affairs.

Another phenomenal personage of whom the world has heard much, was a soldier commonly known as Jacob the Zouave, a healer of remarkable power, and one who during his brief mission performed many wonderful cures.

In 1866 or 1867, he first became publicly known whilst yet attached to his regiment, for his curative as well as clairvoyant powers. From childhood he seemed to have been endowed with spiritual gifts of which those around him had little understanding.

Without any instruction, he often executed beautiful drawings of strange fruit and flowers which he said grew on the planet Venus. He could readily detect the nature of obscure diseases and read the character and lives of strangers—in a word, he exhibited constant proofs of clairvoyant powers up to the time when he became famous amongst his military associates for "curing sick people by magnetism, sympathy, and in other strange ways."

As soon as it was known outside his regiment that he possessed these gifts, he was followed everywhere by solicitations to exercise them. Amongst those who heard of and appealed to the famous Zouave, was a talented young gentleman studying at one of the universities, but who was obliged to relinquish all his hopes of name and fame on account of a confirmed sciatica which settled in the right hip and obliged him to walk painfully on crutches for four years. This gentleman, M. Marney, informed the author he paid but one visit to Jacob who held his hands, stroked his body a few times and then bid him walk—he did so, and never after experienced the slightest sense of pain or lameness. This marvellous cure wrought on the son of a wealthy landowner, attracted so much attention that the barracks at Versailles where M. Jacob was quartered became thronged with visitors.

The officers and men were plied with entreaties for permission to see the healer, and the place—to use the words of one of his superior officers, when describing the scene to a company in which the author was present— "resembled a bear garden." Order and discipline was interrupted, the annoyance was unendurable, and the wonderful Zouave was informed he must either give up his profession of killing or curing, for the two were incompatible. After much effort on the part of his friends and admirers, the Zouave's release from the army was procured, and he commenced his career in earnest as a healing medium. Many of his most astonishing cures were effected whilst he yet remained in the army, but when he was emancipated from that restraint, the enthusiasm which followed him knew no bounds.

Doubtless, many of the reports concerning him were exaggerated, and many understated, according to the predilections of the narrators. Certain it is, that his cures were often remarkable enough to be called miraculous, although he himself told the author in an evening visit paid to her in London, that he never professed to cure every one, and indeed many he felt from the first moment of their approach so strongly repelled from, that he knew instantly they were no subjects for him. On this same occasion he explained to those present, that he saw the diseases of those who came to him, and very often realised that they had sick friends or relatives whose condition, if time had permitted, he could have described accurately. To prove this, he undertook to describe a young lady well known to the author, and then a resident of America.

He gave an excellent account of this lady's personal appearance, but insisted that she was the victim of a disease which would terminate fatally in a given period of time, a prediction which was actually fulfilled, although the disease itself was unknown at the time. He (M. Jacob) added, that he almost always saw spirits busy in ministering to the patients who called upon him, and helping him in his modes of treatment.

Many persons complained that this soldier-doctor was brusque and abrupt in manners, hence that he was not generally popular with those even whom he had most benefited. Whether M. Jacob deemed it prudent to imitate the rough, repulsive, manners adopted by so many of our *most popular* English doctors, under the impression, doubtless, that it is *Abernethy-like and imposing*, or whether the complainants asked too much of an humble private soldier, when they required polished manners, in addition to a GRATUITOUS CURE, we need not take the trouble to enquire. That which we do know is, that the lame walked, the blind received their sight, and the deaf heard, and all this and much more than any ordinary chronicle can record, was done without money and without price, for the Zouave would neither accept of money or presents for his great services, and beyond a paltry franc, paid by those who chose to buy his photograph of his father, who stood at the door with them for sale, this generous and magnanimous creature never received aught for his services, beyond the consciousness of the priceless good he was performing.

Although the readers of the Spiritual journals on both sides of the Atlantic have become familiar with the name of Jacob the Zouave, and the methods of his cures have been too frequently described to need reiteration, it is but justice to this noble and self-sacrificing worker to insert at least one testimonial from a grateful patient, and that in relation to a cure, which may be taken as an illustration of the Zouave's usual mode of procedure.

The letter in question was addressed to the *Patrie* newspaper. It was written by the Count Chateau Villard, residing at 60, Rue St. Lazare, Paris, and was introduced by the editor in the following words :—

"We have several times alluded to the Zouave Jacob, garrisoned at Versailles ; but who comes to Paris to effect his marvellous cures.

"What is the secret of all this, and has he any ? Is he gifted with a degree of magnetic influence unrecognized until now ? How are the various cures of suffering people to be explained ? We can give no opinion ; all we know is, that the house in which he operates is continually attended by invalids; one after the other takes his ticket in order to arrive in turn.

"We must add that the Zouave will receive no money, gifts, or thanks ; he will accept literally nothing ! All these facts are attested by an honourable witness in the person of the Count Chateau Villard, residing at 60, Rue St. Lazare, who writes as follows :—

" 'Sir,—Reading in the newspapers that I had offered a part of my private residence to the Zouave Jacob, I beg of you to be so good as to insert, that I have made the offer only in the event of his being forced to quit his quarters in the Rue Roquette.

" 'God knows that I have no wish to take him away from the poor afflicted who will know well where to find him ; I have made the offer in gratitude, and for the benefit of humanity.

" 'I had heard such extraordinary things of the Zouave, that, paralyzed as I was, I had a desire to attend one of his *séances ;* I took my lady with me, who has been a continual sufferer also, and I here state what actually occurred.

" 'On arriving in the Rue Roquette, where there was a stoppage, I alighted from my carriage with the aid of my valet, and a kind working man who hastened to take my other arm. These two assisted me to the workshop of Monsieur Dufayet. In this condition I arrived at the door, where a person who could not be bribed, refused me admission without a numbered ticket ; my secretary, who by a fortunate accident happened to know the principal clerk of M. Dufayet, beckoned to him, and he seeing my state of impotence allowed me to enter into the court, crowded with sick people. The arrangements of the Zouave are that those who are at the worst, should be treated first.

" 'My lady began to weep at seeing so much misery. There was a lady who had brought her daughter ; she stated that the child was being treated within; that she herself was not allowed to assist, inasmuch as the doors are only open to actual invalids. I observed after, the young girl come out, and walk to the vehicle which had brought her, followed by her mother. This same girl had been taken to the place carried by a man.

"'I also noticed a man with a distorted back, unable to walk, make his exit jumping with joy; whilst the plaudits of the crowd, and persons from that quarter of the town who recognized him, joined in.

"'We were introduced at last to the chamber, which may really be designated the miracle chamber. I saw there a human being frightfully afflicted, paralyzed and incredibly ill, brought in by M. Dufayet and his assistants, and placed in chairs closely packed one against the other.

"'As soon as the apartment was full, the Zouave entered and said, "No one must speak unless I interrogate him, otherwise I leave you." Here the greatest stillness reigned. He then went round telling each one what was the matter with him, and without touching them he said "Rise up!" and those that had been paralyzed arose; I am one of the number and raised myself without the slightest effort.

"'At the end of about twenty minutes, he told us all to retire and amidst profound silence each one left. My wife, more polite than I, wanted to thank him; he immediately imposed silence and said, "Other sufferers await me; you are cured, let that suffice, begone!" On going out I was much crowded upon by persons asking me affectionately of what had occurred, and I regained my carriage without help, walking upon a very badly paved street where the best man might find it awkward.

"'From that time forth, my wife also has been marvellously well.

"'There is an extraordinary fact connected with this strange circumstance which it gives me pleasure to relate; the street is crowded with sick people; not only one is desirous to give a helping hand, but all seem to forget their ailments in their interest to help others.

"'Can it be, that this immense charitable influence spreads itself from one source into the hearts of all?

"'I am, &c,,
"'(Signed),   Chateau Villard.'"

"'Paris, August, 1867. "

More than one half of the columns of the *Petit Journal*, a paper of the largest circulation in Paris, was occupied for several days the following September with Jacob's past and present history. One of the editors of that journal made the Zouave's acquaintance at the camp at Châlons in August 1866, where his fame created as much excitement as it subsequently did in Paris, and the editor vouched for a wonderful cure of a long standing complaint effected for a woman who was a servant in his family.

The crowds that assembled daily round Jacob's tent at Châlons, obliged the officer in command to put an end to Jacob's practice of his great and undoubted gift of healing.

The phenomenon of healing by magnetic or spiritual methods has been by no means an uncommon one in France.

Many mediums less distinguished than Jacob the Zouave, but not less successful in a more limited sphere, have practised their art throughout the land with excellent results. Amongst the records of remarkable cures, it has often been questioned, how far the reports of "healing miracles," attributed to the celebrated shrine, grotto, or fountain of "Our Lady at Lourdes," may be relied on as genuine. As many of our readers may not be familiar with the current accounts rendered of this famous spot, we deem it in order to conclude this chapter with a brief narrative furnished from a distinguished writer, who himself visited the scene of the reputed miracles, brought away with him a small phial of the healing water, and left behind a severe ulcer which for many months had fastened on his arm, without his being able to obtain any relief from the ordinary course of medical treatment. This gentleman who was obliged to conceal the little specimen of the water he carried away, from the watchful eyes of the attendant brothers, who have the sacred place in charge, could only learn from them an account of its miraculous discovery with a mass of attendant circumstances so completely in harmony with ten thousand other legends of Catholic wonders, that he was at much pains to obtain information from somewhat more disinterested sources. These he at length arrived at, and from a young peasant who had been one of the most intimate associates of the favoured Seeress Bernadette, the discoverer of the spring, he received the following particulars. Bernadette was the invalid child of a very poor couple, Soubiroux by name, who lived on the outskirts of the town of Lourdes, a small place but little known till recently, in the Upper Pyrenees. Marguerite, the peasant friend of this family, seemed to imply, that little Bernadette was subject to fits, and on the whole, was what the Scotch country folks would call a little "daft," or at the most, not quite as bright as ordinary children.

With a view of promoting a more rugged condition of health, this little one was permitted to wander round the neighbouring heights, and follow the simple occupation of sheep tending. One day as the child was wandering with some of her other companions on the banks of the river Gave, having lingered behind them to bathe her feet in the clear stream, she was amazed to find herself breathed upon by a sweet wind, although at that time there seemed to be no air stirring. Presently a sense of deep awe fell upon her, and as her companion to whom she confided her experience, informed the narrator, a white angel all radiant and glorious with a halo around her head, and shining white garments, appeared before her, bidding her not to be afraid. When the angel disappeared, the little Seeress hastened to rejoin her companions, and at their suggestion returned to the spot, hoping they too might see the glorious vision. The girl Marguerite, seemed to imply that no one in that neighbourhood believed much that this child said, hence they were neither surprised nor disappointed that no shining white lady appeared to them. It was added, that no one would ever have had faith in these visions although little Bernadette repeatedly averred that she continued to see them, until she one day came home and reported, that the white angel had conducted her to a grotto in the rocks, and there made her bathe her feet in a cold spring, and that then she went on her way lighter and stronger than she had ever been in her life.

This tale induced her protectors, some poor peasants who had the charge of her, to repair with her to the grotto, when one of their number who had a paralyzed hand dipped it into the spring, to try if he too could feel how cold it was. On withdrawing it, great was his astonishment to find that he could use his hand and that in all respects it was entirely restored. Others following the peasant's example, flocked to the newly-discovered spring and each experienced immediate relief of whatever ailment possessed them. Why follow up the narrative farther?

The peasants of Lourdes when separately and cautiously questioned, all unite in confirming the above story in all its general features; all moreover have marvels to relate of the hundreds, and some insist, *thousands*, of miraculous cures that have been effected by these wonder-working waters.

But who may describe the elaborations and embellishments that the Brothers of Lourdes report of the sacred spring? *For there are Brothers there now*, and they not only have charge of the sacred waters, but of little Bernadette likewise, and very good care they take of her—so much so, that she is never seen nor can she be enquired of by the profane, only by select members of Holy Mother Church, and faithful votaries of—not the white angel any longer, but "Our Lady of Lourdes" even "the Blessed Virgin herself," through whose miraculous inspiration—"her adopted child," the Saint in embryo, Bernadette, was also miraculously guided to the sacred grotto, &c.

From this plain narrative of plain facts, the reader is at liberty to draw his own conclusions as we venture to draw ours. If he happen to be a good Catholic, little Bernadette's angelic visitor will of course be the impersonation of "the Blessed Virgin," and the chances are ten to one but he or she will *give a donation* towards the erection of a magnificent church and a full staff of priests and attendant church dignitaries, whose duty it will ultimately become to absorb the healing spring for the sole use and benefit of the said church, of "Our Lady of Lourdes."

If these pages be scanned by medical eyes of the "Lankaster" and "Forbes Winslow" type, the child's visions will be *bosh!* the water's magnetic properties "trash," and the cures—all the effects of that most wonderful of all healers—"imagination." To any Spiritualist readers comment is unnecessary. White angels leading poor mortals to beneficent discoveries are not so rare amongst us as to create wonder or disbelief. All we may have to regret is, that little Bernadette and her angel visitants have not an opportunity to manipulate the healing waters of Lourdes without the aid of a band of highly interested "Brothers.'

CHAPTER X.

SPIRITUALISM IN FRANCE (CONTINUED).

PHENOMENAL AND EXPERIMENTAL MANIFESTATIONS

WE presume our readers are sufficiently informed of the *modus operandi* of Spiritual manifestations, to be aware that their production is due either to the spontaneous action of spirits, or to their evocation through the modern circle.

Some instances of the former mode we have already cited, and hundreds more could be described did space permit.

M. Alphonse Cahagnet has recorded numerous cases of apparitions, stone-throwing, hauntings, visions, prophetic and warning dreams, &c., all occurring spontaneously, in this century, in his appendix to the first volume of "Secrets of the Life to Come." The Baron de Guldenstubbe has made a still more voluminous collection of modern facts in his invaluable work entitled *Pneumatologie Positive.* Some of these have been detailed by Mr. R. D. Owen, in his "Footfalls," and others again are mentioned in Wm. Howitt's magnificent work "The History of the Supernatural." From a large collection of kindred narratives we select the following as an illustration of the beneficent character of spirit influence in respect to spontaneous healing. As the case was fully reported in the *Revue Spirite* of 1877, we take advantage of a translation made by Dr. Carter Blake for one of the London Spiritual journals, which reads as follows :—

" M. Dauzac had both his legs broken by a heavily laden cart passing over them. The doctors in consultation declared amputation necessary, so shattered were the limbs. M. Dauzac's son, who is a medium, retired from the sick room, and prayed fervently that advice might be given him from the spirit world, and in particular that a good spirit, known to him as Dr. Demeure, might be sent to help his father. The following words were then written through his hand :—' Do not consent to the amputation, your father will recover ; he will be able to walk and attend to his affairs again. I will mesmerise him spiritually, and give him strength to bear the operation, which I will perform myself ; after much suffering he will be delivered from this affliction.'

" The doctors came, but pronounced against amputation as useless to save the patient's life. He was in a high state of fever, and already doomed. They replaced the bandages and left the house. Immediately Demeure, aided by a band of spirits, began his operations. M. Dauzac says—

" ' I was placed in a position in which I could not have held myself without iron supports ; I then felt a hand rubbing me so hard that I cried out ; everything seemed to be unwound and displaced ; I believed that I was suffering from cramp, for my son had invoked the beneficent spirit unknown to me. In about ten minutes, when I was quite exhausted with pain and fatigue, I was allowed to rest a little ; and what ease I felt ! Ten minutes later I exclaimed, " There it is again ! It is in the other leg ! Everything is being undone." The watchers declared nothing had happened ; the operation was repeated five times on each leg, at intervals of ten minutes ; after that I slept the whole night.

" The following morning the son consulted his spirit-friends, and Dr. Demeure declared that bones, tendons, veins, and fibres had all been duly laid in proper order, and that the cure would be effected. The legs would be slightly shorter than before, but the patient would not be lame, though he would sometimes suffer pain. A dangerous crisis followed, consequent on the extraction by the doctors of a portion of detached bone ; nevertheless, young M. Dauzac, encouraged by the assurance of his spirit guides, would not give up hopes of his father's recovery. One evening he was told, ' To-morrow he will begin to mend, and will steadily improve until restored to health.' The next morning the doctor inquired of a neighbour, before entering the house, whether M. Dauzac were dead. ' No, he is better,' was the reply. ' I am astonished,' said the doctor, ' this change must be the precursor of death.' A fortnight later he told his patient, ' You may now get up ; but be careful, for only one in a thousand could have lived through this : whether this cure be of God or the devil I do not know, but there is something in it which I cannot understand.' M. Dauzac replied, ' You only see in disease a disorganisation of matter ; when you have learned the part played by the soul and the perisprit in the physiology of man, and the relations between spirit and matter, this fact will be no longer a mystery to you ; and you will make many more remarkable cures.' The doctor had nothing to reply, except that M. Dauzac would certainly never walk again. He went on crutches for a fortnight, and was then able to dispense with them altogether.

" The record from which the above is somewhat condensed is signed by M. Dauzac, his son, and thirteen other persons, and is dated Naujean par Brâme, Gironde, January 18th, 1877, and is published in the June number of the *Revue Spirite.*"

As professional mediumship is little practised in France except when patronage is bestowed upon visitors of that class from other countries, we do not feel at liberty to name the various media through whom the members of private circles have the opportunity of witnessing phenomena, still we have personal evidence of the fact, that hundreds of circles are held in Paris and various parts of France, at which phenomena both of physical and mental types are produced in great abundance.

There can be no doubt that the first well marked impulse which experimental Spiritualism received through the invocatory processes of the circle, in France, as in many other countries of Europe, was due to the visit of Mr. D. D. Home, the celebrated, *non-professional*, physical medium,

D. DUNGLAS HOME

and subsequently to the large influx of professional mediums who found in France an excellent field for the demonstration of their peculiar gifts.

Of Mr. Home's *séances* it would be superfluous to write, he himself having related them in two volumes published at different periods of his career, and his many admiring friends having sufficiently described the marvels of which they were witnesses in numerous magazine and news-paper articles.

Mr. Home's manifestations were given in France almost exclusively to personages of rank or those distinguished by literary fame. He was a guest of royalty, the nobility, and persons of the highest position. During his residence in Paris, under the Imperial *régime*, he was a frequent and ever welcome visitor at the Court of the late Emperor, Louis Napoleon. A record of the manifestations produced through his mediumship was kept by command of the Empress, and frequently read to her favoured friends. Amongst these memoranda is one which went the round of the papers at the time of its occurrence, hence there can be no impropriety in alluding to it now. It stated that on one occasion a *séance* was held at the Tuileries, when none were present save the Emperor, the Empress, the Duchess de Montebello, and Mr. D. D. Home.

On the table were placed pen, ink, and paper, and presently a spirit hand was seen, which dipped the pen in the ink and deliberately wrote the name of the first Napoleon, in a perfectly facsimile of that illustrious monarch's handwriting. The Emperor asked if he might be permitted to kiss this wonderful hand, when it instantly rose to his lips, subsequently passing to those of the Empress, and Mr. Home. The Emperor carefully preserved this precious autograph, and inscribed with it a memorandum to the effect, that the hand was warm, soft, and resembled exactly that of his great predecessor and uncle.

From personal knowledge of Mr. Home, the author is able to testify that his powers were most unique, and his mode of exhibiting them clear, candid, and unaffected.

None but the most wilfully blind or prejudiced observer could attach the idea of fraud or deception to Mr. Home.

The author has been present in brilliantly lighted *salons*, when the spirits have impelled Mr. Home to take burning coals in his hand, and lay his head upon a blazing fire without the slightest injury to the tissues of the skin or hair; when his body was elongated several times, from five to eight inches beyond his usual height without the least perceptible motion on Mr. Home's part; when he was floated in the air above the heads of all present; also, when delightful strains of music were played on an accordion untouched by human hands.

These, together with loud rappings, spirit music, motions of heavy bodies, entrancement, speaking in various languages, the apparition of many hands, in a word every form of spiritual manifestation exhibited through other media, have all been produced through Mr. Home, without the equivocal conditions of darkness, cabinets, or the smallest show of deception, or desire to evade any proposed test. It is no wonder that the phenomena abundantly produced, and freely given under such circumstances, should have created an immense sensation in the circles of privileged witnesses and excited a corresponding amount of bitterness and antagonism amongst the enemies of Spiritualism, especially those who were not favoured with an *entrée* to the scene of the marvels.

Thus it was, that certain disreputable members of the press, scribblers whose speciality it was to pander to the lowest appetites of the vulgar, and slander those whose positions were beyond their reach, began to pelt Mr. Home and his friends with the scurrility peculiar to their calling.

Disgraceful lampoons were directed against him, and libellous charges freely circulated. The total absence of justice which marks all judicial proceedings in which Spiritualists are concerned, deterred Mr. Home from attempting to seek redress for these harassing attacks, meantime their effect was confined to those who wished them to be true, Mr. Home's personal friends being too well satisfied of his work to be affected by scurrility or slander.

Another efficient labourer in the spiritual vineyards of France, was Mr. Rollin Squire, a young American gentleman, now an eminent lawyer in Boston, who visited Europe about 1860, and passed some months on the Continent. Mr. Squire was a physical medium endowed with an extraordinary amount of the power which enables spirits to lift immense weights, and perform feats of strength impossible to a giant, much less to a fragile youth like the medium.

The young American soon became highly popular, and as he never received any payment beyond the pleasure he felt in obliging those who *fêted* him, his motives were of course, placed beyond suspicion of self-interest.

In 1865 the work of experimental Spiritualism was greatly aided by the introduction of the celebrated American mediums, the Davenport Brothers, who were induced to visit Paris at the instance of Mr. Samuel Guppy, a wealthy English gentleman, devoted to the study of Spiritualism and its phenomena.

During their stay in Paris, the Davenports were called upon to give a specimen of their peculiar power in presence of the Emperor of the French. Mr. Benjamin Coleman, a steady adherent of the Spiritual cause in England, furnished the following account of this *séance* for the London Spiritual Magazine :—

THE BROTHERS DAVENPORT AND THE EMPEROR OF THE FRENCH.

"The French special correspondent of the *Star* announced that the Davenports had 'performed at St. Cloud in the presence of the Emperor, Empress, Prince Imperial, and all the Court!' The facts of their visit I have from one who was present, and they are as follows :—

"On the arrival of the Davenports at St. Cloud, accompanied by their *confrère*, Mr. Wm. Fay, they found to their surprise that all the preliminary arrangements had been made for the dark circle. Two strong common chairs were placed in the *salon*, and the fires had been put out to secure the necessary condition of complete darkness. The cabinet being erected in the presence of the Imperial party, under the closest scrutiny, the exhibition commenced; as it proceeded, the Emperor showed that he was not only intensely interested, by repeated ejaculations of 'How extraordinary!' 'How wonderful!' but he readily complied with every condition, and insisted upon perfect order being kept. Two persons who were laughing and making sceptical remarks, were reproved, and reminded by him that if they felt no interest in the exhibition they might find more amusement in the billiard room. The Marquis la Grange having entered the cabinet with the Davenports, he extended his arms, and was fast bound to each of the brothers in the usual way. The instant the doors were closed the noise and confusion which was heard within the cabinet surprised the Imperial party extremely; when the doors were thrown open and the Marquis was seen with his cravat removed, a bell stuck in his waistcoat, the violin and guitar fantastically arranged about his person, and the tambourine upon his head, the Emperor threw himself back in his chair and laughed heartily at the grotesque appearance of the helpless and somewhat frightened Marquis, who on his part seriously and emphatically assured the company that the brothers had not moved a muscle.

"During the dark circle the Emperor and Empress frequently exclaimed, 'A hand is touching me.' A watch being held by the Emperor in the palm of his hand, it was at his request given to the Empress, and upon her asking that it might be taken to the Prince Imperial it was instantly conveyed a distance of 60 feet to the young Prince, who threw it from him exclaiming, 'It was so hot, he could not hold it.'

"When Mr. Fay's hands were tightly bound behind his back, the Emperor gave his seal to impress the wax with which the knots on Mr. Fay's wrists were secured. In an instant Mr. Fay's coat was whisked from his back, and was seen flying through the air. The Emperor satisfying himself that the cords and seal were still intact upon Mr. Fay's wrists, he exclaimed again and again, 'Most wonderful! most extraordinary!'

"At the close of the *séance* the Imperial party asked many questions, the Emperor saying he was not surprised at the excitement which such an extraordinary exhibition created in a large assembly. It was, he thought, imprudent to attempt to show such phenomena to many persons at one time, who could not test for themselves their reality. After many expressions of their entire satisfaction the Imperial party withdrew at half-past one in the morning, and the Davenport party sat down to a sumptuous supper which had been provided for them at the palace.

"On the following day the Emperor marked his further appreciation of the exhibition by sending to the Davenport party an unusually munificent gift for their services.

"*At the Davenports' suggestion* the Emperor sent for M. Houdin, who exhibited his imitations, and without any comment being made by the Emperor, he was dismissed and paid the usual fee of 500 francs, and his expenses."

Since the advent of the Davenports in Paris, many celebrated American and English mediums, such as Messrs. Chas. Foster, Henry Slade, Herne, Williams, Eglinton, Miss Fowler, Miss Nichol, Miss Cook, and others, both in a professional and private capacity have visited Paris and the principal cities of France, and stimulated investigation by their remarkable medial powers.

As there is very little variety in the demonstrations of clairvoyant or physical force mediumship and the public for years past has been fairly surfeited with magazine and journalistic accounts of *séances*, half a dozen of which will exemplify thousands, we forbear to offer the reader any detailed description of the phenomena produced through the various parties above named. Suffice it to say, they have collectively demonstrated beyond a peradventure to many thousands of believers, the solemn affirmative of the question, "if a man die shall he live again?"

There are a few incidents which break the monotony of ordinary circle representations, of which the following examples may not prove unacceptable.

In the *Gazette de France* of 1855, we find a curious anecdote related by the Count de La Resie, Author of *Traité des Sciences Occultes* concerning the mode in which the celebrated violinist Urham, received his charming *morçeau* entitled *Audition*—(hearing). The Count says :—

"Urham was a very pious man, and addicted to devotion ; he divided his life betwixt music and prayer. He had composed a melody to the charming words of the poet Reboul—'Angel at the Cradle of the Sick Infant,' which is, as we know, his *chef-d'-œuvre*. Urham after composing this was walking in the Bois de Boulogne. He was alone in a narrow glade, plunged into profound thought. All at once, he heard in the air a sound which greatly agitated him, and lifting up his head, he beheld a light without form and precision. To the sound which had so startled him succeeded another which was continuous, It was an air commenced—there was no doubt of it, and a voice sang the words of 'The Angel and the Infant,' but to an air totally different to the one he had composed. It was more simple and touching than his own. The melody acquired body in developing itself. Giving an attentive ear, he not only distinguished the air, but also an accompaniment with the accords of an Æolian harp. Astonished, and at the same time seized with a deep sadness at this celestial inspiration, he fell into a kind of ecstasy, and distinctly heard a voice which said to him :—'Dear Urham, write down what I have sung.' He hurried home in a state of mind not to be described, and noted down the air which he had heard with the greatest facility : for the notes, he said, scored themselves on the paper.   He published his inspirations, which he named *Audition*, as we have said, and it is a *chef d'œuvre* of grace, simplicity, and delicious harmony.   It is a similar case to that of the Devil's Sonata, of Tartini, except that it was in a dream that Tartini received it, and that the spirit, the more to strike his attention, had assumed a legendary form of a demon, for assuredly the sonata has nothing diabolic about it, but, on the contrary, is a very good composition for the time."

The author, being deeply interested in the progress of musical art, and learning that the following remarkable incident had occurred in the experience of one of her most intimate musical acquaintances, took much pains during a visit to Paris to ascertain the exact circumstances connected with it.

It was stated by M. C. S. Bach that he had sent the account of his relative's experiences to *Le Grand Journal*, which gave the narrative in terms of which the following is a translation, furnished by Mr. B. Coleman, of England :—

"On the 4th of May, 1866, M. Leon Bach, of No. 3, Rue Castellane, great grandson of the celebrated Sebastian Bach, purchased a spinette of antique fashion admirably carved.   After carefully examining it, he discovered on an interior board an inscription stating that it was made in Rome in 1564.   He passed part of the day contemplating his precious spinette—he thought of it as he went to sleep, and it is no wonder that he had the following dream :—He saw a man stand at his bedside, who had a long beard; shoes rounded at the toe, and large bows at the instep; large full breeches, a doublet with slashed sleeves, stiff collar, and a hat with pointed crown and broad brim.   This person bowed to M. Bach, and spoke as follows :—'The spinette that you possess belonged to me.   It frequently served me to entertain my master, King Henry III.   When he was very young he composed an air with words, which he was fond of singing, and which I frequently played to him.   This air and these words he composed in memory of a young lady that he once met with in a hunt, and of whom he became deeply enamoured.   They took her away, and it is said that she was poisoned, and that the King was deeply distressed at the circumstance.   Whenever he was sad he hummed this song ; and then, to divert his mind, I played on my spinette a saraband of my composition, which he much loved.   Thus I came to confound together these two pieces, for I was continually playing them one after the other.'

"Then the man of the dream approached the spinette, and played a few notes, and sung the air with such expression, that M. Bach awoke in tears.   He lit a candle, noticed the hour—two o'clock—and again fell asleep.   Now it was, that the extraordinary scene took place.   In the morning, on awaking, M. Bach was no little surprised to find on his bed a page of music covered with very fine writing and notes quite microscopic.   It was with difficulty that he could decipher them by the aid of his eyeglass, for he is very near-sighted.

"He then tried the air on the spinette.   The song, the words, and the saraband were exactly as the person of the dream had represented them.   Now M. Bach is no somnambulist ; has never written a verse in his life, and is a complete stranger to the rules of prosody.

"Here are the three couplets as we have copied them from the MS. :—

> " Une jour pendant une chasse lointaine,
> Je aperçus pour la première fois.
> Je croyois voir un ange dans la plaine
> Lors je devins le plus heureux des roys !
>
> " Je donnerois certes tout mon royaume
> Pour la revoir encor un seul instant ;
> Près d'elle assis dessous un humble chaume
> Pour sentir mon cœur battre en l'admirant.
>
> " Triste et cloistrée, oh ! ma pauvre belle.
> Fut loin de moy pendant ses derniers jours.
> Elle ne sent plus sa peine cruelle ;
> Icy bas, hélas ! je souffre toujours.

"In this plaintive song, as well as in the joyous saraband which follows, the musical orthography is not less archäic than the literary orthography. The notes are of a form different from those of the present day. The *basse* is written in one key and the song in another. M. Bach has obliged me by playing to me these two pieces, which have a melody simple, naïve, and penetrating.

"The *Journal de l'Etoile* says that Henry III. had a great passion for Marie de Clèves, the Marchioness d'Isles, who died in the flower of her age in a convent, the 15th of October, 1574. Was she 'la pauvre belle triste et cloistrée,' who is mentioned in these verses? The same journal says that an Italian musician, named Baltazarini, went to France at that epoch, and became one of the favourites of the King. Did not the spinette belong to Baltazarini? Was it not the spirit of Baltazarini who wrote the song and the saraband."

The necessity of passing on to other scenes compels us to limit the closing notices of this chapter to two or three extracts, for which we are indebted to the columns of the journal once so admirably conducted by the late M. Pierart, *La Revue Spiritualiste :*—

"PARAGRAPH 1. M. Debray writes us from Nocé (Orne) that Spiritualism in the experimental mode is making rapid progress. There are, he says, several circles held, at one of which—Mdlle. Hermione P—— being the medium—direct writing is obtained from spirits who address each of the company by name, and write in small but almost perfectly finished characters, resembling copper-plate.

"PARAGRAPH 2. At the trial of Jean Lamenire, for forgery, the Judge gave sentence against the prisoner, but our friends at the *Bordelaise* circle, on the previous night had spelled out the exact words in which the sentence was given, and the number of years of the conviction. Our medium Catalina N—— was present with us; could the Judge have read our minds?

"(Signed)   DR. J. VERNAY.

"PARAGRAPH 3. Our old friend Jobard writes from Metz—'I cautiously sounded my host as to whether there was any *table talking* there.' 'Certainly,' was the answer. 'Metz is a second Paris for novelties; we have here several Nobles, Professors, and other celebrities, who are so unfortunate as to be believers and practisers too of the *table talking* art.' Even old pupils of the Ecole Polytechnic, finished mathematicians, and others, who have never before shown signs of mental derangement, turn religious, and put up prayers to God to send them—what would you think?—*good spirits to be their guardian angels!* What are we coming to next? Some of us may be heard by-and-bye talking of the *Spirit land* instead of Heaven or Hell, and inviting our deceased ancestors, to a *déjeuner à la fourchette.*"

Continuing to write of the Metz Spiritualists M. Jobard says :—

"A collection of communications received by these Metz Spiritualists is just published. The tract I speak of will give you an elevated idea of the mediums here.

"Spiritualism has made an opening at Havre, the medium being a young American lady. In Belgium we have two excellent mediums now—one French, the other English.

"Among other interesting particulars in the correspondence of the *Revue* is the following:—

"'Phenomena of an eminently spiritual order have been long observed in the religious community of La Souterraine (Creuse). Madame Dubourg, the venerable superior, while at prayer, is often raised above a foot from her *Prie Dieu*, remaining suspended in an ecstatic state and unconscious for several minutes. She was raised in this way one day while receiving the communion, to the dismay of the priest, who could not, for his agitation, finish the celebration of the office. Other facts of a similar character take place in this establishment, but they are kept concealed as much as possible, so as not to attract a crowd of curious people to the place.

"At la Châtre (Indre), in the Ursuline community, one of the sisters was disabled with hip disease, in which there was dislocation from disorganization of the joint. She has long been laid up, under the care of Dr. Vergne and others. Given up by them, the lady superior had recourse to prayer. A *neuvaine* was commenced; on the last nine days, the patient, worn out with her long suffering and prolonged recumbent position, was carried on her couch into the chapel. There, in the presence of the statue of St. Joseph, and after prayer, the superior cried out in an inspired tone—'In the name of St. Joseph, arise and walk!' The sister arose and walked perfectly healed.

"Dr. Vergne first denied the possibility; but upon seeing that the girl *is* well, he attributes the necessary healing and reduction to—*emotion!*'"

As an evidence of the wide popularity to which the subject of Spiritualism had attained in 1869, M. Pierart quotes in one of his numbers of that year, an article from the *Siècle*, a leading paper, but one which had hitherto contained many notices inimical to Spiritualism. The writer, M. Eugène Bonnemère, says :—

"Although Somnambulism has been a hundred times annihilated by the Academy of Medicine, it is more alive than ever in Paris: in the midst of all the lights of the age it continues, right or wrong, to excite the multitude. Protean in its forms, infinite in its manifestations, if you put it out of the door, it knocks at the window; if that be not opened it knocks on the ceiling, on the walls; it raps on the table at which you innocently seat yourselves to dine or for a game of whist. If you close your ears to its sounds, it grows excited, strikes the table, whirls it about in a giddy maze, lifts up its feet and proceeds to talk through mediumship, as the dumb talk with their fingers.

"You have all known the rage for table-turning. At one time, we ceased to ask after each other's health, but asked how your table was. 'Thank you, mine turns beautifully; and how goes yours on?' Everything turned; hats and the heads in them. One was led almost to believe that a circle of passengers being formed round the mainmast of a ship of great tonnage, and a magnetic chain thus established, they might make the vessel spin round till it disappeared in the depth of the ocean, as a gimlet disappears in a deal board. The Church interfered; it caused its thunders to roar, declaring that it was Satan himself who thus raised the devil in the tables, and having formerly forbade the world to turn, it now forbade the faithful to turn tables, hats, brains, or ships of huge size. But Satan held his own. The sovereign of the nether world passed into the new one, and that is the reason that America sends us mediums: beginning so gloriously with the famous Home, and ending with the brothers Davenport. One remembers with what a frenzy every one precipitated himself in pursuit of mediums. Every one wished to have one of his own; and when you introduced a young man into society, you did not say, 'He is a good waltzer;' but 'He is a medium.' Official science has killed and buried this Somnambulism a score of times; but it must have done it very badly, for there it is as alive as ever, only christened afresh with a new name."

Amongst the many distinguished adherents of Spiritualism in the department of French literature, none have more bravely asserted and defended their belief than Camille Flammarion, the celebrated astronomer, Messrs. Victor Hugo, Alexandre Dumas, and Victorien Sardou, the renowned writer of French comedy. M. Sardou has been himself a medium of singularly happy endowments. Some years ago he executed a number of curious drawings, purporting to represent scenes in the spirit world, amongst which was an exquisite and complex work of art, entitled "The House of Mozart."

As the author is the fortunate possessor of a fine etching taken from this drawing, we may venture to say it is at once a design of singular imagination and extraordinary execution. The *tout ensemble* of the sketch suggests the face of a highly-ornamented organ, every marking, to the finest hairlines, being made up of musical notes, bars, and staves. The effect of the whole is striking, original, and highly suggestive.

As a writer of comedy, the following tribute, copied from the *Cornhill Magazine*, will give an idea of Sardou's ability, and the mode in which his successes have been aided by invisible dramatists :—

"M. Victorien Sardou is known to many as the drawing medium, through whom were produced, many years back, the *Maison de Mozart*, and several other curious drawings. Since that time he has become, perhaps, the most successful and celebrated of modern dramatists in Paris. The court of France is at this moment entertaining a distinguished company at Compiègne, where a series of theatrical representations are given, and the first play selected, entitled *La Famille Benoiton*, has been written by the hand of Sardou. He has publicly announced that not a line of his comedy is the genuine production of his own brain, but, on the contrary, he asserts that it is entirely the inspiration of the spirits of departed dramatic celebrities, with whom he is in constant communication. If this were not true, why should he deprive himself of the honour of being the author of the most successful of modern dramas, as *La Famille Benoiton* has proved to be?"

We cannot draw this chapter to a better close than by quoting the noble words of M. Jaubert, Vice-President of the Civil Tribunal of Carcassonne, in a letter written by him to the editor of *La Vérité*, in reference to some scandalous slurs cast upon Spiritualism by the Bishop of Barcelona. The letter is dated September, 1864, and reads as follows :—

"I have lately read the charge of the new Bishop of Barcelona on Spiritualism which contains amongst others the following passage:—'*It is thus that we come to create a religion which, renewing the wild errors and aberrations of paganism, threatens to conduct Society—greedy of marvels—to madness, extravagance, and a filthy obscenity.*'

"If I had the honour of speaking with the Bishop of Barcelona I would say to him, 'Monseigneur, permit me to cast a glance backward, perhaps it may carry us a step forward. Spiritualism has launched itself into space; it has passed the sea on a ray of light. France has received its cradle. I have had the honour to assist at some of its first rockings. I have seen it lisp by aid of that instrument known under the name of the *table parlante*. It has spelt through the planchette; to-day it writes with a pen which is at your service and mine. It writes sufficiently well, though it has not been spared chastisement; the child has been mocked, buffeted, covered with mud, crowned with thorns. The hatred shown it, has produced a monstrous alliance, such an one as history has not recorded the like. The Materialists and the "servants of God" are leagued together, the first to disdain or deny it, the second to affirm it, but only to spit in its face, and endeavour to strangle it.

"'And the child has nevertheless suffered no injury. It plants one foot on each world. It embraces in its little arms, France and her colonies; Belgium, England, Russia, Germany, Italy, and even Spain. It has its organs multiplied in Paris, Bordeaux, Lyons; Antwerp, Turin. The domestic hearth serves as a sure and impenetrable asylum to myriads of its friends.

"'In your turn, Monseigneur, enter the lists against it; teach all the world that Spiritualism is only a *resumé* of filthy obscenity. Ah! without doubt, the evil is immense. Descend with us, Monseigneur, into the reformatories and the prisons. The picture of our miseries is vast; 4,990 accused before our courts of assize; 176,456 prisoners judged by our correctional tribunals; 3,767 suicides, and every year the same gulf is opened to receive its fresh prey. Spain undoubtedly, in this point of view, has no reason to envy us. Behold the filthy obscenity! but believe me, Monseigneur, the Spiritualists are not there!

"Do you wish to learn the cause of all these evils? I will tell you. I do not draw my proofs from anger nor from vain declamation, I find them in the general account of the administration of our criminal justice. Misery, reverse of fortune, loss of employ, losses at play, sorrow caused by the ingratitude and misconduct of children, adulteries, jealousy, debauch, drunkenness, idleness, disgust of life, immoderate desire of riches, political exaltations, love of power, ambition, religious terrors. Do you comprehend, Monseigneur? This leprosy which dooms us, Spiritualism destroys; it does what you have not been able to do. You know very well that Spiritualism is not a religion,—it leaves all religions just where they were. The great mission of the dead is to prove that they are not dead; that they live and influence our actions. The spirit is certain of its future life; it expects from the Eternal that justice due to all his works; it combats his enemies not by crushing them but by raising and loving them. It does not sacrifice to the kingdom of this world. Anxious to discharge all its duties, it gives to Cæsar the things which are Cæsar's, and to God the things which are God's. It conspires not in the dark, but in full daylight, and for the happiness of mankind.

"'Reassure yourself, Monseigneur of Barcelona; reassure your friends in France! In your turn become a Spiritualist! Affirm to your people that man never dies, that his immortality is proved, not by books, but by material and tangible facts, of which every one can convince himself; that anon, and our houses of correction and our prisons will disappear; suicide will be erased from our mortuary tables, and nobly borne, the calamities of earth shall no longer produce madness. But if you prefer it, Monseigneur, persist in your insults, strive not to teach as to forget then, the treasures of love and charity." '

CHAPTER XI.

SPIRITUALISM IN FRANCE (CONCLUDED).

THE two extraordinary narratives we are now about to present to our readers are furnished by A. J. Riko, Esq., of the Hague, and although their substance is to be found in several printed records, Mr. Riko's plain unvarnished descriptions correspond so closely with the accounts *given orally to the Author by an eye-witness*, that we prefer to transcribe—as far as possible—our kind correspondent's own words. The first case is headed :—

" The Phenomena at the Abbey of Prunois-sous-Ablis — Arrondisement of Rambouillet—France.

"One of the most interesting records extant on the subject of Spirit power is an account of the disturbances which took place at the above-named Roman Catholic Abbey in the year 1855. On October 1st at eight o'clock in the evening, a great many stones were thrown at the window of the Presbytery. Several witnesses were present, and numbers of others were called by the priest to watch the proceedings. The stones were thrown by no visible agency, and struck the window panes in showers, without breaking any.

"October 2nd. A box filled with dirt and refuse, was found in the place usually kept for the bread, which was thrown on the ground close by. Stones were thrown all that day at intervals, but though the windows were struck in showers, no glass was broken.

"October 3rd. At three in the afternoon, all the doors of the Abbey being shut, a quantity of ashes—salad plants, spoons, coals, and rotten fruit—fell about the floor and furniture of the Presbytery, also in several of the other rooms, every door and window being shut. The showers continued falling till ten o'clock, when one of the witnesses,— the Curé of Alix, said jokingly, that money would have been more welcome than stones. As he spoke, every one in the room was pelted with 'liards.'

" October 4th. The fire irons—brought without noise from the Priest's private room—were found in a locked chest. Pieces of butter and knives used in the larder, were found in another locked chest. As the Abbé was passing out to go to service, a pot full of sand was tossed into a pail of water before his eyes. No disturbance took place in the church, but when he returned, chalk from the walls and ceiling, coals, ashes, fruit, bread, and all sorts of objects were thrown hither and thither through the house, and the stones were flung from outside against the windows all day.

"October 6th.—The bedclothes in the Priest's room, and those of several of the inmates, were pierced with round holes, and the pieces taken out were found in distant closed rooms.

"October 7th.—At nine o'clock the servant maid retired to her room, but found everything displaced, and the furniture in such disorder that she swooned from fear. That night one of the Priest's relatives whom he requested to pass the night in the same room with him, called out in great terror, that his legs were being tied together. When the Priest succeeded in getting a light, he found the young man thrown into a corner, with his legs tightly bound together above the knees with a cord nine feet in length.

"October 14th.—The cook found pieces of coal, sweepings, dust and filth in every article she was using to prepare the meals, in fact she could not put a dish or saucer out of her hand, but what it was instantly but noiselessly filled with rubbish. The same was found in all the pots and kettles. Watchers stationed in all directions failed to find any visible agent.

"October 17th.—Stones were thrown in larger numbers and more inces-antly than ever. Fires were lighted on hearths in empty rooms. The young man before mentioned—the priest's relation—had his cap taken from his head and it was afterwards found in a chimney in a distant part of the house.

"October 18.—A violent noise being heard in the Presbytery, the party who rushed to the spot found a ball of paper containing a large quantity of gunpowder. The ball was tied with a string, and a hole was cut in the wrapping ; close by was a match. Soon after this the disturbances increased, and the garden walks were found indented with marks of huge claws, not belonging to any known animal. Heavy blows and sounds as of tramping feet were now heard during the night in the corridors. As a large number of watchers were stationed day and night within and without the Abbey, it soon transpired that similar disturbances had occurred several times within the last thirty years, though never with such violence as now.

"October 22nd.—The cook was pelted with stones, coal, &c., wherever she went—nothing struck her, though objects fell in showers around her. The Priest, on going to bed, found the wood which had been laid in the grate ready for lighting, taken out and all arranged on his bed in the form of a cross. In the morning, his clothes were found stuffed tightly in a large pitcher full of water—and this, though the door was locked inside, and the window made fast."

Mr. Riko follows up this narrative with a long list of witnesses' names, many of whom were persons of high respectability, holding official situations. It may be added, that in the course of three months, the disturbances died out, though no cause could ever be discovered for their occurrence. M. Riko's next narrative is the well-known case of the disturbances at Cideville—Seine Inferieure, France. The author is in possession of two French newspapers containing reports of the trial in this celebrated case. To save the necessity of a fresh translation, we will again resort to M. Riko's concise narrative. He says :—

"In the spring of the year 1849, the Curate of Cideville having called to see one of his parishioners who was sick and confined to his bed, found at the bedside a man who had the reputation in the neighbourhood of being a "Sorcerer," and was, besides, a fellow of very bad character. As a friend of the Curate's had been attended by him and died under his hands—as the neighbours alleged, by evil practices—the Curate drove him from the house and warned him not to return again. Soon after this "the Sorcerer" was arrested for some mal-practice, and thrown into prison. There he uttered fierce menaces against the Curate, and swore he would be revenged, ascribing his misfortunes wholly to the priest's enmity. Shortly after this, two boys, who were placed with the Curate for education, happening to be at an auction, met there Thorel, a shepherd, who was a friend, and said to be "a disciple" and follower of the Sorcerer. Thorel had been heard to swear he would have revenge for his master's imprisonment. When he met the children at the auction, he approached them, and it was affirmed at the trial, laid his hands on one of their heads, and muttered words they did not understand.

"Immediately after their return to the Abbey, violent poundings were heard on the walls, floors, ceilings, passages, and in every part of the building. Sometimes these blows were so heavy as to make the inhabitants fear the walls would be demolished. Numbers of persons passing near the Abbey stopped to inquire what was the matter. After these blows had been given for several days, and crowds surrounded the building day and night, it was found that the thumpings would keep time to music, and beat correctly the measure of any tune asked for. Windows that could not be reached from without were smashed, crockery broken, and furniture hurled hither and thither with frightful force.

"Officers of justice were sent for, and police stationed everywhere. The furniture flew around them and piled up into curious forms before their very eyes. Some of the heavy furniture seemed to be lifted about as lightly as feathers. Other things were broken into the smallest fragments, and no one was hurt except the Mayor of Cideville, who on one occasion was struck so heavily on the leg, that he feared the bone was broken. As he sat down, he felt a soft hand stroking and patting the affected part, and the pain ceased instantly.

6

"Several of the visitors had their dresses pulled, and their arms and faces gently patted. M. de Mirville, who often attended these wild weird scenes, could hold quite intelligent conversations with the invisible knockers, and get them to answer, or to move any object he wished. All this was done in the light, and in the presence of crowds of witnesses. Meantime the child who had been touched by the shepherd, was always complaining of the shadow of a man following him, and several others described a hand of a grey colour, which seemed to be busy amongst the moving objects. Very often visitors would ask the knockers to spell out their names, ages, and anything they wished to say ; and they afterwards testified in court, the intelligence thus rendered was always correct. In course of time, wreaths of smoke were seen winding through the rooms, and disappearing as suddenly as they came. Footsteps, and the rustling of silk were the next sounds heard. One day, the child touched by Thorel screamed out that there was a black hand coming down the chimney,—no one saw it but the boy, but all in the room heard a smart smack, and the child's face remained red for a long time afterwards. Some one suggested that pointed irons should be driven into the walls at every place where the blows were heard. A large party proceeded to follow this advice. With every blow a stab was made. Immediately upon this, flames burst out from every hole, together with such thick smoke, that the witnesses were obliged to open doors and windows to get rid of it, and desist from all farther attempts of the kind. All the party there assembled testified that they distinctly heard the word 'pardon' cried out in a piteous voice.

"That night all was quiet. The next day, Thorel came to the door of the Presbytery, and asked to see the priest.

"His behaviour was humble, his words embarrassed ; he tried to hide with his hat bleeding wounds in his face. The child saw him and cried, "That is the man who persecutes me." The priest asked him from whence came the wounds he had in his face. Thorel refused to answer, but the priest forced him to fall on his knees and ask pardon, which he at length did ; at the same moment he tried to get hold of the child's frock, in which he succeeded. The priest made him promise to go to the Mayor, and there Thorel in presence of many witnesses fell again on his knees and asked for pardon, trying at the same time to touch the priest, who, in order to defend himself, struck the shepherd with his stick. Thorel on a subsequent occasion confessed that his master the sorcerer was the cause of the disturbances at the Abbey, and that he hated the priest because he had chased him away from a patient ; but he offered to deliver the Abbey of all further disturbances if the priest would offer him something. This was refused, and then Thorel prosecuted the priest for the strokes he had given him in legitimate self-defence. It was on that trial that all the mysterious phenomena at the Abbey of Cideville became generally known, and was commented on in the newspapers of the day. The priest was acquitted and Thorel condemned in all the costs. This verdict was given after the learned discourses of the well-known advocates Vaquier du Traversain for the priest, and Fontaine for Thorel. The latter did not appeal. Several other strange feats performed by Thorel were brought to light during the trial. He predicted several things which happened as he had announced ; he walked through the field with another witness, and said to him, "Every time I shall strike my basket with my fist you will fall," and every time Thorel did so, the witness was seized at the throat by an invisible grip, and thrown to the ground. Others declared that when passing Thorel on the road, they were persecuted by stone throwing, the stones flying towards them from different directions by invisible power, but falling directly before their feet without injuring them. The phenomena began on November 26th, 1850, and ended on February 15th, 1851, at which date the Bishop ordered the two children to be taken away from the Abbey. In the judicial verdict passed against Thorel, the judge in summing up says that '*the cause of the extraordinary facts which occurred at the Abbey of Cideville, as very clearly stated by the testimony of all the witnesses heard, has remained unknown.*'

"It was very remarkable to note the uniformity with which the witnesses related the different strange phenomena observed by them. Some testified with all the simplicity of peasants, others with all the exactness of highly educated people ; but the facts were given by all as identical. Though some of the sceptical newspapers declared all the twenty-five witnesses to be hallucinated, etc., not one had the courage to indicate them as liars ; their good faith was acknowledged by all.

"The phenomena at the Abbey of Cideville stand as one of the best established incidents of the work of an invisible world in our days."

Narrative translated from the *Journal Indre-et-Loire*, dated July 29th, 1882 :—

"A shower of stones has fallen at intervals during the past sixty days, upon the farm-house of Lioniere, near Montbazon (Indre-et-Loire). This farm-house, situated in an open field, is prominent to view, and is approached by two broad thoroughfares, over which persons cannot travel without being seen.

"The stones begin to fall at dusk, and the shower continues until morning. They seem to come from all directions, and their collision leaves deep indentations upon the walls and doors of the farm-house. No one has ever been wounded by them, however, and the intention seems to frighten rather than to seriously injure.

"The rural guards and the armed police of Montbazon have for many nights watched in ambush around the Lioniere without discovering any marauders. The stones fell around them in the darkness in their hiding-places. One of the police, who was crouched upon the roof of the house, was hit upon the shoulder, though very lightly. Companies have been organised, with the assistance of the farm hands and neighbours, to thoroughly beat about and search the place. Nearly a hundred persons gathered at the farm and scoured it in every direction. Nothing suspicious has been seen. During the going and coming, the projectiles have not ceased to whistle by the ears of the investigators.

"The dwellers at the farmhouse of Fontaines, commune of Rouziers, have been awakened almost every night by singular and varied noises. Sometimes it is like the noise of a heavily-laden wagon. The jolting of the wheels in the ruts of the road, the clash of the iron tires against the stony obstructions are heard, as also the prolonged cracking of the whip. The walls of the house tremble as by the passing of some heavy vehicle.

"Sometimes dancing music is heard—sound of a violin accompanied with stamping, like the noise made by iron-nailed boots striking against the floor in beating-time. Again a noise is heard in the well, like the fall of some heavy body, that on striking the surface of the water chops and spatters it about with a splashing sound, but no one has ever been able to discover the cause of these noises. In vain have the farm people, reinforced by their neighbours, placed themselves upon the watch at night—in vain have they used every strategy they can invent; they are still ignorant of the cause of their annoyance. The manager, M. Ronnin, who has been but a short time in this part of the country assures us that he used to hear the same noises and sounds in Vendée."

"An extraordinary medium has been found at Agen. She is quite young—is a Mdlle Honorine—and when the spiritualistic phenomena occur through her, her hands are tied. together with a handkerchief and she is placed upon a bed. Cards are placed under her pillow, or are pinned to the bed-curtains, and mental questions are asked, with the desire that the answer shall appear on said cards; and there indeed the correct answer is found. The '*Marseillaise*' is then drummed out, the '*Dame Angot*,' the '*Chant du Départ*,' the '*Retreat*'—in fact, anything called for. The sound of the horses' feet as the cavalry retreat, is perfectly represented. Musical instruments are played upon and carried about the room. An officer of the army placed a ribbon under the pillow, and invisible fingers tied a knot in it. Money laid outside of a closed tobacco-box was found within it. The bed was drawn across the room, or, as the child-medium said, '*was pushed*.' The direct writing obtained, manifested familiarity with the pen, whereas Honorine can scarcely write or read."—*Revue Spirite, December*, 1881.

"The *Revue Spirite* has from time to time made mention of a young girl residing at Saint Marie-de-Campan, in the province of Bagnères-de-Bigorre, among the Pyrenees mountains, under whose mediumship wonderful phenomena have taken place, and which have attracted the attention of the French secular press generally."

M. Aviragnet, writing to the Editor of the *Revue Spirite*, says :—

"On the 21st of January, 1882, the young girl from Ste Marie-de-Campan, Marie Alexandrine Torné, of whom we have spoken, and who has created a sensation in all this Department, came to me and is with me still. She reads a book without looking at it; she plays dominoes with her eyes closed. I had ha dly formed an idea of tying her hands behind her back than they were tied and untied by invisible hands. I desired to have something brought to me, and yesterday evening I was presented with a flower that does not grow in our gardens. They (the spirits) have manufactured for me a flower of a beautiful red colour, and to-day after dinner, the young girl came to my bedside with a flower in her hand, which immediately disappeared."

It must be stated that M. Aviragnet was a chronic invalid and had been confined to a bed of sickness for a long time. The general impression of this excellent gentleman's friends was, that the medium—quite a young child—who came of her own accord to the house, was sent to redeem a promise of M. Aviragnet's spirit guides that they would cure him. M. Aviragnet continues his narrative as follows :—

"Marie Alexandrine returned to her home shortly after the phenomena that I have detailed to you. At the end of some six days, having received the order to come to me again for an urgent necessity, she set out before day, quite uneasy, fearing to be too late for the operation, which consisted in removing other parasites from my ear.   On Sunday morning she came to my bed, and a hand was formed in her presence.   She made passes over my heart, and infused a mild fluid into my ear and over my eyes. . . . On Monday the medium was forbidden to eat anything.   She was ordered to fast for three days and two nights, and she gave herself up to prayer.   I was told not to be uneasy, that the child would be in no danger ; that the angels would sustain her.   I would fain have shared the sufferings of the child, but loud knocks upon the table made by the friends said ' No.' "

"On Tuesday evening at seven o'clock the child was permitted to take refreshment. Vaporous forms became manifest all around her.   These forms approached me, took me by the hand, patted my face and my breast."

Without following out M. Aviragnet's diary any farther, it is enough to say he was raised from the sick bed he had so long and hopelessly occupied, and testified before a number of officials in his district that without the aid of medicines, or any other means than the presence of this extraordinary medium and her attendant spirits, he was entirely restored to health.   In the issue of *La Revue Spirite*, of December, 1880, is the following :—

"A new writing medium has appeared in France, in the Gironde, who attracts no little attention from the fact that, of himself, he knows nothing about the art of penmanship.   Our friend and brother in the faith does not know how to write, and in opposition to his parents in 1867 he was incited to write mediumistically through the spirits two letters which contain forty-eight lines, have many antique words, and combination of words that must awaken interest, while their sentiments are lofty and impressive.   It seems also that he now speaks as if learned, and has the gift of healing."

"A new rapping medium has also been discovered in the village of Chauvirey, Cote d'Or—a little girl about thirteen years of age.   The noise begins when she retires to bed ; sometimes it is like a scratching with the finger nails ; then it increases in volume till it resembles the sound of revolving mill-wheels.   The clergy and gendarmes have, as usual, been called in, but cannot account for the phenomenon—which continues when the feet and hands of the girl are held fast, and which has now for about two months and a half defied the scrutiny of all her visitors."

In the same journal, of date 1877, we find a large number of cases describing various kinds of phenomenal mediumship.   Amongst them the following :—

"The spirits of the people of the 'barricades' seem not to forget in the spirit world those exciting scenes by which, some of them at least, passed beyond the confines of our sphere ; indeed it is in France, above all other countries with which we are acquainted, stone-throwing by the invisibles is most common.   Some years ago in Paris, near the Pantheon, as reported by the police, a house was pelted with stones, some of which were so large that the doors and windows, secured by heavy timbers, were demolished.   The missiles descended with mathematical precision, but whence could not be discovered by the police, though stationed on housetops in the immediate neighbourhood.   Quite a number of like cases I have since recorded.   Now, M. Parjade writes that at Omet (Haute Garonne), at the house of M. Vimeney, the same phenomena have been taking place ; the furniture, crockery, cooking utensils were tumbled into confusion, while stones flew in every direction.   'These facts,' says the writer, 'have excited all the inhabitants of the canton, but no one but the Spiritualists could discover the cause ; they are identical with those of Tabanac in the year 1872.'

"'The Spiritualists of this region,' he continues, 'evoked the spirits and reasoned with them ; the daughter of M. Vimeney was restored to health, and the phenomena disappeared.'

"In confirmation of the above, Mons. Vimeney wrote himself to the editor of the *Revue*, and says : 'By our appeal and by prayer, these spirits came to us and promised to listen to our counsel ; my daughter has become perfectly well, and the disturbances have ceased completely.'   The letter is signed by sixteen witnesses."

The *Revue* of October, 1880, gives an interesting account of still another physical medium, quite celebrated in the Spiritualist circles of Paris, but known only under the sobriquet of Amélie.

The phenomena obtained in the presence of this young girl are very varied. The following is a brief narrative of one *séance* detailed by Dr. G. L. Ditson, the foreig correspondent of the American *Banner of Light.* This gentleman says :—

"In June, 1875, at a *séance,* the spirits caused the musical box to play, stopping and starting it at will. When visiting a Mme. X., a letter which should have been sent to him some time previous, but had been lying in a receptacle with many others, was brought by the invisibles and placed in his hands. . . . .

"One evening," he says, "Amélie's hands were drawn behind her and fastened very firmly with a cord, whose ends were carried down and 'fixed solidly' to the leg of her chair. The spirits also essayed a duo on the harmonica and tambour, and themselves gave the signal for applause produced seemingly by the hands of little children. The following was given by direct writing : 'We love these *séances,* and will do our best to materialize.' In the next month flowers were brought by the spirits—*une masse des petites plantes*—blue flowers, moist, with fresh earth. Their name however had been forgotten. Amélie took a pencil and rote : 'Forget me not.'"

Dr. Ditson adds the two following narratives, translated from the *Revue Spirite* of the same d te as above :—

"Of Mme. Sardou in lethargic sleep and her voyage in space I must quote a little. Mme. S., sixty-two years of age, made the following statement to the narrator :—

"'About twelve years since I was in the hospital at Lyons, and died, to all appearances, and so remained for twenty-four hours. I had no consciousness of what was passing around me. During this time I went up, up, till the earth appeared blue, like the heavens, and then was out of sight. On I went. Finally I arrived in front of a magnificent chapel, gleaming with indescribable beauty, and in which there was a light of surpassing brilliancy. Attempting to enter, I was warned that I was not yet pure enough ; that I had to return to the earth and suffer much, and then I should be admitted to this paradise. I then went on without knowing what impelled me, till I looked upon a vast, arid, boundless field. There I saw a prodigious quantity of persons all bent towards the ground, which they were scratching vigorously with their two hands, as a dog scratches with his paws. I saw here priests of all ranks ; people well and ill-dressed. I was astonished. Looking on one side I saw *une dame blonde ;* it was a very beautiful woman. There is none upon earth like her. She did not speak to me, so I said : 'Madame, what is this, all this multitude?' 'My child,' she replied, 'this is Purgatory.' 'Where then is hell?' I asked. 'There is none,' was the reply ; 'it is here that penitence is made. See, my child, these had upon the earth all they needed, but were never satisfied, wanting always more, and never doing any good to their fellows. Look yonder,' she said, extending her arm, 'see those down there, down there afar off ; it is two thousand years they are there, two thousand years !' When some dissent was expressed to Mme. Sardou respecting her vision, she replied with much vivacity, '*Oh! but I saw it!*' (She had once before made a like asseveration when some doubt had been expressed.)

"These earnest replies," continues the writer, "prove abundantly the sincerity of her recital. When the spirit of Mme. Sardou returned to her body and awoke it, she found her friends were about enwrapping it for its final disposition. She screamed and drew many persons about her bed. To these she related her voyage and experience, and she was assured that she had seen the Virgin Mary. She suffers, as was predicted by the angel ; and, not unmindful of her vision, she says sadly, when she sees a person in affluence withholding a farthing from the needy, 'See still another who is going to scratch the earth.' . . . .

"Suffice it to say, the woman was persecuted for her faith, and even threatened by the clergy ; and her house, No. 54, Rue de la Reine, was named the 'Folle Bretonne.'"

Within the last two or three years a young person who will quite compare with any of the most powerful physical mediums of America or London, has come prominently before the Spiritual investigators of Paris, by name "Madame Babelin." From a large number of reports of *séances* with this medium, we select the account given by Dr. G. L. Ditson, who writes as follows to the *Banner of Light,* of October, 1882 :—

"Last week, at a Mme. Babelin's, where I was introduced by the courtesy of Mme. Leymarie, I was very satisfactorily entertained. About fifteen of us, joining hands, encircled Mme. B., the medium, who, at her own request, was tied to her chair, 'Universal scepticism,' she said, 'requiring it.' The medium's hands were intricately bound. and as intricately secured to the chair, the ends of the cord being taken by one of the circle, which formed itself around the table, the medium sitting near it. On the table were two musical boxes, three fans, a hand-bell, a child's whistle, a toy barking-dog, and a box of lozenges. On taking seats the candle was extinguished, the circle interlinked little fingers and sang. After a little, there were various manifestations, more than one always occurring at the same time; detonations in, on, or under the table; overhead were heard, moving hither and thither, the musical boxes, the bell, whistle, and barking toy, all in rhythm; the air was kept in motion by the fans, which were also rubbed against our heads; our faces, shoulders, and hands were patted with soft warm hands.

"Each one was also favoured with a large bunch of wild flowers. A bunch of them was forcibly arranged beneath my vest, and later some were put between my neck and collar. Phosphoric lights were then seen floating about, coming sometimes, as it were, from under the table and going into the laps of different parties. There was also seemingly an attempt to illumine a figure that stood close to me—at least, some drab drapery was near me, enveloping apparently a human form. This effort was unsuccessful. A small part of a human figure was however, quite well developed, and there was a persistence in showing me this. At first I thought that only a simple ball of phosphoric light was before me, but as its action was peculiar, I regarded it attentively, and saw unmistakable fingers of two hands that were manipulating the phosphoric ball, taking light from it to show themselves. When I expressed aloud to my neighbour the fact, the two hands separated, one going to the right of the circle, the other to the left—an unmistakable proof that they pertained to no human being. In response to a mental request, some fingers pressed my forehead, and on asking the question mentally, if a loved deceased cousin were present, my cheek was several times smoothed as if by the gentle hand of affection.

"At a sitting last evening, at Mme. Huet's, where I had been presented by M. Lacroix, we had the levitation of a heavy table, and those unmistakable raps which are so very characteristic of the Fox sisters' circles.

"At a *séance* at Mme. Chavée's we were also, through raps, favoured with several interesting messages from the ' promised land.' Though a stranger to almost every one present, I received, in English, the first communication. My brother, who died in Natchez in 1833, not only spelled out his entire name, but expressed his relationship to and supervision of my son, in such terms as to make it a moral certainty that no other than my brother William was actually giving the welcome sentences that at this moment so unexpectedly were being recorded by one (a French lady) who knew nothing of the meaning of the words she penned.

"Paris, France, Oct. 6th, 1882. 　　　　　　　　　　　　G. L. DITSON."

Dr. Ditson subsequently adds the following translation from the *Revue Spirite* :—

"Dr. Chazarain resolved, in order to add to the weight of his testimony, to hold his future *séances* at his own home, with his family and friends, Madame Babelin still being the medium.

"At his first home *séance*, fourteen in the circle, on the light being extinguished the medium described, in minute detail, the appearance of a spirit, whose wife and daughter were present; he had also been well known to Dr. Chazarain.

"'The medium,' says he, ' passed then into the trance; after some rapping sounds, hands touched and pressed us all, the objects placed upon the table floated over our heads, the musical instruments sounding; fresh flowers were laid upon our hands. There were no flowers in the house before the *séance*. Then phosphorescent hands gradually developed themselves as I previously described. The form of a child was then seen upon the table, visible by its own light. It moved about, kissed its hands to us all; we heard the kisses; and as the fingers left contact with the lips they emitted a soft light and whitish vapour. The child disappeared and reappeared three times, but was visible altogether for about ten minutes. When I afterwards showed the photograph of my little Marie all recognised it as that of the child-spirit.

"'Then by my side, appeared the well-defined face of my mother, deceased at seventy-five.

"'I felt then a large hand laid upon my head; in reply to the question, mentally put, Are you he of whom I am thinking? the hand gave three taps. My thoughts were of my deceased brother. Then came sounds of the pencil; these ceasing, we lighted up and found a little writing on two pieces of paper ; on one, "My beloved sisters, I am with you and shall be your guardian.—Marie." On the other, "Seek not thy brother on earth ; he is in God's immensity. I am happy to be able to be with you.—Paul." This was the name of my brother. He was in the Army of Reserve in 1870. After the battle of Chateauneuf no news ever came from him ; his name was neither in the returns of killed nor of prisoners. A spontaneous communication had been received by me through another medium, to the effect that he had been killed for plunder by some dissolute men of his company. I had thereupon written to the authorities to know how I might direct inquiries among the men of his company at that period. As if in reference to my letter came another scrap of paper, "No vengeance, expiation." I received this as a lesson on which I pondered.'"

In an article written for a scientific paper of Paris, by M. Chas. Huc, editor of the journal—*Prospérité Agricole et Commerciale*—there is a long account of a mediumistic couple who have lately excited much interest in Parisian circles. M. and Mdme. d'Alesi are the parties alluded to, and M. Huc says, writing of the husband :—

"The medium is a young Hungarian of brilliant education, but who, through many misfortunes, has been reduced to poverty. His young and estimable wife shares with him heroically his ill-starred existence, and when under magnetic influence, proves to be also a clairvoyant, able to see and describe spirits and give good medical advice. M. Hugo d'Alesi sits at a table in a room so dark that it is almost impossible to see the figure he is sketching. He seems to pay but little attention to what he is doing, executing rapidly, and in the space of a few minutes accomplishes a remarkable work—the head of a woman, for instance—wonderful in respect to *finesse d'execution*. He has thus in pastel produced a striking likeness of Pius IX., and in *aquarelle* a magnificent landscape. The latter bore the signature of Diaz, a fine artist, who passed away about a year since. Most of M. d'Alesi's productions bear the initials T. D., which, on account of the general style, are attributable to Donato, who contributed in his day largely to the resurrection of sculpture in Italy."

It was in the summer of 1882, that the author, then a guest of Madame La Duchesse de Pomar (Countess of Caithness), at Paris, had the pleasure of witnessing M. d'Alesi's remarkable mediumship as an instrument for artistic spirits. The *séance* was given in a brilliantly lighted library, in presence of about half a dozen persons, including the Duc and Duchesse de Pomar, the author, Dr. Britten, Madame and Mdlle. Leymarie. M. d'Alesi occupied about ten minutes in sketching a large crayon drawing. During the performance he was engaged in lively conversation with the company who stood around him, and the author and her friends can all testify that he scarcely ever glanced at his drawing, his hands appearing to move with lightning speed and occasionally with some violent, though unknown impulse, without any apparent volition of his own. When the drawing was finished, M. d'Alesi gracefully presented it to the noble mistress of the mansion, the Duchesse de Pomar. On first regarding this sketch, nothing was discoverable but a mass of uncouth crayon scratches without apparently a vestige of design. On placing the paper against a distant wall, the rude scratches resolved themselves into a fine and spirited likeness of the beautiful Marie Stuart, whom the Duchesse de Pomar not only resembles strikingly in person, but who has been reported through numerous sources to be the "guardian angel" of the Duchesse. This lady had, during the day, expressed to the author her earnest wish that the gracious Scottish Queen would favour her with her likeness through the artistic medium who was that evening expected ; but this wish was entirely unknown to M. d'Alesi, neither could he have had the slightest idea of the spiritual relations existing between the Duchesse and her much-loved spirit guide.

During a recent visit to Paris, the author had the privilege of inspecting the fine collection of spirit drawings, and the splendid library, possessed by the "Psychological Society of Paris," and arranged at their rooms by M. and Madame Leymarie, with the taste and elegance peculiar to the French character. Many of the drawings are as wonderful for their artistic excellence as for their occult mode of production. Amongst these are the drawings of M. d'Alesi, and those of M. Fabre, formerly a blacksmith, who, with a marvellous gift for spiritual art, and a romantic history too long to cite in this place, has produced, amongst other marvels of spirit influence, a splendid copy of Raphael's famous *Bataille de Constantin*, the original of which is now in the Vatican. When it is remembered that the Medium, "Fabre," was an uneducated blacksmith, who, by no possibility could ever have seen Raphael's magnificent picture, and that the work executed by this man is an almost faultless copy of the grand original, something of its real merit may be conceived. The author has only to add, that, through the courtesy of M. Leymarie, one of M. d'Alesi's wonderful crayon sketches, and a fine photograph of Fabre's *Bataille de Constantin*, now grace the walls of the study where these lines are being penned.

The mention of M. Leymarie's name, calls for some notice of the invaluable services rendered to the cause of Spiritual progress in France by that gentleman and his noble wife. Although the author by no means sympathises with the teachings of Allan Kardec on the subject of Re-incarnation, no candid mind can deny the vast ability displayed by that eminent man, nor the wide-spread influence which his writings have diffused over the Continent of Europe.

The Society founded by M. Kardec, and the paper which he so ably conducted, entitled *La Revue Spirite*, are now in charge of M. Leymarie, and it must be owned, that the followers of Allan Kardec have been fortunate in securing such a successor to their great leader in his immense work. M. Leymarie is a man of the most undoubted probity and sincerity. Pure minded, unselfish, wholly devoted to his work of propagandism and the best interests of what he believes to be right, a nobler or more self-sacrificing evangelist, does not live than M. Leymarie, and even the most determined opponents of his belief, among whom the author is one, find their hands stayed, when they would raise them to strike a blow at what they deem to be a stupendous fallacy for fear of wounding the admirable spirit of the Re-incarnationist leader M. Leymarie. It is worthy of note that this noble gentleman has himself been called upon to suffer martyrdom in the trial for fraud, in producing spirit photographs, by a certain pair of conspirators, one of whom claimed to be a medium for spirit photography. Writing on the subject of his trial before its conclusion, the Hon. J. L. L. O'Sullivan, formerly U. S. Consul at Madrid, who was in Paris at the time, and warmly interested in Mons. Leymarie, gives the following version of the case to the London *Spiritualist* :—

"My previous letters will have prepared your readers for a very mockery of justice in the trial of our friend Leymarie before the Seventh Chamber of Correctional Police, but not for the length to which it has been carried. Leymarie, that devoted and conscientious Spiritualist, successor of Allan Kardec as editor of *La Revue Spirite*, and managing director of the *Société des Spirites*, has been sentenced to a year's imprisonment. Leymarie's crime is the prominence of his position in Spiritualism, his zeal, activity, and the usefulness of his labours, to the cause to which his soul is devoted. Happily, imprisonment for opinion and its propagation is too common in France, and has been the penalty paid by too many honourable men for the social crime of having a conscience and a fearless spirit, to involve any real disgrace.

" Lachaud's speech in his defence was one of the most brilliant and convincing efforts of forensic pleading I have ever listened to. His thesis was simple. Leymarie was a sincere zealot, deceived by Buguet, and honestly parading in his Review, as proofs of his doctrine and cause, the spirit photographs produced in hundreds of which the resemblance was recognised and attested by the sitters. He had no complicity with Buguet, and it is impossible to condemn him on the authority of such a manifest liar saying that he had. This, I repeat, was a simple thing, and it was developed in a most masterly manner by Lachaud. He exhibited the man living an honest and honourable life, labouring from rise of sun till the hours of sleep, on a mere pittance of income ; blameless in all domestic relations as husband and father, working off a balance of debt resting on him from an old failure in business which had grown solely out of a too confiding character, and having, with aid from his family, nearly accomplished it, and allowing himself no personal indulgence till he should have fully done so. He then showed how he had not accepted Buguet's spirit photographs until he had put them and him through a series of test investigations with the aid of persons the most competent to detect fraud or error. He referred to the hundreds of letters of attestation of resemblances from sovereign princes down to the humbler strata of society, all of which continued to confirm Leymarie in his sincere conviction of the genuineness of Buguet's pictures. And finally he produced a series of letters from Buguet himself the very day before his arrest, on the face of which stood manifest, as though in large print, Leymarie's perfect good faith and total absence of any sort of complicity in deception. And yet with all this, Leymarie is sentenced for swindling, to the penalty of a year's imprisonment ! It is enough to take one's breath away in the telling of it. I have never known anything more monstrous in the worst courts of injustice."

[The prosecution was initiated by the police, and none of Buguet's customers or dupes appeared in support of it. M. Leymarie had recently written some severe criticisms on the Archbishop of Toulouse, and many think this had something to do with his persecution. The general opinion amongst Spiritualists is, that some of the earlier photographs produced by Buguet were genuine, but a desire to make money prompted him to commence the manufacture of fictitious ones.—Ed. *Spiritualist.*]

Our review of French Spiritualism must end here. Mediums still continue to arise, and in accordance with the spirit of European conservatism thousands of eminent persons become indoctrinated with the truths of Spiritualism, who still shrink from giving their testimony to the world.

La Revue Spirite, like the American *Banner of Light* and *Religio Philosophical Journal*, holds its own against all comers, and many another journal appears and disappears on the hemisphere of public opinion, when its work is demanded and its mission is fulfilled. There are at this present time of writing, about ten Spiritual journals published in the French language, but there are many more that have been the useful and influential ephemera of the hour. It seems certain that M. Leymarie's paper, *La Revue Spirite*, will never go out in darkness, however much it may be eclipsed by circumstances and the force of public opinion, so long as its noble and self-sacrificing editor remains on earth to print and distribute it.

The waves of human thought on the subject of Spiritualism continue to rise and fall, as it is the nature of elastic fluids to do ; but no ebb has yet set in from the shores of earth, and when it does, all things seem to predicate that it will only return with additional force, to ebb and flow between the coast lines of mortality and immortality, till time shall be no more.

It may be asked why in this review of French Spiritualism we have omitted to notice the illustrious name of Eliphas Levi (the Abbé Constant) and his magnificent contributions to the realm of occult literature such as the great work on *Haut Magique*, &c., &c. The attempts which have lately been made by many writers of eminence to draw sharp and even impassable lines of demarcation between the facts and teachings growing out of spirit communion, and the theories put forth in the name of " occultism " render it impossible for the author to combine the two subjects in this work.

Through teachings received also from individuals, who of all others, merited the name of OCCULT ADEPTS, the author has been led to consider that Occultism is in theory the revealment of that which was hidden, or the occult powers and potencies in the animate and inanimate realms of being; whilst Spiritualism is the demonstration of the same occult forces manifested from a super-mundane state of existence. The modern writers who have assumed for themselves the name of "Occultists," are not contented with this position.

Their interpretation of what and who "Spirits" are, and what is the work which this volume has been written to record, will be briefly described in our section on India; it must suffice for the present to say, that the author's definitions would appear in connection with the theories of "the Occultists," as worthless and shadowy as the spirits of whom we write appear, in comparison with the inconceivably *high* presences, or "144th embodiments" of exalted "egos," of whom the "Occultists" write. Eliphas Levi, without soaring into the extraordinary flights of revelation assumed to be authoritative by these same modern "Occultists" still occupies ground that takes no direct part with the spontaneous developments of spirit power manifested in the modern outpouring, nor yet with the simple formulæ of the spirit circle.

The day will come when true Occultism and "common place Spiritualism," will be recognized as being built upon earth and founded in man himself; leading to heaven, and culminating in the personality of angels.

In that day when theories shall be scientifically formulated from facts, and facts will not be scornfully derided to suit theories, Eliphas Levi and many another profound writer, whose words are now "Kabbala" to the multitude, will be recognized as the prophets of the grand Spiritual science of the future. Till then, it would be unphilosophical to give "that which is holy to the dogs."

CHAPTER XII.

SPIRITUALISM IN GREAT BRITAIN.

ONE of the chief difficulties which besets a writer who would attempt to give a faithful account of the Spiritual movement in Great Britain, is the very "embarrassment of riches" with which the subject is loaded, Spiritualistic experiences having become so universal that the author's requisition for evidence is met by an influx of responses which make the task of selection too herculean for the purposes of this volume. Still another subject of perplexity arises from the characteristic reserve of those with whom the phenomena of Spiritualism are very generally associated in this country.

In America, where the sources of popular power are derived from the people, Spiritualism may be found more generally represented by the rank and file of Society, than among the wealthier classes.

In Europe on the contrary, where the governing power centres in an hereditary and influential aristocracy, the people derive their opinions as they do their laws and fashions, from the ruling classes, and it is chiefly amongst these that Spiritualism flourishes.

It is not claimed that this wonderful movement is confined to any class in either hemisphere. It will be found in the hut, and the palace; in the mining camp, and the halls of legislation. Nevertheless its greatest prevalence is ever with the ruling power. Since then Spiritualism in Europe takes the deepest hold of those whose rank and station induces them to shrink from subjecting their personal experiences to public criticism, the author too frequently becomes the recipient of valuable testimony which cannot be made available, because the communicants insist on withholding their true names and addresses. "Miss E." and "Mrs. D.;" "Captain A." and "My Lord X. Y. Z." are impersonals, whom no one puts any confidence in. There is no satisfaction in offering such shadowy testimony to those who are asked to believe in occurrences of an unprecedented and often startling character. Resolving as we have done, not to demand credence for phenomenal incidents upon any testimony open to the charge of unreliability, we feel obliged to relegate an immense mass of interesting matter of this kind to the obscurity which unauthorised statements justly incur.

It would seem as if the Spiritual founders of the great outpouring had been experimenting with the forces at their command, and seeking to open up communion with the two worlds in many places, before they succeeded in systematizing the direct telegraphy which has marked the American phase of the movement.

Those who have perused the author's work entitled, "Modern American Spiritualism," will remember that a statement to this effect was made through the lips of an entranced subject magnetized by Dr. Hallock, of New York. If this hypothesis is admitted, it would account for the great prevalence of Spiritual phenomena which has marked this century in many parts of the world, prior to the disturbances in America known as "The Rochester Knockings." Thus it seems that Scientific Spirits, desirous of founding a Spiritual telegraph between the mortal and immortal realms of being, were instrumental in promoting the phenomena which occurred at Epworth Parsonage, in the family of John Wesley, and influencing Mesmer and his followers in the discovery of the life principle of magnetism.

The wonderful "preaching epidemic in Sweden;" the obsessions in Morzine; the uprising of Mormonism, Shakerism, the gift of tongues amongst the Irvingites, and the great revivals in Ireland, are all unmistakable fruits of the same mighty contagion of Spiritual forces, surging through an age specially prepared for their reception.

Let any candid student of Pneumatology peruse with attention the array of facts collected by Kerner in Germany, Cahagnet in France, and Mrs. Catherine Crowe in her English work, "The Night Side of Nature." Let him remember that these eminent writers contributed their vast mass of Spiritualistic testimony in advance of the "Rochester Knockings," and it will be impossible to evade the conclusion, that the widely separated lines of evidence all diverge from one powerful spiritual centre. Commending to our readers' attention Howitt's exhaustive "History of the Supernatural," the writings of R. D. Owen, Thomas Brevior, Kerner, Ennemoser, and Mrs. Catherine Crowe, for a wealth of detail not attainable in this work, we shall now lay before our readers some of those striking spiritual way marks which antedate the introduction of the modern spiritual telegraph in England.

The first representative case of spontaneous spiritual manifestations we select, occurred in the village of Sandford near Tiverton in Devonshire, about the year 1812. Quoting from an account published by the author some years ago, the particulars of which were derived partly from the newspaper reports of the time, but chiefly from the testimony of Mrs. Floyd—the author's venerable mother who was *an eye witness* of the scenes described, we call attention to the following details which we give in the language before published.

"It was about the year 1812 when my mother, then a young single lady, went with her parents to visit friends at the town of Tiverton, Devonshire.

"It was summer time, and during her first evening's residence she remarked, with surprise, the throng of private carriages which all seemed to be passing one way, and coming forth at one special time. Upon inquiry she learned that the object of this remarkable exodus was to proceed to a village some four or five miles distant, where a number of clergymen—of whom there were many residing in the town—together with the mayor and the principal physician of the place (both personal friends of my mother's family) were going to 'lay the ghost' which had, for a long time, haunted a certain old-fashioned residence in the village of Sandford. The 'trouble' which attached itself to this house, consisted in unaccountable noises, the ringing of bells, pattering of footsteps, lights proceeding from no human source, and other forms of preternatural disturbance.

"The house had been occupied for many years past by different tenants, none of whom had been able long to endure the terrors of their weird surroundings. Every effort made by the owner of the property to detect a mundane source for these annoyances had proved unavailing. At the period when my mother visited the neighbourhood, the house was tenanted by a family who had been induced to occupy it rent free, and who devoted the lower part to the business of a general shop.

"The presence of this family, however, seemed to have no effect, for the disturbances were as constant as ever. Even in open day passers-by could hear the knocking resounding 'like the tap of a shoemaker's hammer.' After nightfall the timid inhabitants of the village carefully avoided even the precincts of the place, whilst doctors, divines, politicians, and officers from the neighbouring garrison, assembled nightly to hold colloquies with the invisible tormentors.

"It seems that the order of these midnight conclaves was as follows. A large wooden table was placed in the centre of the room which the ghosts most commonly affected. Round this the assembled company would seat themselves, and question the rapper in much the same manner as we adopt in our modern investigations.

"For example: Several coins would be placed upon the table, and their number be indicated, *upon demand, and always correctly,* by knocks. At times the number of persons present, even their ages and professions, would be *correctly* told by signal raps. Had the sitters of seventy years ago been instructed how to anticipate the formula of the modern spirit circle, they could not have depicted its *modus operandi* more faithfully. Through the medium of certain signal raps, the sitters were always informed that the knocker was *a spirit, a female,* and one who had terminated an evil career by a violent death.

"Now although the united wisdom of a neighbourhood famous for its learning and piety pronounced through the press the solemn verdict, that 'a tremendous imposture existed *somewhere,*' yet for ten years, during which the house perpetually changed inhabitants, and was the subject of unceasing examination, the said '*imposture*' was never brought to light, nor could any mundane origin for the mysterious disturbance be detected.

"The mixture of ignorance and conservatism which prevailed amongst those who investigated this subject may be judged of from the following circumstances.

"Mr. Colton, a clergyman well known in the literary world as the author of 'Lacon' and other metaphysical works, had been a constant attendant upon the ghostly *séances,* and finally gave it as his opinion 'that the affair could never be cleared up on *mundane* grounds. No sooner was this statement circulated, than the journals of the day inferred, *that Mr. Colton must know something more of the causes than he chose to tell ; in fact, who knew but what the whole thing might have proceeded from him, as a clever ventriloquist ?* Not until Mr. Colton's departure for a foreign land, and the continuance of the hauntings, was the theory abandoned, that he, who dared to hint at a super-mundane origin of the mystery must himself be its source. Again, the magnates of Tiverton pitched upon a poor soldier of somewhat questionable character, who had returned from the war and was glad to share with his parents, the shelter of a place obtainable rent free, as the cause of the trouble. These wiseacres forgot that the disturbances had preceded the soldier's presence for two years ; however, in order to test the validity of their theory, they spirited him out of the village, and shipped him to a foreign land. But all was in vain. Neither the absence of the learned scholar nor the ignorant soldier affected the Sandford invisibles except—as if in mockery—to increase the force of their harassing demonstrations.

"The tenants who had been found bold enough to occupy the haunted mansion at the period when my mother's family came to visit Tiverton, were a poor shopkeeper with his wife and several children.

"Amongst the latter, a little girl of about ten years of age seemed to be the special theme of the ghost's malevolence.

"The child often complained of an *ugly old woman* whom she could see crouching in a corner of the room, making faces at her, and who would wake her up at night, and almost scare her into fits. One day this child was found lying dead upon the hearthstone. A coroner's inquest was held, and the verdict of the jury left it doubtful whether the poor little creature had been struck by lightning, died in a fit, or by the visitation of God. One thing was certain, namely, that the child had perished in the *haunted room*, and that she, above all the rest of the household, had been the victim of the ghost's malignity. A calamity of such a nature was too much even for the hardihood of the present tenant. He resolved upon an immediate removal, and would have put his determination into effect, had he not been delayed by the premature confinement of his wife, whose period of trial was hastened by the tragic circumstances of her little girl's decease.

"Pending the recovery of the sick woman, the physician, at whose house my mother and her family were temporary visitors, was called in to attend the woman. He was also requested to send a nurse competent to assist in such a case. Dr. Guffet, although well acquainted in his professional capacity with all the poor women of the neighbourhood, was unable to induce any one however necessitous to take service in the 'haunted house.'

"Having at length obtained a suitable attendant from a long distance off, the doctor flattered himself that his patient's case was progressing favourably. He soon found however that he was reckoning—in this instance at least, without *his ghost*—for it became evident that the stranger nurse was as much an object of the invisible's malignity as the deceased child had been.

"Having been put to sleep for convenience in the room where the child had so mysteriously died, she became the target for an incessant system of persecution. She was unable to obtain rest by day or night, and one morning when Doctor Guffet was summoned to attend her, he found her confined to her bed, from the effects of the severe beating she had received during the night from invisible hands. Her body was completely black with bruises, and these she testified before a magistrate, she had sustained from some invisible source which came and went without any known means of access to the chamber. The woman affirmed, that she felt a hand belabouring her, as if with a stone. The room was uncurtained, and the brightly shining moon made it as light as day. She testified upon oath in her examination, that no human being was in the room, nor could she discern a single creature near her. When at length her cries for help aroused the other inmates, and brought them to her room, the whole party heard a heavy bumping sound, as if something was falling off the bed, and moving of its own volition across the room, out at the door and down the stairs. The chief witness to the truth of this strange story was the doctor himself, who not only testified to the pitiable condition in which he found the poor nurse's body, but he added, 'the woman whom I sent to that house, hale, hearty, and stout, only a fortnight ago, is now an emaciated object, worn to a very shadow, and so distraught by fear that it would be murder to keep her there one hour longer.'

"The next incident which I have to record of this terrible abode, occurred at the sale of furniture which ensued, the very first hour that the mother of the family became convalescent.

"The auctioneer, who was related to Dr. Guffet, with whom my mother and her parents were visiting, informed them that as he was making an inventory of the goods, previous to the sale, he passed into the 'haunted chamber' about noon, and there found an old lady rummaging a wardrobe which stood partly open near the door. Deeming it one of the members of the family, although her dress pointed her out to be a person of some distinction, he proceeded with his work for some minutes, until he heard the voice of the landlord calling to him to come to dinner. Bowing to the old lady as he passed her, he stood at the door to see if she would go first; but as she continued her occupation without noticing him, he descended the stairs, and having taken the seat placed for him, proceeded with a courtesy peculiar to himself, to put another chair *for the lady whom he had noticed above.* On being questioned why he did so, explanations followed, and the family in haste ascended the stairs to see if any human being could really be found. All was in vain. Every nook and corner was searched without result, and when the auctioneer, at request, described the appearance of the strange visitor, it was universally admitted that the description corresponded exactly to the detestable vision which had tormented the poor deceased child.

"After these persons quitted the house it remained tenantless for many months. The noises could be heard for a considerable distance, and lights were seen flashing at the windows at all hours of the night.

"Workmen were employed to rip up the floors and pull down the walls, in the hope of discovering concealed springs and trap doors. All was to no purpose, however. During these researches, two windows at opposite ends of the long chamber—the principal scenes of the hauntings—were pierced by a bullet or missile of some kind, projected with such skill, that two perfectly round holes were found in corresponding panes of glass. The wind was felt of the passing missile, and the shiver of the glass heard by the workmen, yet nothing was seen, and as the room was on the second storey, without a ledge or the slightest foothold for any human being without, it might be inferred that the haunters desired to prove that no human agency could be at work in these manifestations. At length the sounds became so frightful that neither free tenants nor workmen would enter the place by day or night. It was ultimately abandoned, fell into decay, and what remained of it was pulled down. The papers of the time were full of reports, doubtless much exaggerated. Sages and scientists were alike baffled. Magistrates blustered and threatened, and several officers of the army, who had volunteered to sit up during the night, abandoned their watch, end refused again to enter such a 'veritable *Inferno.*'"

Remembering how many respectable witnesses testified to these facts,—how many years their continuance was a source of horror to a whole neighbourhood, and loss to the proprietor of a once splendid mansion, recollecting moreover, that one of the eye-witnesses is now living, and is a venerable lady incapable of falsehood, we have as good a right to admit this narrative into the category of historical records, as any well attested event of ancient or modern times.

We now turn to another form of haunting, selected from numerous other cases, because some of the witnesses are still living, and holding positions of the highest respectability. We refer to the unaccountable and persistent ringing of bells, which occurred in the house of Major Moor, a gentleman till lately residing at Great Bealing, near Woodbridge. These disturbances commenced on February 2nd, 1834, and continued at intervals with more or less violence till March 27th. The phenomena consisted of incessant ringing, sometimes of two or three, and not unfrequently of a whole row of nine bells at the same time—they rang day and night; at times when Major Moor, his servants, and friends, were facing them, when the doors were locked within, and the house was guarded without; when the wires of communication *were cut*, and nothing but the bells remained. The ceiling and walls were dented by the violence with which the bells were dashed against them, and despite the stringent measures taken to discover imposture or trick, this strange disturbance continued without evidence of human interference, for a period of fifty-three days. At the end of that time, it stopped as suddenly as it had originated, leaving its cause involved in impenetrable mystery. From a pamphlet published by Major Moor on this subject, entitled "Bealing Bells," also from some accounts printed in the Ipswich and other journals, we learn, that during the continuance of this persecution, Major Moor's investigations were assisted by several of his brother officers, some scientific gentlemen, and not a few clergymen who were attracted by the accounts which appeared in the papers of the day.

Amongst the persons who addressed letters to Major Moor, alleging that similar phenomena had occurred in their own houses, were families in

Cambridge, Ramsgate, London, Oxford, Windsor, Ipswich, and numerous other places. Mr. Wm. Felkin, Mayor of Nottingham, and Mr. Ashwell, a gentlemen of high standing in Chesterfield, gave accounts of the mysterious bell ringings occurring at their residences. But one of the most marked cases reported by Major Moor, in addition to his own experience, was that of Lieutenant Rivers, one of the officials of Greenwich Hospital. This witness stated that he had detailed thirty-seven watchers by day and night in the attempt to detect fraud in vain. He employed a bellhanger and his assistant to cut the wires of every bell in and about his premises, and then, in the face of the men and the presence of many neighbours who had come in to witness the wonder, the entire set of bells all over the house began ringing at once, and kept up incessant peals for several hours. The bells in some of the other officers' apartments in the Hospital were rung in the same way, and when Major Moor himself visited the place, he not only received the personal testimony of a large number of witnesses, but examined carefully the locality, and was made aware of the impossibility of the ringing being effected by any human agency.

The publicity which Major Moor gave to these circumstances, called forth a flood of testimony to events of a preternatural character, from various sections of the country. Then it appeared that bell-ringing was not the only form of disturbance prevailing. Hauntings not unlike in character those of the "Sandford Ghost," were reported from many quarters.

The Rev. Mr. Stewart, Incumbent of Sydensterne near Fakenham, Norfolk, wrote in a letter to Major Moor :—

"Our noises are of a graver character. Successions of rappings, groans, cries, sobs, heavy trampings, and thundering knocks in all the rooms and passages, have distressed us here for a period of nearly *nine* years, during the occupancy of my cure. They still continue, to the annoyance of my family, and the alarm of my servants. I am enabled to trace the existence of these disturbances during a period of sixty years past."

Mr. Stewart said that in 1833 and 1834, his predecessors in that house opened the doors to all respectable persons who desired to satisfy their curiosity or wished to investigate the hauntings, but he adds : "Their kindness was abused, their motives misinterpreted, and even their characters maligned. We therefore," he says, "shut *our* doors, and they remain hermetically sealed."

In closing these curious narratives it may not be amiss to give a few extracts from the records of a spirit circle which was held not long since, in which some parties present were commenting severely on the "unmeaning character of such manifestations as bell-ringing and knocking." At this juncture one of the communicating spirits interrupted the conversation with the following pertinent questions :—

"*Spirit*—Pray, sir, what do you do when you want to enter a house and find the door closed ?

"*Mortal*—Well ! If we really want to get in we knock or ring.

"*Spirit*—Then, don't you suppose it probable that those who have been knocking and ringing in your houses for the past half century are trying to get in too ?

"*Mortal*—Why, what can spirits want to get into our houses for ? Having left the earth, it seems strange that they should want to get back to it again.

"*Spirit*—Most of those who knock and ring in your houses have never left the earth, and would far rather get away from it than remain in it. But higher and wiser spirits wish to call the world's attention to the actual facts of spiritual existence, and the real conditions under which life beyond the grave is continued. Spirits of a very ethereal nature cannot affect material substances, and yet, in order to call the world's attention, and waken humanity up to what they have to say, they use the methods so familiar to yourselves—*they knock and ring ;* and those who cannot do this for themselves influence the earthbound spirits, who are magnetically chained to the scenes of their earthly misdeeds, to do this for them.

"*Mortal*—May we regard these hauntings, then, as transpiring under the direction of superintending spiritual wisdom ?

"*Spirit*—Everything in the universe outworks the conditions of the being that belong to its state, and providential wisdom avails itself of different states to convert evil into good, and evolve uses out of the worst of abuses. Ten thousand preachers on the human plane of existence could not demonstrate the fact of spiritual existence so conclusively as a spirit who rings a bell *in response* to a human voice, or *answers a question by knocks,* when no mortal is near to produce the sounds heard." *Verbum sap.*

As a final example of hauntings, especially of that kind which subsequently connected itself with the intelligence manifested at Spirit circles, we shall cite a history furnished to the author some years ago by a party of her personal friends, amongst whom was a gentleman of probity and scientific acumen, well remembered amongst dramatics writers and musicians, as Mr. Lenox Horne. This gentleman being in somewhat embarrassed circumstances about the year 1829, took up his abode temporarily in apartments offered to him at a very moderate rent in an old house near Hatton Garden, long since pulled down. At the period of which we write the house was large, the rooms spacious, especially one, supposed to have been a banqueting chamber, which Mr. Horne used as a music room. As all the lower chambers were either appropriated to the storing of goods, or rented to legal gentlemen as offices, there were no persons sleeping in the house except Mr. Horne and a porter, who occupied a small room on the ground floor. The building had long borne the reputation of being haunted ; it was fast falling to decay, and the former occupants of Mr. Horne's chambers were seldom known to remain long within the gloomy precincts. Report alleged that the place had once been the residence of Sir Christopher Hatton, and the weird reputation that attached to the antique domicile, connected itself with the magical practices attributed to his unfortunate lady.

Mr. Horne had tenanted these apartments some months before he was aware of the phenomena occurring within his own premises. At length he was apprised by Mr. March, a police officer with whom he was acquainted, that for several consecutive nights he and a number of persons invited to share his watch, had remarked that long after the hour when Mr. Horne was accustomed to retire to rest, the great banqueting room, which he had no means of lighting up, and therefore never entered except in daylight, could be seen from the court below *brilliantly illuminated.* Whilst acknowledging that he had often been disturbed by strange noises, odd music, loud laughter, and footsteps, for which he could not account, Mr. Horne—at once the most fearless and least superstitious of beings—strenuously combated the idea of the lights, and it was only when, after watching for several nights with March and his associates, he himself beheld every window of his own apartment, one that he had left closed, locked, and in total darkness, lit up as if by a multitude of gas jets, that he could be brought to believe in the story his friends narrated to him. On several succeeding occasions the same party beheld this spectacle repeated, and whilst some of their number remained below to watch that no intruder passed out from the one entrance of the house, the others would hasten to examine the apartment, to find it enveloped in thick darkness. One of the curious features of this appearance was, the invariability with which the lights disappeared from the eyes of the watchers below, at the moment when the apartment was opened by the searchers above. Only on one occasion was this rule reversed, and that was on a certain night in February, when a larger number of persons than usual had assembled in the court below to watch for the phantom lights.

They blazed out suddenly and in full radiance about one o'clock in the morning, when, after observing them for some five minutes, Mr. Horne, Mr. March, and a nobleman whose name we are not at liberty to mention, determined to ascend the stairs and open the door of the haunted room; and as they did so they agreed to give the signal of a whistle to those in the court below. At the moment when Mr. Horne threw open the large door of the room in question, he and his companions were thunderstruck to perceive that it was full of company.

One of the three observers had given the signal agreed upon of the whistle which he held in his hand, as he gazed upon the extraordinary scene that met the eye. The vast company seemed to be in the act of dancing. They represented ladies and gentlemen, arrayed, not in the Elizabethan style attributed to the Hatton period of the mansion, but in the costume of the reign of Charles the Second, and the whole air seemed to be full of waving plumes, fluttering ribbons, and sparkling jewels. The three witnesses, who subsequently compared notes with each other, and found their own observations fully corroborated by those of the others, affirmed, that the particulars of the whole scene as above related were plainly, clearly defined, in addition to which, all three declared that every one of these splendidly attired revellers wore, or appeared to wear, *a mask, resembling some disgusting animal.*

Before the astounded witnesses could sufficiently collect their senses to take any action on what they saw, the lights began to pale and shimmer, the whole scene quivered, melted out slowly and gradually, as in a dissolving view, and at length, that is, in the space of a few minutes, the apartment was seemingly empty and in total darkness. The watchers below reported to those above, when at last they had sufficiently collected themselves to descend, that the lights were stationary for about five minutes after the whistle sounded, and disappeared *more gradually* than usual.

Immediately after this vision, the house became wholly uninhabitable even to Mr. Horne, and the two friends who volunteered to share his quarters with him.

Heavy poundings were often heard during the day, for which no account could be given. But these were nothing to the Saturnalia which ensued as soon as darkness had set in. Tramping of feet, clashing of arms, the clinking of glasses, the crash of broken china; all the sounds attending drunken revels, rude brawls, and even murderous fights, were heard, at times with horrible distinctness. Low moans, wails, and bitter sobs, were still more frequent, and the rushing as of blasts of winds, from unknown sources, was a frequent feature of these frightful disturbances.

The witnesses, and they were many, represented their experiences to their friends only to encounter the usual sneer of incredulity and scornful derision. Two or three clergymen volunteered to offer prayers, and one zealous Catholic went through the formulæ of exorcism in the possessed mansion; but always to encounter such a storm of blows, laughter, and hideously derisive sounds, as drove them in horror from the place, a retreat in which they were shortly imitated by the tenants, who never after

7

recurred to their painful experiences without a feeling of deep awe, solemnity, and an earnest entreaty that their narration should not be met with the ordinary methods of rude denial, and insulting jest.

Despite what he had already witnessed, Mr. Horne had no knowledge of, or belief in, the reputed modern Spiritual manifestations, the spread of which, since the year 1848, he had noticed but never investigated.

About the year 1853, being invited to spend the evening with some musical friends residing in Holloway, London, Mr. Horne was there introduced to Madame Albert, a French lady who was accompanied by her little daughter, a child of some eleven years of age. During the evening, the hostess proposed that they should try the the experiment of "table turning," which was at that time, the technical expression used for evoking Spiritual manifestations. Madame Albert had it seemed become developed for mediumistic powers, whilst little "Josephine," was reported to be a fine somnambulist or trance medium. When the *séance* was first proposed, Mr. Horne laughingly alleged his entire ignorance of the subject, but at once placed himself *in position* at the table, under the direction of the attendant Sybils, "to see what would come of it." No sooner were the party seated, than Mdlle. Josephine seizing the pencil and paper which had been placed on the table, wrote in an incredibly short space of time, in a large bold hand, the following communication, addressed "To Mr. Lenox Horne," a name which the child up to that moment had never heard. The writing was given in English, a language, it must be remembered, of which the little medium was entirely ignorant.

"You say you know nothing of spiritual existence or the soul's power to return to earth. Oh, my friend! Why will you reject the light that has already dawned upon you? In your own house, you have heard the sounds, and seen the sights, which bore witness to the presence of human spirits. Have you forgotten the phantom dancers, whom you and your companions thought wore animal masks? Those dancers were my companions in vice and wickedness. They and I lived amidst scenes of revelry too shameful to be detailed. We were associates of the frivolous *roué*, that occupied the throne of England,—Charles the Second,—and in the house where you found shelter, we often used to hold such revels as demons alone could take pleasure in. When we became spirits, the base passions with which our lives on earth were animated, became so engraved upon our spirits, that all who looked upon us from a higher plane, beheld us transfigured into the semblance of the animals whose natures we partook of. Shocking as this disclosure of our true natures may be, it haply may help future generations to account for the idea of the doctrine of the transmigration of souls. Unhappily, that doctrine is not true. We might be happier as the animals whose limited instincts we represent, but oh, unhappy that we are! we are at once the human beings we ever were, with the additional humiliation of knowing that we take to others the semblance of the lower creatures, whose passions we have imitated. Friend Horne! Our hell is, *not to pass into other states*, but to live in *our own*, and by the knowledge of what we have made ourselves, to grow into higher conditions. You thought we wore masks. Alas! We had only dropped them, and exchanged the mask of seeming for the face of reality. In the spirit world, all its inhabitants are known for what they are, and the soul's loves take the shape of angelic beauty, or brutish ugliness, according to the tendencies of the life within. On the night when you beheld our revels, we were obliged, by the law of our being, to go through the earthly scenes which we had taken too much delight in. On earth such revels were our heaven ; in the spheres they are our hell. Their enforced enactment was part of our penance ; but thank God! I have seen the errors of the past, and henceforward I am atoning for it, and living my wasted life over again. I am on the road of progress, and even this humiliating confession will help me forward, and aid me to become stronger to save others and myself from the vices, the memories of which still cling to me like a garment. Farewell! My earthly mission is done ; there will be no more haunting spirits in the old house in Hatton Garden."

The signature to this singular communication was, "One who was known in the day and time of Charles Stuart as the finest woman of her age—Lady Castlemaine."

Appended to Mr. Horne's manuscript, entrusted to the author some years ago with a view of publication, were the following words :—

"Great Heaven! If this be indeed a true picture of the life hereafter, should it not make us afraid of doing wrong? But, above all, what a wicked and soul-destroying delusion has been the clerical farce of salvation by a vicarious atonement!—L. H."

CHAPTER XIII.

EARLY SPIRITUALISM IN GREAT BRITAIN (CONTINUED).

REPRESENTATIVE CASES CONSIDERED.

THE circumstances of the following narrative, although they have been frequently referred to in other publications, are too nearly related to the early history of Spiritualism in Great Britain to be omitted. They bear, moreover, so closely upon the hypothesis that wise Spirits have been experimenting during this century in many directions, with a view of establishing telegraphic communications between the two worlds, that our present recital seems peculiarly apposite to this portion of the work.

It seems that a young girl of about 13 years of age, the daughter of Mr. John Jobson, a resident of Bishop Wearmouth, near Sunderland, sometime during the year 1839 became the subject of a severe but inexplicable illness.

Mary Jobson had been a strong healthy girl up to the period named, when she suddenly seemed to collapse under an attack which confined her to her bed for over seven months, during which she became blind, deaf, and dumb. From time to time numerous physicians were called in, by whose directions the poor patient was subjected to all the penalties of the "heroic" system of treatment.

Her case was described as "an abscess on the brain," but whatever the malady might have been, it was obviously increased by the applications resorted to by her medical attendants.

Soon after the most serious features of this case became developed, it was remarked that the whole house, and especially the sick girl's chamber, resounded with unaccountable sounds, consisting of heavy poundings, pattering of feet, the ringing of bells, and the clashing of metallic substances.

As the girl's disease progressed in violence, these disturbances grew more marked ; there were times however when they changed to soft and delightful music which centred in the invalid's chamber, yet resounded through every part of the dwelling. Sometimes it would seem as if a vast crowd of people were ascending the stairs and thronging into the room. *Even the wind that might be occasioned by passing bodies was felt*, when no one but the ordinary attendants were visible. During the progress of these phenomena, the tones of a human voice were frequently heard protesting against the application of leeches and blisters, and recommending mild herb drinks, which, when tried, invariably alleviated the poor patient's sufferings. On one occasion when several members of the family, together with Drs. Clanny and Embleton, were present, this voice spoke clearly and said; "Your appliances will never benefit, but materially injure the girl. She will recover, but by no human means." On several occasions the glasses containing medicines, together with blisters and leeches, were snatched out of the attendant's hands, and thrown to distant parts of the room. Not unfrequently a crooning tone was heard, as of a mother soothing a sick child, and the poor girl's hair was put back and smoothed by tender invisible hands, Dr. Beattie who witnessed many of these scenes, affirms, that it would be impossible either to describe or forget, the angelic expression of the invalid's face at the time when the manifestations of invisible presence were most evident.

About the sixth month of this strange drama, the ceiling of the room in which Mary Jobson lay, was suddenly found adorned with a beautifully painted representation of the sun, moon, and stars.

The father of the patient—who from the first had been determinately hostile to the invisible actors, alleging that they were "demons," and the cause of his child's sickness—no sooner perceived this fresh proof of spiritual agency, than he proceeded to obliterate the paintings with a thick coat of whitewash. His work was in vain however, for the obnoxious paintings re-appeared as soon as the whitewash was dry, only fading out when the child's recovery was established.

On June 22nd, 1840, Mary Jobson regained her speech, hearing, and sight, as suddenly as she had lost them. Her strength too returned, and in a few days, without any apparent cause for the change, she was entirely restored to her usual health and spirits. For several weeks the occasional sounds of music, voices, knockings, and the movement of bodies continued, but these phenomena ultimately ceased, and have never since returned.

The chief witnesses to this wonderful history were the girl's parents, numerous friends and neighbours; Doctors Embleton and Beattie; also Dr. Drury, Messrs. Torboch and Ward, eminent surgeons, and Dr. Reid Clanny, F.R.S., physician in ordinary to the Duke of Sussex, and at the time of these occurrences, senior physician of the Sunderland Infirmary.

Dr. Reid Clanny, who was not professionally called in to attend the child, became informed of her case through the reports that were in circulation concerning it. Like a true and candid scientist, this gentleman, heedless of all the wild rumours that reached him, called on the parents, and subsequently followed up the case with the closest scrutiny, often witnessing the phenomena described, and satisfying himself according to his own published statement, "that the power—come from whence it may—was not only kind and beneficent, but that it manifested all the tokens of human intelligence, and was better able to prescribe remedies and delineate the course of the disease than any of the attendant physicians."

These admissions were made in an account of the case which Dr. Clanny published in pamphlet form, and though he staked his reputation upon the truth of his statements, and cited the testimony of numerous respectable witnesses, including Doctors Drury, Embleton, Ward, and Torboch, his fearless and timely publication was met by the scoff of the press, the ridicule of those scientists *who had not witnessed the phenomena described*, and the special denunciation of the learned and pious.

The pamphlet, nevertheless, was eagerly bought up, and a second edition soon called for. In this Dr. Clanny bravely maintained his position, adding the following earnest words from Mr. Torboch, one of the surgeons who followed the case throughout :—

"I have had lengthened and serious conversations at different times with nearly all the persons who have borne testimony to this miraculous case, and I am well assured they are religious and trustworthy, and, moreover, that they have faithfully discharged their duty in this important affair between God and man."

Since the above account was written the author has been favoured with a perusal of Dr. Clanny's pamphlet, from which the following few additional details are gathered. After commenting on the peculiarity of the voice heard speaking in Mary's chamber, Dr. Clanny says :—

"The phenomena of human voices speaking, did not seem to be special to the sick girl's chamber. Mrs. Elizabeth Gauntlett, a schoolmistress, was suddenly startled by hearing a voice crying to her, 'Mary Jobson, one of your scholars, is ill ; go and see her, it will be good for you.' This person, the child's school teacher, did not know where she lived, but finding the address, she went as directed, and was called by the voice in a loud tone, audible to all those in the house, to come upstairs. On her second visit, delightful music filled the room, and was heard by sixteen persons.

"The voice often declared the child did not suffer, her spirit being away, and her body being sustained by guardian spirits. These voices told many things of distant persons and scenes which came true.

"Before the girl lost her speech she affirmed that she was often visited by ' a divine being who looked like a man, only exceedingly heavenly and beautiful.' Mr. Joseph Slagg, and Mrs. Margaret Watson, friends of the family, who often visited the sick girl, alleged that each of them had at different times beheld the same divine apparition, and had been assured by it that the girl would recover. On several occasions ' the voice' desired that water should be sprinkled on the floor, and when the sceptical father refused compliance, water from some unknown source fell in showers around the witnesses.

"On the 22nd of June, when the poor child seemed to be in the last extremity, the family assembled round her bed united in prayer that God would be pleased to take her and terminate her sufferings. At five o'clock in the afternoon *the voice* cried out, ' Prepare the girl's clothes, and let every one leave the room except the baby.' This was a little child of two years and a half old, who was playing about near the window. When the family at length most reluctantly obeyed, they remained outside the closed door for fifteen minutes ; they then heard a voice calling out, " Come in," and when they entered they found Mary quite well, sitting in a chair with the baby on her knee, smiling and happy."

The report adds :—

"Up to this time, January 30th, 1841, no relapse has taken place, and Mary Jobson seems as well as girls of her age ordinarily are."

Dr. Drury, Dr. Clanny, and Mr. Torboch all assert that many persons of rank and some ministers of the Established Church visited Mary Jobson, and unreservedly testified to the truth of Dr. Clanny's published report.

Few seekers into the evidences which cluster around the history of Spiritualism in England will forget the law suit instituted by a Mr. Webster, the proprietor of a house at Trinity, Edinburgh, for damages done to his property by Captain Molesworth, a gentleman, who with his family, rented Mr. Webster's house, and was accused of causing extensive dilapidations therein, by his attempts to discover the secret of the terrible hauntings which beset the place.

Captain Molesworth entered upon possession of the house in question in June, 1835. Shortly after this, one of his daughters died, leaving a sister of about thirteen years old. This young lady soon after fell into ill health, took to her bed, and after some months of a strange and unaccountable illness, died.

It was generally asserted that the cruel suspicions and harassing investigations, that followed upon the disturbances, the principal scene of which was the poor invalid's chamber, did more to hasten her decease, than either the phenomena, or the course of the disease. In this case as in that of Mary Jobson, delightful music, and audible human voices from unknown and invisible sources were constantly heard around Miss Molesworth's bed.

In other parts of the house, heavy poundings, loud enough to be heard in the street, together with groans, cries, footsteps, and rustlings, were of frequent occurrence.

The sleepers were awakened at night by the beds being heaved up, and rappings, which would respond by given signals to questions asked by the family.

In Mrs. Catherine Crowe's "Night Side of Nature," it is stated, that carpenters, masons, city officials, justices of the peace, and the officers of the regiment quartered at Leith who were friends of Captain Molesworth, all came to aid in his investigations, in the hope of detecting imposture, or exorcising his tormentors, in vain.

Cordons of guards were stationed round the house by day and night, whilst the poor invalid, whose room seemed to be the chief centre of the hauntings, was not only carefully watched, but even tied up in a bag, and subjected to all sorts of harassing annoyances to make sure that she had no hand in producing the disturbances.

Absurd and vexatious as these suspicions were, they were soon put to flight by the suffering girl's decease. Meantime, the evidence called forth by the trial for damages done to Mr. Webster's house, conclusively enough proved to the world the supramundane character of the hauntings, and the impossibility of any human agency accounting for them.

The case of Elizabeth Squirrel, the vision seeress ; of the haunted house at Willington—still in possession of its spiritual occupants, as the latest reports from Newcastle testify—together with many hundreds of well-attested instances of hauntings, ghost seeing, visions, wraiths, and divers other forms of Spiritual manifestations, occurring in Great Britain during this, and the preceding century, have been so minutely described in the works already alluded to, that it would be unnecessary to add to the examples already cited.

In reviewing the narratives thus presented, there will invariably appear to be many striking points of resemblance amongst them. For instance ; they will most generally be found to represent the spirits of human beings, and to manifest human intelligence. Invisible though they may be to mortal eyes—except in rare instances—the actors seem to take cognizance of persons and things in the material world ; to hear speech addressed to them, and to respond intelligently by signal sounds or motions.

In some cases—as in that of the "Sandford ghost"—the invisible presence seems to be malign and mischievous—in others, as illustrated by the bell-ringing at Great Bealing, the demonstrations appear to be simply meaningless and silly.

Intelligence, skill, and kindness, marked the action of the invisible presence that attended Mary Jobson, and lessons of deep import and suggestion grew out of the hauntings detailed by Mr. Lenox Horne.

Could all Spiritual manifestations have been thoroughly sifted, and direct question and answer have taken the place of the foolish exorcisms, threats, and denunciations, with which these hauntings were formerly received, might they not have been explained upon the same hypotheses which are revealed to humanity in the open communion that now exists between the Spiritual and natural worlds?

By these we learn, that haunting spirits are magnetically fettered to the scene of their earthly crimes; that the sounds and sights heard and seen in such places, are projected from the spirit world into the earth's atmosphere by unhappy spirits; the remembrance of their former evil deeds becoming their hell, in which they are compelled to re-enact the deeds that continually recur to their minds.

Other spirits of a higher grade with better intentions, and better guidance, ring and knock to attract attention, and compel enquiry; and still again others, whose love for humanity prompts them to become the guardian spirits of dear relatives still remaining on earth, endeavour to make their watch and word known, as in the cases of Mary Jobson and Matilda Molesworth, by acts of beneficence and tokens of tender ministration.

Could every demonstration of Spiritual presence, whether it comes in the form of haunting or loving ministry, be thoroughly investigated, whilst its phenomena would unquestionably afford to mankind the indication of Spiritual laws now unknown, it would also resolve itself into such strictly human intelligence, that we should marvel how we could have ever relegated it to the dreary horrors of a weird supernaturalism.

Mr. S. C. Hall, the venerable editor of the *Art Journal*, was the first writer we believe who contributed to the literature of Spiritualism the well-known narrative of the spirit calling himself "Gaspar."

This denizen of the other world seemed compelled, in his first attempts to communicate with earth, to manifest his presence by the usual array of terrifying sounds and movements which accompany supernatural agencies; in process of time however he was enabled to converse with the family to whom he was attracted, through the methods of ordinary human speech. For over three years this Spirit took part in the daily life, interests, and welfare of his human friends; talking with them, advising, and counselling them, with all the wisdom and affection of a beloved member of their household, and when at last he left them, in pursuance of some Spiritual conditions which, as he alleged, would aid his progress, but deprive him of the power to hold further audible intercourse with them, they felt "as if they had lost their best friend," and could hardly be reconciled to his absence.

Nothing can more conclusively prove that the darkest shadows of "Supernaturalism" have become dissipated, and given place to light and reason, than the present open communion with the Spirit world. In this, we recognize the men, women, and children of this world over again; the good ascending into angel-hood, the indifferent still lingering on the threshold of the earth, with which their affections have been all too closely interwoven,—and the evil-minded, either exhibiting the first monitions of remorse which impel them forward on the path of progress, or the same hardened adherence to criminal tendencies which await the softening influences of penitence, to lead them into the way of reform.

The great American Seer A. J. Davis, describes in one of his works, a visit he made to the bedside of a man, suffering under an aggravated attack of *delirium tremens.*

On entering the room, Mr. Davis beheld the apparition of a beautiful female Spirit standing at the foot of the bed, scattering visionary flowers over the coverlid, and endeavouring by magnetic passes of her fair hands, to soothe the sufferer's fever-haunted condition.

On describing this celestial visitant to the family present, she was at once recognized as a departed relative, whose pure life corresponded to her angelic appearance. It seemed however that the spiritual perceptions of the unfortunate patient were sufficiently awakened to be conscious of *the presence*, although not of its beneficent character, for in the midst of his frantic ravings, he was perpetually complaining of a *demon, who stood at the foot of his bed, stinging him with thorns, and throwing off fire from her hands. He often appealed to those around, asking if they could not see this demon, whose frightful appearance filled him with horror.* Is not the delirium of ignorance and superstition just as capable of transforming angels into demons, as the delirium of drunkenness?

We must now invite the reader to consider in some detail, the signifi-cance of four well-known movements, each of which, by the wide-spread influence they have exercised over their votaries, demands recognition and earnest attention from the students of psychological philosophy. These are Mormonism; Shakerism, the sect known as Irvingites, and the Irish Revivals; of course the two former, although largely recruited from British sources, belong to the history of American Spiritualism. Neither of these movements may be commended to public acceptance, for their beneficial influence upon mankind.

But, though the CUI BONO of the subject is not the point with which the facts of history are called upon to deal, it will become self-evident to thoughtful students, that there is something wonderfully significant in the lessons which these singular and exceptional movements teach us. For example; Mormonism, which originated through the Spiritual Mediumship of Joseph Smith, illustrates with overwhelming force the depravity into which human beings may be plunged, by seeking authority for their religious beliefs, in the days of ancient barbarism; and setting up for modern example, the old Jehovah system, which not only sanctioned, but even enjoined the horrors of relentless warfare, and the infamies of Polygamy.

On the other hand, we have the religion of Anne Lee, the spiritually-inspired founder of Shakerism, rushing into that opposite extreme of excessive asceticism, which, if Shaker life and practice could prevail over the earth, would depopulate it in a single generation.

Both these movements owe their origin to spiritually-inspired founders; both are advent footprints in the wilderness of modern materialism; but whilst Mormonism illustrates the futility of looking to the past, to find authority for our religious beliefs, Shakerism equally proves the imbecility of attempting to inaugurate in the earthly present, a system of asceticism which only belongs to our condition as pure spirits, in the future.

THE IRVINGITES.

THE third movement to which allusion was made above, is the wonderful Pentecostal outpouring which fell on certain members of a church presided over by the Rev. Edward Irving, from whom the affected persons were called by the name of "Irvingites." The following brief summary of this remarkable demonstration, is gathered chiefly from the history of Edward Irving by Mrs. Oliphant, published in Mr. Thomas Shorter's excellent account of Spiritual manifestations, entitled "The Two Worlds," and a small volume on "The Revivals," written by W. M. Wilkinson, Esq., solicitor, of Lincoln's Inn, London.

The latter in introducing his subject says :—

"Of Mr. Irving himself, it is only necessary to say that he believed and preached that the Church might and ought to have a restoration of the divine gifts which are promised in the gospels, and that the not having such, was a sign of its low state and was in fact its condemnation.

"Whatever may be thought of his theory, he was a great and good man, as all who knew him testify.

"Carlyle, who knew and loved him, says of him—'He was the freest, brotherliest, bravest human soul mine ever came in contact with.

"'I call him on the whole the best man I have ever, after trial enough, found in this world, or ever hope to find.'"

One thing is certain, that panegyrists and detractors alike, attribute to Mr. Irving a character of singular purity and rectitude, whilst it is universally admitted, that his eloquence, and the marvellous power he exerted over his immense and fashionable congregations, were as remarkable even before the Spiritual outpouring with which his name is associated, as any phenomena which occurred during that wonderful visitation.

It was in the magnificent church in Regent Square, erected at a cost of fifteen thousand pounds expressly for Mr. Irving—then the most popular preacher in London—that the outpouring of "the gift of tongues" occurred.

It seems that the first manifestation of this singular power, commenced in Port Glasgow sometime in 1830.

Mr. Irving, a Scotchman by birth, had commenced his ministerial career in Glasgow, and as the reputed demonstrations were of the character which he himself alleged the Church of Christ should possess, he became strongly interested in the tidings that reached him, and forthwith sent one of the elders of his own church to enquire into, and report upon the matter.

The following extracts are condensed from Mr. Irving's own narrative of the "gift of tongues," published in *Fraser's Magazine* (vol. iv.), in which is embodied the report of the agent above alluded to. The latter, writing to his Pastor, Mr. Irving, says :—

"About this time (1830), in the death-bed experiences of certain holy persons, there appeared many and very wonderful instances of the power of God's Spirit, both in the way of discernment and utterance. *They were able to know the condition of God's people at a distance.* In one instance, *the countenance shone with a glorious brightness, as if it had been the face of an angel ;* they spoke much of a bright dawn about to arise in the Church ; and one of them, just before death, signified that he had received *the knowledge of the thing about to be manifested.* . . .

"In March, 1830, on the evening of the Lord's Day, the gift of speaking with tongues was restored to the Church. The handmaiden of the Lord, of whom He made choice on that night to manifest forth in her His glory, had been long afflicted with a disease which the medical men pronounced to be a decline. It was on the Lord's Day, and one of her sisters, along with a female friend who had come to the house for that end, had been spending the whole day in fasting and prayer before God, with *a special respect to the restoration of the gifts.* They had come up in the evening to the sick chamber of their sister, and, along with one or two others of the household, were engaged in prayer, when the Holy Ghost came with mighty power upon the sick woman as she lay in her weakness, and *constrained her to speak at great length, and with superhuman strength, in an unknown tongue,* to the astonishment of all who heard. She has told me that this first seizure of the Spirit was the strongest she ever had ; and that it was in some degree necessary it should have been so, otherwise she would not have dared to give way to it.

"The editor of the *Morning Watch* * writes : 'We have seen eight different individuals who have been eye-witnesses of these manifestations, and who are unanimous in their testimony to the *supernatural, holy, and influential energy of what they there witnessed.*' We subjoin the testimony of one of these, Mr. John B. Cardale, who is now the head of the church. He was specially sent by Mr. Irving to make enquiry, with five others, into these alleged tongues, and he thus gives their observations :—'During our stay, four individuals received the gift of tongues. The tongues spoken by all the several persons who had received the gift are perfectly distinct in themselves and from each other. *J. M'D. speaks two tongues, both easily discernible from each other.* J. M'D. exercises his

---

* A periodical established mainly as an organ of the Irvingites.

gift more frequently than any of the others ; and I have heard him speak for twenty minutes together, with all the energy *of voice and action of an orator addressing an audience.* The language which he uttered is full and harmonious, containing many Greek and Latin radicals, and with inflexions resembling those of the Greek language. The only time I ever had a serious doubt whether the unknown sounds which I heard on these occasions were parts of a language, was *when Mr. M'D.'s servant spoke during the first evening.* When she spoke on subsequent occasions it was invariably in one tongue, which was not only perfectly distinct from the sounds she uttered at the first meeting, but was satisfactorily established, to my conviction, to be a language.

"'One of the persons thus gifted we employed as our servant while at Port Glasgow. She is a remarkably quiet, steady, phlegmatic person, entirely devoid of forwardness or enthusiasm, and with very little to say for herself in the ordinary way. The language which she spoke was as distinct as the others, and it was quite evident the language spoken at one time, was identical with that spoken at another time.

"'*The chanting or singing was also very remarkable.* J. M'D.'s ordinary voice is in singing, harsh and unpleasing ; but when thus singing in the Spirit, the tones are perfectly harmonious. On the morning after the day on which Mrs. —— received the gift of tongues, I heard her singing stanzas with the alternate lines rhyming. The tune was at first slow, but she became more and more rapid in her utterance, until at last, syllable followed syllable as rapidly as was possible, and yet each syllable distinctly enunciated.

"'These persons, while uttering the unknown sounds, as also while speaking in the Spirit in their own language, have every appearance of being under supernatural direction. The manner and voice are different from what they are on ordinary occasions.

"'Their whole deportment *gives an impression not to be conveyed in words, that their organs are made use of by supernatural power.* M. M'D. one morning, having, in consequence of a severe cold, so entirely lost the use of her voice as to be unable to speak out of a whisper, yet, on a sudden, commenced, and from ten a.m. to two p.m. continued speaking in a loud voice—sometimes in intercessory prayer in the Spirit, sometimes in denouncing the coming judgments, *and occasionally speaking in an unknown tongue*— and at the end of that time she relapsed exactly into her former state.'

"When this messenger returned to London with his tidings, it was to find *the tongues of flame sitting on his own wife and daughters.* Still, not rashly, nor arrogantly, was the marvel proclaimed to the world. For some time, only in private meetings was the gift invited to manifest itself.' There, philological learning pronounced the utterances something more than jargon, and observation failed to detect imposture. Prayer-meetings were then held every morning at the church in Regent-square, and were numerously attended. At these meetings, exhortations would be uttered in the 'tongue' by one person, and the interpretation chanted in English by another. Warnings and predictions were sometimes given. On Sunday morning, October 16th, a '*sister*' (*Miss Hall*) *burst forth in the open congregation with an utterance in the tongue.* I calmed the 1,500 or 2,000 people who had risen in alarm, bade the sister console herself—for she had struggled with the power that had possession of her, and hastened her into the vestry of the church, there to give it speech—and expounded to the congregation the 14th chap. of the First Epistle to the Corinthians, as explanatory of the occurrence. In the evening *a 'brother' produced even greater excitement than the morning speaker ;* and in the course of the week all London was talking of this new phase. The 'unknown tongues' continued in the church, and other 'utterances in the Spirit' were also given ; and remarkable cases of healing by spiritual power occurred.

"Those who speak in the tongue always declare 'that the words uttered in English are as much by power supernatural as the words uttered in the language unknown.' But no one hearing and observing the utterance could for a moment doubt it, inasmuch as the whole utterance, from the beginning to the end of it, *is with a power, and strength, and fulness, and sometimes rapidity of voice* altogether different from that of the person's ordinary utterance in any mood ; and I would say, both in its form and in its effects upon a simple mind, *evidently supernatural. There is a power in the voice to thrill the heart and overawe the spirit after a manner which I have never seen.*"

Besides "the tongues," the gift of healing became manifested in the church, and the power extended to other congregations.

At Liverpool and Baldock in Hertfordshire, manifestations similar in character to those of the churches in Port Glasgow and Regent Square, became openly displayed.

Mr. Irving at the earnest solicitation of many interested persons, wrote accounts of the manifestations which were published in *Fraser's Magazine* (vols. iv. and v.); he also contributed largely to the columns of the *Morning Watch*, a quarterly magazine in which the facts and philosophy of the strange movement were freely discussed.

Mr. Irving very highly commends the manner and forms of this "divine speech," and by abundant and earnest reasonings, endeavoured to show that it was a renewal of Apostolic gifts and powers. After some two years continuance of these manifestations, certain members of Mr. Irving's congregation began to utter loud complaints of the disorders that had arisen, the result of which was, that a charge of heresy was ultimately preferred against him.

At the trial that ensued "an utterance in power" came from Mr. David Dow, charging those who were faithful to arise and depart, whereupon Mr. Irving and Mr. Dow made their way out of church, and sentence against the pastor was formally pronounced.

Besides this ruinous division in the excellent and amiable clergyman's congregation, there were other causes of disunion at work with the Revivalists themselves, which militated against the subject, and tended to bring it into ill odour with the world. The principal causes of this division originated with Mr. Robert Baxter, once an enthusiastic subject of the lingual gift, and subsequently a disbeliever in the divine origin of the power which he himself had manifested.

This secession from the Irvingite ranks, was announced by Mr. Baxter himself in a tract which he published entitled, *A narrative of facts characterizing the supernatural manifestations in the members of Mr. Irving's congregation, and other individuals in England and Scotland, and formerly in the writer himself.*

As no description of the subject can depict it in the same vivid light that it borrows from the testimony of witnesses and participators, we shall give the following quotations from Mr. Baxter's pamphlet as the best illustration on record of "the power," and a subsequent condition of disenchantment.

Mr. Baxter says, writing of himself sometimes in the third person, and again in the first:—

"He had heard many particulars of the extraordinary manifestations which had occurred at Port Glasgow, and thought that there were sufficient grounds in Scripture to warrant a fair investigation of them. Being called up to London in August, 1831, he 'had a strong desire to attend the prayer-meetings which were then privately held by those who spoke in the power and who sought for the gifts.' Having obtained an introduction, he attended, and heard 'the utterances,' both in the unknown and in the English tongue. In the latter there was, he says, 'a cutting rebuke to all who were present, and applicable to my own state of mind in particular. *In the midst of the feeling of awe and reverence which this produced, I was myself seized upon by the power; and in much struggling against it, was made to cry out, and myself to give forth a confession of my own sin in the matter for which we were rebuked.* There was in me at the time of the utterance, very great excitement, and yet I was distinctly conscious of a power acting upon me beyond excitement.'

" From this period, for the space of five months, I had no utterances in public; though when engaged alone in private prayer, *the power would come down upon me, and cause me to pray with strong crying and tears for the state of the church.* On one occasion, whilst in my study, endeavouring to lift up my soul in prayer, the power came upon me, and I found myself lifted up in soul to God, and by a constraint I cannot describe I was made to speak a prayer that the Lord would deliver me from fleshly weakness, and graciously bestow upon me the gifts of his Spirit. This prayer was so loud, that I put my handkerchief to my mouth to stop the sound, that I might not alarm the house. When I had reached the last word, the power died off me, and I was left as before, save in amazement at what had passed.

"In January, 1832, when I again visited the brethren in London, the gifts in Mr. Irving's church were now being exercised in the public congregation. The day following my arrival, being called upon by the pastor to read, I opened upon the prophet Malachi, and read the fourth chapter. As I read, the power came upon me, and I was made to read in the power. My voice, raised far beyond its natural pitch, *with constrained repetition of parts,* and with the same inward uplifting which at the presence of the power I had always before experienced. When I knelt down to pray. *I was carried out to pray in the power* for the presence and blessing of God in the midst of the church; in all this I had great joy and peace, without any of the strugglings which had attended my former utterances in the power.

"On the Sunday following, the power came in the form of revelation and opening of scripture; and as I read, the opening of it was just as light flitting across the mind. A passage would be opened in the clearest manner, until portion after portion having been opened, and an interpretation given *which I not only had never thought of, but which wa. at variance with my previous systematic construction of it.*

"If it were convenient here to make particular mention of men's names, I could name you many, who of late years have received such strange preservations, even against the common course of nature, that might convince an Atheist of the finger of God therein.

"*It hath been my own case more than once, twice, or ten times.* When means have all failed and the highest art has sentenced me hopeless, I have been relieved by the prevalence of fervent prayer."

During the prevalence of "the power," a large number of seemingly miraculous cases of healing occurred with those upon whom the spiritual gifts were poured out. Among the most notable was the cure of a Miss Macdonald, an invalid of many years standing, who was entirely restored to health, by the touch, prayer, and command to "arise and walk," of her brother James, one of the Port Glasgow subjects of the "supernatural power." This same man, after raising his sister from the sick bed to which she had been confined for years, addressed a letter to a dear friend, a Miss Mary Campbell, who had just been given up to die by the doctors. In this letter, James Macdonald informed the sick lady, she must instantly arise and go forth to testify for the Lord. Without the least help, "the *dying girl*" arose, dressed herself, walked down to the meeting-room, and entered upon a career which lasted for many months as a prophetess of the new church.

Mrs. Oliphant in her life of Irving, also mentions a sister of Mary Campbell's—Isabella, who was cured in the same way and with the same results.

Still more renowned was the case of Miss Fancourt, the daughter of a clergyman, who for eight years had been a helpless cripple, and whom her father's congregation had been accustomed to see carried to church in the arms of attendants and laid on her back in her pew during the service. The wonderful cure of Miss Fancourt was effected *in a single minute* by the prayers of an eminent subject of the gifts, Mr. Greaves. As the cure has been reported at length in numerous religious as well as secular publications, we must close our notice of it with a brief extract from a letter written by the lady's father, the Rev. T. Fancourt, to the *Christian Observer,* of November, 1831:—

"Her backbone, which was *curved* before, is now perfectly straight, and her collar-bones are quite equal, whereas one of them was previously much enlarged. It is four years since she walked at all, and then it was but for a short time with the assistance of a stick, and subject to a pain in her hip. She now walks stoutly and free from all pain."

It is almost unnecessary to add, that whilst the fact of these, and many other equally marvellous cures could not be disputed, the invariable tone of explanation adopted by the religious journals was, that "the cures were wholly wrought by the name of Jesus;" and "faith in the Lord Christ," &c., &c. These religious writers then, as now, forgot to explain why the millions of earnest Christians that have been done to death and tortured barbarously by other Christians, during the ages of Christian warfare and persecution, were neither saved from death at the stake, or mutilation, by faith in the name of Christ. John Huss, Latimer, Ridley, Joan of Arc, and tens of thousands of devout Christians, have called upon the name of their Lord in their hour of anguish in vain. If the prayer of faith was all that was necessary to save from death and agony, why were the Misses Campbell and Miss Fancourt cured, and ten thousand Christian martyrs unregarded? An equally pertinent question arises in reference to the thousands of cures which have transpired amongst the modern Spiritualists, many of which are recorded in their literature, and some few referred to in this volume. The prayer of faith in these instances is wanting, and the name of Christ is seldom or ever used. Can our Christian friends explain the *modus operandi* of these anti-Christian healing exploits? Even Mr. Baxter, after abandoning the Christian solution of his problematical state, does not deny the facts of healing of which he was an eye-witness, and a subject himself. Can the "Satanic" theory upon which this eminent witness falls back, cover the ground of Spiritual healing as well as the name of Christ? If so, can our Christian friends explain the difference of the power, and the superiority of one source over the other?

As the limitations of our space will permit of no more extended notice of this remarkable movement, nor of the vast multitude of witnesses whose testimony was rendered to the facts of healing as well as of tongues, we must conclude with the following brief extract from the life of Edward Irving by Mr. Wilks, one of his admiring followers.

This writer, after detailing the circumstances of Mr. Irving's trial, and final withdrawal from the church, concludes with the following touching remarks :—

"His public work was over. His flesh became wan ; his raven hair hoary as with extreme age. His eye gleamed with an unquiet light, and the hectic spot on his pale cheek betrayed the fire burning at his heart. On December the 8th, 1834, he passed to that rest for which his weary spirit longed. The last words he was heard to utter were 'If I die I die unto the Lord. Living and dying I am the Lord's.'"

It would be needless to pursue in farther detail the course of the *Catholic Apostolic Church*, an organization which claims the noble-minded and devoted Edward Irving as its founder, although it neither adopts his name, nor conserves "the power" which made that name during four short years a milestone on the highway of immortality.

Numerous records of kindred powers are to be found in the history of Spiritualism, but those which distinguished the uprising at Port Glasgow, and the Irvingites in London, undoubtedly owe a large share of their world-wide renown to the talents, eloquence, and unspotted life of the brave and devoted gentleman who gave all he was, and all he had, even *to his very life*, to uphold the truth and divinity of the mighty outpouring with which his name is associated.

It is one of the triumphs as well as the consolations of Spiritualism, to be assured, that Edward Irving still lives, and though removed from the scenes of earthly trial in which his pure life was consumed, "he being dead, yet speaketh !"

CHAPTER XIV.

EARLY SPIRITUALISM IN GREAT BRITAIN (CONTINUED).

THE IRISH REVIVALS.

THE fourth and last great movement of a Pentecostal character to which we can call attention as occurring during the present century, has been named " The Irish Revival," and though we have no direct account of its unfoldment before 1857—nine years after the commencement of " Modern Spiritualism " in America, the scenes of the Irish drama were so distant from and unconnected with other European centres wherein "spirit circles" were generally held, and the people upon whom " the power" fell, were so far removed in rank and national isolation from the cultured classes amongst whom Spiritualism in Great Britain for the most part took root, that there does not seem even a possibility of tracing any connexion between the two movements, unless we admit the hypothesis of a universal outpouring of the Spirit all over the world and one moving in psychological currents of influence from all points of the compass.

In commencing our necessarily brief review of the Irish Revivals, we must give some account of the place as well as the persons with whom they originated, and this we do in the words of William Arthur, A.M., a learned gentleman who published several voluminous tracts on this subject.

After speaking of the colonies of Protestants from England and Scotland who peopled Ulster, and whose descendants form now its main population Mr. Arthur says :—

" The people are notoriously cool, practical, money-making, strong-willed, and fond of disputation.

" None of the popular religious delusions which took effect in other places found their way into Ulster. Spiritual life was low, but the exaggerated crimes which prevailed in Romish parts of the land were rare. Still many forms of vice were very prevalent. *Drunkenness raged like a plague ; swearing, cockfighting, gambling, and large numbers of illegitimate births, formed its natural train.* A policeman on the streets of Belfast told us that he had lived in Ahoghill for two years, and that it was the 'worst wee place in the world.' On a day when a funeral took place, he said, there was so much drinking and fighting, that the lock-up was always full ; and on a fair day you could not go many yards without hearing drunken men cursing the Pope.

" The origin of the present movement is clearly traced to Connor, a parish seven miles long, peopled by small farmers, weavers, and linen manufacturers, nearly all Presbyterians, mixed only with a handful of Church people, and scarcely any Roman Catholics.

" There was a young man residing at Ballymena, a few miles away, who was zealous for religion after his manner, and stood in his own eyes as a Christian. But he heard a lady from England conversing with some young women, and describing true conversion. Her words reached the heart of the young man. He sought the inward and holy power of religion, and found clear and joyful acceptance with his Father in heaven. Full of this new happiness, he returned to his own parish.

" In the month of September, 1857, *he and three other young men joined together in secret fellowship, to pray for God's special blessing on the people around them.*

" Three months later what is called 'The Spring Communion' came. The parish had been more or less filled with tidings of the prayers that were being offered, and of the happy conversions which had taken place. Their minister had been preaching *on the subject of a great revival,* and telling what the Lord was doing for his vineyard in America, with a strong desire for the like at home. The services of the Communion were crowned with unwonted influence. Life, inquiry, deep convictions, strong crying and tears—these became the familiar tidings of that favoured parish. Prayer meetings sprang up on every hand, and wonderful was it to the staid Presbyterian folk to hear, out of the lips of the unlearned and the ignorant, out of the mouths of babes and sucklings in religion, *prayers of deep import and heavenly power."*

After many fervent expressions of thankfulness for the conversions effected as above shown, Mr. Arthur goes on to say :—

" At a prayer meeting in the meeting-house there were about three hundred persons. All were unexcited, though earnest. At the call of the minister, a young man, one of the recent converts, read a portion of Scripture, and delivered a short exhortation. Then the minister called on them to *spend a little time in silent prayer.* At first it seemed as if the moments would pass in deep silence ; but after a while, *breathings began to be heard, low, subdued, but earnest—no voice, no tone, no words ; but a breathing throughout the place, as if each one apart was breathing out the soul to God. That strange sound rose and came quicker till it almost rushed, and the place seemed all astir with suppressed but outbursting prayer."*

Very different results soon grew out of these peaceful "unexcited" prayer meetings, as the reader will perceive if, passing over a few pages filled with descriptions of similar scenes and individual experiences, he takes up the thread of Mr. Arthur's narrative in June, 1859, two years later than the first "conversion" alluded to. We resume our extracts at the following point of advance :—

" One who had felt the joy of pardoning love filling his own soul, and opening in his breast a little heaven, longed to see his mother, who lived in a neighbouring parish. He got one of his comrades *to join him in earnest prayer for her conversion.* After this, he went home to see if prayer had had any effect, and, to his joy and wonder, found that *just while they had been praying, deep conviction had fallen upon his mother's soul ;* she had sought mercy, and was now rejoicing in hope of the glory of God. This triumph of prayer was no sooner won than came the question, Where was his brother ? *Away at a cockfight.* Thither he followed him : there he found him, and, seizing him, he said, 'I have a message for you from the Lord Jesus.' This went to his heart ; he too fled for refuge to the open arms of the crucified Redeemer. His burden fell off, joy and peace took possession of his soul, and he rushed away to his minister, exclaiming, 'I am saved ! I am saved !'

" Converts from Connor then came to tell the people of Ahoghill what the Lord had done for their souls. It was a strange thing to hear weavers, and stone-breakers, and butchers, and others unskilled in speech, pouring forth reverent and thoughtful prayers. It was more wonderful still to hear them tell how the Lord had sent his arrows through their souls.

" ' You ask,' cries a convert, 'if you did find mercy, how you would know it ? *Ah, you would know it very well, you would feel it.'* And there his argument ended. But something was in these new-born souls—*which went further than ten thousand arguments.* The power of the blessed Spirit attended them. *And then began those overwhelming affections of body and mind together,* which have resounded through the world, and made the Ulster Revival notorious to the religious and the curious alike.

" In an opposite direction to Ahoghill lies the town of Ballyclare. There, one fair day, a slater coming home to dinner, was told by his wife that *there was a man in the fair who had lost his reason ;* for on the 'fair hill,' in his cart, he was praying aloud, and crying for mercy to his soul. The man went to see, and found it even so : it was a man from the neighbourhood of Broughshane, where the Revival had now begun ; and, as he came into the fair, such deep conviction of sin seized upon him, that he cared not for the eye of the crowd or the course of business, but felt he was going down into the gulf ; and he cried, 'Lord, save, I perish !' *There was something in the cry which went to the soul of the slater,* who had come to see the man ' out of his mind.' He felt, It is time for me to seek mercy too.

" And, as if the Lord had said, 'Return to thine house, and show what great things the Lord had done unto thee,' he did return, and told his tale of redeeming love, *and speedily the holy flame was lighted up in Ballyclare.*

" At Hyde Park, a village a few miles from Belfast, I had the happiness of witnessing a wonderful work of revival, and, on inquiry as to its origin, found it traced to a lad from Ballyclare.   He told how the Lord had converted him, and seeing a boy impressed by it, fell upon his neck, and 'the affection of this boy seemed to break down the hearts of the people.'   How slight a cause is followed by wonderful effects, when a mighty power of the Spirit operates !

" *After nearly two years the first converts are steadfast, and the original seat of the revival more and more alive.*   Only within the last two months has it attracted public notice ; but in that time it has spread like fire, among country districts, market towns, and considerable cities.   From Belfast to Coleraine, I have been permitted to see its effects, with wonder and deep adoration.   I never read of anything equal at once in extent and transforming power, and hereafter it will be my endeavour to trace the work through some of those stages in which, instead of the tranquil and gradual progress which marked its early course, it burst forth with such manifestations as filled the newspapers, and became the all-absorbing topic of the country."

As Mr. Arthur's views of revival practices are evidently dictated more in the spirit of orthodox sympathy with the actors than that of philosophic and deliberate investigation, we now turn to the testimony of a still more impartial collator of revival incidents, in the person of Dr. Massie, a writer of eminence, whose excellent account of the Irish Revivals is thus rendered in Mr. W. M. Wilkinson's volume on this subject before alluded to.   Dr. Massie says :—

" We may remark that the first noticeable cases of decided impression appeared in Ballymena, on the morning of Monday, the 16th of May ; and, up till noon of the following Wednesday, the entire number was about thirty.   These cases occurred chiefly in streets of an inferior description, and among the lower classes of the population.   It would be impossible to ascertain the exact number so visited within the town—for cases are now to be found in every street, among all classes of the people.   We know of one house wherein seven persons were impressed in the usual mysterious manner in the course of a single evening ; and the total number in Ballymena alone cannot be reckoned at less than three hundred.   On the evening of Thursday, the 19th instant, the public excitement, particularly in Springwell Street, was intense ; and we visited that locality for the express purpose of witnessing and reporting upon the phenomena.   On one portion of the street we found an assemblage of at least two thousand people engaged in services of prayer and praise under the leadership of laymen, six or seven houses elsewhere in the same street were crowded with people in every spot where standing room could be obtained.   The doors, and in some cases the windows, were open, and besieged by a throng of all classes anxious to hear the proceedings within.   These houses we found to be the homes of ' stricken ' parties, who were then labouring under the influence of the shock in sundry stages of its operation.   Some were in a state of very great weakness and partial stupor ; some were dreadfully excited, calling upon God for mercy, with an earnestness of which no intelligent investigator could doubt the reality for a single moment ; some were uttering exclamations of despairing agony ; others were pouring forth accents of heart-touching and adoring gratitude.   In all cases they were surrounded by crowds of friends or comforters.   They were prayed over, in some cases by a single leader, in others by several persons at the same moment, the stricken person sometimes uniting with them *in language of glowing and continuous eloquence,* and at other times by interjectional exclamations of doubt, hope, faith, or joy unspeakable.   During the earlier paroxysms the sufferers generally experienced considerable relief *from sacred music ;* and hence the devotional exercises were frequently varied by the singing of psalms, in which all who were within hearing appeared to join most cordially.   This description of the proceedings in one house may be regarded as applicable to all the others—for we visited them all, and were favoured with opportunities for investigation in seventeen different cases.

" In the course of the evening we had an opportunity of witnessing cases of ' impression ' in the earlier stages, the scene at one of which we shall attempt to describe. Having made our way up a narrow staircase, crowded with anxious listeners, we entered a small apartment in which about twenty people of both sexes were grouped in various attitudes of deep attention or devotion.   A neatly-attired young woman, apparently about twenty-two years of age, had been stricken an hour previously, and was supported in the arms of an elderly female, who was seated upon a low stool.   The person impressed, appeared to be in a state of partial stupor, from which she was occasionally roused into a feeling of mental agony, depicted in heart-rending expressions of the countenance, and deep, low wailings of terrible despair. *Her face was deadly pale,* and her eyelids closed, except when partially raised by a convulsive paroxysm, *and even then no part of the eye was visible, except a narrow line of white.* Her pulse was intermittent and feverish, and her face and hands covered with perspiration. Occasionally she extended her arms with an action as if groping in the air, and at other times they were elevated high overhead, the hands clasped, and her features rigidly fixed into an expression of supplication, of which no language could convey an adequate idea. Her utterance was interjectional and incoherent, mingled with sobs, moans, and agonizing expressions of despair, like the following :—' Is there no hope ? ' ' Oh, my heart, my heart ! ' ' Pardon, pardon ! ' ' Oh, Jesus, save me ! ' ' Oh, God, have mercy ! ' Beside this poor girl two men were standing and praying aloud alternately.

"In other portions of the room *hands were clasped, and tears silently streaming from many an eye,* but our attention was irresistibly attracted to the movements of a young woman, evidently of the lower classes, who had been ' stricken ' two days previously, but had now recovered, and was bending over the sufferer with emotions exhibiting the deepest and most affectionate solicitude. She told her of Jesus, who was ever willing to save ; she repeated passages of Scripture that spoke of hope and consolation to the penitent ; and then burst forth into *a lengthened and apparently impulsive prayer,* well expressed and perfectly intelligent, but chiefly interjectional.

"Now, it may be asked, who was this earnest suppliant for peace and consolation to the afflicted sufferer ? Four days previous to the evening of which we write, she was a reckless and, apparently, God-forsaken young woman—*a common street prostitute in Ballymena !* Before we left the scene which we had thus attempted to describe, the impressed person had obtained considerable relief, and, at intervals, we observed that her lips were silently moving, as if in inward prayer.

"In the meantime *the movement was progressing with rapidity in every district of the surrounding country.* Soon after breakfast hour on Saturday morning, six or seven young women became suddenly affected with all the usual symptoms, while engaged at work in the spinning factory at Raceview. Intense excitement immediately ensued, *the alarm soon became general,* and within an hour twenty or thirty people of both sexes were found prostrate. The business of the entire establishment was interrupted, and, as a matter of necessity, the factory was closed at twelve o'clock. It was re-opened on Monday, but nearly half the ordinary number of hands were absent, and we understand that the business of Ballygarvy bleachworks has been seriously impeded, owing to a similar course. About six o'clock on the evening of Sunday week, a congregation, numbering fully four thousand people, assembled in the open air, in front of the Presbyterian Church at Broughshane, where services were conducted by the Rev. Mr. Robinson and a number of Revival converts from other localities. Numerous and strongly-marked cases of sudden ' conviction ' occurred among the audience, and several persons were carried into the church, from which place they were not in a condition for removal till midnight. The total number of persons affected on that occasion has been estimated at more than one hundred. On the same evening open-air prayer-meetings were held at Cullybackey and Straid. At Carniney, about a mile from Ballymena, the assemblage numbered fully two thousand, and they separated into large groups, for each of which there was a speaker. Numerous impressions occurred, and some of the parties so affected were removed from the ground on cars, followed, in some cases, by ranks of people singing psalms."

"Dr. Massie gives the following extracts from a Ballymena correspondent : 'Last night, at a prayer meeting in Wellington Street Church, so crowded that the doors and windows were surrounded by a multitude who could not obtain admission, scenes occurred which bowed the heart with awe and solemn fear, as if the invisible world was opening to view. Attempts have been made to describe such scenes, but no one can describe them, they must be witnessed. During the time that Mr. Shaw was speaking, a person labouring under strong convictions of sin was carried out into the session-room. He was a person who had had convictions before, but on this occasion they returned in a manner most distressing to witness. He was a strong, middle-aged man ; but in the mysterious, half-conscious state in which he was, his soul actually seemed to the beholders as the battle-ground between the powers of light and darkness, filling his body with agony unutterable. His cries for mercy, for salvation from Satan, and from his former sins, at first inarticulate, but at last so loud as to be heard over the body of the house—his clasped hands, as he knelt in prayer, with his face turned upwards, his eyes shut, every vein swelled almost to bursting, and the perspiration streaming down his face—his becoming calmer while listening to singing, and at last the torrents of tears running down his face, as he asked the 116th Psalm to be sung, showed the agonizing conflict that had been going on. Would that sceptics and those at a distance would at least suspend judgment until they saw one such case as this ! I would venture to say that if they had stood over that man in his agony and listened to his unutterable groanings for pardon and for peace, if not convinced themselves, they would speak of the present movement, not with sneers or mockery, but with solemn and reverential awe. Further, with respect to this man, he has shown one of the best tests of sincerity, in giving up a lucrative business, when first convinced of sin, about three weeks ago. He feels, as many now do, that a Christian and a whiskey-seller are not compatible terms. During the time that this man was suffering so much last night, others, *all children, were brought in, or were seized with convictions in the room.* The same cries for mercy, for deliverance from Satan, were repeated. During this scene in the session-room, the vast crowd in the church, led by one of the ministers, were praying, great numbers of them audibly, for those under convictions.'"

"On the 18th of June, the *Observer* of Ballymena remarks—'In the town and neighbourhood of Ballymena the mysterious influence continues in unabated operation; and numerous cases, accompanied by all the wonderful phenomena so frequently described, are occurring daily. At the Presbyterian church, the congregation was so numerous on Sunday last, that many persons were unable to obtain admittance, and four or five new cases of "conviction" occurred during public worship. In the evening an immense concourse of the community assembled for united prayer in a grass park to the west of the Galgorm Road. All the churches in Ballymena would not have contained the number present; and the spectacle was one of the most solemn we have ever witnessed.

"'The services were opened by the Rev. S. J. Moore; after which addresses followed in succession from four or five lay converts. Their language was characterized by the unpolished but effective eloquence of nature, for they were thoroughly *in earnest*. Several strongly-marked cases of sudden conviction occurred, while these exhortations were in progress; but the parties had been carried to a remote corner of the enclosure. The services were brought to a conclusion by the Rev. Mr. Moore; but the audience *did not separate*, for strange and most exciting scenes immediately ensued. Suddenly one person, and then another, and another, in rapid succession, *fell to the ground with piercing cries of mental agony. The mysterious influence was at work.* It spread still further among the assemblage; and within half-an-hour we found not fewer than twenty human beings stretched upon the grass, exhibiting emotions, both of soul and body, sufficient to appal the stoutest heart. In all cases it appeared as if *every fibre of the heart, and every muscle of the body were wrung with some excruciating torture.* Then followed loud cries for the Redeemer's mercy, expressed in tones of anguish which no imagination can conceive or pen describe.

"'By some intelligent investigators it is believed that just in proportion to the fairness or immorality of previous character the visitation is more or less severe. *The correctness of that opinion is liable to considerable doubt;* but we know that, from whatever cause, there *is* a great variety in the extent of suffering. Some cases are comparatively mild. But the majority of the cases of this evening were among the *severest* that we ever witnessed—and we have now seen hundreds of them. In general, the stricken parties were carried out from the pressure of the thronging multitude, to localities where they became objects of solicitude to smaller groups in other portions of the enclosure. At about half-past ten o'clock we reckoned nine circles or assemblages of this nature, in a single one of which *we found eleven prostrate penitents, smitten to the heart, and fervently supplicating God, for Christ's sake, to pardon their iniquities.*

"'Over these parties, pious bystanders or some of the converted offered prayer. Other circles laboured to console the sufferers by singing appropriate hymns or psalms. In one of the circles we noticed a case of terrible severity, one in which visions of unspeakable horror must have been pictured to the imagination of the unhappy sufferer. A young woman lay extended at full length, her eyes closed, her hands clasped and elevated, and *her body curved in a spasm so violent that it appeared to rest, arch-like, upon her heels and the back portion of her head.* In that position she lay without speech or motion for several minutes. Suddenly she uttered a terrific scream, and tore handfuls of hair from her uncovered head. Extending her open hands in a repelling attitude of the most appalling terror, she exclaimed, "Oh that fearful pit!—Lord Jesus save me!" "I am a sinner, a most unworthy sinner—but oh, Lord, take *him* away, take *him* away!" "Oh, Saviour of sinners, *remove him from my sight!*" During this paroxysm three strong men were hardly able to restrain her. She extended her arms on either side, clutching spasmodically at the grass, shuddering with terror, and shrinking from some fearful inward vision; but she ultimately fell back exhausted, nerveless, and apparently insensible. How long she remained in that condition we are unable to say; but we understand that she was treated with Christian sympathy, and removed from the field in safety before midnight.

"'This was an extreme case—not without parallel, but certainly the most frightful that we have ever witnessed. We may remark that, three days afterwards, that woman was visited by a Christian friend, who had been a witness of her agony. He found her weak in body, but her mind was thoroughly composed. She was a new creature. *The light of peace and love was beaming from her countenance, and joy reflected in her eyes* as she told him of her perfect reconciliation with God, and her unwavering faith in the Redeemer. Now we do not pretend to explain the moving *cause* of these mysterious convictions ; but we feel bound to say that such have been the *results in every case brought under our notice during the last two months.* In that respect there is not the slightest perceptible distinction in the influence, whether upon the old or the young, the rich or the poor, the learned or the unlearned. Whether the agonies are brief or lengthened, moderate or severe, the *effect* is invariably the same—the fruit is love, peace, joy, temperance, and humility. Some of the "impressed" recovered ability to walk, but the greater number were supported by their friends, or carried away, and the ground was entirely vacated about half-past eleven o'clock.' "

Painful as it is to narrate, and call upon common-sense readers to follow these narratives, it is imperatively necessary that the philosophic student of psychology should trace out the workings of the wonderful modern Spiritual outpouring, in all its various phases. It is not an uninteresting subject of consideration moreover, to observe how the same influx operating upon different grades of religious thinkers, is estimated by the ruling powers of modern society. When an ignorant and half-savage multitude screams and writhes, and, in convulsive agonies, only to be paralleled in the cells of Bedlam, howls forth supplications "that God will pardon them" for *imaginary crimes*, the clergy fold their hands, look reverently on, and cry, "Behold the work of the Lord !" When a broken-hearted mother listens to the telegraphic signals which assure her the child she mourns as lost, still lives and blooms in Paradise, and she dries her tears, and calmly goes forth to proclaim in modest and eloquent terms, the fact of immortality demonstrated—that same clergy holds up its hands in holy horror, and cries, " Behold the work of Satan !"

It is time that a discerning public should have the opportunity of pronouncing judgment upon both sides of these pictures, and of comparing the theologic with the Spiritual influences prevailing during the psychological upheavals of this century.

With this view we shall present a few more examples of the celebrated Revival movement in Ireland.

A Belfast paper, speaking of Messrs. Ewart's mill, Crumlin Road, says :—

"On the morning of Tuesday, in one of the departments of a manufacturing concern, which employs a vast number of workers, male and female, nearly twenty girls were struck down, each in an instant, at their work, several becoming apparently insensible at once, and others uttering agonizing cries for mercy. The scene produced the greatest excitement throughout the entire works, and not a little alarm. Cars were provided for those who could not otherwise be removed to their homes, and the rest were assisted out of the premises, and taken to their respective places of abode. Orders were given that the workrooms should be closed for the day ; *but some additional cases of visitation occurred even as the young women were leaving the place and passing down stairs.* Some of those attacked, have not yet been able to return to work. In most cases, on reaching home, the persons affected, or their friends, *sought spiritual, and some of them medical advice* ; and when prayer had been offered up, in a majority of instances, speedy relief both from physical and mental suffering appeared to be produced. Several of the young women, we have been informed, have found peace, and a number are earnestly seeking it in prayer."

"The Rev. J. O'Brien, writing to the *Dublin Express*, says :—

" 'Mrs. Connor has been one of the most striking cases I have seen. Her bodily affection was very severe. She screamed so as to be heard a quarter of a mile off. She said "she had felt heavy for some days, *and had to hold up her heart*," *putting her hands to her stomach.* She was still in a very weak state. Her husband, who had been a man of very bad character, had been converted also, but was now able to return to his work, and spent all his spare time in trying to convert others.' "

" 'He speaks of another who "complained of a *burning from her throat down to the bottom of her heart*, and said that none but God could do her any good.' '

"The editor of the *Ballymena Observer* writes :—

" ' We went to Ballyclare last night to attend a revival prayer-meeting, and, truly, I cannot understand it. I can only say that " it is the Lord's doing, and marvellous in our eyes." The scene when we arrived baffles all description. Imagine a large meadow, with an immense multitude of people in all attitudes—some praying, weeping, and crying for mercy ; others lying in utter helplessness, only able to utter feebly their entreaties for pardon, surrounded by groups of friends and strangers, all interceding for them, and urging them to call on Christ ; and again, *others with their faces beaming with a more than earthly light*, listening to the speaker, with rapture, eloquently praising God ; fathers and mothers, *tender children and strong men, the infant of a few years, and the grey-haired woman, all equally struck*, all equally earnest and eloquent. I saw stalwart men led away as if they were helpless children ; and during the singing of one of the Psalms, a man beside us suddenly burst out into the most terrific cries, running round and round in circles in such a wild manner that it was dangerous to be in his way—when his cries changed suddenly into calls on the name of Jesus, and in a few minutes, after the most awful suffering, *he fell, unable to stand or even speak*. The public-houses are empty, all through the town. There is a prayer-meeting in almost every second house. Groups about the streets are praying or conversing on the all-engrossing topic. Public works are stopped in consequence of this strange and awful manifestation. All places are alike ; people are struck down while following their daily avocations, resting on their beds, or traversing the streets. Among the people the visitation is sudden. The prayers and supplications for mercy by and for the afflicted are, oh, how awfully solemn and earnest ! *From being one of the wildest towns in the neighbourhood, Ballyclare has become one of the most religious.*' "

" Dr. Carson, of Coleraine, who has written an excellent pamphlet on the Physical side of the Manifestations, gives the following :—

" ' A poor child, I think about *seven or eight years of age*, came to my house one night at a late hour, and asked to see Mrs. Carson, who had gone to her bedroom. The interview was readily granted. The child became affected. Her imploring and heart-rending cries for mercy, for she said *she was a sinner on the brink of Hell*, were so absolutely distressing that I had to leave the house for a time, as I could not bear to listen to the melancholy tones of her infant voice. The expressions of deep despair on her countenance could not be imitated by the best actor I ever saw on the stage. It was a dreadful scene. In a few hours, the poor child got the most perfect relief, and her countenance appeared almost superhuman with delight. She then began to pray, and her prayer would have melted the heart of a rock. It was so powerful, so fluent, and so full of thought, that it almost looked like inspiration in a child so very young.' "

" The Rev. Dr. Spence, of the Poultry Chapel, giving the results of his personal experience, says :—

" ' I saw by the countenance of many of them that they were conscious of an unusual joy. I spoke to several of them individually about their spiritual change and their Christian hope. In some cases I could find *no intelligent foundation for their joy beyond the simple fact that they had been " struck," and by-and-by had found happiness ;* but in other cases I found the most profound sense of sinfulness, and the most loving reliance on the Lord. I endeavoured, when I was brought into contact with those who had been " struck," to test in every case the character of the change which had been experienced. The result was various. Sometimes I could find *no solid scriptural basis for the transition from sadness to joy ;* often, on the other hand, was my own soul refreshed by the simple narrative of a deepening sense of personal unworthiness, and a growing experience of the Saviour's grace. There may be ground, however, to fear that in not a few cases *feeling alone had to do with the change.*' "

" Dr. Massie relates of ' M. Napoleon Roussel, who came to see the revival, that he was full of mistrust, and that he had decided " to surrender his judgment only to evidence, to let no one know his intention of publishing." He describes the physical crisis much as I saw it ; in general consisting ' in wringing of the hands, raising the arms, moving the limbs, *or holding the stomach in the hands*, in a state of violent despair, or at least of great excitement under a sense of sin.' "

" The Rev. Mr. Tocock writes :—

" ' I was requested to come to a young boy, in a most frightful state, *stricken in a moment, and fearfully distracted, throwing out his arms, and kicking with his feet, and dancing and shaking in great agitation.* I told him to be a little calmer, for *he would displease the Lord by his conduct ;* urged him to look to Jesus, and to pray for pardon ; engaged with him in prayer, he repeating the words ; then we sung, and being aided by *two young converts*, he came to Jesus, and found peace very soon afterwards.' "

" From Ballibay it is written :—

" ' The church ministers are beginning to join us. Twenty-five fell in one church *along with the minister.* In another church, there is *a hundred of the congregation and the minister* converted.' "

"The Rev. Mr. Steel, of Dalry, describing a meeting at Glengarnock, says :—

"'About ten o'clock, a person rose and said that we ought to kneel and engage in prayer. A working man then rose, and, with a heart like to burst, poured out a most earnest prayer to Almighty God. At the close of the prayer, the whole meeting seemed to be moved by an invisible power. Here and there were persons crying out for mercy, and strong men crying in such a manner as I had never heard before. I have seen persons suffering under various stages of cholera—I have seen much agony in my day, but never such a sight as this.'"

"The *Ballymena Observer*, describing similar cases, says :—

"'On Sunday evening last, an assemblage numbering 2,000 people, *many of them from Ballymena*, congregated at a prayer meeting in the open air near Kilconriola. The third speaker had nearly concluded his exhortations, when a case of sudden impression, with all the ordinary symptoms, occurred among the audience. The patient was a young woman of the neighbourhood, who had been slightly affected some evenings before, at a meeting near Carncoagh. *Some excitement immediately ensued, and other cases followed in rapid succession. Within half an hour fully twenty people of the audience were laid prostrate;* some of them utterly helpless, and for a time unable to utter anything but incoherent expressions of bodily pain and mental agony. The excitement now became intense, and the scene that ensued baffles all power of description.'"

"Mr. Wilkinson, on p. 91 of his volume, 'The Revivals,' says :—'Let us read the following, which we quote from the *Ballymena Observer :—*

"'The most extraordinary event of that evening occurred in the case of a *mere child, only seven years of age ;* a poor barefooted girl, cleanly but indifferently clothed. Without the slightest appearance of any previous agitation, she was struck prostrate in a single moment. For a time *her body was found to be perfectly rigid,* and her face colourless. On partial recovery she clasped her hands, and, looking up, exclaimed in low accents, "Lord Jesus, have mercy upon me, and bring me to the foot of thy cross !" For a considerable time she continued to repeat—but in an undertone, "Jesus !" "Jesus !" "Jesus !" Her fascinated and soul-absorbing look was fixed, far away beyond all spheres ; *and the mild, unclouded spiritual light of that unwavering gaze into the heavens* will never be forgotten by those who witnessed it. We certainly never saw any condition *so manifestly preternatural ;* nor any result so nearly approaching to a practical illustration of the poet's beautiful, though fanciful, idea of the "Angel's whisper to a slumbering baby." The trance-like attitude of body, and the rapt expression of her eye, appeared to favour the supposition that *a world of glory, invisible to other mortals, had been unveiled to her inner sight, and that, for a temporary period, she had been admitted to communion with the spirits of the just made perfect.* We understand that the girl was restored to nearly her ordinary condition in about an hour. Phenomena analogous to the foregoing came under our personal observation at a house in Alexander Street, in the afternoon of Tuesday last— and it is worthy of special notice that the party affected had *never been at any of the revival meetings.* We there found an interesting girl, *less than eight years of age,* and we ascertained that her general character is that of a shy, intelligent, and truthful child— that she is a pupil in the infant department of Guy's free school. When we first saw her she was extended upon a pallet, and slowly recovering from a *somnambulic trance,* into which she had been instantaneously stricken about five hours previously when in the act of preparation for school. For some time subsequently to the visitation, her eyes were fixed on vacancy, her hands clasped, and her lips moving as in silent prayer. Her arms were frequently elevated, as if to grasp some object immediately in view ; and, on one occasion, she clasped her father's hands, and pointing upward, motioned him to look and pray. At another time she called upon the bystanders to raise her up, in order that she might take hold of some glorious object presented to her imagination. On recovery from this state, she insisted that *she had been in the company of superhuman beings in a world of light and blessedness ; and, to the utter amazement of her parents, she affirmed that she had there intuitively recognized her infant brother, who had died eleven months after his birth, and five years before she was born !'"*

"The following remarkable case is given in a Coleraine paper about the same time. It occurred at Kilconriola :—

"'The person affected was a married woman, of middle age. She appeared to be greatly *excited and feverish ; her pulse was quick, there was a hectic tinge upon the cheeks, her eyes were bloodshot, and her face was streaming with perspiration,* and for the space of fifty-six hours she was unable to taste anything but water. After the first four hours of racking pain and incessant cries for mercy, she remained prostrate for nearly three days in the condition which we have described. During the prostration of this woman her house was visited by hundreds of the neighbouring people. *She had never been taught to read or pray, and was unable to distinguish one letter of the alphabet from another,* yet she prayed with intense fervency, and exhorted the people to repentance with astonishing fluency and accuracy of speech. This case, like many others, was accompanied by visionary scenes — *illusions, certainly, but of a very extraordinary character.* Among other things she maintained that *a Bible, traced in characters of light, was open before her, and that, although unable to read, a spiritual power had endowed her with capacity to comprehend the meaning of every word in it.* It is an undoubted fact that *she repeated with literal accuracy, and as if reading from the volume, a very large number of quotations from the Old and New Testament,* applying them in an appropriate manner in connection with the prayers wherein she was engaged ! but these perceptions gradually faded in her progress towards recovery, and entirely disappeared on restoration to her ordinary health.' "

"The Rev. J. Marrable narrates the following, as occurring under his own eyes :—

" ' I was particularly struck with the following case : N. C., not eighteen years of age, *was in the act of holding a conversation with an invisible Being whom she called an "angel."* I shall not attempt to describe this scene, or the words she uttered ; but when, in about half an hour, she awoke out of the trance, to see many faces looking in amazement at her, *with tears flowing from all eyes,* her tongue, which could scarcely articulate plainly before, became loosened, and *in the most eloquent manner she addressed all present* on the subject of salvation, with an expression of holy joy and gratitude *beaming in her intelligent countenance.* She continued for several minutes in such eloquent strains that all present were compelled to admit that they had *never seen or heard anything like it before. I would myself have gone a thousand miles to see this one case, and did not think it possible that the human countenance could be lit up with so sweet and happy an expression of delight.' "

"Dr. Massie introduces the following narrative in these words :—

" ' On Monday evening we called to visit a little girl in the Commons, called M. E. R. (aged fourteen), who had been labouring under conviction for some days previous. We found her in a melancholy, depressed state, and after conversing with her for a little, we intimated that we would engage in singing and prayer before leaving her. While singing, she fell speechless at our feet, when it was evident to all that she had been deprived of both speech and sight ; her mind, however, was active as ever, and her sense of hearing unimpaired. During the forenoon, Drs. Macaldie and Clarke visited her, and expressed their opinion that none could heal her but the Physician of souls. Later in the day, the dispensary doctor visited her, and endeavoured to restore her by applying remedies to the body, but without effect. About half-past three in the afternoon of the next day, we again visited her, and sung, " Lo ! He comes with clouds descending," and ere this hymn was finished, her tongue was loosed, he reyes we reopened, and she joined us in praising God. This was about four o'clock on the evening of Tuesday—she having been eighteen hours deprived of sight and speech.' "

"Dr. Massie proceeds :—

" ' In compliance with numerous applications upon the subject, we proceed to notice other recent phases of manifestation not less astonishing. Two young unmarried women (whom we shall call Jane, aged eighteen, and Ellen, aged twenty-three) reside at a locality about two miles distant from Ballymena, and within three hundred yards of each other. Both were apparently in good health ; and about a month ago they were stricken with " conviction," accompanied by agonies of conscience and nervous excitement. It would appear, that a species of sympathy became established between them in such a manner, that whatever affected the one party was sure to exercise a corresponding influence upon the other. On Monday, about two o'clock in the afternoon, Ellen, whilst busily engaged at work in her own house, suddenly exclaimed that Jane had become ill—said that *her mind told her so, and that she must go and visit her.* With that intent she left the house ; and on entering that of her companion, found that she had just fallen into a trance— deaf, dumb, and motionless. Within a minute afterwards, Ellen had fallen upon the floor *in a precisely similar condition,* and both remained in that state and position *for fully three hours.* Both recovered *at the same moment,* and immediately on their recovery they were separated ; Ellen being forthwith taken to her own house, where she fell upon her knees, and was engaged in prayer for half an hour. To the great surprise of her relatives, she then affirmed that, precisely at four o'clock on the following evening, she would become deaf, dumb, blind, and without power of motion in one side of her body, for the space of six hours, and that she should be restored to her natural condition at ten o'clock. On being asked how she could know that she would be visited in such a manner, she replied, " I cannot explain how I know it ; but my mind tells me that it will surely be as I have said." Every effort was made to remove the impression from the mind of the party thus affected ; and care was taken that Jane should *have no information of what had been predicted in reference to her companion.* Ellen continued at her ordinary work, and apparently in her usual health, throughout the forenoon of Tuesday ; and the hand of the house clock was secretly put back fifteen minutes in the course of the day. Precisely at the moment when the clock indicated that it wanted a quarter to four, but when the real time *was fifteen minutes later,* Ellen's arms dropped, her eyes closed, and she fell from her chair without speech or motion, and in a state of absolute insensibility ! She was carefully laid upon a bed ; and on examination it was found that the joints of her right arm and leg were perfectly immovable, and rigid as iron. The excitement among the people of the house was naturally very great ; but it was doubled in intensity when intelligence arrived that *Jane had fallen into a state exactly resembling that of Ellen, precisely at the same moment that Ellen had been thus affected.*

" ' In this abnormal condition both women remained for a period of six hours, and both awoke to consciousness, and in the full possession of all their faculties, *precisely at the same moment.* At five minutes before ten, Ellen's rigid arm regained its natural condition, and she was observed to raise her hand and lay it gently across her breast ; but up till the stroke of the predicted hour, no other change became perceptible. Before the remaining strokes of ten had sounded from the clock, she was fully awake ; and her first exclamation, amid a house then crowded with anxious visitors, was, "Christ is my Saviour ! He is all and in all !" It may appear incredible, but the fact is established beyond all controversy, that *these identical words were the first* uttered by Jane in her own house three hundred yards distant, as she awoke to consciousness *at the same moment !* ' "

Dr. Massie relates with great minutiæ of detail, many additional cases of a similar character to those already given, together with instances in which the "stricken ones," both male and female, were poor ignorant people— some of them *very young children,*—servants, and workmen,—who could *neither read nor write,* yet, these persons in their "trances," did intelligently read out consecutive verses, and sometimes whole chapters of the Bible, and exhort, pray, and sing, with a fervency and eloquence, not to be equalled by the best cultured ministers of religion. The last cases which we can cite are as follows :—

"The Rev. R. Gemmell, after saying, 'With regard to the bodily manifestations, I can give no opinion, nor do I like to hear any opinion, as I believe no man can give any satisfactory explanation,' gives the following :—

" ' A young lad about sixteen years of age was struck down in his own house. It took four strong men to hold him, to prevent him from dashing his brains out on the floor. He continued in this state for several hours. When he recovered, he had *lost the power of one of his sides, and was unable to utter a word distinctly.* The third day after, I visited him, about three o'clock ; he was still in the same state, but, to my utter astonishment, when standing at the door at seven o'clock, he came running forward, and shook hands with me, and said, "O Sir, I am now quite well !" ' "

"Dr. Massie says :—

" ' One fearful case was specified to me of an infatuated scoffer, who professed to fall down as an awakened and stricken sinner, while a companion, as depraved, ran to request the attendance of a servant of God. When they came to the spot where the feigned penitent was lying, they found him dead.' "

"The Rev. Mr. Moore says :—

" ' In my own congregation five or six cases—and some of them very painful—have occurred. We hear occasionally *of dreams and visions—the mere drapery of the work, and the effect of its deep and intense reality*—but though beautiful and interesting in themselves, such things are not made much of here, *and the less the better.*' "

"At Paisley, in September, similar cases were frequent. The Rev. Mr. Macgregor says :—

" ' Among the young women affected, two were for a time deaf and dumb, and while in this state, their countenances indicated, from their expression, the most joyous happiness. Many of them had been *dreaming dreams and seeing visions.* It was the case that, *wherever the revivals had arisen, they had dreams and visions,* and they were to be regarded as evidence of the outpouring of the Holy Spirit.' "

"The Rev. Hugh Hunter writes :—

" ' It is now nearly five weeks since the Lord's work commenced in good earnest in this neighbourhood. It was going on amazingly in the neighbouring county of Antrim. Every day brought new tales of *trances, sleeps, visions, dreams and miracles ; such as, that persons who never knew a letter of the alphabet when awake could read the Bible distinctly, sing psalms and hymns, preach, and pray with ease, eloquence, and fluency.*' "

"The Rev. J. Whitsitt, of Drum, Monaghan, writes to a friend :—

" ' It was true the report which you heard. At one of our meetings for prayer, at which there were a number of **convictions,** **a dark cloud** formed on the ceiling, **and,** in the course of a few minutes, a number of forms burst out. One in particular was of human appearance, which passed and repassed across all the lights, and descended to the pew in which a young woman was rejoicing. The appearance lasted for three minutes, or more, produced no terror, but joy, especially among the converts. All present did not see it. Perhaps 300 saw it, and can testify to the reality. I cannot tell what it was; the substance is in heaven, and will not be visible until the time when "every eye shall see Him."' "

CHAPTER XV.

SPIRITUALISM IN GREAT BRITAIN (CONTINUED).

SUMMARY OF CONFLICTING OPINIONS CONCERNING THE IRISH REVIVALS.

IT cannot be supposed that the mighty wave which had surged over the "stricken" subjects of the Irish Revival, could pass away without calling forth an immense array of diverse opinions from various leading minds, concerning the origin and significance of the wonderful movement.

As a general rule the attempts to find an adequate cause for the marvels which flooded the land, during the Revival frenzy, may be classified thus :—

1. The work proceeds from "the Devil."
2. From the Holy Ghost.
3. From interested and artful professional Revival preachers.
4. From mesmerism, hysteria, and other unknown physical agents.

About the time when the Irish Revivals were at their height, some scenes of a kindred character, though conducted on a more limited scale, and promptly checked by the officiating ministers of the time, were proceeding in some of the rural districts of England, and amongst the lowest of the East-end ragged schools of the metropolis. An able writer in the London *Sunday Times* thus comments on scenes of this character, of which he claims to have been an eye-witness in a ragged school in St. Giles' on the preceding Sunday.

"Here are one hundred and fifty ragged, ill-fed, uneducated little boys and girls, from six to fourteen, kept until after ten at night to listen to a 'deeply impressive' account of the doings in Ireland, in all their agonising details. Was there no mercy in the heart of the speaker? No sense of childhood's weakness? No thought of the Divine Justice? And there they were rolling upon the floor, crying out until two in the morning about their sins. Great God! how art thou insulted. Their sins! Why surely, if God arose in His anger it would be, not to crush down and agonise these little friendless, hungry, orphaned children, only six years old, who cannot comprehend the meaning of such subjects, but *He would rise against the high and the mighty*, the men of wealth and statesman power, who, through neglecting their duty, have left these little ones to become the victims of hunger and cold, and hence also the victims of our hard laws, and, to them, cruel institutions. Comments upon such mockery and cruelty are needless."

And again :—" I am not dealing unjustly in thus speaking. I see the poor little girl crying in the Irish churchyard ; I see the young women rolling in agony upon the Irish meadows ; I see the ignorant men, the hysterical women, and the fear-struck children in the Irish churches, with horrible anxiety pictured upon their terror-stricken countenances ; and I see the poor little boys and girls in the St. Giles' refuge rolling upon the floor, their young hearts filled with fear through the story of Irish madness which, without stint or mercy, had been poured into their ears. Yes, I see all this, and more than this—more than can now be told ; and then, while listening to the wild screams which burst from the agonized hearts of an ignorant and frenzied people, I hear also, and blended with the screams, the voices of the ' holy men '—voices of the leaders and teachers in our spiritual Israel—raised as in thanksgiving to God for all this agony, which, either in their blindness or through their hypocrisy, they dare to call ' His great mercy.' I hear them pray that the same ' blessing ' may be granted unto us ; and, from all this, what is it possible to conclude other than that, if they are in earnest, then are they blind also ? but, whether earnest or not, they are endeavouring to inflict upon England one of the heaviest curses that could descend upon a people whose ancestors won freedom alike on the fields of civil and ecclesiastical conflict."

Mr. Wilkinson, in his excellent work on "The Irish Revivals," says :—

"Archdeacon Stopford of Meath is the champion of the physical mode of accounting for the Revival, whose arguments are the best poised, and sufficiently comprehend those of others having the same views. He does not, however, fail to see ' much good in the movement.' He says, ' Even a stranger cannot fail to be struck with the earnest concern about religion which appears to pervade the people ; as I listened to a street preacher—the best sermon which I heard in Belfast—it was impossible not to be impressed with the earnest and reverent expression of countenance in all the working men and lads who gathered round, perhaps one hundred and fifty in number ; faces so earnest I never saw before in any congregation. From house to house I saw much of the same feeling.' "

The question of hysteria has been so widely canvassed, that it is worth while to present the argument as it appears in one of Dr. Carson's excellent letters. Dr. Carson says :—

"I see a good deal of time and labour have been spent in *asserting*, over and over again, that the physical manifestations are neither more nor less than hysteria. Were it not that the public might be misled by the plausible and ostentatious statements which have been put forward on the subject, I would not think of occupying time with its consideration.

"There is no reason why the country should be free from hysterical cases now, more than at any other time. Hence, as might be anticipated, *some cases of hysteria are to be met with in every district where the Revival has appeared.* But the man who will confine his observations to these cases, or confound them with the Revival manifestations, has but a poor capacity for the observation of facts. The fact is, *the Revival and hysteria have scarcely any symptoms in common.* Any person in the Revival district may easily convince himself of this fact by turning to the article ' Hysteria,' in the first work on the 'Practice of Medicine' he can lay his hands on. To enter fully into the distinguishing marks of these two affections would extend this letter to an unreasonable length ; but there are two or three features which require to be noticed, and which are capable of being judged by all parties. . . . Hysteria is *almost entirely confined to the female sex*. It is very common in the female, but so *extremely* rare in the male, that the late Dr. Hooper, and the present Dr. Watson, of London, in their immense practice, have seen only *three cases* each, which they could at all compare to hysteria, and these cases occurred in debilitated subjects. . . . In regard to the Revival, it occurs chiefly amongst the lower and middle classes of society, who are obliged to earn their subsistence by their daily labour. It is to be found as readily amongst the hardy inhabitants of country parishes and mountain districts, as in towns and cities. If all ages are included, there are very nearly as many males affected by it as females. I have seen and known of an immense number of instances in which *the strongest, the stoutest, most vigorous, healthy, and lion-hearted men in the country have been struck down like children,* and have called, with the most agonising entreaties, for mercy for their souls. How could all this be hysteria ? "

Dr. Watson, an eminent medical practitioner of London, who spent some time in personally examining the condition of many of the Revivalists, arrives at the conclusion that the principal source of the movement is a *physical*, though unknown agent, and his views are given in the following remarks :—

"I now fearlessly state, that, in my opinion, *there is a physical, as well as a spiritual, agent concerned in the Revival*. There does not appear to me to be any other rational way of accounting for the facts. Whatever I may have been disposed to think at first, I am now fully satisfied the symptoms of a Revival case do not correspond to the effects which are manifested as the result of mere mental impressions. The unearthly tone of subdued entreaties, and the partial prostration of muscular power in the individual affected, are very different from the wild screams, and convulsive paroxysms, which arise from sudden mental anguish ; and we cannot consistently refer them to a sudden view of spiritual danger, *because the same sudden view of spiritual matters has been revealed to thousands of individuals of different constitutions, at different periods of the history of the world, without producing the like results.*

"The explanation by mere mental impressions will not satisfy a close thinker in regard to them. There must be a special physical agent concerned.

"This view is greatly strengthened by the way in which the Revival has travelled. *It has followed a steady, gradual, and uninterruped course from parish to parish, and district to district. It has travelled almost like a wave.* Again, it was observed that the most illiterate convert, *who had himself been physically affected, had far more power in producing the manifestations in the audience, than the most eloquent speaker who could address them.* There did not seem to be any proportion between the words uttered by the speakers and the results produced. It looked more like a physical effect produced *by individual on individual than anything else.*

"The idea of exclusive spirituality in the Revival would involve us in endless difficulties, which can all be avoided by the simple idea of the double agency. If we do not adopt this view, what are we to do with those *cases of deafness, dumbness, blindness, extraordinary visions, and prophesying,* which have occurred in some localities ? They are not either directly or indirectly the effects of the Holy Spirit. They are entirely owing to the effects of the physical agent on the brain and nervous system.

"In regard to the nature of the physical agent, I have no hesitation in acknowledging my utter ignorance. I know of nothing to correspond exactly with it in the whole range of philosophy.

"No person but the man who has witnessed them could have any idea of the awful effects produced by a number of Revival cases. A scene like the one which took place on the night in which the new hall in Coleraine was first filled with these cases has, perhaps, never been equalled in the world. It was so like the day of judgment, when sinners would be calling on the mountains and the rocks to hide them from the storm of God's wrath, that it struck terror to the heart of the most hardened and obdurate sinner."

As the Evangelical views of the causes operating to produce these Revivals, have already been sufficiently hinted at to make the reader aware that a large number of Ministers of the Gospel attributed the above movement to the direct action of the " Holy Ghost," it only remains to call attention to the very suspicious way in which those peculiar demonstrations were received, which in the form of trances, dreams, visions, and prophecies, seemed to be all too dangerously allied to the *bête noir* of every denomination, namely modern Spiritualism, a development which might well have been unknown to the poor illiterate subjects of the Irish Revivals, but which was by no means *either new or strange* to the better-informed Doctors, Lawyers, Divines, &c., &c., who watched the Spiritual epidemic of the unmanageable Irish Revivals.

Mr. W. M. Wilkinson opens up this question with significant force when he says :—

"What are we to think of that class of phenomena, of which there are so many instances, in which the converts have fallen into swoons and trances, and into those peculiar states of the organism in which they have seen and described visions of angels and devils—of heaven and of hell—and which were so common, 'that almost every girl now struck in Belfast had visions, and would be greatly disappointed if she had not.' 'There are also very many astonishing statements and events which, some years ago, and in other circumstances, would have been called clairvoyance by those who believed that there was such a mode of obtaining knowledge.' Others, again, who could not read a word in their ordinary state, had a faculty or power, when in this wondrous state, of perceiving in letters of light, and reading whole pages from the Bible ; others of seeing things and persons at distances beyond the ken of natural eyes. . . .

"Now, how it has come about we know not, but these phenomenal aspects of the Revival have brought down upon it, its bitterest opponents, and in view of them, the whole movement has been characterised by some religious critics as the direct work of Satan, and by the more sceptical as a work of imposture, or as the product of diseased imagination. Here, again, it is to be noted, that at first there are not so many words used against the calm and quiet part of the awakening ; but when it came to pass that its subjects were seers and seeresses no words are strong enough for its condemnation."

Again, Mr. Wilkinson in commenting on the *pyschical* aspect of this movement, and the various phenomena (far too numerous to admit of farther description) which corresponded with the manifestations of Spiritualism, says :—

" In attempting to gather up facts of this nature at a distance from the places of their occurrence we find, of all those who could not in fairness omit noticing them, there is not one who gives them a kindly welcome. Several suppress them altogether, the others have to apologize for them in the best way they can.

" The excellent Minister at Connor, when in the great excitement of prostrations and ecstatic phenomena, some similar cases were threatened amongst his flock, set his face against them altogether. Others are blamed for not having followed his plan, which had the good effect of preventing them. We shall see that they were amenable to this treatment, and it is a suggestive fact for our consideration.

" In the early days of the excitement arising from these cases, some were made public through the newspapers, and there are others to be found in some of the narratives, but every day they become more difficult of access, as mention of them is seldom made, and it is only from occasional glimpses that we see how common they were—so common, indeed, that they occurred in the majority of the stricken cases, and those who did not have visions, or some of the other extraordinary phenomena accompanying their prostration, complained of the deficiency of the Holy Spirit, and feared that their conversion was not complete. . . .

" We could have wished that these cases had been as fully stated and as largely investigated as the others, for they form a chapter in the book of man that is worthy the most serious and earnest consideration."

We have already extended the notices of this singular movement to so great a length, that we turn, though most reluctantly, from the many suggestive arguments adduced by the author of " The Revival" to show that a great magnetic wave, contagious as magnetism ever is in its effects, world-wide in its centres of evolution, and purely spiritual in its source, underlies these Irish Revivals, just as surely as it does the doings of the *Polter Gheist* in Germany, the manifestations of clairvoyance in France, or the *Rochester Knockings* in America.

Who can doubt that if this Revival had occurred on Mahometan ground, the visionists would have seen Houris and paradises ; screamed for Mahomet, and sought through him reconciliation with Allah? Occurring in a land, the very atmosphere of which was saturated with Calvinistic ideas, and governed by a Calvinistic priesthood, the great magnetic influx which poured into the hearts and minds of a naturally impulsive and susceptible race of people, inevitably partook of the dominant religious idea ; and this was so strengthened by the powerful influence of Revival preachers, that it was only now and then that angel faces could look through the theological veil of terror, in which the peasantry were enshrouded, or in rare cases, that true Spiritual mediumship could be unfolded, and triumph over the unreasoning ecstasies of religious gloom and mystery.

The sunbeam which gives life to the rose and lights up the blue eye of the violet, quickens the heap of corruption into the life of the foul reptile, and stinging insect. The sun of spiritual existence shines on the just and the unjust, and *quickens, but creates nothing.*

Thus we may realise by careful research into the fanaticisms of the Irvingites, the abominations of Mormonism, the unnatural asceticisms of Shakerism, and the frenzied agonies of Irish Revivalism that " all are but parts of one stupendous whole"—*differences of administration, but the same spirit working in all.*

CHAPTER XVI.

SPIRITUALISM IN GREAT BRITAIN.—SECOND PERIOD.

In searching amongst the scattered records of Spiritual manifestations in England, the historian cannot fail to come to the conclusion that there are two well-defined sources of power which antedated in point of time the introduction of that systematic mode of telegraphy practised by the American mediums who commenced to visit this country in 1852.

The first of these was the very general outpouring of Spiritual manifestations noted in preceding chapters, and occurring in the form of haunting isolated phenomena, and Religious Revivals.

The second was Animal Magnetism, which, by preparing the world for the study of occult phenomena, and unfolding in many organisms the potencies of clairvoyance and other Spiritual endowments, paved the way for the more pronounced and comprehensive demonstrations of Spiritual Mediumship.

From the year 1820 to 1840, numerous gentlemen of learning and high social standing, openly avowed themselves disciples of Mesmeric philosophy, and practised with success healing by Animal Magnetism.

As experiments of this character were very often productive of clairvoyance, prevision, trance speaking, and even Spiritual seership, a wide spreading interest began to arise concerning these mysterious potencies. About the year 1851, a Mesmeric Infirmary was established in Wimpole Street, of which Drs. Elliotson, Ashburner, Wilson, Haddock, Mrs. De Morgan, and numerous other ladies and gentlemen became patrons and supporters. In this institution, patients were treated by magnetic processes, and in many instances cures were effected of cases deemed hopeless by the ordinary methods of medical practice.

For some years previous to the formation of this establishment, the advocates of Mesmeric philosophy had conducted an excellent periodical entitled the *Zoist*, in which hundreds of notable experiments were recorded, and the phenomena as well as the facts of magnetic practices were carefully detailed.

In view of the persistence with which the columns of the secular journals are open to all manner of communications antagonistic to new discoveries, and new ideas, and closed against their advocates, the publication of the *Zoist* which was continued for many years, and supported by an able staff of editors and contributors, will be understood to have been the principal means of widening the sphere of knowledge on occult subjects, and preserving many valuable records which would otherwise have been lost to the world.

In the initiatory numbers of this journal, Dr. Elliotson, one of its earliest and most distinguished supporters, alleges, that Mesmerism as a recognised "science," was first established in England in 1828, through the influence of an Irish gentleman, a Mr. Chevenix, who after a long residence in Paris, where he had witnessed, and personally assisted at a number of experiments, finally began to practise on his own account in Ireland, where he found a fine field for his operations amongst the susceptible peasantry of that country.

Drs. McKay, Peacock, Cotter, Gooch; Mr. Smith, surgeon to the Coldstream Guards; Professor Gregory of Edinburgh, Drs. Elliotson and Ashburner of London, Dr. John Wilson, physician at Middlesex Hospital, and many gentlemen of equal standing in their profession, who had avowed themselves advocates of Mesmeric practices, succeeded, both in creating a wide-spread public interest in their philosophy, and in awakening the most relentless spirit of antagonism from those who thought proper to range themselves on the opposite side of the question.

To those who realise with the author, that Mesmerism has been—humanly speaking—the corner-stone upon which the Temple of Spiritualism was upreared, the following notice of some of the curious experiments recorded in the early numbers of the *Zoist*, will be of interest.

Dr. Ashburner, in reviewing a pamphlet written by Dr. John Wilson of Middlesex Hospital entitled, "Trials of Animal Magnetism on the Brute Creation," says :—

> "Dr. Wilson successfully magnetized fish, birds, and savage beasts. I was with him on one occasion at the Surrey Zoological Gardens while honest Mr. Cross was proprietor of the menagerie. The great male elephant was put into a deep sleep by the strenuous and energetic passes of my colleague. The keeper told me, 'The Doctor off with his coat, wrought like a Trojan, and got the old animal into a sound sleep and no mistake.'
>
> "Mr. Cross had a very savage and irascible hyena. Dr. Wilson mesmerised him, and it was amusing to see the delight of the fierce creature at the Doctor's approach."

In the pages of the *Zoist* will be found an answer to the sneer with which those readers will peruse the above-named experiments who—having found their efforts to stamp out unwelcome facts ineffectual—proceed to depreciate their value by the imbecile query, " What is the use of it ?" The *use* of Mesmerism is shown, even in the early stage of the movement of which we are writing, by the facts that the Mesmerisers recorded ; namely ; well attested cures of typhus fever in its last and most hopeless stages; con-sumption, dropsy, bronchitis, all manner of nervous disorders, besides many surgical cases.

Amongst the latter, is described the perfect cure of a woman, employed in the Hospital at Hoddesden, superintended by the celebrated writer Mrs. Ellis,—who was suffering from a severe case of ovarian tumour, for which in fact she was on the point of submitting to a dangerous and doubtful operation. Dr. Ashburner hearing of her dilemma, persuaded her to try Mesmerism, through the instrumentality of which, she became entirely cured. Several other instances of a similar kind are recorded in the *Zoist*, including one, of *malignant cancer*,—a cure so thoroughly well proved, and of such a remarkable character, that we would refer the curious reader to its full details, which may be found given by Dr. Elliotson in the 6th volume of the *Zoist*, page 213. Mesmeric practices received a strong impulse, especially in the unfoldment of remarkable psychological powers, in the year 1849, by the visit to England of two renowned French clair-voyants, Messrs. Alexis Didier, and Marcellet.

Through numerous experiments conducted with these gentlemen, the Magnetizers were enabled to prove, not only that disease could be cured, but that mental power of a highly exalted and wonderful character could be evolved in the magnetic sleep.

The French clairvoyants were adepts in the examination of obscure diseases, in tracing lost, hidden, and distant objects, also in the faculty of mind reading.

The powers thus displayed in the magnetic sleep, were found to be more general than had hitherto been supposed; hence, clairvoyance, in addition to the healing faculty, became another horn of the dilemma with which the materialistic opponents of the new philosophy found themselves compelled to do battle.

To the voluminous writings of Mr. Henry Thompson, Professor Gregory, Mrs. De Morgan, Drs. Barth, Dixon, Elliotson, Ashburner, and Haddock, Mr. Joseph Hands, and above all, to the experiences of Drs. Deleuze and Eisdale, in India, we must refer the readers, desirous to acquaint themselves in farther detail, concerning the origin, practices, and results of Mesmerism in Great Britain.

Quite recently—that is, at the present date of writing—the practice of Mesmerism, whether as a curative process, or an agent for the unfoldment of marvellous psychologic powers, has received a most favourable impulse from the writings, lectures, and private practice of Miss Chandos Leigh Hunt (now Mrs. Wallace), a lady who has thoroughly and philosophically mastered as much of the subject as can at present be known or experimented with. In a scholarly and exhaustive treatise written by this lady on the Science and Art of Organic Magnetism,* the powers and possibilities of this wonderful mesmeric force are admirably described, and the immense range of operations, both curative and psychologic, which the talented authoress delineates, renders it now, as heretofore, a reproach to the age, that no philanthropic as well as philosophic associations should be formed for the study of the stupendous principles suggested by Mrs. Wallace's writings, and practically taught by her, to all who are interested enough to put vague theory into the form of demonstrable proof.

Another valuable work treating of the results, though not of the *modus operandi* of Mesmerism, is Mrs. De Morgan's work, written quite early in the advent of the Spiritual movement, entitled "From Matter to Spirit." Our learned authoress says :—

"Every wonderful effect produced by mesmerism, has since found its explanation or its counterpart in the spiritual phenomena, so that had unseen powers been working for our instruction, they could not have taken a better method of giving the needful elementary knowledge, than by making us acquainted with the processes and results of mesmerism."

Mrs. De Morgan in illustrating the statement given above, cites numerous examples, amongst others, the following experience, recorded by Dr. Jacob Dixon in his published manual, entitled "Hygienic Medicine." This author says :—

"Persons in some of the highest mesmeric states, appear to have gained an insight into the world of spirit. Of this I had striking experiences *long before* the time of raps, seeing mediums, and mysteries of the present day.

"Although I had too many instances of earthly clairvoyance to remain sceptical in that direction, yet I held all belief in intercourse with spirits to be a delusion. This scepticism was first shaken by the following occurrence.

---

* *Private Practical Instructions in the Science and Art of Organic Magnetism.* By Miss Chandos Leigh Hunt. Philanthropic Reform Publishing Office, 2, Oxford Mansion, Oxford Circus, London, W.

"Being invited to see a young lady in a clairvoyant state, in which she professed to see and converse with spiritual beings, I entered the room after she had been put in the mesmeric state, whilst my name was not even mentioned or my presence known. . . . At length my friends asked, whether she could look for any spirit for the party sitting beside her. She would try. I mentioned two names without giving age, sex, or relationship to myself.

"She then said : '*I am now in a garden quite full of flowers. There is a group of children. . . . Two come out of the group. The girl is the oldest. They are ten and eight years' old.*' She then described perfectly every feature of the two children I had asked for, dwelling with animation on their beautiful appearance and surroundings. The ages she mentioned, however, were much in advance of the reality.

"When I remarked this she said : '*They say that I see them as they are now, you must remember, that they have been here some time.*'"

The writer adds—

"It then appeared that the ages she mentioned would have been exactly correct had the two remained on earth."

In the year 1851, there was a society organised in England for the purpose of collecting and examining evidence into the alleged facts of "Supernaturalism." In relation to this society, called in the usual tone of popular derision, "The Ghost Club," Mr. Robt. Dale Owen in his exhaustive work, "Footfalls on the Boundary of Another World," speaks as follows :—

"A society was formed in the latter part of the year 1851 at Cambridge, by certain members of the University, for the purpose of instituting, as their circular expresses it, 'a serious and earnest enquiry into the nature of the phenomena vaguely called supernatural.' The society included some of the most distinguished members of the University, most of them clergymen and fellows of Trinity College, and almost all of them men who had graduated with the highest honours.

"The names of the more active amongst them were kindly furnished to me by the son of a British peer, himself one of the leading members.

"To him also I am indebted for a copy of the printed circular of the Society, an able and temperate document, which will be found at length in the Appendix.* "

Mr. Owen adds in a footnote to page 34 :—

"The Society popularly known as 'The Ghost Club,' attracted a good deal of attention outside its own circle. Its nature and object came to my knowledge through the Bishop of ——, who took an interest in its proceedings, and bestirred himself to obtain contributions to its records."

Although we may often encounter in future chapters some of the individual members of this association of investigators, our notice of their combined researches must terminate here, hence we deem it not entirely out of place to anticipate by a few years the effect which those researches must have produced upon some at least of its members, when we give as the addenda to the subject, the following extracts from the London *Spiritualist* newspaper, dated April 11th, 1879 :—

"An Address by Mr. James Campbell.—Mr. J. A. Campbell, President of the Cambridge University Society for Psychological Investigation, will read a paper next Monday week, April 21st, at one of Mrs. Makdougall Gregory's evening receptions. There will be a large and influential gathering of Spiritualists and non-Spiritualists, the latter of whom will have an opportunity of learning that Spiritualism is not what it is represented to be by daily newspapers. The title of Mr. Campbell's address will be, 'The Record of the Seers concerning the Great Change.'"

---

* *Appendix. Note A.* "Footfalls on the Boundary of another World." By R. D. Owen.

In the *Spiritualist* of the same date, is an address from Mr. Campbell entitled:—THE HISTORY OF THE MOVEMENT KNOWN AS MODERN SPIRITUALISM, AND THE FACTS AND THEORIES CONNECTED WITH IT, *by J. A. Campbell; President of the Cambridge University Society for Psychological Investigation.* Mr. Campbell's speech, although a most excellent one, would only anticipate statements which the progress of the history itself must unfold—but its presentation some twenty years or more after the formation of the society of which he was and we believe is still the honoured President, is noticed now to show that the subject has not proved an evanescent one, or unworthy the consideration of eminent and learned scholars during a period of nearly a quarter of a century.

CHAPTER XVII.

SPIRITUALISM IN GREAT BRITAIN.

SECOND PERIOD (CONTINUED).

AMERICAN SPIRIT MEDIUMS IN ENGLAND.

HITHERTO our history of the Spiritual movement in Great Britain has followed the waymarks made by an invisible host in the production of spontaneous and unsought phenomena. We must now proceed to consider those results which grew out of the invocatory processes of the Spirit circle, and the agency of acknowledged Spirit Mediumship.

Long before the rumour reached England of the American disturbances called the "Rochester Knockings," the practices of "table turning" by what was supposed to be *will power*, were quite popular in many a fashionable circle. That these curious evidences of an unknown force had any connection with the agency of "disembodied spirits" never seemed to enter the imagination of "table turning" *experts*, until the advent in England of Mrs. Hayden, an American lady, who came to this country on a professional tour, in company with her husband and a business agent—as an avowed *medium for communications between earth and the world of disembodied spirits.*

Very shortly after the advent of the "Rochester Knockings" in New York State, America, Mrs. Hayden, the wife of a respectable journalist, found herself the subject of the same strange rappings connected with intelligence, which distinguished the earliest American Mediums. Having been induced to sit for the public as a professional Medium, Mrs. Hayden was visited by a Mr. Stone, an English gentleman on a tour through the United States.

Mr. Stone received such striking tests of Spirit presence through Mrs. Hayden's mediumship, that in 1852 he persuaded her to accompany him to England, never doubting that his own countrymen would become as much interested in the results of her marvellous gifts as he himself had been.

In all the accounts published of early Spiritualism in England, Mrs. Hayden is mentioned as *the Medium* who first introduced the American system of communicating with Spirits through the alphabet and rappings, and strange as it may appear to thoughtful minds that any human beings could do otherwise than hail with delight a system of telegraphy which restored to the mourner his beloved dead, and converted the mere hope of immortality into demonstrated proof, it is nevertheless an historical fact, that an avowed Medium for Spiritual communications no sooner appeared on the scene, than the leaders of the press, pulpit and college, levelled against her a storm of ribaldry, persecution and insult, alike disgraceful to themselves, and humiliating to the boasted liberalism and scientific acumen of their age. From the author's personal knowledge of Mrs. Hayden, she is convinced that her gentle womanly spirit must have been deeply pained, and the harmony of mind so essential to the production of good psychological results constantly destroyed, by the cruel and insulting treatment she received at the hands of many of those who came, pretending to be investigators, but in reality burning to thwart her, and laying traps to falsify the truths of which Mrs. Hayden professed to be the instrument. Sensitively alive—as all mediumistic persons are—to the animus of her visitors, she could feel, and often writhed under, the crushing force of the antagonism brought to bear upon her, without—at that time—knowing how to repel or resist it.

In those early days of the movement, the Mediums had neither the advantage of experience nor precedent in such embarrassing circumstances. Oppressed as they were by the opposing force which was purposely arrayed against them, their distress of mind only served to complicate the mental inharmony of the surroundings, and make it most difficult for Spirits to construct those delicate psychologic batteries, upon which the success of the communion depends.

We all acknowledge that the most carefully prepared and chemically adapted elements are necessary to evolve the force of electricity, and promote a perfect result from the formation of a battery, yet we overlook the fact, that the mental and spiritual telegraph must work through laws just as absolute, and whilst men ruthlessly invade those laws and destroy the equilibrium under which that battery works, they triumphantly regard failure as an evidence that no such battery was in existence at all.

We not only know better now, but with all that tendency to exaggeration which marks the crises of man's ignorance and fanaticism, too many Spiritualists of the present day rush into the opposite extreme, and endeavour to palliate the most daring frauds, by pretending that sceptical minds and antagonistic forces have *compelled* detected impostors to prepare masks and other paraphernalia to personate spirits, when *injurious conditions prevented their materializing*, &c., &c. That the real truth lies between the extremes of antagonism on the one hand, and wilful imposture on the other, none can doubt. In Mrs. Hayden's time, there is good reason to believe that the occasional failures which occurred at her circles, were the result of cunningly prepared traps to involve the inexperienced medium in contradictory statements, and when once the would-be detectives thought they had succeeded in these notable plots, the columns of the public journals were filled with triumphant accounts of "the entire collapse of the Spirit rapping delusion."

As an illustration both of the spirit of the times, and the manifest injury to Mediumship, which determined antagonism can exercise, we give a few

9

extracts from a little work which the writer has wisely bequeathed to posterity in an *anonymous* form. Doubtless "he builded wiser than he knew," and whilst his evil record serves the purpose of preserving both sides of the shield of history, he is spared the disgrace of sending down his name to posterity, branded with the tokens of folly his writings display.

The title of the work is "Spirit Rapping in England and America," and the author after a derisive and perverted account of the American manifestations, goes on to detail the incidents of a *séance* which he professes to have held with Mrs. Hayden shortly after her arrival in London in 1852.

Let the reader picture to himself the poor Medium, leaving the pleasant homes of New England, and establishing herself in the proverbially cold and cheerless shelter of a London lodging-house, in the "pea soup" atmosphere of a London November, and amongst a people not, *at that time*, particularly in favour of "*Yankee speculators.*"

Sneering scoffers of the "gent" order, as described by the late witty writer, Albert Smith; insolent aristocrats seeking for a new sensation and dividing their interest between wrenching off door-knockers at night, and Yankee Spirit rappers" by day; glib press men bound to supply a *funny* item, and not caring if the fun is made out of the souls of their ancestors, so long as they were employed to indite journalistic satire against an unpopular thing—these were amongst the daily visitors of the poor foreigner, whose power to satisfy their demands depended upon the most peaceful and harmonious conditions of mind and body. When we add to this, that the Medium herself was as much a tyro in the means of producing successful manifestations, as those who sought her, the marvel is that any Spirit short of a Mephistopheles or Lucifer, could be enabled to rap out names and dates correctly at all. If the reader has fully possessed himself of the conditions under which the first Spiritual telegraphic messages were produced in London, he need not be surprised at the results obtained, as narrated in the anonymous work which we are now about to quote. After a great deal of circumlocution of an unimportant character, the reader is informed that the visitors were "Brown" and "Thompson;" names no doubt meant to imply that they were assumed to mask two very *illustrious personages*. After all sorts of derisive remarks about the Medium's lodging and surroundings, these *gentlemen* proceeded to hold a *séance*, of which the following extract is a specimen:—

"At length, getting too weary of the scene to pursue it farther, 'I wish,' said Brown, 'to ask some questions concerning the future ; can the spirits answer them without your knowing what they are ?' 'If they cannot, they will be silent,' said the medium, 'sometimes they do so. Try.' 'As they are questions which I should not like to ask in public, will they see them written on paper ?' 'O yes.' Brown wrote down very clearly: 'Shall I soon be married ?' 'Will the spirits answer this question ?' Rat-tat-tat. 'Is "yes" the answer ?' Rat-tat-tat. 'How many children shall I have ?' was written next, Brown saying 'This is a question that must be answered in numbers. Does the spirit see it ?' Rat-tat-tat. 'Can it answer me ?' Rat-tat-tat. And so the spirit answered by the usual process, 'One hundred and thirty-six.' When the 1 was obtained, and then the 3 to go next to it, and then the 6 to go after that, the rapid growth of Brown's family amused Thompson, and the imminent carrying on of the sum into thousands was prevented by his ill-timed mirth. The production of children by Brown stopped, therefore, prematurely, at the number of one hundred and thirty-six.

"The medium, who always asked whether the answers fitted, and who did not clearly know whether she might not be succeeding vastly, although she evidently felt a little puzzled by the sense that she was not doing so well as might be expected, was now re-assured by the reverent tone in which the too explosive Thompson asked whether the spirits of his sisters were in the room. His only sister being in vigorous health, he did not expect her ghost; but it was there, and very prompt to answer him. How long had she been dead ? Two years.

"So the dreary labour was continued ; but we cannot fatigue our readers with the whole monotony of a sitting that was not enlivened by one happy guess."

"Brown" cursorily remarks, among other contemptuous comments on this scene, that Mr. Stone, the party who had undertaken the management of the *séances*, enquired if they were satisfied, *and offered if otherwise to give another séance free*, to which the said Brown only adds in his gracious way, "But we had seen enough," and so there was nothing more to do than to show up the whole thing as "a humbug, through the medium of the press."

The late Judge Edmonds, of New York, assured the author, that he did not dare to make up his mind definitively upon so unprecedented, and important a subject, until he had attended at least one hundred circles, and seen some fifty Mediums for various forms of Spiritual power. "It was through such methods of investigation as these," said this learned jurist, "that I at length became convinced of the fact that the soul of man is immortal, can and does communicate, and that we are even now standing in the dawn of a great and wonderful day of Spiritual science. This knowledge so invaluable, and opening up possibilities so unlimited, is surely worth more than the cost of one hundred hours out of any man's life, however *exigéant* the demands upon his time may be."

"But Judge Edmonds was a crazy Spiritualist," answers Brown. "Thompson and I spent one hour with a *mejium*, and found it all false ; what are *his* hundred hours' experiences compared to our one?"

Shortly after this, a favourable report appeared in the *Leader*, in which a party of ladies and gentlemen who had engaged Mrs. Hayden to attend in their own house, bore testimony to her entire honesty, the excellence of the tests they had received, and the utter impossibility of her agency in producing either the sounds, movements, or intelligence ; whereupon certain gentlemen of the press, who seemed to have made it their special duty "to explode the thing," proceeded to the accomplishment of their creditable work in the way recorded as follows. "Mr. Lewes," the *Leader's* editor, or representative, was the party from whom the annexed report proceeded. He says, in the work on "Spirit Rapping," above alluded to :—

"Before I had witnessed these 'astounding phenomena,' I had formed an hypothesis of the whole process, which turned out to be accurate. It did *not* seem in the least surprising to me that the questioner should be correctly answered, even when asking questions mentally, of which no living soul but his own knew the answer. I invariably said : 'The cause of your delusion is that you direct your attention to the *thing said*, and not to the *way in which it is said*. Whatever the trick may be, it will be just as easy to answer a question of one kind as of another—the nature of the question has nothing to do with it. If you ask where your grandfather died, his death being a mystery to the whole world, the answer is as easy as if you ask where Napoleon died ; because as it is *you* who really give the answer, not the medium, what you have in your mind is what will turn out to be the answer. You assure me solemnly that you do not tell the medium anything ; I declare unequivocally that you *do*. It is the same in cases of clairvoyance : you tell all, and fancy you are told. You do not tell it in so many words, but unconsciously you are made to communicate the very thing you believe is communicated to you.' . . .

"I had formed an hypothesis, and according to that hypothesis I framed certain traps into which the medium would infallibly fall if my supposition were correct ; the hypothesis and the traps I explained to certain friends *before* the experiment was made, and the result not only fully confirmed expectation, but showed what was certainly not anticipated—viz., that the trick was a miserably poor one.

"Our party comprised Mr. and Mrs. Masters, Sir William, Mr. Purcell, and myself (for obvious reasons, the names given are fictitious, except my own). It was after dinner, and we were smoking our cigars, when the footman announced that Mrs. Hayden was in the drawing-room. We soon joined her there, and found her talking to Mrs. Masters about the 'spirits, in the most easy, familiar way—indeed, she always spoke of them without awe, but with implicit confidence—as if they had been pet monkeys. The conversation soon became general, as we formed a circle round the table. It of course turned upon the 'Manifestations,' and Mrs. Hayden was copious in anecdotes (adroitly mingled with aristocratic and well-known names) of the surprising success which had attended her. At last, the rappings having announced that the ghosts were impatient to do something for the money paid, we took our cards, on which the letters of the alphabet, and the numerals from one to ten, were printed, and the *séance* began.

"Sir William was the first. He thought of one dead. On asking whether the person he was then thinking of was present, an alacrity in rapping assured him of the fact. He took his card; the raps were distinct; but the letters were all wrong. He tried another spirit—again the letters indicated were wrong. He tried a third, but a third time nothing came right. I was beginning to get anxious lest repeated failures should alarm the medium, and make her give some evasive excuse; so I suggested that Mr. Masters should try. He tried—but with the same desperate ill success. It was now my turn. Let me pause here to remark that both Sir William and Mr. Masters were determined to give no clue whatever—they remained purely passive, awaiting a result; they passed their pencils along the alphabet with such terrible uniformity that the medium was reduced to vague guessing, and of course in each guess it was thirty-five to one against her. This was what I had anticipated; but it was only negative evidence, and I was to elicit something positive.

"I thought of a relative of mine, and said aloud, 'I should like to know if she is present.' Rapping answered 'Yes.' Observe, the person I thought of was a real person—I was planning no trap this time, because the experiment was to be every way conclusive. I passed my pencil equally along the alphabet without once lingering, until after I had passed the letter J, with which her name began. Finding that I was not to have the *real* name, I thought I would try if I could not make the raps answer where I pleased. I chose N. Raps came; N was written down. What name, thought I, shall it be? Naomi or Nancy? Before I had finally settled, my pencil had passed A, and as I saw E, I determined E should be the letter, and E was indicated. N E, of course, would do for Nelly, and Nelly was spelled! Then came the surname, which ought to have begun with H; but as my pencil did not linger at H, on we passed until we came to S, which was indicated without any intention on my part. I had then to invent some name beginning with S, which was not done at once, from the very *embarras de richesses*; however, I thought O would do, and O was indicated; then R; and after that I resolved the name should be Sorel. It is unnecessary to follow further thus in detail my first trial; enough if I add, that Nelly Sorel informed me she died in 1855, leaving six children, two of whom were boys, the eldest fourteen—every answer being ludicrously wrong, but declared by me to be 'astonishing,' which declaration was accepted in perfect faith by the medium, who thought she had got one good, credulous listener, at all events. That was my object—to make her fall into my trap it was necessary she should believe I was her dupe.

"As far as my hypothesis went, it was confirmed by this conversation. I knew that it was the questioner who supplied the answer, and I made the answer turn out whatever I pleased—not, be it remembered, having that answer originally in my mind, so as to admit of any pretended 'thought reading'—but framing the answer according to the caprice of the moment, and invariably receiving the answer I had resolved on. Now you have only to replace *acted* credulity by *real* credulity, and the trick is explained. What I did consciously, the credulous do unconsciously. I spelled the words, so do they. The medium knows nothing; she guesses according to the indications you give, and only guesses right when you give right indications; therefore, if you ask what you and you alone can answer, she will answer it only on the supposition that you indicate by your manner what the answer is. But if any doubt lingers in your mind, let this my second trial suffice.

"To show how completely the answers are made at random, when no clue is given, but only a 'yes' or 'no' is required, here are four questions I wrote on a piece of paper, and the answers I received :—

"'Had the ghost of Hamlet's father seventeen noses?' Yes.

"'Had Semiramis?' Yes.

"'Was Pontius Pilate an American?' No.

"'Was he a leading tragedian?' Yes.

"I thought Mr. Purcell would have had a stroke of apoplexy, when I showed him these questions; how he restrained the convulsion of laughter is a mystery!

"Let me not forget, that when Mr. Purcell called up a spirit, the answers were tolerably correct, not quite, but still near enough to be curious to one unsuspicious; he confessed afterwards, however, that he had semi-consciously *assisted* the medium; but, in his second conversation, he called up the spirit of an old family servant, who, at an advanced age, married an elderly woman, and who subsequently drowned himself. These were the questions and answers as written down :—

"'Does James miss his children?' Yes. (Never had any.)

"'How many had he?' Yes.

"'How many boys?' Yes.

"'What did he die of?' *Wafer.*

"To explain this 'wafer,' it may be observed, that Mr. Purcell meant the death to be called water on the chest, which was his fallacious hint by way of an explanation of drowning; and, when he said aloud that the word was incorrectly spelled *wafer*, whereas it ought to have been 'water on the chest,' Mrs. Hayden pointed triumphantly to the accuracy, 'Only one letter wrong, you see; *wafer* instead of *water!*' and she referred to this several times in the course of the evening.

"I have not half exhausted my stock of questions and answers written down at the time; but the foregoing will surely suffice; and, should they be deemed inconclusive, perhaps *this* one will close the question. As I had been so very successful in getting correct answers, and was evidently regarded by the spirits with singular partiality, they never declining to answer any question I put, it occurred to me to write this question on my paper, which I showed to Mr. Purcell :—

"'*Is Mrs. Hayden an impostor?*'

"An unequivocating *Yes*, was the answer; and, to make assurance doubly sure, Mr. Purcell affected not to hear that answer; so we repeated the question, and again were assured that she *was* an impostor. This was the most satisfactory answer of the evening, and I felt very sorry that the medium was a woman—not a man, to whom I could have said, 'I asked the spirits if you were an impostor, and you hear them declare you to be one.' For I must plainly say, that a more ignoble imposture than this spirit manifestation never came before me—and that was the opinion of the whole party. It is easy for the reader to convince himself of this by a similar process."

"In the following number of the *Leader* the editor observed: 'Iconoclasts are generally welcomed with abuse from devotees. Entering the temples of superstition and charlatanism, they smite the hideous idols from their pedestals, amidst the howlings of indignant worshippers. It was to be expected, therefore, that in exposing the imposture of spirit manifestations which America has shipped for our gullible market, we should have to bear hard words and worse insinuations from indignant dupes; and what we expected we have received.'

"'Dr. Ashburner, for example, has felt himself personally insulted, and has written an insulting letter, complaining of the "flippant" treatment this "very sacred subject" received at our hands, but as he opposes our experimental *proof* by nothing stronger than his own emphatic assertion, he cannot expect those who reason, to attach much weight to mere declarations.'"

The portion of Dr. Ashburner's letter above alluded to, quoted by the veracious editor of the *Leader*, reads as follows :—

"Sex ought to have protected her from injury if you *gentlemen* of the press have no regard to the hospitable feelings due to one of your own cloth, for Mrs. Hayden is the wife of a former editor and proprietor of a journal in Boston, having a most extensive circulation in New England. I declare to you that Mrs. Hayden is no impostor, and he who has the daring to come to an opposite conclusion must do so at the peril of his character for truth. I defy Mr. Lewes or any one else to prove the acts of imposition or fraud in the phenomena that require the presence of such a medium as Mrs. Hayden for their development. I have calmly, deliberately, and very cautiously studied this subject. It may please superficial thinkers to treat it as they long treated Mesmerism and clairvoyance. The fire from the *Zoist*, the researches of Baron Von Reichenbach, Mr. Rutter's important discovery of the magnetescope, have settled, for posterity, the questions scouted by the twaddling physiologists of this generation. A battle is to be fought for the new manifestations. I have no hesitation in saying that, much as I have seen of Mesmerism and of clairvoyance—grand as were my anticipations of the vast amount of good to accrue to the human race, in medical and physical improvement, from the expansion given to them by the cultivation of their extensive relations—all sink into shade and comparative insignificance, in the contemplation of those consequences which must result from the spirit manifestations. This is a very serious truth, and must and will force its way. Animal magnetism and its consequences appeared marvellous to petty minds. The spirit manifestations have, in the last three weeks, produced *miracles*, and many more will, ere long, astound the would-be considered philosophers, who may continue to deny and sneer at the most obvious facts. I am, Sir, your obedient servant,

"York Place, March 14th, 1853." "JOHN ASHBURNER

No reformers who have attempted to present a new idea to the world, and been compelled to run the gauntlet of ignorance and prejudice, will fail to acknowledge that antagonism is as necessary to ultimate success, as ready acceptance.

So did it prove in the case of Spiritualism and "the American Medium." The attacks upon her so deliberately planned, carried out with utter disregard to all psychological influence, and subsequently so rudely and inhospitably trumpeted abroad as the blow which was for ever to crush out of existence the supernaturalism of thousands of years, had the effect which *wise invisible wire pullers might possibly have foreseen.* It called into print a perfect flood of testimony of a totally opposite character, and so far from crushing out the "delusion" by one fell swoop of the editorial pen, it became a hydra-headed messenger of an established Spirit telegraphy, to thousands of persons, who would otherwise have never known of its existence.

From multitudes of letters which poured in from every quarter in favour of the truth of the manifestations, letters which the press were at that time compelled to place side by side with the opposing testimony, we select the following as specimens of what calm deliberative minds were—even in that early day—impelled to think of the newly-developed telegraphy. Both the following letters were printed in the *Leader*, in connection with reiterated charges on the part of the editor, against "the fraudulent practices of the American Medium."

"Sir,—Having observed in your journal of the 5th instant a statement respecting the alleged spirit manifestations, from a correspondent who appears to have but partially investigated the matter, I take the liberty of transmitting to you a few additional particulars.

"I, upon the first occasion, called the spirit of an old servant—the experiment was unsatisfactory; I then attempted to help him, but got on with difficulty; had I had the inclination, I feel confident answers could have been obtained equally absurd as those your correspondent prides himself with having so ingeniously succeeded in obtaining.

"I, however, did not throw discredit on, or treat with scorn, the experience of others; I, therefore, determined to try again the next evening, believing that the failure rested either in myself or some other unknown cause. I called the spirits of two of my own nearest relations, who might naturally be supposed to be more intimately connected with myself; they both presented themselves, giving proofs of their identity which could never have occurred to me to seek. I tested them in various ways. I was also anxious to ascertain whether by willing strongly, and dwelling upon wrong letters, I could obtain false answers, but failed to influence them in any way whatever, whether the alphabet was placed upon, or concealed under, the table, and at each of the several successive interviews the *rapport* appears to be more thoroughly established; whether I ask questions audibly or mentally, concise and clear answers are given, excepting in some few instances when no reply can be obtained.

"So far as the moving of the table is concerned, I obtained my request, during the second interview, in so satisfactory a manner, that I consider time may be more profitably employed than in seeking a repetition of it; it moved out of reach of Mrs. Hayden, and soon after suddenly regained its former position; it also moved upon its axis in a peculiarly smooth, gliding manner; not the top only, but the whole table, as I particularly observed, commencing with an almost invisible motion until it gained a rapid pace, and stopped suddenly. I immediately endeavoured myself to produce a similar motion, but was unable.

"I will conclude by stating, that I have reason to consider Mrs. Hayden to be a lady possessed of courage, but, having a delicate and sensitive mind, any insults directed against her, whether personally or through the medium of the press, may be likely to have a tendency to disarrange and interrupt that subtle and mysterious agency so intimately connected with our higher nature. May I venture to recommend those who determine to investigate for themselves, to refrain from publishing the crude ideas of one hour's experience, especially should they arrive at conclusions opposite to those of the thousands who have been making the subject their earnest and constant study during the past five years? I am, sir, your obedient servant,

"March 21, 1853."   "C. F. I.*

--- --- --- --- --- --- ---

* Sir Charles Isham.

Another letter makes us acquainted with a novel mode of Spirit writing by medium intervention :—

"Sir,—Permit me, if you conveniently can, the opportunity of affording Mr. Lewes a peg on which to hang a few shreds of additional comments, in defence of his 'hypothesis' relative to the spirit-rapping 'imposture.' Mr. Lewes does not hesitate to impute, by anticipation, imposture to others, nor to 'act' an imposture himself ; why should 'the spirits' be denied their revenge upon him ? Are there no wags out of the body as well as in it ? Are we to dictate to the wag above how he is to treat the wag below ?

"But, further, Mr. Lewes's hypothesis does not cover the whole facts of the phenomena. It does in no way explain the unexceptionably attested cases, recorded in the American literature on the subject, and in the records of private investigation, into which the vulgar notion of imposture, besides being excluded by the very nature of the occurrences described, is, on other grounds, wholly inadmissible. How, for instance, does it apply to the following case ?—A pair of scissors is held, by the points, by a 'medium,' over a sheet of writing-paper. One of the persons present drops a pencil into the thumb-hole of the scissors. Presently, the pencil stands apart from the steel, begins to move, and the hand of the medium is carried across the paper, and the signature of a person known to be dead appears ! The father, or other near relative of the person is present, and, from some peculiarity in it, disputes the genuineness of the signature. The recent letters of the person are appealed to, and there the very same peculiarity is found, and the exact correspondence of the two signatures demonstrated.

"This case is reported in Horace Greeley's paper, the *Tribune*, and he vouches for the honour and capacity of his correspondent, who gives the original letter of the father or relative of the alleged spirit writer. I mention it from memory, but am certain the main facts of the record are as stated. "A.*

"Liverpool, March 21, 1853."

The next sword that was aimed against the new faith was drawn from an unexpected quarter, namely, by the hand of Dr. Elliotson, one of the most prominent writers in the *Zoist*, and a gentleman whose extensive experiences in mesmeric and psychologic phenomena suggested the expectation, that he would be prompt to welcome a phase of power so nearly related to many of the mental revealments that must have come under his own observation.

We do not pause upon the stern and relentless acts of warfare which this gentleman directed against the American Medium, nor is it necessary to say that his adherence to the ranks of the opponents was all the more eagerly welcomed by them, because they had anticipated from Dr. Elliotson's antecedents, a totally different result. It is a far pleasanter task to the author to record, instead of the harsh diatribes published in the *Zoist* by this ever faithful soldier of what he believed to be the truth, a delightful interview which she enjoyed with this venerable gentleman when, nearly sixteen years after the period now under consideration, Dr. Ashburner invited the author to call with him upon an aged and infirm gentleman unable himself to go through the ceremony of the first call, but who, as a *warm and devoted Spiritualist of many years standing, was all anxiety to welcome and converse with Mrs. Emma Hardinge, or any of the well-known American Mediums of the holy faith.*

This "aged and infirm gentleman" was Dr. Elliotson, once the bitter foe, now the warm adherent of Spiritualism, a faith which the venerable gentleman cherished as the brightest revelation that had ever been vouchsafed to him, and one which finally smoothed the *dark passage* to the life beyond and made his transition, a scene of triumphant faith and joyful anticipation.

---

* Mr. Andrew Leighton.

CHAPTER XVIII.

BESIDES the *Leader, Zoist,* and *Household Words,* the columns of several of the London journals began to be filled with *pro* and *con* articles on the subject of Spiritualism, soon after Mrs. Hayden's visit had opened up that topic as a theme of public discussion. Amongst other leading papers in which each side of the vexed question was allowed a fair representation, was the *Critic,* a journal to which Mr. Spicer, the well-known author of "Sights and Sounds," contributed a series of articles on the subject of Spiritualism, from which we give the following excerpts :—

"As Sir Charles Isham has already given his public testimony to the facts witnessed by himself, I need not hesitate to say that I received from him, and other members of his family (including the rector of a parish in Nottinghamshire), the most explicit and positive assurance that they all, together with several others, heard these mysterious sounds at Lamport Hall,* in a perfectly private family circle (neither Mrs. Hayden nor any other *professional* medium being present). They all assured me that there could be no mistake or delusion about it. The rector alluded to also mentioned several satisfactory tests to which he had subjected Mrs. Hayden's spirits—receiving correct answers, through another gentleman present (who held the alphabet), to questions which nobody present could have known by any ordinary mode. I have also received letters from a gentleman of the very highest reputation and authority in the scientific world, and with whose writings and character my Cambridge studies have long ago made me familiar, as those of the most cautious reasoner whom I know.† He is professor of mathematics in a well-known college ; is recognised as one of the first mathematicians in England ; and is pre-eminent for the profound and cautious scrutiny of principles and reasonings which characterises his writings. . . . Well, thus he writes to me :—

" ' Those who can set it down as easily explicable by imposture, are among the easiest believers I know—if they know anything of such facts as I know from a plurality of witnesses to each.'

" The founder of Socialism—the celebrated Robert Owen—has been converted by these rappings, to a belief in a spiritual world, and a future state. He has published a manifesto to that effect. I met him one day last week at Mrs. Hayden's, and heard from his own lips the statement of several of the facts which had produced this conviction in him. This, of itself, is a curious fact, which I presume even the sapient writer of the *Zoist* will not deny. 2nd. The excitement on the subject in the United States, having already existed nearly *five years,* is so far from subsiding or dying away, that it is increasing and spreading wider and faster every day. Only a month or two ago, a Dr. Tyng, one of the episcopal clergy in New York, preached a sermon, at the usual time and place, warning his congregation to have nothing to do with these spirits. The preacher did not for a moment pretend to deny or doubt the facts ; but, like the Rev. Hugh M'Neile in this country with regard to Mesmerism, he considered them of Satanic origin.

" The thing has scarcely begun in England as yet ; but already, within the few months since Mr. and Mrs. Hayden arrived in London, it has spread like wild-fire, and I have good reason for saying that the excitement is only commencing. Persons who at first treated the whole affair as a contemptible imposture, on witnessing these strange things for themselves, become first startled and astonished, then rush blindly into all sorts of mad conclusions—as for instance, that it is all the work of the devil, or (in the opposite degree) that it is a new revelation from Heaven. . . . That it is not imposture I feel perfectly

---

* Lamport Hall, Northampton. Seat of Sir Chas. Isham.
† Professor De Morgan.

and fully convinced. In addition to the tests, etc., above named, I had a long conversation in private with both Mr. and Mrs. Hayden, separately, and everything they said bore the marks of sincerity and good faith. Of course this is no evidence to other people, but it is to me. If there is any deception, they are as much deceived as any of their dupes.

"A word or two as to its being a money-exhibition. In the first place, there are, to my certain knowledge, several persons who are mediums in private life, who, so far from making it public and getting money by it, are only too anxious to keep it quiet; but, of course, such things cannot be altogether hushed up. Of these, one at least is a lady of rank (whose name I could give, if necessary), and others are in a position which renders all such charges as imposture and money-exhibitions perfectly out of the question.

"In the present state of public opinion, however, nobody cares to avow their belief in these sort of things, unless they have a particular wish to be set down by their friends as lunatics, or are desirous of profiting by it in a pecuniary way. But even these are not *fairly* dealt with, I think. Mr. Hayden held a respectable position in America as editor of a newspaper of good repute and circulation; and if he and Mrs. H. believed (as they state) that it was advisable to come over and make these things known here, why should they not be paid for their time and trouble? But this, of course, has nothing to do with the main point—'Are these rappings what they profess to be—the work of spirits?'"

The "manifesto" of Robert Owen, referred to in the foregoing communication, says :—

"I have patiently, with first impressions against the truthfulness of these manifestations, investigated their history, and the proceedings connected with them in the United States—have read the most authentic works for and against them; and although I long continued to doubt, and thought the whole a delusion, *I have been compelled to come to a very different conclusion.*" "While conversing with Mrs. Hayden, and while we were both standing before the fire, suddenly raps were heard on a table at some distance from us, no one being near it. I was surprised; and as the raps continued and appeared to indicate a strong desire to attract attention, I asked what was the meaning of the sounds. Mrs. Hayden said they were spirits anxious to communicate with some one, and she would inquire who they were. They replied to her by the alphabet that they were friends of mine, who were desirous to communicate with me. Mrs. Hayden then gave me the alphabet and pencil, and I found, according to *their own statements*, that the spirits were those of my mother and father. I tested their truth by various questions, and their answers, all correct, surprised me exceedingly." "In *mixed societies* with *conflicting minds*, I have seen very *confused answers* given; but I believe, in all these cases, the errors have arisen from the state of mind of the inquirer."

It would be impossible in this merely compendious notice of Spiritual progress in Great Britain, to pursue the course of Mr. Owen's investigations in farther detail; suffice it to say, they were followed out in the most thorough, calm, and deliberate spirit of enquiry.

Mr. Owen lived to realize many corroborative proofs of Spirit intercourse from other sources than Mrs. Hayden's Mediumship, and in his last days was often heard to declare, the sum of his whole life-long endeavour to bless and improve the condition of his fellow men, paled before that mighty illumination which brought, to him, but especially to earth's toiling martyrs, the assurance of immortality, and the certainty of reunion with all we have loved and lost on earth, "in another and a better world."

Very shortly after the advent of Mrs. Hayden in England, the public were privileged to witness another phase of Spirit power in the person of Miss Emma Frances Jay, a young lady who had quite recently become developed as a trance medium in America, in fact the first phenomenon of this kind that had as yet appeared upon the public rostrum.

Miss Jay's Mediumship consisted of speaking with extraordinary eloquence on metaphysical subjects. She also concluded her addresses by singing; both words and music being improvisations of remarkable beauty and sweetness.

These exhibitions, although singularly interesting, did not furnish the indisputable proof of a Spiritual origin for which the sceptics of the time were seeking ; nevertheless, the wonderful improvisations poured forth by this gifted young sybil, might have convinced any experienced psychologist, that she was controlled by some power far transcending her normal capacity.

After a few months spent amongst the aristocratic circles of England, wherein Miss Jay's interesting phase of Mediumship rendered her the centre of universal admiration, she returned to America, and as Mrs. Bullene soon became one of the most popular *speakers* of the American rostrum.

But the great era in English Spiritualism, from which may be dated unnumbered conversions, was inaugurated by the visit of Mr. D. D. Home, who though of European birth, was brought up by relatives in America, from which circumstance he was at first generally spoken of as an " American Medium." As Mr. Home's wonderful gifts have exercised an unbounded influence upon European society, and his whole career forms an epoch in human history—the effect of which can never be blotted out, we must claim the privilege of dwelling somewhat minutely upon his first introduction to England, and although his own published biography, together with a whole encyclopædia of press notices, are already before the world, the history of the Spiritual movement in Europe would be inexplicable, were we to omit due notice of so important a link in the chain of cause and effect as Mr. Home, and his marvellous Mediumistic career. It has been alleged that Mr. Home came to England in the spring of 1855 for the benefit of his health, which, his friends deemed as a last, but almost hopeless chance, might be restored by an European trip. He was at this time about twenty-two years of age ; had been studying for the medical profession, and though already celebrated in New England for his wonderful medial powers, he would have devoted himself entirely to the practice of medicine, had not the development of consumptive tendencies, compelled him to comply with the wishes of his friends, and seek health in entire relaxation from his professional studies.

Mr. Home never practised his Mediumship professionally. He seldom, if ever, sat in dark circles ; never refused to submit to any tests demanded of him ; was very careful not to sit in any such positions as to warrant the idea that he exercised any personal effort in producing the manifestations, often drawing away from contact with the table, whilst a large amount of the most remarkable phenomena produced in his presence occurred without the agency of tables at all. He never refused to submit to personal examinations, to prove that he carried no concealed apparatus before the commencement of his *séances*, and in every word and act, manifested a spirit of candour and sincerity, which none but the most prejudiced and illiberal bigots could have misconstrued.

We have already given some account of Mr. Home's wonderful Mediumistic endowments in our French section, and the reader will find further illustrations of this gentleman's marvellous gifts in the reports of *séances* in succeeding pages ; it need only be added that Mr. Home's witnesses range from monarchs, princes, statesmen, scientists, and potentates, down to the professional and private grades of life, and throughout them all, it is impossible to find any proven account of fraud, or deception.

It was this marvellous phenomenal being that came in the year 1855 to visit London, and became a guest of Mr. and Mrs. Cox, the noble-hearted proprietors of a fashionable hotel in Jermyn Street, St. James'. Amongst the many distinguished personages that Mr. Home met at Mr. Cox's was the late Lord Brougham, who having became greatly interested in the marvellous phenomena exhibited through the young American, asked permission to bring his friend Sir David Brewster to witness the new and mysterious power.

As the correspondence which grew out of this, and a second visit which Sir David paid Mr. Home, when the latter became a guest of Mr. Rymer at Ealing, exercised a manifest influence upon the progress of Spiritualism in England in divers ways, at the risk of inflicting upon our readers, passages which have already attained to a wide-spread notoriety, we must here give a few extracts that will present a summary of the case in question.

It would seem that the correspondence arose from the circumstance of the *séance* being reported in an American paper, from whence it was copied into the London *Morning Advertiser*, and this called forth from Sir David Brewster the following remarks, from which we only excise some unimportant preliminary words addressed to the editor.

" To the Editor of the Morning Advertiser.

"Sir,—It is quite true as stated by Mr. Home, that I wrote an article in the *North British Review* in which I have denounced 'table-moving and spirit-rapping' in the strongest terms, and it is also true that I saw at Cox's Hotel, in company with Lord Brougham, and at Ealing, in company with Mrs. Trollope, several mechanical effects which I was unable to explain. But though I could not account for all these effects, I never thought of ascribing them to spirits stalking beneath the drapery of the table, and I saw enough to satisfy myself that they could all be produced by human hands and feet, and to prove to others that some of them at least, had such an origin."

The letter concludes with a strong adjuration to Mr. Home to announce himself as the *Wizard of the West* instead of " insulting religion, common-sense, &c., by ascribing his power to the *sacred dead.*"

To this epistle immediately succeeded the following answers from Mr. Cox and Mr. Benjamin Coleman. Mr. Cox, who had been present during Sir David's first investigation, after alluding to his surprise at the letter in the *Advertiser*, and quoting several of its allegations, says :—

"Without unnecessarily alluding to what I understand you saw at the house of an equally-disinterested investigator—for be it remembered all who have received Mr. Home in this country *are above suspicion*, and desire to arrive only at the truth—I beg to recall to your memory what took place at my house when Lord Brougham and you did me the favour to accept my invitation, and I will appeal to your candour to say whether there was a *possibility* of the various acts being effected by the hands or feet of anyone present.

"I have a distinct recollection of the astonishment which both Lord Brougham and yourself expressed, and your emphatic exclamation to me—' *Sir, this upsets the philosophy of fifty years.*'

"If the subject be beyond your powers of reasonable explanation, leave it to others ; for it is not just or generous to raise the cry of *imposture*, in a matter you cannot explain, taking advantage of your character to place humbler men in a false position, by allowing the world to think they were by ignorance or design parties to so gross and impudent a fraud.

" I am, Sir David,
" Your obedient servant,
" Cox's Hotel, Jermyn Street, October 4, 1855." WILLIAM COX."

Mr. Benjamin Coleman—a gentleman of wealth and high social standing—one who subsequently figured largely in the Spiritual movement and against whose honesty, integrity, and acumen as a keen observer, even Sir David Brewster could bring no allegation, next takes up the cudgels by addressing a letter to the *Morning Advertiser*, to the following effect :—

"Sir,— Sir David Brewster has addressed a letter to you, attributing the phenomena which he witnessed in the presence of Mr. Home, to mechanical agency.

"Sir David, although he had at least two interviews, and was invited to further investigation, failed to discover the mechanism by which these marvels were produced.

"I am one of a hundred, who have recently witnessed these manifestations at the house of a friend, and I am sure that they were neither effected by trick, nor were we under a delusion. . . . I was as much astonished at what I saw in . Mr. Home's presence as any man, and when I found that Sir David Brewster had been a witness of similar phenomena, I called upon Sir David, and in the course of conversation he said, that what he and Lord Brougham saw, was marvellous, quite unaccountable.

"I then asked him ; 'Do you think these things were produced by trick ?'

" ' No, certainly not,' was his reply.

" ' Is it delusion, think you ? '

" ' No, that is out of the question.'

" ' Then what is it ? '

"To which he replied, ' I don't know, but Spirit is the last *thing I will give in to.*'

"Sir David then told me what he and Lord Brougham had witnessed : ' The table— a large dinner table—moved about in the most extraordinary manner, and amongst other things, an accordion was conveyed by an invisible agency to his hand, and then to Lord Brougham's, in which, held by his Lordship's right hand, apart from any person, it *played an air throughout.*' Mr. Coleman adds : ' Is it reasonable—astounding as the fact may be—to attribute such a performance to mechanical agency beyond detection, or that it should have been effected by Mr. Home's foot ? ' "

After the perusal of this letter, Sir David published an answer, either denying *in toto* Mr. Coleman's statements, or shuffling out of them in the following way. After alluding to the conversation which Mr. Coleman had with him at the Athenæum Club, he says :—

"I may once for all admit, that both Lord Brougham and myself acknowledged that we were puzzled with *Mr. Home's performances, and could not account for them.*

"Neither of us profess to be expounders of conundrums, whether verbal or mechanical, but if we had been permitted to take a peep beneath the drapery of Mr. Cox's table, we should have been spared the mortification of this confession."

As specimens of the form of denials which Sir David gave to the allegations of Mr. Coleman, the following items may serve :—

"When *all our hands were upon the table,* noises were heard ; rappings in abundance, and when we rose up, the table actually rose, *as appeared to me,* from the ground. This result I do not pretend to explain, but rather than believe that spirits made the noises, I will conjecture that the raps were produced by Mr. Home's toes—or as Dr. Schiff has shown, '*by the repeated displacement of the tendon of the peroneus longus muscle, in the sheath in which it slides behind the external malleolus,* and rather than believe that spirits raised the table, I will conjecture, that it was done by the agency of Mr. Home's feet which were always below it."

It seems sad, nothing short of humiliating indeed, to find a man like Sir David Brewster—one who, as a scientist himself, should have been the first to give a hospitable welcome to a set of phenomena which involved so many hitherto unknown phases of science, as sounds and motions by invisible agency—driven to such rude uncourteous denials, or evasions unworthy of his character either as a gentleman or a man of learning, in order to dispose of facts which transcended the sum of *his* belief, and *his* knowledge.

The whole correspondence however—which we may add was pursued on both sides of the question, in the same spirit as the above,—was shortly after summed up, at least as far as the impartial portion of the public were concerned — by a letter from Mr. T. A. Trollope, a gentleman whose position in the literary and social world is quite as pronounced as that of Sir David Brewster himself. It was addressed to Mr. J. S. Rymer of *Ealing*, and was afterwards published in the papers in connection with the entire correspondence. It is as follows :—

"Florence, October 23, 1855.

"My dear Sir,—I have read with much regret the letters from Sir David Brewster printed in the *Morning Advertiser*, to which you have called my attention ; and although it is extremely painful for me to come out from my tranquil obscurity into the noise and wholly inconclusive bickerings of paper warfare, it is impossible for me when called on, to refuse my testimony to facts of which I was a witness.

"Sir David writes—that when he was present together with Lord Brougham and Mr. Cox at Cox's Hotel—it was *not* true that a large dining-table was moved about in a most extraordinary manner. Further on he states that—'the table was covered with copious drapery *beneath which nobody was allowed to look.*' These italics are Sir David's.*

"I declare that at *your* house at Ealing, on an evening subsequent to Sir David's meeting with Mr. Home at Cox's Hotel, in the presence of Sir David, myself, and of other persons, a large and very heavy dining-table *was* moved about in a most extraordinary manner ; *that Sir David was urged both by Mr. Home and by yourself* to look under the cloth and under the table, *that he did look under it, and that whilst he was so looking, the table was much moved, and while he was looking, and while the table was moving, he avowed that he saw the movement.*

"Sir David Brewster further writes, that on this same evening the spirits were very active, prolific of raps of various intonations, making tables heavy or light at command, tickling knees, male and female, but always on the side next the Medium. I was repeatedly touched on either knee, and on the lower leg, but I experienced no sensation at all akin to 'tickling,' neither did any of those present, who were similarly touched say that they were—or give any token of being 'tickled.' Moreover I affirm that Sir David Brewster, who sat next to me, declared to me at the time of being touched that he was touched on *both knees.* . . . Nor did he then speak of being '*tickled.*'

"Indeed the phraseology of this part of his letter is matter of the greatest astonishment to me. For it should seem wholly impossible that a man of Sir David Brewster's character, standing, and social position, in the grave and public examination of a question on which a young man's honour and character depend, if no yet higher interests are concerned, should intentionally seek to prejudice the issue in the minds of his readers, by a vulgar jest, puerile to those earnest enquirers who disbelieve the Spiritual origin of these phenomena, inexpressibly revolting to those who believe therein, and which, falling from less respected lips, would by all be termed mere ribaldry.

"I must add one more remark on other passages of Sir David's letter. 'The party present at Mr. Cox's,' he writes, 'sat down to a small table, Mr. Home having previously requested us to examine if there was any machinery about his person, an examination however which we declined to make.' A few lines further on he says, with reference to the phenomena which then occurred, '*I conjecture that they might be produced by machinery attached to the lower extremities of Mr. Home.*' Now I submit, that these two statements should not stand together. It appears to me both morally unjust, and philosophically unsound, in the examination of evidence, first to decline the proferred means of ascertaining the absence of machinery, and then to assume its presence.

"I should not, my dear sir, do all that duty I think requires of me in this case, were I to conclude without stating very solemnly, that after many opportunities of witnessing and investigating the phenomena caused by, or happening to, Mr. Home, I am wholly convinced that be what may their origin, and cause, and nature, they are not produced by any fraud, machinery, juggling, illusion, or trickery on his part.

"I am, my dear Sir,

"Always most faithfully yours,

"T. ADOLPHUS TROLLOPE.

"To John Smith Rhymer, Esq., Ealing."

Here this episode in connection with Sir David Brewster must rest. It is of importance that it should be recorded in this place for several reasons. First—Although the correspondence might with more justice to the young gentleman so harshly attacked and condemned without trial or evidence,

---

* This statement is emphatically denied by Mr. Cox in letters preceding Mr. Trollope's.

have been maintained in private, its publication served to obtain for Spiritualism, hundreds of investigators, few if any of whom could be found to duplicate Sir David Brewster's views of common sense, morality, or justice. Next—The position occupied by the disputants, commanded a notoriety for the case which it could scarcely have else obtained, and finally, the palpable animus which could have induced a man in Sir David Brewster's position, to descend to misrepresentation, evoked, as it deserved, a sentiment of indignation, which operated most favourably, both for Mr. Home, and the cause he represented. The young Anglo-American became all the fashion. *Fêted* by potentates and nobles, courted, honoured, and sought for in every direction, it is not too much to allege, as the author can confidently do from many years' knowledge of this famous medium, that he preserved under all circumstances, his integrity and singleness of purpose. He sought no favours, accepted no fees (though he became the recipient of princely gifts and tokens of royal munificence). He was never vain-glorious, conceited, nor presumptuous. At times he was what he himself called "out of power," and though these seasons of incapacity to produce phenomena, sometimes lasted for weeks, the author can positively assert on her own, as well as on the testimony of hosts of the most authentic witnesses, that he was never known to supplement these mediumistic recessions by the smallest attempt at fraud or deception. Thus, though he became the subject of universal attack from those whose interest or predilection determined their antagonistic attitude towards Spiritualism, he also became the centre of attraction to vast multitudes, who owed to him their first demonstrable proofs of the soul's immortality, and restoration to those, whom bereaved mourners had deemed for ever lost to them.

CHAPTER XIX.

SPIRITUALISM IN GREAT BRITAIN (CONTINUED).

MR. D. D. HOME'S MANIFESTATIONS.

IT may appear strange to those who consider how unprecedented in modern experience all the phenomena of Spirit communion are, that their recital excites so little attention and the repetition of spiritualistic narratives so soon palls upon the minds of the recipients ; but the truth is, there exists too little variety amongst these phenomena to render reiteration tolerable.

Then again, Spirit communications are for the most part addressed to individuals, and the innate selfishness of humanity renders personal matter wholly uninteresting except to the parties immediately concerned.

As the intention of this work is to prepare a record for the use of future generations, we feel compelled to avoid the tedium of useless repetition on the one hand, and on the other to send down to posterity a complete set of such representative cases as will display the nature of the spiritual phenomena manifested in the nineteenth century. It is with this view that we select a few of Mr. D. D. Home's remarkable manifestations, as representative cases which it would be difficult to transcend in interest. The following narrative, published in the London *Spiritualist* of March 30th, 1877, was communicated by the charming authoress, Mrs. S. C. Hall, and reads as follows :—

EASTER EVE—IN 1867.

BY MRS. S. C. HALL.

"The near approach of, perhaps, the happiest of our Festivals, sends my memory back to, I think, the most marvellous of all my experiences in Spiritualism : there may be among your readers some who will thank me for preserving and publishing a record of it.

"I did not write concerning it at the time it occurred ; yet I can recall vividly every one of the remarkable incidents : they are as fresh in my mind to-day as they were ten years ago, for they 'happened' on the Easter Eve of the year 1867 : and the Easter Eve of 1877 is now nigh at hand.

"Although my recollection of the scene and circumstances is very vivid, I remembered that my friend Mrs. Henry Senior (the widow of Colonel Senior) had made some notes concerning them. I wrote to her on the subject, and the letter she has written in reply I ask you to print in the number of your publication that you will issue on the Easter Eve of the present year.

"I need do little more than endorse, which I do, every sentence in her letter. I have had more startling experiences in Spiritualism ; but none at once so wonderful and so beautiful, so intensely convincing, so happy in comforting assurance of its holy truth, thoroughly upholding and confirming the faith that has, thank God, been my blessing through the whole of a long life.

"It was not a dark sitting, but the light was subdued, and for a few minutes entirely excluded, when an absolute blaze of light filled the conservatory. We saw shadows (but having forms) pass and repass repeatedly, brought out into distinctness by the brilliancy of the light. When Mr. Home was 'raised' (as he was twice) the gas in the chandelier was lit : although reduced, it was quite strong enough to mark his gradual progress upwards from the chair to the ceiling."

Then follows Mrs. Senior's paper, which is quoted *verbatim*, with a few unimportant excisions :—

"5, Prince of Wales's Terrace, Tuesday.

"Last Saturday (Easter Eve) we had a most wonderful *séance* at Mr. Hall's. I had long been telling him that I was convinced that allowing scoffers and unbelievers to come to our *séances* spoiled them, and that if he would but harden his kind heart for once, and allow us to have a *selfish séance*, I was sure it would be good—and last week he said to me laughingly that I *should* have my wish before I returned to Ireland, that Daniel had promised to come to them on Saturday, and that there should be no one asked but myself and Lady Dunsany—and so it was arranged. Lady Dunsany called for me on her way. We found Mr. and Mrs. Hall alone, but Daniel arrived soon after, and said when he entered the room that he had a very bad headache, which would, he feared, spoil our *séance ;* however, he sat down and chatted a little, and I then asked him to come over to the piano and " croon," as I called it, as I had observed that his doing so always gave us a good *séance.* He played and sang several things, and then Lady Dunsany asked him for a soft Russian air of his wife's. He had not been playing it more than a minute, when a chair, which was at some distance from the piano, *slid* up to it, and placed itself beside him. I was sitting close to the piano on the other side, and saw it move before he did—'Oh !' he said—'Here is Sacha' (his wife, who had left earth), and he went on playing some time longer, though his hands became perfectly stiff, and it was evident that they were not moved by his own volition. After a time his hands were withdrawn from the piano, and he became entranced, turned round the piano stool, and knelt down, and with hands clasped, poured forth a most beautiful prayer. . . . Mr. Home then came out of his trance, quite refreshed and pleased, and asked us to sit down at the table, which at once began to vibrate and 'tremble,' whilst loud and heavy knocks were heard upon it, upon the floor and the furniture. Presently the accordion was touched, and by the alphabet was spelt out ' We will play the earth-life of one who was not of earth.' **Mr. Hall** said 'That's nonsense,' but I answered, ' It must be our Lord's life,' and so it proved. First we had sweet, soft, simple music, like a lullaby, for a few minutes, then it became intensely sad for some time, and then we distinctly heard through the music the *regular tramp* of a body of men marching, and we exclaimed, 'The march to Calvary.' Then the tapping sound of a hammer on a nail, the ringing sound of metal upon metal, then a pause, and afterwards came a *crash*, and a burst of wailing, which seemed to fill the room and the house ; it was followed by the *most glorious* triumphal music we any of us had ever heard ; it thrilled to all our hearts, and we were in tears when it was over—it certainly was not of earth. It evidently meant the resurrection of our Lord. We still sat at the table, but nothing more was done for some time ; then the muslin curtains were draped round Mr. Home ; and he was raised from the ground in them. . . . Then Mr. Hall's face and chest shone like silver, and they spelled out, 'He who giveth shall receive light.' The accordion was carried round the circle, played on Mr. Hall's head, then placed on my shoulder next it, and went to Mrs. Hall, on my right hand, and played on her head ; then played in the air round the circle (Mr. Home's hand not being near the instrument) 'The Last Rose of Summer,' and several other airs. Afterwards a great deal of martial music was played by a cousin of Lady Dunsany's, who had been in the Dragoons, and who had 'passed away' in India, and who always comes to her. After this the spirit of a child, whose mother had sent Mrs. Hall flowers that morning, came and gave us each a flower. Mr. Home was then lifted to the ceiling. We heard his nail against it, and he said, 'Oh, I wish I had a pencil to make a mark.' However, he then came down, and Mr. Hall handed him a pencil, in case he should be again raised ; and five minutes afterwards he was again lifted up, and made a mark on the ceiling, which will remain there as a proof of what was done. When Mr. Home returned to the table we were all touched by hands on our brows and on our hands. Sacha gave each of us her peculiar little pinch, and I was touched by both H—— and E——, and Lady Dunsany's cousin flipped all our hands with a flower. After a little time the spirits spelled out, 'We can do no more. Good night. God bless you ;' and we heard the knocks and sounds die away in the distance out of doors, and *we felt* that it was all over. We were all beyond measure grateful for being allowed to witness what we could never forget as long as our lives lasted. That burst of music was still thrilling in all our hearts—nothing composed by mortal could ever touch it. I should have said that just before Mr. Home was lifted up to the ceiling the first time, his face and his chest shone with a silvery light, as Mr. Hall's had done. But, indeed, I have not told many of the minor things that took place. It was an evening of wonders."

The next illustrative *séance* which we deem it necessary to associate with this record is supplied by the late Henry D. Jencken, Esq., barrister—a gentleman too well known in the *élite* of London professional society as well as among the Spiritualistic ranks, to need any additional proof of the authenticity of his narrative.

Mr. Jencken himself was a witness of the facts narrated, and we may here add that Professor William Crookes in his published work entitled " Phenomena of Spiritualism," alludes to the *séance* about to be detailed, affirming that he received the narrative from the lips of three of the witnesses, namely, Lord Lindsay, the Earl of Dunraven, and Captain Wynne.

Mr. Jencken, writing for the February number of *Human Nature*, says:—

"MANIFESTATIONS THROUGH MR. HOME."

" Mr. Home had passed into the trance still so often witnessed ; rising from his seat, he laid hold of an arm-chair, which he held at arm's length, and was then lifted about three feet clear off the ground ; travelling thus suspended in space, he placed the chair next Lord Adare, and made a circuit round those in the room, being lowered and raised as he passed each of us. One of those present measured the elevation, and passed his leg and arm underneath Mr. Home's feet. The elevation lasted from four to five minutes. On resuming his seat, Mr. Home addressed Captain Wynne, communicating news to him of which the departed alone could have been cognisant.

" The spirit form that had been seen reclining on the sofa, now stepped up to Mr. Home and mesmerised him ; a band was then seen luminously visible over his head, about 18 inches in a vertical line from his head. The trance state of Mr. Home now assumed a different character ; gently rising he spoke a few words to those present, and then opening the door proceeded into the corridor ; a voice then said—' He will go out of this window and come in at that window.' The only one who heard the voice was the Master of Lindsay, and a cold shudder seized upon him as he contemplated the possibility of this occurring, a feat which the great height of the third floor windows in Ashley Place rendered more than ordinarily perilous. The others present, however, having closely questioned him as to what he had heard, he at first replied, 'I dare not tell you;' when, to the amazement of all, a voice said, 'You must tell; tell directly.' The Master then said, 'Yes; yes, terrible to say, he will go out at that window and come in at this; do not be frightened, be quiet.' Mr. Home now re-entered the room, and opening the drawing-room window, was pushed out demi-horizontally into space, and carried from one window of the drawing-room to the farthermost window of the adjoining room. This feat being performed at a height of about 60 feet from the ground, naturally caused a shudder in all present. The body of Mr. Home, when it appeared at the window of the adjoining room, was shunted into the room feet foremost—the window being only 18 inches open. As soon as he had recovered his footing he laughed and said, 'I wonder what a policeman would have said had he seen me go round and round like a teetotum!' The scene was, however, too terrible—too strange, to elicit a smile; cold beads of perspiration stood on every brow, while a feeling pervaded all as if some great danger had passed; the nerves of those present had been kept in a state of tension that refused to respond to a joke. A change now passed over Mr. Home, one often observable during the trance states, indicative, no doubt, of some other power operating on his system. Lord Adare had in the meantime stepped up to the open window in the adjoining room to close it—the cold air, as it came pouring in, chilling the room; when, to his surprise, he only found the window 18 to 24 inches open! This puzzled him, for how could Mr. Home have passed outside through a window only 18 to 24 inches open. Mr. Home, however, soon set his doubts at rest; stepping up to Lord Adare, he said, 'No, no; I did not close the window; I passed thus into the air outside.' An invisible power then supported Mr. Home all but horizontally in space, and thrust his body into space through the open window, head foremost, bringing him back again feet foremost into the room, shunted not unlike a shutter into a basement below. The circle round the table having re-formed, a cold current of air passed over those present, like the rushing of winds. This repeated itself several times. The cold blast of air, or electric fluid, or call it what you may, was accompanied by a loud whistle like a gust of wind on the mountain top, or through the leaves of the forest in late autumn; the sound was deep, sonorous, and powerful in the extreme, and a shudder kept passing over those present, who all heard and felt it. This rushing sound lasted quite ten minutes, in broken intervals of one or two minutes. All present were much surprised; and the interest became intensified by the unknown tongues in which Mr. Home now conversed. Passing from one language to another in rapid succession, he spoke for ten minutes in unknown languages.

"A spirit form now became distinctly visible; it stood next to the Master of Lindsay, clad, as seen on former occasions, in a long robe with a girdle, the feet scarcely touching the ground, the outline of the face only clear, and the tones of the voice, though sufficiently distinct to be understood, whispered rather than spoken. Other voices were now heard, and large globes of phosphorescent lights passed slowly through the room."

Mr. H. D. Jencken, in the March number of *Human Nature*, continues his interesting account of the spirit manifestations through the mediumship of Mr. D. D. Home, as personally witnessed and carefully examined by himself and other competent investigators. He narrates an instance of the elongation of Mr. Home's body, and gives the measurements (carefully made at the time) of the elongation of each part of the body. The most unique and striking portion of the phenomenon in this instance was the elongation and shortening of the hand. Mr. Jencken says:—

"As the weight of the testimony depends much upon the accuracy of the tracing taken, I will describe my method in making the outline. I caused Mr. Home to place his hand firmly on a sheet of paper, and then carefully traced an outline of the hand. At the wrist joint I placed a pencil against the 'trapezium,' a small bone at the end of the phalange of the thumb. The hand gradually widened and elongated about an inch, then contracted and shortened about an inch. At each stage I made a tracing of the hand, causing the pencil point to be firmly kept at the wrist. The fact of the elongating and contracting of the hand 1 unmistakably established, and, be the cause what it may, the fact remains; and in giving the result of my measurements, and the method adopted to satisfy myself that I had not been self-deceived, I am, I believe, rendering the first positive measurement of the extension and contraction of a human organism.

"The phenomenon of elongation I am aware has been questioned, and I do not quarrel with those who maintain their doubt, despite all that may be affirmed. In my

10

own experience I have gone through the same phases of doubt, and uttered disbelief of what I was seeing. The first time I witnessed an elongation, although I measured the extension of the wrist, I would not, could not, credit my senses; but having witnessed this fact some ten or twelve times, and that in the presence of fifty witnesses, from first to last, who have been present at these *séances* where those elongations occurred, all doubts have been removed; and that the capacity to extend is not confined to Mr. Home, was shown some months ago at Mr. Hall's, where, at a *séance* held at his house, both Mr. Home and Miss Bertolacci became elongated. The stretching out and contracting of the limbs, hands, fingers, above described, I have only witnessed on this one occasion, and I was much pleased to have a steady Oxonian to aid me in making the measurements above detailed."

Mr. Jencken also relates the following incident of this *séance*:—

"Mr. Home (in trance), now took a violet and a few leaves, and, kneeling down at the hearth, stirred the fire with his hand. He then showed us the flower, and seizing it with the fire-tongs, placed it in the fire. I distinctly saw the leaves burn away, and, on withdrawing the fire-tongs, only the stem was left. Twice he repeated the burning of the flower, then, handing the fire-tongs to Miss Bertolacci, he stepped on one side, and we saw the flower being replaced between the nippers of the fire-tongs. I asked whether they had re-formed the flower, to which he replied, 'No; the flower has never been burnt, only shielded, protected from the fire; the freshness of the flower has, however, been destroyed.' He then handed me the violet and leaves, which Miss Bertolacci took, and I believe has preserved. Mr. Home then showed his hands, which felt harsher and harder than in their normal state."

Mr. Jencken adds that at a recent *séance* with Mr. Home, tongues of fire formed in an irregular circle round Mr. Home's head, flickering in fits and starts, from one to three inches long.

The author would only add in this connection that she has herself witnessed Mr. Home's elongation several times in circles held at the residence of John Luxmoore, Esq., 16, Gloucester Square, Hyde Park, London, and also been present on occasions when Mr. Home laid his head on a blazing coal fire without injury, handled blazing coals and placed the same in the hands of John C. Luxmoore, Esq.,—the host—Professor Plumtree, Madame Maurigy, of 51, Albion Street, Hyde Park, and the author.

We might enlarge this list of wonderful phenomena to the dimensions of a thick volume and still fail to relate all the marvels that Spirits have been enabled to display through the mediumship of Mr. D. D. Home. We must however conclude our notices of his remarkable powers by the following extracts from the work already referred to, namely "Researches in the Phenomena of Spiritualism," by Wm. Crookes, F.R.S.

This eminent scientist was not only for some time an industrious investigator into the phenomena of Spirit communion, but he was bold enough to publish the result of those researches, and to maintain the purely occult origin of the manifestations he witnessed, in lengthy controversies with his fellow scientists, and divers members of the journalistic fraternity.

Professor Crookes was aided and sustained in his brave and unconservative position, by Dr. Higgins, Sergeant Cox, and others of an equally eminent rank in the realms of science.

Professor Crookes' papers were first published in the *Quarterly Journal of Science*, but it is from the volume of his collected articles that the following excerpts are now taken. He says:—

"That certain physical phenomena, such as the movement of material substances and the production of sounds resembling electric discharges, occur, under circumstances in which they cannot be explained by any physical law at present known, is a fact of which

I am as certain as of the most elementary fact in chemistry. My whole scientific education has been one long lesson in exactness of observation, and I wish it to be distinctly understood that this firm conviction is the result of most careful investigation."

"Among the remarkable phenomena which occur under Mr. Home's influence, the most striking, as well as the most easily tested with scientific accuracy are, first, the alteration in the weight of bodies ; and second, the playing tunes on musical instruments (generally the accordion for convenience of portability) without direct human intervention, under conditions rendering contact or connection with the keys impossible. Not until I had witnessed these facts some half-dozen times, and scrutinised them with all the critical acumen I possess, did I become convinced of their objective reality. Still, desiring to place the matter beyond the shadow of a doubt, I invited Mr. Home on several occasions to come to my own house, where, in the presence of a few scientific inquirers, these phenomena could be submitted to crucial experiments."

Mr. Crookes then proceeds to detail with unnecessary accuracy the precautions he used to surround his experiments with indubitable proofs that Mr. Home had no agency in their production.

The substance of the experiments was as follows. In a large room well lighted with gas, a wire cage was used in which the accordion could freely expand and contract without the possibility of human contact, with the single exception that it was held suspended in the cage by one of Home's hands extended over and resting upon the upper wire of the cage. This was under the table, but in such a position that the company could witness all the proceedings ; Professor Crookes's assistant being permitted even to go under the table and give an accurate report of what was going on. In this position there was first the regular accordion movements and sounds with the instrument suspended from Home's hand ; then it was taken out and put in the hand of the next sitter, still continuing to play ; and finally, after being returned to the cage it was clearly seen by the company generally, moving about with no one touching it. The final paragraph of this description we give in the language of Mr. Crookes himself :—

"The accordion was now taken without any visible touch from Mr. Home's hand, which he removed from it entirely, and placed upon the table, where it was taken by the person next to him, and seen, as were now both his hands, by all present. I and two others present saw the accordion distinctly floating about inside of the cage with no visible support. This was repeated a second time after a short interval. Mr. Home presently re-inserted his hand in the cage and again took hold of the accordion. It then commenced to play, at first chords and runs, and afterwards a well-known sweet and plaintive melody, which it executed perfectly in a very beautiful manner. Whilst this tune was being played, I grasped Mr. Home's arm below the elbow, and gently slid my hand down it until I touched the top of the accordion. He was not moving a muscle. His other hand was on the table, visible to all, and his feet were under the feet of those next to him."

Prof. Crookes occupies quite a considerable amount of his work by republishing the vigorous lines of defence he was compelled to take up against his brother scientists, whose virulent opposition was awakened by the immense importance attached to his (Prof. Crookes') statements, consequently also to the influence which the obnoxious and unquenchable facts of Spiritualism derived from the allegations of so cautious and capable an investigator.

On the multitude and variety of his researches he says :—

"I may at once answer one objection which has been made in several quarters, viz. ; that my results would carry more weight had they been tried a greater number of times, and with other persons besides Mr. Home. The fact is, I have been working at the subject for two years, and have found nine or ten different persons who possess psychic power in more or less degree ; but its development in Mr. D. D. Home is so powerful that having satisfied myself by careful experiment that the phenomena observed were genuine, I have, merely as a matter of convenience, carried on my experiments with him, in preference to working with others in whom the power existed in a less striking degree. Most of the experiments I am about to describe, however, have been tried with another person other than Mr. Home and in his absence."

It would be unnecessary to follow out these experiments, with the result of which most Spiritual investigators are familiar ; we would only show how thorough they were by the following remarks :—

"My readers will remember that, with the exception of cases especially mentioned, the occurrences have taken place *in my own house, in the light, and with only private friends present* besides the medium.

"I have seen luminous points of light darting about and settling on the heads of different persons ; I have had questions answered by the flashing of a bright light a desired number of times in front of my face. I have seen sparks of light rising from the table, and again falling upon the table, striking it with an audible sound. I have had an alphabetical communication given by luminous flashes occurring before me in the air, whilst my hand was moving about amongst them. I have seen a luminous cloud floating upwards to a picture. Under the strictest test conditions, I have more than once had a solid, self-luminous, crystalline body placed in my hand by a hand which did not belong to any person in the room. *In the light* I have seen a luminous cloud hover over a heliotrope on a side table, break a sprig off, and carry the sprig to a lady : and on some occasions I have seen a similar luminous cloud visibly condense to the form of a hand and carry small objects about.

"The forms of hands are frequently *felt* at dark *séances,* or under circumstances where they cannot be seen. More rarely I have *seen* the hands. I will here give no instances in which the phenomenon has occurred in darkness, but will simply select a few of the numerous instances in which I have seen the hands in the light.

"A beautifully formed small hand rose up from an opening in a dining-table and gave me a flower ; it appeared, and then disappeared three times at intervals, affording me ample opportunity of satisfying myself that it was as real in appearance as my own. This occurred in the light, in my own room, whilst I was holding the medium's hands and feet.

"On another occasion a small hand and arm like a baby's appeared, playing about a lady who was sitting next to me. It then passed to me, and patted my arms and pulled my coat several times.

"At another time a finger and thumb were seen to pick petals from a flower in Mr. Home's button-hole and lay them in front of several persons who were sitting near him.

"The hands and arms do not always appear to me to be solid and life-like. Sometimes, indeed, they present more the appearance of a nebulous cloud partly condensed into the form of a hand.   .   .   .   .

"To the touch, the hand sometimes appears icy cold and dead, at other times warm and life-like, grasping my own with the firm pressure of an old friend.

"I have retained one of these hands in my own, firmly resolved not to let it escape. There was no struggle or effort made to get loose, but it gradually seemed to resolve itself into vapour, and faded in that manner from my grasp.

.   .   .   .

"On one occasion I witnessed a chair, with a lady sitting on it, rise several inches from the ground. On another occasion, to avoid the suspicion of this being in some way performed by herself, the lady knelt on the chair in such a manner that its four feet were visible to us. It then rose about three inches, remained suspended for about ten seconds, and then slowly descended. At another time two children, on separate occasions, rose from the floor with their chairs, in full daylight, under (to me) most satisfactory conditions ; for I was kneeling and keeping close watch upon the feet of the chair, and observing that no one might touch them.

"The most striking cases of levitation which I have witnessed have been with Mr. Home. On three separate occasions have I seen him raised completely from the floor of the room, once sitting in an easy chair, once kneeling on his chair, and once standing up. On each occasion I had a full opportunity of watching the occurrence as it was taking place.

.   .   .   .

"As in the former case, Mr. Home was the medium. A phantom form came from a corner of the room, took an accordion in its hand, and then glided about the room, playing the instrument. The form was visible to all many minutes, Mr. Home being seen at the same time. Coming rather close to a lady who was sitting apart from the rest of the company, she gave a slight cry, upon which it vanished."

Such are some of the phenomena obtained by a gentleman who pledges a name and fame standing as high as that of any scientist in the nineteenth century for the truth of all he alleges ; who backs up his own testimony with that of numerous other equally reliable and eminent witnesses, all of whom have everything to lose, and nothing to gain by the assertions they make. It only needs to add, that all the phenomena above alluded to were produced in the light, in private houses, and under circumstances which rendered the interposition of human agency impossible.

If the Spiritualists themselves would but remember that—until Spirit communion is the common experience of the race—the world at large, and investigators seeking for truth in especial, have the right to demand that the records of phenomena shall be placed on equally unquestionable bases, the columns of the Spiritual journals would no longer be desecrated by the unseemly charges of bare-faced fraud from one party and savage recriminations from another. Spiritualism would ascend to the majestic pedestal of immutable truth like a phœnix rising out of the ashes of dead faiths and fleeting superstitions, and ere long it would compel the acknowledgment of humanity that it was the divine science of soul, and the religion of science.*

CHAPTER XX.

SPIRITUALISM IN GREAT BRITAIN (CONTINUED).

THE effect of Mr. Home's presence in England, the wide-spread reports of the marvels occurring through his mediumship, combined with the furious journalistic warfare which these reports elicited, acted like firebrands thrown into the midst of combustible materials, the sparks from which filled the air, and set the entire mental atmosphere ablaze with Spiritual influences.

True it is, that the young medium's marvellous gifts were displayed only amongst that high class of society in which circumstances had contributed to cast his lot, and through whose personal interest he became the guest of many of the nobles and notables of the day.

Still the contagion of the Spiritual outpouring was in the air, and vast numbers of persons to whom Mr. Home's *séances* were but a report, became stimulated to the endeavour to obtain manifestations through private experiments in their own families. The result was—as all experienced Spiritualists would anticipate, that demonstrations of medial power began to arise in vast numbers of family circles, and those who could not enjoy the privilege of investigating through the Transatlantic medium, were soon enabled to prove for themselves the wonderful facts of which rumour had informed them.

---

* For further account of Mr. Home's mediumship and special *séances*, consult his own biography entitled "Incidents of my Life : By D. D. Home," files of the London *Spiritual Magazine*, Owen's "Footfalls on the Boundaries of Another World," and other English Spiritual publications of this century.—(AUTHOR.)

The chances are, that we should very generally find the *modus operandi* of individual investigation exemplified by the experience of Mrs. De Morgan—the wife of the celebrated mathematical professor—who, having been assured by Spirit friends communicating through Mrs. Hayden, that she could have equally good manifestations with those she then witnessed in her own house, at once proceeded to put in practice the instructions given, and form circles, the result of which soon became apparent in the development of remarkable medial powers in Mrs. De Morgan herself, in some members of her household, her friends, and not a few of her servants.

Experiences of this character soon began to multiply. Professor De Morgan, although not avowedly interested to the same extent as his estimable lady, candidly rendered his testimony to the occurrence of the marvellous phenomena which proved Spirit communion. In a short space of time after the advent of Mr. Home in England, the circles known to be held constantly, in various families, might be numbered by the thousand, and those who publicly ranged themselves as advocates of the truth of the communion, included some of the most distinguished and noteworthy persons of the day. Amongst the latter, and especially remarkable as being the earliest of the avowed believers of Spiritualism in England, may be named, Mary and William Howitt and Samuel Carter and Maria Hall; all authors celebrated for their admirable writings, and ladies and gentlemen as much esteemed for their irreproachable private lives as for their eminent literary abilities—Dawson Rogers; a gentleman of high social standing and influential press associations—the Countess, now Duchesse de Pomar, and Countess of Caithness, a lady who takes the highest rank both as an authoress and leader of aristocratic European society; T. P. Barkas, F.R.S.; Lady Otway, Frederick Tennyson, Robert Owen, and his son, Robert Dale Owen; Lord Brougham, Lord Lytton, Archbishop Whateley, the Earl of Dunraven, Lord Adare, the Master of Lindsay, Lady Shelley, Mr. Sergeant Cox; Wm. Wilkinson, Esq., the eminent solicitor, and other members of his family; Sir Edwin Landseer; more than one member of the eminent literary family of the Trollopes; Mrs. Browning, the celebrated poetess; George Thompson, the well known philanthropist; Major Drayson the eminent astronomer; Benjamin Coleman, Esq., and his amiable wife and daughter; John Jones, Esq., of Enmore Park, Norwood; Sir Chas. Isham, Bart., of Lamport Hall, Northampton; the Countess of Paulett; Mrs. McDougall Gregory, widow of the celebrated Dr. Gregory of Edinburgh; Lady Dunsany, Lady Helena Newenham, J. C. Luxmoore, Esq.; Professor A. R. Wallace, the celebrated naturalist; Cromwell Varley, F.R.S.; the renowned electrician; W. F. Barrett, Professor of Physics in the Royal College of Science, Dublin; Lord Rayleigh, F.R.S., Professor of Physics, Cambridge University; the Earl of Crauford and Balcarres, F.R.S., President of the Royal Astronomical Society; Dr. Lockhart Robertson, F.R.S., Editor, *Journal of Science;* Drs. Ashburner and Elliotson, Dr. George Wylde, Dr. Robert Chambers, F.R.S.; Professor Cassel, LL.D.; Captain R. F. Burton, the celebrated traveller; Dr. Fenton Cameron, Henry D. Jencken, barrister; Professor Crookes, the renowned chemist; Mrs. Anna Cora Ritchie, Thos. Shorter, Esq., known under the *nom de plume* of "Brevior;" Dr. Jacob Dixon, the eminent homœopathist; Wm. Tebb, Esq., and his lady; Gerald Massey, the renowned poet; C. C. Massey, the barrister; Hon. J. L. O'Sullivan, Rev. Sir Wm. Topham, A. Gooch, M.P.; Dr. Gully, of Malvern; Chas. Blackburn, Esq., of Parkfield, Didsbury, Manchester;

Jno. Fowler, Esq., of Liverpool, and Jas. Wason, Esq., barrister, of the same place ; Mrs. Honeywood, of Warwick Square, Belgravia ; Dr. Hitchman, LL.D., John Scott, Esq., of Belfast ; John Rymer, Esq., of Ealing ; M. and Madame Maurigy ; W. Cox, Esq., Jermyn Street, St. James', and a long list of other ladies and gentlemen whose names we are not privileged to mention—to say nothing of hundreds of persons in the middle ranks of life, whose advocacy was of equal credit to the cause.

It need hardly be added that since the above-named ladies and gentle· men contributed their influence and honourable names to bear the heat and burden of the early days of spiritual warfare, hundreds of others, scarcely less eminent or noteworthy, have graced the ranks of Spiritualism. Those who have become associated with the moving incidents of the grand historical drama will of course be mentioned hereafter, but a still larger number must necessarily be excluded, though most reluctantly on the author's part, from this over-crowded record.

We recall the few names already cited, chiefly for the purpose of showing the class of individuals against whom the small wits of English journalism amused themselves by directing the shafts of ridicule and contempt, and that simply because they chose to believe what the testimony of their own senses proved to be truth. For this cause and for this only, the above-named parties were virtually branded either as *fools*, incapable of forming correct opinions, or *knaves* wicked enough to join in a world-wide system of imposition upon others. No doubt the *critics* had hardly calculated the sum of the insolence of which they were guilty; still its substance meant neither more nor less than the assertion that the believers in Spiritualism— be they whom they may—were either all deluded or all deluders, however wise or honest they may have been on every other subject but Spiritualism.

Now it must be borne in mind that neither the gifts nor the messages of Spiritualism were limited to the aristocratic circles of Great Britain.

In a great many cases it was found, that some of the best Mediums were developed amongst the poor patients who sought aid at the Mesmeric Infirmary. The servants in great families also, who were often summoned to attend the circles of their masters and mistresses, at the suggestion of the communicating Spirits, frequently proved to be endowed with remarkable mediumistic powers, and these carried the tidings of the new revelation to persons of their own class, by whom quiet unostentatious methods of enquiry into Spiritualism were proceeding, with far more abundant results than the world at large was at all prepared for.

Still there were circumstances tending to limit the earlier manifestations of Spirit power in Great Britain to private families, and the isolation of individual experiences. In the first place, there were no professional Mediums in England, but such as came from America, for some years.

When European Mediums were either called upon or *compelled*—as was often the case—to abandon all other modes of gaining a livelihood, to devote themselves entirely to the exercise of their Spiritual gifts, it became an inevitable necessity that they should be recompensed for the time and labour involved in their services. It is only just to say, that in America—where every description of labour normal to the individual per- forming it, is recognised as natural and honourable—Mediumistic power was—from the incipiency of the movement—classified with every other faculty, and as such acknowledged to be a legitimate means of earning a livelihood.

In Great Britain the attempt to establish a pharisaical distinction between what is sacred and secular, ever has, and still does, stigmatize *professional* mediumship as "a desecration," &c., &c.   Making all due allowance for the fraudulent spirit so common to human nature, and therefore, so certain to be found in the ranks of Spiritualism as well as amongst all other classes of society, we have yet to see why professional mediumship is not as legitimate an occupation as professional editorship, or professional work done in any other capacity for which the Creator has fitted the creature.

We have yet to learn what gifts are specially *sacred* and what—by converse—are *profane.*   When we have sufficiently *proved* these distinctions, we may be in a position to denounce the Mediums who claim the labourers' hire for their work.   It is but justice to the sticklers for "sacred and profane" gifts in humanity, to add, that they never affix these awkward lines of demarcation to the workers of any other denomination than those of Spiritualism; the clergy as a body—from the archbishop who receives his twenty-five thousand pounds a year for Spiritual ministrations, to the poor curate upon his stipend of one hundred per annum — being deemed legitimately entitled to receive *whatever they can get,* unrebuked and unquestioned.   Whether we are to consider the clerical calling as "profane" and therefore entitled to recompense, or "*too sacred*" to be called in question at all, we have not yet been able to ascertain, but we do know for an absolute fact, that many an Englishman who does not hesitate to pay his quota of heavy rates to support the Church, has shrunk back in holy horror from paying a sixpenny fee to hear a fine Spiritual lecture, and excused himself on the ground that Mediumship was a " sacred gift," and should not be made the subject of mercenary traffic, &c., &c.   Whether these assertions are designed to insinuate, that the Spirit Medium's gifts are from the Lord, and should not be paid, and those of the Bench of Bishops are from the other party, and may therefore become the subject of traffic, we cannot exactly determine.   The inference is strong that way, and therefore, were it only for the sake of resisting the wholesale insult which this line of argument hurls against the clergy of all denominations, we ought to disregard such distinctions, or at least hold them in abeyance, until the line between the sacred and profane in human endowments is clearly defined. Meantime, the results of these curious opinions were not favourable to the general dissemination of Spiritualism in Great Britain.   For many years the belief was a close communion affair; the luxurious entertainment of those who could afford to encourage Transatlantic Mediums as their guests, or devote leisure time to the culture of spiritual gifts in small retired family circles.

For a long time, the attempt to disseminate the knowledge thus obtained by aid of professional mediumship was so severely frowned down, that its earliest public exhibitions—as in the case of the Davenport Brothers— became occasions for the display of violence and ruffianism that would have disgraced the darkest of ages.   We may also understand why—with an immense array of titled names and distinguished literary and scientific celebrities as its patrons—Spiritualism remained for many years unrepresented by any public demonstration.

In 1859, Mr. Rollin Squire, the young American gentleman mentioned in our French section, paid a brief visit to Europe, for the purpose of recruiting his health and enjoying a holiday tour.

Both in this country and on the Continent, Mr. Squire exercised his medial powers for the edification of large circles of admirers.   Still, like Mr. Home, Mr. Squire was only known within the charmed limits of aristocracy, or such journalistic commentators as were from time to time invited as witnesses of the marvels enacted in his presence. Mr. P. B. Randolph, an eccentric trance speaker, and Mrs. A. E. Newton, a vision seeress and clairvoyant, were also received amongst the *haut ton* of European Spiritualism, and each contributed their quota as honoured American visitors, in disseminating spiritual light amongst the more favoured part of the community. In 1864 the far-famed Davenport Brothers visited England for the first time. They were the only Mediums except the trance speakers, who had yet appeared in Europe through whom manifestations of spirit power could be given in public audiences.

Professional Mediumship as above suggested, was at that time regarded with so much unreasoning distrust, that the announcement that what had hitherto been regarded as the "most sacred of gifts," was now to be made the subject of paying exhibitions, caused a thrill of horror to pervade even the minds of Spiritualists themselves. It was in deference then to this orthodox view of spiritual power and gifts, that the Davenports and their *Entrepreneur*, were induced at first to tender their inaugural manifestations in private circles, or gatherings convened according to custom, at the houses of the privileged few.

As we feel justified in asserting that no subsequent phases of mediumship exhibited on public platforms, have ever equalled in TEST conditions and clearness, the manifestations produced through the Davenport Brothers in the early days of their public career, we deem it a necessary part of the present record, to give a brief account of the phenomena which ordinarily transpired in their presence, and this we prefer to do, by reiterating a published statement attested by a large number of respectable witnesses, rather than offer the author's own unsustained views of these young men's Mediumship.

Dr. Nichols, author of a sketch of the Davenport Brothers, during the very early portion of their career, says: "On the night of October 11th, 1864, a very distinguished company assembled at the residence of Mr. Dion Boucicault to witness the manifestations which are given in the presence of the Brothers Davenport." An account of the proceedings which transpired, Dr. Nichols alleges to have been drawn up and published by Mr. Boucicault himself. The following is a *verbatim* copy of the report in question :—

" To the Editor of the ' Daily News.'

"Sir,—A *séance* by the Brothers Davenport and Mr. W. Fay, took place in my house yesterday in the presence of Lord Bury, Sir Charles Nicholson, Sir John Gardiner, Sir C. Lennox Wyke, Rev. E. H. Newenham, Rev. W. Ellis, Captain E. A. Inglefield, Mr. Chas. Reade, Messrs. Jas. Matthews, Algernon Borthwick, T. Willes, H. E. Ormerod, J. W. Kaye, J. A. Bostock, H. J. Rideout, Robt. Bell, J. N. Mangles, H. M. Dunphy, W. Tyler Smith, M.D., E. Tyler Smith, T. L. Coward, John Brown, M.D., Robert Chambers, LL.D., and Dion Boucicault.

"The room in which the meeting was held is a large drawing-room, from which all the furniture had been previously removed excepting the carpet, a chandelier, a table and sofa, and twenty-six cane-bottomed chairs.

"At two o'clock six of the above party arrived, and the room was subjected to careful scrutiny.

"It was suggested that a cabinet to be used by the Brothers Davenport, but then erected in an adjacent room, should be removed into the front room, and placed in a spot selected by ourselves.

"This was done by our party, but in the process we displaced a portion of this piece of furniture, thus enabling us to examine its material and structure before we mended it. At three o'clock, our party was fully assembled and continued the scrutiny. We sent to a neighbouring music seller for six guitars and two tambourines, so that the implements to be used should not be those with which the operators were familiar. At half-past three the brothers Davenport and Mr. Fay arrive.d They found we had altered their arrangements by changing the room which they had previously selected for their manifestations.

"The *séance* then began by an examination of the dress and persons of the Davenports, and it was certified that no apparatus or other contrivance was concealed on or about their persons. They entered the cabinet, and sat facing each other. Captain Inglefield then with a new rope, provided by ourselves, tied Mr. W. Davenport hand and foot, with his hands behind his back, and then bound him firmly to the seat where he sat. Lord Bury in like manner secured Mr. Ira Davenport. The knots on these ligatures were then fastened with sealing wax and a seal affixed. A guitar, violin, tambourine, two bells, and a brass trumpet were placed on the floor of the cabinet.

"The doors were then closed, and a sufficient light was permitted in the room to enable us to see what followed.

"I shall omit any detailed account of the Babel of sounds which arose in the cabinet, and the violence with which the doors were repeatedly burst open and the instruments expelled, the hands appearing as usual at a lozenge-shaped orifice in the centre door of the cabinet. The following incidents seem to us particularly worthy of note.

"While Lord Bury was stooping inside the cabinet, the door being open, the two operators seen to be seated and bound, a *detached* hand was clearly observed to descend upon him, and he started back remarking that he had been struck.

"Again, in the full light of the gas chandelier, and during an interval in the *séance*, the doors of the cabinet being open, and while the ligatures of the brothers were being examined, a very white thin female hand and wrist quivered for several seconds in the air above.

"This appearance drew a general exclamation from all the party. Sir Charles Wyke now entered the cabinet and sat between the two young men, his hands being right and left on each, and secured to them. The doors were then closed and the Babel of sounds recommenced. Several hands appeared at the orifice, amongst them the hand of a child. After a time, Sir Charles returned amongst us and stated that while he held the two brothers, several hands touched his face, and pulled his hair ; the instruments at his feet crept up, played round his body, and over his head, one of them lodging eventually on his shoulders. During the foregoing incidents the hands which appeared were touched and grasped by Captain Inglefield, and he stated that to the touch they were apparently human hands, though they passed away from his grasp.

"I omit mentioning other phenomena, an account of which has been rendered elsewhere.

"The next part of the *séance* was performed in the dark. One of the Messrs. Davenport and Mr. Fay seated themselves amongst us. . . . Two ropes were thrown at their feet, and in two minutes and a half they were tied hand and foot, their hands behind their backs, bound tightly to their chairs, and their chairs bound to an adjacent table. While this process was going on, the guitar rose from the table and swung or floated round the room and over the heads of the party, slightly touching some. Now a phosphoric light shot from side to side over our heads. The hands and shoulders of several were simultaneously touched or struck by hands, the guitar meanwhile sailing round the room, now near the ceiling, now scuffling on the head and shoulders of some luckless wight. The bells whisked here and there, and a light murmuring was maintained on the violin.

"The two tambourines were rolled hither and thither on the floor, now shaking violently, now visiting the knees and hands of our circle, all these foregoing incidents being simultaneous. Mr. Rideout, holding a tambourine, requested it might be plucked from him, when it was almost instantaneously taken. At the same time Lord Bury made a similar request, and a forcible attempt was made to pluck a tambourine from his grasp, which he resisted.

"Mr. Fay then asked that his coat should be removed.

"We heard a violent twitch and here occurred a most remarkable fact. A light was struck before the coat had quite left Mr. Fay's person, and it was seen quitting him, and plucked off him upwards.

"It flew up to the chandelier, where it hung for a moment and then fell to the ground. Mr. Fay was seen meanwhile bound hand and foot as before: One of our party now divested himself of his coat, and it was placed on the table. The light was extinguished and this coat was rushed on to Mr. Fay's back with equal rapidity.

"During the above occurrences in the dark, we placed a sheet of paper under the feet of the two operators, and drew with a pencil an outline around them, to the end that if they moved it might be detected.

"They of their own accord offered to have their hands filled with flour, or any similar substance to prove they made no use of them, but this precaution was deemed unnecessary ;

we required them however to count from one to twelve repeatedly that their voices constantly heard might certify to us that they were in the places where they were tied. Each of our own party held his neighbour so firmly that no one could move without two adjacent neighbours being aware of it. At the termination of this *séance* a general conversation took place on the subject of what we had witnessed.

" Lord Bury suggested that the general opinion seemed to be that we assure the Brothers Davenport and Mr. Fay that after a very stringent trial and strict scrutiny of their proceedings, the gentlemen present could arrive at no other conclusion than that there was no trace of trickery in any form, and certainly there were neither confederates nor machinery, and that all those who had witnessed the results would freely state in the society in which they moved that so far as their investigations enabled them to form an opinion, the phenomena which had taken place in their presence were not the product of legerdemain. This suggestion was promptly acceded to by all present.

" Before leaving this question, in which my name has accidentally become mixed up, I may be permitted to observe that I have no belief in what is called 'Spiritualism,' and nothing I have seen inclines me to believe in it—indeed the puerility of some of the demonstrations would sufficiently alienate such a theory, but I do believe that we have not quite explored the realms of natural philosophy—that this enterprise of thought has of late years been confined to useful inventions, and we are content at least to think that the laws of nature are finite, ascertained, and limited to the scope of our knowledge. A very great number of worthy persons. seeing such phenomena as I have detailed, ascribe them to supernatural agency ; others wander round the subject in doubt, but as it seriously engages the feeling and earnest thought of so large a number in Europe and America, is it a subject which scientific men are justified in treating with the neglect of contempt ?

 . . , . . . , .

" I am, &c.,

α Dion Boucicault.

" Regent Street, October 12, 1864."

It may be asked with some point, why we republish accounts of phenomena so well known and which have long since been put into the shade—in the opinion of many Spiritualists—by the marvels of what they term "form materializations ?" On the other hand, there has been a kind of fashion in the assertion, both within and without the ranks of Spiritualism, that the Davenport Brothers are "impostors," and many assume, without any known grounds for the assumption, that they have been *proved* to be impostors. To all classes of objectors we would carefully commend a perusal of the *séance* reported above. Let it be remembered that it is written by one who only admits that his name is "*accidentally*" mixed up in the affair, and who guards that name with unnecessary caution from the charge of *being a Spiritualist*.

All those who have witnessed the Davenports' *séances* know, that their phenomena were performed with lightning speed ; that no singing was called for—"loud, louder, louder still" — during the dreary waiting time when Spirits are "materializing," and all who read the report of these press men, scientists, and sceptics, will observe, how often they insist upon their own caution in examining, and of the utter impossibility of their detecting fraud, or the personal agency of the Mediums in the phenomena.

Now, uninteresting as the facts themselves may be, the above report shows a set of conditions under which human agency or contrivance was simply IMPOSSIBLE. Our aim in dwelling upon this *séance* is to show, that in the case of the Davenports, as in those so often described as occurring with Mr. Home, stringent tests do not hinder the manifestations, neither does the presence of sceptics destroy them.

Here are conditions under which conjurers may be defied and scepticism baffled ; and though imposture is impossible, true Mediumship could not fail to come out of such trials triumphant and unimpeachable. But these conditions are "too degrading for sensitive Mediums to submit to," urge their apologists, "and you who demand it of them, are no true Spiritualists; you are *Spirit grabbers*, Mediums' enemies, the worst foes of Spiritualism," &c., &c., &c.   To this class of talkers and writers, we have no answer to make, neither desiring nor intending to hold intercourse with them; but to the confiding victims whose heart strings are wrung, and whose pockets are so often robbed to sustain impostors, we would say, See what Spirits could do, and did do, through the mediumship of the Davenports, and have no hesitancy in refusing to accord faith to any professions of Spiritual agency that are not equally well guarded round, against possibility of human interference and deception.

That the poor Davenports were often inhumanly, and even brutally treated, we not only admit, but are about to demonstrate; but the tests applied by the party whose record we have given, neither degraded nor insulted the Mediums; on the contrary, they submitted to them cheerfully, and often, to the author's personal knowledge, suggested still more stringent tests, with which their manifestations could readily be given.

The truth is, the Davenports have seldom been fairly dealt with.   The people that could not explain their manifestations, have contented themselves, like Mr. Boucicault, by denying that they could be "Spiritual," because they were too *puerile*, whilst multitudes of Spiritualists who will gaze with rapture upon the tinsel ornaments sewed on to cheap finery by *Mediums*, whilst their masked dummies are contemplated with awe, stretched out on sofas, will turn with disgust from the obvious and unmistakeable proofs of Spirit power, furnished through the Davenports, because they come from "such very low Spirits!"   Had we an opportunity of questioning Mr. Boucicault concerning his opinion as to what becomes of the great mass of mankind that sit nightly to watch his dramas, perhaps we might be in a position to show that the taste of the majority inclines to puerility only, and that anything that was not puerile, would not represent the vanished millions that have passed through the gates of death to the life beyond, where it is exceedingly doubtful, if puerile Spirits become wise in the twinkling of an eye, or low men and women suddenly become exalted angels.   Meantime the question is not one of *quality* but kind. Were the manifestations recorded above, made by the Davenports, if not, by whom and what?

These are the real questions at issue, and those manifestations can no longer be called "puerile," which defy the whole realm of science to explain, nor those Spirits be tabooed as "too low" for pious company, which prove the fact of man's spiritual existence, better than all the sermons that were ever preached from the mere standpoint of belief without knowledge.

Following immediately upon the *séance* recorded above, with the Davenports, were others of a more or less wonderful nature.

These exhibitions were at first confined to private circles held in the houses of the nobility, or of scientific persons; at length however, the Mediums enlarged their borders, and appeared at the Queen's Concert Room, Hanover Square, attracting select and distinguished audiences, by whom they were still esteemed as entirely free from all shadow of fraud or suspicion.   For some time the gentlemen of the press, especially those who were favoured with invitations to attend the more exclusive circles, were fair and candid in their statements concerning what they had witnessed. No sooner did it appear however that the Mediums seemed in a fair way to remunerate themselves for time and service by successful public exhibitions, than the press suddenly became alive to the "impiety," "American audacity," &c., &c., of the whole affair.

Dr. Nichols in his biography of the Davenport Brothers quotes the press utterances of this character at large, and to judge by their general tone, the Davenports had become unmistakably popular, and were very generally *fêted* and patronised by the highest rank of society, whilst their success in "making money" by their public exhibitions, and baffling all attempts of the scientific or learned to "find them out," very *naturally*, and very *justly*, merited the united storm of journalistic indignation from all parts of the country, and the united "anathema maranatha" of every pious professor of Spiritual doctrines, who could not prove what they professed, quite as well as the Davenports. So the storm raged, and so the enemies of the cause contributed to feed the flame by the virulence of the persecution directed against it. The culminating point of these proceedings however was reached, in a demonstration of *popular sentiment* displayed towards the Davenports on the occasion of their visit to the north of England. Although the character of this incident is such an one as no English writer would care much to descant upon, we feel obliged, in the interests of truth, to give the narrative in all its ugly details ; still we prefer to let others tell the tale. We shall therefore place it before the reader in the language of the parties most nearly concerned, and as the following letter from the Brothers Davenport contains published facts which for many years have remained uncontradicted, we cannot do better than reprint it in their own words.

The following quotation, explanatory of the letter, is written by the Rev. J. B. Ferguson, A.M., LL.D., a gentleman from one of the Southern States of America, who having become well acquained with the Davenports, and placing implicit faith in their honesty, and the thoroughly Spiritual nature of their endowments, had consented to accompany them to England, as a travelling companion, and was well advised of all the facts which were published indeed under his own supervision.

Writing to the author Mr. Ferguson says :—"The Brothers Davenport have been subjected to a series of extraordinary outrages in some of the provincial towns of England, which show that the spirit of opposition manifested by a portion of the public press is likely to take more violent form when it falls into a lower stratum of society. The facts connected with the riots at Liverpool, Huddersfield, and Leeds are very clearly stated in the following address of the Brothers Davenport to the British public, which, as a portion of the history of the movement, deserves a place in these records :—"

"THE BROTHERS DAVENPORT TO THE BRITISH PUBLIC.

"We appeal to the free press and the enlightened and fair-dealing people of the British Empire for a candid consideration of the following statement, and for the even-handed justice usually given in this country to all persons, rich or poor, citizens or strangers. We ask, also, as a matter of justice, that journals which have published accounts of the recent riots at Liverpool, Huddersfield, and Leeds, of which we were the victims, should also give the facts contained in this statement.

"We beg, furthermore, most respectfully to commend to the consideration of the Right Honourable Sir George Grey and the magistracy and police authorities of the United Kingdom, the fact that within two weeks, in three of the most important provincial towns in England, without any fault of our own, transgressing no law of the realm, and offering no violence or injury to any person, we have been made to suffer in property, and have been menaced with extreme personal injury, with apparent danger to our lives, as will appear by the following statement of facts :—

"After having given over two hundred public and private *séances*, or exhibitions of physical phenomena, such as have been described in all the leading journals of Europe and America, and in our published biography, at the Queen's Concert Rooms, London, and the mansions of the nobility and gentry of England, we visited Liverpool on the 13th of February, and, as is our custom, gave a private *séance*, to which the members of the press and others were invited, who reported the satisfactory character of the exhibition. February 14th we gave two public *séances* at St. George's Hall with like results ; a private *séance* at a gentleman's mansion and a public morning performance on Tuesday were alike satisfactory.

"On Tuesday evening we were proceeding with another exhibition, when two persons, a Mr. Hulley and a Mr. Cummins, acting as a committee from the audience, in attempting to tie our wrists, caused so much pain that we were compelled to protest against the torture they were inflicting. We were willing to be tied with entire security, as we have been many hundreds of times by riggers, sailors, engineers, and other skilled persons, or to give any reasonable test in proof that we have no active part in the phenomena witnessed in our presence ; we had no fear of a 'Tomfool knot, or of any mode of fastening that did not inflict unbearable torture. We declined to be bound by a committee whose unfairness and even brutality were soon manifest. Hulley and Cummins refused to retire and give place to another committee ; the audience was made to believe that it was the form of a particular knot, and not the cruelty of its application, to which we objected, and we were compelled by an unappeasable tumult to return the money taken for tickets, and postpone further proceedings.

"On the following evening printed regulations were given to every person entering the hall, and read from the platform, in which we distinctly claimed the right of rejecting any person on a committee whom we should find acting with unfairness. This would be our right were we criminals on trial for felony. Before commencing, we invited all persons who were not satisfied with these regulations to retire from the hall, and receive the money they had paid for entrance.

"Messrs. Hulley and Cummins, backed by a crowd of their friends, came again upon the platform, and, from their previous unfairness, were promptly rejected by us as a committee. They insisted upon tying us, and appealed to the audience to support them in their demand. They refused to leave the platform when requested, took possession of our cabinet, and in various ways excited violent manifestations in the audience.

"We were then assured by a gentleman of Liverpool that unless we submitted to the demands of these men there would be a furious riot. He promised that they should not be permitted to injure us, and we finally yielded to his assurances. But they had no sooner placed the cords upon our wrists than they inflicted a degree of pain which could not be endured. We protested against this violence, but in vain, and, refusing to submit to it longer, had the cords cut from our wrists, and left the platform, which was instantly invaded by the mob ; our cabinet was broken in pieces, and Hulley and Cummins, the heroes of this assault of some hundreds of brave Englishmen upon four unarmed, unoffending, and unprotected foreigners were borne from the hall upon the shoulders of their friends, apparently proud of their triumph.

"Our cabinet destroyed and our business interrupted, with heavy pecuniary damage in Liverpool, we returned to London, had a new cabinet constructed, and on the following Monday returned to Halifax, where we gave our usual public and private exhibitions without interruption.

"Our next engagement was at Huddersfield, February 21st. On our arrival we were informed that Hulley and Cummins, the heroes of the Liverpool mob, had been telegraphed to, and were coming with a strong deputation from that town, to break up our exhibition. The infuriated mob was the common talk of the town. We appealed to the police, and we are happy to say that, in this instance, a sufficient force was promptly sent to the hall for our protection. The crowd that assembled gave many indications of being prepared for violence. When our representative had stated the regulations adopted, and that we proposed simply the presentation of certain facts, without any theory, and asked for the appointment of a committee, two gentlemen, instructed, it was said, by Hulley and Cummins, came upon the platform and commenced to tie our wrists together behind us, which they did with needless severity. We bore the pain, however, until carrying the ropes through the hole in the seat, they drew the backs of our hands down upon it with such violence as to threaten dislocation, placing their knees upon the seat, and in one instance upon the hands of one of us to give them greater purchase. This torture, deliberately, and to all appearance maliciously inflicted, we of course could not bear, and at our demand the cords were instantly severed. We exposed our livid wrists, in which every strand of the cord was visibly imprinted, to the audience, who, to the credit of their humanity, cried out 'Shame !' But the mob organized to break up our exhibition had no such feeling, and made a simultaneous rush for the platform, where, however, an efficient police force saved our property from destruction and us from a violence which, under the stimulating addresses of the heroes of the Liverpool outrage, expended itself in hootings and howlings.

"We had engagements for two nights at Hull, but on our arrival we were informed by the gentleman who had engaged us, the chairman of the hall committee, and the police superintendent, that there were such indications of a violent mob, that we could not be permitted to give our exhibition, and we received from the gentleman chiefly interested the following note :—

"'Music Hall, Jarret Street, Hull.
"'22nd February, 1865.

"'Sir,—As I believe there is reason to apprehend a disturbance at the hall this evening, if the *séance* of the Davenport Brothers takes place, I have come to the conclusion that it would be advisable to postpone the *séance*. I am sorry to do this, particularly as yourself and the Messrs. Davenport have arrived in Hull, and are ready to fulfil your engagement ; but I am driven to do so by the *organized attack* which I am given to understand is in preparation. I am also urged to do so by the proprietors of the hall, who are alarmed lest their property should be damaged by any disturbance.
"'I remain, yours faithfully,
"'ROBERT BOWSER.

"'Rev. Dr. Ferguson, Royal Station Hotel, Hull.'

"Failing to find at Hull that protection in our legal rights which we had supposed was extended to every man on English ground, we went to meet our next engagement at Leeds, where the scenes of Liverpool and Huddersfield were re-enacted with increased violence. We were met by an organized mob, and were refused the protection of the police when it was demanded. When the ringleaders or agents of the mob, taking possession of the stage, had subjected us to the same violence that had been planned and practised upon us at Liverpool and Huddersfield—the mob again destroying our property, smashing the cabinet and breaking up or purloining our musical instruments, and we were protected from personal violence, amid the smashing of door panels and the howling of an enraged populace, by the tardy arrival of a detachment of police and the brave and firm conduct of one of its members—our agent, contrary to all justice, was compelled to order the return of the admission money paid by those who had come for the very purpose of making the riot from which we suffered. On the same day we had given a public *séance*, attended by the members of the press and some of the most respectable citizens of Leeds, in which the famous 'Tom-fool knot' was used, and in which, so far as we were able to judge, the phenomena exhibited gave entire satisfaction.

"It remains but to state two or three facts which may throw further light on these proceedings.

"In Liverpool, as reported in the *Mercury*, Mr. Hulley, when accused of acting unfairly to, and being an enemy of the Davenports, said, 'I avow it. I am a bitter foe to the Davenports.' After such an avowal, what right had he to act on a committee whose duty was strict impartiality ?

"We wish to be just to the police. At Huddersfield, though they could not give us order, we were protected from actual violence. At Leeds such protection was withheld until too late to save our property.

"At Liverpool the *Mercury* says :—

"'The appearance of Inspectors Valentine and Southwell, with a force of thirty men, did not stop the process of demolition. The police, indeed, *did not attempt to interfere so long as only the property of the Davenports was threatened.*'

"The *Leeds Mercury*, reporting the violent proceedings against us at Huddersfield, says :—

"'Mr. Walker, not considering that his hands could pull the rope tight enough, *used his knee to assist him*, and the brother he was operating on again protested. . . . . Several persons had at that time gone to the cabinet, and Davenport showed his wrist to some of them. *It had a livid mark fringed with red, about the breadth of a finger, and in the hollow of this mark there were the marks of the individual strands of the rope.*'

"Yet some have been found to insist on inflicting this brutal torture upon us, with howling mobs to back them, as if we were malefactors or wild beasts. It may be doubted if such an amount of violence, wrong, and outrage has been inflicted on any unoffending men in England since Clarkson was mobbed by the slave-traders of Liverpool, and Priestly by the mad bigots of Birmingham. . . .

"(Signed)
"IRA ERASTUS DAVENPORT.
"WILLIAM HENRY DAVENPORT.
"WILLIAM M. FAY."

CHAPTER XXI.

SPIRITUALISM IN GREAT BRITAIN (CONTINUED).

ANOTHER of the abnormal personages who made a deep mark upon tne faith of European society, was Miss Nichol, better known as Mrs. Guppy, the wife of a gentleman of wealth and good social position, who previous to his union with Miss Nichol, had become remarkable in the Spiritualistic ranks as the author of a singular book entitled "Mary Jane." The speciality of this publication, which was issued in two handsome volumes, was to this effect.

Previous to the decease of his first wife, Mr. Guppy's attention had been drawn towards a succession of extraordinary disturbances occurring in his own house, and which continued for many months, in the form of rappings, movements of furniture, direct writings, and at last, when advised by Spiritualistic friends to try and obtain communications with the unseen tormentors through the ordinary methods of the Spirit circle the manifestations changed to intelligent question and answer, rendered through rappings, table tilting, and planchette writings. Being of a somewhat materialistic turn of mind, and greatly interested in the study of the natural sciences, Mr. Guppy—whilst compelled to admit the supra-mundane character of the new development in his household—attributed it to *a species of aromal force, given off unconsciously, from certain human organisms, and combining itself into a sort of magical impersonal personality*, to which he gave the anomalous designation of "Mary Jane." As the said "Mary Jane" manifested a remarkable amount of intelligence, often transcending that of any member of the household, and betrayed moreover, tokens of a strong will of her own, Mr. Guppy conceived such an amount of respect for his "Ariel," that he proceeded to write her history, and completely filled the two volumes above alluded to, with accounts of her strange freaks, varied accomplishments, and demonstrations of preternatural power.

After the death ot his first wife, Mr. Guppy being introduced to Miss Nichol, found in that lady's Mediumship, a very striking counterpart of his invisible friend Mary Jane's performances. The interest thus excited, not only ended in Mr. Guppy's complete conversion to Spiritualism, but also in the transformation of Miss Nichol into the wife of the wealthy scientist, in which position, as a *non-professional Medium*, Mrs. Guppy was enabled to exert a widespread influence both in England and many of the Continental cities.

As Mrs. Guppy's Mediumship is of that representative character which it is the aim of this work to depict, we avail ourselves of the accounts given of Mr. Guppy's *séances*, published by several authoritative witnesses.

The first whose testimony we cite, is the late eminent jurist, Serjeant Cox, who, in a paper read before the Psychological Society of Great Britain, relates in very minute detail, how he one day called 'at Mrs. Guppy's residence at Highbury, and solicited the favour of her company at a Spiritual circle, to be held that evening at his own residence. Serjeant

Cox candidly states, that he desired to take Mrs. Guppy unaware of his invitation, and the lady in her own simple and amiable way, immediately complied with the request preferred.

It was winter time, and the ground was covered with snow. Mrs. Guppy having arranged her dress, entered the hired cab which Serjeant Cox had brought, and drove with him some four miles to his residence. From the time of her arrival at his house, till the period of the *séance*, about five hours later, Serjeant Cox or the ladies of his family never for one moment lost sight of Mrs. Guppy, and yet within three minutes of the time that the circle had assembled, in a room which had been thoroughly searched, the one door locked, and the key deposited in Serjeant Cox's pocket, when the light was extinguished, heavy thuds were heard on the table, the lights were called for by signal, and the table was found to be covered with heaps of pure white snow. When this unwelcome freight of matter had been removed, the party re-formed, and the gas extinguished, more deposits were heard falling, fresh signals were made for lights, and the table was found literally piled up with lovely hothouse flowers, arranged with exquisite taste into divers fanciful groups.

The author on one occasion, in a locked room, too thoroughly searched to admit of the concealment of a single article however small, was presented, at her own request, with a live pigeon, which fluttered down upon her lap, almost as soon as asked for. The bird being released, and flowers asked for, when the signal was given for lights, an immense pyramid of flowers was found tastefully built up around a pot of tulips. The lights—at the request of the Spirits—being again put out, the flowers, including immense branches of ferns, were so completely hidden or removed from the room, that though the one door was locked, and the key in the pocket of one of the company, the strictest search failed to reveal a single leaf. All that was left was the pot of tulips, on which was found a paper with very small writing, presenting the tulips as a gift to the author, "from the Spirits."

One of the most curious narratives in connection with this lady's Mediumship, is given in the following account, which was published as the statement of a *séance*, in which a gentleman present was suddenly, mysteriously, and unconsciously transferred from the locked circle room of Mr. Guppy's house, to the locked and closed premises of a friend of his, two miles distant. Quite twenty reliable witnesses at the two ends of the line, signed their names to an attestation, one party declaring the gentleman was in their midst at nine o'clock p.m. in a locked room, the key of the only door being in the pocket of one of the company, and the other party witnessing that the same gentleman suddenly made his appearance, at nine o'clock also, in a yard, locked, shut up, and enclosed on every side against the possibility of entrance, except by the locked and barred gate; also, that on that night, *when the rain was pouring*, and the streets were covered with mud, this transfer of a human being, through two miles of space, was made, without leaving one trace of dampness or mud upon his clothing.

The names of the twenty witnesses are those of well-known and respectable persons, but as the gentleman himself would not allow his name to be published in connection with the circumstance, we simply allude to it, without ranging it in the category of the narratives given in this volume; indeed we only reprint thus much of the details because the account which was sent to several London papers for publication, was prefaced by a concise summary of a similar event occurring in the experience of Mrs. Guppy, of which the most exaggerated accounts have been put in circulation.

The following brief statement has been pronounced to be so reliable and accurate by all parties concerned, that we deem it in order to republish it. It must be understood, that it was printed in connection with the narrative of the gentleman before alluded to, in the *New York Sun*, from which we give the following extract:—

"Before entering upon particulars, it is desirable to advert to a somewhat similar circumstance that took place on June 3rd, 1871, upon which occasion Mrs. Guppy, the famous medium, was conveyed instantaneously from her breakfast parlour at Highbury (where she was engaged making up her housekeeping accounts) to a locked room at 61, Lamb's Conduit Street, where she was suddenly found in a state of trance or unconsciousness, upon a table around which ten persons were sitting for the investigation of alleged spiritual phenomena, in the presence of Messrs. Herne and Williams, the widely known professional mediums. A minute and circumstantial report of this event appeared in the current spiritual journals, as well as in several newspapers, attesting, not only her unexpected arrival, but also the fact, amongst many others, that she held in her hand her housekeeping book and pen with the ink still liquid—such report being signed by all present at the *séance* in question—viz., N. Hagger, 46, Moorgate Street; Caroline Edmiston, Beckenham; C. E. Edwards, Kilburn Square, Kilburn; Henry Morris, Mount Trafford Eccles, near Manchester; Elizabeth Guppy, 1, Morland Villas, Highbury Hill Park, N.; Ernest Edwards, Kilburn Square, Kilburn; Henry Clifford Smith, 38, Ennis Road, Stroud Green; H. B. Husk, 26, Sandwich Street, W.C.; Charles E. Williams, 61, Lamb's Conduit Street; W.C.; F. Herne, 61, Lamb's Conduit Street, W.C.; W. H. Harrison, Wilmin Villa, Chaucer Road, S.E. Three members of this party (as a deputation), to fully test the circumstance and to prevent collusion, escorted Mrs. Guppy home, and took the testimony of Mr. Guppy and Miss Neyland to the fact of Mrs. Guppy's presence in her home at Highbury, immediately preceding her appearance at Lamb's Conduit Street."

In this case it must be borne in mind that Mr. Guppy—a gentleman of unquestionable probity—his housekeeper, and Mrs. Guppy's maid, testified to her presence in her house at Highbury about half-past eight in the evening, and at or about the same time, ten persons sitting in a third floor room, locked and bolted, in Lamb's Conduit Street, a distance of at least four miles, holding a dark circle, with the window closed, the one door locked, and the key in the pocket of one of the sitters, hearing a sudden noise on the table—struck a light, and found Mrs. Guppy in a state of partial consciousness, arrayed in a loose morning gown, housekeeping book in hand, sitting in their midst, on the table.

Let it be noted also, that the whole of the witnesses were credible, respectable persons, and though their testimony was received with the fool's argument of ridicule, and bald denial, it was of a reliable character, and from persons whose witness thus given, would have been received in any court of judicature as undeniable.

The next and last account we can give of Mrs. Guppy's Mediumship is one published by Miss Houghton in her "Record of Spirit Séances," and confirms numbers of other and similar statements made by Professors Wallace, Varley, Serjeant Cox, the late King Victor Emanuel of Italy, General Garibaldi, Prince George of Solms, Mr. R. D. Owen, and numerous other notables for whom Mrs. Guppy often sat, and who have freely testified to manifestations occurring in their presence of exactly the same character as the following extract from Miss Houghton's book:—

"In October, 1868, a *séance* was held, at which eighteen persons were present, Miss Nichol being the chief medium. Each of the sitters wished for fruit, the wish being in every instance granted. The following were brought and dropped on the table around which the company sat: A banana, two oranges, a bunch of white grapes, a bunch of black grapes, a cluster of filberts, three walnuts, a dozen damsons, a slice of candied pine apple, three figs, two apples, some almonds, dates, pears, a pomegranate, two greengages, a pile of currants, a lemon, a bunch of raisins, which, as well as the figs and dates, were quite plump, as if they had never been packed, but brought direct from the drying ground. While the wishing was in progress a lady said, 'Why does not some one wish for vegetables, such as a potato or an onion?' and even while she was speaking a potato and an onion fell into her lap."

In recalling the phenomenal personages who between the years 1860 and 1880 have contributed most liberally to the diffusion of Spiritual light and knowledge, it would be ungenerous to omit a notice of Mr. David Duguid, of Glasgow, a young man occupying the humble position of an industrious mechanic, and one whose limited means of education entirely precluded the expectation of an exhibition of his powers in the direction of the fine arts. The following account however, furnished to the London *Spiritual Magazine* by Mr. Benjamin Coleman, one of the most persevering as well as dis-interested observers of Spiritual phenomena, will give a fair illustration of the modes by which Spirit influence can evolve latent faculties and cultivate unknown germs of talent, even from the most unpromising sources.

In the *Spiritual Magazine* of June, 1866, Mr. Coleman writes :—

"There are several other mediums in Glasgow, one among them, Mr. David Duguid, a working cabinet-maker, is likely to be distinguished as a drawing medium. One very remarkable and interesting fact connected with this young man it is my purpose to relate, which I do upon the authority of Mr. H. Nisbet and Mr. James Nicholson, with whom I had the pleasure of becoming acquainted whilst in Glasgow.

"After David had been recognised as a medium for the ordinary manifestations, he developed as a drawing medium, but made little progress at first without the aid of a young lady who formed one of the circle. When she placed her hand on the back of his, it would move with great facility, and at this stage his *left hand only* was used.

"At the third sitting David became entranced with his eyes shut before commencing to draw. At each succeeding *séance* his powers increased as the trance condition became more intense, and his eyes more firmly closed.

"The objects usually drawn at first were human heads and flowers; but, when a certain proficiency was obtained, flowers, fruits, and a rough landscape were done in colours, the pencils and brushes being now taken in his right hand.

"At the fifth sitting, a remarkable painting in water-colours was commenced and finished, representing the entrance to an arcade, the archway being surmounted by the figure of Justice, standing upon a globe, around which a serpent is coiled, with the figures on either side of Hope and Charity. These figures are very masterly in concep-tion. The interior of the arcade is panelled with niches, in which figures and vases of flowers are placed. The floor is carpeted, and at the extreme end there is a rotunda, in the centre of which a cross is placed. The picture is a transparency, and, when held up to the light the cross dissolves into a throne, upon which a figure is seated with a halo of glory surrounding the head, supported by twelve figures, six on each side. *Those present were anxious to know the name of the artist, but he declined for the present to satisfy them, giving as a reason that he would ultimately give them the means of establishing his identity.* Subsequently, they were told that he was an artist of celebrity, who had lived in the seventeenth century; that he was born in 1635, and died in 1681; and that he was con-temporary with Steen, the celebrated Dutch painter; that he had not been accustomed to paint figures, but that his delight had been to represent Nature, and that he would attempt at their next sitting a sketch of one of his paintings—his masterpiece.

"Accordingly, on the evening of the 18th of April the promised sketch was pencilled out, and on the 21st it was finished in water-colours, in the short period of four hours, and in the left hand corner the initials "J. R." were placed. This painting is considered a very able production.

"Up to this time, none of the party had the least idea of the name of the spirit-artist, and their curiosity was unsatisfied until Mr. Logan brought an artist friend to see the picture, who was much struck with it, and said he was sure he had seen the painting somewhere, though he could not at the moment name the painter.

"A day or two after, Mr. Logan's friend informed him that he had made the desired discovery, and showed Mr. Logan a volume of Cassell's *Art Treasures' Exhibition*, where, at page 301, there is an engraving, nearly *fac simile* of the spirit drawing, from a painting of 'The Waterfalls,' by Jacob Ruysdael, acknowledged to be his *chef d'œuvre.*

"This circumstance was communicated to the persons forming the circle ; but they determined to keep the medium in ignorance of the fact, being satisfied that in his normal condition he knew nothing of it.

"At the next sitting, on the 28th April, David became deeply entranced, and after the usual short conversation between him and the spirit-artist, the latter spoke through the medium, and informed the company that he was aware of the discovery they had made 'that his name was Ruysdael.' They then placed before the medium Cassell's volume, which also contains a portrait of the painter, and invited the spirit's inspection of it. The spirit remarked that the engraving of the picture was a good copy, and the likeness tolerable when at the age of thirty. They then pointed the spirit's attention to the absence of figures in the new drawing which were in the original. The spirit replied, 'That the figures in his paintings were not by himself. but were put in by an artist friend !' which, upon reference to a biography of Ruysdael, they found to be correct.

"It remains to be stated that Mr. David Duguid, the medium, has no knowledge whatever of drawing, and that he is, as I have already said, a plain working man ; that the drawing was executed in the presence of several persons, including those I have named, in four hours, whilst the medium's eyes were fast closed ; and, further to satisfy the scepticism of some of those present, there was a bandage put over them during part of the time. The medium declares that he had no knowledge of the existence of Ruysdael's picture, nor that such an artist had ever lived, and there is no reason to doubt his asseverations."

For the satisfaction of those who deem that the impelling motive with humanity in general, and Spirit Mediums in particular, is "the greed of gain," and the desire "to make capital" out of the world's interest in Spiritual phenomena, we must here state, that David Duguid, although pursuing steadily the cultivation of his mediumship for many years—up to the time indeed of this present writing—has never done so professionally, but still lives by his mechanical labours, following out his simple unosten tatious career, producing in the brief leisure hours he can afford to give to his mediumship, hundreds of paintings, drawings, and sketches, some of rare merit and others more indifferently executed, but all without the slightest attempt to convert his extraordinary gift to the same means of compensa- tion, which would be freely accorded to any other form of artistic production.

We shall conclude this brief notice of our excellent and self-sacrificing Medium's career, with the following short excerpt, the nature of which speaks for itself. It is taken from *The North British Daily Mail* (Glasgow) of March, 1870, and reads thus :—

"So much has been said and done lately regarding 'the exposure of Spiritualism,' that a few notes may be of interest as to what the writer witnessed the other night at a private *séance* given by Mr. David Duguid. This gentleman was comparatively unknown until publicly challenged by Mr. Bishop during his recent 'exposure of Spiritualism.' Mr. Duguid has never courted publicity, but at the same time he has always been very willing to give every information regarding his manifestations. The *séance* took place in his parlour, and was attended by ten gentlemen, five of whom were rank heretics regarding all Spiritualistic phenomena. Immediately on Mr. Duguid taking his seat at a small table he went into a trance condition, his eyes closing and a smile playing on his counte- nance. A piece of cardboard, about six inches by nine inches, which had been previously examined by the company, was then handed to him. After breathing on it Mr. Duguid made a rough pencil sketch, and then picking up his palette and brushes commenced to paint a landscape with his eyes firmly sealed. To make assurance doubly sure, a hand- kerchief was firmly bound across his eyes, but he did not appear to be the least incon- venienced by this arrangement, and painted away quite briskly, first rubbing in the sky, and then the faint outline of the distant mountains ; and finally boldly dashing in the foreground with a few vigorous strokes. At the suggestion of a gentleman present the light was put out, but this made no difference, the action of the brushes being quite audible in the darkness. After the expiry of half an hour the sketch was complete, and was a most remarkable picture to be produced under such peculiar conditions. What in

Spiritualistic circles is called a 'direct drawing' was then attempted. A common card, coated with iodine, was placed on the table before Mr. Duguid, whose hands and feet were firmly secured with silk handkerchiefs. The gas was turned off, and the company, joining hands, sang the 100th Psalm. After the lapse of about five minutes a rap was heard on the table, and on the gas being lit Mr. Duguid was found sitting as firmly bound as before, and on turning up the card on the table, a nice little miniature landscape was observed, the colours being quite wet and newly painted. Without attempting to give an opinion or explain how such manifestations could be accomplished, we simply narrate the circumstances of the *séance* as they occurred."

Besides the remarkably-endowed Mediums above mentioned, a large number of ladies and gentlemen moving in various distinguished circles of Great Britain have manifested extraordinary spiritual gifts and exercised them freely, in a non-professional way, for the benefit of their friends and acquaintances. Medium power indeed has been exhibited in every class of society throughout the United Kingdom, and for some years it would have been impossible to visit any town or hamlet, without discovering way-marks of Spiritual power in the form of healings, trance speaking, Spirit drawing, writing, seership, or physical force manifestations.

Besides the large number of private Mediums, of whose gifts we are not privileged to speak, except in these general terms, there are a great many excellent and disinterested labourers in the Spiritual vineyard, who *give* their services to the public in the capacity of clairvoyants, and trance speakers. Very few of these persons will receive compensation for their services, and many of them—especially in the North of England—voluntarily travel from place to place each Sabbath day, incurring a vast amount of fatigue and freely bestowing time and service, for the purpose of dis- seminating the glad tidings of Spiritualism, to all who will come to hear them. Throughout the large and thickly-populated districts of Yorkshire, Lancashire, Durham, and Northumberland, scores of these self-sacrificing missionaries may be found. Many of them are miners, pit men, weavers and factory hands, who, notwithstanding the unceasing toils of the week, cheerfully devote themselves to the duties of the Spiritual rostrum on the Sunday; and though they are simply "children of the people," and wholly untrained to such work, their rude natural eloquence, heightened by the afflatus of the spirit intelligences that speak through their lips, produces a much deeper influence upon audiences of their own class, than the metaphysical arguments of more polished speakers could do. The very fact too, that wholly uneducated men and women can give correct diagnoses of disease, make cures that the medical faculty could never succeed in, and pour forth moving strains of exalted eloquence, far in advance of their normal capacity, clearly proves the control of some outside power, and brings conviction to many minds, that could not be reached by all the subtle logic of well-trained orators.

We are not pleading in this category either for the expediency of non- professional Mediumship, or advising the exercise of inspirational powers upon the public rostrum, which are liable to be marred in transmission through illiterate channels, but in reporting the status of Spiritualism as it really exists, we should omit one of the most important factors in Spiritual progress amongst the rank and file of society, if we failed to render justice to the self-devoted labourers who throughout England, but especially in the North, have for years rendered invaluable services as healers and speakers, with few to thank, and none to compensate them, save the consciousness of the good they have performed, and the approbation of the angels whose servants they are. If any readers are curious to learn who these self-sacrificing individuals are, let them turn to the plan of speakers for the Yorkshire districts as advertised in the *Medium and Daybreak*, the reports from the Lancashire, Durham, and Northumberland towns and mining districts, together with a few reports from the South and West, and they will there find a list of humble names recorded, whose place will surely be found, in the day when the MASTER OF LIFE "numbers up his jewels."

Before quitting the subject of non-professional Mediumship in England, we must call attention to the inestimable services rendered in higher and more influential grades of society than those above named—in fact, amongst the most distinguished and aristocratic circles of the metropolis—by Mrs. Everitt, a lady of independent position now residing at Hendon, formerly of Islington, London. Mrs. Everitt's Mediumship has been distinguished by the variety and intellectual character, no less than the force of the manifestations given in her presence. Besides loud rappings and the movement of heavy bodies which have been brought through closed doors and carried hither and thither in broad light, often *without human contact*, Mrs. Everitt is a remarkable Medium for the production of the direct Spirit voice, and writings executed in the most minute form of caligraphy, in an almost incredibly short period of time. The illustration (given on another page) of these spirit writings, purported to come from Dr. Burns, a clergyman of London, and one eminent alike for his noble character, his eloquence as a preacher, and the fearless candour with which he avowed his belief in Spirit communion. Dr. Burns granted the use of his Church to Dr. Newton for the purpose of practising therein his marvellous gift of healing. He attended several of Mrs. Everitt's circles; publicly expressed his entire belief in their supra-mundane character, and after passing into spirit life, returned to those circles, to add his testimony as a spirit, to that which he had borne on earth as a mortal. The writing, of which a facsimile is given, was produced *in nine seconds* upon a piece of marked paper—in the presence of some ten witnesses—honoured guests of Mr. and Mrs. Everitt.

Mr. Everitt has in his possession hundreds of similar writings—most of them produced under the most crucial test conditions. The writing here exemplified was produced by the Spirit of one well known to the parties present, and is of a thoroughly characteristic style.

Sometimes the house in which the *séances* were in session has been shaken as in an earthquake. On other occasions the circle room has been filled with delicious perfumes or strong currents of air.

The intelligence rendered by the direct writings, no less than the Spirit voices conversing with the company, is for the most part of a religious or moral character. The writings have not unfrequently been given in Greek, Latin, and Oriental languages, all of which are totally unknown to Mrs. Everitt. As an example of the preternatural mode in which these writings are produced, the following incident may be narrated. At a *séance* held in a semi-darkened drawing-room, with closed doors, and a company of some twenty persons assembled, a very large and splendidly illustrated book with paper covers, suddenly fluttered down from the ceiling and dropped in view of all present on the table in their midst.

The book had been kept for many previous months in a locked drawer, in a room above that wherein it now appeared, and no human being at that time, *could* have had access to the place from which it was taken.

This book was passed round amongst the company, of whom the author was one, and the illustrations being very fine, it was examined with so much

My dear very dear friends, I greet you on exceeding pleasure and great happiness to meet you here this evening. You are advocates of truth so am I and always have been. I earnestly sought for this one great truth and was willing to pay toil for the truth must be bought, and in never gained except as a sacrifice I have now proved that great truth and here I am able to commune again with those beloved friends who still live on the earth sphere do not think you friends who have stayed over are far away from you no we really are nearer to you because you know now the conditions we given, a clever even with us the early road friend of mine that in spiritual union that it is possible for man to hold eternal with the deported in the one great truth I have refused to what I have found it I wish alone it when you have found it be no only enough to prove what you believe to be true it not such happiness great will denied to proves it herewith a redeemed kingdom that spiritual kingdom which cortege to prove it the kingdom of heaven is a redeemed kingdom looking upon the souls quietly and gently as the clear on the light of heaven whose island movement does not the sleeping dispensing the darkness of the night it comes with such gentleness that it does not disturb the sleeping of the infant the light upraiseth spiritual light must have this nackros loudness and gentleness I live glad my friend do trust I am able to come forward a witness to the great truth

your brethren and fellow laborer

L. Browning

attention by all parties present, that not a leaf could have escaped observation. Whilst the visitors were commenting on the astonishing though by no means unprecedented manner in which this manifestation had occurred, the Spirits spelled out by rappings the request that the lights should be put out. This was promptly done, but in less than twenty seconds another well-known signal was given for the restoration of the lights. Deeming that some preliminary had been forgotten which the Spirits wished attended to, the chandelier was hurriedly relighted, when it was found that the margins of two leaves, at the place where the book was lying open, were covered with very fine pencilled writing. On further examination, it appeared that over twenty of the leaves were similarly marked, thus making in all, nearly three hundred words inscribed upon paper, that, sixteen seconds previously, had been proved to be entirely blank.

It must be added, that although Mr. and Mrs. Everitt's position in the social scale placed them on an equality with all their guests, this excellent lady has ever cheerfully submitted to the most *exigéant* demand for tests, and furnished opportunities for thorough and searching investigation as gracefully, as if she had been a professional medium, or had not been in her own estimable character beyond all possibility of doubt or suspicion. For many years she devoted her varied gifts to the service of her friends, and such guests as could obtain an introduction to her delightful *séances.* Here the noble, the scientific, and the learned, no less than the plain, untitled citizen, were freely welcomed, and ever hospitably entertained by the master and mistress of the mansion, and the author is in a position to affirm, that *thousands* of persons in this generation, owe their assurances of immortality, and their happiest hours of pure communion with blessed ascended ones, to the inimitable gifts of Mrs. Everitt, and the genial hospitality of her noble husband.

Mrs. Everitt was also a seeress, and could readily receive impressions by mental telegraphy, from her friends.

The author has often exchanged messages with this lady, when separated by miles of distance, such messages being invariably found subsequently to be correct. In Mr. Everitt, the cause of Spiritualism has found an equally indefatigable and able champion, Mr. Everitt's eloquent expositions of Spiritualism upon every available opportunity having attracted large audiences, and respectful consideration, whenever presented.

If we speak somewhat in the past tense of Mr. and Mrs. Everitt, it is not because their devotion to the cause of Spiritualism has waned, or the lady's Spiritual gifts have failed, but in the retirement of the family from the busy metropolis to the seclusion of a suburban residence, the opportunities for the exercise of Mediumship to all comers, have necessarily become very infrequent, and it is now only in the family circle and its immediate visitors, that Mrs. Everitt's charming phases of mediumship can be witnessed.

We shall now direct the reader's attention to another wonderful display of Sibylline power manifested in the family of Mr. Bertolacci, a gentleman too well known and esteemed by his wide circle of friends, to incur the slightest shadow of suspicion, either in respect to the disinterestedness of his motives, or the truth of his statements. As Mr. Bertolacci was very free in placing the Mediumistic power of his family at the service of numerous credible witnesses, his testimony is susceptible of full verification in every particular.

After eleven years of astounding and continuous demonstrations of Spirit power, Mr. Bertolacci — at the instance of his friends and numerous interested witnesses,—consented to embody his experiences in a small volume, which—in deference to his devoted adherence to the tenets of the Christian religion, or, it may be assumed, as a line of demarcation between himself and less orthodox believers in Spirit communion—he entitled as follows :—*Christian Spiritualism : Wherein is shewn the Extension of the Human Faculties by the Application of Modern Spiritual Phenomena, according to the Doctrine of Christ.* By William Robert Bertolacci.— Published by Emily Faithfull.

The following extracts are taken from a fine analytical review of Mr. Bertolacci's work by Mr. Thomas Shorter, the learned author of "The Two Worlds," editor of the London *Spiritual Magazine*, &c., &c. Mr. Shorter introduces his subject in these words :—

"The experiences of M. Bertolacci extend over a period of eleven years, and this little volume must be regarded as only a synopsis or sample rather than a complete and elaborate history of them. Previously thereto, M. Bertolacci was, he informs us, a 'complete dis-believer in all miracles,' and he adopted the popular talk of 'laws of nature,' 'priest-craft,' and 'weak-minded credulity,' as all-sufficient to explain them. Under the influence of these derided manifestations this unhappy attribute and tone of mind has become changed to one of earnest and devout Christian assurance, as this book sufficiently evinces. But to come to the facts. M. Bertolacci says :—

"'We have produced most of the manifestations witnessed in other circles, such as table-turnings, and tiltings, raps and many sorts of sounds in different parts of the house. Tables and other objects have been raised from the ground without contact ; and have, when in the air, resisted the efforts of a strong man to force them down again. Tables have been made to adhere so fixedly to the ground as to resist every endeavour to raise them ; and in more than one instance, when five or six persons have combined their whole strength, the wooden top, fixed on with strong screws, has been wrenched completely off, while the light framework and legs have remained adhering to the ground ; whereas these, immediately after, have risen quietly up into the air without being touched on being told to do so. Clocks have passed the hour without striking it on being told not to do so.

. . . .

"'In one circumstance, we obtained direct writing by placing a clean sheet of paper in a drawer overnight, the drawer and room being locked and secured, so that no one could obtain access to them. The next morning, was found written on the paper, as had been foretold through the planchette, "*Christ soit avec vous*," "Christ be with you.'"

"The raps on the table being too slow a process for communicating information, the use of the planchette had been indicated.

"By means of the planchette the author has thus obtained some 1,200 or 1,400 pages of manuscript in English and French, including a work of 500 or 600 pages, explanatory of phenomena of which these writings form a part.

"The *séances* have not been confined to physical manifestations, such as have been already named, nor has the attendance at them been limited to M. Bertolacci and his family ; intimate friends were at first admitted, and these introduced others, and the attendance so increased that after a short time it became requisite to appoint reception days, and on these occasions to hold both morning and evening meetings. These witnesses are, therefore, additional evidence to the facts certified by M. Bertolacci.

"The proceedings of the *séances* were regulated by the planchette writing ; and we learn that—

"'If among those present any one was ailing, or in a state of ill-health, they were generally singled out, and desired to come to the table. When there, they would often be told what their sufferings were, how long they had been ill, &c., although no previous mention had been made of the subject, and while under the surprise which these unex-pected communications generally created, they would be told that if they had faith in Christ they should be cured, which was, in several instances, realized immediately.

"'At other times, the *séance* would begin by first one person and then another being selected among the company, and each in their turn being conversed with by means of the planchette-writing. Then, to the astonishment of many present, persons appearing amongst us for the first time would be called by their Christian names, and others by their familiar nicknames, telling them their peculiarities of disposition, their favourite pursuits, and their thoughts at the very moment. It has constantly occurred that at the very time this was going on, the table on which the planchette was writing would be seen to rise into the air, all its four legs being a foot or more from the ground.' . . .

MRS EVERETT.

"Contagious maladies, and even the action of poison, have been arrested, and organic disease successfully treated. The following is an instance :—

"'At one of our receptions, a Madame G——a, of Pontoise, was, by appointment, introduced by mutual friends. The assembly was very numerous—some twenty persons being present. Madame G——a had, for eleven months previous, lost the use of her legs from a paralysis which extended from her waist downwards, resulting from a premature confinement. It was with difficulty she could move about on crutches upon very even ground, and she had to be carried from the carriage which had conveyed her from the railway station to our reception room on the first floor, in the arms of her friends.

"'The *séance* was a very animated one. Many wonderful things occurred ; the planchette had written at once under the hands of persons who had never witnessed anything of the sort before, &c., &c. Madame G——a was then selected, and during fifteen or twenty minutes, she had it all to herself, much in the same way as it occurred with Mrs. K——d previously to her being cured. Many tears were shed by Madame G——a, who was deeply affected by the words of kind and gentle sympathy and of encouraging hope addressed to her by the sublimely inspired phrases written under the planchette. While this was going on, the rest of the company were conversing quietly among themselves in undertones. Then, all present being desired to give their whole attention, we were exhorted to join our hearts in an act of inward and fervent communion, and implore God to show His mercy upon our suffering sister. During the total silence which ensued, a short and impressive prayer was rapidly written under the planchette, which was read aloud, then the Spirit through the planchette, addressing Madame G——a, wrote, " *Do you believe in Christ's invariable goodness and power ?* " to which she answered, " *Yes, truly I do.* " While she was answering, the planchette was writing, " *Then stand upright !* " As though recollecting her weakness, for a moment she seemed to look round for assistance, and at the same instant the words, " *Alone in Jesus Christ's name !* " were written with such rapidity, that they seemed as if they had been struck off upon the paper ; and they had not time to be read, when Madame G——a sprang on her feet, and she was no longer a paralytic. She was then told to walk up and down the room, which feat she accomplished with unhesitating firmness and perfect ease, and was after that sent downstairs to walk, accompanied, but unassisted, by my wife, for five minutes round the garden, where she was all the time in full view of the company assembled on the balcony and clustered round the windows ; and having come up again, she expressed her gratitude towards God for the mercy she had received, amidst the congratulations of all parties, who by that time had begun to be sufficiently recovered from their first surprise to reflect upon and appreciate the miracle which had been performed. We resumed our places. A thanksgiving to God was written through the planchette, and an hour afterwards, Madame G——a's carriage having been previously discarded, she returned with the rest of the company, going on foot to the railway station, about a mile from our house, and was perfectly cured of her paralysis.'*

"Surgical cases were treated in like manner and with like results. M. Bertolacci says :—

"'When any of my girls cut themselves or met with any other accident, such as bruises, sprains, &c., not only is all pain immediately taken away, but indeed the healing is almost as rapid. One day, one of them, in cutting a loaf of bread, gave herself a deep gash across the left hand, an inch long. The blood was flowing very copiously and had quite wetted a towel, which she had wrapped round it, through and through many folds, by the time she came to me, though she lost no time, however, in so doing. The towel was taken off, and I held the lips of the wound together, while those present joined us, during eight or ten seconds, in communion, the name of Jesus Christ having been invoked. The blood ceased to flow, and the wound was closed. Not more than four hours afterwards, some friends having come to pass the evening with us, she played several long pieces on the pianoforte, and had totally forgotten that she had cut herself in the day. Nevertheless, the wound was sufficiently severe to leave a scar still very plainly to be seen, although it is now somewhere about seven years since the accident occurred. On another occasion since that, one of her sisters cut the top of her thumb from one side to the other, down to the very bone, and was cured in the same manner, as completely and as instantaneously.

"'I have mentioned these two cases in particular to give my reader a notion of the efficacy of the cures ; but, indeed, it is almost of daily occurrence with us, either for one thing or the other—a cut, a bruise, and the blistering of an arm from the effects of a poisonous plant, having, the very day on which I write this narration, been cured, each in the space of eight seconds. A few days back, it was a hand and wrist which had been

---

* Compare this case with the analagous and equally remarkable one of Miss Fancourt, as given in Brevior's "Two Worlds,' pp. 230-235.

pretty smartly scalded with boiling water. Toothaches and caries are as effectually stopped, even to the destroying of the nerve, in order to obviate any recurrence of the pain from extraneous causes. On one occasion, when the request was made that the nerve should be destroyed, the most complete insensibility immediately succeeded; but we were told, that as the tooth was only slightly attacked, if it were stopped within a few days, in order to keep the air and moisture from it, it would be preserved; but that, if that were not done, in ten days it would begin to fall to pieces. It was *not* done, and on the tenth day, a large portion of the tooth fell off, and, in a very few days more, nothing but the bare root was left, which, however, was very easily extracted without occasioning the least pain.'

"There can be no mistake about cases like these, the facts are recent, and are published to the world; the witnesses are living, and well known as persons of credit and integrity. The faculty and the press may ignore or deny the facts; from their antecedents it may be expected that they will do so; but this, though it should affect their own credit, will not affect the facts, which are neither made nor destroyed by the opinions which may be formed about them.

"We omit, from want of space, the magnetic and clairvoyant phenomena related, but the spiritual education of his family, as M. Bertolacci relates it, is something so unique that notwithstanding our already copious extracts we quote it *in extenso*. After a chapter on 'Initiation,' he proceeds :—

"'With this foundation to work upon, and confiding in the revelations and spiritual guidance by which we had already attained the degree of spiritual strength shewn in the preceding narration, I boldly withdrew my two younger daughters from the school they daily attended; and in spite of the opposition and common-place arguments of other parties, began their new mode of education in the manner indicated by our invisible spiritual conductor, which was pursued much in the following order :—

"' LESSONS WERE LEARNT BY HEART BY READING TO MY STUDENTS IN THEIR MAGNETIC SLEEP, ORDERING them to retain in their memory when they awoke, all they had heard. Lessons were next LEARNT BY HEART BY THE PUPILS READING, THEMSELVES, once over, in their MAGNETIC SLEEP, one or more pages of a book. When this began to become familiar, and the organs of memory showed that they were in a fit state of rapid obedience, the action of the organs of outward perception upon the memory was submitted to the strong developing power of the soul's direct influence, and lessons were LEARNT BY THE SIMPLE INSPECTION OF (or staring at) THE OPEN PAGE OF A BOOK,—THE STUDENTS BEING IN THEIR NORMAL WAKING STATE. In the beginning, the inspection, or staring, was made to last a certain number of seconds, and that number being gradually reduced, after a short space of time, the duration of a single second or a mere glimpse at the page was sufficient for the pupils to retain in their memory the whole contents of it.

"' In this manner and in the following, the daily lessons of my children, equal at times to a week's corresponding school tasks, were learnt in the space of a few seconds; lessons that take hours to interrogate them upon, with any degree of detail. LESSONS are ALSO LEARNT BY A SIMPLE ACT OF PIOUS CONCENTRATION FROM BOOKS CLOSED OR TOTALLY OUT OF SIGHT. In this case, we have usually named the page where the beginning of the lesson is to be found, for we have, as yet, had recourse to the process less as a matter of immediate utility than as a practice of the powers of distant clairvoyance. It will be easily conceived that by a slight extension of this faculty, or rather by the special direction being given to it, it may be applied to obtain references from, and even the perfect knowledge of, works one does not oneself possess, but which are known to exist in certain libraries and other places, rendered either by their distance, our own want of time or otherwise, inaccessible to us.

"' DICTATION.

"' DICTATIONS were given by the TEACHER READING FROM A BOOK IN THE ORDINARY MANNER; BUT WITHOUT NAMING THE STOPS OR ANY OF THE OTHER SIGNS, these being seen by the students through their pre-acquired clairvoyant capacities, the phrases becoming visible to them as soon as they are dictated. THE MENTAL DICTATIONS.—In this case the pupils are made acquainted—*by the knowledge of their " inner man," and the perfected obedience of the organs of their " outer man,"* with the contents of the page held open in a position visible alone to the eyes of the teacher—and as the latter desires to communicate a phrase to the pupils, they hear a voice dictating it aloud to them in the air, although no person is speaking at the time.

"' HISTORY.

"' THE DIRECT CLAIRVOYANCE gives the student a correct sight, WITH REGARD TO THE HISTORICAL PERSONS AND FACTS treated of in the lessons learnt by the inspection of books, either open, closed, or at a distance—as explained in the foregoing.

"'NATURAL HISTORY AND PHILOSOPHY.

"'THE SIGHT OF THE PLANTS, FLOWERS, MINERALS, ANIMALS, &c., described or mentioned in their books, as also such other useful details as may have been omitted by the author, or belong to a more minute study of the subject, is enjoyed in the same manner.

"'GEOGRAPHY AND ASTRONOMY.

"'GEOGRAPHICAL AND ASTRONOMICAL STUDIES FROM CHARTS OR GLOBES.—When a locality is named by the teacher, or is to be designated for any purpose in the course of study, the forefinger of the pupil is, *by inspiration*, instantaneously drawn to the exact spot of the map or globe where it is to be found. This action takes place before the reason of the students can have given them the slightest notion of the relative position or bearing of the place, the head following the movement of the hand, instead of directing it. THE STUDENTS ARE ALSO, BY THE FACILITY THEY ACQUIRE FOR RECEIVING INSPIRATIONS, SO PERFECTLY IDENTIFIED WITH EVERYTHING BELONGING TO THE PLACES SPOKEN OF IN THEIR STUDY OF GEOGRAPHY, THAT THEY FEEL AS THOUGH THEY WERE ON THE SPOT. So correct are the impressions made by the ubiquitous power of their souls on all the organs of the body in their temporarily perfected condition, that they appear to themselves to be, not where the lessons are going on, but in the very places therein referred to ; seeing, hearing, and feeling all that they are required or desirous to see, hear, or feel.'

"M. Bertolacci has written in a tone of moderation and a religious spirit ; and he disclaims all idea 'that there is any peculiarity in his nature or that of his children, by which they are exceptionally qualified for the attainment of the gifts they have received.' "*

Whilst no persons who have ever become acquainted with Mr. Bertolacci, or conversed with his witnesses—of whom hundreds are still living—are capable of questioning his veracity or impugning his statements, we know we are drawing heavily on the faith of those readers who are not personally cognizant of the overwhelming mass of testimony which surrounds the case and its narration.

Perhaps in future ages, the substance of what we are now so reticent in offering to the acceptance of modern readers may be deemed trivial or insignificant, in comparison with the soul growth to which humanity may have then attained—meantime, where does our duty lie ? Why, even in turning to the motto of this volume, and accepting practically as well as theoretically the charge to proclaim "THE TRUTH AGAINST THE WORLD."

—

CHAPTER XXII.

SPIRITUALISM IN GREAT BRITAIN (CONTINUED).

BESIDES the merely phenomenal phases of Spiritualism illustrated by the narratives given in the last few chapters, THE MESSAGE which relates to the conditions of life hereafter, and the religious element which grows out of Spiritual communion, has not been lacking in its full share of representation, in England, although there was a strong desire manifested on the part of some of those who stood in the position of "Leaders" in the ranks of English Spiritualism, to keep all questions of a religious and controversial nature in the background.

The author's experience has ever been in this, as in all other departments of human thought and interests, when connected with Spiritualism, that Spirits themselves are at the helm of the new movement, and with or without the sympathy of mortals, they will raise up instruments, and create

* This review may be found in full in the London *Spiritual Magazine* for October, 1865.

opportunities for the impartation of whatever ideas they may determine to communicate. Thus it was, that whilst certain believers in Spirit communion, who were still steadfast in their adhesion to the Christian Church, and its belongings, were constantly deprecating the attempt to incorporate religious ideas with Spiritualism, and protesting—often in no measured terms—against the "infidelities" of the American trance speakers, the Spirits on the other side of the Atlantic were opening up opportunities, and presenting impelling motives to those very speakers, to visit the mother country, and widen the borders of Spiritualism from its conservative position in private families, to the more diffusive arena of the public rostrum.

It has been quite a common practice amongst many European Spiritualists, to endeavour to narrow down the diffusion of Spiritualism to the private circle, or the perusal of such "well digested" literature, as was specially prepared to warn *preaching Spirits* off the sacred preserves of orthodoxy.

All would not do however. The stream whose sources are not on earth, has made its own channels, and swept away all barriers that intervened to check the course laid out for its flow, by higher wisdom than that of humanity.

It was under this special guidance, and in virtue of her commission from a well-tried band of Spiritual guides that the author—a Medium for many phases of Spirit communion, but chiefly recognised as a speaker under Spiritual influence, was impelled after many years' pilgrimage in the New World to return, with her venerable mother, to settle once more in her native city of London. Mrs. Hardinge* reached England in the fall of the year 1865, a period that may truly be called, the blossoming time of Spiritualism in Great Britain. Her intention was to retire from her long and toilsome career as a public speaker into the quiet of home and literary occupations, but her arrival had been already anticipated by generous notices in the London *Spiritual Magazine*, and immediately on landing, she found herself surrounded by hosts of warm sympathizers, who although strangers—in the ordinary sense of social relations—were still one in heart with the new comer, in the desire to promote the interests of a much loved cause. It was in this spirit that Mrs. Hardinge, soon after her arrival in London, found herself compelled to abandon her projected seclusion, and once more to enter upon the vortex of effort to promulgate the truths of Spiritualism, by means of rostrum addresses.

Early in the winter succeeding Mrs. Hardinge's arrival, a series of "winter soirées" were inaugurated, chiefly at the instance of Mr. Benjamin Coleman, Mr. William Wilkinson, Mr. Thomas Shorter, and other leaders of the Spiritual cause, interested in the promulgation of its philosophy.

The scene of these gatherings was the Beethoven Rooms, Harley Street, Cavendish Square, where a splendid suite of *salons*, capable of seating several hundred persons was engaged, and where the guests were admitted in evening costume, by subscription tickets, or introductions permitted by the Committee.

The company included many persons of the highest rank or eminence in literature and science, and at these gatherings Mrs. Hardinge gave weekly addresses in her capacity as an inspirational speaker during a period of many months.

The subjects of the lectures were most generally selected by the audience, and questions on all manner of abstruse, scientific, and metaphysical points, were answered at the close of the addresses.

---

* Now Mrs. Hardinge Britten.

The proceedings were received with tokens of the highest interest, and at the close of each series announced, Mrs. Hardinge was induced to renew her lectures, at the earnest solicitation of the friends of the movement.

How gladly the chief promoters of these meetings welcomed the opportunity of extending phenomenal Spiritualism into the realms of philosophy and mental science, may be gathered from the glowing accounts that were published from time to time in the London *Spiritual Magazine,* especially the numbers for 1865-6. However gratifying these eulogiums might have been to the speaker, they can find no place here, and are only alluded to in order to mark the deep interest which inspirational addresses awaken, even in the minds of those least disposed to sympathize with the speaker's views, and to show how the cause progressed from phenomenal to intellectual phases of the movement.

During her long and arduous career as a speaker in America, Mrs. Hardinge, having taken special interest in tendering the consoling doctrines of Spiritualism to the masses, was unwilling to narrow down her ministry to the exclusive and aristocratic listeners of the Harley Street soirées. She therefore proposed to her friends, that public meetings of a more general character should be inaugurated, the first to consist of three lectures on "America," to be given in St. James's Hall, the next to enter at once and publicly on the subject of Spiritualism in a course of Sunday evening addresses of the same character as those given at the winter soirées, to which all classes of the public should be admitted. To both these propositions Mrs. Hardinge's Spiritualistic friends lent their willing and generous aid.

The secular lectures were at once undertaken, and called forth even from the London *Times* wonderfully complimentary notices of the lady lecturer and her pretensions ; in fact, as these addresses were totally unconnected with the obnoxious, and all too popular Spiritual *bête noir* of the age, they were received with the most laudatory notices from the press in general ; so enthusiastic indeed was the tone of commendation adopted by the leading journals of the metropolis, that Mr. Benjamin Coleman, a *Machiavelli* of strategy, as well as an indomitable general of strategical forces, collected these reports from the various papers, and published them in pamphlet form for general distribution.

As the very next appearance of Mrs. Emma Hardinge's name in the public journals was an announcement of her Sunday evening *Spiritual* lectures, Mr. Coleman was generally thought to have stolen a march on the secular press, which might have induced them to regret that they had contributed so large a share of advertising to "the Spiritualists' new Pythia," as one of the repentant journals now designated the lady, who but a short time ago had been the subject of unqualified laudation.

Not any longer from the columns of the secular press, but in the London *Spiritual Magazine* came the announcement of the next move on the Spiritual chessboard, which was to the effect that the Sunday evening lectures were attracting such immense and enthusiastic audiences, that they would be continued for an indefinite period, or at least, as long as the speaker could remain in the country to give them.

About this time a valuable impulse was communicated to the Spiritual movement by the publication of a new paper called *The Medium and Day-break*—started by Mr. James Burns, now so well known in connection with this and other periodicals, as well as being the founder of the Spiritual Institution, Southampton Row, Bloomsbury. The assistance which an editor of ability and a devoted Spiritualist like Mr. Burns was able to render, in publishing and distributing Mrs. Hardinge's lectures, can scarcely be estimated. The secular journals had obviously entered into a conspiracy of silence in regard to meetings which were attracting immense and over-flowing audiences every Sunday.

In this juncture Mr. Burns—of whom we shall have more to say here-after—devoted himself heart and soul to the work of publishing the addresses, which were issued, some in the columns of *The Medium*, others in tract and pamphlet form, whilst the Harley Street lectures were collected into small volumes, and distributed broadcast by hundreds, and on special subjects by thousands. By the indomitable energy of Mr. Burns, the press found themselves defeated by their own weapons, and from the time when this spirited publisher commenced in earnest his work of literary propagandism, the movement acquired a diffusive popularity which made a deep mark upon public opinion both in the metropolis and in the provinces.

Hitherto, circumstances had not favoured the dissemination of Spiritual teachings through the platform.

English Spiritualists had been honoured with a visit from the celebrated American inspirational speaker and poet, the Rev. T. L. Harris, known in the Spiritual ranks as "The Medium," through whom was communicated the charming poems entitled, "A Lyric of the Morning Land," and "An Epic of the Starry Heavens."

Unfortunately, Mr. Harris's visit failed to promote any interchange of kindly sentiment between the American and English Spiritualists, the former having incurred Mr. Harris's wrath for refusing to install him into the position of a settled ministry. The results of this disappointment he ex-pressed in his English addresses, wherein his former associates and fellow labourers were so roundly abused, that it was evident to his grieved listeners that the ex-reverend gentleman was afflicted with a very *unspiritual* form of Spiritualism; hence his ministrations served rather to retard than advance the cause in England. Mr. B. P. Randolph, another American Spiritual lecturer, had also essayed the platform, but failed to reconcile his hearers to his marked eccentricities. A far more satisfactory expositor of the Spiritual doctrines had been found in the Rev. J. M. Peebles, formerly an American clergyman, but then a speaker on Spiritualism, whose eloquence created a deep impression on audiences gathered to hear him, on both sides of the Atlantic. At the time of Mr. Peebles' first visit, however, there was no available organization to give effect to his public efforts, hence, however valuable, they were not appreciated as they should have been. On several subsequent occasions Mr. Peebles' platform addresses were listened to with deep interest, and his visits to England welcomed with tokens of high appreciation. Time and circumstances combined to favour the effect of Mrs. Hardinge's advent in London, hence the results of her inaugural meetings were most influential in opening up opportunities for platform work in other directions.

Although Mrs. Hardinge could never reconcile herself to a permanent residence in England, and for the last fifteen years has only revisited the country for limited periods of time, the kind greetings and cordial farewells—often accompanied by substantial tokens of interest—which these flying visits called forth, served to create pleasant "revivalisms," which heightened the effect and popularity of her labours.

One of the most talented of the lecturers that succeeded Mrs. Hardinge during her absence in the United States was Mrs. Cora Tappan, a lady whose high reputation as an able and eloquent expositor of the Spiritual philosophy, stands unrivalled on both sides of the Atlantic.

Mrs. Tappan's lectures were not only pronounced to be miracles of eloquence by the *élite* of the London Spiritualists, but by her efficient missionary labours in the provinces, she succeeded in awakening a widespread interest in Spiritualism throughout the country.

We have already alluded to the remarkable test facts of Spirit presence, afforded by the visit of Mr. Charles Foster, an American medium renowned for exhibiting names of deceased persons, and test facts of Spirit presence, by writings in raised letters, on the arm. Besides this remarkable personage, England was visited by Messrs. Redman, J. B. Conklin, and Colchester, all powerful physical test mediums.

The fact that they were professional mediums and demanded liberal fees for their services, was of course a subject of reproach, which the opposition could not afford to pass by unheeded. Not that the English people are grudging in their dealings, whether in trade, commerce, or art ; but, as we have already noted, the orthodox method of regarding Spiritual gifts as " Divine endowments," which must not be desecrated by association with " filthy lucre," threw an absurd and superstitious glamour over the subject, which exempted it from the ordinary methods of justice and common sense. When this unreasonable spirit was met on its own ground, and mediums, visiting the country from foreign lands, refused to take compensation for their services, rich presents were often pressed upon them in greater prodigality than their services could have commanded as payment, but when set fees were required, the whole community was aroused to the iniquity of making *God-like gifts* the subject of traffic, &c., &c.

We shall devote the remainder of this chapter to a brief notice of another Transatlantic visitor whose reputation for the beneficent use he made of his marvellous powers of healing by touch, had long preceded him ; we speak of Dr. J. R. Newton of Rhode Island, U.S., who arrived in this country for a second visit during the month of May, 1870.

Stimulated by the reports of his many wonderful cures, the leading Spiritualists of London met together at the " Beethoven Rooms," Harley Street, on Thursday, May 12th, to tender to Dr. Newton a cordial welcome in the form of a public reception.

The meeting was not only a representative one, the Spiritualists of eminence from the provinces as well as from the metropolis flocking in from all parts of the country, but those who attended were prompt to bear testimony to the excellent services of their distinguished guest, by relating several incidents in connection with his powers as a healer, the recital of which must serve in this place, as a sample of the good work performed by Dr. Newton during his brief residence in England.

In the course of their several addresses, Messrs. Coleman, Tebb, Shorter, the Rev. J. M. Peebles—who happened to be in England at the time— and Mr. S. C. Hall, gave pointed and interesting delineations of the real status of English Spiritualism at the period in question, and the unpre meditated testimony borne by these gentlemen at a time when their utterances were not given for effect on the outside world, may be received as of more value than any elaborately prepared statements.

Mr. Benjamin Coleman, the chief promoter of the meeting, was unanimously called upon to preside, and the exercises of the evening proceeded as follows. The Chairman, after stating that the object of the meeting was to give Dr. Newton a hearty welcome, closed a pertinent speech on the value of the healing power with the following remarks :—

"In America Dr. Newton stands pre-eminent for his healing powers, as proved by recorded facts spread over the last fourteen years, and many of the cures effected by him were of a very wonderful description. When in New York and Boston, I heard of Dr. Newton's powers in this respect. One gentleman told me of a case where Dr. Newton had restored sight to a blind man, who had been unable to see for seven or eight years previously, and who was cured by Dr. Newton in a few minutes. Dr. Newton only arrived in Liverpool last Saturday, May 7th, and he was asked to go on the following day and see Mr. Ashley, of that town, who had been afflicted with a very serious illness for some time, and Mr. Wason, who is present, has given me the following statement of what took place :—

"'Mr. Ashley resides at 5, Catherine Street, Liverpool. On the 27th December last he was at Oxford and broke a blood-vessel in the lungs. A leading medical man, Mr. Freeborn, was called in, who prepared Mrs. Ashley for the worst, and told her that there was no hope ; that her husband would go off in a rapid consumption, and none could say how soon ; he advised that he should not be removed to Liverpool, as his strength was not equal to the journey. Mrs. Ashley prayed fervently for Divine aid, that she might be comforted and directed according to her trial, feeling assured that her husband would shortly depart—and turning to her Bible, opened it at a venture, and found her finger, she knows not how, on the text in St. John, where Jesus, speaking of Lazarus, says, "This sickness is not unto death, but for the glory of God." From that moment she felt assured that her husband would not die, and she told Dr. Freeborn her strong impressions. Some little time after this Mr. Ashley was removed to Liverpool on a bed fitted up in a railway carriage. For about five months he was confined to his room, no one expecting his recovery except his wife. Once Mr. Gardiner carried him like a child down stairs, and had great difficulty in getting him back, and fears were entertained that he would not recover the shock. Last Saturday, May 7th, Dr. Simmons prepared Mrs. Ashley for the worst, and intimated that the great change might take place at any moment. Last Sunday, the 8th of May, Dr. Newton and myself went in a cab to Mr. Ashley's ; the Doctor went upstairs to Mr. Ashley's sick-room, requesting that none should follow but Mrs. Ashley. In about five or six minutes, Dr. Newton brought Mr. Ashley down stairs, and took him into the open air and said he was cured ; he told him that he could walk a mile and a half, which he urged him to do, and to eat a beefsteak and drink a pint of ale for dinner—although his doctor had fed him on slops for the last five months. Mr. Ashley came to the evening service and stood alone a considerable time, whilst Dr. Newton told the audience of the case, which Mr. Ashley confirmed in all respects. Mr. and Mrs. Ashley gave me this account yesterday (Monday), at their house, after Mr. Ashley had been out, and eaten a mutton chop with pudding and ale, and after a long walk. . . . Previous to Dr. Newton's seeing him, *he had not been out of his bed for five months.*'"

Mr. Coleman then went on to say :—

"I cannot in this short address give one-hundredth part of the cases on record, some of which have taken place very recently. Mr. Watson, who has come over from America with Dr. Newton, told me that he had lost the sight of one eye, in consequence of a piece of steel getting into it by accident ; inflammation set in, and he lost the sight of the other eye. Two years ago his wife was impressed to induce her husband to go with her to Montreal from New York, to visit Dr. Newton. They arrived in Montreal as Dr. Newton was on the point of leaving it, and directly Dr. Newton saw the patient, whose eyes were covered with a bandage, he told him that he would do good to one of them, thereby showing a knowledge that both of them were not in the same state. He then removed the bandage, and said, ' You can see, can't you ?' and although he had only been in the room seven minutes, he found that he could read small print. Mr. Watson is present, and can testify to the truth of these facts.

"In London Dr. Newton will doubtless encounter plenty of opposition ; if he does not succeed the medical profession will call him a sharper, and if he does succeed they will call him a lunatic ; they are sure to say that he is mad, because he has announced his intention not to charge a fee to anybody during his stay in England.

"I do not believe that Dr. Newton will cure everybody, nor indeed half of those who call upon him, but there is no doubt that he can effect very wonderful cures, and that he has a great work to do in this country."

After the reading of a cordial, and scholarly address, from the pen of Mr. Thos. Shorter, that gentleman was called upon to speak, which he did in substance as follows :—

"I had the good fortune to make the personal acquaintance and friendship of Dr. Newton on the occasion of a brief visit he paid to this country in the autumn of 1864. I was then deeply impressed, as I think all who know him must be impressed, with his great simplicity and gentleness of character—his ingenuousness of disposition, singleness of purpose, and entire disinterestedness. I allude to this, not for the purpose of compliment, but because I believe that these qualities of character—this large-heartedness and quick active sympathy has had much to do with the marked success as a healer which Dr. Newton has achieved. On the occasion of that visit, as but little previous notice of it had been given, and it was at the time of year when most of our friends were absent from town, there were but few to meet him and hold out to him the hand of welcome. However, a genuine man with a high sense of duty, and who delights in the execution of a noble mission, is not easily discouraged, and I am glad to find that the untoward circumstances to which I have referred, have not deterred Dr. Newton from repeating his visit under happier auspices, and I hope it will be found with more satisfactory results. During the interval that has elapsed since his first visit the position of Spiritualism in England has changed very much for the better ; public opinion on the subject has grown and ripened ; publications and books devoted to its exposition and advocacy have multiplied ; the platform, too, as well as the press, has been called into requisition— lectures have been delivered, conferences held, Sunday services established, various forms of associative effort instituted, and societies and individuals have been stimulated to its investigation ; and thus conviction has spread, and a better understanding of the subject has been reached ; and to-night, instead of the few friends who welcomed Dr. Newton on his first visit, I am glad to see so goodly an assemblage. I trust that the work which Dr. Newton has begun so well in Liverpool will be continued in London, and that he will be as successful in curing disease in England as he has been in America. Many no doubt will think him mad, but looking at the results of this so-called insanity, I can only hope that it may soon become contagious. . . . . Some four or five years since, when Dr. Newton was in Philadelphia, he was brought before a magistrate on some trumpery charge at the instigation of the doctors. Those whom he had cured, naturally indignant at the treatment of their benefactor, came forward unsolicited to the number it is said of about fifteen hundred, thronging the court and all its avenues, eager to tender their unsought-for evidence of the reality of their cure— these included the cures of blindness, deafness, lameness, paralysis, and other chronic maladies, seemingly incurable. Of course the charge was summarily dismissed. I will refer to one other case nearer home. The Rev. Frederick Rowland Young, pastor of the Free Christian Church, Swindon, was not only a minister of the Gospel, but a believer in the gracious word of the Master, 'The works that I do shall ye do also,' and when evidence was brought before him of the cures wrought by Dr. Newton in America, so strong was his faith, that he crossed the Atlantic to be cured by him. His faith was rewarded by an immediate cure. Not only did he return cured of the neuralgia with which he had been afflicted for many years, and which physicians had been unable to remove, but he himself received through Dr. Newton the gift of healing, which he has freely exercised in his own town and neighbourhood, as well as for the benefit of persons living at a greater distance. Last summer, while at Swindon for a few days, I heard much of these cures, and one case came under my notice of a poor woman who had lost her eyesight for many years who had been cured by Mr. Young by the simple laying on of hands and prayer ; and she was then going about her ordinary household occupations. Whether Dr. Newton will be as successful here as in America I cannot say. When I consider the educated prejudice and indurated scepticism with which he will have to contend, I confess my expectations are greatly moderated. All the more credit to Dr. Newton, who, knowing all this, and in the face of these repellent influences, has ventured again to come amongst us. The least we can do is to acknowledge his great kindness in doing so, and by our sympathy and co-operation to aid him all we can in the great and good work in which he is engaged—the relief of suffering humanity, irrespective of all considerations of sect, party, country, class, or creed."

"Mr. William Tebb said : 'I do not rise to make a speech : there are those here, some of whom have already addressed you, who are accustomed to speak in public assemblies, and I am not. I cannot, however, refrain from expressing my concurrence with the sentiments contained in the address just read, and my satisfaction in seeing so many assembled here this evening to do honour to so distinguished a philanthropist as Dr. Newton. It is related of Faraday, that when he made a new discovery he would show it and explain it to his friends, evincing a delight which they could not always appreciate, and the question was frequently put to him, "What is the use of it?" To which the Professor would reply, "Wait, and we'll find some use for it." Now, this question is frequently put with regard to Spiritualism, and I confess that if it was confined, as many seem to suppose, to the phenomena of raps, table-tipping, and the like, one might be puzzled to answer the question satisfactorily. But when it is shown there is a continuous influx from the spiritual world, which is manifested in all the variety of forms witnessed in the Apostolic age, in healing the sick, as illustrated by our guest Dr. Newton; in inspirational speaking, so powerfully instanced in this hall by Mrs. Hardinge; in the power to cast out evil spirits; and when the facts of modern Spiritualism demonstrate the truth of all the most cherished beliefs of humanity, showing the ever-watchful interest which those who have gone before take in those that remain, and giving us clearer and better views of the future as well as of the present life, I think we may affirm that the good is unquestionable. I do not, however, intend to pursue this subject, but permit me before taking my seat to assure Dr. Newton that the kindly feelings he has expressed in his letters to Spiritualists in this country are reciprocated by Spiritualists here towards himself and his fellow-workers. We in England owe a deep debt of gratitude to the earlier advocates of the movement in America, to public men like Governor Tallmadge, of Wisconsin, and Judge Edmonds, of New York; to clergymen like the late Rev. John Pierpont, of Boston, the successor of the celebrated Dr. Channing, and Adin Ballou; to men eminent in the scientific world, like the late Professor Mapes, and Dr. Hare, of Philadelphia; to men like Dr. Willis, and A. E. Newton, who for their faith as Spiritualists have been expelled from college and from church, and many others—with noble women not a few, who have borne the loss of worldly position, the ridicule, vituperation, and all that general hostility which ever seems to follow those who identify themselves with the advent of unpopular truths.'

"Mr. J. M. Peebles said: 'I feel some embarrassment in making any remarks, as this is a meeting of noble-hearted Englishmen to welcome a distinguished friend of my own from America. I am exceedingly happy to be in your midst, and especially to be upon this platform alongside a friend and brother whom I have known, loved, and respected for many years. . . . . Truly it is often asked, "What good does Spiritualism do?" It gives demonstration of a future existence, for even now clear-headed men often ask the question, "If a man die, shall he live again?" Once, as a minister, I attended a funeral of an only child. My text was "Suffer little children to come unto Me, and forbid them not, for of such is the kingdom of heaven." The whole of my sermon was about "faith," but as the mother baptized the coffin with her tears, she turned and said to me, "Tell me what you *know* about the immortal world; my aching heart asks for more than faith—for knowledge." She added, "Tell me what you know of that world; shall I know my child? Will my child know me?"—and *I was dumb*. But now, since I have talked with the angels, and have heard their lute-like voices, I no longer talk only about "faith," for now "We know that we have a house eternal in the heavens." Spiritualism teaches us and proves that there is an immortal life beyond the tomb. Spiritualism is spreading to the ends of the earth. I found its phenomena in Smyrna, in Constantinople, in Athens, and upon the Pacific coast; in fact, wherever thinking men are found, there is this living truth proclaimed. I know much of Dr. Newton, for hundreds have clasped my hand who have been healed by him. To pick out solitary instances from among the large number is like trying to select some specially bright star from the thousands in the midnight heavens. In Buffalo, several years ago, I was present at the house of Dr. Newton, when a gentleman was brought in upon his bed, who for years had had paralysis; Dr. Newton looked at him, simply laid his hands upon him, and said, "Disease, I bid you depart! Arise! you are well;" and the man left the bed and crossed the room, then stood before Dr. Newton weeping with joy. "Stop," said Dr. Newton, "it is not I; it is the spirit power of which I am but the humble instrument." On another occasion a lady could not get near him, and Dr. Newton was impressed to say, "It does not matter, she is well," and she was cured. He has cured the lame, the dumb, and the blind. . . . . As Mrs. Hardinge stands at the head of American inspirational speakers, so Dr. Newton stands at the head of all the healing mediums connected with the movement. Before him disease departs, and when it does not depart at once, it sometimes departs very shortly afterwards, because of its cause being removed—a stream will flow for a little time after its sources of supply have been cut off. I have great faith in Dr. Newton's cures, far more faith than has been expressed by some of those who have spoken before me, because I have seen more of Dr. Newton's work than they have. I know that Dr. Newton will nobly do his work, and that he will be blessed by God and His holy angels: I trust that all present will extend to him love and warmth of soul. Personally, the more time I spend in England, the better I comprehend and love Englishmen, and I wish to bespeak for Dr. Newton cordial welcomes and greetings while he remains in this country.'

"Dr. J. R. Newton then rose amid loud and continued applause. He spoke under spirit influence, with slowness and frequent pauses, and said : ' I feel overwhelmed by your cordial welcome. I stand before you as a plain man, and feel like a little child. I am a practical Christian, and am ready at any time to make a sacrifice of myself for the sake of Christianity. It is a wonder to me that few men ever try to live daily as Jesus lived. When I became Christian in life, spiritual gifts were showered upon me, and this was as wonderful to myself as to those whom I address. I believe in spirit communion, and I even know the names of some of the spirits who control me in the exercise of my gifts. . . . . As to the power of healing, it is merely an illustration of the power of love. When any sick person comes before me, I lay my hands on that person and feel that I love him, and if the patient is not antagonistic, he is almost sure to be healed ; tell them I love them, and when this opens their hearts to me, the disease must depart. I make no profession to be a public speaker. I am entirely under the control of the spirits. . . . . I cannot say that I have come to England at any sacrifice, because it was the will of my Father that I should come. I have not come to London to make money, and I shall receive rich and poor alike. The welcome I have received prevents me from speaking as freely as I wish to do. I have much to say, but I feel overwhelmed at the reception you have given me. I am heart and soul with you. . . . . It is not a matter of belief with me that spirits control me—it is knowledge. Pythagoras, Socrates, and Plato walk the earth to-day, and so do all the great and good men who have gone before us. I shall meet you again next Sunday, and wish you all well, with many thanks and blessings for your kind attention.'

"Mr. S. C. Hall said : Before the meeting closes, I should like to say a few words of congratulation to Dr. Newton. I believe that I express the sentiments of all Spiritualists when I say that it is their desire to give a cordial greeting to all Americans ; and that it is a great duty to bring Americans and Englishmen closer together, that they may understand each other better than they have done. I should not have risen at all except to call attention to one point. I want to tell Dr. Newton that Spiritualism is making great progress in this country among great men and great thinkers, and men who will become great authorities. I rejoice to tell him that a Society the other day called witnesses before them, and made clear and close inquiry ; that that Society is about to send forth a report which will do much good among outsiders. . . . I believe that the report of the Dialectical Society will go far towards the removal of the chief obstacles in the path of Spiritualism, and make it easier to help on our divine belief. We shall then be, I trust, the humble instruments in God's hands of destroying the Materialism of the present age, for this I consider to be the great purpose of Spiritualism. . . . I have myself full knowledge of the truth of Spiritualism, and I hope that many who are not Spiritualists will take my testimony as worth something when I express that certainty of belief. The more Spiritualism has been inquired into, the more its truth has been exhibited ; I thank God for having given us opportunities of proving that which we now believe and know. Dr. Newton has reached London at a good time, with less difficulties than of old to encounter, and with less probability of being considered mad or dishonest.'

"Thanks having been voted to the Chairman, the business part of the meeting then came to a close, and it assumed the character of a *conversazione.*" . . .

· · · · · · · · · · ·

"DR. NEWTON AT THE CAVENDISH ROOMS.

"On Sunday evening at the close of the service, and after a very excellent discourse by Mr. Peebles, Dr. Newton invited all who were afflicted with disease or pain to come forward. Many did so ; and declared themselves either cured or greatly benefited by the Doctor's treatment. These included headache, deafness, stammering, neuralgia, heart disease, &c. His success in one case was very marked ; that of the son of Mr. F. Cowper, 388, Edgware Road, who had been unable to walk without crutches for eight years past. After Dr. Newton's treatment, the lad was able to walk home—a distance of about two miles. On Monday he attended at the Cambridge Hall, and had his spine straightened, which has made him measure about four inches taller. He now walks with a stick, and improves daily. On Sunday, May 22nd, a similar scene was witnessed, and on both occasions the hall was densely crowded."

"DR. NEWTON AT THE CAMBRIDGE HALL.

"The *Medium* says : ' Dr. Newton commenced a regular course of treatment of the poor on Monday morning, May 16th, in the Cambridge Hall, Newman Street, Oxford Street. He attends between the hours of nine and twelve, and will accept no money for his services. A large number came to be healed, and they have steadily increased each day. Many remarkable cures have been made. It would be of little use to fill our columns with an account of the remarkable instances of benefit which could be culled from the Doctor's treatment on one morning only. Dr. Newton commenced on Wednesday morning by removing a curvature from the spine of a young lady, the daughter of Lady Helena Newenham. A lad who had not spoken, except in a whisper, for three years, was enabled to speak, so as to be heard distinctly over the hall. Mr. Hubbard, of Rathbone Place, was cured of asthma of long standing. Mr. Watts, Rathbone Place, was cured of lameness from wounds. Mr. Charles Clutterbuck, 74 years of age, had been totally blind for six years; after treatment, he could see faces and tell the colour of Mr. Watson's beard. Mrs. Anna Crisp, 23, King Street, had been paralyzed for three years; cured by one treatment. She had been affected on one side throughout. Robert Andrews, 151, Metropolitan Meat Market, was blind of one eye, and had pains in the head and hand; after treatment he pronounced himself "all right." James Armstrong, 44, Brindley Street, Harrow Road, was afflicted with paralyzed legs for nearly two years. He could walk with difficulty on a pair of crutches, but he went away with his crutches over his shoulder. Many who were not perfectly cured were much relieved. Some were pronounced absolutely incurable. "It would be as easy to make new eyes as to cure you," said the Doctor to several who were entirely past recovery. Others were benefited, and some were told to come again; others that their diseases were mitigated, and would pass away in a few weeks.'"

"DR. NEWTON AND MR. ASHLEY.

"Since the foregoing was in type, we have received the following communication:—

"'*To the Editor of the Spiritual Magazine.*

"'May 23rd, 1870.

"'Sir,—I have received a letter this morning from Mr. Wm. Ashley, of Liverpool, whose case I alluded to at Harley Street, and which was the first case upon which Dr. Newton tried his healing power after his arrival in England. Mr. Ashley now writes:

"May 22nd.

"You will be pleased to hear that I am gaining strength daily. I generally walk out one or two hours when the weather permits, either alone or with my wife. I enjoy my food as much as ever I did, and have no doubt but in a short time I shall be in robust health—thanks to dear Dr. Newton."

"'You can make whatever use you please of this communication.

"'You will see that the press is in full blast against the Doctor; the *Telegraph* of this day being most violent; the *Echo* of Saturday publishing a letter from a patient who was not healed; the *Advertiser* denouncing him as a humbug.

"The only fair account was given in the *Daily News* of Saturday; but the writer did not half state the facts he witnessed. I was there, and many cases were marvellous—unmistakable!

"Yours truly,

"Benj. Coleman."

"DR. NEWTON AND THE PRESS.

"The *Liverpool Mercury* has a long article on Dr. Newton's proceedings in Liverpool. On Sunday, May 8th, he attended two meetings and operated on from thirty to forty persons, and all, it is admitted, with one exception, professed themselves benefited. A portion of the London press has begun to *Telegraph* false reports and *Echo* dirty insinuations. ''Tis easy as lying,' said Shakespeare, and newspaper scribes well know how easy that is.

"The *Daily News* in a long article gives a tolerably fair account of some of the proceedings during what the writer calls Dr. Newton's morning performance, and this tolerable fairness was so much a surprise to Dr. Newton, amidst the furious blasts of others of the press, that he had the innocence to thank the *Daily News* and even to 'bless' the editor. This was too much for the editor, and he has hastened to repudiate the blessing, and to withdraw all his fairness, saying, with great truth, that such a thing was never in his mind. A great deal more of this is of course in store for Dr. Newton, and he has made up his account to meet it. Perhaps the source of the Doctor's power to heal may itself render him not the most philosophic or prudent person in speaking, and he may not be a good exponent of the philosophy of the subject. In this way additional difficulties may be thrown in his own way, and in that of the public, to prevent their understanding the *rationale* of this power, even to the small extent to which it can be understood. . . . . . . But apart from this, we should be glad to know why a benevolent gentleman cannot assert this power in his own person, and endeavour to exercise it at his own cost, without drawing down on himself the blind ferocity of the press and the public. We do not know why he should be called a blasphemer and an impostor, and have the whole pack of the press, like so many hounds, yelping at his heels. In America, where we have watched his course for many years, he has relieved and cured thousands, and is a poorer man to-day than he was five years ago, though his powers of healing are said to be greater. Already he has been the means of curing many in England during this short visit; and we should have thought the wise plan would have been to watch the result and tabulate his work, and see what it comes to before becoming abusive. It suits the temper of the press, and its ignorance of such matters, to begin by abuse; and so we must be content to let them go on in their own way. Anything above mere physics always produces this unholy rage. We wish that some healer could be found who could cure this public madness."

Our Spiritualistic readers have, no doubt, like the author herself, too often heard the parrot cry of *Cui bono* to marvel why—even with all the excisions of extraneous matter we have made—we should have published the above account *in extenso* from the pages of the London *Spiritual Magazine* of December, 1870.

To non-spiritualistic readers who may perchance glance over these pages we would say, "Read, mark, learn, and inwardly digest" the above account, before you again ask the ten thousand times answered question, "What is the use of Spiritualism?"

CHAPTER XXIII.

SPIRITUALISM IN GREAT BRITAIN (CONTINUED).

OF SPIRITUAL ASSOCIATIONS,

IN 1865 an association was formed under the name and style of "The Association of Progressive Spiritualists of Great Britain," and the following is a brief summary of its aims as reported in the London *Spiritual Magazine* for December, 1865:—

"The 'Association of Progressive Spiritualists of Great Britain,' which recently held its first convention at Darlington, has issued—'A circular respectfully addressed to the friends of Spiritualism and the public generally;' in which, accepting as their definition of Spiritualism the motto of the *Spiritual Magazine*, they state that:—

"'The principal objects we have in view, are, as an association, to meet once a year, or oftener, if it be deemed advisable, for the purpose of social communion, interchange of sentiment; to record our united experiences, and the progress which Spiritualism is making in and around us; to devise means for diffusing among our fellow men and women the principles of this Divine philosophy, by the distribution of the best tracts and books we have upon the subject, and the delivery throughout the kingdom of lectures by persons of approved character and ability.'

"A second convention is announced for the last week in July, 1866, at Newcastle-on-Tyne. The secretary of the Association is Dr. McLeod, of Newcastle."

Of the Convention announced as above, the reports were scarcely as favourable as could have been desired. A general lack of unity seemed to pervade the assembly and the papers presented were not calculated to edify those outside the ranks of Spiritualism, however interesting they might have been to the writers.   The following remarks conclude a report of this gathering furnished by the London *Spiritual Magazine*:—

"Amid much that is crude and undigested in the papers and speeches here reported, there are some well worthy a better companionship, especially one by Mr. Etchells, on The Atmosphere of Intelligence, Pleasure, and Pain ; or a Chapter from the Harmony of Matter, as unfolded in the Circles of Spiritualists who meet at Brothers Chapman, Varley, and Etchells', Huddersfield.' This paper has evidently been prepared with great care ; the facts it relates, especially those concerning the phenomena of 'the Double,' are of great interest ; and the circles named by Mr. Etchells can hardly be better employed in the interest of Spiritualism than in the further prosecution of these investigations."

For a few succeding years, conventions were held either in London or the provinces, but these gatherings were seldom participated in by the majority of the English Spiritualists, nor were they conducive to any very important results.

Conventions appear to be more in harmony with the genius of American than English Spiritualism, and we have but few evidences that their action in England has promoted the progress of the cause or the spirit of unity amongst its supporters.

The invariable struggle between the extremes of Radicalism and Conservatism which so often disturbs the harmony of associative bodies, is a prevailing condition, of which the Spiritualists have had to learn, by painful experience.

One of their most severe lessons in this direction was read to them in the determined opposition manifested by "The Royal Society of Great Britain," against the admission of "Spiritualism" as a theme of discussion worthy the attention of that august body. Several of the Fellows were earnest believers in Spiritualism, and thinking they perceived in its phenomena, subjects quite as worthy the attention of eminent scientists as the genesis of a worm or the precise number of markings on a fossil trilobite, they made strenuous efforts to introduce papers on the subject of the marvellous demonstrations of unknown force which the phenomena of Spiritualism display. It was in the amazing assumptions of contempt and indifference with which these propositions were repelled, that the Spiritualists were led to believe that Societies in general are banded together for the defence of the old against the innovations of the new, and those who presume to try and enlighten the said Societies upon the subject of new ideas, must be taught, that anything a very learned, especially a Royal Society, does not already know, cannot exist, or if it presume to maintain an existence without the pale of such an authoritative body, cannot be worth knowing.

It was doubtless under the influence of this high-toned monopoly of all knowledge worth the having, that Professor Tyndall, Mr. Palgrave, and other members of the Royal Society of Great Britain, maintained a long and acrimonious correspondence with Mr. William Wilkinson, Professors Wallace and Cromwell Varley, Sir J. E. Tennant, and others, on the question of bringing the phenomena claimed to be "Spiritual," before the members of the Royal Society, and although the Mediumship of Mr. D. D. Home was courteously tendered as an illustration of the assertions made by the Spiritualists, the scornful rejection of this offer seemed necessary to convince the zealous propagandists, how useless it is to try and convince those, who neither desire nor intend to be convinced of any facts they do not originate, or any truths they do not themselves already know.

Although the action of Societies as a general rule appears to be ephemeral in connection with Spiritualism, its use being simply available for temporary purposes of propagandism, there have been a vast number of attempts at organization in the ranks of Spiritualism. One of the most permanent and influential associations that has ever been formed in Great Britain has been known under the name of "The British National Association of Spiritualists." It may not be generally understood that this organization owes its first foundation in the metropolis to the steadfast though quiet and unobtrusive efforts of Mr. Dawson Rogers, of Rose Villa, Finchley. This gentleman—one of the veteran Spiritualists of London—has for many years laboured unceasingly to promote the interests of Spiritualism, and both by purse and person has maintained every good work which has tended to advance "the cause." Besides devoting himself with tireless energy to the foundation and conduct of the "British National Association of Spiritualists," the movement owes to Mr. Dawson Rogers the foundation of the admirable periodical entitled *Light*. With the exception of the London *Spiritual Magazine, Light* is unquestionably the highest toned, and most scholarly periodical that has ever issued from the Spiritual Press, and Mr. Dawson Rogers's good services to the cause of Spiritualism have been for many long years pursued so faithfully, so effectively, yet with such a total absence of personal display, that we feel but too happy in offering this humble tribute to one, whose way marks in the path of progress have been far more prominent, than his honoured name. To return to Mr. Rogers's first great public effort in promoting the foundation of the British National Association of Spiritualists. In a brief sketch of this important movement published a few years since in the London *Spiritualist*, the editor says :—

"Some time in 1873 it was resloved to form a national organisation of Spiritualists in Great Britain. This was done at a meeting at Liverpool, to which everybody had been invited by means of advertisements and special letters to well-known men. Thus was the standard raised of "Friendly union among Spiritualists." Fierce attempts were made to kill the organisation, more especially by the press, but the workers fought their way, and succeeded in planting a central establishment in London, and in doing some public work in addition, more especially the founding of fortnightly meetings to consider public questions relating to Spiritualism."

Soon after its first inauguration, the Society issued a well-prepared tract, in which was published the list of distinguished persons who became its members and associates. Although it would be impossible to give *in extenso* a list which includes more than a hundred names and addresses, it may not be out of place to make the following selection from amongst the most noteworthy personages of the association :—

" BRITISH NATIONAL ASSOCIATION OF SPIRITUALISTS (ESTABLISHED 1873.)

PRESIDENT.

Alexander Calder, Esq., 1, Hereford Square, West Brompton, S.W.

VICE-PRESIDENTS.

Blackburn, Charles, Parkfield, Didsbury, Manchester.
Coleman, Benjamin, 1, Bernard Villas, Upper Norwood.
Fitz-Gerald, Mrs., 19, Cambridge Street, Hyde Park, W.
Fitz-Gerald, Desmond G., M.S.Tel.E., 6, Loughborough Road North, Brixton, S.W.
Gregory, Mrs. Makdougall, 21, Green Street, Grosvenor Square, W.
Honywood, Mrs., 52, Warwick Square, S.W.

VICE-PRESIDENTS—*Continued.*

Jencken, Henry D., M.R.I., Barrister-at-Law, Goldsmith Buildings, E.C.
Massey, C. C., Barrister-at-Law, 96, Portland Place, W.
Rogers, E. D., Rose Villa, Church End, Finchley, N.
Speer, Stanhope Templeman, M.D., Douglas House, 13, Alexandra Road, South Hampstead, N.W.
Wyld, Geo. M.D., 12, Great Cumberland Place, Hyde Park, W

COUNCIL.

Isham, Sir Charles, Bart., Lamport Hall, Northampton.
Ivimey, Joseph, Berkeley Mansion, 64, Seymour Street, W.
Joy, Algernon, M.I.C.E., Junior United Service Club, S.W.
Stock, St. George W., M.A., Queen Street, Oxford.
Theobold, Morell, 30, Mark Lane, E.C.

HONORARY OR CORRESPONDING MEMBERS.

His Imperial Highness Nicholas, Duke of Leuchtenburg, St. Petersburg, Russia.
Prince Emile de Sayn Wittgenstein, Lieutenant-General, Aide-de-Camp General de S.M.I. l'Empereur de Russie, Vevey, Switzerland.
Ahmed Rassim Pacha, Khan de Rassim Pacha à Bahdjé Capoussou, Constantinople.
The Baron Von Vay, President of the Spiritual Society at Pesth.
The Baroness Adelma Von Vay, Gonobitz, bei Potschach, Styria, via Gratz, Austria.
The Baroness Guldenstubbe, 29, Rue de Trevise, Paris.
Colonel Don Santiago Bassols y Folguera, Madrid.
El Visconde de Torres-Solanot, Madrid.
The Hon. Alexandre Aksakof, Russian Imperial Councillor, Nevsky Prospect, 6, St. Petersburg.
The Baron von Dirckink-Holmfeld, Pinneberg, Holstein.
M. Gustave de Veh, Bischoffsberger Villa, Interlaken, Switzerland.
Mme. de Veh, Bischoffsberger Villa, Interlaken, Switzerland.
Signor Sebastiano Fenzi, Banca Fenzi, Florence, Italy.
Baboo Pearychand Mittra, 7, Swallow Lane, Calcutta.
James Mylne, Esq., Beheea, East Indian Railway, Bengal.
A. J. Riko, Esq., Oude Molstraat, the Hague, Holland.
M. C. Constant, Smyrna, Turkey in Asia.
Dr. Maximilian Perty, Professor of Natural Science, Berne, Switzerland.
Dr. Franz Hoffmann, Professor of Philosophy, Wurzburg University, Germany.
Gregor C. Wittig, Esq., Kornerstrasse 2B, Leipsic, Germany.
W. H. Terry, Esq., 84, Russell Street, Melbourne, Victoria, Australia.
M. Leymarie, 7, Rue de Lille, Paris.
Epes Sargent, Esq., Box 2,985, Boston, U.S.A.
H. T. Child, Esq., M.D., 634, Race Street, Philadelphia, U.S.A.
E. Crowell, Esq., M.D., 196, Clinton Avenue, Brooklyn, New York, U.S.A.
M. F. Clavairoz, Consul-General de France, Trieste, Austria.
G. L. Ditson, Esq., M.D., Albany, New York, U.S.A.,
W. L. Sammons, Esq., Cape Town, South Africa.
J. H. Gledstanes, Esq., Merignac, Gironde, France.
Rev. Samuel Watson, Memphis, Tennessee, U.S.A.
Luther Cobby, Esq., 9 Montgomery Place, Boston, U.S.A.
M. de Bassompierre, 285, Chaussee St. Pierre, Etterbeck. Brussels.
M. A. Anthleme Fritz, President de l'Union, 67, Rue du Midi, Brussels
Lieut.-Col. P. Jacoby, 11, Rue de Vienne, Brussels.
Le Comte de Bullet, Hotel de l'Athence, Rue Scribe, Paris.
Captain R. F. Burton, F.R.G.S., H.M. Consul, Trieste, Austria.
A. R. Wallace, Esq., F.R.G.S., Rosehill, Dorking.
Isaac B. Rich, Esq., 9, Montgomery Place, Boston, U.S.A.
W. S. Godbe, Esq., Salt Lake City, Utah, U.S.A.
Dr. Grunhut, Waitzner Boulevard, 57, Buda-Pesth, Hungary.
Dr. A. E. Nehrer, Eperjes, Hungary.
Signor Damiani, Salita Pontecorvo, 60, Naples.
Berks T. Hutchinson, Esq., 2, New Street, Cape Town, South Africa.

ALLIED SOCIETIES.

The Liverpool Psychological Society. Secretary, S. Pride, Esq., 8, Grampian Road, Edge Lane, Liverpool.

L'Union Spirite et Magnetique. Secretary, M. Charles Fritz, 121, Rue de Louvain, Brussels.

The Brixton Psychological Society. Hon. Sec., H. E. Frances, Esq., 22, Cowley Road, Brixton, S.W.

The Spiriter-Forscher Society, Buda-Pesth. Secretary, M. Anton Prochaszka, Josefstadt Erzherzog Alexander-gasse, 23, Buda-Pesth, Hungary.

Dalston Association of Enquirers into Spiritualism. Hon. Secretary, T. Blyton, Esq., 74, Navarino Road, Dalston, E.

Cardiff Spiritual Society, Hon. Sec., Mr. A. J. Smart, 3, Guildford Street, Cardiff.

Sociedad Espiritista Espanola, Cervantes 34, 28, Madrid. President, El Visconde de Torres-Solanot.

Sociedad Espirita Central de la Republica Mexicana. President, Senor Refugio T. Gonzalez, 7, Calle de Amedo, Mexico.

Sociedad Espirita di Bogota, Colombia, South America. President, Senor Manuel Jose Angarita.

For several years this Association has maintained its meetings, established a library, held soirées, investigating circles, and social gathings, with an amount of fidelity specially commendable in a movement so fluctuating as Spiritualism. Many internal changes have of course taken place, especially in its officers and directors. Many of its once prominent members have been removed by transition to a higher life; others have been impelled to withdraw from personal motives, and still many eminent persons not enumerated in the first list, have become affiliated with the organization. So much influence for good however has been exerted by the persistent energy of its leaders, that we feel pleasure in adding a notice of the last change that has been effected in its arrangements. The excerpt we are about to subjoin was only published in May, 1882, and is taken from *Light.*

The annexed report is the last announcement of the British National Association of Spiritualists under that name, the society being henceforth destined to be known as "The Central Association of Spiritualists."

The article is headed :—

" BRITISH NATIONAL ASSOCIATION OF SPIRITUALISTS.

" ANNUAL MEETING.—The annual general meeting of this Association was held on Tuesday evening last, at 38, Great Russell Street, Mr. E. Dawson Rogers, vice-president, in the chair. The principal business of the meeting was to receive the annual report of the Council and statement of accounts, and to consider a recommendation involving a change in the name and constitution of the Association. The report was unanimously adopted, as was also a proposition in favour of the adoption of the name 'The Central Association of Spiritualists,' by which designation, therefore, the Association will henceforth be known. The change, we think, is a wise one ; but after eight years' familiarity with the title of the ' B.N.A.S.,' we give it up with some regret."

Then follows an elaborate report of the Council, by which it appears that the society is still in a flourishing condition. The following items, however, may possess some interest to the reader, because they allude to the departture of more than one honoured friend of the Spiritual cause, and give further particulars of the status of the association under its new designation in 1882. The report concludes thus :—

"The following is a concise summary of the history of the Association since the last annual meeting :—

"CHANGES IN THE MEMBERSHIP.—Number of new members elected, 52 ; number of resignations 16. Deaths during the year—M. Léon Favre, Prof. Friedrich Zöllner, Rev. Sir Wm. Dunbar, H. D. Jencken, M.R.I., Alex. Thorn, Mrs. Hook, A. E. Hunter, B.A. (Cantab). Present number of honorary and subscribing members, 294.

"ALLIED SOCIETIES.—The Gateshead Society for the Investigation of Spiritualism, the South African Spiritual Evidence Society, and the Paris Psychological Society have allied themselves to the Association during the year, making a total number of sixteen in friendly union.

"WORK OF THE ASSOCIATION.—A series of Discussion and Social Meetings has been kept up through the season. Many of these have been highly interesting and successful.

"Mr. T. P. Barkas, F.G.S., was appointed as a representative of the Association at the discussion on Spiritualism at the Church Congress held in October of last year. This discussion, and the extent to which the report of it was circulated, has done much to raise the position which the whole subject of Spiritualism occupies in the public mind.

"On the 5th and 6th of January last, conferences of an exceedingly interesting character were held in the rooms of the Association, on the invitation of Professor Barrett, of Dublin. These conferences have resulted in the formation of a 'Society for Psychical Research,' which, while working to some extent on similar lines to those of the B.N.A.S., does not commit itself to a belief in Spiritualism, but aims at approaching the inquiry solely from a scientific standpoint. The Council feels that there is abundant room for such a society without in any way affecting the necessity for a Central Association avowedly for the investigation and propagation of Spiritualism."

The new organization alluded to in the last report sufficiently indicates its aims by its nomenclature—namely, " The Society for Psychical Research."

The announcements put forth by this Society point to the lines of demarcation which separate it from any thoroughly pronounced Spiritual organizations ; in fact, the addresses of its President and Members on the occasion of its first general meeting, which took place in July, 1882, clearly show, that though Spiritualists may and do take part in its researches, a belief in Spirit communion is by no means the leading principle upon which the association is based. To illustrate this position still more forcibly, we append a note which the Society print in connection with their prospectus. It reads as follows :

"To prevent misconception, it is here expressly stated that Membership of this Society does not imply the acceptance of any particular explanation of the phenomena investinated, nor any belief as to the operation, in the physical world, of forces other than those recognised by Physical Science."

After publishing the list of eminent literary and scientific ladies and gentlemen who compose the officers and members of this association, the prospectus gives the following, which may present a satisfactory synopsis of the subjects of proposed research.

"(1) Committee on Thought-reading ; Hon. Sec., Professor W. F. Barrett, 18, Belgrave Square, Monkstown, Dublin.

"(2) Committee on Mesmerism : Hon. Sec., Dr. Wyld, 12, Great Cumberland Place, London, W.

"(3) Committee on Reichenbach's Experiments ; Hon. Sec., Walter H. Coffin, Esq., Junior Athenæum Club, London, W.

"(4) Committee on Apparitions, Haunted Houses, &c. ; Hon. Sec., Hensleigh Wedgwood, Esq., 31, Queen Anne Street, London, W.

"(5) Committee on Physical Phenomena ; Hon. Sec., Dr. C. Lockhart Robertson, Hamam Chambers, 76, Jermyn Street, S.W.

"(6) Literary Committee, Hon. Secs., Edmund Gurney, Esq., 26, Montpelier Square, S.W. ; Frederic W. H. Myers, Esq., Leckhampton, Cambridge."

Besides these well selected subjects for consideration, and the marked ability of the gentlemen who have consented to aid in their investigation, the success of the undertaking is guaranteed by the high standing and literary attainments of the parties under whose direction the work is announced to proceed. Any committee of investigators into psychic phenomena which includes the names of the subjoined officers and Council can scarcely fail to command the respect of the community at large and the sympathy of every earnest investigator into the subjects under consideration :—

PRESIDENT.

Henry Sidgwick, Esq., Trinity College, Cambridge.

VICE-PRESIDENTS.

Arthur J. Balfour, Esq., M.P., 4, Carlton Gardens, S.W.
W. F. Barrett, Esq., F.R.S.E., 18, Belgrave Square, Monkstown, **Dublin.**
John R. Holland, Esq., M.P., 57, Lancaster Gate, London, W.
Richard H. Hutton, Esq., Englefield Green, Staines.
Rev. W. Stainton-Moses, M.A., 21, Birchington Road, London, N.W.
Hon. Roden Noel, 57, Anerley Park, London, S.E.
Professor Balfour Stewart, F.R.S., Owens College, Manchester.
Hensleigh Wedgwood, Esq., 31, Queen Anne Street, London, W.

COUNCIL.

W. F. Barrett, 18, Belgrave Square, Monkstown, Dublin.
Edward T. Bennett, 8, The Green, Richmond, near London.
Mrs. Boole, 103, Seymour Place, Bryanston Square, London, W.
Walter R. Browne, 38, Belgrave Road, London, S.W.
Alexander Calder, 1, Hereford Square, South Kensington, **London, S.W.**
Walter H. Coffin, Junior Athenæum Club, London, W.
Desmond G. FitzGerald, 6, Akerman Road, Brixton, S.W.
Edmund Gurney, 26, Montpelier Square, London, S.W.
Charles C. Massey, 1, Albert Mansions, Victoria Street, London, S.W.
Frederic W. H. Myers, Leckhampton, Cambridge.
Francis W. Percival, 28, Savile Row, London, W.
Frank Podmore, 16, Southampton Street, Fitzroy Square, London. S.W.
C. Lockhart Robertson, M.D., Hamam Chambers, 76, Jermyn Street, S.W.
E. Dawson Rogers, Rose Villa, Church End, Finchley, N.
Rev. W. Stainton-Moses, 21, Birchington Road, London, N.W.
Morell Theobald, 62, Granville Park, Blackheath, S.E.
Hensleigh Wedgwood, 31, Queen Anne Street, London, W.
G. Wyld, M.D., 19, Great Cumberland Place, London, W.

Many other associations besides those already named have been formed with kindred aims. Some have maintained a more or less permanent existence—but whether they still survive or have passed out of being, all have achieved some use as temporary levers in the spiritual progress of the race.

CHAPTER XXIV.

SPIRITUALISM IN GREAT BRITAIN (CONTINUED).

SPIRITUALISM AND THE LONDON DIALECTICAL SOCIETY.

IT now becomes necessary to give a brief account of a movement which has exerted a marked influence over the progress of Spiritualism in Great Britain, namely, the investigations and published report of " The London Dialectical Society," the action of which in connection with Spiritualism arose thus. In January of the year 1869, an association composed of ladies and gentlemen distinguished for their literary and scientific attainments, entitled " The Dialectical Society," determined to investigate the subject of modern Spiritualism.

The minute of the proceedings which inaugurated this investigation reads in their published report as follows :—

" At a meeting of the London Dialectical Society, held 6th of January, 1869, Mr. J. H. Levy in the chair, it was resolved,—' That the Council be requested to appoint a Committee to investigate the phenomena alleged to be Spiritual manifestations, and to report thereon.' "

In consequence of this resolution, the members issued a circular couched in courteous terms, inviting the leading Spiritualists of England to assist them by personal or written testimony in the investigations they proposed to pursue.

One of the first respondents to the call issued by the Council was the author of this work, who happened at that time to be in England, and who, in company with J. C. Luxmoore, Esq., of Gloucester Square, Mr. and Mrs. Everitt, and a few other Spiritualistic friends, waited on the Society at a meeting appointed for that purpose on the evening of March 16th, 1869. After offering such testimony as she felt to be apposite to the place and time, Mrs. Hardinge gave a long address upon the main features of the Spiritualistic movement, the characteristics of Mediumship, the Spirit circle, and the difficulties which beset the path of the investigator, all of which will be found duly recorded in the printed report of the Society. The address closed with a strong recommendation to the Society to conduct their investigations, not in general sessions of the whole body, but to form themselves into groups or sub-committees, of from four to eight, or at most ten persons; selecting the members of these groups on the principle of mutual goodwill, or such cordial relations with each other, as would be most likely to produce harmony of feeling, and psychological equilibrium.

In answer to various queries propounded by members of the Committee at this stage of the proceedings, Mrs. Hardinge described in detail the best and most approved methods of forming circles, founding her advice not on her own opinions, but on the well proved experiences of the Spiritualists with whom she had been associated for many years.

During the entire course of this address, which was occasionally interrupted by appropriate questions, listened to with deep attention, and responded to by a cordial vote of thanks, the Spirits, or invisible audience present, availed themselves of the Mediumship of Mrs. Everitt, who was one of the party, to emphasize the entire speech with loud clear raps which resounded in unmistakable cadence to every sentence, on the uncovered library table, at which the Committee were seated.

Both Mrs. Everitt and the speaker were too far from the table to give rise to the supposition that they had any agency in producing the sounds, yet these manifested an intelligence which was so unmistakable that it must have appeared astounding to the sceptics present. On some occasions, the invisibles emphasized the utterances with the customary signals for "yes" and "no," joining in most vociferously with the applause, and taking part throughout the proceedings with a force, spontaneity, and independence, which was as amusing to the Spiritualists as it was startling and unexpected to the rest of the party.

After the official work of the evening was ended, the company amused themselves for some time by questioning the invisible rapper, and though the meeting did not in any way assume the form of a *séance,* or commit itself by making any report of this informal action of their invisible attendants, the curious proceedings obviously made a deep impression upon some of those present, whilst it called forth from others that involuntary spirit of denial, which would rather discredit the testimony even of the senses than recede from the standard of obstinate and preconceived opinions.

It is more than probable that out of the large number of circulars which were sent to other well-known Spiritualists besides Mrs. Hardinge, not one failed to produce a response of more or less interest to the investigators.

Amongst those respondents whose names will be found in the Society's published report, and who attended in person, to give oral evidence of their faith, are the following persons :—Mrs. Emma Hardinge, Mr. H. D. Jencken, M.R.I.; Mrs. Honeywood, Mr. T. M. Simkiss, Mr. E. Laman Blanchard, Mr. J. Murray Spear, Mr. Benjamin Coleman, Mr. George Childs, artist; Mr. J. Enmore Jones, Miss Alice Jones, Miss Douglass, Lord Borthwick, Mr. James Burns, Mr. Thomas Sherratt, Professor Cromwell F. Varley, Miss Houghton, Mr. Thomas Shorter, Mr. Manuel Eyre, Mr. Lowenthal, Mr. Hockley, Mr. D. D. Home, Mrs. Cox, Signor Damiani, Lord Lindsay, Mr. Chevalier, Mr. Percival, Miss Anna Blackwell, &c., &c.

Letters in response to the Society's circular were received from—Mr. George H. Lewes, Mr. Wm. Wilkinson, solicitor ; Dr. Garth Wilkinson, M.D.; Dr. Davey, Dr. J. Dixon, Mr. Wm. Howitt, Lord Lytton, Mr. Newton Crosland, Mr. Robert Chambers, Dr. Lockhart Robertson, Dr. Charles Kidd, Mr. Edwin Arnold, Mr. J. Hawkins Simpson, Mr. A. Glendinning, Mr. T. A. Trollope, M. Léon Favre, Mrs. L. Lewis, The Countess (now Duchesse) de Pomar, M. Camille Flammarion, &c., &c., &c.

Papers also, though of an antagonistic character, were received and published from Profs. Huxley and Tyndall, Dr. Carpenter, Mr. Bradlaugh, and others.

It would be impossible without giving the substance of a volume of some 400 pages published by the Dialectical Society as their ultimate report, to convey to the reader the least idea of the candour and zeal with which this investigation was pursued, nor the vast sum of testimony which resulted from it ; in short, without any such intention on the part of its authors, the Dialectical Society's report forms one of the best collections of test facts and irrefragible testimony in favour of the Spiritual hypothesis, that has yet issued from the nineteenth-century press.

It seems that the General Committee, acting on the suggestions before named, organized themselves into six groups or sub-committees, at which Mr. Home and other well-known Mediums lent valuable assistance, whilst on many occasions, phenomena of a very convincing character were evolved, no recognised Medium being present. The reports of the Sub-Committees in fact, when read and candidly considered in detail, *are fully sufficient to establish the fact of an unknown super-sensuous and intelligent power communicating with mortals both by physical and intellectual modes, and that without any additional testimony from any other sources."*

"The Dialectical Society's Report on Spiritualism," was first published by the Society, and subsequently reprinted (by permission) with additional matter, by Mr. Jas. Burns, 15, Southampton Row, Holborn, London, where the curious reader can obtain it. Meantime, the following excerpts from the introductory portion of the work will be perused with interest.

The General Council of the Sub-Committee, addressing the Society at large, report as follows :—

"Your Committee have held fifteen meetings at which they received evidence from thirty-three persons who described phenomena which they stated had occurred within their own personal experience.

' Your Committee have received written statements relating to the phenomena from thirty-one persons.

"Your Committee invited the attendance, and requested the co-operation and advice of scientific men who had publicly expressed opinions favourable or adverse to the genuineness of the phenomena.

"Your Committee also specially invited the attendance of persons who had publicly ascribed the phenomena to imposture or delusion.

"Your Committee however, while successful in procuring the evidence of believers in the phenomena and their supernatural origin, almost wholly failed to obtain evidence from those who attributed them to fraud or delusion.

"As it appeared to your Committee to be of the greatest importance that they should investigate the phenomena in question by personal experiment and test, they resolved themselves into sub-committees as the best means of doing so.

"Six sub-committees were accordingly formed.

"All of these have sent in reports from which it appears that a large majority of the members of your Committee have become actual witnesses to several phases of the phenomena, without the aid or presence of any professional medium, although the greater part of them commenced their investigations in an avowedly sceptical spirit.

"These reports hereto subjoined, substantially corroborate each other, and would appear to establish the following propositions :—

"1. That sounds of a very varied character, apparently proceeding from articles of furniture, the floor and walls of the room—the vibrations of which are often distinctly perceptible to the touch—occur, without being produced by muscular action or mechanical contrivance.

"2. That movements of heavy bodies take place without mechanical contrivance of any kind or adequate exertion of muscular force by the persons present, and frequently without contact or connection with any person.

"3. That these sounds and movements often occur at the times, and in the manner asked for by persons present, and by means of a simple code of signals, answer questions and spell out coherent communications.

"4. That the answers and communications thus obtained are for the most part of a commonplace character ; but facts are sometimes correctly given which are known to one of the persons present.

"5. That the circumstances under which the phenomena occur are variable—the most prominent fact being, that the presence of certain persons seems necessary to their occurrence, and that of others, generally adverse—but this difference does not appear to depend upon any belief or disbelief concerning the phenomena.

"6. That nevertheless the occurrence of the phenomena is not induced by the presence or absence of such persons respectively."

Thus far the sub-committees' personal experiences alone are touched upon. The report next proceeds to deal with the testimony of the various witnesses who, orally or by written statements—received as indisputable, in view of the character and standing of the deponents—gave in a vast mass of testimony from which the following numbered extracts are selected :—

"1. Thirteen witnesses state that they have seen heavy bodies—in some instances men—rise in the air, and remain there for some time without visible support.

"2. Fourteen witnesses testify to having seen hands or figures not appertaining to any human being, but life-like in appearance and mobility, which they have sometimes touched or even grasped and which they were therefore convinced were not the result of illusion or imposture. . . .

"4. Thirteen witnesses declare they have heard musical pieces well played upon instruments not manipulated by any ascertainable agency.

"5. Five witnesses state that they have seen red-hot coals applied to the hands or heads of several persons present without producing pain or scorching, and three witnesses state that they have had the same experiment made upon themselves with the like immunity.

"6. Eight witnesses declare that they have received precise information through rappings, writings, and in other ways, the accuracy of which was unknown at the time to themselves or any persons present, and which on subsequent enquiry was found to be correct."

    .   .   .   .   .

"9. Six witnesses declare they have received information of future events, and that in some cases the hour and minute of their occurrence have been accurately foretold, even days and weeks before."

In addition to the above, evidence was given of gratuitously false statements alleged to come from spirits ; of spirit drawings produced under conditions which rendered " human agency impossible," also of " trance speaking, healing, automatic writing, the introduction of flowers and fruit into closed rooms ; of voices in the air, visions in crystals and glasses, and the elongation of the human body.

After a careful and almost exhuastive review of the whole subject, notices of the literature, and the various hypotheses put forth by way of attempted explanation, the preliminary report of the General Committee concludes with the following remarks :—

"In presenting their report, your Committee, taking into consideration the high character and great intelligence of many of the witnesses to the more extraordinary facts, the extent to which their testimony is supported by the reports of the sub-committees, and the absence of any proof of imposture or delusion as regards a large portion of the phenomena ; and further, having regard to the exceptional character of the phenomena, and the large number of persons of every grade of society and over the whole civilised world who are more or less influenced by a belief in their supernatural origin, and to the fact that no philosophical explanation of them has yet been arrived at, deem it incumbent upon them to state their conviction that the subject is worthy of more serious attention and careful investigation than it has hitherto received."

With a recommendation that the entire report together with the detailed reports of the Sub-Committees should be printed, here concludes one of the most remarkable, candid, and noteworthy summaries of a series of investigations into the phenomena of modern Spiritualism that the records of that movement can display.

The very popularity of "the cause," the many honourable and distinguished patrons which it had attracted to its ranks, and the possibility of making easy profits by simulating its phenomena, have doubtless been the superinducing motives which have caused such a vast flood of imposture, fraud and pretension to disgrace its honoured name, *since* the Dialectical Society issued their report. Still that volume remains, and the high character of those who constituted the witnesses, their entire disinterestedness and freedom from bias or motive to pervert the truth, and the care, caution, and indefatigable energy with which the research was pursued, will outweigh with the capable thinker the adverse witness of determined prejudice, or even the soil of ten thousand impure and fraudulent hands laid upon the fair form revealed by the investigations of this brave band of truth seekers. It is only to be regretted that the report of the Dialectical Society has not attained to a far wider circulation than it has hitherto enjoyed—still more that other associations composed of individuals as authoritative in name and place, as capable of judging rightly, and as faithful in seeking for and sifting evidence, have not followed so laudable an example, and by thus formulating and publishing abroad all that was found valuable and important in the movement, they would have tended to repress the atrocious licence, absurd fanaticism, and audacious frauds, that have been foisted upon the name and fame of modern Spiritualism.

CHAPTER XXV.

SPIRITUALISM IN GREAT BRITAIN (CONTINUED.)

IT must not be supposed that the course of Spiritualism in Great Britain moved on to the achievement of its many conquests over materialism and unbelief, without battles to fight, and obstacles to overcome. Besides the persistent opposition directed against this movement from the enemies who may be classified as the would-be monopolists of all knowledge, in religion, science, and literature, many and injurious have been "the foes of its own household," with which Spiritualism has had to contend.

Whether excessive vanity or mercenary motives have been the causes which induced certain individuals, professing to be Mediums for Spiritual phenomena, to supplement the lack of natural endowments by artifice, it matters not now to enquire; but it is an assured fact, that few well-informed Spiritualists would venture to deny, that many manifestations have been exhibited, both by private and professional Media, more or less garbled by fraud, and interpolated by human contrivance.

As our work is understood to record what Spiritualism is, *not what it is not,* we do not feel called upon to dilate farther on the performances of tricksters than to note the fact of their interference, and the injurious effect they have had upon the progress of the Spiritual cause.

It must suffice to say, that Spiritualism, like every other movement in human life worth counterfeiting, has had to endure its share of hindrance and disgrace from the camp followers who are ever found in the wake of the armies of progression.

We know it is constantly alleged by detected impostors, that the frauds they can no longer conceal, were undertaken, "under the influence of *evil spirits,*" generally those, who were attracted to the circle by some *evil-minded sceptic.* As to themselves—poor innocents!—they were *wholly unconscious,* and should be regarded merely as *victims,* not as offenders.

To account for the prepared paraphernalia with which their frauds were perpetrated, they generally fall back upon the theory of *conspiracies to ruin them*, amongst the very sitters whom they have attempted to cheat, &c., &c. To *explanations* of this character, alike insulting to common sense, and common honesty, no answer can be made. Unfortunately however, the heartless impostors who have no scruple in robbing their victims, and imposing on the holiest emotions of the heart, generally find hosts of apologists, who not only seek to excuse their turpitude by the miserable platitudes suggested above, but follow up the detection, with torrents of abuse against those who will not tamely submit to be imposed upon.

"Hard words break no bones," says the Spanish proverb. That may be true, nevertheless they are exceedingly hurtful to the feelings, and hence it is, that many an audacious cheat has been permitted to perpetrate his foul work unrebuked, for fear of the clamorous attacks with which the exposer is sure to be met by ill-judged partisanship, or fanatical credulity.

True Mediums, whether professional or otherwise, deserve the most kind consideration and courteous treatment ; but that is a poor rule which does not apply both ways, and therefore the same consideration and courtesy is due to the investigator, especially when it is remembered that such investigations are generally made under the impulse of the most sacred affections, and therefore deserve to be treated with reverence and respect.

Still the effect of detected imposture has been most injurious to the progress of Spiritualism, and though its publicity may have served the purpose of stimulating the investigator to more caution in his researches, it has turned back many an one from seeking divine truth, in a path bristling with the way marks of deceit and lies.

Other causes too, conspired to produce reactionary tides in public opinion, unfavourable to Spiritualism.

Mr. Sothern, a popular actor, who under the alias of "Stuart," had once been the conductor of the well-known "miracle-circle" of New York, thought proper to amuse his English associates by contriving all sorts of caricature performances calculated to bring ridicule and discredit upon Spiritualism.

Mr. Benjamin Coleman in his zeal for the cause he espoused, in exposing Mr. Sothern's performances, unfortunately republished certain statements copied from the New York papers, which gave the pretext for a prosecution on the ground of libel. A trial ensued. The well-known aphorism that "truth is a libel" obtained with unmistakable force in this case, and Mr. Coleman and his publisher, the editor of the paper called *The Spiritual Times*, were mulcted in heavy damages.

It is worth while in this connection to give a curious episode which may not be unimportant in weighing the statements of those, who—because they find fraud in one direction—pass a wholesale verdict of condemnation against the reliability of all phenomena.

A report has often gained currency, that there was *somewhere*, though rumour never condescended to be explicit on the actual whereabouts, a mechanic who had been employed to manufacture apparatus by which a machine, concealed about the person, could produce the phenomena known as "Spirit rapping."

More than one of the antagonists to Spiritualism have made allusion to this floating rumour, treating it as a well proven fact, and alleging that it fully explained the entire formulæ of the (assumed Spiritual) rappings.

Now these allegations have always been made with an amount of indefiniteness which has deprived them of credit, whether with the advocates

13

or opponents of Spiritualism. For the benefit of both classes, we shall now proceed to give the floating rumour a clear and legitimate parentage.

During the investigations of the Dialectical Society, there was a general flutter of opinion on the part of the antagonists to Spiritualism lest those who were heretofore sceptics, might prove too much and not improbably become themselves converted.

In this direful contingency *some one (whom this record does not care to immortalize)* procured the attendance before the Dialectical Society's Council, of one Mr. William Faulkner, of Endell Street, London, who gave evidence in respect to certain magnets which he claimed to have manufactured, by means of which "artificial raps could be produced," whilst the magnets were concealed about the person of "the Medium."

Being closely plied with questions by the Spiritualists present, this gentleman was unable to show *that he had ever supplied these magnets to a single Medium known to any one in the Spiritual ranks* save a Mr. Addison, the accomplice of Mr. Sothern, and the *gentleman* at whose residence all the tricks were performed, which Mr. Coleman exposed.

It must be remembered that Messrs. Sothern and Addison made it their business to bring Spiritualism into ridicule and contempt by first pretending to produce phenomena and then showing that it was only the result of trickery and deception. It was in aid of this notable work that Mr. Faulkner's magnets were manufactured, and in this way that Mr. Faulkner's testimony was expected to bring discredit on the entire mass of Spiritual phenomena ; in a word, those who contrived to cite this person, before the Dialectical Society's Council, evidently meant to show that because Mr. Addison's house was fitted up with artificial magnets designed to deceive the unwary and bring Spiritualism into ridicule, so all "Spirit rappings," whether occurring in the palaces of emperors and princes, or the homes of clowns and harlequins, must be produced by magnets manufactured by Mr. Faulkner, of Endell Street, London !

Comment upon this very flimsy attempt to destroy a world-wide truth with a harlequin's bat and ball is unnecessary ; in short, a subject so justly relegated to oblivion would not be recalled at this time, were it not desirable to observe, to what desperate and puerile methods of warfare, the opponents of this great cause have been driven.

Shortly after the Coleman prosecution, another of a still more complex and damaging character arose, in connection with Mr. D. D. Home, and an old lady by the name of Lyon.

Although the details of this case may be fresh in the memory of readers of the present generation it is necessary, for the benefit of posterity, to give the following brief abstract of its salient points.

It seems that Mrs. Lyon, an eccentric old lady, took a sudden and violent fancy to Mr. D. D. Home, and being a widow with a large fortune at her own disposal, she induced the young Medium to become her adopted son and heir. Settlements were made, and Mr. Home's name was changed to Lyon, by a formal parliamentary act.

For a time all seemed to promise well for the future happiness of the contracting parties. At length however, the lady grew exacting, the adopted son restive ; she wearied of her fancy, he of his gilded chains. Disputes arose ; then estrangement, and the *finale* was, a demand on the part of the lady, for release from all her promises, and an immediate restitution of the gifts she had bestowed on the creature of her whim.

Unfortunately for Mr. Home, the last-named demand implied an impossibility with which he could not comply. Failing to obtain her exorbitant demands, the whilom *tender mother* had the son arrested, and then commenced a vigorous prosecution against him for the restitution of all the gifts she had bestowed, on the plea, that Mr. Home had worked upon her feelings, and induced her to consent to the act of adoption by *pretended* Spiritual manifestations.

A long trial ensued, in the published reports of which, not one tittle of evidence could be adduced in support of the lady's allegation; on the contrary, her witnesses discredited and contradicted each other, and her own testimony was so silly and unsupported, that the judge was frequently obliged to advise her to be silent, as "her statements were too contradictory to be accepted." On the other hand it was shown by an immense number of the most respectable witnesses, that Mr. Home yielded to this lady's offers slowly and reluctantly, and that he even sent his friend and legal adviser Mr. William Wilkinson to call on her; to place before her the magnitude of her undertaking, and beseech her to take time and good counsel, before consummating her hasty proposal.

During the entire progress of this protracted trial, the balance of evidence was all on the side of the unfortunate Medium, and judging purely by the testimony adduced, not a doubt existed in the public mind, that Mr. Home would be honourable acquitted, and the prosecution anything but honourably quashed.

But great are the uncertainties of the law! Mr. Home was found guilty *of exerting undue influence over the mind of an innocent aged lady*, and ordered to give back all that he could restore, and so the matter was supposed to end. End there however it did not. So long as the details of the case were fresh in the public mind, Mr. Home was regarded as the victim of a very unjust verdict, whilst Mrs. Lyon was regarded as very much more of a wolf in sheep's clothing, than as the representative of her kingly name. When the real facts at issue slipped out of the versatile memory of "the dear public" however, and ancient prejudice was permitted to re-assume her sway, the Spiritualists were constantly reproached with the acts of "that wicked Mr. Home," and the wrongs of that amiable and *truthful* old lady, Mrs. Lyon. Nay, the author in her wide wanderings over the world has frequently been reminded "how that dreadful Mr. Home had been *imprisoned for life*, for plundering and imposing upon his benefactress, and how that dreadful delusion of Spiritualism was all exploded in consequence." It was of no avail to urge that Mr. Home was at that very time the honoured guest of the Emperor of Russia, and Spiritualism exerting more power and influence over the masses than ever. The slanderers "knew all about it," for did not every one "say so," and was it not enough that it was testified of by the authoritative tongue of common report?

At a still later date, other trials and other convictions occurred, and in more than one instance frauds and adventurers received their deserts, and suffered penalties which Spiritualists were as ready to pronounce well merited as were their opponents. Still the result of any judicial trials in which Spiritualism was concerned, invariably ended *unfavourably for the cause*, whatever the merits of the case might be.

It is not to be wondered at then, that antagonistic individuals availed themselves of this mockery of justice in connection with an unpopular movement, and scrupled not to call in the aid of the law to punish the believers whose faith they could not change.

Whatever the present generation may allege, posterity will surely realize that it was the prevalence of an unjust and bigoted public sentiment, and the certainty that the law would uphold that sentiment, which stimulated the vexatious prosecution that was quite recently instituted against the celebrated American Medium, Mr. Henry Slade, who, during a brief visit to this country *en route* to fulfil an engagement in Russia, was becoming all too popular with the visitors whom his limited time permitted him to receive.

It was no doubt in view of this "perversion of public feeling" and "in the highest interests of morality and religion" that two self-styled scientific gentlemen called on the American Medium, and after endeavouring in every possible way to entrap him into some suspicious act, they openly accused him of fraud, caused his arrest and entered upon a vigorous and relentless prosecution against him.

Again the details of the trial were utterly barren of proof that the charge was true. Except that the prosecution could not account for the phenomena produced, and therefore trumped up an imaginary and totally impractical hypothesis as *to how it might or must have been done*, there was not a shadow of evidence to prove fraud on the part of the Medium.

For the defence, a large number of distinguished and respectable persons tendered their witness in favour of Slade's honesty, and the unmistakable character of the supra-mundane phenomena occurring in his presence. Only four of these favourable witnesses were allowed to testify, one of them being the celebrated author and naturalist, Professor A. R. Wallace. Notwithstanding the fact that the magistrate before whom the case was tried, was obliged to acknowledge that the evidence in Slade's favour "was overwhelming," after a most "Dogberry" like summing up, he sentenced Mr. Slade "under the fourth section of the Vagrant Act," to three months' imprisonment with hard labour, "*for using subtile crafts and devices by palmistry or otherwise to deceive*," &c., &c. This notable conviction was soon after "quashed" on appeal to the Middlesex Sessions, for a formal error in the conviction.

But the enemy was not to be deprived of his "pound of flesh." "In the interests of science"—as the prosecutors alleged—they commenced a fresh attack, and although the victim of this pitiful warfare—broken down in health and spirits by the cruel persecution directed against him— insisted upon meeting whatever further proceedings might be taken, his medical attendant declared that "any further attempt to face the storm would kill him outright," and his numerous friends and supporters absolutely forced him to proceed on his way to the Continent, to meet the engagement for which he had come to Europe.

It is but justice to add, that when Mr. Slade's health became sufficiently restored, he wrote to one of his scientific accusers, offering to return to England at his own expense, to give him six *séances* at any place he might choose, under any reasonable conditions he might dictate, entirely free of charge and for the purpose of proving the absence of fraud on his part. This letter, long, clear, and manly as it was, the scientific and gentleman-like accuser doubtless deemed it "in the interests of science" utterly to disregard, even by a single word of reply. The unprejudiced reader may satisfy himself concerning the entire candour and honesty of this letter by perusing it on page 36 of Professor Zöllner's work, "Transcendental Physics."

It might be worth while to compare the facts thus briefly summarized, from already published accounts, with " the lying tongue of rumour," from which source the author has frequently heard, that "Slade had been caught in the act of tricking a party of celebrated professors ; tried, condemned, imprisoned, and that hence, the monstrous delusion of Spiritualism was all exposed and for ever exploded !"

For the rest of Mr. Slade's Continental experiences the reader is referred to the section on " Spiritualism in Germany," and the report of his *séances* with the Leipzig professors.

It only remains to notice one more result of the prosecution, or more strictly speaking, the *persecution*, to which Mr. Slade was subject, and this was, the circulation of a memorial to the British Home Secretary, a few extracts from which will close this chapter.

The Spiritualists of Great Britain probably never expected any other official result from their memorial than a silent smile of contempt from the party whose duty it would be to consign it to the Governmental waste basket—nevertheless they felt that its distribution would serve the purpose of registering the Spiritualists' version of their case, and give the too-trusting public to understand that the Bow Street magistrate's unfavourable verdict, had not yet become the funeral sermon of Spiritualism, also that this irrepressible cause still maintained a vigorous state of being, in which new conversions were effected with each succeeding day and hour.

The *Religio Philosophical Journal*, an old established and excellent Spiritual periodical published at Chicago, U.S., reprinted the above-named memorial, the main points of which, together with the editor's comments, we give in the following extract :—

" The British National Association of Spiritualists has prepared, and is circulating a memorial to the Home Secretary of the British Government, asking that the construction heretofore put upon an Act for the Suppression of Vagrancy, whereby it is made a means of maintaining criminal prosecution against Mediums, may be corrected. The fourth section of the act classes as vagrants, ' Every person pretending or professing to tell fortunes, or using any subtle craft, means or device by palmistry or otherwise, to deceive or impose upon any of his majesty's subjects.' It was under this clause that Henry Slade was prosecuted, and concerning his prosecution the memorial says :

"' As an instance in point your memorialists would refer to the case of Henry Slade, an American Medium, charged at Bow Street Police Court in the year 1876, under the fourth section of the said Act. For the defence the magistrate allowed to be called as witnesses four gentlemen, one of them of great scientific eminence, who were experts in the investigation of Spiritualism, and who had especially tested the Mediumship of the defendant on many occasions. These gentlemen gave evidence of facts wholly inconsistent with the supposition that the defendant was an impostor—evidence which the magistrate himself declared from the bench to be " overwhelming." In attendance were other witnesses prepared to give similar testimony. Yet the magistrate refused to allow them to be called : and, in giving judgment against the defendant, he avowedly put the evidence, which he had described as above, altogether out of consideration, expressly declaring that he based his decision " according to the known course of nature." The law, it is true, does not expressly sanction any presumption against the existence of agencies in nature other than and surpassing those generally known—and these it is, and not " miraculous " or " supernatural " powers that Spiritualists allege—but the persons who administer the law are unavoidably bounded by this common knowledge in dealing with evidence and the probabilities arising therefrom. It results then, that the magistrate who adjudicates " according to the known course of nature " in respect to phenomena which do not conform to such " known course " as interpreted by him, finds it practically unnecessary to hear evidence beyond the mere proof of the alleged occurrence of the phenomena in question in the presence of a certain individual, when no other person also present can be taken to have produced them. The case is therefore prejudged ; and the examination of witnesses to prove that any alleged act of imposture was not really of that character is a superfluous mockery and pretence. It is upon this fact that no tribunal, without going into an exhaustive and impracticable inquiry upon an unfamiliar subject, can do other than take its own knowledge and experience as the standard of probability, that your memorialists chiefly rest their statement of the unavoidable injustice and prejudicial character of these prosecutions.'"

CHAPTER XXVI.

SPIRITUALISM IN GREAT BRITAIN (CONTINUED).

CONCERNING THE LITERATURE OF ENGLISH SPIRITUALISM.

THE first periodical issued in England in connection with the subject of Spiritualism was *The Yorkshire Spiritual Telegraph.* When seeking for authentic information on this pioneer work, the author was referred to the following article which appeared in the year 1882 in the columns of *Light*; and its perusal will perhaps give a better idea than could otherwise be obtained of the regard with which the promoter of this periodical is still remembered :—

" KEIGHLEY.

"An event, unique in character, has recently transpired in this cosy little Yorkshire town, which will long be remembered with pleasure by all concerned, marking as it did the thirtieth anniversary of the introduction of Spiritualism into this country. The celebration, for such in character was the event alluded to, was conceived and executed by the committee and friends of the Keighley 'Spiritual Brotherhood,' Mr. John Pickles, the chairman, working energetically to that end, and being ably assisted by Mr. J. Smith, the hon. secretary. Indeed, so earnestly did all work that a most successful issue was achieved. The proceedings consisted of a public tea and meeting on Saturday, July 8th. The objects the committee had in view were the presentation of the portraits of the three pioneer workers in the movement, viz., Messrs. John Wright, Abraham Shackleton, and David Weatherhead ; the two first-named persons, and the family of the last-named gentleman, who has passed hence, being the recipients of the gifts. In 1853 Mr. David Richmond, from the Shakers, of America, brought the particulars of Spirit phenomena with him to this country, and, paying a visit to Keighley, called upon Mr. David Weatherhead to present the matter to the attention of that gentleman. As a result of the interview, a public meeting was held, at which table manifestations were obtained, through mediums discovered in the audience, by Mr. Richmond, who delivered an explanatory address. Mr. Weatherhead became convinced of the truth of Spirit intercourse, and at once entered heartily into the matter, sparing neither time, pains, nor purse in his zeal. He established the first printing press in the movement, printed the first English Spiritual periodical, the *Yorkshire Spiritual Telegraph,* and caused the circulation of innumerable tracts, pamphlets, &c., throughout the kingdom, and subsequently erected, at his own expense, the comfortable and commodious building used by the society at the present time. He contentedly bore all the expenses involved, and during his residence in the flesh was a true pillar of the cause. Messrs. Wright and Shackleton were the two trance mediums developed in the early days ; they have literally grown grey in the work. Their labours have been free of price, and as speakers, healers, and clairvoyants they have rendered valuable service to the cause. To do honour to these workers, and to express the high esteem in which they were held, the recent presentation was arranged. On Saturday the proceedings were opened by a tea, at which a very large company sat down. At seven o'clock the public meeting was opened by the chairman, Mr. J. Clapham, who said : 'Ladies and gentlemen, we are met here to-night to show our gratitude to the late Mr. Weatherhead, and also to Mr. Shackleton and Mr. Wright, for their past services. Keighley was the place where Spiritualism was first promulgated in this country, being introduced to us by Mr. David Richmond, of Darlington, who, with the assistance of Mr

Weatherhead, was enabled to deliver three lectures upon the subject in the Working Men's Hall, in June, 1853. The issues were, that Mr. Weatherhead took steps which resulted in the formation of the society which exists at the present time ; and soon afterwards the mediums named were developed, and they are still serving us to-day. These gentlemen, with Mr. Weatherhead, were the mainstays of the cause, and Mr. Weatherhead, during his life here, spared neither time nor means in spreading abroad this grand truth. It was he who established the first printing press, and distributed tracts, pamphlets, and other literature broadcast, the materials for which were largely obtained through mediumship. He it was who bore the entire expense of the erection of the Lyceum Buildings, and in many other ways testified his earnestness and devotion to the cause. The outcome of his labours has been that to-day we have here a society in a flourishing condition, having one hundred and fifty members on the roll, some five or six active mediums constantly ministering to us, and a Sunday School composed of upwards of a hundred members. As, therefore, a slight mark of esteem and appreciation to these our pioneer workers, we are to-night to present to them the portraits before us, and all will join with me in saying they are most heartily deserved.' The portraits, in oils, which are excellent specimens of the painter's art, were then presented. That to Mr. Wright was presented by Mr. John Scott, of Belfast ; that to Mr. Shackleton by Mr. D. Richmond, of Darlington ; and that of Mr. Weatherhead to his family, by Mr. J. J. Morse, of London ; and suitable acknowledgments were made in each case. The proceedings were varied by some excellent singing and reciting by a glee party and several friends, and altogether the event was marked by a hearty enthusiasm which evidenced the full sympathy of all present in the event of the day.

"The series of meetings were held in the large Auction Hall of Mr. William Weatherhead, who very kindly placed it at the disposal of the society free of cost. The above events will be long remembered by all present, and constitute an occasion that will be historical in its relations to the progress of Spiritualism in Great Britain."

None but the pioneer of an unpopular cause can understand the value of the good work effected by Mr. David Weatherhead, or the amount of martyrdom he must have incurred in its performance.

In his time, the publication of a Spiritual journal, and the dissemination of Spiritual literature was only repaid by public odium and social ostracism.

Mr. David Weatherhead, as the first publisher of the first Spiritual journal issued from the English press, undoubtedly courted the martyr's cross that was put upon him ; but who can doubt that he is now reaping the reward of the martyr's crown in the better life to which his brave spirit has attained?

After the *Spiritual Telegraph*, the oldest and most important work of the movement was the London *Spiritual Magazine*, which, during a period of nearly twenty years, sent forth its monthly record of Spiritual work and progress in Great Britain in choice language and scholarly form. This magazine was published by the accomplished writer William Wilkinson, Esq., solicitor, of Lincoln's Inn, a gentleman who contributed his wealth and high social position to the advancement of Spiritualism and the promulgation of its teachings, without fear of or favour from men. Mr. Wilkinson's undertaking was promoted and ably sustained by the literary assistance of Mr. Thomas Shorter, who—under the *nom de plume* of "Brevior"—has written, lectured, and laboured for the cause of Spiritualism, with a devotion and zeal that entitle him to the gratitude of every spiritualist in this generation. Quite early in the history of the modern movement, Mr. Shorter published an admirable and compendious work on the Spiritualism of all ages and times, entitled "The Two Worlds." The production of this lucid, and charmingly written work, would in itself have been sufficient to elevate its author to a high rank in the world of letters had the subject been any other than Spiritualism. Working on unceasingly, Mr. Shorter never paused to enquire whether the sublime truths he promulgated met, or opposed the popular taste. From the first opening of the immortal gates to the eyes of humanity in this century, up to the truly *dark day*, when the irreparable loss of sight fell like a pall across the noble gentleman's way, he has laboured with tongue, pen, and influence, to help to plant the standard of the faith and illuminate the path of others with the radiance of that better world, which alone remains to guide his darkened way on earth.

Even since the affliction of blindness has fallen upon him, Mr. Shorter has not relapsed his efforts to *steady the ark of progress* as it moves on its way. His fearless testimony is ever ready, and his clear voice is heard at every public gathering of Metropolitan Spiritualists. A fine collection of choice poems has lately been issued by him, for the consolation and instruction of those *who can see to read them,*—and Mr. Shorter's career gives promise of closing like that of the good sentinel of Pompeian celebrity who died at his post—"faithful unto death."

In addition to the invaluable services of Messrs. Wilkinson and Shorter, the London *Spiritual Magazine* numbered amongst its staff of contributors the flower of European Spiritual literati.

Pre-eminent above all others, stands out the noble name of William Howitt, an author whose works are the pride of every well-informed English reader; a gentleman whom to know was to love and honour, and a Spiritualist whose fearless advocacy shed lustre on his cause, and became a tower of strength to his co-workers. Happily for the better appreciation of Mr. Howitt and his wonderful literary labours, a faithful transcript of his life is just now passing through the press in a volume entitled "The Pioneers of the Spiritual Reformation." Mr. Howitt's biography forms the opening chapters of this interesting work, and how full of valuable information the volume itself will be, may be gathered from the fact, that it is written by the daughter of Mary and William Howitt, Mrs. Watts,—a lady whose charming contributions to Spiritual literature have already become familiar to admiring readers over the signature of "A. M. H. W." It may not be inappropriate in this place to give an excerpt from the London *Spiritual Magazine* in which Mr. Howitt defines, in his own forcible language, the nature of some of his spiritual experiences. He says:—

"We have seen tables often enough lifted by invisible power from the floor; seen them give answers to questions by rising and sinking in the air; we have seen them in the air keep time by their movements to a tune playing on a piano; seen them slide about the floor of a room, laying themselves down when touched. . . . . We have heard bells ring in the air, and seen them thus ringing move about a room; seen flowers broken from plants, and carried to different persons, without any visible hand; seen musical instruments play correct airs apparently of themselves, and even rise up, place themselves on a person's head, and play out a well-known air in fine style. We have heard remarkable predictions given through mediums, and which have come literally to pass; heard wonderful descriptions of scenes in the invisible world made by persons in clairvoyant trance, which would require the highest imaginative genius to invent or embody in words; have seen writing done by pencils laid on paper in the middle of the floor, not within reach of any person present, and innumerable such things."

And in speaking of the drawings made by Madam Hauffé under spirit-influence, he takes occasion to make the following statement of his own experience as a spirit-medium :—

"Having myself, who never had a single lesson in drawing, and never could draw in a normal condition, had a great number of circles struck through my hand under spirit-influence, and these filled up by tracery of ever new invention, without a thought of my own, I, at once, recognise the truth of Kerner's statement. The drawings made by my hand have been seen by great numbers of persons, artists as well as others, and remain to be seen, though the power is again gone from me. Giotto, or any pair of compasses, could not strike more perfect circles than I could under this influence, with nothing but a piece

S C HALL

of paper and a pencil. No inventor of tracery or patterns could invent such original ones as were thrown out on the paper day after day, with almost lightning speed, except with long and studious labour, and by instrumental aid. At the same time the sketches given through me are not to be named with the drawings, both in pencil and colours, produced in this manner through others who are well known."

As an example of the logical yet religious tone of Mr. Howitt's philosophical articles on this subject we call the reader's attention to the subjoined passages, taken from the London *Spiritual Magazine* of April, 1863 :—

"And all this time, in England, thousands and tens of thousands were daily sitting down in their families and circles of intimate friends, and quietly and successfully testing those angels under their own mode of advent, and finding them real. And both in America and here, as well as in most of the Continental nations, this has been the great mode of enquiry and convincement. Public mediums have, in reality, only inaugurated the movement : it has been, of necessity, carried on by private and family practice. In this domestic prosecution of Spiritualism, equally inaccessible to the vulgar sorcerer and the interested impostor—where every person was desirous only of truth, and many of them of deep religious truth—the second stage of Spiritual development, the more interior and intellectual, has been reached by a very large community. For there is, indeed, a very large section of society who are sick of empty profession, or disgusted with the dreary cheat of scepticism, and who have been long yearning for some revelation of the immortal hopes of earlier years, in some substantial and unmistakeable form. They have found this in the daily visits of their departed friends, coming to them with all their old identities of soul, taste, or memory of announcements of Christian truth, and of God's promised felicity. They have listened again and again to the words of their beloved ones, bidding them take courage, for there was no death, but that around them walked their so-called departed, ready to aid and comfort them in their earth pilgrimage, and to receive them to immediate and far more glorious existence."

Besides the voluminous mass of historical and descriptive writings for which both Mr. and Mrs. Howitt have attained a world-wide celebrity, Mrs. Howitt has enriched the répertoire of Spiritual literature with a fine translation of Enmemoser's " History of Magic," whilst Mr. Wm. Howitt's " History of the Supernatural," in two volumes, and his splendid magazine articles, are acknowledged to be amongst the best standard works of which the Spiritual cause can boast.

Amongst the many popular and distinguished writers of the day who have fearlessly avowed their interest in Spiritualism and contributed talent and reputation to its advocacy, were Mr. and Mrs. S. C. Hall, the former well-known as the editor of the London *Art Journal*, whilst Mrs. Hall's charming works of fiction, and other writings, have procured for her a world-wide celebrity. It would be difficult to exaggerate the valuable influence exercised by this accomplished couple upon the cause of Spiritualism.

Moving in the highest ranks of European society, their residence was the scene of delightful *reunions*, where gifted Mediums and persons of the highest literary and scientific culture were brought together and combined to send forth an influence which permeated the ranks of the most intellectual classes of Europe. It is but a few short years since the fair form of the talented authoress, Maria S. C. Hall, vanished from her wide circle of admirers and passed to the land of light to which her hand had already pointed so many of earth's weary pilgrims. And thus after fifty years of heart and soul companionship, the noble octogenarian, S. C. Hall, was left alone on earth, at least so far as mortal sight is concerned ; never have the triumphs of Spiritualism become more manifest than in the fortitude with which this truly " Christian " gentleman sustains the temporary separation between the mortal and the immortal. At a crowded reception tendered to the author by the Central Association of Spiritualists, a few months since, on the occasion of her visit to London, Mr. S. C. Hall—then over eighty years of age—made THE SPEECH of the night, and in a strain of glowing eloquence that thrilled every heart, and brought tears to every eye, he declared that the grave had not separated him from his angel wife. Her constant communications cheered his loneliness, he said; guided his mortal footsteps and gave him unceasing assurance that she in heaven and he on earth were now as ever one in heart, life interest, and undying interchange of loving communion. . . . What a triumphant illustration of immortal life over mortal death, and of the value of the much derided facts and philosophy of Spiritualism !

In addition to these eminent writers, many others of scarcely less celebrity assisted in making the London *Spiritual Magazine* a work as valuable in an æsthetic point of view, as it was interesting to the believers in Spirit communion.

One of the first volumes published in the interests of Spiritualism, and still a standard work with those who desire to trace out the movement from its incipiency, is Mrs. De Morgan's excellent sketch of her own experiences, entitled "From Matter to Spirit."

Another valuable and timely compendium of Spiritual facts and philosophy is, "The Natural and Supernatural," written at an early period of the movement in England, by J. Enmore Jones, Esq., of Norwood.

Mr. D. D. Home has published two interesting volumes at different times, the one called "Incidents of My Life," the other "Lights and Shadows of Spiritualism."

Omitting the long list of smaller volumes, tracts, pamphlets, leaflets, &c., &c., which swell the mass of English Spiritual literature, we next call attention to an admirable work—"Miracles and Modern Spiritualism," written by the celebrated author and naturalist, Professor A. R. Wallace. For the unpretentious size of this volume it would be difficult to find any work which presents a more unanswerable array of facts, logic, and scientific deductions; in short, it is in every way worthy to be regarded as a Spiritualistic manual, of equal value to the well-informed Spiritualist, and the earnest investigator.

Besides the intrinsic value of Professor Wallace's admirable work, the public have appreciated it all the more, from the fact that it emanates from the pen of one so highly honoured in the ranks of science and literature as Alfred Russell Wallace. Dividing honours with the alleged founder of the famous doctrine of "evolution"—Charles Darwin—a world-wide traveller, naturalist, and distinguished author, Professor Wallace has never hesitated to contribute his honoured testimony to the much-abused cause of Spiritualism. His clear logical speeches, unanswerable magazine and journalistic articles, and his noble defence and exposition of true Spiritualism, when and wherever opportunity has permitted, all have combined to render Professor Wallace's adherence to the cause of Spiritualism a tower of strength which can never be too gratefully remembered.

Professor Crookes's record of experiments with Mr. D. D. Home, Miss Cook, and other Media; Professor Zöellner's "Transcendental Physics," and the "Report of the Dialectical Society," have been already noticed.

One of the most esteemed and gifted writers in the ranks of Spiritualism is the gentleman known by the *nom de plume* of "M. A., Oxon."

Amongst this truly inspired author's collected writings, the most popular are, the four volumes entitled severally, "Psychography;" "Spirit Identity;" "The Higher Aspects of Spiritualism;" and "Spirit Teachings."

Nothing in the whole realm of occult literature can surpass the deep insight, and profound mastery of Spiritualistic problems, manifested in these works. And yet they are but a small part of " M. A., Oxon's" contributions. His fine magazine and journalistic articles are to be found in most of the high-toned periodicals of the last few years, whilst his well-known signature invariably attracts every thoughtful reader who desires to be instructed, as well as interested.

Three of the most remarkable volumes that have of late issued from the English Spiritual press, are those, circulated chiefly amongst the publisher's personal friends, entitled, " Angelic Revelations." They are a collection of communications given through the Mediumship of a lady in private life, and received by a circle of ladies and gentlemen whose sessions were continued for several years in the city of Manchester. The *séances* were of the most exclusive character, and were only participated in by such persons as the controlling intelligences elected to receive. Each of these favoured individuals was named by the presiding "angels," according to the qualities of mind that distinguished them. To Mr. William Oxley, the well-known and highly-esteemed Spiritualistic author, was assigned the onerous task of recording the communications spoken in trance by the Medium.

Thus the whole of the three volumes above named, have been written out and prepared for the press, and published in the highest form of mechanical art, by Mr. Oxley "the Recorder," with the permission of the controlling intelligences, and under the auspices of the Manchester circle.* No comment can do justice to the ecstatic style or remarkable views of the future life, indicated in these volumes. They must be read to be appreciated, and then they form but one fragment of the innumerable and diverse revealments of the after life, and man's spiritual genesis and exodus, which the trance utterances of the present dispensation have furnished us with. The volumes above mentioned are not the only ones for which the world is indebted to their accomplished publisher.

Mr. William Oxley has written a remarkably fine poetical adaptation of the celebrated Hindoo *Baghavat Gita;* an excellent metaphysical work entitled " The Philosophy of Spirit;" and he is now enriching the columns of the *Medium and Daybreak* with a graphic account of the ancient monuments of Egypt, which he describes and comments upon in the progressive spirit of an advanced thinker, and from the standpoint of his own personal knowledge, obtained during a recent visit to the wonderful old land of the Pharaohs. Mr. Oxley's name has become so long familiarized to every reader of the best Spiritual literature, by noble and high-toned articles, that many will rejoice in the opportunity of becoming better acquainted with their favourite author, through the accompanying fine illustrations. The introduction to the facsimiles of the spiritually produced flower and the spirit foot are too graphically recorded in Mr. Oxley's own words to need any other comment than their perusal will suggest.

Mr. Oxley, addressing the author of this volume, says :—

"To Mrs. Britten,—I have the pleasure to furnish you with engravings of a materialised spirit's foot, which represents with perfect exactitude the plaster cast, moulded by a professional artist, from the paraffin wax envelope. Apart from any suggestion of trickery and collusion the cast itself tells its own tale, for it has the cuticle marks in the crucial parts, which it would be impossible to produce *under any circumstances* without a

* " Angelic Revelations, concerning the origin, ultimation, and destiny of the Human Spirit, &c., may be had from T. Gaskell, 69, Oldham Road, Manchester.

mould formed of many parts, as any mechanician, or even ordinary person can see at a glance. The cast foot is eight inches long by three inches in the smallest part, and nine inches in the widest part. The opening at the top of the foot is 2¼ inches diameter. And yet through this opening the foot was instantaneously withdrawn. The medium was Mrs. Firman (now deceased). The *modus operandi* was as follows : I prepared the melted hot liquid paraffin, into which the little spirit form dipped her foot several times, so as to make it of sufficient thickness to maintain its figure. After this operation the spirit form—known to us as Bertie—put out her foot *with the wax mould upon it*, and asking me to take hold of it, which I did, the foot was withdrawn (or dissolved, I know not which) and the mould left in my hand. This was at the house of a friend in Manchester, April 11th, 1876, and next morning I took the wax mould to Mr. Bernaditto, who filled it with plaster, and, after melting the wax from the plaster, the result was a beautiful feminine human foot, of which the illustration is a faithful copy. The crucial test of this wondrous phenomenon is seen by reference to Figure II. The ball of the toe (see D C), *half an inch thick*, had to be drawn through an opening only a *quarter-inch deep* (see B A), which, of course, under ordinary circumstances, is a physical impossibility, without destroying the fine bridge (see A C), and it is exactly on this bridge that the cuticle marks are delineated as perfectly as on the human foot. Your space will not permit me to give the means employed to eliminate anything like fraudulent action on the part of the medium, neither is it necessary to do so, as the cast itself—still in my possession—leaves its own stamp of genuineness, for there is not a single mark that betokens anything contrary to what it really is, viz., a cast from a whole and perfect mould, without a division ; and I challenge the world to produce the like, otherwise than by similar agency. I, myself, made the so-called cabinet, which was the recess of a bay window, into which nothing could get without being seen by ten pairs of watchful eyes (there was a good light all through the *séance*). The medium, who was a woman of great size, went inside, and in the course of some fifteen minutes, the little psychic form of Bertie presented herself, and went through the operations as described above. After the performance she disappeared, and in a moment or two I drew the curtain aside, and there was Mrs. Firman entranced, and the sole occupant. Where was Bertie ?

" The other illustration is from a photograph of a plant with flower, produced through the mediumship of Mrs. Esperance, at Newcastle-on-Tyne, August 4th, 1880. The reader must take all accessories for granted, as it is superfluous to enumerate all the precautionary measures to ensure genuine phenomena.

" The cabinet was a plain wooden box, five feet high, closed at top and bottom, with a gauze division in the centre, and a curtain covering the whole front, about six feet wide. The medium sat in one compartment, and the company (about twenty persons) sat round in horse-shoe fashion. In a short time, a little figure, draped in white, known as Yolande, emerged from the other (empty) compartment. That it was not the medium was evident from the fact of the figure being much less in size, and different in outline, and I heard Mrs. E. breathing hard while the figure was outside. Yolande requested my friend, Reimers, to get a glass water-bottle, and some sand and water, which, when mixed, he put into the bottle, and returned to his seat. Yolande then made a few passes over the bottle, and actually *created* a white gauzy cloth before our very eyes. She then retired about a yard from the bottle, and sat down on the floor. Presently we saw—for there was sufficient light to clearly distinguish the operation—the gauze veil gradually rising, as if there was something moving it upwards. In about two minutes, after rising about sixteen inches, Yolande rose to her feet and went to the bottle, from which she removed the covering, and lo ! there was a plant with green leaves grown out of the bottle, with its roots in the sand : but there was no flower on it. After we had somewhat recovered from our astonishment, Yolande took it up, bottle and all, and gave it into my hands. She then retired into the cabinet. After the company had inspected it, I placed it at my feet, and waited for what should come next. In a few minutes raps were heard, and then the alphabet was used. ' Look at your plant ' was spelt out, and taking it up I found, not only that it had grown very considerably in size, but there was a beautiful flower about four inches diameter on it. *This was produced while it was between my feet.* I took it to my hotel, and next morning had it photographed, of which the engraving is an exact copy. The next night Yolande gave me a *small rosebud* on a short stalk, with not more than two leaves on. This I put in my bosom, and kept it there during the time that the *séance* lasted ; but having the impression that something was going on, I put my hand to feel it, and noticing that it felt different I kept my own counsel and did not disturb it. When the *séance* was drawing to a close, I drew forth my rosebud, when, strange to relate, it had developed into a bunch of *three large full-blown roses, with a bud as well !* These I also put away with the plant.

" Extensive as has been my experience—now ranging over many years—with psychic sensitives, there have been no results more satisfactory and pleasing—*i.e.*, on the physical plane—than the above which I have narrated, and curtailed, so as to give only the bald

LE DUC DE MEDINA POMAR.

facts. The top leaves (six inches long), with a part of the stalk and remains of flower plant (preserved under glass), together with the foot—along with other *hand* casts—produced under similar circumstances as told—are before me as I write, and I trust that they may be kept for ages to come as *souvenirs,* or first fruits of that mighty spiritual force and movement—now in its commencement—which is destined to change the face of the whole earth, both as a physical orb, and also the social status of humanity that, from generation to generation, will live and move upon its surface. Without trespassing further on your time and space, allow me to congratulate you on the part which you have been destined to play in this wondrous drama ; and unless I grievously err, the time will come—and at no very distant date—when this new volume, which you are now giving to the world, will be recognised and appreciated at its vastly more than mere money value. Each pioneer has his or her own specific work to perform ; and amongst these, none have laboured more assiduously, and more unselfishly, than the gifted editress of 'Art-Magic' ; 'Ghost Land': and the authoress of the ' History of the Modern Spiritual Movement all over the Earth.' So states

" Your Fellow Workman,

" WILLIAM OXLEY.

" Manchester, August 15th, 1883."

Another of the writers who in any department of human thought rather than that of the " occult," would have achieved a world-wide celebrity, is the noble Countess of Caithness, now Duchesse de Pomar. Besides many fugitive contributions to the journalistic literature of the day, this accomplished authoress has written two remarkable works all too little known ; the one, a volume of nearly 500 pages, entitled " Old Truths in a New Light," the other, " Serious Letters to Serious Friends." These publications are no mere poetical effusions of a high-born lady, but the brilliant, sterling, and philosophic arguments of a master mind, enclosed in one of Nature's fairest and most womanly forms. Soaring far above her compeers in the gay and fashionable world, this truly noble woman maintains her lead in the most aristocratic European *salons,* and yet dares avow herself an " occultist" in the profoundest sense of the term. In the midst of princes and potentates, this brave lady hesitates not to appear in loving companionship with the spirit mediums whom she honours with her friendship, and whilst many of the gay butterflies who crowd her Parisian *fêtes* are spending their time in councilling how to adorn themselves with *modistes* and *friseures,* this high-minded and indefatigable labourer in God's vineyard, is penning sublime lines, which lift the soul up to heaven, and forge the golden links of an universal Brotherhood, for all humanity. Amongst the lesser works that have fallen from the Countess of Caithness's pen, is a charming *brochure* entitled '· A Midnight Visit to Holyrood." It is founded upon the singular relations which attach this lady to her much-beloved guardian spirit, the fair and hapless " Marie Stuart, Queen of Scots." At the request of this angelic guide, the Countess paid a midnight visit to Holyrood, there to listen to the spirit voice of her, whose sighs of anguish had been borne on many a wailing breeze through those grim and mournful towers.

We would fain linger on the Countess's thrilling description of her interview with the presiding genius of the scene, did space permit. Failing this, we must still offer a brief extract from this fascinating little work, were it only to give the world —profoundly ignorant of true spiritual ethics— some idea of the tone in which purified spirits commune with mortals, and the character of the advice which the solemn pedagogues of the pulpit so irreverently assure their gaping listeners, proceed from " demons ! "

The modes in which the spirit and the mortal hold communion is thus described by the Countess of Caithness. She says :—

"It is now nearly eight years since I was first made aware of her (Marie Stuart's) connection with me; or rather, perhaps, I should better describe our relations as my connection with her—but only three, since I have enjoyed the happiness of communion with her. I often feel her presence. She makes it known to me in many different ways; and the oral communications I have received from her, and taken down at various times to the best of my ability, have swollen into the size of a small volume. These interviews have generally taken place in the quietude of my own room, and during the calm silence of the midnight hour. But she has also come to me amongst the wild hills of Scotland, or when seated on the high cliffs of Caithness overlooking the stormy Pentland Firth; but only when its wild waves have been comparatively at rest, and reflecting the intense blue of the sky as serene as that which usually overarches the sunny Mediterranean, and when there has been no sign of life around save the white sea-gull sailing majestically overhead between the earth and sky, and the crisp little white crested waves called '*The Merry Men of Mey*' tumbling over one another as if in mad glee at my feet—have I felt her gentle presence, which is ever bright and soothing as a sunbeam, and heard her precious words, which have appeared to me sublime in their beauty, and in their intent, ever urging me onward in the path of truth and progress, and opening out fresh vistas to me of my pathway in the future."

As a specimen of the communication above referred to, we commend the following excerpt from Marie Stuart to Marie Caithness:—

"Go not alone to the Word for life, but also to those who gave it, for they have added knowledge which is more appropriate, and better adapted to the present hour of spiritual growth and unfoldment. Reverently use the Bible for guidance and instruction. Use Nature's great Bible even as reverently, but remember that the passive soul-inspired one will rise even to the beatitudes, gathering new thought-germs, watching the opening bulb and seed of original heaven-inspired ideas; proving all things, holding fast unto that which will bear all the light which science, art, and reason can bring to bear upon them. You, my child, have a mind capable of grasping truths that are destined to make all nations free and inspired. Aye! and this is accomplishing even now. Stand out before the world as one who dares think—one who courts the wisdom of the ages, and grasps the light of the universe to guide humanity forward. The sweet, ever-living truths given to the world by its inspired ones are to be revered, but let us not go backward with uncovered heads asking wisdom; let us rather press forward even into the inner courts of the temple where Deific harmonies lull the soul into conditions of mind that admit of communion with the Builder of all worlds, the Origin of all life, all forms. Let us rise even to the holy altar where a John carried his gifts, and became filled with power."

There is yet another literary work by the Countess of Caithness, to which we only call attention, without attempting in the present historical compendium to analyze its nature, or do justice to its merits. It was during the closing weeks of the year 1880, that the Countess of Caithness contributed a remarkable series of papers to the London *Medium and Daybreak*, on the signs of the times, and the occult prophecies which, from the most remote ages, had pointed to this period. The inspired writer gave an elaborate review of the Cabalistic interpretation of the Biblical writings. She reviewed the Apocalyptic, prophetic, and Pythagorean systems of numbers, and connected them, and the veiled significance of the mediæval mystical writings with the present discoveries which are revealing the occult meanings in Oriental monuments and myths. From all these sources the the learned writer drew the conclusion that the year 1880 completed one of those cycles of time known to, and defined by the ancient prophets, whilst the year 1881 might be regarded as the commencement of an entirely new era, and one which physically, mentally, politically, and religiously, was destined to be regarded by future ages as the opening up of a new dispensation. The Bible, especially the Apocalypse and prophetic writings, was treated of in these remarkable essays, and their mystic meanings interpreted and brought to bear upon the present singularly disturbed condition of human thought, especially in respect to religious opinions.

In testimony of her own implicit faith that a great world dispensation closed in 1880, and another, foretold by seers and prophets, inscribed in the ancient pyramid of Cheops, and manifest in the universal upheaval of human opinions to-day, was inaugurated in 1881, the Countess has adopted the date of the new era together with divers occult emblems on her letter paper, and in not a few of the ornaments which adorn her toilet, and the furniture of her mansion.

When the mists of the new dawn shall have melted into the sunlight of noonday truth, and the *cyclic* progress of the race shall be fully understood, especially in reference to the present transitional and catastrophic period, the essays of Lady Caithness, though they are now "cabala" to the unthinking multitude, will be then recalled and honoured as the advent voice which proclaimed the coming of the new Messiah, the dispensation of peace on earth and goodwill to all men.

Another remarkable addition to the occult, if not the Spiritual literature of the times, has been made by the son of the noble lady of whom we have been writing—formerly the Count, now the Duke de Medina Pomar. This gentleman whilst yet in his teens, became the author of two beautifully written works of fiction designed to illustrate the doctrine of re-incarnation, a belief with which his mind is strongly imbued, and one which finds a more plausible and fascinating illustration in the young Duke de Pomar's writings, than in any of the abstract treatises yet produced on this subject. The names of the works in question are "The Honeymoon" and "Through the Ages." Both these novels are full of exalted sentiment, vivid description, and thrilling interest. Both are designed to present in the form of what in ancient time would have been termed "parables," and in our own age are simply "works of fiction," grand lessons of ideality and Spiritual philosophy. "The Honeymoon" is a veritable dream of beauty; visionary, pathetic, powerful, and enthralling. If not a direct inspiration, it is such a marvellous feat of writing for a mere boy, that it forms to the candid reader a far better proof of an invisible thinker guiding the pen of a mortal scribe than many a voluminous mass of "communications," labelled with the authorship of "the mighty dead." "Through the Ages" is a novel which—as its name implies—traces the progress of a Spirit through all those phases of mortal trial and discipline, which the re-incarnationists affirm to be essential to round out the full perfection of the soul through human experiences.

It ever stern facts could be superseded by the sophistry of undemonstrated theories, it would be through the fascinating influences of a pen so facile, and an imagination so vivid as that of the Duke de Medina Pomar. The pictures are simply perfect, and if ever re-incarnation could be proved, this brilliant writer's "Through the Ages" would be a veritable modern Iliad of the faith.

Since the production of these *chefs d'œuvre*, the Duke de Pomar has published several dashing works of fiction in which his brilliant pen has been more prompt to lash the vices and follies of society, than to renew his earlier and more exalting task of lifting up the unthinking multitude to a higher standard of life and action. Though still a very young man, the Duke has dropped his prolific pen, and to the deep regret of his many admirers, he floats on the surface of society, but writes, *for the present*, no more. Like all subjects of inspiration the fire of his special literary epoch is burnt out, but that it will be rekindled again none who have studied his peculiarly sensitive nature can question. Whatever the future may call forth, none who read the young Duke de Pomar's first literary productions, can hesitate to pronounce them the work of a very talented man, or a phenomenally inspired boy. If years are to decide the question, the latter position is the only solution of which his writings are susceptible.

CHAPTER XXVII.

SPIRITUALISM IN GREAT BRITAIN (CONTINUED.)

STILL MORE CONCERNING THE LITERATURE OF SPIRITUALISM IN ENGLAND.

AMONGST the most important of the contributions that have been made to the literature of English Spiritualism are the writings of Mr. John Farmer, whose name has achieved a wide-spread popularity on both sides of the Atlantic, as the author of "A New Basis of Belief in Immortality," and the admirable pamphlet entitled, "How to Investigate Spiritualism." In both these works Mr. Farmer has dealt with his subjects in an equally scholarly and exhaustive mode. Both have commanded the respectful notice of the secular press, and hold a deservedly high place in the estimation of every reader of Spiritual literature.

It may be remembered that Mr. Farmer's "New Basis of Belief in Immortality," was deemed worthy of being alluded to in terms of warm commendation by one of the great religious dignitaries of the late Ecclesiastical Congress assembled at Newcastle. We do not cite this as praise of any extraordinary value, but simply to show that the religious tone and authoritative character of that work could command the respect of such men as Canon Wilberforce, Dr. Thornton, &c., &c.

One of the most candid and capable critics of the present day, the book reviewer of the *Truthseeker*, says of this volume :—

"This is an exceedingly thoughtful book ; temperate, earnest, and bright with vivid and intelligent love of truth. Mr. Farmer is no fanatic, if we may judge of him by his book, but a brave seeker after the truth. Incidentally, he conveys a vast amount of information concerning what are called the phenomena of Spiritualism—what these phenomena are, under what conditions they are obtained, and to what they lead ; but his main purpose is to show how Spiritualism explains the Bible, supplies the key to not a little that is mysterious in 'historical Christianity,' and furnishes, as he says, 'a new basis of belief.' We commend his book to the attention of all who are prepared to give serious attention to a very serious subject."

To the above-quoted opinions every intelligent reader, whether Spiritualist or opponent, must say *Amen.*

In noticing the two most popular works that have emanated from Mr. Farmer's pen, it must not be supposed that these are his only contributions to the realm of Spiritual literature.

Mr. Farmer is the author of a fine metaphysical essay on "Present Day Problems," and a work on Mesmerism, the modest title of which—"Hints on Mesmerism"—bears no proportion to the valuable, and truly practical matter it contains. It was to the zeal and enterprise of this gentleman also, that the excellent monthly periodical entitled *The Psychological Review,* after an interregnum of many months, was revived in July, 1881, and carried forward to the current year of 1883.

Since the suspension of this magazine became inevitable, Mr. Farmer has given time and indomitable effort to the editorial management of the fine journal so often referred to in this volume, called *Light*.

Mr. Farmer's devoted and untiring services in the cause of Spiritualism have been rendered in so quiet and unostentatious a manner, and his name has obtained so little prominence, except as the author of the popular works above referred to, that the reader may be surprised to learn how largely the present literary standing of the movement is indebted to him; indeed it is with the view of "rendering honour where honour is due," that the author tenders this brief but well-merited tribute of acknowledgment to one of the best and most philosophic writers, as well as one of the most efficient and faithful workers in the ranks of Spiritualism.

Of the other periodicals connected with the movement, it is only necessary to say, the first metropolitan journal that was issued as a weekly organ was published by Mr. Robert Cooper, and called *The Spiritual Times*.

The unfortunate prosecution incurred by Mr. Coleman, involving in its results the publisher of this paper, occasioned its suspension after a short-lived existence. About 1870, Mr. James Burns commenced the publication of an able, well written weekly paper entitled *The Medium and Daybreak*. Still later the enterprising editor started a fine monthly magazine called *Human Nature*.

This periodical—although filled with the articles of able contributors—maintained only an ephemeral existence compared to its cotemporary *The Medium*, which has continued through a period of thirteen years, and still holds its own against the claims of younger rivals. Its editor, like many of the prominent workers in the divided ranks of Spiritualism, has incurred some amount of both ban and blessing from his fellow labourers. Amongst his most determined antagonists however, none will deny him the credit of indomitable energy, perseverance, and a determination to uphold his paper, and all that he conceives to be his special work in connection with the cause of Spiritualism, at any sacrifice. Mr. Burns is a clever, lucid, and interesting speaker, besides being an expert phrenologist. His lectures on phrenology, temperance, vegetarianism, hygiene, &c., &c., are as creditable to his advanced thought as a practical reformer, as they have been instrumental in lifting up humanity to higher motives of life and action throughout Great Britain. In an excellent speech made at the anniversary celebration of the 31st of March, 1882, Mr. Burns gives the following graphic account of his first attempt at Spiritual journalism:—

"Twelve years ago the Movement was expectant of a change—a widening out of its sphere of action. Some autumn seed had been sown to prepare for the harvest of the year just closed. *Daybreak* had been in existence as a monthly paper, and the *Spiritualist* had been commenced fortnightly. To our great regret it was not weekly, as we shrank from the task of taking up the burden of a weekly paper, and hoped the *Spiritualist* would step in and save us. Sunday services had been started at Cavendish Rooms by Mr. Peebles, and a penny hymn book had been printed. The Spiritual Institution was at work, and means for bringing the phenomena before the public were in operation. There was at that time no public movement; but the elements of such a thing were in a state of combination and development.

"The experienced journalist will smile when told that when we set about the first number of the *Medium* we had no contributors, no means, no experience, no ambition, no end to serve. The spirit world required a 'medium' of the press, and we gave it one, by the aid of a kind lady, now in the spirit-world, who came in and laid a £5 note on the counter. Like a little stream at its fountain head, our first number was insignificant, and contained no specious promises for the future. We felt the shadow of years of suffering and toil enveloping us, and moved in our work, as the hands do on the face of the clock, with no purpose of their own, but obedient to the unseen power within."

Through good and evil report, Mr. Burns has carried his enterprise forward with unflagging energy, and with the exception of the London *Spiritual Magazine* no other English periodical has bravely weathered so many storms, or maintained the flag of the movement it advocates for so long a period, and that under the pressure of the severest trials.

The *Spiritualist* newspaper mentioned by Mr. Burns, and often referred to in these pages, was a very scholarly journal representing the scientific aspect of Spiritualism, and for several years was ably conducted by Mr. Wm. Harrison.

Notwithstanding the unbounded generosity with which Charles Blackburn, Esq., of Didsbury, Manchester, contributed to the support of this paper, it was quite recently suspended, and perhaps forms another evidence, that when the purposes of the Spirit world are accomplished, the instruments are laid aside, and a fresh set of influences are brought to bear upon the progress of a movement—of unmistakably supra-mundane power and purpose.

At the time when this volume was commenced, there were, unfortunately for the best interests of each individual enterprise, four Spiritual journals put before the English public, namely, the two already mentioned, *The Herald of Progress*, published at Newcastle-on-Tyne, and the latest and one of the finest of the Spiritual journals, called *Light*, formerly conducted by Mr. Dawson Rogers, and now under the editorship of Mr. John Farmer. Like the *Spiritualist; Light* represents the scientific and metaphysical phases of the Spiritual movement, and its articles—especially those contributed by " M. A., Oxon," and Mrs. A. H. M. Watts, are of the highest interest and value.

With such a *corps* of contributors as " M. A., Oxon," Hon. Roden Noel, Mr. Spicer, Hensleigh Wedgwood, Prof. Barratt, Dr. Wylde, and many other writers of no less ability, but above all, with Mr. John Farmer in the editorial chair, *Light*, like its veteran cotemporary, *The Medium*, ought to be as nobly sustained as it deserves, and compensate for many of the evanescent ephemera of past years, by an unquenchable and permanent existence. Since this volume was commenced, another monthly journal entitled *The Spiritual Record*, has been issued by the indefatigable veteran publisher of Glasgow, Mr. Hay Nesbit. Report speaks highly of this new venture, and Mr. Nesbit's long and gallant services in the cause of Spiritualism, should alone be sufficient to recommend any publication to which his honoured name and skilful directorship is attached. The mention of Mr. Nesbit's much respected name will necessarily call forth the desire to know how the movement progresses in the city where his valuable services are so faithfully rendered.

Although Spiritualism in its two well-defined phases of religious belief, and phenomenal demonstration, has permeated every part of the United Kingdom and found acceptance from all classes, from the palace to the hut, it has made little or no distinctive mark anywhere *as a public movement* except in England. The following notices concerning the status of the cause in Glasgow may furnish some evidence of exception to this rule, hence their introduction in this place.

In the year 1867, the few believers in spirit intercourse resident in Glasgow, solicited the author to pay them a visit in her capacity of a

Spiritual lecturer. It was represented to her that the unusual phenomenon of a lady speaking on religious subjects *in the city of John Knox*, might awaken popular sentiments of an antagonistic character, especially as Spirit communion was to be the theme; one which, though well known and practised largely in private circles, had hitherto borne but an evil name in the censorship of Glasgow public opinion. Altogether the prospects were not very encouraging, but as the author had ever been accustomed to make choice of such scenes for her public efforts, as her wise and far-seeing Spirit Guides advised, she yielded to their persuasions, and proceeded to fulfil the proposed engagement.

The visit was made; more lectures were demanded than had been covenanted for; and a far more satisfactory impression was produced than could have been anticipated.

Several curious phenomenal occurrences marked this visit, which neither time nor place now permit us to notice.

At the risk of incurring the charge of egotism however, we deem it necessary to the progress of the history, to give the following excerpt from the London *Spiritual Magazine*, of December, 1867, as it records the commencement of an era in Glasgow Spiritualism which our next quotation will bring down to the present day.

The first notice is headed :—

"EMMA HARDINGE IN SCOTLAND.

"Mrs. Hardinge has been delivering a course of lectures at Glasgow, under the auspices of the Association of Spiritualists in that city, and she seems to have created quite a sensation in Glasgow, and to have won the hearts of all who heard her. The newspapers, to their credit, whilst asserting that they do not agree with all she said, have not published, I believe, a word in derogation of the subjects of her discourses, and in some instances they commend her eloquence in unstinted terms of praise. The *Christian News* says :— . . . ."

[Then follows a series of highly eulogistic personal notices, of no moment in the present record.]

"At the close of her course of lectures, the members of the Glasgow Association of Spiritualists presented Mrs. Hardinge with a *souvenir* as an additional mark of their respect, and as Mrs. Hardinge has found a new field by this visit to Scotland for the exercise of her great gifts, I feel sure it will be improved on a future occasion, and will lead to a more general understanding of the truths of Spiritualism."

Since the author's first and only visit to Glasgow, Mr. J. J. Morse, one of the most brilliant and eloquent trance speakers of the new dispensation, and Mr. Wallis, another very able and interesting Spiritual lecturer, have from time to time filled the rostrum most acceptably. The sensationalism awakened by the first public acts of propagandism—especially in consideration of the propagandist being *a lady*—has of course died away, but a steady and healthful growth of public sentiment in favour of the noble philosophy enunciated from the Spiritual rostrum has manifested itself in Glasgow, and still maintains its hold upon the hearts of a large number of the population.

The indefatigable efforts of Mr. Hay Nesbit, the well known printer and publisher, and the sterling work of a large number of brave men and women who have formed and held circles, organized public meetings, and given platform addresses, have kept the lamps which light poor blind mortals to the higher life, well trimmed and burning. And this has been done too, at much disadvantage, the distance of Glasgow from the English metropolis and the places where Mediumistic effort is most rife, rendering the expenses of transit very heavy, and the time consumed in making the journey an obstacle not easily overcome. The following communication to the *Religio-Philosophical Journal of America*, by one of its most esteemed contributors, will give some interesting facts concerning the progress of Spiritualism in Glasgow :—

"A Lyceum was started here last year, and is continued each Sunday afternoon under the supervision of the present writer. The library of the society is well stocked with the literature of the movement, both English and American, and is largely taken advantage of. . . . Through the kindness of one of our most enthusiastic and generous members, Mr. James Bowman, the public library in our city has also been supplied with many volumes bearing on the subject. . . . Meetings are held in the room on several of the week nights, Friday evening being devoted to Mr. David Duguid, so well known for his varied forms of mediumship so ably set down by Hay Nisbet, in his introduction to the volume "Hafid, Prince of Persia." . . . Mr. Duguid is one of the most retiring of men, working every day at his business of a photographer, and giving largely of his spare moments to those who are in earnest to investigate the subject. Numbers come from all parts of the world, who carry with them mementos of their visit in the shape of those marvellous productions, the little direct paintings which are sent forth as missionaries over the world. . . . .

"Only lately we had a visit from Irving Bishop, a conjuror of some note from your side, and this gentleman was taken in hand by all the professors of the Universities of Glasgow and Edinburgh, who presented him with an elaborate address, because he had exposed Spiritualism. Exposures have been most prolific in directing men and women to the subject, and Mr. Irving Bishop's visit was no exception to this.

"Mr. Alexander Duguid, of Kirkcaldy, and a brother of Mr. David Duguid, the trance painting medium, is among the more recent platform workers, and does yeoman's service. In his private sittings, which have extended over many of the towns in Scotland, his clairvoyant powers have been most successful in bringing the fact of Spirit communion home to many hearts. He is largely sought after, and appreciated for his quiet, unassuming manners and hopeful, manly life ; recently he has been in London for the first time, where he met with warm reception from the friends there, speaking at Gospel Hall services, with 'M. A., Oxon' in the chair.

"Professor James Coates, who has resided in Glasgow for over eighteen months, has been quite a tower of strength to the movement since his arrival, ably filling this platform on many occasions, acting as secretary and energetically promoting the progress of the movement in many ways. Mr. Coates is a phrenologist and mesmerist, who has worked up a great reputation in circles outside the spiritual.

"In Dundee the cause has taken firm root among a great number of families. . . . The Secretary of the Glasgow Association is Mr. John Munro, 12, Govanhill-street, Glasgow; the president, James Walker, a veteran in the cause. "J. R."

"Glasgow, Scotland."

It has often been questioned why Glasgow, a merely commercial centre and by no means remarkable for its tendencies to metaphysical speculations, should have taken the palm over Edinburgh, the *reputed* seat of science, learning, and as might be expected from such a reputation, of *good breeding* also. Whether the above-named desirable elements are peculiar to University men in their *presence or absence*, the following excerpts written by Mr. J. Greenwell, now of London, a well known and reliable correspondent of the *Medium*, and a gentleman incapable of falsehood or exaggeration, will sufficiently prove. Mr. Greenwell, writing to the *Medium* about 1878, says :

"Some time ago, Mr. Morse lectured at Edinburgh, and his merits were recognised by one eminent gentleman, whose words of commendation we quoted from the newspapers. As the gentleman in question contrasted Mr. Morse's abilities in the trance with those of men who are public teachers of the fashionable stamp, it might be imagined that revenge would be taken sooner or later. Reports in the *Review* and *Scotsman* have reached us of the meeting held in Upper Oddfellows' Hall, Forrest Road, Edinburgh, on Friday, June 6, at which Mr. Morse was advertised to speak on a subject to be chosen by the audience. A botanical term was voted for by the students, and they would have no other. . . .

Faithfully Yours
J. J. Morse.

" As a supplement to the report, I must say that it was the most disgraceful meeting of any description that it has been my lot to attend. About a quarter of an hour before the lecture was to commence, 100 students, at the very least, came trooping into the hall, with the avowed intention of breaking up the meeting, for as soon as they gained admission, they began their ungentlemanly operations of throwing peas, singing songs, and performing on tin whistles, &c. Thinking they would probably quiet down when the lecturer appeared, Mr. Morse, with Mr. J. T. Rhodes as chairman, made their way on to the platform ; when, instead of abating, the noise was resumed with increased vigour, and neither the chairman nor Mr. Morse were allowed to speak, owing to the unearthly yells issuing from the very refined students. Mr. Morse, in the trance state, was then proceeding to deliver his lecture on ' Is Man Material or Spiritual after Death ?' when the interruption broke out afresh, and continued for two hours, Mr. Morse under control all the time. The guides then declined to proceed further, and left the medium.

" The meeting was then declared closed, when the students in a body made for the platform, and commenced to hustle Messrs. Morse, Rhodes, and myself most unmercifully, throwing the table from the platform, and smashing a form. Some one then got Mr. Morse into the ante-room, where I found him a few minutes afterwards quite overcome and in violent convulsions, which continued for almost an hour. It is really difficult to realise such a state of things in a free and *Christian* country in the nineteenth century, but such is the case ; and I feel more fully persuaded than ever that the power is only wanted to put the existing will in force, and we should soon see the ancient stake, or something more torturing, revived for the benefit of Spiritualists and Free-thinkers.

" I know full well the feelings of indignation that will be evoked from the many friends of Mr. Morse, owing to the cruel treatment he has suffered here ; consequently I need not remind those friends that increased sympathy towards him is necessary on this occasion, the first instalment of which I feel sure would be accorded to him when he arrived in Glasgow. . . .

" I am, yours in the cause of truth,

"Jos. N. Greenwell.

" Edinburgh, June 7."

It is satisfactory to remember that the scenes described above took place some six years ago—since when, the general tides of progress may have even had a contagious influence upon the *gentlemen* of the Edinburgh University, and inspired them with a higher tone, both in the realm of morals and manners.

In the British metropolis, many of the well-known Mediums of past years have retired from public life, Mrs. Mary Marshall, the well-known test and rapping Medium, being almost the only one remaining. Mr. Cecil Husk, a new Medium for the production of materialized forms, is highly reported of; and Mr. Towns, a veteran seer, still astonishes the strangers who visit him with revelations of their most secret thoughts.

Miss Lottie Fowler, the inimitable clairvoyant, trance and test Medium from America, and Mrs. Kate Jencken (*née* Katy Fox)—a name inscribed on the warmest spot of every true Spiritualist's heart—are also ministering most successfully to the investigators who seek for test facts of Spirit communion. It is much to be regretted that the cause of phenomenal Spiritualism has suffered a great loss, in the retirement into private life of Mr. Eglinton, a young gentleman who, though not classed as a professional Medium, was the subject—a few years since—of manifestations, the marvel of which has resounded through many countries of the earth.

The Calcutta *Indian Daily News* publishes in its issue of January 28th, 1882, the following striking communication concerning Mr. Eglinton's Mediumship :—

" *To the Editor of the Indian Daily News.*

" Sir,—In your issue of the 13th January, I stated that I should be glad of an opportunity of participating in a *séance* with a view of giving an unbiased opinion as to whether, in my capacity of a professional Prestidigitateur, I could give a natural explanation of effects said to be produced by spiritual aid.

"I am indebted to the courtesy of Mr. Eglinton, the Spiritualistic Medium now in Calcutta, and of his host, Mr. J. Meugens, for affording me the opportunity I craved.

"It is needless to say I went as a sceptic; but I must own that I have come away utterly unable to explain, by any natural means, the phenomena that I witnessed on Tuesday evening. I will give a brief description of what took place:—

"I was seated in a brilliantly-lighted room with Mr. Eglinton and Mr. Meugens. We took our places round a common teak-wood table, and after a few minutes the table began to sway violently backwards and forwards, and I heard noises such as might be produced by some one thumping under the table. I tried to discover the cause of this movement, but was unable to do so. After this Mr. Eglinton produced two common school slates, which I sponged, cleaned, and rubbed dry with a towel myself. Mr. Eglinton then handed me a box containing small crumbs of slate-pencil. I selected one of these and in accordance with Mr. Eglinton's directions, placed it on the surface of one of the slates, placing the other slate over it. I then firmly grasped the two slates at one of the corners. Mr. Eglinton then held the other corner, our two free hands being clasped together. The slates were then lowered below the edge of the table, but remained in full view (the room remaining lighted all the time). Instantaneously I heard a scratching noise, as might be produced by writing on a slate. In about fifteen seconds I heard three distinct knocks on the slates, and I then opened them and found the following writing:

"'My name is Geary. Don't you remember me? We used to talk of this matter at the St. George's. I know better now.'

"Having read the above, I remarked that I knew of no one by the name of Geary.

"We then placed our hands on the table, and Mr. Eglinton commenced repeating the alphabet until he came to the letter 'G,' when the table began to shake violently. This process was repeated till the name of Geary was spelt.

"After this Mr. Eglinton took a piece of paper and a pencil, and with a convulsive movement, difficult to describe, he wrote very indistinctly the following words:

"'I am Alfred Geary, of the *Lantern;* you know me and St. Ledger.'

"Having read this, I suddenly remembered having met both Mr. Geary and Mr. St. Ledger at Cape Town, South Africa, about four years ago, and the St. George's Hotel is the one I lived at there. Mr. Geary was the editor of the *Cape Lantern.* I believe he died some three years ago. Mr. St. Ledger was the editor of the *Cape Times,* and I believe is so still. Without going into details, I may mention that subsequently a number of other messages were written on the slates, which I was allowed to clean each time before they were used.

"In respect to the above manifestations I can only say that I do not expect my account of them to gain general credence. Forty-eight hours before, I should not have believed any one who had described such manifestations under similar circumstances. I still remain a sceptic as regards Spiritualism, but I repeat my inability to explain or account for what must have been an intelligent force, that produced the writing on the slate, which, if my senses are to be relied on, was in no way the result of trickery or sleight-of-hand.—Yours, &c., "HARRY KELLAR.

"Calcutta, January 25th, 1882."

Without commenting on the illogical position assumed, not alone by Mr. Kellar, but by hundreds of others who are compelled to admit both the supra-mundane character of the phenomena and intelligence displayed, and then wind up by denying emphatically that "either can be Spirits," it is enough to say that Mr. Kellar, the professional conjurer, duplicates the assurance of his Italian *confrère,* Signor Bellachini, in respect to Mr. Slade's manifestations at Leipzig. When two thoroughly skilled professional jugglers acknowledge that they cannot simulate by trickery, the demonstrations performed through Media without any trickery, is it not time that the flimsy pretence of Spiritual phenomena being ALL trickery and fraud, should be abandoned by travelling exposers, even though the petty set of shams they exhibit, of which any tenth rate juggler would be ashamed, were patronized by Scottish Lord Provosts and English Right Reverend Lord Bishops?

Another remarkably-endowed Medium for physical manifestations who has till recently exercised her Mediumship successfully in many parts of England is Miss Wood, a young lady who was developed in private circles at Newcastle-on-Tyne, and subsequently became professionally engaged by the "Newcastle Spiritual Evidence Society," to give *séances* at their rooms for "form materializations." During her sittings with the Newcastle Society, Miss Wood cheerfully submitted to the most exacting tests, and amongst the numerous testimonials that were rendered to the integrity of her Mediumship, are the following—the first being from Mr. H. Kersey, then Secretary to the Society, and the other from the well-known scientist, Mr. T. P. Barkas, F.G.S.

Mr. Kersey says, in writing to the *Medium*, Oct. 25th, 1878:—

"This morning, Oct. 20, I had the pleasure of witnessing some very convincing form manifestations through the medial power of Miss C. E. Wood, at the Newcastle society's rooms. I will spare unnecessary detail, and shortly say that the cabinet, which consisted of a curtain suspended across the corner of the room, was inspected by myself and others, both previous to and after the *séance*. The medium sat *outside* the cabinet in full view of all the sitters, numbering nineteen, the whole of the time, and was never once out of their sight. Three forms successively appeared, the first a woman, who, after several efforts, walked out of the cabinet and passed around the medium, and re-entered the cabinet on the other side of her. At the solicitation of the sitters she repeated this. The next form was a child, who came out of the cabinet, and succeeded in getting about two feet clear of the medium, but could not get around her. The last form was a large one, that of a man, but did not succeed in getting far out.

"'Pocka' controlled and spoke through the medium whilst the last two forms were out. Now the value of this to me, Sir, is that I never lost sight of the medium from first to last, and I am certain none of the sitters left their seats and went into the cabinet.

I am, Sir, yours truly,

"Newcastle-on-Tyne. "H. A. KERSEY.

" We, the undersigned, testify to the correctness of the above report :—

"John Hare, Chester Crescent.
"Martha Hare,   ,,
"Nellie Hare,   ,,
"H. Norris, 59, Newgate Street.
"E. Sanderson,   ,,
"Jane Hammarbon, Northumberland Street.
"Jno. Mould, 12, St. Thomas Crescent.
"James Cameron, Gallowgate Steam Mills.
"W. C. Robson, 8, Brandling Place."

Mr. Barkas, writing to the same paper about a year previously, gives a slight account of Spiritualism in Newcastle and the formation of the first society there. He says :—

"Spiritualism had been investigated in Newcastle-on-Tyne for twenty-five years. Prior to 1872 the manifestations had taken place in private houses and before select circles. In that year a society was formed for the investigation of the phenomena, and in a few months several members of the society became developed as mediums. In the year 1873 it was discovered that two young ladies had very great mediumistic power. The one, Miss Wood, was at that time eighteen years of age, and the other, Miss Fairlamb, was about a year younger. For some trifling remuneration as a compensation for much time spent in the interests of the society, the young women devoted themselves to the work, and soon there were not only trance controls, but extraordinary movements of tables, chairs, bells, and other articles of furniture and musical instruments took place in the dark, under test conditions. In 1874 spectral forms of human faces and hands presented themselves at the openings of the cabinet in which the mediums were enclosed. Then fully developed forms ; and, to make certain of the genuineness of these phenomena, private *séances* were organised in the houses of well known gentlemen. Rigid but friendly tests of many kinds were tried, and the result was that materialisations took place, which nothing but a stubborn prejudice, perfectly inaccessible to the logic of facts, could resist or gainsay.

"I have seen through the mediumship of Miss Wood, in a private house, living forms walk from the curtained recess, which it was utterly impossible for her to simulate. I have seen children, women, and men of various ages, walk forth under her mediumship.

I have seen a materialised form and the medium at the same time. I have had through her mediumship a child-like form standing beside me for about half an hour together; the child has placed its arms around my neck, and permitted me at the same time to place my arm around her neck, and has laid its cheek against mine, breathed upon my face, and, in fact, caressed me precisely as a child would do its parent or guardian. This was not in darkness, but in light, and in the presence of professors and fellows of one of the leading universities in the kingdom. I have, under these conditions, and after having handled the psychic form, seen it gradually vanish or dematerialise, and become invisible in the middle of the room."

A full and elaborate account of Miss Wood and the phenomena occurring in her presence has been published in pamphlet form by W. P. Adshead, Esq., of Belper, a wealthy and intelligent gentleman, who sent for Miss Wood to his own house, wherein he set up a *wire cage*, constructed for the purpose, in which the Medium, firmly secured, was placed, during a given number of experimental *séances*.

The marvellous phenomena of many different materialized forms appearing under these circumstances, is fully detailed by Mr. Adshead, but as the manifestations present little or no variety in effect from those already alluded to, it would be unnecessary to describe them any further. We would commend Mr. Adshead's methods, however, to the attention of the various contending parties who now make the subject of "tests" the theme of warfare—the one side alleging that tests "degrade the Medium," and "ruin the conditions under which spirits manifest;" the other equally pertinaciously insisting that no Medium should claim credence for extraordinary or unusual occurrences without tests of the most crucial and convincing character. Miss Wood was Mr. Adshead's guest for some time. The manifestations were given in his own house, in the presence of scores of the most inveterate sceptics, and under the extraordinary conditions stated above.

Yet Miss Wood felt no degradation in submitting to the tests imposed, and often invited them, nor did they spoil or even interfere with the manifestations, numerous attestations to that effect being given and signed by the parties who attended the *séances*. The following paragraph, taken from page 24 of Mr. Adshead's pamphlet, offers perhaps what the world would deem one of the most striking proofs that can be rendered of Mr. Adshead's unassailable position in reference to these manifestations. He says :—

"For the medium to liberate herself from her bondage, and place herself in such a position that, had she the necessary skill and appliances, she could represent the different forms we had looked upon, and then return to the condition in which we left her—the cage, tapes, and seals being found as when the *séance* commenced—would, to me, be almost as great a marvel as anything else which could be done. Indeed, so profoundly impressed am I with the impossibility of this being done, that unless those who have boasted that it is their mission to stamp out the 'imposture of Spiritualism,' of 'their great charity,' are moved to take the scales from our eyes, I have to say, I am prepared to write a cheque for two hundred and fifty guineas, and my friend, Mr. A. Smedley, will write one for a similar amount, and the FIVE HUNDRED GUINEAS shall at once be paid to any person who will, under similar conditions to those described above, produce phenomena which shall in all respects be like those of which I have just spoken, and so distinctly explain the method by which they are produced that the person to whom the method is made known, or any other person or persons to whom, in turn, the said method may be made known, will be able at any time, or in any place, to produce exactly the same kind of phenomena as those which appeared when Miss Wood was screwed up in the cage. If, as is claimed, the marvels are simply clever conjuring, the above conditions will not be regarded as too stringent. It is also to be understood that those who accept this challenge forfeit a like sum in the event of failing to produce the phenomena under the conditions named above."

Despite all the blatant pretensions of conjurers and their clerical supporters, Mr. Adshead's cheque so freely proferred, still remains unclaimed.

In Cardiff, South Wales, for several years past, circles have been held by a party of earnest Spiritualists, amongst whom was developed Mr. Spriggs, a non-professional Medium for the production of "form materializations." As Mr. Spriggs is now in Australia, placing his phenomenal powers at the service of the "Victorian Association of Spiritualists," we reserve all further accounts of his demonstrations for our Australian section.

In the direction of healing, there are still a much larger number of excellent phenomenal individuals engaged, than we have space to particularize. Not one of the least remarkable, is Mrs. Illingworth, the celebrated seeress and medical trance Medium of Bradford, Yorkshire. Although entirely uneducated, and the wife of a plain Yorkshire mechanic, this wonderful clairvoyant can trace—even by a lock of hair taken from the head of strangers at any distance—the most obscure diseases, prescribing under the influence of medical Spirits the most effective remedies for all complaints of a curable nature. And good Mrs Illingworth is only cited as a representative of many others whose beneficent labours are carried forward with eminent success throughout the North of England. Another of these highly gifted seers practises in the immediate vicinity of the author's residence near Manchester, and scores of Nicodemuses who would treat the openly avowed claim of Spiritual influence with holy horror or scornful derision, resort privately to Mr. Edward Gallagher* to be treated for complaints that baffle all the skill of the faculty—even to trace out— much less to cure. Many are the laudations that the author hears passed upon this quiet unassuming gentleman, who as a "clairvoyant" is permitted to describe hidden diseases and cure them by *occult* power, until his fame fills the country round and attracts even the sacred presence of the very "divines" who devote their next Sabbath's sermons to unsparing diatribes against the impious practices of Spiritualism.

In the metropolis, Dr. Mack, the renowned Spiritual healer; Mr. Younger, the fine mesmerist; Mr. and Mrs. Hagon, Mr. Omerin, and Mr. Hawkins, all pursue their beneficent work with many a secret blessing, and many a public ban, as the reward of their services. These are all professional healers and their services are offered, and their addresses registered in the *Medium*, and that, much to the scandal of those who would cheerfully pay their twenty guineas to a solemn-visaged physician who gives a rough guess, and often an erroneous one, at the seat of their disease, and yet shrink with horror at the idea of paying a modest fee to the clairvoyant and healer because the truths they tell, and the relief they impart, are "the gifts of God, and should not be made the subject of mercenary traffic." And thus it is, that when capable Mediums, and highly gifted seers and seeresses are starved out of their spheres of usefulness, and the sound of their good report is hushed, and for very sordid need of bread they are driven to abandon their Mediumistic calling, the world cries "See how this delusion of Spiritualism has died out," and the Pharisees rejoice that they have succeeded in " crushing out professional Mediumship."

---

* Mr. E. Gallagher, Greenfield Villa, Bloomfield Road, Heaton Chapel, Manchester.

CHAPTER XXVIII.

SPIRITUALISM IN GREAT BRITAIN (CONCLUDED).

IN THE PROVINCES.

SINCE it has been the custom to create an aristocracy of places as well as of classes; to talk of London as the geographical apex from whence the traveller goes *down* to every part of England, whether to the *north* or south; it has also followed, that prestige in every direction must originate in the metropolis, in order to fall into line with the subservience of public opinion.

Whether the immense growth of many of the large provincial towns justifies this traditionary reverence for metropolitan lead, we do not care to enquire.   Certain it is, that Spiritualism is one of the iconoclasts, that has boldly defied this proscriptive deference to "the hub" of the British kingdom, for it has taken a far deeper hold on the common sense and intelligence of thoughtful minds, and exercised a far wider influence on the masses in the provinces, than it has done in the great Modern Babylon.

Whether this may be considered matter of praise or blame, the Modern Babylonians themselves may determine; the fact remains nevertheless, and we are now about to speak in illustration of this position, by citing the experiences of individuals as well as societies, who have only as yet attained to the distinction of being classified as provincial Spiritualists.

At the beautiful estate of Parkfield, Didsbury, near Manchester, till quite recently, resided Mr. Charles Blackburn, a gentleman who by his unnumbered acts of private and public munificence, has exerted a widespread influence upon the growth of English Spiritualism.   Whilst there are but few of the leading Spiritualists who have not become familiar with the lineaments of his kind cheery face, and exchanged pleasant greetings with him in circles, social gatherings, and beneath his own hospitable roof, there are not many who know as well as the author, how much the cause of Spiritualism is indebted to Mr. Blackburn for timely aid in periods of trial.

Mr. Blackburn's generous contributions were the chief support of the excellent periodical entitled *The London Spiritualist.*   Professor Crookes in the closing lines of his authoritative work, entitled " Phenomena of Spiritualism," when writing of his experiences with the celebrated Medium, Miss Florence Cook, says:—

"My thanks, and those of all Spiritualists, are also due to Mr. Charles Blackburn, for the generous manner in which he has made it possible for Miss Cook to devote her whole time to the development of these manifestations, and latterly to their scientific examination."

Few and simple as these words are, their significance is immense to those who follow out in detail, experiments which have obtained a world-wide celebrity, and are still of the highest authority as scientific testimony.

Had Mr. Charles Blackburn's munificence taken no other shape than that of upholding the usefulness of a fine Spiritual journal, and enabling

Professor Crookes, and through him, the entire generation, to profit by the wonderful Mediumship of a young lady in limited circumstances, this Manchester gentleman has done enough. But the waymarks of Mr. Blackburn's good services are to be found in many other directions—amongst scores of poor Mediums, and struggling societies whom he has aided. The investigator will remember him for the ingenious machines for weighing "materialized" Spirits which he has had constructed; in the famous Newcastle "Blackburn Cabinet," and all the associative efforts to which his name has been given, and on which his benefactions have been bestowed.

Family cares and bereavements have thickened around this worthy gentleman's path of late, and compelled his withdrawal from the scenes in which he has so long and faithfully laboured, but he carries with him into his retirement, a philosophy which will be a quenchless light in the darkest hour of trial, whilst he leaves behind him "on the sands of time" footprints of good, that can never be erased from the grateful memories of men or the imperishable records of eternity.

Another of the brave "provincial" Spiritualists, whose fearless advocacy has "helped to shake the world," is Mr. John Fowler, of St. Ann's, Sefton Park, Liverpool, a gentleman whose wealth, and influence, have been freely devoted to the advancement of the Spiritual cause.

Mr. Fowler's name became memorable in the first instance, by the uncompromising faith in Spirit power which led him to stake the sum of one thousand pounds, against the ability of one Cumberland—an itinerant conjurer and "exposer of Spiritualism"—to imitate by trickery, the manifestations which are produced by Spirit power alone, through Mediums. It need hardly be stated, that Cumberland, like the rest of his craft, had taken ample care to make his appearance as an "exposer," just at the time when there were no public Mediums at hand to compete with him. As it is well known that very few Mediums are so peculiarly endowed as to be able to meet large heterogeneous audiences, or furnish the force necessary for Spirits to produce phenomena requiring the most finely balanced psychological conditions in the rude arenas of public antagonism, so Cumberland could safely retort Mr. Fowler's challenge, with the counter demand to place his Mediums and Spiritual manifestations on the same platform with his (Cumberland's) alleged exposures.

As this very indifferent trickster was actually supported by the Lord Bishop of Liverpool, and, besides a right reverend chairman, claimed and advertised the "moral support" of hosts of other clergymen and church dignitaries, who, it thereby appeared, had been unable to find any other means of putting down the *bête noir* of their cloth—Spiritualism—so Mr. Fowler, perhaps moved to a higher concern for the honour of his "Diocesan," than that right reverend gentleman manifested for himself, addressed a letter to his Lordship through the public journals, advising him that he was only being made a tool of by an indifferent conjurer, and that the petty tricks Cumberland could display, bore no sort of relation to the manifold and inimitable phenomena produced by Spirits.

Encouraged by the rich harvest which the poorest tricksters can reap from the "moral support" of English bishops and clergy when they come before the public under the pretence of destroying that cause which a whole bench of bishops could not otherwise assail, soon after Cumberland's disappearance from the scene, still another "exposer" hastened to Liverpool to secure its clerical patronage and pocket the coin of its gullible citizens.

The new "exposer" was Irving Bishop, of American notoriety. Once again Mr. Fowler tried by the offer of the thousand pounds bait to tempt this adventurer into exposing anything that Spirits *could do, under precisely similar conditions.* This time the trickster's chairman and "moral supporter" was the Rev. J. H. Skewes, a clergyman of the Church of England, who after Bishop had utterly failed to expose anything but the credulity of his audiences, changed the base of his attack to his pulpit, where he treated his congregation to a succession of sermons on the demoniac character of Spiritual manifestations in the nineteenth century, and their angelic nature thousands of years ago, in illustration of which, amongst other notable instances of divine power, he cited the case of Jonah's living in the " cold, damp, and uncomfortable habitation of the whale's interior for three days and three nights."

Although there were few platform orators of any standing in the ranks of Spiritualism, who would not have desired to measure swords with an antagonist of a somewhat different description to the Rev. J. H. Skewes, Mr. Fowler's determination to put clerical assumptions to the test, was indomitable, and as the author of this volume was engaged periodically to lecture for the Spiritualists of Liverpool, Mr. Fowler caused answers to Mr. Skewes to be announced, for two successive Sunday evenings, by Mrs. Britten. Mr. Fowler then, by a series of letters published in the Liverpool papers, endeavoured to induce the reverend opponent to meet Mrs. Britten in public debate. Finding all his attempts in this direction only met with repeated evasions, Mr. Fowler requested Mrs. Britten to write out the replies given to Mr Skewes, the authenticity of which could be easily tested by the witness of the immense audiences assembled to hear them.

These replies were subsequently published in several papers, and by the liberality of Mr. Fowler, thousands of copies were scattered broadcast through various English-speaking countries.

The special circumstances which called forth these lectures, were stated in an introductory note which is republished below, as the final conclusion of the whole matter :—

"MRS. HARDINGE BRITTEN AND THE REV. J. H. SKEWES.

"By information received from my Spiritualistic friends in Liverpool, I learn that the faith they profess, and of which I am one of the public exponents, has been repeatedly attacked by certain members of the clergy of that city, in sermons denunciatory of Spiritualism, and by the openly avowed 'moral support' rendered to those travelling conjurers who profess by the exhibition of a few clumsy tricks to imitate and explain the *modus operandi* of Spiritual phenomena. The last, and, as I understand, the most pertinacious of the clerical assailants above named, is a 'Rev. J. H. Skewes.'

"Within the last few weeks, two sermons have been delivered by this gentleman, reported in a paper called the *Protestant Standard*, under the several (editorial) titles of 'Death-Blow to Spiritualism,' and 'Spiritualism in its Coffin !—Nailing Down the Lid ! !' It being the desire of my committee in Liverpool that I should answer these discourses, I proceeded to do so in two lectures, given at Rodney Hall, on the Sunday evenings of February 18th and March 4th, 1883.

"As Mr. Skewes stated in his second sermon that there were still many points in Spiritualism that he had not noticed, my committee followed up my lectures by challenging him to debate the subject with me on a public platform, on conditions honourable to him and beneficial to the charities of Liverpool. In answer to the repeated invitations to accept this challenge, addressed to Mr. Skewes both by public and private correspondence, the reverend gentleman declines, on the ground that he has had no fair report of my Answers to his Sermons.

"As the only report that has been given of my lectures is a series of paragraphs, headed 'Howlings from the Pit,' put forth by the *Protestant Standard*, a report which is not only interpolated by rude and unworthy personal remarks, but is most imperfect, and scarcely touches on half the matter contained in my first lectures, my committee have urged Mr. Skewes to debate the subject of Spiritualism either from the stand-points assumed in his sermons, or any fresh ones he might be able to allege against the Spiritual movement. As Mr. Skewes continues to base his refusal upon the absence of any authentic report of my Answer to his Sermons, I deem it my duty to the cause I represent, to place my Answer to Mr. Skewes's attack on record, and in such a form as cannot be mistaken. It is with this view that I put the annexed statements before the tribunal of public opinion.

"Before entering upon my task, I wish it distinctly understood that I make no profession to repeat, except in general terms, the lectures given by me at Rodney Hall, in answer to Mr. Skewes's sermons. I am not ashamed to avow that I speak in public under the inspiration of those whom I deem to be good spirits, whose wisdom supplies me with the ideas most appropriate to the occasion, and whose power far transcends my own to meet the demands which the spiritual rostrum makes upon me. Under these conditions I find it impossible to recall my lectures by memory, or to transcribe them, as they were originally delivered.

"The following Answer will, however, embody the sum of the arguments before used, and I have only to add, that, for any further elucidation of the question at issue, I still hold myself ready to meet Mr. Skewes in public discussion, under such conditions as may be agreed upon between him and my Liverpool Committee of Spiritualists.

"EMMA HARDINGE BRITTEN."

It must be added that the lectures referred to, being a complete exposition of what Spiritualism is—and what it is *not*, Mr. Skewes's action, supplemented by Mr. John Fowler's indomitable enterprise, has undoubtedly aided in bringing Spiritualism to the notice of vast numbers of the community who would otherwise have remained in profound ignorance of its verities.

Mr. Fowler also was the only individual, outside the ranks of the clergy, privileged to bear testimony to the faith of Spiritualism, before the English Church Congress, held in 1881, at Newcastle-on-Tyne. On this occasion, one or two of the clerical speakers present bore witness to the tone and temper of the times, by speaking unreservedly in favour of Spiritualism, whilst others exhibited the rancour and bitterness which this all too popular element had excited, by vituperation of a *high ecclesiastical order.*

Whilst we could wish that Mr. Fowler's necessarily brief but compendious paper could be read by thinkers of every shade of faith, we can only find space for the following excerpts from his brave utterances :—

"Every man must observe the present indifferent state of the intelligent public to the service and doctrines of the Church. Those who have had opportunities of observing the intellectual state of the country say that infidelity is on the increase. Now, what does the Church propose to do in this matter? Of its seriousness proof is offered by the fact of this discussion. Until the facts of spiritual existence have been demonstrated, like Peter, who denied his Master, we want evidence, and, like Thomas, we want to put our fingers into the prints of the nails. If demonstration was needed to establish the faith in the hearts of the disciples, demonstration is as much needed to-day, to establish its claims in the experience of the present generation. The fabric cannot be maintained. It will fall to pieces without the interior leavening power of the Spirit. Narrow creeds and ceremonies cannot impose on and influence for ever the minds of men. Therefore, Modern Spiritualism has appeared as a Divine necessity of the times. It does not come to destroy the law and the prophets, but to establish that which came aforetime, and to make the possibilities of spiritual growth and strength in the heart of man more possible. . . .

"Therefore we say that a case has been made out on behalf of Modern Spiritualism to be recognised and utilised by the Church itself, that it may become strong to defeat its own doubts, and, in the full reliance of its hope, do battle with the hard foes who deny the immortality of the soul. If Spiritualists do not universally retain their allegiance to the doctrines of the Church of England, it matters but very little. The Church, by fairly and squarely investigating the alleged facts, will bring together into one focus philosophers and thinkers who otherwise might have remained outside the pale of the Church. To shelve the question by saying that Spiritualism is an imposition displays either presumption or ignorance." . . .

The example above given of Mr. Fowler's address, is sufficient to demonstrate its admirable lines of argument. The effect produced upon the community has been marked and healthful. A far more respectful sentiment has been manifested towards Spiritualism by the thinking classes, since the Church Congress was in session, whilst the impulse given to the cause in Liverpool, is sufficiently proved by the large numbers who gather together each Sunday to attend the Spiritualists' services. For the present these meetings are held in Rodney Hall, under the management of an efficient committee, and the presidency of John Lamont, Esq., a gentleman held in the highest estimation by all classes of his fellow-citizens, besides being a seer and inspirational speaker of remarkable power. Mrs. Hardinge Britten is the regular lecturer of the Society for two Sundays in each month during the present season; Mr. W. J. Colville, from America, Mr. and Mrs. Wallis, Mrs. Groom and other speakers of pronounced excellence filling the rostrum on alternate Sundays.

In Belper, Derbyshire, the Spiritualists enjoy the privilege of holding their Sunday services in the pleasant and commodious hall built, and generously placed at the disposal of his Spiritualist friends and associates, by Mr. W. P. Adshead, the gentleman before mentioned in connection with Miss Wood's *séances.*

The kindly sentiments which prevail amongst the Spiritualists of Belper, and the many acts of beneficence towards the poor which are practised in their hall, fill the place with a high and holy influence, and fittingly consecrate it to the ministry of angels, on earth as in heaven.

In Bradford, Yorkshire, a large and zealous society of working men and women have combined to hire a good hall, which they entitle the Walton Street Church, and here, as in Belper, the exalting influence of a specially-consecrated place, and the effect of well conducted and orderly services is felt by every sensitive who visits the meetings. Two other well attended meetings are held every Sunday in Bradford, besides what may be emphatically called "mass meetings" in one of the largest halls in the town, when the author, or other speakers from a distance, are engaged, by the energetic and self-sacrificing Bradford Spiritualists.

A special hall has also been built and devoted to the Spiritual Sunday services, at Sowerby Bridge, Yorkshire, where a fine and well-trained choir of young people adds the charm of excellent singing to the elevating influences which pervade the place.

Those who, like the author, have realised with painful sensibility the injurious or favourable effects produced by the different places where Spiritual services are conducted, will be ready to join with her in the fervent wish that wealthy Spiritualists would emulate the example of good Mr. Adshead, and provide in every town and hamlet of Great Britain a true Spiritual home for the people, and a fitting scene in which to invite the angels to come and participate in holy Spiritual exercises. If there be any truth in Spiritual revelations at all, those who would make such an use of the means committed to their stewardship on earth, would certainly find that they had been

> "Fitting up a mansion
> Which eternally will stand."

In Leeds, Halifax, Keighley, Bradford, and nearly all the principal towns and villages of Yorkshire, well conducted Sunday meetings are held, sometimes aided by renowned speakers from a distance, but in general ministered to by resident Mediums, most of whom—under trance conditions—give discourses far beyond the average of their normal capacity. The speakers are for the most part such devoted men and women as good faithful Joseph Armitage of Batley Carr; Mrs. Dobson, Mrs. Illingworth; Misses Hance, Shipley, and Harrison; Mrs. Wilson, Mrs. Greig; Messrs. Wilson Oliffe, Blackburn, and many others too numerous to mention. All these are working people, toiling during the week in their several vocations, but giving cheerfully, without stint, and often at the cost of labour and fatigue to themselves, their best service every Sunday to platform utterances, and that most commonly with little or no remuneration.

In the meantime, such noble gentlemen as Mr. John Culpan of Halifax, a Spiritual veteran who for thirty years has given means, untiring service, and an honoured name to the advancement of the cause. Mr. B. Lees, Mr. John Illingworth, Mr. Etchells, of Huddersfield, David Richmond, the veteran Spiritualist of Darlington, Dr. Brown, of Burnley, Mr. Foster, of Preston, good John Harwood, of Littleborough, and Peter Lee, of Rochdale, splendid representatives of Yorkshire and Lancashire Spiritualism—these, and hosts of others, with not a few faithful and zealous ladies, devote themselves by purse and person to the best interests of humanity through the noble cause of Spiritualism.

In a crowded record of this character, many a good and honoured name must necessarily be omitted, but none can doubt that they are all engraved in the imperishable types of the higher life to which their noble services so effectually point the way.

In Newcastle-on-Tyne, the residence of the esteemed scientist T. P. Barkas, a "Spiritual Evidence Society" has been formed, which has done good service by maintaining Sunday meetings, and promoting *séances* for the culture of Spiritual gifts, and the investigation of phenomena.

It was at these circles that Miss Wood—the celebrated physical medium mentioned in a former chapter—was developed.

The Newcastle Society has moreover exercised a fostering influence upon that large section of country in the vicinity, devoted to the industries of coal mining. Here, as in Yorkshire, local Mediums and trance speakers keep alive the interest of their various districts, with addresses which produce a deep and favourable impression on their listeners.

The author has herself visited two or three of these collieries, and was deeply moved by the sight of the earnest-looking sons of toil massed in serried groups around her. When no strangers visit them, they are addressed by some of the inspirational speakers who abound in these districts. One of the most eloquent, sincere, and popular lecturers of the Northumberland meetings is Mr. Henry Burton, a good and true man, whose life and preaching are both well calculated to demonstrate the exalting influence of Spirit teachings.

The large manufacturing county of Lancashire, though by no means as thickly studded with zealous Spiritual communities as Yorkshire or Northumberland, is nevertheless a stronghold of the faith. Liverpool has already been noticed; meantime Rochdale, Oldham, Manchester, Burnley, Blackburn, and numerous other places of importance maintain Sunday meetings, where vast multitudes listen with profound interest to the consoling doctrines of Spiritualism, taught by the zealous local Mediums who are to be found in those districts.

In the last named place, Blackburn, a large and busy manufacturing town, the author was instrumental in forming the excellent " Psychological Society," which now holds regular Sunday meetings there.

After the occasion of Mrs. Britten's first visit, the secretary of the Society sent a report to the *Medium* which is reprinted for the sake of the *declaration of principles* it contains—one which might be profitably adopted by other religious societies besides the Spiritualists of Blackburn. Our correspondent says :—

" Spiritualism is looking up at present in Blackburn. During the last few months we have had Mrs. Britten two Sundays occupying the platform of the Exchange : afternoon and evening each visit. The room will hold from 1,200 to 1,800 people, and was packed at each of the four lectures. . . .

" We have also opened rooms for Sunday evening lectures, at the School of Science. There seem to be plenty of fresh faces every Sunday come to listen to what is said. We have a very nice meeting room, and best of all is, that everything is paid for ; we mind that, whatever comes or goes not to run in debt. We are very strong Trinitarians, but the Trinity we believe in is, ' One God ; no Devil, and twenty shillings to the pound.'

" We feel confident if we only had real good speakers like Mrs. Britten, we could without any fear take the Exchange every Sunday. We make no charge for tickets or admission, but trust to the voluntary offerings of the people, and strange to say that although not making much more than bare expenses, we have never come short of meeting the expenses. The people are thirsting for more knowledge on the subject ; the pity is we have no one to give them the knowledge.—Yours, etc.,

"R. WOLSTENHOLME."

In Macclesfield, an earnest and united Society of believers in Spiritualism have hired and furnished a pleasant little hall, where services are generally conducted by the Rev. Adam Rushton, an estimable gentleman, formerly a Unitarian Minister, but one who gave up sect, and even the goodwill of friends and kindred, to throw in his lot with those who believed in the faith of which he became convinced, and to which, in his modest and unostentatious way, he gives his life and able services.

A similarly self-sacrificing profession of the Spiritual faith has been made by the Rev. Mr. Stoddart of Middlesboro', near Stockton-on-Tees. This gentleman was also an Unitarian Minister, but one whose persecutions for the sake of his faith have not as yet, been attended with a settlement as peaceful as that which Mr. Rushton finds in his little Macclesfield Society. Mr. Stoddart however is bound to make his mark, and the good angels he serves have obviously not forgotten their charge over their faithful soldier.

In Nottingham, Mr. Wm. Yates, a gentleman of fine culture, and indomitable energy, together with a few ladies and gentlemen of superior intellectual attainments, have struggled bravely to sustain an unsectarian representation of Spiritualism. Mr. Yates has also commenced the practice of medical electricity combined with magnetism, under the direction of beneficent healing Spirits, and report speaks in enthusiastic terms of the brilliant conquests he is effecting over otherwise incurable forms of disease.

In Birmingham, resides Mrs. Groom, an indefatigable trance speaker, healer, and seeress, who adds to her interesting Sunday lectures, the faculty of seeing and describing the spirit friends of persons in her audience. The labours of this excellent Medium have effected an immense amount of good in the places she visits.

In Birmingham, Walsall, Leicester, and other Midland towns and villages, small Sunday meetings are held, which promise, with good speakers and good management, to swell to large gatherings.

In the West and South of England, less public evidence of progress is demonstrable, although there are many places where it is generally known that good Spiritual meetings have been held, and large numbers of private circles are in session.

One of the most prosperous Spiritual societies in the South-west of England, is that established at Plymouth, where many private circles are held, and regular Sunday services are at present conducted with great acceptance by Mr. Clarke, an excellent inspirational speaker.

The formation of the Plymouth Society, as well as much of the good work which it has achieved, is due to the labours of the Rev. C. Ware, but as this gentleman's experience is modestly narrated in his own statement recently published in the Society's report of their first anniversary celebration, we cannot do better than give the account which we find printed in a recent issue of *Light*, and which is to the following effect :—

"PLYMOUTH.—THE FREE SPIRITUAL SOCIETY.

"The Free Spiritual Society of Plymouth last evening celebrated its anniversary at Richmond Hall, Richmond Street, it being exactly twelve months since its origin. The Rev. C. Ware, having laboured for two years in this town as a minister of one of the Methodist bodies, was suspended in January of last year on account of his belief in Spiritualism ; but a number of persons holding similar views having formed themselves into a Society, invited him to become their minister, in which capacity he has since acted. The Society during the year has considerably increased its membership and extended its operations, and now claims to enjoy the patronage, sympathy, and support of many influential friends beyond its formal membership. The proceedings last evening afforded a fair indication that the community is in a flourishing condition ; about eighty sat down to tea, and at the public meeting that followed, presided over by Mr. W. T. Rossiter, of Torquay, addresses were delivered by several gentlemen from the town and neighbourhood. Several mediums also took part in the meeting.

"The Rev. C. Ware, after making reference to the general aspects of Spiritualism, said it was pretty well known that he had laboured in this town for two years as a minister of one of the Methodist bodies. During that time he became acquainted with Spiritualism, and at the outset it presented itself to him as an astounding and glorious reality. Because he would not deny what he knew to be the truth, and forego the study of the profoundest subject that could occupy the mind of man, he was suspended from the denominational pulpit. There were those, however, who refused to submit to ecclesiastical tyranny and mental slavery, and these formed themselves into a Free Spiritual Society, and invited him to become their minister. The Society was formed twelve months ago in the house of one of their friends ; a few days afterwards they secured a room at the Octagon, and took their stand as a religious body. Soon after this they removed to their present hall. They had had to encounter great difficulties and various forms of opposition. In September, a conjurer, called Irving Bishop, came to Plymouth to give the ' death blow to Spiritualism.' For a time the subject was in everybody's mouth, and of course ' everybody ' went to hear him ; for a time Spiritualists seemed to be objects of commiseration until Irving Bishop proved himself a cheat, by failing to exhibit a single phase of Spiritualism. A correspondence thereupon commenced in the *Western Daily Mercury*, in which a whole galaxy of writers took part ; for a time the battle was tremendous, but he thought they could say without boasting that they poured into the enemy's ranks such a fire of stubborn facts as to leave their opponents ' without a leg to stand upon.' It was impossible for him to give them an idea of the advantage their cause derived from this controversy ; it was certainly the best work ever done for it. Since the year commenced they had placed a splendid harmonium in the hall, and he was pleased to tell them that the past week was a worthy climax to the year's work, for he had not seen such vitality manifested at any time during the year. The fact was, that no cause ever had a brighter outlook than theirs. They had no creed, except the Fatherhood of God and the brotherhood of humanity ; and they enjoyed perfect liberty, their motto being to think and allow others to think ; their aim being simply the natural development of each individual human soul. They could reckon amongst their company that evening some ten mediums, and ere the meeting closed they would, no doubt, hear some of them speak in the trance state, expressing the thoughts of their invisible friends."

Of the few professional speakers who are from time to time engaged in the work of Spiritual revivalism, the limitations of space will only allow us to make very brief mention.

15

Mr. and Mrs. Wallis of Walsall are both highly gifted trance speakers, and their eloquent ministrations are warmly appreciated wherever they go. Of unblemished character and moral worth, the very lives of this noble couple form a sermon, of which any religious denomination might be proud. Mrs. Groom has already been noticed. Several other acceptable speakers of the Spiritual rostrum might take exception to being classified as professionals, consequently, in addition to the author of this volume, it only remains to notice Mr. J. J. Morse, a most admirable lecturer, and a gentleman who has rendered himself worthy of that designation, by Spiritual culture alone.

When the author first knew Mr. Morse, he had risen from an obscure position of drudgery, to one but little better, as the shopman at Mr. Burn's Spiritual Institution. Here his marvellous powers as a trance Medium became unfolded, until at length, by virtue of being made the instrument of exalted and philosophic Spirits, he grew nearer to their level; became one with them instead of simply their automatic mouthpiece, and finally, by force of these educational processes, and his own indomitable perseverance, Mr. Morse has risen to a position of honourable eminence in the realm of Spiritual literature, and occupies the rank of one of the most attractive trance speakers of the day.

In a cause which is still *in transitu*, and amongst a vast number of moving forms who are still *making history*, it would be as unwise to find fault with methods, and criticize the action of individuals, as to complain of the variable clouds which may disappear to-morrow, or the oppressive sunshine which may be modified in the course of a single hour. Every movement in Spiritualism is at present transitional; nearly all the efforts at propagandism now conducted by Spiritualists, are expedients of the hour, whilst to-morrow may call for a widely different course of action. It need be no matter of surprise therefore, that the traditional grumbler finds ample food for his discontent to prey upon, whilst the enthusiast hails every gleam of sunshine that glances across his path, as the advent of the long looked for millennium. On the mountain top, or in the valley, still we repeat we are but *in transitu*, and whilst we pause to criticize, dogmatize, or even attempt to organize, the occasion which seemed to call for our special line of conduct will have passed away, and sweep us along with the current to meet a new emergency of the times.

It is under these ever-changing aspects of the Spiritual cause, that the author's pen has been again and again suspended by an invisible but ever present monitor, when she would have applied in her human blindness, words of censure in one direction, and urgent counsels in another. " God understands," murmurs the angel of guidance in the ear of the scribe. " Write—Behold I make all things new ! " cries another angelic teacher. Satisfied that the movement which seems so confused and heterogeneous in the dazzled eyes of humanity, is dictated by divine wisdom, ruled by Almighty power, and working together for supreme good, our part is to keep our lamps trimmed and burning and wait for the coming of the Heavenly Bridegroom whose name is—DIVINE ORDER.

CHAPTER XXIX.

SPIRITUALISM IN AUSTRALIA.—PART I.

SPIRITUALISM in Australia, like that which pervades the whole world in this modern outpouring, has both a public and private representation. The latter is far more general than the former in every country except America, but although demonstrations of Spirit power are more commonly known in Australia amongst individuals and families, than on the rostrum, or through the columns of the journals, they are less available for the purposes of historical record.

The author is in possession of hundreds of accounts of personal experiences and home circles, whilst ream upon ream of alleged Spirit communications have been tendered, for insertion in this volume.

It must of course become obvious to every sensible reader, that records of this character have no interest for the public, however valuable they may be to individuals.

As Spiritual phenomena are for the most part limited to a few general methods, and family communications—so interesting to the recipients—become monotonous in recital to others, it would be useless to reproduce them in pages designed for the benefit of the world at large.

At the risk therefore of disappointing hundreds of well-meaning correspondents who have sent matter for publication, which the *répertoire* of thousands of Spiritualists could duplicate, we must dismiss this branch of our subject, with the acknowledgment that Spirit power has been far more widely diffused than the public in general is apprised of, and that if a tithe of its doings were given to the world, they would suffice to furnish the shelves of an extensive library.

Aboriginal Spiritualism in Australia has many features of interest, were it within the scôpe of this volume to notice it. As this would not be possible, we must content ourselves by observing modern Spiritual development amongst the white settlers of Australia.

It seems that many Australian colonists had heard of the Spiritual movement before visiting the country, and on their arrival, pursuing the customary methods of unfoldment through the Spirit circle, a wide-spread interest was awakened long before public attention was called to the subject. In Sydney, Melbourne, Ballarat, Geelong, Brisbane, and numerous other towns and mining districts, communion with Spirits was successfully practised in circles and families, up to about 1867. After that epoch it seems to have become the subject of various journalistic reports of the usual adverse, eulogistic, or non-committal character. At or about that period, a large number of influential persons became interested in the matter, and not a few whose names were a sufficient guarantee of their good faith, began to detail wonderful experiences in the columns of the public journals. The debate and denial, rejoinder and defence, called forth by these narratives, served as propaganda for the movement, and rendered each freshly recorded manifestation. the centre of an ever-widening circle of interest.

In Victoria, a gentleman of considerable wealth and learning, writing under the *nom de plume* of SCHAMLYN, entered into a warm controversy with the editor of the *Collingwood Advertiser*, in defence of Spiritualism. This brave advocate of the faith defines his position in unmistakable characters in a letter, from which we make the following pungent extract :—

" I don't like to conclude without adverting to that boast of the editor of the *Collingwood Advertiser*—' That, as he had initiated the controversy, he did not intend to *withdraw* from the arena until he had *thoroughly exposed* the delusion or trickery,' and until he has *shown* that all spiritual publications are ' *sublime rot*,' I wish him to be informed that the moment he has accomplished the feat he has so magnanimously undertaken, he can *draw upon me for five hundred pounds sterling, which sum I have offered for twelve months past* (as our mutual friend Francis Waller can testify) *to any person in or out of the colony, who can do what he, the editor of the Collingwood Advertiser, in his issue of the 21st inst., has offered to do.* The money is in the Union Bank of Australia, Melbourne. The *savans* of the world will have nothing to say to it ; they will not examine it ; which is a strong sign that they don't believe it can be accounted for by any *known* laws of natural science ; the clergy are frightened of it ; it is apt to let *too much light* into the laity ; and the commonality pitch into it venomously, because it pleases their pastors, and gives an occasion for displaying their orthodoxy. Yours ever truly,
" Walwa, 25th November, 1868. SCHAMLYN."

This letter and many others by the same able writer, replete with sound sense and unanswerable logic, will be found printed in the appendix to a small volume entitled " Spiritual Communications." These were given through the mediumship of Mrs. Elizabeth Armstrong, a lady who resides at Melbourne, and in her capacity of clairvoyant physician, has wrought multitudes of cures which, under any other name than Spiritualism, would have been deemed "miraculous."

At the time when the spirit communications were given which form the subject of the above-named volume, Mrs. Armstrong was one of the subjects whom " Schamlyn," a gentleman devoted to scientific research, and a friend of the family—magnetized by way of experiment. In the trance condition thus induced, Mrs. Armstrong's hand was moved to write messages, some of a wonderful test character from spirit friends of those around her—others in various foreign languages utterly unknown to the simple country-bred Medium, and others, ranging through the highest flights of science, philosophy, and metaphysics, but all in a style, entirely beyond the normal capacity of the Medium. To sum up these remarkable productions, we here reprint the short preface of the compiler, the gentleman who sometimes signed his articles by his own initials S. G. W., and sometimes " Schamlyn." It is as follows :—

" The following communications purport to be messages of love and instruction from departed spirits, who, in giving them, have used the hand and mouth of Mrs. Armstrong *mechanically* ; in every instance involuntarily, and often in spite of herself, and of her persevering resistance to their control. Almost all of them were written in the presence of witnesses ; many, unconsciously to herself, when in trance or asleep ; and some were found written in her book, no one knowing when they were written. Some also in shorthand, no variety of which had she, or I, or any of our acquaintance, any knowledge of whatever. These communications are given originally in a great number of handwritings, exactly according to the number of spirits who have influenced her ; and whatever peculiarity of style, chirography, and signature has been adopted by the unseen agent—*claiming to be a spirit*—in his or her first communication through the hand of Mrs. Armstrong, has been uniformly maintained throughout. None of the original writings are in her own hand. The quotations in Greek, Hebrew, Syriac, and Arabic, are given in their respective characters." . . . .

The author of this work—whilst a resident in Melbourne—enjoyed the privilege of an intimate acquaintance both with the clairvoyant, Mrs.

Armstrong, and the gentleman whose initials are given above. From these parties she learned that the Medium's unfoldment did not proceed very smoothly, she being violently opposed to the controlling power, to which in fact she was only induced to succumb by personal methods, of which we give the following curious examples, extracted from "Schamlyn's" book, page 106 :—

"Every night, for weeks past, Mrs. A. has been visited by a spirit whom she knew in his earth life ; he moves the chairs and bed about—pulls her out of her bed, bedclothes and all—takes the comb out of her hair sometimes, and makes her hair a tangled mass. One comb has been taken away about ten days ago, and she was told that when they, the spirits, are satisfied with her conduct, the comb will be replaced in her hair."

And again :—

"Wednesday, 15th.—Excepting Mrs. A.'s nightly trances, there has been nothing done since last writing. I mean nothing that I can report from personal observation. But every night for a month past, she has been visited by a spirit, who pulls her out of bed, sometimes head first, oftener feet first, bedclothes and all ; this sometimes is done four times in one night. She can give no reason for such apparently violent conduct, except her constant refusal to do what he desires her ; and the most unaccountable thing about the matter is, that spirits with whom we have long been conversant, and in whom we have learned to trust, from their uniform goodness and patience, second the advice of the nightly visitant. . . . .

"Friday, 24th.—The nightly visits to Mrs. A. continue, and accompanied with the same apparently unnecessary violent movements of furniture, and pullings of clothes, &c., and still urging her to obey his behests, which she still refuses to do. The only writing that has been done, through Mrs. A.'s hand, for the last week has been the following :—'Did you know how important to your development is every hour you are losing by your indecision, all your hesitation would very soon cease ; and however revolting to your soul the irrevocable step may appear, do not let it stand in your way, or you will one day bitterly repent having done so. We are waiting for you ; so hasten on. Why do you keep lingering on your road ? Be brave, and let no fear daunt your onward progress.' "

If the restoration of hundreds of suffering mortals to health can be accepted as sufficient motive to justify months of similar persecution on the part of spirits towards their recusant Medium, then the strange nature of Mrs. Armstrong's development is explained, and the aphorism—" the end justifies the means"—must be accepted in her remarkable experiences.

Another influential supporter of the Spiritual cause who was an early convert, and for a time became a pillar of strength in its maintenance, was a gentleman connected with the editorial department of the *Melbourne Argus,* one of the leading journals of Victoria, and an organ well calculated to exert a powerful sway over the minds of its readers.

As this early friend of the cause has subsequently retreated from its general advocacy, and allied himself with a small society banded together under an influence inimical to the interests alike of society and Spiritualism, we only allude to his adherence in the incipiency of the movement as one of the subtle springs by which its onward march became so marvellous a success.

As the tides of public opinion moved on, doctors, lawyers, merchants, and men of eminence began to join the ranks. Tidings of phenomena of the most astounding character poured in from distant towns and districts. Members of the press began to share the general infection, and though some would not, and others could not avow their convictions, their private prepossessions induced them to open their columns for debate and correspondence on the subject. To add to the stimulus thus imparted, many of the leading colonial journals indulged in tirades of abuse and misrepresentation, which only served to increase the contagion without in the least diminishing its force.   At length the clergy—moved from their customary apathy by the tidings of conversions amongst their own best supporters, and the obvious fact that the stream of public sentiment was leaving the dull platitudes of old theology far in the rear, began to arouse themselves and manifest their interest by furious abuse, biblical thunders, and ecclesiastical " anathemas."   All would not do.   Denunciation provoked retort ; discussion compelled investigation ; the results of which were, triumphant victories for the FACTS of Spiritualism.   In New South Wales, as in Victoria, the illumination of supernal fires blazed forth—unlit by mortal hands, from every prominent centre.

In Sydney, many converts of rank and influence suddenly appeared upon the scene.

One of the noblest and best of men, one whom all classes and shades of opinion had been accustomed to look up to, honour and respect, now to be named alas, as *the late* Hon. John Bowie Wilson, Land Minister, and a valiant champion of temperance and every good thing that can reform mankind, became an open convert to Spiritualism, and by his personal influence, no less than his public defence of the cause made converts unnumbered, and sustained the work with the grasp of a colossus. Amongst the many others whose names have also graced the ranks of Spiritualism in Sydney, may be mentioned Mr. Henry Gale, an unswerving and self-sacrificing friend both of Spiritualism and Spiritualists.   Mrs. Wilson and Mrs. Gale, Mrs. Woolley and Mrs. Greville, besides a number of other ladies whose names we scarcely feel privileged to mention thus openly ; Mr. Greville, M.P., and several other members of the New South Wales Parliament and Cabinet ; Hon. J. Windeyer, Attorney-General of the Colony, subsequently one of the judges ; Mr. Alfred De Lissa, an eminent barrister ; Mr. Cyril Haviland, a literary gentleman of high standing ; Mr. Macdonald, Captain Barron and his amiable lady ; Mr. Milner Stephen, a barrister of eminence, his lady and family, and many other ladies and gentlemen of the first standing, joined the ranks of Spiritualism, and proved themselves as faithful in its defence, as they were honourable in avowing their unpopular (?) faith.

We must now call attention to a convert who, though neither an M.P. or aristocrat, as regards social position, has yet done as much, we might say more, to advance the cause of Spiritualism, and crystallize its scattered fragments into concrete strength, than any other individual in the ranks. We speak of Mr. Wm. Terry, the well-known and enterprising editor of the Melbourne *Harbinger of Light*, the oldest and best Spiritual organ of Australia.

Although biographical details in general are too prolix and personal for these pages, Mr. Terry's adherence to the cause of Spiritualism became an event of such marked importance, and he has so long and indefatigably identified himself with its progress, that we deem it in this instance only just to depart from the plan of this work and give the following biographical notice of Mr. Terry, as prepared for one of the English Spiritual papers by Hudson Tuttle, of America.

This eminent and careful writer says :—

"Mr. Terry was born in London in 1836, and in 1857 emigrated to Melbourne, Australia.   He was early thrown upon the world, and compelled to labour for a subsistence, and had little opportunity for literary culture.   The boy of seventeen buffetted his way in the rough colonial world almost alone and single-handed.   After the usual vicissitudes incident to the state of society during the early developments of the gold field, he established, in connection with his brother, a general store at Hemington, near Melbourne, on the main road to the principal gold diggings. It was here, in the year 1859, that his attention was first drawn to Spiritualism. It is of deep interest to trace his cumulative experience, and the character of the phenomena presented to him, for they are parallel and identical in character with those so widely witnessed in this country, showing a common origin. The reading of the work by Judge Edmonds and Dr. Dexter on 'Spiritualism,' which chanced to fall into his hand, interested him so much in the subject, that he began to inquire if there were investigators in the colony. Hearing that there were, and that they held *séances* in East Melbourne, he obtained permission to attend. Arriving rather late, he found twelve persons seated around a large loo-table. He took his seat at a small table at the extremity of the apartment, and carefully watched the proceedings. He found the people more than usually intelligent, and after a time the table moved and answered questions. Thus he had at once given him a fact to begin with. He says :—

" ' A supermundane power acted upon the table. The next thing was to ascertain the origin and nature of that power. With that view I obtained an introduction to a private circle, the members of which consisted of one family. I found them firm believers; their conduct was kindly and straightforward, and whilst offering us every opportunity to investigate, they did not seem anxious to proselyte. When we sat at a low table, it soon began to move and respond to the alphabet, to the questions of our hostess. . . . The table then began to imitate the motions of a ship at sea, and on inquiring, the name of a friend who had been lost at sea was given. He was asked to point out any passage in the Bible which would indicate the circumstances of his death, and the chapter and verse were indicated. Altogether the manifestations were demonstrative of an unseen intelligence controlling them. Their respectability and the absence of any motive for deception, forbade the idea of collusion or trickery; moreover our friends were most desirous that we should examine everything for ourselves, and we availed ourselves of the permission.

" ' Never shall I forget the eventful night when I realized the grand truth of man's continuous sensuous existence after death. I felt the presence of my brother, and it was indeed a happy reunion. Death had lost its sting, the grave its victory. My soul was filled with inexpressible joy, and as I wended my way homeward to tell the glad tidings, I could scarcely feel the ground under my feet. Shortly after this I was informed by my spirit friends that I should become a writing medium. I accordingly sat alone, and watched events. The first sensation experienced was a numbness of the hand and arm; then a current, as of mild electricity, passed through it, and my hand began to rotate, drawing circles on paper, and after a considerable time the letters S. B. were written. These I recognized as the initials of a spirit who had communicated before with us by means of the table. In a few days the influence increased, and several messages were written and signed by my brother and many others whom I had known and loved while in the body.

" ' About this time one of our circle received a letter from England, informing him that a ship named the " City of New York," on which an intimate friend of his was an officer, was long overdue and supposed to be lost. At our first meeting afterwards a communication was written through my hand giving an account of the foundering of the steamship " City of Boston."

" ' We said it was the " City of New York" that was supposed to be lost, but the spirit adhered to what he had written, and when the next mail arrived from England the papers contained an account of the loss of the " City of Boston." ' "

Passing over the narrative of many years of steady growth in various phases of mediumship we resume our extracts at the time when Mr. Terry's powers were specially unfolded for the diagnosis and cure of disease.

After describing in graphic terms the commencement and progress of Mr. Terry's work as a Clairvoyant and Medical Medium, the biographer says :—

" About 1869 the necessity for a Spiritualistic journal was impressed deeply on the mind of Mr. Terry. He could not cast it off, but pondered over the enterprise. At this time, an exceedingly sensitive patient described a spirit holding a scroll on which was written, ' *Harbinger of Light*,' and the motto, ' Dawn approaches, error is passing away; men arising shall hail the day.' This influenced him, and in August, 1870, he set to work to prepare the first number, which appeared on the 1st of September of that year, and has continued to be regularly issued to the present.

" There was no organisation in the Australian colony, and Mr. Terry saw the advantage and necessity of associative movement. He consulted a few friends, and in November,

1870, he organised the first Victorian Association of Spiritualists. A hall was rented, and Sunday services, consisting of essays and readings by members, enlivened by appropriate hymns, were held. In October, 1872, impressed with the desirability of forming a Lyceum, he called together a few willing workers, and held the first session October 20th, 1872. It is, and has been from the first in a flourishing condition, numbering one hundred and fifty members, with a very handsome and complete outfit, and excellent library. He has remained an officer ever since, and conductor four sessions. He assisted in the establishment of the Spiritualist and Free-thought Association, which succeeded the original one, and was its first president. He has lectured occasionally to appreciative audiences, and his lectures have been widely circulated. His mediumship, which gave such fair promise, both in regard to writing and speaking, became controlled especially for the relief of the sick. Without the assistance of advertising he has acquired a fine practice. With this he combines a trade in Reform and Spiritualistic publications, as extensive as the colony, and the publication of the *Harbinger of Light,* a Spiritual journal that is an honour to the cause, and well sustains the grand philosophy of immortality. No man is doing more for the cause, or has done more efficient work."

A short but interesting summary of the rise and progress of Spiritualism in Australia is given in the American *Banner of Light* of 1880, in which Mr. Terry's good service is again alluded to, and placed in line with several other pioneers of the movement, of whom mention has not as yet been made. The sketch reads as follows :—

"THE RISE AND PROGRESS OF SPIRITUALISM IN AUSTRALIA.

" The *Harbinger of Light,* published at Melbourne, Australia, furnishes a review of the origin of its publication and the work it has accomplished during the ten years just closed. At its advent in 1870, considerable interest had been awakened in the subject of Spiritualism, by the lectures of Mr. Nayler in Melbourne, and Mr. Leech at Castlemaine. The leaders of the church became disturbed, and seeing their gods in danger, sought to stay the progress of what would eventually lessen their influence and possibly their income. But Mr. Nayler spoke and wrote with more vigour ; the addresses of Mr. Leech were published from week to week in pamphlet form and widely distributed. At the same time, Mr. Charles Bright, who had published letters on Spiritualism in the *Argus,* over an assumed name, openly identified himself with the movement and spoke publicly on the subject. Shortly after, eleven persons met and formed an association, which soon increased to eighty members. A hymn book was compiled and Sunday services began. As elsewhere, the press ridiculed, and the pulpit denounced Spiritualism as a delusion. A number of articles in the *Argus* brought some of the facts prominently before the public, and the growing interest was advanced by a public discussion between Messrs. Tyerman and Blair. In 1872, a Sunday school on harmonial principles was established, Mr. W. H. Terry, the proprietor of the *Harbinger,* being its first conductor. Almost simultaneously with this was the visit of Dr. J. M. Peebles, whose public lectures and work in the Lyceum served to consolidate the movement. A controversy in the *Age,* between Rev. Mr. Potter, Mr. Tyerman and Mr. Terry, brought the facts and teachings of Spiritualism into further notice.

" Soon came Dr. Peebles, Thomas Walker, Mrs. Britten and others, who widened the influence of the spiritualistic philosophy, and aided the *Harbinger* in its efforts to establish Spiritualism on a broad, rational basis. Mr. W. H. Terry is deserving of all praise for his unselfish and faithful exertions in carrying the *Harbinger* through ten years of as hard labour as ever befell any similar enterprise, and we bespeak for him, in his continued efforts to make known the evidences of a future existence and the illuminating truths of Spiritualism, the hearty co-operation and sympathy of all friends of the cause."

The " Mr. Nayler " alluded to in the above-quoted article, as well as his estimable wife, proved invaluable pioneers in the cause of progress as Mediums for speaking, drawing, and other gifts. Both have now passed to their well-earned rest, but the record they have left behind will never pass out of grateful remembrance in this generation, whilst the effects of their good service will endure for all time.

In the palatial Melbourne residence of Mr. William Stanford, an American gentleman who has devoted time, wealth, and noble service to the advancement of Spiritualism, one room is entirely hung with Mrs. Nayler's Spirit drawings, and the hospitable master of the mansion, scorns not to rank amongst his costliest works of art, the Spirit drawings and paintings of the poor Medium. Mr. Stanford never descants more enthusiastically on the glorious pictures which adorn his walls, nor appears in more admirable relief to the time-serving throng with whom the Spirit world and its work is a tabooed subject, than when he conducts his visitors into the cabinet chamber gemmed with the artistic work of the "ancient" lady, now a blessed Spirit, and describes the marvels which attended the production of this complete picture gallery of Spirit art.

Amongst the distinguished workers in early Colonial Spiritualism, we must not omit to mention the Rev. John Tyerman, formerly a clergyman of the Church of England.

Writing to the *Banner of Light* on the subject of Mr. Tyerman's accession to the Spiritual ranks, an esteemed American correspondent says :—

"The Rev. J. Tyerman, of the Church of England, resident in one of the country districts, boldly declared his full reception of Spiritualism as a great fact, and his change of religious faith consequent upon the teachings of Spirits. Of course he was welcomed with open arms by the whole body of Spiritualists in Melbourne, the only city where there was any considerable number enrolled in one association. He soon became the principal lecturer, though not the only one employed by the Association, and well has he wielded the sword of the new faith. He is decidedly of the pioneer stamp, a skilful debater, a fluent speaker, ready at any moment to engage with any one, either by word of mouth or as a writer. So widely, indeed, did he make his influence felt, and so individual was it, that a new society grew up around him, called the Free-Thought and Spiritualist Propaganda Society, which remained in existence till Mr. Tyerman removed to Sydney, when it coalesced with the older Association under the combined name of Melbourne Spiritualist and Free-Thought Association."

Mr. Tyerman is acknowledged to have wrought well and faithfully for the cause of Spiritualism. Though now removed by the Death Angel to the farther shore, his good service is held in grateful remembrance by many of those who were first stimulated to investigate Spiritualism, through his trenchant arguments and fearless example. Like all public labourers in an unpopular cause, Mr. Tyerman had to do battle with personal enemies both within and without the camp, and even now his name is often used as a byword of reproach against Spiritualism. And yet—" He being dead yet speaketh "—and surely " His works do follow him."

Another valuable convert to the cause of Spiritualism at a time when it most needed good service, was Mrs. Florence Williams, the daughter of the celebrated English novelist G. P. R. James, and the inheritor of his talent, originality of thought, and high culture. This lady for a long time officiated at the first Spiritual meetings convened for Sabbath Day exercises, as an acceptable and eloquent lecturer, and her essays would have formed an admirable epitome of Spiritual revelations at the time in which they were delivered.

The visits of several zealous propagandists have been alluded to in previous quotations, amongst whom must be named one of the first to break ground as a public exponent of Spiritualism, the Rev. J. M. Peebles, formerly a minister of Battle Creek, Michigan. Mr. Peebles was well known in America as a fine writer and lecturer, and as such was justified in expecting courteous, if not eulogistic mention from the press of a foreign country, with whom his own was on terms of amicable intercourse. How widely different was the journalistic treatment he experienced may be gathered from his own remarks addressed to the *Banner of Light* some five years after his first visit, and describing in graphic terms the changed spirit which marked alike the progress of the movement and the alteration in the tone of public opinion.

Mr. Peebles says :—

" Relative to Spiritualism and its divine principles public sentiment has changed rapidly, and for the better, during the past five years. Upon my late public appearance in Melbourne, the Hon. John McIlwraith, Ex-mayor of the city, and Commissioner to our Centennial Exhibition, took the chair, introducing me to' the audience. On my previous visit some of the Spiritualists seemed a little timid. They preferred being called investigators, remaining a good distance from the front. Then my travelling companion, Dr. Dunn, was misrepresented and meanly vilified in the city journals ; while I was hissed in the market, caricatured in *Punch*, burlesqued in a theatre, and published in the daily press as an " ignorant Yankee," an " American trickster," a " long-haired apostate," and a " most unblushing blasphemer ! " But how changed ! Recently the secular press treated me fairly. Even the usually abusive *Telegraph* published Mr. Stevenson's article assuring the Rev. Mr. Green that I was willing to meet him at once in a public discussion. The *Melbourne Argus*, one of the best daily papers in the world, the *Australasian*, the *Herald*, and the *Age*, all dealt honourably by me, reporting my lectures, if briefly, with admirable impartiality. The press is a reflector ; and those audiences of 2,000 and 2,500 in the great Opera House on each Sunday for several successive months were not without a most striking moral significance. It seemed to be the general opinion that Spiritualism had never before occupied so prominent yet so favourable a position in the eyes of the public. . . . "

That Australia might not be wanting in phenomenal proofs of the Spiritual authority upon which the doctrines of the rostrum were promulgated, the invisible powers through whose resistless influence the movement has been conducted, impelled the Davenport Brothers, and Charles Foster, the celebrated test and physical Medium, to visit the Colonies on different occasions, subsequently to the establishment of the *Harbinger of Light* in 1870. It was fortunate for the best interests of truth that this was the case, as Mr. Terry's plain account of the phenomena as they really occurred through these Mediums, was essential, to counteract the wilful spirit of misrepresentation indulged in by a large portion of the Colonial press. The reader must now be familiar with the several phases of Spirit power displayed through the Davenports and Charles Foster ; descriptions of what transpired in their presence therefore would be unnecessary. It is worthy of note however, that William Davenport, the younger of the celebrated brothers, closed a life of unnatural toil, cruel persecution, and hardship, in Melbourne, sinking, to what none can doubt to be his well-earned rest, under the premature decay of a worn-out constitution.

To commemorate the blessed transition from the chilling airs which had blighted the young life of his brother, and sped him all too soon to the land of never setting suns, poor Ira, the lonely brother still left, a stranger so far distant from home and friends, determined to leave behind him such a memento of his departed companion, as should (to his conception at least) worthily commemorate the life-long service to which his brother had fallen a sacrifice.

For this purpose, he devised a tombstone, on which he caused to be engraved, the representation of the cabinet, ropes, and other paraphernalia, which constituted the two brothers' stock-in-trade. But when this strange device was about to be set up, the reverend gentleman who claimed rule over the sacred " city of the dead," powerless as he might be to influence the destiny of the enfranchised soul, protested against such a *heathenish* record being introduced into *sacred ground*. In a word, Christian piety was deeply scandalized at Ira's ingenious method of honouring his poor brother, and the holy man in question ruled the unsanctified tombstone out of the cemetery.

It was nothing that stony voices on every side proclaimed such *heathenish* falsehoods, as "gone to God;" "sleeping in the ground;" "waiting for the last trump to sound," &c., &c. These caricatures of the departed soul's condition, were strictly in Christian order, but to tell the actual story of Willie Davenport's life in truthful marble was too direct a perversion of Christian order to be permitted, and so the tombstone was ruled out, and so it would have remained had not a sentiment of reactionary common sense and good feeling so prevailed, that it was ultimately set up in a little nook railed off from the sacred dust, and yet sufficiently near to suggest the inference, that in some distant angelic resurrection day, even Willie Davenport might creep into heaven through some small *side door* whose hinges were oiled by the sanctified remains near which his unsanctified dust was laid to rest. That Willie Davenport's bright and progressed spirit has whispered into his bereaved brother's ear many a time, Laertes' bitter rebuke to the "churlish priest" whom Shakespere represents as cutting short poor Ophelia's funeral rites, we have good reason to believe ; enough that the curtain has fallen on what might have been esteemed a tragedy, had not the cant of Christian ecclesiasticism turned it into a farce. When that curtain rises again on Spirit life, we may find Willie Davenport and the "churlish priest" have changed places.

Of Charles Foster's work in Australia, we can only offer one representative extract. Though written in the *Harbinger of Light* in 1881, it refers to a scene which transpired eight years previously. The author, Mr. H. J. Browne, of Melbourne, is a gentleman whose wealth, influence, and distinguished literary abilities, have been nobly devoted to the advancement of every good work in Spiritualism. Beloved and admired by all who knew them, both Mr. and Mrs. Browne have been pillars of strength to the cause in Melbourne.

Besides being the author of several volumes, pamphlets, and well-written articles, on the facts and philosophy of Spiritualism, Mr. Browne has gallantly maintained the cause in public as well as in private debate. If Charles Foster had made no other converts than this gentleman and his fair wife, his visit to Australia would not have been in vain. In one of his "familiar letters," published in the *Harbinger of Light*, Mr. Browne describes his first interview with Mr. Foster and its consequences, as follows :—

"My first decided experience of practical Spiritualism was connected with the exposition of the phenomena by Mr. Foster, in Melbourne, seven or eight years ago. I received so many assurances of the powerful and convincing nature of his exhibitions from friends who had visited him in Spring Street, that I was induced, in company of a friend, to interview him ; and I must confess I did so with a very strong impression that his exhibitions were based on mere trickery, and that those who visited him were the victims of delusion. However, the evidence he afforded me, the names he mentioned of friends who had been dead years and years, the messages which came through him to me, stamped with a particularity which carried the evidence with them, could not be explained away. I could not conceive that by any process of mind-reading Mr. Foster could tell me circumstances of a private nature, and which for the time had faded from my memory, or indeed that he could tell the name of my father, for I myself was a perfect stranger to him, and he had no opportunity of making enquiry. But in addition to this, he not only quoted names, and gave the cause of the death of several friends long in the spirit-world, describing their characteristics, but I distinctly saw, in the front of *his* face, the materialised features of a friend who had been dead some little time, and of whom he could by no possibility have known anything."

Mr. Browne sums up a long account of phenomena, very wonderful in itself, but too familiar to need re-iteration, with the following urgent question :—

"Is it not sufficient that names, characteristics, appropriate messages, and most accurate description of friends who have been in the spirit-world for so long a time are thus given with accuracy ? "

CHAPTER XXX.

SPIRITUALISM IN AUSTRALIA.—PART II.

WE must now call attention to the efficient service rendered to the cause of Spiritualism by Mr. Thomas Walker, a young Englishman first introduced in the Colonies by the Rev. J. M. Peebles, in whose company Mr. Walker for some time travelled.

Alleging himself to be a "trance speaker" under the control of certain Spirits *whom he named*, Mr. Walker lectured acceptably in Sydney, Melbourne, and other places in the Colonies on the Spiritual rostrum.   At the period of the author's visit to Australia in March, 1878, Mr. Walker was maintaining a public debate with a Mr. M. W. Green, a minister of a denomination termed "the Church of Christ."   This gentleman had acquired some reputation in the Colonies as a preacher, and as one who had bitterly opposed, and taken every possible opportunity to misrepresent Spiritualism.

The debate, which was held in the Temperance Hall, Melbourne, had attracted large audiences, and been extended for several nights beyond the period originally agreed upon.

At the time when the author arrived in Melbourne, and was taken by her new friends to hear the closing arguments, it was evident that Mr. Green had in a great measure abandoned the ground originally assumed for debate—namely, the relative principles of Christianity and Spiritualism—and was now entering upon that most objectionable system of warfare which consists of personal invective, against the characters of those who espoused the cause which he opposed.

This was all the more injurious, as Mr. Green's attacks were chiefly levelled against the American Spiritualists, and the scandalous stories he retailed were not likely to be familiar enough to English listeners to enable them to judge of the truth or falsehood of his allegations.

It was in pursuance of this *very honourable* mode of warfare, that on the last night but one of the debate, Mr. Green, towards the close of the proceedings, launched what he evidently intended to be a final thunderbolt against the whole rank and file of the Spiritualists, by reading a letter, full of the bitterest denunciations against Spiritualism and the vilest charges against Spiritualists—which letter Mr. Green affirmed, emanated " from a physician of high standing in the City of New York."   For the original of this document the reader is referred to the printed report of the Green and Walker debate published in Melbourne and sold by Mr. Terry.

It is only necessary to say to the well-informed American reader, that the said *physician in high standing*—whose name would disgrace these pages, was the notorious individual who was cited by his hapless young wife—one of the most celebrated trance-speaking Mediums of America—to answer for his shameful misdeeds in a New York court of justice; that in passing a sentence which freed the suffering lady from the power of the infamous husband, the latter was branded with a character so vile, that he was virtually expelled—not only from association with every Spiritual society in America—but also from the notice of any respectable members of the community.

It was in revenge for the odium and disgrace thus stamped upon him that the *New York physician of high standing* wrote and printed a vengeful tract, bitterly denouncing the Spiritualists who had repudiated him; and it was this notable and authoritative document by which Mr. Green proposed to deal the final blow that should demolish Spiritualism all over the world.

Although this letter bore in its very wording, evidence of the reckless mendacity and malignity which had dictated it, Mr. Green read it out with an assumption of deep regret that he had been forced to this course "in the best interests of society, morality, duty," &c., &c. The reading of such a document to an audience totally unacquainted with the circumstances under which it was written, of course fell like a thunderbolt on the astonished listeners, and produced a feeling of discouragement even amongst the Spiritualists present, which Mr. Walker could not dispel. But whilst Mr. Green was felicitating himself on the immense advantage his mode of attack had procured for him, he was entirely unconscious of the fact, that two newly arrived strangers from America were in the audience, who *did* know the character of the witness, he had so recklessly cited. Those strangers were the author and her husband, and when on the next evening the closing proceedings of the debate were opened, Mr. Walker and his committee were in possession of a letter signed in full, and stating clearly, the real character and standing of Mr. Green's "New York physician." The circumstances under which this man was universally tabooed by the American Spiritualists were fully detailed, and the vengeance which animated him to retaliate upon them in Mr. Green's *famous* document, made thoroughly manifest. Furthermore, the writer offered in proof of her veracity, to refer a committee of enquiry to twelve respectable residents of New York City. It may well be supposed, the reading of this letter, signed as it was by a party then present in the audience, created a sensation which fully equalled, if it did not exceed that of the former occasion. It is enough to say, the debate on this evening was neither as extended nor yet as spirited as formerly. Every listener felt doubtless with the minister and his party, that the matter had gone quite far enough, and the result was, the affair closed in the usual parliamentary way, that is to say, hollow courtesies were exchanged, the debatants mutually complimented each other; votes of thanks, and a general hand-shaking ensued, and so the proceedings terminated.

Following upon this debate, the author proceeded to fill an engagement to deliver Sunday evening lectures at the Melbourne Opera House, during a period extending over several months. As the audiences at these meetings scarcely ever numbered less than two thousand persons, it may be supposed that the interest as well as antagonism they excited, was very marked. In this, both press and pulpit played their accustomed *rôle*. The columns of the journals became the arena of a perfect guerilla warfare, and the author's pen was kept constantly busy, in refuting erroneous statements, and answering antagonistic opponents. Some of these attacks necessitated answers from the rostrum, which were not unfrequently printed and distributed abroad, as Spiritual propaganda.

Meantime the pulpits thundered forth their customary denunciations, although a few of the more liberal preachers of the day, bore testimony to the immense impulse that Spiritualism had communicated to popular sentiment.

Week evening meetings also were organized in the Melbourne Athenæum and many of the adjacent towns and districts.

During the author's visit to Australia she was induced to publish several lectures, tracts, and two volumes of a still more important character. These works were issued by the large and influential publishing house of Messrs. Robertson and Co., Melbourne, and though several editions were run through, they were so eagerly bought up, that they are now out of print and unobtainable. The first volume published was a manual of Spiritualism designed for the use of investigators, called " On the Road ;" the second was entitled " The Faith's Facts and Frauds of Religious History."

Both will be republished when time and opportunity serves for a future issue.

Mrs. Britten's time being limited, and pressing demands calling her away to other countries, her stay in Australia was comparatively short and terminated in about fourteen months. Mr. Walker, however, remained to reap the fruit of his labours, and after an absence of some months in South Africa, has returned to Melbourne, as a lecturer on avowedly " Free Thought subjects."

It was about this time that the celebrated test and physical Medium, Dr. Slade, arrived in the Colonies, and the marvellous proofs of Spirit power that were exhibited in his presence, contributed not a little to the rapid growth of a deep and intelligent interest in Spiritualism.

How far the insults and sneers of the press had become modified to fair and candid reports of what was transpiring, may be gathered, from the following extracts, taken from the Melbourne *Age*, one of the leading daily journals of the city. They are dated August 20, 1878, and read thus :—

" A SÉANCE WITH DR. SLADE.

" Spiritualism is just now very much to the front in Melbourne. The lectures of Mrs. Emma Hardinge-Britten, delivered to crowded audiences at the Opera House every Sunday evening, have naturally attracted a sort of wondering curiosity to the subject, and the interest has probably been intensified by the strenuous efforts that are being made in some of the orthodox pulpits to prove that the whole thing is an emanation from the devil. The announcement that the famous Dr. Slade had arrived to strengthen the ranks of the Spiritualists has therefore been made at a very critical juncture, and I should not be surprised to find that the consequence will be to infuse a galvanic activity into the forces on both sides. Though I do not profess to be a Spiritualist, I own to having been infected with the fashionable itch for witnessing ' physical manifestations,' as they are called, and accordingly I have attended several circles with more or less gratification. But Dr. Slade is not an ordinary medium, even amongst professionals. The literature of the Spiritualists is full of his extraordinary achievements, attested to all appearance by credible witnesses, who have not been ashamed to append their names to their statements. . . . I see that on one occasion, writing in six different languages was obtained on a single slate, and one day, accompanied by two learned professors, Dr. Slade had a sitting with the Grand Duke Constantine, who obtained writing on a new slate held by himself alone. From St. Petersburg Dr. Slade went to Berlin, where he is said to have obtained some marvellous manifestations in the house of Professor Zöllner, and where he was visited by the court conjurer to the Emperor, Samuel Bellachini. . . . **My object in** visiting Dr. Slade can be understood when I was introduced to him with my friend, whom I shall call Omega. and who was bent on the same errand. Dr. Slade and Mr. Terry constituted the circle of four who sat around the table in the centre of the room almost as immediately as we entered it. There was nothing in the room to attract attention. No signs of confederacy, human or mechanical. The hour was eleven in the morning. The window was unshuttered, and the sun was shining brightly. The table at which we sat was a new one, made especially by Wallach Brothers, of Elizabeth Street, of polished cedar, having four slight legs, one flap, and no ledges of any kind underneath. As soon as we examined it Dr. Slade took his seat on one side, facing the window, and the rest of us occupied the other three seats. He was particularly anxious that we should see he had nothing about him. It had been said that he wrote on the slate by means of a crumb of pencil stuck in his finger-nails, but his nails were cut to the quick, while his legs and feet were ostentatiously placed away from the table in a side position, exposed to view the whole time. He first produced a slate of the ordinary school size, with a wet sponge, which I used to it. A chip of pencil about the size of a grain of wheat was placed upon it on the table ; we joined hands, and immediately taps were heard about the table, and in answer to a question—'Will you write ?'—from Dr. Slade, three raps were given, and he forthwith took up the slate with the pencil lying on it, and held half of it under the table by his finger and thumb, which clasped the corner of the half that was outside the table, and was therefore easily seen by all present. His left hand remained near the centre of the table, resting on those of the two sitters on either side of him. Several convulsive jerks of his arm were now given, then a pause, and immediately the sound of writing was audible to every one, a scratching sound interrupted by the tap of the pencil, which indicated, as we afterwards found, that the t's were being crossed and the i's dotted. The slate was then exposed, and the words written were in answer to the question which had been put by Omega as to whether he had psychic power or not. I pass over the conversation that ensued on the subject, and go on to the next phenomenon. To satisfy myself that the 'trick' was not done by means of sympathetic writing on the slate, I had ten minutes previously purchased a slate from a shop in Bourke Street, containing three leaves, and shutting up book fashion. This I produced, and Dr. Slade readily repeated his performance with it. It was necessary to break the pencil down to a mere crumb, in order to insert it between the leaves of the slate. This done, the phenomenon at once recurred, with this rather perplexing difference, that the slate, instead of being put half under the table, forced itself by a series of jerks on to my neck, and reposed quietly under my ear, in the eyes of every one present. The scratching then commenced ; I heard the t's crossed and the i's dotted by the moving pencil, and at the usual signal I opened the slate, and found an intelligible reply to the question put. . . . . . The next manifestation was the levitation of one of the sitters in his chair about a clear foot from the ground, and the levitation of the table about two feet. I ought to have mentioned that during the whole of the *séance* there was a good deal of by-play going on. Everyone felt the touch of hands more or less, and the sitters' chairs were twice wrenched from under them, or nearly so, but the psychic could not possibly have done it. . . ."

As the messages that were obtained, though of a remarkable test character, would be of no interest to the reader, we omit them. The writer sums up the result of his visit with a candid reiteration of all the conditions, and acknowledges the utter impossibility of attributing the phenomena produced to fraud, collusion, or any known mundane causes.

As personal details are more graphic than the cold narrations of passing events, we deem it expedient in this place to give our readers an *inside* view of Spiritualism in Australia, by republishing one of the many articles sent by the author to the American Spiritual journals during her sojourn in the Colonies. The following excerpt was written as the result of personal experience, and at a time when Spiritualism, in the usual inflated style of journalistic literature, was " in the zenith of its triumphs." It is addressed to the Editor of the *Banner of Light*, and reads as follows :—

" Spiritualism in these Colonies finds little or no public representation outside of Melbourne or Sydney, nevertheless warm friends of the cause are scattered all over the land, and endeavours are being made to enlarge the numerous circles into public meetings, and the fugitive efforts of whole-hearted individuals into associations as powerful as that which exists in Melbourne. At present, the attempt to effect missionary work in any portions of Australia outside Sydney or Melbourne, becomes too great a burden to the luckless individual, who has not only to do the work, but to bear the entire cost of the undertaking, as I have had to do in my visits to various towns in Victoria. Expenses which are cheerfully divided amongst the many in the United States, become all too heavy for endurance when shouldered upon the isolated workers ; hence the paucity of public representation, and the impossibility of those who visit the Colonies, as I have done, effecting any important pioneer work beyond the two great centres I have named. Mr. Walker at Sydney, and I at Melbourne, have been favoured with the largest gatherings ever assembled at Colonial Sunday meetings.

"Having, by desire of my spirit guides, exchanged rostrums, he filling my place at Melbourne, and I his at Sydney, we find simultaneously at the same time, and on the same Sundays, the lessees of the two theatres we occupied raising their rent upon us one hundred and fifty per cent. The freethinkers and Spiritualists had occupied the theatre in Sydney four years at the rate of four pounds per Sunday. For my benefit the landlord raised the rent to ten pounds, whilst the same wonderful spirit of accordance caused the Melbourne manager to increase upon Mr. Walker from eight pounds to a demand of twenty. With our heavy expenses and small admission fees this was tantamount to driving us out altogether. Both of us have succeeded after much difficulty, and fighting Christian warriors with the Christian arms of subtlety and vigilance, in securing other places to lecture in ; and despite the fact that the press insult us, the pulpit curse us, and Christians generally devote us to as complete a prophecy of what they would wish us to enjoy everlastingly as their piety can devise, we are each attracting our thousands every Sunday night, and making such unmistakable marks on public opinion as will not easily be effaced again. . . .

"Dr. Slade's advent in Melbourne since last September has been productive of an immense amount of good. How far his labours here will prove remunerative I am not prepared to say. Frankly speaking, I do not advise Spirit Mediums or speakers to visit these colonies on financial advancement intent. There is an abundant crop of Medium power existing, interest enough in the cause, and many of the kindest hearts and clearest brains in the world to be found here ; but the lack of organisation, to which I have before alluded, and the imperative necessity for the workers who come here to make their labours remunerative, paralyses all attempts at advancement, except in the sensation line. Still I feel confident that with united action throughout the scattered force of Spiritualistic thought in these Colonies, Spiritualism might and would supersede every other phase of religious thought in an incredibly short space of time. I must not omit to mention that the friends in every place I have visited have been more than kind, hospitable, and appreciative. The public have defied both press and pulpit in their unstinted support of my lectures. The press have been equally servile, and the Christian world equally stirred, and equally active in desperate attempts to crush out the obvious proofs of immortality Spiritualism brings.

"In Melbourne, I had to fight my way to comply with an invitation to lecture for the benefit of the City Hospital. I fought and conquered ; and the hospital committee revenged itself for a crowded attendance at the Town Hall by taking my money without the grace of thanks, either in public or private, and the simply formal acknowledgment of my services by an official receipt. In Sydney, where I now am, I was equally privileged in lecturing for the benefit of the Temperance Alliance, and equally honoured, after an enthusiastic and successful meeting, by the daily press of the city in their utter silence concerning such an important meeting, and their careful record of all sorts of such trash as they disgrace their columns with. So mote it be. The wheel will turn some day!

"Sydney is deepening from a lovely spring to a warm summer, just as you in America are collapsing into a freezing winter. Some time soon after Christmas (Midsummer here) I expect we shall begin to turn our thoughts westward, where home duties and private interests imperatively summon us ; if not early in the spring, not later than the ensuing early summer.   "EMMA HARDINGE BRITTEN.

"Sydney, New South Wales, November, 1878."

During the years 1881 and 82 the Australian colonists were favoured with visits from three more well-known American Spiritualists. The first of these was Professor Denton, an able and eloquent lecturer on geology, and one who never fails to combine with his scientific addresses, one or more stirring lectures on Spiritualism. The second propagandist was Mrs. Ada Foye, one of the best test, writing, rapping, and seeing Mediums, that has ever appeared in the ranks of Spiritualism, whilst the third was Mrs. E. L.

Watson, a charming trance speaker, and a lady as much admired for her spotless life and amiable manners as for her eloquent addresses.

Mrs. Watson's stay in the Colonies, like that of Mrs. Foye, was very brief, yet quite long enough to create a profound impression upon her large audiences and establish her memory in the hearts of hosts of friends.

Professor Denton's lectures created a wide-spread interest amongst all classes of listeners. Even the most hypercritical scientists were compelled to admit his claim to equality with themselves.

He lost *caste* it is true, when his fearless advocacy of Spiritualism followed up his scientific lectures ; but even his enemies acknowledged the resistless influence of his eloquence, and the public gladly lent an ear to his common-sense arguments and commanding powers of expression.

Mrs. Foye is one of the few test and physical Mediums whose manifestations can be exhibited in a public audience. For upwards of twenty-five years, this lady has given her wonderful demonstrations of Spirit power in the presence of immense audiences in brilliantly-lighted halls, and under conditions so entirely free from the possibility of fraud that none but the most determined of antagonists could question her good faith. Calm, dignified, and self-possessed, she asks no conditions but quiet attention and keen scrutiny. A Medium of such rare and exceptional powers as this lady possesses, needs none of the apologetic writing and controversial discussion devoted to so many of her compeers, hence it is seldom that her name is mentioned in the Spiritual journals. It might be better for "the cause" were it otherwise. As it would be a disgrace alike to the movement and the generation, to let both pass away without some honourable mention of a Medium whose manifestations have proved convincing to thousands, and are unassailable in any direction, whilst volumes are written on the merits of those whom a considerable proportion of the community denounce as "frauds," we have much satisfaction in giving space to a few reports on Mrs. Foye's work during her short visit to Australia.

The first extract is copied from the New Zealand *Echo*, and reads as follows :—-

"Another visitor (from San Francisco) that gave us a flutter was Mrs. Ada Foye, the celebrated Californian test-medium. Mrs. Foye is a remarkable woman. Evidently without education, she evinces in her addresses a faculty of clear statement, and a quickness and aptness of repartee quite refreshing to listen to. Her public *séances* at the School of Arts were a great success, and it is a pity she only gave three, as she was but just beginning to get known. Her method is as follows : Anyone who chose among the audience—and nearly every one appeared to choose—writes the name of some departed friend on a small piece of paper, and rolls it up. These pellets are then placed on a small table on the stage, and make a pile half a foot high. Mrs. F. then takes a handful of them, and asks, 'Is there present any spirit whose name is on one of the papers in my hand?' If there is no answer, she takes another handful and repeats the question. If raps are given, she desires one of the audience to hold the pellets, and when an affirmative rap is given, she desires the spirit to give the name, the paper being held, still rolled up, by the party who undertook this part of the proceeding. The answer is sometimes spelled out by raps, sometimes Mrs. F. sees it written in the air, and sometimes it is whispered to her, or is written automatically. She then desires the holder of the pellet to open it and see if the name is correctly given. The writer of the name is then asked to declare himself, and to put to the spirit any questions he chooses. Not a single mistake was made, and when it is said that thirty or forty spirits answered each evening, it must be admitted that the *séances* are very wonderful. All possibility of collusion is entirely out of the question, as Mrs. F. was only in Sydney two or three days before the *séances*, and nearly all those receiving answers were well-known citizens, while each time the pellets were held by a different individual, most of them also well-known people. Mrs. Foye is now in Melbourne, and returns immediately to California without visiting New Zealand, having taken the trip for the benefit of her health."

16

As it is quite possible that few of our readers have ever seen any one who can equal Mrs. Foye as a test Medium and it may be long before we shall look upon her like again, at least in this generation, we crave permission to occupy more space than has been usually devoted to individuals in this record and give a summary of the proceedings of Mrs. Foye's opening meeting as reported in the *Harbinger of Light* of August, 1881 :—

"MRS. ADA FOYE'S PUBLIC TEST SÉANCES.

" Mrs. Ada Foye, a lady who has attained a considerable degree of fame in America in consequence of the striking tests of Spirit presence and identity given in public through her Mediumship, has lately favoured this colony with a visit, and gave the first public demonstration of her powers in Melbourne at the Lower Temperance Hall on the evening of Wednesday, the 16th November. The proceedings, which were conducted by the lady herself in an admirably cool and collected way, comprised two portions ; first, a brief address on the subject of Spiritualism, including an account of the development of her Mediumship : secondly, a series of tests given to various members of the audience.

The chairman, W. B. Bowley, Esq., J.P., having in a few words introduced Mrs. Foye to her audience, she gave the following interesting account of the development of her mediumistic powers :—

" ' At the age of twelve and a half years I was living in the suburbs of Boston (my native city). Both my father and mother were very earnest, devoted Christians, and, at my mother's knee, night after night was I taught my prayers ; and I thank God for it. My father being one of the pillars of the church, I was brought up very strictly, and was taught to believe that when the spirit left this world it went either up or down, and there it stayed. This will show how little prepared I was to believe in anything like spiritual manifestations. At the time that I became aware I was a Medium, my father and myself were both singing in the church choir, in Boston, and a lady who was singing with us, after the service, said, "Mr. Hoyt" (my father's name), "Suppose I go home to tea with you to-night. I have been to Rochester, and have heard what they call the Rochester knockings." (They were creating a good deal of excitement at that time.) "I have witnessed those manifestations," continued she, " and the spirits there said I was a Medium, and they could communicate with me, provided I would sit at home. After I got home from Rochester I sat at the table, and sure enough I got the raps. Now if you would like to hear them, we will have a sitting before the evening service." '

" After describing the *séance* that followed, and the amazement which the rappings and the intelligence they gave, created, Mrs. Foye went on to say :—

" ' When I was a little girl, I used to see spirits beside me, and play with them and talk with them. I would give strange ideas to the people about me, and they used to say I was precocious, and going to die. From that time the manifestations continued by rappings and the moving of the table, chairs, and articles of furniture. These movements continued for two years, and after that they began taking my hand to write messages. I could not enumerate all the various phases of Mediumship that were developed day by day and year after year. Suffice it to say that I came before the public when about thirteen, and since then have been giving *séances* nearly all over the United States, and for the last fourteen years in California. For two years after I became aware I was a Medium, I did not believe the manifestations were produced by spirits. This shows that it is not necessary to be a believer to be a Medium. I was very young, and was constantly sitting with men of science, religious men, and people who were forming circles to investigate these matters, and I was expecting every day to get the whole thing explained on some other hypothesis. The scientific men would say that it was electricity. They placed the legs of the chairs and tables in tumblers ; stretched batteries across the table, and completely insulated the table, so that if any raps were produced they would not be electricity, but still they rapped on. The more batteries they put the louder they would rap. Then the ministers came to pray with me, and to exorcise the spirits, and upon one occasion our good clergyman in East Boston came with two or three of the pious brethren, and we all knelt in prayer, to see if we could not stop the rapping ; but the louder Brother Sandford prayed the louder the spirits rapped. So the scientific men could not explain it, the religious people could not " lay " it ; and after two years of earnest investigation, not only by myself, but by scientific and religious men and women from all parts of the country, I made up my mind they were produced by departed spirits, and when any person once makes up their mind in this matter, after careful investigation, there is no backsliding. From that time I have been an earnest worker in the cause. I see spirits, hear them, feel them about me, *know* that they are with me.

MRS ADA FOYE

Some persons may say, "You are crazy." If I am, there is method in my madness. If you would only candidly investigate the subject, you would find something beyond explanation by chicanery, delusion, or even the devil.

"I do not know what will be done here to-night any more than you do. The phenomena which usually occur are rapping, writing, seeing, and hearing. I sit quietly and passively. The raps will be produced upon the platform, the table, the wall, the chairs, or somewhere round about the table. I do not know where they will rap. In writing, spirits take possession of my hand, and write upside down, from right to left, also in other languages, although I know none except English. As to seeing; the spirits sometimes write in the air. The letters look like letters of gold to me. You cannot see them, but the proof that I do is because the names and the answers to questions are given correctly. As to hearing, the spirits whisper to me, and tell me what they want to tell you, and what they tell is always pertinent and appropriate to the circumstances.'

"The speaker concluded her remarks by stating that the only condition she imposed upon her audience was that of perfect stillness. The crying of a child, whispered conversation, or the rustling of persons moving about, would interfere with the manifestations. She then requested each person to write on a slip of paper the name of some departed friend or relative whom they wished to hear from, and fold the slip up. These were collected, forming a large number, and placed upon the table before the Medium. The following are selected as the best, or rather the most striking, since there could hardly be any 'best' where there was not a single failure or inaccuracy, of the tests given :—

"'Are any friends here present ?—if so, please rap to us.' Mrs. Foye touched each of the folded slips or pellets in rapid succession, asking, 'Is this one here ? this ? this ?' until three raps (for Yes) responded. The raps during the whole evening could be distinctly heard throughout the hall, proceeding from the table or platform. Mrs. Foye : 'Will some one take this paper, please, and keep it closed ? I see the name Reeds ; open the paper.' The paper was opened by the gentleman who held it, who read the name, 'Robert B. Reeds.' 'Did anyone know that person ?' A gentleman from the audience replied in he affirmative. Mrs. Foye : 'Ask him any question ; his age, for instance. Call over several numbers, including the right one among them.' The gentleman responded. Mrs. Foye : 'Between 25 and 26 ; I see those numbers right over your head.' The gentleman replied that this was correct. 'Now the cause of death ; call over some diseases.' Gentleman : 'Heart complaint ?' One rap (No). 'Dropsy ?' One rap. 'Apoplexy ?' Mrs. Foye : 'Wait ; they are going to write.' The Medium's hand was controlled to write rapidly the following message, upside down : 'I think it was apoplexy ; my departure was sudden.' The gentleman in the audience replied 'Yes ; it was sunstroke.' 'What part of the world did he die in ?' He called over the names of a few places. 'Melbourne ?' One rap. 'Geelong ? One rap. 'Ballarat ?' One rap. 'Sydney ?' Three raps (Yes). The gentleman stated this was correct. In answer to our reporter's inquiry, this gentleman stated that he had never seen Mrs. Foye before that evening.

"'Some one is going to write in the air ; I can see the lines going to form, and then they go into letters. I can see the name Robert John Williams.' This was recognised by a lady in the audience. Mrs. Foye asked her, 'Are you acquainted with me ?' The reply was in the negative. 'Ask what age' (at time of death). The lady called over— 'Eight months ?' No. 'Nine months ?' No. Mrs. Foye said, 'This spirit cannot write; will some spirit write for him ?' 'Eight months twenty-two days.' The lady who recognised the spirit confirmed this."

Although the tests given on that and other occasions were very various, and the author has heard hundreds of test questions of a striking nature answered through Mrs. Foye's mediumship, the above examples are all that can now be quoted.

It is but justice to this admirable Medium and the effect produced by her flying visit to the Australian colonies, to give the following brief extract from the *Harbinger of Light* concerning her farewell meeting :—

"On the evening of Wednesday, the 23rd November, Mrs. Foye gave, in the Temperance Hall, the last of her public *séances*, the proceeds of which by her desire were to be devoted to the funds of the Victorian Association of Spiritualists. The inclemency of the weather prevented quite as large an attendance as on the previous occasion. W. B. Bowley, Esq., J.P., presided. Mrs. Foye opened with a few remarks, on the conclusion of which Mr. W. H. Terry, on behalf of the Victorian Association of Spiritualists, read the following address :—

" 'VICTORIAN ASSOCIATION OF SPIRITUALISTS.

" '84, Russell Street, Melbourne, November, 1881.

" 'To Mrs. ADA FOYE.

" ' Dear Madam,—On behalf of the Victorian Association of Spiritualists, we desire to congratulate you on the success of your work during your brief stay in Victoria. The able expositions of the philosophy of Spiritualism which have been delivered in this city by such talented speakers as Dr. Peebles, Mrs. E. H. Britten, and Mr. Thomas Walker, supplemented by the efforts of local workers, have stimulated a spirit of inquiry and created a craving for phenomena demonstrative of the alleged facts of Spiritualism, which for some time past we have been unable to supply. Your advent amongst us has therefore been particularly opportune, and the conclusive tests, which your truly wonderful mediumistic power has enabled you to give before large and intelligent audiences, have, to our certain knowledge, brought conviction of the grand truth of Spirit communion to many minds.

" ' Those who have had the pleasure of personal intercourse with you during your brief sojourn, are unanimous in their appreciation of your earnestness and social worth, whilst your last act of placing your valuable services at the disposal of this Association and donating the receipts of this large house to the advancement of its objects, displayed a generosity which is not common.

" 'Wishing you a safe and prosperous voyage, and hoping that circumstances will enable you ere long to pay us a more prolonged visit,

" 'We are, Dear Madam, yours fraternally,

" 'W. B. BOWLEY, President.
" 'S. G. WATSON, } Vice-Presidents.
" 'E. PURTON,   }
" 'W. H. TERRY, Treasurer.
" 'A. VAN RYN VAN ALKEMADE, Hon. Sec.'

[" This address was subsequently beautifully illuminated by Messrs. Fergusson and Mitchell, of Collins Street, and forwarded to Mrs. Foye at Sydney.]

" Mrs. Foye replied in a most pertinent speech. She thanked the members of the Association from the bottom of her heart for their kindness. Coming amongst them as a stranger, she had found herself received with warm hearts and open hands. She would bear back to America pleasant remembrances of her sojourn here, and tell the people there of the kind reception she had met with. She expressed a hope to hear good news of the Association, and to find, on her return to these colonies, that it had doubled its numbers. She had never experienced a prouder or happier moment in her life than this: standing before the Victorian Association of Spiritualists.

" A very beautiful piece of music was then rendered by the choir of the V. A. S., after which the *séance* took place in the manner and with the results before described."

It is only necessary to add that during a period of a few weeks' residence in Australia, several hundreds of persons, all of whom were total strangers to Mrs. Foye, received tests of a similar character to those already mentioned. The narration of these *séances* cannot seem otherwise than cold, dry, and uninteresting. There is nothing to fix the attention of the reader in names, dates, and figures ; and even the messages that are frequently written by Mrs. Foye's hand, or perceived by her in phantom writing, are too personal to the individuals addressed to be of the smallest interest in recital. But let the reader put himself in the place of the recipients of these messages. Let him enter a large thronged public hall, and in imitation of hundreds of strangers around him, write on a piece of paper the name of the most beloved being he has ever known, one whose form has been mouldering in the silent tomb for over a quarter of a century, and of whose continued existence the whole universe has never given the slightest token. Let him watch whilst that name, so tightly folded up, that the writer himself could not pick it out from the heap of similar pellets before him, is yet singled out by a stranger and without even being touched by the Sybil, the name is loudly proclaimed. The relationship, mode and place of death, and events occurring during the long years that have since elapsed are told with unerring accuracy, and perhaps, some message is added, which none but the vanished dead could give; and then—the Sybil passes on to another and another—all is told—all are lost in wonderment; but *to you—you*, who have gone into that place a stranger, to find there—in those few seconds, and by those few commonplace tokens of identity—your dead alive again, and the whole problem of immortality solved beyond a shadow of doubt or denial!! What are not such *commonplaces* worth to those who receive them!!

In the course of her public and private Mediumship, Mrs. Foye—who it may easily be perceived—speaks only American-English—and that in the least adorned methods of phraseology; has written in ten different foreign languages—including even the Sanscrit, Kanaka, and Chinese characters. She has given hundreds of thousands of well-recognised test communications, and besides the incalculable blessings she has showered upon the world by her marvellous Mediumship she is well known in her own private circle of loving friends, as a noble and beneficent woman—a good wife and a faithful mother.

True she is only one of the much-despised class of "Spirit Mediums," but in that day when the books of life are all laid open and each one will be known for what they are, not for what they seem, who would not wish they could present as glorious a record as that which will be found inscribed in the archives of eternity, by Ada Foye, the Spirit Medium?

The latest sensation in the phenomenal line in Australia has been created by Mr. Spriggs, for some years the non-professional Medium of "The Circle of Light" held at Cardiff, South Wales, from whence the remarkable manifestations of "Spiritual materialization," alleged to be produced in this gentleman's presence, have been reported, in terms of high eulogy, in the colums of the English Spiritual journals by various correspondents.

Mr. Spriggs did not appear to have been known by name in England, nor to have given sittings outside the Cardiff circle.

Mr. Terry's arrangements with this Medium are claimed in the *Harbinger of Light* to be wholly independent of what some of the Spiritualists are pleased to term, "filthy lucre," "the greed of gain," &c., &c.

Without attempting in this place to question why the use of time, service, and faculties, as a means of living, should be branded with opprobrium in Spiritualism, but be recognized as legitimate and commendable in every other department of human life, it is enough to render Mr. Spriggs all the justice claimed for him by his Australian friends, and record him as a strictly non-professional Medium.

According to reports published from time to time in the *Harbinger of Light*, Mr. Spriggs's *séances* took place at Mr. Terry's office in Russell Street, an arrangement which Mr. Terry's well-known probity rendered highly satisfactory to the sitters. These latter were reported as being few in number, and elected beforehand by a committee appointed for that purpose. The manifestations were of the same character as those so frequently recorded in the Spiritual journals under the caption of "Form materialization," &c., &c. Not on account of their rarity or novelty, but as a matter of history, we give the following extract from a report of one of those *séances* as published in the *Harbinger of Light*.

We may add, one of its most special points of recommendation to the attention of the reader, is the fact that the report is given by Mr. H. J. Browne, for whose veracity as a gentleman, and capacity as an observer, almost every Australian Spiritualist would be willing to vouch. Mr. Browne says :—

" I will now relate the particulars of another *séance* at which I was present lately, and at which I saw materialised forms walk about, and do several things which are common to intelligent human beings. . . .

" This *séance* was held in a room containing only ordinary office furniture. Across one corner, damask curtains were hung so as to open in the middle and at each end. Behind these curtains there was only a chair standing in the corner of the recess faced by the audience. There were present on this occasion seven persons in addition to myself and the medium, Mr. Spriggs. The only light in the room, a candle, was shaded, but leaving sufficient light to see objects. We had the fullest evidence that behind the curtain there was only the medium, seated on the chair, with no appliances to enable him to personate others ; and during the *séance* we had opportunity for seeing the medium on the chair at the same time that the materialised forms stood before us. . . .

" The *séance* lasted about two hours, and during that time five different forms came out from behind the curtain ; figures of different sizes, and having a different appearance. One of the forms moved a chair, shook hands with one of the audience, and spoke to him. Another, taking a bunch of flowers from the chair, divided them among the visitors, shaking hands with a lady next to myself. Another form, that of a man, walked before us, and had the appearance of a perfect human body, rendering by its opaqueness the objects on the other side from myself invisible. . . . I know that it has been said these forms are no less than the medium in changed clothes, thus accounting for the naturalness of the whole appearance. I can only reply that, for myself, I am quite convinced that while the form stood before me, the medium, in his usual clothing, was behind the curtain in an unconscious state. . . . I was quite satisfied that the medium could not, under the circumstances, personate the departed."

The next report of a *séance* with Mr. Spriggs is written about a year after the commencement of the Medium's acquaintance with his Australian friends, and evidently testifies to the progress that had been made in the Spirit control exercised. It is an editorial report headed :—

" MR. GEORGE SPRIGGS' MATERIALISATION SÉANCES.

" The sittings during the past month have presented the usual features with which our readers are familiar, and also some new and important ones. At the sitting immediately following the close of our last month's report, a lady and gentleman from Chiltern were among the visitors. The Indian spirit, Ski-wau-kie, who speaks ' broken ' English in what is known as the ' direct ' voice, informed the lady that there was with her a ' squaw,' or female spirit-friend, who had passed over a long time since, and who was related to her, of the name of Isabella. The lady recognised an aunt of that name, who had passed away some 28 years ago, and considered it an excellent proof, as no one present but herself knew that she had had an aunt of that name. ' Ski ' also told the gentleman his father was present with him, and gave the name correctly.

" Geordie has manifested with his customary power, in the full glare of the light, walking about freely, approaching the sitters, and placing his face within a few inches of the eyes of the visitors.

" The earlier sittings of the month were marked by an occurrence as striking as any that have been recorded during the progress of these manifestations. This was the recognition, by five different sitters simultaneously, and independently of each other, of a spirit-form as being that of an old colonist and well-known pioneer in the cause of Spiritualism, who passed over some five years ago. Amongst those who recognised this spirit were his son, daughter, and nephew. He came on two occasions, and displayed considerable emotion at being able thus visibly to manifest his presence to his relatives and friends. On the second occasion he shook hands with Mr. Carson, who stood up for the purpose, and who consequently had a better view, not only of the full form, but also of the wrinkled features, and thin beard. The same spirit afterwards transmitted a few words, using the identical phrase which was specially characteristic of him to those who knew him in earth-life, and mentioning (correctly) the incident which led to his investigation of Spiritualism."

Several accounts are published of these *séances* at which the forms presented were "weighed and measured."

For reasons with which many careful investigators will sympathize, we do not attach as much importance to this proceeding as to some other

Geo Spriggs

methods of testing the phenomena. The extract already given, may be accepted as a fair sample of the general class of manifestations witnessed at Mr. Spriggs's circles.

It now becomes necessary to speak of one of the most high-handed and arbitrary acts of tyranny on the part of the Victorian Government towards Spiritualism which the records of the movement can show. This was the interdict promulgated by " the Chief Secretary" against the proprietor of the Melbourne Opera House, forbidding him to allow the Spiritualists to take money at the door for admission to their services, and in effect, forbidding them to hold services there at all. A similar interdict had been issued in the case of Mr. Proctor, the celebrated English lecturer on astronomy. The excuse for this tyrannical procedure in Mr. Proctor's case, *might* have been justified on the ground, that the Chief Secretary was entirely ignorant of the fact, that astronomy had anything to do with religion, or that it was not orthodox to talk about the celestial bodies on a Sunday, except in quotations from Genesis, or Revelations ; but in the case of " the Victorian Association of Spiritualists" it was quite another point. Spiritualism was their religion, and Spiritual lectures their Sabbath Day exercises. Messrs. Walker, Peebles, and Mrs. Britten, had occupied the Opera House for months together, and admission fees had been charged at each of their Sunday services, without let or hindrance. It was, and is, a well-known fact, that the Roman Catholics in most places where their services are conducted, charge a tariff for seats, varying according to the opportunities afforded for witnessing the ceremonies.

It was, and is, also, well known, that pews in churches are a matter of barter and sale, and a thriving trade is driven in the buying and selling of "livings," otherwise called "rectorships," &c., &c. Besides all these precedents, any or all of which might have been—it was thought—of sufficient force to justify the Spiritualists in charging modest fees for the seats which cost them a considerable rent to hire, it might also have been remembered that archbishops, bishops, and all the sacred hierarchy of Christendom, preach *for hire*, and that too, at very costly figures. Not a Christian sermon is preached, that does not cost so much a word ; hence, if the ministry of the Christian Church be a trade, or to put it in its mildest form, a *lucrative profession*, the only conceivable difference between the Christian and the Spiritual Church becomes reduced to the fact, that the Christians do their work on the Sunday but take their pay on the week days, whilst the Spiritualists do theirs on the Sunday, but take their pay as they go. Pew rents and livings it is true are auctioned on week days, not Sundays, but the proceeds of this trade all centre on Sunday work, whilst the sale of Spiritualists' pew rents depends not on the puff of the auctioneer, but on the real value of what the people are going to hear.

In the case under consideration it is quite possible that the Chief Secretary was a shrewd gentleman—one who could read the signs of the times, and mark with sorrow the deluded multitudes who left the Church pews vacant, to throng the seats at the Spiritualists' place of meeting. What better tactics could any Chief Secretary pursue than to force the deluded multitudes back again by closing up the attractions of the Spiritualists' meeting ? The expediency of the thing lay in a nutshell. The people wouldn't go to Church, and would go to Spiritualists' meetings. Close up the latter, and the people may (?) perhaps, turn on their footprints, and go back to the Churches. A doubtful issue, but—worth the trial.

Yet heaven forefend that, we should attribute any such far sighted policy to an Australian Chief Secretary. What that gentleman's motives really were, and how patiently his Australian fellow-citizens endured his policy, will best be understood by the following excerpts, taken from the *Harbinger of Light*, February, 1882 :—

"THE OPERA HOUSE DIFFICULTY.

"GOVERNMENT INTERFERENCE WITH THE SUNDAY SERVICES.

"Intimation having reached the officers of the Victorian Association of Spiritualists too late for advertisement in the papers of Saturday, February 7th, that the Opera House would be closed against them the following day, some handbills were hastily printed for distribution amongst the congregation who began to assemble outside the Opera House at about half-past six p.m. on Sunday. In these they were invited to come up to Mr. Terry's Place in Russell Street, from the verandah of which Mr. Walker would explain the reason of the doors being closed against them. Accordingly, by seven p.m., abo t 800 people were congregated on the road and pavements waiting anxiously for an explanation of the difficulty. At that hour Mr. Walker emerged from the window, and requesting the audience to remove from the footpaths to the road, and to do nothing illegal, briefly explained that through a threat from the Government the Opera House Company were constrained to refuse the use of their house for Sunday services. He therefore requested them to walk in an orderly manner to the Horticultural Hall, where he would more fully explain the position. The progress of this large body through the streets naturally caused considerable excitement, doors and windows along the route being crowded by the inmates of the houses, curious to know the import of it. In a few minutes the hall was densely packed—aisles, platform, and ante-rooms being crowded, and a large number being unable to find even standing room. Mr. Walker, who was greeted with applause, reviewed the circumstances which led up to the present difficulty, characterising the interference as a blow at Freethought and freedom of speech, and urging them to resist it by all legitimate means. The audience heartily applauded the speaker's remarks, and an indignation meeting being suggested, it was announced that one would be held during the ensuing week ; and after a few concluding remarks from Mr. Walker, the meeting dispersed.

"A public meeting was held at the Temperance Hall, Melbourne, on Thursday evening, February 16th, to protest against the interference of the Government with the Sunday lectures. Upwards of nine hundred persons were present. The chairman was supported by representatives of both the Victorian Association of Spiritualists and the Freethought Society."

The speeches, resolutions, &c., which transpired at this meeting were of course strongly denunciatory of the tyrannical procedure of the Victorian Government. Attempts were made to extenuate this action on the part of some of the speakers, but the general sense of the meeting may be gathered from the following extract taken from Mr. Terry's report :—

"Mr. T. Walker moved the first resolution, which read as follows :—

"'That this meeting expresses its indignation at the recent action of the Government, which is calculated to suppress freedom of speech by interfering with the Sunday evening lectures.'

"The chairman considered the word 'indignation' to be 'rather strong,' but numerous cries of 'No, no' from all parts of the audience indicated the contrary.

"Mr. Thos. Walker said he was pleased to see that the meeting agreed with the wording of the resolution, and were disposed to consider it expedient that the word 'indignation' should be retained. When were they to express their indignation if not at the suppression of their liberties ? This was a matter that affected all who had an opinion to give that might differ from the reigning power. He did not think that anyone could become acquainted with the facts of the case without concluding that they had suffered an injustice. . . ."

The final result of this, and other gatherings to the same effect, may be judged of by a perusal of the following paragraph published in the *Harbinger of Light* of March, 1882 :—

" RESUMPTION OF THE OPERA HOUSE SERVICES.

"On Friday last a letter was received from the Government, by the Executive of the Victorian Association of Spiritualists, intimating that the former *had no desire to suppress the lectures*, but endorsed the permit of May, 1879. The directors of the Opera House Company were interviewed, and on the understanding that *no money be taken at the doors*, consented to the opening of the House. The fact being announced in Saturday's papers drew a large audience to hear Mr Walker's lecture on Sunday, 'Lord Macaulay on Roman Catholicism.' The services will be continued as heretofore. *Seats in dress circle or stalls may be hired by month or quarter*, at W. H. Terry's, 84, Russell Street."

It can scarcely be doubted, that if measures at once so oppressive, vindictive, and narrow-minded as those directed by the Victorian Government against the Spiritualists, had been levelled against any of the thousand and one sects of Christianity, the "indignation meetings" resulting therefrom, would have included ALL, and not a petty few of the citizens of Melbourne, whilst the Chief Secretary would have had to learn that he was the servant, and not the slave-driver of the people; but the cause at issue was one which had emptied the pews of many a church and threatened an impending crisis in which the very services of the Church might ultimately be dispensed with altogether. What was to be done? The Church had cried long enough "Great is Diana of the Ephesians!"—but still the contumacious people wouldn't worship the *Ephesian Diana.* What more fitting in such a fearful crisis for highly-paid ecclesiastics, than to call in the authority of the State, to aid the effete power of the Church? And thus it was, that Church and State combined to do that noble work which single-handed they have heretofore been powerless to effect. They have wrought some harm to the Spiritualists, but it may be doubted whether the value of their own pew rents has been raised in the market.

CHAPTER XXXL

SPIRITUALISM IN AUSTRALIA—PART II. (CONTINUED).

IN concluding our notices of Australian Spiritualism we must call attention to a few more noteworthy features of the movement, leaving the minor details in this, as in the Spiritual records of other countries to cluster around the representative cases.

A somewhat unlooked-for episode, of recent date in Colonial Spiritualism, has been the development of remarkable healing powers in the person of Mr. George Milner Stephen, a gentleman of mature age, the father in fact of a family of adults, residing at Sydney.

To the amiable wife of Mr. Stephen the author is indebted for a pamphlet, written by his son Mr. Harold Stephen, in which a detailed account is given of Mr. Stephen's family, Spiritual development, and marvellous cures, the chief circumstances of which will be found summed up in the following extracts, taken from the *Religio Philosophical Journal*:—

"GEORGE MILNER STEPHEN—THE NEW SPIRIT HEALER.

" The people in Australia, and especially in the neighbourhood of Sydney, are greatly astounded at the cures which, within the year past, have begun to be performed by a barrister, Mr. George Milner Stephen. Mr. Stephen is highly connected, a fact which will go far to call attention to his remarkable powers. His father was first *Puisne* Judge at Sydney ; his uncle was a member of Parliament and Master in Chancery in England, &c., &c. . . .

George Milner Stephen entered early on official life in the Colonies, first as Clerk of the Supreme Court at Hobarton, Tasmania, then as Advocate-General in South Australia, and for a brief period as Acting Governor, in which capacity he received the thanks of Her Majesty's Government, and complimentary addresses from the colonists. Soon after, in 1840, he returned to England, married the daughter of Sir John Hindmarsh, acted as Secretary to the Government of Heligoland, and after pursuing his terms at the Middle Temple, was called to the Bar. Refusing the Colonial Secretaryship of New Zealand, he entered on the practice of law as a barrister, first at Adelaide and afterwards at Melbourne. He was Chairman of the Society of Fine Arts and first Vice-President of the Geological Society. In 1853 he returned and settled in London, interesting himself in Art and Mineralogy. He was an honorary member of several Continental scientific societies, and withal was an accomplished musician and painter. Returning to Melbourne in 1856, he resumed his practice as a barrister, sat in Parliament for Collingwood, and finally settled in Sydney, where he now resides.

" He was a member of the Established Church, and had the usual horror of all new and eccentric opinions, until a few years ago, when he came into contact with certain spiritual phenomena, and after protracted study, was satisfied of the spiritual philosophy which lay behind them. Mr. Stephen's son has printed a pamphlet containing an account of his numerous cures.

" It is a singular fact that while Mr. Stephen remained an Episcopalian, he could exercise no healing power whatever ; for on several occasions the spirits having announced that they were about to use him in some great work, he tested his powers as a healer upon various persons and produced no effect. It was not until he had thrown orthodox Episcopalianism to the winds, and became a free Spiritualistic thinker that the power which Jesus promised to believers of the truth came to him. He had expected from his previous training as a barrister and speaker that he would be used as a speaker. The coming of his gift as a healer was a surprise.

" The following may serve as a sample of Mr. Stephen's mode of healing, Mr. Max L. Kreitmayer, of the Waxworks, writes to the Melbourne *Argus* as follows :—

" ' Shortly after entering a saloon carriage on a trip to Sandhurst, on Saturday, April 17, a man was carried in by a clergyman and another gentleman, and laid on the seat. After his friends left him I entered into conversation with him concerning his malady. He informed me that he had been thrown out of a buggy some two months before, and had his spine injured ; that a week previously he took a Turkish bath, and in walking afterwards in Collins Street staggered and fell, and from that time had lost the use of his legs ; that he was going to Castlemaine to get buried or cured, as his friends lived there. I gave one of his legs a good pinch, and he assured me that he did not feel it ; and consequently I put his case down as a decided case of paralysis. I noticed that when he wished to raise himself a little he had to hold on to the rack above, and on several occasions I lifted the legs off and on the couch, to change his position. At Gisborne Station Mr. George Milner Stephen (whom I knew by sight many years ago) entered the carriage, and had to sit close to the sick man for want of room. He offered his rug, to ensure more comfort, and naturally asked what was the matter. The man repeated his story, and Mr. Stephen, in a decided tone said, ' I can cure you.' My curiosity was aroused to fever heat, and I watched events. Mr. Stephen asked the patient to lie on his face, and after making a few passes and breathing on the supposed injured spot, he told him ' to rise,' which summons he obeyed with slight success, and he dropped on the seat again, saying that the pain seemed considerably less. He then rose and walked. After the lapse of some minutes, and after undergoing a similar process as before, the command was given by Mr. Stephen ' to rise and walk across the carriage,' which he instantly did, and returned again to his place without any support. In thirty-four minutes after leaving Gisborne, at Kyneton, I left the carriage for a few minutes, and on returning, to my astonishment the patient had gone. Looking out, I found him on the platform, walking about very carefully, and on arrival at Castlemaine he took his luggage and walked away. Altogether the affair has been so vividly impressed upon my mind that I can recall the most trifling conversation or incident on this ever-memorable journey.'

" The following from the Sydney *Daily Telegraph*, of 24th July last, is less graphic than some of the more minute descriptions, but will suffice to show how strongly the community are stirred by Mr. Stephen's cures :—

"'The scene at the Temperance Hall yesterday afternoon, both inside and in the street, defies description. When Mr. Milner Stephen arrived, shortly after two o'clock, there was a dense crowd collected on the pavement for some yards on either side of the door, which was closed, and it was with difficulty that he could make his way through the mass of people who had been eagerly awaiting his appearance. The lower hall having been taken for the Canary Show, the upper hall was given for the scene of his operations. As on previous occasions, there was a gathering of the "incurables" of the metropolis and suburbs, including "the lame, the halt, and the blind." Many suffering pains more or less violent were clamorously invoking Mr. Stephen's power to relieve their agonies. He appeared to be in great force, as he literally "ordered" pains away right and left ; and as the various subjects of his benevolence invoked blessings upon his head, we may reasonably assume that they experienced relief. The afflicted reached their arms on to the platform, praying him "only to touch them," which he did, and invariably received the grateful acknowledgments of the sufferers. In most of the cases Mr. Stephen simply placed his hands upon the people's heads to drive away rheumatism or rheumatic gout, or the other ills from which they were suffering. Bystanders of all ranks were looking on astonished as people made their way through the crowded hall to the platform, and as they left after being treated by Mr. Stephen, many eager questions were asked as to the number of years' suffering they had endured, whether all their pains had disappeared, and the like. In all, about fifty people were thus sent away, expressing their belief that they were cured, and their astonishment at the wonderful power of the healer.'

"This is probably the first instance in the history of the world in which one born a gentleman, all of whose associations are aristocratic, whose mind is not only cultured but rare in its diversity of accomplishment, and whose whole life has been a social success, has become a minister of healing to the poor."

The editor of the *Religio Philosophical Journal* is in error in respect to the statement contained in his closing paragraph. The experiences of Prince Hohenlohe as detailed in the section on Germany, of Madame Saint Amour in France ; of the late Mr. J. C. Luxmoore, of London, and numerous other ladies and gentlemen of rank and high standing, known to the author as healers of great power, but whose unostentatious benevolence is not publicly recorded—except in rare instances—prove that the gift of healing is not limited to either sex or station, but exists—like all other gifts—as an attribute of specially endowed individuals.

The residents of Melbourne have not yet forgotten the astounding cures of blindness from birth, and of some deaf and dumb lads, who had been born so—effected by Mr. T. W. Singleton, of Melbourne, a gentleman of good professional and social standing. The above-named cures were never designed by Mr. Singleton to be brought before the public, and they never would have been so, had they not obtained inevitable notoriety from the following circumstances :—The cures in question had been performed on patients, some of whom were inmates of the Melbourne Blind Asylum. Early in September, 1877, the editor of the Melbourne *Age*, with great humanity as well as courage, brought forward the fact that one or more of the young men who had been thus marvellously benefited by Mr. Singleton had been maltreated and injured by the asylum superintendent.

The scandal of such a report compelled a public investigation, the details of which do not belong to this history, except inasmuch as the proceedings called forth a letter from Mr. J. W. Singleton, published in *The Age* of September 12th, 1877, in which will be found a concise account of the cures effected on subjects *born blind, deaf, and dumb.*

Mr. Singleton's letter is as follows :—

" To the Editor of The Age.

"Sir,—In justice to myself and some of the unfortunate inmates of our Asylum for the Blind, there is necessity to reply to some uncharitable remarks made respecting me at yesterday's meeting. On the 22nd April last I applied to the committee for permission to continue the treatment of an inmate named Helen Latimer, who, at her friends' request, was treated by me during her holidays last December. The rapid improvement in her case caused a very natural desire to complete the cure, and accomplish so much good to a suffering fellow-creature. I offered at the same time to treat any other inmate the committee selected gratuitously, wishing them to visit me under care of an attendant. I invited one or all the committee, which included Dr. Rudall, to my house to inspect the mode of treatment by the magnetic process, and its result on some of my patients ; Alex. Wilson, in particular, who was well known to Mr. Moss, the secretary of the Deaf and Dumb Institute, as having been an inmate for many years, and was born deaf and dumb. This patient could neither hear nor speak until treated by me, and, although twenty-two years of age, can hear, speak and read aloud now. After two months' consideration I was informed that my offer was respectfully declined. Shortly after my application I was visited by one of the inmates, who asked my opinion on his case, being blind from birth, who expressed a wish to prove for himself whether the deaf heard and the dumb spake, which he proved the following evening ; and the fact of his telling his companions of this made them naturally desire to try if they could be cured. Many came to me, but I only treated the first eight that came, on the understanding that Dr. Rudall was not doing anything for them ; in fact, that they were all incurables. The results were particularly gratifying to me and joyful to the boys, as they will state for themselves, Walker being able to read part of the newspaper, see pictures and objects a mile off, before he was struck in the eye by the superintendent ; and Cockburn could see his way about, tell colours, see large letters, and was progressing well before Mr. Lovell struck him. The other boys have each made more or less progress. I refute Mr. Moss's imputation of inveigling the boys to my house. They came of their own accord, as any other of my patients, and were made aware that I practised as a magnetic healer or psycopath. Walker and Cockburn were among my free patients, and I think it cruelly hard on them to forbid the completion of their cure because they have no friends, or that Dr. Rudall forbids it. Should the committee desire it, I will attend on Friday next and answer any fair and straightforward questions. I have only been actuated by pure motives and real sympathy for the poor young sufferers, and herewith renew my application to the committee to allow me to treat ten out of the 110 inmates, and let Dr. Rudall operate on the balance. My own conviction, from the knowledge of the magnetic power, is that fully one-half of the inmates can be cured, or partially so. With apologies for occupying both time and space, and admiration for your noble action in protecting the helpless, I am, &c.,

"Simpson Street, East Melbourne. J. W. SINGLETON."

Mr. Singleton's methods of cure were practised quietly and without any attempts to bring them before the public, in the privacy of his own office. He himself assured the author the publication of the above letter was enforced upon him by the attendant circumstances, but he expressed a wish that the reprint of his letter as a mere matter of history should be the only notice given of his beneficent work.

As Mr. Stephen's pamphlet fortunately places the cures he has effected before the world without restriction, we are free to add one or two more extracts, and these, the reader will observe, only refer to cases wherein the names and addresses of the parties benefited are given in full :—

" To the Editor of The Sydney Morning Herald.
"June 10th, 1880.

"Dear Sir,—Mr. G. Milner Stephen has asked me to state the circumstances of his late instantaneous cure of my attack of gout, which I had been suffering from ever since laying the foundation-stone of the new lighthouse, South Head, on the 18th of April last. My knees were so very weak that I could not get up from a seat without the assistance of my hands ; and on sitting upon a log with a friend the same morning, at Balmain, whilst waiting for the steamer, I could not rise without assistance. Whilst sitting in a chair in Mr. G. R. Dibbs's room, in presence of Captain Hixson, R.N. (the President of the Marine Board), Captain Heselton, and another gentleman, Mr. Stephen entered the room, and after some joking on my part as to his healing power, he stooped down and breathed into each of my knees, and then made a pass across them (as if driving away the disease), saying, ' Gone !' I instantly rose from the chair without the slightest difficulty, and to the astonishment of myself and friends, I sat down and got up on several chairs in succession, and then sat down on the ground and got up without any assistance. After lunch, the same day, at the Royal Hotel, I raced Mr. J. Pope down the stairs and back again, taking two steps at a bound. On the 24th of last month the stiffness returned for a short time, but I am now as well as I have been for years.

"I am, &c.,

"125, Sussex Street, Sydney, June 3. JOHN BROOMFIELD."

"We witnessed the occurrence referred to, and were assured by Captain Broomfield that he experienced instant relief from a complaint in the knee-joints he had been suffering from.

"Francis Hixson, Thomas Heselton,
"George R. Dibbs, John Pope."

Manly, 19th June, 1880.

"My dear Sir,—At your request I have much pleasure in stating the particulars of my deafness, and the effects of your treatment for the relief of it. For 20 years I have been almost stone deaf with one ear, and I had become so deaf in the other that even with the use of a long telephone tube, I could only distinguish loud speaking, and could not hear a sound of music; and indeed I was obliged to relinquish a valuable appointment in consequence. Since your operation upon both ears I am enabled to enjoy the softest tones of the harp when played by my daughter; and the clearness with which I heard the conversation you addressed to me, without even putting a hand to my ear, in the presence of Messrs. R. Want and A. Allen, the well-known solicitors, and Mr. Larnach, proves the great benefit I have thus far obtained. To myself and friends it is most astounding and gratifying, as at my age I could not have expected such a wonderful improvement in my stone deaf ear. I have also been suffering from asthma a long time, but since you breathed into my chest I have been very greatly relieved. Your simple yet effective mode of operation—viz., the laying on of hands, and breathing into each ear—proves the curative power, or whatever it may be termed, to be most extraordinary, and well deserving the careful study of all scientific men. I hope your good and disinterested labour, to do good and benefit others, may be a source of happiness and blessing to yourself.

"Yours, &c., CHARLES KENT.

"P.S.—I omitted to state that within five minutes after laying on of your hands I heard you speak distinctly with the stone deaf ear. Mr. Russom, J.P., was present at the time.—G. Milner Stephen, Esq."

Besides an immense number of similar cases reported in Mr. Harold Stephen's pamphlet, several of the Australian secular papers as well as the *Harbinger of Light* report numerous others equally well attested. The reader's attention is more especially solicited to these instances of cure by the laying on of hands, first, because Mr. Stephen himself reverently attributes them "to the divine agency of good spirits, and angels," operating through his willing instrumentality; next, because they form a curious commentary upon the position assumed by one of the leaders of the Christian Clergy, in the person of Dr. Moorhouse, the present Bishop of Melbourne. In the Melbourne *Argus* of March 13th, 1880, a sermon preached by Bishop Moorhouse is reported, in which the following sentence occurs :—

"The sacred writer, Saint James, directs that the elders of the church shall anoint the sick and pray over them, encouraging the practice by the example of Elijah. But it is obvious that in an age when miraculous healing was a common gift, such direction was reasonable, and such an illustration apposite. Does any sober Christian believe in the continuance of these miraculous gifts? If they do not so believe, then how can either the exhortation or the illustration apply to the present time?"

In a small pamphlet sent to the author within the current year (1883), entitled "Apparitions and Miracles at Knock," the compiler quotes from the diary of Archdeacon Cavanagh—an eye witness of what he records—a list of nearly 300 cases of divers diseases "miraculously," and in some instances "instantaneously cured," at the Knock Chapel. Are Archdeacon Cavanagh and Mr. MacPhilpin, the compiler of this book, "sober Christians," or what else would Bishop Moorhouse term them?

The author is in possession of over 5,000 certificates of cures effected by the laying on of hands through Dr. J. R. Newton, and other magnetic healers of America, very many of the patients being as "sober Christians" as Dr. Moorhouse.

But as Ireland and America may be deemed by Dr. Moorhouse too far away to enable him to accept of testimony from thence in so grave a matter, here are cases of what in olden times would have been termed "miraculous cures," going on within his own diocese, through Mr. Milner Stephen, and at the very time when he is preaching denials of their possibility! Is it worthy of a Christian Bishop to close his eyes determinedly to great and important facts, because they happen to conflict with his preconceived opinions? or are there no Christians amongst his hearers *sober* enough to advise him against "wresting" and perverting texts of scripture to suit those very erroneous allegations?

There is scarcely a Colonial paper now published but what has had, or still has, some new cases of cure effected by Mr. Milner Stephen—and these cases involve the published testimony of hundreds of living men and women *as sober* and trustworthy as Bishop Moorhouse himself. How can he dispose of all these on his hypothesis?

There is yet another point of testimony to be offered on this subject which proves how determinedly the Schools as well as the Church repel all attempts at innovation upon old established forms, and cry, "Great is Diana of the Ephesians!" when they find *their craft* in danger. It appears that Mr. Milner Stephen tendered service to the Hospital Committee of Sydney, *offering* to treat a given number of obdurate cases by his perfectly innoxious, but often efficacious methods of cure.

As Mr. Milner Stephen did not make this proposal until he had publicly demonstrated to the satisfaction of hundreds of respectable witnesses his ability to perform what he undertook, it was an insult alike to the community, and the cause of humanity, as well as to the gentleman who tendered his services in that cause, when the Hospital Committee returned a sneering answer to the effect that the proposal in question *was too absurd to be entertained.* Regretting that we cannot devote more space to the beneficent work reported of Mr. Stephen, we must pass on to notice other representative phenomena occurring in the Colonies.

At a private circle held in New South Wales by a party of ladies and gentlemen, some of whom were operators in the Magnetic Telegraph Office, the controlling Spirits had been frequently asked if they could not give communications through telegraphic signals. An affirmative promise having been obtained, at the period set for the experiments, the following results ensued, for the strict veracity of which the author has the testimony of a number of respectable witnesses :—

"Friday, August 20th, 1880.—'Met pursuant to adjournment same circle, consisting of four sitters. After sitting around the table, placing our hands on it for fifteen minutes, the key of the instrument was used. All the signals that were given were the same as used in New South Wales, Victoria, and Queensland, and were quite correct. Mr. Johnston named every letter in the alphabet, which were given through the instrument quite correct. Meeting adjourned to Tuesday.'

"Tuesday, 24th August, 1880.—'Met again to-night, half-past eight o'clock ; same circle, same room, instrument in its usual place. Sat an hour and a half. Soon after taking our seats, the armature at the instrument commenced working ; the name of Edward Erskine was spelled out—Mr. Cane says very correctly. There were also very strong raps or knocks given on the table. Darkness was asked for, and given, when strong manifestations ensued ; spirit lights appeared near the key of the instrument ;

hard slaps, which all could hear, were given to three of the sitters several times ; Mr. Johnston was touched on the knee, arm, and head. At this time all hands of the sitters were joined ; a fur cap was also carried from one part of the room and put down in front of Mr. J., passing his face, and falling between his feet ; also a chair, away from any of the sitters, removed and upset. Most of this time the armature at the instrument was working, making considerable noise.' "

Between this date and September 14th, little progress was made ; but on that occasion the record says :—

" Circle met to-night at half-past eight ; all the members present. Within one minute after taking our seats at the table, raps and loud knocks were given ; the armature at the instrument commenced to work strongly, rapidly, and well, spelling the alphabet down to the letter K quite correctly ; then a sound, known as a laugh ; then a short message was given—'We are sorry we could not be present the last two ;' then we asked if the word 'nights' was meant ; three loud raps were given in response. Question asked—'Would they be able to work the instrument perfectly ?' Answer, 'Yes.'"

The next excerpt records an experiment in Spirit photography, the value of which must not be estimated by the slight results obtained, but by the crucial test conditions under which the operations were conducted, and the unimpeachable veracity of the parties concerned.

The narrator is Mr. Cyril Haviland, a gentleman resident in Sydney ; one well known for his literary ability and unexceptionable social standing. Mr. Haviland's testimony carries deep weight with all his large circle of acquaintances. Writing to the *Harbinger of Light* of April, 1882, he says :—

" Dear Sir,—I append for publication a copy of declaration made by me of the particulars surrounding the fact of my taking a photograph of a spirit, and as that will explain the details I need say no more than this, that after my lecture on Tuesday night last, in Sydney, on 'Spiritualism as a Science,' in accordance with an offer made by me to go to anyone's house for the purpose of trying to get spirit photographs, two ladies offered to sit, one having been promised such proof by her spirit friends, and the other stating she had obtained them some years ago in Victoria.

" This latter lady I appointed to meet on Saturday afternoon last, at her own home, and I took with me my own camera, lenses, plates, and apparatus. I exposed eight plates, and on the third only obtained anything beyond those visibly present in the room.

" On this plate appears most distinctly a baby, about two years of age, well dressed, with a toy trumpet in his hand.—Yours faithfully,

"E. CYRIL HAVILAND.
"Sydney, N.S. Wales, 25th April, 1882."

The declaration referred to only reiterates in detail the substance of what is given above, though it is reported that numerous other experiments of a still more important nature in Spirit photography are now in progress. The parties concerned being in private life, and unwilling to allow their names to appear in full, we can only allude hopefully to the fact, although we cannot report it authoritatively.

The following extracts are reports of different writers concerning the progress of Spiritualism in their various districts. They are all taken from the *Harbinger of Light* :—

" Murrurundi, N. S. W., May 2nd, 1877.

" In January last, I and a few friends formed a circle for investigation. We sat for perhaps more than a week without any result, and were beginning to despair of having any manifestations, when we were blessed with results that thoroughly convinced us all of the truth of spirit-communion. We have now, at every sitting, some very remarkable evidences of spirit power. In one instance, we had a message in *direct writing* from a spirit giving the name of 'Flora.' Flowers have been laid upon the table on several occasions, and beautiful lights float about the room. I am already somewhat developed as a writing medium, and receive some very intelligent and useful messages from various spirits through the planchette. But the most remarkable thing in regard to my mediumship, is the writing of messages in French and German—languages of which I am entirely ignorant, and which messages have to be translated for me by those present, who understand those languages. We have had rappings on the top of the table in good lamplight; chairs have moved about the room without human contact, and, on the whole, we have, for a young circle, witnessed some very wonderful phenomena. At our last sitting we had a perfect volley of small pebbles showered about our heads, and some beautiful lights. I may state that these things have been witnessed among a circle of honest investigators, when there could not be the slightest chance of trickery or deception of any kind.—I remain, dear Sir, yours fraternally,

"P. JEFFERSON WALLACE."

"THE CHILTERN CIRCLE.

"Those who read my experiences of Spiritualism in England, published in the *Harbinger* of 1873, will remember that I narrated some very extraordinary phenomena occurring in the presence of private and public mediums. I have had the pleasure lately of being present at the above circle by invitation of the spirits themselves. Our medium is a young married man with a family. He is an engineer, and is employed by the Chiltern Valley Gold Mining Company. His mediumship came upon him unsolicited. The intelligence manifesting through him professes to be his brother ' George,' whose earthly life was cut short by being killed in the mine at which Robert is now engineer. Other spirit friends co-operate with him at *séances.* The circle is generally composed of personal friends and relatives, but the same people do not always sit together, nor do they retain particular seats. They have changed their place of meeting repeatedly without any cessation of the phenomena. The medium, Mr. Robert Brown, is a steady sober man, and his wife is a firm believer in his wonderful intercommunication with the other world. He and wife and two children accompanied us to the house where they have sat for some time.

" We had hardly seated ourselves, all holding hands, when loud raps, as with knuckles, were heard from the table. The alphabet was called for, and 'sing' was elicited. Merry songs were sung the whole evening, and seemed to elicit manifestations of the best kind. I, who had been seated outside the circle, was now made to take a particular seat by the spirit voice. Lights like glow-worms flickered about over our heads. The medium was ordered to stand on the table, and several voices seemed vieing with one another as to who could speak loudest.

" The singing, whistling, and shouting, and all communications were in loud tones, and each different from another. We were all called by name, and towards the end Mr. Pringle, who was present with his wife, was addressed by ' George,' who, as I have already said, was buried in the mine. The spirit said, Keep the laths well ahead, Pringle, for the ground is flaky.' The kind spirit did not desire that Mr. Pringle should leave his family prematurely, and this caution was given because he saw the danger, and remembered his own untimely end.

" After all this had been repeated again and again, George said, 'I will tell you the time if you strike a light. It is four minutes to ten o'clock.' A match was struck, and the clock on the chimney-piece pointed to the exact minute named.

" All present heard the time given, and saw the hands of the clock when the match was struck.

" Chiltern, July, 1877. "W. L. R."

In the *Harbinger of Light* and some of the Australian secular papers, accounts are given of powerful physical manifestations obtained through the mediumship of Mrs. Paton, of Castlemaine. As in the case of Mr. Robert Brown, the demonstrations through this lady occur in the dark, but the doors are invariably closed and locked, and every precaution taken to avoid the shadow of suspicion or the chances of deception. Besides the usual manifestations of fruit, flowers, and other objects being introduced through the well-secured door—on one occasion, a burning hot flat iron was brought in, apparently from the kitchen, the only room in the house where a fire was kindled. The *séance* was being held at a considerable distance from the kitchen; the iron was far too hot to be touched by any one present, and yet the one door of the apartment was carefully locked, and the key inside the pocket of one of the sitters.

Much ridicule was levelled against this manifestation by the editors of certain journals in which it had been reported as a remarkable phenomenon. These sneering critics however seem to have forgotten that the real question at issue was not the dignity of the manifestation, but the utter impossibility of any human agency in its production.

A curious phase of Spiritual writing is reported from Clear Creek, Yackandandah, by a reliable observer, and correspondent of the *Harbinger,* Dr. A. Mueller, who in describing the *séances* of a young lady in private life, Miss Elizabeth H., says :—

" Miss Elizabeth H. is a bright unsophisticated girl of fifteen, whose mediumistic gifts for automatic and direct writing are, considering the short period of her development, of a very high order.   I availed myself of Mr. Chappell's kind invitation to his house on the 29th of last month, and again on Saturday the 19th instant.   . . . .   I purchased a pair of slates on my way to Mr. C.'s house, where I found, at 8 p.m., the medium with Mr. and Mrs. Chappell, a brother of the latter, and Mr. Crambrook, with his daughter, awaiting my arrival.   Evidently to make things as congenial as possible to the medium, we sat, at the special request of the controlling spirit, in a back room of the house, used alike as kitchen and dining-room.   The medium took her seat, facing the brightly burning wood fire, whilst in writing through her the spirit directed me to sit beside her, thus enabling me to observe her closely, even after the candle was put out."

After descriptions of several *séances* in which the ordinary forms of slate writing were produced, together with pertinent answers to questions and messages from deceased friends, the following extraordinary results were reported by Dr. Mueller as occurring at a recent circle.   He says :—

" Placing an open book reversed before the medium I asked her to put the point of her left index finger at random on a line of the print, whilst her right hand held the slate underneath the table as usual, and then shading the page with my own hand, I requested that the word covered by the medium's finger might be written on the slate.   We heard the writing sound almost immediately, and on the slate being raised found the word ' of ' written on it.   On referring to the book, on which the medium's finger had never moved, we found that ' of ' was the word immediately before the point of the finger in the same line.   The experiment was repeated a second time in the same manner, and the word ' for ' found to correspond on the slate and in the book.   In the same manner the words ' spirit,' and ' period,' were written correctly and rapidly.   I then changed the experiment by taking the medium's hand and having mentally selected the words ' the warrior prince,' placing her finger on 'warrior,' but at the same time keeping my own hand between her and the print in order to preclude even the possibility of her seeing it.   Though passive as she was throughout the evening, I felt convinced that she never even attempted to read, and having her right hand fully employed in holding a heavy slate horizontally under a deep-framed table without any support, could not possibly write on it at the same time with the point of the small pencil.   The words ' the ' and ' prince ' came out in succession on the slate ; but simultaneously with the latter, and immediately below it, a plainly-written ' good-night ' announced the conclusion of the sitting.   Looking at my watch I found it was then exactly 10 o'clock, the very hour, either by coincidence, or a kind regard for my wishes on the part of our invisible guest, beyond which, I resolved on sitting down, not to prolong the *séance,* though deeply interested as I was, I had forgotten both my resolve and the lapse of time.
" Yackandandah, 22nd October, 1877."

The same respected and capable observer, Dr. Mueller, gives several other accounts of circles which he attended in different districts, in Victoria, and New South Wales.   As a final representation of how circles were formed and conducted in Australia and how the cause of Spiritualism became popularized in the absence of organized means of propagandism, we give the following extracts from Dr. Mueller's account of THE BARNAWARTHA CIRCLE.   He writes thus, in 1876 :—

17

"The Banawartha Circle has now been in existence for nearly three years. Some experiments in table-turning instituted for mere amusement's sake at a social meeting of two families, the members of which are all more or less mediumistic and now form the majority of the circle— gave the first rise to it. They knew nothing of Spiritualism except by hearsay, but the results at their first impromptu *séance* unmistakeably pointed to some intelligence not their own having been among them. They sat again with even increased manifestations, and then having become acquainted with the mode of conducting Spirit circles, they determined on following up the subject, and sat regularly twice a week. The physical manifestations assumed in the course of the development of the circle a very violent character. At almost every sitting the round table—no matter how tightly fastened to the frame and legs—was broken asunder, and whilst the latter were left on the floor, the round leaf, made of thick pine boards, was whirled about the room over the heads of the sitters, and often out of their reach though standing on tip toe. No injury was ever inflicted on any of the members by this *quasi* animated piece of furniture careering about the room, but on one occasion, whilst rather noisy manifestations were going on, a curious neighbour had slipped into the room unobserved and crouched down in a corner. He had, as he confessed subsequently, scarcely settled in his supposed hiding place, when the table pounced down upon him from the ceiling, where it had been suspended, and belaboured his skull and back so effectively that he had to cry for mercy and beat a precipitate retreat. For a long time manifestations of this kind, convincing certainly, though not very elevating, were carried on, varied at times by levitations of a lady medium. The circle was also much retarded in its development, and at one time nearly broken up by the exigencies of life calling away some of its members. Now, however, they are all together again, and the manifestations have entirely changed in character through the accession of another and very powerful medium. This change was announced by the long and ardently desired spirit raps greeting the circle at the very first *séance* the new medium attended. They were muffled and scarcely audible at first, but are now clear and ringing, and by means of them and the alphabet a running conversation is carried on between the circle, and its mysterious invisible guests. Then came spirit lights floating about the room, shedding a faint whitish light on the objects nearest to them. Soft, velvety, touches, gliding along the heads and faces of the sitters will send a thrill of delight through their frames, hands warm and life-like will grasp theirs. The latest phase of development is the production of the spirit voice."

After describing these and the ordinary physical manifestations which occur at circles of this character, Dr. Mueller gives an account of one *séance* worth narrating, as involving a circumstance by no means of an ordinary character. The wife of the principal Medium before referred to, Mr. Robert Brown, being present with her baby in her arms, the following scene took place :—

"All at once, Mrs. Brown complained that the blanket the baby was wrapped up in was being tugged and pulled away from it, and suspecting this to be done with a view of taking the child from her, declared that she would not let it out of her arms for fear of its being hurt. Raps now came for the alphabet, and the words, " Baby will be given to father " were spelled out. Still Mrs. B. hesitated, when her head and face were touched and stroked so caressingly that, as she stated, almost involuntarily she had to loosen her hold of the child. Immediately she felt the blanket pulled and the child taken from her, and whilst she exclaimed, ' It is gone,' I felt the little head pass my arm in an upward direction. Gone certainly the child was ; but where ? The father declared that it had not been brought to him, and for a few moments all was silence and anxious suspense. We then heard a faint baby's cry coming from the far corner of the room, and high under the ceiling, and after that sounds as if kisses were being showered upon the child, seemed to accompany it in an aerial flight all round the room above our heads, the sounds intermingled with a snuffling noise, evidently made by the child, coming from different and opposite directions successively. Suddenly I felt the little body pressed against my face, and passing on in the direction of the lady on my left, who also felt it distinctly brush her face, and immediately afterwards the father announced that the child had been safely deposited in his arms. Having watched the development of this circle for some years with much interest, and being personally acquainted with its members, it appears to me the height of absurdity to suppose that these people should have met for three years twice a week for the purpose of practising how most effectually to deceive each other, or an occasional visitor. So far from inviting people to their meetings, they are tardy in admitting strangers. after having been told over and over again by their spirit friends, that the presence of most visitors disturbs the harmony and retards the development of the circle. To gain notoriety in an unpopular cause, which must be anything but favourable to their worldly interests, could, therefore, scarcely be alleged as the object they have in view in practising fraud. Moreover, one cannot converse with them for many minutes, see their genuine enthusiasm for the cause of Spiritualism, their firm conviction of the reality of the spirit world, and of their intercourse with it, observe how cordially they are united together by the common cause all have so deeply at heart, and then—however suspicious of human nature—harbour another thought of their producing by deception the marvellous phenomena one witnesses at their meetings."

In Sandhurst, the old mining district, once so familiarly known as "Bendigo," a party of ladies and gentlemen whose characters are beyond reproach or suspicion have met together to hold periodical *séances* under the cognomen of "The Energetic Circle of Sandhurst." How far this gathering has succeeded in enlisting the respect and good will of the outside world may be learned from the following brief paragraph published in the Melbourne *Argus*, as an account of an entertainment given by the members of the circle above named. The editor says :—

"The Sandhurst 'Energetic Circle' of Spiritualists gave an entertainment, under the name of 'An Evening at Home,' at the Masonic Hall last evening, which was of a most enjoyable nature, over 300 guests being present, who appeared to enter heartily into the spirit of the hour, and went in with a keen relish for the good things and various sources of amusement provided for them, under the ardent and courteous direction of the honorary secretary, W. D. C. Denovan.* The 'Circle,' which ranks among its members many well-known citizens, is a private one, the 'Medium' being a non-professional. There is nothing sectarian in its composition, and therefore last night their 'evening at home' was attended by persons professing all shades of religious belief, with whom the circle are popular on account of their quiet unobtrusiveness and good fellowship. Those invited by the circle pay a small amount for their tickets, which is for the most part devoted to the local charities. Their entertainments, therefore, are deservedly in favor, combining, as they do, amusement for their friends, and contributing also to works of charity."

Then follows a list of the visitors present, amongst whom are named some of the most influential and even aristocratic citizens of Sandhurst and its vicinity, including members of Parliament and their families, and a considerable number of literary and political Australian celebrities.

In the conservative and influential city of Adelaide, the late Rev. John Tyerman succeeded in waking up a considerable amount of interest by his stirring lectures, public debates, and newspaper discussions.

In Brisbane, a still more pronounced public interest has been manifested, resulting in the formation of an excellent and flourishing "Psychological Society." From Albury, Newcastle, Beechworth, Ballarat, Geelong, and numerous other places, the author has accounts of well established circles in several of which good Mediums have been developed, and fine phenomena obtained.

We must conclude however with a brief recurrence to the status of Spiritualism in Sydney, of which place, as yet, only incidental mention has been made.

The principal levers for the promotion of Spiritualism in this fair and beautiful city have been the unselfish and indefatigable labours of a few noble propagandists, foremost of whom will ever be gratefully remembered the late Hon. John Bowie Wilson, a gentleman whom all classes of the community united to praise, and whom Spiritualists in especial, regarded, as the father of their cause in New South Wales.

---

* Since this section was written, Mr. W. C. D. Denovan has published a most excellent scholarly, and interesting volume, including many of his own remarkable experiences. It is entitled "Evidences of Spiritualism," and emphatically redeems the claim of its title.

With open purse, hand, and door, seconded by his charming wife and sweet family, this gentleman has supported Spiritualism and all its worthy adherents, until his very name became a pillar of strength to "the cause," in Sydney. Uncounted numbers owed their first introduction to the light and life of Spiritualism to him. Wayfarers from foreign lands have ever found in his home a shelter, and in his association a friend; whilst the opponents of the cause have realized in him, an unassailable garrison against whom their batteries have been levelled in vain. In all ways he has been the stronghold of the faith, and men and angels "rise up and call him blessed."

During the author's flying visits to Sydney, the Hon. J. Bowie Wilson generally officiated as the chairman. The public loved to see him in that post, and listen to his plain speech and rugged eloquence; and the speakers felt as if no harm could befal them, whilst under his protection. Next in fidelity, and the performance of important public service, has stood the good and respected friend of Spiritualism, Mr. Henry Gale. It is not too much to say of this excellent gentleman, as of John Bowie Wilson, that all his good and unselfish work for an unpopular cause, has been nobly seconded by his estimable wife; and in both families, the holy fruits of Spiritualism have borne practical as well as theoretical evidences of their divine influence.

Many others, some of whom have been already named, have contributed invaluable aid to the cause of Spiritual progress in Sydney, but the named and the unnamed, will never murmur because Dr. Wilson, and Mr. Gale, have been selected as the representative men of their cause.

During Dr. Slade's visit to Sydney, a very able and energetic worker in Spiritualism became convinced of its truth, in the person of Mr. E. Cyril Haviland, the author of two excellent pamphlets and many articles, tracts, and good literary contributions on this subject. Mr. Haviland, Mr. Harold Stephen, and several other gentlemen of literary repute in Sydney, combined during the author's last visit, to form a "Psychological Society," the members of which, like the parties above named, represented some of the most accomplished writers and advanced thinkers of the city.

Mr. L. E. Harcus, an able and fluent writer, furnished a report of the origin and growth of this society for the *Banner of Light* of March, 1880, a few extracts from which may not be uninteresting, as bearing upon the present status of the movement in Sydney.

They read thus :—

"The annual meeting of the Psychological Society took place a few days ago, when the following report was submitted and adopted :—

'ANNUAL REPORT OF THE PSYCHOLOGICAL SOCIETY FOR 1879.

'When Mrs. Britten was in Sydney the formation of a Psychological Society was suggested; the suggestion meeting a favourable reception, a list of names for a committee was proposed and adopted. This committee afterwards met at Mr. Alfred De Lissa's rooms, and being materially assisted by Mrs. Britten, they drew up a code of rules and did much other work which has been of great value to the society. The committee then began to form an association, which now numbers nearly eighty members. I think we owe much to that original committee, of which the office-bearers were Mr. Wilson (then absent from the colony), as president; Mr. Greville, M.P., vice-president; Mr. MacDonnell, treasurer; Mr. Haviland, secretary; and Mr. Hosier, librarian.

Mrs. Britten undertook to give the lecture for the first evening, which she did at the New Temperance Hall, which was engaged for the meetings of the society.

'Of the meetings before April I have no record. On the 21st of that month Mr.

Haviland, the then secretary, resigned office, and the society was good enough to entrust me with that office.

'With your leave I will now make a few extracts from the minutes, as they will afford the best insight into the work done by and the progress of the society during the year.

'April 21st, 1879.—Mr. Munro read a paper on clairvoyance, and the president, Mr. Wilson, read from the *Banner of Light* a lecture by Dr. Buchanan, the subject being the discussion, medical and otherwise, on the peculiar and wonderful powers of Miss Molly Fancher.

'May 5th.—Some very interesting incidents were related in connection with clairvoyance. At this meeting the first honorary member, Mr. Bright, was elected. As the society had then more than £31 in hand, £11 11s. was placed in the hands of a sub-committee for the purchase of books. After the meeting a number of tracts and pamphlets, which had been presented to the society by Mr. Haviland, were gratuitously distributed.

'May 19th and June 2nd.—At these meetings Mr. Bright read an extremely interesting series of papers on "Magnetic Education," as received by himself at several sittings in the presence of Mrs. Jackson, of Melbourne.

'June 16th.—At this meeting several members recorded interesting instances of spirit manifestations.

'July 7th.—The business assumed a conversational character, and many interesting experiences were related. At this meeting Mr. Greville presented the society with the complete works of Andrew Jackson Davis.

'August 18th.—First meeting to which the public were admitted. The hall was crowded, and more than sixty people standing. The lecture was "Spiritualism in its Relation to Psychology," and the lecturer Mr. Bright.

'September 15th.—Again a public meeting, with a thoroughly successful lecture by Mr. Harold Stephen, entitled "The Philosophy of Spiritualism."

'October 20th.—A public meeting, at which the president gave the lecture, "Some Proofs of the Reality of Spirit Intercourse."

'November 3rd.—This evening Mr. Haviland read a paper, "Mesmerism, its Uses, and some Hints for its Study," and afterwards showed the way to mesmerize and demesmerize.

'November 17th.—Public meeting, at which Mr. Cavenagh gave a lecture, "Spiritualism and its Future Possibilities," the attendance being nearly two hundred.

'December 1st.—This evening Mr. Rice, the "brain reader" (from America), gave the society some very interesting tests of his wonderful powers.

'J. Bowie Wilson, Chairman.'

"The following officers were elected for the year : President, Hon. J. Bowie Wilson, re-elected ; vice-presidents, Milner Stephen, F.G.S., &c., &c., Hugh Paterson ; treasurer, C. Cavenagh ; librarian, F. Hosier, re-elected ; secretary, Hugh Paterson, jun., re-elected; and a committee of ten.

"The retiring officers were given a vote of thanks, and a very successful session closed.

"L. E. Harcus.

"Sydney, New South Wales, January 19th, 1880."

Should this volume survive the present generation even such simple records as the above may prove milestones on the highway of a great and wonderful movement, the full understanding of which, will be aided by the mere re-echo of the name of those who were its earliest standard bearers. If we now close our notice of Spiritualism on this great Australasian continent, it is for lack of space, not of abundant materials for a far more extended report. Perhaps we should add, that no country of the earth proves more conclusively than Australia how much is due to the unselfish efforts of individuals. To speak of Spiritualism in that country, is to speak of the indefatigable labourers who have given it form and direction.

The all-seeing Spirit alone can determine the future of the movement there, as elsewhere, but if ever it fails in Australia, it will be because future generations are not worthy of it, and fail to produce new recruits equal in courage, devotion, and ability, to the now fast-thinning ranks of the "old guard," to whose gallant endeavour and noble service, the present status of Spiritualism in Australia is due.

CHAPTER XXXII.

SPIRITUALISM IN NEW ZEALAND.

ERE we quit the Southern waters which lave the vast seaboard of Australia, we must take a cursory glance at the progress of Spiritualism in the fair islands which form the brightest gem of the Pacific Ocean—NEW ZEALAND. Here, as in Australia, Spiritualism has made a deep mark, and one that promises to be very permanent; but though the plan of this work does not admit of our lingering upon any nation's Spiritual experiences antecedent to the present century, we are disposed to impinge upon this set purpose, in favour of the fine and singular race whom the white pioneers of the land found in its possession, and who are now known as the "MAORIS." Spiritualism has not only been the religion of this people from time immemorial, but this belief still prevails amongst the broken remnants of the tribes which inhabit the land. There are, moreover, so many features of resemblance between the Maoris' modes of spirit communion, and those with which the Spiritualists of the New Dispensation are familiar, that we deem a few items of information on this subject may be acceptable, and in harmony with our Nineteenth Century Spiritual revelations.

In their ideas of Creation, the Maoris are essentially evolutionists, and Darwin would have found a mental field amongst them, fully prepared for the reception of his plausible philosophy of the *ascent* of man.

The following curious examples of Maori poetry, although greatly marred by translation, will give an approximate idea of the methods of classifying the order of unfoldment as it appeared to the savage mind of uncounted ages ago. The words are given by the Tohungas or Priests amongst the tribes, and after having been handed down from generation to generation, are translated by the various white missionaries who have become familiar with their language. We can only give the following brief extracts from a vast mass of similar legendary recitations :—

"OF THE BEGINNING.

"From the conception, the increase;
From the increase, the thought;
From the thought, the remembrance;
From the remembrance, the consciousness;
From the consciousness, the desire."

"OF THE FIRST LONG, LONG, NIGHT.

"The word became fruitful;
It dwelt with the feeble glimmering.
It brought forth night;
The great night, the long night,
Night, blackness, evermore;
The lowest night, the lofty night;
The thick night to be felt;
The night to be touched;
The night not to be seen;
The night of death, yet alive;
No eyes yet in the world."

"WHEN THE LIGHT COMES FIRST

" From the nothing, the begetting.
  From the nothing, the increase ;
  From the nothing, the abundance ;
  The power of increasing ;
  The living breath,—the world,
  The living breath ; it dwelt with the empty space
  And thence came the air :
  The air above, around, the all ;
  The atmosphere, which floats above
  The great firmament ; the early dawn,
  The glimmering growing light ;
  The atmosphere dwelt with the heat,
  And thence proceeded the mighty sun ;
  And the moon sprung forth,
  And the chief eyes of Heaven, the stars came out.
  Then the Heavens became light ;
  Then the grey earth became light ;
  The early dawn came, the day was born ;
  The mid day,—the blaze of day from the sky."

" The fourth period," gives the names of islands, and the places which were the cradle of the race of men.

The land being formed, " the fifth period " produces the gods of many things, and many creatures. " The sixth period," is assigned to the production of men. Amidst an immense store of legendary description of the heavens, seas, gods, and other evoluted forms, there is another " song," descriptive of how the earth changed from its ancient condition of barrenness :—

" The earth's skin was once the *tutu.*
  Her garment was the *wehe wehe.*
  Her mantle was the bramble,
  The coarse stinging nettle.
  Don't grieve that the earth is covered with **water.**
  Don't lament for the length of time.
  The ocean's reign shall be broken.
  The ocean's surface shall be rough
  With the lands springing up in it ;
  With mountains very high,
  Girdling round the sea.
  Yes, round the sea, and rising through the **waves.**
  The waves shall wash their feet ;
  The high mountains full of fire.
  Broken up shall you be, oh earth ;
  Pierced thro' you white waves ;
  Grieve not earth for your water covered head.
  Lament not seas for your
  Mountains springing up ;—
  Lament not !"

It would require a volume to describe the intricacies of Maori mythology, in which gods, men, demons, monsters, heroes, and spirits of the dead, are the actors. The mythology of these islanders is not less diffuse or complicated than that of the ancient Greeks. But the vivid ideality and poetic fantasies of the Greek mind, are no marvel, *because they emanate from the Greeks.*

The endless convolutions of uncurbed fancy by which the Greeks impersonated the powers of nature, are of course admirable, because they originate in Grecian ideality, and are labelled " classical lore."

The Maori sings, believes, and teaches, all that the Greek classics enshrine, but alas ! his legends only bear the opprobrious name of "savage superstitions." Read however the Rev. Richard Taylor's TE TKA A MAUI, from which our extracts are taken, and the difference between "classical lore" and "savage superstitions" will seem very slight; in fact, the greatest marvel of all is, where either Greek or Maori got their ideality from ? Amidst the mythological personages of New Zealand, "the Spirits of the dead" ever play a very prominent part, and our chief interest in noticing the Maoris at all, lies in the fact, that belief in, and open communion with these Spirits, still exists. The priests or "Tohungas" are unmistakably "Mediums," in the modern sense of the term. Sometimes they are born with their gift, and sometimes they are devoted to the priestly office by their parents, and acquire their powers after the fashion of Eastern ecstatics, by prayer, fasting, and contemplation.

That good prophets exist amongst the Maoris has been abundantly proved, even to the cold materialistic government that has absorbed their country. During the time when Great Britain busied herself in appropriating New Zealand, on the plea of a "discovery," her officials frequently wrote home, that *the Maori would never be conquered wholly ;* information of the parties sent out to attack them ; the very colour of the boats, and the hour when they would arrive ; the number of the enemy, and all particulars essential to their safety, *being invariably communicated to the tribes beforehand, by their prophets or Tohungas.*

The state of preparation in which the English found "the savages," fully verified this claim, and proved the fact of prevision, affirmed to exist amongst them.

The best natural prophets and seers amongst the Maoris are, as amongst the Spiritualists, of the female sex; and although the missionaries try to account for the marvellous powers they exhibit, above all, for the sound of the *Spirit voice*, which is a common phase in their communion with the dead—on the hypothesis that the women who practise "the arts of sorcery," are *ventriloquists*—this attempted explanation rarely covers the ground of the intelligence which is received.

The author has herself had several proofs of the Mediumistic power possessed by these "*savages*," but as her experiences may be deemed of too personal a character, we shall select our examples from other sources. One of these is furnished by a Mr. Marsden, a person who was well known in the early days of New Zealand's colonial history, as a miner, who grew rich "through Spiritual communications." Mr. Marsden was a gentleman who had spent much time amongst the Maoris, and who still keeps a residence in "the King country," that is—the district of which they hold control.

Mr. Marsden informed the author, that his success as a gold miner, was entirely due to a communication he had received through a native woman, who claimed to have the power of bringing *down* Spirits—the Maoris, be it remembered, always insisting that the Spirits *descend* through the air to earth, to visit mortals.

Mr. Marsden had long been prospecting unsuccessfully in the gold regions. He had a friend in partnership with him, to whom he was much attached, but who had been accidentally killed by a fall from a cliff.

The Spirit of this man came unsolicited, on an occasion when Mr. Marsden was consulting a native seeress, for the purpose of endeavouring to trace out what had become of a valuable watch which he had lost.

The voice of the Spirit was first heard in the air, apparently above the roof of the hut in which they sat, calling Mr. Marsden by his familiar name of "Mars." Greatly startled by these sounds, several times repeated, at the Medium's command, he remained perfectly still until the voice of his friend speaking in his well-remembered Scotch accent sounded close to his ear, whilst a column of grey misty substance reared itself up by his side. This apparition was plainly visible in the subdued light of the hut, to which there was only one open entrance, but no window. Though he was much startled by what he saw and heard, Mr. Marsden had presence of mind enough to gently *put his hand through the misty column* which remained intact, as if its substance offered no resistance to the touch. Being admonished by an earnest whisper from the Maori woman, who had fallen on her knees before the apparition, to keep still, he obeyed, when a voice— seemingly from an immense distance off—yet speaking unmistakably in his friend's Scotch accents, advised him to let the watch alone—for it was irreparably gone—but to go to the stream on the banks of which they had last had a meal together; trace it up for six miles and a half, and then, by following its course amidst the forest, he would come to *a pile*, which would make him rich, if he chose to remain so.

Whilst he was waiting and listening breathlessly to hear more, Mr. Marsden was startled by a slight detonation at his side. Turning his head he observed that the column of mist was gone, and in its place, a quick flash, like the reflection of a candle, was all that he beheld. Here the *séance* ended, and the astonished miner left the hut, convinced that he had heard the Spirit of his friend talking with him. He added, that he followed the directions given implicitly, and came to a mass of surface gold lying on the stones at the bottom of the brook in the depth of the forest. This he gathered up, and though he prospected for several days in and about that spot, he never found another particle of the precious metal. That which he had secured, he added, with a deep sigh, was indeed enough to have made him independent for life, had it not soon been squandered in fruitless speculations.

Several accounts are extant of Spiritualism amongst the Maoris, one of the most curious and graphic, being a personal narrative, written by General Cummings, in a small volume called "Old New Zealand."

The party who lent this work for perusal to the author, was well acquainted with General Cummings, and vouched for his truth and reliability in every particular. Although the narrative we are about to quote has often been retailed in magazines and other periodicals, it was so thoroughly authenti- cated by the author's friend that we give it place once more in this volume, as an example of the kind of Spiritualism practised amongst the Maoris.

A popular young chief who had acquired a fair knowledge of the English language, and with whom General Cummings was very intimate, had been appointed registrar of births and deaths.

General Cummings occupied a portion of his office, but they were about to remove to a more convenient place, when the young Maori encountered a violent death. In changing the office, the book of registries was missing, and much inconvenience was occasioned by its loss. A short time after the decease of his friend, General Cummings was informed that his relatives intended to invoke his spirit, and that as the "Pakeha" (white man) had been much beloved by him, he might if he chose, be present.

Notwithstanding his inveterate scepticism, the General accepted this invitation, mentally resolving "to keep his ears and eyes wide open." The narrator then continues as follows :—

"The appointed time came. Fires were lit. The *Tohunga* repaired to the darkest corner of the room. All was silence, save the sobbing of the sisters of the deceased warrior-chief. There were thirty of us, sitting on the rush-strewn floor, the door shut, and the fire now burning down to embers. Suddenly there came a voice out from the partial darkness, '*Salutation, salutation to my family, to my tribe, to you, pakeha, my friend !*' Our feelings were taken by storm. The oldest sister screamed, and rushed with extended arms in the direction from whence the voice came. Her brother, seizing, restrained her by main force. Others exclaimed, 'Is it you ? is it you ? *truly* it is you ! *aue ! aue !*' and fell quite insensible upon the floor. The older women, and some of the aged men, were not moved in the slightest degree, though believing it to be the spirit of the chief.

"Whilst reflecting upon the novelty of the scene, the 'darkness visible,' and the deep interest manifest, the spirit spoke again, 'Speak to me, my family ; speak to me, my tribe ; speak to me, the pakeha !' At last the silence gave way, and the brother spoke : 'How is it with you ! Is it well with you in *that* country ?' The answer came, though not in the voice of the Tohunga-medium, but in strange, sepulchral sounds : '*It is well with me : my place is a good place. I have seen our friends : they are all with me !*' A woman from another part of the room now anxiously cried out, 'Have you seen my sister ?'— 'Yes, I have seen her : she is happy in our beautiful country.'—'Tell her my love so great for her will never cease.'—'Yes, I will bear the message.' Here the native woman burst into tears, and my own bosom swelled in sympathy.

"The spirit speaking again, giving directions about property and keepsakes, I thought I would more thoroughly test the genuineness of all this ; and I said, 'We cannot find your book with the registered names ; where have you concealed it ?' The answer came instantly, 'I concealed it between the *tahuhu* of my house, and the thatch ; straight over you, as you go in at the door.' The brother rushed out to see. All was silence. In five minutes he came hurriedly back, with the *book in his hand !* It astonished me.

"It was now late ; and the spirit suddenly said, '*Farewell, my family, farewell, my tribe : I go.*' Those present breathed an impressive farewell ; when the spirit cried out again, from high in the air, 'Farewell !'

"This, though seemingly tragical, is in every respect literally true. But what was it ? ventriloquism, the devil, or what ! . . ."

The Rev. Richard Taylor, a good and learned missionary, one who, after many years' residence amongst the natives, wrote a valuable treatise on their lives, traditions, and customs, entitled TE THA A MAUI, dilates most ingenuously on the striking similarity of the Maoris' spells, enchantments, &c., &c., with those practised by the ancient Hebrews. He likens the scene of destruction by which a once celebrated *Wharekura*, or Temple, was demolished, and the worshippers scattered, to the destruction of the Tower of Babel. His descriptions of the TAPU, or curse, which attached to certain things and places forbidden to be touched or entered, reads like Leviticus and Deuteronomy, and precisely resembles the *taboo* of the Hebrews, by which certain objects, food, and persons, rendered those that came in contact with them "unclean."

Their prophets officiate and speak oracularly, like the prophets of Israel. They have multitudes of *Karakias*, or *spells*—designed to act as curses or blessings, the translations of which read strangely like the dying words of Israel to his sons, or the curse and blessing on "Ebal and Gerizim." Maoris go up to enquire of the gods, precisely as the Israelites "enquired of the Lord," and the Tohungas, or priests, answer them, in the name of the gods, *by staves, by stones, by lots, by arrows, and a voice,* exactly as the priests of Israel did, as described in Godwyn's "Antiquities of the Jews." This is neither the time nor place to enquire whence this wonderful parity of customs, traditions, and modes of religious observance arose, between nations as widely separated by oceans and continents, as by epochs of time ;

but one of the curious circumstances in this connection which *does* belong to our own time, is the mode in which reverend Christian missionaries comment on these marvellous resemblances, invariably referring the customs, invocations, sacrifices, and other formulæ practised by the Hebrews to Divine command, whilst the almost identical rites and ceremonies practised by a far distant race of Savages, are regarded as evidence of their utter degradation and barbaric superstition.

We regret being unable to pursue the subject of New Zealand *Spirituality* or *Superstition*—let the reader adopt whichever term his predilections incline him to—any farther. Mysterious in their origin, and strongly indicative in their present application of a belief in the potencies of "magnetism" and "psychology," this interesting people illustrate fully, to the very few who are enabled to gain an inside view of their real lives and customs, the astounding fact that the modern Spiritualism, which seems to have fallen upon this century as a new revelation, not only finds a parallel in the Biblical account of the Jewish nation, but in its more subtle phases of science through magnetism and psychology, has been, and still is unconsciously practised by those children of nature whom we contemptuously call "heathens" and "savages." If it be a subject quite worthy of philosophic research to endeavour to find a common origin for language, how much more so would it be to endeavour to find the true root of all religious or Spiritual ideas and customs!

If animal magnetism or the transference of invisible force and influence from body to body be a proven fact, and psychology, or the impress of mind upon mind be a truth, which the poorest experimenter in "electro biology" can demonstrate, then would it not be a subject well worthy the attention of the scholar, especially the psychologist, to trace out the source from whence savage nations have learned the use of these sovereign potencies, and that without books, written language, or philosophic understanding of what they do?

Whilst every phase of Spiritual power now recognised by Spiritualists and attributed to the influence of deceased human beings is known and practised more or less intelligently by the New Zealand Maoris, their Spiritual beliefs, although *not eradicated*, are measurably modified by the new doctrines introduced amongst them by Christian missionaries. A remarkable example of the grafting process by which new forms are being welded into ancient ideas, is found in the person of the celebrated Maori Prophet, "Te Whiti."

This remarkable personage still exercises unbounded influence over the tribes amongst whom he resides, in fact he is considered by them very much in the same light as Christians esteem the Founder of their faith. His word is law, his command is regarded as nothing short of divine, and his prophecies are to the Maori, as the word of fate. We shall conclude this chapter, the only one we can devote to the Spiritualism of a so-called "savage people," with a brief account of Te Whiti, published in a San Francisco paper, the closing paragraphs of which, in especial, we commend to the candid thinker's consideration. The sketch is dated *August*, 1879, and reads thus :—

"A MAORI PROPHET LEADER.

"Erueti, now known as Te Whiti, is the grandson of Paora (Paul) Kukutai, who was chief of the Pautukai tribe when this district was first occupied by European settlers. The chief of the tribe now is Ruakeri, also a grandson of the old chief, though his influence is but nominal, being overshadowed by that of the great prophet leader Te Whiti.

Erueti was in his youth a pupil of the Rev. Mr. Riemenschneider, head of the now defunct Wesleyan mission-station at Warea, and it was here that he obtained his intimate knowledge of the Bible, which it is no exaggeration to say he knows by heart, and his thorough acquaintance with which he displays with so much effect in his public manifestos and orations. He was looked upon by Mr. Riemenschneider as an earnest Christian, and when his pupilage ended, the rev. gentleman presented him with a large Bible, which he still possesses.

"He first came prominently into notice as a leading man among his people in 1862, on the occasion of the wreck of the steamship "Lord Worsley," in Te Namu Bay, Opunake. It was chiefly through the exertions of Erueti that the passengers were allowed to proceed to New Plymouth, and also 1,500 ounces of gold on board the ship were given up. Soon after this Erueti changed his name to Te Whiti; after an old Pah of the tribe, situate in the vicinity of New Plymouth, near the Sugarloaf Peak.

"In 1868, Mr. Parris, then civil commissioner, had an interview with him. Mr. Parris stated that the Parihaka natives were, without exception, Kingites, and Te Whiti was looked up to by them as being little, if at all, inferior to the king; that all he uttered was spoken in a very calm manner, though the man was evidently deeply convinced that he was under supernatural influence, no doubt the result of the secluded life he had then been leading for some years.

"Such is the man who, at the time the Grey Government was trying to purchase the adherence of Tawhaio and Rewhi, again lifted his voice and called on all Maoris to rally round him, and said that their lands should be returned to them, still protesting against fighting, but announcing that the settlers would be removed by some supernatural means. When the survey of the Waimate plains was commenced, it was thought that Te Whiti would make some demonstration, but he still confined himself to prophecy; though, when Maclean, the cook to one of the survey parties in the Waitoturu district, was murdered by Hiroki, and the murderer took refuge at Parihaka, Te Whiti sheltered him and refused to allow him to be given up; and on the chief of the tribe to which Hiroki belonged, proceeding with some of his men to Parihaka to demand that he should be surrendered to them and given over to take his trial, Te Whiti ordered that all the party, with the exception of a European who accompanied them, should be killed if they did not at once retire. In March last the Hon. Mr. Sheenan, native minister, went to the Parihaka meeting and demanded the surrender of the murderer. Te Whiti's reply was that Hiroki was not so guilty as the Government; he had only killed a man, while they had killed the land. He therefore refused to allow Hiroki to be given up, and Mr. Sheenan left Parihaka. The very next day Te Whiti issued orders to his natives to remove all the surveyors and their gangs from the Waimate Plains, but without any shedding of blood, which was accordingly done, men and instruments being carted across the Waingogoro river. Parihaka is now in Alsatia, where any murderer or other criminal of the Maori race is secure from the arm of the law, Te Whiti having proclaimed it a city of refuge. The place is only five miles from the main south road, and barely six miles from the European settlers at Okato. In a speech which Te Whiti delivered at Parihaka in June last, he said that the Government would send large forces to Parihaka, and take him (Te Whiti) and crucify him. He says he will not offer any resistance to the soldiers when they come, but that he will gladly be crucified. He also states that the Government are determined to put surveyors on the plains; but he will not fight them. Te Whiti further stated that he received a telegram from Sir George Grey on the 17th of June, proposing to send a commission to investigate the claims of the natives to the confiscated lands, inviting him (Te Whiti) to employ a lawyer to look after his interests, the Government paying all the expenses. Te Whiti said his answer was that the matter had been delayed too long; that the end of all things was at hand, courts and commissions included. He added: 'When I speak of the land, the survey, the ploughing, and such matters of little consequence their (the reporters') pencils fly with the speed of the wind; but when I speak of the words of the Spirit, they say, "This is the dream of a madman." They are so intent on accumulating wealth, that nothing appears to interest them except what is in some way connected with the acquisition of wealth. The storekeeper who has succeeded in acquiring wealth by short weight and inferior articles, and the numerous ways of picking and stealing known only to the initiated—the men who steal the land of the Maori and acquire flocks of sheep and herds of cattle—the men who would take the bread out of the mouths of the widow and fatherless, and acquire great riches by so doing, are all looked upon as gentlemen of property, while the humble seeker after truth is passed by unknown and unheeded. The time is at hand when their goods will rot in their stores, their ships will rot in their harbours for want of sailors to work them, the merchants will wring their hands in despair when they see all their accumulation of riches melt away like the morning mist before the rising sun.'"

CHAPTER XXXIII.

SPIRITUALISM IN NEW ZEALAND (CONCLUDED.)

WE must now call attention to the earliest attempts of a few earnest investigators in New Zealand, to promote the knowledge of the modern movement known as "Spiritualism."

The first efforts in this direction were made by those who had brought with them from older countries, the tidings of the great Spiritual outpouring.

By these pioneers, circles were formed in private families with the usual results of Mediumistic unfoldment. Amongst the earliest investigators in Dunedin, one of the largest and most flourishing cities in the islands—was a gentleman who now holds a prominent and influential position in the community, Mr. John Logan. Before this esteemed citizen had become publicly identified with the cause of Spiritualism, an association had been formed, the members of which steadily pursued their investigations in private circles and semi-public gatherings. One of the most marked events in connection with the early development of Spiritualism in Dunedin however, was the arraignment and church trial of Mr. Logan, the circumstances of which may be briefly summed up as follows. This gentleman, although holding a high and dignified position in the first Presbyterian church of the city, had not only dared to attend circles and witness Spiritualistic phenomena, but it was currently reported that one of his own near relatives was a very remarkable Medium.

Having become interested in the movement through various influences, Mr. Logan completed the list of his enormities in the eyes of his Christian brethren, by attending the lectures of the Rev. J. M. Peebles, and actually appearing with that arch-heretic on the stage of the Princess Theatre, on "the Lord's day," as the complaint against him set forth. To make matters worse, the offender would neither express penitence nor promise to desist from his desperate acts of heresy for the future, to the committee of church dignitaries who waited on him, with a view of remonstrating on the atrocity of his conduct. On the contrary, the sturdy Scotch gentleman, affirmed his right to visit Spiritual or any other meetings, when and where he pleased, whether on the *Lord's Day*, or any other day, in public or in private.

What was to be done? Mr. Logan was rich and powerful. He had been a pillar in the church, and his example and influence could not fail to lead other sheep astray, besides involving the entire church in the awful scandal of his own dereliction!

On the 19th of March, 1873, Mr. Logan was summoned to appear before a Church Convocation, to be held for the purpose of trying his case, and if necessary, dealing with his grave delinquency.

Up to this time, the noble wife of the accused gentleman had not followed him in his Spiritual researches ; in fact, she had manifested no sympathy in the subject to which they related. In the trying hour of her good husband's arraignment however, she was by his side, and listened attentively to the entire conduct of the high-handed procedure of which he was the victim.

The farce of a modern "star chamber" trial ended, as might have been expected, by Mr. Logan's conviction, and *excommunication* from the heavenly benefits and heavenly hopes of which the Presbyterian Synod claimed to be the appointed dispensers. Before the final breaking up of this most reverend and fraternal assembly of Christians, Mrs. Logan, moved by those tender feminine impulses which rendered the severance of once cherished ties of friendship and religious communion very painful to her, rose up in her place, and with all the dignity and earnestness which mark this estimable lady, she asked in thrilling tones, *if there was no one there to speak for John Logan?* No voice responded. Of all the former friends and associates who had been bound to John Logan by ties of gratitude, as well as companionship in a foreign land, not one held out a hand to sustain him, not one breathed a word to mitigate the insensate tyranny of the sentence pronounced upon him! It seemed as if the ice bolts of a hard and savage theology had shut humanity out of the hearts of those present, even as they would have shut a good man out of heaven, for daring to follow the dictates of his conscience.

Again and yet again the sweet voice of the brave lady rang through the stillness of that guilty crowd, in the pathetic question, "Is there no one here to speak a word for John Logan?" When it was fully shown that not one recreant man present dared to break that solemn silence, the devoted wife taking her husband's arm, passed out from amongst them, saying as she went, in her own calm and touching tones, "This is no place for us; let us go hence." And thus they went forth, that good John Logan and his noble wife; out from the stifling atmosphere of man-made and cruel sectarianism, into the free air of Spiritual life, light, truth, and reason; out from the night of bigotry into the sunlight of God's truth, never more to return, but still better, never more to tread separate paths in life again. From that hour, Mrs. Logan resolved to enquire into the faith that had enabled her husband to withstand the multitude, and prove how one man in a good cause, is mightier than a host. Struck with the base ingratitude of those who had deserted him, and ashamed of the faith which thus disgraced its members in attempting to disgrace their friend, Mrs. Logan sought, and found, the source of her brave companion's strength, and not only found it to be true and good and rational, but she herself came to be a minister of its divine afflatus, and when the author visited Dunedin in 1879 she found Mrs. Logan, not only firm in the faith of Spiritualism, but one of its most marked evidences in her own beautiful and convincing phases of Mediumship.

With the increase of population and development of civilized life in the beautiful islands, even so has Spiritualism grown. It has had its opponents from without, who, by slander, ridicule, and open persecution, have endeavoured to crush its rising influence. It has also had to contend—as usual—with "many foes of its own household." Some of its propagandists, stirred with temporary enthusiasm, have acted, like many other injudicious new converts, with an amount of fanaticism which has laid them open to the charge of folly. Unbalanced minds have ridden it as a hobby to the verge of lunacy. The avaricious have sought to make capital out of it, and failing to do so, turned to revile it; and still others have sought to make it the stalking horse to shield their vicious proclivities, or furnish excuses for the indulgence of their evil propensities; in a word, *human nature* has been represented amongst New Zealand Spiritualists, as fully as elsewhere. Being so remote and self-centered, shut in as it were by its own vast seaboard, New Zealanders are more liable to regard each others failings, than a more cosmopolitan population; hence, whatever shortcomings poor human nature has put upon this noble cause in New Zealand, have had more than the ordinary share of comment. Still "the cause" has grown mightily, and wherever good lecturers have appealed to the candid portion of the community, they have succeeded in awaking a deep and permanent interest.

In many of the principal towns besides Dunedin, circles held at first in mere idle curiosity, have produced their usual fruit of Medium power, and this again has extended into associative action, and organization into local societies.

For over a year, the Spiritualists and Liberalists of Dunedin were fortunate enough to secure the services of Mr. Charles Bright as their lecturer.

This gentleman had once been attached to the editorial staff of the *Melbourne Argus*, and had obtained a good reputation as a capable writer, and liberal thinker. Mr. Bright's lectures in Dunedin were highly appreciated, and by their scholarly style, and attractive manner, served to band together the liberal element in the city, stimulate free thought, and do good in every direction.

In Auckland, the principal town of the North Island, the same good service was rendered to the cause of the religious thought, by the excellent addresses of the Rev. Mr. Edgar, a clergyman whose unconservative and Spiritualistic doctrines, had tended to sever him from sectarian organizations, and draw around him, the Spiritualists and liberal thinkers of the town.

Besides the good work effected by these gentlemen, the occasional visits of Messrs. Peebles, Walker, J. Tyerman, and the effect of the many private circles held in every portion of the islands, all have tended to promote a general, though quiet diffusion of Spiritual thought and doctrine, throughout New Zealand.

During the author's visit to Dunedin, her lectures were given every Sunday evening in the Princess Theatre, and on week evenings, in the Athenæum, and those were attended for several months, with appreciative audiences, filling the buildings to their utmost capacity. Amongst other incidents of this visit, was an extended series of newspaper discussions, not only with numbers of correspondents whose antagonism to the Spiritual doctrines was manifested in the ordinary journalistic fashion, but there were many writers, whose fierce diatribes manifested so obviously their fidelity to the founders of their faith, John Knox, and John Calvin, that the author frequently had cause to felicitate herself upon the fact, that she did not live in the days of those respected ecclesiastics, or in the immediate vicinage of the once *famous* Spanish Inquisition.

Amongst the most keen and persistent of her journalistic denouncers, was the irrepressible M. W. Green, "minister of the Church of Christ," who had somehow managed to close his career in Melbourne and turn up at Dunedin, just in time to hurl his javelins once more at Spiritualism, in the height of its success and popularity.

Mr. Green adopted many modes of attracting to himself the attention of a community, which had hitherto been all too unconscious, that they had so remarkable a personage in their midst. He persisted in writing to the papers, under his full name and style, challenging every statement made at the author's lectures, in which he thought he could pick a flaw, and

when the public began to be tired of him, and the columns of the daily
journals became " too full," to admit of any more of his prosy anathemas
against Spiritualism, he hired an immense new hall, and advertised a series
of lectures to " expose Spiritualism," in which a whole nation of lawyers
might have found employment in libel suits, had not his flaming advertisements been too rude and scandalous to render them worthy of honourable
mention, or notice.   Still the " Free-thought committee," under whose
auspices Mrs. Britten's lectures were given, deemed the gentleman had
gone far enough, if not a great deal too far, and though his atrocious sensational advertisements were obviously put forth to *compel notice*, the committee
deemed their honour involved in putting a stop to them.   The result was,
that the same hall was hired in which Mr. Green's denunciations had been
poured out to the listening few.   On this occasion, the building was
crowded to suffocation.   The Hon. Robert Stout, Attorney-General and
M.P. for Dunedin, was Mrs. Britten's chairman, and a large company of
sympathizers surrounded the minister of the " Church of Christ," a
company who distinguished themselves by hissing, hooting, and stamping,
at the close of every sentence, no matter whether their uproar was in or
out of place.

Once more we deem it in order to give an extract from the author's
American correspondence in which this *coup d'état* of the " Christian
minister " is disposed of in all the paragraphs it merits.   It reads thus :—

"Mr. M. W. Green, one of the most persistent and unscrupulous of clerical opponents,
gave and published, a series of scandalous and disgraceful lectures on the fruits of
Spiritualism, and in proof of his theory of 'Satanic Agency,' drew the entire of his
charges from the lives, writings, opinions and practices of certain so-called Spiritualists
themselves.   His collection of garbage, under the title of 'The Devil's Sword Blunted,' is
now before the world.   The course I finally adopted under the advice and guidance of
good and wise friends from the shores beyond, I mean to stand by. . . .   That course
was as follows :—We procured the largest and finest hall in Dunedin.   The Hon. Robert
Stout, our honoured and talented Attorney-General, was my chairman, and to a mob of
howling Christian followers of my reverend opponent, in his own white, or rather livid
face, and surrounded by a jammed and almost frantic crowd of excited multitudes, I gave
the following definitions of my religion and faith in Spiritualism :—

"1st. Spiritualism proves by a set of obviously supermundane phenomena, that a world
of invisible intelligence is communicating with us.

"2nd. It demonstrates by an immense array of test facts given all over the world, under
circumstances that forbid the possibility of collusion or human contrivance, that the communicating intelligences are identical with the souls of mortals who once lived on earth.

"3rd. It shows by universal coincidence in the communications, that every living soul
is in judgment for the deeds done in the body, and reaps the fruits of its good or evil
life on earth, in happiness or suffering hereafter.

"4th. All the communicating spirits coincide in declaring that the life succeeding
mortal dissolution, is not a final state, but one which manifests innumerable conditions of
progress. . . . and these four propositions I emphatically protest are *the all* of spiritual
facts we know, the all that are absolutely proved. . . . or upon which, all the immense
varieties of persons that make up the ranks of Spiritualism, can absolutely agree.

"The whole of my lecture, printed under the title of 'Spiritualism Vindicated and
Clerical Slanders Refuted,' is now in the hands of thousands of Colonists, and bitter as
the occasion was that demanded it, I thank the Great Spirit, whose instrumentality called
forth so trenchant a plea, for a cause so eminently worthy."

As it will appear, even from this short extract, that the sole aim of Mr.
Green now, as in the debate with Mr. Walker, was to shoulder upon
Spiritualism the shortcomings, follies, and errors of its world-wide
followers, and the basis of Mrs. Britten's lectures was to present the principles of Spiritualism, and redeem them from the misrepresentation which
ever obscures any new movement when it is confounded with the irrespon-

sible doings of its heterogeneous followers, it will readily be perceived that the Christian minister was trumpeting forth to the world the shortcomings of Spiritualists; whilst the author insisted upon recalling him to the only legitimate ground of discussion, namely, the doctrines and principles OF SPIRITUALISM. No further explanation of these movements and counter movements are necessary, and Mr. Green's action was generally recognized as the old strategic method of theological warfare, ever employed by unscrupulous and desperate attacking parties.

Now although neither Mr. Green nor his followers could justify an attack on a great cause by assailing the characters of those who believe in it, especially in a new movement, the wide-spread notoriety of which has necessarily attracted to its ranks all the scum of society, Mr. Green having been industrious enough to hunt up all the scandals which had been cast upon the cause by its camp followers, had of course many facts on his side; facts as cogent to prove the disorder which licentious people can attach to any cause that attracts them, as the records of the Inquisition, the torture chamber, or the night of St. Bartholomew, could prove murder, and barbarity, against Christians. Just in as far as monsters of cruelty have disgraced Christianity, so have examples of vulgarity and profanity, disgraced Spiritualism. When the day comes, in which the community recognizes that principles are eternal truths, and personalities, the transient representatives of certain states of society, such orators as Mr. Green will find their occupation gone, and stick to the endeavour to prove their own forms of belief, instead of throwing mud against the beliefs of others.

During Mrs. Britten's course of Dunedin lectures, the Hon. Robert Stout, as Attorney-General of New Zealand, and member for Dunedin, deemed himself called upon to oppose with all his wide-spread influence, and liberality of sentiment, the introduction of the Bible in the public schools as a necessary element of education. The partisans of this movement had been strenuous in their efforts to effect such an introduction. The opponents, headed by their popular leader Mr. Stout, had been equally persistent in their opposition, and it was in this state of divided opinion, that the Committe of the " Free-thought Association " of whom Mr. Stout was the president, solicited Mrs. Britten to give a lecture on the subject. The attendance on this occasion was overwhelming. The question under consideration was, of course, treated from the Liberalists' standpoint, but the main feature of the occasion was the citation of the Bible itself, *as its own witness*. This was done, by the simple presentation of about seventy or eighty quotations, in which the character and consistency of the Jewish Jehovah, the morality and humanity of the commands issued, and the agreement of the passages cited with science and chronology were fully displayed, and that on Biblical testimony alone, without comment or criticism. At the close of the lecture it was determined to print and circulate gratuitously, ten thousand copies of the Biblical quotations, and this was done without any other notice of the texts presented, than the simple headings which the extracts illustrated. The sensation produced by this procedure, increased the effect of the newspaper and rostrum discussions, and when the author was finally compelled to quit Dunedin to fill other engagements, the ladies who had been her most staunch friends and supporters, organized a farewell meeting, at which they presented her with a splendid set of ornaments formed from the jade or " green stone " so highly prized by the natives, as to be deemed " sacred," set in pure New Zealand gold.

18

Even now, though time and distance have mellowed the enthusiastic influences prevailing on this occasion to regretful and tender memory, the heart swells, the eyes fill, and the hand of the writer becomes nerveless with emotion, as the astral light in which all things are engraved, reveals once more, the images of the beloved faces gazing so earnestly upon the one, and recalls the pressure of the kind outstretched hands, so prompt to sustain, and so loath to unclasp the farewell pressure !

In Wellington, Nelson, and Auckland, important places successively visited by the author, warm friends of the cause were found, many private circles held, and a vast amount of public interest manifested. Fierce newspaper controversies still raged, but these only served to increase the depth of public sentiment, and stimulate investigation.

The great deficiency of railroad accommodation, the remoteness of this lovely land, and its isolation in the midst of the lonely Pacific waters—floating as it were on the tossing billows which lave its rugged volcanic mountain seaboard ; sometimes lashing the rocks with heaving fields of white breakers, and sometimes spouting high in air under the influence of submarine disturbances ; all these physical features of its environment tend to isolate New Zealand from casual intercourse with the outer world, limit its population, and render it far less known than the more distant continent of Australia. Still its internal growth is marvellous, and when the natural charm of its delightful soil, climate, and scenery, shall have produced their legitimate effects upon the characteristics of its inhabitants, New Zealand ought to be, the Paradise—physically, mentally, and morally, of the Southern Seas. Since the author's visit in 1879, two marked events have transpired in the history of New Zealand progressive thought.

One of these, is the publication of a bright spirited " Free-thought " paper, called *The Echo*, in the columns of which, Mr. Robert Stout's incisive logic, forcible argument, and scholarly research, finds frequent expression. Besides this, *The Echo* is graced with numerous scientific and able writers on Free-thought and Spiritualism. The second subject for gratulation by all liberal minds, is the foundation of a noble hall built by free-thinkers, and dedicated to the exposition of scientific and progressive subjects. Meetings are now held every Sunday in this hall.

Its plan and execution are reported to be alike creditable to its founders, and the noble purposes to which it is devoted. A progressive Lyceum or Sunday school, conducted on the principles taught by Andrew Jackson Davis, the " harmonial philosopher " of America, meets in this hall every Sunday, when both children and adults participate in the exercises. Fine music forms part of the religious worship of these Dunedin Liberalists, and already the roof has re-echoed to more sweet strains, elevated thoughts, fine literature, and broad progressive teaching, than has ever been heard within the walls of New Zealand ecclesiastical edifices.

With an account of the memorable scene during which the foundation stone of this fine edifice was laid, our summary of the New Zealand Spiritual movement must terminate. The day has not yet come—and heaven grant that it never may !—when sharp lines of demarcation will be drawn, for the purpose of dividing the ranks of " Free-thinkers " and " Spiritualists." Whatever the former class may profess to accept or reject, the latter are FREE-THINKERS, with RELIGION elevating their free-thought to heaven, and carrying their progress on to a life beyond the grave. In all else, none can transcend the breadth of their thought, or the freedom of its flight. Pending the dark day when this scope of thought shall be deemed *too narrow*, although the hall of which we have been writing was avowedly dedicated to "Free-thought," we dare as Spiritualists to claim the deepest possible interest in its erection and the uses to which it is applied, in token of which, we gladly record the fact, that the corner-stone was laid by a ministering angel on earth, and one who confidently hopes and expects to continue that ministry in a higher life, the Mrs. John Logan, of whom mention has been made in earlier pages of this chapter.

The following extracts from the report of the ceremony in question are taken from the New Zealand *Echo* of October, 1881 :—

" THE LYCEUM HALL.

"LAYING THE FOUNDATION 'STONE.

" The fifteenth of October, 1881, will ever be a memorable day in the annals of Freethought in these Southern Colonies. On that day was laid the foundation-stone of the first hall in the colonies wholly devoted to Freethought, and it was laid with more *éclat* than any foundation-stone ever laid in Dunedin. The morning was bright, but rain seemed threatening, and about eleven o'clock it began to rain. At twelve there was a steady downpour, and many of the committee were afraid that the ceremony would have to be postponed. Between twelve and one o'clock, however, it cleared up, and after that there was no shower till late in the evening. The warm weather and the breeze soon dried up the streets, and from 3 p.m. to 4.30 p.m. the weather was all that could have been wished. Two platforms were erected on the site—one for the band, and one for the children and ladies and the F. T. Choir. Near the north-eastern corner a small space was fenced off, carpeted, and a drawing-room *suite* placed in it. Around the stone and the front of the platform there were numerous flowers and trees in pots, and flags were hung from poles, and evergreen decorations were around the front of the main platform. Mr. Thompson had taken great trouble in decorations, and arranging these nothing could have been better done. Shortly before three, a large crowd gathered in Dowling Street, and the main platform was soon filled with Lyceum children, the choir, and ladies and gentlemen. About three hundred were on the platform. At three Mrs. John Logan arrived, and on her stepping on the platform Mr. Thompson presented her with a splendid white camelia, and she and some other ladies were placed near the stone. The band arrived, numbering about forty performers, many musicians having kindly lent their assistance to the Freethought band, and then the ceremony began. The crowd at this time was not less, we believe, than 3,000 people. The band played the "Star of England Polka," with cornet solos, Mr. Chapman leading, and Mr. Parker conducting. The music was excellently rendered, Mr. Chapman ably executing the cornet solos. The choir and Lyceum children then sang the following version of the " New Zealand National Anthem," composed by Mr. Bracken, one of the members of the Association, namely :—

"God of Nations ! at thy feet,
In the bonds of love we meet,
Hear our voices, we entreat,
    God defend our Freeland !
Guard Pacific's triple star,
From the shafts of strife and war,
Make her praises heard afar,
    God defend New Zealand !

"Men of every creed and race,
Gather here before thy face,
Asking thee to bless this place,
    God defend our Freeland !
From dissension, envy, hate,
And corruption, guard our State ;
Make our country good and great,
    God defend New Zealand !

" Let our Love for thee increase,
May thy blessings never cease,
Give us plenty, give us peace,
    God defend our Freeland !
From dishonour and from shame,
Guard our country's spotless name,
Crown her with immortal fame,
    God defend New Zealand !

" May our mountains ever be,
Freedom's ramparts on the sea.
Make us faithful unto thee,
    God defend our Freeland !
Guide her in the Nations' van,
Preaching love and truth to man,
Working out thy glorious plan,
    God defend New Zealand !

" Mr. Braithwaite, as Chairman of the Building Committee, then stepped forward, and, handing Mrs. Logan a handsome silver trowel, said : I have the honour to ask you to lay in the customary fashion the foundation-stone of a building to be called the Lyceum, which, when erected, is to welcome within its walls people of all shades of opinion, and to be dedicated to freedom of conscience, to intellectual and social liberty, and to that higher morality which we believe results from obeying the laws of Nature. As Freethinkers, we naturally feel proud of the event that brings us together, which in some respects is an auspicious one. To-day we are to lay the foundation-stone of the first Freethought Hall in the Australasian colonies. Old and young are here to take part in the ceremony, each feeling hopeful of the ultimate results of such an unusual occurrence. We have with us— making glad the scene with their clear, ringing, merry voices—the children of the first Lyceum started in New Zealand, an institution fraught with the deepest interests to our movement. We have also with us most of the members who in years gone by initiated and sustained in season and out of season the Dunedin Freethought Association, the first of its kind in this colony. Yourself and your worthy husband are two of the number. What more fitting, then, than that you should lay the foundation stone of a hall to be used for the dissemination of principles for which you have ardently laboured ? I take great pleasure, then, on behalf of the Freethought Association, in presenting you with this silver trowel to perform the work for which we have met. It bears the following inscription :—' Presented by the members of the Freethought Association to Mrs. John Logan on the occasion of laying the foundation-stone of the Lyceum. October 15, 1881.''

Following upon the ceremonial thus auspiciously commenced, were a number of excellent speeches, the most stirring and brilliant of which was one from the President of the Free-thought Society, the Hon. Robert Stout. In this address Mr. Stout defined the noble and unsectarian purposes to which the hall was to be devoted, and in a most eloquent and masterly style, drew pictures of the narrow creeds which chain the soul and erect cruel lines of demarcation between man and man, and the unbounded aspirations for light, love, truth, and kindness, which answer the Free-thinkers' demand for a real religion of life, &c., &c.

Mr. Stout's address deserved to be written in letters of gold. It is something however to know that its characters of ink have met thousands of eyes, and made a deep and healthful impression upon thousands of earnest readers, and now it only remains to add, that the " Free-thought Hall," soon developed its handsome proportions above the foundation-stone laid by the honoured hands of Mrs. Logan. By this time it has echoed and re-echoed to the eloquent strains of many an inspired speaker. It has witnessed weekly gatherings of joyous children, gifted teachers, keen debaters, and unanswerable logicians. Noble strains of music have resounded through its walls, and the place fully realizes the spirit of its dedication, and forms one of the grandest mementos of the value of practical religion stimulated by the exercise of " Free-thought," at present erected in any part of the world.

CHAPTER XXXIV.

SPIRITUALISM IN THE POLYNESIAN AND WEST INDIA ISLANDS.

WHILST it would be in vain to seek for open evidence of the modern Spiritual movement amongst the Polynesian races who inhabit the extensive groups of the Pacific Islands, it is equally certain that Spiritualism is known, and its phenomenal modes of communion more or less practised by the few white settlers who reside there. Doubtless the belief has been imported with the tides of immigration, for few voyagers visit these islands without reporting that Spiritual circles are commonly known wherever a white population is settled. On the other hand, there is a still greater prevalence amongst the aborigines, of that kind of Spiritualism of which we gave a representative sketch in our last chapter.

With varieties special to the natives of various islands, the Spiritualism of the New Zealand Maoris illustrates that of the Kanakas of the Sandwich Islands; the Samoans, Fijieans, natives of the Solomon, Navigator, and other Pacific groups. Senor Gamboa, a Spanish gentleman, having possessions in the Marshall Islands, assured the author that the chief feature in the religion of the natives was belief in many gods, and the influence of the Spirits of deceased ancestors. When accident or disease overtook them, they chanted prayers to some deceased priest who had been known as a healer, or some near and well-beloved relative; then hiding presents of shells or other ornaments near the sick people, they left them for so many hours, in order that the Spirit invoked might come and disclose in a dream, or by whispered communications, the best method of cure. Senor Gamboa declared, he had witnessed remarkable cures made in this way, amongst his own servants. One of these, a cook, had broken his arm by a fall; he insisted on being carried to a native settlement near his master's residence, and though the fracture was a severe one, he returned home in a week, his arm bound up neatly and skilfully with herbs, but so far healed that he could use it, and never after suffered inconvenience from it. On being questioned as to the mode of cure he said, his friends the natives had sung him to sleep, from which he did not wake for three days. During the interval he dreamed that his mother, long dead, but one who had been a famous "medicine woman" in her life, had come and bound up his arm just as he found it on awakening.

When asked who had done this, his friends said they had found him so, and no doubt "the Spirits had healed him." Spirits in these islands are invoked to bless the plantations; curse enemies, give victory, heal the sick, and reveal the future. Mr. James Anson, a good Spiritualist, residing in the Fijis, says:—"It is of no use to try and convert the natives to Christianity, so long as the missionaries deny them their Spiritualism. They will promise for a time to abandon it, but when trouble or danger comes upon them, they *will* invoke the aid of their ancestral Spirits."

Mr. Taylor, the missionary, says that when he reproached those who had "gone back" to their consultation with Spirits, that they were devils, and it was forbidden in scripture to have anything to do with them, the savage to whom he spoke replied, "They make our hearts light, and tell us how to be good; that scripture is a fool, and do not know how to tell bad devil, from good spirit. We know difference; leave bad devil alone, but keep good spirit always."

In the Fiji and Sandwich Islands are scattered many white residents who are good Spiritualists in the modern sense of the term. Some of these worthy friends have sent the author accounts of the phenomena which occur at their circles, and although it is not sufficiently varied to interest the reader, it may be mentioned that several ladies and gentlemen in both groups of islands, speak of the remarkable Mediumistic powers of the natives, and express hopes that *when they become civilized*, and can be made to act in concert with their white employers, through their finely adapted organizations, Spiritual phenomena of a very striking character can be unfolded amongst them.

One gentleman cultivating sugar, and employing a large number of Kanakas on his plantation says:—"Our circles—at which six of my Kanakas sit regularly — are favoured with manifestations of the most stupendous physical force I have ever witnessed. Spirits appear bodily in our midst; lift the children up to the ceiling, tossing them about like nurses. They bring in good-sized bushes, uprooted from the garden, and dash them down in our midst, but never so as to hurt us." . . . . He adds, "If we could but succeed in uprooting the manifold wild superstitions with which these Kanaka heads are crowded; and substitute the calm rational doctrines which our white spirit visitants teach, the magnetic organizations of these natives make them such splendid Mediums, that we might have amongst them a glorious stronghold of the Spiritual faith. Some of my white neighbours"—he adds—"think I practise magic, and are ready to denounce me to the authorities, and this reminds me, how much we have to do in converting Christians *back* to the teachings of their Master, as well as heathens *forward* to the same God."

In the West India Islands, some of which have been visited by the author, we find the belief in Spiritual existence prevailing it is true, but it takes a far lower and more degraded form amongst the native negro population than amongst the high spirited, independent races of the Polynesian Isles. The whites are for the most part, too indolent, luxurious, and enervated by the influence of their tropical climate, to care for any ideas of a Spiritual character, except such as are thought out for them by their ministers.

Here and there a few Spiritualists of the European type may be found, but how much they have to contend with, may be noted from the following paragraph taken from the American *Banner of Light:*—

"Much interest exists in Havana in Spiritualism, but the opposition to the printing and publishing of anything in connection with it acts as a hindrance to the extension of knowledge respecting it. Lately a box of books sent to M. Joseph Mauri was received by him and heavy duties paid on them. They were then submitted to the press censorship, and were ordered to be returned whence they came, because they were adverse to the religion of the State and denied the divinity of Christ. M. Mauri undertook to issue a journal, *La Lumière d'Outretombe;* but its publication was interdicted by the authorities. Yet these efforts to stay the tide of liberalism, and shut out the light of spiritual truth, produce results far different from what were intended, and Spiritualism is progressing with marvellous rapidity in Cuba, the number of converts being constantly on the increase. Several clairvoyant, trance and writing mediums are on the Island, and their services in great demand."

Cuba as a favourite resort of valetudinarians from European countries, fares better than some of the other West India Islands, where the inveterate belief of the black population in "Duppies" or spirits of deceased persons who are supposed to live in the houses they formerly inhabited, and interfere in every thing, communicates an ill odour to the idea of things spiritual, which repels the proud aristocrats of the islands from "such vulgar themes."

These negroes also practise "Obi," and all manner of Fetish rites, and they cannot be persuaded out of them by the commands of their masters or the teachings of the missionaries. A San Domingo priest, a coloured man, and a most eloquent preacher, told the author, that from childhood he had been subject to trances, dreams, and visions. When he preached, he said, he could not even look at his notes, but poured forth the thoughts that rushed into his mind unbidden. He invariably saw the church full of Spirits, both black and white. White Spirits of most beautiful and exalted appearance often brought large bands of dark degraded-looking beings to the church, to hear the preaching, and he knew he was inspired by a circle of Spirits, whose radiant heads he could see filling the air around him; "in short," he added, "I preach to two congregations, and have known from childhood, that the Spirit world was all around us and the veil is very thin which separates us. I regard this Spirit world, as the soul world of this earth, and deem we could no more subsist without it, than the body could exist without soul. When therefore my poor parishioners tell me they see the 'Duppy,' and that 'Duppies,' who were their fathers, mothers, and children, inhabit their houses, and work with, and talk, and help them, my lips are sealed. I believe them, and cannot tell a lie simply because— as a Christian minister—I ought not to encourage Spiritualism."

Such is an *inside* view of the beliefs which prevail amongst some of the most intelligent, and least intelligent, of the West Indian native islanders. The superstitions of the lower classes are as gross, wild, and fetish, as those of their African progenitors, but Spiritualism is slowly but surely, creating a deep impress upon the minds of the higher classes, and converting the disgust and contempt they formerly felt towards the superstitious rites of the people, into a philosophic realization that Spiritualism is one, and Spiritualists many; the manifestation of the power, taking the form and expression of the nation and caste, by whom it is manifested.

The ancestors of the West Indian negroes, the inhabitants of Central Africa, and Guinea, believe in Spirits, but with them, all Spiritual beings, even the souls of their fathers and mothers, when disembodied, are "devils," and must be propitiated, to prevent their working harm; hence, burnt offerings, sacrifices, and even the immolation of human beings.

To the Guinea negro then, the Spirits of ancestors are real, but they are "devils," only to be feared. To the West Indian negro, they are "duppies," household deities, half feared, and half loved, and treated respectfully, in view of *what they might do.* In New Orleans, the negro Vaudoo men and women summon "the Spirits," to heal the sick, and give "good luck," as well as to work harm to enemies. In Baltimore and Washington, educated and intelligent coloured men and women (still negroes) hold circles, invoke Spirits as they would call upon beloved friends and relations, and regard the Spirit world in exactly the same light as did the coloured preacher of San Domingo, whose words were quoted above.

We must now take a glance at the Spiritualism which prevails in South Africa, a section of country which has been bridged over in point of remoteness, by the visits of several good Mediums and Spiritual Propagandists from Europe and America.

For some years past, the open communion with Spirits practised in the modern circle seems to have been anticipated by reports of "hauntings," and supernatural disturbances in various South African districts. Whether attention was drawn to this subject by the contagion of Spiritualism in the air, or the controlling Spirits of the new movement adopted this method of attracting public notice, we need not pause to enquire ; it is enough that the rumour of "supernatural disturbances" began to be circulated in many of the principal towns and villages as early as 1870. The following sketches, detailing the methods of investigation pursued, in the early days of South African Spiritualism, may prove of some interest to the reader, especially as they are related by Aylward in his popular work entitled, "The Transvaal of To-day." This author says there was a certain house in Natal, from which several families—who had successively tried to inhabit it—had been driven, by the prevalence of unaccountable and persistent disturbances. Officials of high position had been called upon to assist in unravelling the mystery, but all to no purpose. At length, a party of persons, some of whom the author hints were Spiritualists, others being experienced "exorcists," and mere lookers on, determined to visit the house in set form, and endeavour to "exorcise" the ghostly inhabitants. Aylward gives the following account of the proceedings that ensued :—

" On the arrival of the party of investigators and exorcists, an armed watch was placed around the house outside. The guard being posted, seven men entered and carefully fastened all the doors and windows. The candles were lighted and in deep silence the watch was commenced. Ten minutes after the arrival of the guests the *séance* commenced by the fall of half-a-dozen pomegranates on the table. This was succeeded by a shower of gravel, the small stones of which I had the curiosity to inspect. No pebbles of a similar nature were to be found within ten miles of the place. One of the guards got up to examine the pomegranates. He had no sooner left his chair than it was flung with great violence after him ; then lumps of ironstone, the smallest of which weighed ten pounds, began dropping from unexpected places, and a mass of clay appeared to tumble through the roof, breaking and scattering about the floor, as if it had come from a considerable height. The remarkable feature about the whole affair was that not one missile struck or injured any of the large party now assembled in the small room. Their excitement was increased by hearing a violent banging at one of the shuttered openings, but which, as we afterwards learned, attracted no attention from the outside guard. McCormyck, who is still a living witness of the facts of this entertainment, being, after his own fashion, a pious man, determined to show the power of his faith and the strength of the exorcisms at his command. He stood up with uncovered head and boldly addressed the ghost in Irish, ordering it in the most solemn manner, and by the most sacred influence known to Christians, to retire to where the wicked ought to cease from troubling, and the weary are presumed—by all but Spiritualists—to take their rest. Whether led on by his subject he went too far or not I cannot say ; but he was stopped in the midst of a torrent of eloquence by what he afterwards described as a 'kick from a three-year-old ;' in fact, a 'young paving stone' brought him to his senses and his seat at the same time. This violent counter-attack was too much for the visitors ; already in a state of high alarm, they flung open the doors, and dashed out into the moonlight, followed by showers of stones, mealie cobs, potatoes, pomegranates, oranges, and all the handy weapons of South African Spiritual warfare that the deceased had accumulated—where ?"

Mr. Aylward adds another sketch of an adventure occurring in the same weird neighbourhood to one of his most intimate friends, from whom he received an account of the occurrence, and for whose veracity and the unquestionable reliance that might be placed upon his statement, Mr. Aylward strongly vouches. He says :—

" My friend was riding one day on a road skirted on the left by high embankments, while the right sloped away into grassy meadows, when a thunderstorm coming up from behind, caused him to look back, that he might calculate whether he could reach the town, two miles in front of him, without being caught in the rain. The horse, as horses will, looked around and backward at the same time. In a moment the brute was madly plunging, striving to bolt up the high bank, and endeavouring with evident terror, to get away from some fearful thing. . . . It was 4 p.m. on an ordinary summer afternoon. . . . Strongly interested by the fear so palpably exhibited by his horse, . . . the rider again turned his eyes towards the rapidly approaching storm. . . . He was not a superstitious man, he was not drunk, or suffering from low spirits, or 'want of spirits,' and yet he saw in the broad daylight, coming floating towards him, with outstretched arms in front of the moving mass of rain, but several feet raised from the earth, a young, fair, ethereal, golden-haired female, whose robes of glittering white trailed just over the highest points of the grass. She spoke not, but came steadily down upon him in advance of the storm. His horse now kicked and plunged more madly than ever, and at length, wild with terror, snapped the strong bridle reins into pieces, and tore away in headlong flight straight down the roadway to the distant village. . . . Twice during the headlong gallop, the rider turned his head to watch the swiftly following rain, which was still preceded by the fair girl and her outstretched arms."

CAPE TOWN.

The progress of Spiritualism in this remote quarter of the globe, strikingly illustrates the possibilities which grow out of the efforts of one determined and earnest mind when bent upon carrying its purpose into practical effect. Spiritualism in Cape Town owes its first unfoldment entirely to the energetic leadership of Mr. Berks T. Hutchinson, a name equally well known and esteemed now, in the annals of the cause, whilst this gentleman's conversion to the belief is due, according to his own statement, to what the world would call a mere passing incident, but one which the Spiritualist recognises as a link in the chain of concerted action forged by the guardian spirits of this mundane sphere.

Mr. Hutchinson informed the author, that the subject of Spiritualism was first brought to his notice by an American gentleman, a Dr. Wilson, who, on his way to the diamond fields in the year 1872, chanced to make Mr. Hutchinson's acquaintance. Being an enthusiastic believer in Spiritualism, Dr. Wilson had much to say on the subject to Mr. Hutchinson, and at parting with him, strongly urged him to subscribe to the *Banner of Light*, one of the chief organs of *the cause* in America. Before Mr. Hutchinson's interest in Dr. Wilson's tidings had time to cool, another earnest propagandist called at Table Bay, in the person of Mr. Holmes, photographer of the United States gunboat Swatara. By this new ally Mr. Hutchinson was induced to experiment in the formation of circles, at one of which Mr. H.'s sister became developed as a fine rapping test Medium. Hence arose the means of furnishing evidence which not only convinced the members of the experimental circles, but many others outside their ranks, of the truth of Spirit communion.

Mr. Hutchinson says of his own sentiments at this time :—

" Being naturally of an enthusiastic turn of mind, I believed that every one would leap for joy at the glad tidings I had to communicate, but to my great sorrow and surprise I found myself shunned and avoided by my nearest and dearest friends, and none but those who have experienced a similar fate can imagine the pain I experienced at being tabooed and reviled for proclaiming my honest convictions, and that on so noble and glorious a revelation as immortality demonstrated."

Mr. Hutchinson's gallant defence of his newly found religion and the devotion with which he promulgated it, may be judged of by the fact, that he built a fine hall capable of accommodating some 500 persons, solely for the purpose of holding Spiritual meetings ; that he organised a psychological society, and indefatigably promoted the formation of circles, at which several good physical Mediums were developed.   In addition to these untiring and costly efforts to promote the advancement of the great truth he realised, Mr. Hutchinson started a paper devoted to the interests of Spiritualism, and although its career was short lived for lack of adequate support, it was a well written and interesting publication, and at a later period in the history of Colonial Spiritualism would have doubtless proved a genuine success.

Undaunted by the vast financial outlay which his efforts entailed upon him, Mr. Hutchinson succeeded in procuring the services of the Rev. J. M. Peebles, who in a fine series of lectures on the Spiritual philosophy, did much to enlighten his audiences on the sublimity and high import of Spiritualism.   Mr. Hutchinson made a trip to England in 1877, and being greatly struck with the manifestations of physical power exhibited through the Mediumship of Mr. Eglinton, a young gentleman much esteemed and admired by the Spiritualists of London, he induced him to come to Cape Town, for the dual purpose of benefiting a fragile constitution and affording the inhabitants of The Cape opportunities of witnessing his (Mr. Eglinton's) unrivalled mediumistic endowments.

Before concluding our brief notice of Cape Town Spiritualism, it may interest the reader to peruse at least one thoroughly well-attested account of Mr. Eglinton's *séances*.   It must be added that although the manifestations of Spirit power through that excellent instrument were very varied, and included nearly every form of intelligence as well as physical power known in the modern dispensation, our space only admits of one narrative, and this must be taken as representative, not only of Mr. Eglinton's Mediumship generally, but also of the crucial modes in which his powers were tested.   The Spiritualists of Cape Town published amongst many other accounts of Mr. Eglinton's *séances* the following report in the London *Spiritualist* of January, 1879:—

"When the reports from Amsterdam reached this town, the local papers of course, made the most of them, and were not choice in their expressions about the deceivers and the deceived.   Some Spiritualists even wavered in their belief ; but the *séance* now described has served to bind them together more firmly than before.   Mr. Eglinton had ceased to be a professional medium, and was not in any way identified with our society. It was proposed to ask him to give a *séance* on purpose to make known if he produced his materialisations as these exposers would have us believe.   Not that we doubted him, for he had been giving *séances* with unvarying success ever since he landed here, and his demeanour, candour, and honesty had much endeared him to us.   We kept our purpose entirely quiet, and not until the circle (a select party of Spiritualists) had met, and the medium arrived, did we place our object before him.

"We desired that a committee of three should search him, to which he at first demurred, but when we explained that it was the wish of his guides that we should do so, he immediately consented.   The room was thoroughly scrutinised, and we aver that there were no cupboards or carpets to conceal any articles, and the most rigid search failed to reveal anything concealed on his person.   The cabinet was simply formed, by suspending two curtains made of black silesia across a corner of the room, the walls of which are very solid, the floor uncarpeted, *and without trap doors.*   The medium, never leaving our sight, retired into the cabinet, seating himself on a chair provided for the purpose.   The sitters, sixteen in number, were arranged in the form of a double horse-shoe around the cabinet.   Shortly after prayer had been offered and a voluntary played on the harmonium by our organist, the tall and graceful form of Abdullah was seen in strong gaslight, clothed in a profusion of snowy drapery, his sparkling jewels flashing out to us the scintillating rays of light.   He bowed gracefully to the sitters, came out from the cabinet, and walked close up to us.   He is apparently five or six inches taller than Mr. Eglinton, slight in figure, with only one arm, and of wholly different physique to the medium.

"Next there appeared in front of the cabinet a small portion of white drapery, and above it a head. It was most strange and weird-like to see nothing but an apparently human head moving about. Very soon two hands materialised, and, taking hold of the white drapery, commenced shaking it out, a voice keeping up an animated conversation all the time. Gradually the mass of drapery grew more profuse, and we noticed that the head then placed itself upon a neck, which soon connected itself with a body, rising, as it were, out of the drapery. It was the form of our dear friend and worker 'Joey,' who remarked, 'There, that's the way I build myself up.' Thus he appeared, formed seemingly out of nothing, in the light, and without the slightest attempt at concealment or mystification, thus solving, to our unbounded satisfaction, one of the most momentous problems of the nineteenth century. Joey's form is wholly unlike that of the sensitive, being smaller, slighter, and of weaker physique altogether. The next form was that of a tall, graceful, good-looking lady, clothed from head to foot in a flowing garment, not unlike a fine Indian mull muslin, and very different in texture to that of the preceding figures. She moved out of the cabinet, and was plainly seen by all, and clearly recognised by several as a Miss Georgina Handley, formerly a sister of mercy in this town. The fourth figure proved to be that of a male, stepping out *immediately* after the last figure. He was recognised as the father of one of the sitters, and the loved husband of another. A marvellous manifestation now took place, for, after bowing to the sitters, he retired to the cabinet, and with the aid of another male spirit, brought the medium right out of the cabinet into full view of the sitters, so that *the medium and two male spirits were distinctly seen at the same time.* They then took Mr. Eglinton back again to the cabinet, and throwing back the curtains showed him reclining in his chair, deeply entranced. The curtains closed on these marvels, and almost instantly the *petite* form of 'Lily,' the much-loved and last plucked flower of our friend, Mr. Hutchinson, came into the circle, and, in childlike confidence, placed her tiny hand on the knee of one of the sitters, and looked up into his face with the touching appeal of "Do you know me?" On her retiring, another female figure appeared of medium height, with flowing garments and light hair, but only for a moment, and was instantly recognised as the sister of a sitter. The difference between this figure and that of Miss Handley was striking, one being tall with somewhat dark hair ; the other considerably shorter and fairer. Six forms had already appeared, yet our friends had not quite done, for suddenly Abdullah drew aside the curtain, and we witnessed the wondrous phenomenon of 'Lily' retiring apparently into the form of Miss Handley, who in turn retired into the body of our faithful medium, followed instantly by the disappearance of Abdullah ; and thus ended the most marvellous manifestation of power and conclusive evidence of Spirit presence and identity yet seen in Southern Africa. Let who will deny these facts, there they remain, and if the evidence of sixteen respectable, intelligent, and *sane* persons, who would unhesitatingly expose trickery (were it possible), is of any value, then we say we have scored a triumph which no amount of deceit or fraud can ever undo.

"That this report is correct we affirm and declare, as witness our signatures :—

<table>
<tr><td>"Berks T. Hutchinson,</td><td>E. Hammick,</td></tr>
<tr><td>Carrie J. Hutchinson,</td><td>F. Williams,</td></tr>
<tr><td>Helene Otto,</td><td>J. F. Marshall,</td></tr>
<tr><td>M. F. Kohler,</td><td>E. Kingsch,</td></tr>
<tr><td>George Silver,</td><td>S. T. Marchant."</td></tr>
</table>

"Cape Town, South Africa, Dec. 3rd, 1878."

We present this statement without comment, except a strong asseveration of the entire honesty, good faith, and reliability of the esteemed narrator, Mr. Hutchinson, and the well-known respectability of his fellow witnesses.

Of course it will be understood that Mr. Hutchinson has secured many noble and effective allies in his arduous undertakings. Mr. Alfred Teague, Mr. Marchant, Mr. C. M. Cogm, and Mr. Simkiss, the latter once known as a devoted advocate of Spiritualism in Wolverhampton, England ; these gentlemen and many others of good repute and standing bravely uphold the flag of the cause in Cape Town, and amidst disadvantages which the cosmopolitan of other countries can never even dream of, maintain its advocacy after the fashion of a single warrior against a host. Mr. Berks T. Hutchinson concludes a brief and modest sketch of his own share in the work of propagandism as follows :—" For the last few years, for various reasons I have taken no active part in spreading the truth, but I never let an opportunity pass of ventilating the subject or lending works out of my library. . . . We have a new Mesmeric and Psychological Society of which I am a member. . . . The light of Spirit communion," he adds, "will never go out in this sunny land "—a conclusion in which he is confirmed by many of the faithful and self-sacrificing men and women whose good names and good services for Cape Town Spiritualism we have been unable to report, but whose efficient labours we feel entire confidence will be found inscribed in the archives of the still brighter land whose sun will know no setting.

CHAPTER XXXV.

SPIRITUALISM IN SOUTH AMERICA, MEXICO, &C.

To the author's work on "Modern American Spiritualism," about the 470th page, will be found a series of communications by Mr. Seth Driggs giving accounts of circles held at Caracas, Venezuela, together with numerous details concerning the status of Spiritualism in the South American Republic. These communications are dated 1865-6, and refer to scenes enacted at a still earlier period. Great changes have been wrought during the succeeding eighteen years, in the Spiritual progress of South America, as the following pages of this chapter will show.

SPIRITUALISM IN MEXICO.

For many graphic accounts of Spiritual progress in Mexico, the author is indebted to the report of Don A. Gamboa, a gentleman residing near the town of Acapulco, and one who although generally too reserved to make his opinions known, has quietly, and generously devoted many years of his life and much of his means, to the advancement of the cause of Spiritualism. Don Gamboa affirms, that there are many earnest and aristocratic supporters of Spiritualism in Mexico, amongst whom he names, General Gonzales, Don Antonio Santago, the president of the Spiritual Society, numbering over one hundred and twenty-five members ; Don E. Alvarez, Don S. Sierra, and Don J. Cordero, an eminent advocate, and the esteemed editor of an excellent paper published in the Spanish language, entitled *La Illustracion Espirita.*

Amongst the contributors to this journal are several ladies and gentlemen of rank and literary ability, whilst the circles held in different parts of the country, although strictly private, are very numerous, and display Mediumship of a high order, especially when the Media are ladies—or as it often happens—very young persons.

Don Gamboa is himself fortunate in possessing a Medium in his own family, in the person of his little daughter, a young girl of fifteen, who, though unfortunately a cripple, and confined to her lonely plantation home by a severe affection of the spine, is still a remarkable clairvoyant, seeress, and Spirit Medium. Under influence, this young lady can read through closed books, tell the nature and colour of any object presented to her blindfolded, has described distant scenes and places, though she has never quitted Mexico, and always predicts correctly what visitors are coming, or any event of importance about to occur in the family.

On account of her invalid condition, the parents refuse to allow their daughter to be visited, or to exhibit her wonderful powers to any but intimate friends, but as her governess is an excellent planchette writer and rapping Medium, Don Gamboa says—to use his own words—"We have for years been living more in heaven than on earth, surrounded and ministered unto by angels, and so radiantly happy, that we shrink from contact with the hard cold world, just as our Amalia mourns and shivers when her Spirit friends return her from flights in the sunny skies, and fragrant airs of the glorious summer land, to the dull grey mists of this weary earth."

Don Gamboa permits the author to mention the fact of the supernal revelations given to his highly-favoured family, but desires it to be added, that no correspondence is answered, nor are visits received from curious enquirers outside his own immediate circle. He mentions Mr. Simonson as a good writing and impressional Medium of Panama; Senora Dolores Portugal, as a fine trance and magnetic Medium; Signor Silvio Pellico, and several other good writing Mediums, and quite a number of others distinguished for their various gifts as trance speakers, pantomimic, tipping, and seeing Media.

Don Gamboa's commercial pursuits have frequently called him to the United States, where he has seen much of American Spiritualism.

He complains of the cold materialistic way in which circles are conducted there, and contrasts them with the solemnity and respect with which Mexican Spiritualists invoke the presence of their "honoured dead." He says: "Our circles never begin without heartfelt prayers, then invocations to Spirits, spoken or sung, with skill and artistic taste. Sometimes voluntaries are played on the harmonium, harp, or other instruments, manipulated with sufficient good taste to satisfy the elevated inhabitants of a higher region; after which, to the ringing of a sweet-toned bell, the members of the circles compose themselves to receive messages from Spirits, in the accustomed way."

From a number of communications on "The divine harmony of the superior regions," given in the Mexican circles, we select one which is a striking confession of a Spirit, who says in reference to the immoral life he had lived on earth :—

"On entering the spirit world the first remembrance that assailed me was of the woman whom I had injured. I returned to the abode of my unhappy victim, and saw her, pale and sad, bending over the cradle of our child. Deeply penitent, I asked forgiveness and sought with tenderness to assuage her tears. I madly fondled the little one I had left upon the earth without a name. But all was silence. No one heard or heeded me. Always at her side and hearing her murmur my name between her sobs and tears, but my penitence and grief reaches her not, and I must seek the aid of the good who practise their virtues in silence and know something of the life beyond the tomb. Could Spiritualists realize that in our selfishness we are making for ourselves a bed that our morally mutilated forms must fit, perhaps the gauge of virtue would be more closely watched."

We now avail ourselves of Dr. G. L. Ditson's scholarly articles prepared each week for the *Banner of Light* to give a farther account of the literature as well as the Spiritual status of the cause in Mexico, and other strongholds of "the faith" in South America.

Writing in 1880 of Don Gonzales' excellent paper, published in Mexico City, Dr. Ditson says :—

"Notwithstanding the troubled waters of the ever unfortunate Mexico, her able exponent of Spiritualism, *La Illustracion Espirita* (August number), has reached me in due time. Don Gonzales's rich, attractive magazine gives no evidence that the political turmoil surrounding him has reached his sanctum, for his pages are, as usual, aglow with all that is valuable to investigators in the realm of our faith and inviting to the scholar who would penetrate the deeper mysteries that underlie the mind's progress.

"The *Illustracion* before me opens with a learned consideration of the 'Doctrine of the Trinity,' by Don Juan Cordero—its literary, historical, and religious aspect. In the course of his remarks Don Cordero says : 'From a historical point of view the dogma in question is a step backward in the career of progress. . . . Why reject the Olympus of the Greeks if you are to substitute for it the Olympus of the Romans ? . . . Why condemn as absurd the *avatars* of Vishnu, yet proclaim the incarnation of the Divine Word ? For what and why laugh at a God with three faces (although monstrous), to substitute one God composed of three Gods, an individual composed of three individuals distinct in themselves ? Why condemn the adoration of the stars and substitute for them a piece of wood ?' After referring to what has been established by religious councils the writer says : 'Without doing injustice to the true value of those venerable " Concilios," we will cite as a simple contemporaneous appreciation of them a passage from a letter directed to Procopius by San Gregorio Nazianceno, who presided at the Grand Council of Constantinople (A. D. 851) : "I have fear of these Councils. I have not seen one that has not done more evil than good, or had a good end ; the spirit of disputation, vanity, and ambition dominates them, and he who among them proposes a reformation of abuses runs the risk of being accused without correcting them." ' "

We conclude this brief notice of Spiritualism in Mexico with an extract from a late number of the American *Boston Herald*, in which we find the following account of a tribe of Indians located at New Mexico, and claiming to be the direct descendants of the most ancient Aztecs, whose customs, traditions, and ceremonials, they affirm they religiously cherish. The accounts of these people, called the "Zuñi Indians," are furnished by a Mr. Cushing, a gentleman who was sent out by the Smithsonian Institution of Washington, America, to report upon the condition of the Indian tribes of New Mexico, and who is now adopted among the Zuñis.

The Editor of the *Boston Herald*, commenting on Mr. Cushing's corres pondence, says :—

"Having made the religion of the Zuñis a subject of close study he has learned that the worship and traditions of Montezuma—so long accepted in all accounts of the Aztecs—have no foundation in fact. He has found the existence of twelve sacred orders, with their priests, and their secret rites as carefully guarded as the secrets of Freemasonry, an institution to which these orders have a strange resemblance. Into several of these orders he has been initiated, and has penetrated to their inmost secrets, obtaining a knowledge of ceremonials both beautiful, profound and grotesque in character. 'But,' adds this correspondent, 'the most marvellous discovery he has made in connection with their religion is the grand fact that their faith is the same thing as Modern Spiritualism. The Zuñis have their circles, their mediums, their communications from the spirit-world, their materializations—precisely like those of the Spiritists of civilised life. Their *séances* are often so absorbing that they are kept up all night. Their belief in the phenomena explains many strange things about their religion which Mr. Cushing was unable to account for until he hit upon it—they had kept it carefully guarded months after he was on most intimate terms with them—by telling them about certain spiritistic phenomena he had himself witnessed, thus gaining their sympathy as apparently a fellow believer.'

"The Zuñis have religious ceremonials, sacred orders and public festivals, in which songs and prayers are employed that have been handed down for very many generations without the changing of a single word. Mr. Cushing's adopted father is the second priest of the tribe, a man of a beautifully loving and gentle nature. Upon the return of one of their number from a dangerous expedition, the following prayer was offered by him :

" 'All spirits ! we ask for your light. Far and in parts unknown, where the world is filled with danger, where things forbidden and the unknown are, thence ye have brought back our child. We thank ye ! In spite of all danger, we now speak to each other again. We now see one another again. Thanks. Therefore your light we ask, and we will meet ye with your own blessing.' "

Dr. Ditson says in connexion with the *Revista Espiritista* of 1877 :—

"*Revista Espiritista*, of Monte Video. This is the oldest, I think, of South American periodicals, and, though containing but eight pages, overflows with fraternal good will, plain truths, such as we need and love, and such as its editor, Don Justo de Espada, invites us to as to a grateful feast." . . . .

"The *Revista Espiritista*, of Monte Video, has always some valuable sentiments from its editor, Don Espada, and the *Angel Guardian ;* it also in the present issue quotes from the ' *Lerida* (suppressed) *Sentido* " what the Bishop of that district has been doing ; but says that after his severe anathemas against this publication and all Liberals, the subscriptions to the *Sentido* had increased, and even a serenade had been given to the Liberals of Bilboa." . . . .

In 1878 Dr. Ditson says of this same paper :—

" The editor of this pioneer in our cause, in a land where Catholicism has held undisputed sway for centuries, has doubtless up-hill work, with not many assistants ; yet he seems to be a host in himself, and brings out regularly his heraldic *Revista*, a kind of red flag, such as is used in the arena in the favourite Spanish amusement of bull-baiting. He relies principally upon his own pen, though he has other able contributors, such as Dona Amalié Soler, who in the present number writes of ' What am I ?' There is also an article from a Belgian paper, which, with the *Revista*, still dwells much upon ' objections to paid mediumship.' " . . . .

Of the leading Spiritual paper of Buenos Ayres, Dr. Ditson gives a number of laudatory notices, and as they contain some interesting mementos concerning the Spiritualistic doings of that important town, we shall give some extended excerpts from the collection in our possession.
The first of 1880 reads thus :—

" Though Mexico formerly furnished us with the finest magazines and spiritualistic literature anywhere to be found, she seems to have abandoned the field to the Spanish-speaking people of the South. Buenos Ayres, which now produces the *Constancia*, has not neglected her opportunity, and the periodical in hand from that fair city vies with our very best. Some remarks on Allan Kardec ; a short discourse delivered by Don H. Mayor before the ' Constancia Society,' ' Observations on Magnetism,' or odic force, in which Baron Reichenbach is frequently referred to, and ' Materialization,' are the first articles that claim attention in the present issue. . . .

" Following an article on ' What there is Positive Respecting Astrology,' and in which the most gloomy forebodings are entertained respecting our immediate future, M. Clavairoz, formerly a French Consul-General, says : ' The Mother Shipton evoked by the London *Spiritualist* declares that at this moment there is not a single true astrologer upon the face of the earth. Now this name of Mother Shipton was the pseudonym under which the celebrated Roger Bacon concealed himself ; this encyclopedic genius, whose investigations in the thirteenth century elicited the admiration of his contemporaries who were occupied with astrology, . . . was in accord with Nostradamus when he said that the world would come to an end in 1881. But it is understood that the end of the world refers wholly to a moral state ; that it signifies the advent of a new reign ; but it is curious to observe at least the coincidence of all these prophecies ; and the conjunction of the four planets. . . .

" Quoting from the *Gaulois* of May 16th, 1869, the *Constancia* has the following : A young lawyer going from Paris to Piedmont was assassinated ; but of this terrible affair, or the whereabouts of the body, nothing was known till a clairvoyant was consulted. This psychic gave a description of the place where the deed was committed, and described the assassin, a well-dressed man who travelled with his victim. The murderer and the murdered youth were thus discovered, and all the minute particulars were verified."

Another journalistic notice of *La Constancia* is given in a recent number of the *Religio Philosophical Journal* of Chicago, and reads as follows :—

"The *Constancia* is a monthly Spiritual review, published in Buenos Ayres, and is now in its fourth year. The September number has reached us, and we find it to be the most satisfactory publication of the kind that we have ever seen from our sister continent. Twenty-four pages of the thirty-two which it comprises, are devoted to a discourse pronounced against Spiritualism by Prof. D. Miguel Puiggari, and its refutation by Senor Hernandez, which latter is the most searching and powerful document that we have ever seen from any source, and we only wish that we had time and space to reproduce it."

"The *Constancia* is not the only Spiritual journal published in Buenos Ayres, for it returns the salutation of a new contemporary called *La Fraternidad* in the following graceful terms :—

"'We accept the salutation with a joyful heart, for we feel the necessity of publications of this sort in a centre so vast as this in order that it may not be supposed that the number of believers is small, but that there are readers for the grand philosophy which we have embraced and that the number of followers is already legion.'"

Writing of Spiritualism in South America in October, 1881, the editor of *Light* (London), says :

"The *Constancia*, a monthly Spiritualist review of Buenos Ayres, dated 30th of July last, contains the report of the General Assembly of the Buenos Ayres Spiritualist Society, including the President's address in which he urges the members of the society not to neglect their attendance at the different meetings, but each to do his share in adding to the brilliancy of Spiritual light. 'The Spirits,' he says, 'understand us thoroughly, and ask our continual assiduous assistance. We, on the other hand, do not comprehend our own selves, while imprisoned in this obscure corporeal dungeon. Let us then accede to the request of those invisible brothers who, with so much interest, invite us to attend these reunions.'

"Then follows the account of the work done by the various sections of the society, and short reports of trance speeches, magnetic sessions, &c. A number of healing prescriptions are mentioned as having been given through the mediumship of Donna Juana de Navajas, a well-known local medium. A series of monthly conferences are held under the auspices of the society, the subject in July being the Theory of Spontaneous Physical Manifestations. The subjects down for discussion in August were : 'Bi-corporeity and Transfiguration,' 'Laboratory of the Invisible World,' 'Places visited by Spirits,' 'Nature of the Communications, &c., &c. A paragraph follows copied from the *Heraldo de San Nicolas*, of the 28th June, 1881, reporting the speech of Don Rafael Hernandez, a leading Spiritualist, at the anniversary banquet of the 'Union' Masonic Lodge. The oration was equally Spiritualistic and Masonic, and was full of sublime sentiments.

"The number before us also contains a communication from the eloquent pen of Amalia Domingo y Soler, a writer and authoress well known to all Spiritualists who are acquainted with the work in Spain. The article was originally written in the *Luz del Porvenir* (Light of the Future), edited by Madame Domingo y Soler, and claims for woman her proper position in society ; to attain which her Spiritual education should be taken in hand, and the blossom of truth gradually unfolded before her eyes."

"THE BRAZILIAN SPIRITUAL PRESS.

"The following Spiritualistic papers have been published from time to time in various parts of the Brazilian empire :—In the Province of Bahia, 1865, *O Monitor de Além Tumulo*—(The Monitor from Beyond the Tomb)—a monthly journal ; at Rio de Janeiro, in 1875, the *Revista Espirita* (Spiritual Review), monthly ; in 1881, the *Revista da Sociedade Academica* ; in San Pablo, at the city of Areas, the *Uniao e Cronca* (Union and Chronicle) ; at Pernambuco in the city of Recife, *A Cruz* (The Cross) ; and we are told that there will shortly be published in this city an organ for the Spiritual circles of the municipality.—*Revista*, of Rio de Janeiro."

The promise contained in the above paragraph, taken from one of the secular papers of Rio de Janeiro, was soon after its publication realised by the appearance of *La Revista*, a title so common amongst these South American journals that their number is hardly appreciated in the confusion of names. Dr. Ditson notices one of the best of these journals, published in the Portuguese language, as follows :—

"The *Revista da Sociedade Academica*, No. 7, of Rio de Janeiro, in the Portuguese language, has come to hand. It is a very handsome magazine of upwards of thirty pages, and contains many articles of the first importance. . . . It was in 1865, in the city of S. Salvador, capital of the province of Bahia, that the first Society of Spiritualists, with a written constitution, was formed ; and for eight years, animated by the salutary doctrines of Spiritualism, it worked and fought for the cause. In 1869 it published a journal entitled, *Echo from Beyond the Tomb.* In 1872 a new society was formed for the exclusive scientific investigation of Spiritualism, and was called the "Associacion Spiritica Brazileira." It adopted as a basis of operations Allan Kardec's works. It started a periodical and a library. In 1880 in Campos, a flourishing city in the province of Rio de Janeiro, there was formed another society—the *S. Campista de Estudos Spiritas,* and many members were added to it, &c., but they had to withstand the usual amount of calumnies.

"*La Luz de Sion* is the name of a spiritualistic periodical published at Bogota, in the United States of Colombia. It has very attractive matter taken from the work, 'Roma and the Evangelio ;' some 'Letters of Lavater,' and some miscellaneous articles.

"*La Revelacion,* of Buenos Ayres, reappears again, 'after a suspension caused by the Jesuits, the principal barriers to modern progress,' says a European paper.

"*La Ley de Amor,* of Merida, Yucatan (July 16th and August 1st), has also reached me. A very sensible article from the 'Circle Peralta' on the historical and present daily proofs of Spiritualism, opens the July number. The *Ley* also says 'that there have been established in our state various "circles" for spiritualistic studies.' From Tobasco have been received notices of the 'rapid advance of the consoling doctrine of Spiritualism.' At the 'circle' of *La Cruz* they have a valuable medium, a *somnambule lucida,* who has made some remarkable cures."

Another notice of this paper says :—

"*La Ley de Amor,* of Yucatan. I have in hand three numbers of this interesting little journal, bearing dates October 9th and 25th and November 10th. The first article that claims attention is from the graceful pen of the poetess, Donna Amalia Soler. Briefly I will report her as saying : 'In a reunion of Spiritualists an elegant youth presented himself, but expressed his incredulity in the alleged phenomena occurring among them ; still he would put a mental question. A young girl took a pencil and wrote some lines in a large hand, exclaiming in innocent surprise : "Oh, what a reply ! What nonsense !" The young man took it and read, growing sober and pale as he did so ; "*En el claustro materno.*" It is true,' he said, 'for I came into the world three months after the death of my father ; and my question was, "Where was I at that solemn event ?" At another spiritualistic gathering was an Englishman who maintained a kind of stolid indifference to all that occurred, but finally, with the rest, promised to attend mass the next day at eight o'clock in the church of St. Paul. All went, and while the rest of the party were grouped around the high altar, he retired to a side aisle, where, seated on a bench, he read a book which he took from his pocket. At the *séance* on the following evening the Englishman said to the spirits (supposed) : "Were you content to see us all at the appointed place ?" "Yes," was the reply, "and I felt very grateful that you prayed for me, but my satisfaction was lessened by seeing one of your number perform an irreligious act—retiring to read a licentious novel." The English gentleman arose as pale as a corpse and said it was even as stated ; and then and there confessed that there must be a *spirit* that could see and feel even as we do, &c. Henceforth he was an earnest Spiritualist. 'Laugh if you will,' says our authoress, 'but that does not destroy facts.' So she continues : 'A physician, a materialist, called on a young man, a medium, and found that he had written quite a learned treatise, much above his normal capacity, on pulmonary affections. "I will believe in this thing," said he, "if my deceased wife will come and in her own handwriting will state to me something of a private nature that occurred between us." The medium soon wrote : "Spirits are not in the habit of satisfying puerile curiosity, but because of my love of you when on the earth I will give you the evidence you seek : As a pledge of my affection, in your secretary you have kept, now yellowed by time, the first letter I ever wrote to you. Some of its lines are now very faint, but the medium will copy them." . . . Julian hastened home and found the original, as copied, that he had preserved for more than twenty years, saying, "I lament the time that I have lost in not devoting myself to Spiritualism."' "

19

"The *Siglo XIX.*, of Guadaloupe, reports in a jesting manner a Spiritual manifestation which occurred to a young girl, religious and much respected, and of a good family in Gaudaloupe. The little medium experienced certain phenomena which were augmented till she saw and heard the phantom of her godmother, or guardian, who came to reproach herself for not having had the child baptized, and to have the ceremony performed. Other manifestations occurred in the child's presence, such as the flying open of doors, which doubtless aided in convincing the bishop, to whom the affair was named, that there was something in it. The baptism took place, and during the ceremony the girl and she who was serving as godmother saw the attending spirit."

"*La Aurora*, of Brazil, and *La Revista*, of Santiago de Chile, have also such communications as tend to enlighten 'all those who through fear and ignorance are still found under the clerical yoke.' Don Rafael Molina in the University has delivered a discourse demonstrating the truths of Spiritualism, as well as the heresies of the Church of Rome, which has elicited much comment."

Writing of Spiritualism in Puerto Rico in November, 1881, Dr. Ditson says :—

"*El Pelegrino* is a quarto of eight pages, and unfurls the banner of our faith with such a firm hand and such force of character that one cannot but heed and respect its pretensions. I have three numbers, dating to September 8th, and I only regret that space will limit me to a brief notice of its forcible articles. One, headed 'El cura de Utuado,' states that the dead body of Don E. Vargas was refused admittance to the Catholic church because Don V. had been a Spiritualist ; and that when the friends had taken it to the cemetery, there intolerance again met them, and it was refused a resting-place in the so-called sacred ground. Again, the conduct of the curate of Caguas in refusing to baptize the child of a Spiritualist is commented upon at great length, and most judiciously."

In the January, 1882, number of *Light*, we find the following article, which we give as our closing notice of Spiritualism in those vast regions where internal interests are so inevitably focalized by distance from other Spiritual centres, that they seem almost *terra incognita*, the fraternal spirit and enterprise which marks the propositions about to be quoted, are equally worthy of respectful attention and sympathetic response, from all quarters of the globe.

They are introduced by the editor of *La Revue Spirite* thus :—

"HOW SPIRITUALISM IS WORKING IN BRAZIL.

"Under the heading of 'Universalisation of Spiritualism,' in its December number, the *Revue Spirite* invites attention to an announcement in the *Revista da Sociedade Academica*, whose publishing office is No. 54, Praça d'Acclamaçao, Rio de Janeiro, Brazil. The *Revista* is the organ of the Brazilian Society of Spiritualists, naïvely calling itself here the Brazilian group of the human family. Having the object in view, it says, of drawing more closely together the bonds of fraternal action among Spiritualists, it proposes to exchange the *Revista* and all its publications for the organ and publications of any and every other Spiritualist society, wishing to place them on the bookshelves and reading tables of the library of the Society, which is open to the public.

" COMPETITIVE THESES.

"Further, in order to attract the attention of all, down to Materialists, to the study of the Spiritual world, we invite—it says—theses to be sent in : the subject to be—*God, the human soul and its immortality scientifically demonstrated*. As an extra inducement to engage in this work, the Society offers the sum of two contos de Reis (about 5,000 francs) to the writer of the accepted thesis, in addition to the prize awarded by the Academy. (What the prize is, is not here specified.) This is the programme :—

"'1. Every thesis sent in to be distinguished by a motto, and accompanied by a letter containing a duplicate of the motto, and the name of author, date, and abode. Theses are receivable up to December 31st, 1882.

"'2. Theses written in a foreign language to be accompanied by a translation in Portuguese. (Translators may be found at any Brazilian or Portuguese legation or consulate.)

" ' 3. The thesis accepted will be printed at the expense of the Society. Those written in foreign languages can be published with the translation.

" ' 4. Every thesis will be numbered correspondingly with the registration of the letters accompanying the theses, which letters will be kept inviolable.

" ' 5. A council will be appointed, consisting of representatives of the scientific and philosophic schools, in due time, which will examine and report upon the theses.

" ' 6. After discussing the council's report, the Academy will appoint a time for opening the letter corresponding to the thesis most approved.

" ' At a formal meeting of the Academy, the author of the thesis most approved, or his representative, will be invited to receive the prize awarded by the Academy. In addition he will receive from the Society the sum before mentioned.'

" The Society will forward a historical summary of Spiritualism in Brazil to every Spiritualist centre which communicates with it, and in this matter reciprocity is expected because the interest is the same on both sides. 'This would lead,' it says, 'to a veritable Spiritualist congress. Animated by the same sentiments, true Spiritualists have little need to meet within four walls for agreement, for generalising an idea ; being one in spirit, and bound together by the same mission, they ought to interchange thought in whatever part of the world they may be.' "

CHAPTER XXXVI.

SPIRITUALISM IN THE EAST INDIES, CHINA, INDIA, &C., &C.

SPIRITUALISM IN CHINA.

THE Spiritualistic beliefs and practices of nearly all Oriental nations commence with their recorded history, and while they assimilate in quality and style of phenomena with the modern methods of Spirit communion, there are lines of demarcation in the processes of invocation, and the uses to which that communion is applied, which separate the East and West, and do not seem likely to be overcome or united.

In a work entitled "Art Magic," edited and published by the author of this volume, and written by a learned gentleman, who had personally witnessed all he described, vivid accounts are given of Spiritual manifestations amongst the Mongolians, including narratives of the marvellous powers exercised by certain "Lamas," or religious devotees, in cutting and mutilating their bodies, and restoring them again without signs of injury, in a single minute.

M. Le Huc, and Mr. McGowan, the well-known Jesuit and Scotch missionaries, testify to having witnessed similar performances, and both add extraordinary narratives of the power acquired by some of the Mongol priests and ascetics in the production of phenomena which transcend description or belief. Besides feats of this astounding character, many of the Chinese practise modes of Spirit communion by rapping, writing, the movement of inanimate bodies ; through trances, prevision and clairvoyance. One of the simplest methods employed in communicating with Spirits is described by M. Le Huc as follows :—

" As a vehicle for spirit communications the Chinese strew a table with sand and on this the written characters are traced by means of a pencil made from the twig of a peach tree. It is said that 'the motions of the pencil are quite extraordinary, and apparently not produced by the medium, on whose open palms the handle of the pencil rests.' Irreverent lookers-on are sharply rebuked by the ministering spirit. After each sentence the sand has to be smoothed, and while this is being done, the whole company unite in praising the poetical talents of the spirit, which responds by tracing on the sand the characters which constitute the message. When wearied it 'jots down as if in a great hurry the two characters, "Excuse me, I am off;"' whereupon the company say, 'If there was any want of respect or attention, great spirit, we beseech thee forgive us this sin,' after which the *séance* comes to an end."

In a recent number of the *Banner of Light*, an able correspondent writes an account of a *séance* which so nearly resembles the descriptions given by many travellers and missionaries, that we transcribe a portion of the narrative, as it will illustrate phenomenal methods, very common in China :—

"The temple of Loi-Sun-Yaong at Canton is one of the many places to which the people resort to receive communications by means of mediumistic writing, and may be described as an illustration of all. In the temple is an altar at which a monk presides. The petitioner for a communication kneels with the monk in front of the altar, and both engage in earnest supplications. Beside the altar stands another monk, in front of whom is a large board covered with sand. There is another officiator near by with pen and paper, prepared to copy the message when it appears, and still another whose office it is to explain it. The writing is done with a stick made of white wood, about one foot long, resembling a large pen-holder, from the under side of which, when it is in position to use, projects a small piece of wood which writes on the sanded board. Mrs. Gray, the widow of Archdeacon Gray, for many years a missionary in China, states that on one occasion she visited the temple to witness the manner of proceeding, remarking that for many centuries spiritual manifestations have been known and believed in, in that empire.

"At the time Mrs. Gray and her husband visited the temple, they were informed that a devotee who was present, was impatient to obtain a written message, and supposing they came for a similar purpose, the person in charge begged them to wait. After the prayers at the altar, the stick of white wood was taken by the chief officiator, balanced on his two fore-fingers, and thus held above the sanded board. In a few moments it began to move, tracing large characters in the sand. When the surface had been entirely covered, the writing was transcribed on paper. The sand was then shaken so that it presented an even surface, and the board was again placed ready for use. This was done three times. The fourth time, the lightly balanced wooden instrument refused to move, and the holder of it said the communicator had left.

"Table-moving has long been known and practised in China. On one occasion some missionaries had a medium in their own house. A large round table was brought and placed, feet upwards, on the floor. Four of their servants were called in, and each was told to place one of his hands on a foot of the table. The medium then began to walk around it with slow and measured steps, holding lighted joss sticks in his hands and invoking the presence of unseen powers. In a few moments, the table began to revolve slowly. Then the medium increased his speed, and the table turned more swiftly, until both table and medium ran round with great velocity. Of course the hands of the servants were not now upon it. They stood speechless in amazement. At length, exhausted, the man stood still, and the table ceased to move. He was asked how he accomplished the feat? In a low, subdued voice, he replied : 'It is Joss that does it ; I pray to him.' It was doubtless a manifestation of some spirit, but the ascribing it to ' Joss' was in keeping with the scriptural accounts of similar events, in which they were said to be performed by God.

"These manifestations have existed among the Chinese for ages, probably to an extent greater than among us, for the reason that a belief in the possibility of their occurrence has formed the primitive or spontaneous faith of the people."

From the author of "Art Magic," Captain Thomas Hunt, of Salem, U.S., and the Hon. Charles Bradley, all of whom have been residents in China, as well as from her own Chinese servants in California, the author has learned that manifestations of similar character to those above detailed, as well as feats of physical strength, and mental forms of intelligence, have been common amongst the Chinese, ages before modern Spiritualism was known.

The latter is practised at times amongst the white residents, and the modes are founded upon European and American experiences; but the

Spiritualists of the white and yellow races, despite their significant resemblance, do not blend, 'and the Chinese—especially the better educated portions of the community—regard the matter of fact, and only partially successful practices of the whites, with some contempt.   Dr. Ah Sin, a very well educated and intelligent medical practitioner of Australia, said to the author when conversing on these subjects :—" You are really behind the times, and ought to call Spiritualism no longer modern, but ancient. Sounds and motions are only made by Spirits to attract notice, but true communion is by words, writings, and speech, such as is uttered, when the Spirit enters the body of another.   All this—besides *siê fa* (evil power) which enables men to cut and hack their bodies, and cure them again on the instant—the Chinese have had amongst them from the beginning of time, certainly since the days of Lao Kuin."

Lao Kuin—the intelligent reader will remember—was a cotemporary of Confucius.   The latter was only a philosopher and a compiler ; Lao Kuin was a " saint," an ascetic, a wonder worker.

He was the founder of the sect *Tao tse*, the votaries of which are all Spiritualists.   It is said by Chinese traditions, that after Lao Kuin had left the earth,—" being translated bodily to heaven in a chariot of fire," one morning, there was found hanging on a tree in the Emperor's garden, a wonderful book full of magical rites, invocations of Spirits, wise sayings, and divine revelations.   The emperor himself carried this book in solemn procession, and with high ceremonial rites, to the principal monastery, and from thence, guidance and direction in all that belongs to Spirit power and communion, has been received for ages.   This book is said by some to have been burned, other authorities claim Lao Kuin as its author, and declare it is still the Bible of the *Tao tse*.   Dr. Ah Sin showed the author a finely illuminated work which is the " Spirit book " of the Lamasery in which as a youth he had been educated.   In this work are forty-six modes of invoking Spirits (gods) for different purposes, and with different powers and functions. Amongst these modes, are the burning of incense, fragrant herbs, gums, paper images, gilt flowers, and pungent perfumes.   Sometimes the votaries employ motions, such as dancing, whirling, and spinning ; at others, they resort to the beating of drums and ringing of bells to induce the " mantic ecstasy " or to invoke certain orders of Spirits.   The most approved modes of summoning " high and holy Spirits," are those employed by religious ascetics, such as prayer, fasting, and silent contemplation.

Spells, enchantments, and amulets are also considered efficacious, but ascetic and devotional processes are preferred above all others, that is, in high ceremonial rites.

Bamboo sticks placed on newly strewn sand or fine ashes, are often used by Spirits through Chinese Media, to draw characters, figures, and landscapes.   They have modes of drawing lots, also of tossing up shells, shooting arrows, setting up staves, and making circles on the ground, in which objects thrown, and falling in certain directions, are accepted as good or evil auguries.   The reader curious in these rites and ceremonies need only consult Godwyn's curious treatise on *The Antiquities and Divination of the Hebrews** to find numbers of the modes practised by the Chinese, but claimed by them to be derived from antique sources, which far antedate the appearance of the Jews on the page of history.

---

* " (Moses and Aaron)—Civil and Ecclesiastical Rites of the Ancient Hebrews." By Thomas Godwyn, B.D., 1628.

Amongst the Chinese, as with every other people, women are considered now—although not in past times—to be the best diviners, augurs, and prophets. Their services in these directions are much more in demand than formerly, and in this respect it is probable that the practices of modern Mediumship have tended to produce this result, even amongst the conservative Chinese.

It would be unnecessary to refer to the religious doctrines, or, if it may be so termed, the theology of the Mongol tribes. It is enough to say that modern Spiritualism honeycombs their ranks, wherever white men appear, or have settlements. This movement makes no visible progress amongst the yellow races, simply because they have Spiritualism already, and that in forms better adapted than ours, to the idiosyncracies of the people, and to their apprehension, far more effective and powerful.

Whilst the Siamese, Japanese, and indeed all the Mongolians indulge in great varieties of speculative doctrines, all are more or less practical Spiritualists, and believe in communion with the souls of ancestors.

The opinion of many intelligent persons who have resided amongst these people is, that their communications transcend in directness, good counsel, and prevision, any that are manifested amongst the Europeans or Americans, and the reasons assigned are, because the modes of invocation are more real and devotional, the trance more profound, and the preparation for such conditions, more in harmony with physiological and psychological laws.

Our highly-advanced civilians would rush through a dozen Spirit circles, whilst the Chinese monk was reverently preparing himself for one. Fasting, asceticism, silent contemplation, ablutions, prayers, and all the formulæ so faithfully observed by these "heathens," would hardly suit the luxurious habits or feverish whirl of life to which civilized nations are habituated; hence modern Spiritualists from Europe and America, are no more likely to convert the Spiritualists of China, Thibet, Siam, &c., than the Christian missionary is likely to convert the true and earnest Buddhist. The world moves *forward*, *not backward*, and Spiritualism and theology move along with it.

SPIRITUALISM IN INDIA.

In the present section of our matter of fact history we must not be expected to catalogue, much less to define, the various doctrinal theories that prevail in India, nor yet to enter at any length upon those subjects of discussion which have of late years occupied the attention of widely-differing parties, under the several captions of "Occultism" and "Spiritualism." Something of both these subjects we shall have to touch upon briefly in this very chapter; for the present however, we must call attention to the definitions under which Spiritual beliefs and doctrines in India may be classified.

As a general rule, the white population settled in India rank themselves under the appellation of "Christians," and believe or deny, only that which their special sect teaches.

There are in these ranks, some few Spiritualists, and some Secularists, but metaphysical thinking in India is fatiguing; hence the rule is, to think only through a paid and duly appointed religious teacher, and leave metaphysics and all its ramifications to Fakirs, Yogis, and restless reformers.

Amongst the native Hindoos, there is almost as great a diversity of opinion upon the questions of religion or theology, as in the ranks of Christianity.

The beliefs of the villagers and lower classes generally, tend to gross forms of "supernaturalism," but the religious devotees of various grades, often attain to high conditions of Spiritual exaltation, and by the peculiar practices enjoined upon them in processes of initiation, achieve the power of working what in olden time would have been deemed miracles, but what is now understood to be the control of matter and material things, by mental and Spiritual forces.

Some of the far-famed religious ascetics of India, are members of secret associations and fraternities; many of them belong to religious orders, and some few are isolated students of occult power, who have acquired their magical potency by research and observance of those practices, which even the highest adept must pass through, if he desires to attain to complete mastery over the realm of sensuous existence.

In the immense wave of immigration which political changes have cast on Hindoo soil during the last century, many things have come to light in connection with this ancient land, which have created a deep impression on public opinion. The partial translation of once unknown and "sacred" books into European languages, has revealed the fact that India has been the cradle of all known theological beliefs. The examination of the wonderful archæological remains of vast temples with which the land is studded, have tended still further to confirm the truth of these revelations, whilst the actual marvels wrought by religious ascetics, in the realms of matter and force, have opened up a new and highly suggestive page in the study of Occultism and Psychology.

As before remarked, the upper classes of the white population in British India are for the most part too much enervated by the influence of its tropical climate to concern themselves very deeply with metaphysical subjects. The continued effort, the patient attention and aspiration required at the Spirit circle, is so rarely attainable amongst the luxurious residents of British India, that the few Spiritualists with whom the author is in communication, express grave doubts if "modern Spiritualism"—in the European sense of the term—will gain any considerable foothold in India during this generation. The religious enthusiast, or even the specious impostor, is sure to command his share of following from all classes, but when the more intelligent Anglo-Indians wish to be informed concerning the alleged possibilities of intercourse with the Spiritual realm of being, rather than subject themselves to the trouble of personal investigation, they send for a Hindoo "wonder worker," and whether he be a genuine Yogi, or a cunning conjurer, it makes but little difference. Provided he can amuse, as well as astonish his employers, the purpose is answered; and as far as his feats bear upon Spiritual verities, the witnesses may be more or less inclined to accept of the generic explanation of a Spiritual agency. There have been of late several movements of a semi-spiritual, as well as religious or metaphysical character attempted in India, and as one in which a large number of European and American Spiritualists have taken a deep interest, and with which many have entered into ties of affiliation, it is in order at this point, to give some brief notice of "The Theosophical Society" of Bombay,* the city in which that society has established its headquarters,

---

* Since this chapter was first indited, the Theosophical Society's headquarters are announced as having been removed to Madras.

and from which it issues its chief literary organ, namely, *The Theosophist*, a monthly journal, avowedly devoted to an exposition of "theosophy," and kindred subjects.

As offering the most impartial information concerning the origin of this Society, that can be laid before the reader, the following extract is given from one of the New York daily journals, subsequently reprinted in the Boston *Spiritual Scientist* of 1876. It reads as follows :—

"A THEOSOPHICAL SOCIETY.

"One movement of great importance has just been inaugurated in New York, under the lead of Colonel Henry S. Olcott, in the organization of a society to be known as 'The Theosophical Society.' The suggestion was entirely unpremeditated, and was made on the evening of the 7th instant, in the parlors of Madame Blavatsky, where a company of seventeen ladies and gentlemen had assembled to meet Mr. George Henry Felt, whose discovery of the geometrical figures of the Egyptian Cabbala may be regarded as among the most surprising feats of the human intellect. The company included several persons of great learning and some of wide personal influence. The managing editor of two religious papers ; the co-editors of two literary magazines ; an Oxford LL.D. ; a venerable Jewish scholar and traveller of repute ; an editorial writer of one of the New York morning dailies ; the president of the New York Society of Spiritualists ; Mr. C. C. Massey, an English visitor ; Mrs. Emma Hardinge Britten and Dr. Britten ; two New York lawyers. besides Colonel Olcott ; a partner in a Philadelphia publishing house ; a well-known physician ; and, most notable of all, Madame Blavatsky herself, comprised Mr. Felt's audience.

"After his discourse, an animated discussion ensued. During a convenient pause in the conversation, Colonel Olcott rose, and after briefly sketching the present condition of the Spiritualistic movement, the attitude of its antagonists, the materialists ; the irrepressible conflict between science and the religious sectaries ; the philosophical character of the ancient theosophies, and their sufficiency to reconcile all existing antagonisms, and the apparently sublime achievement of Mr. Felt in extracting the key to the architecture of Nature from the scanty fragments of ancient lore left us by the devastating hands of the Moslem and Christian fanatics of the early centuries, he proposed to form a nucleus around which might gather all the enlightened and brave souls who were willing to work together for the collection and diffusion of knowledge. His plan was to organise a society of occultists and begin at once to collect a library, and diffuse information concerning those secret laws of nature which were so familiar to the Chaldeans and Egyptians. but are totally unknown by our modern world of science.

"Mr. Felt said, in reply to questions, that communion of mortals with the dead, and the reciprocal intervention of each in the affairs of the other, was not a mere conjecture among the ancient Egyptians, but reduced to a positive science, and he himself had been able to cause the materialization of human forms in full daylight, by magical appliance.

"It was unanimously voted to organise the proposed society forthwith. Colonel Olcott was elected temporary president, and a committee was appointed to draft a constitution and by-laws.

"We hail the movement with great satisfaction, as likely to aid in bringing order out of our present chaos, furnish us a true philosophy of spirit-intercourse, and afford a neutral ground upon which the tired wrestlers of the Church and College may rest from their cruel and illogical strife."

Shortly after the first formation of this Society, in which all the parties alluded to above took part, and filled offices, it was deemed desirable to conduct the proceedings on the basis of a secret society, from which time, the Fellows of the New York Theosophical Society were known to each other by the usual formulæ of passwords, grips, signs, &c. In this, as in all other associations banded together for the study of occult subjects, it may be naturally supposed there are *esoteric*, as well as merely *exoteric degrees*, and results attainable only to those who could, and would pursue, their studies, to the innermost depths of nature's laboratories.

Of the original group of New York Theosophists, several have seceded. Some were removed by mortal death, and others by absence. Madame Blavatsky and Colonel Olcott, the founders of the Society, themselves passed on to England, and after remaining there a short time, and inaugurating a branch Society which still holds its sessions in London, they took up their residence in India, from whence their influence still ramifies to other branch Theosophical Societies, established in different parts of the world. *The Theosophist*—the monthly journal before mentioned—published at Madras—has now entered upon the sixth year of its circulation, and the parent Society is presided over in person by its founders.

There are still many points connected with this Society, of which even its avowed disciples seem to be ignorant.

Questions are constantly propounded concerning *the aims, powers, and scope* of the Association, and it is in view of some misunderstanding that prevails on these points, that we shall give the substance of a correspondence published in *The Theosophist* of October, 1881, the nature of which speaks for itself.

It commences thus :—

"FRAGMENTS OF OCCULT TRUTH.

"We have received from our esteemed Australian brother theosophist, W. H. Terry, Esq., the following interesting and temperate note on some supposed errors of Occultists, when dealing with the phenomena of Spiritualism. The subject is one of universal interest, and we shall require therefore no apology either for reproducing our good brother's communication *in extenso*, or for appending thereto some few fragments of the lessons taught us in the occult schools, which may possibly both help to remove his personal difficulties, and tend to convey to Spiritualists generally, a clearer conception of the causes of many of the phenomena of which they have had experience."

Then follows a long letter written by Mr. Terry, editor of the Australian *Harbinger of Light*, complaining that he, being like a very large number of other Spiritualists in different parts of the world, a member of the Theosophical Society, and a reader of the Society's alleged organ, *The Theosophist*, finds the agency of disembodied human spirits ignored as factors in the production of modern Spiritual manifestations by the leading writers of *The Theosophist*, and the phenomena which Spiritualists are accustomed to attribute to the agency of Spirit friends, who present the most conclusive tokens of their identity, referred to "elementaries, geister, shells," &c., &c. Mr. Terry cites a number of cases occurring in his own experience, and that of numerous friends, clairvoyants, and mediums, all tending to prove the agency of intelligent, living, spirit individualities. After dwelling at great length upon these points, and summing up his testimony in a very clear and logical manner, Mr. Terry desires to be informed, what other explanation than the agency of spirits identical with the men and women who have once lived on earth, the editor of *The Theosophist* can offer him.

To this very reasonable request, the editor appealed to answers, in an article so long, verbose, and incomprehensible, that the author, judging of the majority of her readers by herself, fears it may be "defining night by darkness" to attempt reprinting the same in its entirety.

The following extracts, however, apply to the most salient points of the whole subject, and as they are given with sufficient definiteness of expression to be fairly understood, they are earnestly commended to the reader's attention :—

"It is but fair that we should meet the charge brought, and in the same friendly and frank spirit shown in his letter by our esteemed Australian brother Theosophist. Until some one more competent enters the arena of discussion to pick up the glove flung by

Spiritualism to Theosophy across the oceans, we will take the liberty of saying a few words—not in our defence—but as a matter of courtesy to our correspondent.

"'Those Theosophists who deny to disembodied spirits a legitimate share in the marvellous phenomena' are few, indeed, *for the great majority of Theosophists concern themselves with Spiritualism very little—if at all.* Indeed, our members may be divided into five principal classes and described as follows :—

"1. Men profoundly concerned in the revival of their respective religious philosophies in all their pristine purity—Buddhist devotees outnumbering all others. *These neither know of, nor do they care for, Spiritualism.* (?)

"2. Students of various philosophies, searchers after truth, whencesoever it may come. They neither believe nor disbelieve in spirits. They are open to conviction in any way, but will accept nothing on second-hand testimony.

"3. Materialists, Freethinkers, Agnostics, who care as little for Occultism as they do for Spiritualism. Their only concern is to free the masses from the fetters of ignorance and superstition, and educate them. . . .

"4. Spiritualists and Spiritists who could not well be accused of any such 'heresy.' And finally,

"5. Occultists, who do not number half a per cent. in the Theosophical Society.

"These latter are the only 'Theosophists' who are really open to our correspondent's accusation, and even these, if we look beyond the veil of words which more or less conceals the ideas of both Spiritualists and Occultists, will prove *to differ less widely on these points from our correspondent than he seems to suppose,* . . . and here the conflict of opinions between Spiritualists and Occultists is solely due to the fact that the former (who overrate their quality and character) dignify by the name of 'spirits' *certain reliquiæ of deceased human beings,* while the Occultists reserve the name of Spirit for the highest principle of human nature and treat these *reliquiæ* as mere *eidolons,* or astral *simulacra,* of the real spirit.

"In order to understand clearly the view of the Occultists, it is necessary to glance at the constitution of the living human being. Even the spiritual theory teaches that man is a trinity, composed of (1) a higher spirit, or the "Spiritual Soul" as ancient philosophers designated it ; (2) its envelope—the etherial form or shadow of the body—and (3) the physical body.

"Although from one point of view this is broadly correct, yet, according to Occultists, to render our conceptions of this truth clearer and follow successfully the course of man after death, it is necessary to subdivide further these three entities and resolve them into their constituent principles. This analysis being almost wholly unknown to Western nations, it is difficult in some cases to find any English words by which to represent the Occult subdivisions, but we give them in the least obscure phraseology that we can command.

DIVISIONS OF THE SPIRITUALISTS.	SUBDIVISIONS OF THE OCCULTISTS.
1. The Body.	1. The Physical body, composed wholly of matter in its grossest and most tangible form.
	2. The Vital principle, a form of force, indestructible, and when disconnected with one set of atoms, becoming attracted immediately by others.
2. The Animal Soul or *Perisprit.*	3. The Astral body, composed of highly etherialized matter ; in its habitual passive state, the perfect but very shadowy duplicate of the body ; its activity, consolidation, and form depending on the *kama rupa.*
	4. The Astral shape (*kama rupa*) or body of desire, a principle defining the configuration of—
	5. The animal or physical intelligence or consciousness or Ego, analogous to, though proportionately higher in degree than, the reason, instinct, memory, imagination, &c., existing in the higher animals.
3. The Spiritual Soul or Spirit.	6. The higher or Spiritual intelligence, or consciousness, or Spiritual Ego, in which mainly resides the sense of consciousness in the *perfect* man, though the lower dimmer animal consciousness exists in No. 3.
	7. The Spirit—an emanation from the ABSOLUTE ; uncreated, eternal ; a state rather than a being.

* Italics are the author's throughout.

"Now the change that we call death, only immediately affects the first three constituents; the body decomposes to enter into new combinations, and the vital force is dissipated to help animate new organisms, and the astral human form dies with the body.

"There remain four principles. As a rule (we except the case of the higher adepts) one of two things occurs in accordance with the universal law of affinity. If the spiritual Ego has been in life material in its tendencies, placing its main enjoyment in the gratification of its earthly desires, then at death it continues to cling to the lower elements of its late combination, and the true Spirit severs itself from these and passes away elsewhere. To follow its course is beside the present question, since the remaining principles in which personal or animal consciousness remain *have parted with it for ever.* . . . Suffice it to say now, that it passes away, *taking with it no fragment of the individual consciousness of the man with which it was temporarily associated.* . . .

"But if on the other hand, the tendencies of the Ego have been towards things spiritual . . . then will it cling to the Spirit, and with this pass into the adjoining (so called) world of effects (in reality a state not a place), and there purified of much of its still remaining material taints, *evolve out of itself by the Spirit's aid a new Ego,* to be reborn after a brief period of freedom and enjoyment in the next higher world of causes. . . .

"Now neither during its gestation in the subjective world of effects, nor after its entry on rebirth into the higher objective world of causes—*can the Ego re-enter this present world.* . . . It cannot, even if it would, *span the abyss that separates its state from ours.* . . . Once reborn into the higher world and (independent of the physical impossibility of any communication between its world and ours, *to all but the very highest adepts*) the new Ego has become a new person; it has lost the old consciousness, linked with earthly experiences, and has acquired a new consciousness which, as time rolls on, will be interpenetrated by its experiences, in that higher sphere. . . .

"*Therefore it is that the Occultists maintain that no* SPIRITS *of the departed can appear or take part in the phenomena of the séance-room.* To what can appear and take part in these the Occultists refuse the name of Spirits.*

"But it may be said—what is it that can appear? We reply—merely the animal soul or perisprit of the deceased. . . . Immediately on the severance of the Spirit— whether at death or before death—the spiritual Ego is dissipated and ceases to exist. . . . Thus alike in all cases that remain, all that can appear are *the shells of the deceased,* the two principles which we call the animal, or surviving astral souls, or animal Ego. But there is this to be noted. As the clay, as Sadi says, long retains traces of the perfume of the roses, which once honoured it with their companionship, so the etherialized matter which has been in combination with spirit, long retains a power of resisting disintegration. The more pure the spiritual Ego, the less of the matter which in combination with the Spirit went to form it, does it leave behind clinging to the two principles; the more impure, the greater the mass of such spirit-vitalized matter which remains to invigorate the *reliquiæ.*

"Thus it follows that in the case of the pure and good, the shells rapidly disintegrate, and the animal soul having ever been kept in subjection is feeble and will-less, and it can very rarely, if ever, happen that such should voluntarily appear or manifest themselves— *their* vitality, desires and aspirations almost exclusively existed in what has passed away. No doubt a power exists which can compel even these to appear, a power taught by the evil science of necromancy, rightly denounced by all good men of old. But why evil it may be asked? Because until these shells have dissipated, a certain sympathy exists between them and the departed spiritual Ego which is gestating in the fathomless womb of the adjoining world of effects, *and to disturb the shells by necromantic sorcery is at the same time to disturb the fœtal spiritual Ego.*

"We said that these shells in such cases rapidly decay, the rapidity being exactly proportional to the purity of the departed spiritual Ego; and we may add that similarly the rapidity of gestation of the new Ego is proportional to the purity of the old Ego out of which it is evolved. Happily, necromancy is unknown to modern Spiritualists, so that it is next to impossible that the reliquiæ of the good and pure should ever appear in the séance-room. No doubt, the *simulacra* of some spiritual Egos whose fate trembled in the balance, whose affinities, earthwards and heaven-wards, to use the popular phraseology, were nearly equal, who have left too much of the matter behind that has been in combination to form

* And who may *the Occultists be* who "refuse" to give names and definitions deemed to be correct by millions of their fellow-mortals? The author of this volume claims to be an "Occultist"—and that with as good a right to the cognomen as the editor of *The Theosophist,* and yet she insists that the entire mass of theory presented in these extracts, is *theory* only—and remains wholly undemonstrated, whilst the FACTS of Spirit communion, the identity of the Spirit, the full preservation of that identity, continued progress in sphere life, and *all* the tokens of individuality that made the man, woman, or child of earth, are testified to, and corroborated by tens of thousands independent and reliable communications given in every country of civilization.—AUTHOR.

them, who will lie long in fœtal bonds before being able to develop the new Ego-hood, no doubt, we say such *simulacra* may survive longer and may occasionally appear under exceptional conditions in *séance*-rooms, with a *dim-dazed consciousness of their past lives.* But even this, owing to the conditions of the case, will be rare, and they will never be active or intelligent, as the stronger portions of their wills—the higher portions of their intelligence—have gone elsewhere. . . . . Broadly speaking, as a law, it is only the *reliquiæ* of non-spiritually-minded men, whose spiritual Egos have perished, *that appear in séance-rooms, and are dignified by Spiritualists with the title of ' Spirits of the departed.'*

"These *shells, these animal souls,* in whom still survive the major portions of the intelligence, will-power, and knowledge that they possessed when incorporated in the human combination, invigorated too by the re-assimilation of the spirit-vitalized matter that once combined with the spirit to compose their spiritual Ego, are often powerful and *highly intelligent,* and continue to survive for lengthened periods, their intense desire for earthly life enabling them to seize from the decaying *simulacra* of the good and feeble the material for prolonged existence.

"To these *eidolons,* Occultists are used to give the name of elementaries, and these it is that by the aid of the half-intelligent forces of nature which are attracted to them, perform most of the wonders of the *séance*-rooms. If to these shells, these *eidolons,* which have lost their immortality, and whence the Divine essence has for ever departed, our brothers, the Spiritualists, insist on applying the title of 'spirits of the dead,' well and good—*they are not spirits at all,* they are of the earth, earthy, all that remains of the dead when their spirits have flown—but if this be understood, and it be nevertheless considered desirable to call them that to which they are the precise antitheses—it is after all merely a case of misnomer.

"But let there be no mistake as to what they *are;* hundreds and thousands of lost and ruined men and women all over the globe attest the degradation to which constant subjection to their influence in mediumship,* &c., too generally leads, and we who know the truth should ill discharge our duty if we did not warn all Spiritualists in the strongest terms possible, against allowing this misuse of terms to mislead them as to the real nature and character of the disembodied entities with which they so constantly and confidingly deal.

"Now probably Spiritualists will admit that our views would explain the vast mass of trash, frivolous nonsense and falsehood communicated through mediums, as also the manner in which so many of these, good and honest to begin with, gradually grow into immoral impostors. But many objections will be raised. One man will say—' I have repeatedly conversed with my late father—a better, kinder-hearted, more spiritual-minded man never lived—and on one occasion he told me a fact, unknown to me, and I believe to every one living, which I subsequently verified.'

"Nothing is simpler—the father's image was in the son's mind. Thus put *en rapport,* the disembodied elementary which, if of one of the more intelligent classes, has glimpses of things in the astral light, and can here and there dimly distinguish the pictures which record every deed, word, and thought (pictures which we are all unconsciously incessantly evolving, pictures which survive long after those who originated them have passed away), the elementary, we say, scanning these, easily picks up sufficient facts for its purpose, and by its will materialises itself, partly out of matter drawn from the medium's body, partly out of inert kosmic matter drawn to it by the help of the elementals or half-blind forces of nature which it, and probably the medium also, has attracted and stands forth the counterpart of the dead father and talks of things known only to that dead father.†

"And it must be remembered that these apparently strong and perfect cases are very rare, and that the elementaries who come as A. or B., usually, if they personate people of any note, make gross blunders and almost without exception betray their falsehood in one way or another, Shakespeare and Milton dictating trash, Newton grossly ignorant of his own *Principia,* and Plato teaching a washed-out Neo-platonic *cum* sentimental Christian philosophy, and so on. At the same time undoubtedly in rare cases the ghostly relics of very clever, very bad and very determined men constitute disembodied entities of high intelligence, which survive for a lengthened period, *and the wickeder and more material they are in all their tendencies, the longer do they escape disintegration.*‡

---

* A monstrous libel on unnumbered good and true men and women.—AUTHOR.

† If the father was "the spiritual-minded man" represented above, how comes he to be an "elementary?" And again—is not the above process rather too *clever* a proceeding for a "shell"—with nothing in it—a perfume which a flower has left behind?

‡ Marvellous philosophy! which attributes all the "trash," &c., to the third, fourth, or fifth part of a man whose life was tolerably good, and all the high intelligence to the *emanations* of a man whose life was very wicked! ! !

" Naturally now some Spiritualists will object that this cannot be true since despite the mass of folly and gibberish, or worse, often heard in *séance*-rooms, the purest sentiments and really lofty ideas and teachings are not so very rarely expressed through mediums.

" Several points have, however, to be borne in mind. In the first place, though proved unfit for further development, and, therefore, doomed in most cases by the eternal law of the survival of the fittest to be disintegrated and, losing personal consciousness, *to be worked up again in the lower worlds into new combinations*, all elementaries are by no means actively wicked all round. On the balance, their whole natures proved to have a greater affinity to matter than to spirit, and they are, therefore, incapable of further progress, but when dealing with a pure circle and speaking through a still pure medium (*very few mediums, indeed, continue thus after a long course of mediumship*) the better and less degraded side of their nature comes out, and it is quite possible for elementaries to have a perfect intellectual knowledge and appreciation of virtue and purity and enlightened conceptions of truth, and yet be innately vicious in their tendencies.

" Now it must not for a moment be supposed that all we hear comes from elementaries. In the first place, a great many well-known mediums *are clever impostors*. There are notorious trance mediums, *especially women*, who steadily work up for their so-called trance orations, and these being really clever and working at *good* books, deliver essays of a respectable and at times almost first-class character. There is no spiritual influence at work here, the only apparently abnormal feature in these cases is that persons possessing such fair abilities should be willing thus to prostitute them, and that people who can talk so well and touchingly of truth and purity, should yet live such lives of falsehood and immorality. Alas ! *meliora videor proboque deteriora sequor*, has ever found a response in too many human hearts and has in all ages rung the annihilation-knell of too many Egos.*

Many other similar attempts to account for all the GOOD in trance mediumship are put forth—such as " a seventh principle " being " in rapport " with something, somewhere, and a " sixth principle " fishing up knowledge " out of the astral light," &c., &c., but it can scarcely be doubted that the reader is thoroughly surfeited with such fantastic metaphysics, and such grossly ungenerous and unfounded attacks upon a class of persons who have done more to reform the age, and teach the elements of a pure practical religion, than all the hazy metaphysicians that have essayed to found new sects, on the basis of tobacco, hasheesh, and opium visions. As a final fling at " the Mediums," and a gentle hint at the only road by which heaven can be attained, and final extinction be averted, we commend a study of the closing paragraphs. This modest writer adds :—

" In truth, mediumship is a dangerous, too often a fatal capacity, and if we oppose Spiritualism, as we have ever *consistently done*, it is not because we question the reality of their phenomena, which we know can and do occur (despite the multitudes of fraudulent imitations), and which *our adepts can reproduce at will*† *without* DANGER *to themselves*, but because of the irreparable spiritual injury (we say nothing of the mere physical sufferings) which the pursuit of Spiritualism inevitably entails on nine-tenths of the mediums employed. We have seen scores, nay rather hundreds of, so to say, good, pure, honest young men and women, who but for the cultivation of this evil capacity for the reception of impressions by elementaries, might and would in all probability have lived lives leading to higher things, but who through the gradual pernicious influence of these low, earthbound natures have sunk, from bad to worse, ending, often prematurely, lives that could lead but to spiritual ruin.

" That men bewildered amidst the crumbling ruins of *effete* religions should madly grasp at every clue by which there seems some faint hope of penetrating the cloud-shrouded labyrinth of the mystery of the universe, is neither wonderful nor reprehensible, but it is not through *mediums*, the prey of every *idle spook and elementary* that the great truth is to be reached, but by that rigorous course of study, self-discipline and self-purification *which is taught in the temple of Occultism to which Theosophy is, in the present day, the high road.*" (?)

---

* On what possible authority could any writer presume to bring such allegations against vast numbers of honourable and highly-gifted persons, except he writes from the reflection of a treacherous and deceptive nature ? and having been an impostor himself, deems every one else on the same plane.

† Why does not this Editor produce his adepts ?

There only seems to need one more item added to save the race from final extinction, and the destroying influence of Spiritualism, which is, to give in full, the terms of the initiation fee and membership to the "Theosophical Society," and the price of subscription to the *Theosophical Journal.* Do this! and humanity may be redeemed—Fail! and the world will be full of empty "shells," and heaven a private reserve, inhabited only by the *very high adepts* who have graduated from the schools of Theosophical Occultism. In all seriousness however, it must be said that if the author had any other interests to serve than those of truth, or if she could believe that unsustained and audacious assertions could subvert well-demonstrated truths, she would never have wearied her readers with the "fragments of Occultism" contained in the above-quoted extracts. They have been introduced however for many reasons, one of which is, that the terms "Theosophy," and "Occultism," have of late been repeatedly paraded before the readers of the Spiritual journals, and that with the apparent view of claiming those words as the synonym of divers strange doctrines, the special views put forth above being one.

If to be a "Theosophist," means to have been or still be a member of the Theosophical Society, then the present writer might make that claim, seeing that she was one of the first members ; that the first meetings of the original Theosophical Society were held in her house in New York, and as long as the Society existed in that city *on its original lines*, the author's name was retained as a member of the first council.

If to be an "Occultist" means to be a member of a fraternity that attempts by study and practice, to discover and apply the occult forces of the Universe, then has the author as good a right to be termed an Occultist as any of the "half per cent" which the editor above quoted claims to exist in the Theosophical Society. And yet with some not inconsiderable share of *esoteric* knowledge concerning Theosophy and Theosophists, as well as Occultism and Occultists, the author of this volume, whether as a "Theosophist" or "Occultist," not only repudiates belief in every word of the above article, but insists that it libels most unjustly and unwarrantably a large number of respectable persons, practising "Mediumship" in different countries of the earth, and grossly misrepresents the general aims and worth of the entire movement known as "Spiritualism."

The author does not propose to make these pages the arena of discussion for the propositions put forth by the Theosophical editor, because it would be trespassing on space that should be better employed, wearying the reader, and pitting a stereotyped volume against the unlimited power of retort which the editor of a periodical possesses, and which very few persons in such a position fail to turn to their own advantage.

The article in question has been reprinted, first, as an item of information concerning the environment of the movement which this work is designed to describe.

Next that the readers of the Spiritual journals who must have seen many "fragments" of so-called "Occultism" forced on their attention, might derive from a sufficiently clear statement, a knowledge of what "Theosophical Occultists" teach ; and next, to warn the practical seeker for truth to beware how he leaves the foundation of well-demonstrated facts, to launch out on the ocean of vague, speculative theory.

For the first time in the recorded history of the race, a systematic and practical mode of communicating with the inhabitants of the life beyond the grave has been achieved. All the conditions necessary to establish the identity of the communicating intelligences with the people that once lived on earth, have been manifested to tens of thousands of living and respectable witnesses. But one millionth part of the proof of this position furnished by modern Spiritualism, would be accepted as reliable testimony by all the courts of judicature in the world. Even the very mass of *trash, falsehood*, &c., which *The Theosophist* speaks of, as being communicated through Mediums, is another proof of the strict humanity of the source of *many*, though by no means *all*, of the communications. Without adverting to the false and most ungenerous way, in which this writer attempts to slur over the better part of the communications, it is enough to point to the fact, apparent to the most superficial thinker, that if the ninety per cent of the *communications* between man and man which any modern city could afford, were gathered up, and compared with the mass of "trash," &c., &c., claiming a Spiritual origin, the balance would inevitably be found quite sufficiently manifest in favour of "the Spirits," to show, that they had advanced, to some degree at least, beyond the status of humanity, by their residence in the Spirit world. One thing is certain; less presumptuous, and something more acute writers than this Theosophist, have agreed, that the bulk of the communications, whether for good or evil, or both, are still strictly human and—in at least one-third of their number—are identical with the individuals who have once lived on earth, and whose personalities they represent.

But all this is beneath the "Theosophist's" notice, or if touched on at all is contemptuously disposed of according to *his ipse dixit*—which consists of a mass of metaphysical theorems as trashy as any Spirit communications he can point to, and as false to the probabilities of natural law, as they are irreconcilable with the observed facts of Spiritualism. And finally, the author's sense of self-respect and desire to do justice to hundreds of her fellow labourers, impels her to protest emphatically against the editor's assertions concerning "the mental and physical degradation" which he alleges ensues from the practice of Mediumship. In contradiction of this unfounded statement, and for the information of the candid truth-seeker, the author claims that Mediumship falls on all classes alike; includes the pure-minded and the vicious, the healthful and the sick; that it creates nothing, but simply externalizes the latent germs of individual character, also that multitudes of sane, pure-minded, and healthful men and women, are now living, to testify by their good and virtuous conduct, and their high reverence for their Mediumistic gifts, the wholesale slander hurled against them, by this Theosophical editor:

As for the theories he sets forth, the answer in brief is, that they are all wholly *unproved*—in short, that there is not a statement contained in the article in question, susceptible of verification; not one but what is made on its writer's own responsibility, or at most, on the authority of a "band of brothers," who are of no more authority than any other band of brothers, of whom there are hosts in the East, as elsewhere, and who singly or severally are only authoritative—beyond their particular sphere of discipleship—in as far as their teachings correspond to such laws, principles, and facts, as are already proven, or are capable of being proven.

All knowledge of science has been derived from observation, or when revealed to man by higher intelligences than those of earth, is susceptible of proof by corroborative testimony. Why should Spiritualism—the science of sciences—be exempt from the same reasonable standards of demonstration? It cannot be alleged that we have no means of observing

Spiritual facts, or obtaining corroborative testimony of Spiritual teachings. To deny this, is but the *ruse* of theological dogmatists. We have had in all ages of the past, and we have still more abundantly in the present, opportunities both for observing Spiritual facts and testing Spiritual revelations by corroborative proof; and it is because the Theosophist and his " band of brothers " would have us depart from these rational standards of judgment, and put unquestioning faith in what *they say*, no matter how far it may conflict with what *you have observed*, or what ten thousand Spirits have told you, that none should accept their statements without severely testing and proving the authority upon which they are based. There seems but little difference between " Believe, or go to eternal perdition," and " Believe, or go to eternal extinction." Such dogmatic threats have been the curse of the race, and mankind gains but little in changing the base of these utterances from an ecclesiastical hierarchy to a band of brothers, whose very existence is still to many minds a question of doubt. But it may be urged that belief with the ecclesiastic was enforced by torture and the stake, whilst with the Theosophist it is optional and free. To this we respond, that "Theosophy" and "Occultism," are terms of world-wide import, and when employed to endorse statements which aim at destroying the very corner-stones of proof concerning immortality and the conditions of the life hereafter upon which millions of persons in the present generation base their faith, *they cannot remain unchallenged.* If *they* are true, Spiritualism is the mightiest and foulest delusion that has ever fallen upon the earth. Better that we should believe that those who have come to us, doing us good, watching over, and guarding us like angels, who have for years been our best friends, counsellors, and guides; who have come with all the tokens of identity borne by our fathers, mothers, children, and best beloved, should turn out to be the "devils" of ecclesiastical teachings, than the "ghouls," "gheists," "empty shells," and loathsome *reliquiæ* of *dead bodies*, as taught in Theosophical Occultism. Not to question such doctrines is to assume that there are no sane human beings to be led away by them. But when they come upon our own camp ground and affect to correct the fallacies into which we as Spiritualists have fallen, it not only becomes our right, but our duty to question them. And what is the result?

If we approach the mouthpieces of these *invisible, and only elect*, "adepts," to enquire about our own destiny, we are told, that at death, we are chopped up into seven parts, with a million chances to one against any one of the seven being rescued from annihilation.

If we enquire for the fathers and mothers, husbands and children, that were dearer to us than life, we are told, that they have already melted out, or else, that their graveyard emanations have been very busy, striving to drag us down into mental corruption, and Spiritual ruin!! Are we to receive this, as the culmination of all the long-hidden wisdom of the Orient? Or, supposing we venture to defer to such monstrous asseverations, question their authenticity, and *ask for proof.*

One answers us, " The venerable chief of our Band of Brothers says so." Another, "The God within me affirms it." Still another, "Gautama Buddha says so," or " *Very high* intelligences have revealed this to me." If you humbly question, why "very high intelligences" cannot come to you, as well as to your Occultist informant, you have answers which strongly savour of that ancient pharisaism, which would say, if it dared, "Stand by; I am holier than thou." And if all these are not answers enough you are overwhelmed with the opinions of Hindoo, Egyptian, Aryan, and

Greek sages, whose *opinions* are worth about as much, without corroborative testimony to-day, as the opinions of any other men, whether they lived in the days of antiquity or in the nineteenth century.

That which the Spiritualist asks is reasonable enough. He says : "Give me one shadow of proof to convince me, that the pure and holy spirit with whom I have been conversing is a 'shell,' 'a gheist, a *reliquiæ* of the dead,' and not my mother herself : give me proofs as strong as I can bring to show that it is my mother herself; that death has had no power over her, and that with all the difficulties under which the Spiritual telegraph works, there is not one shadow of evidence to doubt that it is my real veritable mother. Bring me proof for proof ; and testimony for testimony ; or set my facts against your theories, and see which will weigh the strongest; especially when my facts are duplicated by the facts of millions of others and your theories have yet to produce one demonstrable fact to rest upon." The story of Elijah and the priests of Baal may be only an allegory, and one which either party might claim, were it not that Elijah gained his victory by virtue of a demonstrated fact, while the priests of Baal worshipped their ideal only. Time, the great touchstone of truth, sifts all that comes before his tribunal, but whether by the force of a deific will or because truth is the only imperishable element in existence, certain it is that all great truths redeem themselves, and only require time to shake off the mists of error, and take their place as the fundamental principles upon which the Universe is builded. To this unerring touchstone the author can afford to commit the all of the present question. Meantime, at the risk of the threatened extinction with which grovelling minds are liable to be visited who cannot ascend to the airy heights of Theosophical utterances, the author counsels all readers of these passages, "to prove all things"— and then, but not till then, will they be in a position to "hold fast by that which is good."

CHAPTER XXXVII.

SPIRITUALISM IN INDIA (CONTINUED).

PASSING from the realm of controversial discussion concerning the condition of the soul hereafter, we proceed to consider the status of opinion on this subject indicated by the prevailing superstitions amongst some of the lower classes of India.

It will be seen that whilst their ideas of spiritual existence partake largely of ancient superstitions, they still recognize the actuality of intercourse with deceased persons ; in fact, this acceptance of spiritual interposition in human affairs on the part of the souls of men, supersedes in many respects the common belief in Providential agency. The natives of India of low castes, worship the gods whom their Brahminical, Buddhistic, or Mahometan teachers instruct them of, but implicit faith in the direct action and influence of human spirits, especially those whose tendencies are mischievous, is the paramount feature of belief.

The villagers or dwellers in rural districts, are evidently more susceptible of being ruled by fear, than love. At certain periods they hold festivals in

20

honour of the Deities, and the good and true who have passed "into the paradises of the blessed," but they dwell chiefly on the deeds of evil doers whom they believe still preserve their former interest in humanity, and take every opportunity of renewing their earthly propensities to sin and wrong.

They assume that the habitations of these spirits are near, and sometimes upon the earth ; that they haunt desolate places, scenes where great crimes have been committed, deep forests, and lonely dells. They divide these weird beings into three principal grades, the first of which they call *Bhutas*. These are sometimes the spirits of celebrated personages, notorious male-factors, or even kings, provided they were tyrants, or led very wicked lives, but the last qualification is a *sine quâ non* for the office of a Bhuta. They deem these ghosts capable of working illimitable evil to those over whom they rule, and think the greatest aim of mortals should be to placate them by all the means they can devise.

The second class are *Pretas*—supposed to be the spirits of children who have either been deformed, monstrous, or in some way imperfect in mind or body. These beings are represented as frightful, misshapen, and exceedingly mischievous ; not unlike in fact, "the goblin page" of Walter Scott, or "Caliban" of the enchanted isle, so marvellously imaged forth in Shakespeare's "Tempest."

The third class, called *Pisacha*, are supposed to be the spirits of maniacs, drunkards, idiots, or such as represent conditions of mental imbecility.

All these, and others too numerous to particularise are often called by the generic name of "Bhuta ;" all are deemed to be fearsome, more or less monstrous in appearance, and constantly disposed to work ill to man.

It would scarcely be possible to believe that rational beings in the nineteenth century could associate such an array of frightful superstitions as these Hindoos indulge in, with the spirits of those who were once men and women like themselves. Such is the prevalent belief however, and in confirmation of these statements, we shall give a few extracts from a work on "Devil Worship in Western India," by Judge Walhouse, F.R.A.S., an eminent writer, and one who long filled high office in Indian Courts of Judicature.

Mr. Walhouse says, in part 1st of his work above named :—

"The edifices and observances connected with Bhuta worship are both domestic and public. In villages, and very generally in towns, there is in every house a wooden cot or cradle, placed on the ground, or suspended by ropes or chains, and dedicated to the Bhuta of the spot. On these are placed a bell, a knife, or sword, and a pot filled with water, all which are collectively called the Bhandara of the Bhuta, and kept either in a part of the house itself, or in a small separate building. The idea seems to be of placating the spirit that haunts the spot by making a sort of abode for it, much in the same way as the cream-bowl was nightly set for the "drudging goblin," or brownie, in England. On the last day of every lunar month flowers are laid on the cot, and perfume burnt before it ; and once a year, towards the end of April, a ceremony called Tambila is performed. First, a fire is lit on the spot where the cot and paraphernalia stand, to make it "shoodha," *i.e.*, clean ; then fried rice, mixed with coarse sugar and grated cocoanut kernel, is heaped on two plantain leaves, which are placed on the cot, together with some young cocoanuts, pierced ready to drink from. A ball is then formed of boiled rice, coloured yellow with turmeric, and laid on a piece of plantain leaf on a small stool, which is placed before the cot, and a lighted torch stuck on it. A fowl is held above the rice-ball and torch, its throat cut, and the blood let drop upon the ball ; some perfume is burnt, and the ceremony ends. The cocoanuts placed on the cot are then taken and dashed on the ground, or cloven in half. If the pieces fall with the kernel upward, it signifies the Bhuta is pleased with the offering ; if with the kernel downward, the reverse. Should a member of the family be stricken with any unusual attack, such as apoplexy, paralysis, cholera, &c.,

or should disease break out amongst the cattle, it is at once ascribed to the anger of the Bhuta, and a propitiatory sacrifice is offered. A fowl is turned three times round before the patient's face, its neck then twisted, and the blood let fall upon him, and some rubbed on his forehead and joints, the meaning being to offer life for life—the fowl in lieu of the man. Powdered sandal-wood is then sprinkled over the Bhuta's cot, and water from the pot kept there dashed upon the sick man's forehead and eyes. The family priest is then consulted, who, after much grave meditation, usually recommends alms to be given to himself to satisfy the hostile stars, with a promise to perform a special ceremony to the Bhuta, and give a banquet to all the patient's castemen should he recover. Medicine is not neglected, but, in event of recovery, the credit is ascribed to the influence of the Bhuta.

"The general buildings dedicated to these demons are called Bhutastans, and when dedicated to one of the superior, or very popular Bhutas, sometimes of considerable size; but far more commonly a small plain structure, four or five yards deep, by two or three wide, with a door at one end, covered by a portico supported on two pillars, with a thatched roof, and windowless. In front of it there are usually three or four T-shaped pillars, the use of which is not clear. They are said to denote that the building is a Bhutastan, and flowers are placed, and cocoanuts broken on them at ceremonies. It may be worth noticing that pillars of exactly the same shape are found accompanying the mysterious Balearic Talyots, the purpose of which has hitherto baffled antiquaries. Inside the Bhutastan there is usually a number of images roughly made in brass in human shape, or resembling animals, such as pigs, tigers, fowls, &c. These are brought out and worshipped as symbols of the Bhutas on various ceremonial occasions. The Bhutas themselves are usually represented by mere rough stones. Brass basins, bells, a peculiarly-shaped sword, and some other articles used at ablutions are also kept within. These rustic fanes are thickly scattered over the face of the country in very various situations—under a green tree, on hill-sides, down in hollows, in jungles, on plains, by road-sides, in villages, amid rice-fields, but always on a small plot of waste ground, which is kept uncultivated.

"Once a year a festival called Kolla is held at the village Bhutastan, in honour of the local Bhuta, at which all the villagers attend. There is no fixed time for this, but the village priest, after consulting with the principal inhabitants, determines an auspicious day. This being settled, a tall pole is fixed upright in the ground before the Bhutastan, and a flag, that is always kept within, hoisted upon it. The Bhuta's Bhandara, or paraphernalia, and the images, &c., are brought out and cleaned, and a large fire kindled to purify the spot. The festival always takes place at night, and about nine o'clock all the villagers assemble in their best attire, the women wearing all their ornaments, and their heads, as well as often the men's, thickly garlanded with flowers. Tom-toms and drums are beaten, and the Pujari, or Priest, takes the Bhuta-sword and bell in his hands, and whirls round and round, imitating the supposed mein and gestures of the demon. But he does not aspire to full possession, which in aboriginal rites like these, is only given to a representative of the aboriginal tribes, now the lowest castes. A Dhér, one of the slave caste, at other times regarded with contempt, but now advanced to the foremost post, comes forward naked, save a waist-band, and with all his head and body grotesquely and frightfully besmeared with white, yellow, and red paint. Over his head, and tied to his back, there is a sort of an arch, termed Ani, made of green-cocoa-tree leaves, with their ends radiating out. For some time he paces up and down, within a ring formed by the crowd, flinging about his arms, gesticulating wildly, leaping, and shaking his body furiously. Meanwhile a dozen or more tom-toms and drums are beaten incessantly and stunningly, with a continually increasing din; and the Dhér presently breaks into a maniac dance, capering, bounding, and spinning vehemently whilst the instruments redouble their noise, the power of the Bhuta being estimated by the fury and persistence with which the Dhér dances. The multitude around joins in raising a long, monotonous, howling cry, with a peculiar vibration. At length the Dhér stops, he is full of the demon, and stands fixed and rigid, with staring eyes. Presently he speaks, or rather the demon speaks from him, in loud, hoarse, commanding tones, wholly unlike his own, or indeed any natural voice. He addresses the head man of the village first, and then the principal inhabitants in due order, for any neglect of etiquette on this point by the Bhuta would infallibly give rise to great resentment. After thus speaking to the principal villagers and asking whether all the people are present, the possessed Dhér goes on to say that the Bhuta is pleased with the performance of the ceremony, and exhorts all the people to behave justly and charitably to one another. Various disputes and litigated matters, especially when evidence and ordinary means of adjustment fail, are then brought forward and submitted to the decision of the Bhuta, and his award, pronounced through the Dhér, is generally, though not always, submitted to. After this the demon desires to have food, and the Dhér eats fried rice, and drinks the milk of young cocoa-nuts; or if the demon he represents be one of low degree, he eats animal food and drinks arrack. He then distributes areca flowers and pieces of cocoa-nut to all assembled in due order of precedence, and the Bhuta passes away from him, he loses his commanding mien and tones, and relapses into the servile drudge. The assembly then addresses itself to festivity ; there is much drinking of arrack, the drumming and wild music go on vehemently, interminable songs are sung, and at the first dawn the people disperse on all sides to their homes."

The Rev. Mr. Caldwell, who has written an extended account of his mission in Southern India and Siam, gives the following sketch of rites something similar to the above, enacted amongst the natives of Tinnevelly. He says :—

"I have witnessed oracular responses given under the supposed control of a demon, after gesticulatory dances amongst the Todas of the Nilgiri Hills. In Siam spirit-dances are held in a shed built for the purpose, in which offerings are set out for the demon, who is invited by the usual wild music to come down to the dance ; but there is this peculiarity, that there the demon always enters a woman, which is scarcely ever heard of in India. She herself does not dance, but bathes and rubs herself with scent, dresses in a red waistcloth and dark silken jacket, and awaits the descent of the demon, who is incited to come by redoubled din of music and chanted incantations. When he comes she shakes and trembles, and then, assuming the airs and manners of a great personage, all present worship and pay her homage. Sometimes the spirit of one of their ancestors, sometimes a foreign demon, is supposed to have taken possesion of her body. She answers questions, and gives commands and directions in a haughty, imperative tone, and all her words are humbly listened to, and afterwards she partakes of the offerings provided for the demon. An old woman usually plays the part, and after the influence has left her, she declares she knows nothing of what took place, or what she may have said."

Although the methods of inducing trance amongst the ignorant inhabi tants of remote Eastern districts, and the cold unimpassioned dwellers of European cities, are widely different, it is not uninteresting to note the points of similarity which obtain *in the trance*, or during the period when the Mediums of both quarters of the globe are under the controlling influence of the Spirits. Change Mr. Caldwell's nomenclature of " the obsessing demon," for the more familiar phrase " the Spirit control," and we have no very marked difference between the above description, and that of an American or European trance Medium—save in the matter of costume, appearance, and general intelligence. Judge Walhouse's work on "Devil Worship," contains so many suggestions concerning disturbances and hauntings, quite familiar amongst more civilized peoples than the villagers of India, that it may not be uninteresting to follow up his descriptions in the subjoined extracts :—

"Besides numberless local Bhutas, there are some thirty especially feared in Canara, possessing temples and shrines in various parts of the province ; several are females. The most dreaded and malignant amongst them is Kalkatti, or the Stonecutter, reputed to be the spirit of Jackanachari, a famous stone-mason and architect, who, between four and five centuries ago, built most of the exquisitely beautiful Jaina temples that exist in Canara. Much legend has gathered about him, but he undoubtedly lived, and must have been a craftsman of marvellous skill. The tradition runs that he and his wife, having quarrelled with their son respecting a temple then in process of building, they both com- mitted suicide, and became Bhutas so malign and feared, that none dare attempt an exorcism when their presence is suspected. The next most dreaded Bhuta is *Panjurli*, *i.e.*, pig-rider, whose origin is forgotten, but is probably the perturbed spirit of some one once notorious. *Guliga* is regarded as an aboriginal or earth-born demon, and has power during certain minutes on certain days to pass through the air, and strike those he meets with a rod, thereby causing fits, paralysis, or even death. His glance also causes sick- ness, but the hours in which, in Shakspeare's sense, he can take or injure are limited. *Chamundi*, signifying mistress of death, is a female earth-spirit, and when the Kolla ceremony is offered to her, a large pile of wood is kindled, and after it has become a heap of glowing embers, the Dhér who represents and is possessed by her, dances and rolls upon them for some minutes without injury. *Munditaya* is the ghost of a Balala or high caste-man, who died by some accident, and is reputed very troublesome; sandal-wood powder and water, taken from the cot hung up to him, are however believed, when rubbed on, to cure snake-bites without further remedy. Most Bhutas haunt large trees, and it is of this last one, I think, that a story is told regarding a large, solitary Banian tree, near a village in the province. A demon was said to live in its branches, and none dare climb it. Some Mussulmans, however, laughed at the story, and one of them climbed up, but when he had got well up in the branches the goblin was suddenly revealed to him in a monstrous and frightful shape, on seeing which he screeched, let go his hold, fell to the ground, and remained raving with terror for three days; his back was injured by the fall, and he remained humpbacked, but lived to be ninety, and would often tell the story. The tree is now half dead, and limbs and branches often fall from it, but none will go near or pick them up."

In the third part of his work Judge Walhouse says :—

"The Dharmastal Temple, situated in a wild forest track in Canara, is one of the most famous in all that part of the peninsula, and is the abode of seven or eight very powerful Bhutas, who are so dreaded that none will assume their names. In civil suits, when the evidence is balanced or hopelessly contradictory, it is very usual for one of the parties to offer to decide it by taking an oath as to the justice of his contention before one of the Dharmastal deities; this, when accepted and done with certain formalities, is always held satisfactory and decisive; for the litigants know well that no one dare risk abiding the vengeance of those terrible Bhutas by a false adjuration. With respect to assuming their names, it may be explained that it is very common to name children after any Bhuta who may be very popular at the time, probably with the idea that the compliment might induce him to regard the child and family with favour. I remember that a good many years ago a notorious and greatly dreaded dacoit was hung in Trichinopoly, who after death became so fashionable a Bhuta that for some time half the children born were named after him. I may perhaps mention two or three out of the instances of the belief in Bhutas that came before me officially as judge. In a trial for murder before the Sessions Court, the prisoner was charged with having intentionally caused the death of his younger brother, whom he struck down as they were ploughing. In defence the prisoner stated, through his vakil, or pleader, that the deceased, whilst at work in the field, was struck by the eye of a Bhuta, of which he died; and his witnesses deposed that they had known similar instances. In another murder case the evidence of a material witness was objected to because he was well known to be under the curse of a Bhuta, and in consequence a desperate man, whose statements could not be believed. Again, a Potel, or village head-man, was charged with having entered the death of a boy in his register as natural when he had really committed suicide; in defence the Potel asserted that the boy had died from a blow by the village Bhuta, and named several instances. On being punished by the magistrate, he appealed to the Sessions Court, reasserting his plea, and desiring to call witnesses to prove it. These men were far from unintelligent, and the vakils, or native pleaders, acute and well able to conduct a legal argument. But we can hardly ridicule them much, when we reflect that within the last eighteen months a young farmer was sentenced to six months' imprisonment at Dorchester for savagely beating an old woman because she 'hag-rode' him : another man in Somersetshire was charged for twice stabbing a woman who had 'over-looked' him, that he might break the spell with her blood ; and there were four other convictions in Somersetshire and Devonshire alone, for assaults committed, or payment taken, on account of, or to cure, having been bewitched : and all the persons connected may presumably have been at school, and attended some church or chapel.

"Very often Bhutas become a sort of house spirits, such as are heard of in many popular mythologies, more or less mischievous, and delighting in Robin Goodfellow's pranks. Howlings and unearthly shrieks and noises that cannot be traced are attributed to them. Household utensils are thrown about, and stones flung by invisible hands, and pots and cooking vessels found filled with dirt. Women put away their best clothes carefully, and in the morning find them unaccountably on fire and smouldering away. All these are ascribed to the Bhuta, as well as what would now be called a kind of levitation, which is declared to be very frequent. Infants are missed from their cradles, and presently heard crying in the loft of the house, or on stacks of straw outside. Once riding through a village I found the people in great excitement at a prank played by a Bhuta two days before. A woman lying apart in her room expecting her confinement, was suddenly missed, and could nowhere be found, till some children heard her voice proceeding from a dry well in a field hard by. She was drawn up with considerable trouble, quite unhurt, and safely confined the same day. She said she found herself all at once at the bottom of the well, but could not in the least tell how she came there. The people insisted on showing me the well, which was about 100 yards from the house, large and square, one used for irrigation, but then dry, and from 20 to 25 feet deep. Roman Catholics are very numerous in Canara, but quite as subject to these demoniacal annoyances as the Hindus. One clerk of the civil court, a grave, elderly man, affirmed to me that, when passing at evening along a lane near a Bhutastan, he encountered a dark, monstrous, shadowy shape, which grew larger and larger, on which he uttered some religious verses, when it gradually diminished and disappeared. Another story was the talk of the town, and the parties concerned assured me of its truth. Two high native officials, both Roman Catholics, were sitting at noonday in the verandah of the house of one of them, when ashes and earth came pouring in quantities from the roof. The master of the house exclaimed the Bhuta was repeating his tricks, and, bringing a gun, fired it in the air to frighten the goblin away, when instantly, as if in answer, a quantity of powder was exploded in the midst of the open yard before them, and immediately stones and pebbles were flung by invisible agency towards the house from without. These fell on the verandah, and then, my informant asseverated, went "leaping like frogs" into the house, to the great amusement of the children who had assembled, and who would cry out, "one more!" when another stone would instantly fall and go hopping in! This sort of Bhuta annoyance was declared to be not at all unfrequent. It is curious, anthropologically speaking, to observe how general this strange belief in a grotesque sort of goblin, rejoicing in a particular kind of odd, mischievous pranks, has been in widely separated countries and ages. In China such disturbances are common, and ascribed to 'kitchen gods;' in Arabia and Egypt to the jinee or genii, who, Mr. Lane says, are believed to throw stones and furniture about in houses. He also relates that pious and and learned Muslims, on locking the doors of their houses, storerooms, and apartments when going out, habitually repeat, 'In the name of God, the Compassionate, the Merciful,' to secure their property during their absence from the mischief and depredations of the Jinn."

We must now notice a phase of Spiritualism which seems to be even more special to Oriental nations than the hauntings above described; this is the power acquired by some of those religious ascetics called "Fakirs," "Yogis," &c., &c. There are certain individuals styling themselves "Occultists," in contradistinction to the term "Spiritualists," who claim that the wonder-working powers exhibited by these Eastern magicians, are entirely under their own control and proceed from the results of initiation into divers human "Brotherhoods."

The author of "Art Magic," who spent many years amongst religious ascetics in India, and was himself a proficient in their practices, insists, that the Yogis, Fakirs, and wonder workers of India are assisted by the spirits of ancestors, whom they call "Pitris," and whom they almost always claim to be instrumental in the production of their marvellous feats of magical power. M. Jacolliot, for many years a resident in India, makes the same allegation, and M. Le Huc, besides other writers of eminence on East Indian magic, confirms these statements.

M. Jacolliot's articles on "Manifestations with the Fakirs of India," translated by Dr. Maximilian Perty, of Leipzig, will be found to contain a great deal of interesting matter on these subjects.

In a series of papers written for the German Spiritual paper, *Psychic Studien*, M. Jacolliot speaks of a Fakir named Covindasamy with whom he became acquainted under special circumstances, and through whom he witnessed manifestations of power and marvel which almost surpass belief.

Conversing with this wonderful personage on a certain occasion, M. Jacolliot said: "Dost thou know whether any force is developed in thee when these phenomena are produced, and dost thou never feel any peculiar sensation in brain or muscles?"

"It is no natural (or bodily) force which is at work," answered

Covindasamy. "*I call on the souls of my forefathers, and it is they who use their power, and whose instrument I am.*" Dr. Perty says: "Various Fakirs whom Jacolliot had questioned on the same point gave nearly the same answers."

Subjoined will be found one of the experiments recorded by Dr. Perty as occurring with this Fakir and M. Jacolliot :—

"Jacolliot had seen, with some of the fakirs, objects raised from the ground, and asked Covindasamy for this manifestation. The fakir took an ironwood stick, which Jacolliot had brought from Ceylon, rested his right hand upon the knob, cast down his eyes, and began his evocations, when gradually, still leaning one hand upon the stick, and with his legs crossed in oriental fashion, he rose about two feet from the ground, and remained immovable, in a position similar to that of the bronze Buddhas which tourists bring from the far East. Jacolliot could by no means comprehend how the fakir could remain over twenty minutes in a position entirely contravening the law of gravitation. When he took leave of Jacolliot that day, he informed him that at the moment when the sacred elephants in Siva's pagoda should strike the midnight hour on the copper saucers, he would call on the familiar spirits of the Franguys (Frenchmen), who would then manifest their presence in Jacolliot's bedchamber. In order to secure himself against deception, Jacolliot sent both his servants to spend the night in the *dingui*, with the *cercar* (boatman) and other attendants. The palace of the Peishwa has windows on the Ganges side only, and consists of seven stories, whose rooms open on to covered terraces and galleries. The stories communicate with each other in a peculiar way; from the ground floor a staircase leads to the first story, and at the further end of this is another flight of steps to the next above, and so on to the sixth, from which a movable flight, attached with chains like a drawbridge, leads to the seventh story, which is furnished half in oriental, half in European style, and is generally reserved for the foreign guests of the Peishwa.

"After Jacolliot had carefully searched his rooms, and pulled up the drawbridge, all communication with the outer world was cut off. At the given hour he heard two distinct raps on the wall of his room, and as he went towards the spot, a rapping noise seemed to come from the glass bell that protected the hanging lamp from mosquitoes, then a noise in the cedar beams of the roof, and all was still. He then walked to the end of his terrace; it was one of those silvery nights, unknown to our climates. The Ganges lay like a broad carpet at the foot of the sleeping city, and on one of its steps a dark figure was visible; it was the fakir of Trivanderam, praying for the repose of the dead.

"Jacolliot could not feel convinced that the theory of the Hindoos, that the phenomena which he had now so often witnessed were produced by the spirits of their ancestors, was in any sense proved; but he was equally certain that no one in Hindostan understood by what means these enchanters operated; he saw that the Hindoos do not separate material phenomena from religious belief. He said to the fakir, when he appeared the next evening, 'The sounds which you announced were really to be heard; the fakir is very skilful.' 'The fakir is nothing,' answered Covindasamy, quite calmly; 'he says his *mentrams*, and the spirits hear him. It was the manes of thy French forefathers who visited thee.' 'Thou hast power also over foreign spirits?' 'No one can command the spirits.' 'I mean, how can the souls of the Franguys hear the prayers of a Hindoo when they are not of thy caste? 'There is no caste in the world beyond.' It was impossible, as at all other times, to shake Covindasamy's conviction.

"He took a little bamboo stool, without further ado, and seated himself with his legs crossed Moslem fashion, and his arms across his breast. The servant had lighted the terrace to the brightness of day, and presently Jacolliot saw, after the motionless fakir had apparently concentrated his will-power, the bamboo stool begin to glide along the ground, and in about ten minutes arrive at the end of the terrace, and then return backwards to its former place. This happened three times, in accordance with Jacolliot's wish; the fakir's legs being raised above the ground to the level of the seat of the stool. The heat was on this day unusually great, the cool evening breeze from the Himalayas not having yet set in, and the cook was working with all his bodily force, by means of a cocoanut fibre string, an enormous punkah, a sort of movable fan, which was fixed to an iron pole in the centre of the terrace. The fakir took hold of the string, placed both hands upon his forehead, and crouched beneath the punkah, which soon began to swing, without any movement on Covindasamy's part, first gently, then more and more rapidly, as when moved by a human hand. If the enchanter let the string go, the punkah moved more and more slowly, till at last it stood still. Covindasamy next chose one of three flower pots on the terrace, which were so heavy that a man's whole strength was necessary to lift one; he laid the points of his fingers on its edge, causing a regular pendulum-like motion of the base, and at last the pot seemed to Jacolliot to rise off the ground, and to follow the will of the fakir in any direction, a phenomenon that Jacolliot had often seen in broad daylight."

The easiest way for sceptics to dispose of these statements is, to deny their authenticity or their narrator's veracity *in toto.* As we are not prepared to deal in this summary way with the testimony of a respectable and learned witness, especially as his account—however incredible to those who have not familiarized themselves with the records of East Indian Spiritualism—is verified by nearly every writer who has examined the subject, we shall present another extract from Dr. Perty's translation of Jacolliot's Hindoo experiences. It is as follows :—

" At ten o'clock on the evening of this day, Covindasamy came silently, as usual, into Jacolliot's room, having left behind him on the flight of steps his *languty* or small garment which was his only clothing, and having fastened his seven-jointed bamboo-stick to one of his long plaits of hair. 'Nothing impure,' said he, 'must touch the body of the invoker, when he wishes to come effectually into communion with the spirits.' The thought struck Jacolliot at this moment whether the Gymnosophists of the Indus were not similar to Covindasamy.

" The experiments were conducted that evening on the terrace and in Jacolliot's bedroom, both of which, communicating together, were effectually closed from without ; in each was a hanging lamp of cocoa-nut oil, enclosed in a glass globe. All Indian houses are provided with little copper vessels, always filled with glowing coal, in which at intervals it is customary to throw a fragrant powder of sandal-wood, orris root, myrrh, and incense. The fakir placed a similar vessel in the centre of the terrace, and beside it a copper plate covered with powder ; he then cowered down in his usual manner with crossed arms, and began a long incantation in an unknown language, repeated his *mentrams*, and remained immovable, with his left hand upon his heart, and the right leaning on his staff ; from time to time he raised his hand to his forehead, as if to clear his brain by passes. Suddenly Jacolliot trembled, for a faintly luminous cloud began to form in his chamber, from which hands rapidly came out in all directions, and returned to it again ; presently some of the hands lost their shadowy look, and appeared more human and material ; others became more luminous ; the first were opaque and cast shadows, the others so transparent that objects could be seen through them ; altogether Jacolliot counted sixteen. Jacolliot asked whether it would be possible to touch one of the hands ; scarcely had he done so, when one left the group, floated towards him, and pressed his offered hand ; it was small, moist and supple, and like the hand of a young woman. ' The spirit is there, although only one of its hands is visible,' said Covindasamy ; 'thou canst converse with it if thou wilt.' Jacolliot asked playfully if the spirit, to whom this charming hand belonged, would leave him a *souvenir ;* thereupon he felt the hand melt away from his, saw it float to a bouquet of flowers and break off a rosebud, which it threw at his feet ; it then vanished. For two whole hours things occurred enough to bewilder the strongest mind ; hands stroked Jacolliot's face, or fanned him with a fan, showered flowers all over the room, or wrote fiery letters in the air, which disappeared as soon as the last was made ; and flashes as of lightning passed along the terrace and through the chamber. Two of the Sanscrit phrases, which Jacolliot had written first with a pencil, had this meaning—*I have taken on a fluidic body ;* and thereupon the hand wrote—*thou wilt attain happiness, when thou art freed from this perishable body.* By degrees the hands vanished, the mass of cloud in which they seemed to have been materialized was partially dissipated ; and in the place where the last hand had faded away, they found a wreath of those strongly scented yellow *immortelles*, which the Hindoos use in their ceremonies.

" A moment afterwards, whilst the fakir was still earnestly engaged in invocation, a darker cloud formed near the pan of coals, which Jacolliot, at the fakir's wish, had kept replenished ; gradually this cloud took a human form, and appeared as the phantom of an old Brahmin, kneeling and offering sacrifice. He had the sacred sign of Vishnu on his forehead, and the threefold cord of the priestly caste round his body ; his hands were joined above his head, and his lips moved as if in prayer. At a particular moment he took a pinch of the sweet-smelling powder and threw it into the glowing coal, at which a thick smoke filled the air ; when it had dispersed, Jacolliot saw the phantom at two steps from him, holding out its withered hand ; Jacolliot took it in his own, and found it warm and living, though hard and bony. 'Art thou also,' he said aloud, 'a former inhabitant of this earth ?" The question was scarcely put when he saw in phosphoric light on the phantom's breast the word *Am* (Yes) come and go. And when Jacolliot

A HINDOO FAKIR
WORKING MAGIC SPELLS

asked him, ' Wilt thou give me a token of thy passing visit ?' the spirit tore off his girdle, made of a triple woollen twist, and vanished where he stood.

"Jacolliot thought the sitting was ended, but the fakir appeared to have no thought of leaving his place. Suddenly a strange melody was heard, which seemed to proceed from the harmonica previously used, but which the Peishwa had had taken away the evening before, and which was no longer in Jacolliot's apartments. The tones at first sounded as if at a distance, afterwards nearer, and lastly, as if in the bedroom ; but presently Jacolliot perceived the shadow of a pagoda player glide along the wall, holding a harmonica, from which were proceeding the monotonous, plaintive tones peculiar to the religious music of the Hindoos.

"The phantom glided through the room and along the terrace, and vanished, leaving behind him the instrument which was in fact the harmonica belonging to the rajah, and yet the doors were effectually closed. Covindasamy now stood up, bathed in perspiration, exhausted in the last degree. In a few hours he was to begin his journey. "I thank thee, Malabarer," said Jacolliot, addressing him in the name of his beloved country, "and may He who unites the three mysterious powers in his own person (the Brahminical Trinity) protect thee in thy journey to the lovely southern land, and mayst thou find that peace and happiness have dwelt in thy home during thine absence !" The fakir replied with still more emphatic words, took the offered present without looking at it, or returning thanks, paid his last melancholy greetings, and disappeared as silently as was his wont. When Jacolliot looked out on the river in the early morning he saw a black spot, and by means of the telescope discovered it to be the fakir who was crossing the Ganges on his way to Trivanderam, to the blue sea, the cocoa palms, and his own hut, of which he had so often spoken. After a few hours' sleep in his hammock, the past night appeared to him as a dream and a hallucination, but the harmonica was still there, the flowers still strewed the terrace, the wreath of *immortelles* lay upon the divan, and the words he had seen in the writing of flame were written, as at first, upon the slate. Jacolliot could discover as little deception as the Abbé Huc had been able to do in Thibet."

As a corollary to the various accounts which flood the columns of the Spiritual papers of *"form materialization"* obtained only in cabinets, dark *séances*, or under conditions which place the sitter wholly at the mercy of all and sundry who choose to practise on his credulity, the description of the above *séance*, and the conditions under which the phenomena occurred, may prove as *suggestive* as marvellous.

The different degrees of initiation through which the religious ascetics of India pass, to attain to the highest conditions of spiritual power, have too often been described by modern travellers, and are to be found too generally scattered through the pages of popular literature, to need reiteration here ; suffice it to say, the wonder workers of India, despite the halo of extreme sanctity which is traditionally thrown around them, are by no means the *beau idéal* of sublimity and exaltation that they appear in the light of poetical or fervid imagery. Even those who do not attempt to work upon public sentiment by converting themselves into monsters of deformity, are for the most part, lean, emaciated, and unearthly-looking beings ; repulsive in aspect, and so utterly abstracted from the objects of sense, that they move amongst their fellow-men, more like phantoms, or creatures whose only concern with earth is to linger upon its surface as a penance for deeds done in some former state of existence, than mortals having concern with mortal affairs. There are others, and these form the principal sum of the wonder-working devotees, of whom Major Colebrooke, a long resident in India, and one who has written extensively on its modern aspects, says :—

"The Fakirs are ignorant, insolent, and loathsome. The Yogis, who are supposed to give themselves up to meditation, are merely ignorant and superstitious men. There may be, there probably are, exceptions, but from a religion whose high morality and spirituality is lost and buried under a mass of degrading superstitions, what holiness can be expected ? A man who thinks, or is supposed to think, incessantly of one subject, even the highest, only stultifies himself, he cannot evolve out of his own nature anything which that nature does not contain. The proof is in the result. The Yogees or Suniassis, do nothing to make the people better. They receive gifts, and strengthen the dark superstitions which prevent India from rising."

Of modern Spiritualism, as represented by the Mediums of Europe, there is but little to report except in a few special places. Private circles have been successfully established amongst some of the white residents of British India, and one at least eminent Medium has visited the country, in the person of Mr. Eglinton, from London. Of this gentleman's powers as a Medium mention has already been made in connection with his visit to South Africa. During a brief residence amongst Spiritual friends in Calcutta, Mr. Eglinton made many converts, and was honoured by various eulogistic notices of his Mediumship in the public journals. The two following excerpts will suffice as an example of these notices. The first is taken from the *Indian Daily News*, and reads as follows :—

"At Calcutta, Mr. Eglinton's *séances* are attended by the most intelligent classes, and manifestations occur that perfectly astound spectators. On one occasion two 'materialized spirits appeared in the light—one of a Hindu lady, and the other a Hindu gentleman, father and mother respectively of two of the sitters. The *Indian Mirror* of December 17th, says :—

"'One of the sitters was requested to write the name of a departed relative. The name was not shown to Mr. Eglinton, nor did he know it, or was likely to know it. The bit of paper on which the name was written was then folded up and handed over to Mr. Eglinton, who, *as soon as he received* it in its folded state, burnt it in the flame of the lamp before which he sat. It was immediately reduced to ashes, and Mr. Eglinton then rubbed the ashes over one of his arms, which was laid bare and found to be quite clear, and *free from any writing at all*. But scarcely had Mr. Eglinton rubbed the ashes over his arm, when the name of the departed relative of the sitter appeared in a minute or so in *distinctly legible* characters over the very arm, spelt similarly as on the bit of paper itself. But the most striking thing was this. When the materialized spirits had disappeared, a distinct sound of writing was heard in the dark for two or three seconds and immediately, when a light was brought, a card was found stuck up on the edge of a book, near a certain distinguished sitter, and the following Sanskrit text appeared on it in pencil, in pure and excellent Bengali handwriting, with the initials in English of one "P"—"*Tapasha Braham bijigya sumbo*," which, when rendered into English, runs as follows: "By devotion and knowledge of God a person is united with Him, *i.e.*, he attains salvation." '"

For the second extract we are indebted to the *Harbinger of Light*, Melbourne. It is headed—

"ANOTHER CONJUROR NONPLUSSED.

"Many of our readers will remember 'Kellar,' the illusionist, who performed very cleverly the 'Cabinet Trick' and a number of other imitations of spiritual phenomena at St. George's Hall, a few years since. The following letter, extracted from the *Indian Daily News* of January 26th, contains Mr. Kellar's admission of the distinctive nature of spiritual phenomena.

'MR. KELLAR AND THE SPIRITS.

' *To the Editor of the Indian Daily News.*

'Sir, — In your issue of the 13th January, I stated that I should be glad of an opportunity of participating in a *séance* with a view of giving an unbiased opinion as to whether, in my capacity of a professional prestidigiteur, I could give a natural explanation of effects said to be produced by spiritual aid.

'I am indebted to the courtesy of Mr. Eglinton, the spiritualistic medium now in Calcutta, and of his host, Mr. J. Meugens, for affording me the opportunity I craved.

'It is needless to say I went as a sceptic, but I must own that I have come away utterly unable to explain, by any natural means, the phenomena that I witnessed on Tuesday evening. I will give a brief description of what took place :—

I was seated in a brilliantly lighted room with Mr. Eglinton and Mr. Meugens ; we took our places round a common teak-wood table, and after a few minutes the table began to sway violently backwards and forwards, and I heard noises such as might be produced by some one thumping under the table. I tried to discover the cause of this movement but was unable to do so. After this, Mr. Eglinton produced two common slates, which I sponged, cleaned, and rubbed dry with a towel myself. Mr. Eglinton then handed me a box containing small crumbs of slate pencil ; I selected one of these, and in accordance with Mr. Eglinton's directions, placed it on the surface of one of the slates, placing the other slate over it. I then firmly grasped the two slates at one of the corners ; Mr. Eglinton held the other corner, our two free hands being clasped together. The slates were then lowered below the edge of the table, but remained in full view (the room remaining lighted all the time) ; instantaneously I heard a scratching noise, as might be produced by writing on a slate. In about fifteen seconds I heard three distinct knocks, on the slate, and I then opened them and found the following writing : —

'"My name is Geary. Don't you remember me ? we used to talk of this matter at the St. George's. I know better now."

'Having read the above, I remarked that I knew no one by the name of Geary.

'We then placed our hands on the table, and Mr. Eglinton commenced repeating the alphabet until he came to the letter G, when the table began to shake violently. This process was repeated till the name of Geary was spelt.

'After this, Mr. Eglinton took a piece of paper and a pencil, and with a convulsive movement difficult to describe, he wrote very indistinctly the following words :—

'"I am Alfred Geary, of the *Lantern ;* you know me and St. Ledger.'

'Having read this, I suddenly remembered having met both Mr. Geary and Mr. St. Ledger at Cape Town, South Africa, about four years ago, and the St. George's Hotel is the one I lived at there. Mr. Geary was the editor of the *Cape Lantern*. I believe he died some three years ago. Mr. St. Ledger was the editor of the *Cape Times*, and I believe is so still. Without going into details, I may mention that subsequently a number of other messages were written on the slates, which I was allowed to clean each time before they were used.

'In respect to the above manifestations I can only say I do not expect my account of them to gain general credence. Forty-eight hours before I should not have believed any one who had described such manifestations under similar circumstances. I still remain a sceptic as regards Spiritualism, but I repeat my inability to explain or account for what must have been an intelligent force that produced the writing on that slate, which, if my senses are to be relied on, was in no way the result of trickery or sleight of hand.— Yours, &c.,

'Calcutta, January 25th, 1882."   'HARRY KELLAR.'"

The above letter needs no comment to the intelligent Spiritualist. Any other readers may dispose of its contents after their own fashion.

Of religious movements it would be almost impossible to give even a list, so numerous are the cases of enthusiasm, or—as must be admitted in some instances—imposture which lead to the formation of new sects. One of the latest, in which the founder claims to act under Spiritual guidance and inspiration is that headed by the well-known leader of the Bramoh Somaj, KESHUB CHUNDER SEN. This noteworthy personage, although most highly lauded by some and regarded by his immediate followers as something little less than an *Avatar*, but still far beyond the ordinary grade of poor mortality, is nevertheless equally unpopular in other directions, and by many writers is denounced as an audacious impostor.

In a wild rambling discourse given recently to about 1,200 persons in the Town Hall of Calcutta, Baboo Keshub Chunder Sen took for his text the self-propounded question, "Am I an inspired prophet?" Although a full report of his own answer to his own question is in print and before the world, no reader seems yet able to determine whether that answer was given in the negative or affirmative. The speaker represented himself as being in direct communication with John the Baptist, Jesus, and Paul, whose spirits he alleged he had met and conversed with, and from whom he received his commission to lead mankind into the truths of the religion he professes to teach. In some respects this is broad and unsectarian, but in others, the introduction of his own veiled Messiahship, and the strange commixture of old Aryan philosophy, with modern superstition, is curious and perplexing.

The *New York Sun* gives the following notice of the Hindoo Prophet and his self-appointed mission :—

"Kesub Chunder Sen, a high caste Brahmin who for some time has been a rising light in India, has cast aside appearances and become a founder of a new sect. Possibly no man exerts so wide an influence religiously in India to-day as this Hindoo reformer. He was formerly at the head of the Bramoh Somaj, but has progressed—at least so he thinks, beyond them. If to converse with spirits makes a man a Spiritualist, then Chunder Sen is a Spiritualist, for he avows in the most positive manner that Jesus, John the Baptist, and Paul have appeared to and conversed with him. He is considered by his admirers not only as a great reformer, but a prophet sent of God. He has long and earnestly protested against the superstition of his own country, and at times the hearts of missionaries were gladdened by his praise of their works, and his seeming acceptance of the doctrines of Christ. To establish Christianity, however, was not his object. He claims to be a re-incarnation of the divine Bhakti, under the name of Chaitauya, and that he is commissioned to establish the church of the future. He is the Prophet Nadiya ; an organization has been completed at Calcutta ; and the apostles, 'a preaching army,' have been sent forth on their mission to convert the world. This army moves from place to place with banners flying and music, and so great is the enthusiasm that devotees roll themselves in the dust before it.

"The object of the new prophet is to deliver his country from dry rationalism and supply a living faith. Whatever the results may be, the movement is of deep interest to the student of religious history, as an illustration of the rise and progress of sects. Kesub Chunder Sen, with his pretence of being a re-incarnation, in the light of the present, is a sham and a farce ; removed two thousand years into the past, and a few wonder works, would have made good his pretence, and untold millions would have received him as God."

A still more detailed description of the Prophet was recently published in the *Cincinnati Commercial* of July, 1880, by Moncure D. Conway, from which the following extracts may serve to give a graphic idea of the Prophet and his pretensions. Mr. Conway says :—

"It would be worth while for a student of psychology, or of abnormal religious excitements, to visit India just now. The minister of the Brahmos, Keshub Chunder Sen, seems to have had his head somewhat turned by—or at any rate since—his visit to England, and the marriage of his daughter to a prince. He has built a splendid house in Calcutta, and atones for that worldliness by ascetic mortifications."

"He has announced that he is a special agent of Providence ; he is not an incarnation of any deity ; he is not a prophet ; but he is something different from other men. His recent course and preaching have been fruitful of discord and agitations. The more educated of his followers, who have favoured the Brahmo movement as at once a protest against idolatry and a refined theism, have become disgusted and left the church. A large number of the lower-class converts have been offended by the marriage of his daughter with a prince, and they have abandoned him. And this parting with the elements of rational restraint and coolness on the one hand, and of humility on the other, appears to have been the means of revolutionizing a movement to which some had looked for great and beneficial changes in India."

"Keshub Chunder Sen and his followers seem to have taken hints from the revivalists of the West, and formed something like a 'Salvation Army.' They are replacing their lost adherents with fanatics gathered in the highways and byways, the survivals of extinct excitement, and adopting their wild manners and customs, their pilgrimages, shrieks, dances, and superstitions, they are calling the grand totality a 'new dispensation.' But from the mass of evidence before me I should say their star of Bethlehem has a chance of guiding them to Bedlam, or the places in India corresponding thereto. Sen himself has got so far in that direction as accepting a sort of worship from disciples kneeling around him (on the ground that he did not wish to stop the flow of bhatki—that is, devotion or enthusiasm), and holding personal interviews with Jesus, Paul, and John. One consequence of this outbreak of fanaticism is the loss of many of the educated ; but it has secured the results which manifest to Sen a 'new dispensation.' That is, he has raised public curiosity ; thousands go to hear him, and by using Christian phrases in his own sense he has roused the missionaries and made a sensation. They are denouncing him on one side, while the educated theists denounce him on the other ; and the result is that on a recent occasion as many as five thousand people went to hear him. The discourses he now delivers are quite valueless for any moral or religious teaching ; they are merely frantic ejaculations about God and the prophets, among which Jewish, Christian, and pagan are found oddly mixed."

"The last phase upon which this now wild movement has entered appear to be the dance and the pilgrimage. They lately organised a pilgrimage to 'Sinai.' On the 22nd of February they all bathed, put on clean clothes, and followed the minister up into the 'sanctuary ;' here, if one is to believe reports, they passed eight days and nights, and communed with Moses, reading over the Pentateuch and spiritualising each verse : so that on the last day Moses is said to have spoken to them in some mysterious way ; whether he spoke from a burning bush, or whether he materialized personally, cannot be gathered from the mystical narratives of the pilgrims.

"The revelation made by Moses included a transcription of the Ten Commandments, and a proclamation to the modern Israel, in which he stated that Jehovah's voice was his only guide, his only book of wisdom, the only Scripture of salvation ; and promised that 'the Almighty shall lead Bengal out of the bondage of superstition and idolatry into a city overflowing with milk and honey of purity and joy.' "

Amongst the recent literary productions which bear testimony to the spread of the Spiritual faith in India, no writings are more highly esteemed than those of PEARY CHAND MITTRA.

Besides a number of excellent magazine articles contributed by this gentleman to the different Spiritual periodicals of England and America, Mr. Mittra has written an interesting *brochure* entitled "Spiritual Stray Leaves," and a still more profound work on "The Soul ; its nature and development." In the appendix to this publication, there is an announcement of a society recently formed in Calcutta for the study of Spiritual subjects. The author speaks in hopeful terms of the Spiritual outlook in that city, and predicates a grand harvest for "the cause" when the chaotic elements that beset it are sifted away, and Spiritualism can command true *Spiritualists* for its votaries.

Another talented native Spiritualist is Shibchunder Deb, a gentleman who has contributed to the stock of Spiritual literature an excellent compilation from the works of the best American authors. Amongst other undertakings of this character, Shibchunder Deb has translated THE TEN SPIRITUAL COMMANDMENTS, given by the Spirits through the Mediumship of Mrs. Emma Hardinge Britten at one of her London lectures, into the Bengalese dialect. These commandments, hung up in hundreds of houses as Spiritual texts in England and America, are now circulated in India as a valuable missionary tract.

Besides these signs of growing interest in the unfoldment of Spiritual doctrines, Mr. Mittra, in a letter to the editor of the London *Medium and Daybreak* of February, 1881, gives the following items, concerning the present status of Spiritualism in Calcutta. He says :—

"I have found that any one praying and sitting quietly with slate or paper and pencil in hand, and thinking of the departed friend, is gradually developed as a medium. He must not will to move his hand, but it will be moved by the controlling spirit. At first dots and strokes will be formed and replies to questions given. Sometimes instructions will be given. In my family there are several writing mediums. After prayer we have had sometimes writing on the slate, from the spirit of one of my sons, which was of a very soothing nature, and the instruction of my son, who was a Brahmo, was to dedicate ourselves to God, as there was no other means to elevate ourselves or to enjoy true felicity.

"The rapid sale of my 'Spiritual Stray Leaves' is a convincing proof of the growing appreciation of Spiritualism in India. Efforts are being made by certain friends interested in Spiritualism to get a practised medium from England, which will take time. An European brother Spiritualist (who will be happy to give further particulars of other experiences to any earnest investigator), sent a letter to the under-mentioned medium under seal to the address of the spirit of his mother. This letter was not opened. It has come back with a reply to every question from the spirit of the lady who died five and thirty years ago, and the reply bears internal evidence of her identity.

"Another friend has sent a letter to Mr. Mansfield to the address of his father's spirit. We are waiting for the reply. The European brother Spiritualist above referred to is Mr. J. G. Meugens, Member of Messrs. W. Moran and Co., of this city, whose letter published since in the *Banner of Light* of the 22nd ultimo is reproduced :—

" 'I wish to bear testimony to the mediumship of Mr. J. V. Mansfield, of New York. Mr. Mansfield is an absolute stranger to me, and all I know of him was from what I had seen reported in your paper. I wrote a letter to my mother, who has been in spirit-life over thirty years, asking her a number of questions that only my mother could answer ; and this letter I put in a thick envelope, which I carefully gummed, and sealed, and addressed : "To my Mother." I enclosed it in a note to Mr. Mansfield, simply asking him to let me have a reply if he could get one. Last mail brought me a communication from the doctor, returning my letter addressed to my mother, with the seal unbroken, and in precisely the same condition that I sent it, together with a long reply purporting to come from my mother, addressing me by my Christian name, which Mr. Mansfield could have no means of knowing, and which is a very uncommon one, and answering every one of the questions put to her. I have met with a good many tests during my investigations when in England, but I do not know of any more convincing than this.

" 'I wish we had a good medium of Mr. Mansfield's stamp out here, for in that case possibly we might manage to excite a little intelligent interest in this grand philosophy, for it is lamentable to witness the utter ignorance and apathy displayed towards the subject in this part of the world.

" 'J. H. MEUGENS.

" '3, Church Lane, Calcutta, March 24th, 1880.'

"My friend, Baboo Poorna Chunder Mokerjea, Solicitor of the High Court, has received from the spirit of his brother a reply to his letter sent to Mr. Mansfield. The letter was not opened. The reply is satisfactory. Other friends are about to place themselves in communication with Mr. Mansfield.

Mr. Meugens adds a list of Mediums and works on Spiritualism, after which he thus concludes :—

"There are a great many metaphysical, theological works, and works on Buddhism and on the ancient literature of India, which are well worth reading. They are to be found in the Calcutta Public Library."

Now and then a new sensation such as a public debate, and, not unfrequently, the unjust and illiberal action of some interested antagonist, stirs the sluggish waters of mentality when they are disposed to settle in India, as in other great centres of modern thought and civilization. An example of this kind was afforded by the attack of the notorious *Reverend* Joseph Cook, of Boston, mentioned in an earlier chapter of this work, and renowned for his furious onslaught upon the Spiritualists, after having committed himself by parading forth to Boston audiences, the inexplicable marvels wrought through Slade's and Watkin's mediumship.

Mr. Cook has followed up this raid on every possible occasion, determining, as he himself announced in the attack above referred to, "to put himself right on the subject of Spiritualism." How he succeeded in this attempt during a recent visit to India, where, in his diatribes against Spiritualism he took pains to insult some of the most respectable and influential of his listeners, may be gathered from the following letter, published in several European journals :—

"Joseph Cook has been in India. There, as at home, he created considerable commotion. He seems to be so organized that whenever he presents himself, agitation of thought follows, and great good is accomplished thereby, for the friction caused, exposes the errors of the reverend gentleman, and aids at the same time in bringing to the front liberal thoughts, which otherwise might have remained obscured. The following letter alludes to some of his doings in India :—

" ' *To the Editor of the Religio-Philosophical Journal.*

" ' If you will kindly refer to the supplement to the current month's number of the *Theosophist*, you will find therein some account of Mr. Cook's visit to Bombay. You will also learn how he ran down our society and the founders, and how he denounced Spiritualism. There will also be found the challenge issued by us to him, and an account of his backing out. The meeting referred to in the challenge, was held here on the 20th ultimo. After addressing the meeting and convincing the audience about our society and ourselves, Col. Olcott defended Spiritualism. A pamphlet containing a report of the meeting is being printed. As soon as it is published, it will be sent you. In the meantime, Col. Olcott found in the 'Scientific Basis of Spiritualism,' a published testimony signed, amongst others, by Mr. Joseph Cook, vouching for certain phenomena 'not explicable by any theory of fraud.' It was arranged to have it sent immediately to the *Bombay Gazette*, an influential daily Anglo-Indian journal here.

" ' Bombay, India. DAMODAR K. MAVALANKAR."

The editor of *Light* introduces a notice of Colonel Olcott's pamphlets with the following remarks :—

" Colonel Olcott sends two pamphlets from Bombay. One gives 'The whole truth about the Theosophical Society, and its Founders.' It is the outcome of some slanders put about by the Rev. Joseph Cook, of Boston. A specimen of these is the statement that Colonel Olcott and Madam Blavatsky had ' come to India to study the ancient system of magic and sorcery to return to the United States to teach tricks to mediums already exposed !' Mr. Cook is one of the worst products of that offensive alliance between sensationalism and a pseudo-scientific theology which a craving for novelty on the part of audiences and for notoriety at any price on the part of a few professors of the flatulent style of oratory has produced. He seems, however, to have been thoroughly driven out of the field, smitten hip and thigh from Dan even unto Beersheba—from Bombay to Poona. Poor man ! he gave the Society the largest gratuitous advertisement in his power ; and it is open to a casuist to contend that he ought to have had a vote of thanks, instead of being ' posted as a coward and a slanderer.' "

Regretting that so much space has been necessarily devoted to so unworthy a subject as Mr. Joseph Cook's doings, we are happy in bidding him farewell, and now close our summary of the present status of Spiritualism in India with the following expressive lines from " Art Magic :" —

" Spiritism ever has, and ever will find its most fertile soil in the magical East ; that land of Prophets, Saviours, Avatars, and Oriental Mystics ! That land where matter bends and sways in the grasp of mind as a pigmy writhes in the clutch of a giant ; a land where magic shoots up in every plant ; gleams forth in many coloured fires from lustrous gems and glittering minerals ; where the stars tell their tale of eternity undimmed by the thick vaporous airs of equatorial skies, and the sun and moon imprint their magical meanings and solemn glories in beams, the radiance of which goes direct to the inner consciousness of awe struck worshippers.

" Let the magic of the Orient combine with the magnetic spontaniety of Western Spiritism, and we may have a religion whose foundations laid in science, and stretching away to the heavens in inspiration, will revolutionize the opinions of ages, and establish on earth the reign of the true Spiritual kingdom."

CHAPTER XXXVIII.

RÉSUMÉ OF SPIRITUALISM IN THE EAST.

ALTHOUGH the modern works which contain descriptions of Oriental magic are too numerous to catalogue, it is still essential to the completion of this compendium to give a brief *résumé* of the magical *(i.e.,* the Spiritual) practices now prevailing throughout some of the most generally known districts of the Orient.

The methods of inducing the state in which feats of super-mundane power can be accomplished, have already been shown to be dependent in part upon processes of culture which the subject himself can put in practice. The results thus achieved might with propriety be termed "MAGIC," and it is questionable whether the entire of the marvels exhibited in ancient times under this formidable name, might not be resolved into arts in which psychology and magnetism were the principal factors.

The antithesis to the condition attained by the Eastern yogi, or ecstatic, through processes of self-culture, is that of the modern Spirit Medium, whose powers are alleged to require no culture, no self-induced states of preparation, nothing in short but utter passivity, and dependence upon a Spiritual controlling influence. Whether—as suggested in the last chapter—the clue to a true Spiritual science may not yet be found in a judicious combination of both methods, will soon be the question of the age, and on the answer it receives from capable psychologists, will the future status of Spiritualism depend.

Amidst the vague and unproved theories of the day, it is often alleged that the passive "Medium" holds himself in subjection only to beings, who in reality have *no being;* "shells," "*reliquiæ* of the dead," the cast-off garment composed of some imponderable element the Spirit has worn, but which is now represented as being a mere "ghoul;" at once intelligent and powerful enough to deceive and work all sorts of evil, but yet having no distinct intelligence for anything good; a something and a nothing, which will presently fade out and become extinct. In connection with a theory so astonishing to the millions of Spiritualists who have fondly believed they were holding communion with precisely the same individualized men and women they had known on earth, and from whom moreover they persist in affirming they have received untold good, and very little evil, comes another theory, to the effect, that all that the Spiritualists attribute to the agency of their "Spirit friends," together with feats of a still more marvellous character, can be produced by the direct action of *the spirit within man,* that is, provided that Spirit *be still embodied,* its disembodied state being subject to a series of mysterious subdivisions, the only portion which can be known to man, being the malicious, evil disposed, and evanescent "*reliquiæ,*" aforesaid. Of course it will be understood that assertions of so extraordinary a character as these, cannot be accepted upon assertion only, and as the proof of their truth or falsity has yet to be shown, the experienced Spiritualists' faith in the human attributes of his Spirit communicants, remains unshaken. Meantime, and pending the production of *proof*, of more weight and worth than individual assertion, it is necessary to remind the reader, that up to this point, even the mere compendium of the world's latest Spiritual experiences which we have been able to offer in this volume, bears witness to the universal belief of mankind in the strict humanity of the Spirits that communicate with earth, and their agency for great good, as well as for great evil. Of course it must be apparent that there is a wide line of demarcation between the simply passive Medium who makes no effort to cultivate the powers of his own spirit, and the ecstatic who devotes his life to that culture. The former may be termed a "Spiritualist," the other an "Occultist," and both terms may be used in derision or reproach by opposing theorists ; but, if instead of laying down theories, and then distorting the obvious nature of facts to suit them, we were first carefully to formulate our facts, and then deduce logical theories from thence, might we not find Spiritualism and Occultism to be convertible terms, and the accomplished Yogi to be only a highly endowed Medium, whose gifts had been exalted by processes of mental and physical training?

As it is, vague theories are becoming more and more divergent from proven facts, and in the attempt to make them cohere, such wild and incoherent views of Spiritual existence are being promulgated, that the world is sinking into grosser darkness and confusion from the perversion of Spiritual facts, than ever prevailed before those facts were demonstrated.

Advising our readers to recall the accounts of phenomena produced in the East, as given by Le Huc, McGowan, Nevius, Sir J. Barrows, Lane, Salt, Jacolliot, and other writers, we proceed to gather up a few more crumbs of Spiritual evidence, from the well-spread board which Oriental history furnishes forth.

On one occasion when the author was invited to attend a Chinese funeral, it was a remarkable sight to observe the total apathy on the subject of death, displayed by those who were known to be loving and affectionate relatives of the deceased.

An intelligent Chinese merchant present, pointed to the number of garments in which the deceased was arrayed, in evidence that the Spirit was supposed to derive assistance from them in the new country to which he had passed.

Like the rice, and other edibles which the Chinese place on the tombs of their friends, these garments are not assumed to be appropriated materially. It is believed that the spiritual part of all earthly substances is of service to departed ancestors, and by them assimilated in their new state of being, as a welcome tribute of earthly remembrance.

It is proper here to mention, that the Mongolians believe in various spheres of Spiritual existence after death.

A very intelligent Japanese gentleman, a priest, and writer of school books, informed the author, that the general opinion amongst Mongolians was, that the Spirits who throw stones, knock, disturb houses, and haunt trees and woods, are evil minded earth bound souls, who did mischief on earth, and still continue to practice it. Those who play on instruments, write in sand, appear as apparitions, and give good counsel, are Spirits whose affections and interests still draw them to the earth. The very high Spirits, such as Fo, or Joss, Buddha, Lao-Tze, &c. are souls of men who have risen by virtue and purification on earth, to become saints and gods. In that phase of doctrine termed "Lamaism," it is firmly believed that the Grand

21

Lama is an incarnation of Buddha himself; thus with the exception of "the great celestial Emperor of Heaven," the unknown and unknowable of all religions, the Mongolians generally believe that the souls of men constitute an essential part of the Hierarchy of Spiritual existence by which the government of the universe is conducted. They do not teach that the higher intelligences can communicate, except through inspiration, and the agency of lower Spirits, although they do sometimes say they see the gods in the form of brilliant lights, or divine apparitions too glorious for mere mortals to gaze upon. Messrs. Nevius, Doolittle, and other authoritative writers, concur in affirming that the Chinese believe all their gods, except "the Supreme Emperor" were once men, from the idle "kitchen gods," who delight in fun and mischief, to the inspiring deities who rule our mundane sphere.

This deeply rooted faith in human Spiritual agency, is actually assigned as one reason why polygamy has been practised in Mongolian lands. Dr. Eitel, a well-known Christian missionary of Hong Kong, declares, that when he remonstrated with his converts against this custom, they pleaded for its continuance on the ground, that it was necessary to provide an ample posterity to do them honour, and worship them, when they themselves should be Spirits. The same plea was alleged by a man in the service of Captain Thomas Hunt of Salem, Massachusetts. He had taken a second wife whilst his first was yet living, and when Captain Hunt reproved him, he alleged that as his first wife had borne no offspring, he must take a second, or if necessary a third or fourth, otherwise he should leave no one on earth to offer him fruits and flowers, or welcome him back when he wished to revisit the earth as a spirit.

THE KARENS.

Amongst the once unknown people of the far East, with whom the facilities of modern travel have made the Western nations acquainted, is a quiet peaceful tribe of Burmese, called "Karens."

The author of "Art Magic," who spent some time in their villages, gives accounts of their Spiritual belief, from which we make the following extract :—

"In the mountain regions of Burmah reside a people called 'Karens,' who dwell in small settlements or villages, and pass lives of singular purity, temperance, and honesty. Their religious teachers are called *Bokoors*, and their office is to inculcate moral principles, predict the future, and interpret the will of the Supreme Being to man.

"Besides these, there is an inferior class of prophets, called *Wees*, or wizards, who cure the sick by spells and charms, fly through the air, bewitch cattle, exorcise the evil spirit out of them, and perform many other wonderful things. . . . Their faith in the presence and ministry of the spirits of their ancestors is immovable. They declare they often see them by night as well as by day ; they converse freely with them by signal knockings, voices, the ringing of bells, and sweet singing. They perform good offices, and warn their friends of danger, sickness, and death. . . . The Karens believe that the spirits of the dead are ever abroad on the earth ! 'Children and grandchildren,' say the elders, 'the dead are among us ! Nothing separates them from us but a white veil. They are here, but we see them not; only a few gifted ones have eyes to see into the spiritual world, and power to hold converse with particular spirits. . . .'"

Many writers of eminence have given accounts of ancient magic in Egypt, though but few have written on its present status. In Mr. Peebles' interesting sketchy work "Around the World," we have the following items concerning this subject :—

"The *gods*, the guardian angels of the ancient Egyptians, were once mortal men. Sanchoniathon, whom accredited historians place before the time of Moses, wrote in the Phœnician. Philo of Byblus translated a portion of his works into Greek. [Here follow a few lines.] Egyptians and Phœnicians accounted those the greatest gods who had found out things most necessary and useful in life, and who had been benefactors of mankind! Hermes Trismegistus acknowledged that the gods of Egypt were the souls of dead men; and Plutarch informs us that the Egyptian priests pointed out where the bodies of their gods lay buried. Cicero wrote: 'The whole heaven is almost entirely filled with the human race; even the superior order of gods were originally natives of this world!'

"And with these gods, angels, and spirits, the Egyptians of remotest antiquity held constant converse. . . . On their tombs, towers, and obelisks, are pictured mesmerists in the act of pathetising subjects. . . . The angel of Spiritualism has sounded the resurrection trumpet of a future existence in every land under heaven. Madame Blavatsky, assisted by other brave souls, formed a society of Spiritualists in Cairo about three years since. They have fine writing mediums and other forms of manifestation."

From the once beautiful city of Alexandria, so recently reduced to ruins by the barbarisms of war, the author has received a number of interesting communications from the family of Mr. Marcus Temple, a European Spiritualist, several of whose children became Mediums for different phases of Spirit power. This gentleman represented the Medium power manifested in various families of his acquaintance as quite remarkable, but added, that public opinion was against them, most of the Europeans residing in Alexandria being accustomed to associate all subjects of a super-mundane character, with the orgies of howling Dervishes, snake charmers, and the practices of religious mendicants. He fully confirms the descriptions of native Spiritualism as given in "Art Magic," and the sketches of Messrs. Salt, Lane, Mrs. Poole, Miss Martineau, and other writers on Eastern customs.

The tribes of Dervishes in Egypt, Syria, and Arabia, are generally divided into twelve grades, all of whom are more or less trained systematically, and all of whom profess to practise magical arts in connection with super-mundane or Spiritual powers. Their modes of culture include the methods already described, such as silent contemplation, fasting, ablutions, asceticism, chastity, whirling, spinning, violent motions, the use of noise, music, and narcotics. The Dervishes, besides these well-known modes of inducing ecstacy, have many traditionary customs of extreme antiquity, the *modus operandi* of which is known and handed down orally from generation to generation, but never committed to writing or inscription. Sometimes those destined for this strange life pass their initiatory processes in companies ruled over by one highly experienced teacher; sometimes they become solitary Santons, and frequent deserts, mountain passes, savage wilds, or lonely hermitages, from which they only emerge on self-imposed missions, or for special purposes. Many of these solitary Santons as well as individuals amongst the associated companies, are evidently natural Mediums, seers, prophets, and clairvoyants, and these always become the best wonder-workers. They live on the simplest fruits, roots, and herbs, and except for the purposes of stimulating themselves to mantic frenzy, use no intoxicating drinks, or "pleasant food." The five principal classes into which the Dervishes are resolved, out of the twelve grades which are their *religious subdivisions*, are as follows:—The dancing, whirling, or spinning Dervishes. The howlers, shouters, singers, or criers. The fire eaters; the snake charmers, and the illusionists. All these performers save the two last named, work themselves up to frenzy by their peculiar modes, in which condition they prophesy, see visions, predict the future, find lost or hidden things, and work marvellous feats. The snake charmers and illusionists are unmistakable MAGNETIZERS, and exert their powers over the lower animals or man himself, on the principle of electro-biology. Their powers of *fascination*, are simply marvellous, and it is by these that many seemingly impossible feats of wonder are *apparently* effected, before multitudes of people. There are some good healers amongst them, and some, who like the Tartar Lamas, can mutilate their bodies, and restore them instantly.

There are story tellers—or improvisatores—also in their ranks, poets, and visionists. They are skilful in discovering lost property, and very often good diviners. Their prayers, cries, motions, music, and *mentrams* are but means of inducing the psychic state; but question them, and they will one and all declare they are assisted by the gods, and Spirits of ancestors.

Ennemoser in his "History of Magic," gives graphic descriptions of how the Lapps and Siberian Schamanns stimulate themselves to the mantic frenzy, by noise, the beating of drums, cries, leaping, dancing, spinning, &c., &c. Precisely similar rites are attributed by Godwyn to the ancient Hebrews, in their various methods of *enquiring of the Lord.*

The glamour of sectarian superstition, entirely obscures the reason of devout Christians, when the rites of the Hebrews are brought into question, otherwise, they would long since have seen the parity of these Arabian magical practices, with David's "leaping and dancing before the Ark;" Saul catching the contagion of prophecy when he met a company of prophets coming down with tabret and harp, &c.; David expelling the spirit of evil from Saul by playing on the harp; Elisha calling for a minstrel, when he wished to prophesy, and hundreds of other obscure customs, and rites alluded to in the Bible, which have been piously left untouched, and unspeculated upon, but which, in the light of modern travel and observation become too intimately associated with other magical customs of Oriental ecstatics, to be longer misunderstood.

In the modern matter of fact, and very often coldly-material Spirit circle, the use of music as a means of promoting power, has become too familiar to need remark. No philosophical attempt is ever made to explain the connection of music with the production of phenomena, although elaborate treatises are written upon the nature of "Akasa," or the wonder-working life principle which the Eastern ecstatic claims to accumulate, dispense, and manipulate with as much certainty as the electrician can evolve force, by setting his battery in action.

It is well known by the friends of the Davenport Brothers that their controlling Spirit "Morgan," used frequently to beat them, and compel them to wrestle and struggle with him, when he wanted to exhibit power through them of an unusual character. In Mrs. Hardinge's "Modern American Spiritualism," a weird character is described in the section on Spiritualism at St. Louis as "The Color Doctor." This personage, who is known to have effected the most incredible cures simply by will, the effect of his presence, or the laying on of hands, was always accustomed to dance and spin round, and perform extraordinary gyrations, before proceeding to operate on his patients. Sometimes he threw himself on the ground and called upon those he intended to heal to jump upon him, stamp on his ribs, with all the weight of powerful men, and these tremendous feats—often performed in the author's presence—never seemed to produce any other than beneficial effects on both patient and operator. The incredulous reader will remember similar performances recorded by the most trustworthy narrators, as occurring in the cures effected at the tomb of the

Abbé Paris, amongst the *convulsionnaires* of St. Médard. Frail women would implore stout armed men to beat them with heavy mallets, or huge blocks of wood, often screaming out, "Heavier still, good brother; heavier still, for the love of God." All these items of occult power and possibility have yet to be studied, systematized, and their true philosophy discovered, before the first clue is obtained to a true Spiritual science.

When those who claim to be the depositories of all wisdom, and able to enlighten mankind on all mysteries, refuse to do so, because their knowledge is *too sacred to be entrusted to any but the initiated*, humanity is *providentially* perhaps thrown upon its own resources, instructed in the worthless egotism of assertion without proof, and taught to analyze facts, before venturing to hypothecate theories.

It seems clear then from the well-proven and world-wide facts of modern Spirit communion that the occult power by which unseen beings can manifest force, intelligence, and all that constitutes humanity, through a passive and automatic Medium, is just as wonderful as that which enables the Fakir to make sticks and stones come and go at his bidding. The power which floated Mr. Home out of one window, and in at another, in the presence of half-a-dozen unimpeachable witnesses, is no more to be despised or derided, as the work of "shells," or the "cast-off garments of the dead," than the power that enabled Covindasamy to raise himself in the air, before the eyes of M. Jacolliot.

No theorists can explain away such phenomena without discrediting all the rules upon which human testimony is received, neither can they pretend to attribute different causes to similar results, until they are prepared to show cause for their allegations and prove their statements by their facts.

Whatever is possible to one human being through laws and forces inherent in nature is possible to all through the operation of similar laws. But, when humanity is transcended and a super-human world of existence enters upon the scene, human laws are of little or no avail, either to prevent, produce, or account for what is effected. And this is precisely the position in which the thoughtful Spiritualist is now placed.

He sees the Medium wholly passive and inoperative, and yet all the phenomena which demonstrate human intelligence, although invisible, are moving, acting, and manifesting around him. He sees the Fakir enacting even greater marvels, and claiming to do part by his own power, and part by the same Spiritual aid which operates through the Medium. He hears the blatant assertion of the theorist that he knows all about it; "that the Medium is only operated upon by *dead men's emanations; a something which is nothing;* whilst the Fakir effects all his marvels through his own Spirit. If the Spiritualist asks for proof of these assertions, the theorist closes down upon him with the contemptuous assurance that these mysteries are only for "the initiated," and unless he were "an adept," he must be content to swallow whatever "adepts" choose to affirm, with unquestioning reverence.

It would be an insult to common sense to offer any commentary on such a position, although many a really intelligent seeker for Spiritual truth, is obliged to stand in this category, and be derided as "only a Spiritualist,' by the *advanced minds* who were once in the ranks with him. To such we would say, take heart! The world *en masse*, no less than the "advanced ones" in their own esteem, are but as yet standing in the dawning light of the great day when Spiritual science is beginning to illuminate the earth. Continue to seek for your FACTS, before you attempt to found systems, or build up theories. Somewhere the point of contact will be found between the apparently unrelated extremes of the passive Medium, and the whirling ecstatic. "Spiritualism and Occultism" may yet prove to be one, and the Spirit embodied and disembodied, may but represent different degrees of power common to both states, when speculation gives place to knowledge, and assertion to proof.

CHAPTER XXXIX.

SPIRITUALISM IN HOLLAND.

FOR the benefit of those who desire to study the literature of Spiritualism under all aspects of national variety, it is to be regretted that a knowledge of the Dutch language is so limited.

Besides the record of numerous Spirit circles extending over a period of many years, there have been works of rare interest on this subject, published in the Dutch language, which are unattainable to readers not familiar with that tongue.

It may seem surprising to those who are accustomed only to regard the unimpassioned, even phlegmatic element in the Dutch character, to learn that Spiritualism has made a deep mark upon the people, both in Holland and its colonies. Such is the fact however, whether the cause is to be found in some peculiarity of physique, or climatic influence, favourable to the production of psychic phenomena.

For the records which follow, concerning Spiritualism in Holland, the author is chiefly indebted to four good friends whose unsupported statements alone would be sufficient to satisfy any enquirer who had the privilege of their acquaintance; besides which, the author has spared no pains to authenticate every narrative, both from public and private sources, of the most veracious character.

It only remains to add, that three contributors to the following pages, for personal reasons, have deemed it necessary to withhold their names; the fourth, M. A. J. Riko, has generously placed his name and a mass of valuable information at the author's disposal for public use, a favour which both compiler and reader cannot too gratefully acknowledge.

As M. Riko's contributions are rendered into very readable English phraseology we shall commence our present section by giving the opening sketch as nearly as possible in his own words.

SPIRITUALISM IN HOLLAND.

"The introduction of Spiritualism in Holland is due to that well-known supporter of the cause both in England and on the Continent, Mr. J. N. T. Marthese. This gentleman being by birth a Dutchman, naturally desired to aid his countrymen in studying the interesting facts of Spiritualism.

"For this purpose he revisited his native country in 1857-8, bringing with him the young American Medium, Mr. Daniel D. Home. Besides giving several private *séances* at the Hague, Mr. Home was introduced at court, and gave *séances* to the late lamented Queen Sophia, for which he was presented with a splendid ring. Mr. Home also gave a *séance* to a society of Free-thinkers, the publishers of the *Dageraad*, a journal devoted to free-thought subjects. This, and many other *séances* given to distinguished persons at the Hague, created a wide-spread public interest."

Before proceeding further it may not be uninteresting to give Mr. Home's account of his *séance* with the amiable royal lady above named, especially as the communication sent to the London *Spiritual Magazine* is written in the modest and unassuming tone which generally pervades Mr. Home's statements of personal experiences. He says :—

"In the month of January, 1858, Mr. Tiedman Marthese, whose name is so well known in connection with Spiritualism, invited me to accompany him to Holland. He hoped to arouse the attention of his countrymen, and lead them to investigate the important truths which he had, after careful scrutiny, proven to be realities. It is to him that the advent of Spiritualism in Holland is due.

"The day following our arrival at the Hague, a message was sent from the Queen requesting my presence the same evening at the palace. I went as desired at eight o'clock, and as I write to-day the memory of that chill, dreary palace stands before me like some weird dream. I was shown into a drawing-room. On entering, a lady met me, and in .the purest of English accents, bade me welcome. Supposing this to be a lady-in-waiting, I said, 'I believe, Madame, that the Queen is expecting me.' If dark and chill stands the memory of the palace, in bright contrast, and as a ray of blessed sunshine, will ever live the music of that sweet voice, so recently hushed by the birth of her pure spirit into the realms of endless day, as, with a merry laugh, she replied, 'I am the Queen.'

"It was proposed to have a *séance*, and after nearly ten hours of patient expectation not the slightest result had been obtained. The next evening, and indeed six or seven succeeding evenings, were passed in like manner, and I began to fear that for some, to me unknown cause, there would be an entire failure. The last evening but one her Majesty said to me, 'Mr. Home, I have but an imperfect idea of the conditions necessary for what is termed a *séance*, but I am convinced that your surroundings the past evenings have not been congenial. I think if you will follow me we will find just what is required.' Taking a light, the Queen had passed through two rooms, and was about to unlock the door of a third, when I, as it were involuntarily, said, 'It is there the next *séance* is to be held.' Unlocking the door and handing me the light, the Queen said, "I well knew it would be in that room ; go in and see my treasures.' Dimly though it was lighted, I saw at a glance that it had been a room where a child or children had been, for in one corner was a broken toy cart, and near it a toy drum. Other toys were strewn here and there, as if the little ones, weary with play, had left the room for a time, and as if the silence would soon again be broken by their presence. At last my eyes rested on a bunch of faded flowers, and these betokened a lapse of months, or even years, as having been undisturbed. The Queen informed me that this had been the playroom of her child, now in heaven, and that every object had remained just as he left it. The flowers alone had been added, and these had been near the little form after the change we term death.

"The next evening a *séance* was held there, and that sorrowing mother was granted the most perfect and convincing proof that her loved one was still near her. It is impossible to give the details of what took place, for they were of a nature so intimate to the one person, that to recapitulate them to the public would seem almost sacrilegious. There were present relatives of her Majesty and one maid of honour, who, as well as myself, were witnesses, and they cannot have forgotten the tears of joy shed by that most noble and highly-gifted woman as she bowed her head in thankfulness to God for the solace sent to cheer her.

"Taking a sapphire and diamond ring from her finger she placed it on mine, and on a scrap of paper in my possession, and of far greater value to me than gold or precious stones, is this simple memento, whereon is written : '*I will ever remember with gratitude the séance with Mr. Home.*—SOPHIE.'

"No. 6, Nevsky Prospective, St. Petersburg, June 6th, 1877."

If the reader of the above letter chance to be an ordinary marvel seeker, he will be astonished to find a lady, whose rank and station had familiarized her with an ever-ready and prompt compliance with all her wishes, patiently waiting for many successive evenings to obtain something, which after all, might prove of little value to her. Still more remarkable will appear the simple statement of a renowned Spirit Medium, that royalty had to wait through seven *séances* before an exhibition of his powers could be given. To the true and philosophic Spiritual investigator Mr. Home's conduct, and candid acknowledgments, will suggest the earnest wish that every Spirit Medium would imitate his example; then would fraud be at an end, and the world might indeed obtain a clue to a true Spiritual science.

After Mr. Home's departure from the Hague, family circles began to be formed; many Mediums were developed, who obtained remarkable phenomena, so that in process of time, the sitters were favoured with Spirit voices, speaking audibly, direct writing, touches by Spirit hands, musical performances by Spirits on various instruments, together with the movement and transport of ponderable bodies from place to place. These phenomena were given most freely in the house of Mr. T. D. Van Herwerden, "Ancient Resident," of the Indian Government at Java. The Medium in this family was a very ignorant Javanese boy, named "Aridjan," of whom further mention will be made hereafter. Mr. Van Herwerden, a gentleman universally respected, published a work on his wonderful experiences in Spiritualism illustrated by numerous photographs and fac-similes of Spirit writing, which was privately circulated amongst his friends and connections. Remarkable phenomena were obtained in many other families besides Mr. Van Herwerden's, and in many places besides the Hague, but as there were no professional Mediums in Holland, and the manifestations could only be witnessed in private families, the names of the parties, and the marvels enacted in their homes, have been only known by report.

Notwithstanding the reticence attending the investigations, they excited so much interest in the best society, that fresh circles were continually forming, and several associations began to arise for the more orderly and scientific study of the subject. One of the oldest and most numerously-attended of these associations was founded by Major J. Revius, a warm friend of Mr. Marthese before alluded to. Major Revius entered into the investigation of Spiritualism, with great earnestness, and devoted himself for many years to its advancement. He it was who founded the society called "Oromase" (or Ormuzd), of which physicians, officers, government officials, and many distinguished persons formed the members. The aim of this association was to study the phenomena and the laws of their production, without any attempt to fasten upon them, creeds, or religious doctrines. The first regular meeting of this society was inaugurated at the Hague on the evening of December 2nd, 1859. Careful minutes of the proceedings were written down, and entered upon the society's books.

The "Oromase" archives contain many interesting records, and the meetings were presided over by Major Revius until the year 1871, when he was removed from his sphere of mundane usefulness, to the higher life beyond.

We are informed by one of Major Revius's warm friends and admirers, that he was a man universally beloved; one who was respected even by his opponents in belief. He was buried with military honours. The royal band of the King's Guard rendered the music, and a funeral oration, which our informant—who was present—assures us was a most eloquent and touching tribute to the worth of the deceased, was spoken on the occasion by Monsieur A. J. Riko, the secretary of the "Oromase Society." This was the first occasion on which Spiritualism was openly discoursed of at the Hague, and its introduction at so solemn a scene, created not a little interest and sensation.

To return to M. Riko's own narrative, he says :—" The Oromase Society celebrated its three hundredth meeting by a social gathering and supper on February 25th, 1876." He adds : " Besides holding *séances*, the theoretical side of the important subject has not been neglected. 'Oromase' possesses a really splendid library of the principal standard works on Spiritualism in different languages, and an interesting collection of American, English, French, German, and other national periodicals, devoted to the subjects of Spiritualism, mesmerism, psychology, &c."

Amongst the numerous societies for the study of Spiritualism founded in Holland was one in Amsterdam called "Veritas," which commenced its sessions in 1869. This society seems to have specially cultivated trance speaking and Spirit communications obtained through writing Mediums. The doctrines advocated therein, inclined to the belief in re-incarnation, as taught by Allan Kardec, and in this respect it differed from "Oromase," at which the members were more concerned with scientific and inductive methods ; hence, although the investigators of both societies were on friendly terms with each other, the diversity of opinions was fully realized. The society at Amsterdam, like that at the Hague, kept records of its doings, and distributed "leaves," containing the Mediumistic communications given at the *séances.*

At Rotterdam, there existed a small society, the cognomen of which, translated, was—*Research after Truth.* The association did not last long in session, but its members have steadily pursued their researches in private family circles. The same course is adopted in Haarlem, Amsterdam, and many other towns in Holland, besides at the Hague, and everywhere, these *séances* are crowned with more or less success.

Although there has been a general unfoldment of all the phenomenal powers witnessed in England and America, *except form materialization,* there seems to be a great desire for physical phenomena, and an absence of well-developed local Media for that phase of power.

The Hague, Rotterdam, and other large towns have been visited by foreign celebrities such as Henry Slade, the Davenports, Bastian and Taylor, Miss Lottie Fowler, Mrs. Margaret Fox Kane ; Williams, Herne, Eglinton, Rita, "the Bamford Boys," Miss Cook, and several others ; in fact, during the last few years, Holland has formed an invariable scene of attraction to the American and English Mediums visiting the Continent.

So long as Spirit circles were held in private families, wherein many of the Mediums, especially at the Hague and in Amsterdam—were ladies and gentlemen of high social standing, little notice—save in the way of furtive allusion—was taken of the subject by the press, but when foreign Mediums —especially those who made the subject their profession—came before the people, the columns of the newspapers were filled with articles written in the usual spirit of ridicule, denunciation, or grave scepticism.

Respondents were not wanting. Newspaper correspondence, magazine articles, and pamphlets, were published in defence of " the cause." Much talent was called forth, and many admirable expositions of what Spiritualism really was and is, arose out of these newspaper discussions, which else would never have been brought before the world. M. Riko in giving some account of these skirmishes, writes in his own quaint way thus :—

'The defenders however were not lazy in sharpening their pens, and many replies to attacks besides pamphlets and books appeared. Amongst the most able of the defenders was Mr. H. G. Becht, a surgeon ; a logical thinker of *very positive mind* and one whose pamphlets are amongst the best products on Spiritualism which ever saw the light.

Further we had Roorda van Eysinga who is publishing still a periodical devoted to the religious side of Spiritualism (or rather Spiritism), an ex-clergyman of great capacity and a very elegant author. The communications through the medium Rose, an honourable aged man, form the greater part of this periodical. Then we have our admirable and talented authoress, well known for her other literary works, Madame Elise van Calcar who publishes also a monthly periodical. She chiefly defends the study of Spiritualism on biblical and religious grounds.

"Other defenders of Spiritualism and Mesmerism in our country were Mr. A. Hoch, surgeon; Rutgers van der Loeff, ex-clergyman; Dr. Polah, doctor in philosophy; not to forget Major Revius, who first of all put his name to his pamphlets on Spiritualism. A. J. Riko published a history of Spiritualism on the Continent, an analysis of the different explanations of the scientific world, a collection of facts, rules for investigators, etc."

We shall have more to say about the literature of Spiritualism in Holland, especially of the work effected by Madame Elise Van Calcar, at the close of this section; meantime, we may add, as soon as the subject began to be canvassed abroad in the journals, whether the reports were favourable or antagonistic, the dissemination of Spiritual ideas received an immense impulse. Another great factor for moving public opinion was the translation into the Dutch language of the Spiritualistic works of Professors Wallace, Crookes, and Varley. These logical writings, illustrated by engravings, diagrams, and extracts from other authoritative writers, were published in a volume of about four hundred and sixty pages by the liberality of the Hague Spiritualists, whose names have already figured in this chapter. Some five lectures too were given at the Hague by MM. Riko and Wasch, whilst other speakers did good service in various directions; in short, propagandism once commenced, proceeded in earnest, and had the foreign Media who visited the country, all been as free from reproach, and selfish aims, as the Dutch Spiritualists themselves, the cause would now hold a triumphant empire over the intellectual minds of Holland.

A field so inviting as Spiritualism, has of course been traversed by its base imitators, and Holland has been no more lacking in its "Bishops," "Baldwins," and other itinerant "exposers" (of their own tricks) than has England or America. The Dutch, it must be remembered, are neither easily moved to belief, or unstable when once convinced.

They are not to be imposed upon by pretenders, within or without the ranks, and hence imported frauds, and local "exposers," have never shaken the well-grounded faith of the Dutch Spiritualists. Of the colonies, or Dutch Indies, it is enough for the present to say the impulse to regard "supernaturalism" in the light of modern Spiritualism was communicated by several persons of note who were sent by the Government from Holland to fill official positions in the colonies. The prevailing superstitions very much resembled those of the Hindostan provinces, and the introduction of Spiritualism in its modern sense, has effected a most beneficial influence; substituting a rational and scientific system of communion with beloved Spirit friends, for the fantasies of demonism, and the worship of heroes and ancestors.

Hauntings, stone throwing, and other preternatural disturbances have for many years previous to the introduction of modern Spiritualism, been popularly known in Java, Sumatra, Madura, and other districts of the Dutch Archipelago.

A detailed notice of the disturbances occurring at the house of M. Van Kesslinger, the Assistant Resident at Bandong, will hereafter be given, together with the official report of the same preserved in the state archives of the Colonial Government.

Several well-skilled mesmerists have visited different towns of Holland, and given exhibitions of "animal magnetism" through susceptible subjects. One of the most popular lecturers on this subject who visited the Hague, was a Signor Donato, who did much to awaken the attention of the thoughtful to the intimate connection betwen the powers and potencies of the embodied mind, as displayed by the magnetizers, and those of the disembodied, as manifested in the phenomena of Spirit communion.

Many remarkable cases of haunted houses have become notorious of late in Holland, some at the Hague, others in Friesland, Amsterdam, &c., &c. The manifestations in the instances alluded to, precisely resembled those common in Europe and America; in fact, their sameness proves that they emanated from sources universal throughout all countries.

For the present, all reports agree, that there is a quiet steady interest prevailing through the different towns and amongst the circles where Spiritualism has been made manifest in Holland, still public interest is but little stirred on the subject.

The same unanimity of opinion prevails on the belief that the unmistakable frauds that have been perpetrated by certain English and American Mediums visiting the country, have served to bring Spiritualism into public disrepute, and to check the tendency to private investigation amongst the unconvinced.

One of our correspondents, a gentleman holding a high official position in Holland, writes with equal frankness and reason on this subject, to the following effect :—

"Whilst it has been due only to interest and influence in high quarters that we could get a hearing through the journals for our well-attested facts, the rumour of a medium being caught in the very act of tricking runs like a conflagration through every newspaper, and spreads poison through the whole community against us. . . . Yet even this we could endure patiently, because it is the work of our antagonists, and just what we may expect; but the worst stab our cause can receive is dealt by the foes of our own household; those *spiritual* editors who, the moment their tinsel medium is caught at one circle in the act of imposing, straightway begin to defend him, and fill their columns with accounts of all the good things he did at some other circle ! What sort of logic is this ? If these impostors were true on other occasions, why do they prepare—for they must first make their preparations—to cheat us ? But still worse. We who have spent our time, money, and risked our good names, to uphold this cause are by these editors reviled and abused for exposing the frauds. Here in Holland, though the stuffed gloves, wigs, masks, and phosphorus of these deceivers are in our possession, we who bring them here at much expense to prove our faith, are actually accused of a conspiracy to ruin it ! What insanity is this ! Can we wonder that our local press assume that the editors of *spiritual* journals are simply frauds paid to defend frauds, and that we the believers are in league with them, or else are lunatics incapable of judgment.

"If there is yet another thrust which pierces the heart of Spiritualism to the quick it is that excuse of which we read so much in your English papers, which says that when the pretended *form* is seized at a materialization *séance*, it must always be the form of the medium, *as the spirit must needs melt back into the medium's body.* This is a very fine excuse, no doubt, but can those who know this result so well, inform us why the wigs, masks, phosphorus, and drapery so often used on these occasions don't melt back also into the mediums' bodies ? Let them explain, moreover, when the 'form' and medium happens to be a lady why she does not melt back into her clothes, she being very generally found in one place and her clothes in another ! I learned in your country, dear madame, a saying with which I beg to close—it is, 'Tell that to the marines, but not to a Dutchman !'" . . .

As an evidence that the shrewd writer of this communication has never been, and is not now, inimical to true and genuine professional Mediums, it should be added, that he has been largely instrumental in procuring their services in Holland, and forwarded with the above, several laudatory press notices of the Davenports, Slade, Foster, and others, the reprint of which would convey no new impression of those fine Mediums' powers. The following letter, however, from Ira Davenport to Mr. Robert Cooper, of Eastbourne, is copied from the London *Spiritual Magazine*, to show the kindly impression that honest Mediums have received from the true-hearted Spiritualists of Holland. It runs thus :—

"La Haye, Oct. 7, 1866.

"FRIEND COOPER,—In my last letter I promised to write you again shortly. We returned here yesterday from Rotterdam, where we gave three public *séances* to very large and respectable audiences. The people who came to see us were the first people of the city. The admission was four and a half francs. Previous to going to Rotterdam we gave two *séances* in this place, which is the Brighton of Holland. Here, too, the people who came were all of the first society, and were highly pleased with the manifestations—so much so, that we have been invited through the newspapers of the town to return and give more *séances*, as many persons wish to see us who could not avail themselves of the previous opportunity. So, on the whole, we have concluded to repeat our *séances* here for two nights more.

"About a week since we had a paper sent to us, containing an announcement of some sleight-of-hand man ; that he was in possession of our 'secret,' and intended to give public explanations and illustrations. I immediately wrote a reply, warning the public to be careful in paying their money to this man until he had proved himself worthy of their patronage, by accepting a challenge to meet us for five thousand florins a side, and making good his pretensions. We have heard nothing from the gentleman since.

"On the whole, we are very well satisfied with our experience in Holland so far. The probability is, that we shall stay in this country two months yet.—Yours truly,

"I. E. DAVENPORT."

In a still earlier number of the London *Spiritual Magazine*, in the year 1861, the veteran Spiritualist, Major Revius, gives the following interesting account of his son's mediumship. After describing the young man's powers which were similar and scarcely inferior to those of Mr. Home, the Major says :—

"After Mr. Home's departure from the Hague, my son attended many *séances* among our friends, and other mediums were developed. At one of these *séances*, at the house of a physician, the spirits of the late Monsieur and Madame G. announced their presence. Monsieur G. had possessed a considerable fortune, which he had bequeathed in a way disappointing to the expectations of the doctor and his family. After the doctor had expressed his feelings of dissatisfaction on this point, he asked what they wanted there ? The answer was—'To seek a reconciliation with you.' 'Then you go, G.' said he, 'and let your wife speak ; I never thought very well of you ; let her tell me the reason of your leaving the property as you did.' 'You had enough,' was the answer, 'and so I persuaded my husband to dispose of it in favour of my own family, which needed it.' 'Ah ! another proof of your selfishness,' said the doctor, 'of which you gave so many, that nobody regrets you, nor cares to remember you.' 'You mistake there,' was the reply : 'there is a poor widow, now living in —— Street, who remembers me for acts of kindness.' 'Well,' the doctor said, 'we forgive everything ; it's all over now.' Upon which the table pressed itself obliquely against the breast of the doctor, and others of his family who were sitting round it. The communications in this *séance* were by the alphabet.

"The next day, two of the company, determining to enquire into the facts, found out the street so mentioned. It was a small one, inhabited by poor people. The gentlemen ultimately found a widow, who said that she had known Madame G., who had been dead so many years, for which she was sorry, as she had often received from her the tickets of a charity, by which she obtained bread, clothing, and fuel. She said that she lived in another street in the lady's lifetime.

"At a *séance* at my own house, two generals, my friends, were of the company : they wanted proof that they were not under any biological influence or hallucination. The table round which we were seated was strong, and weighed a hundred and ten pounds. At my request, the spirits raised the table free from the ground, and let it fall in such a way as to break the pediment. The gentlemen came the next day, to see if the table was *actually broken, as it appeared to be* the night before ;—for my part, I had still further evidence of it in the cabinet maker's bill.

"The large table being thus broken, we moved to a smaller one. General M. V. asked if this lighter table could turn itself upside down? The table replied by the alphabet—'Turn upside down yourself.' To the General's question, 'Did you ever know me?' the answer was—'Yes, at Bergen-op-Zoom, forty years ago, when you were a subaltern.' The General said this was according to fact. At my request the spirits made this little table feel so heavy, that we could not raise it by our united efforts, and then so light that we could lift it with the little fingers. . . . .

"We have a Medium here, a little girl of ten years of age. On a recent occasion at a *séance* where this Medium was taken, the spirit of the hostess's brother announced his presence. This brother was captain of a merchant vessel, which had not been heard of since the 10th of October, 1854. Through the young Medium's hand it was written that his ship was 'wrecked on the English coast, on the 14th of October, 1854, and all on board perished.' The lady asked as a proof that he would write his name by the hand of this child-medium. The lady was a perfect stranger to the Medium. After some letters were begun and as often rubbed out, the signature of the captain was written, perfectly corresponding to signatures in letters from him, and which she had carefully preserved.

"A few months ago, my wife, myself, and son were passing the evening at a friend's; several young people there proposed to amuse themselves by turning the table. They went into an adjoining room and soon returned with the news that they had turned a work-table and now proposed to try their hands at the large one in the *salon*. Observing twitchings of the hand in one of the young ladies, I got pencil and paper and proposed that she should hold the pencil as if to write. After some objections, she took the pencil, and at the instant of holding it as if to write, fell into the magnetic sleep, and thus wrote with closed eyes four full pages, in which a spirit expressed its happiness at being able by this means to assure his protégée that he was always watching over her. That the young lady was in the magnetic sleep I assured myself, by holding a sheet of paper between her face and the pencil, which did not prevent the lines from being straight and equidistant; the letters were large and like those of a person not in the habit of writing. It was subsequently found that the signature to this singular writing was that of an ancestor of the Medium on the mother's side, a Professor of the University of Gronigen, two centuries ago."

In the same communication as the above, Major Revius furnishes another incident of a circle in which he was himself present, although it occurred at Antwerp, and a report of the occurrence was subsequently published in the *Monde Musical*, of Brussels, Jan. 22, 1865. Major Revius describes it thus :—

"A few evenings ago several persons were at a *séance* at the house of one of the most distinguished inhabitants. Some of them seated at a small table waited gravely, and with confidence that an inmate of the other world would deign to come and communicate. All at once the table was agitated ; there was a spirit. 'My friends,' said the invisible visitant to the attentive group, 'I come to offer you the means of doing a good action and of comforting the unfortunate. In the street *La Cueller*, there is a narrow lane, terminating in a *cul de sac*. In this lane, on the first floor of a house, No. 12, you will find the family of Charles Sorels. Four children, of whom the oldest is but thirteen years, scarcely covered by some wretched rags, are lying in a corner, trembling with cold, on some straw. A fifth child, nearly naked, is pressed by its mother against her breast, dried up by suffering and want—such is the spectacle which I have witnessed. Hasten to relieve them, you have not a minute to lose! This is why I have come to you."

"Every one was astounded by this message, and could scarcely credit it. Nevertheless, interest, curiosity, commiseration excited them to the highest degree. Some of them were quickly on the way. They soon found the narrow street, of which before they had scarcely suspected the existence, and then the blind alley, more squalid still. On enquiring for Charles Sorels, they were soon shown the house, where they found the family exactly in the miserable condition described by the spirit. Need we relate the rest? The family of Charles Sorels, at the moment that I write these lines, is snatched from want, and relates its providential rescue to all who wish to hear it."

The same circumstance will be found detailed by M. A. Malibran in the London *Spiritual Magazine*, of July, 1865. Happily for the belief in Spirits *versus* " astrals, shells, *reliquiæ* of the dead, &c.," " who never tell anything but lies, or do anything but mischief," a large number of such occurrences are recorded in the history of American Spiritualists at the New York Conferences, and in the experiences of Judge Edmonds, Mrs. E. J. French, and many another who firmly believed in the agency of good and kind human spirits before theories arose to sweep them away into the limbo of Ghouls and Hobgoblins.

CHAPTER XL.

SPIRITUALISM IN HOLLAND (CONTINUED).

NARRATIVES OF PERSONAL EXPERIENCES.

As the progress of Spiritualism in Holland has been chiefly confined to private family circles, select associations, and occasional notices of literary works, the exceptions being the publicity obtained by the visits of foreign professional Mediums, it may be expected that we should give a detailed account of a disgraceful exposure of two Englishmen professing to belong to the latter class, for whom their friends and apologists still claim "remarkable Medium powers." In this connection we have only to reaffirm the purpose announced in our opening chapter, whilst promising to give as faithful an account as possible of such manifestations as belong to the history of Spiritualism, we altogether decline to devote time or space to its base counterfeit.

What is not Spiritualism will find no place in these pages. It must suffice then to allege that on more than one occasion the Dutch Spiritualists have been plagued with these pests of every great cause, the tricksters who are ready to become "Mediums for Spirits," or their own sham imitations, whichever is found to pay best. It is due to the Dutch Spiritualists to state, that they themselves, having nothing to fear but falsehood, became the exposers, nor did they shrink from the ridicule heaped upon them and their cause, by their exultant enemies through the columns of the secular press.

In Holland, as in every other place where the veritable truths of Spiritualism have been made manifest beyond a shadow of question, the defalcations of unworthy pretenders, and the lampoons of the press, have never affected the conduct of those, whose faith has deepened into knowledge. Thus it is more than probable that the interposition of the counterfeit and its discovery, would not have affected the progress of Spiritualism injuriously, provided the Spiritualists themselves had united in a stern denunciation of such practices; but unfortunately, the ranks of the movement include a number of worthy persons who in their exceeding charity endeavour to account for what they call *the appearance* of fraud on the hypothesis of "transformation, transfiguration," &c., &c., making a compound of *philosophy* and miracle, of a far more astounding character than all the phenomena of genuine Spiritualism.

It is under such circumstances as these, that public interest in the cause of Spirit communion has obviously declined in Holland, although the belief, founded upon unimpeachable proofs, cherished by the "old line" Spiritualists, remains unshaken.

To the world—which in future generations at least—may be disposed to pass judgment uninfluenced by " the passion and prejudice of that partisanship" which mars the accuracy of philosophic opinion, we now offer a statement of the following facts, all of which the author has carefully scrutinized, proved, and feels justified in recording as testimony founded upon the rock of TRUTH.

The first case to be cited is a notice of the manifestations which occurred in the family of M. Van Brussel, a gentleman of independent means, and highly respectable standing, residing at the Hague.

For some time, M. and Mdme. Van Brussel had noted the occasional production of sounds, and the spontaneous movements of ponderable objects, occurring in the vicinity of their daughter Albertine—a sweet girl, about fifteen years of age—when the attention of the family was first drawn to Spirit manifestations. After they had become convinced that this young lady was a Medium they communicated the following occurrences to the " Oromase" Society.

On a certain night, the father being awake, observed that the bed in which his daughter was sleeping—in the same room with her parents—was moved from its place. The time was mid-summer, and the nights were quite light. On the following night both the father and mother were awakened by an unusual noise, when they observed that the footboard of their daughter's bed was taken away, and placed at some distance against the wall of the chamber. As Albertine was apparently sound asleep, no notice was taken of this circumstance to her; but the father, the next day, not only replaced the footboard, but tied that and the other parts together with strong cords.

The next night the parents were awakened by still more violent noises, when they perceived the cords were being untied by invisible hands, and the pieces of the footboard were placed against the wall. Heavy rappings accompanied these movements through all of which the young girl slept soundly. Besides the sounds above described, the alarmed parents heard the soughing of a wind which seemed to be moaning through all the apartments on that floor. Very shortly after the commencement of these scenes, the beloved young daughter passed to the land of Spirits, leaving her loving parents almost inconsolable for her loss. Very soon after this sad change in the little household, manifestations began to occur which became obviously identified with the Spirit of the loving child they had lost. Portfolios and other objects which had belonged to her were carried about, and her books were moved before the parents' eyes.

In 1873, some few years after their daughter's departure, a book in which as a child she had studied, and which was reverently cherished by the mourning parents, dropped into the mother's lap, and on opening it she read in the daughter's well-known handwriting, the words clearly and freshly written, of which the following is the translation:—" Dear Father, although dead, I live near the good God. When dear mother weeps, oh comfort her by remembering my blessed lot." Within a few years, both the good father and mother passed on to their peaceful rest, but during the brief period of their sojourn on earth, their bereaved hearts were comforted with unnumbered such instances of their child's presence and sympathy as those related above.

Monsieur A. J. Riko gives the following account of the movement of ponderable bodies occurring in the presence of a mesmerized subject. M. Riko had become much interested in mesmeric practices, and was himself a successful operator.

Calling upon a lady of his acquaintance one day, at the Hague, she asked him to mesmerize her, alleging that she could give no reason for the request, except a strong impression that she ought to do so. There were present besides this lady, her daughter and a cousin, and this is what ensued :—

The lady was no sooner placed by passes under the mesmeric influence, than the large table which stood in the centre of the room, moved wholly without contact, and placed itself against the arm of the chair in which the mesmerized subject was sitting. The hour was about three o'clock p.m., the room well lighted, and the whole scene witnessed by three sane persons. It ought to be borne in mind in this connection, that the Baron Dupotet, and M. Billot, the eminent magnetizers of Paris, published, even before the year 1848, accounts of the movement of chairs, tables, and other ponderable bodies in the presence of their magnetized subjects.

Dr. Ashburner and Mr. J. C. Luxmoore of England, both gentlemen of learning, research, and non-professional magnetizers, have affirmed that the same phenomena often occurred in the presence of their magnetic subjects.

These gentlemen were of opinion that the magnetism they gave out in their passes, was analogous in quality to the "force" derived by Spirits from their Mediums, and that its diffusion in the atmosphere, enabled Spirits to make the manifestations so often observed in the presence of mesmerized subjects.

M. Riko, desiring to prove the intimate connection between "the force" employed in mesmeric passes and Mediumism, cites an example which may be selected from many others for its suggestiveness.

M. Siemelink of Amsterdam, well known in Holland as the author of an excellent Spiritual work, entitled, "Immortality Unveiled," to which the good Queen Sophia was the first subscriber—was well known for his remarkable power as a healer by mesmerism.

One of his patients, a young lady of aristocratic rank, residing at the Hague, he could readily affect by passes made at Amsterdam. The father of this patient, a gentleman of unimpeachable veracity, kept a careful record of the phenomena which occurred at the times when M. Siemelink projected this power from a distance on his patient. The exact time when the operations began and ended, were noted, and always found to correspond with the patient's magnetic sleep. Moreover, the young lady noticed, that a Spirit, whom she accurately described, and who was found to have been M. Siemelink's brother, was always present on these occasions, and showed himself in the act of manipulating the fluid or force projected from the mortal magnetizer. And here it is proper to remark, that the author—who on several occasions consented to be the magnetic subject of Drs. Elliotson, Ashburner, and Mr. Luxmoore, of London— always saw Spirits assisting in the manifestations, and as these Spirits were strangers to the seeress, but were invariably recognized by their description as friends of the parties present, it is fair to infer, that the assertions so often made by magnetized subjects is true, and that kind, disembodied Spirit friends, especially physicians and scientists, assist in these experiments, and materially aid the operations of human magnetizers. The Spirit of Benjamin Franklin, speaking through Mrs. E. J. French, of New York, and confirming his statements through the lips of the entranced Medium by loud rappings, alleged that *the force* which forms the life principle of the mortal magnetizer, is the Spiritual body of the enfranchised soul—one and the same element—only that, with the Spirit, it is finer, more subtle, and penetrating, than when in the mortal body ; hence, that the force of the magnetizer on earth, and in the Spirit world, are one and the same thing, differing only in degree, and only requiring special subjects to act upon, and special qualities in the subject, in order to produce analogous manifestations.

At the house of Mr. H. C. Becht, a medical gentleman, well-known and respected at the Hague, but one who at the time of the occurrences about to be detailed, had by no means yielded up his full belief to a Spiritual origin for the phenomena, a *séance* was held when the medium was Mr. G., a Government telegraph officer, whose full name it is not deemed expedient to give. This gentleman had often obtained direct writing for his friends, and at the commencement of the *séance* in question, was promised strong manifestations. Presently M. Becht, as the greatest sceptic of the party, was invited to say, what manifestations he liked best, and he expressed a desire for direct Spirit writing. After this the Medium wrote, that it should be found in the porcelain cup on the small table between the windows.

M. Riko says :—

"Now our friend Becht, left the table ; went and inspected the small table and its immediate surroundings, after which, he took his place opposite the medium with the company. He requested every one in the room to remain quietly at his or her place, which was done. After this he put a question on which he desired the answer by direct writing. It was a question in respect to a history unknown to the medium, in fact M. Becht's private affair. The medium went on to write automatically, and spoke with the company. After a few minutes the medium wrote that the direct writing was done. Nobody had left his or her place and the surgeon had his eyes continually on the medium and the cup. Then M. Becht went himself to the small table and took out of the cup a long piece of paper rolled together, on which was written 20 lines, giving a perfect answer to the question which he had put. It looked as if it were written with lead pencil, but no paper or lead pencil had been near the cup or table. On that same evening two more pieces of direct writing were obtained, while the company named the place where it must be found, viz.—once in a hat on the piano and the second time outside the room, before the door of another room. The hat was first inspected, the door of the room shut after inspection of the corridor. Both times the direct writing was found at the desired spots." . . .

"Spirit lights were very frequently observed at the Hague. At a dark circle at M. Becht's, these lights appeared at spots indicated beforehand by one of the sitters, while nobody left his place. Once they came on the chimney at the greatest distance from the medium, where three lights shone for some minutes observed by all.

"Report 26, October 1st, 1869, of 'Oromase' describes light phenomena on the hands of a lady. It appeared on request several times in the same way."

"Different sounds from instruments came under our personal observation. In a company of several persons we once obtained the playing of a small harp in a degree of light which permitted every one to see the instrument upright on the table, and swaying in different directions while nobody touched it."

"Report 16 B, March 4th, 1869.—Duets were played with an Æolian harp, *lying on the table*, and some porcelain plates *shut* in a chest near one of the walls in the dining-room of Hotel Keisershof, at the Hague, moving in time, and very strongly, to the tune played on the harp. The medium through which these things happened was a young blacksmith."

"At Rotterdam, M. Wasch obtained a great variety of manifestations. Rappings, playing on musical instruments ; tying and untying through the invisibles ; light phenomena, trance speaking, &c."

"In 'Oromase,' at the Hague, where M. Wasch was received as a friend, several *séances* were held with him. Once the medium was levitated to a considerable height while he was held at both hands—at one side M. P., an officer in the army, and at the other through me. We were obliged to climb on our chairs in order not to let the floating medium slip, and several of us felt the soles of his boots rest on their heads. Another time the spirit moved freely round with a phosphorus light, which we had provided for the occasion. In the family circle, M. Wasch obtained still stronger manifestations."

22

Several of our kind Dutch correspondents furnish us with accounts of haunted houses in different towns and cities of Holland, but whilst we take this opportunity of thanking them for their trouble in these transscriptions, we do not find enough diversity from other familiar accounts of the *Polter-Gheist* to warrant our making use of their several narratives. The exception to this rule, will be found in the following chapter, in which we give a condensed report of the manifestations occurring in the Dutch Indies and the official examination into the affair conducted on the part of the Government.

Before inviting the reader to follow us in the perusal of this account, we may relieve our text from the quotation of various authorities by stating that the narrative is condensed from the writings of Mdme. Ida Pfeiffer, Professor A. Wallace, Dr. Hatton, an eye-witness of the scenes described, and a surgeon of a military station in Java, M. Riko, and other correspondents of a trustworthy character.

CHAPTER XLI.*

SPIRITUALISM IN HOLLAND (CONTINUED).

THE following introduction will serve to show the quality and standing of the parties whose experiences will form the subject of this chapter.

M. Riko says :—

" Among the first manifestations observed in Holland, those occurring in the family of M. Van Herwerden at the Hague, belong to the most remarkable, and merit to be preserved for the history of the movement in Europe. M. Van Herwerden himself was a highly esteemed man who during many years occupied with honour the office of President of our Government in one of the principal districts of the Isle of Java. Like many of our Indian officials he after a long service, asked his dismissal, and settled at the Hague. The family was received among the best classes at the Hague. M. Van Herwerden himself was a very positive thinker, an exact observer—in short, a man not to be deceived. The manifestations occurred in his own house, through the mediumship of a young Javanese boy, named Aridjan, 14 years old, ignorant as the Javanese are at that age, and incapable of forming any idea about spiritual manifestations. He inhabited the house in the quality of a servant; was very kindly treated, and felt thoroughly happy. The phenomena lasted several years, and were witnessed by hundreds of the developed class; including professors, clergymen, physicians, etc. M. Van Herwerden at the repeated solicitations of acquaintances interested in Spiritualism, published a volume of notes at his own cost for private use of his friends."

It would seem that strange disturbances in the house and in the vicinage of the boy Aridjan had attracted attention, and suggested the idea of a Spiritual agency for many months prior to the time when the circles commenced. The first sitting was proposed by friends of the family who had been apprised of the disturbances, and was held on the evening of March 16th, 1858. At first the manifestations were slight and unimportant. Still they were sufficiently marked to prove that some foreign though

---

* Our readers will kindly bear in mind the sources claimed for the narratives given in this and the preceding chapters on Dutch Spiritual Manifestations. In order to preserve the simplicity and point to the good faith so clearly manifested in the several translations herewith submitted, the author has preferred to retain as much as possible her correspondents' own phraseology.

invisible power was present, and that the boy Aridjan supplied the force by which the unseen operators manifested. At the seventh *séance* loud rappings were heard, and intelligent answers were spelled out by the alphabet. The table at which the *séances* were held was a large one, and a lamp was kept burning in the room by Spirit direction. The Javanese Medium could neither read, write nor spell, and sat perfectly still in the chair provided for him, unless moved about, as was often the case, by Spirit power. For the rest of the details, we shall refer the reader to M. Van Herwerden's diary, which was published under the title of *Experiences and Communication on a still Mysterious Territory.*

This book numbers over 200 pages, and is profusely illustrated by diagrams and *fac similes* of spirit writing, drawing, &c., &c. Only a few extracts from M. Riko's translation of this curious record can be given, but they will suffice to show the general character of what occurred.

"8th July, 1858.—A young lady got at request strong blows on the table, in the presence of two servants who—after being called in the circle room—gave their testimony. A little later, the door of the room opened ; rappings on the table and scratching at the back of a paper the lady had in her hand, were followed by distinct touchings on her face. Aridjan remained in another room, and no manifestations occurred there in the lady's absence.

"23rd August, 1858.—A frivolous spirit manifested, and one of the ladies present exhorted him about his conduct. The table moved very quickly in the lady's direction and obliged her to retire to the wall by pressing with force against her.

"25th August, 1858.—Besides Aridjan, another medium was present. Rappings and strong blows all round the room. It seemed the spirits attracted by the two mediums, did not sympathise, for the noise and moving of furniture indicated clearly a fight between two spirits. Even the mediums were shaken and their chairs rocked. Once Aridjan was thrown to the floor with chair. At last Aridjan's friend seemed to get the victory ; he showed this by giving a tremendous blow on the table, followed by a strong grip on the keys of the piano which stood at some distance behind the medium. After this all remained quiet.

"22nd September, 1858.—At a *séance* held in another family M. Van Herwerden had made acquaintance with a spirit calling himself Paurellus, and, claiming to have been a Spanish monk who was assassinated in one of the cloisters of this city, about 300 years ago, performed a series of very remarkable manifestations. This evening Paurellus wanted the lamps to be taken out of the room, and paper and pencil put on the table. After about 20 minutes writing was heard on the paper, after which the paper flew like a bird round the circle, which made Aridjan scream for fear. The paper was then thrown on the table and the lead pencil flew to the other side of the room. On getting the lamp again, some Spanish words were found on the paper. There was also direct writing in a tongue unknown to all in the circle. After this, Paurellus wrote some words in Dutch, " Faith, hope, charity," and other small sentences. In the subsequent *séances*, the writing developed more and more, as will be illustrated.

"16th October, 1858.—Aridjan wrote by means of a planchette, a series of extraordinary hieroglyphs, which showed a great likeness to the spirit writing published by Kerner in his ' Seeress of Prevorst.' Of course the ignorant Javanese boy knew nothing about this work published in German and not translated in Dutch. After this, Paurellus touched the keyboard of the piano which he had often done before. . . . In the course of this month very interesting communications in French were obtained through the planchette, by a spirit signing herself Aurelie de B——.

"3rd November, 1858.—Some days previous to this sitting, M. Van Hewerden had put on the table a kind of child's accordion. Paurellus had tried it, but soon threw it away. Another accordion, much better, was provided. At Paurellus' request the lamp was taken to another room and the piano opened, after which, the company, with the boy Aridjan, seated themselves at one side of the table, in close proximity to each other. Aridjan got sleepy, but Paurellus, who didn't like this, kept him perfectly awake by heavy blows under his chair, or by shaking him now and then with force, a perfect remedy against sleep. After having knocked at different distances on the furniture, Paurellus gave several rappings on the instrument with the decided wish to have the attention of the sitters fixed on it, after which, he took the accordion and began to play. Now he floated the instrument high above the heads of the sitters, then again he swiftly moved it near the floor. Sometimes he played with full force, and then again in beautiful pianissimo. After having finished this performance, he put the instrument on the table. Four times he resumed his music, and sometimes held the instrument directly at the ears of the sitters, as if he were afraid to have them miss one tone. In the pauses of his music, he took the piano tabouret and placed it on the table; opened one of the music books and played a slow melody on the piano. To finish the performance of this evening, Paurellus lifted the heavy table several times as high as the sitters' eyes.

"12th November, 1858.—Paurellus began to show for a moment behind the medium a column of light, but it was still weak. After this he showed several times small but brilliant lights in different parts of the room. By direct writing he produced two verses of a religious hymn of the Dutch Protestants.

"29th November, 1858.—One of the sitters mentally wished Paurellus to lift the table and touch the piano, without uttering a single word about it. After a few minutes the table was lifted very high, and directly the keys of the piano resounded with force.

"18th December, 1858.—M. V. H. had made a pair of pasteboard speaking tubes, which were put on the table beside the accordion paper and pencil. Paurellus came at the hour he had announced at a previous sitting, he being always punctual. He played first the accordion. Then he placed a chair at the free side of the table, always kept ready for him, after which he took one of the tubes and spoke through it to each of the sitters. But the excitement of the latter at this first hearing of the direct voice, and the faintness of the sounds, rendered what the good Paurellus said not understood. Still it was learned that he promised to bring on a following occasion some good spirits to assist him. He touched the sitters with the tube, and gave rappings on it to prove that it was he who held it himself.

"7th February, 1859.—At a previous sitting, Paurellus had promised to give direct writing in a shut room. This evening Paurellus said this had been done. One of the ladies took a lighted candle and the door key and went upstairs to the room which had been set aside. However, the paper on the table was untouched, and the lady let it remain where it was, with the pencil. On leaving the room she heard the rustling of a paper, and her dress was pulled. On looking on the floor, she found a sheet of paper on which several characters of spirit writing were found. This manifestation was repeated on the 11th of February, when the paper was found covered with a drawing representing a human figure besides some hieroglyphs.

"19th February, 1859.—This evening Paurellus played the guitar while another spirit accompanied him on the piano, which stood at its ordinary place against the wall. After a while, on Paurellus's request, one of the company 'in the flesh' played the guitar, a lady the mouth harmonica, one of the spirits the piano, while Paurellus himself took his accordion and managed the performance. At the same time many spirit lights danced to the measure of the tune round the Medium Aridjan. After this Paurellus asked one of the ladies in French 'Jouez encore une fois,' and after this had been done, with an accompanying song, he said, ' Merci, jolie chanteuse.' "

"16th May, 1859.—In the meantime Paurellus had succeeded in materializing his hands, and very often he touched the sitters or laid his hand in theirs. He had succeeded also in playing a pair of castagnettes to an accompaniment of the piano.

"20th May, 1859.—Paurellus was presented with a new and beautiful mouth harmonica; there was no end of his playing this evening. Once he accompanied a *quatre main* by the invisibles on the piano. By direct writing he thanked for the new instrument. A lady gave Paurellus a sealed letter. He took it gently from her, broke the sealing wax, after which he wrote for a moment, and placed the answer in the lady's hand. Nobody knew the contents of the letter besides the writer, and the answer was correct. The lady had asked how she could vanquish her fear of the spirits, and Paurellus answered she could do this by praying to God.

"23rd May, 1859.—Paurellus spoke this evening very distinctly and slow, and on one occasion a religious song executed on the piano was accompanied by sweet spirit singing.

"1st September, 1859.—One of the ladies sat at the piano. Mrs. Van Herwerden expressed a wish to have her eau de cologne flaçon. Paurellus took it from her, opened first the golden and then the glass stopper, which he put on the table. He moistened his hand and rubbed one of the gentlemen's foreheads, then he sprinkled the lady at the piano with the scent, and put the glass stopper under Aridjan's nose.

"3rd November, 1859.—This evening, the light streaming in from cracks in the blinds was sufficient to distinguish the furniture in the room, the pictures on the wall, etc. The usual manifestations went on, but no forms could be seen who did them. This was also the case on January 14th, 1860, when the accordion was seen floating through the room sustained by nothing. On the same evening, Paurellus made a lady feel the sleeve of his dress, which she described as very wide and soft.

"16th February, 1860.—Paurellus wished from one of the ladies a lesson on the piano.

He took her by the hand and conducted her to the instrument, after which he put his hands on the key-board. The lady directed this spirit hand, and put the fingers on the right keys. This evening he sang also more than once.

"29th March, 1860.—By the light coming in through cracks in the door of the room, a tall form in long drapery was seen moving through the room.

"11th May, 1860.—Paurellus asked for ink, which was given him, and produced a direct writing in Spanish—a language unknown to the whole family. The writing finished with the words (translated): "Don't believe every spirit, but try the spirits whether they are from God."

"31st May, 1860.—This evening, two spirits were seen in the room, who seemed to be holding an interesting conversation, as could be perceived by their quick gestures.

"15th June, 1860.—Paurellus showed a luminous hand.

"13th July, 1860.—Mr. D. G—— played a grand air from 'Martha' on the piano, accompanied by Paurellus, who moved very quickly, now in the bass, then in the descant, often between the hands of the player, along the key-board.

"23rd March, 1861.—The lamp remained in the room where it was put, in a corner behind a table cloth. By this dim light the accordion was played, and the opening of the keys seen, without a hand touching it.

"30th May, 1861.—Paurellus took the large table from the circle, and placed it near the door, at a distance of 10 or 12 feet. A little one was then put by him in the circle. Some moments later two gentlemen were lifted with chairs and all, and turned in different directions. Paurellus wrote with ink at the large table, at a considerable distance from the sitters. Paurellus played the accordion under the table, and touched the sitters with it. The heavy table floated through the room at a height of 3 or 4 feet, while Aridjan remained in his chair.

"3rd April, 1862.—Within some days we· go to the south of Italy. I told this to Paurellus, and he wrote directly, 'I wish you a good voyage. God be with you! I'll come whenever you'll call me.' Aridjan will accompany us.

"8th July, 1862.—Paurellus manifested every time during our voyage we sat for manifestations. On our return to Paris, he told us one of the servants at home had been ill. This was verified at our arrival at the Hague. Last months of 1862, Paurellus manifested only occasionally. He told us that he in the future wanted permission from higher spirits to come. At the same time Aridjan became suffering, so that we had to cease our sittings.

"So far the few and incomplete extracts from Mr. V. H.'s diary. They are sufficient to show the gradual developing of the manifestations from rappings to playing of different instruments, direct speaking, singing and writing, spirit lights, mind reading, materialisation, etc. The drawings also executed through the spirit, showed a great progress. First he made rough and childish sketches, but after some exercise very good drawings."

CHAPTER XLII.

SPIRITUALISM IN THE DUTCH INDIES.

ALL observers who have had an opportunity of investigating Spiritual phenomena in countries where an aboriginal population is still found, will realize the fact, that the coloured races seem to be largely endowed with that peculiar force through which Spirits from the life beyond can communicate with mortals. That which we now call "Mediumistic power," appears to prevail so largely in the organisms of aboriginal people, that spontaneous manifestations of Spirit presence are far more abundant amongst them, than with Europeans.

It is doubtless the extent and spontaniety of this force amongst savage races, which gives rise to the opinion that they are "very superstitious," and that the phenomena which actually occur, are due to the effects of ignorance and hallucination.

The time is not far distant when such opinions will be visited on the propounders, and "ignorance" in connection with Spiritual manifestations will consist of *incredulity*, rather than honest belief in facts. Still other noteworthy features in aboriginal Spiritualism are violent disturbances and manifestations of a mischievous nature. It need hardly be pointed out, that such specialities are only in accordance with the obviously human character of the source from whence these manifestations come.

The lower and more degraded a human being, or Spirit may be, the more he rejoices in mischief, and delights to rule by fear, and the exercise of tyrannical power.

It must also be remembered that the white races have generally acted as the oppressors of weaker and less civilized nations than themselves; hence, the harassing disturbances attributed by white settlers to aboriginal Spirits, may not improbably arise from a sentiment of racial enmity, and desire for retribution, and although Spirits are rarely if ever known to *inflict bodily injury* upon those whom they harass, and this, when it is evident from their feats of strength and dexterity that they have the ability to do so, it is not unreasonable to suppose they may take pleasure in the performance of such mischief as will astonish and annoy the people whom they regard as the enemies of their race. There are some noble exceptions to this rule, as in the case of many negro slaves whose Spirits often return to do good to the families of their white owners. Still more remarkable is the exception afforded by the North American Indians; "the hapless red man," whose wrongs, inflicted at the hands of his white oppressors, exceed all possibility of belief. And yet the Spirits of these high-souled savages have ever been prominent in returning good for the evil inflicted upon them. In the modern Spiritual dispensation it is well known that there is scarcely an American Medium who has not been attended and generously served by a kind Indian Spirit. These children of nature bring their knowledge of the healing properties of roots and herbs, to the aid of afflicted humanity. Wise in counsel, strong in physical force, and beneficent in healing, the Red Indians hold a special place in the history of modern Spiritual manifestations, which it would be the height of ingratitude to deny or repudiate.

The reader is kindly invited to consider these remarks, before entering upon the details of the following narratives. They are offered as a necessary introduction, to account in some measure for the strange and apparently malignant manifestations which are to be described in the ensuing pages.

Spiritualism has always been rife in the Dutch Indies. As the people with whom its phenomena have occurred, invariably attribute them to an evil and revengeful spirit, *although a human one*, and fear to provoke acts of retaliation by complaint, they are very loath to speak of these things, especially to those who try to investigate them. On the other hand, the writers in the different Colonial journals, who are apprised of supernatural disturbances through popular report, are apt to dismiss the subject with flippant comments on the "superstition of the lower classes," or ridiculous travesties of the occurrences in question. The tone of public opinion has undergone so great a change since those who are in the high places of society have condescended to investigate, and in many instances to endorse, the fact of Spirit communion, that people in the middle ranks of life are encouraged thereby and no longer feel ashamed to acknowledge that which their senses have borne testimony to, and hence, we are flooded with accounts of what has occurred through Spirit power in the Dutch Indies.

From a vast multitude of records we select the following.

A gentleman holding a high official position in Java, writes to the author, describing several rural districts that have been completely abandoned in consequence of certain disturbances which the country people attribute to a *Gendarola* or Spirit of an evil human being.

Our correspondent says :—

"In 1834, at Saehapoesa, there was a much respected family by the name of Teisseire. Mr. T. was a government inspector of indigo. One day, while dining, stones fell upon his table, and for a fortnight fell in every chamber of his house.

"Some years after the above took place, similar phenomena were again recorded at Bandong while M. V. Van Gaasbeck was there as 'assistant resident.' The civilized Javanese regents and the native chiefs affirm that these things often occur in the 'colonies,' but that the Indians seldom mention them, because they are ridiculed by the 'skeptical *Néerlandais.'*

"At one time there came the bones and at another the whole head of a buffalo. The Regent of S., wishing himself to know about these strange occurrences, came to pass the night there, but when he put himself on the bed it was so shaken and finally lifted from the floor, that he quit at once. There was a light burning in the room, and the Regent's son and servants were about him. What was especially wonderful was that the stones, which were marked with a cross or otherwise, and thrown into the torrent of Tjilandoog, which ran near the house and was one hundred and fifty feet deep, were in less than a minute thrown back again.

"A M. Ament, in the district of Beranger, an inspector of the *culture de café*, states that there was a *gendarola* in a little house at Bandong, which manifested as follows: The police having been placed within and without, an old woman led the way to it by its only approach, a narrow lane. She was followed by M. A., an assistant, and the Regent, but the moment she crossed the sill of the door she was seized by the legs, thrown down, and dragged away by invisible hands. M. Ament, entering the premises, received on his breast a quantity of sand thrown with such force that, while telling of the affair in 1870 in Batavia, he declared he did not wish again a like experience.

"In 1825, M. Mertins was Governor of the Moluccas. At Amboina, during his administration, in the Fort Victoria, near the close of the day, a multitude of stones fell from the air. The fort was so far from any inhabited spot, that the missiles could not have come thence. The soldiers were called to arms, but this did not prevent the shower of stones and plaster. This was several times repeated, but not a person was hit. In Banda, in 1842, this same thing was witnessed."

M. Riko describes some manifestations in the Dutch Indies a few years ago, through the Mediumship of an itinerant, who went from place to place exhibiting phenomena which he declared were produced by Spirits, and for which no other account could be rendered.

This man, a half breed, or descendant from mixed castes, would roll up his lithe form into a complete ball. In this state a committee of sceptics previously chosen, would bind him with cords and knots impossible for mortals to loosen, and then sew him up in a strong linen bag. A sheet was then thrown over the immovable mass, but in less than sixty seconds the man would be invariably free, and emerge unbound from the sheet. This performance was given as above stated in numerous towns and districts of the colonies, in the light, and in presence of hundreds of spectators.

As an example of the power of the *Setan*, or *Gendarola*, whose tricks are so constantly performed in the Dutch Indies, M. Riko gives the following narrative :—

"Another remarkable history happened in the dessa Ngalian Regentship, Boys Lalie, Soeraharta. The Javanese Karis Minto, an old weak man, went in December, 1877, on a certain evening to a short distance from his house, on some domestic business. On his way home he met with a *Gendarola*, who took hold of him and put him in less than a second in a very high naugha tree, where he fixed the man between the branches, with his own sarong. The man told afterwards that he could not call for assistance while the

Gendarola was busy with him. After having spent nearly two hours in this disagreeable position, his wife and friends being frightened by his prolonged absence, provided themselves with an 'obor' (light), and found him in the position above described. He could only be liberated by means of a very high ladder, and after much trouble. Similar phenomena have been observed in different parts of the Indian Archipelago."

The following case was communicated to the author by a Javanese gentleman of strict probity. The circumstances were published in all the Javanese papers, but as it involved the credit of a well-known citizen of Madiven, the initials of the parties' names were all that the author was privileged to publish. It may be stated however that the facts as now related, were translated from the *Malayo* of 1878 :—

"On the evening of October 7th, Gretchen, the little seven years' old daughter of M. and Madame S—— came in from the garden seemingly tired of play. In an instant she fell on the *balé balé* (couch) and became unconscious. The parents could not awaken the little one, and neighbours were hastily summoned. One of them advised the calling in of old Anne, who was esteemed in that neighbourhood as a nurse, doctor, and something of a *good witch.*

"Anne comes, when lo ! the child sits up and speaks, though not with consciousness, nor in her own voice, but in that of a man. The nurse takes an herb and puts it into the child's mouth, and says : 'Setan, where do you live ?' The child answers immediately, 'I live eastward in the kampong B——, and my father's name is S——.' The old woman replies, 'Then go away ; you have nothing to do here.' The child cries : 'I will not return, as long as the man who lives here does not pay the debt he owes to my father.' The inhabitant of the house is thunderstruck ! He owes since some time a sum of money to S——, and promises to pay it the following day. The child gives them the directions to burn some perfume, after which she awakes without remembering anything of what had happened."

Numerous cases of stone throwing and the projection of missiles by invisible hands have been sent to the author. The most remarkable however, because the one best sustained by unquestionable evidence, is that of the disturbances which occurred in the house of M. Van Kesslinger of Java. M. Riko having kindly sent a good translation of the official reports printed at the time, we shall again take advantage of his graphic pen, only premising that the reader may compare the narrative here subjoined, with accounts of the same disturbances described in the London *Spiritual Magazine* of 1868 (February number), by Professor A. R. Wallace—mentioned also in Madame Pfeiffer's "Second Voyage Round the World," and several other cotemporaneous publications. M. Riko says :—

"Amongst the spiritualistic phenomena the throwing of stones is one of the most remarkable. A very interesting example occurred on the Isle of Java. An official report was drawn up about the history, and deposited in the government archives of the Netherlands. The report was made by the Assistant Resident and addressed to the General Governor of the Dutch East Indian Colonies, J. C. Band.

"I begin with the document and translate it verbatim.

"'1881. *To his Excellency the General Governor ad interim of the Dutch Indies.*

"'On February 4th, coming home from an inspection, I saw at a distance my house surrounded by a large number of people. Unable to understand what that meant, my wife told me after I had entered, that in the interior gallery and room, there fell a large number of stones, and that it was impossible to discover from whence they came. Hearing this, I got a little angry, saying, that a person with healthy eyes certainly could see through whom the stones were thrown. I went to the interior gallery where most of the stones had fallen, and was soon convinced that it could not be done by human hands, because the stones fell sometimes perpendicularly just before my feet, without moving further, and while nobody was near. I then inspected the boards and the ceiling and found them all fixed and joined together without any opening. After this, I assembled all persons living in or near the house on an open place before the house, and had them watched by some policemen. After I had shut all the doors and windows I went in again, accompanied by my wife. But then the disturbances began still more vehemently and the stones came flying from every direction, so that I soon was obliged to reopen the doors and windows. This continued during 16 days; sometimes there fell in one day about a thousand stones, amongst which there were some of 9 pounds weight. I must not forget to state, that my house is constructed of boards of dry djatiewood, the windows were also shut by a lattice work in wood with spaces of about 2 inches. The throwing began commonly about 5 o'clock in the morning, and continued till about 11 in the evening. I pass silently the particularity that the stones fell mostly near an Indian girl about 11 years old, and seemed to follow that child; this is indifferent to the case, and would make this report too long to dwell upon.

"In confirmation of these facts, I give some names of credible persons who were witnesses of the affair, and who will give their statements under oath :—Michiels, lieutenant-colonel, aide-de-camp; Ermantinger, ex-inspector of the coffee culture; Dornseiff, owner of an inn at Sumadan; Born, surveyor; Adi Pathé Soeria Laga, ex-regent; Rommangong Soeria Laga, now Regent of Sumadan; Soeria Laga, chief djaksa; and several district chiefs.

"(Signed) V. KESSLINGER.
For literal copy,
"(Signed) J. VAN SWIETEN.

" Batavia, 30th December, 1831.

"So far the report. The Assistant-Resident Van Kesslinger lived at Sumadan, in the Preanger districts. The General-Major, A. V. Michiels, was invited also by the Governor-general to hold an inspection *in loco*, which he did with much care. He was a positive minded, and highly esteemed officer. He asserts amongst other points, that he shut himself up, only accompanied by the child named in the report, in the room, while nobody else was admitted. He placed himself against the wall and took the child near him. In this position he observed the fall of the stones during several hours consecutively. They came mostly when his attention was fixed especially on the child. They fell perpendicularly very near her, but never hurt or touched her. The girl was not in the least afraid or astonished. In the Indian Archipelago the inhabitants generally believe the stone throwing by spirits to be a fact. The Javanese call it *Gendarola*.

"Mr. Van Kesslinger had no children. His wife was an Indian lady, and the girl's father was the cook of the family. The house was a service-dwelling. On February the 3rd, 1831, the child played in the room near Mrs. Van Kesslinger; the husband was then travelling. All at once the girl sprang towards Mrs. Van Kesslinger, and showed her white kabaai (an Indian dress), on which a red siri spittle was seen. The chewing of siri is very common in the Indies;* the lady thought at first it might have been done by one of the servants. The girl was given a fresh kabaai, and the affair seemed ended. But a moment afterwards the child was again bespit, and at the same moment a shower of the yolk of an egg fell directly before Mrs. Van Kesslinger's feet. This was repeated several times, so that the lady sent for the Regent Radeen, Natto Koesomo. This government officer was an intelligent and honest man. He came and witnessed the fall of the stones. He had the house surrounded by his people, and sent everybody outside. The siri spittle appeared just the same, and the stones fell also; no cause could be discovered. At length it was resolved to fetch an Indian priest to exorcise the spirit. He came in the twilight, set himself on the floor, with a lamp near him, and opened the Koran. Just as he began to read he got such a heavy blow from an invisible hand that the lamp flew to the left and the holy book to the right side of the room. Mrs. Van Kesslinger feared to pass the night in the house, and went with the girl to the Regent's wife. That night all remained quiet. The following morning, as soon as the lady re-entered her house with the girl, the stone throwing began again, till Mr. Van Kesslinger's return. Very seldom there fell stones in the night, and the bespitting with siri happened only in daytime. When Mr. Michiels, on invitation of the Governor-general, made his investigation on the spot, he sent every one away; placed men on the roof and even in the trees in the neighbourhood. He ordered the inner room to be entirely covered with linen. He remained with the child alone in the house, but the phenomena went on just the same. The stones were such as are found on the roads. When the sun shone they were warm, and when it rained they were wet. Commonly five or six fell directly one after the other, and this was repeated with short intervals. No opening was ever made in the linen with which the walls and ceiling were covered. The stones became visible at the distance of about six feet from the floor. Several trunks were filled with them. Once a papaya fruit was

---

* " Chewing of siri "—chewing the betel nut.

thrown, which after inspection was found to have been plucked from a high tree near the house ; at other times chairs, glasses, plates, &c. were moved, without anybody touching them. At last the impression of a wet hand was seen on a looking-glass which hung on the wall. Mr. Michiels remained several days at Sumadan, and he also sent in a report, likewise deposited in the archives of the government.

"The history remains till this day a profound mystery, and no cause was ever detected, even after large sums had been offered several times to the person who could throw light on the affair.

"General Michiels spoke very seldom about his experiences. In 1847 at a dinner the guests invited him to tell them the history. After some hesitation he did so. General Van Gagern, who was at the table, began to laugh about it, when a vehement scene occurred in which General Van Gagern was obliged to withdraw his remarks 'and apologise.' "

M. Riko concludes his narrative with the following remarks :—

"In Europe, this rain of stones has often occurred. In the street *du Bac* in 1858, and in the street *des Grès*, in 1849, in Paris ; and in 1871 I know myself what happened at the Hague. Capt. O. E. K. occupied the second story of a house in the street Van Hogendorp. A rear room looked out on the dwellings of an adjoining street. After a residence there of some weeks, one afternoon a stone struck the window of said chamber. This was repeated for several days, generally between 2 and 4 o'clock p.m. Pieces of brick, plaster, coal, pottery, and mud enclosed in paper came with such force that the chamber was a mass of ruins. The window curtains were torn, and the glass, the window frames, all the decorations were in pieces. The missiles came over the environing houses, and as if from a distance. The police were actively employed in the matter for several days, and ' *sergents de ville* ' were stationed on the tops of the dwellings, but the source of the mischief was never found out."

It would be impossible to offer any satisfactory comments on the above narrative. The *Polter Gheist* of Germany, and the haunting Spirits of America and England, furnish striking parallels to the stone throwers of Java ; but for the philosophy involved in the phenomena itself, *i.e.*, the passage of stones through a closed room lined with linen, in which no abrasion or rent could be discovered, and the sudden appearance of material objects at points where no human hands could have placed them, all this involves modes of procedure which belong only to the realms of being invisible to man, and laws of which we are at present profoundly ignorant. As to the impelling motives of such manifestations, they are not so difficult of solution. Idle and mischievous men and women, boys and girls, abound in every city and hamlet of civilization, and such persons as delight in ringing door bells, breaking windows, and pelting inoffensive passengers with mud, &c., are not likely to become suddenly reformed by the casting off their outer garments in the material disintegration called death. If the renowned English Marquis of W——, whose chief delight it was to scare respectable citizens out of their beds by midnight pranks, or upset helpless old costermongers' stores, for the pleasure of seeing the distress thus occasioned, had happened to have become a disembodied Spirit in the plenitude of his exemplary modes of passing his time, there is no doubt that he would have rejoiced in associating himself with a company of *Polter Gheists* or *Gendarolas*, and thrown stones, broken plates and dishes, or spat on little girls' clean aprons, to his heart's content.

The world of matter has yet to learn that good and evil, mischief and kind service, are the promptings of the Spirit, not of the body, and until the demons of our city streets are converted into angels, demons they will still remain, whether on earth, or in the Spirit world.

When those who denounce all Spirits as demons, can find a worse demon than a bad man, we shall be ready to join in the cry that "Spiritualism is all diabolism;" until we can find this *rara avis*, we would counsel those who object to the return of "demons" from the other life, to beware how they manufacture demoniac characters on earth.

We must again call attention to the fact, that although much property was damaged, and many persons were annoyed and terrified in these curious Javanese manifestations, *no one was hurt, and the stones hurled at property, were never launched against life.* Would we could say as much for the malignant *Spirits*, who haunt our earthly homes, still clothed in the panoply of flesh.

It now only remains to notice a few of the honoured names which have come prominently before the public in connection with the Spiritual movement in Holland. The first and most worthy of notice is that of Major Revius, to whose good service, attention has already been called, as well as to those of several of his *confrères* and fellow-workers; MM. Van Herwerden, N. T. Marthese, and A. J. Riko, whose valuable contributions to this volume are already known to the reader—in fact the names and services of the eminent Spiritualists already noted, need not be reiterated. Mention has been made of Madame Elise Von Calcar, well-known and highly esteemed throughout Holland, not only for her literary labours, but also for the high and spotless reputation which she has so fearlessly devoted to the service of Spiritualism. This lady, whose name and fame is calculated to shed lustre on any cause, has given her best endowments for many years to Spiritualism. One of her ablest novels has embodied the current ideas of the movement in terse yet eloquent language, and in the shape of a fictional work, entitled, in translation, "Children of the Age," she has enlisted the minds of her readers in the interests of Spiritualism far more forcibly than she could have done by any abstract essays.

Another, and a still more valuable contribution to the literature of Spiritualism, is the well-known journal conducted by Madame Von Calcar, namely, a monthly organ (large book size) of over thirty-two pages, called " *Op de Grenzen van twee Werelden*," " On the Boundaries of Two Worlds."

This fine periodical has been published during the five past years, and its completed volumes contain a mass of literature of the most important character, including descriptions of Spiritual manifestations in every country of the earth. The seers of every age, from Apollonius of Tyana to Andrew Jackson Davis; from Hermes Trismegistus to Jacob the Zouave, are described with graphic force and pleasing ideality. This lady's residence too on *Willemstraat*, the Hague, where with her husband she receives the best literary and Spiritualistic society of the day, forms a rallying point for those in sympathy with her peculiar views, and promotes that friction of mind with mind, which is so valuable a result of well organized social reunions.

At Amsterdam, amongst many Spiritualists of good position and earnest devotion to the cause, may be named, Mr. J. V. Maurik and his amiable lady. Mr. Maurik has won a distinguished place for himself as an author and dramatist, but is now better known amongst Spiritualists, as a warm supporter of their cause.

Dr. H. de Grood, one of the professors at the Groningen University; Dr. I. Van Velzen, secretary of the Synod; Dr. R. Van der Loef, and Herr Schimmel, well-known authors, are names honourably identified with the advocacy of Spiritualism in Holland. Many other gentlemen, besides several ladies distinguished in literary and aristocratic circles, have been reported to the author as possessing fine Mediumistic gifts, or as being the advocates of Spiritualism in the seclusion of their own homes. Not having the privilege of citing these parties as avowed disciples of the belief, we can only cursorily refer to the fact that a far larger number of persons of position in Holland believe in Spiritualism, than those that are willing to incur reproach and public ridicule for its sake. The same may be said of the cause and its disciples in the Dutch Indies.

When it is remembered that the official investigation detailed above, concerning the disturbances in Java, occurred nearly twenty years before the advent of Modern Spiritualism in America, it is no marvel that their cause was wholly misunderstood, and their possible significance disregarded both by the witnesses and the journalistic recorders.

As Spiritualism in its modern sense began to be known, its phenomena discussed and practised in aristocratic circles, and its Mediums patronized by the leading classes of society, the tone of newspaper criticism became gradually changed, and even the counterfeit pretences of itinerant exposers, began to be regarded in their true light, namely, as an evidence that there must be something of genuine worth, to call forth the base imitation, also as a proof how desperate must be the cause of those who vehemently oppose Spiritualism, when they can find no better weapons wherewith to do battle against it than the tricks of poor conjurers.

Spiritualism in Holland, as in every other great centre of civilization, seems to have done the work of ploughing, harrowing, and preparing the ground for the reception of the seeds of truth and Spiritual unfoldment.

Thousands and tens of thousands of invisible hands have been busy in scattering that seed and pressing visible workers into the same beneficent service.

Despite of man's impatience to reap the harvest before the seed has had time to germinate, the Spiritualists find themselves compelled to watch and wait for the natural development which time, and the favouring harvest season, alone can bring forth.

Few there are however who feel that what has been done has been in vain. The marked change which public opinion displays on all subjects relating to Spiritual existence here or hereafter, is the best proof that the work of mortals has been to sow the seed as they have received commission, and trust that the Lord of the Harvest will come in the fulness of time to do the rest. "Be thou faithful unto death," is the watchword which every true Spiritualist obeys, confident that the work well done on earth, is done for all eternity.

CHAPTER XLIII.

SPIRITUALISM IN RUSSIA.

NOTHING can be more difficult to an uninformed observer than the attempt to ascertain the real status of the Spiritual cause in Russia. On the one hand, witnesses of acknowledged credit affirm, that Spirit Communion is a belief prevailing largely amongst both the ignorant peasantry and the highest nobles. In the rural districts it is alleged that every village entertains its pantheon of spectral agencies, whilst the *Schamanns*, or prophet priests of

N. WAGNER.
PROFESSOR OF ZOOLOGY AT THE UNIVERSITY OF ST. PETERSBURG.

Siberia, have proverbially obtained for their wonder-working powers a world-wide celebrity. Amongst the higher classes, one need but cite the well-known opinions of the noble gentleman who but lately ruled the land, Alexander II., who—together with many princely members of his family—was known to have been a warm friend of Spiritualism and Spiritualists.

On the other hand, we are advised by those who claim to speak with authority, that Spiritualism has no open or public recognition in Russia, and that the only journal printed in its interest by a native Russian, is obliged to be published in the German language. The following statement lately given in the *Revue Spirite* of Paris, is also cited as an evidence of the ill odour in which subjects of an occult character are held in Russia. The *Revue* says :—

" Professor Wagner has lately been giving a series of lectures in St. Petersburg on the subject of 'Animal Magnetism.' His audiences numbered about five or six hundred persons, the chief of whom were physicians, university students, or literary men. He had great difficulty in gaining permisssion to give these lectures, as they approached a subject which has been condemned alike by clerical and scientific authorities, the former attributing all psychical phenomena outside of the church to Satan, and the latter to physiological disturbance, to be rectified by orthodox medication. To gain his hearing Professor Wagner called animal magnetism by the less disagreeable name of ' hypnotism.' He quoted facts of history from ancient times down to the present, noticing the discoveries of Van Helmont, Mesmer, Reichenbach, Dupotet, and others, not forgetting Braid, the introducer of the term hypnotism. Professor Wagner solved all the mysteries of the subject by introducing a *psychic principle*, not a resultant of the organism, but a force having individuality and consciousness, whose vehicle is the nerve fluid within the organism and the ether of space without. The lectures were well received, and were frequently interrupted by earnest applause. Professor Wagner concluded by recommending the constitution of a society for the investigation of psychical research."

It is added as a·comment on the covert form in which Wagner attempted to awaken interest in occult subjects, that the formation of any society for psychic investigation will be sternly prohibited. Undoubtedly there must be a median line between the two opposing views of the subject stated above.

To arrive at this, we shall cite the opinions of some of the most reliable authorities who have written concerning Spiritualism in Russia, and the first quotations will be from letters addressed to the *Revue Spirite*, by Prince Adeka, of Russia. This gentleman, an accomplished scholar, a warm Spiritualist, and a member of the royal family of Russia, writes as follows :—

" Spiritualism, as a doctrine, was introduced into Russia in 1854, by M. Boltine and some others who had witnessed Spiritual phenomena abroad, and had become acquainted with the works of Allan Kardec. These prepared the way for the visit of Mr. D. D. Home to Petersburgh about 1861. The wonderful manifestations through his mediumship in the Imperial Palace, as well as in those of some of the Russian aristocracy, gave an impetus to inquiry, and this was strengthened by Mr. Home being received as son-in-law into a good Russian family.

" Unhappily however, Russia not being yet in the enjoyment of a free press, the advocates of Spiritualism have had to keep in the background with the public. ' The State Church does not allow the publication, in the Russian language, of any books, pamphlets, or printed matter discussing it ; it is therefore only a subject of private discussion among those who know other languages besides that of their own country.

" Russia has a penal code in which any Russian who steps outside the pale of the Greco-Russian Church, or who attempts to teach doctrines contrary to it, is punishable by exile to Siberia. Such is the legal situation of the various sects in Russia. Happily, however, laws there are laxly observed. The dogmas of the State Church are by the mass of the people assented to chiefly as a means of keeping themselves clear of the police. But very many, as opportunity comes, throw aside the mask and join some sect ; and sects in Russia are numerous.

"Three years ago, M. Aksakof, who is editor of the *Psychische Studien*, which he,—a Russian of high position, socially and officially, must write in a foreign language and publish in a foreign country,—invited a good many scientific men attached to the University to witness a demonstration of some psychical phenomena, with the object of getting them to acknowledge their reality; but nothing came of it. The gentlemen of science seemed to fear conversion from old opinions. . . .

"But a few professors of the University did join M. Aksakof, and in 1880 the project of a society was drawn up, having for its object the study of psychic science, &c. To this project the authorisation of the Government was formally applied for, and would have been given had not the Church interposed on the ground that no science was wanted to prove the power of Satan, and that the Church needed no help in proclaiming the immortality of the soul.

"Spiritualists in Petersburg are necessarily of the educated classes only. They may be divided into two categories : 1, those who accept the doctrine of Re-Incarnation, from having studied the works of Allan Kardec; and 2, those who belong to the American or English school. M. Aksakof belongs to the second category, which occupies itself with experiments in mediumship and physical manifestations, without concerning itself with the question of Re-Incarnation.

Besides these two categories there are very many individuals who, so to speak, hang on to Spiritualism; who go to *séances* as to an entertainment. There are also many others to whom Spiritualism is a demonstrated science, who study its doctrines and practise its morality. Many of these are foreign residents.

"My remarks have had reference to Spiritualism as it is in the capital, but there is plenty of evidence that it is studied all through the provinces."

Prince Adeka writes at a still later date, namely, April, 1882, to the *Revue Spirite* thus :—

"Since my last communication upon the position of Spiritualism in Russia, it has evidently made favourable progress in the most influential quarters. The censorship has given its sanction to the publication of a weekly paper, the editor of which is Captain Perbikof, of the Imperial navy, who makes no secret of his being a Spiritualist. I may say that his wife is an excellent medium for physical manifestations. They belong to the school of Spiritualism which we here call the American, which does not concern itself about Re-Incarnation. The *Rebus*, for such is the title of the paper, has been out now for six months. Not wishing to jeopardise it, the editor hitherto has dealt with Spiritualism only in an incidental way, having regard to the nominal interest of the paper, which is understood to be in the discussion of rebuses, charades, &c. It announces that the profits, if any, are to go to the funds of a benevolent institution founded last year by Madame Perbikof. This may have smoothed away some of the difficulties encountered by Captain Perbikof in obtaining the sanction to publish. It may also account for the fact that one-half of the subscribers to the paper belong to the clerical ranks. Whatever the reason, the fact is, under all circumstances, significant.

"Here is another item of significance. The *Novoe Vrémya* (*The New Time*), a newspaper of large circulation, is admitting a series of articles based upon R. Dale Owen's 'Debateable Land.' These articles are, under the pseudonym of Poliansky, written by Professor Wagner, who is an earnest Spiritualist and close friend of the Academician Boutlerof, one of our most eminent *savants*. M. Wagner's articles are headed, 'Between Two Worlds.' The censorship has used its scissors more freely than we like, but it is a welcome surprise to Spiritualists that it permits so much to appear in the Russian language. The articles are making quite a sensation among our rising young men.

"But I have yet another welcome piece of news for you; the interdict against translations of Allan Kardec's books into Russian has been removed so far as to allow the publication of his 'What is Spiritualism?' The MS. of the translation has passed the censorship, and is now passing through the printer's office. This gives great cause for congratulation, for nothing has hitherto been published in the Russian language having the least reference to the rational foundation of Spiritualism. The censorship cut out the second part, and insisted that Kardec's name should not appear, for that, it seems, would be too much for our 'Holy Synod' to bear !"

The next quotation is taken from the correspondence of Prince Emil Sayn Wittgenstein (late aide-de-camp, and trusted friend of the Emperor Alexander II.), and the author of this work.

In a private letter to Mrs. Hardinge Britten, dated 1876, Prince Emil Wittgenstein says :—

"The Emperor and most of his household save . . . are not only Spiritualists in belief, but they would be partisans of the faith, did circumstances permit.

"Since Mr. D. D. Home's first visit in—I think—1861, His Majesty has never doubted the truth of spirit communion,—and the rich presents and special favour he has bestowed on Mr. Home, is proof positive of the royal acceptance of his Mediumship. . . . The great enemy of Spiritualism in Russia however is the Church. I think myself it should be the friend of this power,—for without it, the Church may *say*, but it cannot *prove* anything, and with it, it is built upon *facts* which no rival Church can disprove. . . . Perhaps you know that any writing, printing, or words spoken publicly, which offend against the articles of state religion, are punishable by the heaviest penalties—in some cases by exile to Siberia.

"Sects may arise and do, but they are offshoots if not actually a part of the Church,— but as for Spiritualism—why, Great Heaven ! it loosens the chains of ecclesiastical tyranny ; breaks open the doors of the Inquisition, puts out its fires, or uses them to burn up priestly passports to heaven or hell, besides making of every one his own priest. Of course this won't suit the ecclesiastics who live by the people's slavery ; not their freedom,—hence, although Spiritualism is known and believed in, alike by peer and peasant, it must be believed in against authority,—and be assured, my friend, it has a warm place in the hearts of thousands who dare not openly avow their convictions."

From similar friendly communications from Prince Emil Wittgenstein, the author learned that the late Emperor of Russia possessed the most complete library of Spiritual works that the literature of many nations could supply. This noble gentleman was one of the earliest subscribers to a work translated and edited by the author, entitled "Art Magic," and in an autograph letter addressed to the writer of that work, he declared, "that he esteemed it as his most sacred authority, and carried it everywhere with him."

Thus, although Spiritualism has obtained wide recognition in Russia in the hearts and consciences of the thinking classes, its denunciation as a revolutionist, by the Church-ridden members of the community, is quite sufficient to account for the paucity of its literature in the language of the country.

It may not be out of place at this point, to give a few extracts from Mr. Home's autobiography—"Incidents of My Life," in reference to his first introduction at the Russian Court. In order to fulfil his marriage contract with the fair Russian lady who subsequently became his first wife, Mr. Home left Paris for St. Petersburg in company with M. Alexandre Dumas, the celebrated novelist, who had promised to officiate as godfather on the occasion.

Mr. Home says (p. 128) :—

"An amusing account of our journey may be read in Dumas' book, entitled 'De Paris à Astrachan.'

"On reaching St. Petersburg, I was honoured by a kind invitation to be received by the Emperor, but which I was obliged to decline, *not being in power* at the time, and his Majesty having most graciously sent to me to say, that under any circumstances he would be pleased to see me, I excused myself on the plea of having so much to attend, previous to my marriage. A month after this, certain difficulties having arisen, and the papers which were necessary not being forthcoming, the marriage seemed on the point of being postponed.

"I had had no manifestations for several months, but on this evening, I was told by the spirit of my mother to inform the Emperor the next day that my power had returned.

"I did so, and was received by his Majesty at the Palace at Peterhoff, where I spent a week, and all the obstacles in the way of my marriage were removed by his most gracious Majesty, who upon this, as upon every occasion, has shown me the greatest kindness. I have the highest veneration for him, not only as a monarch, but as a man of the most kind and generous feelings.'

In the following chapter Mr. Home gives some interesting details of his manifestations whilst residing in Russia, up to the time when his eldest child was born ; one remark is so pertinent to the diverse opinions that are afloat concerning the appearance of *materialized hands*, that we quote Mr. Home's words *in extenso*. He says (p. 132),—" One evening one of my friends was converted from his previous unbelief, by seeing a hand visible to all of us in the room, slowly forming in the air, a few inches *above* the table, until it assumed the apparent materiality of a real hand." This hand—apparently that of a female—took up a pencil from the table and wrote a communication which deeply affected Mr. Home's visitor, who recognized it as being from his mother. Mr. Home adds—" The general belief is, that spirit hands always appear from *beneath the table, already formed*,—but this is incorrect, for on many occasions in the presence of several persons at a time, they are seen to be formed in the manner I have described, and to melt away in the same way. Often too they have been seen to form high above our heads, and from thence to descend to the table and disappear."

As Spiritualism in Russia owes its status entirely to the individuals who have aided in its promulgation, and the history of their personal efforts is that of the movement also, we shall now call attention to the self-sacrificing and influential labours of a gentleman to whom the cause of Spiritualism is more indebted than to any other person in Northern Europe—namely, the Hon. Alexander Aksakof, the talented editor of the monthly magazine published at Leipsig, devoted to the interests of Spiritualism and entitled— *Psychische Studien.*

As it would be impossible to arrive at a just estimate of Spiritual progress in Russia without including the effect of the vast influence exerted by the indefatigable efforts and high social standing of M. Aksakof, the following brief extracts concerning this gentleman's life and labours, taken from a sketch written for the *Religio Philosophical Journal* of America by Mr. Hudson Tuttle, cannot but prove of interest to the reader.

Mr. Tuttle's article was written in 1881, and headed—

" SPIRITUALISM IN RUSSIA.

" ALEXANDER AKSAKOF, THE PIONEER SPIRITUALIST OF RUSSIA.

" To American—and we may add English Spiritualists as well, the name which stands at the head of this article is familiar, and all who know something of the unwearied efforts of this eminent man to bring to Europe the knowledge of Spiritualism. . . . We have noble and devoted Spiritualists in America, but none who can exceed him. He has counted rank and position as nothing, and without a thought, has sacrificed his health, feeling more than repaid, if the cause he loved prospered, and bestowed on others the happiness he had found.

" Alexander Aksakof was born in the year 1832 at Repiofka, an estate the property of his father in the government of Penza, Russia. After completing his course of studies at the Imperial Lyceum of St. Petersburg, an institution privileged to the ancient nobility of Russia, he entered the service of the government, in which with but little interruption he has remained to the present."

Mr. Tuttle then goes on to notice in detail too diffuse for this place, how M. Aksakof, from becoming acquainted with the writings of Swedenborg, gradually began to study them with an interest so profound, that in course of time they took a deep and permanent hold upon his mind.

After describing at length the earnestness with which M. Aksakof studied the Hebrew and Latin languages, the better to qualify himself for following Swedenborg through his wonderful doctrine of correspondences, the biographer says :—

"The grand design to which all his studies converged, philological and theological, was the translation of Swedenborg's 'Heaven and Hell' into the Russian language. In 1863, his translation of this work was published in Leipzig, but is compelled to wait for more propitious times for its appearance in Russia.

"Swedenborg being the greatest of seers, it was natural that M. Aksakof should take up the study of animal magnetism, and enjoy all works on spiritual revelations obtained in this manner, agreeing, as they all did, in essential points with Swedenborg. In 1854, while searching the libraries, he came unexpectedly on 'Nature's Divine Revelations,' by A. J. Davis. The title did not attract his attention, but the qualification of the author— 'The Seer and Clairvoyant'—at once impressed him. He was rejoiced to find most remarkable proofs of the principal points in the revelation of Swedenborg concerning the Spirit world. These authors differed in dogmas concerning Christianity, it was true, while they agreed in the great facts of Spirit existence.

"In order to form a correct judgment of both physiological and psychological phenomena, M. Aksakof at once saw the necessity of a better understanding of the exact sciences ; the perfect comprehension of the spiritual man, necessitated the understanding of man physically. With this object in view, in 1855, he inscribed himself as free student of the Faculty of Medicine of the University of Moscow, and for two years pursued the studies of anatomy, physiology, chemistry, and physics. He soon departed from the restraints imposed by scientific authority, the result of his experiments in human magnetism being a translation into Russian, and publication in St. Petersburg, in 1863, of Count Szapary's work entitled, 'Magnetic Healing.'

"He readily comprehended in all their bearings, the accounts he received of 'Spiritual Manifestations' in America. The first book on that subject, which reached him was Beechers's 'Review of Spiritual Manifestations,' in 1855. He there received palpable evidence of the truth of the grand doctrine he had accepted by intuition. This, with the French works on magnetism, gave him the first information of the spiritual movement in America, and, with his accustomed habit, he at once sought all works treating on the subject ; but found in Russia, great difficulty in procuring them. Not until the end of 1857, did he obtain the works of Edmonds, Hare, and the 'Gt. Harmonia' of Davis.

"He studied with particular attention the works on magnetism and spiritualism of Cahagnet, whom, in 1861, he met in Paris. The perusal of the consecutive volumes of Davis, and the grand works on Spiritualism, completed the emancipation of his mind. . . .

"The following is an extract from M. Aksakof's preface to the translation of Swedenborg :—

"'The theological works of Swedenborg have engendered a sect—a common occurrence, and unfortunate for the transmission of great ideas—so much does man love the "jurare in verba magistri." Notwithstanding all the spirituality and broadness of his philosophy, his disciples rest with the letter ; astounded by the immensity of his revelations they will not go farther ; for them it is not a step advancing to higher altitudes, but, a finality. In the present work the theologico-dogmatic side is not presented, but the more important information given by Swedenborg in regard to his personal experience in the spirit-world ; for us he is not a theologian, but a seer and medium.'

"This preface drew on M. Aksakof from the little circle of devotees to the doctrines of Swedenborg—of whom he had been a member—the most violent recriminations. He was thus compelled most explicitly to give the reasons for his apostacy. The result of this discussion was the publication of 'The Rationalism of Swedenborg : a criticism of his doctrines on the Bible. Leipsic, 1870.' To this work was attached as an appendix, 'The Gospel according to Swedenborg, five chapters of the Gospel of St. John, and an exposition of their Spiritual Sense according to the Doctrine of Correspondences.' . . .

"With all his studies of Swedenborg M. Aksakof did not cease to investigate the fundamental principles of religion and psychology. One thing he regarded as incontestable, that if the mystery which shrouds the human soul was ever penetrated, and the fact of individual immortality admitted by science, it must be by the study of the phenomena of Spiritualism.

"The works of Kardec began to penetrate Russia, and although in a foreign language they had a wide circulation.

23

"M. Aksakof wished to give his countrymen something more positive. The material-istic tendency of the age led him to place a higher value on facts. With this object he translated Professor Hare's work and published it in Leipzig in 1866. Through this means he discovered the translator of Davis's works, Herr Wittig, who at the prompting of the eminent naturalist and philosopher Von Esenbeck, had translated many of Davis's works though he had not yet found a publisher.

"The impossibility of promoting Spiritualism in his own country induced M. Aksakof to offer M. Wittig to publish some of his translations, and thus began his efforts to propagate Spiritualism in Germany."

Mr. Tuttle then gives a list of the works published at various times as follows :—Davis's " Reformer," " The Magic Staff," " Nature's Divine Revelations," " The Physician"—the principal works of Hare, Crookes, Edmonds, and Owen, and the " Report of the Dialectical Society."

In 1874 M. Aksakof commenced—in addition to all his other magnificent undertakings of a literary character—the publication of the admirable monthly magazine, the *Psychische Studien*, a work which still continues to hold its place as one of the finest periodicals devoted to psychological subjects.

M. Aksakof experienced no obstruction from the Russian censor in promulgating Spiritualism through works or journals, in the German language, and thus it was that he attracted attention from Mr. Yowskevitch, an ardent Spiritualist and a great admirer of Davis's writings. This gen tleman was Professor of Philosophy in the University of Moscow, and he was fearless and candid enough to proclaim his convictions in public as well as in private, and urge the importance of investigating psychological subjects to his colleagues in the university.

When this brave and noble gentleman departed from this sphere to the higher life, M. Aksakof paid a well-deserved tribute to his memory in an article published in the *Revue Russe* in 1876, under the title of " Medium-ship and Science." Continuing Mr. Tuttle's narrative, we find that—

"In 1870, M. Aksakof proposed to M. Boutlerof, Professor of Chemistry in the University of St. Petersburg—whose sister-in-law, the cousin of M. Aksakof, manifested some degree of mediumship—to form a circle for the investigation of Spiritualism in an experimental manner. The circle included the Professor, his sister-in-law, Madame Aksakof, who was endowed with remarkable mediumistic power, and M. Aksakof. The result of twenty *séances* attended by M. Boutlerof was the admission by him of the reality of the phenomena.

"In 1871 Mr. D. D. Home arrived at St. Petersburg. For the first time in his life did M. Aksakof obtain evidence of grand and beautiful Spiritual manifestations. . . . He was not tardy in furnishing M. Boutlerof with an opportunity to assist at similar *séances*, and one *séance* by Mr. Home to the professors of the University of St. Petersburg.

"When Mr. Crookes published his experiences in the *Quarterly Journal of Science*, M. Aksakof immediately translated them, and after long weary years of waiting, had the pleasure of presenting the Russian public with the first book on Spiritualism, entitled ' Spiritualism and Science.'

"In 1874 a zealous Russian Spiritualist, M. Lyof, engaged M. Bredif, a French medium, to visit St. Petersburg. M. Aksakof arranged weekly *séances* for himself, to which Pro-fessor Boutlerof invited his friend and colleague Professor Wagner to participate. After some months Professor Wagner, impelled by the force of evidence, opened the campaign by his celebrated letter, published in the April number (1875) of the *Revue de L'Europe*, one of the best class of Russian monthlies.

"Great offence was taken by the press, and the University, which impelled the Society Physique to nominate a committee to investigate the phenomena of mediumship.

"The honour of the nomination of the first committee, strictly scientific, for the investigation of this question, belongs to Russia. This committee, fully confiding in the ability of M. Aksakof, invited him to make the necessary arrangements for them. He was thus made to act, somewhat, the *rôle* of Dr. Gardner before the famous Harvard committee ; only far more difficult, on account of the total absence of mediums, proper to bring before such a body. He visited England in the autumn of 1875, but was not fortunate in finding mediums whom he considered sufficiently remarkable and reliable.

"Hearing, however, favourable reports of the mediumship of the Petty family at Newcastle-on-Tyne—the manifestations occurring behind a pendant curtain, in front of which the mediums were seated—he visited the family, and his experiences were so satisfactory that he engaged the father and two sons. Unfortunately—by the change of conditions and the absence of the mother, who was the principal medium — the mediumistic forces were not sufficiently powerful to produce any result. After four *séances*, M. Aksakof, seeing the hopelessness of the attempt, discontinued the *séances* and returned the mediums. He then engaged an English lady, with remarkable mediumistic faculties, and offered her services to the committee. This lady, not being a professional medium, desired to remain unknown, and she was presented to the committee under the name of Mrs. Clayer. Mr. Crookes, on pages 38-39 of his 'Researches' relates his experiences with this lady; at his residence, M. Aksakof had the pleasure of making her acquaintance. The production of the physical manifestations in the plain light wholly answered his expectations, and he at last thought that the necessary medium for presentation to the committee had been found. She, at first, declined the offer, but yielded to his urgent solicitation, and arrived in St. Petersburg in mid-winter, accompanied by her two daughters, whom she would not trust to the hands of strangers. This was a most meritorious act, one which the history of Spiritualism in general, and Spiritualism in Russia, in particular, should not ignore.

"The second series of official *séances* commenced, before the committee, in January, 1876. The manifestations began at the first *séance*. The rappings were plain and distinct, and of the same character as those which first arrested the attention of the world, at Rochester, in 1848, in the presence of the Fox family, and witnessed in London, by M. Aksakof, at the home of Mrs. Kate Fox-Jencken. The tipping and levitation of the table were also produced before the committee, being everything he expected for the commencement. Professor Boutlerof, and M. Aksakof, attended these *séances* for the purpose of witnessing the procedures, and being near the medium; but alas! in this case, from the beginning, instead of impartial scientific investigation, the committee were determined to prove that phenomena of mediumship had no existence. Their action put to shame even the methods of the Harvard committee. The medium, in the words of the judges—who had passed judgment before they met at the first *séance*—made all the manifestations, and Professor Mendeleyef, one of the principal personages of the committee, declared that the medium had an instrument, concealed by her skirts, to which she resorted. Thus terminated the scientific history of Spiritualism in Russia.

"Awaiting the report of the committee, M. Aksakof continued his negotiations with different mediums, which resulted in bringing Dr. Slade from London to St. Petersburg, in December, 1878; but when he arrived, the committee had ceased to exist, and Russia was engaged in war with Turkey. The public mind was occupied with other subjects. Although Slade's visit to St. Petersburg was not as productive as it might have been, his sojourn in Germany and its results form a memorable epoch in the history of Spiritualism. The experiences of Professor Zollner, and many other celebrated men of science with him were most marvellous, and are already known round the world. . . . This success fully repaid M. Aksakof for all the sacrifice he had made in Russia, and the long and patient labours by which he had prepared the way in Germany for this gratifying result.

"When we consider the great efforts of Professor Zollner; the advocacy of Professors Perty, of Berne, Hoffman, of Wurzburg, and of Fichte, who not only publicly defended the phenomena, but also the doctrines of Spiritualism, we feel that M. Aksakof must enjoy a deep satisfaction in a result to which he has, more than any one else, contributed.

"After having completed his work with the committee, M. Aksakof demanded, in 1876, permission to publish in St. Petersburg a Russian monthly journal, *A Review of Mediumship*. This was refused by the Minister of the Interior, Timaschef.

"M. Aksakof was not idle, but prepared a reply to the report of M. Mendeleyef entitled 'Materials by which to judge Spiritualism,' a mass of ironical commentaries in which he ridiculed Spiritualism in general, and his colleagues—Professors Boutlerof, Wagner, and M. Aksakof—in particular. On the appearance of this document, M. Aksakof—taking into consideration the bad spirit in which the investigation was conducted—prepared a reply under the title : 'A Monument of Scientific Prejudice.'"

Thus far Mr. Hudson Tuttle; and it may be quite worth while to compare the noble record of literary labour undertaken in the interests of Spiritualism as thus narrated with the simple unaffected account which Mr. Aksakof gives of his own share in Spiritual propagandism in a paper prepared by him to be read at the English International Conference of 1869. This paper was admirably translated by Signor Damiani, a well-known and scholarly Italian gentleman now residing in London, and published in *Human Nature*, from the columns of which are selected the following extracts :—

"As a representative of Russia I ought to give to you a few words concerning the state of Spiritualism in my country. There it is known by the name of Spiritism, because it reached us through the works of Allan Kardec, who has systematised and made that doctrine popular in France, and who has given it this name in order to distinguish it from that which is generally comprehended under the denomination of Spiritualism. Its followers call themselves, regardless of all etymological rules, *Spirites*, instead of Spiritists. Their number in Russia, or rather in the two centres of our civilisation, Moscow and St. Petersburg, can only be counted by dozens ; they certainly would have been more considerable if we were not deprived of the means offered by the press to express publicly our opinions on this subject. One of the most zealous representatives of Spiritualism at St. Petersburg is General Apollon Boltin. He has translated into the Russian language the principal works of Kardec, and has, besides, written much himself upon this matter, but has not had the privilege of being able to print his works. Among the co-operators of the *Revue Spirite* we have here General Foelkner, whose translation of the 'Letters of Lavater to the Empress Marie of Russia,' was published at Paris at the International Library, and also M. H. Stecki, who published at the same library an essay entitled 'Spiritism in the Bible.' We have here, as well as at Moscow, several writing mediums and others, but as to physical manifestations, we are quite wanting in them. By way of recompense however, we have at Moscow, in the person of M. Artemovsky, a very good healing medium. What seems extraordinary to us is, that he holds his *séances* publicly, having had the good luck to receive permission from the authorities. Some mediums here, whose curing functions had commenced to attract sick people to them in crowds, did not meet with the same success ; the police interfered, and these gentlemen were obliged to confine themselves to practising in private.

" Regarding our Spiritism from within, I do not see enough union among its followers, without which no doctrine can become a social and reforming power. If we are going to seek the causes of this disunion, we shall find it in the two following facts :—In the first place stands the onesided study of the subject, inevitable in consequence of its being derived from the one source—the works of Allen Kardec and his Review—a partiality excusable for the Russians, who generally know French and not English, and in consequence imitate the intellectual movement of Europe by the production of French literature ; but wholly inexcusable for Kardec, who holds his lectures exclusively within the limits of his circle, and not only ignores that which is done out of France, but ignores even, or feigns to ignore, what is done in France by that circle of Spiritualists whose organ is the *Revue Spiritualiste*, by Pierart.

"This pretence of ignoring is carried to such a point that M. Kardec, whilst announcing upon the wrapper of his review the Spiritualistic periodicals appearing in Germany and Italy, does not even mention M. Pierart's journal, and this for the reason that the Spiritualists do not accept the doctrine of re-incarnation, as if the source from whence Kardec had derived his system had been another and more authentic one than that of Pierart. Thus it is that dogmatism, that eternal source of discord in religion, threatens to invade Spiritualism, one of whose principal merits is having avoided the rock of sectarianism and not having wished to form a written and obligatory confession of faith. . . .

"In the second place we are disunited and weak because we are deprived of liberty of speech and denied any representation through the press. . . .

"The civil censor has received special instructions not to let anything appear that relates to Spiritualism.

"'A fool throws a stone, says the proverb, 'and seven wise men cannot recover it.' . . .

"Allow me to tell you a few words about myself in particular. Desiring to make the Russian public acquainted with the phenomena of Spiritualism, I had chosen for that purpose the work of Professor Hare, and I had extracted that which principally related to the experimental part of the question. But the censor remained inexorable, and I have been obliged to have my translation printed at Leipzig, where it remains buried in the warehouse of M. Wagner, suffering the same fate as a Russian translation of Swedenborg's work 'Heaven and Hell,' which I had printed some years before. That our learned men are not behind yours in their contempt for Spiritualism I can show by the following example :—We have at the University here a Professor of Logic and Psychology in the person

HON. ALEXANDER AKSAKOF.

of M. Vladislavef—translator into Russian of Kant's *Critique de la Raison Pure*, author of *Doctrines Psychologiques Contemporaines*, &c., &c. Wishing to direct his attention to the psychological phenomena of Spiritualism, I gave him my Russian translation of Hare, some numbers of *Human Nature*, and the autobiography of A. J. Davis in German. Reading this enraged him so much that he could hardly speak. 'All that is only detestable humbug,' he said to me; 'Davis is an impudent man, Hare an unknown person. When I read it I believed I was in a tavern.' This reply deserving immortality, I record it. . . . .

"How much we are restrained in our literary pursuits, I can again show you by the following anecdote :—

"Lately I have been occupied in writing a critique on Swedenborg's 'Doctrine of the Scriptures.' When I had presented my manuscript to the spiritual reviser he sent me to the civil reviser, because I do not examine Swedenborg's system from an orthodox point of view, but only from the logical side, like all other philosophical systems ; and when I gave my manuscript to the civil reviser, he sent me to the spiritual censor, because my work, from the first page to the last, only treated of Holy Scripture.

"Convinced by my own experience and that of others, of the impossibility of serving, at least for the present, the cause of Spiritualism in my own country, I found I had nothing better to do than to transport my activity to a foreign land. In 1863 I learnt for the first time that a German translation of the works of A. J. Davis had been under taken by Mr. Von Esenbeck and his associate Mr. Wittig ; but all my attempts at having more information about this enterprise were fruitless until 1866, when I had the pleasure of becoming personally acquainted with Mr. Wittig, and the displeasure of learning all the difficulties he met with during the publication of his translations. I then offered to become the editor of them, and immediately we set ourselves to the task. In 1867 appeared 'The Reformer,' in 1868 'The Magic Staff,' and in 1869 'The Divine Revelations,' printed by Mr. Wagner at Leipsic. It might appear strange to have commenced the publication of 'The Reformer,' without following the chronological order, upon which Davis himself insisted ; but it is because nearly all the manuscripts were at Bremen with Mr. Ruthman, who had begun talking about their publication, without having, however, caused the enterprise to advance during many years. This is why we commenced by that which was ready at Mr. Wittig's. It is only lately that we have obtained, not without trouble and expense, possession of the manuscripts, and henceforth their publication can be re-established in chronological order. What reception the German public will give them, the future alone can decide. The prejudice of German science against animal magnetism and Spiritualism, and its materialistic tendencies, are, at present, too strong for us to expect a serious and impartial critique. On the other hand, silence still less attains our end, and our first duty is to extricate the public from the ignorance in which they live as to the real value of modern Spiritualism. To attain this result, the works of Davis appear to me the most suitable. Germany requires a philosophical system, which should be in a state to present not only an accordance of facts with a given doctrine, but even with the exigencies of actual science. From this point of view the harmonial philosophy has appeared to me worthy of the attention of German thinkers. Many persons, knowing the works of Davis, have expressed sympathy with their publication in Germany. Thus, one of the best known and most respectable followers of spiritualism in America, Judge Edmonds, in a letter that he wrote me in March, 1869, expresses himself on this matter in the following manner :—' In one respect A. J. Davis and I differ ; he looks upon Spiritualism rather as a philosophy, while I regard it as a religion. Therefore it is that his works must be more valuable in Germany than mine can be. With us and our impulsive nature the religious aspect is the most important ; in Germany the rationalistic must be.' As a psychological phenomenon, the person of Davis offers us one of the most remarkable types of the modern spiritualistic movement, and under this head deserves to be deeply studied. In the German edition of his 'Principles of Nature,' I made it a duty to collect all the proofs which had come to my own knowledge to establish the mesmeric origin of this work, and the further self-development of Davis, by way of pure intuition, like an incontestable psychological fact. . . ."

We can only regret that the limitations of space preclude the possibility of giving more of M. Aksakof's philosophic and interesting comments on the cause he has served so well. Enough has been stated however to show the importance of the work which one individual alone can effect, when animated by devotion to a noble cause, and inspired by the love of humanity rather than the desire for fame, or self-aggrandisement.

Just as this volume is going to press, we hear that M. Aksakof's promised work has been produced, under the title of " A Monument of Scientific Prejudice—*being a history of the committee appointed by the Physical Society of the University of St. Petersburgh for the investigation of so-called Mediumistic phenomena, with all the minutes of the proceedings and other remarks.*"

The volume above named has not only passed through the press, but portions of it have been freely commented on by the English and German Spiritual press, and it is quite evident, that though the reader may form some fair conclusions concerning the action of that committee which pledged itself to hold *forty* Spiritual *séances*, and dismissed the subject after rushing through *eight*, they can form but little notion without reading M. Aksakof's work, of the noble, manly, and philosophic way in which the accomplished writer has dealt with his subject. Another *sign of the times*, and one which promises hopefully for the progress of psychological science in Russia, is the fact, that the same indomitable and devoted worker, Alexander Aksakof is even now publishing in the Russian language (! !) a translation from the German of Baron Lazarus Hellenbach's works, in which—as every scholar acquainted with this great philosopher's writings must know—Spiritual ideas and teachings play a distinguished part. Truly liberty of thought and speech has " moved on " in Russia even within the last decade of months, and the noble triad of Freedom's standard-bearers, Aksakof, Boutlerof, and Wagner, may yet tread with mortal feet the promised land of Spiritual life and light, to which their untiring efforts have helped to conduct the long enslaved consciences of their countrymen.

CHAPTER XLIV.

SPIRITUALISM IN RUSSIA (CONCLUDED).

BEFORE dismissing the subject of " the Russian scientific commission," for the investigation on Spiritualism, instituted chiefly at the suggestion of the Hon. Alexander Aksakof, and reported upon most unfavourably by M. Mendeleyef, it may serve the interests of truth as well as justice to republish the protest which answered the said report. The reader is particularly urged to notice what *conditions* the " scientific commission " was pledged to observe, and how far the pledge was *not* redeemed. The protest was published in the *Journal de St. Petersburg* of May 18th, 1877, and was signed by one hundred and thirty names of influential persons.

It reads as follows in translation :—

" The Scientific Committee formed for the examination of medial phenomena had for its object, if we may judge by a communication from M. Mendeleyef, published in La Voix, No. 137, ' to study with precision ' these phenomena, and to ' render also important public service.' M. Mendeleyef informs us that at the sittings the following phenomena were to be the immediate objects for study on the part of the commission :—' The movement of inanimate objects produced without contact with human hands ; the floating of these objects in the air ; variations in the weight of objects ; movements or noises produced in the said objects, and having the character of being governed by intelligence, as exemplified by the giving of messages or the answering of questions ; writing by inanimate objects, or psychographic phenomena ; lastly, the complete or partial presentation of human bodies, or, in other words, materialization phenomena.'

"The committee promised to hold at least forty *séances* to study these various pheno-
nomena. To-day the committee declares that its investigations are at an end, that 'its
object has been attained,' and that it has arrived unanimously at the following conclusions:
'That Spiritualistic phenomena are the result of unconscious movements or of conscious
imposture, and that the doctrine of Spiritualism is a superstition.'

"This decision of the committee is based—as stated in its report—*upon eight séances.*
in the first four of which no medial phenomena were obtained, and in the last four of
which the committee saw several movements of the table and heard several raps. But
where are the observations of the committee upon the movement of objects without
contact with the hands; on the change of the weight of bodies; on conversational phenomena; and on psychographic and materialization manifestations?

"The committee has not carried out, it will be seen, a quarter of the programme which
it had laid down for itself, but it has decided, without any evidence in that direction,
against the spiritual 'doctrine;' a question which had never been placed in its programme
for consideration. The undersigned think it their duty to declare that, by an examination
so superficial and so rapid, the object of the researches of the committee has not been
attained, and that the committee has not fulfilled its task. It is evident that it has not
collected enough information either to affirm or to deny the existence of the medial
phenomena. After it had sat out eight *séances*, the committee did not hesitate to declare
that its observations were at an end, although it had no right, upon the evidence
collected during those eight *séances*, to come to any absolute decision. The committee
undertook its examination in the name of the interests of a portion of the public, and it
has failed to guard those interests. It has left the public in the same doubt as before in
relation to these medial phenomena, which are so well attested by people of influence and
of good faith.

"The undersigned, consequently, think that they have a right to express the hope
that the examination of medial phenomena, which has been begun in the name of science,
will be continued in harmony with the usual methods of science, and not by persons who
have even given a verdict against that which they have not seen—against phenomena
which have been verified by others after long and minute study. It is not by a partial
examination like this that an 'important public service' can be rendered. . . ."

Then follow the signatures of one hundred and thirty Russian names, the
transcription and reading of which would scarcely repay either author or
reader.

As a sort of corollary to this report, and in evidence first; that each Spiritual
séance should be studied *on its own merits*, and not on the report of previous
occasions; next, that nothing but long-continued and patient investigation
can discover the procedures of a movement so ill understood as that of
Spirit communion; and finally, that the most candid and unprejudiced
frame of mind is necessary to the elucidation of truth in the matter of
Spiritual phenomena—we shall republish the particulars of some *séances*
held by Messrs. Boutlerof and Aksakof with the English Medium Williams;
so often accused of "fraudulent practices," and yet, so inevitably endowed
with rare Mediumistic power.

The article which follows was published in M. Aksakof's fine journal
Psychische Studien, and has been extensively recopied in other Spiritual
papers. It is headed

"SPIRITUALISM IN RUSSIA—EXPERIENCES OF PROFESSOR BOUTLEROF.

"After describing the room (an ordinary hotel apartment without cupboard or
wardrobe), M. Boutlerof says:—

"'I will not describe every *séance* in detail, but will relate only the most striking
manifestations. While we sat at the table, holding Williams fast, various objects were
brought to us from a chest of drawers in the room, which stood behind Williams, at a
distance of about four feet, Williams remaining meanwhile immovable. Even if he had
had his hands free, the objects would have been beyond his reach. At the first sitting
M. Aksakof and myself were both touched on the face with something soft. This, as we
afterwards learned, was M. Aksakof's silk scarf, which was lying in his hat on the drawers,
and had been brought to us with the hat. Immediately afterwards the hat itself was

crushed down on M. Aksakof's head, and then, at my expressed wish, also placed upon my head. At another sitting, we being all in the same position as before, a musical box, which was playing on the table, was raised in the air, and wafted to and fro, as we could tell distinctly by the sound. Presently the box was placed for a moment on my right shoulder, next to Williams, while I still continued to hold him fast. Another time various articles were brought, and placed upon our table or in our hands, such as a match-box, which was also opened, a clothes brush and a travelling strap.

" ' When Williams was placed bound in the cabinet, or rather behind my plaid, which was suspended like a curtain, the phenomena were more powerful, especially at the two last *séances*. As we sat at the table we heard the voices of Peter and of John King. This latter personage is a well-known apparition at Williams's circles, and manifests both audibly and visibly. Peter's voice is quite different from that of King, who speaks in a deep bass and very quickly. These voices suggested that we should have a cabinet *séance*. We lighted a candle for a few minutes, while Williams placed himself behind the curtain. In these last sittings we screwed an iron staple into the wall ; a long tape was fastened round the medium's neck, and another piece was passed three times round the wrists, which were drawn together and securely tied. The long ends of both tapes were then threaded through the iron staple, and drawn across to our table, where I held them all through the sitting with my left hand. After each sitting the tapes were found intact throughout their length ; and I was able, while holding the tapes, to feel the slightest motion on the part of the medium. Only at the beginning did Williams draw in his hands a little, apparently as he was passing into the mediumistic sleep. Later on, while the phenomena were taking place, he did not stir in the slightest degree. We sat at the table, on the side furthest from the cabinet, with our faces turned towards it, at a distance of about three feet from the curtain.

"I will relate a few characteristic occurrences of the last sitting. After the light was put out, we again heard the voices of Peter and John. These voices appeared to come from various parts of the room ; at one moment they were close to us, at another further off, and often on the side opposite to that on which the medium sat. Presently phosphorescent lights were floating in the air, and immediately the form of John King became visible. This apparition is accompanied by a greenish phosphorescent light, which increases in brightness, lighting up John's bust. It is then seen that this light comes from a luminous substance which the form holds in its hand. The manly face, with a thick black beard, is tolerably distinct ; the head is draped with a white turban, and the upper part of the body with white garments. The form was outside the cabinet, and near to us. We only saw it for a moment at a time, the light vanished, and the form retreated into the darkness, but reappeared again as quickly. John asked us what he should do for us. M. Aksakof begged that he would rise to the ceiling and say a few words to us in that position. Accordingly we saw the form appear just over our table, and then gradually rise upwards to the ceiling, which became visible in the light proceeding from the luminous object in the hand of the figure. While up there, John called out to us—'Will that do ?' (*Ist es so recht ?*)

"Peter, in the meantime, although invisible, was busy and loquacious in the darkness, moving various objects through the air and touching us with them. As before mentioned, we sat on the side of the table furthest from the curtain ; behind our backs, about four feet distant, stood the washstand, on which were a water-bottle and glass. Suddenly we heard the ringing of glasses over our heads, as if two pieces were being struck together. Then followed a rapid pouring of water into the glass ; the glass was handed to M. Aksakof, the bottle to myself. As it stood in my hand, I felt sensibly that another hand was holding it above. At this moment we heard the medium move and groan, and the voice of Peter exclaiming that he wanted to give ' his medium ' something to drink. The water-bottle floated away from my hand, we heard the movement and inarticulate murmuring of the awakening medium, mingled with the voice of Peter : then the gurgling of water from the bottle, and in another instant I received the bottle back into my hand. During all that I have described, and indeed throughout the sitting, we were satisfied—so far as our hearing could perceive—that Williams remained in his corner, while the voices of John and Peter were speaking near to us outside the cabinet; occasionally also the sounds proceeding from the medium, and the speaking of John and Peter, were almost simultaneous.

"In conclusion let me remark that it is quite natural if other Russian inquirers regard these phenomena with suspicion. Owing to the scarcity of mediums in our country they have had at present few opportunities of observing them ; nevertheless they have not held back altogether, but took up the investigation so soon as some of their colleagues announced seriously that they had really witnessed the manifestations. On the whole American and English men of science have furnished the most remarkable examples of prejudice and obstinacy. It is easy enough for them to convince themselves of the objective reality of the phenomena ; they have powerful mediums always at hand, and yet with a few honourable exceptions they prefer to ignore the existence of these facts, and to treat as unworthy of credit the testimony of such men as Hare, De Morgan, Wallace, Crookes, Varley, and others. In no far-off future such conduct as this will be pointed at as a glaring example of scientific prejudice and superstition. I am aware that these words can hardly be allowed to appear in conjunction ; the adjective 'scientific,' however, does not refer to true science, which knows neither prejudice nor superstition, but only to such men who may belong to its ranks on the one hand, but who do not work in the true spirit of science so long as they pretend to serve the cause of human knowledge by ignoring facts."

"May the scales soon fall from their eyes, and may they soon enter on the only path to truth, namely, the path of experiment ! "

"I feel constrained to add my testimony to that of my valued friend, Professor Boutlerof, in respect of the manifestations which we witnessed in the presence' of Williams. Besides this, I can testify to having received the confirmation of the appearance of John King from Mr. Crookes in his own house, Mrs. Crookes's hand being on Williams's shoulder, while he was asleep behind the curtain ; also that in the house of Mrs. Macdougall Gregory, the curtain behind which Williams was placed, was nailed over the embrasure of a window so closely that the medium was in a niche almost hermetically sealed ; and that yet John King appeared above the table, round which the company were assembled in front of the curtain !

"ALEXANDER AKSAKOF."

No less striking than the above is the account published in M. Aksakof's journal in 1875 of Professor Wagner's experiences with the French Medium Bredif. The sitters were M. and Madame Aksakof, and other friends, besides Professor Wagner, who himself wrote the account and published it over his own signature. At the *séances* in question the Medium willingly submitted to be tied and tested by methods far more crucial than any of those practised in American or English circles.

M. Bredif never complained of being "degraded" by these tests, nor did they seem to interfere in the least with the phenomena produced, in fact their only result was to assure Professor Wagner and his friends beyond a peradventure that intelligent beings claiming to be Spirits DID—and M Bredif DID NOT make the manifestations observed.

They consisted of the usual results of physical *séances* such as direct voices ; writings of a test character ; the formation of hands ; playing musical instruments and feats of strength accompanied with intelligence.

M. Aksakof complains that as yet physical phenomena have been wanting amongst native Russian Media, although the more intellectual phases of "the power" have been widely manifested in private circles. This may quite possibly be the case in a country where the free investigation of Spiritualism has to be conducted under such stupendous difficulties.

That physical phenomena are not entirely wanting in Russia as in other countries, there is abundant evidence to show, and in proof thereof we cite the accounts which have quite recently appeared in the columns of the *Novoye Vrémya.* The following extract from the above-named journal of January, 1881, has been translated by a Russian gentleman well acquainted with Madame Beetch, and one who has had many opportunities of witnessing the phenomena he describes. The report in the *Novoye Vrémya,* after enlarging upon the great sensation existing amongst all classes of the community on the case reported of, goes on to say :—

"Not far from Petersburg, in a small hamlet inhabited by three families of German colonists, a widow, named Margaret Beetch, took a little girl from the House of Foundlings into her service. The little Pelagueya was liked in the family from the first for her sweet disposition, her hard-working zeal, and her great truthfulness. She found herself exceedingly happy in her new home, and for several years no one ever had a cross word for her. Pelagueya finally became a good-looking girl of seventeen, and was beloved in the house. Notwithstanding her good looks, no village youth ever thought of offering himself as a husband. The young men said she 'awed' them. They looked upon her as people look in those regions upon the image of a saint. So at least say the Russian papers and the district police officer sent to investigate her case, which is as follows :—

"November 3, 1880, accompanied by a farm-servant, she descended into the cellar under the house to get some potatoes. Hardly had they opened the heavy door, when they found themselves pelted with vegetables. Believing some neigbbour's boy must have hidden himself on the wide shelf on which the potatoes were heaped, Pelagueya, placing the basket upon her head, laughingly remarked, 'Whoever you are, fill it with potatoes and so help me !' In an instant the basket was filled to the brim. Then the other girl tried the same, but the potatoes remained motionless. Climbing upon the shelf, to their amazement the girls found no one there. Having notified the widow Beetch of the strange occurrence, the latter went herself, and unlocking the cellar, which had been securely locked by the two maids on leaving, found no one concealed in it. This event was but the precursor of a series of others. During a period of three weeks they succeeded each other with incredible rapidity. When the girl approaches the well, the water begins rising, and soon overflowing the sides of the cistern runs in torrents to her feet ; does she happen to pass near a bucket of water, the same thing happens. Hardly does she stretch out her hand to reach from the shelf some needed piece of crockery, than cups, tureens and plates, as if snatched from their place, begin to jump and tremble, and then fall with a crash at her feet. One day Pelagueya having gone to the shed to do her usual evening work of feeding the cattle, was preparing to leave with two other servants, when the cows and pigs seemed to become suddenly possessed. The former, frightening the whole village with the most infuriated bellowing, tried to climb the mangers, while the latter knocked their heads against the walls, running around as if pursued by some wild animal. Pitchforks, shovels, benches, and feeding trough pursued the terrified girls, who escaped by violently shutting and locking the door of the stables.

"All this phenomena took place not in darkness, but in daytime, and in full view of the inhabitants of the little hamlet ; moreover they were always preceded by extraordinary noises like cracking in the walls, and raps in the window-frames and glass. A panic seized the household and the inhabitants of the hamlet, which went on increasing at every new manifestation. A priest was called, but with no good results ; a couple of pots danced a jig on the shelf, an oven-fork went stamping on the floor, and a heavy sewing machine followed suit. The news ran round the whole district. Men and women from neighbouring villages flocked to see the marvels. The same phenomena took place in their presence. Once when a crowd of men upon entering, placed their caps upon the table, every one of these jumped from it to the floor, and a heavy leather glove, circling round, struck its owner on his face. Finally, notwithstanding the affection the widow Beetch felt for the poor orphan, towards the beginning of December, Pelagueya and her boxes were placed upon a cart, and after many a tear and warm expression of regret, she was sent off to the Superintendent of the Foundling Hospital—the institution in which she was brought up. This gentleman returning with the girl on the following day, was made a witness to the pranks of the same force, and calling in the police, after a careful inquest had a *procés verbal* signed by the authorities, and departed."

Accounts of the officially noted facts above detailed, have appeared in most of the Russian daily organs. Professor Boutlerof also furnishes a long and graphic narrative of Pelagueya and her weird Mediumship for the columns of the *Psychische Studien*. He gives an account of the official investigation, and adds that one half the wonderful things done in the presence of the poor Medium are not stated in the declaration—all parties however he says attribute these occurrences to the agency of evil Spirits, with whom every district in Russia is said to be haunted.

Amongst the many notable personages who aided to maintain the *prestige* of Spiritualism in Russia, not only by his admirable life, but also by his openly avowed interest in the movement, and the unbounded influence which he exercised over the mind of his friend and master the late Czar, was Prince Emil de Sayn Wittgenstein. This noble gentleman not only held high rank in the Russian army and served as aide-de-camp to the Emperor during the unhappy war with Turkey, but few of those who approached His Imperial Majesty's person, enjoyed the royal confidence in the same degree. In a correspondence maintained during some years with the author of this volume, Prince Emil asked for and obtained a number of volumes of the best American literature for the Emperor's library. Previous to the fatal war with Turkey the Emperor and Prince Wittgenstein both received assurances through Mrs. Britten's Mediumship that their lives would be spared during the conflict, but be sacrificed—the one to the insurrectionary spirit at home, the other to the feverish effects of the deadly campaign, into which he was about to plunge. Both these gentlemen placed implicit faith in these prophecies, and Prince Wittgenstein, in acknowledging them to the author, declares—in a letter still cherished in remembrance of her esteemed correspondent—"that the Emperor anticipated his fate and was resigned;" whilst he—Prince W.—should do the best he could to set his house in order, and make provision for his beloved wife and children.

These passages are not introduced to discuss the *rationale* of prophecy, which every experienced Spiritualist must know to be a demonstrated truth, and one, which seems to be singularly rife in Mediumship, but they are named to show that a deep and abiding faith in Spiritualism, was cherished by men, whose talents, education, and political influence, placed them before the world as exemplars of their time. We may conclude a notice which would be far more extended did it not involve personal statements on the part of the author, which she is determined as far as possible to avoid, by giving a brief notice of the departure of good Prince Wittgenstein within a few months after the close of the Turco-Russian war. The lines in question were written to the "Spiritualist" journal of London, by Miss Kislingbury, and speak for themselves. This lady says :—

" To the Editor of ' The Spiritualist.'

" SIR,—I have had sorrowful news this morning. The Baroness von Vay writes to me: 'Our dear, good friend, that excellent and warm Spiritualist, the Prince Emil de Sayn-Wittgenstein, has changed his earthly body for a heavenly one.'

"Having had the pleasure of close personal acqaintance with the Prince during the ten days that I was his guest at St. Valéry two years ago, I wish to add my tribute of regard in respect to his fine social and domestic qualities, in addition to those military honours which, won in fair fight, are a public and standing witness to his valour.

" In affability and courtesy I may say that I never met his equal, and these were evident not only in his treatment of strangers, but shone the most brightly in every detail of his home-life, in his affection for his wife and little children, by whom I need not say he was adored, and who have indeed suffered an irreparable loss. The Prince's official relations with the Russian Court were supplemented by familiar friendship and intercourse with the Imperial Royal family, and often, as we sat sipping our coffee on the balcony in an evening, he would amuse us with little anecdotes about the childhood of the present Duchess of Edinburgh, or harrow us with incidents of skirmishes between Turks and Cossacks, in which he had borne part, long before there was a thought of the late war. . . .

" No doubt there are other English Spiritualists who have experienced, as well as myself, the Prince's urbanity and kindness. I only wish to add my testimony, from personal knowledge, to that of many who will sincerely applaud and deeply lament a man whose benevolence was only equalled by his prowess. " EMILY KISLINGBURY."

Whilst it cannot be denied that the cause of Spiritualism has lost both in Prince Wittgenstein and his illustrious master, warm friends and patrons, it must not be supposed that the interest awakened by these royal converts was confined to themselves or their immediate circle of adherents. Spiritualism has a strong and deep foothold in Russia. It may take the form of the grossest superstition amongst the ignorant classes, but its *facts* are too deeply rooted in their experiences to be ignored, even if they mistake the source of the demonstrations and pervert the modes in which it should be dealt with.   The influence of such men as Aksakof, Boutlerof, and Wagner, *makes public opinion*, and it only requires time to bring the seeds of knowledge they have sown, to ample fruition.   Spiritualism too, still maintains its place "at Court," as the following brief but significant extracts will show. The first is from the *Medium* of May of this year, 1883, and reads thus:—

"The Czar of Russia has become a partial convert to the faith of modern Spiritualism.   It came about in this way.   When the Czar was in some perplexity respecting the measures to be taken for the safe conduct of the coronation ceremonies, it was suggested to him that he should 'ask counsel of the spirits' at the hands of a lady medium who has been practising for some years in London.   The lady (who is an American) was accordingly sent for to St. Petersburg, and gave a 'sitting' to the Czar.   The result of the *séance* was so satisfactory that the preparations for the coronation were hurried forward with greater energy than before, haste being recommended with much emphasis.   Everything having passed off extremely well in Moscow, the Czar has come to think that 'there may be something in Spiritualism after all;" and the lady, on her part, is said to be extremely well satisfied with the results of her visit to the Russian autocrat.—We may add that the medium in question is evidently Mrs. Kate Fox-Jencken, who advertises as having recently returned from St. Petersburg.   The spirits seem to take a great interest in the Czar.   At a circle in Chelsea, messages have been frequently received relative to precautions necessary to be taken during recent events, which have happily passed off without any calamity occurring.   The spirits state that the Czar stands between two spiritual forces: if he incline to the lower, and prove oppressive, he is in danger ; if he incline to liberal reforms his reign will be established, and the higher influences will shield him from danger."

The second notice, which is from the honoured pen of Mr. S. C. Hall, speaks with less confidence of the real mission of "the American Medium" to Russia, but gives a satisfactory inside view of Spiritual progress in St. Petersburgh.   It is as follows:—

"THE VISIT OF MRS. FOX JENCKEN TO RUSSIA.

"BY S. C. HALL.

"MAY, 1883.

"Mrs. Fox Jencken has returned in good health from her visit to Russia, where she had been invited by M. Aksakof, by whom all her arrangements for 'sittings' were made. Her residence in St. Petersburg lasted for seven weeks, on every day of which she met some persons (most of them of high social, professional, or political rank) to whom she manifested the marvels of Spiritualism.   Her mission was entirely successful, although it does not appear that any peculiar 'novelties' attended, or arose out of it.   The result was, however, to *convince* the hundreds who attended her sittings ; and, undoubtedly, belief in Spiritualism and thoroughly confirmed faith in the verity of the phenomena, have resulted from the lady's visit to the Imperial city.

"Mrs. Jencken expresses warm gratitude to M. Aksakof.   Rooms were provided for her at the principal hotel ; a carriage was placed at her disposal ; her two orphan boys, who accompanied her, were placed at a temporary school ; her daily callers were very numerous ; in a word, the result was far more than merely satisfactory to her, while gratifying, convincing, and happy to her sitters, on every occasion for which appointments and arrangements had been made.

"The manifestations were sometimes by night and as often by day—in full light : forms were occasionally visible, messages were written in Russian, both by the hand of Mrs. Jencken and in 'direct writing.'   Several names were communicated of persons 'gone before.'   The raps on the table, floor and walls were even more than usually loud and strong : lights were seen in various parts of the room : a small bell was rung repeatedly in various parts of it : palpable 'touchings' were numerous, with clear evidence as to the identity of the 'touchers:' in short, all the usual phenomena familiar to advanced Spiritualists, were communicated to the sitters—such evidence being fully and entirely accepted by several of the most learned professors of the Russian capital. And, although there does not seem to have been any marked or peculiar manifestations,

PRINCE EMIL DE SAYN. WITTGENSTEIN.

the result was eminently and entirely satisfactory, confirming the very general belief in Spiritualism that prevails in the great city of Northern Europe : the acceptance of Spiritualism as a solemn, impressive, and happy truth. . . . ."

To the Lord of the Harvest whose work Spiritualism is, in Russia, as in every other country, we may confidently commit the results of all that has been said, and done, and striven for, by ministering angels both on earth, and in heaven ; in God's time, if not in man's, the seeds sown by the hands of His faithful labourers will bring forth all the fruit which His divine wisdom deems necessary for the sustenance of His children in the land of the North, as in all other climes and nationalities.

CHAPTER XLV.

SCANDINAVIAN FRAGMENTS OF MODERN SPIRITUALISM.

WERE this work devoted to the record of ancient Spiritual beliefs and manifestations, it would be found that no portion of the earth affords richer fields of observation than the northern lands included under the generic term of Scandinavia.

In Sweden and Norway the Scandinavian cult is so deeply interpenetrated with a sort of Spiritualism corresponding in many respects to that which took form in America about 1848, and there are such frequent reports from those countries of direct interposition on the part of human spirits with human affairs, that the study of this subject, from the "supernatural" and traditional point of view would open up a valuable and instructive theme of research.

During the present century there seems to be but little or no concerted mode of action for the promulgation of Spiritual doctrines, or the study of Spiritual phenomena in Scandinavia. Such manifestations as have occurred, appear to be of the same spontaneous character as those described in Mrs. Catherine Crowe's " Night Side of Nature."

Apparitions, hauntings, healing by occult methods, and second sight, are of common occurrence in Scandinavia, but the organized modes of action practised by the Spiritualists of America and some countries of Europe, are unknown in Sweden and Norway, except in rare instances.

The study of magic antedates the earliest records of Scandinavian history.

Permeating all the popular traditions, whether of history, religion, or social life, Scandinavian supernaturalism is inextricably interwoven with the nature of the people.

As late as the beginning of the eighteenth century, magic was studied as an art, and in still earlier times it was taught as an accepted branch of learning.

Within the last half century, more enlightened and philosophical views of occult power and phenomena have been accepted. It is now generally believed that the spirits of mortals play a more important part in occult manifestations than the " nature spirits," gods, and demons, to whom—in past ages—all inexplicable phenomena were attributed.

It is realized also, that "the true magician is".—as Cornelius Agrippa asserts—"born so ;" in other words, that the seer, prophet, and modern " Medium," is one originally endowed by nature or inheritance, and that magic—as an art—only supplements what nature bestows upon certain exceptional individuals in the form of Spiritual gifts. In writing of the magical practices still common amongst the inhabitants of remote districts in Sweden and Norway, Herr Hansen says :—

"The most essential implement in the performance of magical rites is the famous *quobdas,* or kettledrum. This is cut from the stem of a tree of the required size. The inside is then carefully hollowed out, and covered with the dried skin of some animal, from which the fur has been removed. This skin is painted with images of gods, demons, angels, heavenly scenes, and even fantastic symbols of the Deity. When the sorcerer is called upon to exercise his art, he attaches a mass of bangles or metallic rings to his drum : then kneels on the ground, offers invocations to his chosen saints, and commences to beat his drum—at first gently and with slowly marked rhythm. As he proceeds his strokes fall thicker and heavier, until he seems impelled to strike in the direction of some one of the scenes, images, or figures painted on the drum ; finally he leaps up, shouts, sings, tosses his drum in the air, and strikes it against his head. A chosen circle of his friends gather round him, catch his infection ; dance, leap, sing, and shriek with him, until one or more, and sometimes the whole party, fall to the earth in trance or ecstasy. When the enchanter himself sinks down, the bystanders continue to mutter round him a sort of rhythmical incantation until he regains consciousness, when the visions that have flitted before his entranced eyes, or the scenes which his liberated spirit has beheld, are deemed to be oracular."

Sturleson, Zeigler, Magnus, and other authentic writers on Scandinavian lore, confirm Hansen's statement, and allege that the most marvellous facts of second sight, prophecy, and clairvoyance are revealed in these modes by Lapp and Finnish sorcerers. The methods of incantation are not always as elaborate as those described above, and may be conducted by the enquirer and sorcerer alone, but the professional respondent always consults his drum, and always claims to be directed to some of the images painted upon it, which are used in modes not unlike the spots in which fortune-tellers by cards claim to find direction. Herr Magnus, a Swedish gentleman of considerable learning, connected with Scandinavian journalism, has assured the author, that natural clairvoyance, the faculty of second sight, and the power of prophesying by unpremeditated speech, is far more universal in Norway, Sweden, and Iceland, than in any other countries he has visited in long years of travel. His own young daughter, sent him from Stockholm to California, a perfect description of "the ranche" at which he was staying as a visitor. She added, that two of the cows were sick or would be so, when her letter arrived, and if the proprietor (also a Swede) would bind on their foreheads two scraps of paper she enclosed, covered with little drawings, using them as spells, the animals would recover in three days. The little girl's letter was dated twenty days before its delivery in California. Herr Magnus showed that letter to the author one week later, during which time, the sick animals had been treated as the child had directed, and their recovery took place without the aid of any other medication, just as she had predicted.

It would be difficult to give any other name than "Magnetism" to the healing power thus curiously displayed, whilst the prevision of the sickness and recovery of the animals, might certainly come under the category of "clairvoyance."

SPIRITUALISM IN SWEDEN.

It must not be forgotten that Upsala in Sweden, was the birthplace of the most highly-endowed seer of modern ages, namely, Emanuel Swedenborg. Whilst the limited character of our record forbids any detailed account of Swedenborg's remarkable experiences and doctrines, we should fail to do justice to the Spiritualism of Sweden were we to omit the fact that it gave birth to one whose name occupies so distinguished a place in the shining roll of immortality.

We must also call attention to a curious phase of Spiritualism occurring in Sweden during the dark and iniquitous trials for "Witchcraft" in the middle ages.

Any of our readers who may be fortunate enough to possess a copy of the celebrated work on Witchcraft written by the Rev. Joseph Glanvil, chaplain-in-ordinary to Charles II. of England, will find in his collection of narratives the following striking title-page, printed in clear old English characters:—"*An Account of what Happened in the Kingdom of Sweden in the years* 1669 *and* 1670 *in Relation to the Persons Accused of Witchcraft Tried and Executed by the King's Command. Printed at first in the Swedish dialect by authority; then translated into divers other languages, and now, upon the request of some friends, done into English. By Anthony Horneck, Preacher at the Savoy. LONDON, printed* 1681."

The details of the scenes that follow, bear a striking similarity to those of the New England and Scotch trials for witchcraft, and tend to show, that the unhappy victims who, under the compulsion of torture, threats, or delirium, confessed to wild and impossible practices in the name of witchcraft, were still participators in some acts which proved them to be unconsciously to themselves magnetizers and psychologists.

The horrible rumours of what witchcraft could effect, were in the air, and ignorant though susceptible individuals who felt themselves possessed of the power to impress others for good or evil, often exerted it without any distinct realization of what they did. On the other hand, the parties affected, were involuntarily made aware of the impressions they received and in some instances "the spectre," or living Spirit of the magnetizer became so palpable to sensitive subjects that the phenomena thus mutually produced, ended in accusations and confessions of the most perplexing character.

A careful study of the marvels of psychology and magnetism, especially when these potential forces are exercised under the direction of concentrated WILL, may be found to underlie many of the mysteries ignorantly denominated "Witchcraft," and will afford a clue to explain the stupendous difficulties which beset the conduct of those who were called to sit in judgment upon accused parties. It is obvious also that some of the victims executed for the imaginary crime of witchcraft, were genuine somnambulists, or trance Mediums, whilst others again, especially the unfortunate children implicated in the general horror, shared in the contagion of a deep universal superstition, actually confessing to participation in rites of which they had heard or dreamed, until their susceptible minds succumbed to the delirium of the times, and they came to believe as real, the horrible fictions which popular opinion attributed to them.

It may be asked what could the unhappy accused parties confess to have done or said that should make them worthy of death? In a word, in what was the crime of witchcraft supposed to consist?

It is certainly far easier to propound, than to answer this question.

The trials for witchcraft in Scotland, New England, as in Sweden, abound with such monstrous tales of compacts and intercourse with demons, and the details of the horrible rites, said to have been enacted, are recorded in verbiage, at once so revolting and absurd, that it would be impossible to transfer them to pages designed for the edification of modern readers. As some examples of the style and tone in which the witchcraft accusations were framed, may be instructive to the student of occultism in the nineteenth century, we offer the following selections from Horneck's translation. He says :—

"The news of this Witchcraft coming to the King's ear, his Majesty was pleased to appoint Commissioners, some of the Clergy and some of the Laity, to make a journey to the village of Mohra to examine into the whole business. The examination was ordered to be on the 13th of August, 1669, and the Commissioners met at the Parson's house, to whom both the minister and several people of fashion came and complained with tears in their eyes of the miserable condition they were in, begging them (the said Commissioners) to think of some way whereby they might be delivered from their Calamity.

"They gave the Commissioners very strange instances of the Devil's tyranny among them ; how by the help of Witches he had drawn some hundreds of *children* to him and made them subject to his power ; how he hath been seen to go in a visible shape through the country, and appeared daily to the people ; how he had wrought upon the poorer sort by presents of meat and drink. . . . . The inhabitants of the village added, with great lamentations, that though their children had told all, and sought God earnestly by prayer, they were carried away by him, and therefore begged the Lords Commissioners to root out these Witches, that they may regain their former rest and quietness, the rather, because, the children which used to be carried away in Elfsborg, *since the witches had been burnt, remained unmolested.*"

Then follows a long account of trials, in which obscene details, horrible rites, and utterly impossible crimes were attributed sometimes to adults said to be witches, and sometimes to children, *too young in many instances even to speak plainly.* It is alleged that nearly all the accused persons confessed to that with which they were charged, or rather, that which the ignorant and superstitious imagination of their judges suggested to them as the crimes that they were *supposed* to have committed.

The only sanity manifested in this reign of lunatic superstition, is in the official summing up of the trials, which reads thus :—

"The confession which the Witches made in Elfsborg to the judges there, agreed with the confession made at Mohra, and the chief things they confessed to, consisted in these three points :—

"1st. Whither they used to go.

"2nd. What kind of place it was they went to, called by them *Blockula*, where the Witches and the Devil used to meet.

"3rd. What evil or mischief they had either done, or designed there."

Then followed confessions equally disgusting and absurd, as to how they (the Witches) would go by night to appointed places, wherein by incantations they would summon the Devil, who carried them on brooms, in sieves, on goats' backs, spits, &c., &c., to *Blockula ;* how they generally *saw their bodies left behind*, or something left in their homes resembling them ; also, how in compliance with the Devil's demand, they were obliged to furnish so many children to accompany them.

Amongst the horrors of these details, appears now and then a sentence which speaks of a redeeming touch of sanity such as, "What the real manner of their journey was, God alone knows !" The only marvel is, how men—professing to be Christians, could use the name of God at all in such a record.

Of the nature of the most readable of the confessions, the following paragraph is an illustration :—

"One little girl, of Elfsborg, confessed that, naming Jesus as she was carried away, she instantly fell to the ground, and got a great hole in her side, which the Devil presently healed up again, and away he carried her ; and to this day the girl confessed she had exceeding great pain in her side.

"OF BLOCKULA.

"They unanimously confest that *Blockula* is a large delicate meadow whereof you can see no end.

"The house they met at had before it a gate painted with divers colours. Through this gate they went into a little meadow, where the Beasts went that they used to ride on. But the men whom they rode upon in their journey stood in the house by the gate in a slumbering posture, sleeping against the wall. . . . In a huge room of this house they said stood a long table at which the witches sat down; and that hard by was a chamber where there were lovely and delicate beds.

"The first thing they must do at Blockula was that they must deny all else; devote themselves body and soul to the Devil and promise to serve him faithfully, and confirm all this with an oath. Hereupon they cut their fingers, and with their blood writ their names in his book. They added, that he caused them to be baptized by such priests as he had there, and made them confirm them confirm their baptism with dreadful oaths and imprecations. . . . . ."

Then follow descriptions of their monstrous rites; the evils that the Devil commanded them to do, or that they, the witches, asked permission to do against those they disliked; accounts of their horrid feasts, dances, &c., &c., for all of which consult Goethe's "Walpurgis Night," "The Witches' Sabbath at Blocksberg," *or the annals of Bedlam !*

What sane minds in this age cannot discover, that some malignant atmospheric epidemic had fallen upon the inhabitants of the districts said to be possessed?—that in a certain state of physical weakness and disability, a contagious condition of delirium set in, seizing upon all those who were most negative or most susceptible, such as children, weak, old, or infirm men and women, and that in this state, the wild and ghastly legends of witchcraft which for centuries had prevailed as an article of superstitious belief amongst the peasantry of Europe, became the distinguishing mental feature of their enfeebled minds—that is to say, that some epidemic disorder was in the air, and the result was an universal monomania, of which the belief in Satanic possession and traditional witchcraft were the distinguishing marks?

The introduction of little children into these horrible scenes, especially some of an age so tender, "that they could not even speak plainly enough to answer the simplest questions put to them," of course complicates the horror of the popular madness, and rendered it in the period of its enactment, still more difficult to deal with.

Herr Christian Rumpt, Resident for the States-General in Stockholm, in a narrative of some of the ghastly scenes of the time alleges, that he was obliged to send away his little son to Holland, lest he too should catch the general infection, and become possessed by the prevailing Satanic agency. Herr Rumpt says, the accused children were carried away by the witches to *Blockula*, sometimes by force, and occasionally by promises of fine presents and the prospect of marvellous sights.

Many of the children, he adds, confessed to participation in the horrible rites they were questioned about, and most of them volunteered to tell how "*when they were carried away they saw their own bodies lying in their beds seemingly sound asleep.*"

Report adds, that in several of the districts in the province of Elfsborg the possessed children would at times form themselves into groups and march through the streets and lanes, walking solemnly, praying and preaching with wonderful fervour, and in a style far beyond the years of the oldest of them. Sometimes they would speak in the purest Latin, Greek, and Hebrew, much to the confusion and terror of the grave divines who heard and understood them. The same reports alleged, that "the Devil, their master, would even let them (the children) heal sick folk, and prophesy of coming events correctly, the more surely to win over the souls of the people to the service of Satan, and persuade them the children were not possessed by demons." Anthony Horneck's translation of the Swedish narrative winds up with the statement that, "by order of His Majesty, the convicted ones were sentenced as follows :—Twenty-three adults, *and fifteen children were condemned and executed;* six-and-thirty children between nine and sixteen, less guilty than the rest, were condemned to run the gauntlet ; twenty more were lashed with rods at the church door for three Sundays, and another band of thirty were lashed each Sunday for a whole year." Amidst the unspeakable horrors of these scenes, wherein brutality and ignorance seemed to be struggling for the mastery, it is refreshing to read one beautiful and suggestive paragraph. Horneck says :—"Some of the children talked much of a white angel, which used to forbid them doing what the Devil had bid them do, and told them, that those doings should not last long : what had been done had been permitted because of the wickedness of the people, and the carrying away of the children should be made manifest; and they added that this white angel would place himself sometimes at the door betwixt the Witches and the children, and when they came to *Blockula* he pulled the children back, but the Witches they went in."

Ever *a white angel* to arrest the steps of the helpless or faltering from treading the path of evil, if we will but listen to his warnings !

As a corollary to this shameful narrative, the writer adds :—" The number of the seduced children were about three hundred. . . . On the 25th of August, 1670, execution was done upon the notoriously guilty, the day being bright and glorious, and the sun shining. Some thousands of people were present at the spectacle !"

The heart revolts, the senses sicken, and the mind staggers before the awful tale, and all that it involves ! We gladly close the page, and with convulsive shudders for what *has* been, thank the Supreme Ruler of all times and countries, that we do not live in an age so sunk in ignorance and steeped in barbarity as that in which such scenes could have been enacted.

In closing the detail of this remarkable episode, we acknowledge that some explanation is due to the reader for introducing records of a period which antedates the century, to the annals of which this volume is devoted, by at least two hundred years.

For an anachronism of so marked a character, we have only to plead that our tale of mystery is as yet but half told. Passing over two hundred years after the trials above noted, we find another scene enacted on Swedish ground, which only presents varying features in view of the different stand-points of civilization from which the two narratives are considered. It is chiefly to show how the same influences may recur at different epochs of time and how surely we imprint the characteristics of our own ignorance or enlightenment upon all that befalls us, that we have dwelt so much at length on an illustration of how Spiritual influences were *misunderstood* in the seventeenth century, and forces that must now inevitably take their place in the category of natural law, may be transformed by the glamour of ignorance and superstition into unmixed evil and diabolism. The case which is designed to prove this position and act as a notable corollary to Spiritual influences in Sweden will be found detailed in the succeding chapter.

CHAPTER XLVI.

SCANDINAVIAN FRAGMENTS OF MODERN SPIRITUALISM (CONTINUED).

THE PREACHING EPIDEMIC IN SWEDEN.

FOR a graphic summary of the singular movement which has received the above caption—a movement which took place nearly on the same ground as that traversed in the last chapter, though it occurred about two hundred years later in time—we shall avail ourselves of the description given by Ennemoser, in his "History of Magic," translated by Mrs. Mary Howitt. The narrative commences as follows, and is headed

"THE PREACHING EPIDEMIC OF SWEDEN.

" That portion of Southern Sweden, formerly called Smaland, now comprising the provinces of Kalmar, Wexis, and Jonköping, though one of the poorest parts of the kingdom, is inhabited by a laborious, contented, and deeply religious people. . . . . In 1843, Dr. J. A. Butsch, Bishop of Skara, wrote a long letter to the Archbishop of Upsala concerning the scenes of which he was an eye-witness, then transpiring in his own diocese, and popularly termed by the amazed communities amongst whom they occurred 'the preaching epidemic.' The manifestations described in Dr. Butsch's letter were not confined to the districts he visited and wrote of, but extended throughout a large part of Sweden, especially in the provinces named above. The reader will naturally ask, as the Bishop does himself, what is the preaching epidemic ? . . . The Bishop was of opinion that it was *a disease* originally physical, but affecting the mind in a peculiar way ; he arrived at this conclusion by attentively studying the phenomenon itself. At all events, bodily sickness was an ingredient in it, as was proved from the fact that although every one affected by it, in describing the commencement of their state, mentioned 'a spiritual excitement' as its original cause, close examination proved that an internal bodily disorder attended by pain had preceded or accompanied this excitement.

" Besides, there were persons who, against their own will, were affected by the quaking fits, which were one of its most striking early outward symptoms, without any previous religious excitement, and these, when subjected to medical treatment soon recovered.

" The Bishop in his letter above-named, expresses his opinion that the disease corresponds very much with what he has heard and read respecting the effects of animal magnetism. . . . Speaking of the effect of sulphur and the magnet on the sick persons, he says : 'In these cases there was an increased activity of the nervous and muscular systems ; and further, heaviness in the head, heat at the pit of the stomach, prickling sensation in the extremities, convulsions, quakings, and finally the falling with a deep groan into a profound fainting fit or trance.'

" In this trance, the patient was so insensible to outward impressions, that the loudest noise would not awaken him, nor would he feel a needle thrust deeply into his body. Mostly however, during this trance, he would hear questions addressed to him, and reply to them ; and, which was extraordinary, invariably in these replies, applied to every one the pronoun *thou.* The power of speech too in this state was that of great eloquence, lively declamation, and the command of purer language than was usual or apparently possible for him in his normal state. The invariable assertions of all patients when in this state were, that they were exceedingly well ; and that they had never been so happy before ; they declared that the words they spoke were given to them by some one else who spoke by them. Their disposition of mind was pious and calm ; they seemed disposed for visions and predictions. Like the early Quakers, they had an aversion to certain words and phrases, and testified in their preaching against places of amusement, gaming, drinking, maypole festivities, gay dress, and vanity and display. There was in some families a greater tendency to this influence than in others : it was greater in children and females than in adults and men, and amongst men, prevailed with the sanguine temperament.

"The patients invariably showed a strong desire to be together, and seemed to feel a sort of spiritual attraction to each other. In places of worship, they would all sit together and when questioned they answered *we* instead of *I*. . . . With respect to the conduct and conversation of the patients during the time of their seizure, the Bishop says, he never saw anything improper. . . . In Elfsborg, where the disease prevailed to a great extent, bands of children under the influence went about singing what are called Zion's hymns, the effect of which was singularly striking, even affecting. The Bishop says, that to give a complete and detailed description of the nature of the disease would be impossible, because, like animal magnetism, it seems to be infinite in its modification and form. . . . The *quaking* of which so much has been said, appears to have been the first outward sign, the inward vision and preaching being its consummation; though when this was reached, the fit mostly commenced by the same sign. In some patients, the quakings seem to have come on at the mention of certain words, the introduction of certain ideas, or the proximity of certain persons or things, which in some mysterious manner appeared to be inimical to the patient. . . . One of the patients explained some of these anomalous conditions thus—that according as his spiritual being advanced upwards, he found that there existed in him, and in the world, many things which were worse than that which he had previously considered the worst—and *vice versa* of better things. In some cases the patients were violently affected by the simple words *yes* and *no*—the latter word in particular was most painful and repulsive to them, and has been frequently described by them *as one of the worst demons tied in the chains of darkness in the deepest abyss.*

"It was remarked also that they frequently acted as if they had a strong temptation to speak falsehood, or to say more than they were at liberty to say. They would frequently exhort each other to speak the truth, and so frequently answered dubiously and even said—they did not know, leaving the impression on the minds of the listeners, either that untruthfulness or hesitation was a peculiarity of the disease. . . ."

If our readers have followed Ennemoser's transcript of the Bishop's letter thus far intelligently, they will perceive that the "patients" described above, were unmistakeably magnetic subjects; that they were clearly in magnetic states, though the magnetizers were invisible beings. Furthermore, that the influence was mixed, being both good and bad, truthful and untruthful, the one often prevailing over the other. Also, that all the descriptions given above correspond first to the magnetic states described by Kerner, Cahagnet, Deleuze, Ashburner, Elliotson, &c., &c.; next, that they tally in wonderful parallel lines with the trance Mediums, and especially the inspirational states of the platform speakers of the modern Spiritual movement. Those silly uninformed materialists who are so fond of taunting the Spiritual speakers with the question, *What proof can you give of your abnormal or Spiritually controlled condition?*—if they have not the opportunity of studying the works written by experienced magnetizers, might profitably read the records of the Irish revivals, or the Swedish preaching epidemic, of which we are writing. They might believe in the possibility of an abnormal Spiritual intelligence prevailing with the poor and unlearned inhabitants of Elfsborg, when their case is graphically described in the correspondence between a bishop and archbishop, even if they scornfully ignore the testimony of parallel cases presented before their own eyes. Both examples occur in the nineteenth century, and no doubt explain every other similar visitation recorded as happening at earlier epochs of human history.

There are one or two other points in the testimony presented by the Bishop of Skara to which we cannot omit drawing attention.

The Bishop insists upon calling the subjects of the power "patients," affirms that "bodily sickness" *is an ingredient in it*, and enumerates a few symptoms, not one of which indicates any particular form of *bodily sickness*, though all are more or less suggestive—as he himself allows—of the trance condition induced by magnetism. Without reiterating the summary of results which ensue from the Bishop's so-called condition of "sickness," it must certainly strike any candid observer that such forms of *sickness* are worth cultivating, when they will produce in the patients, sentiments of unwonted happiness ; make them feel *better in health* than they ever felt before, enable them to hear and answer questions, and discourse with an amount of power and eloquence utterly foreign to their normal state. Those "patients" too, were always represented as being in a pious frame of mind ; of denouncing drinking, gaming, and other popular vices. They all exhibited the appearance of speaking the words of others, and not their own, and manifested such remarkable grace, dignity, and exaltation that *the disease* might as well be cultivated as an art of deportment, as for its singular faculty of making orators, preachers, moralists, and saints, out of boorish peasants, and uneducated rustics !

In fine, it seems almost providential that this "disease" only appears at rare intervals, and that generally in places removed from the large centres of civilization. Were it otherwise, our clergymen, statesmen, and orators would have to resort to the hospitals to study eloquence from the victims of the epidemic ; our fine ladies would have to watch "fits," to learn the finest graces of deportment, and moral philosophers would sit around "patients" to discover the true secrets of reform, and derive hints of practical virtue, eliminated from diseased organisms !

In the hope that other bishops besides Dr. J. A. Butsch may study and apply the lessons enforced by this remarkable and strictly novel phase of "disease," we commend the above-named learned gentleman's remarks to the attention of the reader for what they are worth.

We now resume Ennemoser's narrative in which the following descriptions are drawn, as before, chiefly from the Bishop of Skara's letter :—

"The Bishop said he had seen several persons fall at once into the trance without any premonitory symptom.

"Sometimes the parties preached with their eyes open and standing, and sometimes closed, and in a recumbent posture. He gives an account of three preaching girls in the parish of Warnham, of ages varying from eight to twelve. It was shortly before Christmas, 1842, when he went, in company with the Rev. Mr. Zingrist, the Rev. Mr. Smedmark, and a respectable farmer, his friend, to visit the cottage where these children lived. Many strangers besides the Bishop's party were present. The children, though peasants, were well informed, and could read ; they were good and well disposed, and since their seizure were remarkably gentle and quiet. In their normal state they were bashful and timid. When in the trance they declared they were quite well, and had never been so happy before. When *awakened*, they complained of headache, pains in the limbs, and weakness, &c. In the case of one of the children, her symptoms commenced with a violent trembling, and she fell backwards so heavily as to alarm the spectators, though no injury seemed to ensue. The trance lasted several hours, and divided itself into two stages. In the first she rose up violently, and caught at the hands of the people round her. Some she instantly flung aside, as if repugnant to her ; others she held, gently patted, and rubbed softly ; these are called 'good hands." Sometimes she made signs as if she were pouring out something which she appeared to drink, and her father and others present said she could detect any one in the company who was a dram drinker, and even indicate the number of glasses he had taken. She went through the mimic operation of loading, presenting, and firing a gun ; performed most dramatically a pugilistic combat, and went through the action of a person dressing. . . . . "

The Bishop and his commentator, Ennemoser, express the utmost bewilderment concerning the meaning of these signs. Those who have ever seen "the pantomimic Mediums" of the modern dispensation, and remember how graphically they would represent, under the influence of Spirits, the characteristics, or special scenes in the lives of deceased persons, will be at no loss to understand what this little one's "control" desired to depict. The good but uninformed narrator says :—

"What rendered all this so extraordinary was, that although she was but a simple, bashful peasant child, clothed in a sheepskin jacket, yet all her actions were free, full of dramatic effects ; vigorous when representing manly action, and so indescribably graceful and full of sentiment when personating female occupations, as to amaze the more cultivated spectators. She seemed to be far more like an image in a dream, than a creature of flesh and blood. The child next passed into the second stage of the trance, which was characterized by a beautiful calmness and quiet. With her arms meekly folded she began to preach. Her manner was that of the purest oratory ; her tones earnest and solemn, and the language of a high and exalted character, impossible for her to have used when awake. Her appearance was saint-like, and her voice, which in her natural state was hoarse and harsh, had a brilliancy and clearness of tone wonderful to listen to. Many of the assembly wept, and all observed the profoundest silence. . . ."

Ennemoser adds :—

"The number of persons affected in the Bishop's province of Skaraborg alone, where 'the disease' did not prevail as generally as in other places was, in 1843, upwards of 3,000 ! . . . The clergy and doctors used all their endeavours to extinguish the movement, and by the end of 1843 it had almost ceased. Nothing of the kind has since appeared, but the *good effects it produced on the mind of many a hardened sinner remains to testify to its truth and reality,* although no one, whether learned in the science of physical or spiritual life, can yet explain the cause and nature of this extraordinary mental phenomena."

So writes Ennemoser in 1855, giving in the same work several pages to descriptions of phenomena in the United States which in thousands of instances paralleled the preaching epidemic of Sweden and other cases with which his two volumes are full. The good Bishop of Skara called "the power," disease. Ennemoser asserts that "neither physical nor mental science can explain it." "The power" in America and Europe calls itself SPIRITUAL INFLUENCE, and though this assertion is positively demonstrated by uncounted test facts, identifying the said power with the Spirits of men and women who have once lived on earth, *the clergy and doctors* now, as in 1843, "use all their efforts to extinguish the movement," and the fact that they cannot succeed as well with calm, sane, and scientific investigators, as they did when dealing with the simple-minded unlettered peasantry of Skara, is an additional proof that "the power" is an intelligent one, and something too mighty to be extinguished by the particular crafts which it happens to interfere with.

In closing our notices of these curious Swedish phenomena, we have only to point out the numerous records of kindred occurrences in different countries at different periods of time, and suggest the probability, that there are mental upheavals which move with as much regularity, and appear and disappear in connection with unknown laws of magnetism, just as inevitably as those physical disturbances or atmospheric storms which, from time to time, alter the face of our planet. Were the entire scheme known, and the laws of mutual interdependence between mind and matter fully understood, we might prepare for these mental convulsions and Spiritual manifestations, with the same certainty that we expect the trade winds, or the equinoctial storms.

With a few isolated accounts of the phenomena which are recorded from time to time as occurring in certain families in Sweden and Norway, our notices of Scandinavian Spiritualism must be brought to a close.

One sanguine writer in the London *Medium and Daybreak*, gives the following encouraging notice of Swedish Spiritualism as a movement, in 1878. He says :—

"WASA, FINLAND.

" It is about a year and a half since I changed my abode from Stockholm to this place, and during that period it is wonderful how Spiritualism has gained ground in Sweden. The leading papers, that used in my time to refuse to publish any article on Spiritualism excepting such as ridiculed the doctrine, have of late thrown their columns wide open to the serious discussion of the matter. Many a Spiritualist in secret, has thus been encouraged to give publicity to his opinions without standing any longer in awe of that demon, public ridicule, which intimidates so many of our brethren. Several of Allan Kardec's works have been translated into Swedish, among which I may mention his 'Evangile selon le Spiritisme' as particularly well rendered in Swedish by Walter Jochnick. A Spiritual Library was opened in Stockholm on the 1st of April last, which will no doubt greatly contribute to the spreading of the blessed doctrine. The visit of Mr. Eglinton to Stockholm was of the greatest benefit to the cause. Let us hope that the stay of Mrs. Esperance in the south of Sweden may have an equally beneficial effect. Notwithstanding all this progress of the cause in the neighbouring country, Spiritualism is looked upon here as something akin to madness, but even here there are thin, very thin rays, and very wide apart, struggling to pierce the darkness."

The author is in possession of a large number of cases of alleged hauntings, some being attached to houses and others to places, but none of them offer features of sufficient diversity from the ordinary run of similar narratives to make their insertion worth the reader's attention. The same may be said on the subject of dreams, visions, and second sight.

All these phenomena prevail amongst the Swedes, and the tendency to fairy lore manifested in their literature undoubtedly arises from their sentiment of close proximity to "the border land." Frederika Bremer, the celebrated novelist, during a tour through the New England States, frequently alluded to her faculty of dreaming, and prevision. This lady, though neither a Spiritualist nor in sympathy with the Spiritual movement at the time of her visit to America, was undoubtedly a Medium of a high order. She related at a party given by some warm Spiritualists, in her honour at Boston, how often she saw "the images" of her friends at long distances off, engaged in scenes which she afterwards found to have actually transpired. She said that—as in the experience of Hans Christian Andersen—the plot and framework of many of her stories pressed in upon her brain, and haunted her, until she wrote them down, and she often felt as if she was rather transcribing something from memory, than composing, when she wrote her works of fiction. The following short notice of her decease, published in the London *Spiritual Magazine* of 1866, may possess some interest for the admirers of this lady's writings. The editor says :—

" The celebrated Swedish novelist, Fredrika Bremer, passed away, in consequence of a cold, which ended in inflammation of the lungs, at three o'clock on Sunday morning, the last day of the old year, at the seat of Arsta, in the parish of Osserhamminge, some eighteen miles south-east of Stockholm.

" Fredrika Bremer was born at Abo, in Finland, in August, 1801, and had consequently attained her sixty-fourth year. She, herself, expected to die before the end of 1865, owing to a dream which she dreamed thirty years since, and which had left an indelible impression on her mind. It was partly owing to this that she removed to Arsta, the old home of her youth and early womanhood, in the course of last summer, and there she quietly spent her remaining days, in cheerful, resigned preparation. She enjoyed her usual good health to within a week of her decease, and her friends in no wise shared her presentiment. She gave a Christmas tree to the children on the estate, on Christmas eve, and attended service at the Church of Osserhamminge, on Christmas Day, when she took the chill which ended fatally.

"Her writings, which are especially distinguished for their accurate pictures of family life, and for their genial, happy spirit, have made her name known far beyond the boundaries of her native land, and are translated into the principal European languages.

.   .   .   .

"In the closing portion of her life she became much interested in Spiritualism, and read 'From Matter to Spirit' with intense emotion. She says of it, 'It is *the book* I needed to enter fully into the interest and understanding of Spiritualism in its recent form as a science. It is certainly an admirable work, as to its mind and spirit. Its theory and exposure of the natural laws, working in this class of phenomena, deserve the highest attention and appreciation of every intelligent and truth-loving mind.' Still some 'buts' arose in her mind against Spiritualism as the basis for a science and religion. These were fully and ably answered last autumn, by various deep-thinking Spiritualists. Her acceptance of their views has not, however, become known, but of this we are certain, that her mind was thoroughly open to conviction ; a great step—since she had been prejudiced by some of the manifestations she witnessed in America, and which made her declare ' that the spiritual world had its "humbugs," even as our world has,' and it did not seem to her extraordinary that they endeavoured to make fools of us."

SPIRITUALISM IN NORWAY.

Amongst a large mass of literature sent to the author concerning the traditions, fairy lore, and mythology of Norway, Iceland, the Faroe Isles, &c., there is little or no evidence that the inhabitants of these northern lands turn their natural Spiritual endowments to account, or attempt to systematize their powers by holding circles, or taking part in the modern phenomenal movement. The author of " Art Magic," who visited Norway, Iceland, Finland, and other portions of the northern coast during several summers, considers that the superstitious beliefs of the inhabitants in sea gods, sea kings, and the monsters said to haunt the wild caverns and basaltic ranges that fringe the coast lines, render it difficult to separate the facts of direct Spiritual origin, from the legendary lore in which the people of these countries delight. This writer says : "The galleries of mental art are filled with the images of half-formed elementary existences which float like many coloured bubbles over the surface of the mirror in which Spirit friends attempt to reflect their well remembered faces. The people are truly Mediumistic, sensitive, high strung, and nervous, as the result of the climate in which they dwell ; poetical and imaginative, in accordance with their clear skies, studded over with blossoms of fire, and the wild, rugged scenery amidst which they pass untravelled lives. Still it is almost impossible to receive a plain narrative of Spiritual actualities from their lips, without finding it embellished with the mirage of an unformulated supernaturalism. Hanno Steere, the keeper of a lighthouse perched like an eye of fire on a mass of towering crags overlooking the wildest waves that ever swept a fated ship to doom, assured me the voice of his father, now a Spirit, who kept that tower of warning before him, never failed to call him thrice and with solemn earnestness cry 'The lifeboat ! the lifeboat !' before every storm that beat on that coast. And though the sea might be like glass and the winds sighing as softly as an infant's breathing, the voice of that Spirit never called for the lifeboat in vain. 'Sure to be in demand, it is unmoored when the soul of my father has passed by,' said the old man; 'and thus have I been warned to save unnumbered lives.'" A bright young shepherd living in a lonely mountain pass near Bergen, showed the author above quoted the cavern where he used to go to consult a Spirit who appeared to him in the form of a white bird, when he had lost any of his flock, or needed advice in an emergency.

He said he had always been directed right ; that the voice that spoke had warned him again and again of the approach of robbers; directed him how to find lost articles; when and how to buy, sell, and trade.

For miles round, the simple country people came to consult *the white Spirit* through this lad. None could hear the voice but himself, and though he acknowledged that it exactly resembled that of *his dead mother*, the boy was quite sure it proceeded from "the white bird," a large white owl that dwelt in that cavern.

Many of the peasantry can really prophesy correctly and speak oracularly by listening to the murmur of the winds in the pine forests, or the tinkling of small cascades falling over the broken rocks. Ask them the secret of their prevision, and they will tell you, they hear words spoken by *fays* or *kelpies*. Amidst the hoarse roar of the waves lashed into fury by northern storms, the Icelandic fisherman hears the shout of the ancient Viking, or the wail of the Nixie, murmuring a requiem for the ship that shall presently be engulphed in the remorseless ocean grave. The woods, the grasses, the flowers, are full of fairy people to the Norwegian peasant girl, and storm Spirits ride on every meteor that flashes through the blazing midnight skies, in the imagination of every fisher lad. Do they believe in apparitions, the return of the souls of those who loved and left them a while ago? "Oh yes! they all do that—more or less—but spirits of the dead hover round churchyards they think, light up the churches in the still hours of night, or linger around the scenes where deeds of darkness have been performed."

These Northmen and women would make rare clairvoyants and seers of wonderful lucidity, provided they were trained; reserved for occult experiments, and could carry their atmosphere, scenery, and surroundings with them. Remove them from these, and they are but dull, stolid, unimaginative peasants after all.

Within the last few years some attempts have been made to interest the well educated inhabitants of Norwegian towns in reports of the Spiritual movement. Several ladies and gentlemen who have become readers of the Spiritual papers, have formed private circles, and evolved many satisfactory phases of Mediumship. A few American professional Mediums have visited Bergen and Christiansund, and the phenomena exhibited through them has made many converts, although there are few bold enough to openly avow their convictions.

One brave gentleman, Professor H. Starjohann, frequently favours the Spiritual journals of Europe and America with words of encouragement concerning the progress of the faith in which he is himself so deeply interested.

We shall conclude this necessarily brief notice of Spiritualism in Norway with extracts from two communications addressed by this gentleman, the one to the *Banner of Light*, the other to the *Revue Spirite.* The first, dated Christiansund, 1880, reads thus :—

"Spiritualism is just commencing to give a sign of its existence here in Norway. The newspapers have begun to attack it as a delusion, and the ' *exposé* ' of Mrs. C——, which recently took place at 38, Great Russell Street, London, has made the round through all the papers in Scandinavia. After all, it must sooner or later take root, as in all other parts of the world. Mr. Eglinton, the English medium, has done a good work in Stockholm, showing some of the great *savants* a new world; and a couple of years ago Mr. Slade visited Copenhagen. The works of Mr. Zöllner, the great astronomer of Leipzig, have been mentioned in the papers and caused a good deal of sensation.

"Of mediums there are several here, but all, as yet, afraid to speak out. One writes with both hands; a gentleman is developing as a drawing medium. A peasant, who died about five years ago, and lived not far from here, was an excellent healing medium; his name was Knud, and the people had given him the nickname of Vise Knud (the wise Knud) ; directly when he touched a patient he knew if the same could be cured or not, and often, in severe cases, the pains of the sick person went through his own body. He was also an auditive medium, startling the people many times by telling them what was going to happen in the future ; but the poor fellow suffered much from the ignorance and fanaticism around him, and was several times put in prison.

"I am doing all I can to make people acquainted with our grand cause."

The second and more hopeful letter of 1881, addressed to the editor of the *Revue Spirite*, is as follows :—

"My dear Brothers,—Here our science advances without noise. An excellent writing medium has been developed among us, one who writes simultaneously with both hands ; while we have music in a room where there are no musical instruments ; and where there is a piano it plays of itself. At Bergen, where I have recently been, I found mediums who, in the dark, made sketches—were *dessinateurs*—using also both hands. I have seen, also, with pleasure, that several men of letters and of the sciences have begun to investigate our *science spirite*. The pastor Eckhoff, of Bergen, has for the second time preached against Spiritualism, 'this instrument of the devil, this psychographie'; and to give more of *éclat* to his sermon he has had the goodness to have it printed ; so we see that the spirits are working. The suit against the medium, Mme. F——, in London, is going the rounds of the papers of Christiania ; these journals opening their columns, when occasion offers, to ridicule Spiritualism. We are, however, friends of the truth, but there are scabby sheep among us of a different temperament. From Stockholm they write me that a library of spiritual works has been opened there, and that they are to have a medium from Newcastle, with whom *séances* are to be held."

The reader must not suppose that the few fragmentary notices we have been able to give of Scandinavian Spiritualism, especially that which has occurred in the nineteenth century, includes even a tithe of what can be gleaned on the subject. In the *London Spiritual Magazine* of May, 1865, is a long and interesting paper on Swedish Spiritualism, by William Howitt, in which he gives quite a notable collection of narratives concerning Phenomenal Spiritual Manifestations in Sweden, most of which were furnished by an eminent and learned Swedish gentleman--Count Piper. The public have become so thoroughly sated with tales of hauntings, apparitions, prevision, &c., that Count Piper's narrations would present few, if any features of interest, save in justification of one assertion, that Spiritualism is rife in human experience everywhere, even though it may not take the same form as a public movement, that it has done in America and England.

As early as 1864, a number of excellent leading articles commending the belief in Spiritual ministry, and the study of such phenomena as would promote communion between the "two worlds," appeared in the columns of the *Afton Blad*, one of the most popular journals circulated in Sweden. As a specimen of the style in which a rational and deliberate mode of investigating Spiritual phenomena is commended to the readers of the *Afton Blad*, we cannot do better than close this chapter by the following extract from that paper, written by the celebrated German author, Hoffmann :—

"The mysterious spirit world cannot be denied, for it surrounds us, and is continually revealing itself to us by strange tones and marvellous visions. Such tones and visions, and all narratives of the kind, are glibly got rid of under the name of *superstition*.

"But this is a silly way of proceeding. Superstition is only the proper name for weak credulity. But does it not often happen that people include under the general term—superstition—numbers of things which they neither understand, nor are capable of understanding ? The very knowing ones think nothing has ever happened which has not happened to them, and nothing exists which they have not had betwixt their fingers and thumbs. But how far does the circle of man's senses extend, and how imperfect is his knowledge even within that circle ? If then he does not comprehend his own wonderful existence, how does he presume to dogmatize on the eternal laws which are destined by Eternal Wisdom for the spirit-world and its operations ?

" In our day, even learned people treat everything beyond their own immediate sphere of enquiry as matters of sickly fancy and folly, and thereby betray their ignorance. Such men will never solve the great problem of the universe !"

CHAPTER XLVII.

SPIRITUALISM IN SWITZERLAND.

WHILST Spiritualism prevails in every land with more or less phenomenal power, it has assumed no place as a public movement anywhere, save in America, England, Australia, France, and to a certain extent in Spanish America. In Switzerland—where a large number of visitors annually throng the most attractive spots, in pursuit of health, rest, and enjoyment—an universal under-current of Spiritualistic belief prevails with the floating population, although this sentiment with the peasantry, takes the shape of superstitious beliefs or religious enthusiasm.

Experience has shown, that mountain regions, and the clear electric atmosphere of elevated sites, are highly favourable to the development of Spiritual gifts, hence it is not uncommon to find Mediums of various endowments, especially vision seers and healers, amongst the natives of the Swiss mountains. The circumstances to which we shall devote this chapter however, are of a far more remarkable character than the phenomena evolved in the familiar Spirit circle. Two cases of Spiritual outpouring have occurred in the Swiss Cantons during the present century, of so startling a nature, as to attract the eyes of all Europe, and to baffle every attempt at explanation from any other than a Spiritual hypothesis.

These cases are first, the tremendous and universal obsession, which fell upon the inhabitants of Morzine ; the other, an almost unparalleled instance of persecution from the *Polter-Gheist*, or haunting Spirits. Both circumstances have been narrated in many leading publications of Europe, and though treated from different points of view, the very diversity of opinions that prevail on these subjects, enables the candid historian to arrive at a vast array of facts, which do not necessarily require the statement of opposing theories.

The following brief summary of the Morzine epidemic is collated from the pages of the *Cornhill Magazine*, two or three of the London daily journals, the *Revue Spirite*, and Mr. William Howitt's magazine, article entitled, " The Devils of Morzine." The period of the occurrence was about 1860 ; the scene, the parish of Morzine, a beautiful valley of the Savoy, not more than half a day's journey from the Lake of Geneva. The place is quiet, remote, and had been seldom visited by tourists before the period above named. Being moreover shut in by high mountains, and inhabited by a simple, industrious, and pious class of peasantry, Morzine might have appeared to a casual visitor the very centre of health, peace, and good order.

The first appearance of an abnormal visitation was the conduct of a young girl, who, from being quiet, modest, and well-conducted, suddenly began to exhibit what her distressed family and friends supposed to be symptoms of insanity. She ran about in the most singular and aimless way; climbed high trees, scaled walls, and was found perched on roofs and cornices, which it seemed impossible for any creature but a squirrel to reach. She soon became wholly untractable; was given to fits of hysteria, violent laughter, passionate weeping, and general aberration from her customary modest behaviour. Whilst her parents were anxiously seeking advice in this dilemma, another and still another of the young girl's ordinary companions were seized with the same malady.

In the course of ten days the report prevailed, that over fifty females—ranging from seven years of age to fifty—had been seized, and were exhibiting symptoms of the most bewildering mental aberration. The crawling, climbing, leaping, wild singing, furious swearing, and frantic behaviour of these unfortunates, soon found crowds of imitators.

Before the tidings of this frightful affliction had passed beyond the district in which it originated, several hundreds of women and children, and scores of young men, were writhing under the contagion.

The seizures were sudden, like the attacks; they seldom lasted long, yet they never seemed to yield to any form of treatment, whether harsh or kind, medical, religious, or persuasive.

The first symptoms of this frightful malady do not seem to have been noted with sufficient attention to justify the historian in giving details which could be considered accurate. It was only when the number of the possessed exceeded two thousand persons, and the case was attracting multitudes of curious enquirers from all parts of the Continent, that the medical men, priests, and journalists of the day, began to keep and publish constant records of the progress of the epidemic.

One of the strangest features of the case, and one which most constantly baffled the faculty, was the appearance of rugged health, and freedom from all physical disease, which distinguished this malady. As a general rule, the victims spoke in hoarse, rough tones unlike their own; used profane language, such as few of them could have ever heard, and imitated the actions of crawling, leaping, climbing animals, with ghastly fidelity. Sometimes they would roll their bodies up into balls and distort their limbs beyond the power of the attendant physicians to account for, or disentangle.

Many amongst them were *levitated* in the air, and in a few instances, the women spoke in foreign tongues, manifested high conditions of exaltation, described glorious visions, prophesied, gave clairvoyant descriptions of absent persons and distant places, sang hymns, and preached in strains of sublime inspiration. It must be added, that these instances were very rare, and were only noticeable in the earlier stages of the obsession. Considered as a whole, the scenes enacted, and the mental states manifested, were only worthy of originating in Pandemonium.

It is almost needless to say that the tidings of this horrible obsession attracted immense multitudes of witnesses, no less than the attention of the learned and philosophic. When the atttempts of the medical faculty, the church, and the law, had been tried again and again, and all had utterly failed to modify the ever-increasing horrors of this malady, the Emperor of the French, the late Louis Napoleon, under whose protectorate Morzine was then governed, yielding to the representations of his advisers, actually sent out three military companies to Morzine, charged with strict orders to quell the disturbances "on the authority of the Emperor, or by force if necessary." The result of this high-handed policy was to increase ten-fold the violence of the disease, and to augment the numbers of the afflicted, in the persons of many of the very soldiers who sank under the contagion which they were expected to quench.

The next move of the baffled French Government, was a spiritual one; an army of priests, headed by a venerable Bishop, much beloved in his diocese, being despatched in the quality of exorcists, at the suggestion of the Archbishop of Paris. Unhappily this second experiment worked no better than the first.

Respectable-looking groups of well-dressed men, women, and children, would pass into the churches in reverent silence, and with all the appearance of health and piety; but no sooner was the sound of the priest's voice, or the notes of the organ heard, than shrieks, execrations, sobbings, and frenzied cries resounded from different points of the assembly. Anxious fathers and husbands were busy in carrying their distracted relatives into the open air, and whether in the church or the home, every attempt of a sacerdotal character, was sure to arouse the mania to heights of fury unknown before.

On many occasions, the priests and their sacred paraphernalia were driven off by the obsessed, and forced to retreat in fear of bodily harm. Leaping walls, scaling terrific heights, and mocking the exorcists with fierce oaths or frantic sobbings, the last state of these unhappy ones seemed considerably worse than the first. The children affected, acted more like apes than human beings, and although now and then there were signs of exaltation, and the interference of high angelic influences, the general tone of this horrible infection was lunatic, mischievous, and profane.

Sometimes indeed, the women arose in the churches, and prayed with a fervour and eloquence which wrung every heart, and filled the listeners' eyes with tears, but even then, the petitions put up were obviously uttered by an inspiration *foreign* to the speaker, and pleaded in the most pathetic and moving terms for aid in conquering the evil powers that then held sway.

The time came at length, when the good old Bishop thought by a *coup de grace*, to achieve a general victory over the adversary. He commanded that as many as possible of the afflicted should be gathered together to hear high mass, when he trusted that the solemnity of the occasion would be sufficient to defeat what he evidently believed to be the combined forces of Satan.

Our space does not permit the quotation of the Bishop's letter addressed to the French Archbishop; the gist of the document is however, to report an entire failure of his scheme. According to the description cited by William Howitt in his paper on " The Devils of Morzine," the assemblage in question, including at least two thousand of the possessed, and a number of spectators, must have far more faithfully illustrated Milton's description of Pandemonium than any mortal scene before enacted. Children and women were leaping over the seats and benches; clambering up the pillars, and shrieking defiance from pinnacles which scarcely admitted of a foothold for a bird.

Men beat their breasts, tore their hair, and moaned as if in mortal agony. One young man was endeavouring with eyes streaming with tears and face pale as marble, to hold back his young bride from ascending a fluted column, whilst she broke from his grasp, scaled the giddy height, and perching herself on the carved capital, broke forth into peals of laughter, which froze the blood of every mortal to listen to. Whole knots of women, who in their own homes seemed to be healthy, happy, and strictly modest matrons, were lying on the ground with dishevelled hair, and rent garments, or dancing on tombs, and monuments, like incarnate fiends.

The poor Bishop's letter contains but one remark which seems to offer a clue to these scenes of horror and madness. He says: "When in my distress and confusion I accidentally laid my hand on the heads of these unfortunates, I found that the paroxysm instantly subsided, and that however wild and clamorous they may have been before, the parties so touched, generally sunk down as it were into a swoon, or deep sleep, and woke up most commonly restored to sanity, and a sense of propriety."

Good old man! unconsciously to himself a powerful *magnetizer.* Had the clue thus furnished been followed out, the whole tribe of obsessing demons might have been conquered, and their power replaced with a pure, holy, and healthful influence, which would have held possession of the frenzied crowd, until they could have been restored to sanity and individualism.

An earnest and philosophical observer of this frightful drama, a gentleman commissioned by one of the Brussels journals to report what was transpiring, writes of the closing scenes as follows :—

"'I stayed at Morzine until Monseigneur left, that is to say, till half-past six in the evening. The poor bishop was utterly dispirited. Two or three '*possédées*' were brought to him in the sacristy, but he could do nothing. On my return I found one by the side of the road. I questioned her also in a foreign language, but she got angry, and replied by a handful of gravel, which she flung in my face, telling me that I only went once a year to mass, and that I was a busybody.'

"The complete failure of episcopal influence threw the Government back on the help of medical science. Dr. Constans had, since his first visit, published a report, in which he held out hopes of cure if his advice were strictly followed. He was again commissioned to do what he could for Morzine. Armed with the powers of a dictator he returned there, and backed by a fresh detachment of sixty soldiers, a brigade of gendarmes and a fresh *curé*, he issued despotic decrees, and threatened lunatic asylums, and in any case deportation for the convulsed. He fined any person who accused others of magic, or in any way encouraged the prevalent idea of supernatural evil. He desired the *curé* to preach sermons against the possibility of demoniacal possession, but this order could not well be carried out by even the most obedient priest.

"The persons affected with fits were dispersed in every direction. Some were sent to asylums and hospitals, and many were simply exiled from Chablais. They were not allowed to revisit even for a day their homes, except by very special favour. The existing health of the exiles is, of course, not well known, but we have heard of many who have attacks even now when they are far from Morzine. Four or five who were unfortunately kept together in an Annecy hospital, set on the chaplain, a priest who attempted to exorcise them, and ill-treated him after the fashion in which they had dealt with his bishop.

"Whether fear has helped to stay the spiritual plague, as undoubtedly fear helped to produce it, remains to be proved; at present the urgent pressure put by the French Government on the people of Morzine seems to have scotched the snake. There have been no cases of convulsion for four months. The soldiers have been withdrawn. Visitors to the place, curious of information, are, we think wisely discouraged; quacks and charlatans are not allowed admission to the commune."

We should not care to conclude this horrible and apparently incredible narrative without citing some additional testimony of a corroborative and authentic character. We will therefore give a few extracts from Mr. William Howitt's excellent paper on "The Devils of Morzine," published in the London *Spiritual Magazine*, which read as follows :—

"We need not point to the salient facts of our narrative, or discuss the various theories that have been invented to account for them. . . . It is impossible not to see the resemblance of the Morzine epidemic with the demonopathy of the sixteenth century, and the history of the Jansenist and Cevennes convulsionnaires. . . . Some of the facts we have related were often observed in the state o hypnotism, or nervous sleep, with which physicians are familiar. The hallucinations of which we have given instances are too common to astonish us. *But the likeness of this epidemic to others that have been observed, does not account for its symptoms.*

"The resemblance of one set of phenomena to another does not explain any. . . . . In this narrative we notice, that like all the revival and other epidemic phenomena, this of Morzine began with one person, who communicated the infection to her companions. At the commencement, it seemed as if it was about to be a religious revival, but the evil spirits soon got the better and thenceforth maintained their ground. The extreme similarity in small points, such as running up trees and houses, will be best seen by giving some other instances of similar epidemic phenomena which occurred at convents and schools in France, Holland, and Germany during upwards of one hundred and fifty years, breaking out from the year 1494 to the year 1652, each attended with convulsive spasms of the body and mental characteristics, similar in many respects to those of the Morzine possession. It is noticed in that of the nuns at Wertet that it commenced in a notion of witchcraft, and that they were seized with violent fits of sadness and paroxysms of an hysterical kind ; that they fell suddenly to the ground as if dead, *whilst others scrambled up trees, clambering with their feet like cats.* Mr. Madden, in his 'Phantasmata,' gives a description of these cases, and describes that of the nuns of Kintorp as follows :—'At first a few only were seized with convulsions and hallucinations. The symptoms seemed to be communicated, it is said, by contact ; but perhaps it would be more correct to say, by close intercourse and sympathy. When the attack burst out they raved, uttered cries imitating the shrieks and screams of animals, felt a strong desire to bite, and became frightfully contorted.' At the convent of Cologne in 1564, it began with one nun, and was by her communicated to the one whose bed was next to her, and immediately after to the whole convent. In 1566, the foundling children at Amsterdam were attacked with convulsions and delirium, during which '*they spoke foreign languages, and knew what was passing elsewhere, even in the great council of the city ; and they even clambered along walls like cats, and along the roofs of houses.*' The same had happened in Rome in 1555, in the Orphan Asylum in that city, where it is said 'about seventy young girls became demoniacs, and continued in that state more than two years.' Of the Sisters of St. Bridget, who had the disease for ten years, all had the faculty of improvising long discourses under inspirational influence.

"The nuns at Loudun suffered from 'frightful disquietude of mind ; hysterical symptoms, convulsions of extreme violence, producing singular contortions, catalepsy, and hallucinations all bearing on subjects of religious enthusiasm. As to their cries, it was what might be conceived of the bellowing of the condemned.' They also spoke in foreign tongues with which they were not previously acquainted, and by that we come to the knowledge of a curious portion of the Roman ritual, by which they were tried, to 'find any of the three symptoms required by it as a sign of being truly possessed by the Devil ; and which are, divination, *the understanding of languages which the person has not learned,* and a supernatural strength of body.' *Six of the clerical and magisterial functionaries* who had been brought into contact with the nuns as judges, caught the disease. There was an unusual exaltation of some of the intellectual faculties, a power of improvising, and of inner vision or thought reading, as to which Mr. Madden observes, 'that they differ in no respect from the phenomena of magnetism.'

"The cases were all more or less connected with religious ideas, but were also much mixed up, as we might expect, with the prevalent middle age notions of diabolic possession.

"A case similar to those occurring in the middle ages amongst the children of Amsterdam and the nuns in the convents, happened within the last seven years in Piedmont, and went through the Continental papers—'A number of young girls in the district all at once left their schools and homes and went into the fields and woods, roaming, and behaving in the wildest way. Exhortations to return being insufficient, the clergy were called to exorcise the poor girls, who repelled them, calling them devils and sorcerers ; *many of them got up trees and on the roofs of houses, and refused to come down.*'

"Dr. Kerner relates that, 'At the village of Neuhutte, in Wurtemberg, which is situate among the mountains, a sort of St. Vitus' dance becomes epidemic chiefly amongst young people, so that all the children of the place are seized with it at the same time. Like persons in a magnetic state, they are aware of the precise moment that a fit will seize them, and if they are in the fields they hasten home and immediately fall into a convulsion, in which condition they will move for an hour or more with the most surprising regularity, keeping measure like an accomplished dancer, after which they awake as if out of a magnetic sleep."

Mr. Howitt very justly complains that "the resemblance of one set of phenomena to another does not explain any." What then ? Is there no explanation to be rendered of states so utterly abnormal to all *known* procedures of natural law? Speaking authoritatively, we must answer— in our present utter ignorance of Spiritual science and its laws—No; but judging analogically from what we do know of Spiritual potencies, we deem it quite possible that there are mental and magnetic storms, contagions, and epidemics, generated by conditions, and proceeding upon laws of which at present we are in total ignorance, but which assuredly originate in planetary and geologic changes, with just as much regularity and order as do contagious maladies and epidemic diseases. The very fact that they prevail in special districts proves that they obey some unknown but potential physical law; whilst the invariability with which they propagate their effects by contact, proves that the affection is of a nervous, and from thence of a mental type, and that the *malarium*, or pabulum of infection is a *magnetic* one. Awaiting the day when the physiology of mind shall be as carefully studied and its healthful or diseased states as scientifically dealt with as the physiology of the material body, we must for the present quit the realm of hypothesis, and pass on to notice the next representative case of Swiss Spiritualism.

The narrative we are now about to cite has been published in many languages and widely circulated through the Continental journals of the period, 1862-3. The best and most impartial summary of the case is to be found in the London *Spiritual Magazine* of February, 1864, written by Mr. William Howitt, under the caption of—

"PERSECUTION AND EXPULSION FROM HIS PATRIMONIAL HOUSE OF M. JOLLER, OF THE SWISS NATIONAL COUNCIL, BY DISORDERLY SPIRITS."

The extracts which we find most pertinent to this case, taken from Mr. Howitt's narrative, commence as follows:—

"In the third volume of this magazine, p. 499, the reader will find an article headed 'Manifestations at Lucerne.' This article consists of extracts from different Swiss news-papers, giving an account of the extraordinary appearances, noises, and other annoyances going on, from the autumn of 1860 to that of 1862, in the house of M. Joller, at Stans, a village on the borders of the Lake of Lucerne. Some of these newspapers, in the usual style of such journals, were inclined to be witty, if not wise, over these occurrences; but a correspondent well known to us, and one of our most valued contributors, had taken the trouble to go himself to Stans, and ascertain what were the facts on the spot. He tells us that he found M. Joller, a lawyer, a man of middle age, having several children, his eldest son being about twenty. That he bore an excellent character, and was well known. throughout the country. He found Stans a village about an hour's sail by steamboat from Lucerne, standing in a charming valley one or two miles from the shore, fruitful, well peopled, by no means sombre or solitary, and surrounded by magnificent mountains. M. Joller confirmed the supernatural facts which have proved so startling to the public, and so grievous to him. The letter of our correspondent is dated the 4th of October, 1862. On the 22nd of the same month, or only eighteen days later, M. Joller was com-pelled by these unpitying *polter-geister* to abandon his hereditary home, with all his family.

"M. Joller has now published the story of his unmerited sufferings and banishment from his natal hearth by these troublesome intruders, in a small *brochure* of ninety-one pages. This little book now lies before us, and certainly no more extraordinary case of supernatural persecution has yet been put on record.

"Every one familiar with the Lake of Lucerne, must have a pretty good idea of the situation of Stans, when it is said that from M. Joller's house, Mount Pilatus on the one hand, and the Rigi on the other, are in full view. This house and property, M. Joller informs us, had been in the possession of his family for about a hundred years.

"It was in this house that M. Joller, an active and popular lawyer, and member of the national council, lived from the death of his father in 1845, to the summer of 1862, in peace and happiness. Then, suddenly, in the autumn of 1860, uncanny sounds and sights began to show themselves to the astonishment of all, and for some time to the persevering disbelief of M. Joller. 'In my house,' he says, 'bloomed seven healthy children, four boys and three girls. In our abode superstition ever had been a rejected thing; and I may assert that scarcely any family had been brought up with so little fear of ghosts as mine.'

"The troublesome visitations made their *debût* by first rapping on the bedstead of the servant-maid, raps which she said she not only heard but felt, one night in the autumn of 1860. She immediately expressed her belief that this was the token of an approaching death in the family. The maid slept in a room on the third story, so that it could not well be any mischievous person playing a trick; but M. Joller strictly commanded her to keep her superstitious notions to herself, and ascribed the raps to the girl's own imagination, which she would, however, on no account admit. The rapping was not again repeated for some weeks, but after that interval M. Joller came home from a temporary absence and found his family in great alarm. His wife and second daughter, sleeping in his own room, had been awaked by loud rappings on a table in the room. On demanding if it were any living agent, that it should rap again, it did so promptly. They also now entertained the notion that it was the messenger of death, and a letter informing them in a few days of the decease of a friend, confirmed that idea. They were soon, however, to be convinced that it was nothing temporary. In June, 1861, one of the boys, nine years of age, being in a wood-chamber on the third story, was found in a swoon. As he was a stout and fearless lad, great was the wonder, and on coming to himself, he said as he was in the chamber he heard knocks on the door, of which he took no notice, but immediately afterwards a white indistinct figure opened the door and entered, when he lost consciousness. This M. Joller endeavoured to account for by the erudite solvent of all difficulties—imagination. But M. Joller was not to be let off so easily. The other boys in their bedroom heard noises in the night in the rooms above and below them, and called out to know who was making the noise. M. Joller endeavoured to persuade them that they were cats or rats, or birds that made the noises; and yet he now recollected to have heard similar sounds on his own writing table, and that frequently, two years ago.

"In the autumn of 1861, the maid renewed her complaints. She said she was afraid of remaining alone in the kitchen. As she cleaned the shoes in an evening on the steps near the kitchen door, grey shapes appeared from the cellar below. They came upstairs into her chamber, and she heard them sobbing in the fourth story, which was a lumber room. Mrs. Joller scolded her for her fancies. But the same things appeared to the children, and the youngest daughter about eleven years old, at her studies in the day, saw a child enter, walk up to her, and vanish. The maid-servant was dismissed in October of 1862, and a girl of only thirteen taken in her place to do the more common work of the house, the mother and daughters, in Swiss fashion, undertaking the rest. From that time to the summer of 1862 all was quiet, the medium seemed to have gone in the maid; but this was not the case, for two of the boys who slept in a chamber leading by a terrace into the garden, declared that they still heard at nights knocking on the walls; others said that they heard in the rooms above a going to and fro as of a heavy dog, and knockings on the walls and the floors. Still M. Joller endeavoured to persuade his family that these sounds proceeded from merely natural causes.

"On the 15th of August, M. Joller had occasion to visit Lucerne, with his wife and eldest son, and on his return the rest of the children had relations of fresh apparitions to make. This time he threatened them sternly with the rod if he heard any more 'such nonsense;' and the children complained sorrowfully that 'their father would believe nothing.' But the very same forenoon the children were frightened out of the house by knockings, and as they sat down on the doorsteps leading to the gardens, a pebble the size of a man's fist was thrown from somewhere above or from the house, and fell betwixt two of them. Returning to the house they found all the doors of the rooms, drawers, and cupboards standing open. These they closed and locked, only to see them fly open again. They then locked the door of the chamber adjoining the sitting-room, and bolted it with the night bolt, but notwithstanding both, it was thrown open, and all the windows and doors standing open were as suddenly closed. Hearing also a heavy step on the stairs, though nobody was visible, they flew again into the garden. Returning at noon to dinner, they saw a strange spectre on the staircase, and hurried once more into the garden with the dinner apparatus, and took refuge under a large walnut tree. As the girl carried the plates out from the kitchen, she saw doors still opening and shutting and the children from the garden saw all the windows open.

"The disturbances now came thicker and faster. The humming of spinning-wheels was heard in the house; occasionally a strange music; furniture began to move about; then the music was accompanied by the audible singing in a melancholy tone, of Camilla's prayer in Zampa, '*Gleiches Loos,*' &c., and a voice said in the Nidwalden patois, '*Wenn au gar niemer umen isch!*' 'If I should never come again!' Still more extraordinary, not only they, but the woman of the adjoining house, saw on the house floor, drawn with the accuracy of an engraving, a snow-white figure with a death's head, which they watched for some time till it faded quite out. The same evening, on a fire being kindled in the ground story, called the hut, a conical figure surrounded by flames, came down the chimney, and, dissolving into water, drowned the fire out, and raised a wild cry from the maid and children, which brought down the mother, who found the group sitting in the abutting house of the tenant weeping in terror.

"M. Joller now received information of like things going on in other places, from persons of education and intelligence, but he still persisted in ascribing these things to natural causes. But the time was now come for him to meet the enemy face to face. On the 19th of August, as he arrived at home in the evening, his wife called him into the house passage to hear the knocking going on. Then he soon had ample evidence that the stories of the maids and children had foundation enough. The knocking went on briskly on the wall before him; then in the scullery. He followed, putting his ear close to the place, and pretending that it must be a rat, struck some heavy blows on the wall to frighten the rat away. To his astonishment, the blows were returned with equal vigour and in equal number. He then called for a candle, and examined the passage and scullery closely. In vain; so he summoned his family to the sitting-room, declared he would find it all out next morning; and bringing Zschokke's 'Book of Family Worship,' began to read aloud his 28th chapter, namely, 'On the Power of Superstition.'

"The spirit, however, cared neither for M. Joller nor Zschokke, but began pounding on the room door so vigorously, that his reading was soon brought to an end, and the children asked triumphantly, 'Is that a rat, then?'

"Incensed at this, and strongly persuaded that some one was playing the fool with him, he seized a candle, armed himself with a stiletto, and sallied forth to hunt out the villain. The outer doors and windows being fast, he felt sure that he must soon detect him. He descended to the cellar, made a vigorous search amongst the barrels and behind the door. Nothing there! but above his head the knocking was now going on blithely. He ascended, followed the sound from place to place; sometimes with his candle, sometimes without it, stealing along in the dark to pounce on the rogue. Taking nothing by his motion, however, he ordered all to bed. The noises nevertheless became such, that the whole family had flown together into one room, and there the knocking came. The bedstead was seized and banged against the wall till the whole bed shook. M. Joller examined under the bed and into every corner of the room, but in vain, though he found the doors and windows all fast. As he was thus employed, he heard raps on the chairs, and felt a soft stroking on the forefinger of his left hand.

"From this time till that when the family was driven from the house, the haunting was almost incessant; and the knockings, the throwing about of furniture, the visible presentment of spirits has rarely had a parallel in the history of such phenomena. There might have been room to suppose that the maids and children had given way to imaginary fears, but from this time forward the disorders became the subject of incessant public observation. The news flew about, spite of all M. Joller's endeavours to keep it at home; and hundreds and thousands of people flocked from the country round to witness the proceedings—and did witness them in crowds. . . . .

"The next morning he kept his word, and made a thorough examination of the house; and the spirits gave him the amplest opportunity to try his skill. They knocked everywhere, till he saw the very wainscot bend beneath their blows. As he was born in the house, and as an inquisitive lad, had watched all repairs going on at different periods, he says there was not a handbreadth of its wall or roof that was not familiar to him. The knockings were everywhere. Now thumping on a door, he opened it, and held it fast in his hands, when the knocks were given on each side at once. On one occasion he stood with a chamber door ajar, and suddenly pulling it open as the first knock fell on it, saw a dark figure outside; but before he could spring forward, his wife and a daughter who were in the room, simultaneously cried out that they saw a brown bony arm at the moment withdrawn from the door. They did this so completely together that he was convinced that each saw the same thing. The servant flew upstairs to say that she had heard something come down the stairs, and three times groaningly exclaim, 'Take pity on me!' She added that she looked eagerly, but could see nothing; yet soon after she saw a grey transparent little cloud float in at the kitchen window, and pass with a vibrating motion to the chamber door, where it had knocked loudly.

"Driven to a late conviction of what he had to deal with, M. Joller hastened to beg the Commissary Niederberger to come and see these things; but he being absent, Father Guardian came, and watched the phenomena with deep interest, but without being able to suggest a solution of the cause. He thought an investigation by men of authority should take place; but M. Joller, dreading the consequences of publicity, for the present hesitated. The Father bestowed the usual blessing on the house and withdrew. The bewildered M. Joller then drew out his dust-covered college notes on experimental physics, made at Munich, while attending the class of Professor Sieber, but they afforded him no light.

"Neither the blessing of the reverend Father, nor the philosophical enquiry suspended the disturbances for an instant. The next day, as the Court of Justice was sitting at Lucerne, he was obliged to attend on busines, but he was sent for before the Court rose, the house at home being in the most frightful uproar. Arriving, he found all his family in the open air, not daring to stay under the roof. Numbers of people were collected on the high road looking at the house, in great excitement. Having no fear, he entered the house, and found the doors madly flying open and then banging to with a violence that threatened to demolish them. In the kitchen he found the glasses, bottles, and earthenware standing on the table ringing as if struck with a metallic instrument. The knockings were in so many parts of the house at once, that had it been men who did it, it would have required four or five, yet not a man was in the house except himself. He here called in an old friend, the Councillor Zimmermann, Dr. K. von Deschwanden, an accomplished natural philosopher ; the President of the Court of Justice, Obermatt, Judge Schallberger, Master Builder Aloys Amstad, and Drawing Master Obermatt. These gentlemen witnessed with astonishment the phenomena. They sought everywhere for some physical cause, and propounded many theories of Vulcanism, magnetism, galvanism, electricity, &c. But at length they went away as much puzzled as many other scientific men had been in like circumstances.

"The next day, Mr. President Obermatt brought other gentlemen to witness the disturbances, and one of these suggested whether it might not be some electrical machine on the premises which was grown thus riotous, when the eldest son of M. Joller, who had been cautioned by his father to be secret on the real cause, concedingly observed that it might be so. This was enough. It does not appear that there was any electrical machine on the premises, but the frolics of the spirits went on with a violence that no twenty electrical machines in the house could account for. Doors were fiercely flung open, bolts and bars dashed vehemently back. Figures were seen by different people, and the second son fainted and fell at the sight of one. The house was now rarely unoccupied by crowds of people, before whom the manifestations went on in full force and variety. Before the Land-Captain Zelger, the Director of Police Jann, Dr. Christen, the President of the Court of Justice again, and many other persons of condition, the Episcopal Commissary Niederberger, and Father Guardian made a very vigorous examination of the house, and retired advising a thorough physical commission of inquiry ; but believing its origin to be still beyond the scope of such a commission.

"Something was become highly necessary ; the house was crowded from morning to night ; some talked of and hunted for the electrical machine ; others challenged the devil to come out ; and others, who had happened to hear that the eldest son of M. Joller had been seen speaking with an actor in the streets of Lucerne, declared that it was all sorcery, and that young Joller had learned it of the player. The police-director, Jann, sent in two policemen to keep watch that the house was not plundered by thieves amongst the crowds. As the conduct of the visitors, both in the flesh and out of it, grew every day more outrageous, though a number of watchers were maintained throughout the nights ; as the spirits grew bolder and showed themselves more openly ; and as M. Joller seized one of the hands of the spirits and felt distinctly the thumb and fingers, which soon, however, drew themselves away ; he went and demanded a formal examination of the house by the police authorities. This was accorded, and three of the heads of the police were appointed to prosecute the inquiry. Up to this moment the disturbances continued in full play. The directors of police ordered M. Joller to withdraw with his whole family from the house, and take up their quarters elsewhere. They were then left to themselves and profound silence for six days. No knock was heard, no ghost appeared, no door or window opened or shut of itself. The profound Dogberries of the police, therefore, drew up a report that there was nothing at all amiss, and returned to Lucerne in the pride of ignorance of all psychology, and of having shown up the whole affair. These worthy souls knew nothing at all about mediums. M. Joller did not even understand that he had carried the mediums along with him ; but he knew the moment that he recrossed his own threshold that the old ghostly power was there in all its force.

"The tide of popular ridicule was now let loose against the unfortunate Joller. The Press was in a heaven of triumph over the follies of this superstitious man. Though thousands had seen the very things that he asserted to exist ; though police-director Jann, judges, magistrates, and dignified clergy had all witnessed the phenomena, poor Joller and his family were treated as little less than lunatics. The thing was the talk of all Switzerland, and what wounded M. Joller most deeply was, that all his political services and sacrifices to liberal opinion were at once forgotten. His own party, to a man, joined in deriding him ; even those with whom he had stood side by side in battle against political corruptions, threw their sarcasms at him. As is so often the case, however, some of his political opponents, whom he had hit the hardest and spared the least, now stood nobly forward and defended him, as an honourable, meritorious, and trustworthy man.

"In vain did M. Joller protest against the injustice of his neighbours : in vain did he insist on another police examination conducted in whatever manner the authorities pleased, so that the family should be in the house : the one already made was held to settle the whole question. On the contrary, however, the annoyances held their uninterrupted course from this time, the 4th of September, to the 22nd of October, when they finally drove him and his family out. It is still a long story, but we can only notice a few of the most striking phenomena. Chairs and other furniture continued to change their places, apparently at their own pleasure. Broken pots and glass, an old axe, cobs of Indian corn, a sickle, a great iron ring, were repeatedly brought out of the kitchen and cellar, and thrust into a stove in a chamber, locked up and the key in possession of M. Joller. In full sunshine at noon, the eldest daughter saw in the garden, as she thought, the maid servant climbing the lattice-work on the house side to gather grapes. She saw her dress so distinctly, her hair net, smooth hair, and dark neckerchief, that she called aloud to her, when to her astonishment she saw the maid issue from the kitchen below to see what was wanted : and the figure, as if crouching under the vine leaves, disappeared.

"For some days there had been a plucking of leafy branches and flinging of them into the chamber windows, or upon the heads of persons passing below, when on the 12th of September, as the whole family sat at coffee at half-past two in the day, three students being present, and the maid in the room, a great noise was heard in the *salon* above. All rushed up and saw the room in singular disorder. From the wall on the left hand a large engraving was taken down and laid on the floor. Two pier glasses were taken from the wall and laid down in like manner. A parasol that had stood in a corner was spread out over an ornamental hanging lamp. Stools and curtains were thrown confusedly on a heap ; and all the chairs were heaped one upon another around the table. Everything being restored to order, and the room carefully locked, the next morning early, the room was found in a still greater state of chaos, as well as an adjoining chamber.

"M. Joller having to go to Lucerne to pay in some money, heard, on his return, from his family, that they had, in an adjoining chamber, heard the distinct counting out of money, piece by piece, and the rolls of it successively pushed aside, so that they were inclined to believe that there must be somebody there so engaged. On looking, however, they found nobody. On mentioning the time he found it agree exactly with that in which he was then counting his money at the bank. At another time, as he was then at some distance on the estate, watching the felling and cutting up of timber, his wife and children at home heard the chopping and splitting of wood in the cellar. On the 16th of September they were astonished by the hopping and dancing of an apple, which came flying downstairs against the house door, and passed by M. Joller in the passage at several bounds into the kitchen. The servant, busy at her cooking stove, seized it, and laid it on the kitchen table, when it soon sprung away and hopped into the passage. The girl seized it again, and flung it through the window, but it soon came flying back through the same window, bounded on the table, thence into the passage, the sitting-room, and finally into the adjoining chamber, when it flew into a corner and remained quiet. A pear descended from the ceiling, near M. Joller, with such force as to lie smashed on the floor. Other pieces of pear were flung at the girls while at work, and hung in their hair nets.

"The family were repeatedly assailed with showers of stones, both in the house and in the garden. At twelve o'clock in the day, while at the well, a shower of stones fell round one of the daughters without any striking her, and at the same time a sharp-edged wall stone fell down the kitchen chimney, striking the lid of a pan on the fire, and then falling to the floor without bringing a trace of soot with it. A knitting needle took to flying about from room to room, and being thrown out into the garden, it flew back again. There were continually sounds of humming and spinning wheels, and the drawing up of clock chains. On the 16th of September a voice deep and groaning, said distinctly, as out of the wall : "*Jetzt komme ich nimmer*"—"Now I come no more !" but it did not keep its word, or other actors stayed behind, for more variety of annoyances were played off than can be here enumerated.

"During all this time the unceremonious intrusion of people continued, so that there could be no domestic privacy, neither could the family affairs, or the legal business of M. Joller go on. He was, therefore, compelled to seek another home, and abandon this, his natal one, on the 22nd of October, 1862.

"Such is a brief notice of M. Joller's case, undoubtedly, taken altogether, the most extraordinary which has occurred of late years. In closing it, he says, that a great many similar ones, but none so outrageous have been brought to his knowledge by persons of the most unquestionable character. That he could cite a long catalogue of witnesses of his unhappy spirit-persecution, but that it is too notorious to need it. The house, he says, stood empty till the following spring, when he succeeded in letting it, and that up to the time of his writing this account, nothing particular had disturbed the new tenant, nor had the troublers followed him. It may be conceived what a serious affair it had proved to him in interruption of business and family life, in loss of peace of mind, and in infliction of censorious remarks. The nuisance of the invading crowd must, of itself, have been intolerable; for when compelled to lock his doors against them, they procured ladders and broke in at his chamber window.

"The most striking feature of M. Joller's case is the entire ignorance of the nature of haunting spirits both by M. Joller, the police, and the clergy of the neighbourhood. As for M. Joller, evidently a Catholic by faith, he seems to have had no idea of getting rid of his persecutors by prayers and earnest appeal to the God of all spirits. A worthy man, he goes on suffering, and is actually driven from his home, without an idea that these troublesome guests might have been sent away instead. These were evidently unhappy spirits seeking aid from the first mediums they could meet with. They found these in M. Joller's house; but they were mediums without that knowledge which mediums instructed by Spiritualism possess. These unhappy souls were repeatedly heard sobbing and groaning and exclaiming, '*Erbarmet euch meiner!*' 'Have mercy on me!' They wanted the prayers and good offices of M. Joller and his family, and failing to make them comprehend this, they grew desperate; the worst instead of the best feelings of their natures were excited, and in their rage at being able to make these mediums perceive but not to understand them, they grew to resemble fiends in their wild passions rather than miserable supplicants. The consequence was that instead of being soothed by sympathy and gently dismissed on an upward course, as the Seeress of Prevorst often dismissed such, M. Joller was most unnecessarily driven from his own long-loved hearth. M. Joller, with all his worth and secular knowledge, is, in fact, the victim of ignorance—and a standing warning to men of education to pay some little attention to the psychological facts that are daily rising around them.

"It is satisfactory to see that a learned professor of one of the Swiss Colleges has prefaced M. Joller's pamphlet by an assertion of the truth and the real nature of these phenomena, and contends that it is the duty of psychology and natural science, not to ignore these frequent facts, but to throw fresh light on them by honest enquiry."

CHAPTER XLVIII.

SPIRITUALISM IN ITALY.

WERE Spirit communion still fettered by the chains of superstition thrown around it during the early and middle ages of human history, no land would afford a wider or fairer field for occult research than beautiful Italy.

The sunny skies, lovely scenery, and memorable history of Italy, naturally impress its people with a sentiment of romanticism peculiarly favourable to the reception of Spiritualistic beliefs and teachings.

In all lands too, overlaid with the vestiges of ancient civilizations there seems to be an imperishable aura of Magnetism which renders the very ground, and every object it sustains, Mediumistic.

Every foot of Italian soil is charged with the emanations of vanished generations. Rome has her catacombs in the streets as well as beneath them. Milan, Pisa, Florence, once stately Venice, and—in a word—every city and town of this memorable country, is a "psychometric" record engraved with images conserved in "the Astral light," which has been accumulating during the succeeding generations of more than two thousand years.

It scarcely needs the clear eye of the Spirit to recall these images into undying existence. Their mark remains in the conglomerate sphere which pervades the air, and vibrates beneath every footfall. Well may the modern traveller feel the impress of ancient Italy closing around him, and enveloping him in the mysterious shadows of the past ; and this, even when his own imaginative nature affords him no scope for expressing the strange mournful influences which weigh upon his spirit, or the awe which possesses him as the forms which he knows to be commingled with the dust beneath his feet, seem to start into life from every gray ruin, and reappear in the indelible photography impressed on every vestige of the past, by the sunbeam of long succeeding ages.

Our part in this volume however is to deal with the mere actualities of life, both here and hereafter, as revealed through the rifts of that veil of mystery—now happily rent in twain—which has so long enshrouded the soul's destiny beyond " the valley of the shadow."

Speaking then only of the Italy of to-day, we find that the phenomena of modern Spiritualism were believed in amongst many well informed Italians, long before any notice was called to the subject in the public press. It would be difficult at this time to say when or with whom modern Spiritualism originated in Italy, but one of the earliest public accounts that was given of its progress was—as usual—a bulletin issued from the enemies' camp.

This appeared in the form of an article printed in the well-known Roman journal, *La Civitta Catholica.*

The article in question was entitled, "Modern Necromancy," and after describing with remarkable candour the wide-spread influence which the said *necromantic* practices had obtained, and that, "in the best society of Italy," the editor proceeded to draw the conclusions, of which the following is an almost literal translation :—

"1st. Some of the phenomena may be attributed to imposture, hallucination, and exaggeration in the reports of those who describe it, but there is a foundation of REALITY in the general sum of the reports which cannot have originated in pure invention or be wholly discredited without ignoring the value of universal testimony.

"2nd. The bulk of the theories offered in explanation of the proven facts, only cover a certain percentage of those facts, but utterly fail to account for the balance. . . . .

"3rd. Allowing for all that can be filtered away on mere human hypotheses, there are still a large class of phenomena appealing to every sense which cannot be accounted for by any known natural laws, and which seem to manifest the action of intelligent beings," &c., &c.

In the summary drawn from these and similar propositions, the editor satisfies *himself at least* that the agency at work in the production of modern Spiritualism is supra-mundane, Spiritual, and diabolic ; that "the author is *Satan*, and the agents his accredited legions," &c., &c. Now whilst this Italian editor's theory had not even the merit of novelty to recommend it, certain it is, that its publication was most *apropos* and subserved all the purpose that the warmest Spiritual propagandist could desire. It was copied into most of the leading journals of Italy, and formed the best *circulating Medium* that the occasion could have called for.

In all probability the diatribes of the aforesaid editor were principally directed against the friends and converts of the celebrated European Medium, Mr. D. D. Home, who had visited Italy in 1854, and after spending some time in Florence, Rome, and Naples, had been fêted, courted, and honoured by many of the most distinguished royal and noble potentates of the land.

Although Mr. Home does not dwell on his Italian experiences at any great length in his autobiography, the influence he exerted made a deep and permanent mark upon the society he left behind.

Shortly after Mr. Home's departure, circles were formed in numerous families of distinction. Societies for the investigation of the phenomena were organized, in which many persons renowned for learning and literary attainments took part, whilst Mr. Home's friends and enemies both became entangled in journalistic controversies, which kept the subject constantly before the public. Meantime, reports of strange phenomena occurring spontaneously in different parts of the country, filled the columns of the journals, and continued to keep interest in the subject at fever heat. Within the very shadow of the Pontifical walls at Rome, a notorious case of bell ringing occurred which baffled all the efforts of the police to account for. When the law failed, priestly exorcism was tried and proved equally inefficacious. The annoyance ceased as mysteriously as it commenced, but was immediately succeeded by reports of unaccountable stone throwings occurring in three different parts of the city of Rome, and on the premises of persons, whose good standing in society, precluded all idea of deception or fraud. Whilst the public mind was being strongly exercised on these disturbances, whilst priestly exhortations were contributing to excite attention by imploring the people "to resist the wiles of Satan," and tidings were circulated of similar occurrences at Naples, Palermo, and Florence, a strong Spiritual impulse was given to the subject by the publication of a paper issued at Geneva by Dr. Pietro Gatti and Signor B. E. Manieri, entitled *Il Amore del Vero.*

In this journal the editors republished accounts of the Spiritual movement, as it was transpiring in America, France, and England.

As Dr. Gatti, the chief editor, was known to be a man of probity and sound sense, holding moreover the responsible position of director of the Homœopathic Hospital at Geneva, the immense flood of testimony that was disseminated through his journal, served materially to deepen public interest on the subject of Spiritual manifestations.

Against this tide of constantly increasing enthusiasm, the anathemas of the Church and the sneers of the press made no headway; in point of fact, the reiterated thunders of ecclesiasticism only served to awaken the people to a sense of its imbecility, and show the resistless strength of the power against which the clergy launched their impotent threats.

Those who have beheld with astonishment, the political battle for freedom waged so successfully on Italian soil, little know that some of the noblest soldiers in this grand patriotic warfare, were Spiritualists, and that it was from the communications of mighty and exalted Spirits, that such men as Victor Emmanuel, Garibaldi, and their compatriots, received some of their wisest and most encouraging counsels. It is now no longer a secret, that many eminent Italian reformers of the day were and are Spiritualists. When the eye of the soul shall behold no longer "as in a glass darkly" but face to face with actual truth, it will be seen, that the great lever of all the reforms that are agitating the social, political, and religious arenas of human thought, in the nineteenth century, has been Spiritualism, and that in its subtle but irresistible appeals to consciousness and reason, the age has moved forward centuries in advance of the past.

In the spring of 1863, a society was formed at Palermo, entitled *Il Societa Spiritista di Palermo.* The president was Signor J. V. Paleologo. Signor Paolo Morello, professor of history and philosophy, became with many others of equal standing, members of this society, and a regular organ, besides many publications of interest, were put forth under its auspices.

In March, 1864, the attention of the Genevese public was attracted to the case of a young girl residing in Hospital Street, who for several weeks was followed by the phenomena of loud poundings and stone throwing. The police were appealed to. The house was guarded within and without, and though the spectators who watched the girl's residence from the roofs of adjoining houses, could see the stones flying, and those within the dwelling were pelted with them, the agents were all invisible and never discovered. As is customary in such cases, the daily publication of the attendant circumstances, drew forth accounts of similar occurrences all over Italy. Dr. Gatti called attention in his journal to one phenomenon however, which we venture to allege accompanies nearly every well authenticated narrative of stone throwing, and that was *the total absence of any personal injury occurring from the missiles thrown.* "Whilst the stones were flying thickly in every direction," says Dr. Gatti, "no one was struck, although the said stones often fell within a few inches of the observers." The church may scream "Demoniac!" as long as it will. Let it point to any mob of human stone throwers who would be thus careful to avoid injury to their fellow mortals ; or any mortal ruffian who would not aim the stone for the express purpose of committing injury rather than avoiding it !

If this be so, and the histories of Spiritualism and humanity running in parallel lines clearly prove it, then let the Church graciously inform us which class best deserves the name of "demons," the Christian rioters who throw stones for the purpose of murder, or the Spirits whose only object is to compel attention to the fact of their existence? If the Church had only had a few facts, as tangible as the falling of a pebble, to prove its assertions instead of making assertions without a particle of fact to prove them, it would not require the inhabitants of the other world to offer such *striking* proofs of their continued existence, as stone throwing.

It was about the autumn of 1864, that lectures were first given on Spiritualistic subjects in Italy. They were started in Leghorn and Messina, and though of a very mixed character, and often partaking largely of the lecturer's peculiar idiosyncrasies on religious subjects, they served to draw attention to the upheaval of thought going on in all directions, in connection with the revelations from the Spirit world. It could not be expected that a movement so startling and unprecedented as that which opened up a direct communion between the natural and the Spiritual worlds could gain ground in public acceptance without waking up all the latent elements of enthusiasm, fanaticism, ignorance, and bigotry, which prevailed in the Italian as in every other community. In a word, Spiritualism seems to have acted like the summer sunbeam, stirring up malaria and fever from the fetid dust heap, and kindling into bloom and beauty the slumbering life of the blossom. "It is a hothouse process," says the author's most trusted Spirit guide, "which *creates nothing*, but quickens into abnormal activity the latent germs of all that is in humanity whether for good or evil."

In the year 1870, there had been over a hundred different societies formed, with varying success, in different parts of Italy. Two of the most prominent flourishing at that date were conducted in Naples, and according to the French journal, the *Revue Spirite*, represented the two opposing schools which have prevailed in Continental Spiritualism, namely, the "Reincarnationists" whom we have before classified as "Spiritists," and the "Immortalists," or those known in America and England merely as "Spiritualists."

About 1868, an immense impulse was communicated to the cause of Spiritualism—at least in the higher strata of Italian society—by the visit of

Mr. and Mrs. Guppy to Naples, at which place they took up their residence for two or three years.

Mrs. Guppy—*née* Miss Nichol—of London, was renowned throughout Europe for her marvellous powers as a "physical force Medium," and as Mr. Guppy's wealth and social standing enabled him to place his gifted wife's services at the command of the distinguished and princely visitors who crowded his *salons*, it soon became a matter of notoriety that the highest magnates of the land, including King Victor Emmanuel and many of his nearest friends and counsellors, had yielded conviction to the truth of the astounding phenomena exhibited through Mrs. Guppy's Mediumship.

It was about the year 1863, that Spiritualism began to enjoy the advantage of fair and honourable representation in the columns of a new paper entitled, the *Annali dello Spiritismo*, or "Annals of Spiritualism." This excellent journal—now in its twentieth or twenty-first year—was commenced at Turin, and published by Signor Niceforo Filalete, with all the liberality, energy, and talent worthy alike of the subject and its noble editor.

From the columns of the *Annali* we learn that a Venetian Society of Spiritualists, named "Atea," elected the illustrious General Giuseppe Garibaldi their honorary president, and received the following reply by telegraph from the distinguished hero, the liberator of Italy : "I gratefully accept the presidency of the Society Atea. Caprera, 23rd September."

The same issue of the *Annali* contains a verbatim report of "a grand discourse" given at Florence, by a distinguished literary gentleman, Signor Sebastiano Fenzi, in which the listeners were considerably astonished by a rehearsal of the many illustrious names of those who—in Europe—openly avowed their faith in Spiritualism.

The years 1863-4 appear to have been rich in Spiritualistic efforts. Besides a large number of minor associations, the existence of which was recorded from time to time in the early numbers of the *Annali* and *Revue Spirite*, a society which continued for a long time to exert a marked influence in promoting the study of occult forces and phenomena, was formed about this time in Florence, under the caption of "The Magnetic Society of Florence." The members of this association were without exception persons remarkable for literary and scientific attainments, or those of high influential position in society.

The following is a fair translation of the rules, &c., which were printed and circulated in all directions :—

"The object of the Society is to aid in the study and application of animal magnetism, and of all that is connected with it.

"The Society does not wish to occupy itself in persuading the incredulous, in exposing theories, or in polemical discussions. It only offers a *practical field* where each one may verify and produce for himself the well-known phenomena of magnetism, and apply them gratuitously to the moral and physical relief of mankind. Assembling without any ambition, and under the form of simple conversation, it will not have any permanent officer, excepting a general secretary to keep the minutes of the association, to direct the correspondence, and to receive subscriptions.

"The subscription will be two livres, Italian money, per month for each member, leaving him free to continue, to suspend, or to renew his subscription.

"In each week two meetings will be held, the first exclusively for the study and application of magnetism, the second for the study and development of so-called Spiritualism by the help of all that occurs in magnetism.

"Those who desire instruction in the practice of magnetism will have it under the direction of an experienced magnetizer.

"When they have acquired the necessary power to exercise it freely, a certificate to that effect will be given by a committee to be appointed for the purpose.

"All who wish for consultation, or to seek a cure by means of magnetism under the direction of a medical man chosen by themselves, will have gratuitous attendance. As soon as there shall be a sufficient number of members, the Society will be formed, and each will receive a letter of invitation for the first meeting.

"All demands for admission and for further information must be directed per letter, post free, to 'La Società Magnetica di Fiorenze.' May, 1863."

At this time there resided in Florence, a gentleman whose name was very familiar to the early investigators in Spiritualism, Mr. Seymour Kirkup. Mr. Kirkup's communications and records of phenomena, especially such as were frequently printed in the London *Spiritual Magazine*, will ever be remembered with interest and admiration.

Mr. Kirkup was a profound student of magnetism some years in advance of the Magnetic Society's formation at Florence, and as his experiences graphically delineate the gradations, from human to Spiritual magnetism, and the unfoldment of that higher clairvoyance, which quits the realms of earth to ascend into those of the life beyond, we shall give the reader the benefit of one of Mr. Kirkup's instructive papers, written for the London *Spiritual Magazine* in 1863. The writer says:—

"The following is my first perfect and convincing proof of the existence of spirits:—

"My medium had been about two months in training as a *somnambule*, when she was alarmed by a vision, although one very beautiful—the figure of a young child floating in the air. Her alarm was owing to its coming too close to her. Dr. Barzellini and Professor Verati, who were with me, and gave me instructions in magnetizing, drove it away by transverse passes and blowing. They said that such fantastic dreams would be injurious to her lucidity. This happened two or three times, but one day when they were not present, I asked her if it really could do harm, for I suspected that my professor's judgment might be less certain than her own, which had already begun to be very clairvoyant. She answered no, and on the contrary, it would be a great assistance, and as her fears had left her, I determined to encourage and assist the visits of this spirit, who declared himself to be her *angelo custode*—and so he proved. This was on the 27th of July, 1854. On the 5th of January the following year, Professor Puliti was present whilst she slept, making some experiments on her with galvanism; I asked him if he had heard of the rappings in America, and told him I was in doubt respecting some noises in my own house, and I related what had happened, as follows:—One day, while I was writing, Regina and her little sister came running in from the next room, where they were sitting at work: they were in the greatest alarm from a noise of blows against the door of an anteroom, which was closed, and they feared thieves were in the house. We opened the door, and examined every corner in the room, and the rest of the house, under all the furniture, inside closets, and even drawers, behind doors, &c.; nothing was discovered, and I tried to persuade them they were deceived, and that the noise was in the street, or some other part of the house. I did not succeed, and they remained positive. However, Regina was twice alarmed at her mother's house shortly afterwards. I told the professor all this; he said, 'Why do you not ask her and her spirit, now that she is in the magnetic sleep?' I told her to ask her guardian-spirit: she did so. '*Eccolo*, behold him,' he said. She declared that she saw a man—certainly a Florentine—she thought she knew his face, but could not recal him to her memory. 'Ask him his name.' No answer. 'Ask your angel.' He answered, 'Giuseppe.' The truth struck my mind, but not hers. I told her to ask his surname, as Giuseppe is so common. She did, and kept looking up intently; presently she burst into a flood of tears, throwing up her arms, as about the neck of the person she saw in the air. 'Oh, it is my father, my poor father!' She did not remember him at first. He had been murdered in the street six years before, when she was a child, and she thought him much changed and thinner. The crying brought on convulsions, and we wanted to send him away; she begged us not, but as he promised to return and the convulsions increased, I dismissed him. When she recovered I awoke her; she remembered nothing, and we did not tell her. The next day her spirit was accompanied by her father, whom she now knew, and saw without her former excessive grief. She asked him if it was he who had rapped at that door—'Yes'—and why? He wanted to speak to her. Why did he not? Because she was so frightened. 'Will you knock again if I am not alarmed?' 'Yes.' 'And in the presence of Seymour?' 'Yes.' 'When?' 'On Thursday.' 'And at what hour?' 'At the *Ave Maria*.' When she awoke I did not tell her of this, for fear she should mention it to the Italians, and in order not to alarm her at the idea of a ghost. Up to this time I had no belief in the existence of spirits.

Her visions might be mere dreams or imposture for what I could tell ; my own experience had reached nothing beyond witnessing the phenomena common to magnetism, very wonderful certainly, but not owing to the agency of spirits. I was curious to see whether her father would keep his promise to me, but I did not much expect it. I went into the room appointed, having *thoroughly* searched the room adjoining, and bolted every door, and so secured them all that no person could possibly enter. I was fully aware that any imperfect precaution made the experiment entirely useless. I asked her to come and sit down at a distance from the door at the other end of the room, which is very large, above 30 feet square ; I had a paper to make notes, and a candle, as it was getting dusk. I was placing it on the table near the door, expecting nothing at that moment, as I believed I was some minutes too soon, when I was startled by a tremendous blow on the door close to me ; it was as loud as a gun. Regina ran out of the room screaming. I followed her, and had the greatest difficulty in persuading her to return, which at last she did with me, but she cried with terror. I brought her to the dreaded door with safety, and we listened—she said, '*Sento gente*' (I hear people.) I told her to ask who was there—if her angel ?—no answer—if her father ? ' Yes.' 'Why did you knock ?' 'I wished you to hear me and to tell you something.' ' Can you tell me now ?' ' No.' I had told her what to ask, and she told me the answers. I heard the sound of his voice, but could not distinguish all the words, being partially deaf. . . . . The spirit gave her his message ; it was to tell her brother to treat their poor old mother with more respect and kindness, and to leave off swearing. He was a *mauvais sujet*, as bad as Regina was good. I afterwards had manifestations by hundreds. . . . . My Journal has been continued to the present day, and it now fills six volumes. Many prodigies have taken place in my house ; the spirits of four *living* persons have appeared. Some spirits have been seen by my mediums *awake* as well as asleep, and some by myself. But the most remarkable of these manifestations are the numerous *Apports*, as the French call them, which have taken place here—presents of all sorts, which we value highly, brought to us and preserved by us with care, and others which we gave in return—rings, lockets, &c., which have been carried away out of inaccessible, locked-up, and sealed rooms (only a window open), and brought back by appointment by the spirits. . . . .

" 1,309, Ponte Vecchio, Florence."   "SEYMOUR KIRKUP."

Mr. Kirkup's experiences were continued through many years and their publication was always a source of instruction as well as pleasure to his readers.

It is to be regretted however that our space forbids further reprints of his valuable contributions.

About ten years after the establishment of the Magnetic Society of Florence, another was formed in the same city, chiefly by the efforts of the Baron Guitera de Bozzi, an eminent and enthusiastic Spiritualist, who conducted the affairs of the society with zeal and energy until the period of his decease. This association bore the pretentious title of *The Pneumato-logical Psychological Academy of Florence.*

After the departure of the moving spirit for the higher life, the most strenuous efforts were made to maintain the "Academy" on its former flourishing basis, but though Signor Fenzi and many earnest Spiritualists exerted themselves to this effect, "the Florentine Academy" became a thing of the past, although as a *pièce de circonstance*, its actual value to the movement was timely and effective.

The following slight sketch of Spirit circles in Italy will be read with interest, first, because it may be taken as a representation of the mode in which the belief was propagated in private gatherings, and next because it displays in *its best form*, the cherished doctrine of the " Re-incarnationists," whose curious beliefs obtained much favour amongst those Continental " Spiritists," who could find little or no other literature in the French language, save the writings of Allan Kardec.

The sketch was written by the Reverend Thomas Colley, whose lucid and valuable contributions to the English Spiritual journals cannot be too gratefully acknowledged. Mr. Colley's paper is headed

"SPIRITUALISM IN ITALY.

"BY THE REV. THOMAS COLLEY, TEMPORARY CHAPLAIN AT NAPLES.

"Temporarily acting as English chaplain here at Naples, I have the pleasure of studying Continental Spiritualism through the kindness of Signor Damiani, at whose house weekly, and sometimes oftener, we meet the Baroness Cerrapica, a very gifted trance medium, with whom the Signor has, during the course of eight years, had upwards of seven hundred sittings.

"Our circle is a small one, but almost always includes a dignitary of the Roman Church, who, with our host, takes an active part in social converse with the invisible powers that speak through the Baroness. These are numerous beyond calculation, and as varied as they are many; and the linguistical endowments of the Signor, and the classical attainments of the Canon, are frequently in demand to put the circle intelligently *en rapport* with the mental identities that speak through the medium. Three of the domestics also of the Signor's household are mediums, and one, when present, sometimes clairvoyantly perceives, and in a whisper describes, the control that is about to manifest through the Baroness.

"One peculiarity about this lady's mediumship is, that the voices, mind, inner thought, and outer manner of persons yet living sometimes come through her—the dramatic creation to the life of persons she has never known.

"Another characteristic is, that unhappy spirits are suffered to take control, and state their miserable case; and then the Canon, leading them in prayer, directs their minds upward, so that they appear manifestly to progress, and after two or three devotional *séances* are marvellously changed.

"But controls of the highest order, sublime in look and manner, with sweetness and dignity combined, have the normal possession of our friend. Conversation with them is sweet indeed, and most instructive. The problems of this and the higher life are canvassed, and a record is kept of these voices from beyond (which I trust Signor Damiani will publish); the wisdom they convey is in diction perfect, and the language is such as Dante might have used or Cicero speak, if at any time re-incarnated.

"For I must not omit to notice that the doctrine of re-incarnation is upheld and taught here, by spirits *both in and out of the flesh.* The utmost unanimity prevails regarding this. The controls through the Baroness are sometimes astonished to see in the person of some living member of the circle the re-incarnated spirit of one who was perhaps their earth companion ages back. I have been greeted by classical speaking controls, now as a Roman warrior (Aniceto), and now as a Greek philosopher; and one of the controls was sorely puzzled a few weeks ago to see, in one of our company, the spirit of Aristides the Just still tangled up in parcels of fibrine, albumen, and phosphates, that have conspired to build up the body of our living friend; and when the question was put as to the need of one so just to be re-incarnated, the answer was, that though well-nigh morally perfect, yet intellectually it was to his benefit that he should thus return to earth once more, to see, investigate, apprehend, sift, and mentally develope those powers that should balance, with masculine reason, the more feminine qualities of his former virtues. But this question grows under my hand, and I must stop; for though it is a most interesting speculation that the re-incarnation of Elijah in St. John the Baptist should make us deal with patiently and modestly, yet as it is only a speculation (inasmuch as it lacks the physical demonstration which other phases of Spiritualism do not lack), I forbear.

"Since writing the above, and after our usual *séance* with the Baroness to-night, a remarkable matter transpired. Some short time ago, a rustic, patois-speaking spirit manifested through her, and gave the name of Zappacosta, saying that he had been a peasant living on the estate of a gentleman present at our circle, Baron de Riseis. The name Zappacosta is as strange and unusual in Italian as Hedgedigger would be in English (which, by the way, is its literal translation and meaning) and the Baron knew none of his dependents of such a name. But the circle was further astonished when the control declared that he had just been murdered by his own brother, at a place named on the Baron's estate near Chiete, and begged that our friend would write to ascertain the truth of his statement. Baron de Riseis did so, and this evening, just as our sitting was over, he came in with the answer received, giving an account of the sad occurrence, which was found to agree most exactly with what the control had affirmed, all being literally correct. Then, naturally full of the subject, as we were talking about it during supper, the medium was again suddenly controlled by the same power, and a request was preferred that intercession might be made to the authorities on behalf of his murderer, and our prayers also were asked on behalf of the murdered man. Saints Camillus and Urban were named as propitious and helpful to the control (suggestive to the thoughtful of how the creedal mind—in this case Roman Catholic—survives the dissolution of the mind's physical organism), and the Baron recognised these as the patron saints of the place where the man was killed. His estate is across country, about one hundred and twenty miles from here, and the circumstance could not, unconsciously or otherwise, in any way have been known to our friend the medium, the Baroness Cerrapica.

"THOMAS COLLEY.

"Casa Grifeo, Rione Amedeo, Naples, July 19th, 1877."

One of the most accomplished as well as earnest Spiritualists of the present day in Italy is Signor S. Fenzi, a gentleman whose scholarly communications and earnestness in the cause of human progress, have rendered his name as familiar and as much honoured by English and American Spiritualists as by those of Italian nationality. Besides this gentleman's reports, the author has received from a large number of private sources, records of interesting, but by no means *rare* phenomena occurring in various families of distinction in Italy. The strict charge accompanying these letters to withhold the real names, and publish initials only, renders them wholly unsuited to a work of the nature guaranteed to the world by the author.

A few noble gentlemen like Count Caprera, of Naples ; Signori Damiani and Sebastiano Fenzi; Count Ricardo of Rome, Viscount Solanot, and others of similar charcter and standing, hesitate not to avow the belief which they know to be divine truth.

Whatever motives may prevail to the contrary, those who recognize Spiritualism as the pearl of price for which they can afford to sacrifice all the world besides are the only witnesses whose testimony we consider worth acceptance.

One of the last accounts of an authentic character that we can offer to our readers, is contained in a letter from Count Santini, who relates many extraordinary things of a youth in whom he takes a great interest, named "Gino Fanciullacci," whom the Count designates as an extraordinary writing Medium. Two or three less enthusiastic but equally reliable correspondents of the *Revue Spirite* and London *Medium*, have also written of this young "psychic," and as their accounts are more in accordance with the plain statements essential to deliberate investigation we give them the preference in quotation.

"Senex," the London correspondent, writes thus :—

"I lately told you of a young Italian, a Florentine, named Gino Fanciullacci, who had written a long Dantesque poem in the sight of others, in broad daylight, 'without blotting out a line,' like Shakespeare with his plays, as Ben Jonson tells us. I have just got the book. In the commencement he makes the following 'Declaration to the Reader :— I cannot claim the paternity of this poem, although it was written by me. It was dictated to me by a spirit.—GINO FANCIULLACCI.'

"This book contains more than four hundred pages. It is written, not in blank verse, like Milton's great works, but in 'terza rima' or triplet rhyme throughout, like the works of Dante. I have had a letter from this wonderful young medium, who, in answer to my playfully telling him that he should not have told the world about the source of his poem, for that the world only likes inspiration at a distance, returns me the following well-deserved and pertinent rebuke :—

"'I beg you not to write of my ingenuousness in having announced the work as the product of a spirit, it was my duty to speak the truth, the judgment of others being of little importance to me whether favourable or unfavourable ; and besides imagine the ridicule that it might have brought upon me.'

"He tells me that he has 'written other works waiting to be published, obtained by the means of other medianity.'

"In the *Revue Spirite* for June, 1881, there was a critique on this poem by Signor Tremeschini, an Italian engineer and astronomer at the Pantheon in Paris. He says :—

" 'One half of this poem is golden, struck with the seal of Dante ; a quarter is silver ; an eighth is aluminium ; the other eighth is of clay. As a whole it is an immortal work. I defy contradiction.' "

The *Revue Spirite* gives the following in connection with this same Medium :—

"A young Florentine, Gino Fanciullacci, born of poor parents, and with no literary education, has lately written and published a volume in Dantesque metre, called 'A Pilgrimage in the Heavens.' He is employed in the shop of a French antiquary, who has become a Spiritualist through witnessing Fanciullacci writing day after day from twelve o'clock till half past one, this 'wonderful production,' as it is said to be, '*without ever altering a word ;*' because, as he declares, 'he simply writes down what he distinctly hears dictated to him.' According to literary men, this volume is excellent as regards capacity and power, and its prosody is irreproachable. It is well to remark that this young man is said to understand his own language well. Spirits prefer good tools.

"Strange to relate, the young sister of Gino Fanciullacci has lately proved herself, in another way, a medium of as wonderful capacity as her brother. This young girl, who has never played a bar of music in her life, was told by the spirits to seat herself at the piano ; and she then played and continues to play the most elaborate pieces of Beethoven, Mendelssohn, &c., with the mastery of a Thalberg or a Prudent."

Independent of the various groups of persons who—under the afflatus of the modern Spiritual movement—combine to form societies, which in truth represent various phases of thought on Spiritual subjects, rather than the direct teachings of the Spirits in the new dispensation, there are many persons who firmly believe that David Lazaretti, the enthusiast who appeared about ten years ago in Italy, and claimed to be a re-incarnation of Jesus Christ, was indeed a divinely inspired personage, commissioned to re-establish primitive Christianity all over the face of the earth.

The untimely death of this self-styled Messiah in 1879—he being shot in a collision with the Pontifical authorities—served to cool the faith of his adherents, especially as no one of sufficient power and influence to carry forward his mission, has arisen to succeed him. There are no doubt many features of psychological interest to be derived from a study of Lazaretti and his pretensions. Our space however forbids any further notice of the singular movement promulgated under Lazaretti's leadership.

For the last twenty years, the labours of Signor Niceforo Filalete, the indefatigable editor of the *Annali dello Spiritismo* of Turin, have been continued. The devotees of phenomenal Spiritualism may have been disappointed to find in his admirable pages but little to gratify their taste for the wonderful, but the scholars into whose hands his work has passed, have accepted with delight, the learned and philosophical articles with which those pages have been crowded, and which have contributed largely to liberalizing human thought and promote the noblest views of religion, science, and morality. Amongst the many profound and instructive contributions to the *Annali*, none has attracted more respectful attention than the series of articles by Viscount Solanot, on "Catholicism before Christ."

The extracts with which these writings abound, are taken from the Hindoo scriptures, together with an immense mass of Egyptian, Chaldaic, and other ancient traditional lore. The whole series, though by no means a novelty to the student of ancient religious history, is still a marvel of learning and fearlessness, proceeding as it does, from the priest-ridden centre of Catholicism, Italy.

Had the writer of the above-named articles entitled them *Christianity* "before Christ," they would have had a still deeper significance for those who in our time, dare to do their own religious thinking, and base their beliefs upon the authority of truth.

Much of the reading matter of the *Annali* is borrowed from the French, German, Spanish, American, and English Spiritual literature. It is none the less valuable however on that account, and independent of the scholarly articles above referred to, besides others of kindred character contributed by excellent writers, a complete file of the *Annali*, during its twenty years of vigorous life, would form a compendious history of the Spiritual movement.

The lack of any considerable amount of phenomenal record is due to other causes than the editor's unwillingness to print such details.

It must be remembered that there are few if any professional Mediums in Italy, and the manifestations which transpire at private circles, or such as arise spontaneously in the seclusion of the home, are deemed either too sacred or too personal to be paraded before the public. Spiritualism in Italy also, has made a deeper mark upon the higher classes of society than amongst the rank and file ; hence there are a sufficient number of reasons for the exclusion of such records from the columns which are supposed to be open to *vulgar* eyes, as well as to those of society's "upper crust."

Amongst the notices of phenomenal Spiritualism which have been mentioned in the *Annali*, the following excerpts may be considered as of a representative character. They are taken from a series of articles written by an esteemed correspondent of the Magazine, Signor Seffoni, and are entitled, *Vendetta D'Outre Tomba*, "Vengeance beyond the Tomb."

Signor Seffoni says :—

"In February, 1877, Sr. A. P., whom I did not know, came to me recommended by a friend, to ask my counsel and advice concerning a very serious affair in his family. He had two children—a daughter, Carlotta, between sixteen and seventeen years of age, and a son between thirteen and fourteen. His wife being dead, he let a part of his house to an elderly woman, a Marzia N., who was regarded as a neighbour. She was not an educated person, nor yet wholly ignorant, but frank and resolute, and had a certain faith in fortune-telling by playing-cards in respect of matrimony and the like. Though only hospitably received, she sought at once to have a legitimate title as godmother of the family, and there arose an unfriendly feeling between herself and Mdlle. Carlotta. It was finally necessary to turn Madame Marzia from the house. Not long after she sickened and died. Soon after, Carlotta, who had always possessed good health, became very nervous, and ere long had convulsive symptoms. There came great difficulty of breathing, and a feeling as if there was a quantity of hair in her throat. [The writer, here digressing, with an apology, refers to a similar case reported in the *Annali* of 1878, page 241, which had been confirmed to him by the attending physician. The narration appeared under this heading : *Obsession or Hysterics ?*] "Carlotta suffered unremittingly with this terrible sensation of hairs in the throat. Without mentioning to any one anything of this matter, I requested the father to come to my house on a certain evening, when I would have a *sonnambule* present whom I had known to have good and clear communications with the spirits of the departed. The somnambulist came with her magnetizer, and was put into a magnetic sleep. The hair, carefully wrapped up in paper, was placed in her hand, and she was asked to state what she held. 'Heavens ! . . hair ! . . but I cannot comprehend it.' 'Open the paper,' I said, 'and examine the contents attentively, and tell me of the person.' 'But . . . I do not understand. Not of a sick person, not of a man. . . . Oh, my God ! what is it ? Ah ! . . . this hair is not like other ; it comes from the mouth.' 'But of whom is the hair ?' I asked. 'It is of one dead, frankly. See.' She then went on and described the figure of Madame Marzia, and related the enmity that existed between her and Carlotta. The father recognized it all as correct. It seemed clearly a case of obsession. A purely moral course of treatment was recommended, and with care, and with good spiritual influences, a good result was anticipated."

In a still later issue of the *Annali*, Signor Seffoni gives the following additional particulars of the case above mentioned. He says :—

"Our readers will call to mind the young girl Carlotta, the victim of a malign influence, thrown over her by a wicked woman, lately deceased, who had been ejected from her (Carlotta's) father's house. At a *séance* at Sr. Scofini's, subsequent to the one reported, the young girl was invited to attend with her father, as there were to be present several mediums of no little experience and power.   Among the latter was Madame Maddalena Cartoni, who had performed some wonderful cures; and a young man named Luciano, who was greatly respected for gentleness and beauty of character.   During the evening Madame Maddalena essayed to bring under her influence Mademoiselle Carlotta, but produced only sighs or groans. Luciano evoked the perturbing spirit, but it manifested, when it came, only an evil disposition toward all present. A captain in the Roman army, a member of the Turin Society of Spiritualists, a man who had a special gift in ameliorating refractory spirits, took the matter in hand, and by showing the bad aspect of malevolence, by persuasive logic, by virtue of what is right, the efficacy of his reasoning (received at first spitefully), took effect little by little, till a yielding was manifest; still it seemed rather a confusion than a conviction.   In the meantime, a seeing medium, a member of the household of the proprietor, saw clearly the spirit of the malicious Marzia, and described her so exactly, every physical outline, that Carlotta's father confirmed the identity.   With this the *séance* closed.   At a subsequent *séance,* after the usual invocation, Marzia came, and through Luciano made a *voluntary confession.*   To the seeing medium she also presented a very different aspect from that borne at the first interview. Almost covered by a veil, she seemed dejected, mortified, and nearly weeping.   She asked pardon of the family which she had so greatly afflicted through the child, and with remorse of conscience begged the prayers of the sitters to obtain from Omnipotence the necessary force to keep her resolution to do no more evil."

Spiritualism in Italy at the present date presents less distinctive marks of general interest than evidences of an intention on the part of "the powers that be," in the Spirit world, to revive attention to the phenomena.   Accounts are often given of young peasant girls and people of the lower classes, manifesting those gifts of the Spirit that have been heretofore cultivated chiefly by more refined and educated personages.

The literature of the subject is less earnestly studied and phenomenal powers are more regarded.   In this, as in other countries, Spiritualism as a movement is unquestionably in a transitional stage, and whatever the next move on the great chessboard of divinely guided destiny may be, none can doubt, who attentively consider the signs of the times, that Spiritualism has effected for the consciences of the Italian people, what the illustrious Garibaldi has achieved for their political status.

And still the noble work of freedom has but as yet begun.   In the harvest day, when the fruits of true religious and political liberty shall be garnered up for the behoof of posterity, the Spirits of such heroes as Garibaldi, the Italian, and Abraham Lincoln, the American, will be recognized as having aided to finish the work of emancipation for the souls of men, which they began on earth for their material welfare.

CHAPTER XLIX.

SPIRITUALISM IN SPAIN.

WHILST—what our American cousins would denominate as—the *peculiar institutions* of Spain, render it impossible to record public meetings or public gatherings for the promotion of Spiritual progress in Spain—the historian of this volume has been favoured with minutes of a vast number of private circles, and evidences of a wide-spread interest on the subject of Spiritualism existing in nearly all the large centres of Spanish civilization. Without referring to the superstitious beliefs still prevailing amongst the peasantry and lower classes, in that relic of barbarism styled "witchcraft," with all its attendant circumstances of spells, enchantments, signs, tokens, &c., &c., it is enough to say, the people of Spain generally, cherish a broader faith in Spiritual verities than is taught in the "communion of saints," or other church dogmas. It is a remarkable fact also, that in a literary point of view few if any lands can excel Spain in the high tone and abundance of its Spiritualistic writings.

For causes that will become sufficiently apparent even in this brief notice, Spanish Spiritual literature is largely tinctured with the belligerent spirit called forth by clerical aggressions, but independent of this, few countries can boast of a finer *corps* of Spiritual journalists than Spain.

An esteemed writer in the *Religio Philosophical Journal* says on this subject :—

"The language that furnishes the largest number of periodicals devoted to the dissemination of the doctrine and philosophy of modern Spiritualism, is the Spanish. This statement will be somewhat surprising to many of our readers, for we have been accustomed to look upon the Spaniards as non-progressive and conservative in the extreme. Spain, until within a few years, has always been intolerant of any religions except the Roman Catholic, and was the latest of European nations to yield to the spirit of religious progress. Protestantism has with the greatest difficulty obtained a foothold in that country within the last few years, but it has been attended with annoying restrictions and persecutions, while its progress has been exceedingly slow and discouraging.

"The Hispano-American States have been but little behind the mother country in their lack of religious toleration. They have been liberal in everything else more than in matters of conscience, the Romish yoke having been too firmly pressed about their necks to yield to innovations of any sort. But within the last decade a great change has taken place, and in nothing is toleration more manifest than in the progress that Spiritualism has made among them. The religion of Spiritualism appeals more directly to the Spanish heart than does Protestantism, and hence its greater success. In the Spanish dominions and the Hispano-American Republics, there are no fewer than seventeen different spiritual publications, issued at stated intervals, in the Spanish language. There are five at least in the Republic of Mexico ; several in Spain ; one in Cuba ; one in each of the Republics of Peru, Chili, and Uruguay ; two in the Argentine Republic, and others in various Spanish speaking countries."

The above statement speaks within limit. On the author's desk at the present moment, lay specimens of twenty-five journals published in the Spanish language, and devoted to the exposition of Spiritualism. There may have been yet more, for several Spiritual periodicals have been imperiously suspended in Spanish-America by ecclesiastical authority, and at present copies of these ephemera are difficult to procure. We shall however have occasion to allude to them as we proceed.

Spiritualism in Spain commenced, as in many other lands, with a series of disturbances, which took place in a family residing in the outskirts of Cadiz. Stone throwing, bell ringing, and other preternatural annoyances were the first means of awakening attention to the subject, and as they occurred at the house of a Spanish gentleman who had just returned from the United States, full of the marvels of " the Rochester knockings," circles were at once formed, intelligent responses by rappings obtained, and a foothold gained, upon which the edifice of Spiritual progress was upreared. So rapidly did the interest thus awakened spread, that the first promulgators were soon lost sight of, and as early as 1854, a society was formed at Cadiz, which was organized for the sole purpose of publishing the communications received from " the Spirits," during two preceding years. A copy of the tract thus issued is now before us, but its manner and matter are so purely rudimental, that the translation would fail to interest any well-informed reader.

26

From 1854 to 1860, Spiritualism spread through the principal towns and villages of Spain in the usual fashion. Circles were held in private families, and an endless number of "societies" were formed and dissolved, according to the exigencies of the time.

One of the first public events of note in connection with Spanish Spiritualism, was of so remarkable a character, that it deserves special mention. This was no other than an *Auto-da-fe*, perpetrated under the auspices of that Church, so well qualified by centuries of experience to preside at such scenes. The only difference between the occasion under consideration and the fiery executions of olden times being, that the victims were formerly human beings, whereas, in the present instance, they were all the books, pamphlets, and works of a Spiritualistic character that could be procured at that period of the movement.

Amongst the pile thus offered up on the altar of religious *enlightenment*, were the writings of Kardec, Dufau, Grand, and Guldenstubbe; some copies of English and American Spiritual papers, and a large collection of tracts issued by the Spiritualists of Spain. This memorable scene occurred on the morning of the 9th of October, 1861, at the Esplanade, Barcelona.

The executioners were a couple of priests, with torches, crosses, and other "sacred" objects belonging to their occupation, a public scribe and clerk, and several of the city functionaries. The act was performed at the especial command of the Bishop, and an immense gathering of the populace stood around the blazing pile.

If the enactment of such a scene late in the nineteenth century may be regarded as one sign of the times in a religious point of view, it must not be forgotten that another sign was, the murmur of deep indignation that first disturbed the ominous silence of the assembled crowd, and finally broke into a roar of execrations and cries of "Away with the inquisitors," as the priests somewhat hastily gathered up their ecclesiastical paraphernalia, and disappeared from the scene more rapidly than they came. Whilst the pile was yet blazing, the mob began to scatter the burning wreck, and not a few of the bystanders gathered up shrivelled fragments to carry away with them in memory of the nineteenth century *Auto-da-fe.*

Judging by the results that followed, the chief actors in this remarkable scene might have been Mediums, and influenced directly by those powers who have the Spiritual movement in charge, so rapid and efficacious did it become as an instrument of propagandism. "What is Spiritualism?" "What have the Spiritualists done?" and "Where and how can we investigate the subject?" were the questions with which all Spain was ringing immediately after the act above described.

Amongst the well-known residents of Barcelona, was a Senor Navarez, whose daughter Rosa had for many years been the subject of frightful spasmodic attacks, called by the Catholic clergy "the obsession of demons" —by the medical faculty, an aggravated condition of epilepsy. Within two years after the *Auto-da-fe*, Madlle. Rosa was pronounced entirely cured, by the magnetic passes of a gentleman who was the Medium of a private circle held in the city. Shortly after this, Barcelona could boast of its well-approved Spiritual organs, numerous societies for investigation, and several Mediums, who from their exclusive position in private life, would object to their names being mentioned.

Up to the present date, two of the most progressive papers in the Spanish language are published in Barcelona. These are *La Lux del Porvenir* and *Revista de Estudios Psicologicos.*

The former paper—*La Lux*—is edited by Donna Amalia y Soler, an able and brilliant writer, who in addition to her arduous editorial labours, and the delivery of many fine orations on the subject of Spiritualism, has contributed with her tireless pen, elegant diction, and broad humanitary articles, to embellish as well as establish more than a score of the journals and magazines published in the Spanish language. Indeed, it is enough to mention Madame Soler's honoured name to call forth a note of admiration from every Spanish Spiritualist. *El Eco de la Verdad* is another well-written paper published at Barcelona. It will readily be perceived therefore that the Bishop's famous *Auto-da-fe* was so effective in *throwing light* upon the subject of Spiritualism, that it might be desirable to have a repetition of the scene in all the great centres of civilization.

About 1868, there appeared at Madrid, an excellent journal entitled *El Criterio (The Critic)*. At the present date, the editors dare to add a title deemed too dangerous to assume in its earlier issues, namely, *El Criterio Espiritista*. The journal was published by Senor Alcantara, and was warmly supported by the Viscount de Torres Solanot, and numbers of other leaders of science and literature in Spain.

By this publication the opponents of Spiritualism were amazed to learn of the immense progress the cause was making, and the number of distinguished persons who assembled nightly in circles to promote investigation. As an evidence of the enthusiastic spirit which pervaded the various "groups," into which the Spanish Spiritualists began to resolve themselves, we may call attention to the following circular issued by the Viscount Solanot in 1875. It is to the following effect, and was distributed broadcast through Europe in different languages :—

"The great International Exhibition of Philadelphia, 1876, calls together all the efforts made towards improving the physical, intellectual, and moral condition of man. Among these efforts there is none at the present day so powerful and efficient as that which Spiritualism offers, and for this reason we deem that we answer the call of duty in having Spiritualism there exhibited in all its Providential phases, for the enlightenment of the human race. And in order to ensure Spiritualism the due rank to which it aspires from the influence which it exercises in the world, the efforts and co-operation of all the Spiritualists of this planet are necessary.

"Stimulated by this idea, we take the liberty of calling your attention to this subject, sure that if we can realise our project, according to our conception, it will assist great and transcendent triumphs for the truth which we defend. . . . .

"The moment has arrived for forming ourselves into one group, so as to constitute with the unity of doctrine the unity of instruction. . . . .

"We should present to this generation, in order to improve and ameliorate life, our communications with the invisible world, full of hope for the future, full of bright promises for work, for virtue and for knowledge. We will exhibit our books, pamphlets, and journals ; urge the co-operation of all the great mediums and orators, and spread the light as it ought to be spread, lifting it aloft that all may see it. . . . .

"For the accomplishment of our object we have already addressed ourselves to the Spiritualists of Philadelphia, from whom all initiatory action should arise ; and we purpose calling upon all Spiritualist societies to second our proposal to march united to the great meeting to which we are summoned by the superior intelligences which from other spheres watch over the moral and intellectual progress of the planet we inhabit.

"The committee of the society appointed to promote the Spanish co-operation to the Spiritualist exhibition earnestly beseech the brothers of every country to receive this idea with enthusiasm, so that in our united strength we may present in Philadelphia the progress accomplished by the sublime and consoling doctrine which at the present day offers the most powerful impulse in the philosophical, intellectual, and moral improvement of humanity.

"Towards God, by Charity and by Science. Madrid, 31st March, 1875.—Viscount Torres-Solanot, Manuel Corchado, Dr. Huelbes Temprado, Guillermo Martorell, Daniel Suarez, Francisco Migueles, Pablo Gonzalvo, Sanchez Escribano, Eugenio Gouillaut, Jose Agramonte.

The generous and warm-hearted authors of this circular, met with no response worthy of their fraternal intentions. It might have been difficult to define exactly what the Spanish brethren proposed to do, or wished others to unite with them in doing; certain it is, that no tangible results could be expected to follow from a very transcendental address to the scattered ranks of a movement, whose motto might well be Liberty, Inequality, and Disintegration! "Our Spanish friends mean well, but is it possible there can be unity enough amongst them to send a delegation to America?" asked one of the shrewdest of Yankee Spiritualists on perusing this grandiloquent circular.

Nothing daunted by the impossibility of getting an International representation worthy of the cause at Philadelphia, the noble and energetic Viscount Solanot again agitated the subject previous to the Paris Exposition of 1878.

In the articles written for *El Criterio* on this proposition, the Viscount names amongst those societies of Spiritualists prepared to promote an International representation, "La Federation Espirita," of Belgium; "The British National Association of Spiritualists," England; "La Sociedad Central Espirita," of the Republic of Mexico; and "El Central General del Espiritismo," in Spain. Notice is also taken, and with a hope of its ultimate success, of the attempt to form a national association and unite all the discordant elements under the one broad banner of simple Spiritualism.

OF SPANISH MEDIUMS.

In Spain, as in Italy, a considerable amount of attention has been directed towards the unfoldment of Mediumistic power by means of Magnetism. Magnetic societies abounded in Spain up to within the last few years, when many elements of internal discord prevailed in the ranks, and succeeding in dissolving the bonds which had united flourishing associations. Amongst the amateur mesmerists of Spain may be mentioned Don Juan Escudero, of Madrid, a gentleman, who having witnessed some experiments in "animal magnetism" in California, resolved to try its effects in his own family.

On returning to Spain in 1870 from the United States, he found two little twin daughters of eight years old, suffering from what was pronounced to be diphtheria of a malignant and incurable type. Before the afflicted father allowed himself time to exchange greetings with the rest of the family, he commenced making magnetic passes over the little sufferers. The effect was almost electrical. Donna Isabella, their mother, at first deemed the children's hapless state had driven their father insane, but when she saw them sink into a peaceful slumber, fever subsiding, and ultimately every symptom of disease disappear, she became a convert to the efficacy of her husband's apostolic gift.

After the children's recovery, which was rapid and uninterrupted, the delighted parents agreed to hold circles on the approved American fashion. It was soon found that the two little girls were physical Mediums, and their little brother, a child of only five years old, was developed as a clairvoyant and seer of extraordinary lucidity.

Don Juan Escudero, writing to the author of the *séances* that transpired in his house, says :—

"Heaven has descended upon us. We have no more dead. All whom we have ever known and loved fill our house with tokens of their angelic presence. Their voices are heard rebuking our children when they are fractious; joining in our evening hymns;

bringing us fruit, flowers, and presents on our *fête* days and holidays, and by thousands of signals convincing us how near they are to us, and how constantly they watch, guard, and bless us. What is to others the *faith* of angel ministry is to us assured knowledge of angel presence.

This gentleman adds :—

"My dearest wife, who accuses herself of having been of a nervous, irritable temper, is now the most gentle and amiable of women. She says she must live for heaven upon earth, and so she will commence building up her heaven now. My children are veritable little saints under the counsels of their beloved guides,—and for myself,—all I can say is, if I am not a better man under the discipline of this angelic teaching,—I ought to be."

From a number of private circles held in different Spanish towns, the author has received immense files of communications, some given under trance conditions, some rapped out, or written through the planchette. All partake of high and elevated sentiments, although they are in general of too personal a character to interest others than the recipients.

Don Escudero mentions a man who supplied his family with vegetables, whose wife complained, that directly after the birth of her baby, she and the neighbours were continually disturbed with loud and incessant rappings.

Having heard marvellous reports of Senor Escudero's gift of healing, and finding the priest of the vicinity unable to quell the disturbances by virtue of holy water, the poor man, Miguel, solicited the good Senor's advice and assistance.

After calling on his gardener, and ascertaining for himself the preter-natural character of the knockings, Don Escudero and a few friends held a strictly private circle in Miguel's dwelling. On attempting to communi-cate with the knockings by the alphabet, the first sentence spelled out was a charge to bring "the sister babe" in her cradle, and place it upon the table. This was done, when the table rocked to and fro like a ship at sea, and the knockings spelled out, that the infant of six weeks old was the Medium ; that the communicating Spirit was a sailor boy, the child of Miguel by a first wife ; that he had been drowned at sea, and his principal object was, to inform his poor father, who had once been well off in the world, that his brother, a rich planter of Buenos Ayres, had died without a will, and his father must immediately put in his claim for the property, as the Church already held possession of it. Pending the legal steps which the astonished gardener proceeded to take in this matter, it may be stated that all the information thus conveyed was strictly true.

It seems however, that the family were so delighted at the working of the Spiritual telegraph through the new born babe, that they insisted upon continuing the circles night after night, even after they had been strictly enjoined by the Spirits to desist.

The result was, as the Spirits had warned them it would be, that the life principle of the little one became exhausted, and drawn off by the exercises of the eager investigators. The circles which would have been healthful and normal to an adult, well-developed Medium, nearly proved fatal to the growing infant. As the Spirits prophesied, the little Medium became a mere handful of skin and bones, and was obviously fast fading away. Don Escudero then took the case in hand ; commenced magnetizing the babe, and enforcing the commands of the sailor boy, to hold no more circles with "the sister babe." Senor Escudero concludes this little narra-tive by saying, "Marietta," the infant of this adventure, "is now a bonny girl of ten years old, and is playing with my little ones in the garden below my window. Her father has recovered a small part of his brother's property in Buenos Ayres, and very much against my advice, is contesting with the Church for the rest. For my part I would sooner trust to the truth and justice of our rapping Spirits, than to all the reverend fathers in Spain."

Amongst the numerous circles or "groups" formed in the different parts of Spain for the study of Spiritualism and its phenomena, is one of long standing at Tarragona called "*The Christian Circle.*" Quite recently the President of this circle sent the following communication to the *Revue Spirite* of Paris :—

"The convict prison here in Tarragona has 800 inmates sentenced to forced labour. By some means, Spiritualist books have been introduced among the prisoners. The circulation of these books among them has been the means of bringing seventy or eighty of them to be believers in our doctrine. These converts have ceased to regard their miserable position from their old point of view ; they no longer entertain schemes of revolt against the authorities. They endure their lot with resignation under the influence of the teaching that this world is but a preliminary stage to another, where, if repentant of the ill they have done, and seeking the good of others, they will be better off than here.

"Not long since one of these men died ; at his death he declined the established offices of the prison priest, on the ground that he was a Spiritualist and did not need them. The priest then discovered that Spiritualism was a subject of discussion with many of the prisoners. He made a representation of the matter to his bishop, who made formal complaint of it to the commandant of the prison, and the commandant made an investigation. In the end a particular prisoner was selected for punishment in the form of an additional weight of fetters. This coming to the knowledge of the Spiritualists of Tarragona, Barcelona, and Lerida, they had a meeting upon the subject and delegated one of their number, a man of position, to the commandant. The representations which he made, led the commandant to cancel his order as to the additional fetters. The bishop's censure against Spiritualist books placed them under prohibition, which was maintained. It is known, however, that although never found by gaolers, the books are still there.

"A communication has been written through the hand of a medium of the Circle of Christian Spiritualists of Tarragona by the Spirit of the prisoner whose death is mentioned above ; it is as follows :—

"'My Brethren,—Whatever your burdens may be they are light compared to those who suffer under the heavy penalties of the law : wearing fetters, enduring indescribable hardships and the brutalities of coarse and cruel gaolers ; heavy indeed are the burdens of those who have so violated Society's laws as to find themselves inmates of the galleys ! But is Society always equitable ? Does it not sometimes provoke men into criminality ? Does it not sometimes create the evils which it punishes men for doing ? And how many are there who, if equity ruled, would have similar sentences passed upon them ? They seem to escape being called on to pay their moral debts, but the time will come when they will have to do so.'

"Did I know the meaning of the word Love ? Towards my earthly end I learned through the works of Spiritualism to have charity for my enemies—aye, even to love them. Death released me after the new light had penetrated the darkness of the past. By this light I was warned, prepared, and now realise the truths of all it taught me. Brethren of the terrible fetters, have charity for your gaolers. When they would goad you to rebellion conquer them by charity if you can—if not, conquer yourselves. So will you help to plant goodness in humanity and raise for yourselves steps unto heaven. I pray you cherish ever the spirit of Love. Love is God.—Adieu !"

Such are some of the teachings that the Church dominant in Spain continues year by year to denounce with ever increasing bitterness. Complaints are often made that "Spiritualism is aggressive towards the Church." Had the church performed its duty towards Spiritualism, from its first appearance as a supra-mundane fact, Spiritualism would now be the CORNER STONE OF FACT, on which the Church would rest secure from all attacks.

At any rate, as the assumed pattern of all mental, moral, and religious graces, even Spiritualists have the right to look to the Church as its exemplar. Amongst the multitudinous examples which Catholicism in Spain sets to those whom it considers to be stray sheep from its own heavenly fold, the following article from one of the late numbers of the Turin journal, the *Annali dello Spiritismo*, will afford a startling specimen. The editor of the *Religio Philosophical Journal* gives the translation in an issue of 1882, as follows :—-

"In the *Annali dello Spiritismo* we find nothing of interest pertaining especially to Italy, but we make an extract relating to matters in Spain, where spiritual and liberal papers are objects of great displeasure to the Bishops, and which have had the following anathema thundered against their devoted heads :—

"'The Bishop of Santander has demonstrated that in Spain one may go a little too far in the expression of liberal sentiments, and has launched forth an excommunication against all the liberal journals of his diocese, the literal text of which is this : "May God omnipotent and all the saints curse them with eternal maledictions, and may they be hurled to the devil and his angels ; may they be damned with Judas the traitor and with Julian the apostate ; may the Lord judge them as Dathan and Abiram were judged, and may they be swallowed up alive in the earth ; may the few days of their existence be miserable ; may they succumb to the horrors of famine, thirst, nakedness, and all sorts of evils ; may they suffer want, degrading infirmities, and every species of torment ; may everything they possess be accursed ; may they enjoy no blessing nor be benefited by any prayer, and may these rather be turned into curses ; may they be cursed in sleeping or in waking, cursed in fasting, eating, and drinking ; cursed in speaking, and in keeping silence ; cursed in doors and out of doors ; cursed upon the land and upon the water ; cursed from the crown of their heads to the soles of their feet ; may their eyes be blind and their ears deaf ; may their mouths become mute and their tongues cleave to their jaws ; may their hands be palsied and their feet unable to walk ; may all the members of their bodies be accursed ; may they be accursed while standing up or lying down ; may they be cursed from to-day to all eternity ; in the final day of judgment may their light be extinguished before the Lord ; may their sepulture be that of the dogs and asses ; may their corpses be devoured by ravenous wolves ; and may their eternal companionship be that of the devil and his angels."'"

No comments are offered, none are needed we presume on the language of this extract. It is enough to ask, what can we expect from a community whose religious teachers are represented in the above-quoted language ?

How different are the utterances of the poor prisoner's enfranchised Spirit given above ! How different the following quotation from the Madrid paper *El Criterio*, in an article from Senor M. Gonzales on true religion ! He says :—

"Religion was born with man, and man was born with religion . . . That religion ought to be the love of all that is beautiful, good and harmonious—thus approaching God, the author of all good. . . . Religion demands a clean heart, but here on earth it seems that nearly every heart is as black as a coal. It requires a tranquil conscience ; but on this globe, in almost every conscience there is a desolating tempest. It requires an immense love ; but here we can but barely tolerate each other."

Commenting too on the ceaseless war directed by the clergy against the Spiritualists, Madme. Soler writes in her delightful Barcelona paper of what Spain has been and might now be, telling us of what Spain has done for the world, of her ancient splendour, power, learning, but now of her degeneracy, attributable to priestcraft—page after page, in fact, that must stir to their very depths the hearts of all Spain's children not dead, not too deeply steeped in ignorance and bigotry.

Meantime the work progressed bravely under all the opposition brought to bear upon it. In April, 1881, the editor of the Madrid *El Criterio* says :—

"That great progress has been made in Madrid in the cause of Spiritualism ; that the hall of meeting of the Spiritual Society ' is completely full every Thursday evening,' and is not now large enough ' to hold the public who come to the sessions ' ; that Dr. Merschejewski has called the attention of the University of St. Petersburg to a psychometric phenomenon of much importance ; to wit : A young man, deemed from childhood to be an idiot, who will in some seconds solve any mathematical problem, while if a poem be read to him, even of many hundred verses, he will repeat the whole of it without failing in a single word."

Senor Manuel Lopez in the same issue of *El Criterio* says, speaking of the progress of a society of Spiritualists in Madrid :—

"We have received a mediumistic work of extraordinary merit, executed by a medium of the 'Society of Spiritualists' of Zaragoza. It consists of a portrait of Isabel the Catholic, made with a pencil, and is a work truly admirable. It is said by intelligent persons who have examined it to be an exact copy of one preserved in the Royal Museum of Painters of this Court. Many thanks are tendered to the Zaragozan Society for this highly appreciated present.

"From Corunna is announced the formation of a new spiritualistic association.

"Under the title of ' Nicodemo,' Don José Amigo has published a work that is destined to do a great deal of good to the cause of Spiritualism."

It was about the end of the year 1880, that the Spiritualists of Spain sustained another series of attacks from the Church of a highly characteristic nature.

The first of these was the refusal of the clergy to accord the customary rites of interment to the remains of two ladies, both of irreproachable character, and good standing in society, but both guilty of the crying iniquity of having believed in Spiritual manifestations.

The honoured form of one of these ladies had to be carried back to the dwelling of her distracted husband, and await such concessions as could be made, before the Church's vengeance against the silent dead could be appeased. From Alcoy, Seville, Ubeda, and numbers of other places came letters of condolence with the bereaved families whose feelings had been thus outraged, whilst indignant protests of citizens from all quarters were made against what was considered to be a violation alike of decency, humanity, and the noble principles of religion. Of course the Spiritualists did not fail to make good use of this case, and shocked as they were at the pain and insult inflicted upon the survivors, they improved the occasion to call attention to the character of the sacerdotal institutions, to whom the people entrusted their eternal welfare, besides urging forward the demand for civil jurisdiction in the matter of interment, or the still more satisfactory way of disposing of decaying mortality by cremation.

Dr. Ditson, in reporting the remarks of the different Spanish Spiritual papers on this subject, gives the following comments on Donna Soler's article in *El Criterio*. He says :—

"*El Criterio Espiritista* of Madrid contains several contributions of much interest and importance. Mme. Domingo y Soler's caustic pen revels here in another attack upon the Church for assuming the right to consecrate certain parts of God's earth and hold the power to exclude from it certain dead bodies—making in one specified instance a cruel assault upon a family by obliging it to retransport to its old home a decaying form and keep it there for days ; hence the necessity of civil interments, a subject which she illustrates with power. The dignity, beauty, and pathos which breathe through all Mme. S.'s paragraphs are something admirable. A Bishop of Barcelona (to whom she refers) addressing the clergy and urging them to ' arrest the current of civilization that like an impetuous torrent penetrates every portion of the earth,' adds : ' It is one of the true traditions which is in the consciences of generations that the cadavers are a property of the Church'; or, strictly rendered, ' a *propriedad de la religion*.' ' Yes,' replies

Mme. S., ' you are very reasonable, Sir Bishop ; the religions are the cadavers of the ages, and it is just that the bodies of the defunct should have the same resting-place.' Further on among other articles of interest is one on ' Civil Interments.' It was written because another worthy citizen had been refused sepulture in a Catholic burying-ground, on account of his advocacy of Spiritualism. Mme. Soler then takes occasion to describe what she saw and heard on the 18th of May last at a grave where Don Miguel Vives pronounced a memorable and fitting discourse. It being on a holiday many citizens came out of an idle curiosity ; but it seems that the sound words of the orator were largely approved— he 'demonstrating the *conveniencia* of civil interments, for it was now an era when humanity was shaking off the yoke of the religions of the past and adopting a rational faith. He explained that Spiritualism was a school of philosophy *racionalista*, demonstrating to man that only by his good works would he be saved.' . . . And these cemeteries the authoress regards as only to be required for a short time more, for cremation with its sanitary issues is to make them tenantless."

The second raid which the Church in Spain perpetrated about this time to the prejudice of the Spiritualists, was the suppression of a well-written Spiritual paper published at Lerida, entitled *El Buen Sentido*. The Bishop of Lerida had long threatened this step, and warned the fearless editor to beware how he presumed to allow any writings reflecting upon clerical doings to appear in his columns. As some of the principal contributors were Madame Soler, Mdlle. Sans, Don Murillo, and others equally capable of arraigning the intolerant acts which Church policy seemed determined to push against the Spiritualists, it was scarcely likely that the Bishop's threats would produce much effect, or induce *El Buen Sentido's* contributors to pronounce the black doings of the clergy to be white.

The last article which seemed to inflame the oppressors to retaliate was an indignant protest which appeared in the columns of this paper on the condemnation of a working man to three years' imprisonment, leaving a family of children destitute, and all for speaking in public against the intolerance of the Church.

This was enough. To arraign the Church was to deserve the moral death which the time permitted, in lieu of the physical death which only two centuries before, would have certainly ensued, and so *El Buen Sentido* was put to ecclesiastical torture and death. In a fine article written on this subject by the editor of *El Espiritista* of Zaragoza it is said :—

" Some ten years since the respectable head of a family visited Barcelona, where he became convinced of the realities of our faith. On his return he called his family (all of age) together, and told them of the rapid spread of Spiritualism in the aforesaid capital since the *auto da fe*, made by the order of a bishop, of the works of Allan Kardec. . . . And, as has been expressed by the spirit of Marietta, in her immortal book written in Zaragoza, the thoughts that arose from these flames have been spread by the winds over the earth. . . . and thus little by little an air will be created in which all can freely breathe. . . . In the family above referred to were developed several mediums, and all became enthusiastic Spiritualists."

As an evidence that the tactics of the clergy of all denominations, and in all countries, are ever the same, when their craft is in danger, the reader may see in the following extract from a Madrid secular paper how the cry of the American and English clergy, to the effect, "that Spiritualism is all the work of Satan and his imps " is either borrowed from, or repeated by, the clerical *savants* of Spain. *El Criterio*, the journal in question, says :—

" Spiritualism is true enough ; but its facts all proceed from a class of fallen reprobate spirits, who try by every seductive art to alienate Christians from their church, and thus eternally to destroy their souls. In our day, these devils assume the names and personalities of our dearest friends, and by working upon the minds of educated and intelligent converts, thus effectually seek the destruction of nations as well as individuals. Like atheism, Spiritualism leads directly to hell, and mere attendance at a *séance* is a mortal sin."

The editor of the Spiritual *El Criterio*, after a most pungent review of this stuff, says :—

"In Madrid they have put upon the stage (at the theatre Variedades) a play called 'Arturo, the Spiritualist.' This, like several that were presented last year at the minor theatres under the title of 'The Spirits,' and 'The Spirit Lover,' are of course simply to ridicule our cause ; but they in reality aid it wonderfully, for only something of moment is worth such effort."

In the same number of *El Criterio*, dated 1881, is a letter from Don Migueles, in which he gives a somewhat discouraging account of "the cause" as it recently existed in Spain. The editor says :—

"Don Migueles visited many cities to examine into the state of affairs of a spiritual nature, but found many who were only to be enticed by physical phenomena, caring nothing for the esoteric beauties of our faith ; many who were convinced that they knew all there was to be known concerning it, and others who were timid, fearing the dis-approval of neighbours. In some places, however, excellent mediums were discovered. In Santiago, in Oviedo, in Corunna and Valladolid, an exceptional interest was manifest. Near Santiago there was a young girl possessed of wonderful faculties. Two bars of magnetized iron held over her horizontally, half a metre distant, were sufficient to suspend her body in the air.

"The proceedings of the Spanish Society, under the name of the *sesiones de Controversio*, in the month of April last, are spoken of in the *Critic* as markedly impressive on account of the lofty sentiments maintained throughout the discussions, by the various speakers. 'In the past month were given also very interesting *conferencias* by our illustrious brothers, the Sres. Rebolledo and Huelbes.' The able engineer and inventor, belonging to the Society of Santiago de Chili and founder of that of Lima, D. R. Caruana y Berard, has just arrived in Madrid. The *Revista Espiritista* of Barcelona mentions the visit which its editor has made to the central societies of Spiritualists of Sabodell and Tarrasa, where 'a great number of brethren were assembled on the occasion, and which will result in great good to the doctrine.'"

The Barcelona *Lux*, of date 1881, gives encouraging accounts of *séances* held at Cordova, Tarragona, Seville, and many other places. The editor, Madame Soler, also refers to the prohibition to Catholics, by an archbishop to have or to read the Spiritualistic work of Niram Aliv ; of the "Society of Spiritualists" of Tarrasa ; of the circle of Santa Cruz of Tenerif ; of that of "Faith, Hope, and Charity," of Andujar, and of St. Vincent de Bogota. Here is also a brief statement of the intimacy that existed between the widow of Baron Van de Weyer (daughter of the late Mr. Bates of the firm of Baring and Co.) and the Queen Victoria. Lady Van de Weyer lived in a magnificent chateau near Windsor Castle, and it is said that no day passed in which Lady de W. and the Queen were not together ; that, as they both believed in Spiritualism, they counselled each with their respective departed husbands.

The editor also gives extracts from a new Spiritual catechism which has been published by one of the circles in Barcelona entitled *El Progresso Moral*.

Spiritualism in the States of Spanish-America has already been touched upon in a former chapter. No new features of interest have altered the status of "the cause" in South America. Two or three of the journals published in the interest of Spiritualism have been obliged to surrender to the clerical ban. The brave editors of the *Buenos Ayres Constancia* still hold their own, and tidings come from Caraccas, Venezuela, Mexico, and many other places that the organs of the faith still live, and Mediumistic power is rapidly on the increase.

Considering the large share of popular attention bestowed by the European and American nations upon their recent visitor, his Majesty of Brazil, Dom Pedro de Alcantara, and more especially bearing in mind the reputation generally accorded to that illustrious personage for liberality of sentiment and enlightenment of mind, the reader may peruse with some interest and not a little surprise, the following report of a scene which occurred as late as the spring of 1882, the particulars of which were translated into English for the columns of the *Religio Philosophical Journal* of Chicago, and read as follows :—

"The *Academic Society* of Spiritualists holding session in Brazil, have lately suffered much persecution at the hands of the Brazilian authorities. By a public mandate, the society and all branches thereof, were forbidden to hold any more meetings from and after the date of the ordinance, on pain of chastisement. Recourse was had to his majesty, the Emperor Dom Pedro de Alcantara, with whom the following short dialogue took place, one of the commissioners detailed by the society acting as spokesman :—

'Speaker.—The management of the Sociedade Academica beg leave to place in your hands this exposition, corroborated by the numbers of their organ, the *Revista*, which have been published up to to-day, desiring the wise counsel of your majesty.

'Emperor. I do not believe in Spiritism ; I am in accord with the ideas of the Councillor of State.

'Speaker.—We are convinced that your majesty will protect the Academic Society which is suffering persecution on account of its investigation of Spiritism.

'Emperor.—I do not consent to any persecution, but I only protect the ideas with which I sympathise.

'Speaker.—We ask your majesty's protection by causing to be recognised and respected the right of investigation which belongs to us.

'Emperor.—You have the right, gentlemen, to investigate everything ; but I would advise you to investigate something else [than Spiritism].

'Speaker.—We do investigate everything, including even the Constitution of the Empire.'

"Other conversation ensued between his majesty and different members of the committee, and the conference terminated—the former promising to read the 'exposition,' and the latter that after fifteen days they would return to receive the Emperor's 'wise counsel.' At the end of fifteen days the delegation from the society again sought the presence of his majesty, when the following conversation occurred :—

'Speaker.—Sire, we come to receive the wise counsel which we had the honour of soliciting from your imperial majesty in behalf of our rights.

'Emperor.—Seek the Minister of the Empire and have an understanding with him.

'Speaker.—Among the petitions which we have addressed to the government demanding the guarantees which the law concedes to us, some have been treated with indifference and others have received but slow attention ; and now, as some days since we came to consult with your majesty, the Chief of Police judged himself authorised to impose upon us a suspension of our labours. Until then the persecution was dissembled ; but it has now become manifest, and violence has been employed against an association which is beneficent and orderly as all its acts will prove.

'Emperor.—But what is it that the gentlemen desire ? Do they wish the approbation of the statutes ? I agree with the idea of the *Parecer* (some ordinance or legal opinion).

'Speaker.—Your majesty will pardon us, but we have demonstrated in the *Revista*, a collection of which accompanied the representation, that we had the honour of handing to your majesty, that that *Parecer* is not applicable to this society ; and we only ask the approbation of the statutes. . . . The right of re-union is guaranteed to us as a scientific society by the law of December 19th, 1860, which regulates scientific and literary societies.

'Emperor.—But spiritism is not a science.

'Speaker.—We beg that your majesty consider that all the phenomena of the universe being susceptible of observation, and scientific analysis, are facts, and the spirit phenomena, although qualified as metaphysical and supernatural, are none the less facts, and being submitted to investigation by the experimental method, lead us to a knowledge of the laws which govern them, and that constitutes spiritual science.

'Emperor.—Oh! yes, in that way, but it is better to occupy your time with other studies.

'Speaker.—We come to ask your majesty, zealous of the prerogatives of your subjects and the first to give an example of obedience to the law, that you protect us against persecution.

'Emperor.—Nobody shall persecute you, but—you do not wish to be martyrs now.

'Speaker.—We believe that in this enlightened century there is no room for martyrdom. We have no desire to pose as martyrs, but we ask and demand tolerance in accordance with the provisions of the decree 2711.

'Emperor.—The Minister of the Empire is in possession of your papers which I sent him. He will give a solution.'

"The commission took leave of his majesty, convinced that they would have to appeal to the legislative body to have the rights of Brazilian Spiritualists recognized. By this conversation they were satisfied that the Emperor is opposed to Spiritism, and if so, that he will, perhaps, wish to embarrass the progress of the Sociedade Academica, 'but we do not suppose he will do it openly,' says the editor of the *Revista*, 'for by declaring himself frankly against us he will turn over to our camp not only all who are averse to imperialism, but besides all the malcontents of every sort.

"The *Revista* will continue to be published, and by some provision of the law, meetings of the Society and its branches will continue to be held provided no more than twenty persons assemble in one place."

The editor of the Chicago journal containing this report adds in conclusion :—

"The Spiritists of Brazil may be assured of the sympathy of 20,000,000 of Spiritualists in the United States and of all the other millions scattered over the whole globe, upon whom the sun never sets. Dom Pedro will come to his senses one of these days and see the error of his ways. The obstacles in the way of spiritual progress are only apparent, and the advance of the cause will prove to have been all the greater in the end."

To this conclusion there are but few of our readers who will not cordially say Amen !

As a closing salute, and to show that the unhappy warfare waged by the clergy and the Spiritualists of Spain, proceeds from the very source in which Spiritualism *should have found* its warmest friends and supporters, we give a paragraph which has now—in 1883—been going the round of most of the European Spiritual journals. It is as follows :—

"*El Iris de Paz*, of Huesca, March 25th, 'supplement.' This little sheet is nearly all taken up with the document (and response) of the Bishop of Huesca, which is a 'fulmination of excommunication pronounced against all Spiritualists and all subscribers to and readers of spiritualistic papers.'"

"Whom the Gods would destroy they first make mad," says the classic proverb. If that be true, then may the *mad* fury of the Spanish Catholic clergy be considered as *truly divine.*

CHAPTER L.

SPIRITUALISM IN EUROPE (CONCLUDED.)

AUSTRIA, BELGIUM, AND TURKEY.

SPIRITUALISM IN AUSTRIA.

[Written expressly for " Nineteenth Century Miracles " by the Baroness Adelma Von Vay.]

WHEN "American Spirit rapping, and table turning" was first talked of in Austria, we also commenced to experiment.   Everybody tried it.

I was at that time a mere child, but I remember well how splendidly we children could make the table dance ; also, that my help was always required to produce this manifestation.   On one occasion during the table turning I was seized with a swoon, after which the practice was forbidden in my parents' house.

I had a cousin who was a wonderful "Medium."   She wrote with a small table, the fourth leg of which was a pencil (Planchette).

The table would write the contents of sealed letters correctly; discover thefts, and gave the best possible tests.   That young lady was endowed with so much magnetic force that the piano, a heavy dining table, or other large bodies, would move, by her simply touching them with one finger.

In her presence also Spirit forms and lights were seen—still neither she nor her family knew anything about Spiritualism.

After my cousin married, she conceived an aversion to Spiritual manifestations, and when still later, I urged her to read Allan Kardec's writings she declared such studies always made her faint.

In Austria, Spiritualism was first promulgated by M. Constantine Delby of Vienna.   He was a warm adherent of Allan Kardec's, and founded a society under legal auspices, besides starting a Spiritual journal.   The society numbered but few members, in fact Spiritualism never obtained much foothold in Vienna.   At Buda-Pesth it was quite otherwise.

About 1867, there resided in Buda-Pesth a poor woman who had a daughter who was evidently a fine trance Medium.   This girl, when about thirteen years of age, would fall into trances spontaneously, during which she would speak eloquently, and converse on many subjects most wonderfully.   About this time, too, a woman who had resided many years in America returned to Buda-Pesth, and hearing of the young trance Medium, called upon her.   "The American," as she was called, was only in humble circumstances, but she had seen much of Spiritualism, and subscribed to the *Banner of Light* from her small earnings, as a teacher of English. Obscure as these beginnings were, they soon attracted a large number of observers.   Many people went to hear the somnambule, and talk with " the American" about Spiritualism.

In a short time a considerable amount of interest was awakened, and many persons of note began to take part in the circles that were being formed, amongst these were Mr. Anton Prohasker, and Dr. Adolf Grünhut, who was a friend of ours and had become an ardent Spiritist through my influence.

At length a society was formed, legalized by the State, of which my husband, Baron Edmund Vay, was elected president.

Mr. Lishner, of Pesth, built a handsome *séance* room which the society rented. At the present time, we have one hundred and ten members, many of them being Hebrews, though all are believers in Jesus Christ, and better Christians than many other so-called, and professing to be Christians. My husband, Baron Vay, is now the honorary president, Dr. Grünhut is the active president, and these together with myself and Mr. Prohasker were amongst the most devoted and faithful workers.

The principles of the society, indeed the basis of it are—*Geist Kraft Stoff* (Baroness Adelma Von Vay) and the works of Allan Kardec—purely Christian Spiritism. We never encouraged paid Mediumship—nobody takes a fee in our society. All the officers are voluntary and honorary. We have no physical Medium, but good trance, writing and seeing Mediums, and a spirit of true Christian charity and love binds our members together. We lost our dear good worker the excellent Mr. Prohasker in 1879—a great loss indeed it was to our society. The earnest mind and noble spirit of Dr. Grünhut and his indefatigable labours for truth and progress are deserving of all praise.

In my book, "Studien über die Geisterwelt," I related how I myself became aware of my Mediumistic powers.

I had been married some years and was an ardent, and I believe a pious Catholic, when Dr. Grünhut, who was a great mesmerist, came to our house. He told me that he saw the word *seership* imprinted on my brow, and urged me to sit for automatic writing. At first I refused, but after a time curiosity prompted me to try the experiment. Immediately my arm was shaken by a strange force, after which I began to write automatically some wonderful information which was soon verified. As my husband and mother-in-law were deeply interested I tried again, all the while knowing nothing about Spiritism. It was "the saints" who wrote. They told me about the doctrine of Re-incarnation, and wrote homœopathic prescriptions for the poor and suffering, I, at that time, knowing nothing of homœopathy. Very soon my husband and I became the medical attendants of all the people around, mesmerizing and curing them with the aid of homœopathy. The Church remonstrated, but we would not discontinue our practice. Whilst we were living on our estate in Hungary, I was called on by a Mr. Piko who presented me with a copy of Kardec's "Livre des Esprits." Soon after that, I began taking the *Banner of Light*. My first publication was a prayer-book "Betracht für Alle," then came "Geist Kraft Stoff;" "Studien über die Geisterwelt;" "Visionen im Wasserglas;" "Eugählungen des Ewigem Mütterlains;" and now "Tagebuch eines Kleinem Mädchens."

Conjointly with two other Mediums I published "The Four Evangels— An Explanation by the Spirits." Its title "Reformirende Blätter," published by Waigner, Boulvard 21, Buda-Pesth.

After the publication of my books, the Catholic priests would no longer give me absolution. They pronounced me a heretic, and would excommunicate me, upon which, I forthwith became a Protestant, the faith of my mother, husband, and his family; his Excellency the Baron Nicholas Von Vay, being the head of the Calvinist Church in Hungary.

This is but a brief account of Spiritualism in Austria and Hungary.

———

The many readers of the Spiritual journals in America and Europe who have become familiar with articles or quotations from the writings of the Baroness Adelma Von Vay—read and been struck with their purity of tone and exalted religious spirit, however much they may disagree with the amiable and devoted lady, in minor points—will take no exception to the publication of her simple sketch with scarcely any alteration of the diction. The firmness and consistency with which a person in her position, with her education and surroundings, yielded to her honest convictions, and despite the ban of the Church she had been taught to reverence, faithfully gave to the world the published results of her newly-born faith, are circumstances which can only be fully appreciated by those who can or will— " put themselves in her place."

As the Baroness's modesty prevents her from dwelling upon one feature of her life which in itself would be more than sufficient to atone for any diversities of opinion on doctrine or theoretical beliefs, we supplement her little sketch with a brief extract, the nature and authorship of which speaks for itself.   It is as follows :—

"THE BARONESS ADELMA VON VAY A HEALING MEDIUM.

" Our daily programme, although always diversified, was made up of riding, driving, walking, paying visits, entertaining, and last, but not least, for the Baroness is a veritable humanitarian, comforting the afflicted and distressed.

" The peasant population maintain an implacable faith in her power to alleviate pain. From far and near, they bring their sick for her tender ministration ; and, in her boudoir, I found many an offering in token of some great good she had done, some rich blessing she had wrought for those who, if poor in purse, were rich in gratitude towards their noble benefactress.

" It was touching to see this beautiful, high-born lady, tending some poor unfortunate creature, bent and racked with pain.   It was gratifying, too, to remark the growing light come into the hollow, sunken eyes, as they followed each movement of their 'Frau Gräfin,' whilst busy preparing that which would bring relief to the sufferer.   Besides this, the Baroness's bright face is ever a welcome sight in all the homesteads of the poorest and lowliest in the district, and many lips breathe blessings upon her for her goodness and generosity.—*My Visit to Styria*, by CAROLINE CORNER."

SPIRITUALISM IN BELGIUM.

Spiritualism in Belgium seems to have proceeded from much the same cause, and moved onward under the same impulses as those which have been already noticed in other European countries.

Being chiefly under Catholic domination, the Spiritualists of Belgium have had to contend incessantly against the antagonism of that persecuting sect.   Still much progress has been made, and systematic investigation has been carried on very faithfully, whilst the literature of the subject, both in quantity and quality, may be considered as on a par with that of any other country.

M. Jobard, director of the *Musée de l'Industrie* at Brussels, whose name is honourably known to all European Spiritualists, has for many years past exerted himself indefatigably both as a writer and personal propagandist, in the cause of Spiritualism. In the early days of the movement, Mesmerism was largely practised in Belgium, and by many it was regarded as a stepping stone to Spiritualism, and a more reliable mode of obtaining occult knowledge, than through the invocatory processes of the Spirit circle.   Our readers will doubtless remember the case of "Louise Lateau," the so-called "ecstatic," a young girl in the humblest ranks of life, upon whose person, periodical representations of the *stigmata* were found to appear.   As this was the first notorious case of the kind that was known in Belgium, and the clergy were of opinion that it was in order, to call the manifestation *a miracle*, and attribute its occurrence to the interposition of the Virgin Mary, the interest it excited was very favourable to the subject of Spiritual manifestations. Whilst a warm controversy was proceeding between the clergy and the medical faculty, the former crying " Miracle," and the latter " Mesmerism," —although in point of fact the girl had never been mesmerized at all— several kindred cases began to occur in different parts of the country, under circumstances that put both the above-named attempts at explanation, *hors de combat.*

One of these " ecstatics," was thus reported of, in *La Gazette Petrus*, from which we give the following translation :—

"In the commune of Vallengreville there is a young girl eighteen years of age who carries the *stigmates du Christ.* The feet, the hands, the side, the forehead are pierced, leaving wounds two centimetres long by half of one wide. Her head bears the imprint of the crown of thorns. These wounds bleed on Friday at 3 o'clock, and the girl suffers intensely. Physicians have interested themselves in this matter, and found that for three weeks the girl took not a particle of food : that she could seemingly fast indefinitely."

Very soon after the publication of this item, the different journals of Belgium became flooded with accounts of " ecstatics " and fasting girls, from a large number of which we select the following, as being the best authenticated.

Professor Laségue reported in the *Nationale* the case of a servant girl in his own family of whom he says :—" Her lower limbs became paralyzed, her skin became insensible, and she fell into a trance *(une espèce de somno-lence)*, and so remained for *three months* without taking other nourishment than tea. She recovered quite recently, and is now in her usual state of rugged health."

The editor of *L' Univers*, a strictly Catholic organ, not to be outdone by a simply scientific report of an " ecstatic " character, immediately followed up Professor Laségue's statement with the following narrative of religious ecstacy :—

"The Holy Virgin has appeared anew this year to two women of Dietrichswald, Prussia. The vision remains only eight or nine minutes, during which time these two persons are in a complete state of *extase*, pale, insensible as statues. The priests and other pilgrims pass to them pieces of folded paper containing questions addressed to the Virgin. These they read without opening (one in her normal state knows not how to read) and transmit the response of the Virgin, which is always strictly in accord with the questions, and often surpasses enormously the level of the intelligence of these women. '

The *Messager* of Liége, an excellent Spiritual paper, in commenting on this case, shrewdly remarks that the subjects are evidently " Mediums," whilst the " visions " they behold are mainly characterized by the religious influences that surround them.

Anticipating the date of our record by a few years, we may add to our notice of Belgium " ecstatics," a description given in a thoughtful and scholarly work issued in 1880, by Dr. J. Theyskeus, under the title of " On the Abuse of the Supernatural."

It should be stated that Dr. Theyskeus has held the post of inspector of hospitals for the insane in the Arrondissement of Malines, and though not exactly yielding to the Spiritualists' belief of obsession by Spirits, he seems to think that a great number of those persons incarcerated under the sobriquet of "lunatics," are in conditions of hypochondria, which closely conform to what ecclesiastics call "ecstacy," and Spiritualists "obsession." The special case mentioned in Dr. Theyskeu's work, to which attention may be profitably called, reads in translation as follows :—

"Marie van Regemortel, a girl of twenty years, inhabitant of Dussel, near Antwerp, after some hysterical manifestations of great intensity, had frightful fantastic visions, then tableaux of beauty ; a state of syncopy supervening that continued, without her taking any food, for weeks. For the last year, however, this invalid has had no hysterics, properly so called, nor hallucinations, but represents now the phenomenon of a *double life.* There is in her actually *two intellectual existences* well separated ; one normal, ordinary, and another that may be named a second state. When one pays her a visit, no matter at what hour of the day, she is always found in the second state, which has now become the habitual one. Persons not in the habit of seeing her cannot think that she is ill. She converses perfectly well, reasons as do others, and writes better than in her normal state. She executes marvellous work with the crochet needle, which she had never learned and could not do in her former ordinary life. Her hearing is also excessively acute. In a word, her sense and intelligence are intact. A peculiar symptom accompanies this condition ; she *absolutely cannot swallow any liquid,* and with difficulty solids. The œsophagus seems also completely paralyzed. On the other hand, in her first condition, she is more sad, more prostrated ; but she can swallow liquids and solids, though *she absolutely cannot utter a word.* The paralysis is moved from the œsophagus to the larynx. She replies, by writing, to questions put to her. In this state she has no recollection of what has passed in the other, and in the latter nothing of what occurred in the former. *En résumé,* there are with this girl two perfectly distinct existences, and they are never confounded. In the one she recalls perfectly, and no matter at what epoch, what had transpired in the same state previously, no matter if weeks or months have intervened. . . . If asked which of these is her real normal physiological state, one supposes that the second is, in which she talks and reasons lucidly ; and this as she has an aptitude she has not in her normal state ; here, too, her *esprit* is more vivacious, her look more piercing, her language more animated than before her illness. . . ."

Quite recently the author has received from M. Dijon, a surgeon of some eminence at Marseilles, though now residing at Brussels, accounts of two of his patients, sisters, and daughters of a leading public functionary in Belgium, the particulars of which closely correspond with those above detailed.

The girls are twins of about fourteen years of age. They have suddenly given themselves over to prolonged fasts, some of which last for twelve or even fifteen days. When separated at the suggestion of their medical attendants, their fasts and vision-seeing states, exactly correspond with each other in point of time and manner.

Sometimes they speak in unknown tongues with great volubility. Sometimes they not only declare they see "the saints in glory," but, says M. Dijon, "*they affect to personate* these saints, and preach in the most sublime and exalted strain as if they were the holy personages *whose names they borrow.*"

To the author's suggestion that these young ladies may be "Mediums," and if questioned in their trances, might confirm this statement, or explain their own case, the worthy surgeon replied, that the parents were rigid Catholics, and by the advice of their priests, treated the patients to holy water and penitential psalms, whilst he himself prescribed alternations of blue pill and iron tonics.

M. Dijon adds :—"You would be astonished, Madame, to know the number of cases to which I have been called in Catholic families, termed by the priests 'demoniacal obsession,' by you Spiritualists 'Mediumship,' and by my medical associates 'hysteria.' I am quite aware that neither the first nor the last terms mean more than words. When I have seen more of Spiritualism, I may find the solvent in your phraseology of Mediumship, and if I do, I shall consider it to be a *disease*, with which one-third of the young women in Catholic countries are affected. . . ."

About 1870, an important impulse was communicated to the cause of Spiritualism in Belgium, by the first publication of the excellent Spiritual journal known as *Le Messager.* Since that event, several other Spiritual periodicals have been started, all of which have contributed to the dissemination of Spiritual knowledge. At present, besides *La Messager,* there are four other journals devoted to this subject, namely, *La Moniteur*, of Brussels ; *Le Galiléen* and *De Rots*, of Ostend ; and *Le Moniteur de la Fédération Belge.* Although the Spiritual papers of Belgium deal more with the literature of the subject than with records of phenomena, their scholarly style, and the indefatigable efforts that have been made to sustain them, reflect the highest credit upon the Belgian Spiritual Brotherhood.

Amongst the distinguished American Mediums who have visited Belgium, none have excited a greater interest than Mr. Slade, whose arrival in 1877, brought forth the usual amount of controversy from the opponents and defenders of the cause, and in this sense, in addition to his striking Mediumship, performed the good service of wide-spread propagandism.

The following notice from *Le Moniteur* of Brussels, of the year 1880, will show some of the real workings of those means by which itinerant conjurers pretend to *expose* Spiritualism, when they find that exhibitions of true Spiritual phenomena do not pay.

Taking advantage of the eagerness with which the clergy seize hold of any and every occasion, however small, or any means, however contemptible, to deride and misrepresent Spiritualism, many an unprincipled adventurer, endowed with veritable Medium power, has succeeded in gaining that amount of remunerative attention from the public, under clerical patronage, which they could not secure under the clerical ban. Very few of these accommodating itinerants possess the courage or conscientiousness that marks the action of Mr. Verbeck—the subject of the succeeding extract. The reader may judge for himself how closely this exhibitor's case fits that of many others, by perusing the *Moniteur's* account as follows :—

"Mons. Jésupret, writing from Douai concerning an exhibition given there by a Mr. Verbeck, 'a prestidigitateur,' says that he operates without preparation, without boxes with a double bottom, with sleeves drawn back, and that his *direct writing* is his most surprising feat. He first sends a single pair of folding slates among the audience, that all may see that they are wholly free from any marks or characters whatever. Then ten persons, known to be of honourable reputation, are severally asked to write a question, and place it in an envelope. The ten envelopes being collected are presented to some lady who is requested to take one *au hasard*, and keep it. Of the other nine he gives account, which is recognized by each of the writers. The slates, which have not left the audience, are requested to give answer to the question involved in the letter that had been taken by the lady ; and Mr. V. then reads it aloud : '*What is the name of the most celebrated enchanter ?*' One of the most estimable of citizens, placing a bit of pencil between the slates, closing them, and holding them up so that all can see them, hears writing within ; then, after a little shock announcing the completion of the writing, the slates are opened, and the following found therein : 'The name of the most celebrated of *enchanters* is Merlin, of Douai, celebrated jurisconsul, born at Arteux in 1754, died in 1838, Minister of Justice.' The astonishment of the audience at the response obtained under such conditions cannot be described. Mr. Verbeck, with whom the writer was during the exhibition, declared to me, he says, 'that the writing was not the result of his talent, but most assuredly the work of spirits ; that he was a medium, and a Spiritualist ; that for three years he had thus been favoured with communications ; that lately at Lille, among intimate friends (afterwards confirmed by them) he had obtained like results. Indeed, Verbeck declared publicly that the slate-writing was not caused by his *adresse.*' Mons. Jésupret adds that his father, and his friend Bonnefont, had given a private ' conference' at Vitry-en-Artois, and were much commended ; and that a wealthy proprietor, whom they did not know, had offered to them a large hall, where they could give a public lecture on Spiritualism."

Still another case of well-known and even acknowledged Mediumship was ostentatiously announced as an unexplained mental phenomenon by the Belgic *Journal des Beaux Arts* in the following terms :—

"There is at Bruges a wonderful little girl, a child, Louise Van de Kirkhove, who paints with such marvellous skill and rapidity that she attracts vast crowds to her studio. In the presence of more than two hundred individuals who came to see her and be convinced of her powers, she has produced her beautiful works, and nearly all her visitors have received some souvenir of her genius."

It may not be amiss at this point to call attention to a curious incident which has been going the round of the Spiritual papers, copied from a quite new journal started by Dr. B. Cyriax, of Leipzig, entitled *Spiritualistische Blätter*. A notice of Dr. Cyriax's admirable paper, together with the item in question, would have appeared in the German section of this work, had not the latter been completed before the item was published. It is now given in a condensed form, and is suggestive of many cases which might run in parallel lines were there many other professional conjurers as conscientious as Herr Weder. The May number of *Light* for 1883 has the following report :—

"A SÉANCE AT LEIPZIG.

"A new German journal, the *Spiritualistische Blätter*, devoted to popularising and elucidating the reality of modern Spiritualism, contains in a recent number the letter of a medium to the editor, relating the way by which he was led to discover his gift. He says :—

"'I made the acquaintance of Mr. Fox, the prestidigitateur, at Berlin, in 1882. He said he was desirous of extending his professional operations. His representations led me to become his partner, I bringing in 10,000 marks (£500). His intention was to make an extensive anti-spiritualist tour armed with all the latest secrets of the Spiritualists which, he said, we could obtain from dealers in conjurors' tricks, but at high prices. This I found to be the case, for the charge for the cord with which to do what is called the rope-trick, with the secret how to use it, was 300 marks, and so in proportion for other more elaborate contrivance.

"'At the end of six months all was arranged, manager and assistants were engaged, when I met an old acquaintance, Herr Troll, who had been manager to Herr Hansen, the Danish professor of magnetism : he told me of a genuine spiritualist *séance* at Leipzig, the medium, whom he knew, being E. Schraps. I determined to go, for neither I nor my partner had ever been to such a *séance*. I had assumed with him that were called spiritual phenomena were conjuring tricks. I went with Herr Troll. Before the *séance* I was invited to examine the medium. At my request he stripped completely, and I found that beyond ordinary coat, waistcoat, trousers and socks, he had nothing upon him except watch and chain. His boots were put outside the room. I was appointed to tie him, which I did effectively while he sat in an ordinary cane chair. He was tied and the cords sealed to the entire satisfaction of all present. His manager was placed in the centre of those present, bound with a cord, the ends of which were held by an inquirer like myself, whose passivity we also made sure of. I surveyed everything and was satisfied. The light was then turned off.

"'Presently the medium's watch and chain were flung into the circle without being injured ; then followed in succession his coat and his waistcoat ; and finally the medium himself was dropped into our laps. After each separate manifestation light was struck that the knots and seals might be examined. They were all intact. The medium was apparently unconscious and perfectly passive. His manager said he was in a trance. He was carried and placed in his chair.

"'During these manifestations phosphoric lights moved about ; there were raps more or less loud in different parts of the room ; a musical box was whirled rapidly about overhead with other musical instruments playing.

"'A hand touched mine; I took hold of it; it was certainly a living hand, but it melted away in my grasp.

"'Then I had the irresistible conviction that there were forces of which I did not understand the cause and effect.

"'On reaching my hotel with Herr Troll, raps sounded about the table, the bed, the all, everywhere. I went out of the room and ascertained that the noises accompanied le to any part of the building. And it was not illusion, for they also who were with me heard them. I became thus aware that I was myself a medium. Subsequently I learnt that I could hold communication with my departed relatives.

"'I communicated these experiences to my partner in Berlin, and asked him to come to Leipzig, that he might have the same. He came and saw similar phenomena to those which I have described. He said they were beyond his comprehension, but could not believe them to be spiritual. I asked him to reproduce them. He said he could not. Before the public he goes on acting upon the assumption that Spiritualism is trickery, without which assumption he could not maintain his position. Of course my partnership with Mr. Fox is dissolved at the loss of my money. But I am the gainer in happiness, and in the conviction of the truth of spiritual and immortal existence.

"'The magnetic gift with which God has endowed me I purpose to employ in relieving and healing my suffering brethren.

"'Chemnitz, Saxony.　　　　　　　　　　　　　"'WILHELM WEDER.'"

We shall conclude our notice of Belgic Spiritualism by giving a few extracts from the journal of M. Henry Lacroix, a French-Canadian gentleman, whose views, though eccentric, and not in favour with some classes of Spiritualists, nevertheless do not affect the truth and integrity of his statements.

The author has known M. Lacroix for many years, and can thoroughly vouch for the reliability of the following extracts, printed in the *Banner of Light* of 1881 :—

"THE CAUSE IN BELGIUM.

"A small monthly sheet, *Le Moniteur*, is published in Brussels ; Mr. de Turck is the editor. The headquarters for meetings. etc., are in *Rue de l'Empéreur*, 21. Mr. V. Beyns, the generous proprietor, there attends zealously to all wants, and exerts elsewhere a good influence. His reception was most cordial, and I cannot but praise his warm heart and devotedness to the cause. There are several other *Groupes*, in Brussels, beside many private circles ; one is named 'Paix entre Nous,' or 'Peace between Us,' established since 1870. It is composed of twenty-nine members, ladies and gentlemen. The séance-hall is Rue Dupout, 21, in suburb Schaerbeck—meetings twice a week. Direct writing in a closed book was once obtained at this circle. I spent an evening at the regular *séance*, and was influenced to organize the members into different groups, assigning to each medium a suitable *rôle*. I recounted some of my experience, and showed them the American way of proceeding, whereby practical results are obtained. In that consists mainly the object of my two years' mission to Europe ; and, at the very start, I can say that my endeavours are being crowned everywhere by a good cordial reception and a decided will to set to work in the proper way. ⁤ . ⁤ .

"On Sunday, 14th August, I left Brussels for Roux, etc., on a spiritual expedition. I was accompanied by Mr. Alfred Crignier, of Brussels, a most zealous Spiritist. We passed by the battlefield of Waterloo, and saw there some Englishmen, probably, who were climbing up the mound on which is erected the famous English lion. At the village of Roux, about thirty miles south from Brussels, we were warmly greeted, and walked to a scattered neighbouring town, called Gohyssart-Jumet, where I was expected to address, in French, an audience of about four hundred. This place is in the province of Hainaut, and the majority of the people are employed in coal-pits, numerous here, glass factories and foundries, which are many and extensive. In the afternoon I was escorted by a group of friends to a nice, clean hall, and soon after Mr. Crignier introduced me to the audience as 'an American medium who had come to teach them the American way of proceeding, etc.' For two hours I stood on the rostrum, addressing listening ears and eyes that sparkled with lively interest. ⁤ . ⁤ . Mr. B. Martin. of Brussels, comes periodically to address these people, and as he is an able lecturer he has done much toward keeping the ball rolling. But the real soul of this organization is Mr. Alfred Crignier, my companion and friend. After the conference we went—quite a number of us—to the house of Mr. Emile Lefebre, who will assuredly become a successful spirit-photographer. He showed me several plates, on which were very good beginnings of faces, etc. . . . I found here good elements to develop a materializing medium, and described a person suited for such development so accurately that she was recognized at once—the spirits requiring that *absent* person as their medium for that purpose. At this gentleman's house the table was laid and all present partook of the warm, brotherly fare. These Walloons are an intelligent people, the Yankees of Belgium. On leaving I was surprised to find that my hotel bill had been paid, and I was forced to accept the amount of fare from and to Brussels—it being a rule so to do toward all who come to these friends to address them.

"I went next with friend Crignier to another group, which he established and patronizes. It was on our way back to Brussels, at a village called Mont St. Guibert. We were expected, and escorted to the sénnce-hall by six members of the Fraternity. Here I addressed some thirty people for about two hours, and, as at Roux, I found good elements of mediumship, which I individually surveyed and described—to the satisfaction of all—and established several circles on a new plan, *with music*, which is generally omitted in Europe. While we were entertained at supper at Mr. Bouffioux's house, I was influenced to sketch a spirit-picture, which was fully recognized. It startled and pleased every one. The people here are poor, but very tidy. A cotton factory gives employment to a few hundred. The mechanical overseer of it is our host, Mr. Bouffioux, who is a warm intelligent brother, and a great mechanical genius.

"At Mr. Crignier's residence, in Brussels, I organized the select circle held there on a new and quite successful basis, as remarkable manifestations occurred at the second *séance*. Two American spirits, one 'Charlie' (coloured) and 'Red-Skin' (Indian), were brought forward before my vision as immediate controls of this circle. Mr. and Mrs. Verheyen, at whose house this circle is held, are heart and hand in the cause, and so is Mr. R. C. Van Prehn-Wiese, a gentlemanly Hollander residing in Brussels. From what I have seen I feel confident that the cause will gain much in Belgium, when circle-holders and Spiritualists at large are made to understand proper conditions. . . ."

In reference to the present status of Spiritualism in Belgium, the reader will find a perfectly reliable summary of the subject in the two following extracts, the first being taken from *Le Messager*, the second from *Le Moniteur*, both of date 1882 :—

"The number of those who come out each day from the clouds of error to enter by degrees into the light of spiritual truth is relatively so great that the most obstinate of our opponents will soon be under the necessity of making a note of it. . . . Three years ago the annual general meeting of Spiritualists at Brussels numbered only fifty ; this year a meeting called in the same manner was attended by nearly a thousand. The largest proportion came from the great mining district of Charleroi."

"Mons. Jésupret, writing from Douai, says : ' The ideas *philosophiques* of our beloved doctrine have made great progress in our land, where one can now say that he is a Spiritualist without the fear of being ridiculed by those gentlemen who think so much of themselves, but are generally of no great account. The question of Spiritualism is largely agitated among us, awakening public attention, while the press is discreetly silent.' Mons. Jésupret has been invited to lecture in quite a number of towns of considerable population, Vitry, for instance, Vis-en-Artois and Louvain."

SPIRITUALISM IN TURKEY.

Before closing our compendium of European Spiritualism, we must call attention to the first unfoldment of the modern Spiritual movement in Constantinople.

It was as early as 1854, when Mr. Lenox Horne, the author, whose experiences were touched on in our section on English Spiritualism, returned from a sojourn of some months at Constantinople, whither he had been called on commercial business. It was from Mr. Horne's lips, in the city of London, that the author of this work heard for the first time of table turning, and it was in the residences of Mr. Horne's Turkish associates that he himself first witnessed this phenomenon. By some of the Turkish merchants residing at Constantinople with whom Mr. Horne had business relations he was invited to witness a scene which was then as perplexing as it was unprecedented; this was nothing more nor less than the rockings, spinnings, and apparently spontaneous movements of tables and other inanimate bodies which occurred at times in the houses of different individuals, and that without any other visible cause than the presence of any one of three young lads who, in some unknown and mysterious way, seemed to be connected with these motions. The "living principle," or whatever it was, that set chairs and tables dancing was communicated as Mr. Horne found, sometimes by slight contact between the children's hands and the object moved, and sometimes when there was no contact at all, and the boys were several feet from the moving mass.

On one occasion when all the boys were present, and a perfect saturnalia was going on amongst articles of furniture which up to that moment had been perfectly well behaved and quiescent, the youngest of the boys was suddenly lifted up to the ceiling, and after floating for a few seconds above the heads of about a dozen astonished witnesses, was seen to descend and lie at full length upon one of the divans. Mr. Horne remarked, that throughout this wonderful act of levitation, the child was sustained as if he were carried in invisible arms. He was manipulated with the utmost gentleness, declared that his sensations ere full of delightful calmness and peace, and that he distinctly felt the touch of warm, soft hands lifting him up, and at times kindly patting him. One of the merchants present declared that what they had witnessed was nothing new, for that he, a resident of Athens, and a traveller through the East, had heard of, and in some instances beheld, similar marvels enacted in the residences of friends in all directions.

He added, that report had alleged these manifestations to be peculiar to females chiefly, and as Eastern etiquette, especially in Turkey, forbade the intrusion of foreign gentlemen into the sacred precints of female society, Mr. Horne and his friends were obliged for some time to be contented with the phenomena produced through the agency of the boys before alluded to. An opportunity at length occurred, which enabled Mr. Horne to witness these new marvels under another aspect.

Having mentioned the facts above narrated to Signor Orsini, an Italian gentleman, residing in a beautiful villa on the Bosphorus, Mr. Horne, one of his Turkish friends, and his little son, the child who had been levitated, were courteously invited to visit the Orsini family, amongst whom three of the daughters were reputed to have the faculty of making tables or any other inanimate objects dance to any tune, or in any time, which they might sing or play. Several *séances* were held with the Orsinis, in which the facts above stated were not only verified, but wonders of a far more astounding character were displayed.

On one occasion when the party—fourteen in number—were seated around a table, a pencil which had been previously laid on some sheets of paper in the centre of the group, rose up of itself, and after some effort as it would appear, of an invisible hand to steady it, wrote in bold characters the words—"Good evening, friends. *Carl Maria Von Weber.*" The pencil then dropped, and no more writing was produced again that evening. One of the young ladies, who from special circumstances had the privilege of a frequent *entrée* to the Royal Harem, declared that the ladies of that establishment amused themselves night after night with these wonderful practices, and that it was from them that the daughters of Signor Orsini had learned the formulæ of sitting round a table with pencils and paper to procure Spirit writing.

Mr. Horne's departure from the East terminated for him the privilege or attending any more of these weird *séances*, but he found on returning to London that the wonder-working power was more universal than he had deemed, for tables not only turned and kept time to tunes in solitary instances, but soon began to dance all over London, and that to the clarion notes which heralded in modern Spiritualism.

The following account furnished by Monsieur A. J. Riko, of the Hague, will give corroborative details of Mr. Horne's narrative of early Spiritualism in Turkey. Monsieur Riko says :—

"At Constantinople, M. Repos, a well-known advocate, was for several years a warm spiritualist, medium, and zealous defender of the faith of Spiritualism.

"About 1860-61, during *séances* held at his residence, loud rappings, movements, writings, trance, and other communications, besides levitations and floating in the air, were manifested with remarkable power.

"Two young ladies of M. Repos' circle were developed as healing mediums, and performed many cures. They had a very remarkable drawing medium too, who produced life-sized heads without ever having learned drawing ; another composed songs and music under influence.

"Mons. P. Vallarie was also a staunch Spiritualist at Constantinople. At his house strong physical manifestations occurred in 1862. When all sat at a distance from the table, in an ordinary lighted room, it answered by raps, and even by lifting itself without contact, in view of all the assistants. A certain evening a visitor from Alexandria, who came with a walking stick seen by several of the witnesses, missed his stick at the close of the sitting. On arrival at his hotel he found it under his bed covers, in the closed room. When he got to bed he was drawn by the spirits at his request halfway out of the bed. Another evening the spirits carried off the key of his hotel room from his pocket. On coming home he was forced to share the room of a friend. After a while they found the key under the candlestick, and on opening his room the gentleman found everything out of place ; the bed covers, &c. being thrown in a heap in the middle of the apartment. Other similar pranks were often played by the spirits in this gentleman's presence, making it evident that he was what is now called a strong physical medium.

"In May, 1863, an exposition of pictures was opened at Constantinople. Among other works of art was a picture represeting a fine collection of flowers, which attracted general attention by the following inscription : 'Mediumistic drawing executed through M. Paul Lombardo, of Constantinople, unacquainted with the arts of drawing and painting.' It was one of the productions of a medium then sitting with the circle of M. Repos. Among the pictures exhibited none was more generally admired or more eagerly purchased.

"In the capital of the Turkish empire, like other places, the newspapers were filled with controversies about Spiritualism. In March, 1864, the Constantinople journal opened its columns for the defenders, and a protest, signed 'The Spiritualists of Constantinople,' appeared against unworthy attacks. . . . . ."

In the London *Spiritual Magazine* of May, 1861, there is another brief sketch of Spiritualism in Turkey from the pen of the gentleman named by M. Riko, and as it is pertinent to the same *séances* mentioned above, we shall give it in M. Repos's own words. He says :—

"Constantinople, May 1, 1861.

"Our experiments become daily more interesting. We hold several *séances* weekly, sometimes at one's house, sometimes at another's. Every day new believers are made. Tables rise into the air, and the spirits begin to raise persons. Our most remarkable mediums are two young ladies, whom the spirits magnetize direct, and through them they play at the piano—duets sometimes—the music being of wonderful harmony. Then we have trances, visions, and self-magnetizations, the subjects themselves knowing nothing of magnetic science. We cannot make known the subject so much as we would, for these young ladies are in a profession which brings them under the influence of the clergy ; and the priests among us, as elsewhere, are inimical to Spiritualism.

"Some of us, from table mediums, have become writing mediums. I am one of these ; and, under Spiritual influence, I play music ; I being ignorant of even the notes in my ordinary state. I enclose you a piece recently composed through me. The Spirits call the air the 'Song to Eternal Love.'

"One of the spirits of our circle names herself Sophia. At our request she, through my hand (though naturally I know not a line of drawing), has executed her portrait. It is a fine head, and is admired by all, meeting every requirement of artists to whom it has been shown. It has been lithographed by our friend Montani. He is also a medium of the highest order. The spirit Sophia has thanked him for his execution of his part of the work. At the first opportunity I shall send you a few copies of the portrait so produced.

"To tell you what we have obtained in writing is not possible in a letter. I must content myself with informing you that Sophia is writing 'The Theory of Spirits,' a magnificent work which she commenced a year ago. Other scientific treatises are in course of composition—'The Harmony of Colours,' 'Musical Harmony,' &c. All intended to form a compact whole, and showing the direct relation of Spiritualism to external things, and through it an ultimate resolution into universal harmony.

"A spirit of our circle, who is named Angelica, and who is recognised by the other spirits as the head of the spiritual manifestations with us, always addresses us in verse. She has dictated an Ode to Garibaldi. We forwarded it to him three weeks ago : since then she has dictated the words and music of a Hymn to Garibaldi.

"This spirit spoke prophetically in June, 1860, of Garibaldi in connection with the events of Italy. Three fourths of the prediction are already fulfilled.

"B. Repos, Jun."

It can scarcely be said that there is anything very striking or novel in the above details, and were we to enlarge upon them by adding records of circles held in Algeria, Alexandria, Cuba, Jamaica, Yeddo, Hong Kong, and in many other distant parts of the world where European and American civilization prevails, we should simply weary the reader with narratives, any score of which would prove representative of every other score, in whatever part of the world they might have occurred.

And here we must be permitted to say that this very circumstance, or the fact that the generality of Spiritual phenomena consist of a series of— what the superficial observer would call—the same platitudes, is one of the most marvellous features of the entire movement, for it is the one above all others which proves that there is a common origin for the manifestations, and that their appearance and reduplication in various countries, separated from each other by distance, varieties of language, religious beliefs, social customs, and public interests, proves beyond a doubt that the movement cannot have originated in human contrivance, or been propagated by human agency. Any natural products, physical changes, atmospheric disturbances, or even mental impressions, might be traceable to mundane causes, *provided always any mundane conditions were ever known to affect the entire surface of the globe and all its inhabitants at or about the same time.* But the phenomena now under consideration, do not come within any of the above suggested categorical means of explanation. The power exhibited is obviously exerted by some force without, above, or below the mundane sphere, and not in or of it. In all authentic cases, it is accompanied by intelligence, and in at least half the well-attested instances on record, that intelligence transcends the knowledge of the human beings concerned, and in every case refers itself to the Spirits of those the world calls "dead." When the thoroughly supra-mundane character of the phenomena and the intelligence is considered, and it is remembered that the demonstrations occur apparently and spontaneously, at or about the same time in all the countries of Europe, all the States of North and South America ; in the East and West Indies, Australasia and all the centres of civilization in Asia and Africa, what candid mind can evade the conclusion that their source is ONE though the manifestations are various, and that this same source is at once powerful, intelligent, and supra-mundane ?

The "demoniacal" theory, so persistently and stupidly alleged by the clergy, is almost too silly to combat any further, and is at once put to flight by observing that the Spiritual authors of the movement, work for the most part for good, truth, religion, and morality, and where unmistakable mischief or annoyance is manifest, it never seems to be permitted to cause injury to human beings or prove inimical to human life. How different this to the conduct of those human fiends whom a corrupt and evil-minded condition of society tends to manufacture in our city streets! So far from equalling humanity in cruelty, malevolence, and wickedness, there is not a single Spiritual communication ever made, that rivals in malignity the Bishop of Santander's savage "anathema," cited in our section on Spanish Spiritualism, whilst the entire history of Spiritualism fails to produce any criminal record that can match in magnitude the list of crimes reported in a single issue of our London daily journals! It must be added, that the constant use of the term "demons," by the clergy, when they would describe the authors of Spiritual manifestations, is merely a *ruse* to scare the vulgar mind. They strive to make the word odious by associating it with "diabolism," when they well know—unless they are too ignorant for the position they hold—that it signifies only the souls of dead men, without reference to moral qualities at all.

If Spirits are indeed "demons" in the clerical and erroneous sense of the term, they are demons in a state of progression, or the souls of bad men and women no longer in a condition to work the same evils they effected whilst Spirits incarnated in mortal bodies.

Regarded merely as a matter of testimony, we have no apologies to make for the reiteration of phenomena occurring in many lands; in fact, as above stated, it is our best witness for the homogeniety of the power all over the world ; for the strictly human character of the Spirits concerned in the manifestations; for the evidence that those Spirits are either in a state of progression, or that their power for evil is limited by higher laws than those that prevail on earth, and that the whole movement may be looked upon as a handwriting on the wall of Ecclesiasticism, in which the world can read what the clergy seem to be wilfully blind to—the words " MENE, MENE, TEKEL, UPHARSIN."

CHAPTER LI.

SPIRITUALISM IN AMERICA.

RETROSPECTIVE.

IT is now about twenty years since the author of these pages received a series of communications from some of her most honoured Spirit guides, charging upon her to collect from every available source, the materials for a compendious and authentic work on the history of Modern Spiritualism. Preliminary sketches of what that work was to be, were given from time to time, but it was not until the year 1867 that the intention was declared of giving to the world a record of the first twenty years of the Spiritual movement as it had transpired in America.

To the author's objection that such a record might seem premature, and imply the completion of a history still in progress, the communicating Spirits answered by urging many reasons for the adoption of their plan.

Amongst these reasons they alleged that the first twenty years of Spiritualism in America would complete a special cycle in the movement.

During that period it was said, the work of the Spiritualists would be to conduct a stern and unyielding warfare against the world without, to revolutionize old ideas, uproot stereotyped errors, and do battle with priest-craft and schoolcraft, ignorance, and bigotry; and at the close of that epoch it was asserted, that during the ensuing fifteen years many marked changes of a discouraging character would overshadow the cause, but that these would proceed chiefly from within, rather than from without the ranks. *The worst foes of Spiritualism would be those of its own household, and the cruellest stabs directed against it, would be dealt by the hands of Spiritualists themselves.*

Still another fifteen years would be required—said the guides—before the first principles of a true science could be evolved. During that period, the phenomena of Spirit communion would be silently yet surely wrested from the hands of *the spoiler*, and its religious teachings be rescued from the vagaries of speculative theorists in order to ground it on the rock of immutable and well proven truth. At the close of this third epoch, modern Spiritualism would celebrate its year of JUBILEE, and triumphantly enter upon its possession of the promised land, wherein the unity of science and religion should be fully demonstrated. "There will be few, if any, of the veterans of the old guard"—said the communicating Spirits—"who will remain on earth to celebrate the fiftieth birthday of Spiritualism, and the marriage day of the long divorced elements which constitute the Bible of Creation, namely, RELIGION and SCIENCE. Like Moses of old, many of those who have led the modern Israel through the wildernesses of superstition and ignorance, may be permitted to behold the Spiritual Canaan from the far off peaks of distant mountains, but few—if any of them—will ever tread its pleasant paths with mortal feet."

Such were the counsels under which the author was influenced to write the history of the first twenty years of "Modern American Spiritualism;" such the continuous guidance by which she has almost completed the record of thirty-five years of the Spiritual movement throughout the civilized world, and now essays to resume the broken thread of the American record. With an earnest prayer that the prophecy of the Spirit seers may be as surely fulfilled in the promised day of "jubilee," fifteen years hence, as it has been in the night of darkness that has prevailed during the past fifteen years, we resume the American Spiritual history from the point where it was temporarily suspended by the publication of the first twenty years' history.*

As that work is still in print, and fully accessible to the student, we make no apologies for introducing its claims to attention, and commending its careful study to those who desire to acquaint themselves with the full sum of the American record.

Now, as in the earlier portions of this work, we remind the reader that though fidelity to the integrity of history will oblige the author to point to the dark as well as the bright features of the landscape, and uncompromisingly to adhere to the facts of the narrative whether they tell for or against its value to mankind, no prominence will be given to those names that have left the stain of human error and corruption on a movement that but for them, might have been counted as purely divine.

None can follow steadfastly the course of this wonderful history without

---

* "Modern American Spiritualism," a twenty years' record of the communion between mortals and Spirits. Published by Colby and Rich, office of the *Banner of Light*, Boston, Massachusetts, U.S America.

THE THREE FOX SISTERS

LEAH

KATE

MARGARETTA

perceiving that thousands of angular one idea " reformers" (?) have thrust themselves into the ranks of Spiritualism, because they perceived that it was strong, world-wide, and—as they deemed—popular enough to carry all the little hobbies which human pride and egotism desired to harness to its mighty car.

When Spirits first manifested their presence amongst men, their power and functions were so little known, that mortals feared to tamper with them, or pervert their work to human ends or personal aggrandisement. In course of time the awe engendered by the unprecedented character of the new movement wore off, and Spiritualism, like charity, became the convenient cloak which was to cover all the sins which its assumed adherents chose to put upon it. When this line of policy failed, an equally profitably one opened up in the trade of " Spiritual exposers." Those who had once been in the ranks, of course possessed the knowledge of how to work the oracle, and if Spiritualism could not be coined into money and reputation, its alleged *exposure* could, and seeing that the enemies of Spiritualism found themselves so constantly baffled by its almost illimitable means of demonstration, these accommodating exposers gladly availed themselves of the eagerness with which antagonism clutched even at their contemptible agency to destroy the credit or pervert the facts of Spiritualism. And thus, this great cause, like many another of the world's purest Messiahs, has been lifted up on the cross of martyrdom between the thieves of licentiousness and cupidity, and if its quenchless vitality has been again and again manifested in countless resurrections, it is not for lack of every available effort on the part of humanity to sap its integrity by internal corruption, as well as by external antagonism.

As any narrative of events which involve the personal action of the narrator must to some extent demand the fidelity of autobiographical details, the reader must be prepared in the passages which immediately follow, to regard with leniency the seeming egotism of personal testimony, and do justice to the statements of an actor in the scenes described.

It was in the year 1871 that the author returned to America from a short visit to her native country in company with her beloved life companion, and with the addition of " Britten" to her former sobriquet of " Emma Hardinge."

Mrs. Britten soon realized that which she had long anticipated, namely, that what had been entitled the philosophy or doctrine of " social freedom" had expanded from an incipient germ to the full maturity of a wide-spread movement. As the first promoters of what has been emphatically called " Free Loveism" in America, were a concrete order amongst themselves, and only incidentally numbered a few Spiritualists in conjunction with persons of many other denominations in their ranks, there seemed no just cause for associating beliefs and practices as warmly repudiated by many Spiritualists as by any other class of religionists, with Spiritualism at all. On the contrary, as Spiritualism enjoined upon its followers the solemn fact of personal responsibility for all human shortcomings in the life hereafter, and offered no excuse or evasion for sin, sternly alleging that every soul must pay the penalty of its own transgressions, it might have been expected that Spiritualists of all other classes of the community, would be the most scrupulous of moralists and the first to set the example of purity and virtue in thought, word, and deed.

The monstrous flood of licentious doctrine, often illustrated by monstrous licentiousness of life and conduct, which for a certain period of time spread like an evil contagion throughout the United States, and included in its poisonous breathings a certain number of prominent Spiritualists, put the above stated propositions to flight in the opinion of the public at large, and cast a most unjust and ruinous ill odour over the reputation and belief of tens of thousands of innocent persons, who loathed the tendencies of the new philosophy all the more, because they were Spiritualists, and as such, felt horror and aversion at all that could lower the standard of purity in morals or religion.

To account for the epidemic of madness which ruled the time of which we speak, and connected itself so injuriously with the name of Spiritualism, it must be stated, that the questions of social evil and hereditary criminality, together with the abuses which grow out of ill-assorted marriages, had long been the theme of public discussion, and had enlisted many earnest and capable minds in the effort to devise reformatory measures of a salutary character.

It was from about 1850 to 1870 that several worthless and licentious individuals thrust themselves prominently before the world in the attitude of "great reformers," and as some of the iconoclasts who screamed the loudest for "social freedom," the abrogation of the marriage law, and the substitution of licentious will for the restraints of law and order, sought to strengthen their case, by the audacious assumption of being inspired by "great Spirits," the world eagerly caught at the idea that the whole movement was the work of Spiritualists, and that the mass of scum and corruption that ultimately swept like a desolating wave over the realm of public opinion was the instigation of *demoniac spirits*, and owed its detestable prominence to the action of "the Spiritualists." Reviewing this movement not only from the standpoint of bitter experience of the ruin and desolation it effected, but also from the immense mass of literature—now in the author's possession—which recorded the headlong expressions of opinion that were put forth by many who were perhaps maddened by the evil spirit of the time, we may clearly perceive that there were three distinct parties in this ill-omened work, the true nature of which could not be sufficiently discerned in the fever of the hour.

The first of these was a small number of audacious and lawless persons, a few of whom were endowed with sufficient ability to make a mark on public opinion. This band of would-be revolutionists were ready for any change that would bring them into notice, promote their favourite views of unbridled licence, and dignify infamy with the specious name of philosophy.

The author is in actual possession of evidence to show that some of these persons were sustained by certain members of the clergy, and by them induced to promulgate their atrocious doctrines in the name of Spiritualism, and put forth in blatant and unblushing language, the assertion that the spirits of once pure women and holy men, were the promulgators of the infamies taught in some of their published manifestos.

The second, and by far the largest class, were earnest, pure minded, and often estimable persons, who, having regarded the many evils that afflict humanity in its social relations, conscientiously believed that the new movement—of which they knew but little except by report—was really a heaven-born inspiration, designed to reform the wrongs under which society laboured.

The third class, one which included the author of these pages, was constituted of persons who, having assured themselves that the tree from which the assumed reform was to spring was wholly corrupt, never expected it to yield good fruit; and hence opposed with all the power they were possessed of, the entire movement, and above all, determined to repudiate the connection of its name, fame, and teachings with the great Spiritualistic movement. With this view, lectures were given, and articles were published, which called forth angry rejoinders and vituperative denunciations.

Meantime, this unhappy warfare was eagerly fed and stimulated by the craft of worldly antagonism. As an evidence of the use which the clergy made of the deplorable divisions which this terrible fever of wrong occasioned in the Spiritual ranks, it may be mentioned, that when the author some years after the period under consideration was lecturing in New Zealand in her accustomed capacity of a Spiritualistic propagandist, Mr. M. W. Green, the minister of the "Christian Disciples" Church of Dunedin—mentioned in our New Zealand section—made the following use of the all-too-notorious "Free Love movement." This reverend gentleman collected with assiduity a number of printed resolutions in which some of the Spiritualist societies who opposed the author's views, denounced her course, and voted her steady opposition to associating the titles of "Spiritualistic" and "Social freedom" together, as the result of envy, jealousy, and "desire for rule."

Constantly tormented with the idea that those who express opinions opposed to each other, are prompted by the wish to become "leaders," and —to use their favourite expression—"rule or ruin," many Spiritualists in the above-named crisis, affected to believe that the author opposed the "new philosophy" in the spirit of jealous enmity to its founders, and desire for personal leadership. Articles, resolutions, and denunciations to this effect were freely circulated at the time, causing unspeakable grief, heart-break, and mischief. Regarded now as the effervescence of partisanship, and the fever heat of an unseemly contest, they are harmless, and only calculated to inspire lessons of moderation and charity. It would be impossible to describe the evil use which Mr. M. W. Green sought to make of these documents, although none of his listeners could fail to note the craft with which he had collected them, and carefully excised every word which would serve to represent the other side.

With due respect to the author's position amongst hosts of influential friends, Mr. Green affected to sympathize with the martyrdom Mrs. Britten had endured from her "corrupt and infamous associates," and whilst pointing " to the *noble stand* she had taken in withdrawing from them," drew from thence the inference that the entire doctrines of Spiritualism were condemned and repudiated by the very individual who was then publicly advocating them. It is needless to say that sophistry of so flimsy and one-sided a character was not difficult to expose and defeat, but, if it could be made available for the purpose of antagonism in after years, it may well be supposed that those who at the time when the battle was raging were in terrible earnest to put down Spiritualism *at any cost*, did not fail to make effective use of the weapons which Spiritualists thus furnished.

The author still retains the literature of this unhappy period, and those who may deem that even these superficial allusions to the subject are exaggerated, may not only inform themselves to the contrary by consulting those documents, but would read with astonishment the evidences of cruel enmity, bitterness, and fierce antagonism which they display. No candid mind could examine the literature of this terrible time without coming to the conclusion that the same Spirit that lighted the fires of the *auto-da-fe* and directed the horrible mutilations of the torture chamber in past ages, burned just as fiercely in the hearts of humanity at that day, and was just as ready to extinguish its foes in moral fires, or torture its enemies by mental racks, as it was five hundred years ago.

There is one result however growing out of this evil time too remarkable to be overlooked. For a while Spiritualism seemed to furnish its foes with the very weapons which had hitherto been most wanting. But as strangely and suddenly as the warfare had arisen so did it die away. The first promoters have sunk into that obscurity to which society inevitably condemns those who would sap the foundations of its law and order. From time to time they make spasmodic irruptions into temporary notoriety, but their sting has been drawn by experience, and in this generation they will hurt no more.

The true reformers of the second class, whilst realizing their mistake in employing impure tools to effect pure objects, still watch and wait for the institution of salutary reforms, when time and means shall be more favourable. Amazed by the mischief and wild licence provoked by what they deemed would have been a valuable and philosophic movement, they have not abandoned their aim of promoting true social reforms, but they have, as many an one has assured the author, learned not to look for roses from thistles, nor to expect to gather fruit from thorns. The most wonderful result of all however, and the one which excites most astonishment from all classes, is to see how bravely and powerfully Spiritualism has survived the blows that have been levelled against it from friends and foes alike.

The oft-reiterated cry of the clergy, "'Ware Spiritualism! It is all free love," &c., &c., has utterly lost its force, and the steadfast adhesion of fathers and mothers, husbands and wives, of families living in peaceful unity, and characters beyond reproach, seems to have quietly but irrevocably drowned the voice of slander, and testified to the utter fallacy of attempting to fasten on Spiritualism a stigma which belongs to all classes of *individuals*, but to no *special* class of scientists or religionists. In a word, the "Free Love" scare is ended, and although its foundations are far too deeply rooted in the corruptions of society to be destroyed by any exhibition of its ugliness, it has been compelled by a power—assuredly not of earth—to stand aside, whilst Spiritualism passed by, and shook its skirts free of the reproach which never in the remotest sense belonged to the movement, or could have grown out of its pure and elevating teachings.

CHAPTER LII.

SPIRITUALISM IN AMERICA (CONTINUED.)

PHYSICAL AND SPIRITUAL CONFLAGRATIONS.

IT was in the winter of the year 1872 that the terrible conflagration ensued, which swept over a large portion of the city of Boston, destroying whole streets, and desolating the wealthiest and most crowded districts of the city proper.

In the overwhelming ravages of this terrible fire, the premises occupied by the oldest Spiritual paper then in existence, the *Banner of Light*, together with all the stock, valuable library, and other property belonging to the publishing office were destroyed.

It is a noteworthy fact that the *Religio Philosophical Journal*, of Chicago, a paper which occupies in the West the same position as the *Banner of Light* in the East, had also suffered, and that quite recently, in the same calamitous way by the ravages of fire.

When the great north-western city of Chicago was in flames, and the very site once occupied by the office of the *Religio Philosophical Journal* was obliterated, the enterprising proprietor of the paper, Mr. S. S. Jones, together with his high-spirited colleague and son-in-law, Colonel Bundy, set up their "shingle"—to use a familiar American term for *sign*—in the very midst of the smoking ruins, announcing *that the business of the publishing-house would be carried on as usual*—an announcement which was actually verified by the issue of the next and following week's papers, which, though mere sheets, were sufficient to represent the indomitable spirit of the editors, and convey the assurance—since amply fulfilled—of carrying the journal forward on its triumphant mission of enlightening the world, in all its former fair proportions.

Scarcely had the gallant Chicago editors resumed work, and the *Religio Philosophical Journal* smiled in the faces of its friends, in a new and handsome dress, than the report of the Boston fires sent a thrill of horror through the various Spiritual societies which recognized these two papers as the chief standards of their faith. As in the case of the Western fires, the Spiritualists soon began to rally from the shock of this new calamity, and once more testified their high appreciation of the work performed by their well-tried organ, by pouring in contributions with unstinted liberality. The steadfast energy which enabled the citizens of Boston to rise above their great losses, and phœnix-like to erect a new and far more beautiful city amidst the still smouldering vestiges of devastation, seemed to be fully emulated—if it were not actually led—by the resolute publishers of the *Banner of Light*, for their work was resumed before it could be missed, and very soon, large and commodious offices were established at No. 9, Montgomery Place, Tremont Street, in which locality the *Banner* and its publishers have organized headquarters of a satisfactory and permanent character.

It was some six months before the date of the Boston fires that the author became associated with a few ladies and gentlemen, residents like herself of that city, in the publication of a new monthly Spiritual magazine entitled, *The Western Star*.

The motives which impelled this publication and the basis on which it was founded, may be best understood by a perusal of the following extracts from the prospectus, in which it was said :—

"The principal features aimed at in this undertaking are :—First. To present the matter contained in each number in such form and size that any or all the articles can be preserved and bound in ordinary Library volumes. Secondly. To establish a record of the deeply momentous events connected with modern Spiritualism, and to gather up and preserve such material as cannot be included in the columns of the weekly journals devoted to Spiritualism. Thirdly. To open up opportunities for a free and fraternal interchange of facts and opinions with the Spiritualists of foreign countries. Fourthly. To treat all topics of current interest from a purely Spiritualistic stand-point.

In each succeeding number of *The Western Star*, a summary of passing events in the Spiritual arena, both at home and abroad, was given, under the caption of *The Garland*, and as this record was designed to carry forward the historical thread of American Spiritual history from the point where it was interrupted in the publication of the author's twenty years' record, it may not be out of place to quote a few such extracts as will renew the memory of those who formerly constituted the *dramatis personæ* of the great American Spiritual movement :—

"The anniversary festivities of this season were less universally observed and largely attended than at the celebrations of four years ago. The most interesting meetings have been held at Boston, New York, Philadelphia, Providence, Cincinnati, Cleveland, Chicago, Waukegan, Vineland (graced by the presence of A. J. Davis) and Terre Haute, presided over by the Hon. R. D. Owen. . . . .

"The Boston anniversary was chiefly remarkable for the appearance on the Spiritual rostrum of Mrs. Conant, the inspired medium of the *Banner of Light* communications, and Professor Denton, the veteran war-horse of scientific theology. The Spiritualists of Terre Haute were favoured by the presence of Hon. Robert Dale Owen, whose anniversary address was a masterpiece of logical oratory. . . . .

"The *Binghampton Daily Republican* reports the doings of a negro, whom the editor graphically describes as "a black salamander." This man is said to walk on and handle red-hot iron plates with as much impunity as other persons touch the green turf. The *Republican* gives the following item as the account rendered by the man himself, of his own phenomenal gifts :—

'Coleman says that he is no worldly man. Once, while walking in the woods, near the Natural Bridge in Virginia, meditating upon the greatness of the Supreme Being, a small still voice spoke to him from above, saying : "Now will I show this unbelieving age a miration ! I caused Shadrach, Meshac, and Abed-nego to walk through the fiery furnace and I will give you the power to walk on hot iron.

'Coleman thought the voice was trying to get him into a muss, and he had much hesitancy about trying any experiments to test the reality of the "miration," but he finally ventured upon hot pigs of iron from a furnace, and unlike unbelieving Peter, he did not sink.'

"The *Religio-Philosophical Journal* reports that a veritable case of a spirit portrait appearing spontaneously on a pane of window glass, has occured in Virginia City, Nevada. Various other new developments are reported from different parts of the United States, amongst them the advent of a little trance medium of six years old, who resides in the City of Cincinnati, and who, for the last seven months, every night on going to bid her father and mother good-night, has been suddenly entranced, and delivered 'poetic sermons,' which, as her father asserts, for sublimity and piety, he has never heard excelled. This little lady is a seeing medium, also, and frequently pauses in her work, play, or studies, to describe 'the angels' whom she sees in the air. These descriptions have, in every instance, been recognised as applying to some deceased person. . . . .

"Mr. Thomas McGinn, writing from St. Louis, details a case of singular persecution on the part of a 'talking spirit,' who persists in following about his little girl Rosa, aged ten years, and in her presence, but not through her organs, uttering profane and sometimes pious language, purporting to come from a negro who was formerly a slave in his family, of imbecile mind and habits of speaking exactly similar to the words which are heard in the presence of the child.

"Mr. McGinn adds, like our Cincinnati correspondent, that though they communicate these facts for the benefit of Spiritual science, they are unwilling to call the attention of the public to their little mediums, rationally fearing the effect which crowds of heterogeneous minds may have upon their tender youth and susceptible organisms.

"In the realm of spirit art, the veteran mediums already before the public are making steady advances. The most satisfactory accounts are given of pictures produced through the mediumship of Mrs. Blair, N. B. Starr, Wm. Mumler, Willis, of Indiana, and others, whose gifts lie in that peculiar direction.

"The Davenport Brothers have been exposed again for the hundredth time, and for the hundredth time the exposers have been proved to be themselves the humbugs.

"A long and brilliant list of speaking mediums report their good work and indefatigable labours through the columns of the Spiritual papers. Thomas Gales Forster, one of the earliest and most esteemed for high Spiritual endowments, has accepted a call to occupy the New York platform for one year, commencing from last January.

"Mrs. Nellie T. Brigham occupies the Spiritual rostrum at Hartford for the same period of time. J. M. Peebles has been established at Troy, N.Y., and the general tendency to a more stable and permanent order of things amongst the committees having charge of the Spiritual rostrums, is everywhere becoming more and more apparent. . . .

"Several publications of value have been added to the repertoire of Spiritual literature quite recently. The most remarkable of these are Hon. Robert Dale Owen's 'Debatable Land ;' 'The Spiritual Pilgrim,' by J. M. Peebles;' 'Looking Beyond,' by J. O. Barrett;

and 'Flashes of Light from the Spirit Land,' a collection of communications given through the mediumship of Mrs. J. H. Conant, the celebrated medium for the *Banner of Light* circles. Mean time, the columns of the Spiritual periodicals are glittering with a long list of works comprising tracts, essays, poems, and treatises, from A. J. Davis, Lizzie Doten, Prof. Denton, Maria King, Hudson Tuttle, Emma Hardinge Britten, G. L. Ditson, etc., that would reflect lustre on any set of special people and special thinkers. . . . .

"A German Spiritual paper, of high literary tone, has recently been established in Washington, by Dr. Schücking, entitled *The Round Table*. The brilliant ability of its editor, and the splendid staff of contributers who grace its columns, are sufficient guarantee for its superior merits." . . . .

"AUGUST, 1872.—"Since our last issue we have received from England, through a private source, a package of what purports to be photographs of spirits, taken through the mediumship of a photographer of London, and a request accompanies the package, that the editors, 'having had the advantage of American experience in such pictures,' would furnish their European readers with some opinions thereon. With this request we are unable to comply, seeing that our American experiences furnish us with nothing that bears the least similarity to the pictures received. Some of them are placed directly at the side of the sitters, and present an appearance strictly human, and except the fact that they are for the most part veiled, and bear a striking resemblance to one uncomely model, there is nothing to distinguish them from an ordinary attempt to represent two figures on the same plate. In a review of the subject in the *British Journal of Photograghy*, dated May 24th, 1872, we find the following remarks :"—

"'We confess to a feeling of surprise how any photographer could be so blinded as not to see that such productions would be certain to provoke a perfect storm of hostile criticism, for more reckless indifference to the necessity for removing those features from which photographers of ordinary intelligence were certain to deduce imposture, we have never seen.'

"Cordially endorsing the above sentiment, and being unacquainted with any facts which might modify such an opinion, we should here close our remarks on the subject, did we not observe a tendency in the European Spiritual periodicals to associate these pictures with those of Mr. Wm. Mumler of Boston, Mass, a photographer of spiritual forms, whose mediumship has come out triumphantly through the most severe crucial tests that were ever applied to any of the alleged Spiritual phenomena.

"Our space does not allow us to go into details, but it is but justice to Mr. Mumler to remind our readers that the best proof that can be brought forward of a genuine character in spirit photography, is that which so especially distinguishes his pictures : namely, that hundreds of them have been recognised as portraits of deceased persons, and that by strangers visiting Mr. Mumler's studio for the first time. During Mr. Mumler's trial in New York, and all through the bitter persecution which antagonism to his remarkable gift called forth, a perfect cloud of witnesses, including many of the most respectable and veracious persons in America, came forward to bear testimony to the fact, that they had received correct, and clearly defined portraits of their departed friends, and that, when the medium could not have any knowledge of them.

"Another specialty in the Boston pictures, and one which often occurs is, that some portion of the shadowy spirit form is seen behind, and another part in front of the sitter. Take, for instance, the splendidly developed picture of Beethoven as a spirit, standing behind Emma Hardinge Britten, enclosing her with shadowy arms, and placing before her a small lyre wreathed with flowers. This visionary looking lyre is actually seen, as if under the lady's watch chain. Her dress is visible too, through the shadowy arms in front of her, whilst the noble-looking form and head stands clearly erect behind her.

"The last great sensation in English Spiritualism has been the course of spiritual lectures delivered by the renowned poet, Gerald Massey, at St. George's Hall, London. Mr. Massey acted as chairman at the splendid *conversazione* convened to bid farewell and present a noble testimonial to Emma Hardinge Britten, on her departure from England to América, last fall. Gerald Massey's appearance in such a scene and situation, surrounded by the *noblesse* of the land, and supported by a crowd of eminent scientists, literati, and leading men and women, fell like a thunderbolt upon the gaping toadies who are so eager to echo the question, 'What great ones of earth believe in Spiritualism ?' But that Mr. Massey should follow up this *début* by a course of Spiritual lectures has been almost as much of a blow to the fossilized leaders of royal associations for the conservation of opinions and the exclusion of ideas, as to see Professors Wallace, Varley, and Crookes putting on the whole armour of Spiritual faith, and publicly advocating its truth.'

September, 1872.—After excising all the American notices of the September month's "Garland," which are only of personal and temporary interest, we find the following extract from the *Cincinnati Commercial* of July 20 registered as "from an esteemed correspondent" :—

"Mrs. Hollis,* wife of Capt. E. J. Hollis, of Louisville, Ky., says the correspondent, visited his residence several weeks ago, and séances of a remarkable character took place, the manifestations at which he described in a series of letters to the *Commercial*. He invited a large number of people to view them, his visitors being representatives from the most refined circles in the social life of Cincinnati, several holding high official positions. The most remarkable manifestations occurring during her first visit were, slate-writing in the light, of which the narrator says, 'Hundreds of communications have been written in my presence, in Latin, Greek, Hebrew, German, Italian, French, Welch, and English; the showing of spirit hands—from three to five materialized hands being seen at one time, in a room sufficiently light to read in ; and the hearing of audible spirit voices. In proof of this latter phase the writer avers that his mother spoke to him in a strongly defined voice :—' If that voice had simply pronounced my name, I should have fixed it as my mother's. It is only four years since I heard it from her mortal lips. I *know* it was the voice of my mother.' Again it is said :—'The table upon which the music-box was placed stood about ten feet from the cabinet door. After winding it up, I was turning to resume my seat in the circle, in doing which I faced the aperture in the cabinet, when to my utter surprise, *I beheld my mother's face at the opening.* 'Why, mother,' I exclaimed, 'is it possible?' She smiled, *spoke my name,* and retired. The materialization continued for the space of ten or fifteen seconds. All in the room saw the dear face, the Quaker cap, and heard the name pronounced. I was within two feet of the aperture, and others not ten feet off. Not doubting her identity, still I said, 'Mother, dear, can you materialize your left hand, and show it at the aperture?' In less than a minute the left hand was presented for my inspection. I was close to it. The forefinger was permanently closed by contraction of the tendon, from a burn received in childhood. The hand presented had the same peculiarity. The faces of 'Jimmy Nolan,' and those purporting to be Ney and Josephine, together with several unrecognised spirits, were shown at the cabinet aperture. In dark séances, held by direction, Mrs. Hollis was frequently carried over the heads of the party present ; and on one occasion, being provided with a pencil, traced the course of her aerial journey along the ceiling—the walls having previously been examined, and no pencil-marks found thereon—the lead being worn down, and the hand of the medium covered with lime-dust by the operation."

October, 1872.—Besides noticing the suspension of two Spiritual papers, *The American Spiritualist* and *Lyceum Banner*, the writer of the "Garland" adds :—

"The *Religio Philosophical Journal* gives several interesting descriptions of the circles held in Chicago, for physical manifestations. The most candid and intelligent of these reports, are from the pen of Mrs. Annie Lord Chamberlain, herself one of the most gifted physical mediums in the world, and one whose generous recognition of the merits of others speaks more loudly for the nobility of soul which inspires her than all the laudations which could be pronounced upon her. Some of Mrs. Chamberlain's facts are in advance even of the experiences of those most familiar with the power of the invisible world ; for example, she reports that the spirits who keep watch and ward over the wonderful Bangs family, have ministered to the good mother in her domestic duties, laying her cloth, preparing her meals when indisposed, and then serving up the various condiments, cooked in the most approved fashion.

"One of the most interesting reports of Chicago Spiritualism, gives a detailed account of a *séance* with Mrs. Maud Lord, during which the reporter of the Chicago *Tribune*, three other members of the editorial staff, and a Baptist minister were present. Besides the display of lights, the sound of voices, demonstrations of spirit music, and the usual concomitants of a dark circle, several of the witnesses (including the *Tribune* reporter, who testifies of the fact in the *Tribune*) were favoured by the clasp of spirit hands which came and melted, formed again, and again melted in the grasp of the narrators, giving tests of spiritual agency, which put the theories of *stuffed gloves* or mediumistic trickery out of the pale of possibility. Manifestations of a similar kind are increasing on every side. It is scarcely possible to note how numerous and forcible are the proofs which crowd the columns of the Spiritual papers throughout the American continent. Like the miracles witnessed by St. Augustine, 'they are so common that they are hardly worth recording.'

---

* Now Mrs. Billings, the well-known and admired physical medium, of New York.

"December, 1872.—The Boston Music Hall free meetings were inaugurated the first Sunday in October, by a lecture from Miss Lizzie Doten, whose high reputation as a poetess and inspirational speaker gained more in this one splendid discourse than by any of her previous fine efforts.

"Her subject was the 'Celestial Alphabet,' or a description of the immutable fidelity with which nature's language is represented in creation, and the laws which underlie all her forms and forces. . . . .

"Physical manifestations seem to be gaining in power with each returning day. Mrs. Britten's chapter on physical demonstrations makes mention of a Mrs. Libby White, of Sodus Point, N. Y. In the narrative of that lady's mediumship several novel phenomena are described. . . . .

"Not only are spirit faces and forms seen, and that in a lighted room, but visitors have the privilege of shaking hands with their beloved spiritual visitants, whilst warm kisses are pressed on their brows, and kind words of greeting are interchanged as in the days of mortal communion. . . . .

"From Moravia, New York, Boston, Chicago, and every section of the land, media like Dr. Slade, Mrs. Andrews, the Bangs family, Annie Lord Chamberlain, Jennie Webb, Maud Lord, Mrs. Hollis, Mr. Charles Foster, and hosts of others, eliminate through their mediumship more marvels in ten minutes than scientists could explain in ten years ; and yet one of the representative men of the 'scientific' ranks complains that 'for his part he never can see anything in Spiritualism worthy of investigation or notice.'

"This great transatlantic luminary seems to be well up in the nature and properties of metals. We wonder how he would explain the action of iron under the following circumstances.

"The *Religio Philosophical Journal*, giving a description of Captain Winslow, a new physical medium, writes as follows :—'We had the pleasure, a few evenings since, of attending a *séance*, at which Captain Winslow was the medium. The manifestations were very fine. *One very remarkable feat is the union of two solid iron rings, leaving them thus interlinked, and yet the metal perfectly sound.*'

"Something of a scene occurred in Chicago a few days ago, when Mrs. Sawyer, a physical force medium, of that city, was summoned to appear before Mayor Medill, to show cause why she should not be taxed and compelled to pay a license, like other 'exhibitors and vendors of wares ;' indeed, the mayor seemed to think the payment of a one hundred and twenty dollar license was only due to the city authorities for the privilege of allowing mourners to converse with their 'dead,' or the exercise of the gifts which the founder of the Christian religion charged upon Mayor Medill, in common with all his other followers. How the Spiritualists resisted and acted upon this demand may be gathered from a report in the *Chicago Times*, of which the following is an extract :—

"'A day or two since a medium named Mrs. Sawyer was brought before the mayor, and warned by that gentleman that if she did not take out a license she would be arrested. Mr. J. E. Hoyt, of No. 341, West Madison Street, was present, and declared he would continue his *séances*, his sweet communings with angel land, despite the mayor or his staff. Last night was the first occasion on which a stated *séance* has taken place since the mayor gave his warning. There was considerable excitement over the question whether the mayor would seek to carry out his threat, but the *séance* proceeded as usual, and no blue coat made his appearance. The spirits that manifested themselves were in great good humour, and seemed to be as little afraid of Mr. Medill as the temperance committee or the Spiritualists are of his logic.'

"The Massachusetts Supreme Court has given the ignorant and unprogressive officials of Chicago a good illustration of the advanced condition of public opinion on the subject of Spiritualism in the "Athens of America," as the following excerpt from the *Banner of Light* will show.

"'A RIGHT DECISION.

"'The Supreme Court of Massachusetts has reached a just decision in the case of Mrs. A. J. Feital, who had recovered five thousand dollars damages from the Middlesex Horse Railroad Company, in requital of injuries received while on the cars of that company on a certain Sunday, returning from a Spiritualist open-air meeting at Malden. The company contested her claim on the ground that they were not responsible for damages received at their hands on Sunday, the contract on that day with passengers being illegal. It further maintained that a Spiritualist meeting was in no sense religious, and therefore that the plaintiff had no good ground for even a Sunday case.

"'It was bold, if not worse, ground for a public corporation to assume in its defence ; and having been assessed in five thousand dollars damages, the Middlesex Company thought they would resist to the last rather than pay the amount. Hence the hearing before the Supreme Court of the Commonwealth. But justice was not to be thus baffled.

An appeal to its highest seat only brought out its voice with the utmost possible authority. The Supreme Court has decided that the company was obligated to carry the plaintiff, and indeed all other passengers, with as much care on Sunday as on any other day ; and also that a meeting of Spiritualists is as much a religious meeting for such as subscribe to Spiritualism, as any called orthodox.' " ! ! !

With the above extract there falls from the editor's palsied hand the last "Garland" that was ever woven from the blossoms of Spiritual truth for the pages of *The Western Star*. The relentless action of the Boston fires swept off amongst other ravages the warehouses and property not only of the parties who stood related to *The Western Star* as its proprietors and financial guarantors, but also reduced to temporary ruin a large number of its past and prospective subscribers. In this crisis the author issued a circular notice, the following extracts from which will speak for themselves :—

'SPECIAL NOTICE.—THE BOSTON FIRES AND THE INEVITABLE SUSPENSION OF 'THE WESTERN STAR.' "

" It is with the deepest regret that I am compelled to announce to the friends and patrons of this magazine the urgent necessity of suspending its publication,—at least for the present,—in consequence of the heavy losses incurred by its financial supporters in the late calamitous Boston fires.

" As it could not be expected that a new and wholly experimental work could secure a subscription list adequate to its support for the first few months, the actual expenses were guaranteed by the payment of certain sums as shares, with a promise that any deficit which might remain at the end of the year should be provided for by parties interested in the enterprise. . . . .

" Although I have refrained from publishing any of the highly laudatory letters I have received in commendation of this magazine, they have been so numerous and flattering that I could not question but that a steady increase in the subscription list, would have left it at the end of the year on a firm and well established foundation, but pending a climax which I could only hope to arrive at as a process of growth, all my resources and those of my friends and supporters are swept away by the overwhelming losses accruing from the Boston fires.

" My shareholders' and guarantors' property have alike been destroyed.

" I *cannot* add to their heavy losses by pressing my claims, small though they seem in comparison ; and a large number of my books have also been destroyed.

" Considerable sums due on the sale of magazines cannot now be collected from creditors more distressed than myself. The superior claims of *The Banner of Light*, for so many years the justly esteemed standard of the Eastern Spiritualists' faith, now crushed into overwhelming ruin, render all minor claims on the Spiritualists for aid, insignificant and almost unworthy.

" My own resources have been drained to support this (to me) noble labour of love until nothing more is left to give. I have bestowed all my time, night and day, health, rest, ceaseless energy, and every available dollar on the work ; and though I deem the high eulogies that have been passed upon it a meed worth labouring for, these have been the sole recompense I have derived. I can scarcely deem that any one will read this frank and straightforward statement and yet attribute blame, incompetency, or lack of faith to me when I say the work must now—for the present at least—suspend. . . . ."

The next step in the great Spiritualistic movement which claims attention was the first openly recognized dawning of a movement which has generally obtained the name of " Occultism," although in reality that term—*as now understood*—perverts rather than interprets its true significance, or that which it at first promised to unfold.

Mrs. Britten had changed her place of residence after the suspension of *The Western Star* from Boston to New York, and in that city occupied herself in translating and editing a work, since widely known, under the title of "Art Magic." The author of this book, being a life-long and highly-honoured friend of Mrs. Britten's, but—as a foreigner—not qualified to produce a work in the English language, had induced Mrs. Britten to undertake the task of preparing it for the press. Amongst other conditions which this gentleman insisted on, before he would consent to publish his book, was the stipulation that the real author should remain unknown, also that the circulation should be so limited as merely to pay expenses, and so prevent his recondite work from falling into the hands of such heterogeneous readers, as he felt confident would misunderstand, or perhaps pervert its aims to evil uses.

One of the features of this work was indicated in its second title, namely, " Mundane, Sub-mundane, and Super-mundane Spiritualism." It professed to explain the origin of creation ; of all religious systems ; tracing them out from Solar and Sex worship to sects and modern creeds. It defined the Occultist's belief in *Sub-mundane* or Elementary Spirits ; in *Super-mundane* or Planetary Spirits, and ranged between them, the realm of humanity with its spheres of communicating human Spirits, revealed through the order of Nature and Providence in the beneficent Spiritual outpouring of the nineteenth century. A few examples of ancient, mediæval, and present day Oriental magic were given, not as subjects for imitation, but rather as warnings of what to avoid, and in striking contrast to the naturalness and order of the modern Spiritual methods of communion.

As the mechanical details of the publication were likely to be very costly, and the limited circulation rendered it unremunerative, the editor (Mrs. Britten) sent out preliminary notices inviting subscriptions, to which nearly *four thousand answers* were sent in, from different parts of the world. As the circulation was not to exceed a few hundreds, with the addition of a certain number of copies to be prepared as equivalent for losses, &c., it might have been hoped that there was little scope for blame or reproach, singular as the undertaking might have appeared to those who knew nothing of " Occultism."

Far otherwise however were the results. From the first day when the preliminary notices were issued, the author's motives were assailed by a veritable storm of misrepresentation and insult. Articles, prints, and tracts were circulated to warn the public against patronizing the intended work. The unwary were assured it was " a plot of Jesuits," and nothing less than " a cunning conspiracy to uproot Spiritualism, and place Catholicism, witchcraft, magic, and *diablerie* in general, in its place. It would be almost humiliating to recall the folly and absurdity exhibited by the attacking party.

Never in the course of a long career of devotion to the service of humanity, had the author witnessed such a rain of illogical and causeless persecution ; never had she expected to be requited for such service, after such a fashion. And all this while, it must be remembered, the book was yet *unpublished*, and except by its author, editor, and a few private friends, not a line of its MSS. was known, or had ever met the eye of a single creature that denounced it ! It seems to have been the facts that the author insisted on remaining anonymous, wrote on subjects of which the attacking parties were ignorant, and limited his circulation to " a worthy few," which excited the wrath of the belligerents, unless indeed a certain number gladly availed themselves of this opportunity to retaliate upon Mrs. Britten, the opposition they had endured from her, on the subject of the infamous " Social freedom " doctrine.

Meantime it would be ungrateful indeed not to acknowledge, that there was another side to this curious warfare. Those who had personally known, and hundreds of others who had followed Mrs. Britten during her long public career, poured in upon her the most cordial and generous assurances of confidence. Unlimited promises of support and offers of assistance also were volunteered from countless sources. When at length the object of this remarkable warfare was produced, its owners as a general rule had scarcely completed its perusal ere they poured in upon the much-abused editor, letters of the highest eulogy and thankfulness. The receipt of those letters, and the fact that several hundred of such are now in the editor's possession, have more than compensated her for the birthpangs through which this highly-lauded and greatly-abused volume was produced. Amongst other illustrious European potentates who sought and, in some instances only, succeeded in obtaining possession of this book, were the late unfortunate Czar of Russia and his noble *aide-de-camp*, the much-beloved friend of Spiritualism, Prince Emil de Sayn Wittgenstein. These gentlemen were amongst the first European subscribers who applied for "Art Magic," and Mrs. Britten rejoices in the possession of autograph letters from them, not only thanking her for being the instrument of publishing "so glorious a work," but adding commendatory notices of too personal a character to transcribe in this place.

Prince Emil Wittgenstein, who was one of the Russian Emperor's lieutenant generals in the late unhappy Turkish war, wrote to Mrs. Britten that he regarded that book as his "bible," carried it with him wherever he went, and had "often derived consolation and harmony of spirit from its noble teachings in moments embittered by the fever of war, and the cares of State." Many similar tokens of admiration from some of the best minds of the age, soon sufficed to wipe out the stains of mud hurled against the publication by those who knew not what they did, *or whom they denounced*.

Had this episode been of the purely personal character hitherto detailed, it would have found no place here, except indeed to demonstrate the fact that many of those who call themselves Spiritualtists, and claim to be "the friends of progress," have not outgrown the spirit of ancient bigotry, and are just as ready to put those who differ with them to moral death or Spiritual torture as if they were the most zealous adherents of orthodox creeds. The publication of "Art Magic" synchronizes so closely in point of time with the first awakening interest manifested in occult subjects and especially with the foundation of the celebrated "Theosophical Society," of which the author was one of the first members, that it becomes an act of justice due to both subjects, to show, that they were totally unrelated, and that the impression which seems to have prevailed to the contrary, simply arose from the fact that "Art Magic" was published about the time when the Theosophical Society was founded. As there were many persons who —when "Art Magic" was published and the "Theosophical Society" formed—without having the smallest knowledge of the facts, rushed into print to explain to others what they did not understand themselves, and especially to show, that the authors in both cases were combined, and both in a conspiracy to sweep Spiritualism out of existence, and substitute for it Jesuitism, and the *black art*, Mrs. Britten was often compelled to answer these wild and far-fetched attacks by counter statements, one specimen at least of which will do more to enlighten the reader on the true state of the case than all that the lying tongue of rumour could disclose. The article which follows, was printed in the Boston *Spiritual Scientist*, and is prefaced by the following editorial remarks :—

"'ART MAGIC.'

"Emma Hardinge Britten replies to the important caution issued by Dr. B——— against the proposed work on "art magic," advertised in another column of this paper. His insinuations, concerning the unknown author, and also the other objections urged by him, are ably answered. She says :—

"'If the Spiritualists think they know everything that is to be known, of course they need to hear or to read no more. For the few who think with me that we need "light, more light"; to those who are not satisfied that twenty-five years of communion with our beloved ones gone before has explained all of the twenty-five thousand years of life that has gone behind, nor yet exhausted the fountains of revelation on all spiritualistic subjects that may unfold themselves in the future, I say, press on! search on! and take the very Kingdom of Heaven by violence, sooner than sit down in the apathetic rust of "I know enough!" . . .

"'To all whom it may concern, but in strict justice to Col. Olcott, Madame Blavatsky, and any who may unwittingly be confounded with this matter, I emphatically protest that they have nothing whatever to do with it. That the two movements, namely, the publication of my friend's advertisement and the formation of the Theosophical Society, most strangely took place at or about the same time, in fact, within twenty-four hours of each other, is a truth which I admit, but cannot account for.

"'About twelve hours after I had posted the advertisement to the *Banner of Light*, announcing that a book on "Art Magic," &c., was to be published, Col. Olcott and I met for the first time in several years. An old acquaintance was renewed, an introduction to Madame Blavatsky took place, and then, but *not till then*, did I learn the views of these friends, respecting a concerted effort to study faithfully the science which underlies the principles of spirit-communion. So amazed and struck was I with the coincidence of *purposes* expressed in the inauguration of the "Theosophical Society," at which I was present, with some of the ideas, put forth in my friend's work, that I felt it to be my duty to write to the President of that Society, enclose a copy of the advertisement, and explain to him that the publication of the book in question anticipated, without concert of action or even personal acquaintance with the parties concerned, whatever of Cabalistic lore or revelation the said "Theosophical Society" might hereafter evolve. Whilst my Theosophical friends and myself have both been greatly struck with the remarkable coincidence of the two movements, chiming in at precisely the same stroke of the dial from points of action removed from and at the same time unknown to each other, we neither desire to damage the work of the other by being mistaken for or confounded together. The author of "Art Magic" prepared the material for his work many years ago in Europe, and is a total stranger to Col. Olcott or Madame Blavatsky. Praise or blame us all not for each other's sake, but for our own.'"

At this point it may be necessary to explain that the *Spiritual Scientist*, in which the above letter appeared, was a most excellent and scholarly paper published in Boston by Mr. E. Gerry Brown, and although this gentleman never espoused in especial the views of the "Occultists," his unconservative columns were ever open to all who had truths to tell, wrongs to right, or information to impart. It was in this generous spirit, that Mr. Brown reprinted from the columns of the *Banner of Light*, a letter from Colonel Olcott in answer to the many absurd tirades that were levelled against him as President of the Theosophical Society on the subject of "Occultism." Like the *Spiritual Scientist*, the editors of the *Banner* had, without ever writing a word in favour of Occultism, generously opened their columns to both sides of the question; a magnanimous line of conduct which warmly commends itself to the imitation of all seekers for truth. Colonel Olcott says :—

"Occultism is something that *can* be tested and proven by all 'competent' persons, and is not a mere tangle of assertions and theories. . . . .

"Do you want me to name over the authors who corroborate my statement? It would nearly fill every column of this issue of the *Banner*. Do you complain that I have given the public no proofs of the existence of elementary spirits, and their subjection to human control? I could occupy your paper a whole year without exhausting the accessible supply of anecdotes. If you want a perfect reservoir of authenticated cases of magic, read Des Mousseaux's series of volumes in the French language. If you wish to know what the Chinese and Thibetan thaumaturgic priests perform, read Huc and Schlangentweit. If you would know of the power of man to change his corporeal form and assume whatever shape he chooses, read the memoirs of Simon Magus (who is mentioned by St. Luke), and of Apollonius; read Pierre Manor's treatise against the sorcerers; Henry de Coulogue's 'De Lamœis;' the 'Vie des Peres du Desert;' read the stories of magic and sorcery brought back from Mexico and Central America by M. Brasseur de Bourbourg; read about the occultism of the ancient Peruvians, in Prescott and Tscuddi. If you wish evidence of ancient occulist practices, read Pausanias, Plato, Cicero, Iamblichus, Tacitus, Herodotus, Manetho, Sanchoniaton, the Sohar, and the Egyptian and Jewish Kabbalas. . . . .

"Says Eliphas Levi—'There is a true and a false science, a divine magic and an infernal magic. The magician must be distinguished from the sorcerer, the adept from the charlatan. The magician disposes of a force that he knows, the sorcerer endeavours to abuse that of which he is ignorant. The 'devil' submits to the magician; the sorcerer gives himself up to the devil. The magician is the sovereign pontiff of Nature; the sorcerer only its profaner. Magic is the traditional science of the secrets of Natnre, which came to us from the Magi.'

In view of the statements concerning the *character and identity* of the communicating Spirits of the new dispensation, as defined in that number of the *Theosophist* quoted in our section on India, the reader's attention is particularly called to the ensuing paragraph of Colonel Olcott's letter :—

"*Occultism does not rob Spiritualism of one of the comforting features, nor abate one jot of its importance as an argument for immortality. It denies the identity of no real human spirit that ever has or ever will approach an inquirer.*[*] It simply shows that we are liable to the visits, often the influence, and sometimes the absolute control, of a class of invisible but very powerful spirits, whose existence I am the first of American spiritualistic investigators to warn the sect against. Its philosophy clashes in no sense against the basic discoveries of modern science, but, on the contrary, rounds out and completes what without it is a crude magma of the Known and the Unknowable. It completes the demonstration of the law of evolution, and supplies the link that has hitherto been missing from the chain that our philosophical contemporaries have, with so much patience, constructed. Its mission as regards Spiritualism, is to filter, purge, classify, and explain, not to play the part of the iconoclast or the Vandal. Through my unworthy mouth it, for the moment, asks recognition, but soon it will compel the attention of every man capable of thinking for himself, and be taught in every corner of the world by a host of apostles and propagandists."

It would be needless to dwell further upon the "new departures" which divided sentiment upon the now mooted question of "Occultism."

As a sample of the absurdities that were perpetrated by those who in utter ignorance of Occultism, Theosophy, or their aims, wantonly resorted to the schoolboy trick of pelting them with ridicule and insult, we reprint an article sent by the author to the *Banner of Light* on the occasion of the funeral of the Baron de Palm, a Hungarian nobleman who was associated with Mrs. Britten, as a member of the first council established by the Theosophical Society in New York. The funeral services took place on Sunday afternoon May 28th, 1876, and the lampoons and satirical notices of the secular press, and the reticent brief paragraphs of the Spiritual press, called forth from the author the following article, which was published in the columns of the *Banner of Light* :—

"THE LATE BARON DE PALM AND THE NEW YORK THEOSOPHICAL SOCIETY.

"*To the Editor of the ' Banner of Light.'*

"In your issue of June 3rd, I see a very brief notice of the funeral obsequies of the late Baron de Palm, conducted under the auspices of the Theosophical Society. As the

---

* Italics by the author.

New York secular papers have done us the honour of devoting many columns of their 'invaluable journals' in contemptuous ridicule of these two subjects, and as they, with their usual spirit of *fairness* fail to afford us any opportunity of representing ourselves in contradiction to the foolish rumours and childish criticisms volunteered about us, it has seemed meet to the few Spiritualists connected with the Theosophical Society, especially those who were engaged in conducting Baron de Palm's funeral obsequies, to ask if we cannot have a moderate amount of space in the columns of our chief organ of thought for a more fair and complete representation than interested scandal-mongers have hitherto afforded us. The Theosophical Society took its rise in the interest manifested by a party of ladies and gentlemen who had assembled one evening in the parlours of Madame Blavatsky to hear a reading from Mr. George H. Felt, the Egyptologist, and interpreter of the figures of the Egyptian Cabala. I have already stated, whilst defending myself through the courteous use of your columns, from the extraordinary attacks made upon me for the publication of 'Art Magic, that at the reading to which I refer I met Madame Blavatsky and Mr. Felt for the first time in my life, and that it was the astonishment which my husband and I both felt in hearing from the discourse we listened to on the Cabala, so much similarity of ideas and aims to those which we were then busy in translating, and were about to publish in the work of an esteemed friend, that induced us to urge forward the formation of the Theosophical Society, connect ourselves with it, and do all we could to promote its welfare. . . . . The initial meetings of the Society took place as before stated at the rooms of Madame Blavatsky, subsequently at my own house, and after our organisation had been completed at the Mott Memorial Hall. As the most concise and yet comprehensive definition I can render of the aims with which this society entered upon a concrete existence, I commend to the slanderer and candid querist alike, a careful perusal of the following extracts from the printed preamble and by-laws which we have put forth :

" ' The title of the Theosophical Society explains the objects and desires of its founders ; they seek "to obtain knowledge of the nature and attributes of the Supreme Power and of the higher spirits *by the aid of physical processes*." In other words, they hope, that by going deeper than modern science has hitherto done, into the esoteric philosophies of ancient times, they may be enabled to obtain, for themselves and other investigators, proof of the existence of an "Unseen Universe," the nature of its inhabitants, if such there be, and the laws which govern them and their relations with mankind.

" ' Whatever may be the private opinions of its members, the society has no dogmas to enforce, no creed to disseminate. It is formed neither as a Spiritualistic schism, nor to serve as the foe or friend of any sectarian or philosophic body. Its only axiom is the omnipotence of truth, its only creed a profession of unqualified devotion to its discovery and propagation.

" ' The Theosophical Society has been organized in the interest of religion, science and good morals. . . .

" ' The founders being baffled in every attempt to get the desired knowledge in other quarters, turn their faces toward the Orient, whence are derived all systems of religion and philosophy. They find our ancestors practising important arts now lost to us. They discover them dealing with forces whose very names are now unknown, and the simplest demonstration of whose existence is impossible to our scientists. In the Bible occurs a multitude of passages which corroborate inferences deducible from the picture-writings on the architectural remains of the ancient nations ; while every important museum of antiquities augments the proof of their wisdom and enlightenment.

" ' The Theosophical Society, disclaiming all pretension to the possession of unusual advantages, all selfish motives, all disposition to foster deception of any sort, all intent to wilfully and causelessly injure any established organization, invites the fraternal co-operation of such as can realize the importance of its field of labour, and are in sympathy with the objects for which it has been organised. . . .'

" In concluding my necessarily brief notice of this movement, I have only to add, our little gathering has had to contend with all those obstacles which ordinarily hang upon the footprints of new movements. We have been misrepresented in many quarters, not excepting those from whom we had the most right to expect sympathy and support. We have been sneered at as 'attempting to revive the superstitions of the dark ages, and roll back the car of progress,' &c., &c. With the same justice that the author of 'Art Magic' has been denounced as a Jesuit and a Catholic, because he cited as an illustration of mediæval magic the formulæ of Catholic magicians, our society has been denounced as antagonistic to truth and progress, because we are aiming to discover the clue to ancient sciences, as a basis for modern improvements ; hence we had trials to encounter, compelling us at last to shield the truths we could not endure to see misrepresented, by making our organization, if not actually a secret society in its fullest sense, at least an exclusive one, reserving all knowledge of our deliberations and proceedings to our own members, except where we decided amongst ourselves to give them publicity. An occasion of this character occurred in the demise of one of our esteemed associates, the Baron de Palm, whose expressed wish that his obsequies should be conducted under the auspices of the Theosophical Society, and as far as possible in accordance with Oriental customs, obliged us to present ourselves before the world as a subject for such criticism as it has deemed *fitting and decent* to accord to *funeral rites*, conducted on a little out-of-the-common-order plan. The necessary haste in which this ceremonial was got up, and the fact that by the absence of a great many of the fellows of the society, nearly all the onerous duties attending this effort devolved upon our esteemed president, Colonel Olcott, were circumstances which materially interfered with the full representation of our ideas which we so earnestly desired. As it was, on arriving at New York on the Sunday morning, the day fixed for the obsequies, I found every journal full of *funny* writing on the *funny* scene that was expected to take place that afternoon, in the form of a 'Pagan funeral,' and Colonel Olcott harassed, overworked, and thoroughly worn out, first with the severer task of attending his dying friend, and next with the still severer duties which devolved upon him in the attempt to carry out that friend's last wishes.

" As to the scene which the outside of the grand Masonic Temple presented some two hours before that fixed for the ceremonial, it baffles all description. Thanks to the voluntary advertisements which the *comic* writers of the city thought proper to bestow upon us, the Sunday idlers of New York had assembled in vast multitudes to beguile their leisure with something scarcely less entertaining than Barnum's Hippodrome, or Moody and Sankey's hysterical votaries at their confessions. The quiet dignity with which our president reminded the vast assemblage who finally succeeded in pressing into the hall, that they must remember ' they were in the presence of death,' no doubt had its effect in converting the expectations of fun and frolic promised them by their leading journals into a spirit of grave and respectful attention. For a further account of the Baron de Palm, and the ceremonials which actually took place on the occasion, I refer the reader to the following quotations from the *New York Tribune* and *World*, both of which journals did sufficient justice to the historical features of the scene :—

" ' BARON DE PALM'S FUNERAL—SERVICES OF THE THEOSOPHICAL SOCIETY.

" ' At the Roosevelt Hospital in this city, on Saturday, May 21, a man died whose life, character, and religious belief the singular funeral services performed yesterday at the Masonic Temple bring into prominence. Baron Joseph Henry Louis de Palm, formerly Chamberlain of the Duke of Bavaria, was born at Augsburg, May 10, 1809, and was descended from an old baronial family dating back, it is said, to the year 832. . . . . The Baron de Palm was educated in diplomacy, for which his talents fitted him, and for a long time he was in the German diplomatic service. He lived for years gaily and extravagantly in the capitals of Europe, but at last abandoning a life which had become wearisome to him, he came to America in 1862, and spent a considerable time among the Indian tribes in the far West. He often spoke of the time he passed among the Indians as the pleasantest period of his life. Last November, hoping to find in the Theosophical Society of this city a system of religious belief which would commend itself to his judgment and experience, he joined himself to that organization, to which he willed his property, and under its direction his funeral services were conducted yesterday.

" ' The body of Baron de Palm was embalmed immediately after death, and has been lying at the Roosevelt Hospital, whence it was brought by the undertaker, unaccompanied by either priest or pall-bearers, to the Masonic Temple. The casket was of rosewood, with plain silver trimmings, and rested upon a simple undecorated catafalque upon the platform in the large hall. Black tickets of admission were issued in sufficient numbers to fill the hall with people, but as many who received them did not attend, the multitude were allowed to rush into the empty seats just after the beginning of the service. Upon the coffin and on each side of it were placed Oriental symbols of the faith of the dead man, and over the upper end hung the medals and insignia of the Baron's diplomatic service, and his patent of nobility. Seven candles of different colours burned upon the coffin, and these, with the brazier of incense placed at the left, symbolized fire-worship. Upon the right stood a cross with a serpent about it, the cross typifying the creative principle of nature, and the serpent the principle of evolution.

" ' At four o'clock a solemn voluntary was played upon the organ, and a few minutes later, the seven members of the Society who had been selected to perform the service appeared upon the platform in black robes, and carrying in their hands twigs of palm, which, according to Oriental belief, are instrumental in warding off danger and misfortune. Henry S. Olcott, president of the Society, upon whom devolved all preparations for the funeral, and who afterward delivered the funeral discourse, advanced to the front of the platform and requested those present to remember they were in the presence of death, and that as nothing sensational would occur in the funeral services, the Society expected from them a respectful silence. He disclaimed all connection with the Masonic fraternity, and said that the service was not to be conducted according to the Egyptian ritual except in so far as the symbols of immortality were concerned. A choir of three persons then sang an Orphic hymn to organ accompaniment, and this was followed by the invocation, pronounced by T. Frederick Thomas. After the prayer came organ music again, and then the Theosophic Liturgy, Colonel Olcott asking the questions, &c., which were answered by his assistants in the service. The liturgy was followed by another Orphic hymn, and then Colonel Olcott advanced to pronounce the funeral oration.

"'After describing the life and general characteristics which marked his deceased friend and associate, the Baron, the President went on to speak of the Society which he then represented, and denounced in fearless terms the gross misrepresentations with which the press had endeavoured to mislead the public mind, both in regard to the ceremonials now being enacted, and the end and aims of the Theosophists themselves. He described the organization and aims of the Society in substance pretty much as I have given it above, and concluded a long, bold, and very eloquent address in the following terms, which I quote from the *New York World* :—

"'There in that coffin lay a Theosophist. Should his future be pronounced one of unalloyed happiness without respect to the course of his life? No; but as he had acted so should he suffer or rejoice. If he was a sensualist, a usurer, or a corrupter, then the divine first cause could not forgive him the least of his offences, for that would be to plunge the universe into chaos. There must be compensation, equilibrium, justice. Ancient theosophy held immovably to two ideas—the existence of a first cause, and the immortality of the soul. The soul was believed to have emanated from the central soul, and the body had to be subjugated to the spirit. It was no more thought that one could suffer for another's sins than for another's gluttony or other physical wrong doings. The opposite belief was responsible for the condition of the world to-day. The scaffold teemed with ruffians whose sins it was believed muttered words would wash away.

"'Another Orphic hymn followed. Mrs. Emma Hardinge Britten then made a brief address, in which she declared that she, as one who had spoken with the arisen souls of the dead, proclaimed by the revelation of the Great Spirit and his ministering angels, that the dead brother, though enfranchised into the higher life, was with his friends yet. They who were searching for the great mystery of life and death, had been reviled and scoffed at, but here, standing among the emblems of sacred beliefs, they ought to be safe from slanderous revilings and unkind jests. Mrs. Britten thought that in this centennial year, when human enfranchisement was being celebrated, none should attempt to impose chains on the human soul. Then turning toward the coffin she extended her hands bearing flowers, and exclaimed: "Speed home, friend and companion! Thou hast not left us. We know that thou hast passed the golden gates wherein sorrow entereth not, and we bid thee God speed to thy home of light. Although the golden bowl is broken, and the silver cord is loosed, we put on no weeds of mourning, and we offer thee symbols of full-blown human life in these flowers."

"'The High Priest then pronounced the obsequies finished, and the audience slowly dispersed. The coffin was left on the platform, and long after all the spectators and members of the Society had gone away, it remained alone, stripped of its decorations, and with only the roses Mrs. Britten had scattered on it, and three or four green palm branches lying upon it, as if to keep the wood nymphs near and protect the dead Baron from the dreaded elemental spirits. Toward nightfall it was taken by the solitary undertaker to its temporary resting-place in a vault of the Lutheran cemetery.

"'Trusting that the admission of these statements, Mr. Editor, will have the desirable effect of subduing the tone of rancour, contempt, and unworthy misrepresentation which some of our Spiritualistic brethren have thought proper to adopt towards us poor Theosophists, I take my leave, and as one of the Council of the Society, in the name of the President and the Fellows of that Association, tender you, Mr. Editor, our sincere thanks for the space allotted to us in these columns.

"'Very faithfully yours,
"'EMMA HARDINGE BRITTEN.'"

All that now remains to be said on this subject is that to the author's thinking any knowledge that can be gleaned from true "Occultism" ought to be faithfully studied by those who desire to become *scientific Spiritualists*, and any good that has been taught by "Theosophy," *as represented in this chapter*, is equally essential to round out the life here, and prepare for the life hereafter, in the religion of a true Spiritualist.

CHAPTER LIII.

SPIRITUALISM IN AMERICA (CONTINUED).

" PASSED AWAY ! "

IT was in the fall of 1870, that the cause of Spiritualism sustained an irreparable loss in the departure for the higher life of Mrs. Fanny Conant, for many years the Medium through whom were given those communications from all classes of stranger spirits that have formed a leading feature in the columns of the *Banner of Light.*

It was mainly through the influence of wise Spirits communicating through Mrs. Conant, that the *Banner of Light* was established at all, and it was these same far-seeing intelligences who sustained the harassed spirits of its editors, when the cares and embarrassments of its pioneer work would have well nigh overwhelmed them. It was Mrs. Conant also who founded the celebrated *Banner of Light* circle, at which so many thousands of Spirits sent messages of love and consolation to bereaved friends, and afforded the world indisputable proofs of the soul's immortality. This gifted and versatile Medium had lived to see her brother, Mr. Crowell, one of the earliest assistant editors of the *Banner*, Wm. Berry and Wm. White, each in turn, editors and part proprietors of the paper, pass on to the higher life, leaving herself and Mr. Colby all that remained of the original founders of this onerous undertaking. The time came at length when these faithful allies were to part, when the veteran editor Luther Colby was to see the last of his early associates vanish from his side, whilst Fanny Conant, so well beloved throughout the ranks of Spiritualism, gave up her twenty years' trust of the Spiritual standard ; and in the words of the poet—

> " Folded her pale hands so meekly,
> Spake with us on earth no more."

When the first shock of this transition was over, the following correspondence ensued in the columns of the paper so long associated with Mrs. Conant's name. We give it in full, as it speaks in far more graphic language than we could command, of the esteem with which the inestimable services of the departed lady were remembered by some of Boston's most respected and prominent merchants :—

"THE LATE MRS. J. H. CONANT. MEMORIAL SERVICE IN MUSIC HALL, BOSTON, OCTOBER 10TH.

" Mrs. Emma Hardinge Britten,—Madam : The undersigned, friends of the late Mrs. J. H. Conant, appreciating her faithful services in the cause of Spiritualism, so many years a prominent medium of rare power, estimable character, and of unquestioned honesty, feel as if something of the character of a Memorial Service would be but a fitting tribute to her worth, as well as a gratification to us, and to her friends in general, who are the body of Spiritualists all over the world.

" Knowing you to be one of our most gifted speakers and a sister medium, who knew her well, we have thought it would be a pleasure to you, as well as to her friends in general, to undertake such a service, and we therefore invite you to deliver an oration upon her life and work as you are qualified to give on such an occasion.

" You will please select such time as will be most agreeable to you, and when informed we will make all the necessary arrangements suitable for such a service. Hoping this will meet with your approval and acceptance,

" We remain, most truly yours,

" ALLEN PUTNAM,	J. S. LADD,
" JOHN WETHERBEE,	PHINEAS E. GAY,
" DANIEL FARRAR,	ANSON J. STONE.
" DAVID WILDEE,	L. A. BIGELOW,
" J. F. ALDERMAN,	M. V. LINCOLN,
" FRED. A. GOULD,	GEORGE W. SMITH,
" R. H. SPALDING,	GEORGE A. BACON.

" Boston, September 17th, 1875."

" To Messrs. Allen Putnam, Judge Ladd, and others.

" Gentlemen,—Your favour of the 17th inst. has been received by me with feelings of unmixed gratification and interest. From the time when our most excellent and esteemed co-worker, Mrs. J. H. Conant, closed her mortal pilgrimage amongst us I have felt for myself, and all who have participated in the new light and life that Spiritualism has brought us, a sense of pain and humiliation at our lack of opportunity to testify to the whole world how gratefully we remembered her invaluable services, how tenderly we appreciated the martyrdoms her mediumistic life had imposed upon her, and how strongly our sympathies were moved by the obvious fact that in the prime of her early womanhood the faithful and self-sacrificing labourer has sunk beneath the cross she bore, and all too soon for us and for the world, has left us to shoulder the burden too heavy for her to endure longer.

" When some years since I had the honour of representing Spiritualism in the memorial services held in this city, in memory of the venerable John Pierpont, one of the leading journals commented somewhat severely on the fact that this act of grateful reverence to a 'Spiritualistic notable' was remarkable for its rarity on the part of Spiritualists.

" I rejoice to believe that the proposed tribute to one so eminently worthy as Mrs. Conant may afford us the opportunity of wiping away this reproach, and I am especially grateful for the selection which confers on me the gracious task of tendering to the ascended spirit of our beloved friend a just and well-merited recognition of the life-long work of devotion she has performed amongst us. However incompetent I may deem myself to meet the requirements of the great demand you make upon me, I shall not hesitate for one moment to do your bidding. I feel as if every true and honest Spiritualist in America must be with us, and if not in person, at least in the spirit of love and sympathy, so many grateful thousands will join in this memorial service, that my short-comings will be forgotten in the intention of so memorable an occasion.

" Holding myself and my services entirely at your disposal, gentlemen, in the order of the exercises you propose, and only suggesting that you should name the time most suitable for convening an assemblage worthy the subject of the meeting, I am, very faithfully yours, " EMMA HARDINGE BRITTEN.

" 206, West 38th Street, New York, September 18th, 1875.'

---

* The persons moving in this matter of memorial service have arranged to have it take place on Sunday afternoon, October 10th, at 2¾ o'clock, in Music Hall, to which the public are invited free. " JOHN WETHERBEE, for the Committee.

" Boston, September 29th, 1875."

Several of the daily journals of Massachusetts gave brief but respectful notices of "the memorial service" which took place in the Boston Music Hall in the presence of about three thousand deeply moved and interested auditors. The following excerpt from the *Boston Herald* is a fair specimen of the press notices which the occasion called forth:—

" SPIRITUALISM.

" Services in memory of the late Mrs. Fanny Conant were held at Music Hall yesterday afternoon. There was a large attendance of the Spiritualists of Boston and vicinity. The platform was decorated with flowers and autumn leaves. Mr. John Wetherbee presided, and introduced the orator of the occasion (Mrs. Emma Hardinge Britten) in a few felicitous words. Mrs. Britten commenced by reciting an eloquent invocation given through the mediumship of Mrs. Conant, and then gave a brief biographical sketch of the departed. Although her life was a protracted martyrdom, it had been continuously devoted to the service of humanity. As the *Banner of Light* medium for about twenty years, she had been the instrument of receiving more than 10,000 communications from the spirit world, the genuineness of many of them having been tested in the most conclusive manner. To her was due the origin of the *Banner*, and largely to her the moral support which gave strength to the faltering hands of its proprietors and enabled them to continue their great work for Spiritualism and humanity. Mrs. Britten, who was frequently applauded, closed with an eloquent tribute to 'dear, brave little Fanny Conant.' The speaker is a noble-looking, gracious-mannered lady, with a style of oratory at once brilliant, pathetic, and powerful."

To Mr. Allen Putnam's charming biography of Fanny Conant, and the book of her recorded communications entitled "Flashes of Light,"* we must refer the reader for more minute details concerning the life and services of this admirable Medium. The writer who tenders her memory this imperfect but heartfelt tribute of affection can well say of Mrs. Conant what many others all over the world have felt, that in this generation at least, "we ne'er shall look upon her like again."

It would seem almost superfluous in this connection to add expressions either of eulogy or explanation concerning the journal quoted in nearly every chapter of this volume, the name of which, the *Banner of Light*, has become a household word on the lips of every Spiritualist ; and yet for the sake of that posterity to which we dare believe this work will descend, we deem it fitting to add a few brief paragraphs on a subject which now needs no other comment than its name affords. For a period of over a quarter of a century, the *Banner of Light* has redeemed its significant title by carrying the glad tidings of immortality to every land of civilization. Its articles have been translated into every written language, and its glorious standard has been raised wherever reading men and women have congregated together in this nineteenth century.

Of all the original staff that first constituted its strength, and founded its illimitable usefulness, Luther Colby, its veteran editor, alone remains. An experienced "press man," in the outset of the *Banner's* career, Mr. Colby knew how to place it before the world in a practical and acceptable point of view.

It has changed its external appearance from time to time, but always risen in the scale of mechanical excellence and editorial completeness.

It has changed its *corps* of editors and contributors many times, for the harvest angel of death has swept his sickle through the field of effort and transplanted many a shining head from the dull glare of the lamps of earth to the star roads of eternity : but Luther Colby has still kept his place at the helm, firm, faithful, unswerving, in whatever he may have considered to be *his path of duty.* Many have differed from him ; many condemned his course; and many exalted it to the skies. Unmoved by praise or blame, the gallant old standard-bearer has unfurled his flag to the breeze, and waited till the storm passed by, but never departed from the course suggested to him through his own Mediumship, or that of the associates in whom he has placed confidence.

Mr. Isaac Rich, the second proprietor of this grand old paper, with Mr. Colby, although he takes but little part in its editorial conduct, is well-known throughout the Spiritual book trade for the two great though too often dissevered elements, *honour* and *enterprise.* Both these noble qualities have distinguished Mr. Rich in his world-wide dealings. Who then can

---

* Published by Colby and Rich, *Banner of Light* Office, Boston, Mass., U.S.A.

take exception, if the *Banner of Light*, with its well-matched associates and a well-tried corps of assistants, does not always represent the opinions of this or the other party?   Mr. Colby and a large majority of his contributors have incurred the censure of many prominent and earnest Spiritualists, for what they deem to be the all too embracing spirit of charity with which the *Banner* staff have excused the errors and frailties of many a defaulting Medium.   Whilst the author—besides those above alluded to—has taken exception to this position, she *knows* beyond a peradventure, that it has been assumed in the strictest integrity of purpose by the kind-hearted editor and his friends, and that sooner than see those whom they regard as " the pillars of their faith "—*the Mediums*—" abused," they would err on the opposite side of the question, and regard their shortcomings with even too much leniency in consideration of their actual Mediumistic endowments.

Notwithstanding the wide differences of opinion on this subject that have arisen between the editors of the *Banner of Light*, their *collaborateurs*, and others, every Spiritualist in the ranks must admit that the good name of the house so honourably represented by Mr. Rich, and the long and invaluable years of service and devotion contributed by Mr. Colby, call for an earthly acknowledgment, and one which the writer firmly believes is but the faint shadow of that immortal record wherein the *Banner of Light*, and the names of its devoted upholders, will be found inscribed in letters of imperishable gold.

Whilst our attention is attracted to the journalistic department of the movement, we must remind our readers of an event which happily finds no parallel in the entire thirty-five years' history of modern Spiritualism—that is to say, not in connection with any of the immediate actors in that mighty drama.   It was on the 15th of March, 1877, that the tidings flashed over the wires throughout the length and breadth of the United States, that Mr. S. S. Jones, the enterprising and well-known proprietor of the *Religio Philosophical Journal*, had been cruelly murdered in his own office in the city of Chicago, and that the perpetrator of the foul deed had surrendered himself into the hands of justice.

The circumstances of this tragic event are so clearly detailed in the *Banner of Light* of the 31st of March, 1877, that we cannot do better than follow the record, which reads thus :—

" At little past the hour of noon on the 15th inst., William C. Pike called at the Harrison Street Police Station and surrendered himself as the murderer of Stevens S. Jones, whose body, he said, they would find struggling in death at his office, in room 16, in the Religio Philosophical Publishing House Building, No. 394, Dearborn Street, Chicago. An officer was sent to the office in question, examined the premises, found the assassin's words were true, and, after assisting to remove the corpse from the floor, where it had fallen from the chair in which the murdered man sat when he was approached from behind and shot dead without even a warning of danger, returned and reported the startling truth at the station.

" On *post mortem* examination two bullet wounds were found in the body ; one bullet entered the *medulla oblongata* at the junction of the spinal cord, passed upward and forward, and lodged against the *os frontis*.   The ball was found to fit the pistol given up by the assassin ; the other bullet entered the lower portion of the right shoulder, passing upward, and lodged in the muscles.   Dr. Holden testified that consciousness must have ceased on the very second in which the shot was fired.   The assassin claims to be a phrenologist, and had, if the daily papers may be believed, boasted that his knowledge as such enabled him to select that particular point at which to place his pistol (for it was sufficiently close to burn the hair upon the neck) and insure the accomplishment of this most foul murder against all chance of failure.

" According to the indications this sad catastrophe was the result of an effort at black-mailing, at which the high spirit of Bro. Jones rebelled.   It is a singular index in this direction, says the Religio's account, that but a few moments previously to the murder, Mr. Jones 'passed into the business office, and procured a note of 24 dollars, made by the assassin, and *that note has never been seen since,* unless by its maker.'

"The following is the verdict of the jury summoned by the coroner in view of the lamentable occurrence :—

"' We, the jury, find that Stevens S. Jones came to his death on the 15th day of March, 1877, at the Religio Philosophical Publishing House Building, No. 127 4th Avenue, in the city of Chicago, by two pistol shot wounds, one through the head, and the other through the right shoulder, at the hands of Wm. C. Pike, premeditatedly, deliberately, and maliciously, and find it murder in the first degree ; we also find evidence to satisfy us that Genevieve Pike, his reputed wife, should be held as an accessory before the fact, and recommend that both persons be held for the action of the Grand Jury, without bail.'

"The account proceeds, with the parenthetical remark, to the sentiment of which all lovers of humanity will accede a willing agreement :—

"' It may be proper to say in this connection, that the family and friends of the man so cowardly assassinated do not desire the blood of the assassin, nor that of the woman Genevieve, and beyond an honest endeavour to arrive at all the truth (by which they are sure the entire innocence of the murdered man of the charges preferred against him will be established), they are satisfied the law shall take its course, and inflict such reasonable punishment, *short of the death penalty,* as may be thought necessary to protect society.' "

On Saturday, March 17th, the funeral obsequies of the murdered gentleman were conducted at his late residence by his numerous and attached friends, and the members of the Masonic and Oddfellow lodges to which he had belonged. The Rev. R. L. Herbert and Mrs. Cora Richmond were the officiating ministers on the occasion, and the latter, by the pathos and eloquence of her address, served to deepen the impression which the truly Spiritual services produced upon the assembled multitude. It was after giving a detailed account of these interesting services, that the editor of the *Banner of Light* proceeded in the issue above quoted from, to render a just tribute to his talented Spiritual *collaborateur* in a biographical notice, from which we select the following noteworthy items :—

" BIOGRAPHICAL SKETCH OF THE DECEASED.

"Stevens S. Jones, the editor and proprietor of the *Religio Philosophical Journal,* a weekly newspaper devoted to the promulgation of Liberalism and Modern Spiritualism, and the *Little Bouquet,* a monthly magazine adapted to the minds of children and youth, promulgating the same doctrine, was born in Barre, Vt., on July 22nd, 1813. His parents were intelligent, liberal-minded people. His father was a farmer in moderate circumstances. . . . .

"At the age of nineteen Mr. Jones entered upon the study of the law, and was admitted to practice at the November term of Court. He entered upon a successful practice of his profession in Hyde Park soon after he was admitted, and remained there until his removal to St. Charles, Ill., in the spring of 1838. . . . .

"For many years Mr. Jones confined himself to his profession, and ranked high as a lawyer. He was twice elected Judge of the Kane County Court, and discharged the duties of the office to the general satisfaction of the public.

"At an early day in the history of railroads of the Northwest, Mr. Jones was actively engaged as a railroad man. . . . .

"Mr. Jones always belonged to the Liberal school in religion. His parents were Universalists, and he, for many years after arriving at manhood, was an active member of that sect. He was generally the presiding officer at the State conventions, associations, and representative gatherings of the order during the first fifteen years of their history in the State of Illinois.

"He dates his conversion to Modern Spiritualism mainly to the perusal of that remarkable work given through the early mediumship of Andrew Jackson Davis, called 'Nature's Divine Revelations, and a Voice to Mankind.'

"The perusal of that work soon after its publication prepared his mind for the reception of the truth of *spirit communion* as given through the mediumship of the 'Fox girls.'

"Once having been convinced of the truth of spirit communion, he fearlessly proclaimed it on all proper occasions, never obtruding his views, however, upon unwilling ears.

HONBᴸᴱ S.S. JONES,   CHICAGO, U.S

"Often was he heard to speak incidentally of the assurance given him by communicating spirits that he would, at no remote time, be as deeply engrossed in promulgating the truths of spirit intercourse, and the *philosophy of life,* as he was then in his professional business. But not until the spring of 1865 did he fully realise the truth of that oft-repeated assurance. Then it was that he found himself fully committed to the work of promulgating the *philosophy of life* through the columns of the *Religio Philosophical Journal.*

"Mr. Jones's publishing house was entirely consumed in the great Chicago fire of Oct. 9th, 1871. His loss was very heavy, and he received nothing from insurance companies. Some small sums were loaned him, but all was refunded within six months afterwards.

"Most vigorously did he go to work to restore his publishing business. His paper for the week of the fire, fortunately, was mailed, and on its way to the subscribers, when the 'fire-fiend' did its work. While the fire was yet raging he wrote the matter for a new issue—smaller in size—and had it printed and mailed in *advance of time,*'assuring his subscribers that, although burned out clean, the *Religio Philosophical Journal* would be continued without unnecessary delay.

"He then went directly to New York and purchased an entire new outfit, and in five weeks had the *Religio Philosophical Journal,* full size, in the United States mails on its way to its subscribers. In the meantime, between the fire and the printing of the paper in its new dress—full size—he every week greeted his subscribers with the *Religio Philosophical Journal,* small in size, that they might not be in the dark as to the progress being made by him to reinstate his publishing house. None of the publishers in Chicago on that memorable occasion excelled him in enterprise. . . . .

"Mr. Jones, although his locks were whitened with age, was in full vigour of manhood, and devoted his whole time to conducting his business financially and editorially. . . "

The charge of the *Religio-Philosophical Journal* was at once assumed on Mr. Jones's decease by his son-in-law and former business manager Colonel Bundy, and as this gentleman still continues his great and onerous work, and no single individual in the ranks has ever made a deeper and more healthful mark upon the reputation of the Spiritual movement, both as a man and an editor, it seems in order at this point to give an outline of the special place in the work of journalistic propagandism which Colonel Bundy's paper occupies. We have now before us some printed sheets issued from the *Religio-Philosophical Journal* office, which broadly define the general tone, aim, and purpose of that excellent periodical :—

"PLATFORM OF THE 'RELIGIO PHILOSOPHICAL JOURNAL.'

" The old readers of the *Religio Philosophical Journal* know our aims and efforts in the past, and can judge of our future, but a few words may be due to the new readers of the enlarged list that our reduction of terms is bringing. We shall hold steadily on, ' 'bating no jot of heart or hope,' as brave John Milton said when defending liberty of thought, yet enlarging our scope and enriching our pages as the way opens. We shall advocate the Spiritual Philosophy, with its bright outlook toward the life beyond, undimmed by any haze or darkness of Materialism ; yet, while holding firmly to our own ideas, and criticising others fairly, frankly, and strongly if need be, we shall respect all honest opinions, give them fair hearing, and so aim to win the respect of those from whom we may differ.

"Holding that Spiritualism in its broad meaning is THE SCIENCE OF LIFE, we shall aim to supply its facts in a direct and practical way. Such temperance, self-control, and knowledge of physiological law as shall help us to prepare healthy bodies fit for pure spirits to use and inhabit, through long, useful, and happy lives on earth, we shall urge as of high importance. The equality of woman in her social and political relations, in marriage, in the home, and in public affairs, as indispensable to a better state of society and a higher civilisation, we shall continue to advocate. The taxation of church property, the remanding of Bible reading and sectarian prayer from our public schools to the church, the home, and the Sunday school, where there will be no infringement on the consciences of others ; and all that helps a total separation of Church and State, and the truest freedom of thought and conscience, we shall persistently stand for. 'Liberty, but not Libertinism,' is a good motto, and it will be our aim to disapprove all vulgar or immoral writings, especially if in the guise of pretended reform or progress. The pathway of reform must be clean, and true progress leads to purity and self-conquest. In the light of immortality our daily conduct has a new and larger significance. The facts and phenomena of Spiritualism coming mostly, of course, through mediumship, are of priceless value and transcendent interest, and the wisest and kindest of efforts are needed to aid and encourage true mediums. While charitable to the frailties which they have in common with others, we have ever held that persistent and habitual fraud should be exposed, and that those who practise it are unworthy of support and confidence.

"Such frauds we have opposed, and shall continue to do so, and our course has not only been approved by a majority of the best Spiritualists, but by a goodly number of the best and most reliable mediums, as their testimonials in our columns during the past year show.

"Care, accuracy, and truthfulness are indispensable in the investigation of spirit manifestations. We have, therefore, urged that good mediums should at times submit to thorough, yet fair, test conditions, asked and granted in a spirit of mutual good faith and goodwill, and such as many of our best mediums have most willingly granted ; and this not only for the satisfaction of inquirers, but for the good repute of mediums.

"The cry that we are an enemy of mediums is of no consequence to·us, and will not turn us a hair's breadth from our course. We shall go on in the exposure of all persistent fraud, and in the effort to uphold and befriend real mediumship and good mediums. . . ."

"While, no doubt, persons not of high moral qualities may sometimes be good instruments for spirits to use, yet sincerity lies at the base of the finest spiritual gifts. Without willingness to give test-conditions, we can hope for little respect from others, and for little success in convincing careful investigators.

"We feel and are earnestly assured by thousands that our timely exposures of fraud have helped to save the great and precious Spiritual Movement from peril and degradation, and shall go on, if necessary, in that part of our work, trusting to gain in uncompromising fidelity and 'in malice toward none and charity to all.'"

From a large number of press comments which Colonel Bundy's unsparing denunciations of fraud and counterfeit Spiritualism has called forth, both from friends and foes, the following is selected as a fair representative example :—

"The *Religio Philosophical Journal*, of Chicago, as its name implies, is a weekly publication, exclusively devoted to religion and philosophy, and is recognized among its many readers as the boldest, as well as the most sincere and able, journal published in the West, and has for its motto—'Truth wears no mask, bows at no human shrine, seeks neither place nor applause ; she only asks a hearing.'

"While the journal is published mainly in the interest of Spiritual philosophy, it shows no quarter to mediums who will not submit to the most scrutinizing tests of their genuineness. It will not tolerate humbugs, or recommend any travelling mediums, who do not court, and submit to, absolute test conditions, in their exhibitions of mediumship. This rigid scrutiny over the subject of Spiritualism has raised up to the journal some enemies of the gullable kind, but at the same time it has done more to call attention to, and establish the truth of the phenomena than all the other journals together. It is a good and ably edited paper, bold and outspoken on all subjects, but treating mainly upon philosophy, science, and religion, so far as religion can be reduced to philosophy and science.

"It has been a welcome weekly visitor to our desk for several years past, and we propose to so continue it at whatever cost.—*Democrat News*, Xenia, Ohio."

During the author's far and wide wanderings round the world as a Spiritual propagandist, no charge has been more universally preferred against the cause of Spiritualism than that of being allied to the odious doctrines of "Free love."

We have already made our readers aware of the utter falsity of this charge and the concatenation of circumstances which gave the antagonists of Spiritualism an opportunity—which they eagerly embraced—of shouldering the daring licentiousness of the few, upon the entire rank and file of the Spiritualists.

In foreign lands however, and especially when lacking those literary references which would have enabled her to furnish abundant counter statements, the author's denials of this abhorrent stain would have found but slight chance of acceptance, had she not been nobly sustained by the uncompromising denunciations of "Free love" and all its propagandists, which filled the columns of the *Religio Philosophical Journal* during the entire period that this madness ruled the public mind. Here was a well recognized and leading organ of Spiritualism disclaiming all fellowship with the promoters of this doctrine, and protesting against its abominable practices with a trumpet tongue which could neither be mistaken nor denied.

The author is under a debt of deep gratitude to Colonel Bundy for the triumphant refutation which his journal has afforded against the groundless charge that there ever was, or could be, the smallest links of connection between the doctrines of true Spiritualism and "Free love." Allied to the daughter of the late Mr. S. S. Jones, a lady whose brilliant talents well fitted her to be the companion of a leading journalist, and whose eminent virtues, noble character, and sweetness of disposition, are calculated to make her husband's home a paradise, it has been argued that the editor of the *Religio* is not competent to judge of the urgent necessity to reform the wrongs that ensue from unhappy marriages or the miseries of discordant homes.

In answer to this plea it has been abundantly shown that the *Religio* has ever been the champion of true reforms. Its special aim has been to draw the impassable line of demarcation between liberty and licence, moral law and immoral lawlessness, true love and true licentiousness. It is in this sense that its columns have redeemed Spiritualism from the foes of its own household, and furnished the author on countless occasions with a sword which has slain the very arguments that would otherwise have slain Spiritualism.

Another speciality of the *Religio Philosophical Journal* has been its editor's fearless exposure of the frauds practised in the name of Spiritualism and the resolute protection which he has extended not only to *genuine* Mediums, but also to earnest investigators by his unsparing denunciation of sham manifestations, and attempts to simulate genuine Spirit Mediumship.

Before dismissing these journalistic notices, it should be added, that the excellent little paper to which frequent allusion has been made, *The Spiritual Scientist*, so ably edited by Mr. Gerry Brown, as well as the bright Cleveland paper entitled *The American Spiritualist*, established by A. A. Wheelock, were both, after many severe struggles on the part of their editors, compelled to suspend for want of adequate support.

An admirable journal started in New York by the learned writer Dr. Eugene Crowell, entitled, *The Two Worlds*, has also shared the same discouraging fate. At present, besides the two great Eastern and Western journals, the *Banner* and *Religio*, the *Banner of Light* advertises the existence of the following papers devoted to the propagandism of the Spiritual cause :—*The Spiritual Offering*, published in Iowa by Messrs. Fox and Wilson; *Light for All*, San Francisco; Miller's *Psychometric Circular*, New York; and the *Voice of Angels*, claimed to be edited by the spirit of its late editor, D. C. Densmore. Quite recently, two new Spiritual publications have been added to this list, the titles of which speak for themselves. The one is called *The Medium's Friend*, published at Terre Haute, Indiana, proprietor, George R. Moore; and *Light for Thinkers*, Atlanta, Georgia, Messrs. Kates and Bowman, editors.

We are not prepared to state what amount of support is extended to these several periodicals, but none who have entered upon such a field of effort can mistake the fact, that they can only be conducted by an amount of self-sacrifice and personal effort, which amply deserves—even if it cannot command—success.

Many volumes of interest have passed through the Spiritual press since the publication of " Modern American Spiritualism," the most admired and important of which is—in point of scientific research and exhaustive scope —Dr. Eugene Crowell's " Primitive Christianity and Modern Spiritualism." Dr. Crowell's honoured name is a sufficient guarantee for the excellence of this work; it is only necessary to add therefore that the student will find in its two handsome volumes a complete treasury of those facts, ancient and modern, which represent the Spiritual progress of humanity.

Amongst the very last works that have come "as a light to lighten the Gentiles" of modern times, is a book purporting to emanate from the greatest and most exalted of Spirits, through the automatic Mediumship of Dr. Newborough, of New York, entitled, "Oahspe." It is claimed to be "a new bible" and to give an account of the human race, its origin, creation, and history, for twenty-four thousand years, together with a synopsis of what happened during sixteen cycles or forty-eight thousand years previous. Antedating the production of this volume, and amongst a collection of others which would require many pages to enumerate, are three which the author names with a pang of human regret, as they recall the memory of her most esteemed friends Robert Dale Owen, Epes Sargent, and Professor S. B. Brittan.

The most recent works of value bequeathed by these esteemed scholars to the world, are Owen's " Debatable Land," Sargent's " Proof Palpable of Spiritualism," and Brittan's " Battle Ground of the Spiritual Reformation."

Though we cannot introduce any lengthened biographical notices into this volume, we should be unfaithful to the integrity of history if we failed to recall some items of the life work of such eminent champions as in themselves make history.

The best tribute we can offer to Mr. Owen at present then is to select from the eulogistic notices which followed him to the life beyond from every part of Europe, America, and the Colonies, the following brief extracts from the English and American Spiritual journals.

The *Banner of Light* says :—

" DECEASE OF ROBERT DALE OWEN.

" On Sunday morning, the 24th inst., our old friend and valued co-worker passed to the reward which surely awaited him (as it does all who labour for the advancement of every phase of truth on earth) in the land of souls.

" Mr. Owen was in character singularly simple, straightforward, and refined, and he enjoyed the esteem and friendship of a large number of men prominent in literature and public life, outside of as well as within the ranks of the spiritual believers. He was a man of unusually vigorous intellect, honest beyond all question, and animated by a noble-desire to benefit the human race and promote sound principles.

" Robert Dale was born at Glasgow, Scotland, November 7th, 1801, and spent his early years at New Lanark, under the care of a private teacher. He subsequently studied for three years at Hofwyl, in Switzerland, and in 1823 came to this country with his father. He lived several years at New Harmony, Indiana, where his father was engaged in an effort to build up a community in accord with his theories, but from 1828 to 1831 was in New York, conducting a weekly paper called *The Free Enquirer*, in partnership with Miss Frances Wright. He returned to New Harmony in 1832, after his marriage with Mary Jane Robinson, daughter of Samuel Robinson, a prominent merchant of New York.

COL. JNO. C BUNDY

"Mr. Owen after settling at New Harmony, had considerable experience in public life. He served in the Indiana Legislature and in Congress. He introduced the bill organising the Smithsonian Institution, and in 1846 became one of its regents and chairman of its Building Committee. He was a member of the Constitutional Convention in Indiana in 1850, and both in the Convention and the Legislature endeavoured to secure the adoption of measures granting independent rights of property to women. He was appointed Chargé d'Affaires at Naples in 1853 and Minister in 1855, and remained there until 1858. For the last few years Mr. Owen was engaged mostly in literary work.

"His investigations in Spiritualism began some twenty years ago or more, and he became a devout believer in its philosophy and phenomena, passing out of the form in the full assurance of its truth. His first important work on the subject was, "Footfalls on the Boundaries of Another World," published in 1860, and in 1872 appeared "The Debatable Land Between This World and the Next." In these two books an account is given of his studies and observations with mediums, and many marvellous experiences are related.

"He published several books prior to 1860, including a historical drama, entitled, "Pocahontas," and "Hints on Public Architecture," and in 1870 appeared a novel under the title, "Beyond the Breakers." Previous to his illness in 1875 he was engaged on an autobiography, portions of which appeared in the *Atlantic Monthly*. Mr. Owen devoted much thought to social and philosophical questions, and was a vigorous writer and attractive speaker.

"Within a few years he again entered the marriage state, residing with the lady who linked her fortunes with his, at Lake George, N.Y., up to the time of his decease. The army of progress on earth has lost the material presence of a valiant soldier, but the workers in the sphere of causation have, in his transition, won a powerful recruit."

"MR. ROBERT DALE OWEN'S LAST SÉANCE.

The *Boston Herald* says :—

"It was the writer's good fortune, while on a visit to a prominent Spiritualist in Brooklyn, N.Y., three weeks ago, to meet, for the first time, Mr. Robert Dale Owen, and to dwell under the same roof with him for several days. At the same residence was an excellent private medium, and once or twice a day circles would be held. So marked were the demonstrations that other members of the circle could not help becoming sensible that the gathering was one that awaited his coming in the other life. The writer fancies that even Mr. Owen so interpreted it, for at times the language was unmistakable. Among others who came was one who announced himself as "Commodore S., who knew Mr. Owen in Naples, and had many a good time with him." Mr. Owen asked for the full name, and it was given—"Commodore Stringham." "That is very good," said Mr. Owen, "and I know to what he refers. Has he anything to say to me?" The reply came— "Yes, you can't row your boat much longer; it is time for you to go into the cabin." Mr. Owen seemed disposed to take the communication literally, and alluded to his boat at home on Lake George; but the control interrupted, saying, "No, that is not meant; you have sailed a good ship; you have kept a straight course; the voyage is nearly ended, and you will soon come to an anchor. Then I shall meet you on the shore in company with your other friends and relatives who wait your coming. Do you understand?" Mr. Owen replied that he did, and for a time a feeling of sadness fell on the little company, for they knew that Mr. Owen was soon to exchange the corruptible for the uncorruptible, and the mortal would put on immortality. At a later *séance*, when Mr. Owen was taking an afternoon rest on one of the warm summer days in early June, the intelligence was communicated that his mission was nearly ended, and before the autumn leaves fell he would be among those in the spirit whom he longed to greet. This was Mr. Owen's last *séance*, and a pleasant one it was. As a prominent author was also present, it will, undoubtedly, at some time be presented, with all its details."

Dr. Brittan, one of the earliest, most faithful, and most able champions of which the new faith has had reason to boast, seems to have parted from us but yesterday, and so vast is the void that he has left unfilled that we cannot even yet "make him dead," or realize that we can no longer appeal to him as a tower of strength in our hours of trial and discipline.

Dr. Brittan's earthly pilgrimage closed in the beginning of the present year, and on the 9th of January, 1883, his funeral obsequies were celebrated at the residence of his daughter, Mrs. Stryker, in Newark, New Jersey. Amongst the distinguished friends who pronounced addresses of eulogy and farewell on that memorable occasion were Mrs. Cora L. V. Richmond, the celebrated trance speaker; Dr. J. R. Buchanan, the great writer and anthropologist; Mr. A. A. Wheelock; Mr. Henry Kiddle, ex-school superintendent of New York; and Mr. Charles Partridge, Dr. Brittan's early friend and associate in the publication of the first, and still one of the very best Spiritual papers ever printed, namely the grand old *Spiritual Telegraph*, of New York. As a clear and concise account of Dr. Brittan's earliest labours and first connection with the cause of Spiritualism when he was the Rev. S. B. Brittan, an Universalist clergyman, will be found in the twenty years' "History of Modern American Spiritualism," we cannot give a more fitting *résumé* of his later years, than that detailed in the speech of his friend, Mr. Charles Partridge, which we reprint from the report in the *Banner of Light* in full. Mr. Partridge said :—

"Mr. Chairman and Friends : I have been delighted in being here this afternoon, for I know that what has been said of our departed friend, Brittan, is true. I was associated with him as a partner in 1852, and some years afterward, in the publishing of the *Spiritual Telegraph*, the *Shekinah*, and various books on the subject of Spiritualism, written by men who were early investigators of the phenomena. Dr. Gray, Judge Edmonds, and Dr. Hallock were generally with us. We were satisfied that Spiritualism is true; that spirits communicated with us. And when we became thus satisfied, we engaged mediums, and the doors were open, free of charge to anybody who desired to come and investigate the subject; and thousands did so. Many, however, who after investigating exclaimed : 'Oh! I never can doubt again,' often doubted before they reached the next corner. As soon as their prejudices returned, the truth had to go.

"Dr. Buchanan has described to you pretty fully the prejudice of the people against new things. What do you think it must have been when we investigated the fact that spirits communicated with mortals, and pronounced it true? All the churches without exception denied it, and alleged every kind of evil of it, and of us. It was a fraud, or of the devil. They had an abundance of devils then to whom to attribute anything they did not accept, and they had no mercy on Spiritualism. But more recently some have lost the chief of that society; the devil has been expelled from many of the churches, and they cannot thus dispose of the truths that spirits communicate.

"You may understand, after hearing Dr. Buchanan, what the early Spiritualists had to meet. You cannot understand it fully, but you can get an idea. Why! our friends discarded us; they did not desire our acquaintance in society or in business; and even the banks did not want our accounts any more. If they were asked if such a one's credit was good, they would say : 'Well, it used to be; but he is one of these Spiritualists, and we would rather not say anything about it.' That was particularly the case in this city. Dr. Brittan stood firmly throughout, as well as all of the others that I have named, with many others. As to myself, I never cared what people said about me, and I do not now. I often said to them : 'If your slanders do you any good, go on; they do not hurt me.'

"At present you can see what Spiritualism has done in the world—what reforms are going on in the religions of the time, wherever the people are free to think for themselves without being condemned as lunatics. See what freedom Spiritualism has brought into the world already; and it will accomplish still more.

"I want to refer to the practical lesson which this calling us together presents to my mind. It has been said, and truly, that Dr. Brittan was distinguished as an author : he answered very many objections, especially those that came from intelligent sources—clergymen, infidels, and materialists—and I think he never answered them without satisfying their authors that they were wrong. He was a host against all opponents, for he piled fact upon fact, while he had an extensive experience of his own to present, which could not be denied. But here is the lesson that I wish to present : You go out into the world and find antagonism among almost all persons; there is very little sociability, very little care for you among your neighbours—very little kindness or courtesy—but if you look through the published writings and speeches of Dr. Brittan I think you will never find a line or a word that is not gentle, respectful, and truthful, and yet forcible and earnest. That was peculiarly his character. He was peculiarly social, remarkably genial; and this trait of character entered into all his writings—indeed, into everything that he said and did. He was a practical man; and with all the bitterness that was heaped upon us while we were associated, I never heard an unkind word from his lips.

HENRY J NEWTON

"Now here is a lesson for us, and I hope that every one of us will receive it and appropriate it, for it is needed, especially at this time. We are not living under the old dispensation, in which men are condemned to burn for ever if they don't accept church dogmas. We live under the dispensation of love and kindness, which requires us to endeavour to benefit our brother and our sister everywhere. To be free and to be happy, that is the new dispensation. We are witnessing the old Pentecostal manifestations at this time throughout the world. How have they spread throughout the world? Through our efforts? No! They have spread because spirits have opened communion with mortals throughout the entire world, and in the short space of about thirty years. You can scarcely find a record in any part of the civilized world which does not show that spirit influence is potent among the people. What are we to do? These truths are passing into general belief, and they must be reduced to practice. This is inevitable. Spirits are not here simply to talk, but to spiritualize the words and acts of men; we should take in their spirit as far as we can, and emulate the spirit of him whom we have gathered here to commemorate."

We shall conclude this humble tribute to the memory of a true and brave soldier of the Spiritual army by a few extracts from a letter addressed to the president of the occasion by Mr. Henry J. Newton, also one of Dr. Brittan's earliest friends, most constant fellow-labourer, and the present honoured president of the first Spiritual Society of New York. Mr. Newton writes:—

"*Henry Kiddle, Esq., President American Spiritualist Alliance.*

"Dear Sir,—I regret that, in consequence of physical indisposition, I was prevented from doing the part assigned me by the Committee of Arrangements for the memorial services in memory of our brother and co-worker, Dr. S. B. Brittan.

"My intimate acquaintance and friendly relations with Dr. Brittan for many years were of such a character that I felt it a duty which I owed to his honoured memory to contribute my testimony publicly, on that occasion, to his worth and many virtues.

"When a man of genius, and a luminary so brilliant, goes down into the valley and the deep, dark shadow, and we lose sight of his genial and inspiring presence, we seem called upon to bring into active application all our philosophy and knowledge to prevent our being overwhelmed with gloom and sadness. The first impulse is to censure Providence, who at such a time has bereaved us of a dear associate, and when to us, short-sighted as we are, it would seem he could not be spared from his earthly work. But when we reflect how little we know what is best, that our beloved brother is at rest, not from labour, but from the torturing cares and trials which beset him here, we must bow in humble submission to the will of Infinite Wisdom, and try not to complain.

"It is rare that Nature has been so generous of her gifts—of the qualities that constitute a perfect man—as she was in those which she bestowed upon our friend and brother, Dr. Brittan. In him was exhibited our ideal of a perfect gentleman, as understood in our free country, where no inherited title forms the whole or any part of what is essential to the meaning of that term. . . .

"The heroism of our brother was made conspicuous by his daring to face the frowns and censure not only of the public, but also of his best and, at the time, of his dearest friends. What he sacrificed was not that he might gain renown and honour; those gilded treasures, usually so much sought for and coveted, were wholly laid upon the altar, and offered up in testimony of his devotion to the truth of his faithfulness to his convictions and principles. . . .

"With the exception of a few of his most intimate and confidential friends, none knew the thorny path he travelled. A nature like his, sensitive in a marked degree, made capable of suffering more keenly than ordinary men by his peculiar organism— who can describe his sufferings at times? It almost seemed sometimes that Providence was unfavourable to him and to the cause which he had espoused, so greatly was he tried. His four sons were, one after the other, stricken down, torn away from him, and their beloved forms laid away in the cheerless cemetery. One of the brightest jewels of his household, the one of whom he was especially proud, was offered up a sacrifice upon the altar of his country in the war of the rebellion. Yet no word of complaint was ever heard to pass his lips; indeed, the power with which he at all times controlled the fearful tide of emotion, when seemingly overwhelmed with disaster and sorrow, appeared almost superhuman.

"He was sustained by an unbounded, unfaltering faith and confidence in the

goodness of his heavenly Father. This faith never forsook him; it was the rock to which he seemed securely anchored, and from which no storm nor tempest, however fierce or rude, could for a single instant move him.   "Yours truly,
"HENRY J. NEWTON.

"New York, Jan. 24th, 1883."

And last of all, amidst many columns of inspiring records devoted to S. B. Brittan's memory by the editor of the *Banner of Light*, the following lines seem to form a fitting summary of all that human language has to tell :—

"What Dr. S. B. Brittan wrote of William White at the time of his sudden transition may now be aptly applied to himself : 'As we look around us, we miss a faithful soldier who wore the armour of light. "The sword of the Spirit" was in his hand, and he was always on duty. To-day his post seems to be deserted. But when the roll of the faithful is called he still answers to his name, and we learn that he has been promoted from the ranks of mortals. It is well. A worthy champion of the Right and a true lover of his Race—worn with the strife and weary with the march—rests from his labours.' "

CHAPTER LIV.

SPIRITUALISM IN AMERICA (CONTINUED.)

IN MEMORIAM.

As in our last chapter we entered upon the painful task of noting the departure of two of the best and bravest generals who have marshalled the Spiritual army forward through the wildernesses of superstition and materialism, it may be in order to add to the list already commenced, the names of some few others of those, once so familiar in the public records of Spiritualism, but now only mementos of vacant places which none have arisen to fill. Amongst those whose absence has left a deeply-felt void in his wide circle of usefulness, is Dr. H. F. Gardner, of Boston, so often mentioned in the twenty years' " History of Modern American Spiritualism " as the enterprising manager of the Boston Sunday meetings, the undaunted champion of Spiritualism throughout Massachusetts, and the gentleman who gave the celebrated challenge which compelled certain of the Havard professors to institute an investigation into Spiritual phenomena, the promised report on which, the said professors have never thought fit to publish.

Soon after the departure of this noble veteran to his well-earned reward, he was joined in the higher life by a pioneer of no less worth and celebrity, Mr. Horace H. Day, of New York, a gentleman whose many disinterested services to the cause of Spiritualism can hardly be sufficiently eulogized.

Mr. Day founded, and for some years sustained by his own munificence, a library, several circle rooms, and a paid Medium, Miss Kate Fox, at a building hired by himself at 553, Broadway, and entitled, " The Society for the Promotion of Christian Spiritualism."

Mr. Day also published one of the earliest Spiritual papers at that building, and there, public circles—held at this gentleman's expense—were free to all who chose to attend them.

Long after the occupancy of the building was resigned, Mr. Day continued to devote his means, time, and influence to the service of Spiritualism, with an amount of generosity unparalleled in the history of the movement.

Another bright star that has disappeared from the Spiritual hemisphere was E. V. Wilson, the celebrated seer, test Medium, writer, and lecturer.

It is not too much to assert, that thousands of persons have been convinced of the soul's immortality and the facts of Spirit communion by the indefatigable labours of E. V. Wilson. Worn out, even in the meridian of life, by the ceaseless energy with which he followed up his career of speaking, writing, and test Mediumship, the brave soldier presented arms for the last time to the assembled multitudes at Lake Pleasant camp meeting, his favourite sphere of summer labour; then shouldering the musket of duty, he gained his Western home in time to say farewell to earth, leaving a monument behind him inscribed in the grateful hearts of thousands of his fellow mortals. And still another noble worker gone home was the Rev. Thos. Benning, a pioneer Spiritualist as pure, guileless, kind, and true as any that the ranks of Spiritualism could boast of. Many an one has missed his kind face from the New York public gatherings of Spiritualists, wherein for more than twenty years his wise counsels and fearless testimony were esteemed by every listener as bulwarks of the faith.

Good and much-beloved Thomas Benning was soon followed by his old friend and fellow-labourer Dr. John F. Gray, of whom the *Banner of Light* reports as follows :—

"A BRAVE SPIRIT RELEASED.

"Dr. John Franklin Gray passed to spirit-life June 5th, at the Fifth Avenue Hotel, New York City, after an illness of several weeks' duration. He was born in Sherbourne, N.Y., September 23rd, 1804; entered the College of Physicians and Surgeons in 1824, and obtained his degree in 1826. He soon afterward heard of the system of Hahnemann, and upon due experimentation and inquiry becoming satisfied of the superiority of the Homeopathic method, he gave in his adhesion to it, being the first 'regular' physician in America who did so.

"The same degree of manly independence which led him by embracing Homeopathy because it appeared the nearest the truth to him to give up a profitable practice, and all his professional friends, operated to make him equally bold in his religious convictions, and—though we have seen no mention of it in several notices of his death in the columns of the daily press—he became a convert to Spiritualism, being at one time a prominent leader among the friends of the cause in New York. E. Edson, M.D., of White Plains, N.Y., states that Dr. Gray ' hired the first public speaker on Spiritualism in New York— hired and paid for a hall, and warmed and lighted the same gratuitously. He was an eminent physician, and acknowledged he was assisted by the direction of spirit influences in his practice.' He has passed from this sphere of action, where it was his lot to endure ostracism and hardship because of his championship of medical and spiritual reform, to a rich reward in the world of spirits—the world that rights all wrongs."

As the procession of the mighty dead of earth moves on to the realms of life eternal, another illustrious worker appears, one whose name has been sounded as loudly in the ranks of American and European commercial enterprise, as in that of the Massachusetts Spiritual ranks. This is none other than Alvin Adams, the founder of the famous Adams Express Company, and one of the most liberal and untiring friends of Spiritualism.

From a long and intimate acquaintance with Mr. Adams, the author is able to testify that this gentleman frequently acknowledged his deep indebtedness to Spiritualism, both for his religious convictions and worldly prosperity. Mr. Adams on several occasions has detailed to the author how in a great crisis in the affairs of the immense Express Company, of which he was the principal, he was sent for, in the name of his old college companion and early friend, Daniel Webster, *then a Spirit*, and advised, as he valued his name, fame, and fortune, to call upon Mrs. Mettler, a celebrated seeress and clairvoyant of Hartford, Connecticut.

As Mr. Adams at that time had no knowledge of Spiritualism, and Mrs. Mettler's name was utterly unknown to him, he at first disregarded these warnings. In the course of time however they became so urgent that he took an opportunity of calling on Mrs. Mettler, and entering her presence as a total stranger, and unannounced, was greeted by what purported to be the Spirit of his old friend and legal adviser Webster, and assured that he had only just come in time to save his affairs from ruinous entanglements, and perhaps irretrievable loss.

The entranced Medium was then influenced to enter into business details, known, as Mr. Adams supposed, to no earthly being outside of his own official circle. During this, and many subsequent interviews, the Spirit of Daniel Debster counselled Mr. Adams, with more than the legal skill and acumen he had exhibited in earth life, and Mr. A. asserted that he believed he owed to that providential interposition, much of the success and prosperity that placed him on the pinnacle of financial prosperity. Mr. Adams on this, and every other phase of Spiritualism, spoke with perfect freedom, candour, and gratitude.

Although of late years he took a less active interest in the maintenance of the Spiritual meetings in Boston than formerly, we have the assurance that his reticence was the result of ill health and increasing infirmities, rather than any diminution of interest in a cause to which he had so often and so openly owned his deep indebtedness. The following brief extract will suffice to show how the secular papers *noticed* the well-known fact of Mr. Adams's long years of connection with Spiritualism in Boston. It is from the *Banner of Light*, and reads as follows :—

"DECEASE OF ALVIN ADAMS.

"This gentleman, whose name is a household word in all parts of the United States, because of his prominence in a widely useful department of mundane business activities, passed on from his residence in Watertown, Mass., Saturday evening, September 1st, aged 73 years. He was born in Andover, Vermont, on the 10th of June, 1804. The success of the wide and comprehensive system of transportation known as the Adams Express Company was in great part due to Mr. Adams's tact and management. His disease was known to physicans as hydro-thorax. He leaves two sons and one daughter. We have failed to see in any of the city papers which have chronicled his death, reference to his being a Spiritualist in belief, but such is the fact, as we have had the assurance from him personally, during his life, and he has for years past taken occasion to practically prove the force of his faith through pecuniary gifts to assist media. subscribing liberally toward carrying on spiritual lectures in this city, etc."

For many years the Spiritualists of Boston will remember the delightful soirées attended by the *élite* of the faith that were held in Mr. Adams's palatial residence ; gatherings made memorable, not only by the hospitality of the host, but also by the kindness and geniality of the lady of the house, the well-beloved wife of Mr. Adams. For a very brief period only, this much-attached couple survived each other. In the touching words of the poet Wordsworth—

"He first deceased ;—
She tried to live without him ;
Liked it not, and died."

Another venerable pilgrim who has passed to the life beyond during the last fifteen years was Dr. Eliakim Phelps, the Congregationalist minister, in whose house at Stratford, Connecticut, during the very earliest days of the Spiritual movement, occurred those tremendous manifestations, in the shape of hauntings, and disturbances, that transcended in power and continuity any that have been recorded in the history of Spiritualism.

Dr. Hare, Epes Sargent, Owen, and others, have given vivid accounts of these weird manifestations, but the author has often been assured by the venerable gentleman himself that no verbal description could do justice to the stupendous force exhibited by the invisible powers that for ten months possessed his dwelling, causing horror and amazement to the harassed inhabitants, and producing awe and consternation amongst thousands of persons who visited his premises during those stormy times.* As some members of Dr. Phelps's family, connected with high orthodox institutions, have endeavoured to show that the reverend gentleman before his decease had renounced all interest in Spiritual manifestations, and regarded his past experiences only as a proof of Satanic agency, we deem it due alike to the best interests of truth, and to the character of Dr. Phelps himself, whose memory the author cherishes as that of an esteemed friend and frequent correspondent, to give place to the following extracts taken from the *Boston Evening Transcript* of February, 1881, and written by a gentleman well-known and highly esteemed in the Spiritual ranks, Dr. A. S. Hayward :—

"THE LATE DR. ELIAKIM PHELPS.

"To the Editor of 'The Transcript.'

"This earnest labourer in the Christian ministry passed to spirit-life from Weehawken, N. Y., December 29th, at the ripe age of ninety years. His son Professor Austin Phelps, of Andover, Mass., has printed in the *Congregationalist,* for some three weeks past, a series of articles, under the caption, "A Pastor of the Last Generation," intended as a sketch of his father's life-work, religious opinions, etc., and in the course of which he pays his father's memory a high tribute of respect for ability, honesty of purpose, and all that goes to make up a great and good man. . . .

"In Part III. he speaks of his father's belief in Spiritualism in a manner that does not seem to me to convey the views of that gentlemen correctly, and having had myself some facts from Dr. Phelps (the father) as late as 1875—which facts Professor Phelps (the son) had no means of knowing—and believing that they should be made public at this time, in order that he (Dr. Phelps) should be put on record correctly, and that Spiritualism may have, openly, the benefit of this good man's privately cherished opinions, concerning its truthfulness and use, I desire that you will do me the favour of giving these facts publicity in your columns. . . . . I do not think that Dr. Phelps was bold in advocating his convictions as to the truthfulness of Spiritualism, especially among those opposed to it ; therefore it is not strange that his son, the professor, did not know to what extent his father embraced the Spiritual Philosophy and acknowledged the verity of the phenomena ; but if the professor had been present, as I have, at the *séances* attended by his father, and had witnessed with what gratification he recognised his spirit-friends, he might have been led to the use of different language regarding the views of the deceased than he has of late given expression to. . . .

"Dr. Phelps no doubt looked upon the manifestations, as his son states, as 'a visitation from God,' but instead of bowing to them as an affliction 'in sorrow and prayer,' he considered that he was happily blessed with spirit manifestations of a most remarkable character, which convinced him that the two worlds—the material and the spiritual—were one unbroken whole, and that communion between the two spheres of existence was a fixed fact in the nature of things. His conversion to a belief in Modern Spiritualism was of a similar character with that of St. Paul's conversion to Ancient Spiritualism—the result of suddenly presented and overwhelmingly satisfactory proofs in the premises.

---

*For a full description of these manifestations see Dr. Hare's work on "Spiritualism Scientifically Demonstrated."

What Dr. Phelps says himself is quite essential upon the point at issue, therefore we will quote his own words as follows : ' I have seen things in motion more than a thousand times, and in most cases when no visible power was exerted by which the motion could be produced. There have been broken from my windows seventy-one panes of glass — more than thirty of which I have seen break with my own eyes. I have seen objects, such as brushes, tumblers, candlesticks, snuffers, etc., which but a few moments before I knew to be at rest, fly against the glass and dash it in pieces, when it was utterly impossible from the direction in which they moved that any visible power could have caused the motion. As to the reality of these facts, they can be proved by testimony a hundredfold greater than is ordinarily required in our courts of justice in cases of life and death.'

"I met Dr. Phelps at the residence of Dr. Munn, in Philadelphia, Pa., some twenty years ago. He then and there related to myself, and others, his experience in spirit manifestations, and said that the amount of property destroyed by the invisible powers was nothing to him compared to the great benefit he received by and through them ; and that after becoming convinced of the verity of spirit communion, guidance, and protection, he had preached it. 'But.' said he, 'if I had called it Spiritualism, I should not have received support or gained hearers ; while as long as I did not call it by its right name it was received as beautiful teachings.'

"In 1874 Dr. Phelps wrote to me, from New Jersey, asking me to consult a medium for him ; adding that he had not for the past year had an opportunity to visit one— the last one being in Andover—and desiring that I would request that one (if she still continued her mediumship) to enquire if any of his spirit friends had any messages for him. He then remarked : ' I was intimately acquainted with Judge Edmonds. and other prominent Spiritualists now in spirit life.'

"He further spoke of his spirit relatives, and said they used to keep him apprised of important events, sometimes years before they took place. He closed his letter by saying : ' If she should obtain anything, and write me, she will confer on me a special favour.' I laid the doctor's petition before a highly sensitive medium, with the following result."

It would be needless to give the communication which followed, and which Dr. Phelps acknowledged to be characteristic of its alleged Spiritual source. Dr. Hayward's letter to the *Transcript* concludes thus :—

"In the year 1871, Dr. Phelps wrote an interesting essay for publication upon the practical value of clairvoyance in detecting disease, and the practice of 'laying on of hands,' or magnetic treatment, to eradicate diseased conditions from the human system. I caused the essay to be printed, with his consent, but the authorship was, at his request —as far as the public was concerned—to remain a secret until he had joined, by decease, the loved ones in the spirit-world.

"If Dr. Phelps had been brave enough to stem the tide of opposition, and had declared boldly his views to the world, it might have been better ; but still, his blameless life and (acknowledged) marked experiences may, after all, constitute an incentive to inquiry into the important matter which interested him so much, on the part of other religious teachers who have the courage ' to face a frowning world ' in defence of whatever convictions they may arrive at." "A. S. HAYWARD."
"Boston, Mass."

Dr. J. Bryant, a celebrated Spirit Medium and healer ; Mrs. H. M. F. Brown, the well-known and talented editor of the Cleveland *Agitator ;* David C. Densmore, the indefatigable proprietor of the paper called *The Voice of Angels ;* Mrs. M. A. Amphlett, an excellent pioneer trance speaker ; Colonel Danskin, the father of Baltimore Spiritualism, and one of the most philosophic thinkers and writers in the ranks ; kind, good, hospitable Mrs. Maynard, the Medium's friend, in whose genial home in Buffalo every toiler in the Spiritual vineyard found a mother's greeting; good Charles Levy, the devoted friend of Spiritualism in St. Louis ; and Willie Davenport—poor, tired, over-worked, and much-abused Willie Davenport ; these are but a few of the transfigured ones who now begin to muster in serried lines, and pass in the phantom panoramas of memory before their saddened friends' eyes, leaving the ineffaceable marks of their mortal footprints upon the age, although their well-remembered forms lie mouldering in the grave !

Sometimes one or two of these heroic Spirits fall out of line, and stand like a Colossus alone amidst the thronging hosts; and then we pause to note the specialities that distinguish them, and marvel if we who are left behind, shall ever look upon their like again. We are thus attracted to Willie Davenport, the youngest of the celebrated brothers so often written of, so often misunderstood, and misrepresented. He passed away in Sydney, New South Wales. His lonely brother Ira, had much difficulty to obtain leave to erect a monument to his dear companion's memory, because he determined to have upon it a sculptured device representing the time-honoured cabinet and other paraphernalia which recalled poor Willie's earthly work and frequent martyrdoms. Ira succeeded at last, but he might have spared himself the contest. The young man's monument is already set up in the ineffaceable lines which Spiritualism has made on public opinion.

Hear what his fellow-labourers reported of Willie Davenport in the Spiritual journals :—

"William H. Davenport numbered an earth-life of thirty-six years to the present time, and has been a medium for the past twenty-three years. In company with his brother Ira, under the name and style of the 'Davenport Brothers,' or 'Boys,' they have traversed nearly every quarter of the globe: Europe, the East and West Indies, South America, Australia, New Zealand, and other widely separated points being marked on the chart of their wanderings, while there is scarcely a town of any size in the United States where they have not given practical witness of the gifts they possessed. We have had frequent occasion to call the attention of the public to the achievements of these media in the past, and at a time when in all probability the hand of physical change is about to close their labours, at least conjunctively, it is but just to briefly revert to that which they have been privileged to accomplish.

"They have appeared successfully before the kings, queens, and great ones of the Old World, and have created among them a marked impression, which has in some instances been outwrought in action; they have sowed seeds of truth in the minds of the common people which have borne fruit in many cases of more than an hundred fold; thousands having been converted through their mediumship to a belief in spirit return, and a knowledge of the future life awaiting every human soul. As an evidence of the convincing character of their mediumship it is necessary only to refer to the back files of this paper, and particularly to the account of the bigoted and violent treatment dealt out to them in England on their first visit, when they were under the charge of Rev. Jesse B. Ferguson, of Tennessee (since deceased), as agent, and the triumphant victory which they attained at last. May those intelligences with whom he has so long regarded himself as a co-worker—notwithstanding all reports to the contrary—be with the departing member of this celebrated fraternity, and lead his weary footsteps along the green pastures and by the still waters of spiritual peace !"

Two more of the earliest pioneers of the great movement pass singly in the procession of mighty ones, each too distinguished as individualized workers, to be lost in the crowd. They are the Rev. William Fishbough and Dr. Robert Hallock. The last that was heard of good Mr. Fishbough on earth, were these words *in memoriam.*

"DR. WILLIAM FISHBOUGH.

"Funeral services over the earthly remains of Dr. Fishbough took place at his late residence, Brooklyn, N.Y., on the evening of Monday, May 23rd. The *Times* of that city states that although it had been announced that the funeral was to be a private one, the many personal friends of the deceased crowded the house to overflowing. Among well-known citizens present were Rev. Mr. Gunnison, ex-Superintendent Kiddle, and other friends from New York and Brooklyn; and a delegation of forty ladies and gentlemen, members of Phœnix Division Sons of Temperance, of which deceased had been chaplain for some years past. The floral tributes were very handsome, a pillow of roses with the word 'Father' being at the head of the casket; another, the offering of the Division.

having the words 'Our Chaplain.' There was also a column of flowers upon which a star shone prominently, and at the foot were three sheaves of wheat, emblematic of the deceased's age and life.

"We are indebted to Mr. S. B. Nichols for the following tribute to the memory of our departed friend and co-worker, and report of remarks made on the occasion of his funeral obsequies :—

"'IN MEMORIAM—DR. WILLIAM FISHBOUGH.

"'Another veteran Spiritualist, Dr. William Fishbough, passed on to the immortal home, suddenly and under peculiar circumstances, Friday evening, May 20th. He passed the evening away from home, and his wife on retiring for the night left a light burning in the front basement. On waking in the morning she found that he had not returned, and on going to the front basement door she found his lifeless form. Coming home late he had made a miss-step and fell, striking his head against the window sill and crushing his skull—a sad and mournful ending of a long and useful life. On Friday morning when he came to the breakfast table he told a curious dream that he had had in the night. He said he dreamed that the point of his gold pen that he used for his writing was worn out so that he could not use it any more ; and I am informed that he never did write another stroke. Was this a premonition of his sudden transit to the spirit-world ?'"

Amongst many another word of warm eulogy from friends who had known and loved this truly good man none can render him more justice than the statement, that he was *the scribe* that wrote down the famous work of A. J. Davis, then a rustic uneducated lad of sixteen years—"Nature's Divine Revelations ;" that he, William Fishbough, was one of the most patient and able sub-editors of the first Spiritual paper ever published, the New York *Spiritual Telegraph* ; he was also the author of the noble and philosophic work "The Macrocosm and Microcosm," besides innumerable magazine articles, all redolent of the scholarly intellect and pure spirit of a wise and good man.

To do justice to Dr. Hallock, his life of devotion and splendid service to the cause of Spiritualism, would be an attempt so difficult, that we shall leave his name as we find it—enshrined in the hearts of the multitudes who loved and admired him. A few lines of obituary notice we will however reprint from the London *Medium*, Dr. Hallock being scarcely less known and appreciated in England than amongst his own American countrymen. The *Medium* of February 19th, 1879, says :—

"IN MEMORIAM.—ROBERT T. HALLOCK, M.D.

" Translated from Earth to the Higher Life of Spirit, January 18th, 1879.

"One more of the little band, who have laboured in the Cause of Spiritualism, and whose names were associated with the inception of the Movement at the time of the 'Rochester rappings,' has been gathered to his home. Full of years and full of honour, revered and beloved by all who knew him, our departed brother has left behind him the blessed memory of the just, and the memorial of a blameless and well-spent life.

"Dr. Hallock was born seventy-three years ago, of Quaker parentage, at Milton, on the Hudson—his father and grandfather being preachers in the Society. In that faith he was nurtured, but its rigid tenets proved unacceptable to his progressive spirit, and on his arrival at manhood, he cast them aside, and the reaction landed him in Materialism. He was too essentially spiritual, however, to find any rest in negation, and in due time, as his powers developed, Spiritualism claimed him, almost naturally, as an adherent of its elevating philosophy.

"In 1851, having then moved from Utica, where he had practised medicine, to New York, he joined Robert Dale Owen, Judge Edmonds, Dr. Gray, and Mr. Charles Partridge in the investigation of the phenomena which are known to history as the ' Rochester knockings.' He gave to the subject the patient and intelligent care which it was his habit to bestow on everything that engaged his attention, and became convinced that he had found the light for which his spirit longed. From that time to the day when he was emancipated, by a painless and blessed change, from the prison-house of the body, he was a staunch and consistent Spiritualist.

"He founded the first Spiritualist Society of New York, of which he was president, and the Spiritual Conference, from which, during his residence in New York, he was seldom absent, and where his vacant chair, draped in black, tells eloquently of him, who, ' being dead, yet speaketh.' His sympathies were not bounded even by the wide field so open to them. He was a powerful anti-slavery advocate, and a founder and prominent member of the Liberal Club, up to the time when the summons came to him at its meeting on the 17th of January last.

"In his efforts for the emancipation of the slave he stood by the side of Wendell Phillips, Gerrit Smith, and William Lloyd Garrison—names that the world has learnt to honour as foremost in the rank of humanitarian effort.

"The method of his departure was sudden, and not unaccompanied by circumstances of peculiar distress to his sorrowing relatives. He had attended the Friday evening meeting of the Liberal Club, and left his place before the discussion commenced. In the ante-room he was heard to fall, and medical assistance was at once forthcoming from some members in the audience. He was suffering from a sudden spasm of the heart, a malady to which he was liable. He was conveyed to his home, and everything that loving care could do was gladly ministered.

"All, however, was in vain, and in a few hours he had quitted the suffering body and was free."

Still the procession of dearly-remembered faces moves on, and now another star of the brilliant galaxy shoots up rays of light far above the level of the passing groups, challenging—nay, compelling attention. The name of the shining Spirit is Epes Sargent.

Fortunately or unfortunately for Mr. Sargent, his connection with modern literature both in the departments of prose and poetry, procured for him so many complimentary notices from the press of Europe as well as of America, in which his Spiritualistic works were as carefully ignored, as his secular writings were faithfully chronicled, that his name requires the aid of two sets of biographers to render it full justice. Several interesting notices of Mr. Sargent's life work and varied abilities have appeared since he passed from our midst, none of which equals in eloquence and fidelity that given by the celebrated English writer " M. A., Oxon," in the London *Psychological Review*.

As this admirable sketch cannot possibly be transferred *in extenso* to these columns, we must content ourselves with a concise summary of Mr. Sargent's eminent life services, as published in the London *Spiritualist* of May, 1870. The editor says :—

"Mr. Epes Sargent, whose name has long been in the list of our correspondents, was a native of Gloucester, a picturesque maritime town, twenty-eight miles from Boston, U.S.A. While he was yet a child he entered the Public Latin School, where, in the study of Latin and Greek, he stayed five years, with the exception of six months which he passed in making a visit with his father to Denmark and Russia.

"Returning to America, he resumed his place at the Latin School, and soon afterwards was admitted a student of Harvard College. He did not, however, remain there till graduation, but accepted a situation as assistant in the editorial department of *The Advertiser*, a Boston daily paper. Subsequently his services were transferred to the *Daily Atlas*, where he had opportunities of passing a part of the year at Washington, during the sessions of Congress, as political correspondent. Here he was admitted to the familiar personal acquaintance of Webster, Clay, Calhoun, Preston, Chief Justice Marshall, and other eminent public men. With Mr. Clay, senator from Kentucky, and candidate for the Presidency, his relations were especially intimate, and he wrote a life of him, which was largely circulated, and edited with additions by Mr. Sargent's early friend, Horace Greeley. Journalist and man of letters, Mr. Sargent seemed now to have chosen his career. He was for some years a resident of New York, where he edited *The Mirror*, *The New World*, and other publications quite flourishing in their day. He also wrote and edited several works for the Messrs. Harper, which had good success, and led to pleasant relations with that house. He was on friendly terms with Poe, Bryant, Halleck, Washington Irving, N. P. Willis, Longfellow, and also with Charles Dickens during the latter's sojourn there.

"Mr. Sargent wrote several plays which achieved a fair share of success. He edited the *Boston Daily Transcript* several years, and the *Modern Standard Drama.* He put forth the *Standard Speaker,* with three supplementary books of elocutionary selections and translations, the success of which was very marked. These were followed by three series of reading-books, a book of original dialogues, and a much-praised work on etymology, forming twenty-two volumes in all. They are still largely in use in American schools.

"During the civil war he appeared for the first time as a public speaker, and made some spirited speeches, which were widely copied, and served a patriotic purpose. They drew forth letters of warm congratulation from Charles Sumner, one of the friends of his boyhood. Mr. Sargent also wrote a popular novel, entitled *Peculiar,* published by Carleton, New York, and of which sixteen thousand copies were sold.

"In 1868, having suffered from a bronchial affection, Mr. Sargent was advised by his physician to pass the winter in the south of France ; and he established himself at Cannes, on the Mediterranean. During his brief stay in England he made the personal acquaintance of Mr. W. M. Wilkinson, Mr. Thomas Shorter, Lady Caithness, Mr. William White, Dr. Ashburner, and other prominent Spiritualists. He also renewed his acquaintance with Mr. Benjamin Coleman and Mr. D. D. Home, the distinguished medium. Professor Francis W. Newman, author of many much esteemed works, who had long been his correspondent, was also now personally sought out and greeted.

"To Spiritualists Mr. Sargent's connection with the modern Spiritual movement will be perhaps of more interest than his literary career. His attention was drawn to Mesmerism about the year 1837, when he was in his twenty-fourth year. He had witnessed in Boston the experiments of Dr. Collyer. Soon afterwards, in New York, he had opportunities of studying the subject in his own way. Dr. Channing, a well-known physician, introduced him to a sensitive, the phenomena in whose presence he studied for two years under circumstances that precluded the possibility of deception. By the exercise of his own volition he satisfied himself of the mesmeriser's power over his subject. Of clairvoyance, thought reading, insensibility to pain, through Mesmerism, he also became fully convinced. When the phenomena at Hydesville broke out in 1847, he was editing the *Boston Transcript,* and through its columns did much to direct public attention to the subject.

"Having thus become finally convinced of the basic truth of Spiritualism, he omitted no opportunity of passing on the truth-torch to others. In 1867 he published a succinct history of Modern Spiritualism, under the title of "Planchette ; or, The Despair of Science," a title which hardly does justice to a work so earnest and comprehensive as this really is. In spite of its title, however, it has passed through four editions, and is still in demand. The Rev. Austin Phelps, D.D., refers to it as 'written by the most scholarly of the American defenders of Spiritualism.' Mr. William Crookes wrote of it in 1874, "Planchette" was the first book I read on Spiritualism, and it still remains, in my opinion, the best work to place in the hands of the uninitiated.'

"In 1875, Mr. Epes Sargent put forth 'The Proof Palpable of Immortality,' a volume of 288 well-filled pages, devoted chiefly to the materialization phenomena, but also to the discussion of moral and religious questions pertaining to Spiritualism. In 1876 he wrote a reply to Professor Tyndall's severe attack on Spiritualism, a reply which attracted great attention in America, and was hailed as 'the right word at the right time.' He also wrote (1877) the article on Spiritualism for Appleton's new 'Encyclopædia.'

"These works give but an imperfect idea of Mr. Sargent's activity in the cause of Spiritualism. By his contributions, some under his own name, but most of them anonymous, in various journals, English and American, and by a very extensive correspondence, he has been indefatigable in his attempts to convince an unwilling world that there is in and around us something more than Materialists would have us to believe."

Such a record as this needs no comment; it is one of which any individual might be proud ; one which reflects lustre on any cause graced with such an adherent, and which should for ever hush the rude tongue of those who virtually say the Spiritualists are all fools and believe in a delusion, or all knaves, combined in the effort to delude the world.

Last but not least of the shining throng whose name makes many a heart stir with loving and regretful memory is the kind and gentle wife of the celebrated Spirit postmaster, Dr. J. V. Mansfield.

It seems but yesterday since the author parted from this dear friend, then in the prime of a life devoted to unnumbered deeds of good and use. This last February, 1883, brings the tidings that she has passed on, ere the spring flowers could shoot up to adorn her silent bier. She will be missed in the places of gathering, in the dwellings of the poor, in the home she loved so well, and in the hearts of hundreds, who whilst following her bright Spirit to the better world, will realize a void left on earth that none can fill.

Of Mrs. Mansfield more perhaps than of thousands better known, though not less highly appreciated, the homely lines may most truthfully be said—

> "Earth has one angel less,
> Heaven one angel more."

It is only now, as these pages are going to press, that we hear through a private source of the apotheosis of Dr. J. R. Newton, the greatest magnetic healer, and one of the best men that ever wrote his life work on the flesh and blood tablets of grateful loving human hearts.

Extended notices of this beneficent being's manifold services to humanity will be found in another chapter, and presently every Spiritual paper in every land of civilization will teem with eulogies upon his name. But neither single notices, nor world-wide eulogies can chronicle the boundless good that Dr. Newton has done. A mortal pen may record how many blind eyes he has opened, how many crippled limbs he has straightened, and how many diseases that flesh is heir to have departed at his bidding, but to sum up the joy and gratitude with which he has filled thousands of human hearts in this generation, would require the pen of eternity's recording angels—none else should essay the task. It is enough to say he passed away in a ripe old age—ministered to by the most loving of human companions, and his soul has ascended to the spheres of eternal light freighted with the blessings of uncounted multitudes.

After numbering up the leaders of the Spiritual army who have disappeared from our mortal eyes during the last fifteen years, and allowing for many more, less known, whom we cannot catalogue, some of those secular readers whose eyes we confidently expect to glance over these pages, may enquire, after what fashion the Spiritualists are accustomed to celebrate those obsequies which they claim rather to be birthdays of the soul into a higher life, than ceremonials darkened with hopeless gloom or mysterious dread.

As a sample of these services, which time, place, and circumstance of course may often modify, we shall terminate this chapter—written strictly *in memoriam*—with an account of an obituary ceremony which will be long remembered in San Francisco, California.

The subject of this memorable occasion was Captain Francis Connor, commodore of the line of steamers plying between San Francisco and Oregon, a brave and gallant officer, who, though not himself a Spiritualist, was blest with a fair wife who was, and still is, one of the most devoted advocates of the Spiritual cause.

In the beginning of the year 1880, Captain Connor accompanied his wife to Charter Oak Hall, San Francisco, to attend the Sunday lectures of Mrs. Hardinge Britten. On quitting the hall, after the evening service, Captain Connor said to his wife, "If Mrs. Britten should be anywhere accessible when I die, I should like her to preach my funeral sermon."

Within a few weeks from the time when this remark was made, the lifeless form of Captain Connor was brought into San Francisco harbour, by the boat that he had commanded, on board of which he had suddenly breathed his last, on his homeward voyage, after a few hours' illness.

The high character of this noble gentleman, the respect and esteem that

30

he had won from all classes, but especially from the steamship company of which he had been one of the bravest and most devoted captains, were circumstances that created so deep an impression upon the citizens of San Francisco, that every craft in the harbour lowered its flag half-mast high, and the citizens shut their shops, and draped their doors with mourning emblems, as the procession which bore the remains of the gallant commodore passed through the streets.

In a few days, the devoted and high-souled wife of Captain Connor, had applied for, and obtained, the use of the splendid Unitarian Church, built for the late Rev. Thomas Starr King, of which Captain Connor had been an honoured member, as a fitting place in which to celebrate his obsequies. Mrs. Connor, without reserve, announced her intention of fulfilling her beloved husband's wish to the letter, by engaging Mrs. Hardinge Britten to conduct the services. In deference to the kindness of the trustees in granting the use of the church, the regular pastor was invited to assist in the ceremonial, but as sickness confined this gentleman to his bed, he sent a letter of condolence to the noble widow, and appointed the Rev. Mr. Kraig as his substitute.

At the close of the services, the congregation, numbering some three thousand persons, according to the custom prevalent in America, walked in orderly procession round the church so as to pass the bier and altar, both of which were covered with floral emblems and devices wrought with immense masses of the choicest flowers.

Thus the procession moved on, enabling each one to take a farewell look at the calm features of the gallant sailor. When the long files had passed out of the church, vast throngs, to the number of four thousand persons, who had been unable to obtain admittance, were marshalled in order, and permitted to walk round the church, pass through the area filled with blossoms, and silently greet the well-known features of the peaceful dead. Never was such a procession on such an occasion gathered together before in San Francisco. Never a more orderly or deeply-moved crowd marched through those long aisles, or lingered in regretful silence around the remains of mortality.

Thus ended one of the most impressive funeral services ever remembered in San Francisco, the only one wherein the scene was a popular church, the officiating minister a woman, and the day of death celebrated as *the day of new birth.*

The following press report of the ceremonial and the address delivered by Mrs. Britten was published in the San Francisco *Daily Chronicle,* and is given now as a sample of a Spiritual funeral address :—

"SPIRITUAL SERVICES.—FUNERAL OF THE LATE COMMODORE FRANCIS CONNOR, AT SAN FRANCISCO, CAL.

"Eloquent oration delivered by Mrs. Emma Hardinge Britten.

"On March 28th the remains of Commodore Francis Connor, of the Oregon steamship line, were borne into the First Unitarian church by eight uniformed officers of the steamship Oregon and deposited in front of the pulpit, amid a white sea of choice and fragrant floral wreaths and emblems, among which was a steamship, constructed of heliotrope and violets—emblematic of his inviolate devotion to his calling.

"Rev. Dr. Kraig read selections of Scripture, promising spiritual immortality, and the choir chanted Psalm xxiii., 'The Lord is my Shepherd.' Then Mrs. Emma Hardinge Britten, standing in front of the pulpit, at the head of the casket, offered this earnest invocation for divine help and guidance, after which she delivered, under inspiration, the following deeply impressive and touchingly eloquent spiritual address :—

"'O Thou Infinite and Eternal Spirit; Father, God; Lord of life and death; author and finisher of being! Lo, Thine hand is heavy on us in this trying hour. As we stand in the valley of the shadow, we hear Thy voice calling home our heart's beloved, and our spirits fail us, as we listen to the summons which removes from our mortal vision the father, friend, the strength, the consolation of many a pilgrim in earth's rough and rugged pathways. But even now, as we bend beneath the weight of our mighty sorrow, whilst our strength is laid low, and the voice that has spoken the word of power to the weak, and comfort to the helpless is hushed for ever, oh, teach us that Thou art still the strength of our weakness, light to our blindness, the true and unfailing consolation of every heart that trusts Thee. We know it is Thy voice that speaks to us through the eternal silence that has closed these mortal lips, bidding us pause and consider the solemn lessons which death alone can teach. Oh, trusted but most eloquent Teacher! As we stand in the presence of Thy white angel, Death, and still the throbbings of our beating hearts, to hear the message that he brings, we uplift our souls to Thee, Thou only strength and consolation, and learn to lay the burden of our cares and griefs on Thee, who alone canst bear them. Help us, oh, heavenly Father! and clear away the mists of sorrow from our eyes, that we may discern the footprints of the beloved one, in his pathway to the land of light. Help us to retread the tracks of honor, truth, and duty that he has left behind. Captain of our salvation! Pilot of souls! Thou who hast steered Thy beloved one's barque to the port of eternal safety, be with us now!

"'We see, with streaming eyes and arms outstretched in pain, the receding light of the white and flowing sails as his ship of earthly life is fast drifting out of view. The thickening mists of death have closed around him, and we are left alone, straining our failing sight to catch faint glimpses of the glory in which our vanished friend has cast eternal anchor. Oh, thou great spirit! Pole star of every drifting craft freighted with frail humanity! Teach us how to cry out to thee with heart and voice. We trust thee, oh, our father, in life as in death, in darkness as in light, in this, our home of human grief and weakness, as in the more peaceful days of life's full blossoming. We know that all is well with him who has gone before. We know that he has gained the shores of endless day and waves aloft the banner of immortal triumph over death. The veil of mortal being, so dense to us, is luminous to him, and from the Mount of Vision we know that he still watches, with an angel's tender pity, the bereaved and mourning friends who linger yet behind and bear the burdens he has dropped. We know the Immortal still loves, and that He is all—aye, more than all—he ever was or could be to those who love him still. Thou, who dost make the very roses thy preachers, help these faltering lips to tell of the joy and glory he has gained. Show to those mourning ones, the radiant mountain of transfiguration to which the angel Death has raised him. Help us to kiss and bless the rod that smites the human heart, but sets the Immortal free, and once more teach us all to cry in spirit and in truth, 'Thy will be done on earth as it is in heaven, for ever and for ever.'

"'Friends, we meet this day to celebrate the birthday of a soul into the life immortal. Fifty-three years ago there was a birthday of another sort in the home where this ascended soul first saw the light as a helpless, wailing babe. Born into the life of earth, where care and toil are the milestones at every step of the weary way; with all the bitter pangs of humanity's stupendous warfare looming up before him, still he was ushered into being without one tear or sigh to mar his welcome. No prophetic voice of warning spoke of the thorny road those infant feet must tread. The mother's heart was full of joy, and rejoicing friends hailed the young stranger's advent on life's stormy sea, without one sad misgiving.

"'And now, when we know how well, how nobly life's battle has been fought and won, how gallantly he's run the race God set before him, and gained the victor's prize of a well-earned immortality, shall we fail to bid the triumphant soul God speed, or stay with a single murmur the hand of the liberty angel that sets the ripened spirit free? Rather let us strive to follow the shining sails of his true life's ship to that glorious port of rest where the storm is hushed for ever and the sun-lit waves of joy are beating on the shores of eternal light. Whilst he who is transfigured from the clay of earth to the spiritual glory which our dim mortal sight cannot penetrate, the mute and touching eloquence of the form we have beheld in all the panoply of life and strength so strangely still, so dumb and silent now—all, in short, of the solemn mysteries of death—prompt us us to inquire their meaning and pause in the giddy rush of life to ask of God, the quiet dead, and one another, What has death done to this, our friend and brother? The ways of the Infinite One must ever be mysterious to the minds of His finite creatures, but in His mercy he has taught us enough by that we do know to trust Him in all things of which we are yet ignorant, and amongst the brightest revelations of our present day and hour are those that have stripped the grave of all its terror, death of its awe and mystery, and shown to the weeping eyes of bereaved humanity its precious dead in all the glorious reality of life immortal, and death itself to be but the archway to the higher, better, happier spirit land. Another of our Father's gifts to man has been the message of love brought by the very beings nearest to us. They point to the wealth we gather upon earth, the splendour that we fondly lavish upon the crumbling dust of those we've loved, and remind us that all must be left behind, and that the spirit takes not with him the value of death's shroud in material treasure. And yet it is given to us to know there are many mansions in our Father's house; wealth and possessions there; power and strength and noble work to do; joyful duties to fulfil, and life, with all its glorious energies and powers, continuing the woof of being from the point where death has snapt it. If this be so, and these revelations of the life beyond are now re-echoing through the wide, wide world, truly we may lift up our hearts in joy and triumph when we recall the noble record that our friend has made and count up the freight of duties well performed with which his gallant ship has sailed away to heaven. Besides the early years of his brave and useful public service, the lives of thousands have been entrusted to his skill and care, and the fortunes no less than the safety of countless multitudes, have hung upon the faithful performance of his untiring watch and ward.

"'The captain of many a ship destined to plough its way on the roughest seas and brave dangers which none but the well-skilled mariner could conquer, none but those "who go down to the sea in ships" and track their way through the pathless wastes of ocean can understand the perils of the deep—the ceaseless cares and toils, the sleepless vigils of the stormy night, passed neath the rayless skies, 'midst the howling tempest, drenching rain and piercing cold, whilst the lives of multitudes were hanging in the balance on the captain's skill and care. And yet we know that out of *his* brave hands no single life was ever lost. In *his* clear record there's no black mark of duties unfulfilled, no employer wronged, no murmuring crew oppressed, no friend forsaken, no stranger left unaided.

"'Not one soul he ever knew or served with but what would have united in crying, "God speed our gallant captain to his well-earned rest. If ever seaman ploughed his way to heaven he is the man!" Staunch and true! Brave man, great heart, gallant sailor, faithful servant of the King of kings! He watched and waked while others calmly slept. He thought and thought, and battled with the stormy seas, and wrestled with the elements until they became his subjects; and whilst the fiery scriptures of the skies stretched out above his head their canopy of glory, he read their solemn lessons in tireless duty, and worshipped his Creator in noblest service to his fellow men. My friends, the last, best lesson which this wondrous preacher, Death, has taught is, as we thus render the noble record of this gallant life, to emulate its beauty, retread the deep, strong footprints he has made—not in the "sands of time," but in the hewn-out rock of grand endeavour; and the last best lesson which the great outpouring of the spiritual hosts have brought us, is the sweet, consoling truth, that nothing that is good and true and beautiful in manhood can ever be marred by death.

"'God gathers up the beautiful, and He who cares for the falling sparrow and clothes these blossoms with their wondrous beauty, has treasured up the blossoms of his noble life, and only left the dross and dust to death. "We cannot make him dead," the gallant sailor! For mates, companions, friends, he is still the same, though a watcher now on a fairer, calmer sea. For the dear companion, he is still the tender guardian of her precious life; for the earth and man and all he's lived and toiled for, he's a guardian angel now, a ministering spirit, making our path more bright, our way more plain, our lives more holy and nearer heaven, because a good and faithful man has lived and died. He may, he must, have left a void which none can fill again. Many will miss his helpful, outstretched hand, and she—his best beloved one—will miss the coming foot that was ever prompt to hasten to her side; but she knows, as we do, he lives and loves and watches over her now.

"'The veil of earth, transparent to the eye of spirit, is only dense to us who linger yet behind it, but when we know, as God in His mercy shows us through His angels risen, that the form that sleeps the sleep that knows no waking, is not the man we've loved—that death has no power upon him, that he lives and stands in our midst this very hour, with all that made the man, and the added glory of life immortal, why should we weep or sigh, or put on the weeds of mourning? Why should we wish him back, or stay the hands that lay away the garments in the grave, and leave the guardian angel of the home behind? Remembering all we do know of the shining seas our loved ascended brother is sailing over now, surely we can trust our Heavenly Father in the yet veiled realms of mystery hidden from our view. "He doeth all things well," and though the golden bowl of mortal life is broken, the silver cord of earthly duty loosed, the pitcher broken at the fountain and the wheel broken at the cistern, we can bow and lean in calm submission, look back in high emulation at the record of a well spent life, and forward with triumphant joy that he's reached the goal, from which his loving hand will beckon us to follow onward. Oh, may the memory of this hour be ever green amongst us! May the record he has made, the wealth of freight with which his ship of life was laden be a never dying remembrance to us to strengthen us in the hour of trial ; encourage us to speed on amidst thorns and briars to the goal of victory he has gained, until we meet and greet him in the land where the angels have welcomed him with the glorious cry.   "Well done, thou good and faithful servant, enter into the joy of thy Lord."   And now it but remains to put away with all reverence the faded garments an immortal soul has worn. Lay down to rest the crumbling form of clay.   With tender reverence give back to earth the pale, white form of earth. Put out the earthly lamp ; he will not need it more.   Quench the dying flame.   Nor heat shall burn nor biting frost consume the happy dwellers of the summer land. Let dust and blossoms sleep in the tranquil grave, while the shining soul inhales the deathless perfume of the flowers that bloom in the land of never setting suns.   The last rites paid, the last farewell said, the honoured dust closed up from mortal sight, commit we all that's left to the silent grave, and bid God speed to the new-born son of heaven with the sweet, familiar closing words of love: "Our Father which art in heaven, hallowed be thy name.   Thy kingdom come, thy will be done on earth as it is in heaven.   Give us this day our daily bread, and forgive us our trespasses as we forgive them that trespass against us.   And lead us not into temptation, but deliver us from evil.   For thine is the kingdom, and the power, and the glory, for ever and ever.   Amen."'

"After the hymn, 'Rock of Ages,' by the choir, Mrs. Britten again said : 'Before we listen to the benediction, which closes these sacred rites, in the name of the wife and friends of the good and true man whose spiritual birth we celebrate, I tender earnest and heartfelt thanks for the deep reverence, earnest feeling, and kindly sympathy manifested by every friend and stranger gathered together in this hallowed ceremonial.   Above all, I offer on my own behalf, and that of those nearest and dearest to our beloved commander, our grateful thanks to the trustees of this church, who, in their kindness and generosity, have granted us the use of this sacred place for the performance of our last and holiest duty to our honoured dead.

"'Whilst memory lasts we shall ever cherish the tokens of deep sympathy, which, for one brief hour at least, have bound together this vast multitude in the ties of a common humanity.   I know it has been to you, as to me, and all of us, a grateful task to render the best tribute in our power to the memory of a great, good man.   Your presence and kindly feeling have helped to strengthen me in the performance of a sad, though pleasing duty, and almost changed bereavement into gladness.   Let us all go hence cherishing in our hearts the memory of the brave and true ; seeking to shape our lives like his to the line of duty ; striving to bring home to earth's last waymark a record as clear and true as his has been, and commending ourselves to the Father of all with the reverent cry, "Thy will be done on earth as it is in heaven, now and ever more."'

"The services closed with the recitation of a poem, and the benediction by the Rev. Dr. Kraig."

CHAPTER LV.

SPIRITUALISM IN AMERICA (CONTINUED)

SPIRITUALISM IN THE LAW COURTS.

WE must now call attention to a few cases in which prominent Mediums and Spiritualists were cited to appear before those tribunals, too often *falsely* called "the bar of justice."   The two instances narrated in this chapter are the trial of Dr. J. R. Newton, the renowned Spiritual healer, on the charge of "malpractice," and that of Mr. William Mumler, who was tried for "fraud," alleged to have been practised in the production of "Spirit photographs."

The circumstances which led to the charge against Dr. J. R. Newton were these.

It seems that a little girl who had been carried to Dr. Newton's office during his visit to Philadelphia in the hope of obtaining relief for a chronic affection of the spine, had been instantaneously cured, but on quitting the good doctor's presence, she became so excited with the delight of her marvellous restoration, that in running down stairs her foot slipped, she fell, and at the same time sustained a fresh injury to the spine.

It was rumoured that some of the child's nearest relatives were bitterly opposed to Dr. Newton's method of cure, and had been heard to declare, *that they would rather see her in her grave than cured by this Satanic agency.*

Whether the good healer's numerous opponents in the medical profession availed themselves of this opportunity to press home a charge that they could not have attempted to make with more sympathetic persons than those above alluded to, we need not pause to enquire ; certain it is, that the occasion was used by certain members of the faculty for instituting a prosecution against the all too celebrated and popular healer on the charge of "malpractice."

The true animus which stimulated this absurd and wholly untenable charge was soon apparent enough to the whole community and the matter would have terminated with the slight annoyance inflicted upon the beneficent healer, had it not been evident that the mighty powers who have the Spiritual movement in charge, used this opportunity to produce results as acceptable to the friends, as they were unforeseen by the enemies of Spiritualism.

Before the case was concluded, the magistrate in attendance was completely besieged with witnesses who poured in from all parts of the United States to the number of many hundreds, volunteering testimony to the marvellous cures that had been effected in their own persons, or those of their friends, by the *divine*, rather than the *mal*-practice of Dr. J. R. Newton. The court-room, the street, and at last the very city itself, was thronged with these unsolicited and deeply-grateful witnesses, and where personal attendance was impossible, hundred of affidavits testifying to Dr. Newton's marvellous cures, were sent in. Weeks and even months would have been required to receive the evidence thus volunteered. A summary termination of the vexatious prosecution was of course imperatively necessary. Before it could close however, the papers—in reporting the evidence received—had published long lists of cures which but for this malignant attack might have remained unrecorded for ever, except in the experience of private families and individuals.

With the accounts of these cures, came reports of the numerous benefactions which the good healer had performed, many poor people clamouring to be heard, and relating how he had added gifts of money to his healing powers, in cases where the recipients had scarcely dared to expect that so great and celebrated a man would even notice them.

We have suggested that the flood of testimony thus cited must have been unforeseen by the prosecutors. We may venture to add, that it must also have caused the blush of shame to mount to many a cheek when it was found that the very plot designed to crush the great healer was the means of recording his good deeds to an age that would otherwise have been ignorant of them.

Although it would be impossible in this volume to give more than a very small percentage of Dr. Newton's wonderful achievements, the full details of which are in the author's possession, we select from the list of affidavits printed on the occasion above alluded to, a few brief representative examples such as the following :—

" I, Mary Ann Rumer, testify and say that I am twenty-nine years of age, and live in Unionville, Chester County, Pennsylvania ; that for eleven and a half years I had been troubled with a spinal affection, which, with a complication of other diseases, confined me to my bed, and during the whole time I was a great sufferer from constant pain. For the last two years I subsisted almost entirely on water gruel. I had been treated by several physicians without any permanent benefit. On the 22nd of October, 1862, I was brought to Dr. Newton on a litter, in so feeble a condition that it was thought by my friends I could not live to reach the house. I was entirely unconscious, and I was so low that I could not be carried to the Doctor's room, so he treated me at first in the hall. I was then carried to his room, and within half an hour I was able to walk around the room and down stairs. The next day I was treated again by Dr. Newton, and a perfect cure effected. From the time I had the first operation, my appetite has been perfectly good, and I have ever since been able to eat heartily, and am now in good health. I have come to this city expressly to bear testimony to the wonderful cure of myself, for the benefit of suffering humanity. MARY A. RUMER.

" Affirmed and subscribed before me, this 5th day of March, 1863.
" WM. P. HIBBERD, Alderman."

" I, John Corkery, testify and say that I am 72 years of age, and live at No. 1013, Carpenter Street, Philadelphia. I have been partially blind for 22 years ; one eye I could not open at all, with great inflammation of the lids. My eyes had been operated upon by eminent physicians several times with absolute injury, until I became almost entirely blind, when, in the month of October, 1862, I heard of the wonderful cures of the eyes made by Dr. J. R. Newton, and was induced to visit him, when, after two or three operations, the inflammation entirely disappeared, and I was able to open my eyes and could see as well as most men of my age. He also restored my hearing, which I was fast losing, and I am now able to see and hear as well as most folks, and my general health has improved astonishingly, so that I appear twenty years younger than I did four months ago. JOHN CORKERY.

" Affirmed and subscribed before me, this 5th day of March, 1863.
" WM. P. HIBBERD, Alderman."

" My daughter, twelve years of age, had lost the use of her limbs from scarlet fever ; she was perfectly paralyzed. When I took her in my arms her head and feet hung perfectly useless, powerless. I brought her to Dr. J. R. Newton. With three treatments of less than one hour altogether, she was perfectly restored to health, and jumped rope, and came to her mind and intelligence as well as ever. She had many physicians of all kinds of practice, and I paid them a great deal of money, but they could not restore her. During her paralysis she could not keep any food upon the stomach, she is now in perfect health. I live near New Brunswick, N. J., and came here to give my testimony.
" SARAH E. TURQUAND.

" Sworn and subscribed before me, this 4th day of March, 1863,
" WM. P. HIBBERD, Alderman."

" I reside in Harrisburg, Pa. ; have been afflicted with rheumatism since 1820 ; part of the time have been so bad that I was drawn quite crooked ; the least cold I took would so affect me with lameness that I was obliged to use two canes to enable me to walk. I was also afflicted with internal bleeding, and after every other practice had failed of giving me any relief, I was induced to place myself under the treatment of Dr. J. R. Newton, which I did on the 26th of November, 1862, from which time I have enjoyed perfect health. He also cured me of varicose veins at a subsequent treatment, and at this time there is no appearance of any return of the above afflictions.

" I have also witnessed a number of cures performed upon others while I was under his treatment. One case, where a man came on crutches, in a miserable condition, in less than fifteen minutes he was able to walk, and in twenty minutes he ran across the floor and down stairs, leaving his crutches with the doctor.

" Another case : A coloured female was cured of paralysis, her hand being entirely useless. In less than ten minutes she was entirely restored, being able to lift a chair above her head with ease. " C. F. MUENCH.

" Sworn and subscribed before me, this 4th day of March, 1863.
" WM. P. HIBBERD, Alderman."

" I live in Woodbury, New Jersey. On the 21st of August, 1862, I was advised by Dr. Gardiner to call and see Dr. Newton for a cancer on the cheek, just below the eye

I did call as directed, and the doctor (Newton) treated me for it, and it is now perfectly cured. I had the cancer eleven years, and suffered pain all the time ; now there is not even a scar remaining. "WILLIAM V. MANKIN.

"Affirmed and subscribed before me, this 4th day of March, 1863.

WM. P. HIBBERD, Alderman."

"John Herbert sworn : I am forty-six years of age, and reside in West Philadelphia ; am engineer at the Blockley Almshouse. I suffered for weeks at a time with inflammatory rheumatism ; for the last two years, at times, could not turn in bed ; suffered severe pain ; it would pass from one part of my body to another ; had a number of physicians, but had no permanent relief, my feet much swollen. In ten minutes' treatment by Dr. Newton the swelling left my feet, and I was relieved of all pain and swelling. This was in December last ; I had a second operation of about the same time in the fore part of February, I think, and since that have been entirely well, and have no return of the disease. "JOHN HERBERT.

"Sworn and subscribed before me, this 4th day of March, 1863.

"WM. P. HIBBERD, Alderman."

"My son, William Cary, son of Marmaduke Watson, Principal of the Price Grammar School, was for some time afflicted with spinal curvature, being unable to walk without great difficulty. His limbs were very much swollen, and he was rapidly getting worse, until he saw Dr. J. R. Newton, who operated upon him and perfectly cured him. He can now walk six miles without pain or inconvenience.

"MARY E. WATSON, No. 1766, Frankford Road.

"Affirmed and subscribed before me, this 4th day of March, 1863.

"WM. P. HIBBERD, Alderman."

"March 4th, 1863.

"Andrew J. Hay : Live at Manayunk ; my wife for three years was unable to read, write, sew, or anything of the kind, by reason of debility of the optic nerve. Some time in November, 1862, I took her to see Dr. J. R. Newton, who operated upon her eyes. Before leaving his room she read several verses of Scripture, and has been able to read and write ever since ; her general health being also much improved.

"ANDREW J. HAY, Pastor First Baptist Church.

"Affirmed and subscribed before me, this 4th day of March, 1863.

WM. P. HIBBERD, Alderman."

"Peter Manning, being sworn, deposes and says : I live at Bordentown, New Jersey. On the 30th of October, 1862, I called on Dr. J. R. Newton. I was blind two years and three months. When I came to Dr. Newton I was so bad that I could not see a gaslight in front of me ; after ten minutes' treatment, without pain, I was enabled to see to read and write, and have kept my own books ever since. "PETER MANNING.

"Sworn and subscribed before me, this 4th day of March, 1863.

WM. P. HIBBERD, Alderman."

"David Allen, being affirmed, deposes and says : I live in the city of Burlington, N.J.; am in my 67th year of age. I have been troubled many years with spine disease ; and in February, 1861, I had a fall and broke my hip ; had been under the care of an eminent physician for six months ; for a year and nine months could not walk without a crutch ; the limb was stiff, and painful to move. After fifteen minutes' treatment by Dr. J. R. Newton I could use the limb as well as the other, and have never used the crutch since.

DAVID ALLEN.

"Affirmed and subscribed before me, this 4th day of March, 1863.

"WM. P. HIBBERD, Alderman."

We would ask our readers to bear in mind that the cases cited above and selected at random from one of the Philadelphia papers, only constitute about one per cent of the records now in print, many of which—in the author's possession—relate to persons still living, or those whose relatives are ready to give sworn testimony of the most authentic character. We have already alluded to Dr. Newton's beneficent work in England, and must now leave to other records a more detailed account of this great healer's marvellous acts of use and blessing to suffering humanity.

The next instance in which all the powers of wealth, position, and public influence could be brought to bear against Spiritualism and its representatives, was in the prosecution of the well-known Spirit photographer, Mr. William Mumler, at the instance of the proprietors or editors of a New York journal, entitled, *The World*.

As the details of this trial, besides being reported in full in the Spiritual journals, were given "as a curious item of news," in hundreds of the leading journals of America, we present to our readers a brief summary of the case, as reported in one of the most authoritative and widely-circulated of the American "dailies," namely, the New York *Tribune*. The article quoted dated April, 1869, commences thus :—

"In all the annals of criminal jurisprudence, there has seldom, if ever, been recorded a case analogous to that just tried before Justice Dowling, in the Tombs Police Court, in which the People were the prosecutors, and Wm. H. Mumler, of No. 630, Broadway, the defendant. The specific charge against Mumler was, that by means of what he terms Spiritual photographs, he has swindled many credulous persons, by leading the victims to believe it was possible not only to bring back the departed spirit, but to photograph their immaterial forms. . . .

"The announcement that the examination of the case would be continued on Monday last, drew together a large and miscellaneous audience, including a number of the most distinguished of the believers in, and propagators of, the doctrines of Spiritualism, many legal gentlemen, curious to note the points of law which might arise during the trial, and a sprinkling of ladies, believers evidently, who watched the proceedings with an interest scarcely exceeded by that of the party principally concerned. The examination was held in the Special Sessions Court Room ; members of the bar, distinguished Spiritualists (among them Judge Edmonds and Mr. Mc Donald), and the ladies, being accommodated with seats inside the railing.

"The principal defendant, Mr. Mumler, a man of about 40 years of age, with dark hair, beard, and eyes, and olive complexion, was seated next to his counsel, Messrs. J. T. Townsend, and A. Day, and appeared perfectly calm and self-possessed, ready at a moment's notice to whisper to his counsel a question touching some important point which he desired to elicit from the witness. Mumler's face is one of the few from which one fails to gather any trace of character. It is calm and fathomless, and although it would be harsh to say that it is unprepossessing, it is yet a face which one would scarcely be able to believe in at first sight.

"The People were represented by Mr. Eldridge Geary, and the first witness called was Marshall Joseph H. Tooker, through whose instrumentality the spiritual photograph business was brought to the notice of the authorities. He deposed that in consequence of information from Mr. P. V. Hickey, of *The World*, the Mayor had ordered him to 'look up' the case, which he did by assuming a false name, and having his photograph taken by Mumler. After the taking of the picture the negative was shown him, with a dim, indistinct outline of a ghostly face, staring out of one corner, and he was told that the picture represented the spirit of his father-in-law. He, however, failed to recognize the worthy old gentleman, and emphatically declared that the picture neither resembled his father-in-law, nor any of his relations, nor yet any person whom he had ever seen or known. The other portions of Marshall Tooker's testimony were published in *The Tribune* at the time of the alleged swindle, and therefore it would be useless to recapitulate. With this testimony the prosecution rested. . . .

"In the first part of the defence, several photographic experts were called, who testified that without choosing to avow themselves Spiritualists, or having any interest in defending Mumler, they had received spirit photographs from him, and could not either account for the pictures of deceased friends they had received, or find any reason for accusing him of fraud or deception. One of the most notable witnesses summoned, was Judge Edmonds, who gave his testimony to the following effect :—

"'I have known Mr. Mumler some two or three weeks. On the occasion of my becoming acquainted with him, I had gone to his gallery with Dr. John F. Gray and a Mr. Hunt, on the invitation of the former, to have my photograph taken. I had two pictures taken—[Two photographs shown. The photographs were very fair pictures of the Judge, each having near the upper right hand corner, a dim outline of a female face, sufficiently distinct, however, to shew that the lady was very beautiful. It would appear that spiritual manifestations abounded on that occasion, for the faces on these pictures are entirely different, although both are charmingly pretty.]' Judge Edmonds here became retrospective, and detailed several facts and circumstances relative to spiritual photography which had come to his knowledge many years ago. Returning to Mumler he said : 'I know a great many persons who have visited Mumler, some of whom have met with astonishing success in procuring spirit pictures of departed friends. Mr. Livermore, of Wall Street, has been peculiarly successful.' [Another photograph shown, this time a fine-looking young man, seated in a pensive attitude, with his eyes cast downward. Behind his chair, and leaning over his head, is the spectral white-clad form of a lady, whose hands rest on his shoulder. This is the most remarkable of the photographs exhibited in court, from the fact that the photographers present declared that by no means known to them, other than the bodily presence of some one behind the chair, could the picture of the lady's hand be produced.] . . . .

"Cross-examined : 'At the time my picture was taken there were present Messrs. Gray, Hunt and Mumler. I watched the operator closely while he was taking the picture, but could detect no fraud. I believe that the camera can take a photograph of a spirit, and I believe also that spirits have materiality—not that gross materiality that mortals possess, but still they are material enough to be visible to the human eye, for I have seen them. Only a few days since I was in a court in Brooklyn, when a suit against a life assurance company for the amount claimed to be due on a certain policy was being heard. Looking toward that part of the court-room occupied by the jury, I saw the spirit of the man whose death was the basis of the suit. The spirit told me the circumstances connected with the death ; said that the suit was groundless, that the claimant was not entitled to recover from the company, and said that he (the man whose spirit was speaking) had committed suicide under certain circumstances. I drew a diagram of the place at which his death occurred, and on showing it to the counsel, was told that it was exact in every particular.

"'I had never seen the place nor the man, nor had I ever heard his name until I entered that court-room ; the appearance of the spirit was shadowy and transparent.'

"Mr. Jeremiah Gurney, of No. 707, Broadway, testified : 'I have been a photographer for 28 years. I have witnessed Mumler's process, and although I went prepared to scrutinize everything, I could find nothing which savoured of fraud or trickery ; it was the usual process of preparing a plate for taking a photograph, the only thing out of the usual routine being the fact that the operator kept his hand on the camera.'

"Mr. James R. Gilmore, an author whose *nom de plume* is 'Edmond Kirk,' was next called. He testified : 'During last month I was requested by the author of *Harper's Weekly* to investigate this spiritual photography affair, and write an article regarding it. I called on Mr. Mumler, stated my business and desired to investigate the workings of his process.'

"The witness then describes Mumler's method of taking pictures, and concluded by saying :—'I could detect nothing unusual in Mumler's operations, though I watched him closely while preparing the plates and the camera, and finally went with him into the darkened room where the pictures were developed.'" [This witness received three spirit photographs.]

Mr. Elmer Terry, and Mr. Jacob Kingsley, were the next witnesses examined, and both, after the most severe cross-examination testified to Mr. Mumler's entire candour in submitting to be watched at every turn, and to the production of Spirit portraits on their photographic plates, both visiting the artist as total strangers.

Mr. Paul Bremond, a well-known writer, and a gentleman who has held many responsible public positions in the West and South; Mr. David Hopkins, a manufacturer of railway machinery, and a great many other witnesses of respectability and good standing, then testified to the receipt of Spirit portraits recognized by their friends as well as themselves, and all described the searching investigations to which, in their presence, Mr. Mumler not only cheerfully submitted, but often invited. One of the most interesting pieces of testimony afforded in this trial was that rendered by Mr. Charles F. Livermore, a gentleman of wealth and high social standing in New York, and one whose evidence seemed all the more independent from the fact that he was not an avowed Spiritualist. Mr. Livermore said, in the course of his examination :—

"'I sat five times in succession. I think that the first two sittings amounted to nothing but a shadowy background. I made the same examination that I had previously ; I found a screen, made I should think, of white cloth, standing about two feet from the side of the wall. I went behind it, but there was no one there. The screen was directly behind me when I sat down. Mumler was in the room; I accompanied him before the operation into the dark room, and saw him pour the collodion upon the plate. I changed my position each sitting. One showed the picture of a lady standing behind me, bearing a bunch of flowers in her right hand, which was resting upon my shoulder. . . .' He then showed another, which, in answer to the counsel, he said he recognized; [continuing] 'I examined the camera after this, but could see nothing out of the way. . . . I did not discover any fraud or deception, or anything that looked like it. I was cautioned against him as a trickster by some friends in Boston. Mr. Mumler was very polite and gave me every chance of investigation; he said he could not guarantee anything.'

"To Mr. Geary : 'I paid Mr. Mumler $20 ; he only charged me $10, but I gave him $20 because I was so satisfied. These pictures, so far as their identity goes, are satisfactory. It is a very remarkable phenomenon.'

"Q. Who is this figure on the picture ?—A. It is my wife ; she died eight years ago. I have a picture of her in my possession, and I may have seen the picture every day. It is hanging up in my bedroom ; but not in that form. It is a plain figure. I have two portraits besides. I see them every day.

"Q. Do you see anything to cause an identity, except the faces ?—A. Nothing, except the general size.

"Q. Do you recognize any peculiar expression about the face ?—A. Nothing more than the general one—nothing more than the general outline ; the third picture was taken a few minutes after the others.

"What do you recognize in this ?—A. It is unmistakable ; the recognition was perfect, not only with myself, but with all my friends."

Several other witnesses were called, both ladies and gentlemen. Their testimony was all to the same effect as that quoted above. After which,

"Mr. Day said : We can produce many others to show an identification of friends, and that there is no deception, but I suppose there is no necessity for bringing forward any more.

"At the next sitting of the Court Mr. Mumler read the following statement :—

"'In 1861, in the City of Boston, while engaged in business as an engraver, I was in the habit of visiting a young man who was employed in a photographic gallery kept by a Mrs. Stewart, on Washington Street. Occasionally I would experiment with the instrument and chemicals. One Sunday, while entirely alone in this gallery, I attempted to get a picture of myself, and then it was that I first discovered, while developing it, that a second form appeared on the plate. At this time I had never heard of spirit pictures, although I had been somewhat interested in the doctrine of Spiritualism. At first I laboured under what is now the general impression—that the plate upon which the picture was taken could not have been clean, and that the form which showed itself beside my own must have been left on the glass ; and I so stated to my employers and others. Subsequent attempts, however, made under circumstances which preclude such a possibility have confirmed me in the belief that the power by which these forms are produced is beyond human control, and the experts that have been called by the People have failed to produce a picture made in that manner. I wish to state that at the time I developed the shadow or form above alluded to, I was a complete novice in the art of photography, and had no experience whatever in the composition of chemicals used in the business, and that my use of them in my experiments at that time was simply in conformity with what I had seen my friend do, while himself engaged in his business. After getting the form, at the suggestion of several friends to whom I showed the plate, I made other attempts, and generally with most remarkable results ; I then determined to leave my own business and devote myself to photography ; before long the subject of spirit-photography, and particularly my success, became the theme of every tongue, and I was overrun with enquiries, and obliged to go over and over again the routine of taking and developing the pictures. For a long time I never refused any person who came to investigate : it soon became apparent, however, that I must either stop or cease to support myself, for, as a general thing, these *savants*, while greedy themselves for intellectual food, seemed entirely oblivious to the fact that I myself was a material body. (Laughter.) However, I can truly say that I have never refused, intentionally, any person who desired to have a picture taken from making every examination they chose to make, and had I been allowed to have produced evidence from abroad, I could have shown by scientific men, whose names would have satisfied every one, that the most careful and minute examinations have often been made into all the details of my business while I have been engaged in taking pictures ; I solemnly assert here that I have now but comparatively little knowledge of photography or chemicals, or science of any kind, further than is absolutely needed to take ordinary photographic pictures ; I positively assert that in taking the pictures on which these forms appear, I have never used any trick or device, or availed myself of any deception or fraud in producing them ; that these forms have appeared in each and every instance when they have been presented without any effort, except my will-power to produce them.

"'As to my refusal to entertain propositions from the self-appointed committee of photographers who appeared in my room since my arrest, and who desired, as I am informed by Mr. Gray, to make me take pictures for them, whether I would or not, I have only to say that since my arrest I have placed myself entirely in the hands of my counsel, and have been guided by his advice. One of the first cautions he gave me was to refrain, during the examination, from being led into any trap of that kind ; having been charged with a crime which, temporarily at least, placed me before the public in the same category with gamblers and men of that ilk, I have been deprived of the privilege of having my utensils examined at the time of my arrest.' (Here Judge Dowling said : I was applied to to have your tools seized, but refused to have it done because I disapproved of such proceedings.) Mr. M. continued : 'If I had been engaged in such nefarious proceedings as I am charged with, the implements themselves would have been the strongest evidence against me. They have stood ever since in the position they have always occupied in my gallery.'

"Mr. Townsend, on behalf of the defendant, first addressed the Court. After an able introduction, Mr. Townsend directed his Honour's attention to what appeared to be the legal aspect of the case. He then entered into the evidence given by the respective witnesses for the defence. 'Mr. Mumler has obtained spirit pictures in strange places, on other instruments, and with strange chemicals. The pictures thus obtained have been recognized by the sitters, in many instances, as deceased friends and relatives. Mr. Gray has been present many times when they were recognized. Judge Edmunds recognized one.' (Here the learned counsel gave a synopsis of the testimony, making commentaries as he proceeded.) He continued : 'Five hundred persons could have given similar testimony to those who had been called for the defence. Mr. Mumler has been here but a few months, and it is wonderful that so many respectable people would come without demand. He obtained pictures of persons dead, who had no pictures taken during life. He took these pictures sometimes without even touching the camera. He took his pictures through a yellow light, with no gas. There is no evidence that Mumler pretended to do what he knew to be false, and consequently the whole element of the crime is wanting. Mumler may be wrong in saying he can give a spirit picture, but that does not constitute a crime, unless he knew he could not give one. Upon the prosecutor's own showing, this case must be dismissed. It will not change a believer, or prevent one from believing. Spiritualists will stand by him at all hazards to the utmost extremity. The case in a Court of Justice should be looked upon simply as one of law. But suppose these defences should fail, we come to our affirmative defence, namely (1), that spirit pictures can be taken. It has been proved that pictures of the dead have been taken. (2) That such pictures have been taken where there was no picture of the deceased in existence. These two things have been distinctively, positively sworn to by unimpeachable witnesses, and in a judicial proceeding such as this, that testimony must control, unless it has been overborne by countervailing evidence. Now let us look at this countervailing evidence. It is proved that shadowy, ghost-like pictures can be produced by other photographers. Everybody acquainted with photography knows that to be so ; it has never been denied by us ; Mumler's circular says that. But still the question remains—and it is the real question in the case—can such shadowy pictures as produced by others be pictures of the dead ? But even against the testimony for the prosecution, which was theory, we have direct practical evidence. . . . .'

"Mr. Townsend then remarked, that if all Spiritualists were insane, there must be a great deal of insanity in America, for statistics showed that in the United States there were 11,000,000 of Spiritualists to 10,000,000 of other denominations. After pursuing his arguments in a theological light, Mr. Townsend concluded his most able and eloquent peroration.

"Mr. Geary then rose ; and after expressing his admiration of his adversaries' argument, said : 'This is no private prosecution. One of the gentlemen connected with a public journal of this city examined into these so-called spirit photographs, satisfied that a large swindle was being perpetrated ; he called to it the attention of the Chief Magistrate of this city, who at once directed his Chief Marshal to make a personal investigation. Hence any assertion that private malice instigated these charges is as baseless as it is untrue.' He then elaborately reviewed the whole of the evidence for the defence.

"After criticising the testimony of other witnesses, Mr. Geary continued : 'Now what does all this prove? Why, that the trick was so cleverly done that not even photographers could discover how it was done. That very many persons of ordinary intellect, competent to conduct the every-day business of life, went to the prisoner, paid their money, received these spirit photographs, and (Polonius like) fancied they recognized likenesses of their departed friends, and therefore believed the prisoner's statement. There is no proof of any spiritual agency, only evidence that certain persons believe it to exist. Man is naturally superstitious, and in all ages of the world, impostors and cheats have taken advantage of credulity to impose on their fellows less sharp than themselves.' Mr. Geary then accounted for the testimony of Judge Edmonds and Paul Bremond on the theory of hallucinations, which affected Lord Byron, Cowper, and Goethe. He then showed the application of the principle in the present case. He asserted that probable cause had been shown to warrant the commitment asked for.

"At the close of the address the Judge said, after careful attention to the case, he had come to the conclusion that the prisoner should be discharged. He would state that however he might believe that trick and deception had been practised by the prisoner, yet as he sat there in his capacity of magistrate, he was compelled to decide that he should not be justified in sending the defence to the grand jury, as, in his opinion, the prosecution had failed to prove the case."

The following letters have appeared in the *Tribune* on the same subject:—

"CAN A SPIRIT BE PHOTOGRAPHED?

To the Editor of the Tribune.

"Sir,—It is sometimes a thankless task to expose villany. It is always a thankless task to throw yourself against a popular belief with nothing in your hand but a new truth. Mr. Mumler may be a villain. I do not know the man. I never saw him. If he is a trickster his villany is of the darkest hue, for he speculates on the holiest instincts of men. I have nothing to do with Mr. Mumler. He may be honest, or the court may find him a swindler. The questions raised in this trial do not turn on the innocence or guilt of one man.

"Can a spirit be photographed? Whether Mumler be acquitted or convicted, most intelligent men will say 'No.' Ask them why, and they cannot tell you. They have certain vague ideas of a spirit as something incorporeal. They dismiss the question with an *à priori.* One day, in a conversation with Herbert Spencer, I told him of certain facts which had led Alfred Wallace to a belief in the nearness of a world of spirits, and the communion of spirits with mortals. Mr. Spencer met the facts by saying that he had settled the question on *à priori* grounds. Wallace is one of the first naturalists of Europe. He tells me he has seen and heard certain things; and I, making my own experience a measure of the universe, dismiss his testimony as contradicting nature. Is that the method of modern philosophy? . . . .

"In February, 1867, I formed the acquaintance of a photographer living in the Connecticut Valley. I had gone to his rooms for a photograph. While sitting for the picture, I saw that the artist was strangely agitated. When the plate was developed a bright but vapory female form appeared, standing at my side. I had never heard of Mumler or spirit photography. I asked the photographer how that form got on the plate; he did not know; he could only say that while he was photographing me he saw that woman standing at my side. He did not want the picture taken from his gallery, and wished me not to speak of it. He told me that now and then, for years, he had taken such pictures; that they came through no agency of his; that he could take them almost any time by yielding to the control of beings which he believed to be spirits, but he wanted nothing to do with it. 'He would not have his name mixed up with Spiritualism in any form.'

"I had such confidence in my friend's honesty, that I wished to make an investigation of this strange power. It was only after many interviews and much urging that he consented to give me sittings, and yield to the 'invisibles.' I offered to pay him generously for his time, but he declined any consideration, saying that he could not be tempted to use this mysterious gift for gain. He gave me every facility in making the investigation. I took a friend to assist me. We had his time for four afternoons. We had the utmost confidence in him, but made the investigation as if he were a trickster. I assisted in preparing the plates, and stood by while the pictures were developed. We took *every* precaution to prevent or detect trickery. At almost every sitting we got the photograph of a woman—the same bright, vapory form that appeared when I went alone, or *thought* I was alone! And at almost every sitting the photographer was partially entranced. What shall we say? He is a man of position and character. I would as soon think of flinging the charge of falsehood against the Chief Justice. He had no motive to deceive. He would not sell his gift for money. If I believed him capable of falsehood, still I should be unable to account for the pictures. . . . . The photographer, myself, and my friend were the only persons in the room. Could we have been deceived for four days by shallow tricks? And if we were deceived, how did the confederate who personated the spirit make herself transparent? How did she suspend herself in the air? for one of these photographs is the picture of a woman floating down through the air. . . .

"Another case came under my notice. A young girl in Chelsea called on one of the leading photographers of the city to have some tintypes taken. He was about to close his rooms for the day. The girl sat, and while the picture was taking, she felt a blur coming over her eyes. She spoke of it to Mr. A., who was standing by the camera. He told her she might wink, but she must sit still. When he developed the plate, a pair of hands appeared on each face! There were eight faces on the sheet. This photograph is very remarkable. I have examined four of the impressions, and have one of them in my possession. The hands are clasped around the girl's neck. They are shown up to the wrist, where they fade away into a formless vapor. They are transparent. One hand comes down over the girl's chin, and you see right through it the perfect outlines of the chin. There is a wonderful family likeness to all these pictures. Judge Edmonds testifies that the spirits he sees are transparent; and one of the leading Doctors of Divinity of New England (Orthodox) tells me that he sees spirits in the same way.

"Now you cannot suppose that these hands had been photographed on the tin before. The photographer tells me that he used a new sheet. Suppose I do not believe him. How, then, did the hands appear *over* the face? Can you suppose the hands were photographed *after* the girl? You will see that the little finger and the ring finger on the left hand are thrust under the girl's collar. You must say, then, that the girl and hands were all taken together. And now, did some one steal in and clasp her hands around the girl's neck, and still elude the eye of the artist? He tells me that no one was in the room but himself and the girl. Suppose some one did steal in—how did she make her hands transparent, and conceal the rest of her body? The photographer is a man whose word no one will doubt. He tells me that he had never thought of spirit photography; that he has no theory; that he only knows the hands came through no agency of his.

"Now, gentlemen—you have not settled these questions on *à priori* grounds—can you escape the conclusion to which I have been driven?

"That men and women—spirits, but not incorporeal—can, under certain conditions, clothe their persons with elements sufficiently tangible to reflect light.

"While reading a report of the the trial of Mumler, and finding lawyers trying to break the testimony of witnesses because of their belief in spirits, I thought of the words of a living German philosopher: 'No one who has eyes to see can fail to remark that the belief in the immortality of the soul has long been effaced from ordinary life.' We swear a witness on the Bible, and then impugn his testimony if he believes in spirits!—believes that the writers of the New Testament were not mistaken when, on almost every page, they speak of spirits, and admonish us 'to *try* the spirits!' Whither are we drifting? How would an item like this appear in *The Tribune*?

"'The Bishop of Rhode Island has written to the Bishop of New York that three men whom he had known in Providence appeared to him, and talked with him, after their decease. The Rhode Island Bishop thinks that bad spirits can personate good ones and deceive us; but he is confident these three spirits were really his friends.

"'Our table-talk over such an item would be a measure of our departure from the faith of primitive Christianity. For the Bishop of Rhode Island put Exodius, a Bishop in Africa, and for the Bishop of New York put Augustine, and for the nineteenth put the fourth century, and you have an historical truth." "W. D. L.

"Boston, Mass., April 26, 1869."

The closest attention is called to the following still more important letter:—

"*To the Editor of the 'Tribune.'*

"Sir,—The question has been frequently asked during the Mumler trial, 'Why, if it be not a deception, cannot he produce his pictures in some other establishment than his own?'

"In answer, I beg space for a brief statement of facts within my own knowledge and experience. With a desire to fully investigate this subject, I invited Mr. M. to visit Poughkeepsie. He accepted, and on the 30th of March last came to our rooms.

"I had, previous to his visit, made every arrangement possible for a full investigation, removing all old negatives from my operating rooms, preparing fresh plates from glass never before used, and putting everything in a shape to prevent or detect any attempt at imposture. A reward of $50 was offered by me to any of our employés who should succeed in detecting any trickery or deception.

"Mr. M. entered our operating room without any previous preparation or appliances whatever, and with the camera, chemicals, &c., in daily use by us, and under the closest scrutiny of my operator and myself, produced at once his so-called spirit pictures. In three instances during our experiments my operator performed all the manipulations himself, from the coating of the plate to the developing of the pictures; the result in each case being the same, a second figure appearing upon the plate. In one instance the camera was taken into the developing room by him, the plate-holder there removed and thoroughly examined, and the picture developed. Result the same, no second negative or mechanical arrangement whatever being discovered. One fact is worth more as evidence than all the theories in existence, and it is a fact that Mr. Mumler's pictures were produced in our rooms, with our instruments, chemicals, &c., without his touching the plates or taking any part in their production whatever; save only that of laying his hand upon the camera box during the time of exposure. The theories advanced by so-called experts all involve previous preparation of cameras, plate-holders, &c., none of which was it possible for Mr. M. to have made upon this occasion. The different processes described by them, by which Mr. M.'s pictures may be imitated, are known to most photographers. They may prove a satisfactory explanation to the minds of said experts, none of whom have investigated Mr. M.'s operations themselves, but are far from satisfying those who have. Messrs. Gilmore, Gurney, Silver, and myself, with a host of others, know they utterly fail to afford a solution of the problem, or account for the facts within our knowledge. I will pay $100 to any *expert* who will come to my rooms, and under the same circumstances that Mr. Mumler's pictures were produced there, do the same by natural means without detection. If he succeeds, and can give a satisfactory explanation of the matter, I will promptly acknowledge the fact to the world, and thank him for the solution of a mystery beyond my comprehension.

"My operator was present at the trial on Friday last, ready to give his sworn testimony to the facts stated. His testimony was not admitted, on the ground that what occurred in Poughkeepsie was foreign to the case; and yet the question is asked, why cannot Mumler produce his pictures in some other gallery than his own? It would seem, if the desire was to arrive at the facts in the case, and not to condemn the man, innocent or guilty, that any evidence tending to a solution of the matter should not have been ruled out upon mere technical grounds. A sworn statement of the facts mentioned has been made by my operator, and is now in the hands of Mr. M.'s counsel. Mr. M., while here, was not only thoroughly watched by those immediately about him, but also by our printers, who, stimulated by the reward offered, and believing the whole thing a deception, had loopholes prepared, looking from the printing room above into the developing and dark rooms below; and during the little time Mr. M. was left unwatched, or supposed himself to be, his every movement was noted by them. They failed to detect anything in his operations different from the ordinary process. I have no personal interest in Mr. M., and had no acquaintance with him, previous to a casual visit made to his rooms in New York, where, at his invitation, on learning I was a photographer, I investigated the subject as far as possible. Not being fully satisfied there, although unable to detect any sign of imposture, I induced him to visit my rooms, with the above result.

"Poughkeepsie, N. Y.   WM. P. SLEE."

The editor of the London *Spiritual Magazine,* in the issue of June, 1869, says of this case :—

"We observed that several of the London daily papers published with great alacrity the report of the early days of the trial, but so far as we have seen, not one has published the conclusion of the case, which ended in the acquittal of Mr. Mumler. The evidence given on his behalf is most interesting, and appears to be of the strongest kind to prove the facts. We invite the London press to publish this evidence, and the Judge's decision."

As well recognized photographic portraits of deceased persons form one of those phases of Spiritual phenomena which itinerant conjurers cannot *expose* by jugglery, and priestcraft cannot anathematize by biblical quotations, as Mr. Mumler in especial has been one of the most candid Mediums for the production of this interesting phenomenon, and one who seemed the last person to become open to the charge of trickery or deception, we deem it not out of place to cite still another witness to the test facts which generally accompanied the production of his Spirit photographs. The testimony with which we propose to close our case is an excerpt from a letter written by the author herself to her friends in England, when complying with their request to send them some specimens of American Spirit photographs.

The letter is dated from Chicago, January 20th, 1872, and was published in the columns of the *Religio Philosophical Journal.* The extract pertinent to our case reads as follows :—

"In 1870, during a brief residence in London, I was engaged to write a series of musical articles, amongst which was an analysis of Beethoven's celebrated C Minor Symphony. Whilst I was occupied in this work, I was made aware that the spirit of the noble composer was present, and that he desired me to frame my analysis after a certain fashion, the specialities of which he himself undertook to dictate. I had always been a passionate admirer of Beethoven's music, and as I was frequently called upon to write analyses of his works, I must admit that I was too much disposed to become enthusiastic in my methods of expression to suit my matter of fact employers.

"I had been warned previous to the occasion of which I write, not to indulge in any 'high-flown strains of eulogy,' but the presence of the grand old master's spirit seemed so completely to conquer all tendencies to common-place expression that forgetful of the warning I had received, I wrote out the spirit's ideas in language of my own, and that of a character which on any other occasions I should have been certain would be rejected for its unqualified and enthusiastic tone of eulogy. When my work was ended, the keen-sighted spirit, addressing me, said : 'Presently, when I am gone, you will doubt my identity and rebuke yourself for fancying that Beethoven has been your visitor. I will give you three convincing tests of my presence, the first of which is, that your employer *shall* accept your article and declare it is the best you have ever written on this subject. The other two tests *will come.'* *Test number one* was realised that very same day, my employer expressing unusual satisfaction with my article, and declaring it to *be the best I had ever written,* &c., &c.

"The following evening I had the privilege of being one of a party of twelve persons who were holding a *séance* at the residence of Mr. and Mrs. S. C. Hall, Mr. D. D. Home being the medium. During the progress of the manifestations, which were very powerful and interesting, I suddenly beheld the spirit of Beethoven standing by my side, and heard clairaudiently the words, 'I have come to give you the second test.' No one saw the spirit or heard the voice but me, and whilst I was relating to the company what I had seen and heard, and the circumstances which rendered the presence of that spirit peculiarly significant, an accordion, which was lying on the table, was carried by unseen hands beneath it, and instantly was played in clear and stately measures a remarkable and very prominent passage in the C Minor Symphony. It is necessary to remember that this passage is repeated in every movement of the Symphony, and it is rendered still more memorable from the fact that when Ferdinand Reis, Beethoven's pupil, commented upon its frequent recurrence to the composer. the latter seized a pen and wrote beneath the passage in question in the German language : 'So knocks fate at my door.' These words will be found in the original score in Beethoven's handwriting, and from this circumstance the name of "The *Geist Symphony*" has been commonly given to this magnificent work. All this I had commented upon in the analysis before referred to. The passage itself, played by no mortal hands, was at once recognized by several of the party present besides myself, and hence formed, as may be imagined, a second and striking test of the identity of the great master's spirit. A few weeks after the occurrence of this circumstance, I was in Boston, America, and a few days after I had landed a lady friend called on me and asked if I would accompany her to the spirit photographer's (Mr. Mumler). As we were both entirely unacquainted with Mr. Mumler, we deemed that our improvised visit might be the means of eliciting some good tests. After waiting a considerable time to take our turn we were admitted, and my friend, who was the first sitter, was overjoyed by procuring a striking spirit photograph of her deceased brother. I had no intention of sitting at the time when I entered the room ; indeed Mr. Mumler had remarked that it was so late that he would rather make a fresh appointment with us than give a sitting at that time. But this we were resolved not to do ; we would have our sitting then or never. After my friend's sitting was ended, Mr. Mumler, addressing me, said he very much wished I would let him take my picture. There seemed to be such a strong spirit influence present, he said, that he would rather take my picture without payment than suffer me to depart. Thus urged, I sat down before the camera entirely unprepared as I was. Whilst Mr. Mumler was developing the plate, which he did in our presence, we having accompanied him, by his own request, to the darkened room, I heard the voice of the spirit Beethoven saying, 'I have come to give you the third test.' When Mr. Mumler withdrew the negative from the bath, we all remarked a large head on the plate, and the appearance of a lyre composed of flowers, held before me. I observed that I thought the spirit must be a musician, and that the head resembled that of Handel, Immediately upon this Mr. Mumler caught up a pencil and wrote the name BEETHOVEN. I have only to add that my custom of writing musical articles, or being in any way interested in musical matters, was at that time unknown to my friends in America. This fact, together with the circumstances attending my unprepared visit to the photographer, and his entire ignorance of my name, should all be considered as links in the chain of evidence, tending to prove that the veritable spirit of Beethoven was the agent in producing the whole series of tests, the last of which so transcendently proves the genuine character of Mr. Mumler's mediumship. Permit me to add that I have had many tests through this same medium subsequently ; also, that I am cognisant of numerous parties who have received well-defined spirit portraits of their deceased friends through Mr. Mumler, but I do not remember any case that demonstrates more conclusively the agency of an individualised spirit than the incident I have narrated, taken in relation to all its attendant circumstances."

CHAPTER LVL.

SPIRITUALISM IN AMERICA (CONTINUED.)

THE next case in relation to Spiritualism before the bar of human judicature which we propose to notice, forms a marked example of the mode in which medical monopolists endeavour to stamp out of existence the beneficent gift of healing by the laying on of hands ; a power—which of all others—should be manifested by those who rejoice in the title of Christians, and claim to be followers of the Great Healer of Nazareth.

The subject of the trial we are about to describe was Dr. J. D. MacLennan, a gentleman who was first widely known as a healer, by the marvellous cure which he effected of Dr. Slade, when the latter was carried to his office paralyzed and helpless.

The celebrity which this case obtained was amply justified by Dr. MacLennan's subsequent successes, and the invariable kindness and liberality with which his great gift was exercised.

The nature of the charges brought against Dr. MacLennan will be best understood by perusing the following summary of the trial to which he was subjected, the report being taken from the San Francisco *Evening Post*, dated March 22nd, 1881. It is headed

"MAGNETIC HEALING.—TRIAL OF J. D. MACLENNAN FOR MISDEMEANOR IN PRACTICING IT.

"There was a very interesting case on trial in the Police Court yesterday afternoon before Judge Rix. In December last J. D. MacLennan, the magnetic healer, whose office is at 114, Geary Street, was arrested at the instance of A. A. Stoneburger, charged with violating section 11 of the law regulating the practice of medicine in this state. There were quite a large number of ladies present ; also the officers and many of the members of the First Spiritual Union, who seemed to take great interest in the case. It was claimed by the prosecution that Mr. MacLennan was a physician and practiced as such, and should procure a certificate to practice from one of the three examining boards appointed under the law. The defendant claimed, on the contrary, that he was no doctor, but was a healer, alleviating pain and disease by God-given, vital magnetic force. The complaining witness, Stoneburger, who is a medical student at the Medical College of the Pacific, when sworn, related how, on the 20th of December last, provided with money given him by Dr. Plummer, he had sought Mr. MacLennan's office, then on Stockton Street, and pretended to be seeking relief for an affection of the spine. Dr. Plummer had cautioned this stool-pigeon to be sure and address Mr. MacLennan as 'Doctor,' which he did ; and the healer, not noticing that he was so addressed, allowed Stoneburger to use that title. The witness related how the defendant had assured him that he was suffering from rheumatism (which proved to be the case), and then assured him that he could cure him in three weeks. Stoneburger agreed to the terms mentioned, and gave the healer three dollars of the money provided by Dr. Plummer. He was then subjected to a course of manipulation by hand-rubbing, which the witness was forced to acknowledge had a very salutary effect on him. When cross-examined by Daniel J. Murphy and Judge Collins for the defence, Stoneburger admitted that the money paid MacLennan came from the college where he was studying, and that he went to the healer's office simply to 'put up a job' on him. The witness did not see any medical appliances in the healer's room, his process of curing being simply by manipulation ; was not offered any medicine, nor did the healer use any ointment or oils. Witness felt a slight shock during the manipulation. He thought it was not electricity. Witness was positive that it could not have been electricity ; yet when asked if he knew the difference between electricity and animal magnetism said that there was none ! After thus leading off weakly, the prosecution called Dr. C. M. Bates, who defined ponderable and imponderable elements of medicine.

"The witness defined the difference between electricity and animal magnetism. The former could be generated—the latter was that force in a person which, when he has a positive individuality, he can produce and use to alleviate pain in others. After adroitly getting this acknowledgment from the witness, Mr. Murphy put this question to him.

"Q. This principle of relieving pain by rubbing has existed for all time, has it not ?—A. Yes.

"Q. Now, then, would you call every mother who uses these methods to relieve pain in her children a practitioner ?—A. No ; for sometimes they fail to relieve pain.

"Mr. Murphy : And do not your medicines sometimes fail ?

"This was a poser, and the witness was obliged to confess that they sometimes did. Witness admitted that rheumatism could often be cured by the application of hands, and he did not deny that some people were endowed with this mysterious gift.

"Mr. Murphy : What is medicine, doctor ?

"Dr. Bates : Medicine is anything that will cure disease or relieve pain. A practitioner can use any and all means to alleviate pain or cure disease.

"After this witness had claimed that a mother giving her child a mustard bath, or rubbing its body, or a barber brushing a customer's hair, to alleviate pain, was a practitioner and 'M.D.,' Dr. Ellinwood was called for the prosecution.

"Witness knew that there was such a force as animal magnetism, but could not define what it was. It was something no one could understand. He defined it as something like heat. He thought that the application of this magnetism was practicing medicine. Anything,' said the witness, ' used to alleviate pain or cure disease is a medicine.'

"Mr. Murphy : Then, doctor, everything and anything that has healing properties—such the air, light, heat, the sun's rays—all belong to the medical fraternity ?—A. Well, yes ; in the ordinary acceptation of the word.

"Mr. Murphy : Then anything that has curative properties is medicine ? Witness (promptly) : Yes, sir.

"Q. And any one who uses these to benefit others is a physician ? A. Yes, sir.

"Q. Well, then, if I should take a man out of a dungeon, where he was dying for want of air and sunlight, and bring him out into the light, I would be giving him medicine— I would be practicing medicine ?

"Witness (after a pause) : Well, I think that you would be. (Suppressed merriment.)

"Mr. Murphy : That's all, doctor. I do not know what the honorable fraternity would not claim after that !

"The prosecution, seeing how they had utterly failed to make out their case, had little argument to make. Judge Collins, for the defence, asked the court to instruct the jury to acquit the defendant, as the prosecution had failed utterly to show that Mr. MacLennan had practiced medicine. In support of the motion he defined the term physician, as meant by the law. It was that any person shall be regarded as practicing medicine, within the meaning of the act, who shall publicly profess to be a physician, or shall append ' M.D.' to his name. ' No proof,' said Judge Collins, ' has been adduced that our client has professed to be a physician or a doctor, nor has he prescribed medicine, as it is ordinarily understood, for any one. The section that covers the case of the defendant reads as follows: " Any itinerant vendor of drugs, nostrums, ointments, or appliances tending to cure disease, or any person who shall, by the use of any writing, printing, or by manipulation, profess to cure disease, shall pay a license of $100 per month." That is where the defendant comes in. He does not profess to be a physician, but he does profess to cure disease by this animal magnetism, by the laying on of hands. No medical board can order him to procure a doctor's certificate. How can he, when he has not studied medicine?'

" Mr. Murphy : 'This clause in the law, requiring a license and not a certificate, was made for that class of men who can throw the powers of the unseen world into others. When a man has this God-given gift would you bar him out from benefiting mankind? The men that would do this would have prosecuted Christ for healing the sick and for raising the dead.' After making a very able and logical argument, Mr. Murphy again asked the court to instruct the jury to acquit. At the conclusion of Mr. Murphy's remarks, Judge Rix, addressing the jury, said : 'The prosecution has failed to show that the defendant claims to be a physician. They only show that he professes to be a healer. He himself admits and claims that he is a healer by animal magnetism. I think that the prosecution have failed to substantiate this charge, and therefore will instruct you to acquit.' When the jury promptly returned a verdict of not guilty, the many friends of Mr. MacLennan crowded around him and congratulated him on so ably proving to all that while he did heal the sick by his great powers, those powers were in-born, God-given, and that no college of medicine could debar him from using them for the benefit of suffering humanity. Owing to the granting of the motion to dismiss, a large number of witnesses for Mr MacLennan, who had volunteered in his behalf, were not called upon to testify."

It need hardly be added that there were more persons than the parties named above who were personally rejoiced in the issue of this trial ; the principles of liberty and equity being even more deeply involved in its results than the simple fact that justice was due to the benevolent healer who was the enforced defendant in the case. It is worth while also to take note of the arguments used by the prosecution, and observe how grossly ignorant the present generation appear to be on the subject of Spiritual gifts, and powers in general.

We call attention to this case, not only because the verdict established the rights of the Spiritualists in the above-mentioned directions, but because it affords a noteworthy illustration of the wide difference in the administration of justice between the courts of judicature in England and America. In every instance in which Spiritualists have been cited to appear before the tribunals of justice (?) in England, the verdicts have been given against them, and yet none can ever peruse the trials of Sothern *versus* Coleman, and Lyons *versus* Home, without coming to the conclusion that the most flagrant injustice was exercised in each case by verdicts against the defendants.

It will be remembered also, that when the Australian Spiritualists petitioned through the "Victorian Association of Spiritualists," for leave to take a modest admission fee at the door where their religious exercises were held Sabbath by Sabbath; where hymns were sung, prayers said, and no perversion of bigotry could twist the exercises into an appearance of show, or attempt at gain, the Government unrelentingly forbade the continuance of the meetings, so long as the admission fee was taken, and that notwithstanding the fact, that the same Government tolerated a regular tariff of payment for seats in every Catholic place of worship, and allowed church pews, aye, and the sacred office of rectorship to be sold by auction to the highest bidders in the reverend (?) State Church of England.

It now becomes necessary to refer to a matter that has hitherto been left to oral representation or, more correctly speaking, no representation at all, save such as originated with the "lying tongue of rumour." This is, the amount of influence said to be exerted by Spirits upon the mind of the martyred President, Abraham Lincoln, in issuing the famous "emancipation proclamation," by which the chains of that slavery—so disgraceful to the nation in which it was practised—were struck from the necks of four millions of human beings.

The narrative in substance was given to the author, together with the several printed extracts quoted, by Colonel Kase, one of the principal actors in the scenes which follow. It should be stated, that Colonel Kase is a noble-hearted, philanthropic gentleman, whose warmest efforts have ever been given to the advancement of Spiritualism, and whose residence in Philadelphia is open to all comers who plead "Spiritualism" as their claim for hospitality. It cannot be expected but that this munificent spirit is often abused by the unworthy. Colonel Kase however, as well as his amiable wife, evidently deems that it is " better to be the wronged, than the wronger."

Meantime, to return to Colonel Kase's part in the famous deed which caused the whole world to ring with blessings on the name of Abraham Lincoln.

It was during the progress of the fatal civil war which raged in America from 1861 to four years later, that Colonel S. P. Kase, of Philadelphia, being deeply interested in railroad undertakings, was compelled to visit the Capitol in 1862, with a view of making interest in Congress in favour of some of his enterprises. Whilst Colonel Kase was one day strolling in the Capitol grounds, his eyes were attracted to a house where he had formerly boarded, and on which he now saw the sign of " J. B. Conklin, writing and test Medium." Colonel Kase had some slight knowledge of this Medium, then widely celebrated as one of the most reliable of instruments for Spirit communications. To continue the narrative in the Colonel's own language. He says :—

"Just as the name attracted my attention I *heard a voice* at my right side say : '*Go see him : he is in the same room you used to occupy.*' I looked to see who spoke, but there was no human being within a hundred yards of me. The question passed through my mind—'Who knows that I ever occupied a room in this house?' Twelve years had passed since that time. An indescribable feeling came over me ; I seemed rivetted to the spot. It was only the work of a moment. However, I concluded to enter the building, and upon ascending the stairway, passed into the room which had been occupied by me in 1850, and here Mr. Conkling sat, just having finished a letter to President Lincoln, and which he was enclosing as I entered. 'Here, Mr. Kase,' said Mr. Conkling, 'I want you to take this letter to the President ; you can see him, but I can't.' 'O, sir,' I replied ; 'I cannot take your letter ; send it by mail ; I have just arrived in this city and am not acquainted with the President ; besides, I am here on important business and must be formally introduced to him. I cannot take your letter.' Mr. Conkling said : 'You *must* take this letter ; you are here for this purpose ; if you do not take it he will never see it.' At this moment a voice again said to me : '*Go and see what will come of this.*' This voice seemed just behind me. I was startled, dumbfounded ; I stood fixed to the spot. Finally I said : 'Give me the letter.' 'Will you go along?' 'Yes ; but I can't see him.' 'You can,' was the medium's reply. 'Well, here's an omnibus just turning ; we'll get in that.' The sun was just then setting behind the distant hills. We arrived at the Presidential mansion in the dusk of the evening ; rang the bell ; a servant appears. 'Is the President in?' 'Yes,' was the reply, 'he is at tea.' 'Can I see him?' 'What is the name?' I gave him my name. He soon returned, saying, 'The President will see you after tea. Step up into the gentlemen's parlour.' Conkling and myself seated ourselves in the parlour to which the servant had directed us. Soon after the servant appeared at the door, beckoning me forward, and opening a door leading to the President's room. The President was approaching the door as I entered. He stopped, somewhat disappointed, and stepped back one or two steps as I approached, I saying to him, 'My name is S. P. Kase, of Danville, Pa.' 'The President expected to meet S. P. Chase, then Secretary of the Treasury,' his response was, 'you are from Pennsylvania,' showing me to a chair upon the opposite side of a long table. He took a seat directly opposite, and for some time drew me out respecting Pennsylvania. I told him that I lived in the town where the first anthracite pig-iron was manufactured, and where the first T rail was made in the United States. And for a full half-hour various questions pertaining to the war and the prosperity of Pennsylvania were discussed, when I handed him the Conkling letter. He broke it open, read it, and seemed a little surprised, saying ; 'What does this mean?' My reply was, 'I do not know what the letter contains, but I have no doubt that it means just what it says.' 'You do not know,' responded the President, 'what this letter is, and yet you think it means just what it says?' 'Yes, sir, I think so,' I replied. 'Well, then,' said the President, "I will read it for you.' Here is the letter :

"'I have been sent from the city of New York by Spiritual influence pertaining to the interest of the nation. I can't return until I see you. Appoint the time. Yours, etc.,
"'(Signed) J. B. CONKLING.'

"The President then said, 'What do you know about Spiritualism?' 'I know very little, but what I do know you are welcome to.' 'Let me hear.' I then rehearsed my first interview in New York, in the year 1858, as hereafter stated."

It would be unnecessary to follow Colonel Kase's narrative which, though sufficiently interesting to be worthy of recital, has been doubtless duplicated in every Spiritualistic reader's experience many times over.

It must be observed however, that although the President of the United States was not at that time, and is not now, easily accessible to strangers, there were special circumstances attending Colonel Kase's visit, which were peculiarly favourable to the interview in question.

In the first place, he was no doubt admitted because his name was mistaken for that of the Secretary of the Treasury.

When he met the President he was at once known as a gentleman of influential position, whose connection with railroads—then of the utmost importance to the Government in the transport of troops—secured attention for whatever he might have to say. It must be added, that no stranger, however high his position may be, who once looks into the kind face and clear honest eyes of Colonel Kase, can treat him with *hauteur*, or even indifference. There are some individuals whose very presence is a letter of recommendation. Such an one is Colonel Kase, and as such, the reader must remember, that the Spirits full well understood the characteristics of the messenger they had selected to do their work. At the conclusion of Colonel Kase's narrative of personal experiences, he adds :—

"President Lincoln seemed very much interested and said : 'Tell Mr. Conkling that I will see him on Sunday, between 9 and 10 a.m.' 'Oh, no,' was my reply ; 'write him a letter.' 'Very well, I will write him a letter,' was the reply of the President. I then said I thought my mission was ended—shook hands, and left ; called for Conkling in the gentlemen's parlour, and we returned to our respective lodgings."

In a condensed account of what followed this interview, the editor of the *Spiritual Scientist* says :—"For four succeeding Sundays Mr. Conkling was a guest at the Presidential mansion." Mr. Conkling has himself alleged to the author, that the Spirits not only urged the subject of the emancipation proclamation, but that they, in the name of the Independence Fathers, spelled out, *letter by letter*, the preliminary draft of that famous document. The result of these interviews was the President's proposition to his Cabinet to issue such a proclamation, and the final success of the stupendous work, as recorded in the national archives of the country. The influence exerted by the celebrated test Medium Conkling, was not the only one brought to bear upon the good President, as the following incident will show. Again we give it in the simple words of Colonel Kase, as narrated to the editor of the *Spiritual Scientist*, and confirmed through his own lips, in recent interviews with the author. He says :—

"Four weeks after I first carried the Conkling letter to President Lincoln, I was standing in the gallery of the House, when I saw an old lady leave her seat and come walking across the gallery toward me ; and as she got opposite me she turned and handed me her card, saying, 'Call when it suits you,' and immediately turned and went back to her seat. l stood, thinking it very strange that a lady l had never seen, should give me her card and tell me to call. In looking around I saw Judge Wattles, and immediately inquired of him who that lady was. He replied, 'That is Mrs. Laurie.' 'And who is Mrs. Laurie?' was my quick response. 'She gave me her card and said I should call.' The judge replied, 'She is a medium. I have been twice to her house ; she lives in Georgetown, and has a daughter who plays the piano with her eyes closed, and the piano raises up and beats time on the floor as perfectly as the time is kept upon the instrument, and they call it Spiritualism.' I replied I would like to witness that very much. 'Well, you have a card of invitation, if you wish I will go with you this evening.'

"The arrangement being perfected we went, and arrived there about eight o'clock in the evening. Who should we meet there but President Lincoln and his lady. After passing the courtesies of the day, perhaps ten minutes intervening, I saw a young girl approaching the President, with a measured step, with her eyes closed, and walking up to the President, accosted him as follows : 'You, sir, as President of the Republic, are called to the position you occupy for a very important purpose. The world is not only groaning under the weight of mental and spiritual bondage, but four millions, made in God's image, are enduring physical slavery. Their yokes must be broken, the fetters must be severed, and the physically enslaved must be set free, before your nation can be restored to its proper station. Freedom was germinally planted in the forest lands of the West in Washington's time, and is now about to bud and bear precious fruitage. This Republic has heretofore led the van of nations in its line of free-thought, but the dark plague-spot of slavery stains its banner. This national evil must be removed. There is a spiritual congress supervising the affairs of this nation. This civil war will never cease ; the shout of victory will never ring through the North, will never reverberate along the valleys of the South ; the olive-branch of peace will never wave over your fields, and lakes, and mountains, till you issue a proclamation of freedom—a proclamation that shall set for ever free the enslaved millions of your distracted country.'

These were only the opening words of an address which Colonel Kase comments on in the following terms :—

"This being her text, she lectured the President for a full hour and a half upon the importance of emancipating the slave, saying that the war could not end until slavery was abolished ; that God destined all men to be free, that they may rise to their proper status. Her language was truly sublime and full of arguments, grand in the extreme ; that from the time his proclamation of freedom was issued there would be no reverses to our army. As soon as this young girl (who I thought could not be out of her teens, but who I afterwards understood was the celebrated trance medium, Nettie Maynard, of New York State) came out of the trance, she ran off, frightened to think that she had been talking to the President."

Colonel Kase's description of what followed this remarkable speech is too *naïve* to be omitted. He says :—

"Immediately Mrs. Miller commenced playing the piano, and the front side of it commenced to beat the time, by raising off the floor and coming down with a heavy thud. I got up and requested the privilege of sitting on it that I might verify to the world that it moved. Yes, the medium says : 'You and as many more as see proper may get on it.' Judge Wattels, the two soldiers who accompanied the President, and myself, got on the instrument ; the medium commenced to play, the instrument commenced to go with all our weight on it, raising four inches at least ; it was too rough riding, so we got off it, whilst the instrument beat the time until the tune was played out. This brought 11 o'clock and we all returned to our respective homes. Two evenings after, I went back to Mrs. Laurie's and again I met the President and his lady there. Again the medium was entranced and lectured the President upon the same subject, for a full hour and a half, when Mrs. Miller played the piano, and the time beat as before described in the presence of the President and his lady and a number of persons who were in attendance. Thus it was that President Lincoln was convinced as to the course he should pursue ; the command coming from that all-seeing angel world, was not to be overlooked ; so like a faithful servant, when convinced of his duty, he feared not to do it, and to proclaim freedom by the Emancipation Proclamation to four millions of slaves. That proclamation was issued on September 22, 1862, to take effect the First day of January, 1863. In the intermediate time the Union army had in divers places twenty-six battles, every one of them was a success upon the Union side. Thus the prediction of the medium was verified."

It now becomes necessary to take a general review of the phenomenal facts that have occurred in America since the publication of the work so often referred to as the history of the first twenty years of the movement. In so doing, we shall step aside to a certain extent from the plan of confining our notices to the last fifteen years, the author having collected a large mass of material for the compilation of a second volume of the American Spiritual History, some of which is too remarkable to be consigned to oblivion, even though it may be out of the chronological order adopted in this section of the work. The first narrative seems strangely enough to form a well-defined corner stone for uprearing the structure of " Nineteenth Century Spiritualism," as it dates back to the year 1800, and in this respect, no less than in its marvellous character, forms the basis of a distinct epoch in the history of what has been called " Supernaturalism."

We shall give the narrative with some excisions, as it was printed by the author in the pages of the *Western Star* magazine. The article is headed

WONDERFUL SPIRITUAL MANIFESTATIONS IN MAINE IN THE YEARS 1800-1806.

One of the most extraordinary manifestations of Spirit communion that is to be found on authentic record occurring in America prior to the date of the Rochester knockings, took place in the year 1800, in the State of Maine, and a general account is given of it in a pamphlet written by the Rev. Abraham Cummings, an eye-witness of the phenomena he describes. The title of the pamphlet is "Immortality proved by the Testimony of Sense," etc. The publisher adds on a fly leaf: "Immortality proved by phenomena that were witnessed by hundreds in the town of Sullivan, Maine, in the year 1800. Published by an eye-witness, the Rev. Abraham Cummings, a man eminent in learning and piety; a graduate of Harvard University."

The pamphlet, which is a series of letters, arguments, allusions to portions of the history supposed to be already known to the reader, and affidavits of various witnesses—contains circumstantial details of the apparition of a Mrs. Butler, who manifested her presence to hundreds of people by rappings, preternatural lights, singing, speaking with an audible voice, and frequent appearances in her own as well as other forms.

Besides Mr. Cumming's pamphlet, the author has gathered up a mass of information on this subject from various publications of the time, as well as the oral testimony of several persons whose nearest relatives were residents in Sullivan, and themselves eye-witnesses of the extraordinary scenes here related. From all these sources, it appears that a certain Captain Butler, residing near Sullivan, Maine, married Miss Nelly Hooper, who, ten months after her marriage, gave birth to one child, and passed with her infant into the spirit world. Shortly after this lady's decease, Captain Butler became the accepted lover of a Miss Blaisdell, whose father, like his own, was violently opposed to the match.

In this state of things, and whilst the lovers were vainly attempting to soften the obduracy of their parents, the spirit of Mrs. Nelly Butler became an active participator in the scene. She manifested herself in the various modes before described, in the houses of Mr. Blaisdell, Mr. Butler, and her own father, Mr. Hooper. She appeared to, and audibly conversed with her mother and sisters; urged her father to visit Mr. Butler, with a view of persuading him that the manifestations that now began to astound the whole country, were not, as he wilfully persisted in asserting, the artful contrivance of Miss Blaisdell, but were in reality produced by herself, the spirit of his daughter. Her father, mother, and sisters, became so entirely convinced of the spirit's identity that they published circumstantial details of her visitation, attested by their solemn affidavits. One of the purposes alleged by the spirit to have influenced her appearance, was to procure the consent of the parents to the marriage of her late husband with Miss Blaisdell. To the latter she seemed to manifest an extraordinary attachment, and constantly declared that the union was destined by Heaven, and should take place.

It appears that after the decease of Mrs. Nelly Butler, strong suspicions were entertained of foul play, and a trial, attended with circumstances of much suspicion and many curious allegations, took place, to ascertain the manner of her death. The "spectre" herself, as the phrase went, made several communications to different parties on the subject, and the general impression which prevailed in the community was, that the frequent apparition of this unresting spirit was attributable to the fact that her life was cut short by violence.

As the immediate descendants of the three families involved in this dark scandal are still living, and reside at the scene of the hauntings, we do not feel justified in entering into any further details. The Rev. Abraham Cummings alludes but slightly to the trial, the decision of the grand jury, and the persecutions which attended the various members of the families connected with the entire transactions.

One thing is certain : the lapse of over seventy years since the period of these strange occurrences, has not been sufficient to erase the impression that Mrs. Nelly Butler was murdered, and that to this cause was attributable her pertinacious visitations to the scene of her earthly wrongs.

Mrs. Butler's spirit often walked by the side of Miss Blaisdell in the light of day, and the full sight of astonished witnesses. She was frequently seen in the fields, lanes, and woods, besides the houses which she frequented, where she would pass from room to room, and when the inmates, terrified by her apparition, fled from the apartment, she would kindly assure them she would not intrude upon their presence, but meet with them whenever they wished to see or converse with her in the cellars of their dwellings. In the cellar of Mr. Blaisdell's house she conversed for several hours on different occasions with the crowds who flocked thither to witness the manifestations. Sometimes she appeared to a number of persons at a time, occasionally in the likeness of her former self, but still oftener in a fleecy mass of white shadowy light. When the parents of the lovers, awed by the preternatural interference of this wonderful apparition, finally gave their consent to the union, the spirit presented herself at the wedding festivities, and there foretold the death of the bride within ten months, together with the birth and death of one child. These dark predictions, like many other of her prophecies, proved correct, but the decease of the second Mrs. Butler seems to have had no effect in laying the spirit of her predecessor. From the pertinacity with which she urged on the marriage, and her frequent appearance in the house and about the person of Miss Blaisdell, suspicion had attached to the latter as having simulated the phenomena for the purpose of effecting a union with Captain Butler; but when it was found that her appearances after the marriage were more frequent than before, whilst her visitations continued with equal force and intensity after the second Mrs. Butler's death, this hypothesis became untenable; neither would the facts of the case conform with the assumption that Miss Blaisdell's mediumship was essential to the production of the phenomena, which continued, as we have stated, long after her decease.

Mention is made in Mr. Cumming's pamphlet of a singular act, enjoined in the most solemn manner by the "spectre," namely, the digging up and re-interment of her child's body, which she desired to be buried in a different place. At the re-interment, which caused great scandal in the neighbourhood, the spirit attended in person, singing and chanting in a voice which was audible to over eighty people who were present at the ceremony. She appears to have been very piously disposed, singing hymns, quoting Scripture, praying, exhorting, and representing herself as "in heaven, with Jesus and the angels." Hundreds of witnesses saw and heard this spirit, many of them people of the first standing, whose veracity and candor was unquestioned; notwithstanding this, the three families chiefly concerned became the subject of the most cruel calumnies, bitter persecutions, and finally of the trial above alluded to, during the course of which upwards of forty affidavits were given by some of the most respectable persons in the community, confirmatory of the statements above alleged, and descriptive of the various modes in which the "spectre" had manifested herself. As the Rev. Abraham Cummings has given several very interesting and minute details of the modes in which the ghostly visitant's presence was regarded, besides having published in full the affidavits of the whole forty witnesses examined on the trial, we shall refer our readers to the following quotations from this pamphlet, for the better understanding of the marvellous circumstances narrated:—

"The times, places, and modes of her appearing were various. Sometimes she appeared to one alone, sometimes to two or three, then to five, six, ten, or twelve, again to twenty, and once to more than forty witnesses. She appeared in several apartments of Mr. Blaisdell's house, and several times in the cellar. She also appeared at other houses, and in the open fields. There, white as the light, she moved like a cloud above the ground in personal form and magnitude, and in the presence of more than forty people. She tarried with them till after daylight, and vanished; not because she was afraid of the sun, for she had then several times appeared when the sun was shining. Once in particular, when she appeared in the room where the family were, about eleven o'clock in the day, they all left the house; but convinced of the impropriety of their conduct, they returned.

"At another time, when several neighbours were at the house, and were conversing on these remarkable events, a young lady in the company declared that, though she had heard the discourse of the spectre, she would never believe that there had been a spectre among us, unless she could see her.

"In a few minutes after, the spectre appeared to several persons, and said she must come into the room where the company was. One of those who saw her, pleaded that she would not. The spectre then asked, 'Is there a person here who desires to see me?' The young lady was then called, who, with several others, saw the spectre. 'Here I am,' said she, 'satisfy yourselves.' The lady owned that she was satisfied. It was now about two o'clock in the day. In short, the ghost appeared or conversed almost as frequently in the day as in the night.

"In all the appearances of the spectre she was as white as the light, and this whiteness was as clear and visible in a dark cellar and dark night, as when she appeared in the open field and in the open day. At a certain time, August 9th, she informed a number of people that she meant to appear before them (for she frequently conversed without appearing at all), that they must stand in order, and behave in a solemn manner: 'For the Lord,' said she, 'is a God of order.' Accordingly she appeared and vanished before them several times. At first they saw a small body of light, which continually increased till it formed the shape and magnitude of a person.

"This personal shape approached so near to Captain Butler, that he put his hand upon it, and it passed down through the apparition as through a body of light, in the view of thirteen persons, who all saw the apparition, which rose into personal form, face and features, in a moment ; returned to a shapeless mass, resumed her personality, and vanished again directly. They saw that which was not *afraid* to be handled by them, for she passed slowly by them, near enough for that purpose.

"As to the witnesses, not one of them has ever been accused or even suspected of being concerned in an artifice. Some of them are aged, others young. They had, and still have, professions, employments, and interests widely different, and belong to different families. . . . .

"She mentioned several incidents of her past life, known only to her husband, as he declared, and asked him if he remembered them. He said yes. She asked him if he had told them. He answered no ; and of such a nature were those incidents as to render it utterly improbable that he ever should have mentioned them before. This was at the time when he attempted to handle the apparition.

"Once, when she conversed with about fourteen persons, Mr. Blaisdell, having heard that his father was sick, asked the spectre whether she knew anything, or not, concerning him. 'Your father,' she replied, 'is in heaven, praising God with the angels.' He afterwards found that his father, two hundred miles distant, died three days before this answer of the ghost, and his friends at York, where his father lived, utterly deny that they sent the news in the course of these days. . . . .

"At the time when fifty people heard her discourse, while more than forty saw her, to some of them—who no more believed these extraordinary events than mankind now do in general—she mentioned several occurrences of her past life, known to them and her, in order to satisfy them that she was the very person she professed to be. Almost all this company had been acquainted with her in her life-time, and a considerable number of them very intimately. She desired that any of them would ask what questions they pleased, for the removal of any doubts respecting her. Accordingly certain persons did propose several questions respecting a number of events in her past life. To all these inquiries, she gave completely satisfactory answers.

"She foretold what the opinion and conduct of mankind would be with regard to her, and the ill-treatment which Mr. Blaisdell's family would receive on her account. She not only declared the necessity, but foretold the certainty of the marriage at an hour when both the parties and both the families opposed it.

"Within thirty hours after Mrs. Butler's marriage, the spectre predicted that she would become the parent of but one child, and then die. Ten months after this her child was born, and she died the next day. The safe return of one bound to the West Indies was also foretold and accomplished.

"These predictions are all fulfilled, and were previously and sufficiently known in this vicinity for evidence that they were such. She uttered several other predictions now accomplished. . . . .

"Some time in July, 1806, in the evening, I was informed by two persons that they had just seen the spectre in the field.

"About ten minutes after, I went out, not to see a miracle, for I believed that they had been mistaken. Looking towards an eminence twelve rods distant from the house, I saw there, as I supposed, one of the white rocks. This confirmed my opinion of their spectre, and I paid no more attention to it. Three minutes after, I accidentally looked in the same direction, and the white rock was in the air ; its form a complete globe, white, with a tincture of red, like the damask rose, and its diameter about two feet.

"Fully satisfied that this was nothing ordinary, I went toward it for more accurate examination.

"While my eye was constantly upon it, I went on four or five steps, when it came to me from the distance of eleven rods, as quick as lightning, and instantly assumed a personal form with a female dress, but did not appear taller than a girl seven years old. While I looked upon her, I said in my mind, 'You are not tall enough for the woman who has so frequently appeared among us.' Immediately she grew up as large and as tall as I considered that woman to be. Now she appeared glorious. On her head was the representation of the sun diffusing the luminous rectilinear rays everywhere to the ground. Through the rays I saw the personal form, and the woman's dress. Then I recollected the objection of the Encyclopædia, that 'ghosts always appear to one alone.' Now, said my mind, I see you as plainly as ever I saw a person on earth ; but were I to converse with you an hour, what proof could I produce that I ever conversed with you at all ? This, with my fear, was the reason why I did not speak to her. But my fear was connected with ineffable pleasure.

"Life, simplicity, purity, glory, all harmonizing in this celestial form, had the most delightful effect on my mind. And there appeared such a dullness afterwards upon all corporeal objects as I never perceived before. I went into the house and gave the information, not doubting that she had come to spend some time with us, as she had before. We went out to see her again; but to my great disappointment, she had vanished. Then I saw one of the great errors of my life. That I had not spoken to her, has been the matter of my regret from that hour to this."

. . . .

"Some time in March, 1806, she talked a few minutes without appearing, at eight o'clock in the morning, and promised to come again that day; at two o'clock she performed her promise, and talked with four people two hours. It was then she uttered these words: 'Though my body is consumed, and all turned to dust, my soul is as much alive as before I left the body.' This conversation was indeed in the cellar, but the place was enlightened with her radiance.

"May 21st.—At ten o'clock, she appeared to two persons, and sent a message to another.

"May 25th.—Ten o'clock. Appeared and conversed with two witnesses, while a third person heard the conversation; and revealed that by which the same was proved to others.

"May 26th.—She appeared at eight o'clock in the morning, and talked with four persons an hour and a half. In half an hour after, she appeared and talked with the same four persons, while two others heard a voice, without knowing what was said.

"May 27th.—Talked with two persons, and promised to be present at a meeting of about twenty people, which was to be held the next day in the evening. Accordingly she appeared at this meeting to persons who were ignorant of the promise. The assembly was immediately interrupted by the declaration that 'the spirit is come.' The next evening after, she conversed with a couple of persons, and told them by her inimitable voice to whom she had appeared. . . .

"Her conversation was always with grace, seasoned with salt, very affecting and delightful.

"August 13th.—At ten o'clock, she talked with three persons invisibly. At two o'clock the same day, she appeared and talked to three people in the hearing of five other persons."

———

"Of forty depositions and affidavits given by as many different persons in reference to this remarkable affair, we insert the following as specimens. The first is from one who appears to have been constitutionally sceptical, and whose very circumstantial testimony is on that account all the more valuable.

"TESTIMONY OF MISS HANNAH BATCOMB.

"August 9th, 10th.—I was at the house of Mr. Blaisdell by the persuasion of others; for as to myself, I made very light of the matter, supposing that the whole was the contrivance of certain persons.

"We heard rappings, and these sounds were spoken to, but no answer obtained. After much altercation (which is needless to rehearse), we all came out of the cellar, and all went off, except a few persons, of whom I was one. Some of Mr. Blaisdell's family uttered severe expressions against those who went off and did not believe. 'What do you want they should believe,' said I; 'for my part, I see nothing to believe.' Immediately Mrs. Butler came in from the entry, very much affrighted. 'If any one desires to be convinced,' said she, 'let him look there in the entry.' I looked there and saw nothing. Soon after this, while Mrs. Butler was sitting on the foot of a bed, we heard a sound right against her on the outside of the house. Mr. Butler told her to speak to it. At first she refused. They told her she must. Then she said to it, 'If I am guilty, stay away; if I am clear, in the name of the Lord, clear me.' The spirit then rapped very hard, so as to shake the house. Some of the company said she must go into the cellar. 'So I must,' said she; 'if I do not, she will come into the room; and if she does, I shall die. Who will go with me?' D—— A—— said she would go. They went, and soon after we all went down. Then I plainly heard the voice say to Mrs. Butler, 'Go up, that the people may not think it is you who speak.' I saw her go up into the room, and heard at the same time the voice in the cellar. Mr. Blaisdell asked the spirit whence she came. She answered, 'I am from heaven. I am with God and Christ, angels and seraphim, praising God. Glory, glory, glory!'

"Mr. Blaisdell asked why she did not manifest herself in the forepart of that night to all the people. She answered, "I was not permitted to come where there was so much sin.'

"The spirit then said to Mr. Blaisdell, 'Ask the people if they are convinced.'

"He did so; and I among the rest answered that I was.

"Then the spirit said, 'I must appear; and by her direction we placed ourselves in order. Then I saw a white appearance, at first not more than a foot in height, but it appeared larger and larger, and more plainly; and when it came nearer to me, I was struck with fear, and left the cellar; but others told me that afterwards they saw the spirit plainly.

"August 13th, 14th.—I again went to Mr. Blaisdell's with forty-seven persons.

"The spirit now told us again that she was from heaven, and that she was once Nelly Hooper. After much conversation, the spirit said that some of the people were faint, and could not hear all that was to be said, and that we must go up and refresh ourselves.

"'You must go with me to two places this night,' said she, 'and you must be ready at one o'clock.'

"'What o'clock is it now?' said Mr. Blaisdell.

"She said, 'Twelve, twelve, twelve!'

"We went up immediately and looked on the watch, and it was exactly twelve.

"In a short time, hearing the usual sign, we returned. Among many other words which I do not remember, Mr. Downing asked the spirit if she knew him; she answered, 'Yes,' and called him by name. He asked her if she was ever at his house. She answered that she had been once there with her mother. At length she told us that we must go up, and she would walk with us behind, with Mrs. Butler. 'But you must walk in order, two and two,' said she, 'singing a psalm; for God is a God of order.' Some person asked when she would be ready. She said, 'I will let you know.'

"Some person again asked what o'clock it was. She answered *one*. We went up and again looked on the watch, and it was one. We attended prayer, and immediately after she knocked. A psalm was chosen, which the greatest number of us could best remember, and it was sung as we walked. I was now far forward, and did not see the spirit. When we came to Captain Millar's the spirit rapped there, and Captain Millar, with Captain Paul Blaisdell, and some others, went into the cellar, and I heard them talk, but could not understand what was said to them. Then word came to us that we must stand out in the field before the house—that she would appear before us, and walk with Mrs. Butler, that the people might be convinced that Mrs. Butler had told the truth in relating that she had walked with her before. Then we all stood before the house. Mrs. Butler put on a black cloak, and when she had walked a little distance from us, as before directed by the spirit, I heard her groan bitterly, and soon after I saw the appearance of a woman in white walking with her. Suddenly Mrs. Butler sung a part of that hymn called 'New Jerusalem.' Then she came to us, and we all went back in order to Mr. Blaisdell's. I then looked back and saw a person in white, walking with Mrs. Butler. After we returned to the house, Mrs. Butler appeared very weary and exhausted.

"I asked her at what time the spirit came to her. She told me it was after she had walked a little distance from the people. 'When you heard me groan,' said she, 'then I saw it coming towards me; I am always more afraid when I only see it than I am after it has spoken to me; and she then told me not to be scared, that she was not come to hurt me, and that if I would sing a hymn it would expel my fears.'

———

"The following is the testimony of Captain Millar, whose house was the scene of the remarkable visitation above mentioned:—

"TESTIMONY OF CAPTAIN JAMES MILLAR.

"August 7th.—Mr. Blaisdell came to my house, and desired me to go to his own, where I might hear and see for myself. He also went to Capt. Samuel Simson's with the same request. Capt. Simson and his wife, S—— B——, and N—— G——, who were there, came with him to my house, and we all went to Mr. Blaisdell's. When we had been there some minutes, Capt. Simson, by desire, prayed. His prayer was immediately followed by a knocking, and we all went into the cellar. Mr. Blaisdell asked what was wanted, and who it was. It answered, 'I was once Nelly Hooper.' I asked, 'How was man made?' 'Out of the dust,' said the voice; 'dust thou art, and unto dust shalt thou return. You have the Bible, and that is God's truth, and do you abide by it. Love God, and keep His commandments.' After some conversation with Mrs. Simson and others, she said, 'I must go,' and we heard no more. It was now broad daylight, the outer cellar door being open, and utterly impossible that any living person should be there but those whom we could see and know. The voice was about six feet from me.

"August 9th.—I went to that house with many people, among whom I observed much disorderly behaviour. The spirit spoke but little, and I returned with a resolution to go no more to that house on such an errand.

"August 14th.—Just before daylight, I heard singing as I lay in bed, approaching to my house. Presently, by my leave, my house was filled with people, and I heard knockings on the floor. By the desire of certain persons, I went into the cellar with Capt.

Paul Blaisdell. After some discourse of the voice with him, which I understood not, I heard sounds of knocking near me. I asked, 'What do you want of me?' It answered, 'I have come to let you know that I can speak in this cellar as well as in the other. Are you convinced?' I answered, 'I am.' 'Now,' said the voice, 'the company must be solemn, and stand in order before your door; I am going to appear. Now, do you remember that I was once Nelly Hooper?' We went up, and complied with her direction, and I saw a personal shape coming towards us, white as the light. By the spectre's order, as I was informed, Mrs. Butler went towards her, 'Lydia,' said the spectre, 'you are scared, you must sing.' Then she sung a hymn. The spirit came almost to us, then turned, and Mrs. Butler with her, and went several rods towards Capt. Simson's, and appeared to take her by the hand, to urge her on further, and disappeared in our sight. Mrs. Butler returned, and informed the company, as I was told, that if they would walk to Mr. Blaisdell's solemnly, as to a funeral, the spirit would walk with Mrs. Butler, behind them. The company did so. But I, being far forward, saw nothing.

"JAMES MILLAR."

TESTIMONY OF MRS. MARY JORDAN.

"On the 4th of August, 1800, about two hours before daylight, while I slept at Mr. Blaisdell's house, I was awaked by the sound of knocking. I got up, and with about twenty others went into the cellar. There I heard a voice speaking to us, as I never heard before nor since. It was shrill, but very mild and pleasant.

"Mr. Blaisdell, addressing the voice, said that several persons (of whom I was one) had come from a distance to obtain satisfaction, and desired that she would tell us who she was, and the design of her coming.

"She answered that she was once Nelly Hooper, and after she was married became Nelly Butler.

"After much conversation of a religious nature, she appeared to us. At first the apparition was a mere mass of light; then it grew into a personal form, about as tall as myself. We stood in two ranks, about four feet apart. Between these ranks she slowly passed and repassed, so that any of us could have handled her. When she passed by me, she was so near that if she had been a substance I should certainly have felt it. The apparition had a constant tremulous motion. At last the personal form became shapeless, expanded every way, and vanished in a moment.

"Nothing more being now seen or heard, we were moving to go up, when the voice desired us to tarry longer.

"We did so, and the spirit talked with us another hour, even till broad daylight. She mentioned to us the ill-treatment which Mr. Blaisdell's family had suffered by reproach and false accusation, and told us they would on her account be yet more despised and ridiculed.

"Her discourse concluded by a solemn exhortation. After speaking much more that I cannot remember, she sang praises, and left us. Her notes were very pleasant. Her words were no higher than common, yet they were exceedingly impressive.

"MARY JORDAN."

"TESTIMONY OF MRS. WENTWORTH (SISTER OF THE APPARITION).

"On the 2nd of January, 1800, Hannah Blaisdell came to Mr. Butler's house, and informed me that the extraordinary voice which they had heard, had declared itself to be that of my sister, and that I must go to her father's house.

"I replied to her face that I did not believe it. The next day I received the same message from three other persons of other families, to whom I returned the same answer.

"Nevertheless, I was at last persuaded, and accompanied Capt. Butler and my husband to Mr. Blaisdell's house. Capt. Butler and I examined the cellar with a candle. Capt. Simson and some others went with us.

"I held Lydia (Mrs. Butler) by the arm, when we heard a loud knocking, and the sound of a voice which brought fresh to my mind my sister's voice.

"This voice spoke several sentences, which were such as my sister used to utter, and from this time I cleared Lydia of the voice, and accused the devil.

"August 8th.—Was there again with about thirty others, and heard much conversation. The voice was still hoarse and thick, like that of my sister on her deathbed, but more hollow. Sometimes it was clear and pleasant.

"August 14th.—I heard the same voice in the same place, and did then believe it was my sister. She talked much with Capt. Simson, and exhorted the people. I heard a private conversation which I had with my sister in her life-time, and which I had never repeated to any one. We were alone together; but may it not have been overheard by some evil spirit who now personates my sister? I know of no reason for her coming.

"SALLY WENTWORTH."

"TESTIMONY OF MR. JAMES SPRINGER.

"August 13th, 1800.—After much conversation with the spectre, she told us that she must talk and appear at the house of Capt. Millar, because he had reported that she could not be anywhere but at Mr. Blaisdell's house. 'And Lydia must walk with me,' she said, 'that you may all see that she is one person, and I another.'

"We walked in order, two and two, to the house, and I saw the spirit appear and disappear several times.

"Whilst we were at Capt. Millar's house, we stood in the field, whilst Mrs. Butler, in great fear, walked with the spirit, before our eyes, a few rods towards Mr. Simson's.

"Then Mrs. Butler came to us and said we must return to her father's house, two and two, singing a hymn, and she and the spectre would walk with us. We did so. Mr. Paul Simson and I walked behind, if possible to see the apparition. When we had walked about fifteen rods, I saw a white appearance to the left hand. As we passed it, it fell into rank, and walked with Mrs. Butler. Mr. Downing and I turned and looked upon them, and heard them talk. We kept walking on, then stopping to look at them, all the way. We heard them speaking all the time, but in a low voice. The spirit appeared in a personal form, with arms locked, as white as snow, and about as tall as Mrs. Butler.

"Soon after daybreak I saw it plainly vanish.   "JAMES SPRINGER."

Most of the affidavits are to the same effect as the above. Many of them state that the spirit often appeared, bearing a very small child in her arms. That the particles of luminous matter that seemed to compose her were tremulous, in constant motion, presented no resistance to the touch, and were always white and shining.

All the witnesses saw her with more or less distinctness, and all heard her voice, and bore testimony to its remarkable shrillness, and "inimitable" peculiarity.

Mr. Cummings' pamphlet concludes with the following summary of the manifestations.

"At first, the terror of the persons who beheld her was excited by the idea of beholding a 'ghost,' yet after a little discourse with her, their fears were entirely dissipated, and succeeded by a singular pleasure, so delightful was the mode of her address and conversation.   .   .   .   .

"The spirit was always extremely disposed to piety; sang hymns, uttered prayers, exhorted, quoted Scripture, and joined with her wonderfully sweet but indescribable voice in the singing of hymns with others.

"This same voice, though inimitable, most nearly resembled her own as she was remembered when she lay dying.

"This apparition impressed all witnesses with feelings of pleasure and reverence, except in rare instances, one of which occurred at that assembly held in the cellar on the night of August 9th, when, as I have said, there were gathered some of the best of people, who conducted themselves with order and reverence; but others there were, who uttered such profanity and derision as rendered them unworthy to obtain conviction; and thereby, as the spirit afterwards declared, she could not manifest herself amongst them, so that save some knockings and a few sentences spoken, no tokens of her presence could be given.

"The spectre gave a number of extraordinary messages, of which the marriage was but one, and that a subordinate one to other ends of far superior magnitude and importance.

"These superior ends you will know hereafter, but they cannot, they must not be written.   .   .   .   .   "

No doubt can exist that if the parties interested in these strange phenomena could have considered and investigated them with the same practised coolness that characterizes the visitors of our modern spirit circles, most valuable and important views of spirit life, its laws and conditions, might have been gathered from such unusual opportunities for the enquiry; but amidst the fear, ignorance, and superstition which have for centuries obscured man's views of spiritual existence, it was next to impossible that even one risen from the dead should be able to bring conclusive evidence of her presence, or inform the prejudiced and bigoted concerning the true conditions of spirit life.

Still, the details of this remarkable case are too circumstantial and well attested to leave room for doubt concerning its main facts, and they unquestionably form one of the most singular and authentic evidences of direct spirit communion that the annals of history can furnish in America, prior to the great outpouring from which the modern movement of Spiritualism dates in 1848.

CHAPTER LVII.

SPIRITUALISM IN AMERICA (CONTINUED).

FURTHER ACCOUNTS OF EARLY MANIFESTATIONS IN THE NINETEENTH CENTURY,

THE following case though well known, and frequently cited in the literature of Supernaturalism, may not be deemed—in a condensed form—out of place in this record :—

"A TRANCE SPEAKER.

"In 1811, 'Miss Rachel Baker, the Sleeping Preacher,' recorded at the time as 'a remarkable case of *Devotional Somnism*,' attracted much attention. While sitting in a chair, apparently asleep, she began to sigh and groan, as if in excessive pain. She talked incoherently. These conditions came at brief intervals for two months. The talking then became understandable. The account says : 'Her body is as motionless as a statue. The only motion the spectator perceives is that of her organs of speech. She commences and ends with an address to the throne of grace, consisting of proper topics of acknowledgment, submission, and reverence; of praise and thanksgiving, and of prayer for herself, her friends, the church, the nation, for enemies, and the human race in general. Between these is her sermon or exhortation. She begins without a text, and proceeds with an even course to the end; embellishing it sometimes with fine metaphors, vivid descriptions, and poetical quotations.' These 'fits,' as the entrancements were then termed, occurred always at night. They each continued from thirty-five to ninety-eight minutes. At the close of the address follows 'a state of body,' continues the account, 'like groaning, sobbing, or moaning ; and the distressful sound continues from two minutes to a quarter of an hour. This agitation, however, does not wake her ; it gradually subsides, and she passes into a sound and natural sleep, which continues during the remainder of the night. In the morning she wakes as if nothing had happened, and entirely ignorant of the scenes in which she has acted. She declares she knows nothing of the nightly exercises, except from the information of others.' But they did not look upon these things in those days as they do in our own more enlightened time. Every conceivable form of medical treatment failed to 'cure' her, until, in 1816, Dr. Sears of New York drugged her so completely with opium that he put a stop to her power to pray, preach, and exhort."

The voucher for the next narrative being "the Rev. Giles B. Stebbins," a name recognized by American Spiritualists as a synonym for judgment and acumen, as well as the strictest integrity, needs no other introduction than Mr. Stebbins's own words. Writing to the Detroit *Post* he says :—

"The following narrative of a wonderful experience I noted down carefully when it was related to me by Henry Willis, of Battle Creek, whom I have known for years as a man of integrity, uncommon energy in business, clear intellect, strong nerve, and fine physical health. He came from Pennsylvania to oversee the building of the Michigan Central Railroad, has been well known in this region since, enjoys good health at seventy years of age, as a result of his Quaker temperance, and has a fair competence, which might have been much larger had not his hospitality and public spirit been generous and active. The reference to well-known residents of this city makes this narrative of additional interest. M. W. Baldwin was the first locomotive builder in America, and gave name to the great locomotive works of Baldwin and Co., in Philadelphia. He was an intimate friend of Mr. Willis all his life, connected with him in business, and on cordial and familiar terms. I give the words of Henry Willis as given to me by himself. He has seldom told this strange story, and could only be induced to allow its publicity as a possible help to psychological and spiritual research. He said:

"'In July, 1838, M. W. Baldwin, of Philadelphia, Penn., came with me to Detroit, intending to start a branch locomotive shop on Cass wharf. We remained nearly three weeks in Detroit altogether. I was at that time engaged to build a railroad from Kalamazoo to Allegan. I think it was on a Thursday morning I left my friend Baldwin for Allegan; he was to leave by a steamboat at ten o'clock of the same day for his home. As I passed through Marshall on Friday, Ketchum requested me to go to Sandusky, Ohio, and purchase provisions for our railroad men, as there were none to be had on our route, the country being new. I came on and stopped at Battle Creek to visit. On Saturday and Sunday I became very uneasy. I was frequently asked if I was unwell. My mind was much depressed, but I bore up and endeavoured to be cheerful, and after meeting left for Sandusky in company with friends living near Adrian. At Tecumseh I stopped to take the stage, and paid my fare to Sandusky. The stage drove up within fifteen or twenty feet of the door of the hotel. I handed the driver my carpet-bag; and as I put my foot on the step to get in I felt a heavy blow on the back of my neck, and the words, "Go to Detroit" were as audibly, but inwardly, heard as I ever heard anything. I turned to see who struck me. No one except the driver before me, was nearer than the hotel, twenty feet off. I stood astonished, and passengers and driver shouted, "Why don't you get aboard?" I said, "Driver, hand me my bag." I took it, went to the hotel, and asked the landlord who it was that struck me on the back of my neck. "I saw you," said he, "give a bound as you put your foot on the step, but no one struck you, I know, for I was looking directly at you. What is the matter?" he asked. "I must go to Detroit," I said, "and cannot imagine why, or for what. I have no business there." The Chicago stage drove up in a moment or two. I mounted the seat with the driver, handed him fifty cents to drive as fast as he could. I repeated it with the next driver. I felt as though I wanted to fly, so anxious was I to reach the station. As we turned out of Main Street I saw an engine on the track. The engineer said to the fireman, as I afterwards learned, "Let us go; we can't find Willis." The fireman looked around, saw the stage, and said: "Stop; Willis must be in that stage." He jumped down, ran and met us some 300 feet off. I knew him and said: "Why, Jack, what on earth is the matter?" and he answered: "Baldwin fell down sick in the hotel two or three hours after you left last Thursday. His great wish has been to have you with him. We have been out for days to try and find you. This morning when we left it was doubtful if he lived till night." We went to Detroit as fast as the engine could go. I ran to the hotel, and as I reached the head of the stairs the landlord and wife, Mr. and Mrs. Wales, Dr. Hurd, and five or six of the servants were at the door. Dr. Hurd said, "He is gone." I pushed into the room, threw off my coat, and applied my hands over his head and down the sides of his face and neck as vigorously as I could for some five or six minutes, when he spoke: "Henry, where have you been? where have I been? Oh, how much I have wanted you with me!" Dr. Hurd said, "Well, if that is not bringing a man to life, what is?" This action of mine, like magnetizing, I cannot account for. I never did it before or ever saw it done. He was in a trance or spasm, but not dead. Dr. Hurd told me his symptons were those of a dying man. I remained seven weeks with him, never sleeping in all that time on a bed, except about four or five hours when C. C. Trowbridge and Augustus Porter relieved me. I took him home on a cot to his family in Philadelphia, he not having been able to sit up for some eight or nine weeks. I think it was in 1844 or 1845 I was at work in my nursery of fruit trees, at Battle Creek, with my mind then, as it often had been, on this strange and to me unaccountable matter—how I was some sixty miles from Detroit, going directly away to the South, and on important business; and why I should have changed my course, and a voice said to me: "The spirit of Baldwin's father was after you to go and save his son and take him to his family." Down to this time I had never told a living being about this singular affair, not even Baldwin himself. From the moment that I was thus notified in my nursery why I went to Detroit, I ceased to wonder, and was, and still am, convinced that there was an invisible power that followed me from the time I arrived at Battle Creek until I took Baldwin to his home.'

"Any comments on these remarkable facts would be superfluous. They give, surely, abundant food for thought.

"Detroit, March 27, 1877.   "G. B. STEBBINS."

Whilst making collections of narratives in New York city some years ago, the author was favoured with the receipt of the following account, furnished by a gentleman of the strictest veracity and a man "whose word has been as good as his bond," for over half a century of time to all his friends and neighbours. The account is given in a letter to Dr. Mitchell, of New York, and has recently been admitted into "Day's Historical Collections of Pennsylvania." It runs as follows :—

"Meadville, Penn., June 21st, 1816."

"Dear Sir :—I now give you an account of a very singular case; possibly you may have met with something analogous to it in your researches, but so far as my inquiries have extended, it is without parallel.

"Mr. Wm. Reynolds, his wife and children, a respectable family, originally citizens of Birmingham, in Great Britain, settled in the vicinity of Oil Creek, twenty-seven miles from this village, in the year 1797. Miss Mary Reynolds, one of his daughters, is the subject of this communication, upon which I shall be happy to see your animadversions. For five years, she has exhibited the phenomenon of a person vested with two distinct consciousnesses. I became acquainted with Miss Reynolds soon after my removal to this place, in May, 1815, when she was in exercise of her original consciousness, the last evening of which she spent at my house. The following evening I was at her brother's, where there was considerable company, of which she was one. To my surprise, when I spoke to her, she had no knowledge of me; I was, therefore, introduced to her anew. My curiosity was excited; and it was gratified by a history of her singular case.

"After arriving at adult age, she was occasionally afflicted with fits. In the spring of 1811, she had a very severe visitation of this kind; her frame was convulsed, and she was extremely ill for several days, when she became totally blind and deaf. During twelve weeks she continued in a very feeble state; but at the end of five weeks, the use of her visual and auditory faculties was perfectly restored. A little before the expiration of the twelve weeks, one morning when she awoke, she appeared to have lost all recollection of everything which she ever knew.

"Her understanding, with an imperfect knowledge of speech, remained; but her father, mother, brothers, sisters and neighbours, were altogether strangers to her. She had forgotten the use of written language, and did not know a single letter of the alphabet, nor any domestic employment, more than a new born babe; she, however, presently began to regain various kinds of knowledge. She continued five weeks in this way when she suddenly passed from this 'second state' (as for distinction it may be called) into her first. All circumstances of the five weeks just elapsed, were totally gone, and her original consciousness was fully restored; now the cloud which had overspread her mental hemisphere, was dissipated; her kindred and friends were all at once recognized. Every kind of knowledge which she had ever acquired was as much at her command as at any former period of her life, but of the time and of all events which had transpired during her second state, she had not the most distant idea. For three weeks she continued in her first state, but in her sleep the transition was renewed, and she awoke in her second state. As before, so now, all knowledge acquired in her first state was forgotten, and of the circumstances of her three weeks lucid interval, she had no conception; but of the small fund of knowledge she had gained in the former second state, she was able to avail herself, and she continued from day to day to add to this.

"From the spring of 1811 Miss Reynolds has been in this wonderful condition, frequently changing from her first to her second, and from her second to her first state; more than three-quarters of her time she has been in her second state. There is no periodical regularity as to the transition. Sometimes she continues several months and sometimes a few weeks, a few days, or only a few hours in her second state, but in the lapse of five years she has been in one instance more than twenty days in her first state. Whatever knowledge she has acquired at any time in her second state is familiar to her whenever in that state; and now she has made such proficiency, she is as well acquainted with things, and is in general as intelligent in her second as in her first state. It is about three years since an attempt was first made to reteach her chirography. Her brother gave her a name, which he had written, to copy. She readily took a pen, agreeable to his request, and it is a fact that she actually began to write it, though in a very awkward manner, from the right to the left in the Hebrew mode. It was not long before she obtained a tolerable skill in penmanship, and in her second state often amused herself by writing poetry, yet in her first state this is an exercise which she seldom if ever attempts. It may be remarked that she acquires all kind of knowledge in her second state with much greater facility than would a person never before instructed. In her second state she has now been introduced to many persons whom she always recognizes when in that state, and no one appears to enjoy the society of friends better than this young lady ; but if ever so well known to her in her first state, she has no knowledge of them in her second till an acquaintance, *de novo*, is formed ; and in like manner, all acquaintances formed in her second state, must be formed in her first also, in order to be known in that.

"This astonishing transition, scores of times repeated, always takes place in her sleep. In passing from her second to her first state nothing is particularly noticeable in her sleep ; but in passing from her first to her second state, her sleep is so profound that no one can wake her, and it not unfrequently continues eighteen or twenty hours. She generally has some presentiment of the change, and frequently for several days before the event. Her sufferings formerly, in the near prospect of the transition from either the one or the other state, were extreme. When in one state, she had no consciousness of ever having been in the other ; but of the wonderful fact she was persuaded on the representation of her friends, hence when about to undergo the transition, fearing she would never revert so as to know again in this world those who were dear to her, her feelings in this respect were not unlike the feelings of one entering the valley of the shadow of death ; but she has now so often passed from one state to the other, that she does not anticipate the change with that horror or distressing apprehension with which for a considerable time she used to do.

"As an evidence of her ignorance in her second state, at an early period, she was once walking at a little distance from her father's house, and discovered a rattlesnake. She was delighted at the beautiful appearance of this, to her unknown, dangerous reptile, and sprang forward to catch it. Fortunately, the serpent lay near a hole under a log, and as she seized it by its rattle it thrust its head in, and she was not able to draw it out. At another time she was riding in a narrow path alone in the woods, and met a bear, which did not seem disposed to give her the path. She boldly rode up to the huge animal, and in a very imperious style ordered him out of her way ; and she was upon the point of dismounting to belabour him with her whip when he peaceably 'cleared off.'

"This young lady is naturally of a cheerful disposition, but thoughtful. In her second state her imagination glows, her wit is keen, her remarks are often shrewd and satirical, and her prejudices, conceived without cause, against her best friends, are sometimes very strong. "TIMOTHY ALDEN."

As it may assist the student of psychological physiology to observe the relations, as well as the differentiation of two very remarkable instances of abnormal existence, we shall introduce in this place a brief notice of a case which has excited the attention of thousands of persons both within and without the ranks of the medical profession, and one which has called forth more remarks from the secular papers, than any other instance of the kind known to modern science.

We speak of Miss Mollie Fancher, of Brooklyn, N.Y., whose condition may be found summarized in the following extracts from the columns of the London *Spiritualist* of June, 1879. The details are given in a letter addressed to a lady from Dr. C. E. West, of Brooklyn Heights Seminary, the former preceptor of the unfortunate invalid. Dr. West says :—

"Brooklyn, October 8th, 1878."

"Dear Madam,—You request me to write a brief sketch of Miss Mollie Fancher, in answer to the many inquiries which have been made by those who have examined the beautiful specimens of her needlework sent to your loan exhibition, and which were wrought during a most extraordinary illness of more than twelve years' duration. To give anything like an adequate account of this remarkable girl would require a treatise. This I cannot attempt.

"Miss Mary J. Fancher was born in Attleboro', Mass., Aug. 16th, 1848, and was educated at the Brooklyn Heights Seminary under my care. She was a sweet girl, of delicate organization and nervous temperament, and was highly esteemed for her pleasing manners and gentle disposition. She was an excellent scholar, excelling in *belles lettres* studies ; but her delicate health led to her removal from school a short time before the graduation of her class in 1864. For three years I lost sight of her, till I learned from a Brooklyn paper of her singular condition, which resulted from a remarkable accident.

"Her aunt soon after called and invited me to visit 'Mollie,' as she is familiarly called. I did so, March 4th, 1867, and from that time until the present I have been an intimate visitor of the family. I have kept a journal of my visits and noted all that was important which came under my observation. I have used all the sagacity I possess to discover any fraud or collusion ; but I have never seen anything to excite my suspicion or shake my confidence in her integrity. She is a Christian girl, and shrinks from any public exhibition of herself. Spiritualists and curiosity-seekers have sought access to her, but have failed. The power of discriminating character is so great that she is rarely ever imposed upon.

"The facts to which attention is called can be fully verified. They are as follows :—

"May 10th, 1864.—She was thrown from a horse and severely injured.

"June 8th, 1865.—In attempting to leave a street car her skirt caught, and she was dragged for a block over the pavement.

"Feb. 2nd, 1866.—She was taken seriously ill. Her nervous system was completely deranged. Her head and feet coming together, she would roll like a hoop. She would also stand on her toes and spin like a top. Several persons were required to prevent her from doing personal injury to herself.

"Feb. 8th, 1866.—She went into a trance, and was, to all appearance, dead.

"Feb. 17th.—She lost her eyesight.

"Feb. 18th.—She lost her speech.

"Feb. 19th.—She lost her hearing.

"Feb. 22nd.—She saw, she spoke and heard for half-an-hour, and then for a time she lost these faculties.

"Feb. 23rd.—She lost the sense of sound.

"Feb. 24th.—The fingers closed.

"Feb. 25th.—The jaws locked.

"Feb. 26th.—The legs took a triple twist.

"March 7th.—The spasms were violent.

"May 20th, 1866.—She asked for food, ate a small piece of cracker, and took a teaspoonful of punch—it being the first food she had taken in seven weeks.

"May 27th, 1866.—She was shocked by thunder, and again lost her speech.

"May 28th, 1866.—She went into a rigid trance at 2.30 o'clock, which lasted till 11.30 A.M., the next day. She then passed into a trance till June 1st.

"June 2nd, 1866.—Nourishment was forced by a pump into her stomach, which threw her into convulsions. She was unconscious and suffered intensely till Sunday evening, June 3rd, when her throat closed, and she was unable to take any nourishment or utter a sound.

"These items are taken from the diary of Mollie's aunt, who made a daily record of her condition. I have copied but a few of them, to show the beginning of her remarkable illness.

"My first visit, as I have said, was March 4th, 1867. I found her lying on her right side, with her right arm folded under her head. Her fingers were clenched in the palm of her hand. The right hand and arm were paralyzed, as was her body generally, excepting her left arm. She was in a trance, and seemed to be in pain. She remained in this trance till the 8th, a shorter time than usual at this period of her illness, her trances often lasting from ten to twelve days. . . . .

"I now speak of her physical condition. For twelve years she has lain in one position on her right side. For nine years she was paralyzed, her muscles only relaxing under the influence of chloroform. For the last three years her muscles are so relaxed that her limbs can be moved without the aid of chloroform. While passing into this state her sufferings were intense. For days it did not seem possible that she could live. Her eyes were open and staring. For nine years they had been closed. Now they were open, never closing day nor night. They were sightless. She could swallow, but take no food ; even the odour of it was offensive. During these twelve years' illness there have been times when for many days together she has been to all appearance dead. The slightest pulse could not be detected—there was no evidence of respiration. Her limbs were as cold as ice, and had there not been some warmth about her heart she would have been buried. During all these years she has virtually lived without food. Water, the juice of fruits, and other liquids have been introduced into her mouth, but scarcely any of them ever make their way to her stomach. In the early part of her illness it collapsed, so that by placing the hand in the cavity her spinal column could be felt. There was no room for food. Her throat was rigid. Her heart enlarged. When I first saw her she had but one sense—that of touch. With that she could read with rapidity. This she did by running her fingers over the printed page. With the finger she could discriminate the photographs of persons, the faces of callers, &c. She never sleeps, her rest being taken in trances. The most delicate work is done in the night. The circulation is sluggish, and, as a consequence, there is very little animal heat. She longs to die, but says she cannot, as there is nothing to die. Such is a brief statement of her bodily condition.

"To me her mental state is more extraordinary. Her power of clairvoyance, or second sight, is marvellously developed. All places in which she takes any interest are open to her mental view. Distance imposes no barriers. No retirement, however secluded, but yields to her penetrating gaze. She dictates the contents of sealed letters which have never been in her hands without the slightest error. She visits the family circles of her relations and acquaintances in remote places, and describes their attire and their occupations. She points out any disorder of dress, however slight, as the basting thread in the sleeve of a sack which to ordinary sight was concealed by the arm. Any article which has been mislaid she sees and tells where it may be found. She discriminates in darkness the most delicate shades of colour with an accuracy that never errs. She works in embroidery and wax without patterns. She conceives the most beautiful forms and combinations of forms. She never studied botany or took a lesson in waxwork, and yet she never mistakes the forms of leaf or flower. Holding a pen or pencil in her left hand, she writes with extraordinary rapidity. Her penmanship is handsome and legible. She once wrote a poem of ten verses in as many minutes—her thought flowing with the rapidity of lightning. In cutting velvet leaves for pin-cushions, like the sample sent you, she held the scissors by the knuckles of thumb and fore-finger of the left hand, and bringing the velvet with thumb and finger of her right hand, she cut the leaves as shapely and without ravel, as though they had been cut with a punch. These leaves do not differ in size or form more than leaves growing on tree or shrub. In the early part of her sickness she cut more than two thousand such leaves. In April, 1875, she worked up 2,500 ounces of worsted; to December, 1875, she had written 6,500 notes and letters. She has kept an account of all the expenses of the family during her sickness. She keeps a daily journal except when in trances of longer duration than twenty-four hours. In passing into the new condition three years ago, of which I have spoken, she forgot everything that had occurred in the previous nine years. When she was able to speak, she inquired about matters that occurred at the beginning of her illness—the nine intervening years were a perfect blank to her.

"But I must take leave of this subject. The incredulous will not accept it—and it is not surprising. Miss Fancher is not be judged by ordinary laws. The state is abnormal—a species of modified catalepsy, which has deranged the ordinary action of mind and body. It is a rich mine for investigation to the physiologist and the psychologist, and with them I leave the case. "Very respectfully,
"CHARLES E. WEST."

The following additional particulars of this wonderful case have since been published by Dr. West's permission in several of the local papers. We commend them to the Spiritualistic reader as being specially worthy of attention.

In a conversation between Dr. West and a party of Brooklyn clergymen, the former says :—

"To my knowledge she never has made a penny by her gifts, although having many opportunities to do so. . , . She knows who her visitors are long before they are ushered into the hall below, and she allows them to see her, or refuses, just as the whim takes her. I took Kossuth's sister there just before her departure for the Old World. Miss Mollie refused to see her. Afterward I asked Mollie for an explanation. 'Why, I didn't like her looks when she entered the door,' was the reply. The door is on the floor below. Another time I took a gentleman of reputation as a scholar. She directed that he be kept from her room, for the same reason—she did not like his looks. While she was blind I took a large man with a great black beard to her, and said, 'What do you think of this little man with a smooth, sharp chin?' and without turning her face, which was from us, she answered, 'He is very large, and has full whiskers. I can see him.' She knows what is going on all over the country, but whether from her marvellous sight-seeing, or because she reads it, I am unable to say. She is not willing to talk to visitors about her gifts. The topic is painful to her. To her friends, however, she is more free, and she is quite willing at times to explain her sensations. She tells them where she goes and what she sees.

"To the question asked by Dr. Channing, then present—'Does she see friends who have gone before her?'—the answer, given with great apparent reluctance, was ; 'Yes ; she sees many of them. She sees her mother ; she longs to be with her mother. She says her mother comes to her.'"

The following extract from the *Western Times* refers to the testimony of a physician well known in New York and highly esteemed for learning and truthfulness :—

"From the first, Dr. R. Fleet Speir, of 162, Montague Street, Brooklyn, has been **Miss** Fancher's physician. He has watched her case with unrelenting vigilance, and has made full memoranda of every symptom and every change. After she had declared that she could not partake of food, that it was nauseating and distasteful, he introduced nourishment through a silver tube. When she was to all appearances dead, he worked over her and restored her. One day he received a note from this curious patient, warning him that an attempt was to be made to rob him. He paid not more than passing attention to it ; but the next day some one entered his house and took therefrom a valuable case of surgical instruments. When he has rung the door bell Miss Fancher has almost invariably called out : 'Aunt, please go down and let in the doctor.' Once or twice he has halted on the landing at the stair top, while some other visitor who accompanied him entered the room with Mrs. Crosby. Miss Fancher, after greeting the new-comer, has said : 'Why does the doctor wait outside ? Ask him to come in." She has been aware of his presence in the neighbourhood, and has told, when he was starting from his Montague Street residence, a mile away from her, that he was going to call upon her. Dr. Speir has taken Dr. Mitchell, Dr. Kissam, Dr. Crane, Dr. Ormiston, and many others of Brooklyn's best known physicians to see Miss Fancher.

"It was Dr. Speir who, in the earlier stages of Miss Fancher's illness, tested whether she had partaken of food by going in suddenly upon her and administering an emetic. The drug gave her much pain, while the result was convincing that her stomach was empty. The nature of the medicine was well known to Miss Fancher, although it had been carefully kept from her. This event was just before she went into the rigid condition that lasted nine years. As soon as she emerged from this condition into that of relaxation, three years ago, her memory of the nine years was gone, and she remembered only incidents of previous years. So nine and a half years after the administering of the test, as Dr. Speir entered the room Miss Fancher broke out with : 'You thought I didn't know why you gave me that medicine, but I did. You wanted to see whether food was in my stomach, and you learned that none was there. You won't do so again, will you ?'

The editor of the *Western Times* adds :—

"Miss Fancher longs to die, yet she tells her friends she is afraid she cannot die. 'There is nothing of me to die,' she says. Once, after a most death-like trance, in which it required hours of vigorous efforts to restore her, she uttered : 'Why did you not let me alone ? I think I might have died, had you allowed me to.' . . .
"Some of her friends have seriously said : 'If death is the parting of the spirit from the body, and if Miss Mollie's spirit has been released from the bondage of the flesh, can she indeed ever die ?'"

That which the above narrative ought to suggest to every intelligent reader is the revelation which Miss Fancher's condition makes, of the latent powers within every human soul. The Spiritual powers manifested by this poor invalid must necessarily prove what is the normal condition of the Spirit, when the abnormal state of the physique permits that Spirit to act alone or in a manner independent of the body. Let it be observed that most of the effects manifested in Miss Fancher's case, are often witnessed in mesmerized or entranced subjects. Miss Fancher exhibits the power of the Spirit when the physical organism is subdued by sickness. The mesmerized subject displays the same Spiritual powers when his body is controlled by the magnetic fluid of a human operator, whilst the automatic trance Medium exhibits kindred, if not precisely similar states, when his mortal body is put to sleep by the magnetism of an invisible Spirit.

These states are all graduated degrees of one condition ; to wit, the temporary suspension of bodily powers and the exaltation of the Spirit, or —as in the latter case—the substitution of a foreign intelligence for that of the entranced subject. It is unphilosophical on the part of the many scientific observers who have visited Miss Fancher, that they do not search out and examine kindred cases amongst the mesmerists and Spiritualists. The correlation of a multitude of cases drawn from different sources, would do far more to promote the best interests of science, and explain the mysteries of soul life and powers, than ever can result from the childish experiments now so rife amongst would-be scientists called "thought reading." It is not an uncommon thing to see a travelling mountebank who offers "to expose Spiritualism," placed on a rostrum with a lord bishop for his chairman, and a party of grave deans and vicars, &c., &c., as his "moral supporters."

Presently, one of the grave ministers of Christ is requested to hide a pin, a child's doll, top, or ball, or some such respectable toy, when the mountebank seizing hold of his reverence, drags him hither and thither in the dignified attitude of a pair of schoolboys playing at hide-and-seek, and when the mountebank succeeds in finding the toy, a large audience of grave professors cry, "Oh, how wonderful!" and a chorus of pious Christians send up hymns of praise to God because Mumbo Jumbo has exposed that wicked Spiritualism that has emptied the pews of the churches, and done so much harm to the world by telling it, that it would have to atone for its own sins, instead of having "a Saviour" to make atonement for it.

Poor Miss Fancher! Her life is in truth but a living martyrdom, but if science demands its martyrs, and this poor girl's case is properly considered by science, when she herself becomes an enfranchised Spirit, she will scarcely deem that she has paid too heavy a penalty for her glorious crown.

Returning once more to the few additional narratives we can give of Spiritualism in America prior to the Rochester knockings, we invite our readers' attention to the following extracts from the August, 1872, number of the *Western Star.*

The following narrative, from the pen of Dr. Joseph Warren, D.D., of Tennessee, is not only vouched for on the authority of its venerable author, but has been carefully investigated and testified to by several living witnesses, one of whom (Squire Fisher) was actually present at the *séances* described in the narrative. Dr. Warren, now a resident at Rome, favours the author with permission to publish his narrative in full, reserving only the real name of the family chiefly interested, for reasons which will appear sufficiently obvious to every intelligent reader.

We shall endeavour to preserve, as far as possible, the phraseology of our esteemed correspondent; but as the narrative occupies more space than would conform to the limits of our record, we must content ourselves by giving such quotations as will be found of the most interesting character.

It was in the year 1830 that Dr. Warren was solicited to fill the pulpit of a dear old friend, and former college companion of his, who had been suddenly struck with paralysis. The doctor had secluded himself from his ministerial duties for several months from an ardent desire to devote his time to literary pursuits; but deeming that the change from his city residence in N——, to the quiet of his friend's country parsonage might prove congenial to his present condition, he determined to comply with the invitation in question.

The Rev. Mr. W——, the friend whom he designed to oblige, had been the father of a son, whose wild and dissolute career had recently been terminated by self-destruction. Rumour alleged that if the unhappy young man had not put an end to his life by a deed of violence, the law was prepared to avenge upon him more than one act of murder, perpetrated, as it was currently reported, on the victims of his lawless passions. It was the shame and anguish of mind occasioned by the iniquitous career of this wretched son, that had reduced Mr. W—— to that condition of helplessness in which the aid of his kind and sympathizing friend, Dr. Warren, had been solicited.

On arriving at the scene of his intended labours, Dr. Warren found that the mansion and grounds formerly occupied by Mr. W——'s family had been abandoned since the tragic death of his son ; in fact, the parent and child had long been estranged from each other, and the latter had pursued his course of riot and dissipation in the once stately family mansion, whilst his justly offended father had removed to a small cottage, situated as far as possible from the home thus desecrated.

Here Dr. Warren took up his abode, and here for some months he continued to minister to his suffering friend, and rural parishioners, with ever increasing acceptance.   Dr. Warren goes on to say :—

"After a few weeks' residence in the parish which I had taken under my care, I began to be aware that strange rumours were prevalent concerning the house formerly occupied by my old friend, and of late abandoned to the occupancy of his profligate son.   I was informed that the most unaccountable sounds and ghostly sights had been recently manifested there.   The house was a large, handsome Southern residence, closely embosomed in thick pine woods, and removed about two miles from any other habitation.

"Despite its secluded situation, and the evil reputation which attached to it, the lovely woods and shady forest paths that surrounded it had become a favourite resort of the children in the neighbourhood ; and it was from the fearful disturbances that they encountered in their sports near the mansion, that the first tidings of hauntings had been derived.

"In a little while the rustics, who had occasion to pass through the woods, and now and then the sportsmen pursuing their game in its well-stocked preserves, encountered, as they alleged, ghostly forms and fearful apparitions, whilst shrieks, groans, and concussive sounds of tremendous power, echoed and re-echoed from the path-like avenues that surrounded the building, 'making night hideous,' and compelling a strict but fruitless search to discover the source of these disturbances.   On more than one occasion I was informed, by reliable witnesses, that the mansion had been seen through the woods at night brilliantly illuminated ; figures had been discerned passing before the windows, and flitting along the terraces ; but when a determined body of the villagers sallied forth to ascertain who had thus invaded the solitude of the place, the lights vanished, the forms disappeared, and the most profound stillness succeeded to a loud hum of voices, and a chorus of sobs.   'The next morning, when I and four of my most sceptical acquaintances visited the house,' added one of my informants (Deacon Harvey), 'I pledge my honour there was not a footprint to be found in the dust that covered the rooms, passages, and stairways, and that, too, in the very chambers and galleries which I had with my own eyes seen blazing with lights, and crowded with forms of men and women passing and repassing.'

"As time rolled on, the reports of the hauntings became more frequent and circumstantial.   Numbers of persons, in whose good sense and veracity I had entire confidence, visited the place, and gave me accounts of their alarming experiences.   The affair at length began to assume a serious aspect, and this was confirmed by a cautiously written account which appeared in the *G—— Citizen*, in which the editor detailed his experiences in visiting the possessed mansion, in company with Reuben Jacobs, Esq., a magistrate, and Mr. Stephen Moss, an engineer.   As both these gentlemen were personally known to me, and their statements respecting the sights and sounds they had encountered were boldly affirmed over their own signatures, I began to attach a degree of importance to the case which I should never else have associated with a tale of the so-called 'supernatural.'   My final resolve to enter upon an investigation of these mysteries for myself, was confirmed by an account given me of several days' exploration in the haunted dwelling, by my friend and parishioner, Mr. Fisher, ex-mayor of N——, and a man upon whose calm judgment and power of observation I felt able to rely.   This gentleman assured me he had several times confronted the spirit of young W——, and the forms of two girls supposed to have been murdered by him, and that in the open light of day, and with a tangibility of appearance which admitted of no doubt or question.   He affirmed that he himself, with Reuben Jacobs, and Deacon Harvey, had sat in a deserted chamber, and all of them had simultaneously seen two women, in garments stained with blood, rise up from the floor and flee across the apartment, pursued by the shadowy form of young W——.   As the apparition disappeared, the loud report of a musket was heard, and that not only by themselves, but also by a crowd of persons who had followed the gentlemen to the house, but feared to enter with them.   They added, that as they sat on that floor, they heard many knocks, the number of which they counted, sounding on the very planks beneath them, and proceeding with just as much force when they stationed Squire Fisher in the room below, in which he and two other watchers testified that they heard the knocks but could not find any cause to account for them. . . . .

"Now, although I heard all this, and more to the same effect, from persons whose veracity I esteemed at the same rate as my own, I determined to visit the scene of the hauntings, and investigate their nature *alone,* before I felt justified in abandoning what I deemed to be the safe ground of incredulity, on the possibility of the dead revisiting the earth and causing their presence to be known through the strange and occult means here detailed.

"As a minister of religion myself—as one who had ventured to assert the fact of man's immortality, but who could only prove it from the traditions of the past or the hearsay of the fathers, I deemed it my solemn duty to avail myself of any clue which could open up to me an assurance of the doctrines I taught, and transmute faith into actual know-ledge.   Besides these pleadings of duty, I remembered with some awe, and perplexity, certain experiences I had gone through in a visit to Europe, amongst some French *savants,* much given to the practices of animal magnetism.   These gentlemen, at a pleasant assem-blage where occult philosophy was the theme of our conversation, had assured me I was a 'fine magnetic subject,' and begged me to allow myself to be put into the mesmeric sleep. As a mere matter of curiosity, I consented to their request; but the results were such as I little anticipated, and can never forget.   I became lost to this earth and its surroundings, and found myself in realms of beauty, joy, and harmony, the memory of which I can never recall even now without tears.   On every side of me I saw multitudes of radiant people with glorious forms, shining apparel, and beautiful faces.   Some of these divine-looking beings I perceived wore the identity of those I had once known on earth, but whom I had long since regarded as dead.   Amongst them was the form of my blessed and much loved mother ; also a lovely little sister, who, marvellous to relate, still preserved her identity, and was known to me, although she had grown up into a peerless and angelic-looking woman.   There were several other well-remembered and dearly loved sojourners of earth, none of whom I should have ever looked to meet again.

"These glorious beings filled me with a wondrous sense of delight, and one or two of them spoke to me, though it was the misfortune of my after life that I could not remember what they said.   I beheld one wonderful thing in this scene of paradise which perplexed me more than all others.   At times I saw human beings of a most horrible and repulsive appearance, and of different degrees of blackness and density.   These wretched-looking objects were all surrounded by an atmosphere which seemed to correspond in color and thickness to their own bodies ; and what was most astonishing, was the fact that I often saw them, and the bright beings surrounded by light and bloom, advance towards each other with inconceivable swiftness, and such a terrific momentum, that I looked to see them shivered to pieces by the shock ; but instead of this, I perceived that they literally passed through each other's forms, and that without betraying the least consciousness of meeting, seeing, or even being aware of the others' presence. . . . .

"In subsequent *séances*—for I practiced with these mesmerists for several months—I saw the solution of this singular problem.   I perceived that the degrees of density of every world or atmosphere corresponded to the beings who dwelt within it, and that finer and more sublimated spheres and spirits penetrated and inhabited the grosser and denser ; thus a vast number of spheres and spirit people inhered together invisible to each other, yet related like water in a crystal, microscopic creatures in water, gases in the creatures, electricity in the gases, and the innermost invisible life principle in all.   I could see world within world, spheres of sublimated refinement, brightness, and beauty, penetrating within and within and still within the grosser and denser.   I could see the forms of the dwellers in these interlacing atmospheres piercing each other, invisible all to each other ; but for me to look upon them in this interior unfoldment, was very wonderful and very awful. . . . .   But to return.   It was on a quiet summer's evening that I found myself, after a long ramble in the pine woods, standing before a melancholy-looking, deserted mansion, the park-like approach to which, with its broad verandahs, open courts, and shattered appearance, convinced me I had chanced upon the very spot which I had so often designed to visit.

"The occasion seemed propitious ; and as no human being appeared to be within or about the place, I resolved to explore it at once, and to do so in the thorough spirit of a fearless investigator.

"I had no sooner made my way through the open doors and halls into a suite of apart-ments which had once been used as reception rooms, than I experienced a sensation of fear, dislike, and repulsion, which I had never known before.   A sudden chill pervaded my whole frame, and a strongly-defined impression, almost as clear as a voice, bore these words in upon my mind : There is a gulf between the living and the dead which humanity cannot endure to fathom.

"Again I thought, or something seemed to make me think: How terrible is the approach of unbodied spirit ! The mortal cannot stand in the presence of the immortal and live. Such sentiments as these oppressed me with a nameless and indescribable sense of horror. I would have given all I possessed, aye, even years of my life, to fly the place, and yet I could not move. The whole atmosphere seemed to be full of *spirit*, and that of a horrible and repulsive character. 'How dreadful is this place !' was the thought which at length shaped itself into words, and with their shuddering utterance, I knew that I had broken some spell. Instantly I perceived that a woman, young, once fair, but hateful and antagonistic to my mortal being, had entered the hall and was gliding swiftly towards me. Had no relief interposed to save me from waking conscious contact with this being, the horror of that moment would, I am certain, have terminated my earthly existence ; but just then, as if by a providential interposition, three gentlemen of the neighbourhood, one of whom was my intimate friend, Squire Fisher, entered the apartment from a long gallery which they had been traversing on the opposite side to that from which the spirit had borne down upon me. The pang of horror on the one hand, and the relief of mortal companionship on the other, served to produce a shock which threw me instantly into the mesmeric condition to which I have above alluded, and one which my French experiences had rendered familiar to me.

"My friends subsequently informed me they were horror-struck to perceive me lying on the ground cold, and as they at first deemed, lifeless, but when one of the party strove to raise me, I threw him off, and standing upright, I began to speak in a decided and unfamiliar manner, bidding them have no fear, for that I was 'entranced,' and should converse with the spirits who inhabited that possessed mansion. By my command, some rude seats were improvised, and, lighted only by the rays of the full moon streaming in brightly through the broken panes of the shattered windows, the amazed visitors remained listening to the revelations which I poured forth under what purported to be the influence of the risen soul of the unhappy suicide, the son of my friend Mr. W——.

"Speaking not as myself (Dr. Warren), but as Marcus W——, I declared that I was as much a living man as I had ever been, and moreover that I dwelt in that same house still, and should continue to do so until my spirit was freed from the bonds which chained me to it. I desired my visitors to speak to me, and when, in awe and confusion, they at first began imperfectly to question, but finally to press their queries with eagerness and intelligence, they learned from me, still speaking as the spirit of the unfortunate suicide, that there is no real death, only a change of bodies, or outward coverings to the soul ; that with every one of these changes the soul enters upon an inner sphere to the place, scene, and surroundings which it formerly occupied ; that its ability to change its *locale*, or place of abode, depended wholly upon the power it had acquired in its previous state of existence. That where the moral excellence of the soul was great and exalted, its condition was correspondingly pure, beautiful, and refined ; that where the spirit was mighty in intellectual and moral worth, its powers were almost unbounded ; whilst its capacity to roam through and master the various conditions of many spheres of being were so enlarged, that such spirits appeared to men like gods, and were in reality, tutelary spirits, or 'Guardian Angels.'

"Being urgently questioned why the spirit of Marcus W—— continued to haunt and disturb that place, I replied, in his name, that *I was compelled to do so*. That the strongest part of my earthly magnetism had been poured out in that place ; that crime was strong passion ; strong passion ever liberated strong magnetism ; and that human magnetism formed 'tractors,' or magnetic points, which drew the spiritual body and bound it as forcibly as chains forged of the magnetism of the universe. They asked of the possessing spirit if it had companions, and who were the female forms so often described by affrighted watchers ; also what produced the frightful noises that pierced the awful solitude. The possessing spirit replied that thousands of wretched beings like himself were attracted to his society, and that it was a part of the law of their lives that, as the remembrance of their crimes returned to them (and when was it ever absent ?) they were surrounded by the images called up by their thoughts, and seemed madly impelled to deal blows at those images, and repeat again and again, in frenzied misery, all the scenes which crowded in upon their minds. It was at such times, he said, that their cries, groans, and acts resounded through the heavy atmosphere of their prison house into the atmosphere of earth, and became palpable alike to the sense of sight and hearing.

"When asked if he was sorry for the wrongs he had committed, he replied he was, *sometimes*, but at other times he was possessed by an uncontrollable desire to repeat it all again and again, and that that was hell, and he could not escape from it. Here he was questioned as to whether the Catholic idea had any foundation in fact that prayers and penances performed by others could avail him. He answered eagerly in the affirmative, assuring his hearers that the strong sympathy of human spirits, when directed towards the earth-bound soul, gave it psychologic strength, and aided it to pray for itself, and ultimately to repent, and rise out of its bonds into a condition of change analogous to death ; that when the imprisoned spirit had passed through this second death, it entered into a finer, purer, inner sphere, and he believed would have the opportunity to progress, as he had been told, eternally ; but he didn't know ; he was not ready for death for his part. He kept on repeating and repeating the scenes of earth, and he supposed, until he had outgrown them, he could not escape from the horrid necessity of going over them. He only knew he was infinitely wretched, and longed for, but could not die, this second death.

"One of the interlocutors here asked if he and the unhappy spirits around him had any teachers with them, any guardian angels to help them progress. Here a violent shuddering shook my frame, and the obsessing spirit replied, with bitter curses, that often and often they saw bright lights flashing amidst them, and they knew they were the spirits of purer and better spheres, come to try and reform them. Sometimes, he added, they heard celestial voices urging them to pray, and strive to banish the horrid desires that oppressed them.

"There were some, the spirit added, who followed these lights with weeping, wailing, and penitential tears ; then they laid down to sleep, and melted out of that sphere—that is, they passed on higher. But others, like himself, saw the lights, and heard the voices ; and though for a moment they felt remorse, and a wild aspiration to overcome their miserable propensities, they generally returned to them with added fury, and then they mocked and gibed at the angels, and bid them go hence with curses. He added, all such angels as penetrated into the sphere in which he dwelt were called ' Christs,' but he believed they were only good and pure souls of men and women that had once lived on earth, and many wise, though wicked spirits he conversed with had said that was what ' Christ,' ' Mediator,' and ' Saviour ' meant ; also that the great love and pity which good men felt towards poor earth-bound spirits did at last give them strength, and help them to rise ; ' and so,' said this intellectual but morally degraded spirit, ' this is what is meant by a Saviour, bearing the transgressions of many, and thus it is that " with His stripes we are healed." ' . . . .

"It was far in the night when I awoke in that place of dread. My three friends were kneeling around me, praying fervently, with streaming eyes, and hearts wrung with anguish, for pity on the miserable spirits who were there bound in-the prison-house of their eartuly crimes. As for me, I neither comprehended their pious occupation, nor my own share in the terrible revelations to which they had been listening. They led me to my home, but it required several days of rest, and calm communion with my deeply-moved companions, to restore my mind to its wonted peace, and make me apprehend the full force of what had transpired, the memoranda of which they had made from their joint recollections of the scene.

"The fearful and loathsome impression produced upon me by that one night's inter-course with ' the spirits in prison ' never became modified, or faded out of memory. Within a few days of its occurrence, I succeeded in procuring a substitute, and imme-diately upon his arrival I quitted the neighbourhood of the hated dwelling. The friends who had been sharers in my painful experiences in vain urged me to renew them, and devote myself to the reform of the unhappy spirits who dwelt in the bonds of earthly crime within that awful mansion. No sense of duty, however strong, could persuade me again to renew the loathsome, and as I still deem it, unnatural intercourse between the mortal and the spirit. I know that what I have written is true. I know that the experiences and revelations of the movement known as modern Spiritualism can add nothing to the terrible revelations of that night of horror ; but though I believe in the truth of spirit communion, and doubt not that the intercourse with purer spheres and higher existences may be fraught with pleasure and instruction, I can never again consent to place myself in such a position as to overstep the boundaries of the sphere in which I have been mercifully limited by the providence of my all-wise Creator."

The narrative of Dr. Joseph Warren proves to us conclusively that there are certain grand central truths, revealed to us through Spirit communion, concerning the condition of the soul hereafter, which do not change nor become modified by time, place, nor Mediumistic idiosyncracies. If the above narration contains no philosophy startling from its novelty, it impresses us forcibly with the fact that prior, as well as subsequent to, the celebrated era we designate the Rochester knockings, well attested communications ¨om the realm of soul life invariably teach the stupendous lesson that we carry our own doomsday book within us, and that life hereafter is not only a continuation, but an inevitable result of the good or evil deeds we have sown in the rudimental sphere of mortality.

Of the following two cases (the first occurring in 1834, the second in 1836) a vast mass of published testimony exists, variously written, and profusely attested.

The most concise and authentic accounts that we can select, are to be found in a little volume written by Mr. Henry Spicer, entitled " Sights and Sounds," and published in England, in 1853.

This work is professedly an account of " all the modern Spiritual manifestations" which have occurred in America; and one of its chief points of interest is derived from the exceeding care which the author has taken to verify all he relates.

"The first regularly recorded American manifestations commenced in the year 1834, at Canandaigua, New York, and recurred in 1836, in various parts of Pennsylvania.

" It is stated that the witnesses, now living, who have it in their power to attest the details which follow, are numerous and respectable, besides being persons who were in the highest degree incredulous, and who repaired to the theatre of operations in order to detect, if possible, the means by which they were effected.

" Mr. Dods was a resident in the village of Levant, Penobscot County, Maine. The first intimation that gentleman or his family received, that they were to be made the subject of any unusual manifestation, was conveyed in certain rappings, sometimes on the outside door of his house, sometimes within, on the walls, in the chambers, in fact, in every part of his dwelling. Coming from the village late one evening, he observed the school-house brilliantly lighted, and forms of men and women moving to and fro. As he drew near, the lights were suddenly extinguished. Fancying, however, that the scholars had assembled for a dance, he crept silently to the door, and, opening it suddenly, stepped within. All was darkness and silence—not a human being was to be found !

"On other occasions, noises like the rolling of a heavy metal ball were heard to reverberate from one end of the house to the other; bedsteads were lifted and turned round, tables moved across the room, lights danced up and down the road before the house, or assembled in an open space, and then mingled in what suggested to the astonished watchers the idea of some fantastic dance !

" The scene of these extraordinary phenomena was visited by so many persons, that the clerk of the county courts deemed it his duty to visit the spot, with his assistant, and endeavour to detect and expose the trick.

" Mr. Dods was perfectly willing to receive them, and permitted them to select their own apartment, to which, about nine o'clock in the evening, they withdrew.

" They fastened the door, secured the windows, searched the room, closet, and bed, and were confident that no human being was in the room, or could get in without their knowledge. Placing the candle on the table, unextinguished, they went to bed.

" Soon after they retired, they felt the bedclothes move. They immediately caught hold of the quilts, and braced themselves against the footposts of the bedsteads. The clothes continued to move until they relaxed their hold, when the quilts and sheet hopped six feet from the bed on to the floor. The candle was burning, but no visible power could be detected. The bed was again searched, but nothing was found. They replaced the clothes, and once more got into bed.

" In a very few moments the feather-bed started out from under them, and fell on the floor, notwithstanding their united exertions to retain it in its place.

" The adventurers never succeeded in obtaining the slightest clue to these disturbances. The like fortune attended other inquiring friends of Mr. Dods.

" At length, a company of gentlemen from various parts of the country, assembled at the house, in the hope of witnessing the manifestations. Nor were they disappointed.

" They were conversing freely on various topics, when a noise was heard, like the rumbling of distant thunder. It continued to increase in loudness, drawing nearer and nearer, and at last burst directly over the house, shaking the whole structure to its very foundation. This took place in winter, and the stars shown out clear and cold. Soon after this, a noise was heard in the attic like the trundling of iron balls, and it continued for ten minutes, when the company were startled by a heavy weight falling apparently from the ceiling to the floor. It immediately commenced rolling about the room ; would glide under the chairs without touching them, jump over the table, strike the four sides of the room, bounding, without touching the floor, and at last it hopped upon a bed which stood in one corner of the room, and moved from the head to the foot.

"The clothes were distinctly seen to settle under it, as if some heavy weight was pressing them down. A gentleman in the room walked towards the bed, with the seeming intention to take hold of, or arrest its progress; but one of the company caught hold of his arm, and said, 'Do not touch it *for your life.*' It then dropped on the floor, and rolled out of the side of the house.

"During all these phenomena nothing could be seen. That which made the noise was invisible.

"It would appear that the spirit was by no means of a communicative disposition, since, after indulging in many similar manifestations, it ultimately withdrew from the house and neighbourhood, leaving all parties in total ignorance as to its character and object.

"Eighteen years since, in 1834, the *Newark Advertiser* published a curious narrative of a rapping case, into the truth of which its agents had previously inquired.

"It appeared that on a certain night the family of a Mr. Joseph Barron, living in the township of Woodbridge, about three miles from Rahway, Newark County, were alarmed, after they had retired, by a loud thumping against the house. Mr. Barron's first impression was, that some person was attempting to break in; but further observation soon undeceived him. The thumping, however, continued at short intervals, until the family became so alarmed, that Mr Barron called in some of his neighbours, who remained up with the family until daylight, when the thumping ceased.

"The next evening, after nightfall, the noise recommenced, when it was ascertained to be mysteriously connected with the movements of a servant girl in the family, about fourteen years of age.

"When passing a window on the stairs, for example, a sudden jar, accompanied with an explosive sound, broke a pane of glass, the girl at the same moment being seized with a violent spasm. This, of course, very much alarmed her, and a physician (Dr. Drake) was sent for, came, and bled her. The bleeding, however, produced no apparent effect. The noise still continued as before, at intervals, wherever the girl went, each sound producing more or less of a spasm; and the physician, with the family, remained up during the night. At daylight the thumping ceased again. On the third evening the same thing was repeated, commencing a little earlier than before, and so every evening.

"The circumstance rapidly spread, and produced a vast excitement, the house being filled and surrounded from morning till night. All imaginable means were resorted to in order to unravel the phenomenon. At one time the girl would be removed from one apartment to another without effect. Wherever she was placed, at uncertain intervals, the thumping noise would be heard in the room.

"She was taken to a neighbour's house; the same result followed. When carried out of doors, however, no noise was heard.

"Dr. Drake, who had been constant in his attentions during the whole period, on one occasion, in company with the agents of the paper, made a variety of experiments with the girl, who was placed in an upper room with some members of the family. The noises would be produced five or six times in succession, jarring the house, ceasing a few minutes, and then resuming as before. The girl appeared to be in perfect health, cheerful, and free from everything like the apprehension she had on former occasions exhibited. The noise, however, continued; and in order to ascertain more satisfactorily that she was not herself the author of it, she was placed on a chair upon a blanket, in the centre of the room, the chair being bandaged with cloth, the girl's feet fastened, and her hands confined.

"All these precautions produced no change, the thumping continuing as before, though the girl moved neither limb nor muscle.

"She was then placed in the doorway of a closet, the door being ajar. In less than a minute it flew open, as if violently struck with a mallet, accompanied with precisely such a noise as would be produced in such a case."

The records of this century, and the experience of numerous persons still living, furnish many more cases strictly analogous to that of the modern movement, yet lacking the scientific explanation which has been so generally received since 1848.

Spiritual beings who appeared *eighteen centuries ago* are regarded by modern Christianity as "Angels," sometimes as "God" in person; while trance speakers of the same period are spoken of as "Prophets," "Men of God," and considered to be plenarily inspired by the Almighty himself.

The very same persons who make these enormous claims for ancient Spiritualism, write of Spiritual appearances in the eighteenth and nineteenth centuries as necessarily being the work of human imposture, or if genuine, at the very most, of "evil spirits," while the trance speakers whose utterances they can neither ignore nor account for, they pertinaciously denounce as "diseased" or "insane."

It is to mark the vast and important change in public opinion which the advent of modern Spiritualism with all its scientific facts has wrought, and show the flood of light which it has poured upon the subject of man's Spiritual nature and life beyond the grave, that we have ventured to inflict upon the reader narratives with which the experiences of the last twenty-five years have completely familiarized us.

"The people that walked in darkness" have indeed "seen a great light;" and nothing more conclusively proves this truth, so wonderfully illustrated in our own time, than these brief notices of the early Spiritualism of the nineteenth century.

CHAPTER LVIII.

SPIRITUALISM IN AMERICA (CONTINUED).

WONDERFUL PHENOMENAL MANIFESTATIONS.

[Written by the Author of "Nineteenth Century Miracles," and first published in the "Western Star," Boston.]

PASSING on to the manifestations which succeeded the famous "Rochester knockings" in 1848, and selecting from hundreds of wonderful narratives a few only, of what may be considered as representative cases, we call attention to two or three well-attested examples of *the direct Spirit voice.* The first notice cited, is borrowed from the June number of Mr. Stephen Albro's excellent Spiritual journal entitled *The Sunbeam.** In this Mr. Albro gives a condensed account of certain manifestations transpiring at Medina, the report of which was of so extraordinary a character, that Mr. Albro was at much pains to ascertain the real facts. The result of his enquiries he publishes as follows :—

"Our informants are several of the most respectable inhabitants of Medina, amongst them a young lady, educated, intelligent, and truthful, who visits in a wealthy and distinguished family who are constantly annoyed with the presence of a badly brought up, uncivil 'spirit.' This spirit began to 'cut up' about two years since. First it commenced 'rapping' in the bedroom of two young ladies, members of the family. It 'rapped' on the walls, the floor, the ceiling, above, below, all around, and finally commenced pulling the bedding from the bed. The young ladies, nearly frightened out of their senses, ran down-stairs and reported the terrible phenomenon to their parents. The spirit followed, and the entire household were smitten with terror.

"But after they had become satisfied that the noise and other demonstrations proceeded from a 'spirit,' and when their excitement had partially subsided, they determined to hold a circle by way of ascertaining who their invisible tormentor might be. No sooner did they commence their enquiries, than to their horror they received *vocal responses.*

"The spirit informed them in audible, but not very polished English, that his name was 'Josh;' that he died about thirty years since in South Carolina; that when on earth he was ignorant and debased, so that when he passed into the spirit world he was confined to the lowest spheres; that he finally wandered off, and had now concluded to become a

---

* Published at Buffalo, N.Y., now suspended.

resident in the family where he made himself 'manifest;' that he should remain with them, because he found them congenial, and that he intended to stay with them for years to come ; that no power could drive him away ; and if he was not used well he would 'knock things endwise,' and make himself generally disagreeable.

"From that time to the present, 'Josh' has been a fixture in the family, and laughs, talks, cracks jokes, etc., as if he was still occupying his fleshly tenement.

"He is somewhat passionate, and frequently breaks crockery, or mars furniture, when he is offended.

"But he is easily coaxed. When company is expected, 'Josh' is importuned to keep quiet. Upon one occasion the young ladies were expecting company, and were particularly desirous that 'Josh' should keep perfectly still during the sojourn of the visitors.

"After receiving a thorough outlay of flattery and coaxing, he agreed to keep 'mum,' 'but,' said he, 'I shall remain here upon this end of the piano. There is no need of my leaving the room.'

"The next day he stated that he sat upon the piano during the visit, and to prove what he said, he repeated a portion of the conversation between the young ladies and their 'company.'

"At one time, when the laundress was ironing in the kitchen, 'Josh' seized one of the flat-irons and ran upstairs with it, where he was heard in high glee after the feat was accomplished. The iron was very hot, and by being placed momentarily on several of the stairs, left its imprint wherever it stood. Writing is a favourite amusement with this remarkable 'spirit.' He writes messages and throws them upon the floor quite frequently. His chirography is awful, and his orthography of the same pattern.

"'Josh' is very fond of children, and treats them with becoming consideration.

"When the adult members of the family leave the house, the children are entrusted to the special care and guardianship of the said spirit, and he, like a worthy ghost, leads them from all harm.

"This is only a meagre beginning of the story of 'Josh,' the spirit. It comes direct from a family of the highest respectability, and is corroborated by the statements of several 'neighbours,' who have also been favoured with frequent conversations from the disembodied individual above described."

The author is in possession of several other reports furnished by different individuals who were moved by curiosity to visit the haunted family at Medina, but as 'they contain but little variety, and the head of the family at last emphatically declined to furnish any farther information on the subject, the above extract will suffice. About the same time as these marvels were transpiring in Medina, a similar visitation occurred at Williamsport, Penn., and the extraordinary resemblance that appears between the two cases has led to the supposition that they both referred to the same phenomena.

The author's personal knowledge of the family who were the subjects of the following details, enables her to refute this statement, and to allege that the Williamsport talking Spirit was known and listened to by hundreds of curious visitors, and that the witnesses of this fact are numerous, respectable, and still living. We shall cite the report furnished by the *Penn. Bulletin* of June 16, 1859.

" TALKING SPIRITS.

"Williamsport has, through all times of excitement on Spiritualism, remained quiet and undisturbed. But our city is destined to have its share, even on this subject. . . .

"We suppress names for the present, because the family do not wish to be troubled by being made the centre of curiosity, or to have people rushing in at all hours to learn the truth. The facts are briefly these : In the west ward of this city reside a quiet family, exemplary in all respects, the heads of which are, and have been for a long time, members of the Pine Street M. E. Church. A short time ago they were surprised at certain, or, perhaps we should say, very uncertain sounds, as of rapping with the fingers or knuckles, and sometimes a scraping or scratching noise on the floor or wall.

"These sounds seemed to follow a young girl, about sixteen years of age, a daughter of the gentleman of the house. For a time they paid no attention to them ; but they increased in such a manner as to compel attention, and were apparently determined to be heard. What was more strange, was the fact that the spirit—or whatever it is—now *speaks in an audible voice.* At first it called the name of the young girl, and of other persons. The pious head of the family betook himself to prayer in order to lay the spirit, but it would not down.

"On Saturday evening last the pastor was sent for, and he, after convincing himself that there was no fraud on the part of the family, called in another aged and well-known clergyman. They both prayed, and the unseen visitant spoke audibly during the prayers of each. On Sunday morning the girl attended church with the family. There the rapping was heard by several, and the girl's name was called. Fearing to attract attention, she left the church. At a class-meeting, the same day, the same phenomena occurred.

"This much and a great deal more had occurred up to Sunday morning last. It seems to follow the girl, yet some demonstrations have occurred when she was out of the house. They have talked and rapped at her, or with her, while in the street, and on the gate, the door-steps, and other places ; and, as we understand, the talking has continued while the girl was absent from the house.

"The members of the family, with whom we conversed, say they are all satisfied that there is no possibility of trick or collusion in the matter on the part of any human being. The two clergymen pronounce the whole thing entirely inexplicable, and we are told that they also are satisfied that no member of the family has any agency in producing the sounds or the talking.

"The parties are too respectable to admit of the theory of collusion. Indeed, they are all greatly pained at the occurrences, and would gladly be rid of them.

"We await further developments, and will report if anything more definite transpires."

In the *West Branch Bulletin* of Williamsport, of February, 1860, are the following additional particulars : —

"MORE ABOUT THE 'TALKING SPIRITS.'

"We have taken some trouble to ascertain the facts connected with the singular case of noises and strange sounds which we reported last week. It seems that the girl, who appears to be the medium for these manifestations, is not of a robust constitution, but is quite nervous, and has, at times, been extremely ill.

"About a year ago she was playing with another girl about her own age, when both fell into a well. The subject of the present excitement was rescued alive ; but the other lost her life. The voice which speaks to the medium makes frequent allusions to this circumstance, generally in a trifling and taunting way. It will say, ' How would you like to be down in that well again ?' or 'How did you like it when you fell into the well ?'

"After the family had been greatly annoyed by strange sounds, knocking, thumping, etc., for several days, the girl said : 'In the name of God, what do you want ?'

"To their utter consternation, a voice replied, plainly and distinctly : 'You, you, you ! I want you !' and from this time talking was common.

"Not only would it follow the girl, but when she was up-stairs, and the other part of the family down, and in a different part of the house, the voice would speak to them. This seems to preclude the hypothesis of some specialty attaching to this girl. Men of candour and judgment, who were there and heard for themselves, have no idea that there was a possibility of any deception on the part of any of the family. If it is a spirit, it must be a mischievous one, or be among what Swedenborg calls the 'infernals.' At one time it said : 'I was in heaven once, but I did not like it there. I climbed over the battlements and came down here ; I am in hell now, and will have you there. We have to gnash our teeth some, but that don't hurt ; anybody can do that.'

"When a clergyman was spoken of, it expressed great contempt for him, and paid very little respect to him while in the attitude and act of prayer, in which all the family joined, as the voices and talking were irreverently continued.

"It said if the clergyman came again it would show him a cloven foot.

"We have conversed with a gentleman who sat near the 'medium' in church on Sunday morning week. He says the sounds were as loud as if made with a mallet, and the calling of the medium's name was heard by all in that part of the church. The officiating clergyman also heard the sounds at the same time.

"Since that Sunday evening or the Monday morning following, we learn that there have been no manifestations. The girl, from the effects of fright, and other exciting causes, is prostrated, and her case is considered very critical."

The following narrative is equally well known, and has been thoroughly investigated by the author. It is on the subject of the life, times, and doings of Bill Dole, both as a mortal and a Spirit, and we are furnished with numerous affidavits from the parties who have conversed with his invisible ghostship by the hour together. We have visited the scene of the hauntings too, and though the parties in whose house the marvels occurred have moved away, numerous residents of Logansport still bear their testimony to the facts, which we must briefly sum up as follows :—

It was very soon after the first commencement of the disturbances at Hydesville that a family named Lewis, German by birth, residing at Logansport, were annoyed by singular and unaccountable noises and erratic movements of their furniture. A sound too was often heard in their midst like the whining of a small animal, and this would taper off (to use their own expression) into low whisperings. The family were religiously disposed persons, and at no time were favourable to the idea of Spirit communion.

Greatly disliking publicity, and repelled from every attempt to communicate with their invisible tormentor, they endured these hauntings for some time without mentioning their occurrence, until, as the newspaper accounts relate, they were startled with distinctly audible vocal sounds.

At first their names only were called, then connected sentences were spoken, and finally an invisible personage established himself in the family, conversing with them as freely as any mortal inmate could do, and though annoying them greatly in respect to his supermundane character and ubiquitous presence, yet manifesting all the attributes, predilections, and characteristics of a regular member of the family. His own account of himself was, that he had been in earth life a tailor by trade, his name William, or as he chose to style himself, "Bill Dole."

Some accounts represent him as having been a man addicted to drink, and dying under the influence of delirium tremens; but the most authentic history of his exit from the mortal sphere, represents it as occurring through an act of suicide by drowning.

He affirmed that he had dwelt some time in the Spirit world, but found his position there very far from satisfactory; in fact, so contrary to his inclinations, that he had resolved not to stay there, and finding from some power in and about that family that he was unable to define, that he could make himself at home amongst them, he had resolved to take up his residence there; and "there he meant to stay," and *did stay*, for a period extending over upwards of two years.

Bill Dole's adventures in his self-elected home would occupy volumes, but we need not dwell on details which present a very great similarity of character, save to notice that the invisible performer was, as in each of the preceding instances, a person of entirely different habits and temper from his earthly associates. Bill Dole interlarded his conversation with rude oaths and profane remarks, besides manifesting extreme self-will, and when thwarted, propensities to violence, and even mischief. He would knock, pound, stamp his feet, run about the house with a great clatter, and "knock things around generally." He manifested a great contempt for orthodox religion, and on one occasion, when a clergyman, who frequently conversed and remonstrated with the Spirit, offered up a fervent prayer in his behalf, Bill Dole called out, in hearing of the minister and all assembled, "Well, I don't feel a d——d bit better for that."

On two or three occasions he accompanied the family to church, where his remarks were clearly heard by the whole congregation, who affirm that he pronounced the sermon preached at him, "all d——d stuff."

On other occasions he was heard to vociferate "Amen!" and "Good for you, old fellow!" (meaning the clergyman) with great unction.

Generally however, during religious service, at church or "to hum," as he called the house he favoured with his presence, he contented himself with making tremendous poundings, always giving two knocks for "Amen," or else calling out the Christian names of the lady or her daughters who were supposed to be the Mediums.

At times the cloth and every article necessary for a meal was laid suddenly, whilst the family were absent from the dining-room for the space of a minute or two. Bill would sometimes carry heavy loads about for them, and when in a good humour, perform many little kindly offices. He was especially fond of the children ; would guard and watch over them with wonderful power, and obvious affection ; indeed, their mother complained that Bill spoiled them, as he would get for them whatever they asked of him.

On one occasion, when the mother was preparing their lunch to take to school, Bill, in his usual authoritative way, desired that they should have some jam spread over their bread.

This they had asked him to procure for them, but the mother refused, alleging that it was not good for them. Bill swore they should have it, and during the recess in school time kept his word, by dropping down a pot of jam before them.

On several occasions when one of the daughters, to whom Bill seemed especially to attach himself, was indisposed, he would demand, with no gentle oaths, that she should not be sent out in the rain, or made to exercise herself in household work. On one occasion, when her throat was tied up with a severe cold, Bill lifted her into the house from the garden, carried out a basket, and gathered all the fruit and vegetables he could lay hands on ; then bringing it swiftly into the house, he set it on the hearth, lifted up the cover of a large saucepan, and tumbled the things he had gathered indiscriminately into the boiling water. At times he would attend when visitors were present, horrify them by moving things around without any visible agency, and scare them almost into fits by taking part in their conversation, and reminding them that he was the Bill Dole they had formerly known when he lived among them. On one occasion a lady, making a visit to the distressed family, incautiously expressed her disgust that a wretch of the well-known bad character of Bill Dole should, as report alleged, come back to make Spiritual manifestations.

She openly expressed her disbelief of the popular rumours, alleging that it must be some trick of the neighbours, which would ultimately be discovered. Whilst speaking, the family became extremely uneasy, judging from the kicks and poundings on a bureau in the apartment that the subject of the visitor's unfavourable criticisms was himself listening to them. Nor were they mistaken. In a few minutes the voice of the Spirit was heard in clear and distinct tones, saluting the visitor as "my dear," and asking affectionately after her little boy Arthur, "whom you know, my precious one," the mischievous imp added, "I am the real father of, though you do try to hide it by abusing me."

The tricks, gambols, and sometimes the mischief enacted by this monstrous persecutor were beyond all description weird and powerful.

By night and day his pranks were continued, and though he always yielded to the remonstrances of kindness or gentle entreaty, opposition and abuse only seemed to convert him into a being little short of a fiend. The little ones of the family dearly loved Bill Dole, and some witnesses of the scene informed the writer they had seen the children visibly carried, lifted, danced, and jumped about by their invisible attendant.

33

Mrs. Lewis, or "mother," as Bill called his hostess, had a log-house at some distance from her home, which was occupied by a tenant from whom it was impossible to obtain the rent. Bill, who became familiar with all the family affairs, and volunteered his advice on all occasions, offered to clear them out, if "the mother" would take him along to pay them a visit. This being agreed to, the landlady called on her tenants, together with her invisible ally.

The house had two doors at opposite sides of the building, which consisted of only one room. On these doors Bill kept up alternate successions of raps or poundings, which had no sooner summoned the inmates to one door, than the blows were exchanged for the other; and in this way he kept up a distracting noise all night, varying the performance by projecting missiles down the chimney, and dislodging portions of the roof.

The harassed inmates, at last comprehending that the "ghost of Bill Dole" had made a dead set against them, consented to vacate the premises, much to the delight of the injured owner, who desired, next to the payment of her rent, that the obnoxious inmates would quit.

Bill Dole spent his time in this way, performing services for the family, and especially for the children, with all the rough fidelity of a household demon.

It seemed that the attachment he conceived for his entertainers might have become mutual, and actually reconciled them to the strange and mysterious guest who had forced himself upon them, but the weird reputation which "Bill Dole's ghost" brought on the household, the influx of marvel seekers that intruded on their privacy, and the scandal and reproach that the circumstances entailed upon them, at last so wearied the family that they positively refused to communicate for, or with the Spirit any longer.

They broke up, and changed their household and all their plans of life, until they finally succeeded in driving their unwelcome visitor from them.

The voice ceased, and even the loud knockings and erratic movements of furniture were discontinued. Bill Dole was driven away, and his weird voice and mystic presence at last past from human observance, but not from memory. There are still hundreds of persons in Logansport who remember to have heard him converse, and can contribute items of hearsay evidence to this brief notice, which would, if published, swell the narrative to the full extent of the volume.

We have only to add, that all which our space has permitted us to publish can be vouched for on the most undeniable authority. Beyond this, much more might be given which we cannot as readily prove, but which no doubt would throw light on its extraordinary details. Something of a sequel, however, we will add to the history which may not prove uninteresting.

After conversing with a gentleman from Logansport who was well acquainted with the whole transaction, and had frequently held conversations with "Bill Dole," a Spirit purporting to be that individual presented himself one night to the author, and desired to make a communication to her concerning his present situation.

He affirmed that when driven away, as he called it, from his earthly refuge, he wandered around for a long time, in the vain hope of finding another home in the same sphere. Not succeeding, he fell into a state of bitter anguish of mind, during which he received consolation and assistance from kind and wise Spirits, who counselled him to lift his thoughts above the earth, and strive to elevate his aspirations to the better land, to which, as a Spirit, he now belonged. At first the task seemed hopeless, as his grovelling tendencies and earth-bound nature rendered aspiration almost impossible. He loathed the sphere to which, as a profane and undeveloped Spirit, he had formerly gravitated, and yet, though longing for a higher condition, he found it almost impossible to earn admission to those brighter realms.

At length, and by the divine aid of blest angels from the land of light, he attained once more to a happy and peaceful home, and one moreover where he was a welcome guest, and assimilated with the Spiritual existence of which he was a part.

In short, he had passed on to a higher life, and when idly solicited by some who had witnessed his marvellous performances to repeat them for their amusement, he gently but kindly replied, that though his life was now devoted to the task of pleasing and obliging others, yet he had lost the physical aura which had once bound him to earth, and enabled him in its gross atmosphere to perform the material feats which had distinguished him as an earth-bound Spirit. "Bill Dole," such as he was, exists no more. The sunlit butterfly has arisen from the chrysalitic shell of the earthly worm, and he now "sings with the angels," instead of astounding the marvel seekers of earth with the dread sound of his ghostly merriment and terrible Spirit voice.

The credibility of this part of the narrative depends on the fact that the author's description of the Spirit's appearance, tallied exactly with the facts, and that some tokens of identity were given by her to a party who had been personally acquainted with him, which rendered it more than probable that the above statements were made by the progressed Spirit of the terrible "Bill Dole."

SPIRITUAL EXPERIENCES OF MR. JOHN LOWE OF MASSILLON, OHIO.
CARDS WRITTEN UPON BY THE HANDS OF SPIRITS.

In the author's possession are some twenty or thirty small cards, ranging from two to three inches, square and oblong square. Some are plain white, others pink, blue, and green enamelled ; the white cards are written upon with a pencil or black ink, the coloured ones chiefly in silver or gold letters. The writing consists of brief sentences containing words of encouragement, counsel, Scriptural phrases, prophecy, and rebuke. Occasionally there are short communications addressed by name to different members of a circle, of a personal and private nature, *apropos* to the time.

The chirography of these cards is extremely fine, and executed apparently by the same hand. They all purport to come direct from Spirits, and were dropped under the most convincing conditions, in the presence of numerous witnesses, sometimes, though rarely, in the dark, but still oftener in the broad day or lamp light. It appears that these manifestations originated with a circle of sincere and earnest believers in Spiritualism, who were in the habit of holding private *séances* amongst themselves at Canton, Ohio. Of the members of this circle, the principal Mediums were Mr. George Baugh, an excellent physical Medium now residing in Wilmington, Delaware ; Mr. John Lowe, an Englishman, a good writing test Medium ; and Mr. Peter Jones. There were from twelve to twenty members of the original circle, and the whole party consisted of honest, respectable tradesmen and mechanics, persons who had nothing to gain by their reputation as Spiritualists, but very much to lose, in point of custom and credit, with their neighbours.

After two or three years' session in Canton, some of the members removed to Massillon, Ohio, where the circle was re-organized, and the manifestations continued with increasing success for a considerable time longer.

The records of these circles were occasionally published in the local papers, and contain accounts of truly astonishing phenomena, both in the direction of physical force, and intelligence.

Mr. Lowe and his associates are well known and highly esteemed by all who know them.

They frankly admitted sceptical inquirers to their sittings, and the author has received the testimony of over twenty of the most prominent citizens of Massillon to the perfect good faith, sincerity, and respectability of all the parties concerned.

One or two of these witnesses attribute the manifestations to "evil spirits," although they acknowledge that some of the fruit was good, and all "generally harmless." Others say the whole thing was fanaticism and delusion, though they exculpate the members of the circle from the charge of being the deluders, and believe them to be strictly honest. Who the real executants were, these sage witnesses cannot say, although they are quite sure they cannot be Spirits, for the very obvious reason "that they don't believe in Spirits;" further deponent sayeth not.

In respect to the manifestations, we find that besides the usual phenomena accompanying physical force Mediumship, the circle were continually in the habit of receiving cards written as above described, and dropped down on their table whilst in session, or hidden away in the most singular and uncomeatable places, where different members of the circle were desired to look for them.

Sometimes cards and direct Spirit writings would be dropped down in the stores or houses of the sitters.

A manifestation of this kind is described by Mr. Henry Schneider, of Massillon, one of the circle, who, though a firm believer in the agency of Spirits, strangely enough deemed that they were all evil in character, and of Satanic origin. Mr. Schneider writes to the author that being one day in the store of Mr. Lowe (who is a tailor), he and another friend turned the conversation upon his favourite theory of "evil Spirits," when, his companions being each quietly engaged in their several avocations, and all in the full light under his own immediate observation, he saw a small card within a few inches of the solid ceiling, from whence it fluttered down through the air, falling on the floor at Mr. Schneider's feet.

On one side of the card was written, "Be ye faithful, and ere long your cause shall triumph. Ye shall find wealth in the earth, and wonderful revelations shall be made known unto you."

"YOUR 'GOOD SPIRIT.'"

On the other side of the card were mystical characters claimed by the Spirits to be Spiritual language.

On another occasion a card was dropped down before Mr. Lowe on which was inscribed, "Spirits are with you; let them communicate."

This remark was appropriate to the special occasion, but Mr. Lowe himself had some unpleasant doubts respecting the identity of the communicating power.

He however placed the card, after a thorough examination by himself and all present, in his waistcoat pocket. On arriving at his home and taking out the card for the purpose of showing it to others, he found on the reverse side, written in the same Spiritual chirography as the rest of the cards, " Lowe's Spirit."

This writing greatly perplexed him. He knew it had come whilst he carried it home, for it had been carefully examined by every one present at the circle before he placed it in his pocket ; again, he questioned whether these words might not signify that his own double or living Spirit was indicated by the words, " Lowe's Spirit."

On a subsequent occasion he was informed that his father's Spirit was the executant, and the words were meant as a rebuke to himself for questioning the good intent and individuality of those who made these manifestations.

As a specimen of the poetry received through these direct writings, we quote the following stanzas, which purported to be written, as well as dictated, by the Spirit of the English poet, Cowper:—

" TRUTH.

" Truth is like a flowing river,
Flowing on and flowing ever ;
Ever spreading, ever rising,
With its waves the heart baptizing ;
Ever soothing, ever healing,
Banishing each troubled feeling ;
Entering in the willing soul,
Making the broken-hearted whole.

" Stay not thou the flowing tide,
Turn not thou its waves aside ;
Let it ever freely enter
To thy bosom's inmost centre,
Let it warm the heart of ice,
Purifying guilt and vice,
Till the soul redeemed from sin,
To God and heaven shall enter in."

The chirography of this fragment is bolder and wholly different from the cards, although it is remarkably clear and elegant.

It was " fluttered down " from the ceiling in the light, and in full view of the whole circle. We shall conclude by a quotation from the Buffalo *Sunbeam* of 1861, in which the editor gives a slight account of the Canton circle and its doings, compiled by a gentleman whose prominent position as a well-known editor, and strict truthfulness of character, places his statement beyond question.

The Canton editor says :—

" We have long known that our town contained a large number of downright, manly, and sincere Spiritualists, who for years have been pursuing their investigations quietly, and following their respective avocations in their own way.

" We ave frequently conversed with them on the subject of the spiritual manifestations that have from time to time been had during their sittings, and have always admired the truthfulness of their statements, and the sincerity with which they were made. . . . .

" Communications were frequently given by writing on cards. We copy the description of one of the first messages :—

" ' On producing a light, a card about three inches in length, one and one half inches in width, one side of a light pink colour and enamelled, and the other side white, was found on the table. On the enamelled side was written in pencil, in skilful and delicate chirography : " The hands of spirits are now lifting the veil fold by fold. Be not afraid."

" On one occasion the circle, or some members of it, were sent to a public hall, with instructions where to find the key, which no one present, it is affirmed, knew anything about at this time. The following is the message written on a card like the one described above :—

" ' On the south-west window of Madison Hall there is a message,—depart ye hence and receive it. Take no light but the light of your faith. The key you will find hanging on a nail to the right, first door entrance, about four feet from the floor.'

" Two persons went to the place as directed without a light, and failing to find the key, the arm of one of the parties was moved without his will, and his hand placed upon it. We quote a portion of the message there found :—

" ' A PROPHECY.—Some of you are to be to this earth as Elisha and Elijah were in golden days that long since have flown. Return to-morrow eve, at the same hour, half-past eight.'

" March 6th.—The circle met at half-past eight o'clock ; a card was dropped on the table inscribed. At 'half-past eight' Dr. M——, Mr. C——, and Mr. Lowe, went to Madison Hall. Mr. Lowe unlocked the door at the foot of the stairs leading directly to the hall, and the three ascended the stairs to the door opening into the hall, when it swung open untouched ; the three were close together, and all saw a light in the south end of the room, at a platform there erected, and called the speaker's stand ; at seeing which Mr. Lowe gave an exclamation of surprise, and immediately there arose at the desk on the speaker's stand a figure which, after the manner of Leigh Hunt, we shall call 'a presence,' in white drapery, of full size and features, plainly seen by all. It was surrounded by a halo of soft mellow light, which was so brilliant that Mr. Lowe assures us he could have seen a half-dime on the floor.

" At this juncture Mr. C—— became alarmed, and sought safety in flight ; Mr. Lowe was about to follow, when Dr. M—— took him by the collar, and told him ' he must see it through.' During all this time ' the presence ' stood facing the visitors, with its right arm extended, the right hand clasping a roll, similar to a sheet of paper rolled to an inch or two inches in size.

" Immediately to the right of ' the presence,' and toward the southeast corner of the room, rose a second volume of light, accompanied with a slight hissing sound. As the sound increased, the latter light faded away. Then came a rumbling noise like the heavy rolling of far-off thunder. On hearing that, Mr. Lowe broke for the door, the doctor following, and both making the best of the time.

" At the foot of the stairs, on the sidewalk, stood Mr. C——, and the three went to Mr. B——'s, and resumed the sitting. In a short time came another card of the same kind of paper, inscribed, ' O, ye of little faith ! how it saddens our hearts that ye should flee at the critical moment when important revelations were about to be made.' The circle was then informed that further developments would be made at some future day.

" Much else is detailed of a very interesting character, but we can make room for only the following messages, the first being given February 24th.

" ' Be of good cheer, for brighter days are about to dawn, and a new light shall envelop the world. Prepare for the coming glory by purifying your lives and conquering your evil passions. Let pure water be your only beverage. Let your raiment be plain and comfortable, without regard to fashion. Truth is light, and truth shall triumph.

" ' (Signed)   MARY.'

" We copy from another card, received by a circle at Mr. B——'s on the 26th of February :—

" ' Be ye faithful and proclaim to the world the things ye have seen and heard, for in the fulness of time men will believe.'

" ' I am the voice of one crying in the wilderness, Repent, for the kingdom of heaven is at hand.'

" The parties to whom these messages were delivered, still doubting the propriety of publishing them, met again on Thursday night the 28th, at Mr. Lowe's, and again they were ordered ' to publish to the world the things which they had seen and heard,' as appears from the following message, which we copy from the original, precisely as it was received, and which was handed to us by Mr. Lowe.

" ' O, ye faithless ones, how long must we bear with your unbelief ? Have we not manifested ourselves unto you ? And have not some of you witnessed things which but few mortals are permitted to behold ? And yet ye turned and fled at the moment when great revelations were about to be made. Have we not commanded you to publish these things to the world, and ye have not done it ?

" ' Have we not commanded other things which ye have not done ?

" ' If ye cannot keep these light commandments how can we trust greater ones to your keeping ? Obey our directions at once, or we must seek another and more faithful circle through which to make our revelations to the world.

" ' (Signed)   YOUR GUARDIAN SPIRITS.' "

Direct writing from Spirits is by no means a rare phenomenon, but the Spirit cards presented to Mr. Lowe and his associates were continued for such a length of time (a space of several years) and occurred, without the least shadow of suspicion attaching to the parties concerned, in the presence of so many respectable witnesses, that it renders the whole transaction one of peculiar and noteworthy interest.

The original circle is now broken up, and its members scattered far and wide over the country, but from many of them the author has received the assurance that the good counsel, directing wisdom, comfort, and consolation conveyed in those precious scraps of writing, formed a gift beyond all price to those who were favoured with them. Also, that during the continuance of these inestimable messages, the recipients were " all better and purer men ;" the time employed in this communion, "the best spent of their lives," and the result, an enduring testimony in each one's heart that mankind has "entertained angels unawares."

It has often been asserted that the manifestations occurring in the form of hauntings, or what the Germans call the *Polter-Gheist* or *the ghost which throws*, are the work of "evil Spirits," the result of "Satanic agency," and should be treated with all the formulæ of exorcism, &c., &c., but never admitted as legitimate proofs of the relations subsisting between the mundane and super-mundane spheres of being. It is a remarkable fact that these sage opinions are never shared by the parties who have received the manifestations. On the contrary, they invariably acknowledge, as good Dr. Eliakim Phelps has done to the author, that stupendous and violent demonstrations of Spirit presence are doubtless absolutely necessary to convince some sceptical minds, that many persons could never be otherwise moved, and that there seems no just cause for supposing that the Spirits who are the agents in such riotous proceedings, act without due guidance and supervision from higher intelligences, in fact, there are many careful observers who contend, that without the obvious and super-mundane demonstrations produced by Spirits of a very corporeal nature, the world in this sceptical age would never have believed in the fact of Spirit communion at all. The following curious history was communicated to the author by the gentleman in whose experience it happened, and beneath the very roof made memorable by the occurrences narrated. This gentleman subsequently embodied the main facts in a small pamphlet, entitled, "The Oakland Ghost," his aim in publication being, as he stated ; first, to put on record circumstances liable to be misrepresented when left to the mercy of the local press or the tongue of rumour ; next, to advise all who were acquainted with him—and, as a public man, his circle of acquaintances is a very large one—that he was not ashamed to testify to the truth as he understood it ; and finally, he wished to draw a parallel between his own experiences, with other cases narrated in history, deemed far more authentic —because they are antiquated, and cannot be verified—than when they occur under the immediate supervision of scores of living and thoroughly reliable witnesses. We shall avail ourselves of Mr. Brownell Clarke's pamphlet to record his statements rather than draw upon the mere remembrance of his oral descriptions.

The occurrences about to be narrated took place at the Clarke Mansion, Oakland, California, in the month of April, 1874.

The proprietor of the house is a gentleman holding a high and honourable official position, and one who previous to the ensuing occurrences, was a devoted member of a Christian church in which his good standing and that of his family were beyond all shadow of doubt or question. Two ladies and two gentlemen occupied rooms in Mr. Clarke's house, and as he did not feel at liberty to cite their opinions in support of his own, he alludes to these parties only by their initials.

It may be proper to add however, that they are all as well known as the author of the pamphlet, Mr. Thomas Brownell Clarke, himself, and being alluded to as residents in his house, they have had every opportunity of refuting his published statements had they been so disposed. We shall now give such quotations from Mr. Clarke's pamphlet as relate strictly to the phenomena occurring, omitting for the sake of brevity the observations and reflections of the observers concerning those phenomena about which all parties were at that time profoundly ignorant.

THE OAKLAND GHOST——ACCOUNT OF MANIFESTATIONS.

[*By Thomas Brownell Clarke.*]

"That the reader may form an intelligent idea of the manifestations, it will be necessary first to give a brief description of the house and its occupants. It is a one and a half story house, situated in Oakland, California. The first floor has five rooms——the second four. The house for a number of years previous to becoming my residence, had been occupied by a purely orthodox family. No murders had ever been committed within its walls at the time previous to these manifestations. Myself, wife, and son of eight years, occupied as private room, one in the ell opening from the dining room ; Mrs. F—— and sister and my daughter, the two front rooms in the second story; Mr. B—— and Mr. O—— the two in the rear. The evening in question, April 23rd, 1874, the family had been at home as usual. Mr. B—— and Mr. O—— had been at a neighbour's and did not return until a quarter past eleven o'clock. Having retired, but hearing them come in, I requested them to lock the doors and put out the lights. When the gentlemen had been up stairs about fifteen minutes, I heard a noise that seemed to be at the front door as though the gong upon it had been lightly struck. I went immediately there, but found no one. I closed the door and returned to bed. Hardly had I laid down, before that same noise was repeated, but much louder ; again I went to the door, and found no one— I stepped out on the porch, it being a bright moonlight night, looked in all directions for any one who could have rung the bell, but saw no one, and so returned in doors—as I did so I spoke to Mr. B—— whose room was at the head of the stairs, asking him if he was making any noise with his clock. He replied, no—and asked who is ringing that bell—I replied, that is what I wish to know. Immediately he came rushing down the stairs with pistol in hand, and said "that is some boy's work," and out of the door he went and around the house, but found no boy. When he came in, we had quite a conversation as to who had been the cause of this sound, but had to give up any solution and again retired ; but a few moments, and there was a tremendous shaking of furniture in the dining-room, as though some one was rattling the upright piano that stood there. Mr. B—— hearing this, pistol in hand, came rushing down. We met to see no one, and were still more astonished than ever. While talking, Mr. B—— walked into the hall, and when opposite the parlour door, he exclaimed in an excited manner, 'Clarke, bring a light, quick !' I was there in about one second, when Mr. B—— rushed over behind the sofa, and then to the bay window. Finding one fastening unclasped, he said, 'That fellow has gone out at the window.' Turning around, and seeing a small reception chair lying in the centre of the parlour, I said, 'How came it there?' B—— replied, 'I know nothing about it, I did not touch it, but there was a man struck me on the back when I called you.' Our astonishment is better imagined than described. Meantime I had dressed myself, lighted some lamps; the people above were aroused and conversation as to who or what was doing these things became general. As we again retired to our separate rooms, we heard a loud rattling noise in the parlour, as though bundles of sheet iron had been slammed down on the floor. In about two seconds I was there, and only found the blower lying in the centre of the room. The gentlemen hearing the noise came rushing from their rooms, with 'What made that noise?' My daughter, who had slipped on a morning dress and come from her room, stood talking to the gentlemen, each of whom had a lamp in his hand; I was standing in the hall below; she started to come down stairs, and when about two-thirds down Mr. B—— saw a basket of silver belonging to him, valued at about three hundred dollars, rise from a bureau standing in the extreme end of the hall. He instantly exclaimed, 'Take care, Nellie!' Having some instinctive knowledge of danger, she screamed, and turned the newel post just in time to escape the basket, that coming down in a half circle, fell with a thud on the floor at the foot of the stairs. All supposed the silver ruined as a matter of course; I picked up the basket and contents and carried them to the dining-room, where we all assembled to examine, which we did, piece by piece, finding no injury on coffee or tea pots, creamer or bowl, save only one very thin silver vase which was slightly bruised.

"Presently Mr. O—— went outside to take a little fresh air, to strengthen his nerves, when we heard a noise in his room, directly over us as though a person was jumping with all his might upon the floor. Mr. B—— and myself rushed up into the room, but found no one—neither anything disturbed. While there, Mr. O—— came up to his room—walked to a chair in which lay a towel rolled into a bunch. He picked it up as though to wipe his hands; as he did so, he, as well as we, discovered his watch and chain lying on the chair. His amazement cannot be described. He exclaimed, 'How came that watch in the chair?' I said, 'I suppose you placed it there.' He said, 'I tell you I left it with the chain run through the button hole, hooked back into the pocket, and on that bed.' As he took the watch from the chair it sprang up, clipping Mr. B—— on the elbow, and landed in the centre of the bed. It now seemed that wonders would never cease, so we descended to the dining-room, and commenced an inquiry meeting as to the causes of these wonderful phenomena.

"While thus speculating, one of the solid oak chairs rose about one foot, and with the velocity of a boy's top, went revolving across the room some ten feet, and sat down as still as though it had never moved. . . . .

"While still in the dining-room, there came a great crash in the hall; we rushed to see what new development had occurred, and found a box 15 × 15 inches square, 6 deep, that had contained about twenty lbs. of coal, which stood in the upper hall, had been thrown over the baluster and down stairs. I picked up the box with what coal I could, and carried them to the kitchen. Then came another of our scientific discussions upon electrical, magnetic, natural, supernatural, and occult forces. While thus engaged, another most frightful noise came from the parlour. Rushing in there, we found the same blower lying in the middle of the room bottom up, which, when I picked it up previously, I had placed on the hearth face downwards.

"Some one had gone upstairs to tell the ladies what had happened, and while thus talking, a large upholstered chair, standing in the hall, went whirling around, and down in full view of all. Hardly was this new fact well settled, before from the parlour came another racket. Upon going there we found the same small reception chair that once before had been laid in the centre of the room again lying in the same place. In the mean time the family had assembled in the dining-room, discussing this phenomena. While thus engaged, another heavy oak chair rose and spinning like a top, crossed the room in a contrary direction from the previous one. It now being about one o'clock, Mr. B—— had taken his lamp in his hand, and standing in the hall door leaning against the casing, said, 'Well, I am going to bed, and I won't get up again if they take the end of the house out.' No sooner had the words ceased than a large upholstered chair rose a few inches, and spinning around, fell out in the middle of the room.

"After a while, wearied with this display of legerdemain by an unseen power, peace and quiet seeming to have come again, we retired to our various rooms in hopes to get a little rest. We were hardly there, however, when the whole house was shaken, as by a wave of the sea against a ship. Mr. B—— came rushing out, calling, 'Was that an earthquake?' While we were talking of this new phenomenon, heavy raps began all over the house, which continued for some minutes, appearing to some to be inside the house, and to the others outside. It may well be imagined that to a sleepy household at that time of night, the novelty soon wore off, and again we scattered in various parts of the house with the determination not to get up again, come whatever might. Hardly had I laid down when I heard a few low, sharp raps, appearing to be in the dining-room. Mrs. Clarke also heard the same, and noticed them because of their peculiar sound. In a few moments more, we heard the same kind of raps. As I had made up my mind not to be disturbed any more, I declined to get up, or even look to see the cause. For a while everything remained quiet, and we felt encouraged that peace had again come to our household; but in a few minutes there came a crashing sound from the parlour, as though some one was making kindling wood of the furniture. The ladies directly overhead, remarked, 'There goes over that marble-top table in the parlour, and everything upon it is ruined.' This noise brought me out in about one second, and the gentleman downstairs in the same time.

"We found, lying in the centre of the parlour, that same reception chair, for the third time—this time a long shawl, that had been folded and lying in the parlour, was opened and spread very carefully over the chair. Two large upholstered chairs had been turned around and laid on their backs—the same blower was again laid in the centre of the room, and a dining chair, face down, was lying upon one end of the table. Upon further examination I found another dining chair laid upon its side, and a small goblet I had drank out of only a short time before, and set down where the chair now lay, had been moved to the other end of the table, and turned bottom up. There seemed to be no end to the diversity of demonstrations. Being tired of putting things to rights, which had been my occupation now about two hours, I said, for the benefit of these unseen powers, that I should put up no more furniture, and they could go on and throw around as much as they pleased; and thus I left the furniture as it lay. As morning was drawing near, all well tired out one by one, scattered to obtain some little rest. But in a few moments there came the sound of a terrible crash in the hall that seemed as though Mr. B——'s request had been granted, and the end of the house had been torn bodily away. As quick as thought I was in the front hall. The two gentlemen made their appearance at the top of the stairs about the same time. We found the front door had been lifted or removed from its hinges without withdrawing the bolt, and now stood leaning against the newel post, and we had the opportunity of looking upon a beautiful moonlight through where the door ought to be. Locks, bolts, and even the door itself seemed no impediment to this power. Thus ended the first act of occult demonstrations in the 'Clarke Mansion.'

"The morning of the 24th, Mr. B—— arose about half-past six o'clock, and went over to his place across the street to attend to personal business matters. My daughter came downstairs soon after and requested that we would let the furniture remain, as she wished to go and invite a neighbour to come in and see what had been done. Very soon after we heard considerable noise. Mrs. Clarke went to the kitchen and questioned the boy as to whether or not he had upset a table or made noise otherwise—finding nothing she returned; when immediately Miss B—— came in and said, 'Why, you didn't tell me that the sofa had been turned over.' To which I replied neither has it. 'Oh, yes, it has, and lies flat on its back.' Upon going into the parlour, we found not only the sofa wheeled around in front of the grate, and then laid on its back; but also a zinc safe that weighed eleven pounds, had been taken from a whatnot and placed upon the back of one of the chairs thrown down the night before. Three books were taken from the whatnot on the floor; a pair of gloves were lying side by side; also a small wooden puzzle had been moved to the middle of the room, and a paper covered book was standing on end among the sundries. At about a quarter past seven o'clock, my daughter returned with her friends to see the midnight orgies, but was much astonished at the new display of furniture scattered about the floor. Another convention was held, including our outside friends, which discussion culminated in eating our breakfast, and enjoining secrecy upon all within the house. By some oversight the young man that came with my daughter was not told to keep silent on this scene, so that while we three inmates of the household passed to San Francisco in silence about the matter, this young man thought it a good joke, and going over on the boat told a few friends about it. From this the story spread. About twelve o'clock, I was requested to enlighten a gentleman in regard to it, but turned the subject by telling him that he was 'sold' by some one and passed on. About two o'clock a reporter called to get particulars; I did not wish to tell a falsehood, and neither could I imagine how the rumour had got about town. I said to the reporter that it was true that a few chairs moved quite singularly, that I supposed that would be the last of it, and I hoped they would not give it public notice. Lest I should be visited by other reporters, I immediately left for Oakland. The *San Francisco Chronicle* having heard of the rumour, and as it calls itself a 'live paper,' could not bear to go to press without improvement of the opportunity for a sensational article. Consequently one of their reporters who had a vivid imagination, wrote a two-column article, in regard to dancing silver ware, crockery, furniture, &c., at the 'Clarke mansion,' in Oakland, which article appearing on the morning of the 25th, as might have been expected, set the town in a perfect uproar, discussing the 'Oakland Ghost.' . . . .

"April 24th.—The family remained the same as the previous night, except that I had sent our litttle boy in the country. Mr. O—— had gone out to spend the evening, and did not return until quite late. At about half-past eight, while we were sitting in the dining-room, my daughter remarked that after the previous wakeful night, she felt tired and thought she would retire. When she was about half way up stairs, recollecting the scene of the basket of silver coming at her the night before, I said jokingly, 'Nellie, look out for your head.' She replied, 'Oh! it is not time for them to begin yet.' Instantly a large upholstered chair standing at the head of the stairs, went revolving and lay down across the stairway preventing her getting up. I came to the rescue immediately, and picking up the chair put it again in its place. The ladies became very much excited, much more so than on the previous night, and especially Mrs. F——, who declared that she could not live through another such night of horror as the previous one, especially as this had commenced so early. During our rambling conversation of what had been, and what we must do, especially in regard to Mrs. F——, Mr. R—— came from his room and went out of doors. While my family were in the dining-room talking of these things, there came another crash as though a dozen chairs had been crushed in pieces in the hall. As I reached the foot of the stairs, I found one of a set of reception chairs that had been standing in the hall above. Upon examination, though a very delicate chair, I found no injury, not even a scratch; I then proposed to go for a friend, but the ladies all said, No, you must not leave us alone. So I waited for Mr. B——, who soon came in, and while we were standing near the head of the stairs my daughter stepped a short distance into Mr. O——'s room. Hardly had she done so when the chairs went flying around that room. I then left for a friend, whom I found at the City Hall. He with four others returned to the 'haunted house,' where we found everything had been quiet during my absence. These gentlemen after sitting for about half-an-hour began to get tired, and were about to leave, when a rattling was heard at the top of the stairs. Upon examination we found that a large upholstered chair had been going through its accustomed evolutions, and again laid down on the floor. It was but a few moments when there came another crash in the hall, one of the gentlemen exclaiming, 'There is a chair crushed all to pieces.' Upon examination they found a duplicate of the chair that had previously been thrown over the balusters down at the foot of the stairs entirely uninjured. Upon further examination they found that when it came over it struck the wall with such force as to make two indentations in the plastering with the two hind legs. To our agreeable surprise this was the last manifestation of the night, and though watching the entire night no more demonstrations came.

"The sensational article appearing in the *Chronicle* of the 25th, created so much excitement, that our residence was surrounded by hundreds of curious people, looking at the 'haunted house,' during the following day. Friends came and went, wondering how and who, or by what power had these things been done. The 'Oakland Ghost' became the general theme of conversation.

"Having remained at home, I was visited by the *Chronicle* reporter, who had procured a letter of introduction from a friend, and came for further information. Seeing that I was already notorious in connection with this mysterious affair, I thought best to tell him the truth about it, and consequently, gave to the press the items, as they had occurred.

"As evening came on, with it also came the crowd in increased force. Mr. B—— and Mr. O—— went out soon after dinner, and did not return till after ten o'clock.

"Early in the evening, friends and acquaintances began to call, and of course every one was anxious to know of this new wonder.

"While sitting in the parlour engaged in conversation with various callers from Oakland and San Francisco, at about nine o'clock, we all heard distinct rapping, that appeared as though the sills under the dining-room had been struck by a heavy sledge-hammer.

"Upon going into that room, we found Mrs. F——and my daughter, quite excited. They said those heavy raps were directly under Mrs. F——'s feet. As a matter of course, this was interesting to our visitors, however annoying it might be to us. During this examination we had nearly all gone into the dining-room. One gentleman remained, and while standing in the hall, the large chair at the head of the stairs went whirling around in a most mysterious manner, and down on its side as on the previous evening. This evolution was made in full view of the two ladies up stairs.

"This renewed the interest of our visitors, and created an intense excitement among the crowd outside, who had heard the noise made by the falling chair. Visitors, in the meantime, had increased, and conversation upon the new wonder became general. While thus engaged, a continuous sound, as though proceeding from a silver tea bell in the china closet in the dining-room, was heard all over the house. The sound continued for a moment after the door was opened, but no striking of the hammer was made.

"A few moments after this, an old bell in the kitchen rang quite violently. Hardly had we returned from the kitchen, when over the balusters was thrown down into the hall, two paper boxes ; one empty, the other containing a lady's hat, a covered willow basket, and a small leather bag, which were stored in the hall, making so much noise as to be heard outside, making the crowd almost furious to get into the house. The basket I laid in the hall below, and carried the boxes and bag upstairs, putting them on the floor in the hall. Very soon after this performance, one of the small reception chairs was thrown over the balusters and down stairs, without harm.

"About this time Mr. B—— and Mr. O—— came in.

"While people walked to and fro, not knowing from where would come the next development, as quick as a lightning flash, which was the character of all the movements, the same upholstered chair at the head of the stairs, went revolving in mid air and down, in the presence of Mr. F——, who stood in Mr. B——'s door talking to him, and in the presence of Miss B——, who stood in the door of her room directly opposite.

"A great rush was made for this point by the friends in the house, not even respecting the privacy of the ladies' room where Mrs. F—— was constantly in bed. This chair having been the means of great annoyance to us thus far, I placed it in Mr. O——'s room where it would be less likely to disturb us. The ladies at the time protested, saying ' If you do not leave it, who can tell that they will not throw the bureau down,' referring to a large, old-fashioned mahogany bureau with mirror on top, that stood in the hall at the head of the stairs close to the wall, and close in the corner. Quiet having followed this last demonstration, and the house getting nearly full of acquaintances, we were compelled to have some one constantly at the door to prevent strangers from entering, for this thing of having our yard overrun with the crowd, and our house overflowing with friends on such an errand, was to us a great nuisance. While the crowd were scattered in parlour, dining-room, and hall, Mr. S——, who was standing at the foot of the stairs, looking directly up at the bureau, saw it begin to jump about, and in an instant, fall forward, being caught on the turn of the baluster, falling so hard, that it indented the mahogany rail a quarter of an inch, and jarred the uprights of the balusters loose in their sockets, making so much noise, that it was heard by the hundreds outside. The gentlemen in the hall rushed up to right the bureau ; but before so doing, were careful to look for springs or contrivances of any kind, by which this could have been done, and found none ; but they did find that this heavy bureau had been moved forward about one foot, and endwise about one foot, before being tipped ; also, that notwithstanding the force that could indent a mahogany rail, the marble of the bureau was not broken ; and more remarkable still, the mirror upon the top was unharmed.

"At this time, five gentlemen well known to me, came to the door, and requested to be admitted with the privilege of remaining in the house all night. I acceded to their request and have their evidence to close the mouths of all vilifiers of their neighbours' characters. At the request of the ladies, I again brought out the chair as the lesser evil, and set it at the end of the bureau in the hall, where it had previously stood, and from whence it had performed its various evolutions. As usual, between the acts, quiet in good measure reigned. Mr. S——, who stood at the foot of the stairs, in a few moments, saw this same upholstered chair going through its accustomed evolutions, but this time it started down stairs, end for end, and was caught by him. Inthis descent, one of the legs was broken, being the first harm that had happened to any one or anything, save the small, thin, silver vase. Soon after this, the chairs in Mr. O——'s room were heard moving about, and upon examination were found lying on the floor in a promiscuous manner. As it was getting late, one by one our friends were leaving, until the house seemed again at rest. A number of us were sitting in the parlour, among them Mr. O—— sitting in a large Turkish chair reading a newspaper. While thus sitting, to the great astonishment of us all, he sprang from the chair, landing on the other side of the room, exclaiming, 'Heavens, that chair was going up with me!' My daughter saw the chair rise from the floor before he sprang ; I saw it immediately after. This was followed by a good hearty laugh at Mr. O—— for his fright ; this being the first time his calmness had deserted him ; in fact, fear is not a quality of any of that household, including Mrs. F——, the invalid, for when she did leave, it was that she might get rest—not from fear. After this, Mr. O——, thinking that this thing would never end, and that he must have rest, retired to his room with the intent of remaining for the night. The balance of our friends, save those expecting to spend the night, had all left. Myself and four of the gentlemen were seated in the parlour ; one was standing in the hall. Almost imperceptibly to us all, the hat-box containing the lady's hats that I had put on the floor in the hall above, was silently set directly in the parlour door. Again I carried it up stairs, but for safe keeping, placed it in a ladies' room. It now being about twelve o'clock, the crowd outside, well tired of looking at the 'haunted house,' and seeing nothing, had nearly all left. Mr. O——, feeling somewhat nervous while in his room, changed his mind, and concluded he would not retire, but again go down stairs and sit awhile longer. As he came from his room he closed his door. Looking directly up the stair-way, to my utter astonishment, I saw a trunk strike the wall, fly past me, and set down at the foot of the stairs. Upon getting in the hall, Mr. O—— exclaimed, 'That is my trunk.' I rushed upstairs, found my daughter and Mr. B—— looking down, who asked what it was that had made that noise I said it is O——d's trunk. 'Nonsense,' said Mr. B——, 'why his door has not been opened.' My daughter repeated the same words, and said, 'Why, look at the door; it is now closed, and has not been opened since Mr. O—— went downstairs.' Immediately the trunk was brought up, and the door found closed, and Mr. O—— declared that he closed it when he went down but a few minutes before. The trunk weighed ninety pounds, contained a large glass tube, a dozen small glass tubes, a quantity of glass bottles, containing artist's oils, a palette, brushes, pictures, papers, &c., and though the trunk was quite upset, not a single thing in the inside was injured. In its flight the trunk did not revolve, and was set down at the foot of the stairs the same as it had stood in Mr. O——'s room. An afghan, that had been spread over the trunk, was found spread over the balusters, as though it had been left by the trunk sliding out from under it. After the excitement of this last unexplainable demonstration had died away, we assembled in the dining-room as headquarters. Quiet continued for about one hour, which being longer than the usual intervals between the manifestations, we had made up our minds that there would be no more this night, and one by one the chamber lodgers had retired to their separate rooms, leaving Mrs. Clarke upon the lounge in the dining-room. Col. V——, C. T——, H. P——, F. P——, and myself, sitting about the dining-room. Two of the five thought best to go home after the trunk performance. I learned since that at that eventful moment, Mr. B—— was nearly if not quite asleep; Mr. O—— stood with his hand on the thumb screw of his lamp, having at that instant turned the light out; the ladies were all in a semi-sleep—ourselves as above stated, when in an instant the whole house was illuminated, as by the flash of a powerful drummond light, and there came a long, terrible scream of a female voice, that filled the whole house. It appeared to me as the last wail of despair from the regions of hell itself. Every one of us were on our feet instantly, and white with horror at the sound of this voice. Mention it to this day to any one who heard it, and the cold chills creep over their mortal frame. In a moment I flew to the ladies' room, and found them in a state of excitement exceeding our own. My daughter screaming, 'Oh, that dreadful scream; that horrid face.'

"The illumination seemed to have the effect of causing the partitions of the whole house to vanish for all of us, both up stairs and down; the centre of the light was in the hall, from which centre the visible woman was seen, and from which centre came the scream.

"Though accustomed to all this for three nights; regarding the revolution of a chair, as calmly as the waving of a tree in the breeze, our frames trembled, and every face was blanched as we saw and heard the phenomenon that closed the scene.

"I have made record of the facts. The honest philosopher that shall investigate and give to the world the cause, if within material philosophy, can immortalize himself

"That the reader may be assured that I was not deluded by the phenomena called modern Spiritualism, I will give an account of my first *séance*. It was held at my residence in the haunted house, Sunday evening, the 26th day of April, 1874. I returned from San Francisco at nine o'clock, finding my residence surrounded by about five hundred people; inside the house, some twenty or thirty. The dining-room I found occupied by a *Chronicle* reporter, who, with Mr. and Mrs. Foye, were holding a *séance* for the purpose of allowing the Spirit world to come and control Mrs. Foye, who is a Spiritual Medium of great note, and explain all these wonderful manifestations. After I had assured myself that there were police enough on the outside to keep the four or five hundred people from destroying the real property, garden, &c.; spoken a word or two to the twenty or thirty inside, hunted up my wife whom I found occupying an 'upper chamber' (made vacant by the two ladies whom I had taken to town, and my daughter, who had gone to a neighbour's), I returned to the dining-room, and joined the Spiritual circle.

"We sat in a quiet condition until twelve o'clock without the least manifestation of Spirits to either move the furniture, or Mrs. Foye. I then said to Mrs. Foye, that it was a very singular phenomenon; that I could always bring spirits, and that she could not, and that I still had faith in my ability to continue to do so. This made their eyes brighten. I remembered that there was some choice whisky in the closet, and being much exhausted, I stepped to the closet, brought out the bottle, some glasses, and a dish of cake as a real manifestation of Spirits. This was all the Spirits we saw or heard that *séance.* Justice to Mr. and Mrs. Foye demands that I add, that neither touched the whisky. But it is no slander to add, that the reporter drank enough for all three. It is also justice to add, for the honesty of Mrs. Foye as a Medium, that though her Spiritual theory was here put to a public test and failed, she proved an honest, true woman and Medium, to write only as moved by the unseen.

"This account, I claim, should stand as it came, as involving philosophical facts, capable of investigation upon the plane of tangible realities. There was no dark seance, no secret, no humbug, no fraud, but eternal truth, to stand when all the actors of this day, shall have passed on. . . . ."

The names of the gentlemen who shared with the Clarke family the horrors of the weird watch nights detailed above, although mentioned by Mr. Clarke in initials only, were soon revealed in the newspaper articles that flooded the country for many weeks after these startling occurrences had ceased.

A lady residing at Oakland, in the immediate vicinity of the possessed mansion, wrote to her sister in New York, who, being a Spiritualist, sent the letter to the *Banner of Light* for publication. As it contains the off-hand observations of a wholly disinterested neighbour of the Clarke family, its perusal may be of some interest to the candid inquirer. This lady, writing under date of April 28, 1874, says:—

"Great excitement has prevailed here for the past few days, and people are all waiting for further developments. Spirits have been so unquestionably at work that I think there is hardly a person in Oakland, even the most sceptical, but admits that these remarkable occurrences are the result of supernatural agencies. Last Thursday night a family, consisting of three or four gentlemen and as many ladies, living in a house only four or five blocks from us, retired, as usual, and at about one o'clock were wakened by a noise as though Bedlam were let loose. The gentlemen, going downstairs and lighting the gas, witnessed the proceedings. The piano, *shut* and *locked,* was playing itself, and the furniture moving around in the liveliest manner. One chair edged up to Mr. Bayley, and, springing up, hit him in the eye. Suddenly they were startled by a great crash, and found that the *door,* which was strongly bolted, had been carried seven feet from the doorway, without a single bolt being slid or hinge broken. Similar manifestations continued through Saturday night. On Friday a large trunk lifted itself over the railing and came crashing down the stairs. Subsequently several chairs came down in the same way. This is no newspaper sensation, for on the second and third nights a great many people were at the house and witnessed these things. I can't begin to tell you all. Henry is acquainted with a good many of the gentlemen who saw these performances—men who could not have any reason for making misstatements. Saturday night the phenomena ended with the most fearful, blood-curdling shriek that ever greeted mortal ears. Strong men, to whom fear was unknown, were perfectly unmanned, and Mr. Clarke, the tenant of the house, said that if all Oakland were his he would willingly give it for the sake of having that shriek effaced from his memory, for it haunted him night and day. We have heard no more lately, and very likely nothing more will happen, but this has been enough to set us all thinking, for, although I have never been a believer in Spiritualism, I do think spirits have been at work here."

Notwithstanding the fact that a large number of credible witnesses all testified to the same occurrences, that those occurrences were calculated to produce indescribable distress, annoyance, loss, and injury to the subjects of them; that their health was affected, and their house turned into a Babel to which the curious resorted as to a menagerie for months after the phenomena had ceased, the papers soon began to insinuate the old story of trickery, and some even ventured to hint that the whole thing was got up for—none could pretend to say why or wherefore—but still "got up," because the parties who said so *didn't believe in such things themselves.*

We shall conclude, in justice to Mr. Clarke, also as an illustration of what kind of a community Spiritual gifts and powers have been obliged to struggle with to obtain acceptance at all, by a few closing quotations from his pamphlet.

In reference to the committee of citizens for the investigation of the subject alluded to above, Mr. Clarke says:—

"The evidence, given at the solicitation of respectable citizens, was obtained only by the agreement that names should not be made public; for every member of the family was already disgusted with notoriety, and only in the interest of science did we consent to the tax upon our time, and the expense made. The gentlemen selected to make examination, and take the evidence that could be obtained for the purpose of establishing the presence of a power not known in physical sciences, consisted of the Rev. J. K. McLean, pastor of the First Congregational Church of Oakland, Joseph Le Count, Professor at the University of California, and W. W. Crane, Esq.

"The positions of these gentlemen seemed to guarantee an honest examination, and a truthful verdict; but when this verdict, 'We find the evidence insufficient to indicate the action or presence of any supernatural, or of any occult natural agency whatever,' was rendered, Jesus Christ was not more surprised when Pilate said, 'I find no fault in this man,' and yet ordered him to the crucifixion, than we and the intelligent people of Oakland were on receipt of this 'Bunsby' verdict.

"The witnesses were twenty in number, composed of gentlemen holding the highest offices of trust, foreign consuls, doctors of divinity, lawyers, bankers, merchants, and ladies professing and living the Christian religion.

"Every demonstration recorded in this volume was proved to the entire satisfaction of the men sitting as judges. Each witness went before them alone, and told the story, submitting to as much cross-questioning as in the hardest contested case in court, and with no opposing council, until the reporter's volume reached the enormous amount of three hundred and twenty pages; to which the committee added forty pages of summary, endeavouring to show that Mr. B—— was the cause of all the manifestations, instead of attempting to arrive at simple truth."

Mr. Clarke adds: "These gentlemen, after assuring me in the most Christian spirit that they exonerate Mr. O——, the ladies, and all my family, and, at the same time, knew that *Mr. B——. was absent during many of the manifestations*, still repeat: 'We find no *evidence* of a supernatural or of any occult natural agency whatever.'" If any proof were wanted to show, that Christian Divines are not always honest, or learned scientists not always wise, the above sage verdict would furnish that proof, rendered as it was, in defiance of reason, justice, probability, and all the grounds upon which human testimony is received by experienced juries all over the world."

34

CHAPTER LIX.

SPIRITUALISM IN AMERICA (CONTINUED).

SPIRITUAL PHENOMENA OF VARIOUS KINDS.

THE following chapter will present to the reader examples of the phenomena still frequently occurring in different parts of America.

When the manifestations of Spirit presence, or the unfoldment of Spiritual powers in special directions, were first witnessed during the earlier periods of the new dispensatiou, it was customary to send full details of the same to the Spiritual journals, and thus it was that phenomenal demonstrations appeared to be more prevalent than at the present time. We have reason to believe this is not the case, but rather that the exhibitions of Spirit power having become more familiar, excite less attention and are less carefully chronicled than formerly. Still the records of preternatural events already in print are so extensive, that the author finds her chief difficulty in selecting well-attested representative cases from the immense mass of material in her possession. Following out the plan steadily pursued throughout the earlier chapters of this volume, we shall give invariable preference to those narratives for which the author can personally vouch, and relate such incidents as present the most varied aspects.

The following sketches refer to a young man who has come forward as a remarkable writing and test Medium within the last few years in America.

Although the author has received personal evidence of Mr. Phillips' Mediumship of the most convincing character, it may be more satisfactory to offer the testimony of two gentlemen of such authoritative standing and unquestionable veracity as Professor J. R. Buchanan and the Hon. J. L. O'Sullivan. It is to the statements of these gentlemen therefore that we refer, in the following proofs of Spirit agency.

In lectures given in aid of different Spiritual enterprises by Mr. J. L. O'Sullivan (late American Minister to Portugal), that gentleman stated, that in company with Professor Buchanan, of New York, he had had three testing sittings with a young man named Phillips, who was a pleasing honest youth and afforded grand instances of psychographic mediumship. Writing was plentifully obtained on two joined slates placed on the top of the table under their hands. On one occasion the slates were placed at a distance of twelve feet from the Medium, and when taken up contained six messages— two in Latin, the rest in French, Italian, English, and Oriental characters.

The first in Latin was: "Homines damnant quod non intelligunt" (Men condemn what they do not understand); the other was a quotation from Horace of the two hexameter lines:

> "Rusticus expectat, dum defluat amnis, at ille
> Labitur et labetur in omne volubilis ævum."

> (The countryman looks on awaiting the flowing away of the river,
> But it flows, in its whirling course, and will flow on for ever.)

After Mr. O'Sullivan had placed the joined slates in position under the distant chair (all in full light), the Medium handed him a paper containing a quantity of corn-flour, suggesting to him to place it by the slates, as sometimes it was found strewed over them.

When the three raps on the table at which they were sitting gave the signal for examining the slates, the under slate was found covered with six different communications, and also with the impress in flour (over the writing) of the ends of the four fingers and thumb of a large hand. The flour had to be blown or lightly brushed away to get fully at the underlying writing. In the little heap of flower in the paper alongside were found the corresponding indentations left by the invisible hand. Both slates and flour had been under the keen vigilance of the two gentlemen who sat at the table with Mr. Phillips.

A piece of paper was placed between two slates on the table, and there was found written on it an elegant and almost literal Latin translation of the well-known child's hymn, " Twinkle, twinkle, little star." The Medium does not know a word of Latin, nor would such knowledge have availed in this case, as the paper was inaccessible to him, being securely placed between two slates. With Mr. Phillips neither slate nor lead pencil was ever placed between the slates. Those who did the writing brought or made their own pencils. The translation was as follows —

> " Mica, mica, parva stella,
> Miror quanam sis tam bella,
> Splendens eminus in illo
> Alba velut gemma cœlo."

The small piece of paper on which it was written had been torn by Dr. Buchanan from a large sheet, at the moment of placing the slates, from which the hands of the sitters never stirred. The torn edges, of course, identified the paper. It was said to have been written by Dr. Buchanan's father.

On the third evening, a piece of paper was placed by Mr. O'Sullivan between slates, which were allowed to remain under a chair some six or eight feet from the sitters. On examination after some time no writing was found on either slate or paper.

It was accordingly removed by Mr. O'Sullivan (the medium never quitting his seat at the table) and the slates left in the same place. On being taken up soon afterwards a large green leaf was found between the slates, bearing an inscription in Chinese characters, written with a reddish brown pigment.

Mr. O'Sullivan produced this leaf itself to his audience, framed and protected under glass, and bearing date " June 14, 1880." The leaf is in a perfect state of preservation, and the Chinese characters are well-formed and quite distinct, though now blackened, presumably by the action of the light. A Japanese gentleman made the following translation : " The doctrine of Christ is in the centre of our true heart and not the external adornment."

In answer to an inquiry from what spirit this had proceeded, the reply, by psychographic writing, was " Confucius."

Several accounts have been written of this remarkable phenomenon, and the author has been presented with a fine copy of the photographed leaf, the plate of which was carefully prepared by Mr. Henry J. Newton, of New York—President of the First Society of Spiritualists, and an amateur photographer of considerable skill.

The edges of the leaf, originally perfect, are now somewhat torn, having been gummed by Dr. Buchanan to the paper on which it was laid when framed under glass. The drying of the leaf has also wrinkled it and torn it a little apart in one place. The Japanese gentleman who translated the inscription said that the leaf was of a tree from which silkworms are fed in Japan.

This phenomenon makes intelligible and no longer incredible the stories told by travellers of the holy tree at the sacred city, Lassa, in Thibet, the leaves of which are said to contain certain sacred names or phrases. Since a Spirit has thus written on one leaf, why not on many?

Another phase of Spirit art quite as marvellous as the above, is that displayed by the Mediumship of Mrs. L. M. Blair, a lady who paints large groups of flowers, shaded and coloured with remarkable skill, whilst carefully *blindfolded* by sceptical persons selected from the audiences before whom she exhibits her marvellous powers.

When first the author became a witness of this lady's extraordinary Mediumship, she was giving a public *séance* in the town of Oswego. Entering the room before the commencement of the exercises, Mrs. Hardinge Britten and her party watched the operations of the two sceptics who had been named by the audience to blindfold the Medium. This work was evidently accomplished with *a will* which left no chance of admitting the smallest ray of light to the closed eyes of the entranced artist. Directly afterwards Mrs. Blair commenced painting with astonishing rapidity, dipping her one brush now into this colour, now into that, without making the smallest mistake in the selection. When the picture was completed, the Medium, still entranced, stated that it was an allegorical representation of the life and work of a lady then present, and having explained in choice language the meaning of the flowery group, and detailed most minutely the design expressed in every petal and colour, she commanded it to be carried "to the stranger who sat so thickly veiled," in such a part of the hall, that even had the veil been raised, the distance from the platform would have utterly precluded all chance of recognition. The party who received the picture had never before seen Mrs. Blair. The interpretation of the allegory as given through the entranced lips of the Medium exactly fitted the recipient's life woof, and as Mrs. Blair has never met that stranger, and even the small recompense sent for this wonderful test of Spirit power was conveyed anonymously, the author rejoices in this opportunity of doing justice alike to the Spirit friends and the Medium through whom they worked, by acknowledging, that Mrs. Hardinge Britten was the well-pleased but greatly surprised recipient of this fine test. We deem it right to add another illustrative account of Mrs. Blair's powers, succinctly given in the following extract from a narrative furnished to the *Banner of Light* by one of its most esteemed and reliable correspondents. This gentleman says :—

"It was at Montpelier I first saw Mrs. L. M. Blair, now Mrs. Murdock, who resides near the village of Rockbottom, some thirty miles west of Boston, Mass. I think she is one of the most remarkable mediums in this country. She was deeply interested in our *séances,* and attended them in Montepelier, Barre, and Northfield, Vt. She was born with only one arm, and that one is often controlled by what claims to be an Italian artist who lived on the shores of the Mediterranean, and passed to spirit-life about seventy years ago. I have in my parlour a painting, some twelve by sixteen inches. It represents a delicate hand holding a few branches of a rosebush which contain twelve full-blown roses, a number of buds, leaves, etc., so placed as to partially cover a motto : 'We'll bless you for ever.' This painting was executed by Mrs. Blair while she was effectually blindfolded, and in the brief time of eleven minutes. I have taken it to at least half-a-dozen prominent artists in Boston, and asked them how long it would take them to paint a duplicate, and the shortest time given by any one of them was five hours.

"During the time that her hand is controlled to paint, her brain and vocal organs are controlled by another spirit who talks very fluently on almost any subject you mention. He said to me that he had to keep the medium unconscious during the time the artist was painting, as she was so sensitive to any sceptical remarks that might be made in her presence that the other spirit could not control the hand satisfactorily.

"Her paintings are all in water colors, and she, or the spirit, uses only one brush, which is cleansed in a tumbler of water as soon as one color is used. I have seen her painting on many different occasion, but I have never seen her return to the same color after she has rinsed the brush. All the red, green, yellow, or other color she uses, is laid on before she commences with another color, and any of her paintings when half done are greater curiosities than when fully completed.

"One day as I sat watching her, and talking with the spirit that controlled her speech, I called attention to another part of the room, and although her eyes were blindfolded she turned her head for a moment in the opposite direction, and I picked up the tumbler and held it directly at the back of her head. As soon as it became necessary to wash the brush again, the controlling spirit brought the hand of the medium over her shoulder and washed out the brush as readily as if the tumbler was in its accustomed place, and proceeded at once with another color.

"While I have been talking with one of her controlling spirits the other would answer my questions in writing at the same time. He assures me that he paints more beautiful pictures in the spirit-world than have ever been seen on earth. I asked what use he made of paintings in his country, and he replied that they were used there, as here, to adorn their homes which are in every respect as real as are our homes in this life."

We have already given one representative account of Spirit photography, and some of the friends to whom these chapters have been shown, have objected that Mr. Mumler's case might seem exceptional, were it not duplicated. The author is in possession of a large number of well-attested evidences that Spirit photographs have been taken under circumstances that admitted of no chance for deception. Amongst these—since it seems desirable to duplicate cases of so remarkable a nature—we offer the following example, testified to by witnesses of the most undoubted veracity.

Mr. Julius Plaetz, photographer, Kansas City, Missouri, writing to the Spiritual papers under date March, 1882, says :—

"No. 618, Main-street, Kansas City, Missouri, March 11th, 1882.

"Concerning the phenomena of Spirit-Photography, although I do not profess to be a Spiritualist, I deem it just and right to state that while Mrs. Lizzie Carter, the spirit-photographer, was taking spirit-photographs at my gallery, she prepared the plates in my presence and the presence of my operators in the same manner, using the same chemicals as used by myself in taking photographs ; she used the same camera, the same furniture which I use daily, and which has been used at my gallery during the last ten years. And on all the photographs she took, from two to eight human faces and frequently full forms besides that of the sitter did appear, in fact two-thirds of all the plates she used while at my gallery, from January 20th to March 6th, 1882, were prepared and developed by myself or my operators, always with the same result.

"And I desire to further state that myself and my operators have frequently, without the knowledge of Mrs. Carter, tested her so-called mediumship in various ways, by exchanging plates which she had handled and prepared from the plate-holder, replacing others prepared by ourselves such as she had never seen nor handled before, but still the result was the same ; human faces and forms would appear in addition to the sitter on every photograph she took. I further state that she has taken photographs of a number of persons strangers to her, and known to me to be sceptics, but still the result was the same—spirit faces on every photograph.

"I have been a practical photographer for over twenty years, am well acquainted with all the details of the business, and I declare that there is no chemical process known by which the phenomena, such as produced by Mrs. Carter, can be duplicated.

"The only observable difference in the process of taking a photograph between Mrs. Carter and other photographers is, that Mrs. Carter generally lays her hands on the camera while she takes the photograph ; this, and only this, is the difference I have been able to discover in the operation during about six weeks of daily observation at my

gallery. Of course myself and many other experts in photography, among other experiments made, did not fail to lay our hands on the camera, stood on the same spot in the
same position generally occupied by herself, &c., but all was of no avail, the spirits would
not and did not come for any or either of us.—Yours, &c.,

"JULIUS PLAETZ, Photographer."

In addition to the statements of one more Spiritualist, we offer those of
a physician, a well-known and highly respected resident of Kansas City,
who writes to the London *Medium and Daybreak* in the following terms :—

"Kansas City, Mo., U.S.A., March 11th, 1882."

"Allow me to state briefly through your paper my experiences, had lately, relative to
the phenomenon known as Spirit-Photography, through the mediumship of Mrs. Lizzie
Carter, at the Photographic Gallery of Mr. Julius Plaetz, No. 618, Main Street, this city.
I notice your comments in your number of the *Medium and Daybreak*, of February 11th,
1882, entitled, 'Chronicles of Spirit-Photography,' and as this beautiful phase of mediumship has recently elicited much interest among investigators of this city and vicinity
during the last six weeks, it was proposed to Mrs. Carter to give a sitting under test
conditions, to which she cheerfully consented. Consequently on the 4th inst., Messrs. W.
W. Judson, Fred Meyers, H. M. Johnson, John E. Fleming, and your humble servant
constituted ourselves a committee to investigate this phase of mediumship, and I take
pleasure in laying before your readers the details of its results.

"We procured a plate-holder in Mr. Plaetz's gallery, fitting the camera through which
Mrs. Carter took photographs, and proceeded with it to the photographic gallery of Messrs.
Williams and Thomson, 612, Main Street ; requested Mr. Thomson, one of the proprietors,
to place in our presence a prepared plate for taking an ordinary photograph in that plate-
holder. The plate was prepared and placed in the plate-holder, in the dark room at the
gallery of Messrs Williams and Thomson, in our presence, the plate-holder then wrapped
in a covering to exclude the light and carried by Mr. Thomson ; thus we returned
together to the gallery of Mr. Plaetz. Mr. Thomson was here introduced to Mrs. Carter
and requested to hand her the plate-holder. Mrs. Carter requested that the camera be
examined, which was accordingly done by Mr. Thomson, he being an expert in his profession as photographer, next your humble servant was requested to sit for a photograph.

"Mrs. Carter then placed the camera in position, removed the covering from the plate-
holder and, without opening the same, placed it in the camera. After the lapse of eight
seconds, during which time Mrs. Carter held her hands on the camera, she removed the
plate-holder from the camera, and without opening it, handed it back to Mr. Thomson
with the request to go to his gallery and develop the plate. The committee returned with
Mr. Thomson to his gallery in the dark room, when Mr. Thomson handed the plate-holder
to his operator, requesting him to remove the plate and develop it in our presence. The
operator admitted that this was the same plate he had placed in that plate-holder a few
minutes before, that it had not been taken out, but was there just as he himself had
placed it.

"He applied the necessary chemicals generally used by photographers to develop the
negative and nothing more, and on presenting the negative to the light, there appeared
on it five human faces distinctly outlined in addition to the face of the sitter. Mr.
Thomson after making several proofs, delivered the negative to me, which I handed to
Mr. Plaetz, to be printed.

"These are the facts and the result of our investigation, and I lay them before your
readers as they occurred in our presence.—Respectfully yours, H. F. BUNGARDT, M.D.

"The undersigned spectators present at the time the photograph mentioned was taken,
and members of the committee as above referred to, having carefully examined the foregoing statement of the proceedings, acknowledge the same to be true and correct in every
particular :—

VIRGINIA J. JUDSON ;	W. W. JUDSON ;
H. M. JOHNSON ;	JUSTIN ROBINSON ;
FRED MEYERS ;	JOHN E. FLEMMING ;
D. P. THOMSON, Photographer ;	JACOB SHERMAN.
	JULIUS PLAETZ, Photographer."

Both the following cases are well known to the author, and being
narrated by highly respected citizens of Troy and Chicago, will be read
with interest by the many parties acquainted with Mr. Vosburgh, and the
Rev. M. H. Forscutt

The first article is copied from the *Troy Standard*, and reads thus :—

"In the year 1850 I was engaged in business and resided at West Troy. There lived in the town a family named Thalimer. The family was composed of father, mother, three sons, Peter, James, and Henry, and Elizabeth, the daughter. James desired very greatly to embark on a sea voyage. His parents opposed him for some time; but he finally, without their knowledge, ran away one day and shipped for a three-years' voyage in the whale fishery, from New Bedford, Mass. About this time the Fox girls visited Troy, and there was considerable excitement in reference to the claims set forth by them. The opposition by the press and people was very marked against them. James had been absent about one year and a half, when Elizabeth, his sister, was entertaining a party at the family residence one evening.

"In the midst of their sport one of the party said by way of a satirical sally at Spiritualism, ' Oh, let's form a circle !' No sooner said than done; the table was moved out into the middle of the room and several of the company, Elizabeth among the number, gathered around it. They had not rested their hands on it more than a moment or two when Elizabeth's was seized by a power foreign to her own, which very much frightened her. She tried to extricate herself, but without avail. The intelligence moving her hand motioned as though it desired to write. One of the company procured paper and pencil; her hand instantly caught up the pencil and wrote as follows : ' I fell from the yard-arm of the ship to the deck and was killed; this will be verified by letter from the captain of the ship.—James Thalimer.'

"The company was very much excited and broke up at once, going to their respective homes. The next morning Henry Thalimer, the father, knowing me to be a Spiritualist, called on me and related the circumstances, and wanted my opinion. I replied that I honestly believed James had fallen, as stated, and that it was a genuine spiritual manifestation. I advised him to be patient and await the verification which I assured him would no doubt come by mail. In about ten days after, Mr. Thalimer received a letter from the captain of the vessel confirming the truth of the communication through his daughter's hand.

"After a lapse of thirty years, in August, 1880, I was at Lake Pleasant camp-meeting. One afternoon while seated on the stoop fronting the hotel, two Troy gentlemen approached and invited me to take a walk with them. I accepted, and we walked wherever inclination led us, not having in view any particular place we desired to visit. We were passing along by what is called the open square, and discovered under a large tent a great throng of ladies and gentlemen, who seemed intently interested in what was taking place. Being desirous of learning what it was, we drew near, and discovered a lady under what was claimed as spirit-control, giving tests of spirit-identity to the people assembled. This lady, I desire to state, neither my friends nor myself ever met before. She was an entire stranger to us. We noticed that she gave a number of tests, names, dates, circumstances, and events which were corroborated by different persons in the audience. All at once she exclaimed under great excitement : ' I see an immense ship nearing me ; this vessel seems to be labouring in a terrible storm. It seems as though this vessel would come upon me. Now I see a young man going aloft. My God !' she said, ' this man will fall and will be killed.' She watched him with intense interest, and then she suddenly shrieked so loud as to be heard in all the surroundings : ' Oh ! my God ! he falls to the deck and is killed.' Her eyes were riveted to the spot for a moment in perfect silence.

"She then said, ' This young man gives me his name. He says he is James Thalimer, of West Troy, N. Y.' I at once replied, raising my hat, ' Yes, that is correct.' The lady then moved from the platform, and motioning with her hands for the people to make way for her, she came to where I was standing, and threw her arms around my neck, exclaiming, ' Vosburgh, God bless you ! I am glad to meet you here. This is the second time I have been able to return and identify myself. First through my sister, which you knew of, and second through this lady, a stranger to us both. God bless you, Vosburgh !'

"Troy, N. Y., Sept. 4th, 1882. "W. H. VOSBURGH."

The *Chicago Times* of 1880, has the following statement :—

"It will be remembered that there was published a few weeks since an account of the death of Mr. Frank Culver, of 606, West Jackson Street, who died on July 7th, from sewer gas poisoning. Almost immediately after, Mr. Culver's little daughter passed on, as the medical attendants alleged, from the same cause. At the funeral of the child, the Rev. Mr. Forscutt, who only a short time previous had attended the interment of Mr. Frank Culver, made the following remarkable and startling statement. The narrative is furnished by the *Times* reporter, who was sent to call on Mr. Forscutt, with a view of correcting any mistakes that might have arisen by giving publicity to the subject on the strength of rumour alone. The reporter says :—

"'Mr. Forscutt was found in his study at No. 619, West Lake Street. He had the appearance of a man who is guided by plain common sense, and answered the questions put to him in as matter-of-fact a way as could be desired. He said that he was sitting in his study just one week after the death of Mr. Culver, quietly reading. His thoughts were on a subject entirely foreign to anything pertaining to Mr. Culver, when he was suddenly impelled to look up—Mr. Culver stood before him, not more than six feet distant, and as natural as he had seen him dozens of times in his study. It did not occur to him that Mr. Culver was dead, and that his body had been buried. As soon as he looked up, Mr. Culver said in his familiar tones, "I want Pearl. I want her to come with me." Mr. Forscutt says that he asked, "Do you think it would be better for her to go than to stay here ? Have you any knowledge of future evils which might befall her on earth ?" "No, I have not," Mr. Culver replied, "but I want her with me. I went to her to-day and called her, and she lifted up her hands and cried for ' Papa.' I know she wants to come."

"'Mr. Forscutt says he replied to the effect that it was a question which should predominate, fatherly or motherly affection, but he would advise that the matter be submitted to the Lord, and say, "Thy will be done." He would go to the mother and encourage her to submit to the affliction if it should seem best for Pearl to die.

"'In a moment the apparition was gone, and it was not for some minutes afterwards that Mr. Forscutt was able to realize that Frank was dead, and that it was his disembodied spirit with which he had been talking.

"'Pearl, Mr. Culver's little girl, had been sick a few days previous to this, but it was not yet believed by any one that she must die.

"'The attending physician had said nothing to indicate that she would not recover. As Mr. Forscutt realized what had taken place in the interview between himself and the father, he became convinced that the child's death was assured. He put on his hat and went immediately to the house of Mrs. Culver to prepare her for the worst. He called her aside, and said that he feared Pearl must go. Immediately the mother said : "I am afraid so, too, for Pearl threw up her hands this morning as she lay in bed, opened her eyes, and called ' Papa, papa, papa !' I believe she saw him, as she seemed unusually pleased."

"'Mr. Forscutt then told her that Frank had paid him a visit and said that he had called Pearl, and that she replied to him precisely as she described.

"'The reporter called at the house of Mrs. Culver, and learned that the circumstances were as Mr. Forscutt had repeated them. It was also learned that the child and father were very fond of one another. Pearl was only 14 months old, but was unusually precocious, and the father had often spoken of the pride he should take in giving her superior training. This seems, in the mind of Mr. Forscutt, to account for his solicitude after his death.

"'During the day of the occurrence narrated, the child seemed much better, apparently happy over the recognition of her father. On that night and the succeeding days she began to grow worse, and died on Friday.

"'Mr. Forscutt is pastor of a congregation which worships under the appellation of Latter Day Saints in the Crystal block, at 619, West Lake Street. He believes, in accordance with his denomination, that spirits are permitted by God to assume mortal shape and reveal themselves to their friends, but says this is the first experience of his in receiving one who had departed this life. Mr. Culver had come to be quite intimate with him before his death, and on that ground he accounts for his appearing before him. Mr. Forscutt maintains that he never had a more real experience in his life, and laughs at the idea that it could have been imaginary.' "

In several parts of the United States accounts are given of the appearance of Spirit-pictures being photographed upon the window panes of houses ; the forms appearing and disappearing so suddenly that the parties to whom the pictures were visible had scarcely time to call in a sufficient number of witnesses to associate the manifestation with authentic testimony.

About fifteen years ago the author being engaged to speak at a grove meeting held at Milan, Ohio, under the auspices of Hudson Tuttle and the Spiritualists of that district, was taken with several other persons to see the pictures mysteriously photographed upon the window panes of a house rented by a person who stood high in one of the churches at Milan, and who was entirely opposed in belief and sentiment to Spiritualism and all its advocates.

This person acknowledged that the pictures had come in the most mysterious and unaccountable way; that some, that had already faded out, closely resembled relatives of his who—as he said—had "long been in their graves," whilst those yet remaining were recognised by scores of residents in the town as representing deceased parties well known by many who went to investigate them.

As the proprietor of the house in question only permitted the author and her friends to inspect the pictures on condition that his name should not be reported, we feel obliged to keep faith in this respect, and merely allude to the fact, which will be remembered by any readers acquainted with that locality. Another well attested case of this kind of phenomenon was published in the *Banner of Light* of August, 1875, by a venerable resident of West Woodstock, Vermont, Mr. J. D. Powers, who says :—

"The demonstration took place at the house of Mr. Chaney Richardson, a farmer, now seventy-five years of age, and who has been a Spiritualist for a long time. It appears that Mr. R. had retired to his room during the daytime to rest, and while lying on the bed, wide awake, his attention was attracted to the white curtain on the window in his room, which was lowered about half way down the window. At first he noticed the gradual appearance on the curtain of three dark lines, some two inches apart and about six in length. He eagerly began to scrutinize this strange circumstance and to observe what followed. Soon he noticed that the spaces between the lines began to fill up and interblend, presenting a cloudy appearance, in which immediately there came the figure of a child in a laughing mood. Mr. Richardson arose and approached the curtain, when the figure disappeared, and in the same place he saw another scene, representing houses, and men, women and children in citizens' dress. Mr. R. considered this singular phenomenon too good to be enjoyed by himself alone, so he called in his neighbours as witnesses, some of whom could see the pictures as distinctly as he did. By invitation of my friend Mr. J. P. Cobb, an infidel of fifty years' standing, I rode with him to Mr. Richardson's to witness the unaccountable occurrence. He was quite astonished at the result, for he saw all that any one did ; but what surprised him most was the appearance on the curtain of an officer whom he had known, holding in his hand a flagstaff and waving the flag to the breeze. He disappeared, and on coming again the flag was furled. Still more ; on his arrival home he saw on one of the curtains of his own house, and also on one in his neighbour's house, pictures similar to what he had seen at Mr. Richardson's. I saw but two figures ; one was small featured and wore spectacles ; the other was my father's face, plainly daguerreotyped on the curtain. . . . .

"Another correspondent writes : 'Spirit-photography without material aid ! A new phase of spirit manifestation has appeared in Woodstock, Vt. Pictures representing men, women, and children, buildings, &c., have appeared on a window curtain. They come and go in the presence of spectators, some of whom recognise genuine likenesses of deceased friends. The curtain was taken down and washed, but still the phenomenon would occur. Many persons have visited the house where the occurrence took place, but no one can account for it except as a phase of spirit power.' "

We frequently read accounts of "the summer land" and visits to the bright spheres of the hereafter, as narrated by Spirit Seers and Mediums. These accounts are so entirely in harmony with each other, that it has been suggested by sceptics, that if the narrators do not actually repeat each other's statements, there is at least *a contagion of psychology* which is liable to affect certain individuals whose minds come into relation or mental contact with each other. It is with a view of meeting and repelling this highly strained hypothesis that we give place to the following narrative, furnished by a medical gentleman well known in the West, in relation to a family of wealth and respectability, whose statements speak for themselves. The case, after being reported in numbers of local papers, was republished in the *Harbinger of Light*, Melbourne, in 1879, and is now cited as an independent and impartial witness for the conditions of life in the spheres of Spiritual existence. The narrative is as follows :—

"Mrs. Diana Powellson, widow of the late Thomas Powellson, resides seven or eight miles south-west of Kansas City. She is forty-one years of age, and the mother of nine children. Up to three years ago she had been a remarkably vigorous woman. On the 1st of August, 1876, a premature labour induced the disease which culminated in what was supposed to be death. At one time, Dr. Thorne, supposing his patient would soon die, remained with her. The symptoms were cold, clammy perspiration all over the body ; eyeballs thrown upward ; no action of the diaphragm ; she had been blind for several days ; things continued in this course until one o'clock in the morning, when she apparently died. A current of electricity passed from the base of the brain to the lower portion of the back failed to revive her. She did, however, finally revive, and gave this statement to our reporter, in company with Dr. Thorne :—

"'I have been a professed Christian for many years. Some time in 1877 I joined the Methodist Church. I am a full believer in Christianity. The statement that I am about to make is stranger to me than it can be to you.

"'On the night I died, I was so happy at going ; felt no misery of any kind ; pain in the head all gone ; it seemed that I lost all consciousness but for a moment ; when I came to my senses again I knew I was dead, but everything was very dark to me. I thought I was still blind. I became filled with terror, anticipating the worst. My husband (who died a short time ago) soon, however, took hold of me. Others of my departed friends and family did the same. The darkness suddenly vanished. I saw all my friends and millions of others. I saw hills and valleys, trees and flowers, rivers, seas, lakes and birds, and heard such music as I cannot describe. The people were not what I expected to see. They were ordinary men and women. Some were bright and beautiful, and others were lean and miserable looking. I saw their homes. They lived in communities. All were much more beautiful than any we have, but some were not so beautiful as others. I saw many bright spirits, but was very much surprised that they had no wings. My friends led me from the dark place into the light. I did not come through this dark place any more, either in coming back or returning at any time. I saw many meetings or congregations, but did not learn what they were doing. I was told that I must return to my body again. My husband told me this. I cried and was very much angered at him and still am for sending me back. I long to be in that beautiful home that they told me was mine. My husband sent a message to his son and to my children by me.

"'Messages were also sent by many others. I was afraid of some spirits, who looked dark and forbidding, while others were bright, beautiful, and kind. When I was there a large concourse gathered around me. I did not know I should return to earth till I was told so by my husband. He was sixty-seven when he died, though he now looks in the prime of life. My two children were with their father. I was very much surprised at this ; I had known only one ; one child was born dead, prematurely, in August, 1876 ; it was quite rejoiced to see me. I cannot compare it to any age, it differs from earth, but is still a small child. I felt all a mother's love for that child, which I did not think I possessed. My boy, one year old, died fifteen years ago ; he is now a young man and knew me.

"'Spirits do not sing like we do ; much nicer. The clothing of all was of the flowing or robe kind. No voice is used by spirits. I understood them more perfectly without words. I read their thoughts ; it is more perfect language than ours. They told me to come back to earth for three or four years with my little children who are here. I promised to do so. I expected to meet Christ, but did not do so. They told me that this was why I was in the dark. I know now that I must depend upon myself. We are over there as we are here. We make our own happiness. I did not find any heaven or hell, only life, more perfect and beautiful than this. This is not life at all. What I now relate is as clear to my memory as anything in life can be.

"'In dying, I did not lose consciousness. I seemed to fade from one life into another. I now often see spirits around me, but cannot speak to them or they to me. They show me flowers which are more beautiful than ours. Spirits told me that they had to repent of their sins over there before they could advance. Till they did this they were unhappy. I was much surprised when I first went there at seeing a spirit which I took to be God, and I afterwards supposed it was Jesus Christ, but who was only a bright spirit teaching the others. I saw many such afterwards ; they don't seem to belong to the rest at all. Everybody is engaged in learning and growing brighter, so they told me. . . . .'

"The facts and particulars of this strange death were verified by the people of Rosedale generally. More particularly was the account substantiated by Mrs. Kittie Powellson, sister-in-law to the lady, and Miss R. Powellson, the daughter ; Mrs. John Haddock, Mrs. Jas. Wilson, Mrs. Callenburgher, Mr. Baird, practising physician in Rosedale, and many others who have been constantly attending her.

"Dr. Thorne called in consultation Dr. Halley, of Kansas City, who made a thorough investigation of the case.

" Philadelphia, Pa., July 9, 1879."

Amongst the locally-celebrated Mediums of America is a family or children residing at Chicago where their manifestations, although given in the privacy of a plain domestic circle, and without the slightest desire for display, have yet attracted hundreds of curious and sceptical investigators, not one of whom has ever made the least suggestion of fraud or failed to bear testimony to the apparent truthfulness of all parties concerned. The following account of this Mediumistic household, now celebrated as " the Bangs children," is printed in the *Religio Philosophical Journal*, of 1871, with these editorial remarks.

"We have on three occasions been invited to witness the wonderful physical manifestations of departed spirits in the presence of the Bangs children. These manifestations take place in a fully lighted room, and yet musical instruments have to be enclosed in a box or dark room, in order to enable spirits to play upon them. This family all seem to be mediumistic, but two little girls, aged respectively eleven and seven years, are considered the best mediums. The manifestations were so varied in our presence, that we can give but a faint outline of them in this article. A long, heavy, extension dining-table is brought out, and an ordinary table cloth is spread over it. The family are seated along on one side, and as many as is convenient fill up the circle around the table, excepting a space of about three feet between two of the children, which is left vacant. In this vacancy is placed a chair. The audience who may be present are seated around the room. It is then quite usual for some one of the family to ask a little spirit—son of the Bangs parents—if all is right. This little son passed to spirit-life when only fourteen months old, but is now plainly seen and talked with by the other children. In response to that inquiry, an affirmative or negative answer is given by a certain number of raps or tips of the table, or by the tipping of the vacant chair above referred to. If the answer be in the negative, one of the children puts a slate under the table, upon which a pencil is laid. Immediately the sound of writing is heard on the slate, and yet the hand of the child and the slate where she holds it is in plain sight. As soon as the sound of writing ceases, the slate is placed on the table, and thereon is found, in plain *English*, such corrections as are required to be made in the circle to improve conditions for better manifestations. Sometimes, some one plays the piano; then the chair above referred to, dances (apparently with delight) keeping time to the music without anything or any one touching it. The table, also, often hops and skips about like an intelligent being, keeping time with delight to the music. The children are also *clairaudient*. They hear the spirits talk, and give what they say to the members of the *séance*, whereupon the spirits in return give their assent to the truth thereof by raps on the table, or by forcibly tipping the vacant chair. This chair seems to answer a very important purpose. It is always ready to respond to any one's inquiries when requested. For instance, one directing an inquiry to the chair, says, Chair, is John Smith (or some less noted character) present? The chair immediately responds by one, two, or three emphatic tips, which are understood to mean respectively, no—I don't know—yes. One wants to have a spirit friend write something on the slate, whereupon one of the little girls holds the slate under the table, as before described, or on the top of her head. Immediately the pencil is heard writing, and as soon as the sound ceases, she takes down the slate, and the inquirer finds a short message to him or her, and sometimes, as is claimed, in the *fac simile* hand-writing of the deceased person while in this life. In all these cases, as hundreds of sceptics can testify, the writing is done without the touch of any mortal hand.

"A little box is fitted up, and a number of musical instruments are placed in the same. One of the little girls will sit by the side of the box, with one hand inserted through a little hole, only to the wrist joint, all in plain sight of the audience. Then the musical instruments will be played, several at a time, keeping time with a piano played in the room. Dancing will also be heard, &c., &c. Hands are often presented at a little diamond shaped hole in the box, moving things which have been deposited in the box. These last manifestations are most perfect when a little seven year old girl is tied fast and placed inside of the box.

"Another most interesting phase is also witnessed. While you are looking right at one of these little girls, you will hear her cry out, ' oh !' in a child-like voice, as if she were hurt. She will push up her sleeve, and there will be found plain and deep indentations in the muscle of the arm of a set of children's teeth—upper and lower—indeed, in some instances, almost drawing blood. She will slip down her sleeve, and no sooner down than she cries out again as before, and again slips up her sleeve, and other indentations similar to the first are to be seen, and this will be repeated for a half-dozen times or more, while you are looking right at her all the time. She says it feels exactly as if she was being bit by a child, and, indeed, the arm presents that appearance.

"We might go on and recite the varied manifestations which are daily astonishing the beholders, in the presence of these children, would space admit it. We will content ourselves, for the present, by giving the following narrative, written for this paper, by Mrs. Bangs, the mother of the children, under the approval of Mr. Bangs, their father.—

"MRS. BANG'S REPORT.

"I will commence by saying that up to September 30th, 1874, none of our family had ever seen any spirit manifestations, and were not thinking about them. All at once, on September 30th, about five o'clock in the evening, hard coal was thrown in at the door. I thought it to be the neighbours' children, and requested them to stop. They answered that they had not thrown any coal; but of course I did not believe them, and closed the door.

"The kitchen window was dropped about six inches at the top, and after I closed the door, coal commenced to come in at the top of the window. When my husband, Mr. Bangs, came home to supper, about seven o'clock in the evening, I told him the children had been throwing coal into the house. While he was at supper the coal kept coming in all the time. After supper Mr. Bangs went out around the house and concealed himself, with the expectation that he could find out who it was that threw the coal, but failed to see any one, but he could see the coal pass in at the window, and hear it fall on the floor. It was a pleasant evening, and the moon shone very bright. If there had been any one near by he would have seen them. Mr. Bangs then came into the house and shut the window. Several pieces fell in the room after that. The next morning, about seven o'clock, coal commenced to come in at the pantry window on the other side of the house, and next it came into the dining-room. From seven to eleven o'clock nearly a peck was thrown in. We were not disturbed during meal hours, nor after eight o'clock in the evening. Coal continued to come in for four days. It made no difference whether the windows and doors were open or not. One large piece was dropped in the front room, weighing eight to ten pounds, when all the doors and windows were closed. Several other large pieces were brought in and scattered in different places. Several of the neighbours were called in and can testify to the truth of this statement. They said it was some evil spirit that had got into the house.

"The next day, chairs and other articles of furniture were piled up together in plain view in a moment, and then returned to their places again. Dishes were put on the children's heads. A brick, and a tumbler full of water, was placed on the head of one of the girls several times. Nearly every dish and small article in the house was put on their heads, and kept me busy all day taking them off.

"When evening came, they took the ribbon off the eldest girl's head, and tied her fast to the chair with it, and did many other things. They tipped the chair she was sitting in. I had the impression to give her a piece of paper and pencil, and I asked the question, who it was making those demonstrations. Immediately they controlled one of the girl's hands, and wrote, 'good spirit'—the girl not having any control of her hands. In a day or two after that, she saw the spirit of Mr. Bangs' sister, and described her form and features perfectly. She never saw her in life. The spirit spoke in an audible voice several times, calling Mr. Bangs, 'Brother Edward, brother Edward!' one time when the children were not in the house, at another time when the children were asleep in bed.

"The lamp was trimmed every day, for two weeks, by spirit hands, the wick being cut each time. Dishes were washed, knives were scoured by them in a few moments, and beds were made. The pantry floor was washed, and another floor was swept. One day while the eldest girl, Elizabeth, was ironing one part of a garment, a spirit took another iron and ironed the other part and helped until all the clothes were ironed. I saw the iron move about on the cloth, but could not see the spirit. Presents were brought for the girls, and carried into the schoolroom and given to them. They had each a new circular comb and neck ribbon given to them in the schoolroom. The combs were put in their hair and the ribbons tied around their necks. They did not know anything about it till some of the scholars asked them where they got their new combs and ribbons.

"The spirit wrote through our daughter Elizabeth's hand, that she wanted our family to hold a circle every evening for development. We did so. The first evening, they tipped the table, and telegraphed by raps, our daughter hearing the voice of the spirit at the same time, giving directions what they wanted us to do next. We sang, and they kept time to the music, by raps and dancing on the floor. We heard the sound of their feet plainly. That evening the children saw other spirits of our departed friends. Among them was our little boy, who passed away when only fourteen months old. Since that time he seems to be constantly with us. He has drawn pictures on paper and on the slate, and writes on the slate without the aid of natural hands, giving very intelligent communications. One evening, while all the family were sitting at the supper table, with a full light, our little girl Mary had her dress changed in a few moments by spirit power. We are all positive she did not move from her chair during the meal, and yet her dress was changed, and the dress they took off from her was carried and hung up, in her room. Quite often the girls have had their dresses thus changed, and their hair curled before our eyes; that is, we could see that their clothes were changed, and their hair curled, but could not see any one doing it, but we do know the girls did not do it. The spirits have bought toys and other useful articles, and brought them into the house. They use their own money. Several times they have given the children small pieces of silver money and currency. I said to the spirits one day, that I wished them to put a piece of money on the girl's head, if they could. I kept looking at her all the time. In a few moments they put twenty-five cents on her head. I know she did not have any money about her, and could not have put it there while I was watching. One day I put an apron in a bureau drawer, and locked the drawer. In a few moments the same article was thrown out from a little cabinet or box in another part of the sitting-room. I put it back in the bureau drawer, and locked it in the drawer three times in succession, with the same result. The spirits have written many times on a slate placed on the girl's head, without using any visible pencil, or anything but their own hands. Some of the best communications that we have had, have been written on the slate, as it lay on the head of the medium. There are many other manifestations of a startling nature which I omit to mention.

"This article being already longer than I thought it would be when I commenced it, in conclusion I will say that we have a large band of spirits with us all the time—some of them our near relations, who seem ever ready to manifest their presence. They say all our family are mediums. I will give the names and ages of the children. Elizabeth is eleven; Mary is eight; William is six; and Edward is fourteen years of age.

"Chicago, March 10th. MRS. M. L. BANGS."

The author would scarcely have ventured to print a narrative so full of *almost incredible commonplaces*, were it not that several persons of undoubted credit have testified to being present in Mrs. Bang's house when invisible servitors laid the dinner table, and brought in one after another the articles necessary for the meals, whilst the witnesses sat by and watched the proceedings in the full light of day.

As in many other instances on record, a large number of residents of Chicago who have visited this wonderful family as mere acquaintances, affirm, that the spontaneous demonstrations, occurring in the routine of private family life, are far more wonderful than any which can be obtained in circles, or through processes of invocation. This is a phase of phenomenal power testified to by all who have had the privilege of visiting Mediumistic persons in their own homes.

The act of waiting in expectancy of phenomena, although it is most generally responded to by the kind guardian spirits of circles, seems to be less favourable to the production of demonstrations, than the totally unprepared conditions which the routine of busy home life furnishes. Mrs. Coleman, an authoress of repute from Massachusetts, who made a quiet visit to the Bangs family, under a pretext of a slight business nature, reported that in one week's occasional visitation in that family, she saw more wonders spontaneously performed than she could dare to publish, and far more than any related of the circles wherein phenomena were anticipated. These statements should be remembered, as they tally closely with the experiences of all other cautious investigators in the modern Spiritual movement.

CHAPTER LX.

SPIRITUALISM IN AMERICA (CONTINUED),

SPIRITUAL CAMP MEETINGS.

THERE are two features of the American Spiritual movement both of which seem to have grown out of local customs until they have attained to the proportions of what are popularly called "American Institutions." These are, the anniversary celebrations of the famous "Rochester Knockings," taking place on or about the 31st of March, and the annual gatherings, called "The Spiritual Camp Meetings." The latter are generally held about the last of July and extend through August, and occasionally up to the end of September.

The custom of holding camp meetings in woods and rural scenes has not originated with the Spiritualists, many religious denominations having instituted such assemblages long before Spiritualism was known. It would seem as if the rigour of the severe American winters and burning summers, had rendered the custom of seeking a pleasanter temperature in shady groves or in the vicinity of cool lakes, in the fall of the year, an absolute necessity with the denizens of American cities. The extreme reserve and *caste* spirit of Europeans which induces each family to go forth in its own exclusive circle for autumn recreation, finds but little favour in the democratic life of America. On the contrary, the first idea of enjoyment which prevails in the land of the West is that of social gatherings, and these have gradually grown from pleasant pic-nics or grove meetings into annual encampments where all the portable conveniences of city life are associated with the charms of rural scenery and out-of-door amusements.

And thus it is, that these assemblages, so foreign to the spirit of European conservatism, and so attractive to American republicanism, have been adopted by the Spiritualists until their annual meetings in different sections of the country have far outstripped in magnitude those of any other sect or association in the United States. The Spiritual camp meetings also have become an integral part of the movement in America, and whether they are open to unfavourable criticism or may yet become so, certain it is, that at this time tens of thousands of persons sympathising with the belief in Spiritualism look forward every year with as much eager anticipation to these gatherings, and prepare to attend them with as much regularity, as the lower classes in England look forward to the inevitable roast beef and plum pudding of the Christmas festivities. In many localities, Spiritualists invest large sums in the purchase of land and build or rent cottages which they furnish for family use during the camping season, and close up for the rest of the year. Hotels are fitted up on the camp grounds for the accommodation of transient visitors, and an immense trade is carried on in the hire of tents which are put up in streets, avenues, and squares in regular city fashion, and named after the thoroughfares of the adjacent towns. In some encampments all sorts of amusements are provided. Large halls or tents are erected for dancing, music, and various exhibitions, but the "auditorium" or space fitted with seats, together with a speaker's stand, and accommodation for a choir, form an invariable feature of every encampment.

To a visitor who has never before beheld, or taken part in such a scene, a Spiritualistic camp meeting produces an indescribable feeling of strangeness and bewilderment, which scarcely allows him to determine whether he is under the influence of pleasure or pain. The gatherings are so vast, the scenes so new, and each member of the busy crowd seems so intent on pursuing his own special avocation, that a sense of loneliness, even of desolation, such as is often experienced by strangers in thronged cities, almost invariably possesses the sensitive mind. Gradually, the multitude of objects crowding in upon view on every side, arrange themselves into order, and then the sight is one of endless interest and amusement. To a lounger passing through the various groups, some arranged in picturesque knots at the tent doors, others reclining beneath shady trees, or stretched out upon grassy knolls, the fragments of conversation that meet the ear are as curious and heterogenous, as the objects that appeal to the sense of vision. From the first peep of day, the campers are astir, lighting gipsy fires, preparing breakfast, and trading with the various hawkers who ply with their provisions regularly through the white-tented streets. After the morning meal, visits are exchanged, and the business of the day proceeds with as much energy and order as in the cities. Sailing parties, *séances*, amusements, and business, all proceed in due course, until the hour for speaking arrives, when thousands assemble at the speaker's stand, to partake of the solid intellectual refreshment of the day. Lectures, balls, parties, illuminations, public discussions, &c., &c., fill up the time until midnight, when the white tents enclose the slumbering hosts; the fires and lamps are extinguished, and the pale moonbeam shines over rocks, groves, and lakes, illumining scenes as strange and picturesque as ever the eye of mortal gazed upon. Resembling to some extent a martial camp, but adorned with flowers, wreaths, and emblems of taste and beauty, instead of the grim paraphernalia of war, the stern sentinel with musket in hand is exchanged for watching angels. Instead of the savage password, "Death and glory," "Life eternal" is whispered in every breeze that stirs the tree tops, and the white tents, instead of sheltering the fever-racked forms of mailed victims, only waiting for the shrill cry of the bugle to marshal them to murder or death, shade the peaceful slumbers of those who know no death, and who are tenderly guarded by the glittering rank and file who have triumphed over the grave, and risen as immortal victors from life's cruel battlefields.

Amongst those who greet you as you take your morning's walk from street to avenue, or linger on rocky pinnacles to contemplate the busy hive of life thronging below, are strangers from States a thousand miles off, and neighbours from the next village. You may talk politics with a white-haired knot of grandsires sunning themselves on a social bench, around an ancient elm; talk metaphysics with a group of lecturers assembled "from the four corners of the earth," hear some merry "Indian maid" pouring out through the lips of her entranced "medy," shrewd philosophy, mingled with clairvoyant tests, and comical jokes, interspersed with startling proofs of super-mundane intelligence. Glancing down the avenues of gaily decorated tents, with wreaths, banners, inscriptions, and all manner of fanciful devices adorning them, the visitor cannot but be struck with the multitude of signs which almost every habitation exhibits. The shrewd

practical spirit of " the Yankee," evidently knows how to combine business
with pleasure, and turn each shining hour into profit, as well as amusement.
Bookstalls abound, photographs of spirits and mortals are on sale, and
literature is rapidly changing hands.   Healing, trance, test, and physical
Mediums, put out their signs, and ply their professional avocations as
industriously here as at home.   In a word, every one who has anything to
say, says it here, and the " dear public " need be at no loss to find all they
want to see, hear, purchase, or take part in, just as readily as in the midst
of the busiest cities.   The Spiritual camp meetings are in all respects such
thoroughly practical illustrations of American life, that any visitor may
glean more knowledge of popular institutions in a single day's ramble
through " Lake Pleasant," than he could gain in many weeks of far and
wide travel.   As a general rule, there is a fine choir and a good band of
music engaged for the camping season.   Most commonly too, besides an
efficient corps of officers and managers, there is a staff of police at hand, to
ensure order.   To the credit of the Spiritualists' gatherings be it said, this
last addendum is generally a superfluity, for unless some " roughs " from the
" world's people " gain admission, a more orderly and generally well conducted set of people cannot be found, than a gathering of Spiritualists.
They are most commonly also total abstainers, and whatever their private
views of morality may be, they are never permitted, at least on the best
ordered camp grounds—like Lake Pleasant for example—to pass obnoxious
opinions on others, or work mischief and disorder.   It must, of course,
be understood, that there are many diverse views amongst people so hete-
rogeneously brought together by a few generic points of agreement; but it
is tacitly resolved amongst them, that persons of widely different grades of
thought shall assemble themselves in different directions, and hold
gatherings where their special views shall be permitted free expression
without infringing on the rights and privileges of others.   Thus it is quite
common to find those who hold directly opposing views, calling their
sympathizers around them in special gatherings, whilst at the very large and
well conducted meetings, ultra-radical or obnoxious opinions on any subject
are not heard.

Those who may be curious to learn what are the prevailing themes of
discussion at these meetings will soon find that metaphysics and personal
experiences with Mediums are on every lip.   That scandals may abound,
both in speech and manner, among such vast multitudes none can deny,
but as far as strict regulations can prevail, no such disorders are manifest
to the public eye or ear.   The visitor is never shocked by the sound of the
profane oath, the ribald jest, or unseemly language.   Modest women may
walk the camp at night without fear of molestation, and the impure or dishonest must at least wear the mask of decent seeming before they can be
permitted to remain.

As an example of the wide-spread popularity to which some of these
Spiritualistic camp meetings have attained, the author may cite her own
experience when engaged as a speaker at Lake Pleasant, in Montague,
Mass., and at Neshaminy Falls, Pennsylvania, in 1880.   At the first of these
gatherings Mrs. Hardinge Britten addressed an almost breathlessly attentive audience of nearly eighteen thousand persons, and at the second there
were twenty thousand people on the ground, many of whom, of course,
could not approach near enough to the auditorium to hear the speaker.

The usual number of stationary campers at Lake Pleasant, Neshaminy
Falls, and other of the largest gatherings, varies from one to ten thousand

DR JOSEPH BEAL.

Artotype.

persons. The officers in charge make arrangements with the railroad companies to bring passengers at reduced rates, and on Sundays and special excursion days the visitors often amount to twenty thousand persons. Meantime, refreshments are provided, and when it is remembered that means of entertainment both mental and physical are arranged in due proportion for such vast assemblages, and that the most perfect order, harmony, and goodwill invariably prevail, too much credit cannot be given to the managers and the denomination that can attract, and successfully conduct, such meetings.

As Lake Pleasant camp meeting is now the oldest, and, on a general average, the largest of these gatherings, we shall continue our description, by giving some extracts from the managers' circular put forth by the Lake Pleasant Camp Meeting Association, in 1880 :—

"NEW ENGLAND ASSOCIATION OF SPIRITUALISTS.

"Dr. Joseph Beals, President.

"Lake Pleasant is situated in the town of Montague, Mass., on the Hoosac Tunnel Line, six miles south-east of Greenfield, and midway between Troy and Boston. Its attractions are manifold—embracing every variety of inland scenery—everything possible for the comfort and convenience of visitors, and ample facilities for amusement and recreation. The lake is a beautiful sheet of about one hundred and eight acres, and is within a mile of another lake of sixty acres. Bath houses are located at convenient points on the shore, a commodious wharf lies near the foot of the stairs leading to the grove from the railroad station, and a flotilla of boats is always in readiness to take out pleasure or fishing parties. An elegant Pavilion stands on an elevated plateau overlooking the grove on the one side, and the railroad station on the other, accessible from each by easy flights of stairs. The dancing assemblies held here each week-day afternoon and evening during the camp meeting, are conducted with the utmost order and decorum, and have become exceedingly popular. . . . .

"August, 1880."

Under the head of

ARRANGEMENTS FOR 1880.

The management print a long list of the various railroad companies—whose lines run over thousands of miles—that are prepared to carry passengers to and from the camp at half-fares, together with directions for bringing camp equipage, and the following curious, because eminently practical

"ITEMS OF INTEREST."

"The Grocery Store this season will keep a large line of goods of the best quality, including tin ware, crockery, fruits, vegetables, etc., which will be sold at regular market prices. No peddling of any kind will be allowed on the grounds, except by permission from the Committee. Table board, $4 per week ; dinners, 50 cents. A large stock of Ice was stored on the grounds last winter, and will be sold to campers at reasonable rates. All Campers are requested to register at the Secretary's Tent on their arrival. Parties driving to the Lake will find ample provisions for their teams. *Lodgings.*—Parties will be prepared to furnish lodgings in tents or cottages at 25 and 50 cents per night. Cot beds, mattresses and blankets can be hired on the grounds. The Post Office and Telegraph Office will be opened on the 4th of August. Fish, lobsters, oysters, etc., will be received fresh, daily, and will be sold at lowest prices. Meats and poultry will be brought on the ground every morning by Montague and Turners Falls dealers, and fresh vegetables, berries, milk, etc., by the farmers of the surrounding country."

Then follows an order of musical exercises, including the times of performance for the Fitchburgh Military Band (one of the best in the country, by the way), and the vocal exercises of the Grattan Smith Family,

35

a charming and accomplished choir of vocalists, whose entertainments in themselves are sufficient to command large and appreciative audiences.

The following plan of speakers may not be uninteresting for future reference :—

"The first regular exercises will be held on Sunday, August 8. Speakers—Captain H. H. Brown and E. V. Wilson ; Tuesday, August 10, Mrs. Lizzie Manchester, Inspirational Singer, Randolph, Vt. ; Wednesday, August 11, Giles B. Stebbins, Detroit, Mich. ; Thursday, August 12, Mrs. E. S. Watson, Titusville, Pa. ; Friday, August 13, Mr. E. A. Stanley, Leicester, Vt. ; Saturday, August 14, Bishop A. Beals, Versailles, N.Y. ; Sunday, August 15, Mrs. E. S. Watson and Cephas B. Lynn ; Tuesday, August 17, Louis Ransom, Stratford, N.Y. ; Wednesday, August 18, Rev. J. H. Harter, Auburn, N.Y., and Elder Evans, Mt. Lebanon, N.Y. ; Thursday, August 19, Mrs. N. J. T. Brigham, and Professor Henry Kiddle, New York City ; Friday, August 20, Dr. Anna M. Middlebrook, Bridgeport, Ct. ; Saturday, August 21, Mrs. Emma Hardinge Britten ; Sunday, August 22, Ed. S. Wheeler and Emma Hardinge Britten ; Tuesday, August 24, C. Fanny Allyn, Stoneham, Mass. ; Wednesday, August 25, Ed. S. Wheeler, Philadelphia, Pa., and Mrs. R. Shepard, Washington, D.C. ; Thursday, August 26, W. J. Colville, Boston, Mass., and Rev. Samuel Watson ; Friday, August 27, Mrs. Sarah Byrnes ; Saturday, August 28, Professor William Denton ; Sunday, August 29, Dr. J. M. Peebles, and Professor William Denton.

"Some of the best Mediums in the country will be present, and the phenomenal phases of the Spiritual Gospel will be invited to full manifestations through circles and *séances.*"

To this list should be added the following names of the officers for 1880 :

"President : Dr. Joseph Beals, Greenfield, Mass. Vice-Presidents : M. V. Lincoln, Dr. H. H. Brigham, and Mrs. M. A. Lyman. Clerk : J. H. Smith, Springfield, Mass. Treasurer : Wm. C. Bryant, Greenfield, Mass. Directors : Dr. Joseph Beals, M. H. Fletcher, D. B. Gerry, W. H. Gilmore, Harvey Lyman, J. S. Hart, A. Bullens, and W. F. D. Perkins. Committee on Grounds and Tents : N. S. Henry, Chairman, Montague, Mass ; W. F. D. Perkins, and John Patterson. On Transportation : J. H. Smith, D. B. Gerry, and Dr. E. A. Smith. On Speakers : Dr. Joseph Beals, Dr. N. D. Ross, and Mrs. M. A. Lyman. On Police, Lights, and Sanitary Regulations : J. S. Hart, P. H. Babbitt, and T. T. Greenwood. On Renting Privileges : T. W. Coburn, W. H. Gilmore, and M. H. Fletcher. On Music and Dancing : Dr. Joseph Beals, J. H. Smith, and A. Bullens."

The following summary of one week's exercises at "Lake Pleasant" may also prove acceptable, especially as it represents fairly the ordinary routine of camp life pursued at this favourite place of resort.

The notes are taken from the report of the *Banner of Light* for August 28, 1880.

"LAKE PLEASANT CAMP MEETING.

"This busy little city among the pines is the scene of constant and varied attractions. The great congregation of Sunday dispersed in an orderly manner, and left the campers to enjoy a quiet Sunday evening. The addresses of the day were discussed, private *séances* were held, and fraternal calls were made among the occupants of the camp. Following is the record of the week ending August 22nd :—

"Monday.—The officers and board of directors were elected for the ensuing year. In the evening, Lizzie J. Thompson, of Boston, gave a reading to a select and appreciative audience.

"Tuesday.—Louis Ranson, of Troy, N. Y., delivered the regular address. He chose for his theme : "Christianity as a Force in Civilisation." At 3-30 p.m. Jennie B. Hagan's friends convened in the hall and were well entertained. Miss Hagan improvised with her accustomed ability. In the evening the Grattan Smith family held a concert, which was largely attended.

"Wednesday.—The Shakers were present in force, and conducted the exercises both morning and afternoon. Elder Evans, Elderess Doolittle, and other members of the party spoke. The singing was a novel portion of the exercises. Elder Evans is a radical speaker, and some of his remarks were loudly applauded. The audiences were very large during the day. Charles Sullivan's entertainment in the evening was very successful. The hall was crowded, and Mr. Sullivan was in good 'form.' He was enthusiastically received.

"Thursday.—Rev. J. H. Harter, of New York, delivered the regular address of the forenoon session. His wife read a lengthy poem (original) on 'True Religion.' Mr. Harter then proceeded with his sermon. He said substantially :—'I was once a member of the Dutch Reformed Church ; then I changed to the Methodist ; then I moved forward to the Universalist ; my last jump was into Spiritualism. I sing hosannas of praise for Spiritualism. It is a glorious religion. I shall preach a sermon on "Coming, Doing and Going."' In the afternoon the Regular Address was prefaced by some remarks from that veteran Camp-Meeting-worker, Dr. A. H. Richardson, who was cordially welcomed by the audience. Dr. H. B. Storer, the well-known lecturer, who has officiated in such an acceptable manner at the Onset Bay meetings this summer, was next introduced by President Beals. As Dr. Storer advanced to the front of the platform a storm of applause greeted him. He spoke substantially as follows :—'I thank you, my dear friends, for your cordial greeting. I have just left Onset Bay, where we have had the baptism of the spirit. We all rejoice at your success here. May our meetings increase. One spirit animates us all ; one impulse moves us onward. It is a high honour to be an humble worker in this great movement. Our veteran workers leave us : E. V. Wilson has gone. Blessed thought, however, that our sainted and heroic dead are still in sympathy with us. They inspire us ; they lead us on to noble works.' Mrs. Nellie J. T. Brigham, of New York City, delivered the regular address. Her topic was, 'One Lord, one Faith, one Baptism.

"Friday.—Rev. J. H. Harter of New York, spoke in the forenoon, continuing his former address :—The Regular Address was delivered at 1.45 P.M., by Dr. Anna M. Middlebrook-Twiss, of Manchester, N. H. Her theme was 'Fact and Philosophy.'

"Saturday.—Capt. H. H. Brown spoke by special request in the forenoon. The discourse was preceded by a song from Mrs. Mason and daughter and Chas. W. Sullivan. Capt. Brown's topic was 'The Mission of America, or the Place of Spiritualism in History.' In the afternoon at 1.45 P.M., Mrs. Emma Hardinge Britten delivered a splendid address on 'The New Bible.' Mrs. Britten is a speaker of world-wide celebrity. Her discourses are grand and lucid, delivered with dramatic fire, and reflect credit upon the cause of Spiritualism. She was attentively listened to and loudly applauded.

"Sunday, Aug. 22nd.—There never was a fairer day than this. At an early hour crowds began to enter the camp ground. The excursion trains were larger than ever before. It was an interesting sight to witness the arrival of the constantly incoming host. At 9-30 the Fitchburg Band began a very fine concert. The vast amphitheatre was well filled with an appreciative audience. In the afternoon Mrs. Emma Hardinge-Britten was greeted by an immense audience, which she held spellbound, as in a stately and impressive manner she replied to Joseph Cook's recent coarse imputations upon Spiritualists. This discourse will soon be issued in tract form, hence the writer will not attempt to give a digest here. Suffice it to say that the eminent and able defender of Spiritualism, Mrs. Emma Hardinge-Britten, who honours any cause by her advocacy of it, subjected Joseph Cook to a scorching criticism and answered in a lucid manner the current objections to Spiritualism. The lecturer was congratulated by thousands at the conclusion of her address.

"Monday, Aug. 23rd.—At 1.30 p.m. a memorial service was held in honour of E. V. Wilson, the veteran lecturer, who passed to spirit-life Aug. 8th. The grand stand was beautifully decorated, and a very large audience convened to listen to the speeches. President Beals said : 'We have met to hold a memorial service to our dear brother, E. V. Wilson, who has gone to the spirit-land. He was a brave and noble worker. Let us show our respect for him to-day.' Capt. H. H. Brown was the first speaker. He paid an eloquent tribute to the memory of Mr. Wilson. Ed. S. Wheeler followed in a touching speech, filled with reminiscences of personal relations with Mr. Wilson. He also made a very forcible plea for practical work in direction of liquidating the indebtedness upon the home of Mr. Wilson's family. Mrs. Emma Hardinge-Britten made the closing speech, which was one of great power. She asked the question, What does death do to us ? and proceeded to argue that death transfigured us ; that the noble warrior in whose honour the meeting was held had been transfigured since the episode of death, which was, in reality, his spiritual birth. The speaker in closing adverted to the question of assisting the wife and children of Bro. Wilson, and directed President Beals to put her name down as the first one to purchase E. V. Wilson's book : 'The Truths of Spiritualism.'

"CEPHAS."*

Having rendered all the justice our space will permit to the colossal camp meeting of the present day, we must follow with just at least a few

---

* Cephas B. Lynn, a young and highly-inspired speaker, writer, and thinker. Cephas Lynn's addresses are amongst the brightest, most original, and scholarly that can be heard on the American Spiritual rostrum, and his admirable reports for the *Banner of Light* contribute largely to its popularity.

extracts from the *Religio Philosophical Journal* of August 28th, 1880, touching the "Neshaminy Falls Camp Meeting," a much younger organization than that of "Lake Pleasant," but one which in point of numbers seems likely to rival the immense gatherings of Massachusetts. Neshaminy Falls is a beautiful place about ten or twelve miles from Philadephia, and its attractions and methods of management may be gathered from the following stirring remarks :—

CAMP MEETING OF THE FIRST ASSOCIATION OF SPIRITUALISTS OF PHILADELPHIA, AT NESHAMINY FALLS GROVE.

"There were, as I have informed you, some ten or twelve thousand persons at Neshaminy Falls Grove on Saturday, August 1st, and, in consequence, Monday was a day of quiet and repose there. . . . .

"On the day to which we refer, there was some dancing by the regular citizens of the camp in the pavilion, our orchestra always being ready to discourse sweet music, whenever the lads and lasses wish "to trip the light fantastic toe," which is pretty often. By the way, these small social parties, among acquaintances, are fast becoming very enjoyable. . . . .

"On Tuesday, Mrs. Shepard, ever ready to gratify those seeking for truth and instruction, answered questions from an audience gathered in the pavilion, the weather being unfavourable. In the afternoon H. H. Brown discoursed upon the text : "He went up into the mount of Olivet," etc. The lecture was considered an excellent essay by those who heard the same. . . . .

"On Thursday, August 5th, Mrs. R. Shephard spoke in the forenoon, in answer to interrogations from her hearers. In the afternoon, Mrs. Emma Hardinge-Britten, so long and extensively known among Spiritualists all over the world, was the speaker announced, and she came duly from the scene of her present labors in the city of New York.

"In order to encroach as little as possible upon the time of so busy a person as Mrs. Britten ever is, the committee had engaged her to speak on consecutive days. And so it came about, that on Friday, August 6th, Mrs. Britten spoke again. To attempt a report in half-a-dozen lines, would be but an impertinence deserving resentment. It is better to say the two lectures of Mrs. Britten gave great satisfaction, being grandly instructive, and only made all concerned the more regret the accident, which prevented us from placing her before our great Sunday audiences. The ensuing Saturday was one of our quiet days, such as have been described before, but the camp gradually filled, until every nook was occupied and new comers were quartered among hospitable friends and accommodating strangers for miles around.

"But Sunday, August 8th, was not a quiet day. The morning dawned brilliantly. The speakers were A. B. French, of Clyde, Ohio ; Samuel Watson, of Memphis, Tenn. ; and Mrs. R. Shepard. By arrangement with the railroad company several extra trains were secured, and, warned by the immense throng of the last Sunday, other enlarged accommodations were provided. Early in the morning the people began to gather, and by the time for opening the meeting for the forenoon the camp had more people than at the same time on the Sunday previous.

"A. B. French spoke to a magnificent audience upon the subject, 'What of Death, and what of our Dead ?'

"Long before the time for the Rev. Samuel Watson to speak, it was seen that the audience, as on the last Sunday, must be divided. Two meetings were arranged, but three were needed, as on the former Sunday, but there were not so many speakers at hand competent for such crowds, and in the evening a fine audience heard Mrs. Shepard once more upon 'Woman and her relation to Spiritualism.' Last Sunday there were one thousand or more carriages came to this ground—this Sunday the gatekeepers told me they passed over fifteen hundred teams, some of them four-in-hand. There were many more cars, and all, as I am informed, came full. There was 'a great company which no man could number," but order and peaceful enjoyment reigned supreme, without an accident to mar the occasion at Neshaminy."

Lake Pleasant and Neshaminy must suffice to inform our readers of what Spiritualistic camp meetings are like, and what Spiritualists do and talk about when they go into camp. There are multitudes of similar gatherings ; some less it is true in numbers, but not very much less. Let the following list of such gatherings, selected like the above extracts, from the *Banner*, and the *Religio Philosophical Journal*, of August, 1880, speak for themselves.

"CAPE COD CAMP MEETING. [By H. B. S.]* The charm of a delightful summer lingers in the groves and over the odorous fields basking in the sunlight. The air is vocal with the twitter of birds and hum of insects, and a morning walk over the hills seems a fit preparation for that natural worship which we hope to enjoy in larger measure by the aid of this first Sunday's exercises at the camp. The dead leaves have been swept away, the speakers' stand newly painted, and the seats, all comfortably backed, await the coming audience. After the deluging rain of Saturday, the sandy roads of the Cape are comparatively hard, and on foot and by vehicles of all sorts, the good people stream toward the camp. Baggage is unloaded, and soon the semi-circle of cottages are occupied by their annual tenants, who greatly enjoy their social reunions under the trees."

"LILY DALE CAMP MEETING.—The sessions of this Camp Meeting have been productive of great good in the western portion of the State of New York. The principal speakers have been Mrs. Stearns, Lyman C. Howe, C. Fannie Allyn, Prof. Wm. Denton, Judge McCormick, and W. J. Colville. With this array of talent the meetings have been well sustained twice daily. In addition to the regular exercises, every evening has been profitably employed, either by a scientific lecture or a concert. Prof. Denton's geological course has been intensely interesting and instructive, and Mr. James G. Clarke's ballad concerts have been a very pleasing feature."

"BUSWELL'S GROVE, ME.—Mrs. Mattie E. Hull writes :—' Extensive preparations are going on for the prospective camp-meeting in Buswell's Grove, commencing the 8th of September. In all probability it will be the largest gathering of Spiritualists ever convened in the State. The committee have engaged the services of J. Frank Baxter, Dr. H. P. Fairfield, Moses Hull, and the writer.'"

"NOTES FROM ONSET BAY.—Our camp meeting has had another week of uninterrupted success, save by the very dry weather. The meetings during the past week have been largely attended by an earnest and thinking people, who are ready for the bread of life. Saturday, W. J. Colville, of Boston, occupied the platform in the afternoon, while your correspondent, with the rest of the Committee on Entertainments, was busy in caring for the parties arriving in large numbers to spend Sunday at the grove. Sunday, August 6th, opened clear and dry, and with, by far, the largest number of people at the grove that ever stayed over night at one time. The trains from Boston and New Bedford on the north, and the trains from Provincetown and Oak Bluffs on the south, with the steamer Monohanset from New Bedford, all came loaded, swelling the numbers to nearly 7,000. Mrs. Sarah A. Byrnes, of Boston, spoke at 10.30 a.m., subject, 'The Practicality of Spiritualism.'"

"LAKE CHAMPLAIN SPIRITUALIST CAMP-MEETING.—To be held at Queen City Park, Burlington, Vt., under the auspices of the Forest City Park Association. Commencing August 21st, and continuing until September 11th, 1882."

"SUNAPEE LAKE SPIRITUALIST CAMP-MEETING.—The Spiritualists of New Hampshire will hold their fifth annual camp-meeting at Blodgett's Landing, Newbury, N. H., commencing September 8th and closing September 25th."

"MICHIGAN CAMP-MEETING.—There will be a grand camp-meeting at Lansing, on the Central Michigan Fair Ground, commencing August 25th and closing September 4th, held under the auspices of the State Association of Spiritualists and Liberalists of Michigan."

"A LIBERAL LEAGUE CONVENTION AND SPIRITUALIST AND SECULAR CAMP-MEETING.— Will be held at Tama, Tama County, Iowa, September 7th, 8th, 9th, and 10th."

"THE ANNUAL STATE CAMP MEETING of the Kansas Liberal Union will begin on Sunday, Aug. 27th, and continue till and close on Sept. 4th, 1882, at Bismarck Grove, Lawrence, Kansas.—ANNIE L. DIGGS, Secretary."

"CAMP MEETING AT ETNA, ME.—The Spiritualists of Eastern Maine will hold their Annual Camp-Meeting at Etna, Penobscot Co., in Daniel Buswell's Grove, commencing August 25th, and continuing ten days, ending Sunday, Sept. 3rd, 1882. Dr. H. B. Storer, J. Frank Baxter, Miss Jennie B. Hagan and others are expected."

"THE ADJOURNED MEETING (being the first annual) of the Fourth District Spiritual-Liberal Association, will be held on Orion Park Island, Saturday and Sunday, Aug. 26th and 27th.—Mrs. F. E. ODELL, Secretary, Farmer's Creek, Mich."

---

* Dr. Storer, of Boston.

"GROVE MEETING.—The Spiritualists of Paulding County, O., and vicinity, will hold their Annual Grove-Meeting in Daniel Wentworth's Grove, north of Antwerp, on the 19th and 20th of August.—R. B. CHAMPION, Secretary."

"THE NIANTIC (CT.) CAMP MEETING.—The grounds will be open on and after June 12, 1882. The regular Camp Meeting will commence with public speaking, July 12, 1882, and will continue until August 20th."

"SPIRITUALIST CAMP MEETING.—The 5th Annual Solomon Valley Spiritualist Camp Meeting will be held under the direction of the Delphos Society at Delphos, Ottawa County, Kansas, from September 22nd to October 1st inclusive."

"THE PEOPLE'S CAMP MEETING will be held on the grounds of the Cassadaga Lake Free Association, from July 28th to August 28th inclusive."

"SPIRITUALIST CAMP MEETING at Lake George, N. Y., from July 15th to August 20th."

Several new Camp Meetings have been started within the last two years of which the author has no authorized accounts, in addition to those named above ; nearly all of which are old established gatherings. Besides these, there is a long list of Grove Meetings, and Conventions, announced to continue for two, three, or more days ;—all and each of which command full gatherings, never falling below six or seven hundred, and often reaching to several thousand persons.

Quite recently, a blatant minister of the Church of England, who found his pew rents like his congregation, sadly in need of replenishment, commenced, by way of effecting his object, a series of Sunday Evening Sermons "against Spiritualism,"—to be preached in the Church of the Holy Trinity, Liverpool, England.

The *religious* paper that reported these sermons, announced them as " Spiritualism in its coffin " ;—" Nailing down the lid " ; and, " Death blow to Spiritualism," &c., &c. One of the correspondents of this same *religious* paper, called upon the clergyman aforesaid, to do his duty, and *crush out the obnoxious reptile—Spiritualism—at once.* Other writers followed in the same strain ; but all agreed, that the clergyman in question, whose name was never heard till then beyond his dreary range of empty pews, and a few solemnly sad looking worshippers, scattered by twos and threes, through the church, *could soon do the business*, and presently the whole thing would collapse beneath the lightning of the minister's eye, and the thunder of the ecclesiastical sheet engaged in " Nailing down the lid " of Spiritualism's *coffin.*

Although Mrs. Hardinge-Britten was called upon during several weeks by the Liverpool Spiritualists to answer this monstrous bombast, her controls never deemed it worth while to do more than use these occasions to describe what Spiritualism was not, as well as what it was.

Could the reverend orator and his clerical abettors have glanced over the foregoing chapter before entering upon their pitiful crusade, is it not more than probable that they would have paused to draw breath before they entered upon their work ? and measuring their own exceeding littleness against the multitude whom their vain gloriousness presumed to attack, would they not have prudently waited until they had found another Samson before they attempted to slay their thousands and tens of thousands with " the jaw bone of an ass ? "

E Buffum
New Church College
Devonshire St
London   Islington

I love this little Child
God bless him advise
his father to f to back
to London on Monday
by all means
Susan

W Cason

K. F. Jencken Jr

the mark of
the nurse who held
the Child +

SPECIMEN OF WRITING EXECUTED BY MRS. FOX JENCKEN'S BABY, AGED NINE DAYS.
ALSO, FACSIMILES OF THE SIGNATURES OF THE WITNESSES AND MARK OF THE NURSE WHO HELD THE BABY.

CHAPTER LXI.

CONCLUSION.

It need scarcely be stated to the readers of this volume, that its limits no more admit of a record which would include all the memorable names which have figured in the history of American Spiritualism, than it would serve to catalogue all the noteworthy personages who have been instrumental in planting the standards of the Spiritual cause in other countries of the earth. Of the vast number of influential actors in the great nineteenth century Spiritual drama mentioned in the author's Twenty Years' History of Modern American Spiritualism, few indeed are now remaining on earth. Amongst those still spared to the present generation are the three Fox sisters, whose eminent services in founding the first Spiritual telegraph of the present age, have been fully described in "Modern American Spiritualism," as well as every other work written on the subject of the present Spiritual dispensation. The eldest of the far-famed sisters known as "The Rochester Knockers," Mrs. Leah Fox Underhill, though retired from her long and arduous duties as a professional test Medium, is ever gratefully remembered by the Spiritualists of this country, as well as by the many personal friends who throng her pleasant *salons* in her private New York residence. Margaretta Fox—now the widow of Dr. Kane, the eminent Arctic discoverer—and Mrs. Kate Jencken—also unfortunately deprived by the death angel of her good companion Henry Jencken, barrister, of London, England—still pursue their avocations as professional Mediums, the former in America, the latter in England. Mrs. Jencken is the mother of two lovely and promising boys, the eldest of whom, at the immature age of five months, whilst held in his nurse's arms, began toying with a pencil lying on the table near the babe, and in the presence of reliable witnesses, his tiny hand—moved by an invisible but irresistible power—wrote several lines in clear bold caligraphy, the facsimile of which will be found on the opposite page.

Still another of the most celebrated and esteemed of the Spiritual "old guard," who remains at the post of duty, is Mr. J. V. Mansfield, the Spirit postmaster, whose powers as an unrivalled writing Medium will also be found described in ample detail in "Modern American Spiritualism." Though the snows of many winters have bleached the once raven locks, the heart and hand of the good "postmaster" are as devoted to the service of the angels, as in days of yore.

During a period of nearly thirty years, Mr. Mansfield calculates that he must have written over one hundred thousand answers to sealed letters at the dictation of Spirits! He has seen one after another of his early friends and associates vanish from his side, and last, and best beloved of all, the fair and faithful companion of his youth, the friend and counsellor of his mature age, has disappeared amidst the golden mists which enshroud the radiant summer land, from the dazzled eyes of mortality; but despite of care and change, bereavement, and the stealthy approaches of life's wintry season, for which earth knows no returning spring, James V. Mansfield has still kept his seat at the mystic Spirit table; waiting—and seldom in vain—for the invisible dictators who should send messages of consolation and proofs of immortality from land to land, and despatch tidings from the post-office of the soul across the silent sea, bounded by the coast lines of earth and the realms of immortality.

In a copy of the *Banner of Light* some eighteen years old, is a long list of speakers, healers, test Mediums, &c., &c., very few of whom now remain on earth to fill the posts of duty they then occupied.

In the midst of this decimation of the Spiritual ranks, it is indeed pleasant to see the standard of the faith still upheld in the great city of New York, by Mr. Henry J. Newton, a noble gentleman, who, with his devoted and accomplished wife, as far back as a quarter of a century ago, dared to proclaim himself a Spiritualist in the face of the most bitter and relentless sentiment of public antagonism to the faith.

Professional gentlemen and merchants *may now* walk the streets of New York, and though they may be openly avowed Spiritualists, they are no longer in danger of being mobbed or maltreated. Not so when Mr. Henry J. Newton became a Spiritualist. Of a rich and flourishing firm of pianoforte makers, Mr. Newton was still dependent on public opinion for his standing amongst his fellow men, and this, and much more he fearlessly risked, for the sake of the cause which he had espoused. During all the stormy scenes of warfare and persecution which Spiritualists had to endure, ere their faith could obtain general recognition, Mr. and Mrs. Newton never faltered. Their hospitable doors were ever open to the harassed Mediums, and their aid, support, and countenance, ever extended to the advocates of the cause. They helped to sustain the public meetings both with purse and person, and Mrs. Newton's beautiful soprano voice has been a feature of interest for many a succeeding year in the Sabbath day gatherings of the Spiritualists.

And now this noble couple have lived to realize the fruits of their self-sacrifice and untiring devotion. For many past years Mr. Newton has held the post of President of the First Society of Spiritualists in New York, and with the admirable ministrations of Mrs. Nellie T. Brigham as the regular speaker, Mr. Newton has had the happiness of seeing the faith he advocates grow into such honour and respect with the public, that few meetings in the city are better attended, and few Sabbath day gatherings are more prolific of divine and salvatory teachings than that presided over by Mr. Newton.

Besides Mr. Newton, Mr. Charles Partridge, the veteran father of New York Spiritualism, and the founder of the first and best Spiritual paper ever published, *The Spiritual Telegraph*, still maintains his place in the foremost ranks, as in the respect and honour of the New York Spiritualists. Dr. J. M. Buchanan, the learned and philosophic discoverer of the marvellous power of reading character by touch—a power which he himself has named "psychometry"—with his fair and gifted wife, one of the best psychometrists of the age, are also residents of New York. There too resides Mr. Henry Kiddle, ex-school superintendent of New York, a gentleman who has sacrificed name, place, and position, for the faith he advocates, and one whose learning and ability would reflect honour on any cause. It must be added, also, that although many of the grand "old guard" have performed their last act of good service for Spiritualism on earth, young, fresh, and aspiring men and women have not been wanting to infuse new vitality into the ever-advancing march of the army.

Hosts of "materializing Mediums" follow in the track of Conklin, Redman, &c., &c. Mrs. Richmond, Lizzie Doten, A. B. French, Dr. Storer, and F. L. Willis, already stretch out the hand of welcome to their younger

W^{M.} EMMETTE COLEMAN

sisters and brothers in the persons of Mrs. Nellie T. Brigham, Mrs. Shepherd Lillie, Mr. W. J. Colville, Captain H. H. Brown, and a constantly increasing succession of brave Spirits who are springing up on every side to fill the gaps that the death angel has left in the ranks.

We cannot close these personal notices without a few words of grateful recognition of the invaluable services rendered to the cause of truth and knowledge by Mr. William Emmette Coleman, a Western gentleman, whose admirable and scholarly essays appear for the most part in the columns of the *Religio-Philosophical Journal*. Mr. Coleman has had a strange and varied life—one that will form a deeply interesting page of biography in some future volume devoted to such records. Meantime, it is enough to say at present, that like many another "self-made" American, this man, still young in years, but old in rich experience, has studied so deeply and well the lore of ancient myth and Oriental literature, that his journalistic articles are a perfect treasury of research and valuable information. An untiring and devoted advocate of Spiritualism pure and unadulterated, the shams, frauds, and fanatics have found an unrelenting censor in Mr. Coleman. Indeed, if it were not for the well-known worship of truth which animates his busy pen, his best friends would regret the unsparing severity with which he is prompt to rebuke the charlatan, and expose the pretender. As the hammer of the "iconoclast" is often more necessary to shatter the idols within the ranks of reform than without them, so the work of such determined censors as Colonel Bundy and his learned contributor, William Emmette Coleman, have unquestionably been equally necessary to purge away the rank weeds of falsehood and sham, that have grown up on the fertile soil of Spiritualism. If all things are now being brought into judgment, both old and new, and "all that was hidden" is at this time destined to see the light, and face the broad sunshine of reality, then no one has done a better work in promoting such a result than Mr. W. E. Coleman, of San Francisco, California.

It will be remembered that the avowed aim of the author in producing this volume has been to compile a compendious history of the great Spiritual movement, and whilst endeavouring as far as possible to chronicle the leading events of the moving drama, to limit the notices of the individuals who appear from time to time upon the scene, to their connection with one or two of those cases which may serve to illustrate the chief characteristics of the phenomena, which make up the sum of the Spiritual system of telegraphy. Keeping this purpose strictly in view, the author has recorded well-attested examples of every description of phenomena by and through which Spirits have manifested their presence on earth, but, both for the sake of brevity, and in accordance with the plans laid down for her by her invisible prompters and assistants, she has been compelled to eliminate all merely personal histories or biographical details, save and except such as were essential to the clearer understanding of the progress of the movement. Thus there are at this very period throughout America, scores of admirable Mediums for the production of "form materialization" and marvellous dark circle phenomena, whose faithful services keep alive the world's faith in Spiritual presence on earth, but whose only record at present is to be found in the columns of the Spiritual journals. To these eminent workers, besides the numerous speakers, writers, and faithful labourers in the great vineyard of effort, of whom it would be impossible now to give detailed notices, we have only to say, the plan of another work, including the biographies of Mediums and renowned Spiritualists, has been sketched out by the author's Spirit friends as her next literary undertaking, and will be put into execution at the earliest available opportunity. Until this arrives, the faithful and self-sacrificing labourers who toil so often and so long without other reward than that which scant courtesy, a paltry meed of recompense, or the satisfaction which their own consciousness of work well done affords, must be content to wait for that earthly word of remembrance which the author herewith pledges herself to give them to the utmost of her power, in a forthcoming volume.

One only departure from the enforced silence of these closing lines can we now make, and that is to assure our readers that the first as well as one of the noblest of the phenomenal personages who has made this century memorable with Spiritual footprints, namely, Mr. Andrew Jackson Davis, is still in the mortal form, and doing a noble and untiring work in preaching the "harmonial philosophy" to weekly gatherings of devoted followers in New York.

Those who best know the author of this volume are aware, that there are many points of divergence between the opinions she has received from the teachings of trusted Spirit friends, and those enunciated, and often written, by Mr. Davis; but there are none more than the author, who can fervently admire the nobility of mind, purity of life, and wonderful Spiritual endowments that have distinguished Mr. Davis's whole career, and made him and his revelations the very corner-stone upon which the great Spiritual reformation of the nineteenth century is upreared.

We have been given to understand that Mr. Davis has quite recently passed through a University course which has qualified him to take his place amongst the secular scientists of the day, as one of the medical faculty, and that he is now Dr. A. J. Davis.

It is indeed gratifying to be able to add that the renowned and well-beloved couple Hudson and Emma Tuttle, now in the prime of life, continue to exercise their unmeasured usefulness in every good work. Dr. Slade, Charles Watkins, Mrs. Simpson and Maud Lord, A. H. Phillips, and hosts of others scarcely less famous, maintain the phenomenal department of the movement to admiration, whilst as the only representative of the numerous *corps* of American trance speakers to whom we can now call attention, we would name Mr. W. J. Colville—himself a phenomenon of intellectual Spirituality, never yet excelled, even if his peer can be found within the ranks of Spiritualism. *Petite* in person, and with no special educational or natural advantages, this young gentleman when on the rostrum and under control of his Spirit friends, is capable of dealing with, and mastering any point of science, metaphysics, or history, that may be spontaneously presented to him. If the present decade had produced no other evidence of inspiration from supra-mundane sources than Mr. W. J. Colville, he alone might suffice to prove its continued existence and ministry. Mr. Colville has quite recently made a visit to England. Allusion has before been made to his invaluable services on the Spiritual rostrum of the old country; in fact, his marvellous style of oratory, besides his capacity to improvise poems on any theme that his audiences may suggest, all combine to render him one of the most remarkable evidences of Spiritual influence that the ranks of Spiritualism can display.

It can scarcely be possible for any thinking person to peruse the foregoing pages, without coming to the conclusion that the movement they treat of is one of a truly supra-mundane nature. Never before in the history of the race has any belief of a religious character obtained so wide and deep a foothold amongst men, or established its standards of faith at so many distant points at once, appealed successfully to so many classes of society, and wrought such a vast revolution in human opinion—and that in less than half a century of time.

Let the reader consider the different and widely-separated nationalities treated of in this record, the vast numbers already engaged in the work, and then, even without allowing for the fact that where one case has been recorded, at least a hundred parallels remain untouched, the above assertions must be accepted without reserve or qualification.

Fifty years ago, the destiny of all the countless millions that have vanished from the earth through the mysterious portals of death, was utterly unknown. Whether they were sleeping in the ground, annihilated, living, some in eternal torment, others in eternal bliss, or when, or how, if ever, we should meet them again, was all an unsolved mystery. Now the sea has given up the drowned mariner; the fire has restored its perished myriads; the earth has yielded up her buried treasures; the ages have not blotted out from view a single creature that has ever drawn the breath of life. On the night of the 31st of March, 1848, we found beyond a shadow of doubt or peradventure, that death had no power over the Spirit, could never touch the soul, or destroy one attribute or property of soul life. In a word, we found our so-called *dead* were all living, aye, and living so near to us, that they breathe our very atmosphere, share our very thoughts, and do us a thousand times more good as blessed inspiring guardian Spirits than they ever could effect as poor weak mortals like ourselves.

On the 31st of March 1848, we discovered that we had never lost a friend; only parted with those that had vanished behind the veil of mortality as far as our mortal vision is concerned. On that momentous night, all our vague dreams of " Supernaturalism " were swept away like cobwebs, and in their place came the realities of a rational living human Spirit naturalism. All our doubts and denials concerning " miracles " were blown to the winds, and a new and wonderful array of powers for the soul, possibilities for the man of the future, and germs of new sciences, took their place. We found besides matter and force, a new element, called "Spirit." We discovered the existence of a new country; one as much more capacious and extensive than earth, as the generations of the past are more numerous than those of the present.

We were enabled to locate that country and map it out as existing in and about the planet, and holding the same relation to it, as our souls hold to our bodies. We discovered that night, a new phase of physiology in the existence (in some individuals) of a force which can animate inanimate bodies—make dumb things speak, and blind non-intelligent matter deliver wonderful messages. We saw founded that night, a telegraph, which outstrips that of electricity, and without wires, batteries, or needles, carries messages between heaven and earth, and exchanges ideas with all the vanished ones of past ages in the twinkling of an eye. We found in the Spirit rappings, a new page in the science of acoustics; in the apparition of living Spirit people, a new page in the science of optics. We found in " dancing tables " a new motor power. We discovered in the formation of Spirit hands, a page of chemistry that puts all other chemical operations known to man utterly in the shade; and above and beyond all this, we found the complete solution to our own fate hereafter. We saw the judgment upon all our works, words, and thoughts.

We learned how to build our own heaven or avoid our inevitable hell.

We saw the results of every moment of our lives in the doom of those that had gone before us. Their past, and our present and future throughout all *time*, if not through *eternity*, was all so clearly revealed to us, that henceforth we never need say more " we take our leap in the dark." We know we are making or marring our life hereafter—and thus the chains of fear, doubt, error, ecclesiastical pretentions, priestly ignorance, with all the fictions of the past, and mysteries of the future, fall like ropes of sand from our necks, and we stand in the light of a scientific religion and a religious science, emancipated souls, newly born into the divine and unshackled liberty of truth. For the present the author and reader must part company. The former will not insult the intelligence of the latter by pretending that she offers to the world's acceptance a work upon which she herself does not set a high value; and yet, who can be so conscious as a patient world-wide investigator into the marvels of Spiritualism, how impossible it is for any mortal hand to chronicle one tithe of what the Spirits have done amongst men in this century, or for any one volume to contain the record.

And still, humble and reverent acknowledgments of human incapacity must be accompanied with earnest and grateful recommendations to study out the record, such as it is, with all fidelity, were it only as an incentive to extend the field of exploration to the end of the reader's mortal career. Without attempting to shoulder upon " the Spirits" the many shortcomings which the execution of so mighty a record as this must necessarily manifest, the author can at least claim that it was undertaken, and continuously assisted, by the wise intelligences by whom her life labours have been for many years past consciously guided, and whether they selected her as their scribe from choice, or in the absence of a more suitable instrument, it is for them alone to decide. It is enough for the author to claim that her portion of the work has been fulfilled with the most inviolable regard to truth and justice, and at the same time in a spirit of charity towards all, and malice to none. For the rest—whether it concerns the opinions of men, or the future issues of her work, the author rests secure upon the strength of her life's motto—

GOD UNDERSTANDS.

JOHN HEYWOOD, Excelsior Steam Printing and Bookbinding Works, Hulme Hall Road, Manchester.

CPSIA information can be obtained
at www.ICGtesting.com
Printed in the USA
LVHW061245140623
749653LV00016B/1634